D0110616

Discover the California Road Trip

Take a look at a map of California, and you'll discover that some of the top destinations in the country are within a day's drive of one another: San Francisco, Yosemite, and Los Angeles. Push past the state's borders and add Las Vegas and the Grand Canyon, and you'll have the road trip of a lifetime.

That's because the West *is* larger than life. The boisterous cities seem bigger, redwood forests and snow-capped mountains loom taller, and sandy coastlines stretch longer than anywhere else. California was a dream before it was a place, before its boundaries existed on any map. People have long headed west seeking natural beauty and wide-open space. And despite an ever-growing population, that open space still exists. It's there in Yosemite's lofty peaks, or the depths of the Grand Canyon, or the primal collision of land and ocean along the Pacific coastline. This is nature at its best, just a few hours away from the cosmopolitan pleasures of the most intriguing cities anywhere. San Francisco, Los Angeles, and Las Vegas all offer high art, frenetic nightlife, and gourmet dining, but the choices are as different as the distinctive personalities of the cities themselves.

The pace of life in the American West is as diverse as everything else. Life in the fast lane is an apt metaphor for Los Angeles, where California

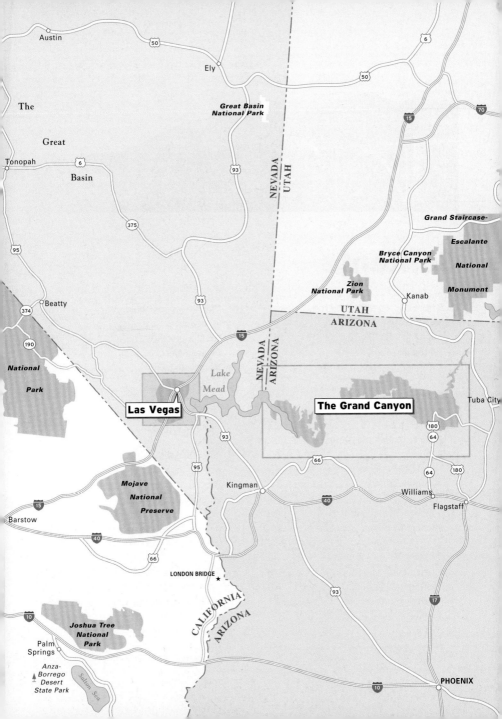

Contents

car culture reaches its zenith. Yet the quiet frenzy of San Francisco sometimes seems just as quick, and Las Vegas has made living fast into almost a new art form (not to mention big business). Outside the major urban areas, the hectic speed diminishes. California's wine regions invite visitors to relax and enjoy life a sip at a time. Beyond the vineyards, an even more venerable and variable pace emerges – that of nature. The gushing waterfalls of Yosemite, towering redwoods and delicate native wildflowers along the coast, even the imperceptible flow of the Colorado River as it carves the Grand Canyon...all contribute to the unique rhythms of the West.

So choose your own pace. If you don't mind spending hours at a time behind the wheel, it's possible to experience the best of the West in two weeks. Gawk at Hollywood movie stars, wander Old West ghost towns, and explore the Magic Kingdom. Hike the Grand Canyon and hit the slots in Vegas. Or just lie on the beach and soak up the sun. Let your interests determine your routes and itineraries. No matter who you are or what you're into, the West awaits.

Planning Your Trip

▶ WHERE TO GO

San Francisco

The weather, the politics, the technology, the food—these are what make San Francisco world-famous. Come to the City by the Bay to dine on cutting-edge cuisine, tour avant-garde museums, bike through Golden Gate Park, and stroll Fisherman's Wharf. Venture beyond the Bay to explore wine country.

Yosemite

The work of Ansel Adams and John Muir have made Yosemite a worldwide icon. Thousands crowd into Yosemite Valley to view the much-photographed Half Dome, Yosemite Falls, and El Capitan. On the eastern side of the Sierra, Mono Lake and Mammoth Lakes provide more scenic wilderness to explore.

Las Vegas

Glorious excess is the lifeblood of Las Vegas. Even strict dieters simply *must* sample a lavish buffet. Wallflowers gyrate themselves into a lather under pulsing strobes. And even non-gamblers, horrified at the thought of throwing away their hard-earned money, often break down and slide $20 into a slot machine—hey, you never know, right? Dine, drink, dance, and double down, then do it all again. Some 36 million visitors a year can't be wrong.

The Grand Canyon

River-cut more than a mile deep into the Kaibab Plateau is one of the world's most sought-after landscapes—the only canyon on earth deserving of the grand title. Looking into the Grand Canyon can be a truly life-altering experience. Its brash vastness

the Golden Gate Bridge and San Francisco

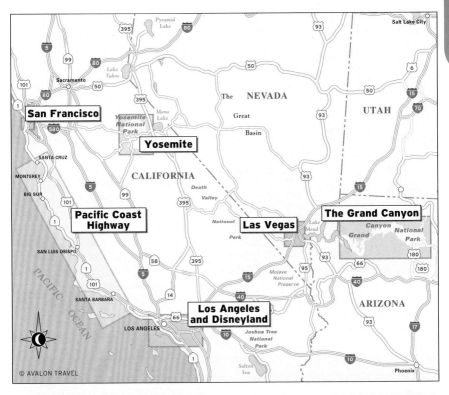

Las Vegas skyline

Santa Monica Pier

Los Angeles and Disneyland

For a taste of the iconic California dream, you can't beat Los Angeles. From the glitz and glamour of Hollywood and Beverly Hills to the camp and kitsch of Santa Monica's Pier, L.A. is all California culture, all the time. Kids of all ages come to visit Walt's original Disneyland, while sun and surf worshippers ride the waves or relax on the sugar-sand beaches.

Pacific Coast Highway

Some of the most beautiful, most adventurous coastline in the world lies along Highway 1 between Los Angeles and San Francisco. Go beach-combing and wine-tasting in Santa Barbara. Tour grandiose Hearst Castle in San Simeon. Witness gray whales and sea lions off rugged Monterey Bay. Camp and hike the unspoiled wilderness of Big Sur. Where to stop—and how long to stay—is up to you.

inspires you to respond to all of the big questions about life, humanity, and meaning. How to answer? Just stare.

Old Mission Santa Barbara

Bridalveil Fall in Yosemite

▶ WHEN TO GO

The West's best feature is its all-season appeal. That said, this trip is best in the summer and early fall, when Highway 120 through Yosemite will most likely be open, although Las Vegas and the Grand Canyon will be quite warm. It's possible to bypass Highway 120 in the winter and spring by taking a different route, but it will add hours and miles to the trip. Be aware that summer brings the most visitors, whether to sweat through the crowds at Disneyland, experience San Francisco charm or Las Vegas glitz, or take in the natural wonders of Yosemite and the Grand Canyon.

▶ BEFORE YOU GO

Even though this is a road trip, it's good to book hotels and rental cars in advance for the best rates and availability, especially in the summer which is high tourist season. If you plan to rent a car in one city and return it in another (for example, rent the car in San Francisco and return it in Los Angeles), you should expect to pay an additional fee, which can be quite high.

High-season travelers should also plan ahead for the big-name attractions. If you have your heart set on visiting Alcatraz in San Francisco, purchase tickets at least two weeks in advance. You'll save money buying advance tickets for Disneyland online as well. Reservations are pretty much essential at campgrounds near the Grand Canyon and Yosemite. If you plan to stay at Yosemite's

a vineyard in the green hills of San Luis Obispo

historic Ahwahnee Hotel or dine in its restaurant, make reservations as far in advance as possible.

The easiest places to fly into are San Francisco, Los Angeles, and Las Vegas. If you're flying into San Francisco, you can avoid some of the hassle of San Francisco International Airport (SFO) by flying into nearby Oakland or San Jose. Similarly, Los Angeles offers several suburban airports—Burbank, Long Beach, and Ontario—which are typically less congested than Los Angeles International Aiport (LAX).

Coming to the United States from abroad? You'll need your passport and possibly a visa.

Bring layered clothing. Expect desert heat in Las Vegas and the Grand Canyon in the summer, but also be prepared for cooler temperatures. Summer fog is likely along the California coast, and is pretty much guaranteed in San Francisco, making the air damp and chilly. No matter what, bring (and use!) sunscreen; that cold fog doesn't stop the rays from burning unwary beachcombers.

Hit the Road

▶ THE 14-DAY BEST OF THE WEST

You can hit the top destinations in fourteen days by driving in a rough loop. The day-by-day route below begins in San Francisco, but you can just as easily start in Los Angeles or Las Vegas if that works better for you. For detailed directions for each leg of this road trip, including advice on where to stop for a meal or to spend the night, see the *Driving Directions* at the beginning of each chapter.

Days 1-3
SAN FRANCISCO
Three days are perfect for a whirlwind romance with the city of San Francisco (see details and more suggestions on page 28). Extend the love affair with side trips to wander the redwoods in Marin (see page 37) or

imbibe from the venerated grapes of wine country (see page 44).

Days 4-5
DRIVING TO YOSEMITE
FROM SAN FRANCISCO
170 MILES / 4 HOURS
Head to Yosemite via Highway 120 from the west. The 170-mile drive to the Big Oak entrance takes at least four hours; however, traffic, especially in summer and on weekends, can make it much longer.

YOSEMITE
Leave San Francisco by 8 A.M. to reach Yosemite by noon. Plan to arrive midweek so that you can camp overnight (there are

Half Dome, Yosemite

four first-come, first-served campgrounds on Tioga Pass Road), or book a room ahead of time at the park's Awhahnee Hotel. Spend your days getting back to nature, and hit all of the park's world-class photo-ops: El Capitan, Bridaveil Fall, or Half-Dome (see details and more suggestions on page 113).

Days 6-7
DRIVING TO LAS VEGAS FROM YOSEMITE
415 MILES / 8 HOURS

For most of the year, the best route is via Tioga Pass (if you're traveling in winter or spring, check to make sure that it's open before heading out). The Nevada route is the most direct: the 415-mile drive to Las Vegas takes 7 hours, 45 minutes. Follow Highway 120 east to U.S. 6 in Benton. Take U.S. 6 northeast to Coaldale, where it shares the road with U.S. 95 south to Tonopah, which makes a good stopover. It's then a 210-mile straight shot on U.S. 95 south to Vegas.

The California route is more scenic. It's only a few miles farther but 45 minutes longer,

traversing Mammoth Lakes, Bishop, and Lone Pine. East of Lone Pine, Highway 136 becomes Highway 190, which winds through Death Valley. A right turn onto the Daylight Pass Road leads to the Nevada border and Highway 374 just before Beatty, which makes a good place to stop. From Beatty, U.S. 95 leads southeast to Las Vegas.

LAS VEGAS

Sin City makes a lively, somewhat surreal stop-over between the natural wonders of Yosemite and the Grand Canyon. This is the place to overindulge: try your hand at blackjack, take in a show (Blue Man Group, anyone?), sample gourmet food, and drink more than your share of exotic adult beverages (see details and more suggestions on page 200).

DRIVING TO THE GRAND CANYON
FROM LAS VEGAS
280 MILES / 5 HOURS

The 280-mile drive to the Grand Canyon takes about five hours. Head south on U.S.

the Grand Canyon

Tourists walk the Hollywood Walk of Fame.

Los Angeles skyline

93, breezing over the new Hoover Dam Bypass, and stop over in Kingman, Arizona. Then take I-40 east to Williams (115 miles), where you pick up Highway 64 for 60 miles to the Grand Canyon's South Rim.

Days 8-9
THE GRAND CANYON

Overnight in Kingman, in Williams, or in Grand Canyon National Park itself. Spend the day exploring the Canyon. Hike the Rim Trail, enjoy the views from Yavapai Observation Station, and visit Bright Angel Lodge (see details and more suggestions on page 292).

DRIVING TO LOS ANGELES
FROM THE GRAND CANYON
494 MILES / 8 HOURS

The 494-mile drive to Los Angeles takes 7–8 hours. Take I-40 west to Barstow. From Barstow, take I-15 south, then take I-10 west into the heart of L.A. Be prepared to slow

down when you hit the L.A. traffic, which may extend your driving time exponentially.

Days 10-12
LOS ANGELES

With three days in Los Angeles, you can focus a day on Hollywood glitz, a day on the kind of fun only Disneyland can provide, and still fit in some relaxation on the beach in between (see details and more suggestions on page 337).

Days 13-14
DRIVING TO SAN FRANCISCO
FROM LOS ANGELES
500 MILES / 9 HOURS

This scenic route runs almost 500 miles and can easily take 8–9 hours to drive (without stops). From Los Angeles, take U.S. 101 north. You can alterate between U.S. 101 and Highway 1 (which are sometimes the same road) depending upon where you want to stop and linger.

Pacific coastline in Big Sur, California

PACIFIC COAST HIGHWAY

While it's possible to make the coastal drive from Los Angeles to San Francisco in one long 9-hour day, this is one stretch of your western road trip that you won't want to power through. Stay longer depending upon where your interests lie. Soak up surf culture in Ventura or experience fine living in Santa Barbara. Spend at least one night along the way; Pismo Beach and San Luis Obispo are around the midway point and make good stopovers. Then take in either Hearst Castle, Big Sur, or Monterey Bay on your way back to San Francisco.

Options for Shorter Trips

If you have less time, you can eliminate a day here or there, or spend some days driving farther without stops. One option is to follow the shorter, inland route via I-5, which compresses the drive between Los Angeles and San Francisco to around seven hours. Ignoring the Las Vegas and the Grand Canyon legs and driving directly from Yosemite to Los Angeles (eight hours) will allow you to hit the highlights of the Golden State in about a week. In a long four-day weekend, it's possible to combine San Francisco and Yosemite. With just four days, you can also plan a great Pacific Coast Highway road trip, including San Francisco and Los Angeles. And four days is all you need to see Los Angeles, the Grand Canyon, and Las Vegas—a road trip that Southern California natives have perfected.

SAN FRANCISCO

Famed for its ethnic diversity, liberal politics, and chilling dense fog, the San Francisco Bay Area manages somehow both to embody and to defy the stereotypes heaped on it. Street-corner protests and leather stores are certainly part of the landscape, but family farms and friendly communities also abound. English blends with languages from around the world in an occasionally frustrating, often joyful cacophony. Those who've chosen to live here often refuse to live anyplace else, despite the infamous cost of housing and the occasional violent earthquake.

San Francisco perches restlessly on an uneven spit of land overlooking the Bay on one side and the Pacific Ocean on the other. Refer to the City as "San Fran," or worse, "Frisco," and you'll be pegged as a tourist immediately.

To locals, the City is the City, and that's that. Urban travelers can enjoy San Francisco's great art, world-class music, unique theater and comedy, and a laid-back club scene. Many visitors come to the City solely for the food; San Francisco functions as a culinary trendsetter that competes with the likes of Paris for innovation and prestige.

The Golden Gate Bridge leads into the North Bay, with its reputation for fertile farmland, intense material wealth, windswept coasts, and towering redwoods. An adventure here can be urban and touristy or rural and outdoorsy. The far more locally used Bay Bridge leads to the East Bay, with an emphasis on ex-military and pro sports culture, especially in Oakland and in more residential Alameda, formerly occupied by the Navy.

© KATHRYN OSGOOD

HIGHLIGHTS

◖ Cable Cars: Get a taste of free-spirited San Francisco – not to mention great views of Alcatraz and the Bay – via open-air public transit (page 23).

◖ Ferry Building: The 1898 Ferry Building has been renovated and reimagined as the foodie mecca of San Francisco. The Tuesday and Saturday farmers market is not to be missed (page 29).

◖ Alcatraz: Spend the day in prison...at the historically famous former maximum security penitentiary in the middle of the Bay. Audio tours bring to life the cells that Al Capone, George "Machine Gun" Kelly, and Robert "Birdman of Alcatraz" Stroud called home (page 31).

◖ Exploratorium: Kids and adults alike love to explore the Exploratorium, San Francisco's innovative and interactive science museum. The exhibits here are meant to be touched, heard, and felt (page 36).

◖ The Presidio: The original 1776 El Presidio de San Francisco is now a dormant military installation and national park. Tour the historic buildings that formerly housed a military hospital, barracks, and fort – all amid a peaceful and verdant setting (page 37).

◖ Golden Gate Bridge: Nothing beats the view from one of the most famous and fascinating bridges in the country. Pick a fogless day for a stroll or bike ride across the 1.7-mile span (page 39).

◖ de Young Museum: The revamped de Young has become the showpiece of Golden Gate Park. A mixed collection of media and regions is highlighted by the 360-degree view from the museum's tower (page 48).

◖ California Academy of Sciences: Wander a self-contained rainforest in this state-of-the-art museum with a decidedly ecological bent (page 48).

◖ City Lights Books: The bookstore that ignited the Beat movement in the 1950s still fuels San Francisco's independent literary spirit today (page 65).

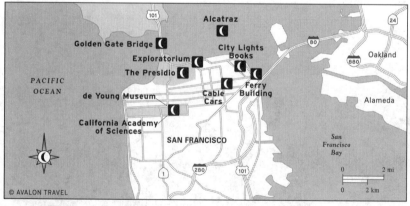

LOOK FOR ◖ TO FIND RECOMMENDED SIGHTS, ACTIVITIES, DINING, AND LODGING.

But it's also home to erudite, progressive (and sometimes aggravating) Berkeley—the birthplace of many liberal political movements from the 1960s all the way up to today. The original University of California sits in Berkeley, offering protest groups for liberals and top-flight technical educations to multitudinous engineers.

South of the City, Silicon Valley is all about the technology. With the likes of Hewlett-Packard, Apple Computer, Google, and eBay headquartered here, it's no surprise that even the museums run to technology and the residents all seem to own the latest iPod. Visitors gravitate toward the rarified landscape of Stanford University and the multicultural wonderland of San Jose.

For a more relaxed, outdoorsy experience, the Coastside region has a small-town feel with big-time extreme ocean sports. Locals know that this is not Southern California, and pack sweatshirts and parkas as well as swimsuits and sun hats for a day at the beach in Half Moon Bay or Pescadero.

Driving to San Francisco

DRIVING TO SAN FRANCISCO FROM LOS ANGELES

From Los Angeles, the quickest route to San Francisco is north on **I-5**. This route runs just under 400 miles and takes about six hours of drive time (without traffic). The drive on I-5 is straight and flat, and not particularly scenic, filled with trucks and highway patrol cars that can slow traffic considerably. On holiday weekends, the drive time can increase to 10 hours.

From Los Angeles, most freeways lead or merge onto I-5 north and ascend through the Grapevine. This hilly, high-elevation section of the freeway, between LA and Bakersfield can close in winter due to snow and ice (and sometimes in summer due to wildfires). From November to March, tule fog (thick, ground-level fog) can also seriously impede driving conditions and reduce visibility to a crawl. Before you hit the road, check the Caltrans website (www.dot.ca.gov) for weather and fog reports for the Grapevine and I-5.

The multilane I-5 eventually narrows to two lanes north of Los Angeles and remains so for the next 300 miles until splitting off onto I-580 west (Tracy and San Francisco) to the Bay Area. Merge onto I-580 west and then merge (right) again onto I-80 west. Follow signs for San Francisco and the Bay Bridge/I-80 (toll $6) for the next 45–50 miles.

The coastal route from Los Angeles is known as the **Pacific Coast Highway** (U.S. 101 and Highway 1). This scenic route runs almost 500 miles and can easily take eight hours to drive. What you may lose in time and expediency on I-5, you more than make up for in gorgeous coastal scenery that takes in Santa Barbara, Big Sur, and Monterey. U.S. 101 is long, narrow, and winding; in winter rock slides and mud slides may close portions of the road entirely. Always check Caltrans (www.dot. ca.gov) for traffic conditions before starting your journey.

From Los Angeles, take U.S. 101 north (past Oxnard, U.S. 101 also follows Highway 1). At Gaviota, U.S. 101 turns inland toward Buellton and Santa Maria before rejoining Highway 1 again at Pismo Beach. At San Luis Obispo, U.S. 101 and Highway 1 split again: Highway 1 continues west along the Big Sur coast; U.S. 101 moves inland through Paso Robles up toward Salinas, Gilroy, and San Jose. Note that U.S. 101 is a more direct route to San Francisco; Highway 1, while scenic, is longer and will end at Highway 17 in Santa Cruz, which is often clogged with traffic and can be dangerous in winter.

DRIVING TO SAN FRANCISCO FROM YOSEMITE

Yosemite National Park is 200 miles from San Francisco, a drive of 4–4.5 hours. The trip

SAN FRANCISCO

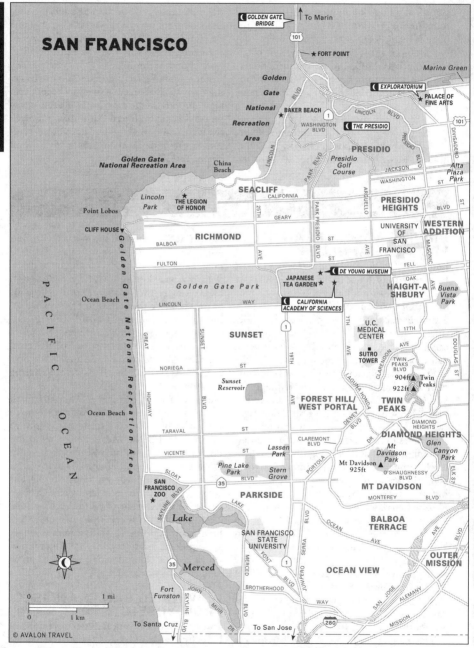

☾ GOLDEN GATE BRIDGE

To Marin

101

★ FORT POINT

Golden

Gate

National

Recreation

Area

Marina Green

☾ EXPLORATORIUM

★ PALACE OF FINE ARTS

101

BAKER BEACH ★

WASHINGTON BLVD

1

LINCOLN BLVD

☾ THE PRESIDIO

PRESIDIO

Golden Gate National Recreation Area

China Beach

Presidio Golf Course

JACKSON

WASHINGTON ST

Alta Plaza Park

SEACLIFF

CALIFORNIA

PRESIDIO HEIGHTS

BLVD ST

Lincoln Park

★ THE LEGION OF HONOR

Point Lobos

25TH

GEARY

PARK PRESIDIO BLVD

ARGUELLO

UNIVERSITY OF SAN FRANCISCO

WESTERN ADDITION

MASONIC

CLIFF HOUSE ▽

RICHMOND

BALBOA

AVE

ST

ST

FELL

FULTON

OAK

Golden Gate National Recreation Area

Golden Gate Park

JAPANESE TEA GARDEN ★

★ DE YOUNG MUSEUM

HAIGHT-ASHBURY

Buena Vista Park

Ocean Beach

LINCOLN

WAY

☾ CALIFORNIA ACADEMY OF SCIENCES

7TH

U.C. MEDICAL CENTER

17TH

AVE

DOUGLAS

SUNSET

19TH

GREAT HIGHWAY

SUNSET BLVD

ST

NORIEGA

ST

AVE

LAGUNA HONDA

CLARENDON

SUTRO TOWER ■

TWIN PEAKS BLVD

904ft ▲

922ft ▲

Twin Peaks

TWIN PEAKS

Ocean Beach

Sunset Reservoir

FOREST HILL/ WEST PORTAL

DEWEY BLVD

DIAMOND HEIGHTS

TARAVAL

ST

CLAREMONT BLVD

PORTOLA DR

Mt Davidson Park

Glen Canyon Park

VICENTE

ST

DIAMOND HEIGHTS

ELK ST

Lassen Park

Mt Davidson ▲ 925ft

O'SHAUGHNESSY BLVD

SLOAT

Pine Lake Park

Stern Grove

BLVD

MT DAVIDSON

SAN FRANCISCO ZOO ★

35

SKYLINE BLVD

PARKSIDE

LAKE

MONTEREY

BLVD

BALBOA TERRACE

Lake Merced

SAN FRANCISCO STATE UNIVERSITY

MERCED

FONT BLVD

1

OCEAN

AVE

SERRA

JUNIPERO

BLVD

AVE

OUTER MISSION

35

Merced

OCEAN VIEW

SAN JOSE

ALEMANY

Fort Funston

JOHN MUIR DR

SKYLINE BLVD

BROTHERHOOD

WAY

280

MISSION

To Santa Cruz

To San Jose

PACIFIC OCEAN

0 ___ 1 mi
0 ___ 1 km

© AVALON TRAVEL

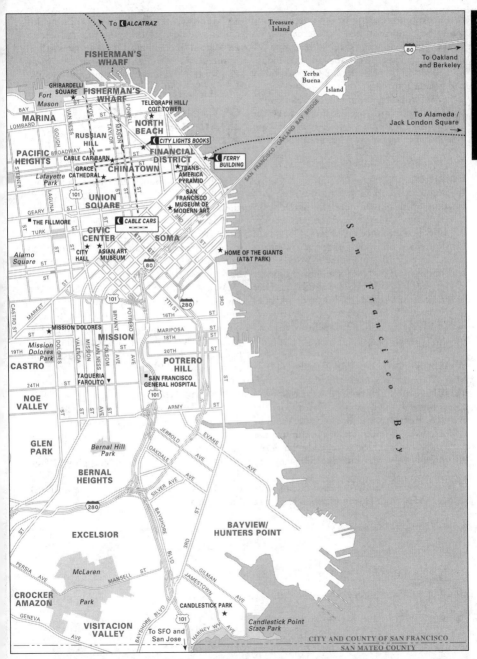

To ☾ALCATRAZ

Treasure
Island

FISHERMAN'S
WHARF

80
To Oakland
and Berkeley

Yerba
Buena
Island

To Alameda /
Jack London Square

GHIRARDELLI
SQUARE
Fort
Mason
FISHERMAN'S
WHARF

MARINA
BAY

LOMBARD

TELEGRAPH HILL/
COIT TOWER

NORTH
BEACH

PACIFIC
HEIGHTS
BROADWAY
RUSSIAN
HILL

VAN NESS

GOUGH

CITY LIGHTS BOOKS

CABLE CAR BARN

FINANCIAL
DISTRICT

FERRY
BUILDING

SAN FRANCISCO OAKLAND BAY BRIDGE

GRACE
CATHEDRAL
Lafayette
Park
CHINATOWN
TRANS-
AMERICA
PYRAMID

STEINER

UNION
SQUARE

SAN
FRANCISCO
MUSEUM OF
MODERN ART

LAGUNA

GEARY

THE FILLMORE

CABLE CARS

TURK

CIVIC
CENTER

SOMA

Alamo
Square

CITY
HALL

ASIAN ART
MUSEUM

80

HOME OF THE GIANTS
(AT&T PARK)

S
a
n

CASTRO ST

MARKET

101

POTRERO

7TH ST

280

3RD

MISSION DOLORES

16TH

BRYANT

MISSION

MARIPOSA

18TH

Mission
Dolores
Park
19TH
DOLORES
VALENCIA
MISSION
VAN NESS
FOLSOM
AVE

20TH

F
r
a
n
c
i
s
c
o

B
a
y

CASTRO

24TH

POTRERO
HILL

TAQUERIA
FAROLITO

SAN FRANCISCO
GENERAL HOSPITAL

101

NOE
VALLEY

ARMY

ST

GLEN
PARK

Bernal Hill
Park

JERROLD

EVANS

BERNAL
HEIGHTS

OAKDALE

AVE

AVE

280

SILVER AVE

BAYSHORE

3RD

BAYVIEW/
HUNTERS POINT

EXCELSIOR

PERSIA AVE

McLaren

MANSELL ST

BLVD

GILMAN AVE

CROCKER
AMAZON

Park

JAMESTOWN

AVE

GENEVA

BAYSHORE BLVD

101

CANDLESTICK PARK

Candlestick Point
State Park

VISITACION
VALLEY

AVE

HARNEY WY

AVE

To SFO and
San Jose

CITY AND COUNTY OF SAN FRANCISCO
SAN MATEO COUNTY

may require navigating heavy traffic in and out of Yosemite National Park (especially on weekends), the annual closure of Highway 120 (a.k.a. Tioga Pass), twists and turns on mountain roads, and traffic in the Central Valley and greater Bay Area.

For information about current road conditions and standard road closures, check the Yosemite park website (www.nps.gov/yose/planyourvisit/conditions.htm) or call 209/372-0200.

Summer

In summer, park roads and surrounding freeways are open, but they are also heavily trafficked. From Yosemite, exit the park via the Big Oak Flat entrance on Highway 120 west to Manteca. Follow Highway 120 west for about 100 miles as it merges with Highway 49 and Highway 108. Near Manteca, Highway 120 merges into I-5. Take I-5 south for about two miles, then take I-205 west for 14 miles to I-580 west. In about 45 miles, I-580 merges with I-80 onto the Bay Bridge (toll $6) and into San Francisco.

Winter

Many Yosemite park roads are closed in winter. Tioga Pass and Highway 120—the east–west access through the park—are closed from the end of September until May or June. In addition, Highway 120 west and north through the park and into San Francisco can also be closed due to snow. In winter, chains can be required on park roads at any time.

If traveling from Yosemite September through May, your surest access is Highway 140 and the Arch Rock entrance. From this entrance, follow Highway 140 west to Merced. In Merced, merge onto Highway 99 north to Manteca. At Manteca, merge onto Highway 120 west, then continue the summer route to I-5, I-205, I-580, and I-80 in San Francisco.

GETTING THERE BY AIR, TRAIN, OR BUS
Air

San Francisco International Airport (SFO, 800/435-9736, www.flysfo.com) isn't within the City of San Francisco; it is actually about 13 miles south in the town of Millbrae, right on the Bay. You can easily get a taxi ($35) or other ground transportation into the heart of the City from the airport. Both Caltrain and BART are accessible from SFO, and some San Francisco hotels offer complimentary shuttles from the airport as well. You can also rent a car here.

As one of the 30 busiest airports in the world, SFO has long check-in and security lines much of the time and dreadful overcrowding on major travel holidays. On an average day, plan to arrive at the airport about two hours before your domestic flight, three hours before an international flight.

Train and Bus

Amtrak does not run directly into San Francisco. You can ride into San Jose, Oakland, or Emeryville stations, then take a connecting bus into San Francisco.

Greyhound (200 Folsom St., 415/495-1569, www.greyhound.com, 5:30 A.M.–1 A.M. daily) offers bus service to San Francisco from all over the country.

Sights

UNION SQUARE AND NOB HILL

Wealth and style mark these areas near the center of San Francisco. Known for their lavish shopping areas, cable cars, and mansions, Union Square and Nob Hill draw both local and visiting crowds all year long. Sadly, the stunning 19th-century mansions built by the robber barons on Nob Hill are almost all gone—shaken then burned in the 1906 earthquake and fire. But the area still exudes a certain elegance; restaurants are particularly good on Nob Hill.

If you shop in only one part of San Francisco, make it Union Square. Even if you don't like chain stores, you can just climb up to the top of the Square itself, grab a bench, and enjoy the views and the live entertainment on the small informal stage.

◖ Cable Cars

Perhaps the most recognizable symbol of San Francisco is the cable cars (www.sfcablecar.com), originally conceived by Andrew Smith Hallidie as a safer alternative for traveling the steep, often slick hills of San Francisco. The cable cars ran as regular mass transit from 1873 into the 1940s, when buses and electric streetcars began to dominate the landscape. Dedicated citizens, especially "Cable Car Lady" Friedel Klussmann, saved the cable car system from extinction, and the cable cars have become a rolling national landmark.

Today, you can ride the cable cars from one tourist destination to another throughout the City for $6 per ride. A full day "passport" ticket (which also grants access to streetcars and buses) costs $14 and is totally worth it if you want to run around the City all day. Cable car routes can take you up Nob Hill, through Union Square, down Powell Street, out to Fisherman's Wharf, and through Chinatown. Take a seat, or grab one of the exterior poles and hang on! Just be aware that cable cars have open-air seating only, making a ride chilly on foggy days.

© ROBERT HOLMES/CALTOUR

San Francisco's cable cars are a rolling landmark.

Because everybody loves the cable cars, they get stuffed to capacity with tourists on weekends and with local commuters at rush hours. Expect to wait an hour or more for a ride from any of the turnaround points on a weekend or holiday. But a ride on a cable car from Union Square down to the Wharf is more than worth the wait. The views from the hills down to the Bay inspire wonder even in lifetime residents. Or make your way to the foot of Beach and Hyde Streets and board the Powell-Hyde cable car for gorgeous bay views as you crest Russian Hill around Filbert Street. A ride through Chinatown feels long on bustle but in fact reveals the lifestyle in a place that's unique.

Cable car aficionados can ride on the cars to **The Barn** (1201 Mason St., 415/474-1887, www.cablecarmuseum.org, 10 A.M.–6 P.M. daily Apr.–Sept., 10 A.M.–5 P.M. daily Oct.–Mar., free), a museum depicting the life and times of the San Francisco cable cars.

Grace Cathedral

A local icon, Grace Cathedral (1100 California St., 415/749-6300, www.gracecathedral.org, 7 A.M.–6 P.M. Mon.–Sat., 8 A.M.–6 P.M. Sun.) is many things to many people. The French Gothic–style edifice, completed in 1964, attracts architecture and beaux arts lovers by the thousands with its facade, stained glass, and furnishings. The labyrinths—replicas of the Chartres Cathedral labyrinth in France—appeal to meditative walkers seeking spiritual solace. Concerts featuring world music, sacred music, and modern classical ensembles draw audiences from around the Bay and farther afield.

But most of all, Grace Cathedral opens its doors to the community as a vibrant, active Episcopal church. The doctrine of exploration and tolerance matches well with the San Francisco community, of which the church remains an important part.

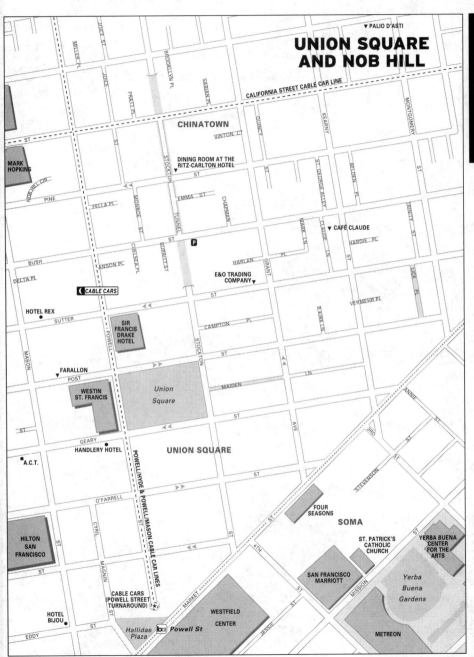

UNION SQUARE AND NOB HILL

▼ PALIO D'ASTI

CALIFORNIA STREET CABLE CAR LINE

MILLER PL

JOICE

PRATT AL

BROOKLYN PL

SABIN PL

MONTGOMERY

CHINATOWN

QUINCY

KEARNY

ST GEORGE ALLEY

BELDEN

ST

VINTON C

MARK HOPKINS

NOB HILL CIR

PINE

FELLA PL

MONROE

STOCKTON

TUNNEL

ST

DINING ROOM AT THE
RITZ-CARLTON HOTEL ▼

EMMA ST

CHAPMAN

MARK LN

CLAUDE LN

▼ CAFÉ CLAUDE

HARDIE PL

TRINITY

ST

P

BUSH

ANSON PL

CHELSEA PL

BURRITT ST

HARLAN

GRANT

PL

DELTA PL

E&O TRADING
COMPANY ▼

ST

VERMEHR PL

LICK PL

🌙 **CABLE CARS**

• HOTEL REX

SUTTER

POWELL

SIR FRANCIS DRAKE HOTEL

CAMPTON PL

STOCKTON

KIRK LN

ST

LN

MASON

▼ FARALLON

POST

WESTIN ST. FRANCIS

Union Square

MAIDEN

AVE

ANNIE

3RD

ST

ST

ST

ST

GEARY

• HANDLERY HOTEL

POWELL/HYDE & POWELL/MASON CABLE CAR LINES

UNION SQUARE

ST

STEVENSON

■ A.C.T.

O'FARRELL

CYRIL

ST

FOUR SEASONS

SOMA

ST

HILTON SAN FRANCISCO

ST

MAGNIN

4TH

ST

ST. PATRICK'S CATHOLIC CHURCH

MISSION

YERBA BUENA CENTER FOR THE ARTS

SAN FRANCISCO MARRIOTT

Yerba Buena Gardens

CABLE CARS
(POWELL STREET
TURNAROUND) 🚃

MARKET

• HOTEL BIJOU

EDDY

ST

Hallidae Plaza 🚃 *Powell St*

WESTFIELD CENTER

JESSIE

ST

METREON

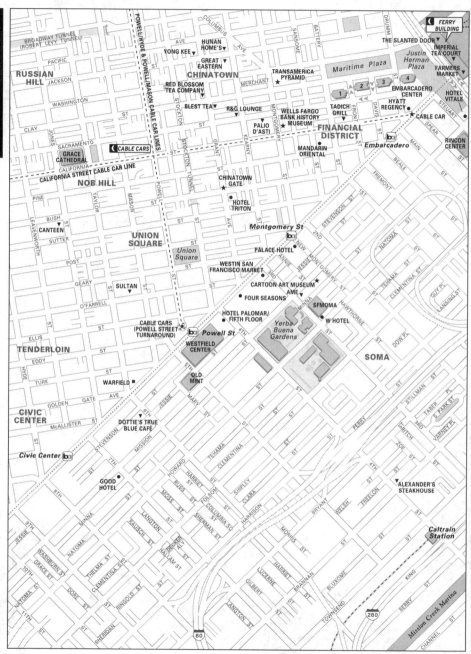

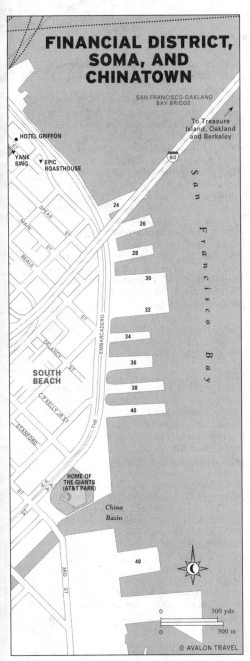

FINANCIAL DISTRICT AND SOMA

The skyscrapers of the Financial District create most of the San Francisco skyline, which extends out to the waterfront, locally called the Embarcadero. It's here that the major players of the San Francisco business world make and spend their money. The Stock Exchange sits in the middle of the action, making San Francisco not just rich but important on the international financial scene. But even businesspeople have to eat, and they certainly like to drink, so the Financial District offers a wealth of restaurants and bars. Hotels tend toward expensive tall towers, and the shopping here caters to folks with plenty of green.

SoMa (local shorthand for the South of Market area) was once a run-down postindustrial mess that rented warehouses to artists. Urban renewal and the ballpark have turned it into *the* neighborhood of the 21st century, complete with upscale restaurants and chichi wine bars.

Transamerica Pyramid

The single most recognizable landmark on the San Francisco skyline, the Transamerica Pyramid (600 Montgomery St.) was originally designed to look a little like a tree and to be taller and prouder than the nearby Bank of America building. Designed by William Pereira, the pyramid has four distinctive wings, plus the 212-foot aluminum-plated spire, which is lit up for major holidays. Visitors can no longer ride up to the 27th-floor observation deck (a post-9/11 precaution), but a "virtual observation deck" can be viewed via cameras in the lobby.

Wells Fargo Bank History Museum

One of a number of Wells Fargo museums in California and the West, the Wells Fargo Bank History Museum (420 Montgomery St., 415/396-2619, www.wellsfargohistory.com, 9 A.M.–5 P.M. Mon.–Fri., free) in San Francisco boasts the distinction of sitting on the site of the original Wells Fargo office, opened in 1852. Here you'll see an 1860s Concord stagecoach,

THREE DAYS IN SAN FRANCISCO

San Francisco may only be roughly seven miles long and seven miles wide, but it packs in historic neighborhoods, one of the West Coast's most iconic landmarks, and dozens of stomach-dropping inclines within its small area. Exploring all its hills and valleys takes some planning.

DAY 1

Start your day with breakfast at the **Ferry Building** (page 29). Consider sitting down for a meal at **Boulettes Larder** (page 86), or graze from the many vendors, including **Blue Bottle Café, Cowgirl Creamery,** and **Acme Bread Company.**

After touring the gourmet shops, catch the Muni F line (Steuart St. and Market St., $2) to Jefferson Street and take a stroll along **Fisherman's Wharf** (page 31). Near Pier 39, buy tickets for the ferry to **Alcatraz** (page 31). You can save some time and frustration by reserving tickets to Alcatraz before your trip.

After you escape from Alcatraz, make your way back to the foot of Beach and Hyde Streets and board the Powell-Hyde **cable car** ($6). Watch for gorgeous bay views as the cable car crests Russian Hill around Filbert Street. Hop off at Sutter Street and walk three blocks east past **Union Square** to lunch at **Café Claude** (page 85), a classic French brasserie. After lunch, window-shop around Union Square, meandering down to the Powell Street Muni station at Market Street.

Take the N Judah line ($2) to 9th Avenue and Irving Street, then follow 9th Avenue north into **Golden Gate Park** (page 46). The fabulous **de Young museum** (page 48) is directly across from the **California Academy of Sciences** (page 48). Art lovers and science geeks can part ways here – or squeeze in a trip to enjoy both.

Leave Golden Gate Park by walking east along John F. Kennedy Drive to the **Haight,** the hippie enclave made famous in the 1960s. Enjoy the finely crafted cocktails and nibbles at **Alembic** (page 55). Or catch a cab to the splurge of your choice: **Tadich Grill** (page 88) or **Farallon** (page 85). Consider ending your day with martinis at the swank **Top of the Mark** (page 51), with its view of the SF skyline.

DAY 2

Head to North Beach for brunch at **Mama's on Washington Square** (page 91), whose specialty "m'omelettes" have made this joint a local favorite for decades. Then explore the neighborhood. Be sure to stop in **City Lights** (page 65), the legendary Beat Generation bookstore, and enjoy an old-school cappuccino at **Caffé Trieste** (page 93). You might also want to climb to the top of **Coit Tower** (page 36) to catch a great view of the city skyline – look west to find crooked **Lombard Street** (page 35).

Drive or take a cab to the Mission district for the afternoon. If you're hungry, enjoy an authentic Mission burrito at **Papalote Mexican Grill** (page 96). For something sweeter, try **Tartine Bakery** (page 96) or **Bi-Rite Creamery & Bakeshop** (page 97). History buffs will want to visit 18th-century **Mission Dolores** (page 44). End your stay in the Mission with thin-crust pizzas and classic cocktails at **Beretta** (page 54) before hitting the clubs.

DAY 3

Start your day with dim sum at **Great Eastern** (page 90) before exploring **Chinatown.** If you'd rather get an early start, try breakfast at **Dottie's True Blue Café** (page 84).

From there, drive to the **Palace of Fine Arts** (page 36), one of the city's top photo-ops. Spend a few hours exploring the world of science at the **Exploratorium** (page 36). Or if the weather cooperates, explore **The Presidio** (page 37) and take a hike along Crissy Field. Stop for coffee and a snack at **Warming Hut Bookstore & Café,** then it's off to the ultimate San Francisco photo-op, the **Golden Gate Bridge** (page 39).

Here, you might consider crossing the Bridge to head north on U.S. 101 to explore **Marin** (see page 37), including **Muir Woods** and **Muir Beach.** Stay the night at the **Pelican Inn** or **Cavallo Point Lodge** before getting up early the next morning to continue on to **Wine Country** (see page 44).

gold dust and ore from the Gold Rush era, and an exhibit called "Wells Fargo CSI Officers in Pursuit." Enjoy the history of the stagecoach line that became one of the country's most powerful banks.

◖ Ferry Building

In 1898, the City of San Francisco created a wonderful new Ferry Building to facilitate commuting from the East Bay. But the rise of the automobile after World War II rendered the gorgeous construction obsolete, and its aesthetic ornamentation was covered over and filled in. But then the roads jammed up and ferry service began again, and the 1989 earthquake led to the removal of the Embarcadero Eyesore (an elevated freeway). Restored to glory in the 1990s, the San Francisco Ferry Building (1 Ferry Bldg., 415/983-8030, www.ferrybuildingmarketplace.com, 10 A.M.–6 P.M. Mon.–Fri., 9 A.M.–6 P.M. Sat., 11 A.M.–5 P.M. Sun., check with businesses for individual hours) stands at the end of the Financial District at the edge of the water. You can get a brief lesson in the history of the edifice just inside the main lobby, where photos and interpretive plaques describe the life of the Ferry Building.

Inside the handsome structure, it's all about the food. The famous **Farmers Market** (415/291-3276, www.ferrybuildingmarketplace.com/farmers_market.php, 10 A.M.–2 P.M. Tues. and Thurs., 8 A.M.–2 P.M. Sat.) draws crowds. Accompanying the fresh produce, the permanent shops provide top-tier artisanal food and drink, from wine to cheese to high-end kitchenware. Local favorites Cowgirl Creamery and Acme Bread Company maintain storefronts here. For immediate gratification, a few incongruous quick-and-easy restaurants offer reasonable eats.

Perhaps surprisingly, out on the water side of the Ferry Building, you can actually catch a ferry. Boats come in from Larkspur, Sausalito, Tiburon, Vallejo, and Alameda each day. Check with the Blue and Gold Fleet (www.blueandgoldfleet.com), Golden Gate Ferry (www.goldengateferry.org), and Bay Link Ferries (www.baylinkferry.com) for information about service, times, and fares.

AT&T Park

The name changes every few years, but the place remains the same. AT&T Park (24 Willie Mays Plaza, 415/972-1800, http://sanfrancisco.giants.mlb.com/sf/ballpark) is home to the San Francisco Giants, endless special events, several great restaurants, and arguably California's best garlic fries. From the ballpark, you can look right out onto the Bay. During baseball games, a motley collection of boats float beside the stadium, hoping that an out-of-the-park fly ball will come sailing their way.

Cartoon Art Museum

The Cartoon Art Museum (655 Mission St., 415/227-8666, http://cartoonart.org, 11 A.M.–5 P.M. Tues.–Sun., adults $7, seniors and students $5, children $3) offers a fun and funny outing for the whole family. The 20-year-old museum displays both permanent and traveling exhibits of original cartoon art, including

© RAFAEL RAMIREZ LEE/123RF

the Ferry Building

international newspaper cartoons, high-quality comics, and Pixar Studios' big-screen animated wonders. Even young children are captivated by the beauty and creativity found here.

San Francisco Museum of Modern Art

SFMOMA (151 3rd St., 415/357-4000, www. sfmoma.org, 11 A.M.–5:45 P.M. Fri.–Tues., 11 A.M.–8:45 P.M. Thurs., adults $18, seniors $12, students $11, children under 12 free), as it's fondly called, is a local favorite. Even if modern art isn't your favorite, SFMOMA has a wonderful array of pieces to suit every taste. Amazing permanent collections include works by Ansel Adams, Henri Matisse, and Shiro Kuramata. Enjoy the paintings and sculptures in the fine arts collections, the wonderful photography, the funky modern furniture, and some truly bizarre installation art. SFMOMA brings in a number of special exhibitions each year, featuring the works of the hottest current artists and retrospectives of post-1900 legendary figures.

CHINATOWN

The massive Chinese migration to California began almost as soon as the news of easy gold in the mountain streams made it to East Asia. And despite rampant prejudice and increasingly desperate attempts on the part of "good" Americans to rid their pristine country of these immigrants, the Chinese not only stayed but persevered and eventually prospered. Many never made it to the gold fields, preferring instead to remain in bustling San Francisco to open shops and begin the business of commerce in their new home. They were basically segregated to a small area beneath Nob Hill, where they created a motley collection of wooden shacks that served as homes, restaurants, shops, and more. This neighborhood quickly became known as Chinatown. Along with much of San Francisco, the neighborhood was destroyed in the 1906 earthquake and fire. Despite xenophobic attempts to relocate Chinatown as far away from downtown San Francisco as possible ("back to China" was one suggestion), the Chinese prevailed, and

San Francisco Museum of Modern Art (SFMOMA)

the neighborhood was rebuilt where it originally stood.

Today, visitors see the post-1906 visitor-friendly Chinatown that was built after the quake. Beautiful Asian architecture mixes with more mundane blocky city buildings to create a unique sky-scape. Small alleyways wend between the broad touristy avenues, creating an atmosphere that speaks of the secrecy and closed culture of the Chinese in San Francisco.

Chinatown Gate

Visible from the streets leading into Union Square, the Chinatown Gate (Grant Ave. and Bush St.) perches at the southern "entrance" to the famous Chinatown neighborhood. The gate, built in 1970, is a relatively recent addition to this history-filled neighborhood. The design features Chinese dragons, pagodas, and other charming details. The inscription reads "All under heaven is for the good of the people," a quote from Dr. Sun Yat-sen. Its gaudy colorful splendor draws droves of visitors with cameras each day; on weekends it can be tough to find a quick moment to get your own picture taken at the gate.

Chinatown truly is a sight in and of itself. Visitors stroll the streets, exploring the tiny alleys and peeking into the temples, admiring the wonderful Asian architecture on occasionally unlikely buildings. Among the best known of these is the **Bank of America Building** (701 Grant Ave.)—an impressive edifice with a Chinese tiled roof and 60 dragon medallions decorating the facade. The **East West Bank** (743 Washington St.) is even more traditional in its look. The small, beautiful building that acted as the Chinatown Telephone Exchange was constructed in this ultra-Chinese style just after 1906, when the Great Earthquake demolished the original structure. The Bank of Canton purchased the derelict building in 1960 and rehabilitated it; like many banks, it has changed hands since then. The **Sing Chong Building** (601 Grant Ave. at California St.) was another 1906 quick-rebuild, the reconstruction beginning shortly

after the ground stopped shuddering and the smoke cleared.

NORTH BEACH AND FISHERMAN'S WHARF

The Fisherman's Wharf and North Beach areas are an odd amalgam of old-school residential neighborhood and total tourist mecca. North Beach has long served as the Italian district of San Francisco, reflected in the restaurants in the area. Fisherman's Wharf was the spot where 19th-century Italians came to work; they were a big part of the fishing fleet that provided San Francisco with its legendary supply of fresh seafood.

Today, Fisherman's Wharf is *the* spot where visitors to San Francisco come to visit and snap photos. If you're not into crowds, avoid the area in the summer. For visitors who can hack a ton of other people, some of the best views of the air show during Fleet Week and the fireworks on the Fourth of July can be found down on the Wharf.

◖ Alcatraz

Going to Alcatraz (www.nps.gov/alcatraz), one of the most famous landmarks in the City, feels a bit like going to purgatory; this military fortress turned maximum-security prison, nicknamed "The Rock," has little warmth or welcome on its craggy forbidding shores. The fortress became a prison in the 19th century while it still belonged to the military, which used it to house Civil War prisoners. The isolation of the island in the Bay, the frigid waters, and the nasty currents surrounding Alcatraz made it a perfect spot to keep prisoners contained with little hope of escape and near-certain death if the attempt was ever made. In 1934, after the military closed down their prison and handed the island over to the Department of Justice, construction began to turn Alcatraz into a new style of prison ready to house a new style of prisoner: Depression-era gangsters. A few of the honored guests of this maximum-security penitentiary were Al Capone, George "Machine Gun" Kelly, and Robert Stroud, "the Birdman of Alcatraz."

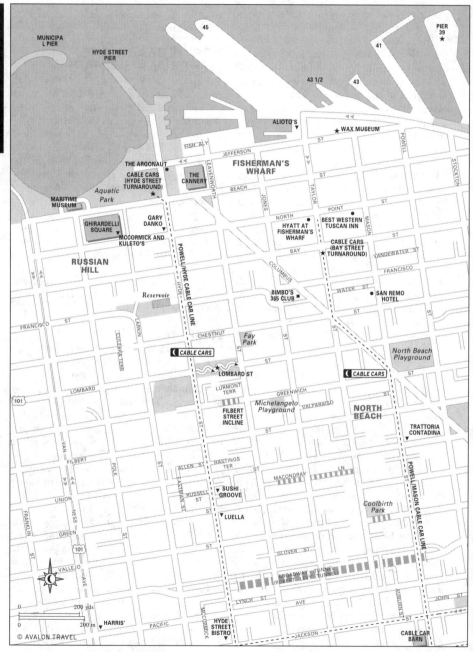

MUNICIPAL PIER

HYDE STREET PIER

45

PIER 39 ★

41

43 1/2

43

ALIOTO'S ▼

★ WAX MUSEUM

POWELL

FISH ALY

JEFFERSON

FISHERMAN'S WHARF

ST

STOCKTON

THE ARGONAUT

CABLE CARS (HYDE STREET TURNAROUND) ★

THE CANNERY

BEACH

LEAVENWORTH

JONES

TAYLOR

ST

POINT

MASON

ST

Aquatic Park

MARITIME MUSEUM

GHIRARDELLI SQUARE ▼

GARY DANKO ▼

NORTH POINT

HYATT AT FISHERMAN'S WHARF ●

BEST WESTERN TUSCAN INN ●

ST

MCCORMICK AND KULETO'S

CABLE CARS (BAY STREET TURNAROUND) ★

VANDEWATER ST

RUSSIAN HILL

HYDE

COLUMBUS

BAY

FRANCISCO

Reservoir

LARKIN

CULEBRATER

BIMBO'S 365 CLUB ■

WATER ST

SAN REMO HOTEL ●

ST

FRANCISCO ST

CHESTNUT

Fay Park

ST

ST

North Beach Playground

☾ CABLE CARS

LOMBARD

101

ST ★ LOMBARD ST

LURMONT TERR

GREENWICH

☾ CABLE CARS

ST

NORTH BEACH

FILBERT STREET INCLINE

Michelangelo Playground

VALPARAISO

TRATTORIA CONTADINA ●

VAN

FILBERT

POLK

ST

ALLEN ST

HASTINGS TER

ST

MACONDRAY LN

POWELL/MASON CABLE CAR LINE

UNION

EASTMAN ST

RUSSELL ST

SUSHI GROOVE ▼

Coolbirth Park

FRANKLIN

NESS

GREEN

▼ LUELLA

101

ST

ST

GLOVER ST

VALLEJO

AVE

BROADWAY TUNNEL (ROBERT C. LEVY TUNNEL)

AUBURN ST

0   200 yds

0   200 m

LYNCH ST

AVE

JOHN ST

© AVALON TRAVEL

▼ HARRIS'

PACIFIC

HYDE STREET BISTRO ▼

MCCORMICK

JACKSON

CABLE CAR BARN

POWELL/HYDE CABLE CAR LINE

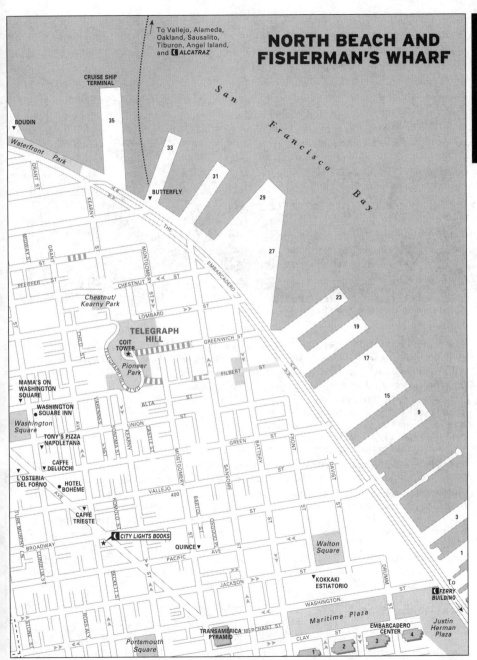

NORTH BEACH AND FISHERMAN'S WHARF

To Vallejo, Alameda,
Oakland, Sausalito,
Tiburon, Angel Island,
and ◗ *ALCATRAZ*

San Francisco Bay

CRUISE SHIP
TERMINAL

35

BOUDIN
▼

Waterfront Park

33

31

29

BUTTERFLY
▼

27

THE

EMBARCADERO

MIDWAY ST

GRANT ST

PFEIFFER ST

GRANT ST

KEARNY

MONTGOMERY ST

CHESTNUT

*Chestnut/
Kearny Park*

LOMBARD

CHILD ST

ST

23

19

**TELEGRAPH
HILL**

COIT
TOWER
★

*Pioneer
Park*

GREENWICH ST

17

FILBERT ST

15

TELEGRAPH HILL BLVD

9

MAMA'S ON
WASHINGTON
SQUARE
▼

VARENNES ST

ALTA ST

ST

WASHINGTON
SQUARE INN
●

*Washington
Square*

AVE

KEARNY

UNION ST

GREEN ST

BATTERY ST

FRONT ST

DAVIST

TONY'S PIZZA
NAPOLETANA
▼

SONOMA ST

CASTLE ST

ST

SANSOME ST

CAFFE
DELUCCHI
▼

MONTGOMERY ST

L

L'OSTERIA
DEL FORNO
▼

HOTEL
BOHÈME
●

ROMOLO ST

VALLEJO

400

BARTOL ST

ST

CAFFÈ
TRIESTE
●

★ ▼ *CITY LIGHTS BOOKS*

OSGOOD ST

ST

3

QUINCE ▼

PACIFIC

*Walton
Square*

ST

ST

1

TURK MURPHY LN

BROADWAY

CORDELIA ST

ST

BECKETT ST

ST

JACKSON

ST

DRUMM ST

ST

To
◗ *FERRY
BUILDING*

▼ KOKKAKI
ESTIATORIO

WASHINGTON ST

STONE ST

ROSSI ALLY

*Portsmouth
Square*

TRANSAMERICA MERCHANT ST
PYRAMID

Maritime Plaza

CLAY ST

1

2

EMBARCADERO
CENTER

3

4

*Justin
Herman
Plaza*

Alcatraz, also known as "The Rock"

© ROBERT HOLMES/CALTOUR

The prison closed in 1963, and in 1964 and 1969 occupations were staged by Indians of All Tribes, an exercise that eventually led to the privilege of self-determination for North America's original inhabitants.

Today, Alcatraz acts primarily as an attraction for visitors to San Francisco. **Alcatraz Cruises** (Pier 33, 415/981-7625, www.alcatrazcruises.com, 9:10 A.M.–3:55 P.M., 6:15 and 6:45 P.M. daily, adults $28–35, children $17–20) offers ferry rides out to Alcatraz and tours of the island and the prison. Tours depart from Pier 33. It's a good idea to buy tickets at least a week in advance, especially if you'll be in town in the summer and want to visit Alcatraz on a weekend. Tours often sell out, especially in the evening. Be carefully after dark; the prison and the island are both said to be haunted!

Fisherman's Wharf

Welcome to the tourist mecca of San Francisco! Just don't go looking for an actual wharf or single pier when you come to visit Fisherman's Wharf. In fact, the Fisherman's Wharf area (Beach St. from Powell St. to Van Ness Ave., backs onto Bay St., www.fishermanswharf.org), reachable by Muni F line, sprawls along the waterfront and inland several blocks, creating a large tourist neighborhood. The Wharf, as it's called by locals, who avoid the area at all costs, features all crowds, all the time. Be prepared to push through a sea of humanity to see sights, buy souvenirs, and eat seafood. Fisherman's Wharf includes many of the sights that people come to San Francisco to see: Pier 39, Ghirardelli Square, and, of course, **The Wax Museum of Fisherman's Wharf** (145 Jefferson St., 800/439-4305, www.waxmuseum.com, 10 A.M.–9 P.M. daily, adults $14, seniors and ages 12–17 $10, under age 12 $7), the presence of which tells most serious travelers all they need to know about the Wharf.

Pier 39

One of the most-visited spots in San Francisco, Pier 39 hosts a wealth of restaurants and shops. If you've come down to the pier to see the sealife, start with the unusual **Aquarium of the Bay** (415/623-5300, www.aquariumofthe-bay.com, 9 A.M.–8 P.M. daily summer, call for winter hours, adults $17, seniors and children $10). This 300-foot clear-walled tunnel lets visitors see thousands of species native to the San Francisco Bay, including sharks, rays, and plenty of fish. For a special treat, take the Behind the Scenes Tour or sign up for a Sleeps with the Sharks family sleepover. Farther down the pier, get personal (but not *too* close) to the local colony of **sea lions.** These big, loud mammals tend to congregate at K-Dock in the West Marina. The best time to see the sea lions is winter, when the population grows into the hundreds. To learn more about the sea lions, head for the interpretive center on Level 2 of the **Marine Mammal Center** (415/289-7325, www.marinemammalcenter.org, free).

A perennial family favorite, the **San Francisco Carousel** ($3 per ride) is painted with beautiful scenes of San Francisco. Riders on the moving horses, carriages, and seats can look at the paintings or out onto the pier. Kids also love the daily shows by local street performers. Depending on when you're on the pier, you might see jugglers, magicians, or stand-up comedians on the **Alpine Spring Water Center Stage** (show times vary, free).

San Francisco Maritime Museum

The Maritime Museum (900 Beach St., 415/561-7000, www.nps.gov/safr, 10 A.M.–6 P.M. daily, adults $5, children free) comprises two parts—the visitors center museum on the bottom floor of the Argonaut Hotel and the ships at permanent dock across the street at the Hyde Street Pier. While the visitors center museum presents some of the long and amazing maritime history of San Francisco, the fun comes from puttering up the Pier and climbing aboard the historic ships. The shiniest jewel of the Museum's collection is the 1886 square-rigged *Balclutha,* a three-masted schooner that recalls times gone by. There are also several steamboats, including the workhorse ferry *Eureka* and a cool old steam paddle-wheel tugboat called the *Eppleton Hall.* Be careful if you're tall—as with most

ships, these all have very short doorways and sometimes low ceilings. Ranger-led tours and programs, included in the price of a ticket, make this inexpensive museum more than worthwhile. Check the website for the fall concert series.

Ghirardelli Square

Jammed in with Fisherman's Wharf and Pier 39, Ghirardelli Square (900 North Point St., www.ghirardellisq.com), pronounced "GEAR-ah-DEL-ee," has recently reinvented itself as an upscale shopping, dining, and living area. Its namesake, the famous **Ghirardelli Chocolate Factory** (900 North Point St., 415/775-5500, www.ghirardelli.com, 9 A.M.–11 P.M. Sun.–Thurs., 9 A.M.–midnight Fri.–Sat.) sits at the corner of the square. Here you can browse the rambling shop and pick up truffles, wafers, candies, and sauces for all your friends back home. Finally, get in line at the ice cream counter to order a hot-fudge sundae. These don't travel well, so you'll have to enjoy it here. Once you've finished gorging on chocolate, you can wander out into the square to enjoy more shopping (there's even a cupcake shop if your teeth haven't dissolved yet) and the sight of an unbelievably swank condo complex overlooking the Bay.

Lombard Street

You've no doubt seen it in movies, on TV, and on postcards: Lombard Street, otherwise known as "the crookedest street in the world." The truth is, Lombard Street is a major artery running through San Francisco. So why bother braving the bumper-to-bumper cars navigating its zigzag turns? For one, you can't beat the view from the top. With its 27 percent grade, Lombard Street offers unobstructed vistas of San Francisco Bay, Alcatraz Island, Fisherman's Wharf, Coit Tower, and the City.

The section that visitors flock to spans only a block, from Hyde Street at the top to Leavenworth Street at the bottom. Lombard was originally created to keep people from rolling uncontrolled down the treacherously steep grade. Brave pedestrians can walk up and down the sides of the brick-paved street, enjoying the hydrangeas and Victorian mansions that line the roadway. For convenience during the peak summer months, take a cable car directly to the top of Lombard Street and walk down the noncurvy stairs on either side.

Coit Tower

It's big, it's phallic, and it may or may not have been designed to look like a fire-hose nozzle or a power station. But since 1933, Coit Tower (1 Telegraph Hill Blvd., 415/362-0808, 10 A.M.–6:30 P.M. daily, elevator ride adults $7, ages 11–17 $5, under age 11 $2, call for tour times) has beautified the City just as benefactor Lillie Hitchcock Coit intended when she willed San Francisco one-third of her monumental estate. Inside, murals depicting city life and works of the 1930s cover the walls. From the top of the tower on a clear day, you can see the whole of the City and the Bay. Part of what makes Coit Tower special is the walks up to it. Rather than contributing to the acute congestion in the area, consider taking public transit to the

area and walking up the Filbert Steps to the tower. It's steep, but there's no other way to see the lovely little cottages and gardens that mark the path up from the streets to the top of Telegraph Hill.

MARINA AND PACIFIC HEIGHTS

The Marina and Pacific Heights shelter some of the amazing amount of money that flows in the City by the Bay. The Marina is one of the San Francisco neighborhoods constructed on landfill (sand dredged up from the bottom of the ocean and piled in what was once a marsh). It was badly damaged in the 1989 Loma Prieta earthquake, but you won't see any of that damage today. Instead, you'll find a wealthy neighborhood, a couple of yacht harbors, and lots of good museums, dining, and shopping.

Palace of Fine Arts

The Palace of Fine Arts (3301 Lyon St., 415/567-6642, www.palaceoffinearts.org, 6 A.M.–9 P.M. daily) was originally meant to be nothing but a temporary structure—part of the Panama Pacific Exposition in 1915. But the lovely building won the hearts of San Franciscans, and a fund was started to preserve the Palace beyond the Exposition. Through the first half of the 20th century, efforts could not keep it from crumbling, but in the 1960s and 1970s, serious rebuilding work took place, and today the Palace of Fine Arts stands proud and strong and beautiful. It houses the Palace of Fine Arts Theater, which hosts events nearly every day, from beauty pageants to conferences on the future of artificial intelligence. It also houses the Exploratorium.

◖ Exploratorium

Kids around the Bay Area have loved the Exploratorium (3601 Lyon St., 415/561-0360, www.exploratorium.edu, 10 A.M.–5 P.M. Tues.–Sun., also some Mon. holidays, adults $15, students and seniors $12, ages 4–12 $10) for decades. This innovative museum makes science the most fun thing ever for kids of all ages; adults are welcome to join in on the interactive

Coit Tower

exhibits too. You can learn about everything from frogs to the physics of baseball, sound, and seismology. The Exploratorium seeks to be true to its name and encourage exploration into all aspects of science. For an utterly unusual experience, pay an extra $5 and walk bravely (and blindly) into the Tactile Dome, a lightless space where you can "see" your way only by reaching out and touching the environment around you.

Fort Mason

Once the Port of Embarkation from which the United States waged World War II in the Pacific, Fort Mason Center (Buchanan St. and Marina Blvd., 415/345-7500, www.fortmason.org, 9 A.M.–8 P.M. daily, parking up to $10) now acts as home to numerous nonprofit, multicultural, and artistic organizations. Where soldiers and guns departed to fight the Japanese, visitors now find dance performances, independent theatrical productions, art galleries, and the annual **San Francisco Blues Festival** (www.sfblues.com). At any time of year, a number of great shows go on in the renovated historic white and red buildings of the complex; check the online calendar to see what's coming up during your visit.

Other fun features include installations of the **Outdoor Exploratorium** (www.exploratorium.edu/outdoor, dawn–dusk daily). Ranging all over Fort Mason, the Exploratorium exhibits appeal to all five senses (yes, even taste) and teach visitors about the world around them—right there around them, in fact. You'll taste salt in local water supplies, hear a foghorn, and see what causes the parking lot to crack and sink. It's free, and it's fascinating—download a map from the website, or grab a guide from installation 5, Portable Observatories.

◖ The Presidio

It seems strange to think of progressive, peace-loving San Francisco as a town with tremendous military history, yet the City's warlike past is nowhere more evident than at the Presidio (Montgomery St. and Lincoln Blvd., 415/561-4323, www.nps.gov/prsf, visitors center

DAY TRIP TO MARIN

Muir Woods National Monument (Panoramic Hwy. off Hwy. 1, 415/388-2596, www.visitmuirwoods.com, www.nps.gov/goga, daily 9 A.M.-sunset, $7) comprises acres of staggeringly beautiful redwood forest nestled in Marin just north of San Francisco. The **Muir Woods Visitors Center** (daily 8 A.M.-4:30 P.M.) is a great place to begin your exploration. The visitors center abuts the main parking area and includes a bookstore and a café where you can purchase souvenirs and sustenance. The **Main Trail** (1 mile, easy) leads from the visitors center on a paved boardwalk through the beautiful redwoods; pick up a self-guided trail leaflet at the visitors center and follow the interpretive numbers along the trail to learn about the flora and fauna of this unique ecosystem.

After your hike, fill up on a hearty lunch of British comfort food at **The Pelican Inn** (10 Pacific Way, Muir Beach, 11:30 A.M.-3 P.M. and 5:30-9 P.M. daily, $15-30). Dark wood and a long trestle table give a proper Old English feel to the dimly lit dining room. It's just a short drive from the restaurant to lovely **Muir Beach** (www.nps.gov/goga, daily sunrise-sunset), perfect for wildlife-watching and beachcombing.

End the day with oysters and drinks at the Farley Bar at **Cavallo Point Lodge** (601 Murray Circle, Fort Baker, Sausalito, 415/339-4750, www.cavallopoint.com, 11 A.M.-11 P.M. Sun.-Thurs., 11 A.M.-midnight Fri.-Sat., $20). Snag a blanket and a seat on the porch to watch the fog roll in over the Golden Gate Bridge.

10 A.M.–4 P.M. Thurs.–Sun., trails dawn–dusk daily, free). This sweeping stretch of land running along the San Francisco Headlands down to the Golden Gate has been a military installation since 1776, when the Spanish created their El Presidio del San Francisco fort on the site. In 1846 the United States army took over

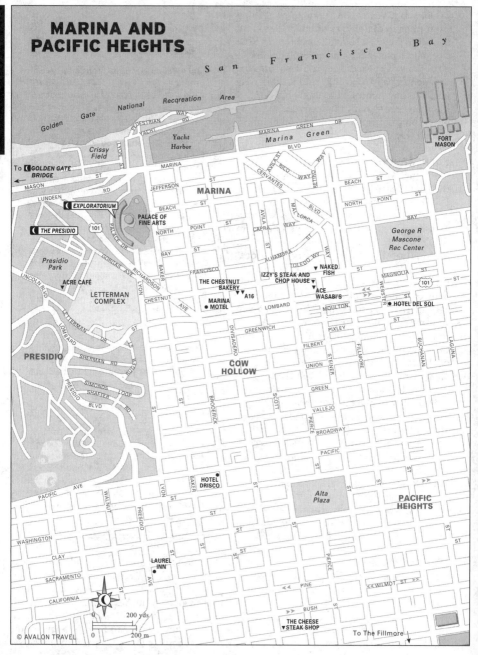

MARINA AND PACIFIC HEIGHTS

San Francisco Bay

Golden Gate National Recreation Area

Crissy Field

Yacht Harbor

Marina Green

FORT MASON

To GOLDEN GATE BRIDGE

EXPLORATORIUM

THE PRESIDIO

PALACE OF FINE ARTS

MARINA

George R Mascone Rec Center

Presidio Park

ACRE CAFÉ

LETTERMAN COMPLEX

NAKED FISH

THE CHESTNUT BAKERY

IZZY'S STEAK AND CHOP HOUSE

A16

ACE WASABI'S

MARINA MOTEL

HOTEL DEL SOL

PRESIDIO

COW HOLLOW

HOTEL DRISCO

PACIFIC HEIGHTS

Alta Plaza

LAUREL INN

THE CHEESE STEAK SHOP

To The Fillmore

0   200 yds
0   200 m

© AVALON TRAVEL

the site (peacefully), and in 1848 the American Presidio military installation formally opened. It was finally abandoned by the military and became a national park in 1994. The Presidio had a role in every Pacific-related war from the Civil War through Desert Storm.

To orient yourself among the more than 800 buildings that make up the Presidio, start at the visitors center or the **Warming Hut Bookstore & Café** (983 Marine Dr., 415/561-3040, 9 A.M.–5 P.M. daily). As you explore the huge park, you can visit the pioneering aviation area **Crissy Field,** Civil War–era fortifications at **Fort Point,** and the **Letterman Digital Arts Center** (Chestnut St. and Lyon St., www.lucasfilm.com), built on the site of the Letterman Army Hospital, which served as a top-notch care facility for returning wounded soldiers over more than a century's worth of wars.

Golden Gate Bridge

People come from the world over to see and walk the Golden Gate Bridge (U.S. 101/Hwy. 1 at Lincoln Blvd., 415/923-2000, http://goldengatebridge.org, cars $6, pedestrians free). A marvel of human engineering constructed in 1936 and 1937, the suspension bridge spans the narrow "gate" from which the Pacific Ocean enters the San Francisco Bay. On a clear day, pedestrians can see the whole Bay from the east sidewalk, then turn around to see the Pacific Ocean spreading out on the other. Or take in the stunning bridge view from the Marin Headlands barracks, looking down from the northwest and in toward the City skyline.

The bridge itself is not golden, but a rich orange color called "international orange" that shines like gold when the sun sets behind it on a clear evening. But newcomers to the City beware—not all days and precious few evenings at the bridge are clear. One of the most beautiful sights in San Francisco is the fog blowing in over the Golden Gate late in the afternoon. Unfortunately, once the fog stops blowing and settles in, the bridge is cold, damp, and viewless, so plan to come early in the morning, or

© ROBERT HOLMES / CALTOUR

The Golden Gate Bridge links San Francisco to Marin County.

pick spring or autumn for your best chance of a clear sight of this most famous and beautiful of artificial structures.

CIVIC CENTER AND HAYES VALLEY

Some of the most interesting neighborhoods in the City cluster toward its center. The Civic Center functions as the heart of San Francisco; the beautiful building actually houses the mayor's office and much of San Francisco's government. Visitors who last visited San Francisco a decade or more ago will notice that the Civic Center has been cleaned up quite a lot in the last few years. It's now safe to walk here—at least in the daytime.

As the Civic Center melts toward Hayes Valley, the high culture of San Francisco appears. Near the border you'll find Davies Symphony Hall, home of the world-famous San Francisco Symphony, and the War Memorial Opera House. And serving these, you'll find fabulous Hayes Valley hotels and restaurants.

City Hall

Look at San Francisco's City Hall (1 Dr. Carlton B. Goodlett Place, 415/554-6079, www.sfgov.org, 8 A.M.–8 P.M. Mon.–Fri.) and you'll think you've somehow been transported to Europe. The stately building with the gilded dome is the pride of the City and houses much of its government. Enjoy walking through the parklike square in front of City Hall (though this area can get a bit sketchy after dark). The inside has been extensively renovated after being damaged in the Loma Prieta earthquake in 1989. You'll find a combination of historical grandeur and modern accessibility and convenience as you tour the Arthur Brown Jr.–designed edifice.

Asian Art Museum

Across from City Hall is the Asian Art Museum (200 Larkin St., 415/581-3500, www.asianart. org, 10 A.M.–5 P.M. Tues.–Fri., adults $12, seniors $8, ages 13–17 $7, under age 13 free). Yup, that's it right there with the enormous Ionic columns and Eurocentric facade. But

SAN FRANCISCO CONVENTION & VISITORS BUREAU PHOTO BY PHILLIP H. COBLENTZ

the beautiful row of "painted ladies" in Alamo Square

inside you'll have an amazing metaphorical window into the Asian cultures that have shaped and defined San Francisco and the Bay Area. The second and third floors of this intense museum are packed with great art from all across Asia, including a Chinese gilded Buddha dating from A.D. 338. Sit down on a padded bench to admire paintings, sculpture, lacquered jade, textiles, jewels, and every type of art object imaginable. The breadth and diversity of Asian culture may stagger you; the museum's displays come from Japan and Vietnam, Buddhist Tibet, and ancient China. Special exhibitions cost extra—check the website to see what will be displayed on the ground floor galleries when you're in town. Even if you've been to the museum in the past, come back for a browse. The curators regularly rotate items from the permanent collection, so you'll probably encounter new beauty every time you visit.

Alamo Square

Possibly the most photographed neighborhood in San Francisco, Alamo Square (Hayes St. and Steiner St.) is home to the "painted ladies" on "postcard row." This is a row of stately Victorian mansions, all painted brilliant colors and immaculately maintained, that appear in many images of the City. Stroll in Alamo Square's green park and enjoy the serenity of this charming residential neighborhood.

MISSION AND CASTRO

Perhaps the most famous, or infamous, neighborhoods in the City are the Mission district and the Castro district. The Castro is the heart of gay San Francisco, complete with naughty shops, leather bars, and all sorts of, uh…adult festivals. It has become pretty touristy, but you can still find the occasional jewel here. Just don't expect the Halloween party you've heard about—the City has cracked down, and Halloween has become sedate in this party-happy neighborhood.

With its mix of Latino immigrants, working artists, and SUV-driving professionals, the Mission is a neighborhood bursting at the

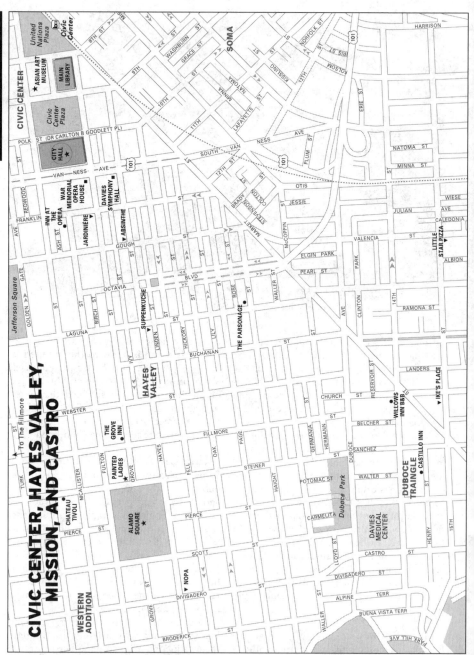

CIVIC CENTER, HAYES VALLEY, MISSION, AND CASTRO

DAY TRIP TO WINE COUNTRY

The Napa Valley lies less than 100 miles north of San Francisco, making it an ever-popular day-trip destination for visitors from San Francisco.

If you plan to tour the wine country, choose one region to explore. Napa and Sonoma are closest to San Francisco, about one hour's drive north. Traffic on the winding two-lane roads in these regions can easily become clogged with wine-tasting day-trippers, especially on weekends. To avoid the crowds, try to get an early start and visit on a weekday. Note that most wineries close by 4 P.M., and some are open only by appointment.

MORNING

From San Francisco, take the Golden Gate Bridge north to U.S. 101. From there, pick up Highway 37 east in Novato, then follow Highway 121 north and west through the Carneros wine region. Stop off for a bit of bubbly at gorgeous **Domaine Carneros** (1240 Duhig Rd., Napa, 707/257-0101, www.domainecarneros. com, 10 A.M.-5:45 P.M. daily), where the views and gardens are almost as impressive as the sparkling wines. Just down the road, stop at the unique **di Rosa Preserve** (5200 Carneros Hwy., Napa, 707/226-5991, www.dirosaart. org, 9:30 A.M.-3 P.M. Wed.-Fri., by appointment Sat.), filled with modern art galleries and an outdoor sculpture garden.

Highway 121 continues east to Highway 29, which leads north to Napa.

AFTERNOON

In downtown Napa, get your bearings at **Top Flight Wine Tasting** (1285 Napa Town Center, Napa, 707/253-9450, http://napavintages.

com, 1-8 P.M. Sun.-Wed., 2:30-10 P.M. Thurs.-Sat.) and sample some Napa vintages. Have lunch, or just pick up some picnic supplies, at **Oxbow Public Market** (644 1st St., Napa, 707/226-6529, www.oxbowpublicmarket.com, 9 A.M.-7 P.M. Mon.-Sat., 10 A.M.-6 P.M. Sun.) before hopping back on Highway 29.

Drive north to Rutherford and the **Rubicon Estate** (1991 St. Helena Hwy./Hwy. 29, Rutherford, 800/782-4266, www.rubiconestate. com, 10 A.M.-5 P.M. daily), owned by film director Francis Ford Coppola. The "Daniel" tasting ($25 pp) includes a 30-minute tour of the château, museum, and winery as well as five tastings. Also in Rutherford, **Grgich Hills** (1829 St. Helena Hwy./Hwy. 29, Napa, 707/963-2784, www.grgich.com, 9:30 A.M.-4:30 P.M. daily, tasting $10) offers a less-showy tasting experience.

Continue north on Highway 29 to St. Helena and the palatial estate of **Beringer Vineyards** (2000 Main St., St. Helena, 707/967-4412, www.beringer.com, 10 A.M.-6 P.M. June-Oct., 10 A.M.-5 P.M. Nov.-May, tours $20-30, tasting $15). Many of Beringer's wines are only available here.

EVENING

It's time to give your taste buds a different treat (and to let the traffic die down before your drive back to the City). Stop for dinner at the **Culinary Institute of America** (2555 Main St., St. Helena, 707/967-1010, www.ciachef. edu), where America's top chefs are trained. The Greystone Restaurant (11:30 A.M.-9 P.M. Sun.-Thurs., 11:30 A.M.-10 P.M. Fri.-Sat., $9-30) is where that food is served; you can even watch as it's prepared in the open kitchen.

---

seams with idiosyncratic energy. Changing from block to block, the zone manages to be blue-collar, edgy, and gentrified all at once. The heart of the neighborhood is still very much Latin American, with delicious burritos and *pupusas* around every corner. It's a haven for international restaurants and real bargains

in thrift shops, along with the hippest (and most self-conscious) clubs in the City.

Mission Dolores

Mission Dolores (3321 16th St., 415/621-8203, www.missiondolores.org, 9 A.M.–4:30 P.M. daily May–Oct., 9 A.M.–4 P.M. daily

From St. Helena, the drive back to San Francisco will take 1.5-2 hours. Alternately, spend the night at the aptly named **Zinfandel Inn** (800 Zinfandel Lane, St. Helena, 707/963-3512, www.zinfandelinn.com, $195-350) just down the road.

TOUR OPERATORS

Getting to and from Napa – not to mention driving up and down the valley in dense traffic – can be a headache. Tour companies offer vans, limos, minibuses, and even the occasional full-size charter bus that will pick you up from a predetermined San Francisco location. Depending on the tour company, you may stop at anywhere from two to six wineries for tastings in the Napa, Sonoma, or Russian River wine regions. Some tour operators run only prearranged itineraries, while others let customers request stops at specific wineries or even set a custom itinerary for the whole tour. Because it's a full day, most tour companies include a stop for lunch – usually a picnic at one of the wineries.

• **Platypus Tours** (707/253-2723, www.platypustours.com, $99 pp) is one of the most popular Napa tour companies.

Pickup: From the Ferry Building in San Francisco, take the Baylink Ferry at 8:30 A.M. to Vallejo (1 hour). A Platypus shuttle picks customers up in Vallejo at 9:40 A.M. Sunday, Tuesday, and Thursday; call 707/927-0669 for pickup any other day.
Length of trip: Daylong tours of Napa, Sonoma, or the Russian River wine regions run 8-10 hours (10:30 A.M.-4:30 or 5 P.M.).
Wineries: The number of wineries visited is

customized by the driver; a sample list of Napa wineries includes Cuvaison, Hill Family Estate, Jessup Cellars, Miner Family Vineyards, Mumm, Opus One, Peju, and Rubicon Estate.
Tasting fees: Not included; a picnic lunch is provided.

• **A Friend in Town** (AFiT, 800/960-8099, www.toursanfranciscobay.com, $600 per group) offers a more personalized experience. Travel by minivan in one of seven preset Wine Country tours, or create your own.

Pickup: Anywhere in the Bay Area
Length of trip: 9-10 hours
Number of wineries: The Discover Napa and Sonoma Tour includes 3-5 wineries (Benzinger, Kuleto, Domaine Carneros, and smaller wineries on the Silverado Trail).
Multilingual options: Available with advance notice for a fee
Tasting fees: Not included; lunch is included on some tours.

• **All San Francisco Tours** (866/654-1410, www.allsanfranciscotours.com, $73-145 pp) provides standard package bus tours of the wine country. The company lists eight wine tours, including a combo package with a stop at Muir Woods, and a smaller-group tour in a luxury van.

Pickup: Free from Downtown San Francisco, Fisherman's Wharf, and San Francisco Airport (8-8:50 A.M.)
Length of trip: 9 hours (8 A.M.-6 P.M.)
Number of wineries: 3-4; the Napa and Sonoma Valley Wine Tour includes Nicholson Ranch, Madonna Estate, and Sutter Home.
Tasting fees: Included; lunch is included in the Napa Valley Wine Country Tour.

Nov.–Apr., donation adults $5, children $3), formally named Mission San Francisco de Asís, was founded in 1776. Today, the Mission is the oldest intact building in the City, survivor of the 1906 earthquake and fire, the 1989 Loma Prieta quake, and more than 200 years of use. You can attend Roman Catholic services here

each Sunday, or you can visit the Old Mission Museum and the Basilica, which house artifacts from the Native Americans and Spanish of the 18th century. The beauty and grandeur of the Mission recall the heyday of the Spanish empire in California, so important to the history of the state as it is today.

GOLDEN GATE PARK AND THE HAIGHT

Perhaps the most spectacular sight in Golden Gate Park is, well, Golden Gate Park (main entrance at Stanyan St. at Fell St., McLaren Lodge Visitors Center at John F. Kennedy Dr., 415/831-2700, www.golden-gate-park.com). Acres of land include forest, desert, formal gardens, museums, and buffalo pasture. Enjoy a free concert in the summer or a walk under the trademark fog in the winter.

Haight-Ashbury

The neighborhood surrounding the intersection of Haight and Ashbury Streets (known locally as "the Haight") is best known for the wave of countercultural energy that broke out in the 1960s. The area initially was a magnet for drifters, dropouts, and visionaries who preached and practiced a heady blend of peace, love, and psychedelic drugs.

The door to the promised new consciousness never swung fully open, and then it swung

shut with a resounding bang. Today, thousands of visitors stand at the iconic intersection, and what they see is Ben & Jerry's. The district is still home to plenty of independent businesses, including vintage stores, lots of places to get pierced and tattooed, and, of course, head shops. Plenty of chain stores are interspersed with the indies, reminding visitors that the power of capitalism can intrude anywhere—even in a countercultural center.

A prettier aspect of local gentrification appears in the form of restored Victorian houses in the Haight. You can actually stay in a bright, funky Red Victorian, or check out the private homes on Page Street and throughout the neighborhood. To learn more about the history of the Haight and to walk past the famed homes of the Grateful Dead and Jefferson Airplane, take the **Flower Power Walking Tour** (starts at intersection of Stanyan St. and Waller St., 415/863-1621, www.hippygourmet.com, 9:30 A.M. Tues. and Sat., 11 A.M. Fri., $20).

GREENING THE CITY

Encompassing more than 1,000 acres of meadows, lakes, forests, and exotic gardens, Golden Gate Park provides plenty of refreshing green space and amusements for the urban dwellers and visitors it serves. Extending from Haight-Ashbury for more than three miles to the Pacific Ocean, the park makes a great spot for a long walk or bike ride; plenty of marked trails and paved pathways link the park's highlights. On weekends especially, the entire place is a hub of recreational pursuits, with softball teams and Frisbee tossers sharing grassy stretches with picnicking families.

Incredibly, this lushly landscaped haven, set aside by the city in 1870, was coaxed out of barren, wind-swept sand dunes. While the park's founder, William Hammond Hall, was the first to bring the dunes under control using innovative sand-reclamation techniques, it was his handpicked successor, John McLaren, who devoted most of his life to the landscaping and development of the park. Thanks to his foresight, winding pathways discourage speeding traffic, rich foliage attracts birds and wildlife, and more than a million trees shelter visitors from harsh winds.

Some of the park's most popular attractions – the **Japanese Tea Garden,** the **Music Concourse,** and the **Bison Paddock** – were part of the 1894 Midwinter International Exposition, Golden Gate Park's official opening extravaganza. A century later, the park became famous for its "Summer of Love" spectacles, including the 1967 Human Be-In, and a few decades later, Jerry Garcia's memorial. The popular **Conservatory of Flowers** (JFK and Conservatory Drs., 415/666-7001, www. conservatoryofflowers.org) reopened in 2003 after an eight-year renovation. The treasured Victorian landmark houses hundreds of exotic plants and flowers. A highlight is the Aquatic Plants exhibit, where beautiful pools of water feature floating flowers and giant lily pads.

de Young Museum

Haven't been to the City in a while? Take some time out to visit the completely rebuilt de Young Museum (50 Hagiwara Tea Garden Dr., 415/750-3600, http://deyoung.famsf.org, 9:30 A.M.–5:15 P.M. Tues.–Thurs. and Sat.–Sun., 9:30 A.M.–8:45 P.M. Fri., adults $10, seniors $7, children $6) in Golden Gate Park. Everything from the striking exterior to the art collections and exhibitions and the 360-degree panoramic view of San Francisco from the top of the tower has been renewed, replaced, or newly recreated. The reason for the recent renewal was the 1989 earthquake, which damaged the original de Young beyond simple repair. The renovation took more than 10 years, and the results are a smashing success. For a special treat, brave the lines and grab a meal at the museum's café.

The collections at the de Young include works in various media: painting, sculpture, textiles, ceramics, and more modern graphic designs and "contemporary crafts." Some collections focus on artists from the United States, while many others contain art from around the world. The exhibitions that come through the de Young range from the William Morris art nouveau art from Britain to the exquisite glass of the Chihuly collection. There's something for just about everyone—even classic art purists who eschew SFMOMA will find a gallery to love inside the de Young.

California Academy of Sciences

A triumph of the sustainable scientific principles it exhibits, the California Academy of Sciences (55 Music Concourse Dr., 415/379-8000, www.calacademy.org, 9:30 A.M.–5 P.M. Mon.–Sat., 11 A.M.–5 P.M. Sun., adults $30, ages 4–11 $20, students and seniors $25) drips with ecological perfection. From its grass-covered roof to its underground aquarium, visitors can explore every part of the universe. Wander through a steamy endangered rainforest contained inside a giant glass bubble, or travel through an all-digital outer space in the high-tech planetarium. More studious nature lovers can spend days examining every inch of the Natural History Museum, including favorite exhibits like the 87-foot-long blue whale skeleton, from the older incarnation of the Academy of Science. Though it might look and sound like an adult destination, in fact the new Academy of Sciences takes pains to make itself kid-friendly, with interactive exhibits, thousands of live animals, and endless opportunities for learning. How could kids not love a museum where the guards by the elevators have butterfly nets to catch the occasional "exhibit" that's trying to escape?

Japanese Tea Garden

The Japanese Tea Garden (7 Hagiwara Tea Garden Dr., 415/752-4227, http://japaneseteagardensf.com, 9 A.M.–6 P.M. daily Mar.–Oct., 9 A.M.–4:45 P.M. daily Nov.–Feb., adults $7, seniors $5, children $2) is a haven of peace and tranquility that's a local favorite within the park. The planting and design of the garden began in 1894 for the California Exposition. Today the flourishing garden displays a wealth of beautiful flora, including stunning examples of rare Chinese and Japanese plants, some quite old. As you stroll along the paths, you'll come upon sculptures, bridges, ponds, and even traditional *tsukubai* (a tea ceremony sink). You can visit the tea house, the brilliant pagoda and temple, and the gift shop as well.

San Francisco Botanical Gardens

Take a bucolic walk in the middle of Golden Gate Park by visiting the San Francisco Botanical Gardens (1199 9th Ave. at Lincoln Way, 415/661-1316, www.sfbotanicalgarden.org, 9 A.M.–6 P.M. daily Apr.–Oct., 10 A.M.–5 P.M. daily Nov.–Mar., adults $7, students and seniors $5, ages 5–11 $2, families $15, under age 5 and city residents with ID free). The 55-acre gardens play home to more than 8,000 species of plants from around the world, including a California Natives garden and a shady redwood forest. Fountains, ponds, meadows, and lawns are interwoven with the flowers and trees to create a peaceful, serene setting in the middle of the crowded city. The

© ROBERT HOLMES/CALTOUR

Conservatory of Flowers

Botanical Gardens are a great place to kick back with a book and a snack; the plants will keep you in quiet company as you rev up to tackle another round of touring.

Conservatory of Flowers

Lying at the northeastern entrance to Golden Gate Park, the Conservatory of Flowers (100 John F. Kennedy Dr., 415/831-2090, www.conservatoryofflowers.org, 10 A.M.–4:30 P.M. Tues.–Sun., adults $7, students and seniors $5, ages 5–11 $2) blooms year-round. The exotic flowers grow in several "galleries" within the enormous glassy white Victorian-style greenhouse. Rare, slightly scary orchids twine around rainforest trees, eight-foot lily pads float serenely on still waters, and cheerful seasonal flowers spill out of containers in the potted plant gallery.

If you're traveling with small kids, be aware that strollers are not permitted inside the conservatory; wheelchairs and power chairs are.

The Legion of Honor

A beautiful museum in a town filled with beauty, the Legion of Honor (100 34th Ave. at Clement St., 415/750-3600, http://legionofhonor.famsf.org, 9:30 A.M.–5:15 P.M. Tues.–Sun., adults $10, seniors $7, students and ages 13–17 $6) sits on its lonely promontory in Lincoln Park, overlooking the Golden Gate. A gift to the City from philanthropist Alma Spreckels in 1924, this French beaux arts–style building was built to honor the memory of California soldiers who died in World War I. From its beginning, the Legion of Honor was a museum dedicated to bringing European art to the population of San Francisco. Today, visitors can view gorgeous collections of European paintings, sculpture, and decorative arts, ancient artifacts from around the Mediterranean, thousands of paper drawings by great artists, and much more. Special exhibitions come from the Legion's own collections and museums of the world. If you love the living arts and music, visit the Florence Gould Theater or come to the museum on a Sunday for a free organ concert on the immense Skinner Organ, which is integral to the building's structure.

San Francisco Zoo

Lions and tigers and bears…and lemurs and meerkats and penguins, oh, my! Located farther out in the Sunset "avenues," the San Francisco Zoo (Sloat Blvd. at 47th Ave., 415/753-7080, www.sfzoo.org, 10 A.M.–5 P.M. daily summer, 10 A.M.–4 P.M. daily winter, adults $15, seniors $12, ages 4–14 $9) has them all and more, making it a favorite excursion for locals and visitors all year long. Over the last several years the zoo has undergone a transformation, becoming an example of naturalized habitats and conservatory zoo practices. Today, animal lovers can enjoy the native plants and funny faces in the lemur habitat, the families of meerkats, and the bird sanctuary. Families come to check out the wealth of interactive children's exhibits as well as the various exotic animals. However, it's wise to bring your own picnic as the food offerings at the zoo have not improved as much as the habitats. But watch out for seagulls—they fly low and love to steal snacks.

Note that the official address is 1 Zoo Boulevard, but if you put that address into a GPS system, it will take you to the zoo's service entrance. Go to the gate at the corner of Sloat Boulevard and 47th Avenue instead.

Entertainment and Events

NIGHTLIFE
Bars
UNION SQUARE AND NOB HILL

These ritzy areas are better known for their shopping than their nightlife, but a few bars hang in there, plying weary shoppers with good drinks. Most tend toward the upscale. Some inhabit upper floors of the major hotels, like the **Tonga Room and Hurricane Bar** (950 Mason St., 415/772-5278, www.fairmont.com, www.tongaroom.com, 5–11:30 P.M. Wed.–Thurs. and Sun., 5 P.M.–12:30 A.M. Fri.–Sat., $5–7), where an over-the-top tiki theme adds a whimsical touch to the stately Fairmont Hotel on Nob Hill. Enjoy the tropical atmosphere with a fruity rum drink topped with a classic paper umbrella.

Just outside the Union Square area in the sketchy Tenderloin neighborhood, brave souls can find a gem: **Café Royale** (800 Post St., 415/441-4099, www.caferoyale-sf.com, noon–midnight Sun.–Thurs., noon–2 A.M. Fri., 3 P.M.–2 A.M. Sat.) isn't a typical watering hole by any city's standards, but its intense focus on art fits perfectly with the endlessly eclectic ethos of San Francisco. Local artists exhibit their work in Café Royale on a monthly basis, and plenty of live performers grace the space. Live music tends toward the folksy and indie unplugged. In among the artwork, some liquor lurks—think trendy sake and *soju* cocktails, good glasses of wine, and imported beers. The menu includes French sandwiches, gourmet salads, and small plates.

Part live-music venue, part elegant bar, **Top of the Mark** (InterContinental Mark Hopkins, 999 California St., 415/616-6940, www.intercontinentalmarkhopkins.com/top_of_the_mark, 5–11:30 P.M. Sun.–Mon., 2–11:30 P.M. Tues.–Thurs., 2 P.M.–12:30 A.M. Fri.–Sat.) has something for every discerning taste in nighttime entertainment. Since World War II, the views and drinks in this wonderful lounge at the top of the InterContinental Mark Hopkins Hotel have drawn visitors from

around the world. The lounge doubles as a restaurant that serves breakfast and lunch, but the best time for cocktails is, of course, at night. That's when live bands play almost every night of the week. The dress code is business casual or better and is enforced, so leave the jeans in your room. Have a top-shelf martini, and let your toes tap along.

The cocktail craze is alive and well at the **Rickhouse** (246 Kearny St., 415/398-2827, 5 P.M.–2 A.M. Mon. and Sat., 3 P.M.–2 A.M. Tues.–Fri.). Voted one of the best bars in the world by *Food & Wine* magazine in 2010, Rickhouse excels in the creative and classic cocktail. Grab a seat upstairs or down, and sample a Rye Maple Fizz or go in on a massive rum punch, served in a hollow clam shell. Just get here before the after-work crowd, or you may not get in at all.

FINANCIAL DISTRICT AND SOMA

All those high-powered business suit–clad executive types working in the Financial District need places to drink too. One of these is the **Royal Exchange** (301 Sacramento St., 415/956-1710, http://royalexchange.com, 11 A.M.–11 P.M. Mon.–Fri.). This classic pub-style bar has a green-painted exterior, big windows overlooking the street, and a long, narrow barroom. The Royal Exchange serves a full lunch and dinner menu, a small wine list, and a full complement of top-shelf spirits. But most of all, the Exchange serves beer. With 73 taps pouring out 32 different types of beer, the hardest problem will be choosing one. This businesspeople's watering hole is open to the public only on weekdays; on weekends they host private parties.

The Cosmopolitan (121 Spear St., Suite B8, 415/543-4001, http://cosmopolitansf.com, 3:30 P.M.–midnight Mon.–Tues., 11:30 A.M.–2 A.M. Wed.–Fri., 5:30 P.M.–2 A.M. Sat.) offers the best of both worlds: a bar and piano lounge serving top-shelf liquors and reasonably priced well drinks, and a large dining room serving an ever-changing menu of California cuisine. You're more than welcome to enjoy drinks only at the bar, or make a reservation for a complete upscale dinner in the restaurant. If you're lucky, you might even get some live entertainment from a local musician plying the lounge piano.

In urban-renewed SoMa (meaning South of Market), upscale wine bars have become an evening institution. Among the trendiest you'll find is **District** (216 Townsend St., 415/896-2120, http://districtsf.com, 4 P.M.–2 A.M. Mon.–Fri., 5 P.M.–2 A.M. Sat.). A perfect example of its kind, District features bare brick walls, simple wooden furniture, and a big U-shaped bar at the center of the room with wine glasses hanging above it. While you can get a cocktail or even a beer here, the point of coming to District is to sip the finest wines from California, Europe, and beyond. With more than 30 wines available by the glass each night, it's easy to find a favorite, or enjoy a flight of three similar wines to compare. While you can't quite get a full dinner at District, you will find a lovely lounge menu filled with small portions of delicacies to enhance your tasting experience (and perhaps soak up some of the alcohol).

The **House of Shields** (39 New Montgomery St., 415/284-9958, www.thehouseofshields.com, 2 P.M.–2 A.M. Mon.–Fri., 3 P.M.–2 A.M. Sat.–Sun.) has been in the City since 1908. The original incarnation was an illegal speakeasy during the prohibition era (it even has an under-street tunnel to the neighboring Sheraton Hotel). After an extensive remodeling in 2010 by celebrity chef Dennis Leary, the House of Shields has reopened serving upscale cocktails (with upscale prices) in the gorgeous interior. Expect a huge crowd during happy hour, which thins out after about 8 P.M. or so.

Secret passwords, a hidden library, and an art deco vibe make **Bourbon and Branch** (505 Jones St., 415/346-1735, www.bourbonandbranch.com, 6 P.M.–2 A.M. Mon.–Sat., reservations suggested) a must for lovers of the brown stuff. Tucked behind a nameless brown door, this resurrected 1920s-era speakeasy

evokes its prohibition-era past with passwords and secret passages. A business-class elite sips rare bourbon and scotch in secluded booths while those without reservations step into the hidden library.

CHINATOWN

Nightlife in Chinatown runs to dark, quiet dive bars filled with locals. Perhaps the perfect Chinatown dive, **Li Po Lounge** (916 Grant Ave., 415/982-0072, 2 P.M.–2 A.M. daily, cash only) has an appropriately dark and slightly spooky atmosphere that recalls the opium dens of another century. Cheap drinks and Chinese dice games attract locals, and it's definitely helpful to speak Cantonese. But even an English-speaking out-of-town visitor can get a good cheap (and strong!) mai tai or beer. The hanging lantern and Buddha statue behind the bar complete the picture. Another great local hangout worth checking out is the **Buddha Cocktail Lounge** (901 Grant Ave., 415/362-1792, 1 P.M.–2 A.M. daily, cash only).

NORTH BEACH AND FISHERMAN'S WHARF

For a good time down on the Wharf, you can choose from a number of popular bars. **Rosewood** (732 Broadway, 415/951-4886, 5 P.M.–2 A.M. Mon.–Sat.) glows with its namesake wood paneling and soft lighting. Join the young, hip, urban crowd and sip a specialty cocktail, or quaff a draft beer inside the bar or out on the bamboo-strewn patio. A popular hangout, Rosewood can get crowded (and service can get spotty) on weekends.

One of the oldest and most celebrated bars in the City, **Tosca** (242 Columbus Ave., 415/986-9651, http://toscacafesf.com, 5 P.M.–2 A.M. Tues.–Sun.) loves its unpretentious yet glam 1940s style. Hunter S. Thompson once tended bar here when the owner was out at the dentist. The jukebox plays grand opera to the patrons clustered in the big red booths. Locals love the lack of trendiness, the classic cocktails, and the occasional star sightings.

Almost across the street from Tosca is **Vesuvio** (255 Columbus Ave., 415/362-3370, www.vesuvio.com, 6 A.M.–2 A.M. daily). Jack Kerouac loved Vesuvio, which is why it's probably North Beach's most famous saloon. This cozy bi-level hideout is an easy place to spend the afternoon with a pint of Anchor Steam.

Dress up a little for a night out at **15 Romolo** (15 Romolo Place, 415/398-1359, www.15romolo.com, 5:30 P.M.–2 A.M. daily). You'll have to hike up the steep little alley (Fresno St. crosses Romolo Place, which can be a little hard to find) to this hotel bar, but once you're here you'll love the fab cosmos, edgy jukebox music, and often mellow crowd. The bar is smallish and can get crowded on the weekend, so come on a weeknight if you prefer a quiet drink. 15 Romolo also serves brunch (11:30 A.M.–3:30 P.M. Sat.–Sun.).

MARINA AND PACIFIC HEIGHTS

Marina and Pacific Heights denizens enjoy a good glass of vino, and the wine bars in the area cater to local tastes. The **Bacchus Wine Bar** (1954 Hyde St., 415/928-2633, 5:30 P.M.–midnight daily) is a tiny local watering hole that offers an array of wines, sake cocktails, and even delivered-to-your-table sushi from nearby Sushi Groove. DJs sometimes spin on Thursday and Friday nights.

Another favorite bar is the **City Tavern** (3200 Fillmore St., 415/567-0918, www.citytavernsf.com, 3 P.M.–2 A.M. Mon.–Fri., 11 A.M.–2 A.M. Sat.–Sun.). Here you'll get a mix of sports, drinks, and good company. Good solid American food comes at reasonable prices, while weekend brunch features an array of tasty classics as well as some health-conscious fare. The full bar pours an array of beers, wines, liquors, and cocktails.

All that's really left of the original Matrix is the ground you stand on, but the **MatrixFillmore** (3138 Fillmore St., 415/563-4180, www.matrixfillmore.com, 8 P.M.–2 A.M. daily) does claim huge mid-20th-century musical fame. The Matrix, then a live music venue, was opened by Marty Balin so that his freshly named band, Jefferson Airplane, would have a place to play. Subsequent acts included the Grateful Dead, Janis Joplin,

and the Doors. Today, the MatrixFillmore's Lincoln-log fireplace and top-shelf cocktails appeal to the quiet drinking crowd on weeknights and the bridge-and-tunnel singles scene on the weekend. DJs spin techno most nights, though you can catch an occasional live act here too. There's valet parking at the Balboa Cafe down the street.

CIVIC CENTER AND HAYES VALLEY

Hayes Valley bleeds into Lower Haight (Haight St. between Divisadero St. and Octavia Blvd.) and supplies most of the neighborhood bars. For proof that the independent spirit of the Haight lives on in spite of encroaching commercialism, stop in and have a drink at the **Toronado** (547 Haight St., 415/863-2276, www.toronado.com, 11:30 A.M.–2 A.M. daily). This dimly lit haven maintains one of the finest beer selections in the nation, with a changing roster of several dozen microbrews on tap, including many hard-to-find Belgian ales.

The bar scene heads upscale with the **Pause Wine Bar** (1666 Market St., 415/437-1770, www.pausesf.com, 5 P.M.–midnight Tues.–Sat.), in the former site of Cav. The focus is on the food as much as the wine—the small plates menu is pleasantly diverse, and the bar closes at midnight, encouraging an earlier night for a slightly older crowd.

Longtime classic bar Jade has given way to the hipster-tiki-cocktail stylings of **Smuggler's Cove** (650 Gough St., 415/869-1900, http://smugglerscovesf.com, 5 P.M.–2 A.M. daily). Yes, it's all about the rum.

If what you really want is a dive bar, **Place Pigalle** (520 Hayes St., 415/552-2671, http://placepigallesf.com, 2 P.M.–2 A.M. Wed.–Sun., 5 P.M.–2 A.M. Mon.–Tues.) is the place for you. This hidden gem in Hayes Valley offers beer and wine only, a pool table, lots of sofas for lounging, and an uncrowded, genuinely laid-back vibe on weeknights and even sometimes on weekends. The too-cool-for-school hipster vibe somehow missed this place, which manages to maintain its friendly neighborhood feel.

FESTIVALS AND EVENTS

No town does a festival, holiday, or parade like San Francisco. If you're in town for a big event, prepare to check your inhibitions at the airport. Nudity, sex displays, and oddity abound. Even the "tame" festivals include things like fireworks and skeletons.

GAY PRIDE

Pride parades and events celebrating queer life have sprung up all over the country, spreading joy and love across the land. But the granddaddy of all Pride events still reigns in San Francisco. San Francisco Lesbian Gay Bisexual Pride (Market St., 415/864-3733, www.sfpride.org) officially lasts for a weekend – the last weekend of June of each year. But in truth, the fun and festivities surrounding Pride go on for weeks. The rainbow flags go up all over the City at the beginning of June, and the excitement slowly builds, culminating in the fabulous parade and festival. Everyone is welcome to join the wall-to-wall crowds out in the streets to stroll the vendor booths and pack in to see the Dykes on Bikes and cadres of magnificent drag queens.

BAY TO BREAKERS

Are those naked people you see trotting through the fog? Yes! But why? It must be Bay to Breakers (www.ingbaytobreakers.com)! On the third Sunday of May every year since 1912, San Franciscans have gotten up early to get to the starting line of the legendary 12K race. But Bay to Breakers is like no other race in the world. Sure, there are plenty of serious runners who enter the race to win it or to challenge themselves and their abilities. And then there are the other racers...San Franciscans and visitors who turn out by the thousands wearing astonishing outfits, pulling carts and wagons, and stripping down to the buff as they make their way along the course without any care for their pace. A huge audience packs the racecourse, eager to see costumes and conveyances that may well be recycled for Pride the following month. If you want to participate in B2B, check the website for all the details you'll need. Spectators can also scope out the course location and best spots to find a place to watch.

CHINESE NEW YEAR

When Chinese immigrants began pouring into San Francisco in the 19th century, they brought their culture with them. One of the most important (and most fun) traditions the Chinese gave us is the Southwest Chinese New Year Festival and Parade (www.chineseparade.com, $30 parade bleacher seating). Cast off the weari-

MISSION AND CASTRO

These neighborhoods seem to hold a whole city's worth of bars. The Mission, despite a recent upswing in its economy, still has plenty of no-frills bars, many with a Latino theme. And, of course, men seeking men flock to the Castro's endless array of gay bars. For lesbians, the Mission might be a better bet.

Dalva (3121 16th St., 415/252-7740, 4 P.M.–2 A.M. daily) is a small but sophisticated oasis in an ocean of overcrowded Mission hipster hangouts. You'll find dramatic high ceilings, modern paintings, and a jukebox stuffed with indie rock and electronica. Way back in the depths of the club, the Hideaway bar serves up a delectable array

of cocktails poured by a rotating staff of local celebrity mixologists.

Excellent draft beers, tasty barbecue plates, and a motorcycle-inclined crowd give **Zeitgeist** (199 Valencia St., 415/255-7505, http://zeitgeistsf.com, 9 A.M.–2 A.M. daily) a punk-rock edge. This Mission favorite, though, endears itself to all sorts, thanks to its spacious outdoor beer garden and Friday barbecues.

The cocktails at **【 Beretta** (1199 Valencia St., 415/695-1199, www.berettasf.com, 5:30 P.M.–1 A.M. Mon.–Fri., 11 A.M.–1 A.M. Sat.–Sun.) consistently win raves from locals and visitors alike. Order a Rattlesnake—and a pizza to suck up the venom of that bite.

You'll have no trouble finding a gay bar

ness and bad luck of the old year, and come party with the dragons to celebrate the new! Chinese New Year is a major cultural event in San Francisco – schoolchildren of all races are taught the significance of the dancing dragons and the little red envelopes. The parade, with its costumed fan dancers and stunning hand-made multicolored dragon's heads, is one of the most beautiful in the world. It's got more history than almost any other California cele-bration; the parades and festival events began in the 1860s, helping to bring a few days of joy to a Chinese population feeling the hardships of a life thousands of miles from home. Today, crowds in the tens of thousands join to help bring in the new year towards the end of Janu-ary or the beginning of February each annum (on the Western calendar).

DIA DE LOS MUERTOS

On the other end of the thematic spectrum, the Hispanic community turns out into the so-often marched upon San Francisco streets each autumn to celebrate their ancestors. The dead ones, that is. The Dia de los Muertos and Festival of Altars procession takes place as close as possible to All Saint's Day (also Hal-loween, Samhain, and other cultures' harvest festivals) in the Mission District. Walkers are encouraged to bring flowers, candles, and spe-cial items to create altars in honor of their de-ceased loved ones, and artists create beautiful murals and signs to celebrate those who have come and gone. You'll note a distinct theme to the artwork: skulls and bones, mostly, though roses also tend to twine through the scenes. Unlike a funeral, Dia de los Muertos truly is a celebration, so expect music and dancing and a genuine sense of joy in the lives of the dead, rather than somber mourning.

FOLSOM STREET FAIR

Celebrating the uninhibited side of San Fran-cisco each year, the Folsom Street Fair (www. folsomstreetfair.com) brings sex out of the bedroom and into the street. Literally. This fair pays homage to the best perversions and fetishes of consenting adults. You can watch a live BDSM show, shop for sex toys, get some-thing pierced, or just listen to the top alter-native bands rocking out on the main stage. The fair takes place at the end of September each year on Folsom Street between 7th and 12th Streets. To say too much more about this major leather event would do damage to the rating of this book; check the fair's website, or better still, head on down to find out what's really going on.

in the Castro. One of the best is called sim-ply **Q Bar** (456 Castro St., 415/864-2877, www.qbarsf.com, 4 P.M.–2 A.M. Mon.–Fri., 2 P.M.–2 A.M. Sat.–Sun.). Just look for the red neon "Bar" sign set in steel out front. Inside, expect to find the fabulous red decor known as "retro-glam," delicious top-shelf cocktails, and thrumming beats spun by popular DJs almost every night of the week. Unlike many Castro establishments, the Bar caters to pretty much everybody: gay men, gay women, and gay-friendly straight folks. You'll find a coat check and adequate restroom facilities, and the strength of the drinks will make you want to take off your jacket and stay awhile.

GOLDEN GATE PARK AND THE HAIGHT

Haight Street crowds head out in droves to the **Alembic** (1725 Haight St., 415/666-0822, www.alembicbar.com, noon–2 A.M. daily) for artisanal cocktails laced with American spirits. On par with the whiskey and bourbon menu is the cuisine: Wash down beef-tongue sliders with a Sazerac.

Club Deluxe (1511 Haight St., 415/552-6949, www.sfclubdeluxe.com, Tues.–Sun.) is the perfect place to discover your inner Sinatra. Pull up a stool at this dark retro-style bar and order something classic while listen-ing to live jazz or watching burlesque. A pizza menu gives patrons something to buffer those strong drinks.

The **Beach Chalet Brewery** (1000 Great Hwy., 415/386-8439, www.beachchalet.com, 8 A.M.–11 P.M. Sun., 9 A.M.–11 P.M. Mon.–Thurs., 9 A.M.–midnight Fri., 8 A.M.–midnight Sat.) is an attractive brewpub and restaurant directly across the street from Ocean Beach. Sip a pale ale while watching the sunset, and check out the historic murals downstairs.

Clubs

Some folks are surprised at the smallish list of San Francisco clubs. The truth is, San Francisco just isn't a see-and-be-seen, hip-new-club-every-week kind of town. In the City, you'll find gay clubs, vintage dance clubs, Goth clubs, and the occasional underground Burner rave mixed in with the more standard dance floor and DJ fare.

If you're up for a full night of club-hopping and don't want to deal with transit headaches, several bus services can ferry your party from club to club. Many of these offer VIP entrance to clubs and will stop wherever you want to go. **Think Escape** (800/823-7249, www.thinkescape.com, from $30 pp) has buses and limos with drivers and guides to get you to the hottest spots with ease.

UNION SQUARE AND NOB HILL

Defying San Francisco expectation, **Ruby Skye** (420 Mason St., 415/693-0777, www.rubyskye.com, 9 P.M.–2 A.M. Thurs.–Sat., cover $15–20, dress code enforced) books top DJs and occasional live acts into a big, crowded dance club. The building, built in 1890, was originally the Stage Door Theatre, but it has been redone to create dance floors, bars, DJ booths, and VIP spaces. Crowds can get big on the weekend, and the patrons tend to be young and pretty and looking for action. The sound system rocks, so conversation isn't happening, and the drinks tend toward overpriced vodka and Red Bull.

For a chic New York–style club experience, check out **Vessel** (85 Campton Place, 415/433-8585, www.vesselsf.com, 10 P.M.–2 A.M. Wed.–Thurs. and Sat., 9:30 P.M.–2 A.M. Fri., cover $10–30). With old-school bottle service at some tables, Vessel caters to an upscale crowd that likes postmodern decor, top-shelf liquors, and a bit of dancing to round out the evening. Dress up if you plan to get in.

Down the brightly lit staircase in the aptly named **The Cellar** (685 Sutter St., 415/441-5678, http://cellarsf.com, 5 P.M.–2 A.M. Mon.–Fri., 10 P.M.–2 A.M. Sat.–Sun., cover from $25), you'll find a combo bar and club. Two dance floors share the space with pool tables favored by the after-work happy hour crowd (beer is $2 during happy hour, 5–9 P.M. Mon.–Fri.). With regular theme nights, this red-and-blue plush velvet club often attracts a slightly older crowd. An online guest list, reserved tables, and bottle and cocktail service are available through the website. The Cellar is a favorite with many local urbanites.

Harry Denton's Starlight Room (450 Powell St., 21st Fl., 415/395-8595, www.harrydenton.com, 6 P.M.–2 A.M. Tues.–Sat., cover up to $20) brings the flamboyant side of San Francisco downtown. Enjoy a cocktail in the early evening or a nightcap and a bite of dessert after the theater in this truly old-school nightclub. Dress in your best to match the glitzy red-and-gold decor and mirrors. Whoop it up at Sunday's a Drag shows (noon and 2:30 P.M. Sun.). Reservations are recommended.

FINANCIAL DISTRICT AND SOMA

111 Minna Street Gallery (111 Minna St., 415/974-1719, www.111minnagallery.com, noon–11 P.M. Wed., noon–2 A.M. Thurs.–Fri., 5 P.M.–2 A.M. Sat., cover $5) really is an art gallery, but it's also one of the hottest dance clubs in SoMa. Art lovers who come to 111 Minna to enjoy the changing exhibitions of new art in peace and quiet do so during the day. After 5 P.M. the gallery transforms into a nightclub, opening the full bar and bringing in DJs who spin late into the weekend nights. While it may sound pretentious, the mix of modern art and lots of liquor really feels just right. Check the website for special events, including '80s dance parties and art-show openings. Guests must be 21 and older due to the liquor license and because they often showcase explicit artworks.

It's dark, it's dank, and it's very, very Goth. The **Cat Club** (1190 Folsom St., 415/703-8964, www.sfcatclub.com, 9 P.M.–3 A.M. Tues.–Sun., cover $6–10) gets pretty energetic on '80s dance nights, but it's still a great place to go after you've donned your best down-rent black attire and painted your face deathly pale, especially on Goth-industrial-electronica nights. In fact, there's no dress code at the Cat Club, unlike many local night spots, which makes it great for travelers who live in their jeans. You'll find a friendly crowd, decent bartenders, strong drinks, and easy access to smoking areas. Each of the two rooms has its own DJ, which somehow works perfectly even though they're only a wall apart from each other. Check the website to find the right party night for you, and expect the crowd to heat up after 11 P.M.

Looking for *the* DJs and dance parties? You'll find them at the **DNA Lounge** (375 11th St., 415/626-1409, www.dnalounge.com, 9 P.M.–3:30 A.M. Sun.–Thurs., 9 P.M.–5 A.M. Fri.–Sat., cover varies). With Bootie twice a month, '80s parties, and live music, the DNA Lounge has been one of the City's perpetual hot night spots for decades (it even has its own entry in Wikipedia). It's also one of the few clubs that's open after hours.

NORTH BEACH AND FISHERMAN'S WHARF

The North Beach neighborhood has long been San Francisco's best-known red-light district. To this day, Broadway Avenue is lined with the neon signs of strip clubs and adult stores, all promising grown-up good times. Do be aware that cover charges at most of the strip clubs tend to be on the high side, and lone women should approach this area with extreme caution after dark.

If you're just looking for a good time at a PG-rated (OK, maybe R-rated if you get lucky) dance club, check out the **Bamboo Hut** (479 Broadway, 415/989-8555, www.maximumproductions.com, 8 P.M.–2 A.M. Mon., 5 P.M.–2 A.M. Wed.–Fri., 7 P.M.–2 A.M. Sat.). It's part tacky tiki bar, part impromptu dance club, and has a cheerful vibe and friendly scene that

can be hard to come by in this part of town. You'll see the tiki god, the bamboo decor, and the fun umbrella-clad fruity rum drinks. The house specialty is the Flaming Volcano Bowl—yes, it's really on fire, and it's probably a good idea to share one with a friend—or three. DJs spin on weekends at the Bamboo Hut; they might not be the hippest in town, but regulars have a great time dancing anyhow.

MARINA AND PACIFIC HEIGHTS

Clubs in the Marina are all about the trendy and the spendy. The **Hi-Fi Lounge** (2125 Lombard St., 415/345-8663, www.maximumproductions.com, 8 P.M.–2 A.M. Wed.–Sat.) personifies the fun that can be had in smaller San Francisco venues. This one-floor wonder with a tiny dance floor gets incredibly crowded. Yet even the locals have a good time when they come out to the Hi-Fi. The decor is funky and fun, and the patrons are young and affluent. Most visitors find the staff friendly and the bartenders attentive. It being the Marina, come early to get decent parking and to avoid the cover charge. On Thursday and Friday, early birds get $1 draft beer.

CIVIC CENTER AND HAYES VALLEY

Not your slick, shiny nightclub, the **Rickshaw Stop** (155 Fell St., 415/861-2011, www.rickshawstop.com, 5 P.M.–midnight Wed.–Thurs., 5 P.M.–2 A.M. Fri.–Sat., cover $5–18) in the Hayes Valley neighborhood welcomes one and all with a cavernous lower bar, stage area, and dance floor, and a quirky balcony area complete with comfy old sofas. Up-and-coming live acts play here, DJs spin, and special events and parties add to the action almost every week. Have a drink, enjoy the music, and get comfortable! You'll feel almost as though you're in a friendly neighborhood coffee shop (albeit a really big one) than some fancy nightspot. Check the website for events and club hours—the schedule varies widely.

The most famous gentlemen's club in the City is **Mitchell Brothers O'Farrell Theatre** (895 O'Farrell St., 415/776-6686, www.ofarrell.com, 11:30 A.M.–1:30 A.M. Mon.–Thurs.,

11:30 A.M.–2:30 A.M. Fri.–Sat., 5:30 P.M.–midnight Sun., cover $20 before 7 P.M., $40 after 9 P.M.). The O'Farrell started out as an adult movie house in 1969, featuring its own productions on the silver screen. Live shows began in 1976, though films still run in the CineStage room. Today, patrons can choose between five different show rooms, plus VIP booths. Unlike many City strip clubs, Mitchell Brothers offers full nudity and features live shows. Many of the performers and dancers are major adult film stars who perform limited engagements at the O'Farrell. The catch? No liquor.

MISSION AND CASTRO

The Mission and the Castro are popular clubbing districts in San Francisco, and as the urban renewal continues, SoMa is making its own play to create a hot nightlife rep. Naturally the biggest concentration of gay clubs is in the Castro.

Fans of the hipster lounge scene flock to the **Fluid Ultra Lounge** (662 Mission St., 415/385-2547, www.fluidsf.com, 9 P.M.–2 A.M. Thurs.–Sat., cover varies). The second you walk in, you'll probably feel you're not chic enough for this David Oldroyd–designed postmodern wonderland. Gleaming metal meets fascinating floral-esque accessories in a series of rooms that boast really uncomfortable white chairs. If you're not up for lots of young and ultra-cool clubsters, you may find the decor to be the best part of Fluid. You can definitely dance on an interestingly lit floor, though it can be tough to pry a drink out of the bartenders at times. Come early or get your name on the guest list (you can sign up online) to avoid the hefty cover charge.

GOLDEN GATE PARK AND THE HAIGHT

In the infamous Haight, the club scene is actually an eclectic mix of everything from trendy to retro. **Milk** (1840 Haight St., 415/387-6455, www.milksf.com, 9 P.M.–2 A.M. Mon.–Sat., from 3 P.M. Sun., cover up to $5) counts itself among the trendy. It's tiny, and it's often empty on weekdays and packed solid on weekends. The music ranges from reggae to hip-hop to

'80s, depending on the night and the DJ. Milk attracts more locals than out-of-towners, but if that's what you're looking for in your visit to the City, a night of Milk might be just what the doctor ordered.

Gay and Lesbian

San Francisco's gay nightlife has earned a worldwide rep for both the quantity and quality of options. In fact, the gay club scene totally outdoes the straight club scene for frolicsome fabulous fun. While the City's queer nightlife caters more to gay men than to lesbians, there's plenty of space available for partiers of all persuasions. For a more comprehensive list of San Francisco's queer bars and clubs, visit www. sfgaybarlist.com.

Looking for a stylin' gay bar turned club, Castro style? Head for **Badlands** (4121 18th St., 415/626-9320, www.sfbadlands.com, 2 P.M.–2 A.M. daily). This Castro icon was once an old-school bar with pool tables on the floor and license plates on the walls. Now you'll find an always-crowded dance floor, au courant peppy pop music, ever-changing video screens, and plenty of gay men out for a good time. Any number of local straight women count themselves among the regulars at this friendly establishment, which attracts a youngish but mixed-age crowd. Do be aware that Badlands gets incredibly crowded, complete with a hot and packed dance floor, especially on weekend nights. There's a coat check on the bottom level.

The **Lexington Club** (3464 19th St., 415/863-2052, www.lexingtonclub.com, 5 P.M.–2 A.M. Mon.–Thurs., 3 P.M.–2 A.M. Fri.–Sun.) calls itself "your friendly neighborhood dyke bar." In truth, the Lex offers a neighborhood dive environment and cheap drinks—think $1 margaritas on Friday nights and Pabst on Mondays. Friendly? Depends on how dyke you are—tats, piercings, short hair, and tank tops make for a better Lex experience.

Unlike some of the harder-core Castro gay clubs, **Truck** (1900 Folsom St., 415/252-0306, www.trucksf.com, 4 P.M.–2 A.M. Tues.–Fri., 2 P.M.–2 A.M. Sat.–Sun.) offers a friendly neighborhood vibe. Truck lures in patrons with cheap drinks, friendly bartenders, and theme nights every week. Food is served 4–9 P.M. weekdays and 2–9 P.M. weekends, when the bar tends to be quieter. Oh, and yes, that's a shower. Stop by late on Friday night for the Truck Wash to see it in action.

The Lookout (3600 16th St., 415/431-0306, www.lookoutsf.com, 3:30 P.M.–2 A.M. Mon.–Fri., 12:30 P.M.–2 A.M. Sat.–Sun., cover $2–5) gets its name and much of its rep from its balcony overlooking the iconic Castro neighborhood. Get up there for some primo people watching as you sip your industrial-strength alcoholic concoctions and nibble on surprisingly edible bar snacks and pizza. Do be aware that the Lookout hosts quite a few "events" that come complete with a cover charge.

Yes, there's a Western-themed gay bar in San Francisco. **Cinch** (1723 Polk St., 415/776-4162, until 2 A.M. daily) has a laid-back (no pun intended), friendly, male-oriented vibe that's all but lost in the once gay, now gentrified Polk Street hood. Expect fewer females and strong drinks to go with the unpretentious decor and atmosphere.

For after-hours dancing on weekends, many SF clubsters end up in SoMa at **The EndUp** (401 6th St., 415/646-0999, www.theendup.com, 10 P.M.–4 A.M. Thurs., 11 P.M.–9 A.M. Fri., 10 P.M.–4 A.M. Sat.).

Live Music
ROCK AND POP
Opened in the late 1960s, **The Fillmore** (1805 Geary Blvd., 415/346-6000, www.thefillmore.com, 7 P.M.–2 A.M. daily) ignited the careers of legendary bands such as Santana and the Grateful Dead. This popular venue now hosts everything from concerts to theme parties.

Started by rock veteran Boz Scaggs in 1988, **Slim's** (333 11th St., 415/255-0333, www.slims-sf.com, $15–60) showcases everything from the Subhumans to Billy Bob Thornton. Dinner tickets are the only way to score an actual seat.

The **Warfield** (982 Market St., 415/345-0900, http://thewarfieldtheatre.com, prices vary) is one of the older rock venues in the City. It started out as a vaudeville palace in the early 1900s, booking major jazz acts as well as variety shows. The Warfield's configuration is that of a traditional theater, with a raised stage, an open orchestra section below it, and two balconies rising up and facing the stage. There's limited table seating on the lowest level (mostly by reservation), reserved seats in the balconies, and open standing in the orchestra below the stage. The Warfield books all sorts of acts, from Bill Maher to alternative rock; the likes of Evanescence, Lyle Lovett, and Death Cab for Cutie have played here. The downsides include the total lack of parking—you'll need to hunt for a spot at one of the local public parking structures, and you'll pay for the privilege.

Given the dense crowd of tourists in the Fisherman's Wharf area, it's no surprise that a few bars and clubs offer live music to entertain the masses and keep them buying drinks late into the evening. Despite its locale, **Bimbo's 365 Club** (1025 Columbus Ave., 415/474-0365, www.bimbos365club.com, tickets $15–35, cash-only bar) retains its reputation as a favorite venue for locals. Bimbo's was opened in 1931 by an Italian immigrant looking to create a fun and fabulous club to help San Francisco residents take their minds off the gloom of the Depression. The club moved to the Columbus Avenue location in 1951 and became a favorite of San Francisco legend Herb Caen as well as many other local socialites. Today, major accessible acts such as Chris Isaak and the Brian Setzer Orchestra play Bimbo's. You might even luck out and catch Robin Williams working up new stand-up material here. The club itself, with its shabby chic interior and atmosphere, remains a beloved elder statesman with a heavy local following.

Mezzanine (444 Jessie St., 415/625-8880, www.mezzaninesf.com) brings top acts to San Francisco. This vast club inside a renovated warehouse showcases a veritable who's who of DJs and live acts, from Public Enemy to the Chemical Brothers. Art parties, fashion shows, and film installations round out the monthly calendar.

BLUES AND JAZZ

The neighborhood surrounding Union Square is one of the most fertile areas in San Francisco for live music. Whether you're into blues, rock, or even country, you'll find a spot to have a drink and listen to some wonderful live tunes.

Biscuits and Blues (401 Mason St., 415/292-2583, www.biscuitsandblues.com, 6 P.M.–2 A.M. daily) is a local musicians' favorite. Just around the corner from the big live drama theaters, this house dedicates itself to jazz and blues. Headliners have included Joe Louis Walker, Jimmy Thackery, and Jim Kimo. One of the best things about this club is that you can, in fact, get biscuits as well as blues. Dinner is served nightly and features a surprisingly varied and upscale menu combining California cuisine with the mystical flavors of New Orleans. Yum! So when you plan for your night of blues, consider showing up early to enjoy a jam session and a meal, then stay on for the main acts and headliners (and, of course, cocktails).

At the **Boom Boom Room** (1601 Fillmore St., 415/673-8000, www.boomboomblues.com, 4 P.M.–2 A.M. Tues.–Sat., 2 P.M.–1 A.M. Sun.), you'll find the latest in a legacy of live blues, boogie, groove, soul, and funk music.

In the same neighborhood is **Yoshi's** (1330 Fillmore St., 415/655-5600, www.yoshis. com). Both a restaurant and live music venue, Yoshi's attracts some big names—Natalie Cole, Hiroshima, and the Bad Plus—as well as Fillmore locals for drinks and sushi in the stunning lounge.

Comedy

San Francisco's oldest comedy club, the **Punch Line** (444 Battery St., 415/397-7573, www.punchlinecomedyclub.com, shows 8 P.M. and 10 P.M. Tues.–Sun., cover varies) is an elegant and intimate venue that earned its top-notch reputation with stellar headliners such as Robin Williams, Ellen DeGeneres, and Dave Chappelle. An on-site bar keeps the audience primed.

Cobb's Comedy Club (915 Columbus Ave.,

415/928-4320, www.cobbscomedy.com, shows 8 P.M. and 10:15 P.M. Thurs.–Sun., cover varies, 2-drink minimum) has played host to star comedians such as Jerry Seinfeld, Sarah Silverman, and Margaret Cho since 1982. The 425-seat venue offers a full dinner menu and a bar to slake your thirst. Be sure to check your show's start time—some comics don't follow the usual Cobb's schedule.

THE ARTS
Theater

For a great way to grab last-minute theater tickets, walk right up to the **Union Square TIX** booth (Union Square, 415/430-1140, www.tixbayarea.com, 11 A.M.–6 P.M. Tues.–Fri., 10 A.M.–6 P.M. Sat., 10 A.M.–3 P.M. Sun.). TIX sells same-day, half-price, no-refund tickets to all kinds of shows across the City. If you've got your heart set on a specific musical or play in a big theater, get to the booth early in the day and steel yourself for possible disappointment—especially on weekends, when many top-shelf shows sell out. If you're flexible, you'll almost certainly find something available at a reasonable price. It might be lesbian stand-up comedy, Beach Blanket Babylon, or the San Francisco Vampire Tour, but it'll be cheap and it'll be fun. TIX also sells half-price tickets to same-day shows online—check the website at 11 A.M. daily for up-to-date deals.

If you really, really need to see a major musical while you're in San Francisco, check out **SHN** (www.shnsf.com). SHN operates the Orpheum, the Curran, and the Golden Gate Theater—the three venues where big Broadway productions land when they come to town.

UNION SQUARE AND NOB HILL

Just up from Union Square, on Geary Street, the traditional San Francisco theater district continues to entertain crowds almost every day of the week. The old Geary Theater is now the permanent home of **A.C.T.** (415 Geary St., 415/749-2228, www.act-sf.org, shows Tues.–Sun., $22–82). A.C.T. puts on a season filled with big-name, big-budget productions. Each season sees an array of high-production-value musicals such as *Urinetown,* American classics by the likes of Sam Shepard and Somerset Maugham, and intriguing new works; you might even get to see a world premiere. Don't expect to find street parking on Geary. Discount parking is available with a ticket stub from A.C.T. at the Mason-O'Farrell garage around the corner. Tickets can be reasonably priced, especially on weeknights, but do be aware that the second balcony seats are truly high altitude—expect to look nearly straight down to the stage, and take care if you're prone to vertigo.

The **Curran Theater** (445 Geary St., 888/746-1799, www.curran-theater.com, $105–250), next door to A.C.T., has a state-of-the-art stage for classic, high-budget musicals. Audiences have watched *Les Misérables, Phantom of the Opera,* and *High School Musical* from the plush red velvet seats. Expect to pay a premium for tickets to these musicals, which can sometimes run at the Curran for months or even years. Check the schedule for current shows, and leave children under age five at home—they won't be permitted in the Curran.

NORTH BEACH AND FISHERMAN'S WHARF

There's one live show that's always different, yet it's been running continuously for three and a half decades. This musical revue is crazy, wacky, and offbeat, and it pretty much defines live theater in San Francisco. It's **Beach Blanket Babylon** (678 Green St., 415/421-4222, www.beachblanketbabylon.com, shows Wed.–Sun., $25–100). Even if you saw *Beach Blanket Babylon* 10 years ago, you should come to see it again; because it mocks current pop culture, the show evolves almost continuously to take advantage of tabloid treasures. While minors are welcome at the Sunday matinees, evening shows can get pretty racy, and liquor is involved, so these are restricted to attendees 21 and over.

The hats. Oh, the hats. You'll never forget the hats.

MARINA AND PACIFIC HEIGHTS

Beyond the bright lights of Geary and Market Streets lie any number of tiny up-and-coming (or down-and-going, depending) theaters, many of which produce new plays by local playwrights. One of the best known of the "small" theaters, the **Magic Theatre** (Fort Mason Center, Bldg. D, 415/441-8822, http://magictheatre.org, $30–60) produced Sam Shepard's new works back before he was anyone special. They're still committed to new works, so when you go to a show at the Magic you're taking a chance or having an adventure, depending on how you look at it.

At the **Palace of Fine Arts Theatre** (3301 Lyon St., 415/567-6642, www.palaceoffinearts.org, cover varies) you'll find accessible avant-garde performing arts pieces, live music performance, dance recitals, and the occasional children's musical recital or black-and-white film.

CIVIC CENTER AND HAYES VALLEY

Down on Market Street, the **Orpheum Theater** (1192 Market St., 888/746-1799, www.shnsf.com, $50–200) runs touring productions of popular Broadway musicals. At the **EXIT Theatre** (156 Eddy St., 415/673-3847, www.theexit.org), down in the Tenderloin, you'll see plenty of unusual experimental plays, many by local playwrights. The EXIT also participates in the annual San Francisco Fringe Festival (www.sffringe.org).

MISSION AND CASTRO

Take care getting to **Theatre Rhinoceros** (2926 16th St., 415/552-4100, www.therhino.org, $15–35), as it's in a less-than-ritzy part of town. But it's worth it: The Rhino puts on a wonderfully entertaining set of gay and lesbian plays and has branched out to explore the whole spectrum of human sexuality, especially as it's expressed in anything-goes (even conservative Republicans!) San Francisco.

Focusing on short works by new writers, **Three Wise Monkeys** (415/776-7427, www.bayoneacts.org, $19–25) productions usually run at the **Eureka Theater** (215 Jackson St.). Each year

Three Wise Monkeys hosts the Bay One Acts (BOAs) as well as the Short Leaps Festival, where all plays read last 10 minutes or less.

Classical Music and Opera

Right around the Civic Center, music takes a turn for the upscale. This is the neighborhood where the ultrarich and not-so-rich classics lovers come to enjoy a night out. Acoustically renovated in 1992, **Davies Symphony Hall** (201 Van Ness Ave., 415/864-6000, www. sfsymphony.org) is home to Michael Tilson Thomas's world-renowned San Francisco Symphony. Loyal patrons flock to performances that range from the classic to the avantgarde. Whether you love Mozart or Mahler, or you want to hear classic rock blended with major symphony orchestra, the San Francisco Symphony does it.

The **War Memorial Opera House** (301 Van Ness Ave., 415/621-6600, www.sfwmpac.org, performances Tues.–Sun.), a beaux arts–style building designed by Coit Tower and City Hall architect Arthur Brown Jr., houses the **San Francisco Opera** (415/864-3330, http://sfopera.com) and **San Francisco Ballet** (415/865-2000, www.sfballet.org). Tours are available (10 A.M.–2 P.M. Mon.).

Cinema

A grand movie palace from the 1920s, the **Castro Theatre** (429 Castro St., 415/621-6120, www.castrotheatre.com, adults $10, children and seniors $7.50, matinees $7.50) has enchanted San Francisco audiences for almost a century. The Castro Theater hosts everything from revival double features (from black-and-white through 1980s classics) to musical movie sing-alongs, live shows, and even the occasional book signing. Naturally, the Castro also screens current releases and documentaries about queer life in San Francisco and beyond. Check the calendar online to figure out what's going to be playing when you're in town before buying tickets. Then plan your Muni route to the theater, which doesn't have a dedicated parking lot. Once inside, be sure to admire the lavish interior decor.

Expect an upscale moviegoing experience at the **Sundance Kabuki Theater** (1881 Post St., www.sundancecinemas.com/kabuki.html, adults $9–17, seniors $9–15, children $8.25–15). The "amenity fee" pays for reserved seating, film shorts rather than commercials, and bits of bamboo decor. The Kabuki has eight screens, all of which show mostly big blockbuster Hollywood films, plus a smattering of independents and the occasional filmed opera performance. The Over 21 shows, in the four theaters connected to the full bars, encompass the most compelling reason to see a typical first-run movie for several dollars extra.

Shopping

UNION SQUARE AND NOB HILL

For the biggest variety of chain and department stores, plus a few select designer boutiques, locals and visitors alike flock to Union Square (bounded by Geary St., Stockton St., Post St., and Powell St.). The shopping area includes more than just the square proper: More designer and brand-name stores cluster for several blocks in all directions.

Department Stores

Several big high-end department stores call Union Square home. **Macy's** (170 O'Farrell St., 415/397-3333, 10 A.M.–9 P.M. Mon.–Sat., 11 A.M.–7 P.M. Sun.) has two immense locations, one for women's clothing and another for the men's store and housewares. **Neiman Marcus** (150 Stockton St., 415/362-3900, www.neimanmarcus.com, 10 A.M.–7 P.M. Mon.–Wed. and Fri.–Sat., 10 A.M.–8 P.M.

Thurs., noon–6 P.M. Sun.) is a favorite among high-budget shoppers and PETA fur protesters, while **Saks Fifth Avenue** (384 Post St., 415/986-4758, 10 A.M.–7 P.M. Mon.–Wed. and Fri.–Sat., 10 A.M.–8 P.M. Thurs., 11 A.M.–6 P.M. Sun.) adds a touch of New York style to funky-but-wealthy San Francisco.

Clothing and Shoes

Levi's (300 Post St., 415/501-0100, www.levi.com, 10 A.M.–9 P.M. Mon.–Sat., 11 A.M.–8 P.M. Sun.) may be a household name, but this three-floor fashion emporium offers incredible customization services while featuring new music and emerging art. Guys should head to the outpost of **Ben Sherman** (55 Stockton St., 415/593-0671, www.bensherman.com, 10 A.M.–8 P.M. Mon.–Sat., 11 A.M.–7 P.M. Sun.) for stylish threads from the British-based outfitter that has been dressing cool mods for almost five decades.

A gem of a boutique is the original shop of the San Francisco designer **Margaret O'Leary** (1 Claude Lane, 415/391-1010, www.margaretoleary.com, 10 A.M.–5 P.M. Tues.–Sat.), who launched a knitwear-inspired line in her name. Women's fine sweaters—from sleeveless to cardigans—and chic fabric designs are featured in the cozy, European-inspired space.

An elegant space on boutiquey Maiden Lane houses **Wolford** (115 Maiden Lane, 415/391-6727, www.wolford.com, 10 A.M.–6 P.M. Mon.–Sat.), the top name in hosiery. Stockings laced with elegant seams and zigzag patterns usually run $65, but sales can offer bargain prices. Upscale and inventive lingerie at **Agent Provocateur** (54 Geary St., 415/421-0229, www.agentprovocateur.com, 11 A.M.–7 P.M. Mon.–Sat., noon–5 P.M. Sun.) promises a most unique and memorable souvenir to go with those Wolford stockings.

Fluevogers unite! There's an outpost of the popular **John Fluevog Shoes** (253 Grant Ave., 415/296-7900, www.fluevog.com, 10 A.M.–6 P.M. Mon.–Thurs., 10 A.M.–7 P.M. Fri.–Sat., noon–6 P.M. Sun.) here. The Canadian designer's artistic creations have appeared on the pages of *Vogue* and on the feet of notable celebrities like Scarlett Johansson and the White Stripes.

Gift and Home

Britex Fabrics (146 Geary St., 415/392-2910, www.britexfabrics.com, 10 A.M.–6 P.M. Mon.–Sat.) draws fashion designers, quilters, DIYers, and costume geeks from all over the Bay Area to its legendary monument to fabric. If you're into any sort of textile crafting, a visit to Britex has the qualities of a religious experience. All four floors are crammed floor-to-ceiling with bolts of fabric, swaths of lace, and rolls of ribbon. From $1-per-yard grosgrain ribbons to $95-per-yard French silk jacquard and $125-per-yard Italian wool coating, Britex has it all. It's the place to shop if you're planning to hand-create an all-silk wedding gown with beaded lace trim and a matching cathedral-length veil. Or if you're very, very serious about your Renaissance fair outfit.

Health and Beauty

Another thing the elite of the City do down at Union Square is attend to their hair, faces, nails, and general beauty. One of the most rarified salons in Union Square is the **Elizabeth Arden Red Door** (126 Post St., Suite 4, 415/989-4888, 9 A.M.–7 P.M. Mon.–Wed. and Sat., 9 A.M.–8 P.M. Thurs.–Fri., 10 A.M.–6 P.M. Sun.). You'll definitely need an appointment to get a trim or a color touch-up here.

FINANCIAL DISTRICT AND SOMA

Is there any place in San Francisco where you *can't* shop? Even the Financial District has plenty of retail opportunities. Antiques, art, and design lovers come down to **Jackson Square** (Jackson St. and Montgomery St.) for the plethora of high-end shops and galleries. Don't expect to find much in the way of cheap tchotchkes—the objets d'art and interior accessories find places in the exquisite homes of the wealthy buyers who can afford such luxuries.

QUAKING AND SHAKING

The single most famous event ever to occur in San Francisco happened at 5:12 A.M. on Wednesday, April 18, 1906, when the ground beneath the City jolted violently as the result of a magnitude 7.8 earthquake. Buildings shook and tumbled and a great crack opened along the San Andreas Fault. Gas and water mains ruptured all over the City, and even as the trembling earth settled down, fires broke out. It was the fires that caused the widespread devastation of San Francisco – with the water mains broken, firemen couldn't adequately fight the conflagrations that engulfed whole neighborhoods. Neither rich nor poor residents were spared as the mansions on Nob Hill and the slums of Chinatown felt equal destruction and desolation.

Despite $235-400 million in damage (well over $5 billion in today's dollars), the City persevered. Rebuilding quickly (and with a shocking lack of concern for earthquake safety in construction), San Francisco was back on its feet by the time the 1915 World Exposition rolled around.

Then, in 1989, right in the middle of a San Francisco-Oakland World Series game, another major earthquake struck the Bay Area. Known as the Loma Prieta Quake (the epicenter was down by Loma Prieta near Santa Cruz), this quake registered 6.9 on the Richter scale and was not nearly as destructive as the 1906 monster. Still, a section of the arterial Bay Bridge collapsed, as did part of an Oakland freeway. The disused Embarcadero freeway was badly damaged (and later torn down). Much of downtown Santa Cruz was destroyed, and the quake affected the lives of almost all Bay Area residents – but again rebuilding started almost before the ground stopped quivering.

Today, it's hard to find evidence of the Loma Prieta quake anywhere in the Bay Area. Meanwhile, earthquakes continue to remake the land, reminding us that the only constant here is change.

But as always, it's free to look, to imagine, and to dream.

Kathleen Taylor–The Lotus Collection (445 Jackson St., 415/398-8115, www.ktaylor-lotus.com, 10 A.M.–5 P.M. Mon.–Fri., 11 A.M.–4 P.M. Sat.) specializes in antique textiles from around the world. Whether you fancy a medieval tapestry for your wall or an ancient Asian table runner, this is the place to find it. A more classic but intensely high-end and well-known gallery sells works of fine art to the cream of West Coast society.

The **Montgomery Gallery** (406 Jackson St., 415/788-8300, www.montgomerygallery.com, 10 A.M.–5:30 P.M. Tues.–Fri., 11 A.M.–5 P.M. Sat.) seems like a museum, displaying works of the old masters as well as the top tier of more modern artists.

CHINATOWN

Chinatown is one of the most popular shopping districts in San Francisco. Shopping in Chinatown isn't about seeking out a specific store; instead, it's an experience of strolling from shop to endless shop. It can take hours just to get a few blocks up Grant Street, and a thorough perusal of all the side streets might take days. Narrow, cluttered T-shirt and tchotchke shops stand between jewelry stores offering genuine gems and antiques shops crammed with treasures. Clothing boutiques run to slippery silks, while home-decor stores offer table linens made out of real linen as well as statuary, art, tea sets—everything a dedicated shopper could dream of and more.

Good ideas for shoppers who want to bring home gifts and souvenirs that cost less than $10 and fit easily in a carry-on bag include small China silk brocade items like wallets and jewelry pouches, colorful paper lanterns, small hand-painted china planters, chopsticks, and Chinese candies. Be aware that in Chinatown shops, you're not just allowed to ask for discounts—haggling is expected and is part of the fun of shopping here. No matter what you're buying, ask for the special discount. You'll actually get it!

If you've only got a short time to shop, the epic **Chinatown Bazaar** (667 Grant Ave., 415/391-6369, chinabazaarsf@gmail.com, 10 A.M.–9:30 P.M. daily) has pretty much everything you can imagine coming from Chinatown and a lot of things beyond imagination. They've got some of the best prices in the district for pottery items, Chinese and Buddhist-inspired statuary, chopsticks, tea sets, and much more. Prices for small, pretty items run $2–10.

Fine jewelry stores abound in Chinatown— you'll have no trouble finding a strand of matching pearls if that's to your taste. **Royal Fine Jewelry** (730 Grant Ave., 415/397-8868, 11 A.M.–6:30 P.M. daily) has a particularly fine selection of semiprecious and precious jewelry, some of it fairly unusual in style.

Gourmet Goodies

For a sense (and a scent) of the more local side of Chinatown, head off the main drag to Stockton Street and seek out the local food markets. Or visit the **Red Blossom Tea Company** (831 Grant Ave., 415/395-0868, www.redblossomtea.com, 10 A.M.–6:30 P.M. Mon.–Sat., 10 A.M.–6 P.M. Sun., $10–20). You'll find top-quality teas of every type you can think of and probably some you've never heard of. Red Blossom has been in business for more than 25 years importing the best teas available from all over Asia. For the tea adventurous, the blossoming teas, specific varieties of oolong, and *pu-erh* teas make great souvenirs to bring home and share with friends. And if you fall in love, never fear; Red Blossom takes advantage of Bay Area technology to offer all their loose teas on the Internet. (Sadly, their website isn't scratch-and-sniff, or they'd probably run out.)

The **Golden Gate Fortune Cookie Company** (56 Ross Alley, 415/781-3956, 9 A.M.–midnight daily) makes a great stop, especially if you've brought the kids along. Heck, even if you're alone, the delicious aromas wafting from the building as you pass the alley on Jackson Street may draw you inside. Expect to have a tray of sample cookies pressed on you as soon as you enter. Inside the factory, you'll see the cookies being folded into their traditional shapes by workers, but the best part is checking out all the different types of fortune cookies. Yes, there are lots of kinds you'll never see on the tablecloth at a restaurant: chocolate and strawberry flavors, funky shapes, various sizes, and don't forget the cookies with the X-rated fortunes, perfect to bring home and share with friends. Bags of cookies cost only $3–4, making them attractive souvenirs to pick up—although with their lovely scent, they might not make it all the way home.

NORTH BEACH AND FISHERMAN'S WHARF

The best thing about the 40 zillion souvenir stores in the Fisherman's Wharf area is that they know what tourists to San Francisco really *need*: sweatshirts, hats, gloves, and fuzzy socks. For last-minute warm clothes on foggy days, you don't need a specific store. Just take a walk from the cable car turnaround down Hyde Street to Jefferson Street and then over to Mason Street. You'll find the heavy sweatshirt you need or cheap-and-cheesy gifts for friends—fridge magnets, snow globes, and pewter replicas of cable cars. For more unusual souvenirs, try **Pier 39.** Funky boutiques crowd both sides and both stories of the buildings that line the pier.

The North Beach district is filled with fun, beauty, and great Italian restaurants and cafés. The Italian district also boasts some of the hippest shops in the City, so it's a great place for shoppers who eschew chains to seek out thrift shops and funky independents.

◖ City Lights Books

One of the most famous independent bookshops in a city famous for its literary bent is City Lights (261 Columbus Ave., 415/362-8193, www.citylights.com, 10 A.M.–midnight daily). It opened in 1953 as an all-paperback bookstore with a decidedly Beat aesthetic, focused on selling modern literary fiction and progressive political tomes. As the Beats flocked to San Francisco and to City Lights, the shop put on another hat—that of publisher. Allen Ginsberg's *Howl* was published by the erstwhile independent, which never looked back. Today, they're still selling and publishing the best of cutting-edge fiction and nonfiction. The store is still in its original location on the point of Columbus Avenue, though it's expanded somewhat since the '50s. Expect to find your favorite genre paperbacks along with the latest intriguing new works. The nonfiction selections can really make you take a step back and think about your world in a new way, which is just what the founders of City Lights wanted.

Music

For the ultimate hip North Beach stop, head to **101 Music** (1414 Grant Ave., 415/382-6369, 10 a.m.–8 p.m. Tues.–Sat., noon–8 p.m. Sun.). This independent shop is short on copies of the latest pop CDs and long on vintage vinyl and secondhand instruments and musical equipment. Expect to see turntables, keyboards, and all sorts of fun arcane stuff as soon as you walk in the door. The vinyl collection hides downstairs. The organization of the records and CDs could be better, but isn't browsing for treasure in the bins part of the fun at such a shop? Customer service, much of it provided by the owner, keeps locals coming back.

Clothing

For hip dressers who prefer classic style to the latest stuff fresh out of the sweatshops, **Old Vogue** (1412 Grant Ave., 415/392-1522, 11 a.m.–6 p.m. Mon.–Tues. and Thurs., 11 a.m.–8 p.m. Wed., 11 a.m.–10 p.m. Fri.–Sat., noon–6 p.m. Sun.) is the perfect North Beach destination. Stop in at the funky little storefront and plan to spend a little while browsing through the racks of vintage apparel: one floor dedicated to comfy old jeans and pants, the other to coats, blouses, dresses, and accessories. Old Vogue can provide you with just the perfect hat to top off your favorite clubbing outfit.

Eye-catching **Alla Prima** (1420 Grant Ave., 415/397-4077, www.allaprimalingerie.com, 11 a.m.–7 p.m. Tues.–Sat., 12:30–5 p.m. Sun.) sells nothing but lingerie from the likes of Cosabella, La Perla, and Dolce & Gabbana. Pieces range from delicate and frilly to sturdy and functional. Hayes Valley boasts a second location (539 Hayes St., 415/864-8180, 11 a.m.–7 p.m. Mon.–Sat., noon–5 p.m. Sun.).

MARINA AND PACIFIC HEIGHTS

Pacific Heights and its neighbor Presidio Heights, two quiet residential areas, are connected by Sacramento Street, home to interior design and clothing boutiques that display high-end wares that appeal to the well-heeled residents of this area. With 12 blocks' worth of shops, galleries, salons, and eateries, the main trouble folks have is getting through all of it in one shopping session.

Clothing

There are plenty of high-end boutiques to choose from. For the latest outfits, try **Bettina** (3615 Sacramento St., 415/563-8002, www.bettinasf.com, 11 a.m.–7 p.m. Mon.–Fri., 11 a.m.–6:30 p.m. Sat., noon–5 p.m. Sun.). If you prefer fashions from earlier decades, browse through **GoodByes Consignment Shop** (3483 Sacramento St., 415/674-0151, www.goodbyessf.com, 10 a.m.–6 p.m. Mon.–Wed. and Fri.–Sat., 10 a.m.–8 p.m. Thurs., 11 a.m.–5 p.m. Sun.). GoodByes also has a men's store (3464 Sacramento St.) just across the street.

Gift and Home

It takes a ritzy San Francisco neighborhood to support a six-days-a-week orchid store. **Beautiful Orchids** (3319 Sacramento St., 415/567-2443, www.beautifulorchids.com, 10 a.m.–9 p.m. Mon.–Fri., 10 a.m.–5 p.m. Sat.) specializes in rarified live orchid plants. Every color of the rainbow, amazing shapes, and waterfall figures spill from elegant planters. Expect to pay a premium for these rare hand-tended flowers, and to spend even more to ship them home. You can also find elegant home accessories here, most picked to complement the orchids rather than the other way around.

CIVIC CENTER AND HAYES VALLEY

In the Hayes Valley neighborhood adjacent to the Civic Center, shopping goes uptown, but the unique scent of counterculture creativity somehow makes it in. This is a fun neighborhood to get your stroll on, checking out the art galleries and peeking into the boutiques for clothing and upscale housewares, and then stopping at one of the lovely cafés for a restorative bite to eat.

Clothing and Shoes

Ver Unica (437B Hayes St. and 526 Hayes St., 415/431-0688, www.verunicasf.com, 11 A.M.–7 P.M. Mon.–Sat., noon–6 P.M. Sun.) is a vintage boutique that attracts locals and celebrities with high-quality men's and women's clothing and accessories dating from the 1920s to the 1980s, along with a small selection of new apparel by up-and-coming designers.

The corset takes center stage at unique **Dark Garden** (321 Linden St., 415/431-7684, www. darkgarden.net, open daily, call for hours). Custom fitting and design doesn't come cheap, but you'll get quality. An assortment of lingerie is also sold here.

Paolo Iantorno's boutique **Paolo Shoes** (524 Hayes St., 415/552-4580, http://paoloshoes. com, 11 A.M.–7 P.M. Mon.–Sat., 11 A.M.–6 P.M. Sun.) showcases his collection of handcrafted shoes, for which all leather and textiles are conscientiously selected and then inspected to ensure top quality.

On the same street is **Bulo** (418 Hayes St., 415/255-4939, http://buloshoes.com). Italian for hip, fresh, and attractive, Bulo caters to the fashion- and quality-conscious foot fetishist.

Gourmet Goodies

Those with a sweet tooth flock to **Miette** (449 Octavia St., 415/626-6221, www.miettecakes. com, noon–7 P.M. Sun.–Fri., 11 A.M.–7 P.M. Sat.), a cheery European-inspired candy shop, sister store to the Ferry Plaza bakery (415/837-0300). From double-salted licorice to handmade English toffee, the quality confections include imports from England, Italy, and France.

MISSION AND CASTRO

In the 21st century, the closest you can come to the old-school Haight Street shopping experience is in the Mission. The big shopping street with the coolest selections is definitely Valencia Street, which has all the best thrift shops and funky stuff.

On Castro Street, shopping is sexy. Whether you want toys or leather, fetish or lace, or just a pair of fabulous spike-heeled boots, you can find it in one of the racy shops found in the City's notoriously "everything goes" district.

Books

There's a **Books Inc.** (2275 Market St., 415/864-6777, www.booksinc.net, 10 A.M.–10 P.M. daily) in the Castro. This small independent Bay Area bookseller's chain hosts numerous author events and stocks plenty of local authors. You can also find your favorite paperbacks. At this location, the managers stock lots of great gay fiction and nonfiction, in keeping with the neighborhood. You're welcome to stay as long as you like, browsing through the books.

Clothing and Shoes

A local favorite vintage and secondhand clothing store in the Mission is **Schauplatz** (791 Valencia St., 415/864-5665, 1–7 P.M. Wed.–Mon.). It might be a bit more expensive than your average Goodwill, but you'll be wowed by the fabulous and unusual apparel. Surf the racks for everything from 1940s dresses to vintage sunglasses.

At quirky designer boutique **Dema** (1038 Valencia St., 415/206-0500, www.godemago. com), you'll find a range of cotton goodies that include Velvet, Blended, and Orla Kiely as well as fine cashmere blends and silk dresses.

Sunhee Moon (3167 16th St., 415/355-1800, www.sunheemoon.com, noon–7 P.M. Mon.–Fri., noon–6 P.M. Sat.–Sun.) showcases San

Francisco designer Sunhee's own line of classic separates with a twist, which fit petite gals perfectly. Her boutique also carries jewelry, bags, sunglasses, and other accessories from local designers.

Therapy (545 Valencia St., 415/865-0981, www.shopattherapy.com) surpasses the nearby competition with its well-priced mix of clothing, accessories, and goofy gifts.

Need shoes? One of the few honest-to-goodness local family-owned shoe stores, **De La Sole** (549 Castro St., 415/255-3140, www.delasole.com, 11 A.M.–7 P.M. daily) in the Castro proffers both men's and women's foot fashions. You'll find the shop friendly to all shoppers, even those who come in often, if you know what I mean. The shoes shine with the latest fashions, from sneakers to formals. Even the shop's interior carries on the theme of fun, fashionable modernity, making visitors feel hip just by walking in the door.

Gift and Home

Five and Diamond (510 Valencia St., 415/255-9747, www.fiveanddiamond.com, noon–8 P.M. Mon.–Thurs., 1–9 P.M. Fri.–Sat., noon–7 P.M. Sun.) can bring you every aspect of the stereotypical San Francisco experience all in one storefront. Inside this unique space, you'll find off-the-wall art, unusual clothing, and downright scary jewelry. Those who make an appointment in advance can also get a tattoo here, or purchase some keen body jewelry. A trip inside Five and Diamond can be an exciting adventure for the bold, but might be a bit much for the faint of heart. Decide for yourself whether you dare to take the plunge.

Author Dave Eggers's tongue-in-cheek storefront at **826 Valencia** (826 Valencia St., 415/642-5905, www.826valencia.org/store, noon–6 P.M. daily) doubles as a pirate supply shop and youth literacy center. While you'll find plenty of pirate booty, you'll also find a good stock of literary magazines and books. Almost next door, **Paxton Gate** (824 Valencia St., 415/824-1872, www.paxtongate.com, 11 A.M.–7 P.M. daily) takes the typical gift shop to a new level with taxidermy. This

quirky spot is surprisingly cheery, with garden supplies, books, and candles filling the cases in addition to the fossilized creatures.

Cliff's Variety (479 Castro St., 415/431-5365, www.cliffsvariety.com, 8:30 A.M.–8 P.M. Mon.–Fri., 9:30 A.M.–8 P.M. Sat., 11 A.M.–6 P.M. Sun.) is no ordinary hardware store, though it does carry jigsaws and wrenches. Check out its delightful array of bric-a-brac, including toys, wigs, and lava lamps.

Good Vibrations (899 Mission St., 800/289-8423, www.goodvibrations.com, 10 A.M.–9 P.M. Sun.–Thurs., 10 A.M.–11 P.M. Fri.–Sat.) is a woman-owned, woman-operated, woman-centric sex shop. The well-lit house of sex succeeded in creating a sex-positive cultural center in the Mission, then expanded to two more stores in San Francisco (603 Valencia St. and 1620 Polk St.) and one in Berkeley. In addition to selling every kind of sex toy you can imagine, and probably a bunch you'd never even fantasized about, Good Vibration hosts classes and seminars aimed at improving the human sexual experience. And GV prides itself on its sex-positive, female-friendly, hand-picked collection of adult videos.

GOLDEN GATE PARK AND THE HAIGHT

The Haight-Ashbury shopping district isn't what it used to be, but if you're willing to poke around a bit, you can still find a few bargains in the remaining thrift shops. In Golden Gate Park, the Museum Stores at the de Young and the Academy of Sciences sell high-priced but beautiful and unusual souvenirs—true remembrances of a visit to San Francisco.

Want to get yourself a new tattoo, a split tongue, or a Prince Albert as a unique souvenir of your trip to San Francisco? Head down to **Mom's Body Shop** (1408 Haight St., 415/864-6667, www.momsbodyshop.com, noon–close daily).

One relic of the 1960s counterculture still thrives on the Haight: head shops. Items from these shops will delight any teenagers on your gift list—their parents may be somewhat less delighted by the hemp clothing, Bob Marley

T-shirts, and lava lamps. All pipes, water pipes, and other paraphernalia are *strictly for use in smoking legal tobacco,* you understand. For legal reasons, be sure not to mention anything else when you're browsing in shops like **Ashbury Tobacco Center** (1524 Haight St., 415/552-5556, 10 A.M.–9:30 P.M. daily).

Books and Music

Music has always been a part of the Haight. To this day you'll find homeless folks pounding out rhythms on *doumbeks* and congas on the sidewalks. Located in an old bowling alley, **Amoeba** (1855 Haight St., 415/831-1200, www.amoeba.com, 10:30 A.M.–10 P.M. Mon.–Sat., 11 A.M.–9 P.M. Sun.) is a larger-than-life record store that promotes every type of music imaginable. Amoeba's staff, many of whom are musicians themselves, are among the most knowledgeable in the business.

The award-winning **Booksmith** (1644 Haight St., 800/493-7323, www.book-smith.com, 10 A.M.–10 P.M. Mon.–Sat., 10 A.M.–8 P.M. Sun.) boasts a helpful and in-formed staff, a fabulous magazine collection, and Northern California's preeminent calen-dar of readings by internationally renowned authors.

Technically in the Richmond neighborhood, **Green Apple Books & Music** (506 Clement St., 415/387-2272, www.greenapplebooks.com, 10 A.M.–10:30 P.M. Sun.–Thurs., 10 A.M.–11:30 P.M. Fri.–Sat.) is worth the trek. Locals head to this fog belt location to get their fill of thousands of titles that include staff picks, new releases, and used nonfiction. Friendly

sales staff are on hand to assist with navigat-ing the myriad stacks.

Clothing

Join the countless bargain shoppers who prowl the racks for fabulous forgotten garments, but don't expect to pay $0.25 for that great 1930s bias-cut dress or $0.50 for a cast-off Dior blouse; the merchants in the Haight are experi-enced used clothiers who know what the good stuff is worth. The same is true at the **Buffalo Exchange** (1555 Haight St., 415/431-7733, www.buffaloexchange.com, 11 A.M.–8 P.M. daily), another Haight institution filled with a mix of new and used überhip clothes.

Originally a vaudeville theater, the capacious **Wasteland** (1660 Haight St., 415/863-3150, www.wastelandclothing.com, 11 A.M.–8 P.M. Mon.–Sat., noon–7 P.M. Sun.) has a traffic-stopping art nouveau facade, a distinctive assortment of vintage hippie and rock-star threads, and a glamour-punk staff.

For more upscale (and unworn) threads, head to **Ambiance** (1458 Haight St., 415/552-5095, 10 A.M.–7 P.M. Mon.–Sat., 11 A.M.–7 P.M. Sun.). The two-level store is packed with every-thing from evening dresses to jeans—and tons of customers.

From the grungy, make for the glam at **Piedmont Boutique** (1452 Haight St., 415/864-8075, www.piedmontsf.com, 11 A.M.–7 P.M. daily). The narrow store is a riot of color, filled with feather boas, sequined shorts, fantastic wigs—and those who wear them. This is where San Francisco's drag queens shop. (Tip: Avoid the crowds during Halloween.)

Sports and Recreation

PARKS

The largest park in San Francisco is **Golden Gate Park** (main entrance at Stanyan St. and Fell St., McLaren Lodge Visitors Center at John F. Kennedy Dr., 415/831-2700, www.golden-gate-park.com). In addition to popular sights like the Academy of Sciences, the de Young, and the Japanese Tea Garden, Golden Gate Park is San Francisco's unofficial playground. There are three botanical gardens, a children's playground (Martin Luther King Jr. Dr. and Bowling Green Dr.), tennis courts, and a golf course. Stow Lake offers paddleboats for rent (415/752-0347, 10 A.M.–4 P.M. daily, $13–17 per hour), and the park even has its own bison paddock (off John F. Kennedy Dr.). Weekends, find the park filled with locals roller-skating, biking, hiking, and even Lindy Hopping. Note that the main entrance at John F. Kennedy Drive off Fell Street is closed to motorists every Sunday for pedestrian-friendly fun.

Crissy Field (1199 E. Beach, Presidio, 415/561-7690, www.crissyfield.org, 9 A.M.–5 P.M. daily), in the Golden Gate National Recreation Area, is a park with a mission. In partnership with the National Park Service, ecology programs are the centerpiece. Check the website for a list of classes, seminars, and fun hands-on activities for all ages. Many of these include walks out into the marsh beyond the center and the landscape of the Presidio and beyond. Just check the address before you head for Crissy Field—the visitors center is currently housed in a temporary location while a long-term road construction project is underway.

Expect to see lots of locals when you visit **Mission Dolores Park** (Dolores St. and 18th St., 415/554-9529, http://sfrecpark.org/MissionDoloresPark.aspx), usually called Dolores Park and a favorite of Mission district denizens. Bring a beach blanket to sprawl on the lawn, enjoy the views, and do some serious people watching; wear walking shoes and stroll on the paved pedestrian paths; or take your racket and balls and grab a game of tennis up at one of the six courts. On weekends, music festivals and cultural events often spring up at Dolores Park.

Note that Dolores Park is undergoing construction on a new playground, set to open later in 2012. Most facilities and access may be closed until then.

Many people who like to hike prefer it with some semblance of solitude. That can be tough to come by in the ever-crowded Golden Gate Park and Presidio. **McLaren Park** (Mansell St. between Excelsior District and Visitacion Valley, 415/239-7735, www.jennalex.com/projects/fomp/homepage) is something of a hidden gem in the busy City—a crowd-free park with miles of hiking trails, dozens of picnic tables, athletic fields, an indoor pool, and even a nine-hole golf course. You can enjoy a set of tennis, swim some laps, or play a quick round. But most of all, you can walk. Seven miles of trails are asphalt paved, and plenty of undeveloped trails wend off into the brush and trees all around. If you've got the stamina, you can circle the whole park by following its trails. Feel free to bring your canine companion with you to this dog-friendly park. On the other hand, take care walking here if you're a woman alone; McLaren Park is generally quite safe in the daylight hours, but at night it becomes much less safe, so plan to finish up your hiking, picnicking, and playing by sunset.

BEACHES

San Francisco boasts of being a city that has everything, and it certainly comes close. This massive urban wonderland even claims several genuine sand beaches within its city limits. No doubt the biggest and most famous of these is **Ocean Beach** (Great Hwy., parking at Sloat Blvd., Golden Gate Park, and the Cliff House, www.parksconservancy.org/visit/park-sites/ocean-beach.html). This five-mile stretch of sand forms the breakwater for the Pacific Ocean along the whole west side of the City.

© LUCIE ERICKSEN

view of the Golden Gate Bridge from Baker Beach

Because it's so large you're likely to find a spot to sit down and maybe even a parking place along the beach, except perhaps on that rarest of occasions in San Francisco: a sunny, warm day. Don't go out for an ocean swim at Ocean Beach: Extremely dangerous rip currents kill at least one person every year.

The beach at **Aquatic Park** (Beach St. and Hyde St., www.nps.gov/safr) sits right in the middle the Fisherman's Wharf tourist area. This makes Aquatic Park incredibly convenient for visitors who want to grab a picnic on the Wharf to enjoy down on the beach. The coolest part of Aquatic Park is its history rather than its current presence. It was built in the late 1930s as a bathhouse catering to wealthy San Franciscans, and today, one of the main attractions of Aquatic Park remains swimming: Triathletes and hard-core swimmers brave the frigid waters to swim for miles in the protected cove. More sedate visitors can find a seat and enjoy a cup of coffee, a newspaper, and some people watching.

Baker Beach (Golden Gate Point and the Presidio, www.parksconservancy.org/visit/park-sites/baker-beach.html) is best known for its scenery, and that doesn't just mean the lovely views of the Golden Gate Bridge from an unusual angle (from the west and below); Baker is San Francisco's own clothing-optional (that is, nude) beach. But don't worry, plenty of the denizens of Baker Beach wear clothes while flying kites, playing volleyball and Frisbee, and even just strolling on the beach. Baker Beach was the original home of the Burning Man festival before it moved out to the Black Rock Desert of Nevada. Because Baker is much smaller than Ocean Beach, it gets crowded in the summer. Whether you choose to sunbathe nude or not, don't try to swim here. The currents get seriously strong and dangerous because it is so close to the Golden Gate.

BIKING

In other places, bicycling is a sport or a mode of transportation. In San Francisco, bicycling is a religion (the concept of mountain biking originated here). As a newcomer to biking in the City, it may be wise to start off gently, perhaps with a guided tour that avoids areas with dangerous traffic. The fabulously named **Blazing Saddles** (2715 Hyde St., 415/202-8888, www.blazingsaddles.com) rents bikes and offers guided bicycling tours all over the Bay Area. If you prefer the safety of a group, take the guided tour (10 A.M. daily, 3 hours, reservations required) through San Francisco and across the Golden Gate Bridge into Marin County. You'll return to the City by ferry. Blazing Saddles can also supply intrepid cyclists with bike maps of the City and the greater Bay Area. For a sedate introductory ride, you can take the popular self-guided tour of the waterfront. With five Blazing Saddles locations, most in the Fisherman's Wharf area, it's easy to find yourself a cruiser and head out for a spin.

If you're not a serious cyclist, or you're a serious cyclist who's new to the City, take the easy and flat nine-mile ride across the **Golden Gate Bridge** and back. This is a great way to see the Bridge and the Bay for the first time, and it takes only an hour or two to complete. Another option is to ride across the bridge and into the town of Sausalito (8 miles) or Tiburon (16 miles), enjoy an afternoon and dinner, and then ride the ferry back into the City (bikes are allowed on board).

If you've got a bit more time and leg strength, consider a scenic ride on the paved paths of **Golden Gate Park** (main entrance at Stanyan St. and Fell St., McLaren Lodge Visitors Center at John F. Kennedy Dr., 415/831-2700, www.golden-gate-park.com) and the **Presidio** (Montgomery St. and Lincoln Blvd., 415/561-4323, www.nps.gov/prsf). A bike makes a perfect mode of transportation to explore the various museums and attractions of these two large parks, and you can spend all day and never have to worry about finding parking.

Looking for some great urban mountain biking? Miles of unpaved roads and trails inside the city limits provide technically challenging rides for adventurous cyclists willing to take a risk or two. Check out the website

for **San Francisco Mountain Biking** (www.sfmtb.com) for information about trails, roads, routes, and regulations.

GOLF

A number of golf courses hide in the parks of San Francisco. The premier golf course in the City, the **Presidio Golf Course** (Arguello St., 50 yards from Arguello Gate, 415/561-4653, www.presidiogolf.com) was once reserved for the exclusive use of military officers, government officials, and visiting dignitaries. Since 1995 the 18-hole, par-72 course, driving range, practice putting greens, and clubhouse have been available to the public. Reserve your tee time by phone or online. Lessons are available, offered by the Arnold Palmer Golf Academy (the Arnold Palmer Management Company operates the course).

Lincoln Park Golf Course (34th Ave. and Clement St., 415/221-9911) is an 80-year-old public 18-hole, par-68 course in the Outer Richmond district. It hosts the annual San Francisco City Golf Championships. For tee times at any municipal course, call 415/750-4653.

HIKING

Yes, you can go for a hike inside the city of San Francisco. Most of the parks in the City offer hiking trails to suit various tastes and ability levels. The City also boasts some longer and more interesting trails that present serious hikers with a real challenge.

For an easy nature walk in the Presidio, try the easy **Lobos Creek Trail** (Lincoln St. at Bowley St., www.bahiker.com/sfhikes/loboscreek.html, dawn–dusk daily). Less than a mile long, this flat boardwalk trail is wheelchair-accessible and shows off the beginning successes of the ecological restoration of the Presidio. You'll get to see restored sand dunes and native vegetation, which has attracted butterflies and other insects, in turn bringing birds to the trail area. While it's still in the City, this trail gives walkers a glimpse of what the Presidio might have been like 500 years ago. Another easy Presidio hike goes way

TWIN PEAKS

Twin Peaks rises up from the center of San Francisco, and is the second-highest point in the City. Twin Peaks divides the City between north and south, catching the fog bank that rolls in from the Golden Gate and providing a habitat for lots of wild birds and insects, including the endangered Mission Blue Butterfly.

While you barely need to get out of your car to enjoy the stunning 360-degree views of the City from the peaks, the best way to enjoy the view is to take a hike. If you want to scale the less traveled South Peak, start at the pullout on the road below the parking lot. You'll climb a steep set of stairs up to the top of the South Peak in less than 0.2 mile. Stop and marvel at man's industry: the communications tower that's the massive eyesore just over the peak. Carefully cross the road to access the red-rock stairway up to the North Peak. It's only a 0.25 mile, but as with the South Peak, those stairs seem to go straight up! It's worth it when you look out across the Golden Gate to Mount Tamalpais in the north and Mount Diablo in the east.

If it's the view you're seeking rather than the wildlife and exercise, head to Twin Peaks only on a sunny day. If the fog is in, as so often happens in the summertime, you'll have trouble seeing five feet in front of you. Oh, and don't expect a verdant paradise up there – the grass doesn't stay green long in the spring, so most visitors get to see the dried-out brush that characterizes much of the Bay Area in the summertime and fall.

To get there, drive west up Market Street (eventually turning into Portola Dr.), and turn right onto Twin Peaks Boulevard and past the parade of tour buses to the parking lot past the north peak. Parking is free and Twin Peaks is open year-round.

---

back into the region's history. The one-mile (one-way) **Lover's Lane** (Funston Ave. and Presidio Blvd., www.nps.gov/prsf/planyour-visit/lovers-lane.htm) once served soldiers stationed at the Presidio who beat down the path into the City proper to visit their sweethearts. Today, you'll have a peaceful tree-shaded walk on a flat semipaved path that passes the former homes of the soldiers, crosses El Polin Creek, and ends at the Presidio Gate.

Want to hike the whole **Bay Area Ridge Trail** (415/561-2595, www.ridgetrail.org)? Prepare to get serious—the whole trail runs more than 325 miles and grows longer annually. It crosses the City of San Francisco from south to north. The easy Presidio section (Arguello Blvd. and Jackson St.) runs 2.7 miles from the Arguello Gate to the foot of the Golden Gate Bridge. If you've been trudging the sidewalks and climbing the hills of the difficult seven-mile section from Stern Grove (Wawona St. and 21st Ave.) to the Presidio's Arguello Gate, you'll be happy to find the gently sloping dirt footpaths through unpopulated forests and meadows of the Presidio. Round out the City section of the trail with the moderate 3.2-mile (one-way) section from Fort Funston (hang glider viewing deck off Fort Funston Rd.) to Stern Grove. If the weather is right, you can watch the hang gliders fly at the fort before pointing your boots north to hike the paved trails through protected glens and residential neighborhoods that most visitors to San Francisco never see.

The **Land's End Trail** (Merrie Way, 415/561-4323, www.parksconservancy.org/visit/park-sites/lands-end.html) winds, drops, and rises from the ruins of the Sutro Baths, past the Legion of Honor, and on out to the rugged cliffs and beaches where the North American continent ends. At low tide, you can stand out in the wind and see the leftover bits of three ships that all wrecked on the rocks of Point Lobos. Smaller side trails lead down to little beaches, and the views of the Golden Gate are the stuff of legend. The **El Camino Del Mar** trail intersects Land's End, creating a big mostly paved loop for enthusiastic hikers who want to take on a three-plus-mile trek that hits most of the major landmarks of Land's End. Seriously, bring a camera on this hike, even if you have to buy a disposable one. The views from this trail may be some of the most beautiful on earth.

It isn't surprising that Golden Gate Park is riddled with paved pedestrian paths. The surprise is that most of them aren't named, and residents don't go to the park for serious hiking. One exception is the **Golden Gate Park and Ocean Beach Hike** (trailhead at Fell St. and Baker St., www.traillink.com/trail-maps/golden-gate-park-and-ocean-beach.aspx). Almost seven miles long, this trail runs from the Golden Gate Park Panhandle all the way to the ocean, then down Ocean Beach to the San Francisco Zoo. You'll pass close by the Conservatory of Flowers, the de Young Museum, Stow Lake, Bercut Equitation Field, and several children's play areas.

Probably the closest thing to a true serene backwoods hike in San Francisco can be found at the easy 0.5-mile trail at **Mount Davidson** (Dalewood St., West Portal, 6 A.M.–10 P.M. daily, www.bahiker.com/sfhikes/davidson.html). Park in the adjacent West Portal residential area and wander through the gate and into the woods. Take the main fire road straight up the gentle slope to the top of the mountain, then find the smaller track off to the left that leads to the famous "cross at the top of the mountain." To extend your stay in this pleasant place, either walk down the other side of the mountain or head back to find the smaller branch trails that lead off into the trees.

For a more vigorous and better-known walk, take the moderate one-mile trail at **Glen Canyon** (Bosworth St.). Feel free to bring your canine companion on this trail through an unlikely but lovely little urban canyon. It only takes about half an hour to explore Islais Creek, the nonnative eucalyptus and blackberries, and the attractive if unspectacular views. Take care to avoid the prolific poison oak that spreads throughout the canyon.

The difficult 10.5-mile **California Coastal Trail** (Golden Gate National Recreation Area, www.californiacoastaltrail.info) runs through the city of San Francisco on its way down the state. Originating beneath the Golden Gate Bridge, the trail meanders all the way down the west side of the City. It passes by many major monuments and parks, so you can take a break from hiking to visit Fort Point, the Palace of the Legion of Honor, and the site of the Sutro Baths. You'll get to walk along the famous beaches of San Francisco as well, from Baker Beach to China Beach and on down to Ocean Beach, which account for five miles of the Coastal Trail. You can keep on walking all the way down to Fort Funston; the San Francisco portion of the trail terminates at Philip Burton Memorial State Beach. You can enter the trail from just about anywhere and exit where it feels convenient. Get a current trail map to be aware of any partial trail closures.

KAYAKING

For the adventurous, kayaking on San Francisco Bay is a great way to experience the famous waterway on a personal level. **City Kayak** (415/357-1010, www.citykayak.com) has locations at South Beach Harbor (Pier 40, Embarcadero and Townsend St., 10 A.M.–7 P.M. daily), with rental equipment available, and at Fisherman's Wharf (Pier 39, Slip A21). Beginners can take guided paddles along the shoreline, getting a new view of familiar sights. More advanced kayakers can take trips out to the Golden Gate and around Alcatraz Island.

WHALE WATCHING

With day-trip access to the marine sanctuary off the Farallon Islands, whale watching is a year-round activity in San Francisco. **San Francisco Whale Tours** (Pier 39, Dock B, 800/979-3370, www.sanfranciscowhaletours.com, tours daily, $60–89, advance purchase required) offers six-hour trips out to the Farallons almost every Saturday and Sunday, with almost-guaranteed whale sightings on each trip. Shorter whale-watching trips along the coastline run on weekdays, and 90-minute quickie trips out to see slightly smaller local wildlife, including elephant seals and sea lions, also go out daily. Children ages 3–15 are welcome on boat tours (for reduced rates), and kids often love the chance to spot whales, sea lions, and pelicans. Children under age three are not permitted for safety reasons.

YOGA

It's tough to walk two blocks in San Francisco without tripping over a yoga studio. The best way to find one that has the right kind of classes to keep your practice up while you're on the road is to ask a friend, or your current yogi, which studio they'd recommend in San Francisco. The second-best option is to check out listings in the *Yoga Journal* (www.yogajournal.com/directory). The magazine is based in San Francisco, and the editors not only recommend local studios, they practice in them.

The chain **Hiking Yoga** (1 Ferry Building Plaza, 888/589-2250, www.hikingyoga.com, $20 per hike, 3 hikes $50) has a facility in the Ferry Building. While it's not a traditional yoga class, Hiking Yoga gets you stretching, working out, and hiking around the City all in one 90-minute package. Bonus: Because it's an outdoor hiking thing, you don't need to figure out how to lug a yoga mat along.

SPECTATOR SPORTS

Lovers of the big leagues will find fun in San Francisco and around the Bay Area. The City is home to the National Football League's **San Francisco 49ers** (www.49ers.com). The 49ers play at **Candlestick Park** (490 Jamestown Ave., tickets 415/656-4900, parking 415/656-4949, parking $30), far from the center of the City on Candlestick Point. This doesn't seem to matter to "the Faithful," the loyal fans who've seen the team through their dismal beginnings, rejoiced in their domination of the NFL through the 1980s and 1990s, and continued to cheer as the team "rebuilds" (that is, loses a lot) in the 21st century. Check the website for current single-ticket prices. And be sure to bring a coat to the games—the fog rolls in off the Bay and makes the park chilly and windy. (Note that as of press time, the team is planning to move to a new—and hotly debated—stadium in Santa Clara.)

Major League Baseball's **San Francisco Giants** (http://sanfrancisco.giants.mlb.com) play out the long summer baseball season at **AT&T Park** (24 Willie Mays Plaza, 3rd St. and King St., 415/972-2000). Come out to enjoy the game, the food, and the views at San Francisco's still shiny and new ballpark. Giants games take place on weekdays and weekends, both day and night. It's not hard to snag last-minute tickets to a regular season game. Oh, and be sure to check out the gourmet restaurants that ring the stadium; it wouldn't be San Francisco without top-tier cuisine to complement a midsummer ball game.

Accommodations

San Francisco has plenty of accommodations to suit every taste and most budgets. The most expensive places tend to be in Union Square, SoMa, and the Financial District. Cheaper digs can be had in the neighborhoods surrounding Fisherman's Wharf. You'll find the most character in the smaller boutique hotels, but plenty of big chain hotels have at least one location in town if you prefer a known quantity. In fact, a number of chain motels have moved into historic San Francisco buildings, creating a more unusual experience than you might expect from the likes of a Days Inn.

Be aware that many hotels in San Francisco are 100 percent nonsmoking—you can't even light up on your balcony. If you need a smoking room, you'll have to hunt hard. Be aware that many motels are cracking down on green smoke as well as on cigarettes.

Free parking with a hotel room is rare in the City, existing mostly in motor lodges and chain motels down by the wharf. Overnight garage parking downtown can be excruciatingly expensive. Check with your hotel to see if they have a "parking package" that includes this expense (and possibly offers valet service as well). If you don't plan to leave the City on your trip, consider saving a bundle by skipping the rental car altogether and using public transit. On the other hand, to explore outside the City limits, a car is a necessity.

UNION SQUARE AND NOB HILL

In and around Union Square and Nob Hill, you'll find approximately a zillion hotels. As a rule, those closest to the top of the Hill or to Union Square proper are the most expensive. For a 1–2-block walk, you get more personality and genuine San Francisco experience for less money and less prestige. There are few inexpensive options in these areas; hostels appear in the direction of the Tenderloin, where safety becomes an issue after dark.

Under $150

While the best bargains aren't in these neighborhoods, you can still find one or two budget-conscious lodgings in the Union Square and Nob Hill area. Just off Union Square, the **Handlery Hotel** (351 Geary St., 800/995-4874, www.handlery.com, $135–330) offers a wide variety of guest rooms for all different price ranges. Value rooms in the historical section of the hotel tend to be small and the appointments a bit sterile, but the amenities are as good as those in the newer, pricier Club section of the complex. For a serious splurge, rent the Rooftop Garden Suite, complete with an outdoor patio overlooking the City. A heated outdoor pool is available to all, and the Daily Grill restaurant serves up large portions of standard California cuisine all day long. The **Hotel Bijou** (111 Mason St., 800/771-1022, www.hotelbijou.com, $116–200) might be the most fun of the inexpensive lot. Whimsical decor mimics an old-fashioned movie theater, and in fact a tiny "movie house" downstairs runs double features, free to guests, every night—with only movies shot in San

Francisco. The guest rooms are small, clean, and nicely appointed.

Should you find the need for a full-service professional recording studio in your hotel, head straight for **The Mosser** (54 4th St., 800/227-3804, www.themosser.com, $79–189, parking $35). The Mosser's inexpensive guest rooms have European-style shared baths in the hallway and spare Asian-inspired interior decor. Pricier options include bigger guest rooms with private baths; on the other hand, solo travelers can trim their costs by getting a teensy room with a single twin bed. With a rep for cleanliness and pleasant amenities, including morning coffee and comfy bathrobes, this hotel fulfills its goal—to provide visitors to the City with cheap crash space in a great location convenient to sights, shops, and public transportation.

$150-250

Hotel Rex (562 Sutter St., 800/433-4434, www.jdvhotels.com/rex, $190–430) has a classic feel, evoking a hotel in San Francisco early in the 1900s. Guest rooms are comfortable and spacious, decorated with the work of local artists and artisans. The dimly lit lobby bar is famous in the City for its literary bent—you may find yourself embroiled in a fascinating conversation as you enjoy your evening glass of wine. Amenities include a small elevator (not all boutique hotels in SF have them), access to a nearby gym, and valet parking packages for an additional fee. The attached Café Andrée serves dinner each night; ask at the desk about reservations.

The **Hotel Monaco** (501 Geary St., 415/292-0100, www.monaco-sf.com, $179–300) shows the vibrant side of San Francisco. Big guest rooms are whimsically decorated with bright colors, while baths are luxurious and feature cushy animal-print bathrobes. Friendly service comes from purple-velour-coated staff, who know the hotel and the City and will cheerfully tell you all about both. Chair massage complements the free wine and cheese in the large open guest lounge. Be sure to check out the Grand Café and the dining room as well. Because the Hotel Monaco is located a couple of blocks from Union Square, you get more, and more fun, for your money.

Only half a block down from the square, the **Sir Francis Drake** (450 Powell St., 800/795-7129, www.sirfrancisdrake.com, $220–360) has its own history beginning in the late 1920s. Here at the Drake you'll find a bit less opulence in the lobby, compared to the St. Francis, and a bit more in the guest rooms. The Beefeater doorman (almost always available for a photo), the unique door overhang, and the red-and-gold interior all add to the character of this favorite.

Over $250

A San Francisco legend, the **Clift** (495 Geary St., 415/775-4700, www.clifthotel.com, $315–500) has a lobby worth walking into, whether you're a guest of the hotel or not. The high-ceilinged, gray industrial space is entirely devoted to modern art. Yes, you really are supposed to sit on the antler sofa and the metal chairs, though most folks avoid the seriously oversize vintage seat. By contrast, the big Philippe Starck–designed guest rooms are almost Spartan in their simplicity, with colors meant to mimic the City skyline. Stop in for a drink at the Redwood Room, done in brown leather and popular with a younger crowd. For dinner, a branch of Jeffrey Chodorow's Asia de Cuba restaurant is located inside the hotel. The Clift is perfectly located for theatergoers, and the Square is an easy walk away.

The opulence of the lobby at the **Westin St. Francis** (335 Powell St., 415/397-7000, www.westinstfrancis.com, $295–370) matches its elegant address. With more than a century of history as San Francisco's great gathering spot, the St. Francis still garners great prestige. Guest rooms are attractive but small. The cost of a stay pays mainly for the decadent fixtures of the common areas, the four eateries (including Michael Mina, the executive chef's signature restaurant), the state-of-the-art gym, top-quality meeting and banquet spaces, and the address on Union Square.

Certain names just mean luxury in the hotel world. The **Fairmont San Francisco** (950 Mason St., 415/772-5000, www.fairmont.com, $270–420) is among the best of these. With a rich history, above-and-beyond service, and spectacular views, the Fairmont makes any stay in the City memorable. Check online for package specials or to book a tee time or spa treatment, and note that some of the guest rooms in this rarified hostelry actually allow smoking.

Another Nob Hill contender with a top name, the **Ritz-Carlton** (600 Stockton St., 415/296-7465, www.ritzcarlton.com, $430–560) provides patrons with ultimate pampering. From the high-thread-count sheets to the five-star dining room and the full-service spa, guests at the Ritz all but drown in sumptuous amenities. Even the "standard" guest rooms are exceptional, but if you've got the bread, spring for the Club Floors, where they'll give you an iPod, a personal concierge, and possibly the kitchen sink if you ask for it.

FINANCIAL DISTRICT AND SOMA

Top business execs make it their, well…business to stay near the towering offices of the Financial District, down by the water on the Embarcadero, or in SoMa. Thus, most of the lodgings in these areas cater to the expense-account set. The big-name chain hotels run expensive; book one if you're traveling on an unlimited company credit card. Otherwise, look for smaller boutique and indie accommodations that won't tear your wallet to bits or laugh at your checking account.

Under $150

No, really, there's a place to stay in SoMa that's cheap, fastidious, and safe. It's the surprisingly eponymous **Good Hotel** (112 7th St., 800/444-5819, www.thegoodhotel.com, $139–159). The guest rooms here are small and are starting to turn shabby around the edges of the eyeball-searing modern decor, but they've got scrupulously clean private baths, and it's hard to beat the location at the corner of 7th and Mission Streets, an easy walk to the Civic Center or the Asian Art Museum, places to enjoy good cheap food, and quick access to BART. Just don't wander up one block to 6th Street, because the "safe" thing comes to an abrupt halt between the two numbered streets. If you're slightly suicidal, you can borrow one of the cruiser bikes in the lobby from the friendly desk staff. The Good Hotel is noisy at night, but if you're going to stay at a major intersection in a major city, you have to expect some traffic noise.

$150-250

An unlikely hotel in the middle of the stuffy suit-clad Financial District, the **[** **Hotel Triton** (342 Grant Ave., 800/800-1299, www.hoteltriton.com, $160–300) welcomes guests with whimsical decor and an ecological theme. Jerry Garcia and Carlos Santana both decorated guest rooms here, and the environmentally friendly practices developed at the Triton are being adopted by sister hotels all over the world. You'll find the guest rooms tiny but comfortable and well stocked with ecofriendly amenities and bath products. The flat-panel TVs offer a 24-hour yoga channel, and complimentary yoga props can be delivered to your room on request. For the most eco-zany experience at the Triton, book a Celebrity Eco-Suite. Or if you're traveling alone, consider reserving a Zen Den—specially designed for solo travelers and offering the finest Buddhist-inspired amenities. And don't forget to adopt a rubber ducky for the duration of your stay!

For something posh but not overwhelmingly huge, check out **Hotel Griffon** (155 Steuart St., 800/321-2201, www.hotelgriffon.com, $245–350). A boutique business hotel with a prime vacation locale, the Griffon offers business and leisure packages to suit any traveler's needs. They're a bit pricier, but the best guest rooms overlook the Bay, with views of the Bay Bridge and Treasure Island.

Over $250

Le Méridien San Francisco (333 Battery St., 415/296-2900, $300–570) stands tall in the Embarcadero Center, convenient to shopping,

dining, and the streetcar and cable car lines to all the favorite downtown destinations. This expensive luxury hotel pampers guests with Frette sheets, plush robes, marble baths, and stellar views. Expect nightly turndown service, free newspapers, and 24-hour room service.

It may be part of a chain, but at the **Westin San Francisco Market** (50 3rd St., 415/974-6400, www.westinsf.com, $260–670) you'll find plenty of San Francisco charm at your doorstep. Guests stay in pleasant rooms with pretty cityscapes at this large hotel (formerly known as the Argent). Amenities mimic the more expensive SoMa hotels, and seasonal special rates dip down into the genuinely affordable. The attached restaurant, Ducca, serves three meals daily, and the lounge is open until midnight for nightcaps.

Hotel Vitale (8 Mission St., 888/890-8688, www.hotelvitale.com, $300–520) professes to restore guests' vitality with its lovely guest rooms and exclusive spa, complete with rooftop hot soaking tubs and a yoga studio. Many of the good-size guest rooms also have private deep soaking tubs. If you happen to reside in the greater Bay Area, check out the deeply discounted "Sunday Locals Only" package.

The only problem with staying at the **[** **Mandarin Oriental San Francisco** (222 Sansome St., 415/276-9888, www.mandarinoriental.com, $520–860) is that you may never leave your room. Redefining decadence, the Mandarin Oriental includes raised beds in all rooms so guests can enjoy the panoramic city and bay views while snuggling under the covers. In the swank corner guest rooms and suites, raised bathtubs let bathers enjoy stunning sights (such as the Transamerica Pyramid, Alcatraz, and the Golden Gate Bridge) from the warmth of the bubbly water. All guest rooms boast top amenities and Asian-inspired decor, and families are welcome. You can find the best room rates on the hotel's website (the prices will make a budget-minded traveler's eyes bleed) along with various stay-and-play packages with an emphasis on golf and spa treatments.

For a unique San Francisco hotel experience, book a room at the famous **Hotel Palomar**

(12 4th St., 866/373-4941, www.hotelpal-omar-sf.com, $250–575). You'll find every amenity imaginable, from extra-long beds for taller guests to in-room spa services and temporary pet goldfish. The overall decorative motif evokes M. C. Escher, and whimsical colorful touches accent each room. Be sure to make reservations for dinner at the award-winning Fifth Floor restaurant during your stay. Check the website for special deals, some quite reasonably priced, that focus on shopping and spa-style relaxation. You can even book a spa package with your dog!

The **Palace Hotel** (2 New Montgomery St., 415/512-1111, www.sfpalace.com, $260–600) enjoys its reputation as the grande dame of all San Francisco hotels. The original Palace was the dream of William Ralston, who bankrupted himself creating the immense hotel. The rich history of the Palace began when its doors opened in 1875. It was gutted by fires following the 1906 earthquake, rebuilt and reopened in 1909, and refurbished for the new millennium during 1989–1991. In 1919, President Woodrow Wilson negotiated the terms of the Treaty of Versailles over lunch at the Garden Court. Today, guests take pleasure in beautiful bedrooms, exercise and relax in the full-service spa and fitness center, and dine in the Palace's three restaurants. If you're staying at the Palace, having a meal in the exquisite Garden Court dining room is a must, although you may forget to eat as you gaze upward at the stained-glass domed ceiling.

NORTH BEACH AND FISHERMAN'S WHARF

Perhaps it's odd, but the tourist mecca of San Francisco is not a district of a zillion hotels. Most of the major hostelries sit down nearer to Union Square. But you can stay near the Wharf or in North Beach if you choose; you'll find plenty of chain motels here, plus a few select boutique hotels in all price ranges.

Under $150

The **San Remo Hotel** (2237 Mason St., 800/352-7366, www.sanremohotel.com,

$70–100) is one of the best bargains in the City. The blocky old yellow building has been around since just after the 1906 earthquake, offering inexpensive guest rooms to budget-minded travelers. One of the reasons for the rock-bottom pricing is the baths—you don't get your own. Four shared baths with shower facilities located in the hallways are available to guests day and night. The guest rooms boast the simplest of furnishings and decorations as well as clean white-painted walls and ceilings. Some rooms have their own sinks, all have either double beds or two twin beds, and none have telephones or TVs—so this might not be the best choice of lodgings for large media-addicted families. Couples on a romantic vacation can rent the Penthouse, a lovely room for two with lots of windows and a rooftop terrace boasting views of North Beach and the Bay.

$150-250

Hotel Bohème (444 Columbus Ave., 415/433-9111, www.hotelboheme.com, $175–195) offers comfort, history, and culture at a pleasantly low price for San Francisco. The Bohème's long history has included a recent renovation to create an intriguing, comfortable lodging. Guest rooms are small but comfortable, Wi-Fi is free, and the spirit of the 1950s bohemian Beats lives on. The warmly colored and gently lit guest rooms are particularly welcoming to solo travelers and couples, with their retro brass beds covered by postmodern geometric spreads. All guest rooms have private baths, and the double-queen rooms can sleep up to four people for an additional charge.

The **Washington Square Inn** (1660 Stockton St., 800/388-0220, www.wsisf.com, $195–350) doesn't look like a typical California B&B. With its city-practical architecture and canopy out on the sidewalk, it's more a small, elegant hotel. The inn offers 16 guest rooms with queen or king beds, private baths, elegant appointments, and fine linens. Some guest rooms have spa bathtubs, and others have views of Coit Tower and Grace Cathedral. Only the larger guest rooms and junior suites are spacious; the standard guest rooms are "cozy" in the European urban style. A few of the amenities include a generous continental breakfast brought to your room daily, afternoon tea, a flat-screen TV in every guest room, and free Wi-Fi. To stay at the Washington Square Inn is to get a true sense of the beauty and style of San Francisco.

It may be part of a chain, but the **Hyatt at Fisherman's Wharf** (555 North Point St., 415/563-1234, www.fishermanswharf.hyatt.com, $210–390) still merits a visit. The brick façade, unusual for San Francisco, hides an ultramodern lobby and matching guest rooms. Although not too big, guest rooms are elegantly appointed with lots of decadent white linens. Many packages aim at both business travelers and visiting families. Perhaps the best of these is the Summer Parking Package, which includes overnight valet parking in the room rate.

Another great upscale hotel in the heart of San Francisco's visitors' district is the **Best Western Tuscan Inn** (425 North Point St., 800/648-4626, www.tuscaninn.com, $200–290). This luxurious Italian-inspired hotel offers great amenities and prime access to Fisherman's Wharf, Pier 39, Alcatraz, and all the local shopping and dining. The attractive and very modern exterior gives way to earth tones and country-style charm in the common areas. The guest rooms boast bright colors and up-to-date furnishings—much fancier than you might be accustomed to from a Best Western. All guest rooms have private baths. They've also got Internet access, cable TV, and limo service to the Financial District three times daily. Check online for discount rates if you're coming during the middle of the week or booking more than two weeks in advance.

Over $250

For an ultra-luxurious stay in the City, save up for a room at **The Argonaut** (495 Jefferson St., 800/790-1415, www.argonauthotel.com, $250–350). With stunning Bay views from its prime Fisherman's Wharf location, in-room spa services, and a yoga channel, The Argonaut is

all San Francisco, all the time. Bold patterns in blues, golds, and black and white dominate guest-room decor. Guest rooms range from cozy standards up to posh suites with separate bedrooms and whirlpool tubs. The hotel is located steps from the Maritime Museum and Ghirardelli Square.

MARINA AND PACIFIC HEIGHTS

These areas are close enough to Fisherman's Wharf to walk there for dinner, and the lodgings are far more affordable than downtown digs.

Under $100

For an unexpected, bucolic park hostel within walking and biking distance of frenetic downtown San Francisco, stop for a night at the **Fisherman's Wharf Hostel** (Fort Mason Bldg. 240, 415/771-7277, www.sfhostels.com/fishermans-wharf, dorm $26–30, private room $75–125). The hostel sits on Golden Gate National Recreation Area land, pleasantly far from the problems that plague other SF hostels. The best amenities (aside from the free linens, breakfast, and no curfews or chores) are the views of the Bay and Alcatraz, and the sweeping lawns and mature trees all around the hostel.

Few frills clutter the clean, comfortable guest rooms at the **Redwood Inn** (1530 Lombard St., 800/221-6621, www.sfredwoodinn.com, $80–110), but if you need a reasonably priced motel room in ever-expensive San Francisco, this is a great place to grab one. From the location on Lombard Street, you can get to points of interest throughout the City.

Another one of the many motels lining Lombard Street is the **Lombard Motor Inn** (1475 Lombard St., 415/441-6000, www.lombardmotorinn.com, $90–150). It's got the standard-issue amenities: reasonably sizable guest rooms, dark 1990s-era motel colors, free parking, and location, location, location. Of course, the location means there's plenty of nighttime noise pouring in through the windows, especially on weekends.

The **Marina Inn** (3110 Octavia St., 800/274-1420, www.marinainn.com, $80–130), built in 1924, exudes old-fashioned San Francisco charm but boasts pleasant modern amenities. This small family-friendly hotel offers continental breakfast, concierge services, and free Wi-Fi. The Inn is within walking distance of major City attractions, including Fisherman's Wharf, Ghirardelli Square, and the cable cars. And if you're feeling a bit scruffy and want to freshen up before your big night on the town, visit the Inn's attached barbershop or salon.

The **Francisco Bay Inn** (1501 Lombard St., 800/410-7007, www.franciscobayinn.com, $80–125) offers good motel lodgings at reasonable-for-San Francisco rates. The stellar location provides easy access to the Golden Gate Bridge, famously crooked Lombard Street, and Fisherman's Wharf. Best of all, the Francisco Bay offers free parking—a City rarity worth upward of $50 per day.

$100-150

The stately **Queen Anne Hotel** (1590 Sutter St., 800/227-3970, www.queenanne.com, $130–230) brings the elegance of downtown San Francisco out to Pacific Heights. Sumptuous fabrics and rich colors in the guest rooms and common areas add to the feeling of decadence and luxury in this boutique hotel. Small, moderate guest rooms offer attractive accommodations on a budget, while superior rooms and suites are more upscale. Continental breakfast is included, as are a number of high-end services such as courtesy car service and afternoon tea and sherry.

The exterior and interior amenities of the **Hotel Majestic** (1500 Sutter St., 415/441-1100, www.thehotelmajestic.org, $120–140) evoke the grandeur of early-20th-century San Francisco. The Edwardian-style 1902 building boasts antique furnishings and decorative items from England and France. Cozy guest rooms, junior suites, and one-bedroom suites are available. If you're in the City on business or just want to go shopping, take advantage

of free car service to Union Square and the Financial District on weekday mornings. The Cafe Majestic serves breakfast and dinner, with a focus on local, healthful ingredients.

$150-250

The guest rooms at the ◖ **Marina Motel** (2576 Lombard St., 800/346-6118, www.marinamotel.com, $150–200) may be small, but the place is big on charm and character. This friendly little motel, decorated in French-country style, welcomes smokers, families with kids, and dogs. Just ask for the room type that best suits your needs when you make your reservations. Guest rooms are pleasantly priced for budget travelers, and several vacation packages offer deep discounts on tours, spa treatments, and outdoor adventures.

Pack the car and bring the kids to the **Hotel del Sol** (3100 Webster St., 877/433-5765, www.thehoteldelsol.com, $150–180). This unique hotel-motel embraces its origins as a 1950s motor lodge, with the guest rooms decorated in bright, bold colors with whimsical accents, a heated courtyard pool, and the ever-popular free parking. Family suites and larger guest rooms have kitchenettes. The Marina locale offers trendy cafés, restaurants, bars, and shopping within walking distance as well as access to major attractions.

A small, cute inn only a short walk from the Presidio, the **Laurel Inn** (444 Presidio Ave., 800/552-8735, www.jdvhotels.com/laurel_inn, $215–250) provides the perfect place for people with pets or for travelers who want to stay a bit longer in the City. Many of the guest rooms have kitchenettes, and all are comfortable and modern. The G Bar lounge next door offers a nice place to stop and have a cocktail, and the exclusive boutiques of Pacific Heights beckon visitors looking for a way to part with their cash.

Another Pacific Heights jewel, the **Jackson Court** (2198 Jackson St., 415/929-7670, www.jacksoncourt.com, $210) presents a lovely brick facade in the exclusive neighborhood. The 10-room inn offers comfortable, uniquely decorated queen rooms and a luscious continental breakfast each morning.

Over $250

Tucked in with the money-laden mansions of Pacific Heights, **Hotel Drisco** (2901 Pacific Ave., 800/634-7277, www.jdvhotels.com/drisco, $300–475) offers elegance to discerning visitors. Away from the frenzied pace and noise of downtown, at the Drisco you get quiet, comfy guest rooms with overstuffed furniture, breakfast with a latte, and a glass of wine in the evening. Economy rooms have detached baths, and lavish suites have stellar views.

CIVIC CENTER AND HAYES VALLEY

You'll find a few reasonably priced accommodations and classic inns in the Civic Center and Hayes Valley areas.

$100-150

The Grove Inn (890 Grove St., 800/829-0780, www.grovinn.com, $138) offers simple, quiet guest rooms with double-paned windows, fluffy feather beds, TVs, and phones. A continental breakfast is served every morning. You can walk from the Inn to "postcard row" (ask the innkeepers for directions), take a longer stroll down to the Civic Center, or take public transit or a cab to any of the City's attractions.

Take a step back into an older San Francisco at the **Chateau Tivoli** (1057 Steiner St., 800/228-1647, www.chateautivoli.com, $114–340). The over-the-top colorful exterior matches perfectly with the American Renaissance interior decor. Each unique guest room and suite showcases an exquisite style evocative of the Victorian era. Most guest rooms have private baths, although the two least expensive share a bath. With a reasonable price tag even for the most opulent suites, this B&B is perfect for families (though there are no TVs in any room) and for longer stays. Try to get a room for a weekend so you can partake of the gourmet champagne brunch.

$150-250

Located in Hayes Valley a few blocks from the Opera House, the **Inn at the Opera** (333 Fulton St., 888/298-7198, www.shellhospitality.com/hotels/inn_at_the_opera, $205) promises to have guests ready for a swanky night of San Francisco culture. In fact, overnight shoeshine and clothes-pressing services count among the inn's many amenities. French interior styling in the guest rooms and suites once impressed visiting opera stars and now welcomes guests from all over the world.

It might seem strange to stay at an inn called **The Parsonage** (198 Haight St., 415/863-3699, www.theparsonage.com, from $210). But this classy Victorian bed-and-breakfast exemplifies the bygone elegance of the City in one of its most colorful neighborhoods. Guest rooms are decorated with antiques, and baths has stunning marble showers. Enjoy pampering, multicourse breakfasts, and brandy and chocolates when you come "home" each night.

MISSION AND CASTRO

Accommodations in these neighborhoods are few and tend to run toward modest B&Bs.

Under $100

For a sweet, affordable little Castro inn experience, try the **Castillo Inn** (48 Henry St., 800/865-5112, $95). With only four guest rooms and shared baths, you'll imagine you've found a family pension in Tuscany transported to San Francisco. In the midst of the Castro, you've got all sorts of queer-life entertainment options only a short stroll way.

$100-150

For a romantic visit to the Castro with your partner, stay at the **Willows Inn Bed & Breakfast** (710 14th St., 800/431-0277, www.willowssf.com, $114–220). The Willows has European-style shared baths and comfortable guest rooms with private sinks and bent willow furnishings, and serves a yummy continental breakfast each morning. Catering to the queer community, the innkeepers at the Willows can help you with nightclubs, restaurants, and festivals in the City and locally in the Castro. One of the best amenities is the friendship and camaraderie you'll find with the other guests and staff at this great Edwardian B&B.

At the **Inn on Castro** (321 Castro St., 415/861-0321, www.innoncastro.com, $145–230), you've got all kinds of choices. You can pick an economy room with a shared bath, a posh private suite, or a self-service apartment. Once ensconced, you can chill out on the cute patio, or go out into the Castro to take in the legendary entertainment and nightlife. The self-catering apartments can sleep up to four and have fully furnished and appointed kitchens and dining rooms. Amenities include LCD TVs with cable, DVD players, and colorful modern art.

GOLDEN GATE PARK AND THE HAIGHT

Accommodations around Golden Gate Park are surprisingly reasonable. Leaning toward Victorian and Edwardian inns, most lodgings are in the middle price range for well above average guest rooms and services. However, getting downtown from the quiet residential spots can be a trek; ask at your inn about car services, cabs, and the nearest bus lines.

Out on the ocean side of the park, motor inns of varying quality cluster on the Great Highway. They've got the advantages of more space, low rates, and free parking, but they range from drab all the way down to seedy; choose carefully.

$100-150

The Summer of Love seems endless to guests at the **Red Victorian Bed, Breakfast, and Art** (1665 Haight St., 415/864-1978, www.redvic.com, $114–220). The Red Vic serves up peace, love, and literature along with breakfast, while community and color (but absolutely no TVs) decorate the guest rooms. Part of the economy of this B&B includes shared, named baths for some guest rooms, although many guest rooms have their own

private baths. Enjoy the intellectual, peaceful conversations over breakfast, browse the Peace Arts Gift Shop, and if you can, get in a chat with owner Sami Sunchild.

To say the **Seal Rock Inn** (545 Point Lobos Ave., 888/732-5762, www.sealrockinn.com, $130–200) is near Golden Gate Park pushes even the fluid San Francisco neighborhood boundaries a bit. In fact, this pretty place perches near the tip of land's end, only a short walk from the Pacific Ocean. All guest rooms at the Seal Rock Inn have ocean views, private baths, free parking, free Wi-Fi, and recent remodels that create a pleasantly modern ambiance. With longer stays in mind, the Seal Rock offers rooms with kitchenettes (two-day minimum stay to use the kitchen part of the room; weird but true). You can call and ask for a fireplace room that faces the Seal Rocks, so you can stay warm and toasty while training your binoculars on a popular mating spot for local sea lions. The restaurant downstairs serves breakfast and lunch; on Sunday you'll be competing with brunch-loving locals for a table.

$150-250

The **Stanyan Park Hotel** (750 Stanyan St., 415/751-1000, www.stanyanpark.com, $175–230) graces the Upper Haight area across the street from Golden Gate Park. This renovated 1904–1905 building, listed on the National Register of Historic Places, shows off its Victorian heritage both inside and out. Guest rooms can be small but are elegantly decorated, and a number of multiple-room suites are available. For a special treat, ask for a room overlooking the park.

Way over on the other side of the park, the **Great Highway Inn** (1234 Great Hwy., 800/624-6644, www.greathwy.com, $150–200) sits across the street from Ocean Beach. Actually an old motor-lodge style motel, the Inn has big clean guest rooms, decent beds, road noise, some language problems with the desk when checking in, and a short walk out to the Pacific Ocean. Guest rooms have standard-issue floral bedspreads, industrial-strength carpets, and private baths. A better option for travelers with cars, the Great Highway Inn has free parking in an adjacent lot. An on-site coffee shop offers decent food but weird hours. The motel offers discounted rates to families visiting patients at the nearby UCSF Medical Center.

SAN FRANCISCO AIRPORT

Because San Francisco Airport (SFO) is actually 13 miles south of the City on the peninsula, there are no airport hotels with a San Francisco zip code. If you're hunting for an urban chic boutique hotel or a funky and unique hostel, the airport is *not* the place to motel-shop. SFO's hotel row has many mid-priced chain motels.

Under $100

Don't expect ritzy accommodations at the **Ritz Inn** (151 El Camino Real, San Bruno, 800/799-7489, www.ritzinnsfo.com, $58–70). At this cheap plain Jane you'll get a bed with an uncomfortable mattress and a loud floral spread, a bathroom, a microwave, a fridge, and a TV. The neighborhood is mediocre but not actually awful—many other businesses along the El Camino are other airport motels.

$100-150

The **Villa Montes Hotel** (620 El Camino Real, San Bruno, 650/745-0111, www.ascend-collection.com, $143–170) offers mid-tier accommodations and amenities on a fairly nice block. Both the exterior and the interior are attractive and modern, complete with slightly wacky lobby decor and an indoor hot tub. Guest rooms have one or two beds, complete with bright white duvets and pillow-top mattresses. Focusing on business travelers, the motel has free in-room Wi-Fi, multiline phones with voicemail, and copy and fax machines for guest use.

Millwood Inn & Suites (1375 El Camino Real, Millbrae, 800/516-6738, www.mill-woodinn.com, $125–150) offers contemporary decor and big guest rooms designed for the comfort of both business and vacation travelers. Amenities include free Wi-Fi and satellite TV with an attached DVD player. Gorge on a bigger-than-average free buffet breakfast in the morning. Perhaps best of all, the Millwood Inn offers a complementary airport shuttle—not all airport motels near SFO do.

$150-250

A generous step up both in price and luxury is the **Bay Landing Hotel** (1550 Bayshore Hwy., Burlingame, 650/259-9000, www.bay-landinghotel.com, $165–185). Updated guest rooms include pretty posted headboards, granite sinks in the baths, tub-shower combos, in-room safes, and free Wi-Fi. Free continental breakfast is served in the lobby, which has a lending library for guests and, frankly, too much decoration.

Food

One of the main reasons people come to San Francisco from near and far is to eat. Some of the greatest culinary innovation in the world comes out of the kitchens in the City. The only real problem is how to choose which restaurant to eat dinner at tonight.

UNION SQUARE AND NOB HILL
American

Looking for a good old-fashioned American breakfast? Walk on down to **Dottie's True Blue Café** (28 Sixth St., 415/885-2767, 7:30 a.m.–3 p.m. Wed.–Mon., $6–12). The menu is simple: classic egg dishes, light fruit plates, and an honest-to-goodness blue-plate special for breakfast as well as salads, burgers, and sandwiches for lunch. The service is friendly, and the portions are huge. So what's the catch? Everyone in San Francisco knows that there's a great breakfast to be had at Dottie's. Expect lines up to an hour long for a table at this locals' mecca, especially at breakfast on weekend mornings.

Asian

It seemed unlikely that anything worthy could possibly replace Trader Vic's, but **Le Colonial** (20 Cosmo Pl., 415/931-3600, www.lecolonialsf.com, 5–10 P.M. Mon.–Thurs., 5 P.M.–2 A.M. Fri., 11:30 A.M.–2 A.M. Sat., 11:30 A.M.–10 P.M. Sun., $25–40) does it. This Vietnamese-fusion hot spot takes pride in its tiki lounge, which features live music acts and house DJs six nights a week. Cocktails are big and tropical, and they pay proper homage to the building's illustrious former occupant. But don't skip the food; the lush French-Vietnamese fare comes family-style and blends flavors in a way that seems just perfect for San Francisco.

You'll find all of Southeast Asia in the food at **E&O Trading Company** (314 Sutter St., 415/693-0303, www.eosanfrancisco.com, 11:30 A.M.–10 P.M. Mon.–Thurs., 11:30 A.M.–11 P.M. Fri.–Sat., 5–9:30 P.M. Sun., $12–26). This fusion grill serves up small plates like Indonesian corn fritters, mixed in with larger grilled dishes such as black pepper shaking beef. Enjoy the wine list, full bar, and French colonial decor. Reservations are recommended.

It may not be in Chinatown, but the dim sum at **Yank Sing** (101 Spear St., 415/957-9300, www.yanksing.com, 11 A.M.–3 P.M. Mon.–Fri., 10 A.M.–4 P.M. Sat.–Sun., $39) is second to none. The family owns and operates both this restaurant and its sister location (49 Stevenson St., 415/541-4949), and now the third generation is training to take over. In addition to the traditional steamed pork buns, shrimp dumplings, egg custard tarts, and such, the "Creative Collection" offers unique bites you won't find elsewhere in the City. Note that it's open for lunch only.

California

Make reservations in advance if you want to dine at San Francisco legend ◖ **Farallon** (450 Post St., Suite 4, 415/956-6969, www.farallonrestaurant.com, 5:30–9:30 P.M. Mon.–Thurs., 5:30–11 P.M. Fri.–Sat., 5–10 P.M. Sun.,

$30–55). Dark, cave-like rooms are decorated in an under-the-sea theme—complete with the unique Jellyfish Bar. The cuisine, on the other hand, is out of this world. Chef Mark Franz has made Farallon a 10-year fad that just keeps gaining ground. The major culinary theme, seafood, dominates the pricey-but-worth-it menu. Desserts by award-winning pastry chef Emily Luchetti round out what many consider to be the perfect California meal.

Another local mainstay of San Francisco haute cuisine is Wolfgang Puck's **Postrio** (545 Post St., 415/776-7825, www.postrio.com, 6 A.M.–10:30 P.M. daily, $30–40). Here you'll find everything from Puck's famed pizzas to the best of rarified local sustainable fare. The restaurant has three levels, all of which see their share of celebrities. Not surprisingly, reservations are strongly recommended if you want to dine chez Puck.

French

The famed **Fleur de Lys** (777 Sutter St., 415/673-7779, www.hubertkeller.com, 6–9:30 P.M. Tues.–Thurs., 5:30–10 P.M. Fri.–Sat., prix fixe $72–95, reservations strongly recommended) is one of the longest-running and finest dining establishments in San Francisco, and chef Hubert Keller (Keller may be *the* best name in Bay Area dining ever) continues to create delectable and inventive dishes. The dining room is magnificent, with its elaborate tented ceiling, lushly upholstered chairs, and perfect glass accent pieces. But the reason people flock to Fleur de Lys is, and has always been, the food. The absolutely cream-of-the-crop menu isn't really à la carte—instead, you're encouraged to peruse the items and create your own three-, four-, or five-course feast. Vegetarians aren't left out, since Keller creates vegetable-only (and fish-only) dishes with the same love he dedicates to his meats. You'll probably want wine with your meal, which means it's going to cost a bundle. But it's worth the money to splurge at this world-famous spot.

Tucked away in a tiny alley that looks like it might have been transported from Saint-Michel in Paris, ◖ **Café Claude** (7 Claude

Ln., 415/392-3505, www.cafeclaude.com, 11:30 A.M.–10:30 P.M. Mon.–Sat., bar until 2 A.M., $18–28) serves classic brasserie cuisine to French expatriates and Americans alike. Much French is spoken here, but the simple food tastes fantastic in any language. Café Claude is open for lunch through dinner, serving an attractive postlunch menu for weary shoppers looking for sustenance at 3 or 4 P.M. In the evening it can get crowded, but reservations aren't strictly necessary if you're willing to order a classic French cocktail or a glass of wine and enjoy the bustling atmosphere and live music (on weekends) for a few minutes.

Coffee

With a monopoly on the coffee available in the middle of Union Square, business is brisk at **Emporio Rulli** (333 Post St., Union Square, 415/433-1122, www.rulli.com, 7:30 A.M.–7 P.M. daily, $10–20). This local chain offers frothy coffee, pastries, and upscale sandwiches, plus wine and beer. Expect everything to be overpriced at Rulli. In the summer, sitting at the outdoor tables feels comfortable. In the winter, it's less pleasant, but it's fun to watch the skaters wobble around the tiny outdoor ice rink in the square.

Blue Bottle Café (66 Mint St., 415/495-3394, www.bluebottlecoffee.net, 7 A.M.–7 P.M. Mon.–Fri., 8 A.M.–6 P.M. Sat., 8 A.M.–4 P.M. Sun., $5–10), a popular local chain with multiple locations around the city, takes its equipment very seriously. Whether you care about the big copper thing that made your mocha or not, you can get a good cup of joe and a small if somewhat pretentious meal at the Mint Plaza. Other locations include the Ferry Building (1 Ferry Bldg., Suite 7) and the SFMOMA (151 3rd St., 5th Fl.).

FINANCIAL DISTRICT AND SOMA
California

A local favorite, especially for weekend brunch, **Butterfly** (Pier 33, 415/864-8999, www.butterflysf.com, 11:30 A.M.–10 P.M. Tues.–Thurs., 11:30 A.M.–11 P.M. Fri.–Sat.,

11 A.M.–3:30 P.M. Sun., $19–40) attracts a young, hip crowd with its ultramodern decor and cocktails for both lunch and dinner. You can sit at a window table enjoying the Asian-inspired California cuisine and watching the city-size cruise ships dock next door. The brunch menu offers fun breakfast-type dishes. Butterfly can draw a crowd, so make reservations to get a seat at your favorite time.

From an impossibly small kitchen, chef Dennis Leary turns out some of the biggest flavors in town at **Canteen** (817 Sutter St., 415/928-8870, www.sfcanteen.com, 6–9:15 P.M. Tues.–Fri., 8 A.M.–9:15 P.M. Sat., 8 A.M.–2 P.M. Sun., $20–27). Sidle up to the lime-green counter or squeeze into one of the tiny booths to enjoy his eclectic menu—from black cod with couscous to velvety vanilla soufflé. Reserve early: Seats are in short supply.

French

There's no question that **Fifth Floor** (12 4th St., 415/348-1555, www.fifthfloorrestaurant.com, 5:30–10 P.M. Tues.–Sat., $30–40) is one of the top French restaurants in San Francisco. Which is saying something. The restaurant sits on the fifth floor of the Hotel Palomar and has both a casual café and a full-scale formal dining room to serve as many diners as possible. The cuisine exemplifies the best of southern France—the chef specializes in Gascon food and loves to create dishes that show off his early life and training. An ultra-expensive dinner at Fifth Floor is the perfect excuse to dress to the nines. Don't worry, the dining room decor can take it.

For breakfast or lunch with a view of Treasure Island and the Bay Bridge, consider sitting down at the communal table at **Boulettes Larder** (1 Ferry Bldg., Suite 48, 415/399-1155, www.bouletteslarder.com, 8 A.M.–6 P.M. Mon.–Fri., 8 A.M.–2:30 P.M. Sat., 10 A.M.–2:30 P.M. Sun.). Chef Amaryll Schwertner creates breakfast and lunch menus that change daily, dependent in part on what's available from local farms. Many of the key ingredients are also available to purchase to take home to your own kitchen.

For the lower end of the French cuisine

DELECTABLE DUNGENESS

They don't have a top-rated reality show, but Dungeness crabs enjoy local celebrity status in San Francisco. Dungeness start to appear on local menus in mid-November, delighting diners and sending chefs into paroxysms of joy. Dungeness season in Northern California usually runs November–June, but the freshest crabs are caught and cooked from the start of the season (usually the second Tuesday of November) through New Year's.

This crab has firm white flesh that has a delicate, sweet flavor; it tastes lovely dipped in only a little drawn butter, but it also has enough oomph to stand up in complex and spicy Asian preparations. Mature male Dungeness crabs measure 7-10 inches across their carapaces (the big, meaty body of the crab) and weigh several pounds, about one-quarter of which is meat.

Dungeness crabs scuttle up and down the Pacific Coast; crab fishers catch Dungeness from Washington State down through central California. Although Dungeness crabs no longer live in San Francisco Bay, the fishery as a whole is remarkably well managed. Even the famously strict Monterey Bay Seafood Watch program (www.montereybayaquarium.org/cr/SeafoodWatch) rates Northern California-caught Dungeness crab as a "Best Choice," citing the stringent rules that permit only mature males to be harvested, a fishing season that avoids the crabs' mating months, and crab traps that allows bycatch to be released unharmed.

Although the crabs are named for a place on the Washington coast, the Dungeness came to fame in San Francisco, where Italian immigrant fishers caught crabs in and around the Bay, cooked them up in steaming cauldrons, and sold the meat in paper cones as "crab cocktail." These entrepreneurs also sold whole cooked crabs to families, who took them home and held crab feeds for their families.

You can still buy Dungeness crab cocktails and whole-cooked crabs from crab shacks along Fisherman's Wharf. Famed Italian seafood restaurant **Alioto's** (8 Fisherman's Wharf, 415/673-0183, www.aliotos.com, 11 A.M.-11 P.M. daily, $17-48) serves whole cracked Dungeness in the traditional style. They've also got crab soups, salads, sandwiches, and stews; there are more than a dozen different preparations on Alioto's menu. Locals particularly love the Dungeness preparations by Chinese and Vietnamese chefs. In Chinatown, **R&G Lounge** (631 Kearny St., 415/982-7877, http://rnglounge.com, 11:30 A.M.-9:30 P.M. daily, $12-40, reservations suggested) offers deep-fried and salt-and-pepper crabs. In the Outer Sunset, **Thanh Long** (4101 Judah St., 415/665-1146, 4:30-9:30 P.M. Sun.-Thurs., 4:30-10:30 P.M. Fri.-Sat., $20-30), is famous for its roast crab soaked in garlic and butter.

spectrum, check out **Crepes A Go-Go** (350 11th St., 415/503-1294, 11 A.M.–10 P.M. daily, $3.50–6) in SoMa. Believe it or not, the tiny but clean premises, lone guy working the crepes, and late-night hours (call to check what the *real* closing hours are) are all quite reminiscent of Paris. Crepes A Go-Go can make you some quick and hearty nighttime sustenance or perhaps a fruity dessert. The house special is the turkey, egg, and cheese—a great way to fuel a full night of drinking and clubbing.

Indian
On the more affordable end of the Indian food

spectrum you'll find **Chutney** (511 Jones St., 415/931-5541, www.chutneysf.com, noon–midnight daily, $3–10). With a menu emphasizing curries and masalas—some vegetarian and some meat-laden—Chutney offers a good quick bite, especially late at night.

Italian
Palio d'Asti (640 Sacramento St., 415/395-9800, www.paliodasti.com, 11:30 A.M.–2:30 P.M. and 5:30–9 P.M. Mon.–Fri., 5:30–9 P.M. Sat., $15–33) is one of the City's elder statesmen. The restaurant has been around since just after the 1906 earthquake,

and the decor in the dining areas recreates another bygone era in the old country. Try either lunch or dinner, and enjoy the classic Italian menu, which includes wood-fired handmade pizzas as well as homemade pastas and classic Italian entrées. If you're in the City in the fall, be sure to stop in and sample the luscious, expensive, and exceedingly rare Piedmont white truffles.

For fine Italian-influenced cuisine, make a reservation at **Quince** (470 Pacific Ave., 415/775-8500, www.quincerestaurant.com, 5:30–10 P.M. Mon.–Thurs., 5:30–10:30 P.M. Fri.–Sat., $25–95). Chef-owner Michael Tusk blends culinary aesthetics to create his own unique style of cuisine. It's best to arrive at Quince hungry; the menu is divided into four different courses, or you can try the chef's tasting menu ($125). Once you've had a look at the dishes, made with the finest local and sustainable ingredients, you'll want to try at least one from every course.

Japanese

In these neighborhoods you'll find plenty of sushi restaurants to choose from, from the most ultracasual walk-up lunch places to the fanciest fusion joints. **Ame** (St. Regis Hotel, 689 Mission St., 415/284-4040, www. amerestaurant.com, 6–9:30 P.M. Mon.–Thurs., 5:30–10 P.M. Fri.–Sat., 5:30–9:30 P.M. Sun., $35–40) is one of the latter. Appropriately situated in stylish SoMa, this upscale eatery serves a California-Japanese fusion style of seafood. Raw fish fanciers can start with the offerings from the sashimi bar, while folks who prefer their food cooked will find a wealth of options in the appetizers and main courses. The blocky, attractively colored dining room has a modern flair that's in keeping with the up-to-date cuisine coming out of the kitchen. You can either start out or round off your meal with a cocktail from the shiny black bar.

Forget your notions of the plain Jane sushi bar; **Ozumo** (161 Steuart St., 415/882-1333, www.ozumo.com, 11:30 A.M.–2 P.M. Mon.–Wed., 11:30 A.M.–2 P.M. and 5:30–10:30 P.M. Thurs., 11:30 A.M.–2 P.M. and 5:30–11 P.M.

Fri., 5:30–11 P.M. Sat., 5:30–10:30 P.M. Sun., $28–46) takes Japanese cuisine upscale, San Francisco style. Order some classic *nigiri,* a small-plate *izakaya* pub dish, or a big chunk of meat off the traditional *robata* grill. The high-quality sake lines the shelves above the bar and along the walls. For nonimbibers, choose from a selection of premium teas. If you're a night owl, enjoy a late dinner on weekends and drinks in the lounge nightly.

Seafood

One of the very first restaurants established in San Francisco during the Gold Rush in 1849, the **(Tadich Grill** (240 California St., 415/391-1849, www.tadichgrill.com, 11 A.M.– 9:30 P.M. Mon.–Fri., 11:30 A.M.–9:30 P.M. Sat., $20–40) still serves fresh-caught fish and classic miner fare. The menu combines perfectly sautéed sand dabs, octopus salad, and corned beef hash. Mix that with the business lunch crowd in suits, out-of-towners, and original dark wooden booths from the 1850s and you've got a fabulous San Francisco stew of a restaurant. Speaking of stew, the Tadich cioppino enjoys worldwide fame—and deserves it, even in a city that prides itself on the quality of its seafood concoctions.

Steak

Alexander's Steakhouse (448 Brannan St., 415/495-1111, www.alexanderssteakhouse.com, 5:30–10 P.M. Mon.–Sat., 5:30–9 P.M. Sun., $35–200) describes itself as "where East meets beef." It's true—the presentation at Alexander's looks like something you'd see on *Iron Chef,* and the prices of the *wagyu* beef look like the monthly payment on a small Japanese car. This white-tablecloth steak house that's managed to succeed even in beef-loving SoMa is the very antithesis of a bargain, but the food, including the steaks, is more imaginative than most, and the elegant dining experience will make you feel special as your wallet quietly bleeds out. Console yourself with a cone of cotton candy after dessert—the delicate spun sugar will help make you feel like a kid who blew his allowance at a carnival.

How could you not love a steak house with a name like **Epic Roasthouse** (369 Embarcadero, 415/369-9955, www.epicroasthouse.com, 5:30–9:30 P.M. Mon.–Thurs., 5:30–10 P.M. Fri., 11 A.M.–3 P.M. and 5:30–10 P.M. Sat., 11 A.M.–3 P.M. and 5:30–9:30 P.M. Sun., bar 3 P.M.–midnight Mon.–Fri., 11 A.M.–1 A.M. Sat., 11 A.M.–midnight Sun., $20–50)? Come for the wood-fired grass-fed beef; stay for the prime views over San Francisco Bay. The Epic Roasthouse sits almost underneath the Bay Bridge, where the lights sparkle and flash over the deep black water at night. On weekends, the steak house offers the hipster City crowd what it wants—an innovative prix fixe brunch menu complete with hair-of-the-dog cocktails. Epic!

Vietnamese
Probably the single most famous Asian restaurant in a city filled with eateries of all types is **The Slanted Door** (1 Ferry Plaza, Suite 3, 415/861-8032, http://slanteddoor.com, 11 A.M.–2:30 P.M. and 5:30–10 P.M. Mon.–Sat., 11:30 A.M.–3 P.M. and 5:30–10 P.M. Sun., $20–30). If all you know of Vietnamese cuisine is rubbery summer rolls and tripe-and-tendon *pho,* you are in for some seriously tasty reeducation. Owner Charles Phan, along with more than 20 family members and the rest of his staff, pride themselves on welcoming service and top-quality food. Organic local ingredients get used in both traditional and innovative Vietnamese cuisine, creating a unique dining experience. Even experienced foodies remark that they've never had green papaya salad, glass noodles, or shaking beef like this before. The light afternoon tea menu (2:30–4:30 P.M. daily) can be the perfect pick-me-up for weary travelers who need some sustenance to get them through the long afternoon until dinner, and Vietnamese coffee is the ultimate Southeast Asian caffeine experience.

Bakeries and Cafés
One of the Ferry Building mainstays, the **Acme Bread Company** (1 Ferry Plaza, Suite 15, 415/288-2978, 6:20 A.M.–7:30 P.M. Mon.–Fri., 8 A.M.–7 P.M. Sat.–Sun.) remains true to its name. You can buy bread here, but not sandwiches, croissants, or froufrou pastries. All the bread that Acme sells is made with fresh organic ingredients in traditional style; the baguettes are traditionally French, so they start to go stale after only 4–6 hours. Eat fast!

For a quick bite, stop in at **The Grove Café** (690 Mission St., 415/957-0558, 7 A.M.–11 P.M. Mon.–Fri., 8 A.M.–11 P.M. Sat.–Sun.), in Yerba Buena. This local chain offers fresh soups, salads, and sandwiches as well as coffee and Wi-Fi in an airy and relaxed setting.

Coffee and Tea
For their daily caffeine, local workers rely on the usual Starbucks and Peet's shoved into every convenient small storefront. If it's tea you favor, try the **Imperial Tea Court** (1 Ferry Plaza, Suite 27, 415/544-9830, www.imperialtea.com, 10 A.M.–6 P.M. Sun.–Fri., 9 A.M.–6:30 P.M. Sat.) at the Ferry Building. This intensely Chinese tea shop sells black teas in bulk, beautiful Asian tea ware, and, of course, serves hot tea at its six Chinese rosewood tables. If you want to get into the tea experience, consider signing up for a class with owner Ray Fong, who is a published author and tea consultant. You'll learn about the traditions of tea from plant to cup, including the Chinese ceremonial modes of serving.

Farmers Markets
While farmers markets litter the landscape in just about every California town, the **Ferry Plaza Farmers Market** (1 Ferry Plaza, 415/291-3276, www.ferrybuildingmarketplace.com, 10 A.M.–2 P.M. Tues., 8 A.M.–2 P.M. Sat.) is special. At the granddaddy of Bay Area farmers markets, you'll find a wonderful array of produce, cooked foods, and even locally raised meats and locally caught seafood. Expect to see the freshest fruits and veggies from local growers, grass-fed beef from Marin County, and seasonal seafood pulled from the Pacific beyond the Golden Gate. Granted, you'll pay for the privilege of purchasing from this market—if you're seeking bargain produce, you'll

be better served at one of the weekly suburban farmers markets. Even locals flock downtown to the Ferry Building on Saturday mornings, especially in the summer when the variety of California's agricultural bounty becomes staggering.

CHINATOWN
Chinese Banquets
The "banquet" style of Chinese restaurant may be a bit more familiar to American travelers. Banquet restaurants offer tasty meat, seafood, and veggie dishes along with rice, soups, and appetizers, all served family-style. Tables are often round, with a lazy Susan in the middle to facilitate the passing of communal serving bowls around the table. In the City, most banquet Chinese restaurants have at least a few dishes that will feel familiar to the American palate, and menus often have English translations.

The **R&G Lounge** (631 Kearny St., 415/982-7877, www.rnglounge.com, 11:30 A.M.–9:30 P.M. daily, $12–40, reservations suggested) takes traditional Chinese American cuisine to the next level. The menu is divided by colors that represent the five elements, according to Chinese tradition and folklore. In addition to old favorites like moo shu pork, chow mein, and lemon chicken, you'll find spicy Szechuan and Mongolian dishes and an array of house specialties. Salt-and-pepper Dungeness crab, served whole on a plate, is the R&G signature dish, though many of the other seafood dishes are just as special. Expect your seafood to be fresh since it comes right out of the tank in the dining room. California-cuisine mores have made their way into the R&G Lounge in the form of some innovative dishes and haute cuisine presentations. This is a great place to enjoy Chinatown cuisine in an American-friendly setting.

Another great banquet house is the **Hunan Home's Restaurant** (622 Jackson St., 415/982-2844, http://hunanhome.ypguides.net, 11:30 A.M.–9:30 P.M. Sun.–Thurs., 11:30 A.M.–10 P.M. Fri.–Sat., $10–15). It is a bit more on the casual side, and it even has

another location in suburban Los Altos. You'll find classic items on the menu such as broccoli beef and kung pao chicken, but do take care if something you plan to order has a "spicy" notation next to it. At Hunan Home's, and in fact at most Bay Area Chinese restaurants, they mean *really* spicy.

Dim Sum
The Chinese culinary tradition of dim sum is literally translated as "touch the heart," meaning "order to your heart's content" in Cantonese. In practical terms, it's a light meal—lunch or afternoon tea—composed of small bites of a wide range of dishes. Americans tend to eat dim sum at lunchtime, though it can just as easily be dinner or even Sunday brunch. In a proper dim sum restaurant, you do not order anything or see a menu. Instead, you sip your oolong and sit back as servers push loaded steam trays out of the kitchen one after the other. Servers and trays make their way around the tables; you pick out what you'd like to try as it passes, and enough of that dish for everyone at your table is placed before you.

One of the many great dim sum places in Chinatown is the **Great Eastern** (649 Jackson St., 415/986-2500, 10 A.M.–midnight daily, $15–25). It's not a standard dim sum place; instead of the steam carts, you'll get a menu and a list. You must write down everything you want on your list and hand it to your waiter, and your choices will be brought out to you, so family style is undoubtedly the way to go here. Reservations are strongly recommended for diners who don't want to wait 30–60 minutes or more for a table. This restaurant jams up fast, right from the moment it opens, especially on weekends. The good news is that most of the folks crowding into Great Eastern are locals. You know what that means.

Another well-known dim sum spot, **Yong Kee** (732 Jackson St., 415/986-3759, www.yongkeecompany.com, 7 A.M.–6 P.M. Tues.–Sun., $10, cash only), offers a completely different dim sum experience. This Cantonese-only hole-in-the-wall caters primarily to locals, but if you've ever had dim sum or even just Chinese steamed buns before, you'll want to try them here. They're famous for their enormous fresh-made chicken buns *(gai bow)*, which is what the Chinese women lined up at the take-out counter have come for. You can also get a great pork bun, and the rest of the dim sum nibbles are tasty too. Reservations are not taken, but they aren't necessary. Do be aware that Yong Kee isn't a good beginner's dim sum place un-less you've got a Cantonese-speaking friend to guide you. But if you're already a fan of the cuisine, you'll love Yong Kee even if you can't understand the menu or the staff.

Tea Shops

Official or not, there's no doubt that the world believes that tea is the national drink of China. While black tea, often oolong, is the staple in California Chinese restaurants, you'll find an astonishing variety of teas if you step into one of Chinatown's small tea shops. You can enjoy a hot cup of tea, and buy a pound of loose tea to take home with you. Most tea shops also sell lovely imported teapots and other implements for proper tea-making.

One option is **Blest Tea** (752 Grant Ave., 415/951-8516, http://blesttea.com, tasting $3), which boasts of the healthful qualities of their many varieties of tea. You're welcome to taste what's available for a nominal fee to be sure you're purchasing something you'll re-ally enjoy. If you're lucky enough to visit when the owner is minding the store, ask her lots of questions—she'll tell you everything you ever needed to know about tea.

NORTH BEACH AND FISHERMAN'S WHARF
American
Smack-dab in the middle of North Beach, **◖ Mama's on Washington Square** (1701 Stockton St., 415/362-6421, www.mamas-sf.com, 8 A.M.–3 P.M. Tues.–Sun., $8–10) is the perfect place to fuel up on gourmet omelets, freshly baked breads—including a delectable cinnamon brioche—and daily specials like crab Benedict before a day of sightseeing. Arrive early, or be prepared to wait…and wait.

California
San Francisco culinary celebrity Gary Danko has a number of restaurants around town, but perhaps the finest is the one that bears his name. **Gary Danko** (800 North Point St., 415/749-2060, www.garydanko.com, 5:30–10 P.M. daily, prix fixe $69–102) offers the best of Danko's California cuisine, from the signa-ture horseradish-crusted salmon medallions to the array of delectable fowl dishes. The herbs and veggies come from Danko's own farm in Napa. Make reservations in advance to get a table, and consider dressing up a little for your sojourn in the elegant white-tablecloth din-ing room.

European
With a culinary style perhaps best described as European fusion, **Luella** (1896 Hyde St., 415/674-4343, www.luellasf.com, 5:30–10 P.M. Mon.–Sat., 5–9 P.M. Sun., $13–28) brings the flavors of Italy, France, and Spain to the City. The tasty original dishes, most with a distinc-tive splash of California style that complements the European roots, are best enjoyed with a glass of wine from the extensive wine bar. If you're out late or on the run, dinner is served at the wine bar, and a bar menu offers tasty treats after the dining room closes.

French
The **Hyde Street Bistro** (1521 Hyde St., 415/292-4415, www.hydestreetbistrosf.com, 5:30–10 P.M. Sun.–Thurs., 5:30–10:30 P.M. Fri.–Sat., $27) definitely belongs in San Francisco, what with the cable car clanging by outside the front door and the fog blowing past overhead. But in romance and cuisine, it's all Parisian splendor. A prix fixe menu offers economy, while the à la carte menu provides a variety of traditional French bistro fare, includ-ing snails, foie gras, and coq au vin. This is a perfect place to bring a date for romantic night out, or to celebrate an anniversary.

Greek
In the Greek fishing village of Kokkari, wild game and seafood hold a special place in the

local mythology. At **Kokkari Estiatorio** (200 Jackson St., 415/981-0983, www.kokkari.com, 11:30 A.M.–2:30 P.M. and 5:30–10 P.M. Mon.–Thurs., 11:30 A.M.–2:30 P.M. and 5:30–11 P.M. Fri., 5–11 P.M. Sat., 5–10 P.M. Sun., $22–42), patrons enjoy Mediterranean delicacies made with fresh California ingredients amid rustic elegance, feasting on such classic dishes as zucchini cakes and grilled lamb chops.

Italian

North Beach is San Francisco's own version of Little Italy. Poke around and find one of the local favorite mom-and-pop pizza joints, or try a bigger, more upscale Italian eatery.

At busy **Caffe Delucchi** (500 Columbus Ave., 415/393-4515, www.caffedelucchi.com, 11 A.M.–10 P.M. Mon.–Wed., 11 A.M.–11 P.M. Thurs., 8 A.M.–11 P.M. Fri.–Sat., 8 A.M.–10 P.M. Sun., $12–24), down-home Italian cooking meets fresh San Francisco produce to create affordable, excellent cuisine. You can get hand-tossed pizzas, salads, and entrées for lunch and dinner, plus tasty traditional American breakfast fare with an Italian twist on the weekends. Drinks run to *soju* cocktails and artisanal Italian and California wines.

Trattoria Contadina (1800 Mason St., 415/982-5728, www.trattoriacontadina.com, 5:30–9:30 P.M. Sun.–Thurs., 5:30–10:30 P.M. Fri.–Sat., $17–27) presents mouthwatering Italian fare in a fun, eclectic dining room. Dozens of framed photos line the walls, and fresh ingredients stock the kitchen in this San Francisco take on the classic Italian trattoria. Kids are welcome, and vegetarians will find good meatless choices on the menu.

A teensy neighborhood place, **L'Osteria del Forno** (519 Columbus Ave., 415/982-1124, www.losteriadelforno.com, 11:30 A.M.–10 P.M. Sun.–Mon. and Wed.–Thurs., 11:30 A.M.–10:30 P.M. Fri.–Sat., $10–18) serves up a small menu to match its small dining room and small tables and small (but full) bar. The delectable northern Italian–style pizzas and pastas paired with artisanal cocktails go a long way toward warming up frozen fog-drenched visitors from the Wharf and the beach. Locals love

L'Osteria, which means it's next to impossible to get a table at lunchtime or dinnertime, and doubly impossible on weekends. Your best bet is to drop by during the off-hours—L'Osteria stays open all afternoon and makes a perfect haven for travelers who find themselves in need of a very late lunch.

Want a genuine world-champion pizza while you're in town? Nine-time World Pizza Champion Tony Gemignani can hook you up. **Tony's Pizza Napoletana** (1570 Stockton St., 415/835-9888, www.tonyspizzanapoletana.com, noon–11 P.M. Wed.–Sun., $15–30) has four different pizza ovens that cook eight distinct styles of pizza. You can get a classic American pie loaded with pepperoni, a California-style pie with lamb and eucalyptus (if you really must), or a Sicilian pizza smothered in meat and garlic. The chef's special Neapolitan-style pizza margherita is a simple-sounding pizza made of perfection. The wood-fired atmosphere of this temple to the pie includes marble-topped tables, dark woods, and white linen napkins stuck into old tomato cans. The long full bar dominates the front dining room—grab a fancy bottle of wine or a cocktail to go with that champion pizza.

Japanese

Even in a town with hundreds of sushi bars, **Sushi Groove** (1916 Hyde St., 415/440-1905, www.sushigroove.com, 5:30–10 P.M. Sun.–Tues., 5:30–10:30 P.M. Fri.–Sat., $15–23) stands out. With an immense sushi bar, friendly chefs, and innovative sushi that blends traditional Japanese fish with unusual California touches, the Groove finds favorites with locals and visitors alike. For a treat, order one of the chef's choice specials.

Seafood

It's tough to walk down the streets of the Wharf without tripping over at least three big shiny seafood restaurants. You can pick just about any of the big ones and come up with a decent (if touristy) meal. A good way to choose is to stroll past the front doors and take a look at the menus.

It has the look of a big tourist trap, but at **McCormick and Kuleto's** (900 North Point St., 415/929-1730, www.mccormickandschmicks.com, 11:30 A.M.–10 P.M. Sun.–Thurs., 11:30 A.M.–11 P.M. Fri.–Sat., $20–35), the chefs know how to cook seafood to satisfy even the pickiest foodie. In the grand dining room, with slightly scary light fixtures and stellar views out to the Bay, you'll find an array of fresh fish and a list of innovative preparations.

Steak

A New York stage actress wanted a classic steak house in San Francisco, and so **Harris'** (2100 Van Ness Ave., 415/673-1888, www.harris-restaurant.com, 5:30 P.M.–close Mon.–Fri., 5 P.M.–close Sat.–Sun., $43–54) came to be. The fare runs to traditional steaks and prime rib as well as a bit of upscale, with a Kobe rib eye and surf-and-turf featuring a whole Maine lobster. Music lovers can catch live jazz in the lounge most evenings.

Bakeries and Cafés

Serving some of the most famous sourdough in the City, the **Boudin Bakery & Café** (Pier 39, Space 5-Q, 415/421-0185, www.boudinbakery.com, 8 A.M.–8 P.M. Sun.–Thurs., 8 A.M.–9 P.M. Fri.–Sat., $6–8) is a Pier 39 institution. Grab a loaf of bread to take with you, or order in one of the Boudin classics. Nothing draws tourists like the fragrant clam chowder in a bread bowl, but if you prefer, you can try another soup, a signature sandwich, or even a fresh salad. For a more upscale dining experience with the same great breads, try **Bistro Boudin** (160 Jefferson St., 415/351-5561, 11:30 A.M.–9:30 P.M. Sun.–Thurs., 11:30 A.M.–10 P.M. Fri.–Sat., $18–30).

Widely recognized as the first espresso coffeehouse on the West Coast, family-owned **Caffé Trieste** (601 Vallejo St., 415/392-6739, www.caffetrieste.com, 6:30 A.M.–10 P.M. Sun.–Thurs., 6:30 A.M.–11 P.M. Fri.–Sat., cash only) first opened its doors in 1956. Sip a cappuccino, munch on Italian pastries, and enjoy Saturday afternoon concerts by the Giotta family at this treasured North Beach institution.

MARINA AND PACIFIC HEIGHTS
Italian

The name **A 16** (2355 Chestnut St., 415/771-2216, www.a16sf.com, 5:30–10 P.M. Mon.–Tues., 11:30 A.M.–2:30 P.M. and 5:30–10 P.M. Wed.–Thurs., 11:30 A.M.–2:30 P.M. and 5:30–11 P.M. Fri., 5–11 P.M. Sat., 5–10 P.M. Sun., $13–30) refers to the major road cutting through the Campania region of southern Italy. At A 16 in San Francisco, you'll find fabulous southern Italian food. Handmade artisanal pizzas, pastas, and entrées tempt the palate with a wealth of hearty flavors. Pasta dishes come in two sizes—a great thing for those with smaller appetites. A wonderful wine list complements the food.

For a southern Italian meal with a soft touch, **Capannina** (1809 Union St., 415/409-8001, 5–10 P.M. Mon.–Thurs., 5–10:30 P.M. Fri.–Sun., $17–30) is the place. Soft green walls with marble and glass accents provide a sense of peace. The menu features classic Italian with an emphasis on the fruits of the sea. Many of the ingredients are imported directly from Italy, enhancing the authenticity of each dish.

Japanese

For a super-hip San Francisco sushi experience, strut on down to **Ace Wasabi's** (3339 Steiner St., 415/567-4903, http://acewasabisf.com, 5:30–10:30 P.M. Mon.–Thurs., 5:30–11 P.M. Fri.–Sat., 5–10 P.M. Sun., $6–13 per item). Advertising "rock 'n' roll sushi" and created with the atmosphere of an *izakaya* (a Japanese bar and grill), Ace Wasabi's appeals to a young, fun crowd. Be aware that the party can get loud on weekends.

On the other hand, the **◖ Naked Fish** (2084 Chestnut St., 415/771-1168, www.nakedfishsf.com, 11:30 A.M.–2:30 P.M. and 4:30–10 P.M. Mon.–Fri., noon–2:30 P.M. and 4:30–11 P.M. Sat., 4:30–11 P.M. Sun., $5–12 per item) proffers an upscale Japanese dining experience. In a fine dining room, taste the sushi, *robata* grill skewers, Hawaiian-style tapas, and spicy appetizers. Don't skip the sake—Naked Fish has a stellar menu of premium brands, including unfiltered and high-quality bottles rarely found outside of Japan. Consider bringing a date for dinner to start an elegant night on the town.

If you're in Pacific Heights, give **Kiss Seafood** (1700 Laguna St., 415/474-2866, 5:30–8:30 P.M. Tues.–Sat., $30–60) a try. This tiny restaurant (12 seats in total) boasts some of the freshest fish in town—no mean feat in San Francisco. The lone chef prepares all the fish himself, possibly due to the tiny size of the place. Obviously, reservations are a good idea. When it comes to the menu, anything seafood is recommended, but if you're up for sashimi, you'll be in raw-fish heaven. Round off your meal with a glass of chilled premium sake.

Seafood

Located in the somewhat grimy Polk Gulch area, tiny **Swan Oyster Depot** (1517 Polk St., 415/673-1101, 8 A.M.–5:30 P.M. daily, $10–20, cash only) packs in the lunchtime crowd with the freshest oysters, crab, and lobster you can eat.

Steak

The Marina is a great place to find a big thick steak. One famed San Francisco steak house, **Bobo's** (1450 Lombard St., 415/441-8880, www.boboquivaris.com, 5–10 P.M. daily, $30–50) prides itself on its dry-aged beef and fresh seafood. In season, enjoy whole Dungeness crab. But most of all, enjoy "The Steak," thickly cut and simply prepared to enhance the flavor of the beef.

Another great house of beef is **Izzy's Steak and Chop House** (3345 Steiner St., 415/563-0487, www.izzyssteaks.com, 5–10 P.M. Sun.–Thurs., 5:30–10:30 P.M. Fri.–Sat., $20–32). Here you'll find an array of tasty steak preparations, seafood, and selected nonsteak entrées. Be sure to save room for one of Izzy's classic desserts.

Bakeries and Delis

Just looking for a quick snack to tide you over? Drop in at **The Chestnut Bakery** (2359 Chestnut St., 415/567-6777, www.chestnut-bakery.com, 7 A.M.–noon Mon., 7 A.M.–6 P.M. Tues.–Sat., 8 A.M.–5 P.M. Sun.). Only a block and a half from Lombard Street, this small family-owned storefront is a perfect spot for weary travelers to take the weight off their feet and enjoy a cookie, pastry, or one of the bakery's famous cupcakes. If you come in the morning, you'll find scones, croissants, and other favorite breakfast pastries. Be aware that this is a favorite local spot, which means that some items sell out each day.

CIVIC CENTER AND HAYES VALLEY
California

Housed in a former bank, **Nopa** (500 Divisadero St., 415/864-8643, http://nopasf.com, 6 P.M.–1 A.M. daily, $18–25) brings together the neighborhood that the restaurant is named after with a whimsical mural by a local artist, a communal table, and a crowd as diverse as the surrounding area. A creative and inexpensive menu offers soul-satisfying dishes—and keeps tables full into the wee hours. The cocktails are legendary. On weekends Nopa also serves brunch (11 A.M.–2:30 P.M. Sat.–Sun.).

French

◖ **Jardinière** (300 Grove St., 415/861-5555, www.jardiniere.com, 5–10:30 P.M. daily, $20–40) was the first restaurant opened by local celebrity chef Traci Des Jardins. The bar and dining room blend into one another and feature stunning art deco decor. The ever-changing menu is a masterpiece of French California cuisine, and Des Jardins has long supported the sustainable restaurant movement. Eating at Jardinière is not only a treat for the senses, it is a way to support the best of trends in San Francisco restaurants. Make reservations if you're trying to catch dinner before a show. If you can wait until after the symphony or opera for dinner, Jardinière takes late-night diners on a first-come, first-served basis.

Absinthe (398 Hayes St., 415/551-1590, www.absinthe.com, 11:30 A.M.–midnight Tues.–Fri., 11 A.M.–midnight Sat., 11 A.M.–10 P.M. Sun., $23–35) takes its name from the notorious "green fairy" drink made of liquor and wormwood. Absinthe indeed does serve absinthe—including locally made St. George Spirits Absinthe Verte. It also serves upscale French bistro fare, including what may be the best french fries in the City. The French theme carries on into the decor as well—expect the look of a Parisian brasserie or perhaps a café in Nice, with retro-modern furniture and classic prints on the walls. The bar is open until 2 A.M., so if you want drinks or dessert after a show at the Opera or Davies Hall, just walk around the corner.

German

Suppenküche (525 Laguna St., 415/252-9289, www.suppenkuche.com, 5–10 P.M. Mon.–Sat., 10 A.M.–2:30 P.M. and 5–10 P.M. Sun., $15–20) brings a taste of Bavaria to the Bay Area. The beer list is a great place to start, since you can enjoy a wealth of classic German brews on tap and in bottles, plus a few Belgians thrown in for variety. For dinner, expect German classics with a focus on Bavarian cuisine. Spaetzle, pork, sausage—you name it, they've got it, and it will harden your arteries right up. Suppenküche also has a Biergarten (424 Octavia St., http://biergartensf.com, 3–9 P.M. Wed.–Sun.) two blocks away.

MISSION AND CASTRO

The Mission has become the next big thing in San Francisco's fanatical food scene. Parking is a bitch, but the food is sent from heaven above.

California

Range (842 Valencia St., 415/282-8283, 6 P.M.–close Mon.–Thurs., 5:30 P.M.–close Fri.–Sun., $20–26) may have lost its Michelin Guide star in 2011, but it's no less popular. Consistently rated one of the top Bay Area restaurants, Range serves up expertly crafted California cuisine such as coffee-rubbed pork shoulder and halibut cheeks à la nage. An inventive cocktail list doesn't hurt either.

French

Frances (3870 17th St., 415/621-3870, 5–10 P.M. Sun.–Thurs., 5–10:30 P.M. Fri.–Sat., $26–28) has been winning rave reviews ever since it opened its doors. The California-inspired French cuisine is locavore-friendly, with an emphasis on sustainable ingredients and local farms. The short-but-sweet menu changes daily and includes such temptations as caramelized Atlantic scallops and bacon beignets. Reservations are strongly advised, especially since Frances received its Michelin Guide star.

Italian

Sometimes even the most dedicated culinary explorer needs a break from the endless fancy food of San Francisco. When the time is right for a plain ol' pizza, head for **Little Star Pizza** (400 Valencia St., 415/551-7827, www.littlestarpizza.com, 5–10 P.M. Tues.–Thurs. and Sun., 5–11 P.M. Fri.–Sat., $10–15). A jewel of the Mission district, this pizzeria specializes in Chicago-style deep-dish pies, but also serves thin-crust pizzas for devotees of the New York style. Once you've found the all-black building and taken a seat inside the casual eatery, grab a beer or a cocktail from the bar if you have to wait for a table. Pick one of Little Star's specialty pizzas, or create your own variation from the toppings they offer. Can't get enough of Little Star? They've got a second location (846 Divisadero St., 415/441-1118).

Delfina (3621 18th St., 415/552-4055, www.delfinasf.com, 5:30–10 P.M. Mon.–Thurs. and Sun., 5:30–11 P.M. Fri.–Sat., $18–26) gives Italian cuisine a hearty California twist. From the antipasti to the entrées, the dishes speak of local farms and ranches, fresh seasonal produce, and the best Italian American taste that money can buy. With both a charming, warm indoor dining room and an outdoor garden patio, there's plenty of seating at this lovely restaurant.

Mediterranean

La Méditerranée (288 Noe St., 415/431-7210, www.lamednoe.com, 11 A.M.–10 P.M. Sun.–Thurs., 11 A.M.–11 P.M. Fri.–Sat., $9–14) serves delicious Greek and Middle Eastern dishes at reasonable prices. You can get kebabs or baba ghanoush, tabbouleh and baklava, vegetarian dishes, and meatballs. Locals love La Méditerranée for the quality of the food, the quantity provided, and the flexible hours. In warm weather, ask to be seated outside.

Mexican

Much of the rich heritage of the Mission district is Hispanic, thus leading to the Mission being *the* place to find a good taco or burrito. **Farolito Taqueria** (2950 24th St., 415/641-0758, www.elfarolitoinc.com, 10 A.M.–12:45 A.M. Sun.–Thurs., 10 A.M.–2:45 A.M. Fri.–Sat., $10) has found favor with the ultra-picky locals who have dozens of taqueria options within a few blocks. It seems that every regular has a different favorite—the burritos, the enchiladas, the quesadillas. Whatever your pleasure, you'll find a tasty version of it at Farolito. A totally casual spot, you order at the counter and sit at picnic-style tables to chow down on the properly greasy Mexican fare. (Don't confuse this Farolito with the taqueria by the same name on Mission Street.)

La Taqueria (2889 Mission St., 415/285-7117, 11 A.M.–9 P.M. Mon.–Sat., 11 A.M.–8 P.M. Sun., $5–10) is a local Mission favorite for burritos.

For a famous iteration of the classic Mission district burrito joint, join the crowd at **Papalote Mexican Grill** (3409 24th St., 415/970-8815, www.papalote-sf.com, 11 A.M.–10 P.M. Mon.–Sat., 11 A.M.–9 P.M. Sun., $5–12). Build your own plate of tacos or a burrito from a list of classic and specialty ingredients—carne asada, *chile verde*, grilled vegetables, and tofu—whatever makes you happy. What will make you even happier is the price: It's possible to get a filling meal for less than $10.

Seafood

For great seafood in a lower-key atmosphere, locals eschew the tourist traps on the Wharf and head for the **Anchor Oyster Bar** (579 Castro St., 415/431-3990, www.anchoroysterbar.com, 11:30 A.M.–10 P.M. Mon.–Fri.,

noon–10 P.M. Sat., 4–9:30 P.M. Sun., $15–30) in the Castro. The raw bar features different varieties of oysters, but not so many as to be overwhelming or pretentious. The dining room serves seafood, including local favorite Dungeness crab. Service is friendly, as befits a neighborhood spot, and it sees fewer large crowds. This doesn't diminish its quality, and it makes for a great spot to get a delicious meal before heading out to the local clubs for a late night out.

Vietnamese

Even casual international food aficionados find that the *banh mi* (Vietnamese sandwiches on French-style baguette bread) at **Dinosaurs** (2275 Market St., 415/503-1421, 10 A.M.–10 P.M. daily, $5) makes the grade. Dinosaurs makes good sandwiches, it makes them fast, and it sells them cheap. Diners love the barbecued pork, but the vegan crispy tofu gets mixed reviews. Dinosaurs is a great idea if you don't need a huge meal but want a taste of something you might not be able to get elsewhere.

Bakeries and Cafés

Need to grab a quick sandwich before heading off on another San Francisco adventure? Get it at **Ike's Place** (3489 16th St., 415/553-6888, http://ilikeikesplace.com, 10 A.M.–7 P.M. Mon.–Sat., $10). An independent deli, Ike's serves big hearty homemade sandwiches that will fuel up even the most energetic travelers. Ike's is the perfect place to buy your daily take-out lunch.

Locals love the artful pastries and fresh breads at █ **Tartine Bakery** (600 Guerrero St., 415/487-2600, www.tartinebakery.com, 8 A.M.–7 P.M. Mon., 7:30 A.M.–7 P.M. Tues.–Wed., 7:30 A.M.–8 P.M. Thurs.–Fri., 8 A.M.–8 P.M. Sat., 9 A.M.–8 P.M. Sun., $4–13). Tartine's bakers use organic flour, sea salt, and locally sourced produce and cheeses to craft their culinary creations, and the French-Italian-Californian fusion pastries and paninis have brought this bakery its word-of-mouth success. With hours that extend into early evening,

Tartine makes an attractive alternative for a light dinner or fixings for an evening picnic.

Speaking of dinner, sister property **Bar Tartine** (561 Valencia St., 6–10 P.M. Tues.–Thurs., 6–11 P.M. Fri., 10:30 A.M.–2:30 P.M. and 6–11 P.M. Sat., 10:30 A.M.–2:30 P.M. and 6–10 P.M. Sun., $10–25) serves gourmet dinners and weekend brunches.

Satisfy your sweet tooth at **Bi-Rite Creamery & Bakeshop** (3692 18th St., 415/626-5600, 11 A.M.–10 P.M. Sun.–Thurs., 11 A.M.–11 P.M. Fri.–Sat.). The ice cream is made by hand with organic milk, cream, and eggs; inventive flavors include maple walnut, salted caramel, and white chocolate raspberry swirl. Pick up a scoop to enjoy at nearby Mission Dolores Park.

GOLDEN GATE PARK AND THE HAIGHT
American
For visitors from parts east who long for a taste of home, **The Cheese Steak Shop** (1716 Divisadero St., 415/346-3712, www.cheesesteakshop.com, 10 A.M.–9 P.M. Mon. and Sat., 9 A.M.–9 P.M. Tues.–Fri., 11 A.M.–8 P.M. Sun., $10) provides a welcome respite from the endless California cuisine. Heck, no one can live on bean sprouts all the time. This small franchise serves up hearty cheesesteak sandwiches, Philadelphia style, to order. You can even get a Tastykake, a goodie you won't find many other places in California.

Cafés
The Sunset lends itself to a proliferation of cafés. Among the best of these is the **❰ de Young Museum Café** (50 Hagiwara Tea Garden Dr., 415/750-2613, http://deyoung.famsf.org, 9:30 A.M.–4 P.M. Tues.–Sun., 9:30 A.M.–8 P.M. Fri., $10–20). Situated inside the museum on the ground floor, with a generous dining room plus outdoor terrace seating, the Café was created with the same care that went into the de Young's galleries. From the day it opened, the focus has been on local sustainable food that's often organic but always

affordable. Service is cafeteria-style, but the salads and sandwiches are made fresh daily on the premises. Just be sure to get lunch early, or pick an off-hour to eat; the lines at lunchtime can extend for miles.

Visitors to the Presidio can enjoy a quick bite or a leisurely lunch at the **Acre Café** (1013 Torney Ave., 415/561-2273, 7:30 A.M.–3 P.M. Mon.–Fri., $10). This simple café serves up fresh food for almost (but not quite) reasonable prices. Open for both breakfast and lunch, it's also a good spot to grab a cup of coffee to enjoy with a morning walk along the paths of the Presidio. Just keep in mind that this is a walk-up style café, so don't expect much by way of customer service.

California
One of the most famous restaurant locations on the San Francisco coast is the Cliff House. The high-end eatery inhabiting the famed facade is **Sutro's** (1090 Point Lobos Ave., 415/386-3330, www.cliffhouse.com, 11:30 A.M.–3:30 P.M. and 5–9:30 P.M. Mon.–Sat., 11 A.M.–3:30 P.M. and 5–9:30 P.M. Sun., $18–36). The appetizers and entrées are mainly seafood in somewhat snooty preparations. Although the cuisine is expensive and fancy, in all honesty it's not the best in the City. What *is* amazing are the views from the floor-to-ceiling windows out over the vast expanse of the Pacific Ocean. These views make Sutro's a perfect spot to enjoy a romantic dinner while watching the sun set over the sea.

The Cliff House also houses the more casual **Bistro** (9 A.M.–3:30 P.M. and 4:15–9:30 P.M. Mon.–Sat., 8:30 A.M.–3:30 P.M. and 4:15–9:30 P.M. Sun., $15–30).

Japanese
Sushi restaurants are immensely popular in these residential neighborhoods. **Koo** (408 Irving St., 415/731-7077, www.sushikoo.com, 5:30–10 P.M. Tues.–Thurs., 5:30–10:30 P.M. Fri.–Sat., 5–9:30 P.M. Sun., $30–50) is a favorite in the Sunset. While sushi purists are happy

with the selection of *nigiri* and sashimi, lovers of fusion and experimentation will enjoy the small plates and unusual rolls created to delight diners. Complementing the Japanese cuisine is a small but scrumptious list of premium sakes. Only the cheap stuff is served hot, as high-quality sake is always chilled.

Thai

Dining in the Haight? If the touristy cafés don't appeal to you, check out the flavorful dishes at **Siam Lotus Thai Cuisine** (1705 Haight St., 415/933-8031, 11 A.M.–10 P.M. daily, $7–13). You'll find a rainbow of curries, pad thai, and all sorts of Thai meat, poultry, and vegetarian dishes. Look to the lunch specials for bargains, and to the Thai iced tea for a lunchtime pick-me-up. Locals enjoy the casually romantic ambiance at Siam Lotus, and visitors make special trips down to the Haight just to dine here.

Behind its typical storefront exterior, **Marnee Thai** (1243 9th Ave., 415/731-9999, www.marneethaisf.com, 11:30 A.M.–10 P.M. daily, $10–20) cooks up some of the best Thai food in San Francisco, with a location convenient to Golden Gate Park. The corn-cake appetizer is a must.

Vietnamese

Thanh Long (4101 Judah St., 415/665-1146, www.anfamily.com, 4:30–9:30 P.M. Sun.–Thurs., 4:30–10:30 P.M. Fri.–Sat., $20–30) was the first family-owned Vietnamese restaurant in San Francisco. Since the early 1970s, Thanh Long has been serving one of the best preparations of local Dungeness crab in the City—roasted crab with garlic noodles. This isn't a $5 *pho* joint—expect white tablecloths and higher prices at this stately small restaurant in the outer Sunset neighborhood.

Coffee and Tea

One of the prettiest spots in Golden Gate Park is the Japanese Tea Garden. Within the garden is the famous **Tea House** (7 Hagiwara Tea Garden Dr., 415/752-1171, http://japaneseteagardensf.com, 9 A.M.–6 P.M. daily Mar.–Oct., 9 A.M.–4:45 P.M. daily Nov.–Feb., $10–20), where you can purchase a cup of hot tea to take with you on a soothing walk through the beautiful and inspiring garden.

Information and Services

INFORMATION
Tourist Information

The main San Francisco **Visitor Information Center** (900 Market St., 415/391-2000, www.sanfranciscotravel.com, 9 A.M.–5 P.M. Mon.–Fri., 9 A.M.–3 P.M. Sat.–Sun. May–Oct., 9 A.M.–5 P.M. Mon.–Fri., 9 A.M.–3 P.M. Sat. Nov.–Apr.) can help you even before you arrive. See the website for information about attractions and hotels, and to order a visitors' kit. Once you're in town, you can get a San Francisco book at the Market Street location as well as the usual brochures and a few useful coupons.

If English is not your first language, you'll find materials at the Visitor Information Center in 12 different languages along with multilingual staff.

Media and Communications

The major daily newspaper in San Francisco is the *San Francisco Chronicle* (www.sfgate.com). With an appropriately liberal slant on the national political news, a free website, and separate food and wine sections, it's the right paper for its city.

San Francisco also has about a zillion alternative papers, free at newsstands all over town. The *San Francisco Bay Guardian* (www.sfbg.com) and the *SF Weekly* (www.sfweekly.com) are the best-known and most reputable of these. The alternative rags often have the best up-to-date entertainment information available, so if you're looking for nighttime fun, be sure to pick one up while you're out and about.

Need **Internet access?** You got it! This is San Francisco, after all. Most hotels have Internet access of some kind, the jillion Starbucks locations (sometimes two on the same block) often have Wi-Fi for a fee, and plenty of other restaurants and cafés also make it easy to get online.

SERVICES
Banks and Post Offices
Every major national bank and many regional and international banks have branches in San Francisco. ATMs abound, especially in well-traveled areas like Fisherman's Wharf and Union Square. Ask at your hotel or restaurant for the location of the nearest branch or ATM.

Post offices and mailing centers are common in San Francisco; again, ask the concierge or desk clerk at your hotel for the nearest facility. The **main post office** (1300 Evans Ave., 415/550-5501, 7 A.M.–8:30 P.M. Mon.–Fri., 8 A.M.–2 P.M. Sat.) boasts of its short lines and friendly employees. If you've been shopping for things that don't easily fit into the overhead bin, hit the well-placed post office branch in the basement of Macy's (170 O'Farrell St., 415/956-0131, 10 A.M.–5:30 P.M. Mon.–Sat., 11 A.M.–5 P.M. Sun.). Yes, you read that right—it's open on Sunday.

Luggage and Laundry
If your hotel doesn't have valet service, you can take your dirty linen down to a coin laundry. The most entertaining laundry in the City is **BrainWash Café and Laundromat** (1122 Folsom St., 415/255-4866, www.brainwash. com, 7 A.M.–10 P.M. Mon.–Thurs., 7 A.M.–11 P.M. Fri.–Sat., 8 A.M.–10 P.M. Sun.). Enjoy a BrainWash salad or a Burger of Doom with a cold beer and kick back to the sounds of live bands and open mike (7–8 P.M. most nights).

Store your bags through the **Airport Travel Agency** (650/877-0422, 7 A.M.–11 P.M. daily, no reservations necessary) on the Departures-Ticketing Level of the International Terminal at the San Francisco Airport, near Gates G91–G102. Fees vary by the size of the object stored, from $3 for a purse to $6–10 for a suitcase, up to $15 for surfboards or bicycles. All rates are for 24 hours' storage. If traveling by bus, rent a locker at the **Greyhound** bus terminal (200 Folsom St., 415/495-1555, www.greyhound. com, 5:30 A.M.–midnight daily).

Medical Services
The **San Francisco Police Department** (766 Vallejo St., 415/315-2400, www.sf-police.org) is headquartered in Chinatown, on Vallejo Street between Powell and Stockton Streets.

San Francisco boasts a large number of full-service hospitals. The **UCSF Medical Center at Mount Zion** (1600 Divisadero St., 415/567-6600, www.ucsfhealth.org) is renowned for its research and advances in cancer treatments and other important medical breakthroughs. The main hospital is at the corner of Divisadero and Geary Streets. Right downtown, **St. Francis Memorial Hospital** (900 Hyde St., 415/353-6000, www.saintfrancismemorial.org), at the corner of Hyde and Bush Streets, has an emergency department.

SAN FRANCISCO

Getting Around

Car

The Bay Bridge (toll $6) links I-80 to San Francisco from the east, and the Golden Gate Bridge (toll $7) connects Highway 1 from the north. From the south, U.S. 101 and I-280 snake up the peninsula and into the City. Be sure to get a detailed map and good directions to drive into San Francisco—the freeway interchanges, especially surrounding the east side of the Bay Bridge, can be confusing, and the traffic congestion is legendary. For traffic updates and route planning, visit **511.org** (www.511.org).

A car of your own is not necessarily beneficial in San Francisco. The hills are daunting, traffic is excruciating, and parking prices are absurd. If you plan to spend all of your time in the City, consider dispensing with a car and using cabs and public transit options. Rent a car when you're ready to leave San Francisco, or turn your rental in early if the City is your last stop.

If you absolutely must have your car with you, try to get a room at a hotel with a parking lot and either free parking or a parking package for the length of your stay.

CAR RENTAL

All the major car rental agencies have a presence at the San Francisco Airport (SFO, 800/435-9736, www.flysfo.com). In addition, most reputable hotels can offer or recommend a car rental. Rates tend to run $90–160 per day and $250–550 per week (including taxes and fees), with discounts for weekly and longer rentals. If you're flying into Mineta San José Airport (SJC, www.flysanjose.com) or Oakland Airport (OAK, www.flyoakland.com), the cost can drop to $110–250 per week for budget agencies. Premium agencies like Hertz and Avis are much pricier—you'll pay $375–650 for the same car. Off-site locations may offer cheaper rates, in the range of about $375 per week.

DRIVING

Driving in San Francisco can be confusing.

Like most major metropolitan centers, one-way streets, alleys, streetcars, taxis, bicycles, and pedestrians all provide impediments to navigation. Touring around the City to see the sights means traffic jams filled with workers on weekdays and travelers on weekends. It means negotiating the legendary steep hills without crashing into the cars behind and in front of you.

PARKING

To call parking in San Francisco a nightmare is to insult nightmares. Every available scrap of land that can be built on has been built on, with little left over to create parking for the zillions of cars that pass through on a daily basis. Parking a car in San Francisco can easily cost $50 per day or more. Most downtown and Union Square hotels do not include free parking with your room. Expect to pay $35–45 per night for parking, which may not include in-and-out privileges.

Street parking spots are as rare as unicorns and often require permits (which visitors cannot obtain, as a rule, unless they're friends of Danielle Steel). Lots and garages fill up quickly, especially during special events. You're more likely to find parking included at the motels along the edge of the city—Fisherman's Wharf, the Marina, the Richmond, and the Sunset district have the most motor inns with parking included.

RV and RV Rental

In California there are three functional "seasons" for RV rental prices: winter, summer, and Burning Man. If you want to rent an RV for the week before, the weekend of, or the week after Labor Day, plan to book a year or more in advance, and expect to pay extra-super-premium rates for the privilege. If you're renting from a small lot or a private party, you'll also be asked for a larger-than-average cleaning deposit.

The Bay Area location of **El Monte RV**

WALKING TOURS

The best way to see San Francisco is to get out and take a walk. You can find dozens of companies offering walking tours of different parts of the City. Here are a few of the best and most interesting:

One of the most popular walking tour companies in the city is **Foot** (800/979-3370, www.foottours.com, $30-45/person). Foot was founded by stand up comedian Robert Mac, and hires comics to act as guides for their many different tours around San Francisco. If you're a brand-new visitor to the City, pick the two-hour *San Francisco in a Nutshell* tour for a funny look at the basics of San Francisco landmarks and history, or the three-hour *Whole Shebang*, a comprehensive if speedy look at Chinatown, Nob Hill, and North Beach. For visitors who are back for the second or third time, check out the more in-depth neighborhood tours that take in Chinatown, the Castro, or the Haight. You can even hit *Nude, Lewd, and Crude*, a look at the rise of 18-and-up entertainment in North Beach. Tour departure points vary, so check the website for more information about your specific tour and about packages of more than one tour in a day or two.

San Francisco is famous for its incredibly steep hills. Logic suggests that residents would build stairways to make getting to their homes and businesses easier. And so it went. Today, some of the best and most beautiful walks in the City run up and down these stairways. A great guide to these walks is **Stairway Walks in San Francisco** (http://wilderness-press.com/book148.htm); with this book, you can plan routes through beautiful residential neighborhoods filled with lush gardens and attractive vintage homes. At the tops of the hills you'll be rewarded for your efforts with amazing views out over the City — one of the big reasons residents are willing to deal with

all those steps and slopes. Just be aware that you'll need to be in reasonably good shape to tackle the stair walks.

For an inside look at the culinary delights of Chinatown, sign up for a spot on **I Can't Believe I Ate My Way Through Chinatown** (650/355-9657, www.wokwiz.com, $90/person). This three-hour bonanza will take you first for a classic Chinese breakfast, then out into the streets of Chinatown for a narrated tour around Chinatown's food markets, apothecaries, and tea shops. You'll finish up with lunch at one of Chef Shirley's favorite hole-in-the-wall dim sum places. For folks who just want the tour and lunch, or the tour alone, check out the standard Wok Wiz Daily Tour ($50/person with lunch, $35/person tour only).

To check out another side of Chinatown, take the **Chinatown Ghost Tour** (877/887-3373, www.sfchinatownghosttours.com, Fri.-Sat. 7:30 P.M., adults $48, children $24, tour lasts 1.5 hours). It's hard to find a neighborhood with a richer history rife with ghost stories than San Francisco's Chinatown. The whole thing burned down more than a century ago, and it was rebuilt in exactly the same spot, complete with countless narrow alleyways. This tour will take you into these alleys after the sun sets, when the spirits are said to appear on the streets. You'll start out at Kan's Restaurant (708 Grant Ave.) and follow your loquacious guide along the avenues and side streets of Chinatown. As you stroll, your guide will tell you the stories of the neighborhood spirits, spooks, and ancestors. The curious get to learn about the deities worshipped by devout Chinese to this day, along with the folklore that permeates what was until recently a closed and secretive culture. This information delights all walkers, whether or not they actually get to see one of the legendary spirits.

(6301 Scarlett Ct., Dublin, 888/337-2214, www.elmonterv.com, $2,100-3,300 per week summer) has the great advantage of offering a shuttle from San Francisco proper out to their lot in Dublin. Of course, you've got to meet the shuttle at the Westin St. Francis Hotel (111 Mason St.) and pay a fee for the shuttle, and a fee (discounted, but still expensive) to park in the hotel garage. El Monte's RVs tend toward the big and shiny.

CruiseAmerica (796 66th Ave., Oakland, 800/671-8042, www.cruiseamerica.com, pickup 1–4 P.M. and drop-off by 11 A.M. Mon.–Sat., $1,520–1,875 per week summer) has a location near San Francisco. Beware of the base rates advertised by CruiseAmerica—they don't include mileage, kitchen equipment, or towels. You can bring your own towels, but you're on the hook for the mileage. CruiseAmerica does not offer shuttles from San Francisco to its lot in Oakland.

Adventure Touring (866/672-3572, www.adventuretouring.com/pages/rv-rent-als-san-francisco,8 A.M.–4 P.M. Mon.–Fri., 8 A.M.–noon Sat., $2,100–4,300 per week summer) has an even more interesting range of rental options. They rent everything from compact 18-foot RV vans to 40-foot monster buses. All Adventure Touring vehicles are recent models with plenty of amenities like air-conditioning, satellite radio, and bathrooms. Be sure to check the options before you rent—Adventure Touring has some unusual "package deals" for mileage. AT permits pets with a big cleaning deposit.

Muni

Local opinion about the Muni (www.sfmta.com, adults $2, $0.75 youths and seniors) light rail system isn't printable in guidebooks. The truth is, Muni can get you where you want to go in San Francisco as long as time isn't a concern. A variety of lines snake through the City—those that go down to Fisherman's Wharf use vintage streetcars to heighten the fun for visitors. See the website for a route map, ticket information, and (ha-ha) schedules.

To buy tickets, use one of the vending machines placed near some stops. Muni ticket machines are also outside the Caltrain station. See the website for more information about purchasing tickets.

Muni also runs the bus lines, which require the same fares; they can be slightly more reliable than the trains and go all over the City.

BART

Bay Area Rapid Transit, or BART (www.bart.gov, $3–10 one-way), is the Bay Area's late-coming answer to major metropolitan underground railways like Chicago's L trains and New York's subway system. Sadly, there's only one arterial line through the City. However, service directly from San Francisco Airport into the City runs daily, as does service to Oakland Airport, the cities of Oakland and Berkeley, plus many other East Bay destinations. BART connects to the Caltrain system and San Francisco Airport in Millbrae. See the website for route maps, schedules (BART usually runs on time), and fare information.

To buy tickets, use the vending machines found in every BART station. If you plan to ride more than once, you can "add money" to a single ticket, and then keep that ticket and reuse it for each ride.

Caltrain

This traditional commuter rail line runs along the peninsula into Silicon Valley, from San Francisco to San Jose, with limited continuing service to Gilroy. Caltrain (www.caltrain.com, $2.75–13 one-way) Baby Bullet trains can get you from San Jose to San Francisco in under an hour during commuting hours. Extra trains are often added for San Francisco Giants, San Francisco 49ers, and San Jose Sharks games.

You must purchase a ticket in advance at the vending machines found in all stations, or get your 10-ride card stamped before you board a train. The main Caltrain station in San Francisco is at the corner of 4th and King Streets, within walking distance of AT&T Park and Moscone Center.

Taxis

You'll find plenty of taxis scooting around all the major tourist areas of the City. Feel free to wave one down or ask your hotel to call you a cab. If you need to call a cab yourself, try **City Wide Dispatch** (415/920-0700).

YOSEMITE

Of all the wondrous sights, natural and otherwise, that California has to offer, none is more breathtaking or iconic than Yosemite National Park. One of our earliest national parks, this 1,200-square-mile playground has been immortalized in the photographs of Ansel Adams and in the words of naturalist John Muir, who called it "the grandest of all the special temples of Nature I was ever permitted to enter." It was Muir who introduced Yosemite to President Theodore Roosevelt, and that meeting resulted in its national park designation in 1890.

No one seems to visit Yosemite without being profoundly affected by it. If this is your first visit, prepared to be overwhelmed. If you're a regular visitor, then you already know you're going to see something new this time that will knock your polar-fleece socks off. Whether you scale a legendary granite precipice, wake at dawn to watch bear cubs frolic in a glistening meadow, hike under a crashing waterfall, or sit by the fire in one of the park's rustic lodges and watch the snow fall in the moonlight, you'll be different by the time you leave; enjoy the transformation.

East of the great park, Mono Lake greets visitors with an eerie stillness. This treeless, alkaline, and salt-filled lake, with tough desert scrub on its shores, is home to odd calcite (tufa) formations—mute testament to the extraordinary mineral content of the water. The rough High Sierra climate, with its deep winter snows and summer heat, attracts few year-round residents, although the mining town of Bodie—now California's biggest ghost

© GEORGE JEN

HIGHLIGHTS

◖ **Half Dome:** Even in a park filled with iconic monuments, Half Dome towers over all others. Whether you come to scale its peak or just to see the real-life model for all those wonderful photographs, Half Dome lives up to the hype (page 131).

◖ **Bridalveil Fall:** One of the most monumental – and the most accessible – of Yosemite's marvelous collection of waterfalls (page 131).

◖ **Mist Trail:** The best way to experience Yosemite Valley's grandeur is on one of its many scenic trails. A hike along the Mist Trail

to the top of Vernal Fall, or even Nevada Fall, brings the waterfalls and valley views alive (page 133).

◖ **Badger Pass Ski Area:** California's first-ever downhill ski area is as popular as ever, with affordable downhill and cross-country skiing, sledding hills for the kids, and full-moon snowshoe walks (page 142).

◖ **Tuolumne Meadows:** Explore the wonders of the park's high elevations at this rare alpine meadow. Numerous hiking trails thread through Yosemite's backcountry while the adjoining campground gives weary hikers a place to rest their heads (page 147).

◖ **Bodie State Historic Park:** A state of "arrested decay" has preserved this 1877 gold-mining ghost town. Tours of the abandoned mine provide background on the settlement's sordid history (page 159).

◖ **Mono Lake Tufa State Natural Reserve:** Freestanding calcite towers, knobs, and spires dot the alien landscape of Mono Lake. Several interpretive trails provide history and access to what is undoubtedly one of the most unusual lakes you will ever see (page 167).

◖ **Ancient Bristlecone Pine Forest:** The oldest trees on earth are on view in this quiet, fascinating section of the Inyo National Forest. Take a self-guided nature trail past Methuselah, a 4,750-year-old tree (page 173).

◖ **Devils Postpile National Monument:** One visit to these strange natural rock formations and you'll understand how they got their name. A mix of volcanic heat and pressure created these near-perfect, straight-sided hexagonal posts that have to be seen to be believed (page 178).

LOOK FOR ◖ TO FIND RECOMMENDED SIGHTS, ACTIVITIES, DINING, AND LODGING.

town—once sheltered 10,000 gold-hungry adventurers.

South of Mono Lake, the picturesque town of Mammoth Lakes supports the Mammoth Mountain ski area. Winter tourism plays a big part in the local economy, but there's much more to do around Mammoth than just skiing and snowboarding. Hiking, mountain biking, fishing, backpacking, and sightseeing are great in this part of the Eastern Sierra, and you can find bargains on lodging in the summertime "off-season."

As if that wasn't enough, the Ancient Bristlecone Pine Forest in the White Mountains of the Inyo National Forest lies to the east of these ski destinations, near the California-Nevada border. Here you can see the oldest living things on earth in a dramatic and remote wilderness area.

Driving to Yosemite

Yosemite's regions are accessible via five park entrances: Big Oak Flat, Arch Rock, South, Tioga Pass, and Hetch Hetchy. The **Arch Rock** entrance (Hwy. 140) and the **Big Oak Flat** entrance (Hwy. 120 west) are usually open year-round. The **Tioga Pass** (Hwy. 120 east) entrance is just a few miles from Tuolumne Meadows and is the eastern access to Yosemite from U.S. 395. Tioga Road closes in November or December each year and reopens in the spring, usually in May or June. The **Hetch Hetchy** entrance is to the northwest of the park and also closes in winter. The **South** entrance is open year-round.

In winter it is always possible that roads can close unexpectedly and chains may be required on any road at any time. Check the park website (www.nps.gov/yose) or call 209/372-0200 for current road conditions.

DRIVING TO YOSEMITE FROM SAN FRANCISCO

The **Big Oak Flat** park entrance is the closest to San Francisco, accessed via Highway 120 from the west. The drive to Big Oak Flat is about 170 miles from San Francisco and takes at least four hours; however, traffic, especially in summer and on weekends, has the potential to make it much longer. Try to time your drive for weekdays or early mornings to avoid the biggest crowds. From the Big Oak Flat entrance, it's about another 45 minutes to Yosemite Valley.

For the most efficient route to Yosemite from San Francisco, take I-580 east to I-205 east. In Manteca, take I-5 to Highway 120 and follow it south to Big Oak Flat Road.

The **Arch Rock** entrance is another option. From San Francisco, take I-580 east to I-205 east. In Manteca, take Highway 99 south for 56 miles to Merced. In Merced, turn right onto Highway 140 east. Highway 140 will take you right to the Arch Rock entrance.

DRIVING TO YOSEMITE FROM LOS ANGELES

Yosemite is a pretty straightforward drive north from Los Angeles. The **South** entrance is closest to Los Angeles and is open year-round via Highway 41. This is also the nearest entrance to the Badger Pass Ski Area, Glacier Point, and the Bridalveil Creek campground. You can reach Yosemite Valley from the South entrance in about one hour.

Plan about six hours to drive the 300 miles to the park. From Los Angeles, take U.S. 101 north, then Highway 170 north, and finally I-5 north, following signs for Sacramento. Once past the Grapevine, merge onto Highway 99 and follow it through Bakersfield and Fresno (about 130 miles). Once in Fresno, take Highway 41 north for 60 miles to the South entrance of the park.

DRIVING TO YOSEMITE FROM LAS VEGAS

If there's any chance Tioga Pass will be closed (and between October and May there's a good

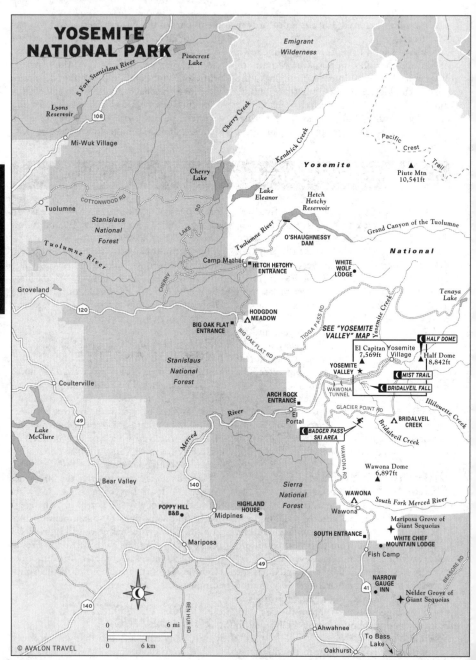

YOSEMITE NATIONAL PARK

Emigrant Wilderness

S Fork Stanislaus River

Pinecrest Lake

Lyons Reservoir

108

Mi-Wuk Village

Cherry Creek

Kendrick Creek

Yosemite

Pacific Crest Trail

Piute Mtn 10,541ft

Tuolumne

COTTONWOOD RD

Cherry Lake

Lake Eleanor

Hetch Hetchy Reservoir

Grand Canyon of the Tuolumne

Stanislaus National Forest

LAKE RD

Tuolumne River

Tuolumne River

O'SHAUGHNESSY DAM

National

Tenaya Lake

Groveland

120

CHERRY RD

Camp Mather

HETCH HETCHY ENTRANCE

WHITE WOLF LODGE

TIOGA PASS RD

HODGDON MEADOW

Yosemite Creek

SEE "YOSEMITE VALLEY" MAP

BIG OAK FLAT ENTRANCE

BIG OAK FLAT RD

HALF DOME

Stanislaus National Forest

El Capitan 7,569ft

Yosemite Village

Half Dome 8,842ft

YOSEMITE VALLEY

★

MIST TRAIL

Coulterville

49

WAWONA TUNNEL

BRIDALVEIL FALL

Illilouette Creek

ARCH ROCK ENTRANCE

River

GLACIER POINT RD

BRIDALVEIL CREEK

Lake McClure

El Portal

Merced River

BADGER PASS SKI AREA

Bridalveil Creek

Bear Valley

140

Sierra National Forest

WAWONA RD

Wawona Dome 6,897ft

POPPY HILL B&B

HIGHLAND HOUSE

WAWONA

South Fork Merced River

Midpines

Wawona

Mariposa Grove of Giant Sequoias

Mariposa

SOUTH ENTRANCE

WHITE CHIEF MOUNTAIN LODGE

49

Fish Camp

41

NARROW GAUGE INN

BEASORE RD

Nelder Grove of Giant Sequoias

140

BEN HUR RD

0   6 mi

0   6 km

Ahwahnee

To Bass Lake

© AVALON TRAVEL

Oakhurst

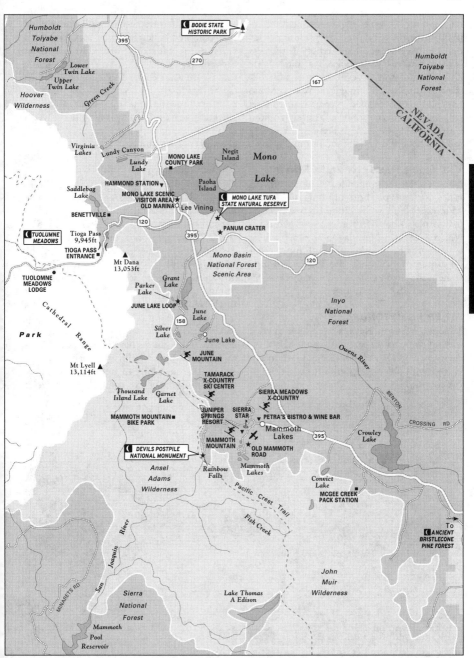

YOSEMITE

one), call the National Park Service at 209/372-0200, then press 1 twice at the prompts for the latest weather and roads report. If the pass is open, you have your choice of a couple fairly direct routes into Las Vegas. Both start by rolling west on SR 120 through the pass to Mono Lake. If the pass is closed, prepare yourself for a tedious 8.5-hour sightseeing trip through central California (SR 41 south to Fresno, then SR 99 south to Bakersfield and SR 58 east to Barstow).

Via Tioga Pass–Nevada Route

The quickest recommended route covers 415 miles, with a typical driving time of 7 hours, 45 minutes. Follow SR 120 to US 6 in Benton, California (3 hours, 15 minutes). Take US 6 west to Coaldale, Nevada (35 minutes), where it shares the road with I-95 south for another 40 minutes to Tonopah. It's then a 210-mile straight shot (more or less) to Las Vegas via I-95 as it leaves US 6 (3.5 hours).

STOPPING IN TONOPAH

Tonopah is a great Nevada crossroads town, a natural stop that rewards pit-stopping travelers with colorful mining history and overnight visitors with one of the darkest starry skies in the country.

Tonopah's few restaurants specialize in good old fashioned American food and American versions of Mexican fare. The menu at **Sidewinders** (222 Main St., 702/482-8888, 6 A.M.–10 P.M. Sun., Mon., Wed., Thur., 6 A.M.–midnight Fri.–Sat., $10–20) runs the comfort-food gamut—spaghetti, burgers, chicken fingers, and fries (especially the fries!) for lunch, along with nightly specials such as chicken marsala and crab legs. Tequila, beer, and spice lovers will revel in the cheesy chiles rellenos at **El Marquez** (348 North Main St., 775/482-3885, 11 A.M.–9 P.M. Tues.–Sun., $10–20). If you're in a hurry but still jonesing for Mexican, hit the drive-through at **Cisco's Tacos** (702 N. Main St., 775/482-5022, $5–10). It has burgers, pizza, and ribs, as well.

New owners have faithfully restored the **Mizpah Hotel** (100 Main Street, 775/482-3030, www.mizpahhotel.net, $69–84), the "Grand Lady of Tonopah." The rooms at **Jim Butler Motel** (100 S. Main St., 775/482-3577, www.jimbutlerinn.com, $40–75) are bright and inviting, with wood furniture and faux hearths. Some rooms have fridges and microwaves; all have free WiFi.

The marquee and an understated plaque on the room door are the only overt jester

© GEORGE JEN

line-up at Tioga Pass entrance, on the east side of Yosemite

references at the **Clown Motel** (521 N. Main St., 775/482-5920, $35–50), where rooms are clean and smoke smell-free, with much-appreciated refrigerator and microwave. They feature basic twin double beds at a decent price, and no juggling, grease-painted harlequins to keep lodgers up at night.

Via Tioga Pass–California Route

Only a few miles farther but 45 minutes longer, an arguably more scenic route traverses Mammoth Lakes, Bishop, and Lone Pine, California, and sets up the trip to include views of Mt. Whitney and an overnight stay at Death Valley National Monument. Leaving Lone Pine, California, SR 136 becomes SR 190, winds through Death Valley, and turns into Nevada SR 374 just before hitting Beatty. From Beatty, I-95 leads 117 miles southeast to Las Vegas.

STOPPING IN BEATTY

Once the center of one of Nevada's most productive mining districts, Beatty is a microcosm of western history, the town having served as a Shoshone settlement, ranching center, and railway hub.

The fajitas and fish tacos at **Ensenada Grill** (600 US 95 S., 775/553-2600, 8 A.M.–7 P.M. daily, $10–15) comes up aces. They pride themselves on their family recipes and regional cuisine. The Harleys and half tons in the parking lot at the **Sourdough Saloon and Restaurant** (106 W. Main St., 775/553-2266, noon–9 P.M., $10–20) correctly suggest that you'll find charred meat and malted barley on the menu. While the food isn't particularly memorable, the friendly folks and the desert dive bar experience certainly are.

Several motels offer clean, cheap, and sometimes eye-opening accommodations. The **Stagecoach Hotel Casino** (900 US 95 N., 775/553-2419, $65–85), is the only true casino in town. Rooms are larger than average with sturdy if not overly stylish furnishings. The on-site **Rita's Café** gets high marks from travelers for the satisfying portions and food quality. The **Atomic Inn** (350 S. First St., 775/553-2250, $50–70) is a park-outside-your-room throwback to the 1950s, and plays up the Cold War theme with a small museum. Rooms are inviting, with lots of golds and honey blonde wood.

Bypassing Tioga Pass

If Tioga Pass is closed—ugh. The only way to Las Vegas is an ugly 8.5-hour, 490-mile ordeal. Take SR 41 south to Fresno (95 miles, 2 hours and 20 minutes), then follow SR 99 south to Bakersfield (1 hour and 45 minutes). Continue on SR 58 east to Barstow (2 hours and 15 minutes), before catching US 95 north to your destination (2 hours and 20 minutes).

STOPPING IN BAKERSFIELD

While far from a tourist destination, Bakersfield is at least a bit of a diversion on the otherwise dreary winter Yosemite-Las Vegas route.

Plenty of vanilla Holidays, Hamptons, and Hiltons in the $90–130 range, as well as America's Best Values, Super 8s and Rodeways for half as much, can be found in Bakersfield. They all serve their purpose, but travelers looking for a bit of personality in their lodgings will have to look a little harder. The rewards are substantial at the **Padre Hotel** (1702 18th Street, 888/443-3387, $109–199), rescued in 2009 and restored to its 1930s grandeur. The hotel's vaguely Spanish colonial exterior gives way to sleek staterooms with ultra-modern furniture. The hotel's fifth-floor Prospect Lounge earns high marks as well, but road-weary travelers fear not; sound walls and thick insulation insure a peaceful rest.

A few blocks west, the rooms at **Hotel Rosedale** (2400 Camino Del Rio Court, 661/327-0681, $60–120) lure guests with their springy umber, burnt orange and green décor. The oversized pool is surrounded by plenty of shade and shrubbery. A small playground will keep little tykes busy, while an arcade ensures older children don't lose their video-game dexterity while on vacation. At the on-site **Bull Shed Bar & Grill** (3 P.M.–2 A.M. Mon.–Fri., noon–2 A.M. Sat, noon–midnight Sun., $8–15), you can fill up on burgers, pizza, beer and deep-fried peaches.

YOSEMITE

A bit more highbrow, **Uricchio's Trattoria** (1400 17th St., 661/326-8870, 11 A.M.–2 P.M. and 5–9 P.M. Mon.–Thurs., 11 A.M.–2 P.M. and 5–10 P.M. Fri., 5–10 P.M. Sat., $15–25) serves the best lasagna in town and the lobster ravioli in clam sauce is no slouch, either.

It's tough to decide among the Caribbean-style chicken, steak, and seafood at **Mama Roomba** (1814 Eye Street, 661/322-6262, 11 A.M.–10 P.M. Mon.–Fri., 5–10 P.M. Sat., $10–15). Insist that someone opts for the calamari and another goes for the tri-tip.

GETTING THERE BY TRAIN OR BUS
Train
It is possible to reach Yosemite via **Amtrak** (800/872-7245, www.amtrak.com, $37–68 one-way from San Francisco, $56 from Los Angeles). From San Francisco (7 hours), you must take a bus to the Amtrak station in the East Bay (5885 Horton St., Emeryville, 45 minutes) and connect to the San Joaquin line to Merced. From Los Angeles (8.5 hours), take the bus from Union Station downtown (800 N. Alameda St., Los Angeles, 3 hours) to Bakersfield and then the Amtrak San Joaquin line to Merced.

All trains terminate at the Merced Amtrak station (324 W. 24th St. at K St., Merced, www.amtrak.com, 7:15 A.M.–9:45 P.M. daily).

From Merced, the YARTS bus takes passengers into Yosemite (2.5 hours), making stops at Curry Village, the Ahwahnee Lodge, the Yosemite Valley Visitors Center, and Yosemite Lodge (year-round); and Crane Flat, White Wolf Lodge, and Tuolumne Meadows (summer only).

Bus
Greyhound (Merced station 209/722-2121, reservations 800/231-2222, www.greyhound.com, Merced station 8 A.M.–5:30 P.M. Mon.–Fri., $39–50 from San Francisco, $40–50 from Los Angeles) can get you as close as Merced. From the **Merced Transportation Center** (710 W. 16th St., Merced), you must then catch the YARTS bus into Yosemite.

The **Yosemite Area Regional Transportation System** (YARTS, 877/989-2787, www.yarts.com) runs daily buses into Yosemite. The Highway 140 bus ($12–25) picks up passengers in Merced, Mariposa, Midpines, and El Portal on the way into Yosemite. The Highway 120 bus (daily July–Aug., Sat.–Sun. June and Sept., $3–20) runs in summer only, picking up passengers at Mammoth Lakes, June Lake, and Lee Vining on the way to Tuolumne and Yosemite Valley. Schedules vary and change often; check the YARTS website for the most up-to-date information before your trip.

Visiting the Park

Yosemite National Park (209/372-0200, www.nps.gove/yose, $20 per vehicle, $10 pp pedestrians, bicycles, motorcycles, non-commercial buses) is open daily year-round. There are five park entrances, two of which close in winter, and entrance fees are valid for seven days. Your many questions can be answered through the menu of recorded messages on the general park phone number, although it's difficult to speak to a live person. The park website provides the best source of comprehensive, well-organized, and seasonal

information along with the downloadable *Yosemite Guide.*

SEASONS
Yosemite is gorgeous any time of year. **Summer** is traditionally high season, and during the height of summer, traffic jams and parking problems plague the park, making it hard to get around. Consider parking at the visitors center in Yosemite Valley and using the free shuttles to travel around the park. Tuolumne and Tioga Pass are less congested than the

© HC LISTON

Yosemite in winter

valley, and parking is more available, making it a good summer option (it's closed in winter).

Spring is best for waterfalls and wildflowers, and there are fewer crowds, as in **fall**. **Winter** dusts the park with snow; roads close and crowds are minimal, but the park is still enchanting. The Badger Pass ski area offers a fun and affordable winter getaway.

LODGING IN YOSEMITE

If you plan to spend the night in the park, advance reservations for overnight accommodations are essential. All lodgings, including campsites, fill up quickly—up to months in advance. For reservations and details on lodging in the park, you must contact Yosemite's concessionaire, **Delaware North Companies** (DNC, 801/559-5000, www.yosemitepark. com). DNC books reservations for Yosemite as well as many other national parks, but they are not located near Yosemite and cannot answer park-specific questions. The website list lodging rates, but always confirm prices and other details with a reservation agent.

Camping in Yosemite

Yosemite has 13 campgrounds, seven of which are available by reservation. Campground reservations are required March 15–November and are absolutely necessary April–September.

Yosemite National Park campgrounds are managed by **Recreation.gov** (877/444-6777, www.recreation.gov, 7 A.M.–9 P.M. daily Mar.–Oct., 7 A.M.–7 P.M. daily Nov.–Feb.). Campsite availability is released in one-month blocks, and you can book up to five months in advance. Only two site reservations at a time are permitted per booking.

When reservations become available in the campgrounds, booking can become competitive. You'll want to be online, or to start calling, first thing in the morning the day sites become available. Note that the reservation system works on eastern time. If you're on Pacific time, and new sites become available at 10 A.M., you need to get on the phone at 7 A.M. to get a shot.

The following campgrounds are available by reservation:

- Lower Pines (Yosemite Valley, Mar.–Oct., reserve 5 months in advance)
- North Pines (Yosemite Valley, Apr.–Sept., reserve 5 months in advance)
- Upper Pines (Yosemite Valley, Mar.–Nov.)
- Crane Flat (Big Oak Flat Rd./Hwy. 120, July–Sept., reserve 5 months in advance)
- Hodgdon Meadow (Big Oak Flat Rd./Hwy. 120, mid-Apr.–mid-Oct.)
- Tuolumne Meadows (150 sites available by reservation, Tuolumne Meadows/Tioga Rd., mid-July–late Sept.)
- Wawona (Wawona, Apr.–Sept.)

The following campgrounds are available first-come, first-served:

- Camp 4 (Yosemite Valley, open year-round)
- Upper Pines (Yosemite Valley, available first-come, first-served Dec.–Mar. 15 only)
- Bridalveil Creek (Glacier Point, July–early Sept.)
- Hodgdon Meadow (Big Oak Flat Rd./Hwy. 120, available first-come, first-served mid-Oct.–mid-Apr. only)
- Tamarack Flat (Tioga Rd., June–Sept.)
- White Wolf (Tioga Rd., July–Sept.)
- Yosemite Creek (Tioga Rd., July–Sept.)
- Porcupine Flat (Tioga Rd., July–Oct.)
- Tuolumne Meadows (150 sites available first-come, first-served, Tuolumne Meadows/Tioga Rd., July–late Sept.)
- Wawona (Wawona, available first-come, first-served Oct.–Mar. only)

From May to September, first-come, first-served campgrounds often fill up by noon or earlier.

ENTRANCES
Big Oak Flat

The most popular route into the park, particularly for those coming from the Bay Area, is through the Big Oak Flat entrance. **Highway 120** leads directly to this portal after taking drivers through Modesto, Manteca, and Groveland. Inside the park, Highway 120 becomes Big Oak Flat Road; if you follow it to the right (southeast), it will lead you into the famed Yosemite Valley. The trip from the entrance to the valley is only about 25 miles, but allow at least 45 minutes. Speed limits in the park are set low to protect animals and people, and they are strictly enforced.

If you're headed for **Tioga Road** or Tuolumne Meadows, the Big Oak Flat entrance is a good way to get there. About nine miles into the park, take the left fork east off Big Oak Flat Road onto Tioga Road (closed in winter). This scenic mountain road winds across the higher elevations of the park, past White Wolf, Yosemite Creek, and Porcupine Flat campgrounds; Olmstead Point, Tenaya Lake, and Cathedral Peak; and on to one of the park's most popular areas, Tuolumne Meadows. **Tuolumne Meadows** is 38 miles from the Big Oak Flat entrance, and it will take about 1.5 hours to reach (maybe a little less if traffic is light). If you continue on Tioga Road another eight miles past Tuolumne, you'll get all the way to Tioga Pass, the east entrance to the park.

Arch Rock

The most direct route into Yosemite Valley is through the Arch Rock entrance. This gateway, south of the Big Oak Flat entrance, is reached via **Highway 140** from Merced and Mariposa. After you enter the park you're on El Portal Road, which follows the Merced River.

Tioga Pass

The Tioga Pass entrance is on the east side of Yosemite, 12 miles west of **U.S. 395.** The entrance road is **Tioga Road** west of the entrance, and Tioga Pass Road to the east. The town of Lee Vining is near the east entrance. Tioga Pass is closed in winter (usually Oct.–May or early June), but closing dates can vary depending on the weather. To check on weather and road closings in Yosemite, call 209/372-0200.

ONE DAY IN YOSEMITE

If you only have one day, spend it in Yosemite Valley. The sights, waterfalls, and hikes here are enough to fill a lifetime, but we'll squeeze what we can into one day.

MORNING

Arrive at Yosemite National Park through the Arch Rock entrance (Hwy. 140), only 11 miles from Yosemite Valley. Stop at **Bridalveil Fall** (page 131) for a photo op, then continue on to the Valley Visitors Center, where you'll leave your car for the day. At the visitors center, check for any open campsites or tent cabins at Curry Village, and make reservations now for dinner later tonight at the Ahwahnee. Explore **Yosemite Village,** stopping for picnic supplies and water, then board the Valley Shuttle Bus. The shuttle provides a great free tour of the park, with multiple points to hop on and off.

AFTERNOON

Choose one of the valley's stellar day hikes (tip: not Half Dome). Take the Valley Shuttle Bus to Happy Isles (shuttle stop 16) and the trailhead for the moderately difficult **Mist Trail** (page 133). This hike is best done in spring when the waterfalls are at their peak but is still gorgeous at any time of year. Hike 1.5 miles round-trip (1-2 hours) to the Vernal Fall Footbridge and gaze at the Merced River as it spills over Vernal Fall. Hardier souls can continue on the strenuous trail to the top of Vernal Fall (3 miles round-trip, 2-4 hours) and enjoy a picnic lunch soaking in the stellar views of the valley below. Return via the John Muir Trail back to the Happy Isles trailhead and the Valley Shuttle.

EVENING

With all that hiking, you probably built up an appetite. Fortunately, you have reservations at the **Ahwahnee Dining Room** (page 141). Change out of your shorts and hiking shoes (and maybe grab a shower at Curry Village), and then catch the Valley Shuttle to the Ahwahnee (shuttle stop 3). Grab a drink in the Ahwahnee Bar and spend some time enjoying the verdant grounds and stellar views of this historic building. After dinner, take the shuttle back to Yosemite Village, where your car awaits – and immediately start planning your return.

EXTENDING YOUR STAY

If you have more time to spend in the park, you can easily fill up two or three days just exploring **Yosemite Valley,** with an excursion to **Glacier Point.** With a week, add the **Tuolumne** (summer only), **Hetch Hetchy,** and **Wawona** sections of the park.

To explore the Eastern Sierra, visit in summer and plan a full weekend to explore **Mono Lake** and **Bodie State Historic Park.** **Mammoth Lakes** makes a great ski getaway in winter, but you'll need a three-day weekend at the very least.

South

Yosemite's South entrance, which leads to Mariposa Grove, Wawona, Badger Pass, and Glacier Point, is accessed from **Highway 41,** coming north from Fresno and Oakhurst. Inside the park, Highway 41 becomes Wawona Road. The road is open year-round, although chains may be required in winter. The smaller Mariposa Grove Road, which leads off to a giant sequoia grove to the east, is closed to vehicles in winter (but you can walk it). You can take Wawona Road farther north to Yosemite Valley (from the South entrance to the Yosemite Valley Visitors Center is about 35 miles, or 1.25 hours); or you can make a right turn from Wawona Road onto Glacier Point Road and reach the Badger Pass Ski Area (about 17 miles from the South entrance). At the end of that road is Glacier Point.

Hetch Hetchy

The northernmost route on the west side of

Hetch Hetchy Reservoir

Yosemite is the Hetch Hetchy entrance. This is the entrance for Hetch Hetchy Reservoir, and it accesses much of the vast backcountry in the less developed section of the park. To get here from **Highway 120,** make a left (north) onto Evergreen Road before the Big Oak Flat entrance. After about seven miles, Evergreen Road passes through the tiny town of Mather and becomes Hetch Hetchy Road, which leads right through the entrance and on to O'Shaughnessy Dam, Hetch Hetchy Reservoir, and the Hetch Hetchy Backpackers Camp. Note that this entrance, and Hetch Hetchy Road, are open year-round but only at limited times. The road tends to be open sunrise–sunset; in summer (May 1–Labor Day) that translates to 7 A.M.–9 P.M.

VISITORS CENTERS
Yosemite Valley
The busiest visitors center is the **Valley Visitors Center** (209/372-0299, 9 A.M.–7:30 P.M. daily late May–mid-Oct., 9 A.M.–5 P.M. daily mid-Oct.–late May), just west of the main post office in Yosemite Valley. Shuttle stops 5 and 9

are near the visitors center, so it's easy to get here even without a car. Here you can catch one of the nearly continuous free showings of the 23-minute film *Spirit of Yosemite,* shop at the bookstore, and enjoy the extensive exhibits about the park. Many ranger talks and walks begin from here throughout the year. For details on the schedule, check the official *Yosemite Guide.*

Wawona
The **Wawona Visitors Center at Hill's Studio** (209/375-9531, 8:30 A.M.–5 P.M. daily mid-May–mid-Oct., 9:30 A.M.–4 P.M. Fri.–Sun. mid-Oct.–late Nov.) is right next to the Wawona Hotel, in the former studio and gallery of Thomas Hill, a famous landscape painter from the 1800s. The visitors center is perfect for information gathering; you can also get free wilderness permits (self-register outside in the off-season) and rent bear-proof canisters ($5 for 2 weeks).

Tuolumne Meadows
The **Tuolumne Meadows Visitors Center** (209/372-0263, 8 A.M.–7 P.M. daily summer,

9 A.M.–6 P.M. daily fall) is in a rustic build-ing not far from the campground and the Tuolumne Meadows Store. Frequent ranger talks are held in the parking lot throughout the summer; details on upcoming programs are available in the *Yosemite Guide*. Wilderness permits are available year-round, and a separate structure across the parking lot houses large handicapped-accessible restrooms.

Soon after entering the park through the west entrance, you'll come to the **Big Oak Flat Information Station** (209/379-1899, 8 A.M.–5 P.M. daily mid-May–mid-Oct.) on the right. You can get a free wilderness permit here in the summer when it's open; in winter you can self-register for a permit right outside.

Wilderness Permits

There is a wilderness center near each of the visitors centers (at Big Oak Flat, both are in the same building). The Tuolumne wilderness center closes at the end of September, and the others close at the end of October; they all re-open in April or May. In summer, you can get a free wilderness permit in any of the wilder-ness offices. The permit allows access to back-country trails anywhere in the park. When the wilderness centers are closed, you can get per-mits in the visitors centers. And when the visi-tors centers are closed, you can self-register for permits right outside each visitors center. To self-register during the off-season, you need to go to the office in the district where you plan to hike. When wilderness offices and visitors centers are open, they rent bear-proof canisters ($5 for up to 2 weeks, $95 security deposit re-quired), which are required in the backcountry. Separate campfire permits are not necessary in Yosemite, but no fires are allowed above the tree line.

INFORMATION AND SERVICES

To accommodate the high density of visitors in Yosemite Valley, the National Parks Service has put in place a number of guest services beyond those found in most other national parks.

A Roman Catholic mass (209/372-4729) is held at the Valley Visitors Center at 10 A.M. Sunday in summer. After October 1, mass moves inside to the theater on Northside Drive.

Media and Communications

The print guide you absolutely need as you tour Yosemite is the official **Yosemite Guide,** pub-lished several times a year by the park. This paper provides general information about the park and its services. More important, it has a detailed schedule of all classes, events, pro-grams, and so on for the upcoming weeks. You'll receive a copy when you enter the park at one of the entrance stations; you can also download it (www.nps.gov/yose) ahead of time or pick it up at the California Welcome Center (710 W. 16th St., Merced, 209/724-8104 or 800/446-5353, www.visitmerced.travel or www. visitcwc.com, 8:30 A.M.–5 P.M. Mon.–Thurs., 8 A.M.–4 P.M. Sat., 10 A.M.–3 P.M. Sun.).

Internet access is available in a few spots in Yosemite Valley. The only place you can con-nect your own laptop is inside Yosemite Lodge. If you're an overnight guest of the lodge, you can use the wireless service at no extra charge. If not, it's $5.95 for up to seven log-ins or seven days. In Curry Village, wireless Internet ac-cess is available in the lounge for Curry Village guests only. Similarly, guests of the Ahwahnee Hotel have access to wireless Internet service at no additional cost. Internet kiosks are available in Degnan's Deli (209/372-8454, 7 A.M.–5 P.M. daily year-round, $0.25 per minute, summer only), and free Internet access is available at the Yosemite Valley Branch Library (Girls Club Bldg., 9000 Cedar Ct., 209/372-4552, www. mariposalibrary.org/yosemite, 2–5 P.M. Mon., 8:30 A.M.–12:30 P.M. Tues., 2–6 P.M. Wed., 4–7 P.M. Thurs.) in Yosemite Valley.

Banks and Post Offices

A number of ATMs are available through-out Yosemite, making it easy to extract cash for souvenirs, food, and more souvenirs. Specifically, **Citizens Bank** (www.citizens-bank.com) maintains cash machines inside the park at the Village Store, Degnan's Deli, the

YOSEMITE

lobby of Yosemite Lodge at the Falls, the Curry Village Gift and Grocery Store, the Wawona Pioneer Gift & Grocery, the Crane Flat Store, the Ahwahnee Lodge, the Tuolumne Meadows store (seasonal), and the Badger Pass Ski Area (seasonal). In addition, there is a **Yosemite Credit Union** ATM in Yosemite Village at the Yosemite Art & Education Center.

Several **post offices** provide mailing services. Look for a post office in Yosemite Village (8:30 A.M.–5 P.M. Mon.–Fri., 10 A.M.–noon Sat.), inside Yosemite Lodge (12:30 P.M.–2:45 P.M. Mon.–Fri.), in El Portal (8:30 A.M.–12:30 P.M. and 1:30–5 P.M. Mon.–Fri.), and in Wawona (9 A.M.–5 P.M. Mon.–Fri., 9 A.M.–noon Sat.).

Gas and Automotive Services

There is no gas available anywhere in Yosemite Valley. The nearest gas stations in the park are at **El Portal, Wawona,** and **Crane Flat,** and at **Tuolumne Meadows** (June–Oct.). All gas stations are open 24 hours and are pay-at-the-pump with debit or credit cards. There's gas in Mariposa at **Pioneer Texaco** (5177 Hwy. 140, Mariposa, 209/966-2136), which also has a minimart.

If your car breaks down, you can take it to the **Village Garage** (9002 Village Dr., off Northside Dr., Yosemite Village, 209/372-8320, 8 A.M.–5 P.M. daily, towing 24 hours daily). Because it's the only game in town, expect to pay a high premium for towing and repairs.

Laundry, Groceries, and Showers

There are laundry facilities available at the **Housekeeping Camp** (8 A.M.–10 P.M. daily Apr.–Oct.) inside the Curry Village complex.

Several expensive, crowded, and limited-stock grocery stores are located in the park: the **Curry Village** Gift and Grocery (8 A.M.–9 P.M. daily), the **Yosemite Lodge** Gift and Grocery (8 A.M.–8 P.M. daily), the **Crane Flat Store** (9 A.M.–5 P.M. daily), and the **Wawona Store and Pioneer Gift Shop** (8 A.M.–6 P.M. daily). In summer, you can also get groceries in the **Housekeeping Camp** grocery (8 A.M.–6 P.M. daily Apr.–Oct.) and the **Tuolumne Meadows** store (9 A.M.–6 P.M. daily spring–late Sept.).

Showers are available at **Curry Village** (24 hours daily year-round, $5) and **Housekeeping Camp** (8 A.M.–10 P.M. daily Apr.–Oct., $5).

Medical Services

The park maintains its own clinic, the **Yosemite Medical Clinic** (209/372-4637) in Yosemite Village at the floor of the valley. It's got a 24-hour emergency room, other services available 9 A.M.–7 P.M., and a domestic violence crisis center. **Dental services** (209/372-4200) are also available adjacent to the medical center.

The nearest hospitals to the park are the **John C. Fremont Hospital** (5189 Hospital Rd., Mariposa, 209/966-3631, http://jcf-hospital.com), west of the park; and **Mammoth Hospital** (85 Sierra Park Rd., Mammoth Lakes, 760/934-3311, www.mammothhospital.com), which is southeast of the park and is not accessible from Yosemite in winter, when Tioga Road is closed.

GETTING AROUND

Once you've reached Yosemite, most of the popular sights, attractions, and trailheads are accessible by road, at least in the summer. However, summer traffic and parking in Yosemite can be every bit as frustrating as it is in a big city. Preserve your good mood and help save the air by leaving your car behind and relaxing on one of Yosemite's free, comfortable, and efficient shuttle buses.

In winter (Nov.–May), Tioga Road, Glacier Point Road, and Mariposa Grove Road are closed, and chains may be required on any park road at any time. Check the park website (www.nps.gov/yose) or call 209/372-0200 for current road conditions.

Shuttle Services

Yosemite runs an extensive network of free shuttle buses in various areas of the park. The system works extremely well and frees up visitors to enjoy the park and decrease the traffic.

• **Yosemite Valley** shuttle (7 A.M.–10 P.M. daily year-round, free) provides access to numbered shuttle stops in the valley, including Yosemite Lodge, the Valley Visitors Center, Curry Village, all campgrounds, and the Happy Isles trailhead. Shuttles run about every 10–20 minutes; check the map in the *Yosemite Guide* for stops.

- **El Capitan** shuttle (9 A.M.–6 P.M. daily mid-June–early Sept., free) runs during the summer season and stops at the Valley Visitors Center, El Capitan, and the trailhead for Four Mile.
- **Wawona-Mariposa Grove** shuttle (spring–fall, free) transports travelers between Wawona and the Mariposa Grove, picking up passengers at the South entrance, the Wawona Store, and the Mariposa Grove gift shop.
- **Wawona to Yosemite Valley** shuttle (Memorial Day–Labor Day, free) leaves the Wawona Hotel at 8:30 A.M. for Yosemite Valley. The shuttle picks up passengers at Yosemite Lodge at 3:30 P.M. for the return trip to Wawona.
- **Badger Pass** shuttle (Dec.–Mar., free) runs twice daily between Yosemite Valley and the Badger Pass ski area during the winter ski season.
- **Tuolumne Meadows** shuttle (7 A.M.–7 P.M.

daily June–mid-Sept., free) runs along Tioga Road, making multiple stops between Olmstead Point and the Tuolumne Meadows Lodge.

In-Park Bus Tours

Separate from the Yosemite shuttle system, a few commercial operators provide bus services in the park for a fee. **Glacier Point Tours** (209/372-4386, www.yosemitepark.com, 8:30 A.M., 10 A.M., and 1:30 P.M. daily spring–fall, adults $25 one-way, $41 round-trip, discounts for children, seniors, and groups) runs daily trips from Yosemite Valley Lodge to Glacier Point (4 hours round-trip). A popular choice for the hardy is to take the bus one way and then hike back to the valley.

July–September, Glacier Point Tours offers a luxurious guided bus tour between Yosemite Valley and Tuolumne Meadows. The coach makes multiple stops from Curry Village (8 A.M.) all the way to Tuolumne Meadows Lodge (arriving at 10:35 A.M.). It departs Tuolumne Meadows again at 2:05 P.M. and heads back. You don't have to take the whole journey; you can travel any segment and get off when you like. Round-trip fares range $5–23 for adults, depending on the distance traveled, and children ages 5–12 are half price.

Gateways to Yosemite

If you want a small inn or inexpensive motel for your visit to Yosemite, consider staying outside the park proper and driving in each day. A wealth of inns, lodges, and B&Bs cluster near both the west and south entrances to the park. If you prefer a standard chain motel, Oakhurst (south of Fish Camp on Hwy. 41) and Mariposa (to the west on Hwy. 140) have most of the usual suspects.

MODESTO

The archway welcoming visitors to the city of Modesto (I St. near 9th St.) reads, "Water, Wealth, Contentment, Health." The motto celebrates Modesto's history as an agricultural center with an abundance of natural resources. Located along Highway 99 in the fertile San Joaquin Valley, Modesto still produces large quantities of dairy products, nuts, and wine grapes. Modesto functions as a stopping place on the way to Yosemite. Travelers pull off the road here to get a cup of coffee or a meal or to stretch as they make the pilgrimage to the park.

The hometown of film director George Lucas, Modesto was immortalized in his 1973 film *American Graffiti,* about 1950s-era juvenile delinquents, teen angst, and cruising.

These days, Modesto is pretty quiet; you'd never guess the city has 210,000 residents. The town is making an effort to attract visitors, and much of the downtown area has gone through some renewal. Attractive restaurants and coffee shops intermingle with storefronts that have gone out of business. In the heart of downtown, a section of 10th Street has been blocked to traffic, creating a pleasant, brick-inlaid pedestrian mall. E&J Gallo Winery is the largest employer in Modesto, but the company does not offer tours or tastings. Modesto is where they age, blend, and bottle their wines, and make bottles (2.4 million per day!) to ship for tasting and sales in Napa and Central California.

The Gallo family invests in the city, and their **Gallo Center for the Arts** (1000 I St., Modesto, 209/338-2100, www.galloarts.org) is a large and impressive modern facility that brings a rich variety of performing arts to the area. The Modesto Garden Club maintains lavish floral displays downtown (K St. between 10th St. and 11th St.), and large, complex fountains add to the civic beauty while serving as

© HC LISTON

Gallo Center for the Arts, Modesto

a reminder to the residents of the part water played in their city's development.

Accommodations

A large and modern **Doubletree Hotel** (1150 9th St., 209/526-6000, www.doubletree. com, Sun.–Thurs. $124–149, Fri.–Sat. usually $99) towers over the downtown area, making Modesto a welcoming place for conventions and business meetings. With a gym, pool, and valet parking, this place has all the amenities you expect in an upscale hotel. Since it is primarily a business hotel, the weekend rate is lower than weekdays. Internet access costs extra, but ask about their Executive Package, which bundles use of the Internet with parking privileges and a full breakfast for a bargain price. The hotel is within easy walking distance of Gallo Center for the Arts as well as the restaurants, shops, and the visitors center downtown.

Food

The best restaurant in Modesto, and maybe in the whole Central Valley, is **Galletto Ristorante** (1101 J St., 209/523-4500, www. galletto.biz, 11:30 A.M.–9:30 P.M. Mon.–Thurs., 11:30 A.M.–10:30 P.M. Fri., 4:30–10:30 P.M. Sat., 11 A.M.–9 P.M. Sun., $12–30). The Sunday dinner menu is available all day; other days, dinner service begins at 5 P.M. The owners, Tom and Karyn Gallo of the Gallo winery family, take pride in running a "farm-to-fork" restaurant that buys from local purveyors, thereby ensuring the freshest possible meals, reducing their carbon footprint, and supporting local businesses. The atmosphere in this ivy-covered 1930s art deco building, formerly a Wells Fargo bank, is just right for the offbeat elegance of the place.

If you love Italian food but are on a bit of a budget, try **Carino's Italian Restaurant** (3401 Dale Rd., 209/578-9432, www.carinos. com, 11 A.M.–9 P.M. Sun.–Thurs., 11 A.M.–10 P.M. Fri.–Sat., $14–18). It's part of a small California chain, so the Modesto branch is not one of a kind, but the food is tasty, dependable, and generously portioned, and the atmosphere is warm and friendly.

The British-style pub **Firkin & Fox** (1111 I St., 209/575-2369, www.firkinfoxmodesto. com, noon–1 A.M. Sun.–Thurs., noon–2 A.M. Fri.–Sat., $10–20) is across the street from the Gallo Center for the Arts, welcoming concert-goers and other arts patrons for some bangers, beans, and mash before or after the show. If you're not an Anglophile, don't worry—Firkin & Fox has an extensive menu that includes everything from steaks and chops to quesadillas and Italian subs.

Modesto has a certified farmers market (16th St. between H St. and I St., 209/605-8536, www.modestocfm.com, 7 A.M.–1 P.M. Thurs. and Sat. Apr.–Nov.) where you can sample and purchase local produce.

Information and Services

The **Modesto Convention & Visitors Bureau** (1150 9th St., Suite C, 209/526-5588 or 888/640-8467, www.visitmodesto.com, 8 A.M.–5 P.M. Mon.–Fri.) operates a friendly visitors center downtown.

ALONG HIGHWAY 120
Manteca

If you're traveling to Yosemite from the Bay Area, the best way to jump in and start enjoying the abundant treasures of the region is to begin eating locally. The little town of Manteca, 76 miles east of San Francisco and about 80 miles from Yosemite's north entrance, is a great place to stop for a break. Depending on the season, the area is ripe with almonds, cherries, strawberries, spinach, peaches, watermelons, walnuts, and more. And it's all available for sale, at reasonable to low prices, in a series of farmers markets right by the side of Highway 120. One of the largest is **Nature's Country Corner** (18033 Jack Tone Rd., 209/239-5901, 8 A.M.–7 P.M. daily), which offers a few vacation staples like soda and chips in addition to luscious piles of fresh produce and a large selection of dried fruits and nuts that have been grown and prepared locally. Other stands in the vicinity sport homemade signs touting the harvest of the moment: "Cherries!" "Apricots!" "Honey!" Stop and stock up now

on California's fresh bounty—from here on, the towns get smaller and the shopping opportunities sparser.

Groveland

The little town of Groveland, 26 miles outside the north entrance to Yosemite National Park on Highway 120, is the perfect place to stop for a last fill-up of gas, food, coffee, and anything else you may need before you immerse yourself in the wonders of nature (and the limitations of campground stores and captive-audience prices). Groveland is a mix of the down-home ordinariness of small-town America (with its Friday night bingo games at the Lion's Club, mediocre pizza parlors, and bulletin boards advertising handyman services and used washers and dryers for sale) and savvy marketers catering to urban travelers (yes, cappuccino and latte are available some 140 miles beyond the Bay Area).

If you're trying to avoid rush hour traffic or getting a jump on your weekend trip to Yosemite by driving up late the night before, it can be a great idea to sleep in Groveland and enter the park the next morning, rested and ready to go.

ACCOMMODATIONS

The most elegant option is Groveland is the historic **C Groveland Hotel** (18767 Main St., 800/273-3314, www.groveland.com, $145–339), built in 1849, the year before California became a state, which is located right in the center of town. The proprietor, Peggy A. Mosley, a former Silicon Valley executive, oversees a seamless blend of historical intrigue that includes gold miners, gambling, and ghosts along with the modern comfort of the hotel's 17 guest rooms, each furnished with down comforters, feather beds, and charming touches like flocked floral wallpaper, hand-sewn quilts, and china chamber pots—and large flat-screen HD TVs, discreetly mounted on the wall.

Nods to the foodie and pet-loving Bay Area clientele include fresh coffee beans, ready for the grinders on the in-room coffeemakers;

YOSEMITE

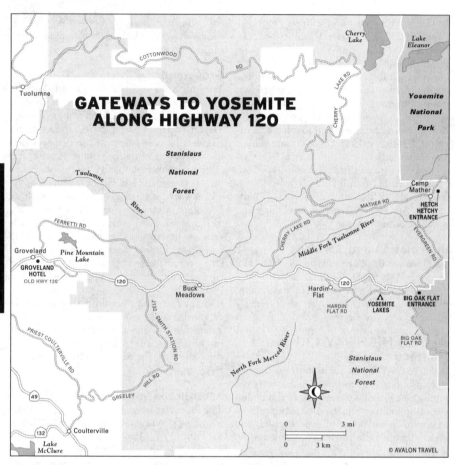

GATEWAYS TO YOSEMITE ALONG HIGHWAY 120

© AVALON TRAVEL

private-label chocolate chip cookies waiting on the beds; and an open-door policy for dogs and cats in all guest rooms. Free wireless Internet service throughout the facility also helps work-aholics ease gradually toward their wilderness vacation.

Those itching to get outside will love the Groveland Hotel's elegant front porch, cool and shady with an upper level from which you can watch all the goings-on in the village. There is also a quiet patio courtyard in back, where breakfast (included with the room) and dinner are served by the hotel's upscale restaurant.

CAMPING

Camp in Big Oak Flat along Highway 120 at the Thousand Trails Campground at **Yosemite Lakes** (31191 Harden Flat Rd., 800/533-1001, ranger station 209/962-0103, www.1000trails. com, RVs $49, tents $59). Yes, as odd as it sounds, it costs more to pitch a tent here than to rent an RV site. This sprawling wooded campground be-side the water has more than 250 RV sites with full hookups, 130 tent sites, a few dozen cab-ins, tent cabins, yurts, and a 12-bed hostel. It's only five miles from the park entrance, and it has a full slate of recreational amenities, laundry facilities, and Internet service. It is right on the Tuolumne River, has great access to the boating opportunities on Lake Don Pedro, and Moaning Cavern is only a few miles away.

FOOD
The **Iron Door Saloon** (18761 Main St., 209/962-6244, www.iron-door-saloon.com, 11 A.M.–9 P.M. daily year-round, $11–20) claims to be the oldest bar in California, and it definitely has a lively history. It served gold prospectors sometime in the 1850s, and through the early 20th century it was the saloon of choice for the engineers who built the O'Shaughnessy Dam at Hetch Hetchy. Presently, folks young and old don't consider a trip to Yosemite complete unless they stop here for a drink on the way. With live music every weekend, it's still arguably the center of nightlife for many miles around. It's hard to recommend the food, which arrives suspiciously fast, but the drinks and atmosphere seem to make everyone happy. The Iron Door never wants for a crowd. The bar stays open till 2 A.M. if it's busy, but may close earlier in the off-season.

If quaint is more your style than raucous, stop in at **Dori's Tea Cottage** (18744 Main St., 209/962-5300, www.doristeacottage. com, 11 A.M.–3 P.M. Mon. and Wed.–Thurs., 11 A.M.–7 P.M. Fri.–Sat., $9–16). Dori and Greg Jones run this sweet little place, which promises a "traditional English tea luncheon in a quaint and comfortable atmosphere." The elegant offerings include tuna tarragon; blue cheese, walnut, cranberry, and pear sandwiches; and tea cookies. Wine, champagne, and dessert are always available, there are vegetarian options, and there's also a special menu for "little princes and princesses." Reservations are recommended if you want to come for lunch in the summer. There's a gift boutique (10 A.M.–4 P.M. Wed.–Sun.) where you can get drinks and lunches to go.

As you approach Groveland from the west, you'll pass through the tiny community of Big Oak Flat. The **Big Oak Restaurant and Bar** (17820 Hwy. 120, 209/962-6015,

7:30 A.M.–2:30 P.M. daily, $8–10) is near the junction of Highways 120 and 108. Dark, cool, and quiet by day, the place feels more like a bar than a restaurant. The food is nothing special, but quantities are generous. If you have a choice, breakfast here is better than lunch.

Stop in Groveland at **Mar-Val's Main Street Market** (19000 Main St., Groveland, 209/962-7452, 8 A.M.–9 P.M. daily summer, 8 A.M.–8 P.M. daily winter) to pick up some last-minute groceries before you head into the park. It's not large, but you'll find more choices here and at lower prices than anywhere in the park. Watermelon and other seasonal produce are often featured outside at good prices.

The **Cellar Door** (18767 Main St., 800/273-3314, www.groveland.com, 8–10 A.M. and 5:30–9:30 P.M. daily, Dec. hours shorter, $17–27, reservations suggested in summer) is the excellent restaurant at the Groveland Hotel. Outdoor tables are equipped with sun umbrellas and surrounded by lush gardens of roses and local flora. On cool evenings, propane heaters ensure that the patio stays comfortable, and indoor tables are also available in the hotel's oak-paneled dining room. The Cellar Door has been selected for the Award of Excellence by *Wine Spectator* magazine in each of the past 10 years.

MERCED
Merced is a small, lively city of just under 80,000. It has the beautiful Merced River, for which the city was named, flowing nearby, and since 2005 it also has the newest branch of the University of California. Merced has a strong agricultural sector producing dairy products, nuts, and fruit, and there is visible evidence of an elegant past in the well-preserved Victorian homes and 19th-century courthouse building. But Merced knows what it's really all about, as its motto proudly proclaims: It's the "Gateway to Yosemite."

Even if you think you've seen enough gracious and lovely historic buildings, take a quick drive over to the **Merced County Courthouse Museum** (21st St. and N St., 209/723-2401, www.mercedmuseum.org, 10 A.M.–4 P.M.

© H C LISTON

Merced County Courthouse Museum

Wed.–Sun., free). This truly gorgeous building, dedicated in 1875 and now listed on the National Register of Historic Places, is maintained to the point it practically sparkles in the sun. Inside you'll find exhibits about the early history of Merced County and the Central Valley.

Right across the small parking area from the Courthouse Museum is a peaceful, grassy park encompassing the **Merced County Veterans Memorial.** With separate monuments to local soldiers from a long list of wars, this is a well-managed oasis in the middle of town: cool, shady, and quiet.

If the day isn't too hot, pick up a brochure at the **California Welcome Center** (710 W. 16th St., 209/724-8104 or 800/446-5353, www.visitmerced.travel or www.visitcwc.com, 8:30 A.M.–5 P.M. Mon.–Thurs., 8 A.M.–4 P.M. Sat., 10 A.M.–3 P.M. Sun.) and follow a self-guided walking tour of Merced's impressive collection of Victorian houses. Whether you're an architecture buff or you just like a pleasant stroll through a gracious part of town, this walking tour of about 20 blocks can make for a memorable afternoon.

Accommodations

Merced is a modest small American city without a lot of expensive hotels or resorts. It has all the usual low to moderately priced chain hotels and motels, many of which are situated right on Highways 140 and 99 so you don't have to go a minute out of your way if you're just stopping off for the night on your way to Yosemite.

For something a little more special, try the **Hooper House Bear Creek Inn** (575 W. North Bear Creek Dr., 209/723-3991, www.hooperhouse.com, $139–169). This colonial-style bed-and-breakfast has three suites in a preserved mansion that was handed down from the owners' gentleman-farmer ancestors. There is also one private cottage on the grounds nearby. All guest rooms have private baths and down comforters as well as full breakfast in the dining room.

Food

In keeping with its American working-class image, Merced has the full gamut of standard fast food and moderately priced restaurants. For breakfast, lunch, and baked goods, one standout is **Toni's Courtyard Café** (516 W. 18th St., 209/384-2580, www.toniscourtyardcafe.com, 7 A.M.–3 P.M. Mon.–Fri., 7:30 A.M.–2 P.M. Sat., $7–10). Although located in an unimpressive little strip mall, Toni's is a cute café with appealing seating options both inside and out. They make omelets, sandwiches, and salads, but it's the bakery items that really make this place special. The homemade pumpkin bread alone is worth a trip.

For a genteel lunch or dinner, your best choice is **Fernando's Bistro** (510 W. Main St., 209/381-0290, www.fernandosbistro.com, 11 A.M.–9 P.M. Tues.–Sat., $16–27). This upscale restaurant, located in attractive Bob Hart Square, serves California cuisine at patio tables right beside the pleasant Susie Rossi Memorial Fountain—just the right level of white noise to give outdoor diners a sense of intimacy. Entrées include salmon, sirloin, and lamb complemented by selections from the martini bar menu (espresso, pomegranate, and chocolate martinis; ask the waiter for a recommendation). Fernando's also hosts the occasional wine tasting event ($10, including appetizers).

If you're passing through on Saturday, visit the **Merced Farmers Market** (19th and M St., www.mercedcfm.org, 7 A.M.–noon Sat. June–Oct., 8 A.M.–noon Sat. Nov.–May), which takes place weekly near the Courthouse Museum.

Don't forget one of the main functions of a gateway city like Merced: to stock up on supplies before you dive into the wilderness. Merced makes grocery shopping easy with two mega-stores right across the street from each other. The **Save Mart** (1136 W. Main St., 209/723-0449, www.savemart.com, 7 A.M.–midnight daily) and **Grocery Outlet** (1125 W. Main St., 209/384-0441, www.grocery-outlet.com/Merced-CA, 8 A.M.–9 P.M. daily) both have huge selections, reasonable prices, and long hours.

Information and Services
Merced has a large and welcoming **California Welcome Center** (710 W. 16th St., 209/724-8104 or 800/446-5353, www.visitmerced.travel or www.visitcwc.com, 8:30 A.M.–5 P.M. Mon.–Thurs., 8 A.M.–4 P.M. Sat., 10 A.M.–3 P.M. Sun.). In this exceptionally well-stocked showroom you can pick up brochures and maps for attractions all over California, not just the local area. Nearly everything is free, and you're welcome to take as much literature as you need. Mention you're headed to Yosemite, and the staff will pull out a special packet with helpful items like a map of the park and a copy of the *Yosemite Guide* (hold onto it; you're going to appreciate it when you get there). They no longer sell tickets for the buses here, but they can tell you anything you need to know about schedules, prices, and logistics.

Getting There
As the last major city on the way to Yosemite, Merced is a transportation hub; it's served by Amtrak, Greyhound, Yosemite Area Rapid Transit, and the local Merced Transit system. The **Merced Transportation Center** (710 W. 16th St.) is home to both the **Greyhound** bus station (station 209/722-2121, reservations 800/231-2222, www.greyhound.com, 8 A.M.–5:30 P.M. Mon.–Fri.) and the **YARTS** depot (877/989-2787, www.yarts.com). The **Amtrak** station (324 W. 24th St. at K St., www.amtrak.com, 7:15 A.M.–9:45 P.M. daily) is where you'll stop when taking the train to Yosemite. From the Amtrak Station, you catch the YARTS bus, which stops at the Merced Transportation Center before continuing on to Yosemite.

For local transportation in and around Merced, take **The Bus** (209/725-3813, www.mercedthebus.com, 7 A.M.–6 P.M. Mon.–Fri., 9:30 A.M.–5:30 P.M. Sat., adults $1, seniors $0.50, children under 46 inches free).

ALONG HIGHWAY 140
Mariposa
Mariposa is a little over one hour (44 miles) from Yosemite Valley via the Arch Rock entrance.

ACCOMMODATIONS
You can't miss the **River Rock Inn and Deli Garden Café** (4993 7th St., 209/966-5793,

www.riverrockncafe.com, $65–159) with its vivid orange-and-purple exterior in the heart of Mariposa. What was once a rundown 1940s motor lodge is now a quirky, whimsical motel with unusually decorated guest rooms that make the most of modern Pottery Barn–esque wrought-iron and wood styling in the spaces the decorators had to work with. Never fear: The colors become softer inside the reasonably priced guest rooms. Two suites provide enough space for families, while the other five guest rooms sleep couples in comfort. The River Rock is a 45-minute drive from the west entrance to Yosemite, at the southern end of the long chain of Gold Country towns, making it a great base of operations for an outdoorsy, Western-style California vacation.

If you prefer cozy seclusion to large lodge-style hotels, stay at the **Highland House** (3125 Wild Dove Lane, 209/966-3737, www.highlandhouseinn.com, $115–150), outside Mariposa and west of Yosemite. The house is set deep in the forest far from town, providing endless peace and quiet away from civilization. This tiny B&B has only three guest rooms, each decorated in soft colors and warm, inviting styles. All guest rooms have down comforters, sparkling clean bathtubs and showers,

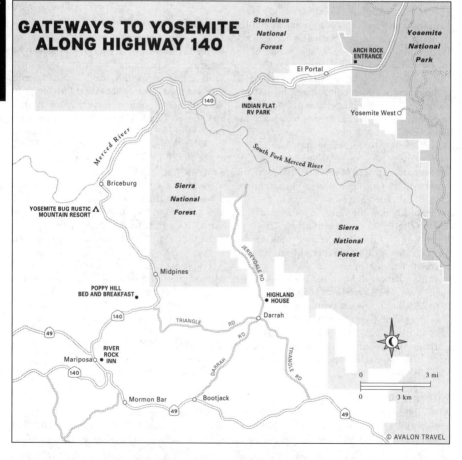

GATEWAYS TO YOSEMITE ALONG HIGHWAY 140

free wireless Internet access, and TVs with DVD players.

Another lovely small B&B, **Poppy Hill Bed and Breakfast** (5218 Crystal Aire Dr., 209/742-6273 or 800/587-6779, www.poppyhill.com, $135–150) is 27 miles from the west entrance to the park. The four airy guest rooms are done in bright white linens, white walls, lacy curtains, and antique furniture. No TVs mar the sounds of birds from the expansive gardens surrounding the old farmhouse, but you can take a dip in the totally modern hot tub any time. A full gourmet breakfast served on your schedule gives the right start to a day spent exploring Yosemite or the Mariposa County area. This inn can be hard to find, especially at night. Double-check the directions on the website, and consider using a GPS device if you have one.

CAMPING

Several campgrounds surround the Arch Rock entrance near Mariposa. The **Yosemite Bug Rustic Mountain Resort** (6979 Hwy. 140, 209/966-6666 or 866/826-7108, www.yosemitebug.com, dorm $22–25, tent cabin $45–75 for 2–4 people, private cabin $75–155 for 2–4 people) is part hostel, part rustic cabin lodge. This facility includes five hostel dormitories, a number of attractively appointed tent cabins with real beds (but bring your own sleeping bag), and a few cabins with private guest rooms, some with private baths. Solo travelers and families on tight budgets favor Yosemite Bug for its comfortable and cheap accommodations. It's not the Ritz, but the baths are clean and the linens fresh when you arrive, and the location is great for Yosemite visitors who want to exit the park each night.

FOOD

For a better selection of groceries at much lower prices than inside the park, check out **Pioneer Market** (5034 Coakley Circle, Suite 104, 209/742-6100, www.pioneersupermarket.com, 7 A.M.–10 P.M. Mon.–Sat., 8 A.M.–9 P.M. Sun.).

El Portal

El Portal lies only 14 miles from Yosemite Valley via the Arch Rock entrance, about a 30-minute drive.

ACCOMMODATIONS AND CAMPING

RVers aiming for the Arch Rock entrance flock to the **Indian Flat RV Park** (9988 Hwy. 140, 209/379-2339, www.indianflatrvpark.com, tents $20–25, RVs $32–42, tent cabins $30–59, cottages $65–109, pet fee $5). This park is a full-service low-end resort, with everything from RV sites (with water and electricity; some with sewer hookups) to tent cabins and full-fledged cottages. Showers are available ($3), and you can stop in for a shower even if you're not spending the night. The lodge next door has extended an invitation to all Indian Flat campers to make use of their outdoor pool. Because Indian Flat is relatively small (25 RV sites and 25 tent sites), reservations are strongly recommended for May–September. You can book up to a year in advance; this kind of planning is a good idea for summertime Yosemite visitors.

ALONG HIGHWAY 41
Fish Camp

Fish Camp is 40 miles from Yosemite Valley via the South entrance, a little over an hour's drive. At **Bass Lake Water Sports and Boat Rentals** (North Shores Pine Village, Bass Lake, 559/642-3200 or 800/585-9283, www.basslakeboatrentals.com, 8 A.M.–8 P.M. daily year-round), you can rent all sorts of watercraft, such as a six-passenger patio boat ($118 for 2 hours, $249 per day) or a Jet Ski ($99 per hour, $389 per day), or make a reservation for a three-hour guided fishing trip ($195 for up to 4 people). If you bring your own boat, you can dock it here too ($35 per night).

ACCOMMODATIONS AND FOOD

Near the South entrance, the **Narrow Gauge Inn** (48571 Hwy. 41, 559/683-7720 or 888/644-9050, www.narrowgaugeinn.com, $79–195) recalls the large lodges inside the park, only in miniature. This charming 26-room mountain inn offers one- and two-bed nonsmoking guest rooms done in wood

YOSEMITE

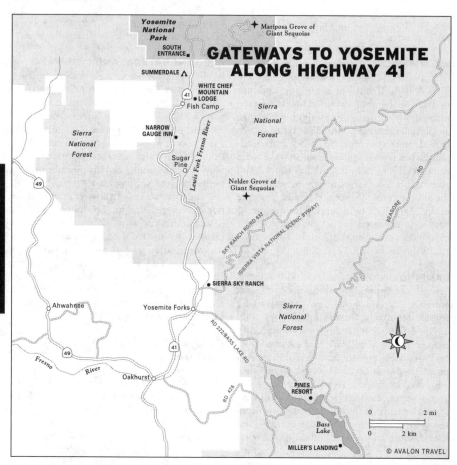

Yosemite
National
Park

SOUTH
ENTRANCE

SUMMERDALE

WHITE CHIEF
MOUNTAIN
LODGE

Fish Camp

NARROW
GAUGE INN

Sugar
Pine

Ahwahnee

Yosemite Forks

Oakhurst

Fresno   River

Mariposa Grove of
Giant Sequoias

GATEWAYS TO YOSEMITE
ALONG HIGHWAY 41

Sierra

National

Forest

Lewis Fork Fresno River

Nelder Grove of
Giant Sequoias

SKY RANCH RD/RD 632

(SIERRA VISTA NATIONAL SCENIC BYWAY)

SIERRA SKY RANCH

Sierra

National

Forest

RD 222/BASS LAKE RD

RD 426

BEASORE   RD

PINES
RESORT

Bass
Lake

MILLER'S LANDING

0   2 mi

0   2 km

© AVALON TRAVEL

paneling, light colors, white linens, and vintage-style quilts. Each guest room has its own outdoor table and chairs to encourage relaxing outside with a drink on gorgeous summer days and evenings. The restaurant and common rooms feature antique oil lamps, stonework, and crackling fireplaces. Step outside your door and you're in the magnificent High Sierra pine forest. A few more steps take you to the Yosemite Mountain Sugar Pine Railroad—the narrow-gauge steam train from which the inn takes its name.

For inexpensive lodge-style accommodations east of Fish Camp, check in to the

White Chief Mountain Lodge (7776 White Chief Mountain Rd., 559/683-5444, www.whitechiefmountainlodge.com, $120–160). The basic guest rooms feature light wood paneling and tribal-design textiles. Small TVs offer in-room entertainment, but the woods outside your door invite you outside to enjoy all that the rich Sierra range has to offer. The lodge offers packages that show off the best of the Wild West heritage of the area. Guest rooms in the main lodge have wireless Internet access, but the cottages do not.

The **Tenaya Lodge** (1122 Hwy. 41, 559/683-6555 or 888/514-2167, www.tenayalodge.com,

$245–400) sits just outside the South entrance of Yosemite, offering plush lodge-style accommodations at a more reasonable price than comparable rooms inside the park. Prices vary considerably by season (or, as one front-desk worker explains it, "The higher the temperature, the higher the rates."). Guest rooms in the lodge are styled with rich fabrics in bright oranges and other bold, eye-catching colors; the three dozen cottages have a Native American-themed decor. The modern wall art evokes the woods and vistas of Yosemite. The beds are comfortable, the baths attractive, and the views forest-filled. Tenaya Lodge focuses on guest care, offering five dining venues on-site, from pizza to deli to fine dining, with three meals daily; a full-service spa that specializes in facials; and daily (and nightly) nature walks complete with costumed guides. Check at the desk for events during your stay.

If you plan to do some fishing during your trip to the Yosemite area, the **Pines Resort** (54432 Rd. 432, Bass Lake, 559/642-3121 or 800/350-7463, www.basslake.com, June–Aug., $159–299) is perfectly located for your angling convenience right on the shores of Bass Lake; bring your boat! You can choose a suite (a split-level king room with dark floors, light walls, fireplaces, some with spa tubs) or rent a chalet (a two-story cabin in rustic mountain style that sleeps up to 6, with a full kitchen, a deck, and an outdoor mini barbecue). The Pines is a full-service resort, with a lake-view restaurant, **Ducey's on the Lake** (7–11 A.M. and 4–9 P.M. Mon.–Fri., 7 A.M.–noon and 4–9 P.M. Sat.–Sun., $18–37), a grocery store (8 A.M.–9 P.M. Mon.–Fri., 8 A.M.–10 P.M. Sat.–Sun. June–Aug., shorter hours Sept.–May), all-weather tennis courts, a swimming pool (in summer), hot tubs (year-round), massage services, a fitness room overlooking the lake, shaded lakefront chaise longues, parking for trailers, and wedding and meeting facilities.

CAMPING

A mile and a half south of the South entrance, in the Sierra National Forest down by the spread-out forest town of Fish Camp, you can book a site at the small, attractive **Summerdale Campground** (Hwy. 41, northeast of Fish Camp, 877/444-6777, www.recreation.gov, $20). This lovely spot has a two-night minimum on weekends and a three-night minimum on holiday weekends, only 29 campsites, and a strict limit on RV size (24 feet), making it a bit quieter and less city-like than the mega-campgrounds. You'll have a fire ring and a grill at your site, plenty of room under mature shade trees, and maybe even a water spigot (although boiling the water before drinking it is recommended).

Yosemite Valley

The first place most people go when they reach the park is the floor of Yosemite Valley (Hwy. 140, Arch Rock entrance). From the valley floor, you can check out the visitors center, the theater, galleries, the museum, hotels, and outdoor historic exhibits. Numerous pullouts from the main road invite photographers to capture the beauty of the valley and its many easily visible natural wonders. It's the most visited place in Yosemite, and many hikes, ranging from easy to difficult, begin in the valley.

GETTING THERE
Car
From the San Francisco Bay Area, Yosemite Valley is about 195 miles, and the drive takes about 4.5 hours. The most efficient way to get to the valley from the Bay Area is to take I-580 east to I-205 to I-5 to Highway 120, and enter through Groveland and the Big Oak Flat entrance on the west side of the park. After you enter the park, it's another 25 miles to the valley, which takes about 45 minutes.

If you plan to drive to most places in

YOSEMITE

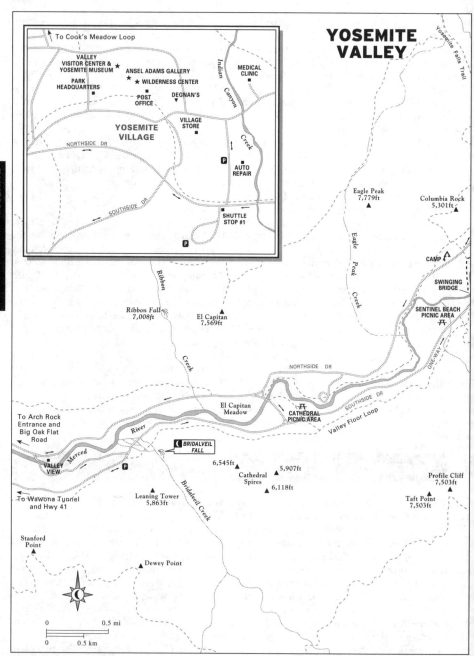

YOSEMITE VALLEY

To Cook's Meadow Loop

VALLEY VISITOR CENTER & YOSEMITE MUSEUM ★
★ ANSEL ADAMS GALLERY
PARK HEADQUARTERS ■
★ WILDERNESS CENTER
■ POST OFFICE
DEGNAN'S ■
MEDICAL CLINIC ■
VILLAGE STORE ■

YOSEMITE VILLAGE

NORTHSIDE DR

P
■ AUTO REPAIR

SOUTHSIDE DR

■ SHUTTLE STOP #1

P

Indian Canyon Creek

Yosemite Falls Trail

Eagle Peak 7,779ft ▲

Columbia Rock 5,301ft ▲

Eagle Peak Creek

CAMP 4 ⚕

SWINGING BRIDGE

SENTINEL BEACH PICNIC AREA

Ribbon Creek

Ribbon Fall 7,008ft

El Capitan 7,569ft ▲

NORTHSIDE DR

ONE-WAY

SOUTHSIDE DR

El Capitan Meadow

CATHEDRAL PICNIC AREA

Valley Floor Loop

To Arch Rock Entrance and Big Oak Flat Road

Merced River

BRIDALVEIL FALL

VALLEY VIEW

P

To Wawona Tunnel and Hwy 41

Leaning Tower 5,863ft ▲

Bridalveil Creek

6,545ft ▲

Cathedral Spires 6,118ft ▲

5,907ft ▲

Profile Cliff 7,503ft ▲

Taft Point 7,503ft ▲

Stanford Point

Dewey Point ▲

| 0 | | 0.5 mi |
| 0 | | 0.5 km |

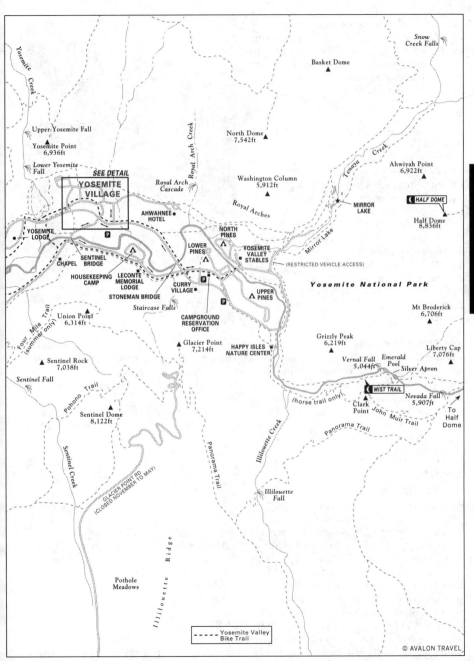

YOSEMITE

© AVALON TRAVEL

YOSEMITE

Yosemite Valley, be aware that in summer—especially on weekends—traffic and parking can be slow and stressful. If possible, it's a good idea to leave your car parked somewhere during those busy times and use the free shuttle buses to get around.

Bus

The **Yosemite Area Regional Transportation System** (YARTS, 877/989-2787, www.yarts. com) runs daily buses from Mariposa ($8–12 round-trip, $4–6 one-way) and Merced ($18–25 round-trip, $9–13 one-way) to Yosemite Valley. If you enter the park on one of these buses, you won't have to pay the entrance fee ($20). You can buy tickets on the bus, as well as from several businesses in the area. No reservations are necessary, and children under 12 ride free. You can also take your bicycle on the bus, making a complete no-car vacation a real possibility. Buses run more frequently in summer. Check the YARTS website for current schedules.

© HC LISTON
Half Dome

Shuttle Services

The free Yosemite Shuttle is particularly active in Yosemite Valley. The **Yosemite Valley** shuttle (7 A.M.–10 P.M. daily year-round) runs every 10–20 minutes, stopping at Yosemite Lodge, the Valley Visitors Center, Curry Village, all campgrounds, and the Happy Isles trailhead. Check the map in the *Yosemite Guide* for a list of numbered shuttle stops.

SIGHTS
Valley Visitors Center

After the scenic turnouts through the park, your first stop in Yosemite Valley should be the visitors center (Yosemite Village, off Northside Dr., 209/372-0299, www.nps.gov/yose, 9 A.M.–7:30 P.M. daily late May–mid-Oct., 9 A.M.–5 P.M. daily mid-Oct.–late May). Here you'll find an interpretive museum describing the geological and human history of Yosemite in addition to all the usual information, books, maps, and assistance from park rangers. The complex of buildings includes the **Yosemite Museum** (9 A.M.–5 P.M.

daily, free) and store, the **Yosemite Theater LIVE,** the **Ansel Adams Gallery** (209/372-4413, www.anseladams.com, 9 A.M.–6 P.M. daily), and the all-important public restrooms.

A short, flat walk from the visitors center takes you down to the recreated **Miwok Native American Village.** The village includes many different types of structures, including some made by the later Miwoks, who incorporated European architecture into their building techniques. You can walk right into the houses and public buildings of this nearly lost group. One of the most fascinating parts of this reconstruction is the evolution of construction techniques—as nonnative settlers infiltrated the area, building cabins and larger structures, the Miwok took note. They examined these buildings and incorporated elements that they saw as improvements.

El Capitan

The first natural stone monument you encounter as you enter the valley is El Capitan

(Northside Rd., west of El Capitan Bridge), a massive hunk of Cretaceous granite that's actually named for this formation. This 3,000-foot craggy rock face is accessible in two ways: You can take a long hike westward from Upper Yosemite Fall and up the back side of El Capitan, or you can bring your climbing gear and scale the face. El Cap boasts a reputation as one of the world's seminal big-face climbs.

◖ Half Dome

At the foot of the valley, one of the most recognizable features in all of Yosemite rises high above the valley floor. Ansel Adams's famed photographs of Half Dome, visible from most of the valley floor, made it known to hikers and photography lovers all over the world. Scientists believe that Half Dome was never a whole dome—the way it appears to us now is actually its original formation. This piece of a narrow granite ridge was polished to its smooth dome-like shape tens of millions of years ago by glaciers, giving it the appearance of half a dome.

◖ Bridalveil Fall

Bridalveil Fall (Southside Dr., past Tunnel View) is many visitors' first introduction to Yosemite's famed collection of waterfalls. The **Bridalveil Fall Trail** (0.5 miles, 20 minutes) is a pleasantly sedate walk up to the fall. Although the 620-foot waterfall runs year-round, its fine mist sprays most powerfully in the spring—expect to get wet!

The trailhead has its own parking area, which is west of the main lodge and visitors center complex, so it's one of the first major sights people come to on entering the park. It's a great first stop as you travel up the valley.

Yosemite Falls

Spring and early summer are the best times to view the many waterfalls that cascade down the granite walls of Yosemite. Most of the major waterfalls require at least a short hike to the best viewing points. Yosemite Falls, however, is visible from the valley floor near Yosemite Lodge. Actually three separate waterfalls—Upper Fall,

© HCH LISTON

YOSEMITE

Bridalveil Fall

Lower Fall, and Middle Cascade—this dramatic formation together creates one of the highest waterfalls in the world. The flows are seasonal; if you visit Yosemite Valley during the fall or the winter, you'll see just a trickle of water on the rocks or nothing at all. The best time to see water gushing is the spring, when the snowmelt swells the river above and creates the beautiful cascade that makes these falls so famous.

Mirror Lake

Past the end of Southside Drive in Yosemite Valley lies still, perfect Mirror Lake. This small lake offers a stunningly clear reflection of the already spectacular views of Tenaya Canyon and the ubiquitous Half Dome. A short, level hiking and biking path circumnavigates the lake (2 miles round-trip, 1 hour). But come early in the season—this lake is gradually drying out, losing its water and becoming a meadow in the late summer and fall. Take the shuttle from anywhere in Yosemite Valley to stop 17 to get to the start of the paved pathway to the lake.

YOSEMITE

RECREATION
Hiking

Yosemite Valley is the perfect place for a day hike, no matter how energetic you feel. Valley hiking maps are available at the Valley Visitors Center (Yosemite Valley at Valley Village, Northside Dr.). Talk to the rangers about trail conditions and be sure to bring you map—and water—on the trail with you.

In addition to the easy hikes to **Bridalveil Fall** (0.5 miles, 20 minutes) and **Mirror Lake** (2 miles, 1 hour, shuttle stop 17), there are several other valley hikes that provide a good sampler of what's available in Yosemite—plenty of other trails wind through this gorgeous area. Be aware that many people love the valley trails, so you likely won't be alone in the wilderness.

LOWER YOSEMITE FALL

If you're staying at Yosemite Lodge and want an easy, gentle walk with a great view, take the Lower Yosemite Fall loop (1.1 miles, 30 minutes, shuttle stop 6). Enjoy the wondrous views of both Upper and Lower Yosemite Falls,

© HC LISTON

Mirror Lake

complete with lots of cooling spray. If you can, hike this trail in the spring or early summer, when the flow of the falls is at its peak. This easy trail works well for families with children who love the water.

COOK'S MEADOW

Soak in quintessential Yosemite Valley views from the easy Cook's Meadow Loop (1 mile, 30 minutes, shuttle stop 5 or 9), a short walk through the heart of the valley. The main point of this hike is to observe Ansel Adams's famous view of Half Dome from the Sentinel Bridge, and then to gaze up at the Royal Arches and Glacier Point. You can extend this hike a bit by making it the Sentinel–Cook's Meadow Loop. By circling both meadows instead of just one, you'll make the whole trip about 2.25 miles and increase the number of angles for your photo ops. Trail signs, and the plethora of other hikers doing these trails, make it easy to find the turns.

VALLEY FLOOR

If you've got several hours, take the Valley Floor Loop (Northside Dr. and Southside Dr., paved path beside the road). The moderate **half loop** (6.5 miles, 3 hours, shuttle stop 6) traverses the El Capitan Bridge, following the path of many old wagon roads and historic trails. The **full loop** is 13 miles long and takes about six hours to hike. It's a great moderate day hike, and you'll see the most beautiful parts of the valley while escaping the crowds on the roads. If you want to hike the Valley Floor Loop, it's a good idea to talk to the rangers at the visitors center; the route is not entirely clear on the trail map, and getting lost in the meadows or forests is a distinct possibility.

UPPER YOSEMITE FALL

Naturally, some of the more challenging hikes in Yosemite Valley are also the most rewarding. One of these is the strenuous trek up to Upper Yosemite Fall (7.2 miles, 6–8 hours, shuttle stop 7). You can start this hike from the Upper Yosemite Fall trailhead or walk from Lower Yosemite Fall. The trail starts getting

© HC LISTON

Nevada Fall

steep right away—you'll climb 2,700 vertical feet in three miles to reach the top of America's tallest waterfall. Your reward will be some of the most astonishing views to be had anywhere in the world. You can look down over the fall and out over the valley, with its grassy meadows far below. Plan all day for this hike, and bring plenty of water and snacks to replenish your energy for the potentially tricky climb down. This trail is well marked and much used, and the steep parts are made passable with stone steps, switchbacks, and occasional railings. But much of the trail tends to be wet and slippery, so hold on and take it slow.

◖ MIST TRAIL

Starting at the Happy Isles Nature Center (shuttle stop 16), the moderate-strenuous Mist Trail leads first to **Vernal Fall** (3 miles, 3 hours) over much steep, slick granite—including more than 600 stairs—up to the top of Vernal Fall. Your reward is the stellar view of the valley below while relaxing on the flat granite boulders that abut the Merced River.

If you packed a lunch, stop and eat here before returning back the same way. Hardier souls should continue another steep and strenuous 1.5–2 miles of switchbacks to the top of **Nevada Fall** (5.4 miles, 5–6 hours) and return via the John Muir Trail. Plan six hours for this hike, with a 2,000-foot elevation gain, and consider taking a lightweight rain jacket since this aptly named trail gives hikers a shower in the spring and early summer months.

Note that the Mist Trail is closed in winter due to ice and snow and can be dangerous in the spring months when the river is at its peak; hikers have been lost in the waters here. Exercise caution in extreme conditions, and obey all trail signage.

HALF DOME

The most famous climb in Yosemite Valley takes you to the top of monumental Half Dome (14–16 miles, 10–12 hours, May–Oct. only, shuttle stop 16). But before you start, a word of warning: This hike can be dangerous. With a round-trip distance of 14 miles by

THE BEARS OF YOSEMITE

Although the official California state flag shows a majestic grizzly bear on the prowl, grizzlies, a.k.a. North American brown bears, have not been seen in California since 1922. We do, however, still have quite a few of the smaller but still impressive black bears (*Ursus americanus californiensis*). Black bears do not seek out humans as prey, and they're usually not looking for trouble. They are, however, looking for food, and this often leads them into campgrounds and other places frequented by humans. To protect both people and bears, National Park and State Park rangers are very strict about enforcing rules to minimize contact between the species.

In most areas with bear populations, the parks provide metal storage lockers. Under California state law, you must store all food, ice chests, and anything that looks or smells like food in these lockers when staying overnight. Even if you're in a park only for the day, you must use the lockers or at least put all your food in the trunk of your vehicle, out of sight. Remember that garbage, toothpaste, shampoo, deodorant, beer, and soda all smell like food even if they don't seem like it to you – don't ever put any of these items in your tent.

Yosemite is particularly vigilant about its bear rules. Bears do not hibernate in Yosemite during the winter; the visitors center and lodge display disturbing videos of bears tearing apart car doors and rooftops to get at food inside. Visitors have been known to get expensive tickets for having even an empty grocery sack within view inside a locked car. If it looks like food to a bear, it can lead to trouble. For camping and backpacking, the old rule about hoisting your food up and hanging it from trees is mostly out of favor now (although it's still allowed in the Desolation Wilderness). Many parks, including Yosemite, Sequoia, and Kings Canyon, require the use of approved bear-resistant canisters instead. You can buy these at any outdoor supply store, and sometimes you can borrow or rent one at a trailhead or visitors center. Note that bear spray and pepper spray are not permitted in the park.

If you see a bear at least 50 yards away, be quiet and keep your distance. If the bear approaches you or your campsite, actively discourage it by banging on pots and pans, yelling, and waving your arms. If you're carrying food or a backpack or other parcel, drop whatever you're holding and get away from it. The bear will probably switch its attention to the pack and leave you alone.

Note any distinguishing characteristics of the bears you see and report any sightings to park staff (209/372-0322).

the Mist Trail or 16 miles by the John Muir Trail, and with a very strenuous 4,800-foot elevation gain, this arduous, all-day hike is not for small children, the elderly, or anyone remotely out of shape. The trek is significantly riskier in rain, snow, high wind, or other adverse conditions, and rangers will not be able to rescue you should you become stranded at the top. Attempt this hike only in the summer (Memorial Day–Columbus Day) when the cables are up (you must hold onto cables to help pull yourself up the last 400 feet of steep granite to the top of the dome). Most importantly, obey all signage on the trail. If the park posts that the trail is closed or unsafe, heed the conditions and turn back. Continuing on when conditions deem otherwise risks your life and others, including those who will have to try to rescue you.

For many people, Half Dome is a life-list kind of experience, not to be missed, but that does not mean everyone should try it. Before you commit to Half Dome, make sure you're ready, mentally and physically, for a long and sometimes treacherous challenge. Check weather conditions and sunrise and sunset times before you hike, and establish a turn-around point so that you aren't hiking back in darkness. Take a well-organized pack with water (1 gallon pp), food, a topo map and compass, a headlamp or flashlight (with batteries), and other safety essentials. Wear hiking shoes that have been broken in and bring a hat.

From the Happy Isles shuttle stop, follow the Mist Trail to Nevada Fall (or, alternately, take the John Muir Trail instead), and then follow the signs for Half Dome. Once you stagger to the top, you'll find a restful expanse of stone on which to sit and rest and enjoy the scenery.

Yosemite requires all hikers to have a **permit** (877/444-6777, www.recreation.gov, $1.50 pp) to climb Half Dome. There are 400 permits issued per day; 300 permits are allotted for day hikers, and the rest are for backpackers. You can reserve up to four permits during each phone call or online visit. Reservations must be made in advance; permits are not available first-come, first-served, so don't show up at the trailhead expecting to get lucky. However, there are a few almost-last-minute options: Check the website at 7 A.M. Pacific time the day before you want to climb. If the next day's allotment of permits isn't all taken, a batch of permits will be released. If someone cancels their permit at the last minute, the park will continue issuing permits to replace those canceled until midnight the night before.

Backpacking

If you're a serious hiker and you have time for just one big hike in Yosemite, you can't go wrong with the **Snow Creek Trail** (13 miles round-trip, 5–7 hours, shuttle stop 17) from Mirror Lake to the granite domes above Tenaya Canyon. From the shuttle stop, walk 350 yards on a paved sidewalk to Tenaya Bridge. Here the trail splits; keep left and cross the bridge to take the northern trail. In another 0.5–0.75 miles you'll see Mirror Lake. Look straight down into this aptly named pool and you'll notice that the view of Half Dome and the other natural wonders nearby is stunningly clear. Eventually, you'll leave Mirror Lake behind and continue walking northeast, following a wide trail for about a mile through a cool, swampy forest. The terrain is mostly easy, but soon the trail joins the Tenaya Lake and Tuolumne Meadows Trail and begins a long series of switchbacks,

backpackers on the Mist Trail

climbing up through rocks, streams, redwoods, ponderosa pines, and manzanitas. In the spring, gradual snowmelt seeps across the trail, making for a few shallow water crossings and an abundance of wildflowers.

The trail is a little steep but never impassable. The switchbacks keep the grade reasonably consistent, discreet rock stairs help you over the rough spots, and water bars and contouring guide water off the trail, helping to contain erosion as well as keeping your feet dry and your footing secure. As you climb, take in the hillside teeming with forest life, and vast sweeping views of the mountains and rock faces to the east and south.

Just when you've had enough of climbing (about 2.5 miles of switchbacks and nearly 3,000 feet of elevation gain), you'll notice that the trail flattens out and enters a forest. Look for a clearing to your right after about 0.25 miles and head in that direction through fallen trees and low brush. In just a couple of minutes you'll find yourself on top of a massive granite slab, the end of the hike. This enormous rock provides a perfect lunch spot with 360-degree views of Mount Watkins to the east with Clouds Rest beyond it, Snow Creek Falls across the valley, and the rarely seen north side of Half Dome. When you're ready, return by the same route.

Yosemite Valley Stables

Two different rides begin at the Yosemite Valley Stables (end of Southside Dr., 209/372-8348, www.yosemitepark.com/Activities_MuleHorsebackRides.aspx, 7 A.M.–5 P.M. daily May–Oct., $64–85). The sedate two-hour trek to Mirror Lake works well for children and beginning riders. Along the way, your guide will explain the geologic forces that are slowly drying out the lake. A half-day ride takes you out to Clark Point, from where you can admire Vernal Fall, Nevada Fall, and the valley floor. This ride takes about four hours but isn't terribly difficult.

Biking

Biking is a great way to get out of the car, off the crowded roads, and explore Yosemite at a quicker-than-walking (and sometimes even quicker than driving) pace. Twelve miles of paved trails are mostly flat. You can bring your own bike, or rent one in Yosemite Village from the in-park concessionaire, Delaware North Companies (209/372-4386, www.yosemitepark.com, 9 A.M.–6 P.M. daily, $10 per hour, $28 per day). Check at Yosemite Lodge (801/559-5000, shuttle stop 8) for more information about rentals and to get a bike trail map.

Rock Climbing

The rock climbing at Yosemite is some of the best in the world. **El Capitan,** the face of **Half Dome,** and **Sentinel Dome** in the high country are challenges that draw climbers from all over. If you plan to climb one of these monuments, check with the Yosemite park rangers and the Mountaineering School well in advance for necessary information and permits.

Note that many of the spectacular ascents are not beginners' climbs. If you try

to scale El Capitan as your first-ever climb, you'll fail (if you're lucky). The right place to start climbing in Yosemite is the **Yosemite Mountaineering School** (209/372-8344, www.yosemitepark.com/activities_mountaineeringschool.aspx). Here you'll find "Go Climb a Rock" classes for beginners, perfect for older kids or adult team-building groups. You'll also find guided climbs out of Yosemite Valley and Tuolumne Meadows, and if you're looking for a one-on-one guided climb experience, you can get it through the school. Also available are guided hikes and backpacking trips as well as cross-country skiing lessons and treks in winter.

Ice-Skating

Curry Village (end of Southside Dr., 209/372-8319, www.yosemitepark.com, 3:30–6 P.M. and 7–9:30 P.M. Mon.–Fri., 8:30–11 A.M., noon–2:30 P.M., 3:30–6 P.M., and 7–9:30 P.M. Sat.–Sun. mid-Nov.–Mar., adults $8, children $6, rentals $3) has an ice-skating rink in winter.

ENTERTAINMENT AND EVENTS

LeConte Memorial Lodge (Southside Dr., 10 A.M.–4 P.M. Wed.–Sun., shuttle stop 12) hosts evening programs (8 P.M. Fri.–Sun. summer, free) and has a library, a children's play area, and seasonal exhibits. Check the *Yosemite Guide* for a list of programs.

Ranger Programs are popular with the kids. Park rangers give talks, lead guided walks, and host evening programs throughout the valley; check the *Yosemite Guide* for a list of programs.

Theater and Music

The **Yosemite Valley Auditorium and Yosemite Theater** (Northside Dr.) share a building behind the visitors center in the heart of Yosemite Village. Check the copy of *Yosemite Guide* you received at the gate for a list of what shows are playing during your visit. The John Muir Performances (209/372-0731, 7 P.M. Wed.–Thurs. May–mid-Nov., adults $8, children $4), starring Yosemite's resident actor

YOSEMITE AT NIGHT

Yosemite National Park does not roll up its meadows and trails at sunset. In fact, some aspects of the park come alive only at nightfall. Many of the animals that live in the park are crepuscular by nature – they're most active in the twilight hours of dawn and dusk. Take a quiet stroll in the park early in the morning or just as darkness is falling and you're likely to see more wildlife than you'll run into during the day.

If you prefer a guided tour, come in the spring or early fall to join the **Night Prowl** (209/372-4386, www.yosemitepark.com/Activities_EveningPrograms_NightProwl.aspx, 90 minutes, $5). This guided tour takes you along easy trails near Yosemite Lodge at the Falls and explains the nightlife of the valley floor's inhabitants. Night Prowl takes place once or twice a week, starting at various times and places, and is good for both children and adults. Purchase your tickets at any activity desk in Yosemite, or call 209/372-4386, and you'll get all the information on where and when to meet.

In winter, take a **Full Moon Snowshoe Walk** (Badger Pass Day Lodge, reservations 209/372-1240, weather conditions 209/372-1000, Jan.-Mar., $18.50 includes snowshoe rental, $5 if you bring your own, reservations required, not recommended for children under 10). This two-hour trek from the Badger Pass ski lodge takes you out into the sparkling white wonderland that is Yosemite in winter. These walks are offered five days per month: the four days leading up to the full moon and the day of the full moon itself. Also be aware that the Badger Pass shuttle does not run in the evenings, so you must drive to and from the lodge on your own (chains may be required).

If astronomy is your interest, join experienced guides for the **Starry Skies** (209/372-4386, summer-fall, $5) program. Equally well suited for beginners and more experienced stargazers, this 90-minute program takes you out to the meadows to look at the stars and the moon free of light pollution. You'll learn about constellations, comets, and meteors and enjoy the myths and legends about the night sky. Starry Skies happens several times each week in Yosemite Valley and once a week in Wawona.

For families tired after a long day of running around the park, more sedentary evening programs are available. The **Campfire Program** (209/372-4386, summer-fall, 90 minutes, $5 pp or $20 per family) does it old-school – groups gather around a nice big campfire (bring blankets and bug repellent) for stories, singing, and marshmallow toasting. You might need to take a short walk to get to the fire near Camp Curry. If you're out at one of the more primitive lodges or campsites, check with the local rangers or office for campfire programs at the site, since many spring up in the summer and early fall months. **Fireside Storytelling** (fall-spring, free) focuses on, well, telling stories around the big fire inside the Ahwahnee Great Lounge. Take refuge from the bugs and the cold and listen to great tales in a comfortable indoor environment during the off-season. Check the *Yosemite Guide* for more information about these and other programs.

Lee Stetson, have been running for 25 years. Stetson's repertoire includes *Conversation with a Tramp: An Evening with John Muir* about Muir's battle to preserve Hetch Hetchy, *The Spirit of John Muir, John Muir Among the Animals,* and a two-person show, *The Tramp and the Roughrider,* about Muir's relationship with Theodore Roosevelt. Any or all of these may be offered during a given season in the park. Other programs in the theater and auditorium include presentations by Shelton Johnson (who appeared in the Ken Burns documentary *The National Parks: America's Best Idea*) about the Buffalo Soldiers, films about climbing, and—on Monday evenings—Tom Bopp singing historic songs of Yosemite. For more details on upcoming programs, visit www.yosemiteconservancy.org; for background on Lee Stetson and John Muir in particular, visit www.johnmuirlive.com.

Photography and Art Classes

The unbelievable scenery of Yosemite inspires visitors young and old to create images to take home with them. Knowing this, Yosemite offers art and photography classes to help people find their inner Ansel Adams. In summer, free art classes are offered by the **Yosemite Art and Education Center** (Yosemite Village, 209/372-1442, www.yosemiteconservancy. org, 10 A.M.–2 P.M. Tues.–Sat. Apr.–Oct., $5 per day donation), a program of the Yosemite Conservancy. Check the *Yosemite Guide* or the website for a list of classes during your visit. You must bring your own art supplies, a chair or cushion to sit on, and walking shoes (you'll take a brief walk out to a good location to see the scenery). If you don't have supplies, you can buy them at the Village Store (9 A.M.– 4:30 P.M.) just before class. Also check the *Yosemite Guide* for guided tours of the **Ansel Adams Gallery** (Yosemite Village, 209/372-4413, www.anseladams.com, 9 A.M.–5 P.M. daily) and walks throughout the park led by staff from the gallery.

ACCOMMODATIONS

All lodgings, including campsites, fill up quickly—up to months in advance. In Yosemite Valley, **Delaware North Companies** (801/559-5000, www.yosemitepark.com) handles reservations for the lodgings at Curry Village, Housekeeping Camp, Yosemite Lodge at the Falls, and the Ahwahnee Hotel.

Curry Village

Curry Village (801/559-5000, www.yosemitepark.com) offers some of the oldest lodgings in the park. Often called Camp Curry, this sprawling array of wood-sided and canvas-tent cabins was originally created in 1899 to provide affordable lodgings so that people of modest means could visit and enjoy the wonders of Yosemite. At Curry Village, you can rent a tent cabin or a wood cabin, with or without heat and with or without a private bath, depending on your budget and needs. You can also reserve a motel room if you prefer. Curry Village has showers ($5) and several eateries (most open in

summer), so you won't lack for food choices. The Curry Village breakfast buffet (7–10 A.M.) is included in some special "hiker's packages"; it can also be added to any accommodations option for $12. You won't find any TVs or telephones in the Curry Village lodgings, which is part of the appeal for many people.

The 56 **Yosemite Cabins** (year-round, $171 d) are hard to come by, and they're usually booked far in advance. These wood structures include one or two double beds (some have a double and a single) that sleep up to five. Cabins have private baths, electricity, decks or patios, and maid service. There are 14 cabins without private baths; these share a central bathhouse instead.

In addition, there are 319 **Canvas Tent Cabins** ($70–120), the most affordable option. These are small, wood-frame, canvas-covered structures that sleep 2–4 in a combination of single and double cot beds. A small dresser, sheets, blankets, and pillows are provided, but there is no electricity or heat. Bear-proof lockers are available outside each tent cabin. Shared showers and restrooms are found within Curry Village. A few **Heated Tent Cabins** (801/559-4884, late Sept.–mid-May, $120) are available on a limited basis, and the **Curry Village Signature Tent Cabins** ($120) include insulation panels for warmth.

The 18 guest rooms in the **Stoneman Motel** ($192 d) sleep 2–6 and have heat, private baths, and daily maid service. There's an extra charge of $10–12 for each person beyond the first two.

Dining options include the **Pavilion Buffet** (209/372-8303, 7–10 A.M. and 5:30–8 P.M. daily Mar.–Nov., $10–12); **Coffee Corner** (6 A.M.–10 P.M. daily summer, 7–11 A.M. Sat.–Sun. winter); the **Curry Village Bar** (noon–10 P.M. daily summer); **Pizza Deck** (noon–10 P.M. daily summer, 5–9 P.M. Fri., noon–9 P.M. Sat. winter); and the **Taqueria** (11 A.M.–5 P.M. daily summer).

Housekeeping Camp

Want to camp, but don't want to schlep all the gear into the park? Book a tent cabin at

Housekeeping Camp (801/559-5000, www. yosemitepark.com, mid-Apr.–mid-Oct., $100). Located on the banks of the Merced River, Housekeeping Camp has its own sandy river beach for playing and sunbathing. Cabins have cement walls, white canvas roofs, and a white canvas curtain that separates the bedroom from the covered patio that doubles as a dining room. Every cabin has a double bed plus two bunks (with room for two additional cots), a bear-proof food container, and an outdoor fire ring. You can bring your own linens, or rent a "bed pack" (no towels, $3). No maid service is provided, but you won't miss it as you sit outside watching the sunset over Yosemite Valley.

Yosemite Lodge at the Falls

 Yosemite Lodge at the Falls (801/559-5000, www.yosemitepark.com, $192–219), situated near Yosemite Village on the Valley floor, has a location perfect for touring all over the park. The motel-style rooms are light and pretty, with polished wood furniture, bright-colored bed linens, and Native American design details. Lodge rooms with king beds offer romantic escapes for couples, complete with balconies overlooking the valley, while the standard rooms can accommodate singles, couples, or families. Enjoy the heated pool in the summer and free shuttle transportation up to the Badger Pass ski area in winter. The amphitheater at the middle of the lodge runs nature programs and movies all year. The lodge is central to the Yosemite shuttle system and has a post office, an ATM, the on-site **Mountain Room Restaurant** (209/372-1499, 5:30–9:30 P.M. Sun.–Fri. May–Oct., 5–8:30 P.M. Sun.–Thurs., 5–9 P.M. Fri. Oct.–May), the **Mountain Room Lounge** (4:30–11 P.M. Mon.–Fri., noon–11 P.M. Sat.–Sun.), and a food court (6:30–11 A.M., 11:30 A.M.–2 P.M., 5–9:30 P.M. daily summer).

Ahwahnee Hotel

If you're looking for luxury among the trees and rocks, check in to the **Ahwahnee Hotel** (801/559-5000, www.yosemitepark. com, $493–1,102). Built as a luxury hotel in the early 20th century, the Ahwahnee lives up to its reputation with a gorgeous stone facade, striking stone fireplaces, and soaring ceilings in the common rooms. The guest rooms, in both the hotel and the cottages, drip with sumptuous appointments. The theme is Native American, and you'll find intricate, multicolored geometric and zoomorphic designs on linens, furniture, and pillows. The Ahwahnee includes 24 cottages and 99 hotel rooms in the main building. All bedrooms come with either one king bed or two doubles; guest rooms in the main hotel may be combined with a parlor to make a suite. The cottages come with small stone patios as well as TVs, telephones, small refrigerators, and private baths. Whether you're seeking a romantic getaway or a family vacation, you're likely to find a room that feels just right.

A bonus is the on-site **Ahwahnee Dining Room** (Ahwahnee Hotel, 209/372-1489, www.yosemitepark.com, 7–10:30 A.M., 11:30 A.M.–3 P.M., and 5:30–9 P.M. Mon.–Sat., 7 A.M.–3 P.M. and 5:30–9 P.M. Sun., $27–46).

CAMPING

There are four campgrounds in Yosemite Valley, and they are deservedly popular. Upper Pines, Lower Pines, and North Pines require reservations (877/444-6777, www.recreation. gov), sometimes up to five months in advance; leashed pets are permitted at these three campgrounds. Campground reservations in Yosemite Valley are very competitive. At 7 A.M. eastern time on the 15th of each month, a new batch of campsites become available for a period up to five months in advance. A few minutes after 7 A.M., choice sites and dates—maybe even all of them—will be gone. If you need a reservation for a specific day, get up early and call or check online diligently starting at 7 A.M. eastern time.

If you're in the valley and don't have a campsite reservation, call the campground status line (209/372-0266) for a recording of what's open, what's closed, what's full, and what's available

YOSEMITE

that day. Or try one of the first-come, first-served campgrounds (but get there early).

Lower Pines

The Lower Pines campground (60 sites, Mar.–late Oct., $20) is across from Curry Village. Sites accommodate tents and RVs up to 40 feet and include fire rings, picnic tables, a bear-proof food locker, water, flush toilets—and very little privacy. Supplies and showers ($5) are available in Curry Village. Reservations are required and are available up to five months in advance.

Upper Pines

Upper Pines campground (238 sites, year-round, $20) is the largest campground in the valley. It lies immediately southwest of Lower Pines and is encircled by the park road. Sites accommodate tents and RVs up to 35 feet and include fire rings, picnic tables, a bear-proof food locker, water, and flush toilets. Supplies and showers ($5) are available in Curry Village. Reservations are required March 15–November and are available up to five months in advance. Sites are available first-come, first-served December–March 15.

North Pines

Set along the Merced River and Tenaya Creek, North Pines (81 sites, Apr.–Sept., $20) offers slightly more privacy than its Upper and Lower Pines siblings. Sites accommodate tents and RVs up to 40 feet and include fire rings, picnic tables, a bear-proof food locker, water, and flush toilets. Supplies and showers ($5) are available in Curry Village, and the Yosemite Valley Stables are right nearby. Reservations are required and are available up to five months in advance.

Camp 4

Camp 4 (35 campsites, first-come, first-served, $5) stays open year-round. Yes, you can camp in the snow! Bring a tent—no RVs or trailers are allowed. You'll find showers nearby at Curry Village, and food and groceries at Yosemite Lodge. Sites include fire pits, picnic

tables, and a shared bear-proof food locker. Restrooms with water and flush toilets are nearby. Pets are not permitted.

Reservations are not accepted. Spring–fall, hopeful campers must register with a park ranger. Plan to wait in line at the campground kiosk well before the ranger arrives at 8:30 A.M. Sites are available first-come, first-served and hold six people each, so you may end up camping with new friends.

FOOD

There's plenty to eat inside Yosemite National Park. In Yosemite Valley, you have a number of dining options, but if you leave the valley floor, you'll need to plan for meals.

Casual

For more casual food options, head to Yosemite Village for **Degnan's Loft** (209/372-8381, noon–9 P.M. daily June–Aug., 5–9 P.M. Mon.–Fri. and noon–9 P.M. Sat.–Sun. Apr.–May and Sept.–Oct., $8–20) for hot pizza, soups, and appetizers. **Degnan's Deli** (209/372-8454, 7 A.M.–5 P.M. daily year-round, $6.50–7.50) offers an array of sandwiches, salads, and other take-out munchies, and **Degnan's Cafe** (Apr.–Sept.) has coffee and baked goods. The **Village Grill** (11 A.M.–5 P.M. daily spring–fall, $5–15) offers standard burgers and grilled food.

Curry Village is where to go for relatively cheap fast food. Hiking clothes are expected! The Curry Village **Pavilion Buffet** (209/372-8303, 7–10 A.M. and 5:30–8 P.M. daily Mar.–Nov., $10–12) hosts an all-you-can-eat buffet for breakfast and dinner. There is also **Coffee Corner** (6 A.M.–10 P.M. daily summer, 7–11 A.M. Sat.–Sun. daily winter), the **Curry Village Bar** (noon–10 P.M. daily summer), a **Pizza Deck** (noon–10 P.M. daily summer, 5–9 P.M. Fri., noon–9 P.M. Sat. winter), the **Taqueria** (11 A.M.–5 P.M. daily summer), and the **Happy Isles Snack Stand** (11 A.M.–7 P.M. daily summer) at shuttle stop 16.

The **Yosemite Lodge Food Court** (Yosemite Lodge, 6:30–11 A.M., 11:30 A.M.–2 P.M., and 5–9:30 P.M. daily summer, $5–15) offers basic meals in a cafeteria-style setting. A casual bar menu is available at the **Mountain Room Lounge** (4:30–11 P.M. Mon.–Fri., noon–11 P.M. Sat.–Sun., $5–21), immediately across from the Mountain Room Restaurant.

Fine Dining

The ◖ **Ahwahnee Dining Room** (Ahwahnee Hotel, 209/372-1489, www.yosemitepark.com, 7–10:30 A.M., 11:30 A.M.–3 P.M., and 5:30–9 P.M. Mon.–Sat., 7 A.M.–3 P.M. and 5:30–9 P.M. Sun., $27–46) enjoys a reputation for fine cuisine that stretches back to 1927. The grand dining room features expansive ceilings, wrought-iron chandeliers, and a stellar valley view. The restaurant serves three meals daily, with dinner the highlight. The California cuisine of an Ahwahnee dinner mirrors that of top-tier San Francisco restaurants (with a price tag to match). Reservations are recommended for all meals, though it's possible to walk in for breakfast and lunch. For dinner, "resort casual" attire is requested, which means something like semiformal. Specifically, all the dress code really says is no shorts on anyone, and men should wear collared shirts with their long pants, but some people dress up quite a bit more than that, and it's fun to join in and make an elegant evening of it.

At the other side of the valley, you can enjoy a spectacular view of Yosemite Falls at the **Mountain Room Restaurant** (209/372-1499, 5:30–9:30 P.M. daily May–Oct., 5–8:30 P.M. Sun.–Thurs., 5–9 P.M. Fri.–Sat. Oct.–May, $16–32), part of Yosemite Lodge at the Falls. The glass atrium lets guests at every table take in the view. The menu runs to American food, and drinks are available from the full bar.

Glacier Point

The best view of Yosemite Valley may not be from the valley floor. To get a different look at the familiar formations and falls, drive up Glacier Point Road to Glacier Point (16 miles from Chinquapin junction). The trail from the end of the road to the actual point is an easy one—paved and wheelchair accessible—but the vista down into Yosemite Valley is anything but common. The first part of Glacier Point Road stays open all year, except when storms make it temporarily impassable, to allow access to the Badger Pass ski area, but chains may be required.

In summer, park rangers host evening programs at Glacier Point. Check the *Yosemite Guide* for specific listings.

GETTING THERE
Car

Glacier Point is in the southwestern quadrant of the park, about an hour's drive from Yosemite Valley. From the Valley Visitors Center, drive 14 miles south to Chinquapin junction, and then make a left turn onto Glacier Point Road. Drive another 16 miles to the end of the road, and park in the lot on the left.

If you're driving from San Francisco directly to Glacier Point, allow at least five hours; it's 213 miles. The most efficient route is to enter through Big Oak Flat, and once you're inside the park, turn right (south) onto Wawona Road (Hwy. 41). In 9.2 miles, you'll come to Glacier Point Road. Turn left and take it 16 miles to the point itself.

If you enter through the South entrance (Hwy. 41), drive 20 miles to Chinquapin junction, make a right turn onto Glacier Point Road, and take it all the way to the end, about 16 miles.

Glacier Point Road is closed approximately November–May. You can get as far as Badger Pass Ski Area (5 miles) on the road whenever the ski area is open, which is usually December–March; chains may be required.

Bus

The Yosemite Shuttle system does not serve Glacier Point, but during the season when conditions allow, the park's official concession-aire, Delaware North Companies, operates four-hour trips from Yosemite Valley to Glacier Point and back: **Glacier Point Tours** (209/372-4386, www.yosemitepark.com, 8:30 A.M., 10 A.M., and 1:30 P.M. daily spring–fall, adults $41 round-trip, $25 one-way, discounts for children, se-niors, and groups). Tickets can be purchased by telephone (209/372-4386) or in person at the tour desks in Yosemite Lodge, Curry Village, or the Yosemite Village Grocery Store.

SIGHTS
Badger Pass
Five miles east of Wawona Road on the way to-ward Glacier Point is Badger Pass, a beautiful section of Yosemite and probably the only one that's actually busier in winter than in summer. This is the site of the Badger Pass Ski Area, which was California's first-ever downhill ski hill; it is one of only three areas with ski lifts in any national park. In winter, Badger Pass is bustling with downhill skiers, cross-country skiers, ice skaters, sledders, and people drinking hot chocolate. In summer, it's a good starting place for hikes to Glacier Point and nearby.

RECREATION
◖ Badger Pass Ski Area
Downhill skiing at Badger Pass (Glacier Point Rd., 5 miles from Chinquapin turnoff and 15 miles from Wawona, www.yosemitepark.com, 9 A.M.–4 P.M. daily mid-Dec.–mid-Mar. or early Apr.) is a favorite wintertime activity at Yosemite. Badger Pass was the first downhill ski area created in California, and today, it's the perfect resort for families and groups who want a relaxed day or three of moderate ski-ing. With plenty of beginner runs and classes, Yosemite has helped thousands of children and adults learn to ski and snowboard as friends and family look on from the sundecks at the lodge. There are enough intermediate runs to make it interesting for mid-level skiers as well. Double black-diamond skiers may find Badger Pass too tame for their tastes since there are just a few advanced runs. But everyone agrees that the prices are more reasonable than at Tahoe's

big resorts, and the focus is on friendliness and learning rather than showing off and extreme skiing. Downhill ski lessons are available (1 lesson $44–83). Lift tickets run $23–42 for a full day and $18–34 for a half-day. Season passes are also available ($169–434). Ski rent-als are available (adults $32.50–42, ages 13–17 $30–37, ages 7–12 $18–22, under age 7 free with a paying adult, over age 64 $30–37, free nonholiday weekdays).

And here's a snowshoe adventure to remem-ber: If you're lucky enough to be in Yosemite during a full moon, or the four days leading up to one, do your best to reserve a spot on one of the **Full Moon Snowshoe Walks** (Badger Pass Day Lodge, reservations 209/372-1240, weather 209/372-1000, Jan.–Mar., $18.50 in-cludes snowshoe rental, $5 if you bring your own, reservations required). These two-hour treks into the snowy forest, not recommended for children under 10, include an expert guide who can help you with your snowshoes and also discuss survival techniques, winter wild-life, folklore about full moons, and more.

Cross-Country Ski School
Glacier Point Road is the only place in Yosemite with groomed tracks for cross-country skiing, but the park has more than 800 miles of trails, and nearly all of them are skiable when the snow gets deep enough. In fact, many places in Yosemite are accessible in winter only on cross-country skis or snowshoes. The Cross-Country Ski School (www.yosemitepark.com/badger-pass_crosscountryskiing.aspx) has classes, rent-als (adults $19–23, youths $15–17, under age 13 $7–11), and guided cross-country ski tours. Skiers of any level can have a good day out in the snow on the groomed trails from Badger Pass to Glacier Point. This 21-mile run is wide and well maintained; much of it is flat, so be-ginners can enjoy it slowly while experts fly past at top speed on skating skis or carry back-packs for overnight hut-to-hut ski trips. Many tributary trails branch off into the backcountry from this main trail; they're much less crowded and can be very beautiful. Just make sure you have a trail map if you decide to explore them,

and don't go alone. Conditions can change rapidly in the woods, and things can get hazardous when frozen streams start melting, tree branches block a trail, or darkness falls faster than expected.

Cross-country skiing lessons ($35–49, with rental $46–60) are available, and tours and packages ($120–350 pp) include an overnight trip to **Glacier Point Hut.** The school also offers guided hikes and winter camping trips. In winter, guides from the Nordic Center lead group snowshoe walks to Dewey Point (9 A.M.–3 P.M. Wed. and Sun., $50, with snowshoe rental $60).

Hiking

If you love the thrill of heights, head up Glacier Point Road and take a hike up to or along one of the spectacular and slightly scary granite cliffs. Hikes in this area run from quite easy to rigorous, but note that many of the cliff-side trails aren't appropriate for rambunctious children.

SENTINEL DOME

The two-mile round-trip hike up Sentinel Dome starts at the trailhead just southwest of the end of Glacier Point Road. It is a surprisingly easy walk; the only steep part is climbing the dome at the end of the trail. You can do this hike in 2–3 hours, and you'll find views at the top to make the effort and the high elevation (over 8,000 feet at the top) more than worthwhile. On a clear day, you can see from Yosemite Valley to the High Sierras and all the way to Mount Diablo in the Bay Area to the west. Be sure to bring a camera! Be aware that there are no guardrails or walls to protect you from the long drops along the side of the trail and at the top of the dome.

TAFT POINT AND THE FISSURES

Another not-too-long walk to a magnificent vista point is the hike to Taft Point and the Fissures. To get here, park 1–2 miles southwest of Glacier Point on Glacier Point Road. This two-mile round-trip hike takes you along unusual rock formations called the Fissures,

through the always lovely woods, and out to Taft Point. This precarious precipice does not have any walls, only a rickety set of guardrails to keep visitors from plummeting off the point down 2,000 feet to the nearest patch of flat ground. Thrill seekers enjoy challenging themselves to get right up to the edge of the cliff to peer down. Happily for more sedate hikers, the elevation gain from the trailhead to the point is only about 200 feet.

FOUR MILE TRAIL

If you're looking for a mid-level or challenging hike, plus the most spectacular view of all of Yosemite Falls in the park, take the misnamed Four Mile Trail (9.6 miles round-trip) that connects Glacier Point to Southside Drive in Yosemite Valley. It's actually 4.8 miles each way, but who's counting? In summer, the easiest way to take this hike is to start from Glacier Point and hike down to the valley. You can then catch a ride back up to your car on the **Glacier Point Tour Bus** (209/372-4386, www.yosemitepark.com, 8:30 A.M., 10 A.M., and 1:30 P.M. daily spring–fall, adults $25 one-way, discounts for children, seniors, and groups), but be sure to buy tickets in advance. The steep climb up the trail from the valley can be much harder on the legs and the lungs, but it affords an ascending series of views of Yosemite Falls and Yosemite Valley that grow more spectacular with each switchback.

OSTRANDER LAKE

For a longer high-elevation hike, take the 12.5-mile walk to Ostrander Lake and back. The trailhead is approximately two miles past Bridalveil Creek Road on Glacier Point Road. You can also cross-country ski to the lake in the winter and stay overnight at the local ski hut. This trek can take all day if you're going at a relaxed pace—especially if you're visiting during June–July and stopping to admire the wildflowers in bloom all along the trail. The lake itself is a lovely patch of shining clear water surrounded by granite boulders and picturesque pine trees. Consider starting up the trail in the morning and packing a picnic lunch to enjoy beside the serene water. And remember to bring bug repellent since the still waters of the lake and nearby streams are mosquito breeding grounds during hiking season.

ACCOMMODATIONS

If you're planning an extended stay at Yosemite with friends or family, it might be convenient and economical to rent a condo or house with a full kitchen, privacy, and the comforts of home. You can find these through Yosemite Four Seasons Vacation Rentals at the **Yosemite West Condominiums** (Yosemite West Community, 7519 Henness Circle, 800/669-9300, www.yosemitelodging.com, $135–155), 0.5 mile from Glacier Park Road. Modular buildings can be divided into a number of separate units—or not, if you want to rent a large space for a big group. The studio and loft condos sleep 2–6 and have full kitchens and access to all complex amenities. Luxury suites are actually one-bedroom apartments with full kitchens, pool tables, hot tubs, four-poster beds, and all sorts of other amenities. Two- and three-bedroom apartments sleep 6–8. And a duplex house ($1,180) can actually fit up to 22 guests, so you could fit an entire family reunion or college ski party into one huge house.

CAMPING AND FOOD

Bridalveil Creek (110 sites, first-come, first served, mid-July–early Sept., $14) is halfway up Glacier Point Road, eight miles from Chinquapin junction and 45 minutes south of the valley. Its season is fairly short due to the snow that blankets this area, but its location along Bridalveil Creek makes it an appealing spot. Sites permit tents and RVs up to 35 feet and include fire pits, picnic tables, a shared bear-proof food locker, and a bathroom with water and flush toilets nearby. In addition, there are three equestrian campsites (877/444-6777, $25, reservations required) and two group sites (www.recreation.gov, $40, reservations required).

The **Glacier Point Snack Stand** (9 A.M.–4 P.M. daily Memorial Day–Oct., $5–10) sells snacks and hot chocolate.

Wawona

The small town of Wawona is only four miles from the South entrance of Yosemite. The historic Wawona Hotel was built in 1917 and also houses a popular restaurant and a store.

GETTING THERE

Enter the park at the **South** entrance (year-round) and continue four miles up Highway 41 (Wawona Rd.) to Wawona. From Wawona, it's another 1.5 hours to Yosemite Valley.

Wawona is well served by the Yosemite Shuttle bus system. The **Mariposa Grove & Wawona** shuttle (9 A.M.–6 P.M. daily spring–fall, free) takes passengers among the Wawona Store, the South entrance, and the Mariposa Grove of Giant Sequoias, where it drops them off at the Mariposa Grove Gift Shop. The **Wawona to Yosemite Valley** shuttle (daily Memorial Day–Labor Day, free) leaves the Wawona Hotel at 8:30 A.M. and the Wawona Store at 8:35 A.M., delivering passengers to Yosemite Valley. It returns to Wawona in the afternoon, leaving Yosemite Lodge at 3:30 P.M.

SIGHTS
Pioneer Yosemite History Center

Wawona is home to the Pioneer Yosemite History Center (near Wawona Store parking lot, daily year-round). The first thing you'll see as you enter this outdoor display area is a big open barn housing an array of vehicles used over a century ago in Yosemite, including big cushiony carriages for wealthy tourists and oil wagons once used in an ill-conceived attempt to control mosquitoes on the ponds. Farther along, walk under the Vermont-style covered bridge to the main museum area. This rambling, uncrowded stretch of land contains many of the original structures built in the park. Most were moved here from various remote locations. Informative placards describe the history of Yosemite National Park through its structures, from the military shacks used by the soldiers who were the first park rangers through homes lived in by early settlers in the area presided over by stoic pioneer women.

In summer, visitors can take a 10-minute tour by horse-drawn carriage (adults $4, ages 3–12 $3). If you want more help understanding it all, you can also buy a self-guided tour brochure ($0.50) nearby. Check your *Yosemite Guide* for listings of living history programs and live demonstrations held here during the summer.

Mariposa Grove of Giant Sequoias

One of three groves of rare giant sequoia trees in Yosemite, the Mariposa Grove (Wawona Rd./Hwy. 41, dogs and bicycles not permitted) offers a view of these majestic trees even to visitors who aren't up for long walks or strenuous hikes. During high season, a one-hour open-air tram ride meanders through the grove, complete with an audio tour describing the botany and history of this area. You can also walk throughout the grove, taking your time to admire the ecology of the giant sequoia forest. The **Wawona to Mariposa Grove Trail** entails a moderate walk of about six miles from the Wawona Hotel; there are also shorter loop walks that allow you to see some of the most impressive trees in a mile or less. The **Mariposa Grove Museum** (Upper Mariposa Grove, 10 a.m.–4 p.m. daily May–Sept.) is another good place for visitors interested in Sequoias. The museum building is a replica of the cabin of Galen Clark, a former Guardian of Yosemite National Park who is credited as the first non-native to see Mariposa Grove.

It's best to take the free **Mariposa Grove & Wawona shuttle** (9 a.m.–6 p.m. daily spring–fall, free) to the grove from Wawona or Yosemite Valley in high season to cut down on auto traffic and minimize use of the limited grove parking areas. Note that you cannot drive all the way to the museum. Either take a short walk to it from the grove's parking lot or take the tram.

RECREATION
Wawona Stable

You'll find more horses than mules at Wawona Stable (Pioneer Yosemite History Center, Wawona Rd., 209/375-6502, www.yosemitepark.com/Activities_MuleHorsebackRides_WawonaStable.aspx, 8 a.m.–5 p.m. daily May–Oct., $64–128), and more travelers too—reservations for the rides out of Wawona are strongly recommended. From Wawona you can take a sedate two-hour ride around the historic wagon trail running into the area. Or try the five-hour trip out to Chilnualna Falls—you'll get to tell your friends about a waterfall that few Yosemite visitors ever see. Be sure to bring a camera! Both of these rides are fine for less experienced riders, and the wagon-trail ride welcomes children with its easy, flat terrain.

Hiking

It's not quite as popular (or crowded) as Yosemite Valley, but the hikes near Wawona in southern Yosemite can be just as scenic and lovely. From the trailhead at the Pioneer Yosemite History Center, start with the easy **Wawona Meadow Loop** (3.5 miles, 2 hours), a flat and shockingly uncrowded sweep around the lovely Wawona meadow and a somewhat incongruous nine-hole golf course. This wide trail was once fully paved and is still bikeable, but the pavement has eroded over the years, and you'll find much dirt and tree detritus. It is best in late spring because the wildflowers bloom in profusion. For a longer trip, you can extend this walk to five miles, with about 500 feet of elevation gain, by taking the detour at the south end of the meadow.

If you're up for a hard-core hike and a waterfall experience few who visit Yosemite ever see, take the difficult 8.5-mile trail to **Chilnualna Falls**, with a 2,300-foot elevation gain. The trailhead is near the Pioneer Yosemite History Center. Plan for 4–6 hours and bring water, snacks, and a trail map. You'll see a few fellow hikers and many tantalizing views of the cascades. Sadly, there's no

YOSEMITE

viewing area, so you'll need to peek through the trees to get the best looks and photos of the falls. The trail runs all the way up to the top of the falls, but be careful to avoid the stream during spring and summer high flow—it's dangerous, what with the waterfall and everything!

Other hikes in the area include the easy **Swinging Bridge Loop** (4.8 miles, 2 hours), from the trailhead at the Wawona Store, and the more strenuous **Alder Creek Trail** (12 miles, 6–8 hours) from the trailhead on Chilnualna Falls Road.

Snowshoeing and Cross-Country Skiing

Mariposa Grove maintains winter trails for snowshoeing and cross-country skiing in winter. A popular trail is the **Loop Road** (8 miles round-trip) from the South entrance to the Mariposa Grove of Sequoias. Pick up a copy of the *Mariposa Grove Winter Trails* guide ($0.50) at the visitors center, or download a copy from the park's website (www.nps.gov/yose).

ENTERTAINMENT AND EVENTS

It's worth making an evening trip out to Wawona to listen to the delightful piano music and singing of the legendary Tom Bopp. He plays vintage camp music (and requests, and whatever else strikes his fancy) in the **Piano Lounge at the Wawona Hotel** (209/375-1425, Tues.–Sat. Apr.–Dec.) five nights a week throughout Wawona's season. Older visitors especially love his old-style performance and familiar songs, but everyone enjoys the music and entertainment he provides. Even if you're just waiting for a table at the restaurant, stop in to say hello and make a request.

Ranger Programs include "Coffee with a Ranger" (8–8:45 A.M. summer) at the Wawona Campground Amphitheater, and a nightly campfire. Check the *Yosemite Guide* for specific listings.

ACCOMMODATIONS AND FOOD

The charming **Wawona Hotel** (801/559-5000, www.yosemitepark.com, Mar.–Nov. and Dec.

14–Jan. 1, $225, $148–168 shared bath) opened in 1879 and has been a Yosemite institution ever since. The black-and-white exterior of the hotel complex may remind visitors of a 19th-century Mississippi riverboat. The interior matches the outside well, complete with Victorian wallpaper, antique furniture, and a noticeable lack of in-room TVs and telephones. The Wawona feels more like a huge European pension than an American motel, including guest rooms with shared baths for the more economically minded traveler.

The ◖ **Wawona Dining Room** (Wawona Hotel, 209/375-1425, 7–10 A.M., 11:30 A.M.–1:30 P.M., and 5:30–9 P.M. daily Apr.–Dec., $19–30) serves upscale California cuisine for reasonable prices to all comers. No reservations are accepted—all seating is first come, first served. The large, white-painted dining room is family-friendly, and the menu offers options for vegetarians as well as devout carnivores; breakfast is always a lavish buffet. You'll probably have to wait for a table on high-season weekends, but the large common area offers seating, drinks, and live piano music (Tues.–Sat.). Note that dining hours for each meal may be slightly shorter in the off-season (late Oct.–Dec.); if you plan to eat at the beginning or the end of a shift, call ahead to make sure they're open.

The **Wawona Golf Shop & Snack Stand** (9 A.M.–5 P.M. daily in season) and the **Wawona Store & Pioneer Gift Shop** (8 A.M.–8 P.M. daily in season) fill the gap when the Wawona Dining Room is closed.

CAMPING

Camp at the lovely and forested **Wawona Campground** (93 sites, 877/444-6777, www.recreation.gov, reservations required Apr.–Sept., $20; first-come, first-served Oct.–mid-Apr., $14), one mile north of Wawona. RVs are welcome, although there are no hookups on-site. If you want to camp with your horse, Wawona offers two equestrian sites. The small grocery store in town can provide a few basics, but most services (including showers) can't be found closer than Yosemite Valley.

Tioga Pass and Tuolumne Meadows

Tioga Road (Hwy. 120), Yosemite's own "road less traveled," crosses Yosemite from west to east, leading from the more visited west edge of the park out toward Mono Lake in the eastern Sierra. Along the road, you'll find a number of developed campgrounds, plus a few natural wonders that many visitors to Yosemite never see.

GETTING THERE AND AROUND
Car

Tuolumne Meadows is located along Tioga Road (Hwy. 120), which runs all the way across the park to the eastern boundary. At Tioga Pass, the east entrance, Highway 120 becomes Tioga Pass Road. Although you'll sometimes hear it referred to as Tioga Pass Road, technically that name does not apply within Yosemite.

From the west, Highway 120 becomes Big Oak Flat Road at the Big Oak Flat park entrance. In nine miles, at Crane Flat junction, the left fork becomes Tioga Road. The Tuolumne Meadows Visitors Center is 38 miles from the west entrance. To get to Tioga Road from Yosemite Valley, take Northside Road to Big Oak Flat Road. At the Tioga Road junction, turn east.

Tioga Road is always closed in winter, and remember that "winter" can come at almost any time at this elevation. To check weather conditions and road closures, call 209/372-0200.

Shuttle and Bus

In summer, the free **Tuolumne Meadows** shuttle (7 A.M.–7 P.M. daily June–mid-Sept., weather permitting) runs along Tioga Road between Olmstead Point and the Tuolumne Meadows Lodge. Trips begin at 7 A.M. at Tuolumne Meadows Lodge and run every half hour, stopping at the Dog Lake Parking area, the Tuolumne Meadows Wilderness Center, Lembert Dome, Tuolumne Meadows Campground and Store, Tuolumne Meadows Visitors Center, Cathedral Lakes Trailhead,

Pothole Dome, the east end of Tenaya Lake, Sunrise Lakes Trailhead at the west end of Tenaya Lake, May Lake Trailhead, and Olmsted Point. Going the other direction, the first bus leaves Olmstead Point at 7:30 A.M. daily. Limited service is available to the Mono Pass Trailhead and Tioga Road–Gaylor Lakes Trailhead, on the east end of this route.

July–September, Delaware North Companies offers a **guided bus tour** (209/372-4386, www.yosemitepark.com, adults $5–23, children half price) between Yosemite Valley and Tuolumne Meadows. The coach makes multiple stops, starting from Curry Village (8 A.M.) and ending at Tuolumne Meadows Lodge (arriving at 10:35 A.M.). It departs Tuolumne Meadows again at 2:05 P.M. for the return trip. Fares are prorated if you only want to travel part of the way.

SIGHTS

In the spring, walk out to view the wildflowers at **White Wolf,** about 15 miles east of the Tioga Road junction (turn north on a dirt road to get to the parking lot). Another 12 miles east along Tioga Road, bring out your camera to take in the vista at **Olmstead Point.** Stroll along the sandy beach at **Tenaya Lake,** two miles east of Olmstead, while staring up toward **Clouds Rest.** Nearby Tuolumne Meadows is bracketed by **Pothole Dome** on its west end and **Lembert Dome** to the east.

⟨ Tuolumne Meadows

Tuolumne Meadows lies along Tioga Road (summer only), about 40 miles from the Crane Flat junction. After miles of soaring rugged mountains, it's almost surprising to come upon these serene grassy High Sierra alpine meadows. In tones of brilliant green, and dotted with wildflowers in spring, the waving grasses support a variety of wildlife. Stop the car and get out for a quiet, contemplative view of the meadows. Or if you prefer a long trek, Tuolumne Meadows serves as a good base camp for high-country backpacking. The short, easy

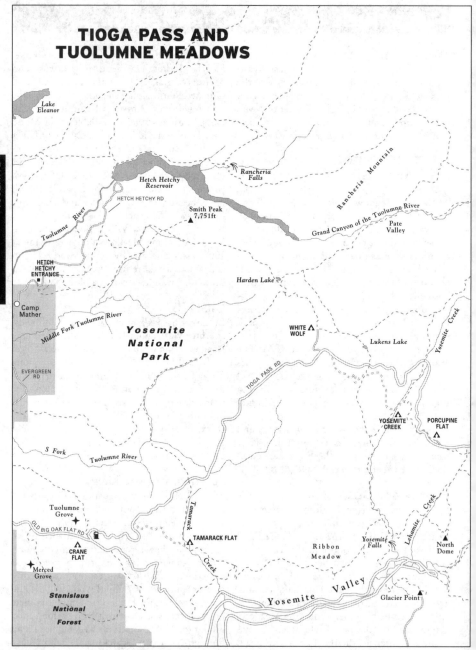

TIOGA PASS AND TUOLUMNE MEADOWS

Lake Eleanor

Tuolumne River

Rancheria Falls

Rancheria Mountain

Hetch Hetchy Reservoir

HETCH HETCHY RD

Smith Peak
7,751ft

Grand Canyon of the Tuolumne River

Pate Valley

HETCH HETCHY ENTRANCE

Harden Lake

Camp Mather

Middle Fork Tuolumne River

Yosemite National Park

WHITE WOLF

Lukens Lake

Yosemite Creek

EVERGREEN RD

TIOGA PASS RD

S Fork

Tuolumne River

YOSEMITE CREEK

PORCUPINE FLAT

Tuolumne Grove

OLD BIG OAK FLAT RD

Tamarack Creek

TAMARACK FLAT

Ribbon Meadow

Yosemite Falls

Lehamite Creek

North Dome

CRANE FLAT

Merced Grove

Stanislaus National Forest

Yosemite Valley

Glacier Point

YOSEMITE

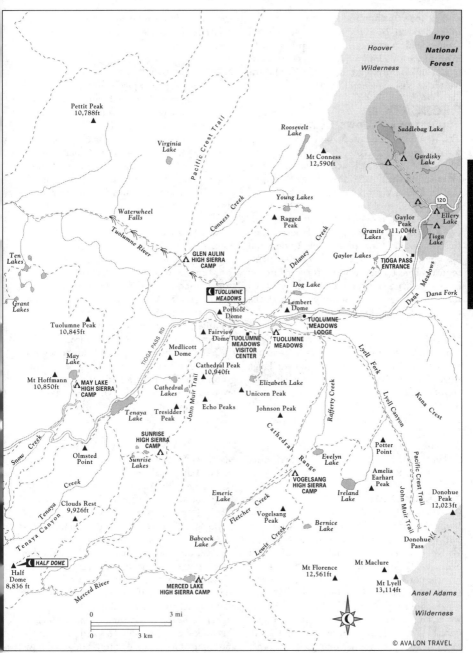

Pettit Peak
10,788ft

Virginia
Lake

Pacific Crest Trail

Inyo
National
Forest

Hoover
Wilderness

Roosevelt
Lake

Saddlebag Lake

Gardisky
Lake

Mt Conness
12,590ft

Waterwheel
Falls

Conness Creek

Young Lakes

Tuolumne River

Ragged
Peak

Delaney Creek

GLEN AULIN
HIGH SIERRA
CAMP

Gaylor Lakes

Granite
Lakes

Gaylor
Peak
11,004ft

Ellery
Lake

120

Tioga
Lake

TIOGA PASS
ENTRANCE

Ten
Lakes

Grant
Lakes

Dog Lake

Dana Meadows

Dana Fork

TUOLUMNE
MEADOWS

Lembert
Dome

Tuolumne Peak
10,845ft

Pothole
Dome

TUOLUMNE
MEADOWS
LODGE

Tioga Pass Rd

Fairview
Dome

TUOLUMNE
MEADOWS
VISITOR
CENTER

TUOLUMNE
MEADOWS

May
Lake

Medlicott
Dome

Lyell Fork

Kuna Crest

Mt Hoffmann
10,850ft

MAY LAKE
HIGH SIERRA
CAMP

Cathedral Peak
10,940ft

Cathedral
Lakes

Elizabeth Lake

John Muir Trail

Unicorn Peak

Rafferty Creek

Lyell Canyon

Tenaya
Lake

Tresidder
Peak

Echo Peaks

Johnson Peak

Pacific Crest Trail

Olmsted
Point

SUNRISE
HIGH SIERRA
CAMP

Sunrise
Lakes

Cathedral Range

Evelyn
Lake

Potter
Point

Snow Creek

Amelia
Earhart
Peak

John Muir Trail

Donohue
Peak
12,023ft

Creek

Clouds Rest
9,926ft

VOGELSANG
HIGH SIERRA
CAMP

Ireland
Lake

Tenaya Canyon

Emeric
Lake

Fletcher Creek

Vogelsang
Peak

Bernice
Lake

Donohue
Pass

HALF DOME

Babcock
Lake

Lewis Creek

Half
Dome
8,836 ft

MERCED LAKE
HIGH SIERRA
CAMP

Mt Florence
12,561ft

Mt Maclure

Mt Lyell
13,114ft

Ansel Adams

Merced River

Wilderness

0   3 mi

0   3 km

© AVALON TRAVEL

YOSEMITE

trail to **Soda Springs** and **Parsons Lodge** (1.5 miles, 1 hour), from the trailhead at Lembert Dome, leads past a carbonated spring to the historic Parsons Lodge (10 A.M.–4 P.M. daily in season) before leading to the Tuolumne Meadows Visitors Center.

RECREATION
Tuolumne Meadows Stable
The Tuolumne Meadows Stable (209/372-8427, www.yosemitepark.com, 8 A.M.–5 P.M. daily May–Oct., $64–85) is accessible on a short dirt road on the north side of Tioga Road past the Tuolumne Visitors Center. You can get the perfect overview of the Yosemite high country by taking the introductory-level two-hour ride. For a longer ride deeper into the landscape, do the four-hour trip that passes Twin Bridges and Tuolumne Falls. An all-day ride with a variable route beckons the adventurous traveler, but you need to be in good shape and be an experienced rider for this one. To customize a longer pack trip, call 209/372-8348.

Hiking
For smaller crowds along the trails, take one or more of the many scenic hikes along Tioga Road. Just be aware that they don't call it "high country" for nothing; the elevation starts at 8,500 feet and goes higher on many trails. If you're not in great shape, or if you have breathing problems, take the elevation into account when deciding which trails to explore.

Trailheads are listed in west-to-east order along Tioga Road.

TUOLUMNE GROVE OF GIANT SEQUOIAS
If you're aching to see some giant trees but were put off by the parking problems at Mariposa Grove, try the Tuolumne Grove of Giant Sequoias. Parking and the trailhead are at the junction of Tioga Road and Old Big Oak Flat Road. This 2.5-mile round-trip hike takes you down about 400 vertical feet into the grove, which contains more than 20 mature giant sequoias. (You do have to climb back up the hill to get to your car.) While you'll likely see other

visitors, the smaller crowds make this grove an attractive alternative to Mariposa, especially in the high season.

OLMSTEAD POINT
For nonathletes who just want a short walk to an amazing view, Olmstead Point (Tioga Rd., 1–2 miles west of Tenaya Lake, shuttle stop 12) may be the perfect destination. The trail is only 0.5 mile round-trip from the parking lot to the point, and it exists to show off Clouds Rest in all its grandeur. Half Dome peeks out behind Clouds Rest, and right at the trail parking lot, a number of large glacial erratic boulders draw almost as many visitors as the point itself.

TENAYA LAKE
A great place to start your high-country exploration, the loop trail to Tenaya Lake (Tioga Rd., 12 miles west of the east entrance, shuttle stop 9) offers an easy walk, sunny beaches, and possibly the most picturesque views in all of Yosemite. The trail around the lake is about 2.5 miles, and the only difficult part is fording the outlet stream at the west end of the lake, since the water gets chilly and can be high in the spring and early summer. If the rest of your group is sick of hiking and scenery, you can leave them on the beach while you take this easy 1–2-hour stroll. Just remember the mosquito repellent.

MAY LAKE AND MOUNT HOFFMAN
May Lake (May Lake Trailhead, 1 mile southwest of Tenaya Lake on Tioga Rd., shuttle stop 11) sits peacefully at the base of the sloping granite of Mount Hoffman. While the hike to May Lake is only two miles round-trip, the elevation gain from the trailhead up to the lake is a steady, steep 500 feet. One of Yosemite's High Sierra camps is located here, which makes this hike popular with the sort of visitors who enjoy the lesser-known high-country areas. For more energetic hikers, a difficult trail leads from the lake another two miles and 2,000 vertical feet higher to the top of Mount Hoffman. Much of this walk is along granite slabs and rocky trails, and some of it is cross-country, but you'll have

Tenaya Lake, seen from Clouds Rest

clear views of Cathedral Peak, Mount Clark, Half Dome, and Clouds Rest along the way. As you pass May Lake, you'll see May Lake High Sierra Camp at the lake's southeast corner. The final part of the climb to Mount Hoffman's summit, at 10,850 feet, is very rocky, but there is a narrow trail through the boulders. On top is a nice flat plateau where you can relax and stay awhile, enjoying outstanding vistas of the entire park. Mount Hoffman is right in the center, so all of Yosemite is laid out around you.

ELIZABETH LAKE

The trail to Elizabeth Lake, from the trailhead at Tuolumne Campground and John Muir Trail (shuttle stop 5), begins at Tuolumne Meadows and climbs almost 1,000 vertical feet up to the lake, with most of the climb during the first mile of the 4.8-mile, 4–5-hour roundtrip. Evergreens ring the lake, and the steep granite Unicorn Peak rises high above it. This stunning little lake makes a perfect photo op that your friends won't necessarily recognize as Yosemite.

GAYLOR LAKES

Hikers willing to tackle somewhat longer, steeper treks will find an amazing array of small scenic lakes within reach of Tioga Road. Gaylor Lakes Trail, from the trailhead on Tioga Road at the Yosemite Park border (seasonal shuttle), starts high, at almost 10,000 feet, and climbs a steep 600 vertical feet up the pass to the Gaylor Lakes valley. Once you're in the valley, you can wander around the five lovely lakes, stopping to admire the views out to the mountains surrounding Tuolumne Meadows or visiting the abandoned 1870s mine site above Upper Gaylor Lake. The total hike is about three miles (2 hours) if you don't wander around the valley. The crowd-averse will enjoy this trek, which is one of Yosemite's less-populated scenic hikes.

NORTH DOME

For an unusual look at a classic Yosemite landmark, take the strenuous North Dome Trail from the trailhead at Porcupine Creek, through the woods, and out to the dome, which is right across the valley from Half Dome. You'll hike almost nine miles round-trip, with a few hills thrown in, but getting to stare right at the face of Half Dome and Clouds Rest just beyond at what feels like eye-level makes the effort worth it.

CATHEDRAL LAKES

If you can't get enough of Yosemite's granite-framed alpine lakes, take the moderate to strenuous long walk out to one or both of the Cathedral Lakes (7 miles round-trip, 4–6 hours) from the trailhead at Tuolumne Meadows Visitors Center. From Tuolumne Meadows, you'll climb about 800 vertical feet over 3.5 miles, depending on which lake you choose. These picture-perfect lakes show off the dramatic alpine peaks, surrounding lodgepole pines, and crystalline waters of Yosemite to their best advantage. Be sure to bring your camera, water, and food for a lovely picnic.

GLEN AULIN TRAIL

The strenuous Glen Aulin Trail, from the trailhead at Tuolumne Stable to Tuolumne Fall and White Cascade, is part of the John Muir Trail, and several of its forks branch off to pretty little lakes and other nice spots in the area. From Tuolumne Meadows to Tuolumne Fall and back is 11 miles round-trip (6–8 hours), with some steep and rocky areas. But if you've got the lungs for it, you'll be rewarded by fabulous views of the Tuolumne River alternately pooling and cascading right beside the trail. This hike may get a bit crowded in the high season. In the summer, many trekkers trade their dusty hiking clothes for swimsuits and cool off in the pools at the base of both White Cascade and Tuolumne Fall. A great way to do this hike is to enter the High Sierra Camp lottery, and if you win, arrange to stay the night at the Glen Aulin camp. If you do this, you can take your hike a few miles farther, downstream to California Fall, Le Conte Fall, and finally Waterwheel Fall.

Snowshoeing and Cross-Country Skiing

Crane Flat has a variety of ungroomed winter trails for snowshoeing and cross-country skiing. Pick up a copy of the *Crane Flat Winter Trails* guide ($0.50) at the visitors center or download a copy from the park's website (www.nps.gov/yose).

ACCOMMODATIONS AND FOOD

Tuolumne Meadows Lodge (801/559-5000, www.yosemitepark.com, early June–mid-Sept., $104) offers rustic lodgings and good food in a gorgeous subalpine meadow setting. Expect no electricity, no private baths, and no other plush amenities. What you will find are small, charming wood-frame tent cabins that sleep up to four, with wood stoves for heat and candles for light. Central facilities here include restrooms, hot showers, and a dining room. The location is perfect for starting or finishing a backcountry trip through the high-elevation areas of the park.

The **Tuolumne Meadows Lodge Restaurant** (5:45–8 P.M. daily early June–mid-Sept., $7–27) serves dinner nightly in a rustic central building near the tent cabins. The quality of the food is better than you'd expect in what feels like a summer-camp mess hall, and it's priced accordingly. Order the Sierra flatiron steak, wild salmon linguine, or the chef's special nightly creations; everything comes with generous sides of salad, potatoes, and vegetables. Seafood is selected in accordance with the Monterey Bay Aquarium's recommendations for health and sustainability, and the vegetables are locally grown and organic. If you don't want a big meal, or don't want to spend too much money, the good news is that anyone, not just children or early birds, can order from the "Lighter Eaters" menu, with its low-priced small-portions of hot dogs, hamburgers, and macaroni and cheese.

Right next to Tuolumne Campground, **Tuolumne Meadows Grill** (8 A.M.–5 P.M. daily June–Sept., $10) offers sustenance for hungry campers. Breakfasts include filling egg and

© HC LISTON

Tuolumne Meadows Lodge

biscuit sandwiches and pancakes, while lunch offers burgers and chili. Eat outside on the accompanying picnic benches with views of Tuolumne Meadows across the road.

Another rustic high-country lodging option, the **White Wolf Lodge** (801/559-5000, www.yosemitepark.com, mid-June–Sept., $95–115) sits back in the trees off Tioga Road. Here you can rent either the standard wood-platform, wood stove–heated tent cabin with use of central restroom and shower facilities, or a solid-wall cabin with a private bath, limited electricity, and daily maid service. All cabins and tent cabins at White Wolf include linens and towels. Breakfast and dinner ($20, reservations required) are served family-style in the White Wolf dining room; they'll also make you a box lunch to take along on your day hikes. Amenities are few, but breathtaking scenery is everywhere. Take a day hike to Harden Lake or a horseback ride through the backcountry. White Wolf works well for visitors who prefer smaller crowds, since the lodge has only 24 tents and four cabins.

CAMPING

Yosemite visitors who favor the high country tend to prefer to camp rather than to stay in a lodge. Accordingly, most of Yosemite's campgrounds are north of the valley, away from the largest crowds (excluding the High Sierra Camps, which are also up north).

 Tuolumne Meadows (304 sites, Tioga Rd. at Tuolumne Meadows, 877/444-6777, www.recreation.gov, July–late Sept., reservations strongly advised, tents and RVs $20, equestrian sites $25) has one of the largest campgrounds in the park, with more than 300 sites, including four horse sites. Half of the sites are available by reservation; the remaining half are first-come, first-served. Tuolumne can be crowded for the whole of its season, and the campground does tend to fill up every night, so don't just show up and assume you will find a spot. Tuolumne is accessible for RVs up to 35 feet, although it does not have electric, water, or sewage hookups. Sites include fire rings and picnic tables, and there are bear-proof food lockers, water, and flush toilets. Leashed pets are permitted. Food is available at nearby Tuolumne Meadows Lodge and the Tuolumne Grill, but the closest showers are in Yosemite Valley. Tuolumne Meadows is at about 8,600 feet elevation, which means nights can get quite chilly even in midsummer; you're might wake up to frost on your tent by the end of the season in late September.

If you're entering the park from the west side on Highway 120, the first campground you'll come to is **Hodgdon Meadow** (102 sites, 877/444-6777, www.recreation.gov, reservations required mid-Apr.–mid-Oct., $20; first-come, first-served late Oct.–early Apr., $14). This can be an excellent choice for people who drive up Friday night after work; you can set up camp right after entering the park and won't have to drive for miles in the dark. At 4,900 feet, Hodgdon Meadow can accommodate tents or RVs, although there are no hookups for electricity, water, or sewage. Sites include fire rings and picnic tables, and there are bear-proof food lockers, water, and flush toilets. Supplies are available at Crane Flat, and the closest showers are in Yosemite Valley. Pets are permitted.

Another good-size campground near Tioga Road is **Crane Flat** (166 sites, reservations required, 877/444-6777, www.recreation.gov, mid-July–Sept., $20). Crane Flat is 17 miles from Yosemite Valley on Big Oak Flat Road at 6,200 feet elevation. Although it does allow RVs up to 35 feet as well as tents, there are no electric, water, or sewer hookups. Sites include fire pits and picnic tables, and there are bear-proof food lockers, water, and flush toilets. Pets are permitted. There is a small grocery store down the road at Crane Flat gas station; the closest showers are in Yosemite Valley.

Serene **White Wolf** (74 sites, first-come, first-served, late July–early Sept., $14) is at 8,000 feet elevation on Tioga Road; the turnoff is on the left down a narrow side-road. Sites accommodate tents and RVs up to 27 feet and include fire pits and picnic tables, and there are bear-proof food lockers, water, and flush toilets; pets are permitted. Crane Flat is the closest place for supplies.

If you're looking to ditch the RV traffic and crowded central visitor areas, head for **Yosemite Creek** (75 sites, first-come, first-served, late July–mid-Sept., Sat.–Sun. only mid-Sept.–mid-Oct., $10). Yosemite Creek flows right through this tent-only campground, a perfect spot for cooling off on a hot day. Yosemite Creek offers few amenities—fire pits, picnic tables, and bear-proof food lockers but no groceries, showers, or water, and only vault toilets. It's just what many outdoors visitors want.

At **Tamarack Flat** (52 sites, Tioga Rd., first-come, first-served, July–early Oct., $10), you'll be reasonably close to Yosemite Valley but still in a fairly primitive environment. Tamarack Flat is at 6,300 feet elevation and is a tent-only campground. Although there are picnic tables and bear-proof food lockers, there are no restroom facilities except pit toilets, and you must bring your own water or be prepared to treat the water you find.

The ◖ **High Sierra Camps** (801/559-5000, www.yosemitepark.com/accommodations_highsierra_howtoapply.aspx, June or July–Sept., lodging, dinner, and breakfast adults $151, ages 7–12 $91, sack lunches adults $15.25, children $7.75) at Yosemite offer far more than your average backcountry campground. Want to get into the wilderness, but don't want to carry a heavy pack with all your stuff? The High Sierra Camps provide tent cabins with amenities, breakfast and dinner in camp, and a sack lunch to take along during the day. Choose from among the Merced Lake, Vogelsang, Glen Aulin, May Lake, and Sunrise Camp—or hike from one to another if you're lucky enough to get a spot. Why do you need luck? Because you can't just walk up to a High Sierra Camp and expect to find a bed. Starting September 1, a lottery takes place for spots at High Sierra Camps through the following summer. You must submit an application to join the lottery; even if you get a spot, there's no guarantee you'll get your preferred dates. Check the website during the high season (June–Sept.) to see if any dates are available. The High Sierra camps have a limited number of spaces available for hikers looking for dinner and breakfast (801/559-4909, adults $46, ages 7–12 $23), but not for overnight campers.

The bottom line? If you want to take advantage of the Yosemite backcountry, it's best to plan for a summer when you can be flexible with your dates, and start making your arrangements a year in advance.

Hetch Hetchy

One of the most politically controversial areas in California, Hetch Hetchy (Hetch Hetchy Rd. past the Hetch Hetchy park entrance), about 30 minutes north of Highway 120, was once a valley similar to Yosemite Valley. It is now Hetch Hetchy Reservoir, with 1,972 acres of surface area, a maximum depth of 312 feet, and a capacity of 117 billion gallons. Hetch Hetchy supplies famously clean, clear water (plus some hydroelectric power) to the city of San Francisco and other parts of the Bay Area. But many environmental activists—beginning with the patron saint of Yosemite himself, John Muir, who opposed the project before it had even begun—see the reservoir's existence as an affront, and lobby to have O'Shaughnessy Dam torn down and the valley returned to its former state of natural beauty. For those of us who didn't have the privilege of seeing this spot before the dam was built, it's almost difficult to imagine how it could be even more beautiful than it is today. The water is deep and blue, the trees around its perimeter cast stunning reflections into its calm surface, the gushing waterfalls along the sides are some of the most gorgeous in the whole park, and the hikes surrounding Hetch Hetchy are outstanding.

GETTING THERE

Hetch Hetchy is in the northwest corner of Yosemite National Park. The Hetch Hetchy entrance is about 10 miles north of the Big Oak

© GEORGE JEN

Hetch Hetchy Reservoir

YOSEMITE

YOSEMITE

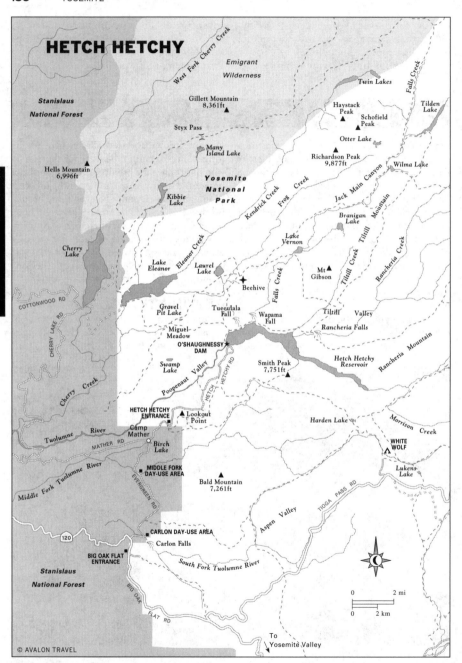

HETCH HETCHY

Stanislaus National Forest

West Fork Cherry Creek

Emigrant Wilderness

Gillett Mountain
8,361ft

Twin Lakes

Falls Creek

Styx Pass

Haystack Peak

Schofield Peak

Tilden Lake

Many Island Lake

Otter Lake

Hells Mountain
6,996ft

Richardson Peak
9,877ft

Wilma Lake

Yosemite National Park

Kibbie Lake

Kendrick Creek

Frog Creek

Jack Main Canyon

Branigan Lake

Tiltill Mountain

Cherry Lake

Lake Vernon

Rancheria Creek

Lake Eleanor

Eleanor Creek

Laurel Lake

Falls Creek

Mt Gibson

Tiltill Creek

COTTONWOOD RD

Beehive

Gravel Pit Lake

Tueeulala Fall

Wapama Fall

Tiltill Valley

Rancheria Falls

CHERRY LAKE RD

Miguel Meadow

O'SHAUGHNESSY DAM

Rancheria Mountain

Swamp Lake

Poopenaut Valley

HETCH HETCHY RD

Smith Peak
7,751ft

Hetch Hetchy Reservoir

Cherry Creek

Tuolumne River

HETCH HETCHY ENTRANCE

Lookout Point

Harden Lake

Morrison Creek

Camp Mather

MATHER RD

Birch Lake

WHITE WOLF

Middle Fork Tuolumne River

MIDDLE FORK DAY-USE AREA

EVERGREEN RD

Bald Mountain
7,261ft

Lukens Lake

120

CARLON DAY-USE AREA

Carlon Falls

Aspen Valley

TIOGA PASS RD

Stanislaus National Forest

BIG OAK FLAT ENTRANCE

South Fork Tuolumne River

BIG OAK FLAT RD

0   2 mi

0   2 km

To Yosemite Valley

© AVALON TRAVEL

Flat entrance on Highway 120. From Highway 120, take the Hetch Hetchy turnoff onto Evergreen Road, then follow Evergreen Road north for 7.2 miles. At the town of Mather, turn onto Hetch Hetchy Road and proceed another 16 miles through the gate and to the parking lot near O'Shaughnessy Dam.

If you're already in the park, you have to leave through the Big Oak Flat entrance and onto Highway 120 before reentering at the Hetch Hetchy entrance. It takes about 1.25–1.5 hours to get to Hetch Hetchy from Yosemite Valley, a distance of about 40 miles.

Hetch Hetchy Reservoir is about 185 miles from San Francisco, and the drive takes about four hours. The road to Hetch Hetchy is open year-round, except in extreme weather conditions, but the park gate is only open 8 A.M.–7 P.M.

SIGHTS
O'Shaughnessy Dam

Named for Michael M. O'Shaughnessy, the original chief engineer of the Hetch Hetchy Project, O'Shaughnessy Dam is a massive curved gravity dam that turns part of the Tuolumne River into Hetch Hetchy Reservoir. It originally opened in 1923 at 344 feet high; a later phase of construction, completed in 1938, raised it to its current size of 426 feet high and 900 feet long.

RECREATION
Hiking

At less than 4,000 feet in elevation, Hetch Hetchy is one of the lowest parts of Yosemite; it gets less snow and has a longer hiking season than many other areas of the park. It's also warmer here in summer, so you may want to plan a spring or fall visit. The relative warmth, combined with the abundance of water, may be one reason rattlers and other snakes seem particularly common in this area. Do not let that deter you—snakes really, really do not want to mess with people, and they'll get off the trail in time to avoid an encounter as long as they sense you coming.

In addition to the hikes listed are the moderate-to-difficult trails to **Lookout Point** (2 miles, 1 hour) and the more strenuous **Smith Peak** (13.5 miles, 6–8 hours) and **Poopenaut Valley** (3 miles, 2 hours), all starting from the Hetch Hetchy Entrance Station.

WAPAMA FALLS

If you like waterfalls, you'll love the easy-to-moderate hike to Wapama Falls (5 miles round-trip, 2 hours). Begin by crossing O'Shaughnessy Dam and then follow the Wapama Falls Trail (also known as Rancheria Falls Camp Trail) through the tunnel and along the shore of the reservoir. Along the way, you'll also see close-up views of the spectacular **Tueeulala Falls.** Tueeulala is set back in the hillside a little, so you can get some great photos of it. Wapama Falls comes splashing down right onto the trail, so you'll experience it in a whole different way— and you'll probably want to keep your camera safely packed away. For a longer hike, bring a large poncho or rain gear to protect yourself and your pack before stepping onto the wooden bridge that crosses under these falls. On a hot day, the shower could be a very welcome treat.

A word of warning: The amount of water flowing over Tueeulala and Wapama Falls varies greatly with the season and recent precipitation in the park. In spring, water can be especially abundant and powerful. Although thousands of hikers have passed through here safely over the years, and many families with young children enjoy playing in the falls, there are times when they can be quite dangerous. In June 2011 two experienced male backpackers were killed when they tried to cross under the falls during an unusually high runoff. If you go, follow any posted restrictions and use good judgment to stay safe.

RANCHERIA FALLS

A longer day hike, also a recommended backpacking trip, is the 13.4-mile round-trip (6–8 hours) Rancheria Falls Camp Trail, which begins at O'Shaughnessy Dam and continues past Wapama Falls along the shore of Hetch Hetchy Reservoir. This trail can be done comfortably in one day by fit hikers. The terrain is rolling, with

YOSEMITE

Tueeulala and Wapama Falls

some up and some down each way, and the total elevation gain is less than 700 feet. Along the way, you'll pass Tueeulala Falls and become one with Wapama Falls (remember to bring your rain gear). You'll continue along the same path, but with far fewer people around as you complete the journey to Rancheria Falls. Beautiful views of Hetch Hetchy Reservoir continue most of the way. You'll walk through pine forests, on stone stairs, across creeks, and past sunny overlooks. Large flat granite slabs beside Rancheria Falls make a great place for lunch before you turn around to return the same way.

Backpacking

A great backpacking destination from Hetch Hetchy is Rancheria Falls. This 6.5-mile (one-way) trek along the **Rancheria Falls Camp Trail** begins at O'Shaughnessy Dam and continues past Wapama Falls along the shore of Hetch Hetchy Reservoir. The terrain is rolling, meaning there's some up and some down each way, but no major mountains to climb on the way to your destination. The total elevation gain is less than 700 feet. When you get to

Rancheria Falls, you'll find a beautiful woodsy area with plenty of space for multiple visitors to set up tents and enjoy some peace. The sense of privacy and seclusion here is enhanced by the sound of the nearby falls, which muffles the noise of human activity. Rancheria Falls isn't the kind of waterfall that crashes down from high atop a mountain; it's a wide expanse with water flowing gradually over massive rocks. You can wade in and fill your water bottle as long as you treat the water before drinking it. This area makes a good base camp for challenging day hikes.

CAMPING

There are no developed campgrounds in the Hetch Hetchy region of the park. The **Hetch Hetchy Backpackers' Campground** is next to the overnight parking lot at the end of Hetch Hetchy Road. To backpack overnight in the Hetch Hetchy area, you need a bear canister for your food and a wilderness permit (reservation $5 plus $5 pp) from the Hetch Hetchy Entrance Station (209/372-0200, 7 A.M.–9 P.M. daily May 1–Labor Day).

Eastern Sierra

🌙 BODIE STATE HISTORIC PARK

Bodie State Historic Park (end of Hwy. 270, 13 miles east of U.S. 395, 760/647-6445, www.parks.ca.gov, 9 A.M.–6 P.M. daily Memorial Day–Labor Day, 9 A.M.–5 P.M. daily Oct., 9 A.M.–3 P.M. daily winter, adults $7, ages 6–16 $5) is the largest ghost town in California and possibly the best-preserved in the whole country. Its preservation in a state of "arrested decay" means you get to see each house and public building just as it was when it was abandoned. What you see is not a bright shiny museum display; you get the real thing: dust and broken furniture and trash and all. It would take all day to explore the town on foot, and even then you might not see it all. If you take a tour, you can go into the abandoned mine and gain a deeper understanding of the history of the buildings and the town.

The town of Bodie sprang up around a gold mine in 1877. It was never a nice place to live at all. The weather, the work, the scenery, and, some say, the people all tended toward the bleak or the foul. By the 1940s mining had dried up, and the remote location and lack of other viable industry in the area led to Bodie's desertion.

A visit to Bodie takes you back in time to a harsh lifestyle in an extreme climate miles from the middle of nowhere. As you stroll down the dusty streets, imagine the whole town blanketed in 20 feet of snow in winter and scorched by 100°F temperatures in summer with precious few trees around to provide shade or a hint of green in the unending brown landscape. In a town filled with rough men working the mines, you'd hear the funeral bells tolling at the church every single day—the only honor bestowed on the many murder victims Bodie saw during its existence. Few families

YOSEMITE

© STAN NESTER

Bodie State Historic Park, California's largest ghost town

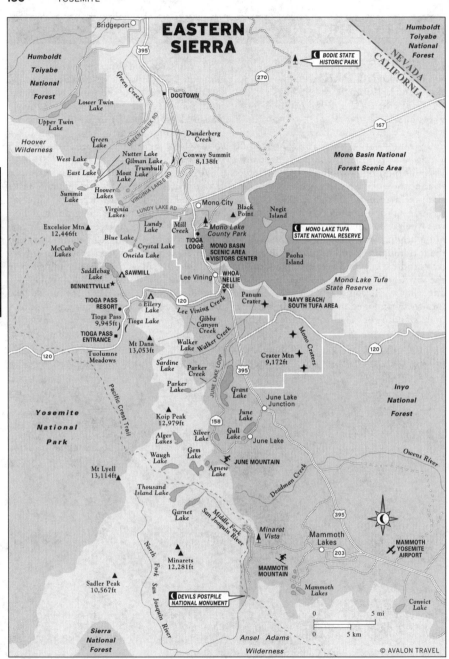

EASTERN SIERRA

Bridgeport

395

Humboldt
Toiyabe
National
Forest

NEVADA
CALIFORNIA

Humboldt
Toiyabe
National
Forest

BODIE STATE
HISTORIC PARK

270

DOGTOWN

167

Green Creek

GREEN CREEK RD

Lower Twin
Lake

Upper Twin
Lake

Dunderberg
Creek

Mono Basin National

Forest Scenic Area

Hoover
Wilderness

Green Lake

West Lake

Nutter Lake
Gilman Lake
Trumbull
Moat
Lake

Conway Summit
8,138ft

East Lake

VIRGINIA LAKES RD

Hoover
Lakes

Summit
Lake

Virginia
Lakes

LUNDY LAKE RD

Mono City

Black
Point

Negit
Island

Excelsior Mtn ▲
12,446ft

Lundy
Lake

Mill
Creek

Mono Lake
County Park

MONO LAKE TUFA
STATE NATIONAL RESERVE

Blue Lake

Crystal Lake

TIOGA
LODGE

McCabe
Lakes

Oneida Lake

MONO BASIN
SCENIC AREA
VISITORS CENTER

Paoha
Island

Saddlebag
Lake

SAWMILL

Lee Vining

BENNETTVILLE ★

WHOA
NELLIE
DELI

Mono Lake Tufa
State Reserve

TIOGA PASS
RESORT ●

Ellery
Lake

Panum
Crater

NAVY BEACH/
SOUTH TUFA AREA

Tioga Pass
9,945ft

Tioga Lake

Lee Vining Creek

TIOGA PASS
ENTRANCE

Gibbs
Canyon
Creek

120

Mt Dana
13,053ft

Walker
Lake

Walker Creek

Mono
Craters

120

Tuolumne
Meadows

Crater Mtn
9,172ft

Sardine
Lake

Parker
Creek

Inyo

Pacific Crest Trail

Parker
Lake

JUNE LAKE LOOP

Grant
Lake

National

Yosemite
National
Park

Koip Peak
12,979ft

June Lake
Junction

Forest

June
Lake

395

Alger
Lakes

158

Silver
Lake

Gull
Lake

June Lake

Waugh
Lake

Gem
Lake

Mt Lyell
13,114ft

Agnew
Lake

JUNE MOUNTAIN

Owens River

Thousand
Island Lake

Deadman Creek

Garnet
Lake

Middle Fork San Joaquin River

Minaret
Vista

395

Mammoth
Lakes

MAMMOTH
YOSEMITE
AIRPORT

North Fork San Joaquin River

Minarets
12,281ft

MAMMOTH
MOUNTAIN

203

Sadler Peak
10,567ft

DEVILS POSTPILE
NATIONAL MONUMENT

Mammoth
Lakes

Convict
Lake

Sierra
National
Forest

Ansel Adams

Wilderness

0   5 mi

0   5 km

© AVALON TRAVEL

came to Bodie (though a few hardy souls did raise children in the hellish town), and most of Bodie's women earned their keep the old-fashioned way: The prostitution business boomed while mining did.

Today, most of the brothels, stores, and houses of Bodie aren't habitable or even tourable. Structures have been loosely propped up, but it's dangerous to go inside, so doors remain locked. You can peer in the windows at the remains of the lives lived in Bodie, however, and get a sense of hard-core California history.

HOOVER WILDERNESS

The Hoover Wilderness (Bridgeport Ranger District, 760/932-7070, www.fs.usda.gov) is a 48,600-acre section of Mono County within the Inyo and Humboldt-Toiyabe National Forests. It's a narrow strip of wild land east of Yosemite and west of Mono Lake that runs into the Ansel Adams Wilderness and Tioga Pass to the south, near the Emigrant Wilderness and Sonora Pass to the north. Hoover is what the U.S. Forest Service calls a Class I area, which means it is one of 88 places in the country given the highest level of protection from air pollution under the Clean Air Act Amendments of 1977.

Travertine Hot Springs

A delightful treasure in the Eastern Sierra, Travertine Hot Springs (www.monocounty.org) is a naturally occurring series of spring-fed pools hidden in the hills. Only one of the pools has a concrete bottom, added by human hands. The rest are pretty much the way nature made them, with uneven rocky sides. They can be slippery with moss or smelly from sulfur, but if you like to relax outdoors in a peaceful setting, especially under a full moon, you'll find a visit a memorable experience. Temperatures in the small pools vary from warm to extremely hot, so explore the area until you find one that's just right for you. The population varies too: It's not uncommon to have the whole isolated backcountry spot to yourself, but around sunset on a summer weekend you might find the pools crowded with people. And not everyone who visits here wears a bathing suit; if naked strangers aren't your cup of tea, avoid peak times, or at least be prepared to walk a little beyond the first pools.

The pools are accessible by car, although finding them can be tricky. To reach Travertine Hot Springs, drive north from Lee Vining on U.S. 395. In about 24 miles, just south of the town of Bridgeport, you'll see a ranger station

YOSEMITE

Travertine Hot Springs

on the right-hand side, and then a sign that says "Animal Shelter." Turn right at that sign onto Jack Sawyer Road. After a few hundred yards, make a left onto a dirt road and follow it for about a mile until you come to the springs.

Hiking

The strenuous hike from **Glines Canyon to Virginia Pass** (10 miles) starts at an elevation over 8,000 feet and climbs more than 2,500 vertical feet, making it a pretty serious workout among wildflowers, waterfalls, and mountain lakes. Start by walking alongside Green Creek for about 2.5 miles to Green Lake. On the north side of the lake, begin climbing Glines Canyon all the way to Virginia Pass (about 10,500 feet), which is between Yosemite National Park and Hoover Wilderness. From here, you can see Twin Peaks, Matterhorn Peak, and Camiaca Peak, the two small Par Value Lakes, and Soldier Lake, all spread out in various directions far below.

Another strenuous hike that's not quite as long is **Lundy Canyon Trail** (7 miles), although it still gains more than 2,000 feet of elevation. The trail begins by crossing Mill Creek and continues up above Lundy Lake. From here, continue climbing alongside Mill Creek until you reach Blue Lake, then Crystal Lake, and then Oneida Lake. Along the way, you'll see remains of the May Lundy Mine as well as a beaver pond, two waterfalls, and plenty of alpine lakes. This is an out-and-back hike, so turn around when you start to get tired. The trailhead is at the end of Lundy Lake Road; to get here, drive seven miles north of Tioga Pass on U.S. 395. Turn right on Lundy Lake Road and go 6.3 miles, passing the Lundy Lake Resort along the way.

Accommodations

Soon after exiting the Tioga Pass entrance on the east side of the park, you'll come to the rustic ◖ **Tioga Pass Resort** (85 Hwy. 120 W., Lee Vining, www.tiogapassresort.com, summer only, $105–210, cash or check only), which offers both charm and convenience. Whether your plan is to play in Yosemite itself, explore the treasures of the Eastern Sierra like Bodie and Mono Lake, or do some of both, this is a great spot. Tioga Pass Resort offers 10 cabins and four guest rooms. The noncabin guest rooms do not have kitchens or showers but do have access to showers in a shared facility. One thing the resort does not have on a reliable basis is telephone and Internet access. This means you can't contact them directly; someone from the staff has to go to Mammoth once a week to check the resort's email. They cannot accept credit cards because they can't transmit card information. Technology has a way of changing quickly, of course, so things may be different by the time you read this.

The manager recommends this method of making reservations: Send an email to tiogapassresortllc@gmail.com with the requested dates. If you don't get an answer within a week, email again. When you receive a reservation confirmation, print it out and bring it with you. The resort has closed in recent winters, but they hope to get their infrastructure back up to snuff so they can be a year-round resort once again.

Camping

There's plenty of room for camping throughout the Hoover Wilderness, but you do need a wilderness permit. Pick one up in either of the two National Forests (Humboldt-Toiyabe and Inyo) that share management of the Hoover. Closest to Lee Vining, and much of the rest of this area, is the **Bridgeport Ranger Station** (U.S. 395, Bridgeport, 760/932-7070, www. fs.usda.gov, 8 A.M.–4:30 P.M. Mon.–Fri.). If the Bridgeport Ranger Station is closed, you can self-register there. You can also order a permit by mail up to three weeks in advance of your trip. You can also contact the Inyo National Forest Permit Reservation line (760/873-2483, 8 A.M.–4:30 P.M. daily summer, 8 A.M.–4:30 P.M. Mon.–Fri. winter) or download an application (www.fs.usda.gov) and fax it in (760/873-2484).

Food

The **Bridgeport Inn** (205 Main St., Bridgeport, 760/932-7380, 8 A.M.–9 P.M. Thurs.–Tues.

mid-Mar.–mid-Nov., $10–30) offers the most genteel dining experience around here, with steaks, fish, and salads in a historic-inn sort of atmosphere.

For something more youthful and budget-friendly, the place to go is **Rhinos Bar & Grille** (226 Main St., Bridgeport, 760/932-7345, 11 A.M.–9 P.M. Sun.–Thurs., 11 A.M.–10 P.M. Fri.–Sat. Mar.–Dec., $10).

Tioga Pass Resort's simple diner-restaurant, the **Tioga Pass Resort Café** (85 Hwy. 120 W., Lee Vining, www.tiogapassresort.com, 8 A.M.–8 P.M. Mon.–Fri., 7 A.M.–9 P.M. Sat.–Sun. summer, $20), offers breakfast, lunch, and dinner, served with plenty of good cheer.

Information and Services

In this northern section of the Eastern Sierra, the best place for information is the **Bridgeport Ranger Station** (U.S. 395, Bridgeport, 760/932-7070, www.fs.usda.gov, 8 A.M.–4:30 P.M. Mon.–Fri.). There's also the small **Bridgeport Museum and Visitors Center** (123 Emigrant St., 760/932-7500, www.bridgeportcalifornia.com, 8 A.M.–6 P.M. daily May–Oct.) in downtown Bridgeport, run by the local Chamber of Commerce.

Getting There and Around

Green Lakes, Bodie, and the Hoover Wilderness are all on the east side of Yosemite National Park. If you're traveling from the Bay Area in summer, you have a choice of routes. You can cut through Yosemite on Tioga Road (closed in winter); or you can take the northern route along Sonora Pass, also known as Highway 108 (closed in winter). The route along Tioga Road takes about six hours. From San Francisco, take I-580 east to I-205 east to Highway 120 east. Enter the park through the Big Oak Flat entrance and drive south to the junction with Tioga Road. Take Tioga Road east for almost 60 miles to U.S. 395. Drive north on U.S 395, and in 26 miles you'll come to the town of Bridgeport, the most significant town of any size near the Hoover Wilderness.

To travel via the Sonora Pass, when Highway 108 splits from Highway 120, east of Oakdale, stick with Highway 108 and head north. When you get to U.S. 395, turn right and drive south. After a total of about 228 miles (5 hours), you'll reach Bridgeport. To get from Bridgeport to Bodie, take U.S 395 south another seven miles, then make a left onto Highway 270, also known as Bodie Road. Bodie is 12.8 miles down this partly unpaved road.

In winter, when Tioga Road and Highway 108 are closed, take I-80 east from the Bay Area for about 80 miles before turning onto U.S. 50 east for about 100 miles. Turn right onto Highway 89/88 and drive about 30 miles until you reach U.S. 395. Turn right (south) onto U.S. 395, and you'll arrive in Lee Vining in another 93 miles. The total distance is about 300 miles, a travel time of about six hours, depending on traffic and weather.

LEE VINING

Visitors can rent affordable rooms at several motels and lodgings in the lakeside town of Lee Vining.

Accommodations

For clean, comfortable, affordable lodgings, try **Murphey's Motel** (51493 U.S. 395, 760/647-6316 or 800/334-6316, www.murpheysyosemite.com, $58–123). Open all year, this motel provides double-queen and king beds with cozy comforters, TVs, tables and chairs, and everything you need for a pleasant stay in the Mono Lake area. Its central location in downtown Lee Vining makes dining, shopping, and trips to the visitors center and chamber of commerce convenient. If you plan to make a winter trip to Mono Lake, call to find out about Murphey's discounts for ice climbers.

El Mono Motel (1 3rd St. at U.S. 395, 760/647-6310, www.elmonomotel.com, late May–Oct. 31, depending on weather) offers comfy beds and clean guest rooms at very reasonable prices. Enjoy the location in downtown Lee Vining, and start each morning with a fresh cup of organic coffee from the on-site **Latte Da Coffee Café** (7 A.M.–8 P.M. daily summer).

At the junction of Highway 120 and U.S. 395, stay at the comfortable and affordable

Lake View Lodge (51285 U.S. 395, 760/647-6543 or 800/990-6614, www.lakeview-lodgeyosemite.com, $122–255). This aptly named lodge offers cottages, which can be rented in summer only, and motel rooms, available year-round. Whether you choose a basic guest room for a night or two or a larger option with a kitchen for more than three days, you'll enjoy the simple country-style decor, the outdoor porches, and the views of Mono Lake. All guest rooms have TVs with cable, and Internet access is available in the motel rooms but not the cottages. Pick up supplies at the local market for a picnic on the lawns of the lodge, get yourself a latte at the on-site coffee shop, or enjoy one of the nearby restaurants in Lee Vining.

Camping

There are a number of campgrounds in the Inyo National Forest on the east side of Yosemite, near U.S. 395 and Tioga Pass. You can stay at **Ellery Campground** (Hwy. 120, Upper Lee Vining Canyon, ranger station 760/873-2400, www.fs.fed.us/r5/inyo, $19), which has 12 campsites at an elevation of 9,500 feet with drinking water, pit toilets, and garbage cans. It's not possible to reserve these sites, so get here at dawn if you want a site on a weekend.

Another option is **Sawmill Walk-In** (Saddlebag Rd., on Forest Rd. 04, 1.6 miles north of Hwy. 120, ranger station 760/873-2400, www.fs.fed.us/r5/inyo, June–Oct., $14). This primitive hike-in campground, at an elevation of 9,800 feet, has 12 sites and no water, so walk in slowly. It's not possible to reserve these sites.

Food

The best way to kick off any vacation in the Eastern Sierra is with a memorable meal (and a tank of gas) at the ◖ **Whoa Nellie Deli** (Hwy. 120 and U.S. 395, 760/647-1088, www.whoanelliedeli.com, 6:45 A.M.–9 P.M. daily end of Apr.–end of Oct., $12–14) at the Tioga Gas Mart. The Whoa Nellie and Tioga Gas Mart are right at the east entrance to Yosemite, so it's the perfect place to stop when leaving the

park or heading in. Stock up on food and fuel as you prepare to spend some time in its wilderness. Yes, the deli is inside a gas station, but this is not typical gas-station minimart food. You'll get a full hearty meal of fish tacos, buffalo meatloaf, or pizza; a pleasant place to eat it all; and an all-around friendly, festive atmosphere. Expect to wait in line for a while at the counter to order, as Whoa Nellie is justifiably popular. Seating is available both inside and out, so there are usually enough tables to go around—but heaven help you if you get there at the same time as a tour bus. There's a fairly large grocery store and souvenir shop, and the large, clean restrooms are also a draw, especially for those who've been camping for a while. The place is closed in winter, though, since Tioga Pass tends to be closed.

Where can dedicated outdoors lovers get their morning coffee to begin a great day of hiking, climbing, or kayaking? Lee Vining has several charming independent coffee shops just for this purpose. The **Latte Da Coffee Café** (1 3rd St. at U.S. 395, 760/647-6310, 7 A.M.–8 P.M. daily summer) uses organic coffee and local fresh water to create delicious coffee drinks at the El Mono Motel.

Over at the Lakeview Lodge, enjoy a cup of joe at the **Garden House Coffee Shop** (51285 U.S. 395, 760/647-6543, www.lakeview-lodgeyosemite.com, 7–11 A.M. daily summer–fall). To get a great start to your day, you can pick up a smoothie or a fresh pastry in addition to your favorite espresso drinks.

Information and Services

There's a fine visitors center in the middle of Lee Vining, the **Mono Lake Committee Information Center & Bookstore** (U.S. 395, 760/647-6595, 9 A.M.–5 P.M. daily). It's got a big selection of free maps and brochures and helpful staff.

You can use mail services at the **Lee Vining Post Office** (121 Lee Vining Ave., 760/647-6371, www.usps.com, 9 A.M.–2 P.M. and 3–5 P.M. Mon.–Fri.). Lee Vining has few ATMs, but you can find one or two places to get cash (which you'll need, because many places out here don't take plastic). Try the gas stations, the visitors center, and the local grocery-minimart.

Getting There
AIR
The nearest airport to Lee Vining is the **Mammoth Yosemite Airport** (MMH, 1200 Airport Rd., Mammoth Lakes, 760/934-3813, www.ci.mammoth-lakes.ca.us). Alaska Airlines serves this airport year-round; United and Horizon fly in December 15–April 30. For more options at a major hub, book a flight to **Reno-Tahoe International Airport** (RNO, 2001 E. Plumb Lane, Reno, NV, 775/328-6400, www.renoairport.com). From Reno, drive south on U.S. 395; Lee Vining in about 137 miles (3 hours).

From the **Sacramento International Airport** (SMF, 6900 Airport Blvd., Sacramento, 916/929-5411, www.sacramento.aero) you can get to Lee Vining in about four hours. From the **San Francisco International Airport** (SFO, U.S. 101, San Francisco, 650/821-8211 or 800/435-9736, www.flysfo.com) it takes approximately 5.5 hours.

Angelenos like to play in the Eastern Sierra almost as much as their Northern California neighbors do. If you fly into **Los Angeles International Airport** (LAX, 1 World Way, Los Angeles, 310/646-5252, www.lawa.aero), or if you live in that general area, budget at least six hours to drive to Lee Vining.

CAR
Lee Vining is located just north of the junction of Highway 120 (also known as Tioga Pass Rd.) and U.S. 395. In summer the drive is quite beautiful, if not always fast. From the Bay Area, take I-580 east to I-205 east to Highway 120. Follow Highway 120 east as it becomes Tioga Road and across Yosemite National Park. When you reach U.S. 395, turn left, and you'll find yourself in Lee Vining. Expect the trip to take about 5.5 hours, but don't be surprised if it's longer. Traffic near and through Yosemite can be intense—especially on summer weekends—and many of the other travelers are enjoying the scenery, stopping to take photos along the way. When the snow comes, Tioga Road is closed.

To reach Lee Vining by car, you can also drive up U.S. 395 from the south; it is 336 miles or about six hours from Los Angeles International Airport. From the Bay Area or Sacramento, you can take an alternate route to avoid Tioga Road, which is closed in winter. Take I-80 east for about 80 miles before turning onto U.S. 50 east for about 100 miles. Turn right onto Highway 89/88 and drive about 30 miles until you reach U.S. 395. Turn right (south) onto U.S. 395, and you'll arrive in Lee Vining in another 93 miles. The total distance is about 300 miles, a travel time of about six hours, depending on traffic and weather.

MONO LAKE
Mono Lake, eerie in its stillness, is the main attraction in the northern part of the Eastern Sierra, just east of Yosemite. This unusual and beautiful lake is 2.5 times as salty as the ocean and is 1,000 times more alkaline. The reason for Mono Lake's odd appearance? It is fed by only about seven inches' worth of rain and snowfall each year; the rest of the water inflow is from various streams. No streams or tributaries flow out of Mono Lake, but it loses about 45 inches of water each year to evaporation. Meanwhile, any salt and minerals that have been carried into the lake stay in the lake as water evaporates. Over time, the lake has collected huge stores of calcium carbonate, which solidifies into strange-looking tufa towers.

The lake surrounds two large islands: **Negit Island,** a volcanic cinder cone and nesting area for California gulls, and **Paoha Island,** which was created when volcanic activity pushed sediment from the bottom of the lake up above the surface. Mono Basin, where the lake is located, is part of the Inyo National Forest. In 1984 the U.S. Congress designated Mono Basin a National Forest Scenic Area, which gives it additional protections.

If you're visiting the Eastern Sierra, you won't want to miss this natural wonder. It's large enough that you can see it from a

YOSEMITE

distance—in fact, you can get a pretty good view just by driving by on U.S. 395, but stop to take a closer look if you can. One of the best viewpoints is on the grounds of the **Mono Basin National Forest Scenic Area Visitors Center** (U.S. 395, 0.5 miles north of Lee Vining, 760/647-3044, www.monolake. org, May–Nov.). Another good spot for looking through binoculars and taking photos is the lookout area on the east side of U.S. 395 near the junction with Highway 120, right across from the Whoa Nellie Deli. Look for a grassy hill with a parking lot, a large American flag, and a "Mono Lake" sign with a big hunk of volcanic rock hanging from it. If you want to do more than just look, come in summer and enjoy an oddly buoyant swim in its heavily salted waters or a boat trip around the silent, uninhabited islands.

Mono Basin National Forest Scenic Area Visitors Center
The large building that houses the visitors center for Mono Lake is only a short drive

from the highway. The Mono Basin National Forest Scenic Area Visitors Center (U.S. 395, 0.5 mile north of Lee Vining, 760/647-3044, www.monolake.org, 8 A.M.–5 P.M. daily May–Sept., 9 A.M.–4:30 P.M. Thurs.–Mon. Oct.–Nov.) is the perfect place to learn about Mono Lake, to take a walk around the lake, and to photograph the landscape. The interpretive museum inside this distinctive building describes in detail the natural and human history of the lake, from the way tufa towers form to the endless litigation involving the lake. Original films, interactive exhibits, a bookstore, and friendly staff are all available to help get you up to speed on this beautiful and unusual area. Walk out the back of the building to take one of several brief interpretive walks through the landscape or to sit on a bench and gaze down at the lake for a while. Talk to the staff to learn about the best hikes and spots to visit, swim, launch a boat, or even cross-country ski.

At the visitors center, you can also learn about various guided walks and hikes at Mono

sign at Mono Lake overlook, with volcanic rock

© HC LISTON

Lake, which can give you a more in-depth look at the wonders of the area.

◖ Mono Lake Tufa State Natural Reserve

The tufa formations—freestanding calcite towers, knobs, and spires—make Mono Lake one of the most unusual lakes you'll ever see. The Mono Lake Tufa State Natural Reserve (U.S. 395, just north of Lee Vining, 760/647-6331, www.parks.ca.gov, 24 hours daily, free) educates and amazes visitors. Free tours are offered at 10 A.M. daily in summer. Among other reasons to visit, the California State Parks service has declared it the "best place to watch gulls in the state." About 85 percent of the entire population of California gulls nests here in the spring.

A boardwalk trail provides access to the North Tufa area. Enjoy wandering through the different chunks of this preserve, which appear along the shore all the way around the lake. Be aware that much of the land adjacent to the State Reserve areas is restricted—help take care of this delicate terrain by not venturing out of the designated visiting areas. Also, to access some of the reserve at the east side of the lake, you'll need either a boat or a 4WD vehicle, since no paved roads circle Mono Lake.

South Tufa

The South Tufa area (off Hwy. 120, 11 miles east of Lee Vining, $3 pp, free with Federal Parks Pass) on the—where else?—south shore of Mono Lake is one of the best places to view the spectacular tufa towers and a good place for newcomers to start exploring. This area is managed by the U.S. Forest Service, which charges a fee even though most of the state-run areas around here do not. But the good news is that all summer long, naturalists lead a one-mile, one-hour **walking tour** (6 P.M. daily summer) around South Tufa, and it's free.

If you're hiking on your own, a good place to start is the one-mile **interpretive trail** (southeast of the visitors center, adjacent to Navy Beach) that winds through the South Tufa area and describes the natural history of the area and the formations.

YOSEMITE

© MARINA TROOST

Mono Lake's tufa formations

Old Marina

Years ago, the stillness of Mono Lake was broken by quite a bit of boat traffic. Private boats and small tour operators still travel the lake in the summer, but no major commercial water traffic remains. The hub of this activity was the marina north of Lee Vining. Today, the Old Marina (1 mile north of Lee Vining, off U.S. 395, www.monolake.org/visit/oldmarina, $3 per car) is a good spot to take a short stroll down to the edge of the lake and to enjoy outstanding views of the lake's two large islands and several nearby tufa towers. There's a 1.5-mile trail from the Mono Basin Scenic Area Visitors Center to the Old Marina, and an even shorter boardwalk trail that's wheelchair-accessible.

Panum Crater

Even if you aren't a professional geologist, the volcanic Panum Crater (Hwy. 120, 3 miles east of U.S. 395) is worth visiting. This rhyolite crater, accessed from a parking area down a short dirt road off Highway 120, is less than 700 years old—a mere baby on geologic time scales. Take a hike around the rim of the crater, and if you're feeling up to it, climb the trail to the top of the plug dome. Be sure to slather on the sunscreen, since no trees shade these trails and it gets quite warm in the summer. Check the Mono Lake website (www.monolake.org) for occasional guided tours of Panum Crater.

Hiking

Mono Lake is not like Yosemite and its clusters of trailheads everywhere. But the hiking near Mono Lake is usually quieter, with fewer other travelers around, and the scenery is unlike anything you'll find anywhere else. Note that the trails around the Mono Basin National Forest Scenic Area Visitors Center and the South Tufa area are open year-round, even when the visitors centers are closed.

You can get a quick and informative introduction to the ecosystem around the lake by taking the 0.25-mile **Secrets of Survival Nature Trail** right outside the Mono Basin National Forest Scenic Area Visitors Center (U.S. 395, 0.5 mile north of Lee Vining, 760/647-3044,

www.monolake.org). This trail offers interpretive signage and long views of the lake.

For an easy walk along the lake, go to the **Mono Lake County Park** (Cemetery Rd.), where the trailhead is 0.5 mile east of Cemetery Road, and take the boardwalk trail 0.25 mile down to the tufa formations. Wandering through the tufa will add distance to your walk, but the ground is flat and the scenery is diverting.

A lovely interpretive trail, the **Tioga Tarns Nature Walk** (Hwy. 120, east of Tioga Lake) is about 0.5 mile long and includes numerous signs describing the flora, fauna, and geology of the area.

A nature walk that offers both gentle exercise and increased knowledge is the **Lee Vining Creek Trail.** This easy-to-moderate 1.6-mile (one-way) walk stretches from the Mono Basin National Forest Scenic Area Visitors Center (U.S. 395, 0.5 mile north of Lee Vining, 760/647-3044, www.monolake.org) to the south end of Lee Vining, following Lee Vining Creek, which is currently under restoration to return it to its natural state after decades of diversion. If you start at the visitors center, you can pick up a free trail guide. The total round-trip walk is just over three miles and takes an hour or two, depending on how much time you spend admiring the revitalized ecosystem.

You can find any number of moderate hikes in the Mono Lake vicinity. The **Lundy Canyon Trail** (Lundy Lake Rd.), from the trailhead at the dirt lot, can be anywhere from 0.5 mile of fairly easy walking through Lundy Canyon to a strenuous seven-mile hike all the way out to Saddlebag Lake. Another trail leads out to **Parker Lake** or **Parker Bench** (Parker Lake Rd., off Hwy. 158). This hike is a minimum of four miles round-trip, and it can be 10 miles if you take the left fork of the trail out to Silver Lake and Parker Bench. Steep sections make this trek a bit demanding, but you'll love the scenic, shady trail that follows Parker Creek along the shorter right fork to Parker Lake. If one or two lakes just aren't enough, take the longish but only moderately tough **20-Lakes Basin Trail** (Saddlebag Lake Rd.) from the parking area across from the dam. This six-mile loop trail will take you out past many of the lakes for which the basin is named. If you're tired of all that water, take a moderate two-mile round-trip pilgrimage out to the remains of the mining town at **Bennettville** (Junction Campground Rd.). You can prowl around the abandoned mine, but be careful—old mine shafts and abandoned buildings can be extremely hazardous.

Boating and Swimming

Go ahead and bring your powerboat, canoe, kayak, or even a sailboat out to Mono Lake. You can launch from **Navy Beach** (0.5 mile east of South Tufa), although there's no direct access to the water from the parking lot, so you'll have to carry your canoe or kayak about 30 yards to get it into the water. If you're putting a heavier boat into the lake, check with the staff at the **Mono Basin National Forest Scenic Area Visitors Center** (U.S. 395, 0.5 miles north of Lee Vining, 760/647-3044, www.monolake.org, 8 A.M.–5 P.M. daily May–Sept., 9 A.M.–4:30 P.M. Thurs.–Mon. Oct.–Nov.) for directions to the launch ramp near Lee Vining Creek. Also note that, for the protection of nesting California gulls, you cannot beach any kind of boat on the islands April 1–August 1. Outside that protected timeframe, the islands of Mono Lake can be a great destination for boaters. You can even camp on the islands as long as you first get a letter of authorization from the Mono Basin National Forest Scenic Area Visitors Center.

Swimming is allowed (and even encouraged) in Mono Lake in the summer. You can swim from your boat or from any of the unrestricted shore access points. You'll find yourself floating easily since the salt content of Mono Lake is several times higher than the ocean. But take care and watch kids closely: No lifeguards patrol the area, and you're swimming at your own risk.

Bird-Watching

The birds of the Eastern Sierra are so varied and abundant that three organizations—the Eastern Sierra Audubon Society (www.es-audubon.org), the Mono Lake Committee (760/647-6595, www.monolake.org), and the Owens Valley Committee (760/876-1845, www.ovcweb.org)—got together to produce the wonderful *Eastern Sierra Birding Trail Map*. The map covers 200 miles of territory from Bridgeport Reservoir (near the junction of U.S. 395 and Hwy. 182) in the north to Cactus Flat and the Haiwee Reservoir in the south (near Olancha and the junction of U.S. 395 and Hwy. 190). Along the way, 38 stops identify good birding habitats, and callouts provide details on the natural habitat of each area and the species to look out for. For an online version of the map, visit www.eastsierrabirdingtrail.org. To get your own free hard copy, contact the Mono Lake Committee (707/647-6595, birding@monolake.org).

Entertainment and Events

It's called the **Ghosts of the Sagebrush Tour** (760/647-6461, www.monobasinhs.org, late Sept., $25 per day), but this annual education-and-entertainment weekend event, produced by the Mono Basin Historical Society, is much more than just a tour. Friday evening, there's a dinner at **The Historic Mono Inn** (U.S. 395, Lee Vining, 760/647-6581, www.mononinn.com) with a presentation by a living history interpreter. Saturday is a full day of activities that include walks, talks, special exhibits, and lunch from the **Tioga Lodge at Mono Lake** (54411 U.S. 395, Lee Vining, 760/647-6423, www.tiogalodgeatmonolake.com). This special weekend is a great way for the whole family to learn more about the intriguing history of the Mono Lake area while having some fun.

Accommodations

You won't see any five-star resorts in the Mono Lake area. Most of the outdoorsy and naturalist types who come to this region find the no-frills motels, lodges, and campgrounds perfectly suitable for their activities. There is no camping allowed on the shores of Mono Lake.

Just across the freeway from Mono Lake, the **Tioga Lodge** (54411 U.S. 395, Lee Vining,

760/647-6423, www.tiogalodgeatmonolake. com, late May–mid-Oct., $99–139) offers a view of the lake from every room. This old lodge at the center of the town of Lee Vining offers the perfect location for sightseeing and outdoor adventures, plus heated rooms and comfortable beds. Guest rooms are simple and appealingly decorated, each with tile floors and a full private bath. Some rooms sleep two, and others have room for up to four. The two-bedroom suites are perfect for families. Don't expect to find TVs or other digital entertainment—in keeping with the area, you're encouraged to get outside to find your entertainment. Friendly, helpful staff can assist with everything from room amenities to local restaurants and great places to visit in the area.

Named for its main claim to fame—its proximity to the park, only 14 miles from Yosemite's east gate—the **Yosemite Gateway Motel** (51340 U.S. 395, Lee Vining, 760/647-6467, www.yosemitegatewaymotel.com, $99–159) offers a charming rustic experience for travelers to the Eastern Sierra. The red and white exterior is echoed in the decoration of the guest rooms, which are supplemented with gleaming wood, new furnishings, and clean baths. TVs and Internet access provide entertainment on chilly evenings, and the wonderful outdoor recreation opportunities of the Eastern Sierra are just outside the door. Enjoy the views of Mono Lake, or take a day trip to Bodie or indulge in some skiing at Mammoth Lakes or June Lake. Room rates are deeply discounted in the winter.

Food

Your food choices around the Mono Lake area might feel limited if you're coming right from Los Angeles or San Francisco. You won't see many five-star restaurants, nor will you run into the standard fast-food chains. However, the town of Lee Vining offers a number of respectable eateries, plus adequate groceries for campers and picnickers.

The **Hammond Station Restaurant** (54411 U.S. 395, Lee Vining, 760/647-6423, reservations 619/320-8868, www.tiogalodgeatmono-lake.com, 7:30–10 A.M. and 5–9:30 P.M. daily

late May–early Oct., $10–24), at the Tioga Lodge, offers an excellent variety of good food. Choose from the health-conscious vegetarian and spa menu, which includes a number of vegan, gluten-free, and dairy-free options; the California Casual menu; or the Drinks & Desserts menu. If you're planning a day out hiking or sightseeing, request the "Picnic to Go" menu and get a sandwich or wrap to take with you. If you're dining in, expect a small dining room with attractive wrought-iron furniture plus an ample outdoor seating area perfect for warm summer evenings. The food is tasty, and the service makes you feel like a local even if you're from far out of town.

A classic American diner, **Nicely's** (U.S. 395 and 4th St., Lee Vining, 760/647-6477, 7 A.M.–9 P.M. daily summer, 7 A.M.–9 P.M. Thurs.–Mon. winter, $10–20) offers friendly service and familiar food. Inside, you'll find a large dining room with half-circle booths upholstered in cheerful red vinyl. The cuisine includes eggs and pancakes in the morning; salads and sandwiches for lunch; and steak, trout, and salmon in the evening. Portions are more than generous. Nicely's is open earlier in the morning, later in the evening, and more in the winter than most places in the area, making it a very viable dining option, a very welcome thing in such a small town. This is a good place to take the kids for comfort foods like burgers, fries, and macaroni and cheese.

If you're looking for a Wild West atmosphere and a good spicy sauce, have lunch or dinner at **Bodie Mike's Barbecue** (51357 U.S. 395 at 4th St., Lee Vining, 760/647-6432, 11:30 A.M.–10 P.M. daily June–Sept.). Use your fingers to dig into barbecued ribs, chicken, beef, brisket, and more. A rustic atmosphere with rough-looking wood, red-checked tablecloths, and local patrons in cowboy boots completes your dining experience. Just don't expect the fastest service in the world. At the back of the dining room is the entrance to a small, dark bar populated by local characters.

A great place to get a to-go breakfast or lunch is the **Mono Market** (51303 U.S. 395, 760/647-1010, 7 A.M.–10 P.M. daily summer,

7:30 A.M.–8 P.M. daily winter). Breakfast sandwiches and pastries are made fresh daily, as are the sandwiches, wraps, and messier napkin-requisite entrées you can carry out for lunch or dinner. In addition to prepared food, the market offers standard grocery staples and a liquor section.

Information and Services

The **Mono Basin National Forest Scenic Area Visitors Center** (U.S. 395, 0.5 mile north of Lee Vining, 760/647-3044, www.monolake.org, 8 A.M.–5 P.M. daily May–Sept., 9 A.M.–4:30 P.M. Thurs.–Mon. Oct.–Nov.) is an excellent resource for information about the area. It includes an interpretive museum that describes the creation of Mono Lake and the strange tufa formations that define it. This visitors center also has a ranger station with knowledgeable staff who can help you with the best seasonal trail and lake advice.

Right in the center of Lee Vining is another fine visitors center that's about much more than just the lake. The **Mono Lake Committee Information Center & Bookstore** (U.S. 395, Lee Vining, 760/647-6595, 9 A.M.–5 P.M. daily) is a pleasant and welcoming place, with endless free maps and brochures, helpful staff, and souvenirs available for purchase.

The nearest medical facility to Mono Lake is to the south in Mammoth Lakes at **Mammoth Hospital** (85 Sierra Park Rd., Mammoth Lakes, 760/934-3311, emergency services 760/924-4076, www.mammothhospital.com), which has a 24-hour emergency room.

Getting There and Around

Mono Lake is very close to the junction of Tioga Pass Road and U.S. 395. Getting here from San Francisco, Los Angeles, or anyplace else in California with a major airport usually requires a long drive.

Tioga Road is closed November–May each year, sometimes longer if snows are heavy. Check the Yosemite National Park website (www.nps.gov/yose) or call 209/372-0200 for updates on road closings in and around Yosemite. U.S. 395 remains open all year,

although storms can close it briefly until the plows do their work. But accessing U.S. 395 from the north or south involves long drives from most places. You might want to consider flying in Reno or even Las Vegas and approaching Mono Lake from the north or east. From the **Reno-Tahoe International Airport** (RNO, 2001 E. Plumb Lane, Reno, NV, 775/328-6400, www.renoairport.com), you can drive 140 miles south on U.S. 395 and get to Mono Lake in about three hours. From **McCarran International Airport** (LAS, 5757 Wayne Newton Blvd., Las Vegas, 702/261-5211, www.mccarran.com), the 350-mile trip takes about six hours, mostly on U.S. 95 north.

Very little public transit of any kind gets as far as Lee Vining and Mono Lake. To adequately explore this region, you need a vehicle of your own. On the bright side, parking in Lee Vining and around the lake tends to be both easy and free.

JUNE LAKE

Like so many other parts of the Eastern Sierra, June Lake as a vacation destination is largely about skiing. Although the lake and the others nearby make lovely summer recreation spots, most people who come here are headed for the snow.

June Lake Loop

The 15-mile scenic June Lake Loop (Hwy. 158), accessible from U.S. 395 south of Lee Vining, takes you away from the high-traffic, heavily visited areas of the Eastern Sierra. Along the way, you get the full-fledged alpine experience. Once you get out of the car, the loop's namesake—June Lake—offers good recreation. You can take a hike, go fishing, or even plan to stay overnight at one of the campgrounds. Next you'll come to Gull Lake, and then to Silver Lake, two other popular boating and angling waterways. As you drive north on the loop, stop at least once to admire Reversed Peak, a 9,500-foot Sierra mountain. Finally, you'll come to Grant Lake. There are no resorts or major trailheads here, but you'll find a boat launch and some spectacular alpine trout fishing. Finally, take a break at the Mono Craters Monument before heading back out to U.S. 395 toward Lee Vining or Mammoth Mountain.

June Mountain

One of the most popular places to hit the slopes in this area is the **June Mountain Ski Resort** (3819 Hwy. 158, 760/648-7733, www.junemountain.com, lifts 8:30 A.M.–4 P.M. daily, adults $72, seniors $36, ages 13–18 $54, ages 7–12 $20). About 20 miles north of Mammoth Lakes, June Mountain offers seven lifts (two quads, four doubles, and a carpet) and more than 2,500 feet of vertical drops on 500 skiable acres. The resort caters to beginners and intermediate skiers, and 80 percent of its trails are green or blue. Beginners can even take a lift up to the top of Rainbow Summit and enjoy a long run down the Silverado Trail. However, a number of black and double black-diamond slopes make a trip to June Mountain fun for more advanced skiers and boarders as well. Thrill-seeking experts and adventurous intermediates head up to the top of June Mountain Summit and then plummet down the bowl (hard-core double black diamond) or slide along the ridge-line (blue). Be sure to check your trail map before going up this way unless you're very sure of your abilities. For a cup of coffee or hot chocolate, stop at the June Meadows Chalet (top of Chair J1, breakfast and lunch from 8 A.M. daily) at the center of the ski area.

Accommodations and Food

June Lake has plenty of cabins and lodges available. One particularly nice one is the **Double Eagle Resort and Spa** (5587 Hwy. 158, 760/648-7004, www.doubleeagle.com, year-round, $199–349). Its 15 two-bedroom cabins ($349) sleep up to six, and all come complete with decks and fully equipped kitchens. The 16 luxurious lodge rooms ($199–229) come with breakfast, free Internet access, and whirlpool tubs. The on-site Creekside Spa includes an indoor pool and a fitness center, and the resort's **Eagle's Landing Restaurant** (7 A.M.–9 P.M.

daily, $20–30) helps make this an everything-you-need destination, whether you're seeking an active trip or a relaxing getaway.

A little more rustic but also very pleasant is **The Four Seasons** (24 Venice St., 760/648-7476, www.junelakesfourseasons.com, late Apr.–Oct., $129–195), which, ironically, is only open in summer. The five A-frame cabins each sleep up to six, with a master bedroom and a sleeping loft as well as a full kitchen, a living room, and a large deck. The resort is just two miles from the town of June Lake and a short drive to all the lakes.

Camping

The U.S. Forest Service maintains several campgrounds near June Lake in the Inyo National Forest. A particularly good one is **Silver Lake Campground** (Hwy. 158, 7 miles west of U.S. 395, reservations www.recreation.gov, mid-Apr.–mid-Nov., $18). Each of the 39 sites has a bear-proof food locker, a picnic table, and a fire ring; the campground has flush toilets, drinking water, and even a small store. The best part is that the campground is right on the shore of lovely Silver Lake, which is a good place to fish, watch for wildlife, or just sit and enjoy the view.

Information and Services

The small **June Lake Visitors Center** (U.S. 395 and Hwy. 158, 760/648-1917, summer only) is staffed by volunteers, so there's no guarantee of when it is open.

Getting There

June Lake is located east of Yosemite, west of U.S. 395, south of Lee Vining, and north of Mammoth Lakes. To get to June Lake, take U.S. 395 and turn west onto Highway 158 at the June Lake Loop. June Mountain Ski Resort is about four miles west of U.S. 395.

BISHOP
Laws Railroad Museum and Historic Site

If you've got a railroad buff in the family (and who doesn't?) make time to visit the Laws

Railroad Museum and Historic Site (Silver Canyon Rd., off U.S. 6, 760/873-5950, www.lawsmuseum.org, 9:30 A.M.–4:30 P.M. daily summer–Labor Day, 10 A.M.–4 P.M. winter, donation), 4.5 miles north of Bishop. There's more here than just trains—in fact, there's a whole historic village with artifacts from the area's history well preserved and on display. But the center of the village is the railroad depot, which is pretty much how towns were organized back when residents depended on the railroads not only for transportation but also for commerce and communication with the outside world. Come and see the self-propelled Death Valley Car from 1927, a caboose from 1883, model railroad displays, and more.

◖ Ancient Bristlecone Pine Forest

Directly to the east of Bishop near the Nevada border is yet another amazing California wilderness area. Little visited but worth a trip on its own, Ancient Bristlecone Pine Forest is a section of the Inyo National Forest in the White Mountains where the world's oldest trees reside. The bristlecone pines can be even older than the coastal redwoods and sequoias. The most famous bristlecone pine, **Methuselah,** at the ripe age of about 4,750, is believed to be 1,000 years older than any other tree in the world. To protect the tree, the Forest Service has chosen not to mark it or produce maps directing people to it, but don't worry—almost all the trees around here are beautiful to behold.

There are two main groves of trees that you won't want to miss. The **Schulman Grove** is where you'll find the **Bristlecone Pine Forest Visitors Center** (Hwy. 168, 23 miles east of Big Pine, 760/873-2500, www.fs.usda.gov/inyo, 10 A.M.–5 P.M. daily Memorial Day–Sept. 30, $3 pp or $6 per car). The tentative opening date for the new, larger visitors center in the Bristlecone Pine Forest, replacing the one that burned in 2008, is July 2012.

The second notable grove, 12 miles north of Schulman on a dirt road, is the **Patriarch Grove.** Here you'll see the Patriarch Tree, which is the world's largest bristlecone pine. A self-guided nature trail in the Patriarch Grove enables you to get out among the trees and learn more about them.

Three hiking trails begin right outside the Bristlecone Pine Forest Visitors Center. The **Discovery Trail** is an easy one-mile loop with helpful signs along the way. The **Methuselah Trail** is a loop of about 4–5 miles, also easy. Yes, you will see the world's oldest tree if you take this walk—you just won't know exactly which tree it is. Its secret identity is protected, but you can have fun admiring *all* the noble specimens here and guessing which is most ancient. Finally, the **Mexican Mine Trail** is an out-and-back hike of about five miles in total that leads past some abandoned mine buildings made out of tough bristlecone pine wood, of course, in addition to still more living trees.

You can get to the Ancient Bristlecone Pine Forest by car from the town of Bishop in about an hour. Take U.S. 395 south to Big Pine and turn left (east) onto Highway 168. Take Highway 168 for 13 miles to White Mountain Road. Turn left (north) and drive 10 miles to the visitors center in Schulman Grove.

Horseback Riding

Operating out of Bishop, **Rainbow Pack Outfitters** (off Hwy. 168, west of Bishop, 760/873-8877, www.rainbowpackoutfit.com) offers a wide range of options for horse lovers. At the stables, small children can enjoy their "Li'l Cowpoke" ride ($20) on a pony or horse with an expert leading. Options for bigger kids and adults include the Rainbow Meadow Ride (1 hour, $35), the South Lake Vista Ride (2 hours, $50), the Long Lake Scenic Ride (4 hours, $75), the All-day Ride (9 A.M.–5 P.M., $105), and the All-day Fishing Ride (9 A.M.–5 P.M., $125), which is a mini–pack trip. If you're looking for a longer horseback vacation, check into Rainbow's options for full-service multiday riding trips, with hunting, fishing, photography, birding, and more. Rainbow provides service into the John Muir Wilderness, the Inyo National Forest, and Sequoia and Kings Canyon National Parks.

YOSEMITE

Another part of Rainbow's business is displaying the historic side of packing. Free facility tours are available during the summer season when the pack station is open. Reservations are recommended for any of the rides. The best way to reach Rainbow is by telephone; since the pack station has no electricity, they don't get their email until they head into town for a break.

Snowmobiling

Given the heavy snows, great scenery, and wide-open spaces, snowmobiling in Bishop is a given. To rent equipment and get some help getting started, stop into **Bishop Motosports** (107 S. Main St., 760/872-4717, www.bishopmotosports.com, daily, $225–275 for 3 hours, $400–500 full day). Maps, helmets, and trailers (for off-road vehicles) are included with all rentals. The management at Bishop Motosports declines to list hours since they make themselves available to customers from early in the morning till late at night every day of the week. If you make an appointment, they'll be there. Another location in Mammoth offers similar services.

Entertainment and Events

Each September for more than 20 years, the Inyo Council for the Arts has put on the sort of music festival you'd expect to find in a much larger metropolitan center. The **Millpond Music Festival** (Millpond Park, Sawmill Rd., 5 miles northwest of Bishop, 760/873-8014, www.inyo.org, day pass $25–35 adults, K–12 students $15, weekend pass $75–90 adults, K–12 students $25) has performers as varied as Los Lobos, Ray Bonneville, and the Marc Atkinson Trio. In addition to amazing music in a beautiful mountain setting, you'll find work by local artists, arts and crafts activities for children, food and drink booths, and musician workshops.

If an hour or three at the slots or the blackjack tables sounds like a good way to unwind, go to the **Paiute Palace Casino** (2742 N. Sierra Hwy., 888/372-4883, www.paiutepalace.com, 24 hours daily), owned by the Bishop Paiute Tribe. You can play more than 300 slots

plus table blackjack and poker. Look for Texas hold 'em tournaments every Wednesday and Sunday. The in-house restaurant, **TuKaNovie** (7 A.M.–midnight Sun.–Thurs., 7 A.M.–10 P.M. Fri.–Sat., $8–15), serves steak, pork chops, and liver and onions, with a prime rib special on Friday and Saturday nights starting at 5 P.M.

Shopping

Bishop isn't known for its shopping opportunities, but the town does have one very special shop, the **Mountain Light Gallery** (106 S. Main St., 760/873-7700, www.mountainlight.com, 10 A.M.–6 P.M. daily), which showcases the wild and scenic photography of Galen and Barbara Rowell, world adventurers who died in a plane crash in 2002. At the gallery, you can view and purchase photographic prints as well as calendars, note cards, posters, and books. The guest gallery features the work of other landscape photographers. You can even take classes in nature photography and attend other special events.

Camping

A nice place to stay near Bishop is **Keough Hot Springs** (800 Keough Hot Springs Rd., 760/872-4670, www.keoughshotsprings.com, $20–115). The 100- by 30-foot swimming pool is heated by natural hot springs, so it's open year-round, as is the campground and other facilities. Lodging options include "dry" tent or RV sites ($20), campsites with water and electricity ($25), four tent cabins ($75), and a mobile home ($115). To get to Keough, travel six miles south of Bishop on U.S. 395. When you see the big blue sign on your left, turn right. You'll be there in less than 10 minutes.

A number of campgrounds are available in the Inyo National Forest near Bishop. One of the most popular is **Bishop Park** (Hwy. 168, 12 miles west of Bishop, 760/872-7018, www.fs.usda.gov, 20 sites, first-come, first-served, Apr.–Oct., $21). It's right on the banks of Bishop Creek with flush toilets and space for RVs. Another nice option is **Intake Two** (Hwy. 168, 16 miles west of Bishop, 8 sites, first-come, first-served, Apr.–Oct., $21), located

© STAN NESTER

YOSEMITE

Keough Hot Springs

near Intake Two Lake. Swimming is not advised because the water is so cold, but you can catch trout here. **Sabrina Campground** (Hwy. 168, 18 miles west of Bishop, 18 sites, first-come, first-served, late May–Oct., $21) is at 9,300 feet elevation, making it low on oxygen but high on views. Lake Sabrina is nearby, and it's a good trout-fishing destination. Showers are not available at any of the National Forest campgrounds, but you can buy a shower at a couple of places nearby: **Bishop Creek Lodge** (2100 S. Lake Rd., 760/873-4484, www.bishopcreekresort.com, Apr.–Oct., $6 for a 10-minute token, $1 for soap and towel) and **Parchers Resort** (5001 S. Lake Dr., 760/873-4177, www.parchersresort.net, Memorial Day–Oct., $6 for a 10-minute shower, $1 for soap and towel).

Food

Even if you don't usually like casinos, consider having a meal at **TuKaNovie** (2742 N. Sierra Hwy./U.S. 395, 888/372-4883, www.paiutepalace.com, 7 A.M.–midnight Sun.–Thurs.,

7 A.M.–10 P.M. Fri.–Sat., $8–15), the restaurant at the Paiute Palace Casino. The food, service, and prices are all better than you might expect, and the restaurant is smoke-free. Expect basic American food, with a prime rib special on Friday and Saturday nights starting at 5 P.M. The absence of sales tax on Native American land makes the place even more affordable.

Another hopping place to eat in Bishop is **Whiskey Creek** (524 N. Main St., 760/873-7174, 11 A.M.–10 P.M. Mon.–Thurs., 11 A.M.–10:30 P.M. Fri., 7 A.M.–10:30 P.M. Sat., 7 A.M.–10 P.M. Sun. summer, 11 A.M.–9 P.M. Mon.–Thurs., 11 A.M.–10 P.M. Fri., 8 A.M.–10 P.M. Sat., 8 A.M.–9 P.M. Sun. winter, $11–30). This branch of the popular Whiskey Creek in Mammoth serves burgers, steaks, salads, and a full menu of beer and wine.

Information and Services

The **Bishop Chamber of Commerce and Visitors Bureau** (690 N. Main St., Bishop, 888/395-3952, www.bishopvisitor.com, 10 A.M.–5 P.M. Mon.–Fri., 10 A.M.–4 P.M.

Sat.–Sun.) offers friendly advice on lodgings, local attractions, and more.

Getting There

AIR

The nearest airport to Bishop is the **Mammoth Yosemite Airport** (MMH, 1200 Airport Rd., Mammoth Lakes, 760/934-3813, www.ci.mammoth-lakes.ca.us). Alaska Airlines serves this airport year-round, and United Express and Horizon fly in December 15–April 30.

CAR

Bishop is not located near a major city, so expect it to take a while to get here from almost anywhere else. Bishop is located at the junction of U.S. 395 and U.S. 6, west of Sequoia National Forest and east of the Inyo National Forest's Ancient Bristlecone Pine Forest. From the San Francisco Bay Area, in summer, cross through Yosemite on Highway 120 (Tioga Rd., closed in winter), or drive north and cross on Highway 108 via the Sonora Pass (closed in

winter). Once you get to U.S. 395, follow it south to Bishop, about 64 miles from Tioga Pass or 107 miles from Sonora Pass. Plan on at least 6.5 hours to drive the 300–320 miles. Since both mountain passes are closed in winter (usually Nov.–May), the only way to get here during those months is to take I-80 to U.S. 50 all the way to Lake Tahoe, then cross over into Nevada on Highway 88/89 and connect with U.S. 395. From this point, the trip south to Bishop is 157 miles. Altogether, this winter route is about 370 miles and will take at least seven hours.

The route from Sacramento to Bishop is shorter than the winter route from San Francisco. Take U.S. 50 to Lake Tahoe, then turn onto Highway 88/89. Go south on U.S. 395 for the final 157 miles. The total trip is 285 miles and takes about 5.5 hours.

Getting to Bishop from Los Angeles is pretty direct. From I-5 north, just take Highway 14 north, which eventually becomes U.S. 395. Under good conditions, it takes about five hours to drive the 265 miles.

Mammoth Lakes

SIGHTS
The Village at Mammoth Lakes

Like many large ski resort areas, the Village at Mammoth Lakes (www.thevillageatmammoth.com) is a hybrid of a real town, an overly planned shopping mall, and a clean, upscale amusement park. Its central purpose, of course, is to provide support services for people who come to enjoy Mammoth Mountain, most of whom are skiers. To that end, the Village offers lodging (including the Juniper Springs Resort), dining (the standard chains plus a few local places), and shopping—all organized around a central pedestrian plaza. In summer, the plaza is sprinkled with outdoor benches, tables with umbrellas, and recently planted greenery as it tries to impersonate an actual village square. Concerts and outdoor movies are presented here in the warmer months.

Gondola Rides

Mammoth Mountain, like all ski resorts, has plenty of gondolas, chairlifts, and other ways to get up to the mountain while relaxing and enjoying the view. Of the two main gondolas, one is open only in winter: **Village Gondola** takes you from the Village at Mammoth Lakes to Canyon Lodge. The other gondola, **Panorama Gondola,** sometimes called the Scenic Gondola Ride, operates in summer and winter. Panorama runs from the Main Lodge at Mammoth to McCoy Station and then, after a stop there, goes all the way to the top of the mountain. In winter, the gondola is extremely popular with skiers: Intermediate-level skiers get off at McCoy to access the trails there; the top of the mountain is for experts only. In summer (9 A.M.–4 P.M. daily June–Sept., adults $21, ages 13–18 $17, under age 13 free

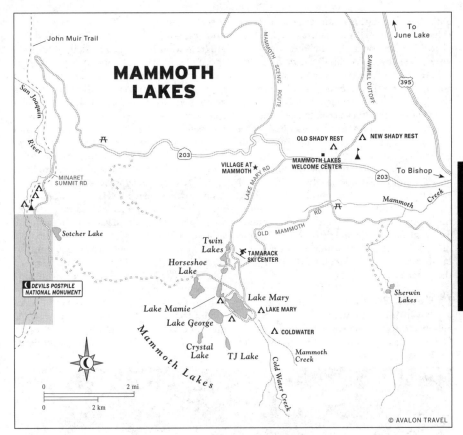

MAMMOTH LAKES

© AVALON TRAVEL

with an adult) it serves sightseers, mountain bikers, hikers, and anyone else who wants to get to the top of the 11,053-foot mountain. From the top, you can see as far as 400 miles on a clear day.

The ride all the way to the top takes about 20 minutes. Some people do it just for the thrill of the ride; others stop for a meal or a snack at the **Top of the Sierra Café** (9:30 A.M.–4 P.M. daily summer, 8:30 A.M.–3:30 P.M. daily winter, $8–20), open when the gondola is running.

One of the most popular reasons to ride up is to ride down—on your mountain bike. In summer, 70 miles of trails are open for biking and 25 miles of hiking trails are available. You

can buy a day pass (over age 12 $43, under age 13 $22) to bike the trails, which includes all-day access to both the Panorama Gondola and the shuttle. Hikers only pay to ride the gondola, and then they're free to walk down.

If you're not a skier, you can still ride the Panorama Gondola to the top and back in winter (ages 18–64 $24, over age 64 $20, ages 13–17 $19, ages 7–12 $8).

The Panorama Gondola is usually closed only in October for maintenance between the two big seasons.

Inyo Craters

California is full of volcanic action, and some

YOSEMITE

of the most interesting results to behold are the three Inyo Craters (www.fs.usda.gov). These phreatic craters on and near Deer Mountain were created by explosions of steam. Scientists believe that all three craters came into being at about the same time, around A.D. 1350. Two of the three craters are about 200 feet deep and large enough that they actually have lakes inside them. The third crater is smaller, but all are worth seeing. If you can, make time for this geologic side trip.

To reach Inyo Craters, drive five miles north of Mammoth Lakes on Highway 203. Turn right (east) onto the Mammoth Scenic Route (Dry Creek Rd.) and continue about 3.2 miles until you see the sign for the Inyo Craters. Turn right at the sign and drive about 1.3 more miles on a dirt road (not plowed, or advised, in winter). Park in the lot and walk 0.3 mile to the crater site.

◖ Devils Postpile National Monument

Compared to the area's other national parks, Devils Postpile National Monument (Minaret Vista Rd., 760/934-2289, www.nps.gov/depo, mid-June–mid-Oct., park 24 hours daily, ranger station 9 A.M.–5 P.M. daily, adults $7, ages 3–15 $4) is small, but what you'll see is worth a visit. The park is named for the strange natural rock formation called the Devils Postpile. It's hard to fathom that the near-perfect, straight-sided hexagonal posts are a natural phenomenon created by volcanic heat and pressure; you have to see it to believe it. Less heavily traveled than many other parks, Devils Postpile has hikes to serene meadows and unspoiled streams, and you're likely to see the occasional deer or maybe even a bear meandering through the woods. Free guided ranger walks are held at 11 A.M. most days throughout the summer, starting from the ranger station.

Also part of the monument is the beautiful crystalline **Rainbow Falls.** The thick sheet of water cascades 101 feet down to a pool, throwing up stunning rainbows of mist. For the best rainbows at the waterfall, hike the three miles (round-trip) from Red Meadow near the middle of the day when the sun is high in the sky.

The $7 park entry fee includes the Reds

Devils Postpile

© HC LISTON

Meadow–Devils Postpile Shuttle. Visitors are required to access the park via the shuttle, which runs hourly 7–11 A.M. daily from the Village at Mammoth Lakes and every 15–30 minutes 7 A.M.–7 P.M. daily mid-June–early September from the Mammoth Mountain Adventure Center and Main Lodge area. When the shuttle stops running for the season in September, visitors may drive their cars into the park, but the $7 fee still applies, unless you have a Federal Parks Pass.

Old Mammoth Road

Like most of the Eastern Sierra region, Mammoth Lakes became of interest to miners in the 19th century after the gold rush began—miners got out this far in 1877. Along Old Mammoth Road (south off Hwy. 203/ Main St.) you'll find a number of old mining sites. At the height of the short-lived boom, about 20 different small mines operated in the area. Along this road, you can see the grave of a miner's wife, a stamp mill's flywheel, and then the meager remains of Mammoth City and the nearby Mammoth Mine. The highlight of this summertime half-day trip is the ruins of the Mammoth Consolidated Mine. You can still see some bits of the camp and its housing buildings, the assay office, the mill, and mining equipment. The mine shaft is also visible, but do not attempt to get around the security features to head down there. Old mine shafts are unbelievably dangerous and should not be entered for any reason.

SPORTS AND RECREATION

Even beyond skiing and snowboarding, outdoor activities are a central focus of life in and around Mammoth Lakes. People come from all over to hike, bike, fish, and more.

Ski Resorts

The town of Mammoth Lakes exists primarily to support the winter sports industry. The downhill skiing, snowboarding, and cross-country skiing here attract sports enthusiasts of all ages and ability levels. If you don't own your own equipment, you can rent skis, snowboards,

and all the necessary accessories at a dozen different shops in town.

MAMMOTH MOUNTAIN

The premier downhill ski and snowboard mountain is, aptly, Mammoth Mountain (1 Minaret Rd., information 760/934-2571, lodging and lift tickets 800/626-6684, snow report 888/766-9778, www.mammothmountain. com, lift 8:30 A.M.–4 P.M. daily, 2011–2012 rates adults $96, ages 7–12 $30). Whether you're completely new to downhill thrills or a seasoned expert looking for different terrain, you'll find something great on Mammoth Mountain. More than two dozen lifts, including three gondolas and nine express quads, take you up 3,100 vertical feet to the 3,500 acres of skiable and boardable terrain; there are also three pipes. If you're staying at Eagle Lodge, Canyon Lodge, Mammoth Mountain Inn, or the Village at Mammoth Lakes, enjoy the convenience of a lift or gondola right outside your door. All these, plus the Mill Café and McCoy Station halfway up the mountain, offer hot drinks, tasty snacks, and a welcome spot to rest during a long day of skiing.

The easiest runs on the mountain mostly cluster around the ski school and the lower area near the Mammoth Mountain Inn; they are recognizable by their cute nursery-school names. If you're an intermediate skier, runs swing down all over the mountain just for you. Build your confidence by taking the Panorama Gondola up to Panorama Lookout at the top of the mountain then skiing all the way down the east side of the mountain along the intermediate-to-harder ridge runs. Advanced skiers favor the bowls and chutes at the front of the mountain, and hard-core experts go west from Panorama Lookout to chase the dragon.

TAMARACK CROSS-COUNTRY SKI CENTER

Here's your chance to explore the snow-covered Mammoth Lakes Basin in winter. Tamarack (163 Twin Lakes Rd., 760/934-2442, www. tamaracklodge.com, 8:30 A.M.–5 P.M. daily mid-Nov.–Apr., adults $22–27, youths and

YOSEMITE

seniors $17–21, children $12–15) offers 19 miles of groomed cross-country ski tracks, some with groomed skating lanes, for all abilities and levels. This lovely resort also has a restaurant, a lounge, and a bar where you can enjoy a nice cup of hot chocolate and good book if you get tired of skiing. And getting here from Mammoth Lakes is free: Just take the Orange shuttle line from Mammoth Village hourly on the half-hour 8:30 A.M.–5 P.M. daily in winter.

BLUE DIAMOND TRAILS

The Blue Diamond Trails (www.mammoth. us/winter/blue_diamond_trail.shtml) system starts just behind the Mammoth Lakes Welcome Center (Hwy. 203, 3 miles west of U.S. 395, 760/924-5500, www.visitmammoth. com, 8 A.M.–5 P.M. daily), at the entrance to Mammoth Lakes, and winds through 25 miles of Inyo National Forest, marked by signs bearing a blue diamond on the trees. Pick up a free trail map in the Welcome Center before you set out. Some trails are not groomed, so be prepared to deal with varying snow conditions and unbroken trails. There's plenty of relatively flat land here for beginners, however. The Shady Rest Trails (Hwy. 203, just before the Welcome Center) might sound like a cemetery, but in fact it's a group of beginner loops with plenty of shade trees to keep skiers cool through their exertions. The Knolls Trail (Mammoth Scenic Loop, 1.5 miles north of Hwy. 203) makes a good intermediate day out, passing through lovely stands of lodgepole and Jeffrey pines. Beginners beware of the deceptively named Scenic Loop Trail (Mammoth Scenic Loop, across from Knolls Trail); this reasonably short trail—about four miles long—includes steep descents and some difficult terrain.

Hiking

Hikers will find plenty of worthwhile terrain around Mammoth Lakes for both short day hikes and longer backpacking adventures. The **Mammoth Mountain Bike Park** (1 Minaret Rd., 800/626-6684, www.mammothmountain.com/bike_ride, 8 A.M.–6 P.M.

daily summer) includes a number of great hiking trails. For an all-downhill walk, take the Panorama Gondola (9 A.M.–4 P.M. daily June–Sept., adults $21, ages 13–18 $17, under age 13 free with an adult) up to the Panorama Overlook and hike back down to town. Just be sure to get a trail map at the **Mammoth Adventure Center** (1 Minaret Rd., 800/626-6684, www.mammothmountain.com/bike_ride, daily 8 A.M.–6 P.M. June–Sept.) so you can keep to the hiking areas and avoid being flattened by fast-moving mountain bikers.

Mammoth Lakes also acts as a jumping-off point for adventurers who want to take on the **John Muir Wilderness** (south of Mammoth Lakes to Mount Whitney, www.sierranevadawild.gov/wild/john-muir). John Muir pioneered the preservation of the Sierra Nevadas, and more than 500,000 acres in the area have been designated national wilderness areas in his honor. Day hikers are welcome, and there's plenty to see. Check with the Inyo and Sierra National Forests (www.fs.usda.gov) for trail maps of the area. The main attractions to the John Muir, as it's called locally, are the **John Muir Trail** (JMT, 215 miles Yosemite–Mount Whitney, www.johnmuirtrail.org) and the **Pacific Crest National Scenic Trail** (PCT, 2,650 miles Mexican border–Canadian border, www.pcta.org), both among the holiest of grails for backpacking enthusiasts from around the world.

If you're planning an overnight camping trip in the John Muir, Ansel Adams, Dinkey Lakes, or Kaiser Wilderness areas of the Sierra National Forest, you must first obtain a wilderness permit. You can apply for these up to one year in advance by downloading an application from www.fs.usda.gov/sierra or by calling 559/297-0706. If you reserve in advance, there is a charge of $5 pp for the permit. On the other hand, if you're willing to be flexible, you can just show up at a ranger station no more than 24 hours before your trip begins and apply in person. There is no charge for these "walk-up" permits, although their availability is not guaranteed. The main office is the **High Sierra Ranger District Office** (29688

Auberry Rd., Prather, 559/855-5355, 8 A.M.–4:30 P.M. daily).

If you're planning an overnight in the Inyo National Forest, you can apply for your permit in person at the **Mammoth Lakes Welcome Center** (Hwy. 203, 3 miles west of U.S. 395, 760/924-5500, www.visitmammoth.com, daily 8 A.M.–5 P.M.), at the entrance to Mammoth Lakes, or apply online (www.fs.usda.gov/inyo).

Biking

Come summertime and melting snow, Mammoth Mountain transforms from a ski resort to a mountain bike mecca. The **Mammoth Mountain Bike Park** (1 Minaret Rd., 800/626-6684, www.mammothmountain.com/bike_ride, 8 A.M.–6 P.M. daily, $10 for trail access, $43 for trail, gondola, and shuttle access) spans much of the same terrain as the ski areas, with almost 90 miles of trails that suit all levels of biking ability. The park headquarters is at the **Mammoth Adventure Center** (Main Lodge, 1 Minaret Rd., 760/934-0706 or 800/626-6684, 8 A.M.–6 P.M. daily June–Sept.), at the Main Lodge at Mammoth Mountain. You can also buy bike park tickets at the Mountain Center at the Village (760/924-7057).

You can take your bike onto the Panorama Gondola and ride all the way to the top of Mammoth Mountain, then ride all the way down (3,000-plus vertical feet) on the single tracks. Be sure to pick the trails that best suit your fitness and experience level. Several other major lodges offer rider services, including the Village at Mammoth Lakes, Juniper Springs, the Panorama Lookout, and Outpost 14. If you value scenery as much as extreme adventure, pack your camera and plan to rest at the various scenic overlooks throughout the trail system.

If you need to rent a bike or buy park tickets, go to the **Mammoth Adventure Center** (Main Lodge, 1 Minaret Rd., 760/934-0706) or to the **Mammoth Mart at the Village** (6201 Minaret Rd., inside the Village, 760/934-2571, ext. 2078). Both locations offer new high-end bikes for adults and kids. These shops can also help

with parts and repairs for bikes you've brought up with you, and they sell accessories.

Horseback Riding

Perhaps the most traditional way to explore the Eastern Sierra is on the back of a horse or mule. Early pioneers to the area came on horseback, and you can follow their example from several locations near Mammoth Lakes. From the **McGee Creek Pack Station** (2990 McGee Creek Rd., Crowley Lake, June 1–Sept. 30 760/935-4324, Oct. 1–May 31 760/878-2207, www.mcgeecreekpackstation.com, $35 per hour, $125 9 A.M.–5 P.M.), 10 miles south of Mammoth Lakes on U.S. 395, you can ride into McGee Canyon, a little-visited wilderness area. Other day-trip destinations include Baldwin Canyon and Hilton Lakes. Standard rides range from one hour to a full day, but McGee's specialty is multiday and pack trips that let you really get out beyond the reach of paved roads to camp for a number of days by one of the many pristine lakes dotting the mountains. If you love the outdoors and really want a vacation as far away from it all as you can get, consider a few days' camping in Convict Basin or near Upper Fish Creek in the John Muir Wilderness. The McGee Creek guides will help you pack your gear and guide you through the incredible backcountry of the Eastern Sierra.

Snowshoeing

If you prefer walking to all that sliding around on planks, rent or bring your own snowshoes to Mammoth and enjoy a snowy hike through the mountains and meadows. Check the cross-country ski areas first—many have specifically designated snowshoe trails. Or head out to the backcountry and explore Mammoth Lakes Basin or the Sherwin Range. Groomed trails start right behind the Mammoth Lakes Welcome Center.

ATVs and Snowmobiles

ATVs, dirt bikes, and snowmobiles are a big no-no in most national parks and wilderness areas; not so at Mammoth Lakes. Here you'll find miles of trails set aside for motorized fun. Eighty miles of groomed trails and 75,000 acres of snow-covered meadows and mountainsides await snowmobilers each winter. Much of the same territory is open to ATV and dirt-bike traffic in the summer. Get a copy of the *Mammoth Lakes Winter Recreation Guide* for a complete trail and area map to find the best (and legal) places to play. The guide is available at local hotels and businesses and at the **Mammoth Lakes Welcome Center** (Hwy. 203, 3 miles west of U.S. 395, 760/924-5500, www.visitmammoth.com or www.fs.usda.gov/inyo, 8 A.M.–5 P.M. daily) at the entrance to Mammoth Lakes.

To rent snowmobile equipment, ATVs, and other sporty vehicles in Mammoth Lakes, visit the Mammoth location of **Bishop Motosports** (58 Commerce Dr., 760/872-4717, www.bishopmotosports.com, by appointment early morning–10 P.M. daily, $225–275 for 3 hours, $400–500 full day). Maps, helmets, and trailers for off-road vehicles are included with all rentals.

Golf

If you're in the Mammoth Lakes area in the summer, you can enjoy a round of golf at a beautiful course with stunning mountain views. The 18-hole, par 70 **Sierra Star Golf Course** (2001 Sierra Star Pkwy., 760/924-4653, www.mammothmountain.com, $99–129) is open to the public. Walk this wonderful course for the best views of the surrounding Sierra Nevadas, or concentrate all your efforts on the game. Amenities include a full-service pro shop, a PGA golf pro on-site, and a café with a full bar.

Spas

If you want to enjoy some pampering after a hard day of skiing, book a treatment at one of Mammoth Lakes's day spas. The **Bodyworks Mountain Spa** (3343 Main St., 760/924-3161, www.bodyworksmountainspa.com, $60–95 for a 1-hour Swedish massage), located upstairs at the Luxury Outlet Mall, offers massage therapy, spa treatments, and facials, plus a wide

range of combination packages to maximize your time and money at the spa.

The **InTouch MicroSpa** (3325 Main St., 760/934-2836, www.intouchmicrospa.com, $85 for a 1-hour massage) offers a full menu of treatments with a focus on the four elements of earth, air, fire, and water. Exclusively using Aveda products, InTouch caters to spa-goers who care about what's put on their skin. A number of different styles of facials and aesthetic treatments are available. If you're in town with a group, InTouch offers several spa-party options that get everyone great treatments at discounted rates.

Located inside the Best Western Hotel, the day spa **BellaDonna** (3228 Main St., 760/934-3344, www.belladonnamammoth.com, $85 for a 1-hour massage) offers a crackling fireplace, a serene setting, and all sorts of massages, facials, manicures, and pedicures. If you're looking for romance, check out the couples side-by-side fireside massage.

ENTERTAINMENT AND EVENTS
Bars and Clubs

What would a ski resort town be without a selection of après-ski activities? Mammoth Lakes has a number of bars that open their doors to chilled and thirsty skiers.

For possibly the best evening in Mammoth, try the **Clocktower Cellar Pub** (Alpenhof Lodge, 6080 Minaret Rd., 760/934-2725, www.alpenhof-lodge.com, 4:30 P.M.–midnight daily winter, 5 P.M.–midnight daily summer, food service 4:30–10 P.M. daily, $3–12). This happening nightspot offers a full bar with more than 125 whiskeys, 26 brews on tap, and 50 different bottled beers. They also provide glasses of fine wine cadged from Petra next door, and a casual atmosphere complete with sports on TV, vintage video games, and a pool table. Instead of an obnoxious pickup joint, the Clocktower acts as a refuge for locals looking for some after-work relaxation and a pint or two. Expect informal dress and friendly conversation up at the bar, along with the delicious and unusual variety of beers. The location is perfect—in the basement of the Alpenhof just across the street from the

Village. Note that the Clocktower closes for a few weeks in what they call the "shoulder seasons." If you're visiting in October or May–June, call ahead to be sure they're open.

If you prefer a French-style wine bar experience to a noisy British-style pub, try the vintages at the **Side Door Bistro** (100 Canyon Blvd., Suite 229, 760/934-5200, www.sidedoormammoth.com, 7 A.M.–10:30 P.M. Sun.–Thurs., 7 A.M.–midnight Fri.–Sat. winter, 11 A.M.–9 P.M. daily summer, $8–11). Not only can you enjoy glasses of California's top wines in the evening, you can order up a delicious dinner or dessert crepe to go with your favorite varietal. Or you can show up in the morning in the winter and enjoy a breakfast crepe with your coffee. The crepes are excellent, and the wine list is often called the best in the Village. Note that the hours at many places in Mammoth Lakes, including the Side Door, can vary considerably with the seasons. The manager of the Side Door notes that they're open "till 9 P.M. or later" in summer and winter, and also that they often close a few days a week during spring and fall; but they're always open on weekends.

Didn't get enough sports during your day at Mammoth? Spend the evening at **Grumpy's** (361 Old Mammoth Rd., 760/934-8587, www.grumpysmammoth.com, 11 A.M.–1:30 A.M. Mon.–Thurs., 11 A.M.–1:30 A.M. Fri.–Sat., 10 A.M.–1:30 A.M. Sun., food service until 10 P.M., $10–24). This sports bar has the usual array of TVs showing major sporting events, along with pool tables and an arcade. Grumpy's has a full bar and serves up a lunch and dinner menu of Mexican and American specialties. Come for the big-screens, stay for the surprisingly tasty food and drink.

The **Lakanuki Tiki Bar** (6201 Minaret Rd., 760/934-7447, www.lakanuki.com, 3 P.M.–2 A.M. Mon. and Thurs., 10 A.M.–2 A.M. Fri.–Sun., food service until 10 P.M., $6–22) serves fresh fish, steaks, and stir-fries, but it's the nightlife in the tacky tiki bar that packs the place, especially on weekends, with the young male snowboarding crowd. Note that hours may vary, so call ahead to be sure they're open.

Live Music

For an exceptional evening of classical music in the mountains, check out a performance of **Chamber Music Unbound** (760/934-7015, www.felicitrio.com, late July–early Aug., adults $25, seniors $17, students $10, season passes $190). This nonprofit group mixes the familiar with out-of-the-way classical pieces and performs at several locations in Bishop and Mammoth Lakes. Most of the annual festival takes place at Cerro Coso Community College (101 College Pkwy.).

Festivals and Events

Whatever the season, Mammoth is about vacations and recreation, and locals plan plenty of special events each year to celebrate. In late September, the Village at Mammoth Lakes throws an **Oktoberfest** (760/924-1575, www.villageatmammoth.com). "Roktoberfest" is 6–9 P.M. on Friday night and features concerts, food, and drink, and there are events all day Saturday—keg-tossing, Bavarian food tasting, and children's activities.

We probably don't need to tell you when **The Village 4th of July Festivities** (760/924-1575, www.villageatmammoth.com) take place. This all-weekend party includes concerts and rubber ducky races; everyone is welcome. The town's official Independence Day event is the **Mammoth Lakes 4th of July Celebration** (888/466-2666, www.mammothfestivals.com), which features a Lion's Club Pancake Breakfast, a parade, fireworks, and Pops in the Park.

If music is your thing, check out the **Sierra Summer Festival** (760/935-3837, www.sierrasummerfestival.org, $20–30, discounts for students) in August. The Eastern Sierra Symphony Orchestra, under musical director Bogidar Avramov, performs during this weeklong festival, along with special guests. For art enthusiasts, the **Labor Day Arts Festival** (760/937-2942, www.monoarts.org) has been going on for more than 40 years, showcasing both fine artists and craftspeople.

Not surprisingly, there are plenty of special sporting events around here too. Late August

YOSEMITE

brings the **Mammoth Mud Run** (Village at Mammoth, 100 Canyon Blvd., 800/626-6684, www.mammothmountain.com, adults $49–60, ages 5–12 $15), a 6K race for adults and a 1K for kids, both full of obstacles and chances to get dirty.

A Saturday in August brings the **Mammoth Lakes Challenge Triathlon** (415/335-0179, www.sierra-nevada-races.com, $40), and the next day the same organization—that is, Bay Area schoolteacher and runner Gail Pavlich, whose passions include triathlons and Mammoth Lakes scenery—puts on the **Quake & Shake 10K & Half-Marathon** ($30). The Quake & Shake takes place in Inyo Crater, three miles north of Mammoth Lakes. It's a beautiful but not-too-hilly course through changing scenery. Pavlich's third event each year is called **George's Tri** ($40), which she believes may be the highest-elevation triathlon anywhere. It's run at 9,000 feet, with a 0.25-mile swim in Horseshoe Lake, three laps of the lake on a mountain bike, and a two-mile run on a loop trail up and down Mammoth Pass. The event is a benefit for the town of Mammoth Lakes, in honor of the late George Fowler, who was both a runner and a pillar of that community. Wetsuits and mountain bikes are strongly recommended in this rugged region, but if you're concerned about your abilities in one area, don't worry: Families and friends often do this event as a relay, so one person bikes, one swims, and one runs.

On the Sunday of Labor Day weekend, the High Sierra Triathlon Club puts on the **Mammoth Rock Race 10K** (760/717-0176, www.highsierratri.org, $30–40), which it claims is California's highest-elevation 10K. The race starts and ends in Mammoth Creek Park and has an average elevation of about 8,000 feet. For cyclists, there's the **High Sierra Fall Century** (760/914-0396, www.fallcentury.org, $60) held on a Saturday in September. This gorgeous 100-mile course with its autumn scenery is almost entirely free of stop-and-signs; the entry fee includes a lavish lunch, five rest stops, and plenty of snacks.

And what's a festival roundup without beer?

In early August, the annual **Mammoth Festival of Beers and Bluespalooza** (888/992-7397, www.mammothbluesbrewsfest.com, $35 individual events, $135 weekend pass) gives attendees the chance to sample the work of more than 60 craft breweries and listen to major performers like Robert Cray and Blues Traveler.

SHOPPING

While it's not a big shopping town, Mammoth Lakes has some upscale boutiques and galleries and a small outlet mall that allows weary adventurers to take a day off the slopes and engage in some retail therapy.

In downtown Mammoth Lakes, visit the **Mammoth Gallery** (501 Old Mammoth Rd., 760/934-6120 or 888/848-7733, www.mammothgallery.com, 10 A.M.–5 P.M. daily) to see the work of a number of local photographers and watercolor artists plus a large collection of vintage ski poster reproductions. Another photo gallery in Mammoth Lakes, formerly located in Bishop, is the **Vern Clevenger Gallery** (220 Sierra Manor Rd., Unit 4, 760/934-5100, www.vernclevenger.com, 1–5 P.M. Mon. and Wed.–Sat., and by appointment), which features only the nature photography of Mr. Clevenger himself. What you see in his work is all natural, with no digital enhancement to the images or colors. Inexpensive note cards and posters are available for purchase in addition to the lovely framed fine-art prints. You can also take a workshop to learn how to create these gorgeous images yourself.

ACCOMMODATIONS

Accommodations at Mammoth are often luxurious ski condos with full kitchens, perfect for spending a week on the slopes with family or friends. But comfortable motels and inns are available as well, often for a little less money and with shorter minimum-stay requirements.

Under $100

Want to ski the slopes of Mammoth, but can't afford the hoity-toity condo resorts? Stay at the **Innsbruck Lodge** (Forest Trail between Hwy.

203 and Sierra Blvd., 760/934-3035, www.innsbrucklodge.com, $95–165). Economy rooms offer twin beds, a table and chairs, and access to the motel whirlpool tub and lobby with a stone fireplace at very reasonable nightly rates. Other rooms have queen or king beds, some can sleep 2–6, and some include kitchenettes. The quiet North Village location is on the ski area shuttle route for easy access to the local slopes. It's also an easy walk to most restaurants and other Village attractions, making this a great find for budget travelers.

The inexpensive **Boulder Lodge** (2282 Hwy. 158, 760/648-7533 or 800/458-6355, www.boulderlodgejunelake.com, Oct.–May $88–265, June–Sept. $98–365) provides an array of options, from simple motel rooms for short stays to multiple-bedroom apartments and even a five-bedroom lake house for longer trips and larger groups. The Boulder Lodge takes guests back a few decades with its decorating style—the browns, wood paneling, and faux leather furniture recall the 1950s. But the views of June Lake, the indoor pool and spa, and the wonderful outdoor recreation area surrounding the lodge are timeless.

$100-150

The **Sierra Lodge** (3540 Main St., 760/934-8881 or 800/356-5711, www.sierralodge.com, $119–129) offers reasonably priced all-nonsmoking guest rooms located right on the ski shuttle line, and only 1.5 miles from the Juniper Ridge chair lift. This small motel's rates are rock-bottom in the off-season and on weekdays in winter. Guest rooms have either a king or two double beds, a kitchenette with a microwave and dishes, and plenty of space for your snow and ski gear. The decor is simple motel styling in cool, relaxing blues. Breakfast, cable TV, and Internet access are included with your room.

$150-250

From the outside, the ornate, carved-wood, fringed **Austria Hof** (924 Canyon Blvd., 760/934-2764 or 866/662-6668, www.austriahof.com, $150–170) might be a ski hotel

tucked into a crevice of the Alps. But on the inside, you'll find the most stylish American appointments. Winter is high season for these peaceful, sea-green motel rooms—some with king beds and spa bathtubs—and rates can be considerably more on weekends and holidays. In summer, however, guest rooms can be rented for less than $100. If you've got a large party or want to cook your own meals, check out the one- and two-bedroom condos ($220–310). Austria Hof's location adjacent to the Canyon Lodge and the free gondola to the Village make it a great base camp for winter skiing or summer mountain biking. In the evening, head down to the Austria Hof Restaurant ($25) for some hearty German fare. Or if you prefer, slip into a swimsuit and enjoy the views from the large outdoor spa.

Over $250

It's not cheap, but the **Juniper Springs Resort** (4000 Meridian Blvd., reservations 760/924-1102 or 800/626-6684, www.mammothmountain.com/lodging/juniper-springsresort, $300–900 winter, $119–269 off-season) has absolutely every luxury amenity you could want to make your ski vacation complete. Condos come in studio, 1–3-bedroom, and townhouse sizes, sleeping up to eight. The interiors have stunning appointments, from snow-white down comforters to granite-topped kitchen counters and 60-inch flat-screen TVs. Baths include deep soaking tubs, perfect to relax aching muscles privately after a long day on the slopes. The resort also features heated pools year-round and three outdoor heated spas—there's nothing like jumping into a steaming hot tub on a snowy evening, and then jumping back out to find the cold perfect and refreshing. The on-site **Talons Restaurant** (760/934-0797 or 760/934-2571, ext. 3797, 7:30 A.M.–5 P.M. daily Nov.–Apr.) serves breakfast and lunch in winter only, and the **Daily Grind** (7 A.M.–1 P.M. daily summer, 7 A.M.–10 P.M. daily winter) provides coffee and snacks year-round. Juniper Springs is located next door to the Eagle Lodge, which serves as one of the Mammoth Mountain base lodges, complete with a six-seat express chairlift up to the main ski area. You can rent skis right inside the hotel, and ski back down to Juniper after a day on the slopes. In the summertime, Juniper Springs's proximity to local golfing and the Mammoth Mountain bike park make it a perfect retreat.

The company that owns Juniper Springs also owns the luxury condo complex at **The Village Lodge** (1111 Forest Trail, 760/934-1982 or 800/626-6684, www.mammothmountain. com, $349–900 winter, $139–429 off-season), which is even a little closer to the ski mountain. Check them out if you can't get the condo of your dreams at Juniper.

For another fine condo rental, check out **Mountainback** (435 Lakeview Blvd., 800/468-6225, www.mountainbackrentals.com, $265–420 winter, two-night minimum, $35 booking fee). This complex has an array of all-two-bedroom units, some of which sleep up to six. Every individual building has its own outdoor spa, and the complex has a heated pool and a sauna. Every condo is decorated differently (you might even be able to buy and redecorate one if you have the cash). Check the website for photos to find what you like—big stones everywhere, wood paneling, gentle cream walls, or even red-and-green holiday-themed furniture. Walk to the ski lifts, or enjoy a round of golf or a day of fishing in the summer.

FOOD

Plenty of dining options are available in Mammoth Lakes. You can get your fast-food cheeseburger and your chain-store double-latte, but why would you, with so many more interesting independent options around? There's lots of American food and pizza, with a few international options thrown in for variety.

American

The very popular **Whiskey Creek** (24 Lake Mary Rd., 760/934-2555, 4 P.M.–close daily Nov.–Mar., 5 P.M.–close daily Apr.–Oct., $12–30) offers fine food and good drinks on two levels. The menu is the same whether you eat in the elegant dining room downstairs or the

homey nighttime bar above. Order a fine steak or a simple burger, and sample the wide selection of wines and beers. Whiskey Creek maintains its own small on-site brewery, so some of the beers they serve really are as local as it gets. The crowd, both for dining and for drinking, feels warm and friendly, as do the hearty dishes served to hungry après-skiers. Be sure to make reservations on winter weekends as it can get crowded. If you've just come for a drink and a good time, enjoy a DJ in the bar (Wed. and Fri.–Sat. winter, Wed. summer). The music starts around 9 P.M. and usually keeps playing long past midnight. Whiskey Creek is only half a block from the Village, so you can walk over from most places.

California

Petra's Bistro and Wine Bar (6080 Minaret Rd., 760/934-3500, www.petrasbistro.com, 5:30 P.M.–close Tues.–Sun.) brings a bit of the California wine country all the way out to Mammoth Lakes. This eatery offers a seasonal menu that's designed to please the palate and complement the wine list. That wine list is worth a visit itself—an eclectic mix of vintages highlights the best of California while giving a nod to European and South American wines. Wine lovers will recognize many names but still might find something new on the unusual list. The by-the-glass offerings change each night, and your server will happily cork your unfinished bottle to take home. Two dining rooms and a wine bar divide the seating nicely, and the atmosphere succeeds in feeling romantic without being cave-dark. Petra's stays open all year, so if you're visiting in the off-season, you'll get a pleasantly uncrowded treat. Reservations are a good idea during ski season.

The popular gourmet establishment **Skadi** (587 Old Mammoth Rd., Suite B, 760/934-3902, www.skadirestaurant.com, 5:30–9:30 P.M. Wed.–Sun., $24–32) describes its menu as "alpine cuisine." The restaurant, co-owned by a chef and a rancher, offers a creative menu of fresh local meat (venison, for example) and plants (macadamias) to their best advantage. Everything on the list looks tasty, but if you're not ready for a heavy entrée, consider ordering a couple of items from the ample selection of appetizers for a "small plates" experience. Oh, and don't skip dessert! Whatever you choose, the European-heavy wine list will have something perfect to pair with it. If you're in town in ski season, make reservations in advance, especially on weekends.

Mexican
Even Californians who eat Mexican food on a regular basis tend to agree on that **Roberto's Mexican Café** (271 Old Mammoth Rd., 760/934-3667, www.robertoscafe.com, 11 A.M.–close daily, $7–15) is special. This casual spot serves classic California-Mexican food in great quantities but includes specialty items like lobster burritos and duck tacos to shake things up. Whatever you order, it's perfect for skiers and boarders famished after a long day on the slopes. For a quiet meal, stay downstairs in the main dining room. To join a lively younger crowd, head upstairs to the bar, which has tables and serves the full restaurant menu.

INFORMATION AND SERVICES
Visitor Information
The town of Mammoth Lakes has an awesome visitors center at the entrance to Mammoth Lakes, the **Mammoth Lakes Welcome Center** (Hwy. 203, 3 miles west of U.S. 395, 760/924-5500, www.visitmammoth.com or www.fs.usda.gov/inyo, 8 A.M.–5 P.M. daily). The facility is jointly run by the U.S. Forest Service, the town of Mammoth Lakes tourism bureau, and the National Parks Service, so they can help you with everything from condo rentals and restaurant reservations before you arrive to the latest bar openings and best seasonal recreation options when you get here. They're also your best resource for camping information, weather travel advisories, updates on snowmobile trails, and even backcountry passes for your backpacking trip.

Note that the Welcome Center anticipates a possible reduction in hours due to future budget cuts. If you're counting on visiting in person, call ahead to make sure they're open. In any case, you can call any time for recorded messages on any number of relevant topics.

Media and Communications
Mammoth Lakes has its own weekly newspaper, the **Mammoth Times** (www.mammoth-times.com), which comes out on Thursday and serves the whole of the Eastern Sierra region. Check for local events and good nightspots, and visit the website for up-to-date weather and road conditions.

Despite its small size, the town of Mammoth Lakes has a cosmopolitan atmosphere that includes plenty of Internet access. Many of the condos and hotel rooms have some form of Internet access, and you can find a couple of Starbucks (481 Old Mammoth Rd., 760/934-4536, and 6201 Minaret Rd., 760/934-0698) with dependable wireless service.

Banks and Post Offices
Plenty of ATMs crowd Mammoth Lakes at gas stations, minimarts, and bank branches. Check the Village, Main Street, and Minaret Road for banks and cash machines.

Mammoth Lakes has a **post office** (3330 Main St./Hwy. 203, 760/934-2205, www.usps.com, 8 A.M.–4 P.M. Mon.–Fri.).

Gas and Automotive Services
Mammoth Lakes is a great place to gas up before hitting the wilder parts of the Eastern Sierra. Gas stations are clustered at the eastern edge of town, where Highway 203 becomes Main Street, and more gas can be found throughout the downtown area. Be prepared to pay a premium: This is a resort town, and they know how far the next gas station is.

Many gas stations, as well as big-box stores and even pharmacies and supermarkets, sell tire chains in the winter.

Medical Services
Need medical service beyond that offered at the ski resorts? You can get it at **Mammoth**

Hospital (85 Sierra Park Rd., 760/934-3311, www.mammothhospital.com), which has a 24-hour emergency room.

GETTING THERE AND AROUND
Air
The nearest airport to Mammoth Lakes is the **Mammoth Yosemite Airport** (MMH, 1200 Airport Rd., 760/934-3813, www.ci.mammoth-lakes.ca.us). Alaska Airlines serves this airport year-round; United Express and Horizon fly in December 15–April 30. In winter, nonstop flights run to Mammoth from Los Angeles, San Francisco, and San Jose. For a major transportation hub, fly to the **Reno-Tahoe International Airport** (RNO, 2001 E. Plumb Ln., Reno, NV, 775/328-6400, www.renoairport.com). From there, you can drive 166 miles south on U.S. 395 and get to Mammoth Lakes in about 3.5 hours.

Car
U.S. 395 is the main access road to the Mammoth Lakes area. To get to the town of Mammoth Lakes from U.S. 395, turn onto Highway 203, which will take you right into town.

Mammoth Lakes and most of the rest of the Eastern Sierra isn't near any of California's major cities. Expect a six-hour drive from Los Angeles and at best a seven-hour drive from San Francisco if the traffic and weather cooperate. If you fly into Reno, the drive out to Mammoth takes about 3.5 hours.

In the winter, be aware that it snows at Mammoth Lakes more than it does in almost any other place in California. Carry chains! Even if the weather is predicted to be clear for your visit, having chains can prevent a world of hurt and the need to turn back in a sudden storm. The longer you plan to stay, the more you should stock your car with items such as ice scrapers, blankets, water, food, and a full tank of gas whenever possible. For the latest traffic information, including chain control

areas and weather conditions, call Caltrans (800/427-7623).

Parking in Mammoth Lakes in the off-season is a breeze. In the winter, it can get a bit more complicated, as constant snow removal means that parking on the street is illegal throughout town. Most of the major resorts and hotels offer heated parking structures, and many of the restaurants, bars, and ski resorts have plenty of parking in their outdoor lots. If you're concerned about parking, call ahead to your resort and restaurants to get the lowdown on how best to get there and where to leave your car.

Shuttles and Buses
The **Eastern Sierra Transit Authority** (ESTA, 760/924-3184, www.estransit.org) runs a number of bus lines, including the CREST line, which takes passengers from Lone Pine through Bishop, Mammoth, Lee Vining, and other stops on the way to the Reno Greyhound station and the Reno-Tahoe International Airport. The trip from the Reno Airport to Mammoth Lakes takes 3.5 hours (adults $50, children and seniors $44). The ESTA also operates local bus routes around Mammoth Lakes, including the **June Mountain Express** ($11.50–13.25 round-trip), which takes skiers from Mammoth Lakes to the June Lake ski area.

The **Mammoth Transit System** (www.visitmammoth.com, Nov.–May, free) offers complimentary rides all over town in the winter, freeing visitors from their own cars most of the time. You can download a copy of the transit map from the website.

Devils Postpile National Monument (760/934-2289, www.nps.gov/depo, adults $7, children $4) runs a shuttle that's mandatory for all visitors during high season (vehicles with handicap placards excepted). The shuttle runs hourly 7–11 A.M. daily from the Village at Mammoth Lakes, and every 15–30 minutes 7 A.M.–7 P.M. daily mid-June–early September from the Mammoth Mountain Adventure Center at the Main Lodge area.

LAS VEGAS

Pack your dancing shoes, your hiking boots, and your flip flops, but leave your sensible shoes at home. Las Vegas is where New Year's resolutions come to die. From the first glimpse of neon glowing in the middle of the empty desert, Las Vegas seduces the senses and indulges your appetites. An oasis of flashing marquees, endless buffets, feathered showgirls, chiming slot machines, and grand recreations, the city surrounds visitors—all 35 million of them each year—as a monument to fantasy. Here, you can stroll the streets of Paris, float down a Venetian canal, lie on a tropical beach, soak up Rat Pack swank, and most of all dream that tremendous riches are a slot pull away.

After a brief attempt to pawn itself off as a family destination, the Neon Jungle has stepped into its sequins, ordered a Jäger Bomb, and hollered, "Hit me, baby!" But no one back home has to know you've succumbed to Vegas's siren song. After all, "What happens in Vegas . . . . "

With odds overwhelmingly favoring the house, jackpot dreams may be just that: dreams. The slim chance at fortune is powerful enough to have lured vacationers into the southern Nevada desert for more than 75 years, ever since the Silver State legalized gambling in 1931. At first, the cowboy casinos that dotted downtown's Fremont Street were the center of the action, but they soon faced competition from a resort corridor blooming to the south on Highway 91. Los Angeles nightclub owner Billy Wilkerson dubbed it "The Strip" after his city's Sunset

HIGHLIGHTS

◖ Caesars Palace: Las Vegas is an apt heir to the regality and decadence of ancient Rome, and Caesars Palace carries on the empire's excesses with over-the-top statuary, testosterone-dripping centurions, toga-clad cocktail servers, gluttony-inducing restaurants, endless jugs of wine, and dancing till dawn (page 207).

◖ Fremont Street Experience: Part music video, part history lesson, the six-minute shows presented in "Viva Vision" – a four-block-long, 12-million-diode, 550,000-watt sensory overload – are the star of this downtown Las Vegas promenade. Caricature artists and strolling musicians add to the street fair atmosphere (page 222).

◖ Gondola Rides: Just like the real Grand Canal, only cleaner, the Venetian's waterway meanders beside quaint shops, under intricate frescoes, and along the Las Vegas Strip. Gondoliers singing Italian ballads provide the soundtrack (page 225).

◖ Secret Garden and Dolphin Habitat: Trainers and caretakers don't put on shows with the big cats and marine mammals at the Mirage's twin habitats, but the tigers, lions, and leopards can often be seen playing impromptu games, wrestling, and cavorting in the water, and the bottlenose dolphins can never seem to resist the spotlight (page 226).

◖ Las Vegas Springs Preserve: Natural springs attracted early Native Americans and inspired visiting Mormons to establish a settlement here. Las Vegas's birthplace now displays the area's geological, anthropological, and cultural history along with what very well might be its future: water-conserving landscaping, solar and wind energy, and other "green" initiatives (page 228).

◖ Atomic Testing Museum: Commemorating Las Vegas's unique position as the almost literal ground zero of the atomic age, the museum celebrates the science and technology of nuclear power while also taking a sobering look at its sometimes dreadful consequences (page 228).

◖ *Jubilee!:* The showgirl has outlived the mob, the Rat Pack, and the Stardust. This show at Bally's pays tribute to one of Las Vegas's

Strip, and together with Bugsy Siegel built the Flamingo, the first upscale alternative to frontier gambling halls. Their vision left a legacy that came to define Las Vegas hotel-casinos. This shift to "carpet joints," as opposed to the sawdust-covered gambling floors of frontier Las Vegas, was only one of the many reinventions Las Vegas has gone through—from city of sleaze to Mafia haven, family destination, and finally upscale resort town—each leaving its mark even as the next change takes hold.

Today, each megaresort offers more to do than many a small town. Under one roof you can indulge in a five-star dinner, attend spectacular productions, dance until dawn with the beautiful people, and browse in designer boutiques. If there's still time, you can get a massage and ride a roller coaster too. The buffet, a fitting metaphor for this city with an abundance of everything, still rules in the hearts of many regulars and visitors, but an influx of celebrity chefs is turning the town into a one-stop marketplace of the world's top names in dining. Similarly, cutting-edge performers such as Blue Man Group and Cirque du Soleil have taken up residence alongside such beloved showroom fixtures as Elvis impersonators and *Jubilee!* These hip offerings are drawing a younger, more stylish crowd that harks back to the swinging '60s, when Las Vegas was a pure adult recreation and celebrity magnet.

Some say Old Vegas is as hard to find as a

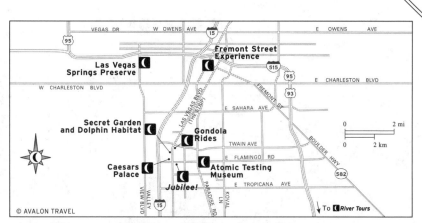

LOOK FOR ◖ TO FIND RECOMMENDED SIGHTS, ACTIVITIES, DINING, AND LODGING.

most enduring icons in all her sequined statuesque grandeur. Dozens of feathered femmes fatales strut their way through intricate production numbers amid juggling, contortionist, and aerial acts (page 231).

◖ **River Tours:** Motorized rafts give riders a trout's-eye view of the Colorado River as it rolls through Black Canyon downstream from Hoover Dam. Guides lead rafters through slot canyons to hot springs and bracing wading pools. On the other side of the dam, the Desert Princess plies the waters of Lake Mead, coming within a few dozen feet of the dam wall and exploring peaceful coves (page 277).

game of single-deck blackjack. It's true that you can no longer have your picture taken in front of Binion's million-dollar display, but the King and the Rat Pack can still be found in impersonators and tribute shows, torch singers still croon in low-lit lounges, and showgirls still prance in sequined headdresses (and little else).

That's not to say the city wholeheartedly relishes its reputation as Sin City. Downtown's art district, Broadway productions, gourmet restaurants, and a few top-notch attractions for kids balance sin with sophistication and

sanity. And despite the go-go reputation, Las Vegas really is a small city surrounded by idyllic retreats and world-class recreational activities.

Lounge beside a gurgling snowmelt stream on Mount Charleston and feel last night's hangover wash away. Skim across Lake Mead on a rented Jet Ski, and soon you'll forget all about that bad beat at the hold 'em table. Gaze at mesmerizing Red Rock Canyon long enough, and your swivel-hipped karaoke rendition of "Viva Las Vegas" seems almost résumé-worthy.

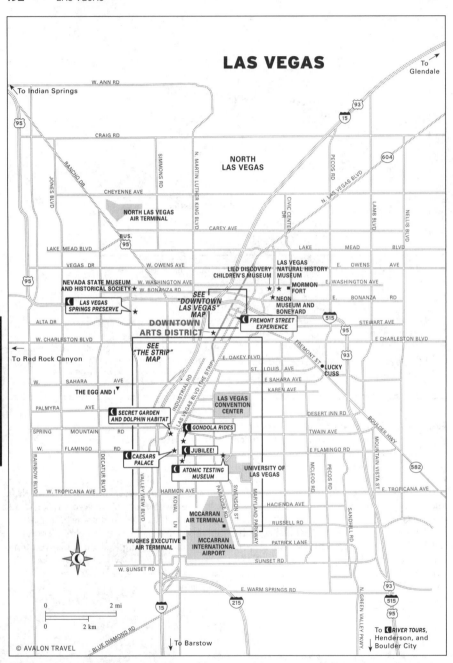

LAS VEGAS

To Glendale

To Indian Springs

W. ANN RD

CRAIG RD

CHEYENNE AVE

NORTH LAS VEGAS

NORTH LAS VEGAS AIR TERMINAL

CAREY AVE

LAKE MEAD BLVD

VEGAS DR

W. OWENS AVE

LAKE MEAD BLVD

E. OWENS AVE

LIED DISCOVERY CHILDREN'S MUSEUM

LAS VEGAS NATURAL HISTORY MUSEUM

NEVADA STATE MUSEUM AND HISTORICAL SOCIETY

W. WASHINGTON AVE

E. WASHINGTON AVE

MORMON FORT

W. BONANZA RD

E. BONANZA RD

LAS VEGAS SPRINGS PRESERVE

NEON MUSEUM AND BONEYARD

SEE "DOWNTOWN LAS VEGAS" MAP

DOWNTOWN ARTS DISTRICT

FREMONT STREET EXPERIENCE

ALTA DR

W. CHARLESTON BLVD

E CHARLESTON BLVD

SEE "THE STRIP" MAP

To Red Rock Canyon

E. OAKEY BLVD

ST. LOUIS AVE

LUCKY CUSS

W. SAHARA AVE

E SAHARA AVE

THE EGG AND I

KAREN AVE

PALMYRA AVE

LAS VEGAS CONVENTION CENTER

DESERT INN RD

SECRET GARDEN AND DOLPHIN HABITAT

SPRING MOUNTAIN RD

GONDOLA RIDES

TWAIN AVE

W. FLAMINGO RD

E FLAMINGO RD

CAESARS PALACE

JUBILEE!

ATOMIC TESTING MUSEUM

UNIVERSITY OF LAS VEGAS

W. TROPICANA AVE

E. TROPICANA AVE

HARMON AVE

HUGHES EXECUTIVE AIR TERMINAL

McCARRAN AIR TERMINAL

HACIENDA AVE

RUSSELL RD

McCARRAN INTERNATIONAL AIRPORT

PATRICK LANE

W. SUNSET RD

SUNSET RD

E. WARM SPRINGS RD

0   2 mi

0   2 km

To Barstow

To RIVER TOURS, Henderson, and Boulder City

© AVALON TRAVEL

BLUE DIAMOND RD

Driving to Las Vegas

DRIVING TO LAS VEGAS FROM LOS ANGELES

Multilane highways ensure that the drive from L.A. to Las Vegas is smooth, if not especially visually appealing. Smooth doesn't mean easy, fast, or non-nerve-racking, however. Even traffic that is mild by L.A. standards can easily add an hour or more to the 270-mile, four-hour-plus drive from Los Angeles to the Las Vegas Strip. The last 220 miles is a northeasterly cruise on I-15 that moves at a pretty good clip through Victorville, Barstow, and Baker. The first 50 miles, however, can put drivers in a bad mood long before they lose their bankrolls on an inside straight draw. On paper, at least, the way to I-15 is simple. Either take I-10 east past Ontario or Highway 134/I-210 east past Rancho Cucamonga.

STOPPING IN CALICO

About two hours outside the L.A. environs, the restored boomtown of Calico is tourist-trappy, but can make for a fun stop. It's just four miles off I-15 (take Exit 191 between Barstow and Yermo). The building exteriors at **Calico Ghost Town** (36600 Ghost Town Rd., Yermo, 800/86-CALICO—800/862-2542, 9 A.M.–5 P.M. daily, $6, ages 6–15 $5, under age 6 free) are restored to their 1880s appearance, and they now house shops, restaurants, and attractions. The small museum, located in an original adobe building, contains original furnishings and gives a thorough overview of the town and its mining history. Pretend you're back in the Wild West: Pan for gold, ride the train, watch a shootout, tour a mine, and flirt with brazen women.

The dining options stick to the ghost town theme, of course, offering hot, hearty breakfasts and meat-and-potatoes dinners. At **Calico House Restaurant** (760/254-1970, 8 A.M.–5 P.M. Sun.–Fri., 8 A.M.–7:30 P.M. Sat., $10–20), the meat is smoked, and the chili simmers all day. **Lil's Saloon** (760/254-

2610, 11 A.M.–5 P.M. Mon.–Fri., 9 A.M.–5 P.M. Sat.–Sun., $8–15) is full of Western ephemera—roulette wheels, a manual cash register, and gun collections. Munchies, including pizza, hot dogs, and giant pretzels, dominate the menu. Offering a bird's-eye view of the town, **Old Miners Cafe** (760/254-3323, 9 A.M.–5 P.M. daily, $10–15) also deals in sandwiches, salads, and daydreams of striking the mother lode.

Calico offers no indoor accommodations, so it's not the best place to spend the night. There are 265 camping sites ($25–30, $5 discount for seniors) for tents and with full and partial hookups, cabins ($38), and a mini bunkhouse ($80).

DRIVING TO LAS VEGAS FROM THE GRAND CANYON
From the West Rim

The good news is that the West Rim is the closest canyon point to Las Vegas—only about 120 miles, or 2.5 hours, even with the big detour south around the White Hills. The bad news is there's almost nothing to see along the way. If you parked and rode the shuttle from Meadview (highly recommended), simply take Pierce Ferry Road 39 miles down past Dolan Springs, Arizona, to U.S. 93 north for another 76 miles to Las Vegas.

From the South Rim

The National Park portion of the canyon is on the South Rim and is the most visited, most developed, and most scenic portion. It is 4.5 hours or 275 miles from Las Vegas. Take U.S. 180/Highway 64 south for 55 miles to Williams, then I-40 west for 116 miles to Kingman. Here you'll connect with U.S. 93 north for the final 100 miles of the journey to Las Vegas. Most summer weekends, you'll find the route crowded but manageable, unless there's an accident; in that case you'll likely be stuck where you are for some time.

STOPPING IN KINGMAN

Proving ground for the manifest destiny of the United States, training ground for World War II heroes, and playground for the postwar middle class, Kingman preserves and proudly displays this heritage at several well-curated museums, such as the Historic Route 66 Museum and the Mohave Museum of History and Arts.

The best restaurant for miles in any direction is **Mattina's Ristorante Italiano** (318 E. Oak St., 928/753-7504, 5–10 P.M. Tues.–Sat., $13–25), where you can get perfectly prepared Italian food and outstanding beef medallions and rack of lamb. It's difficult to choose from the diverse and outlandishly appetizing selection of pasta dishes, but it's equally difficult to pass up the lobster ravioli or the thick, creamy fettuccini alfredo. Don't leave without trying the tiramisu or the key lime pie, and consider sampling liberally from their well-stocked wine cellar. **Redneck's Southern Pit BBQ** (420 E. Beale St., 928/757-8227, 11 A.M.–8 P.M. Mon.– Sat., $10–20), in Kingman's small, often quiet downtown, serves some of the best Southern-style barbecue this side of Memphis, with delicious baked beans and coleslaw on the side. The pulled pork and the brisket should not be missed by connoisseurs of those heaven-sent dishes. It is widely known throughout this flat and windy region that the retro Route 66 drive-in **Mr. D'z Route 66 Diner** (105 E. Andy Devine Ave., 928/718-0066, www. mrdzrt66diner.com, 7 A.M.–9 P.M. daily, $3–17) serves the best burger in town, but they also have a large menu with all manner of delectable diner and road food, including chili dogs, pizza, hot sandwiches, baby back ribs, chicken fried steak, and a big plate of spaghetti. Breakfast is served all day. The portions are big, but save room for a thick shake or a root-beer float. Don't leave your camera in the car; the turquoise-and-pink interior and the cool old jukebox here are snapshot-ready.

There are several very affordable basic hotels on Andy Devine Avenue (Route 66) in Kingman's downtown area, some of them with retro road-trip neon signs and Route 66

themes. There are many chain hotels in town as well. The **Ramblin' Rose Motel** (1001 E. Andy Devine Ave., 928/753-4747, $35–42 d) isn't much more than a highway-side place to park and snooze. It's inexpensive, clean, and has big comfy beds. You can check your email using the free wireless Internet, chill your soda in the mini fridge, and warm up a burrito in the microwave. For the price, you can't ask for more. The small, affordable **Hill Top Motel** (1901 E. Andy Devine Ave., 928/753-2198, www.hilltopmotelaz. com, $47–55) has character, with a 1950s-era neon sign that calls out to Route 66 road-trippers, striking something in the American memory, convincing them to stop and stay. Built in the 1950s but since refurbished, the Hill Top has comfortable standard guest rooms with refrigerators and microwaves as well as free wireless Internet access. Although it's located in the city center, the motel's guest rooms command views of the surrounding Hualapai Mountains and are set back from the main streets, making use of block walls to deflect city noise. Outside is a stylish pool and a well-kept cactus garden.

From the North Rim

The route from the Grand Canyon's North Rim to Las Vegas may appeal to Canyon lovers, as the journey takes drivers through Utah's Zion National Park for another opportunity to view nature's handiwork with stone, wind, and water. If you figure that if you've seen one canyon, you've seen them all, you can skip the North Rim and its 5.5-hour, 281-mile drive to Vegas. We recommend attempting this route only during good weather; Highway 67 is subject to closure early November–late May, and all facilities at the North Rim are closed mid-October–mid-May. From the North Rim, take Route 67 north for 44 miles to Jacob Lake, and then head east on U.S. 89-Alt for 37 miles. It becomes the main U.S. 89 after crossing into Utah. Stay on it for 17 more miles. Passing Silver Spring RV Park, turn left onto Highway 9 for 12 miles to the junction with I-15 south. It's then 125 miles to Las Vegas.

STOPPING IN OVERTON

Crossing into Nevada and approaching Glendale, look for the Overton exit. Twelve miles off the highway, Overton is a compact agricultural community whose downtown is strung along several blocks of Highway 169, also known as Moapa Valley Boulevard and Main Street. Surprisingly for such a small town, Overton offers two strong lunch options. **Sugars Home Plate** (309 S. Moapa Valley Blvd., 702/397-8084, $7–15) serves $7.50 bacon and eggs, $8–9 burgers, including the Sugar Burger, a cheeseburger with polish sausage, and homemade pie. There's also a sports bar with bar-top video poker and sports memorabilia. The other food pick is just a block away: **Inside Scoop** (395 S. Moapa Valley Blvd., 702/397-2055, $10–20) has 30-plus ice cream flavors and filling sandwiches. The baked potatoes come with whatever toppings you can come up with. You can also stop at the Red Rooster Bar, a pizza place, and the Chevron station.

Best Western North Shore Inn (520 N. Moapa Valley Blvd., 866/538-0187, $65–130) provides basic guest rooms.

DRIVING TO LAS VEGAS FROM YOSEMITE

If there's any chance that the Tioga Pass is closed, which happens October–May, call the National Park Service (209/372-0200) and press 1 twice at the prompts for the latest weather and roads report. If the pass is open, you have your choice of two fairly direct routes to Las Vegas; both start by heading west on Highway 120 through the pass to Mono Lake. If the pass is closed, prepare for a tedious 8.5-hour trip through central California: Highway 41 south to Fresno, Highway 99 south to Bakersfield, and then Highway 58 east to Barstow.

Via Tioga Pass–Nevada Route

The quickest recommended route covers 415 miles, with a typical driving time of 7 hours, 45 minutes. Follow Highway 120 east to U.S. 6 in Benton, California (3 hours, 15 minutes).

Take U.S. 6 northeast to Coaldale, Nevada (35 minutes), where it shares the road with U.S. 95 south for another 40 minutes to Tonopah. It's then a 210-mile, 3.5-hour straight shot on U.S. 95 to Las Vegas.

STOPPING IN TONOPAH

Tonopah is a great Nevada crossroads town, a natural pit stop that rewards travelers with colorful mining history and overnight visitors with one of the darkest starry skies in the country.

Tonopah's few restaurants specialize in good old-fashioned American food and American versions of Mexican fare. The menu at **Sidewinders** (222 Main St., 702/482-8888, 6 A.M.–10 P.M. Sun.–Mon. and Wed.–Thurs., 6 A.M.–midnight Fri.–Sat., $10–20) runs the comfort-food gamut—spaghetti, burgers, chicken fingers, and fries (especially the fries!) for lunch, along with nightly specials such as chicken masala and crab legs. Tequila, beer, and spice lovers will revel in the cheesy chiles rellenos at **El Marquez** (348 N. Main St., 775/482-3885, 11 A.M.–9 P.M. Tues.–Sun., $10–20). If you're in a hurry but still jonesing for Mexican, hit the drive-through at **Cisco's Tacos** (702 N. Main St., 775/482-5022, $5–10). It has burgers, pizza, and ribs as well.

New owners have faithfully restored the **Mizpah Hotel** (100 Main St., 775/482-3030, www.mizpahhotel.net, $69–84), the "Grand Lady of Tonopah." The guest rooms at **Jim Butler Motel** (100 S. Main St., 775/482-3577, www.jimbutlerinn.com, $40–75) are bright and inviting, with wood furniture and faux hearths. Some guest rooms have fridges and microwaves; all have free Wi-Fi.

The marquee and understated plaques on the guest room doors are the only overt jester references at the **Clown Motel** (521 N. Main St., 775/482-5920, $35–50), where guest rooms are clean and free of smoke smells and have much-appreciated refrigerators and microwaves. They feature basic twin double beds at a decent price, and there are no grease-painted juggling harlequins to keep you up at night.

Via Tioga Pass–California Route

Only a few miles farther but 45 minutes longer, an arguably more scenic route traverses Mammoth Lakes, Bishop, and Lone Pine, California, and includes views of Mount Whitney and the possibility of an overnight stay at Death Valley National Monument. East of Lone Pine, California, Highway 136 becomes Highway 190, which winds through Death Valley. A left turn onto the Daylight Pass Road leads to the Nevada border and Highway 374 just before Beatty. From Beatty, U.S. 95 leads 117 miles southeast to Las Vegas.

STOPPING IN BEATTY

Once the center of one of Nevada's most productive mining districts, Beatty is a microcosm of Western history, having served as a Shoshone settlement, a ranching center, and a railway hub.

The fajitas and fish tacos at **Ensenada Grill** (600 U.S. 95 S., 775/553-2600, 8 A.M.–7 P.M. daily, $10–15) come up aces. They pride themselves on their family recipes and regional cuisine. The Harleys and pickups in the parking lot at the **Sourdough Saloon and Restaurant** (106 W. Main St., 775/553-2266, noon–9 P.M. daily, $10–20) correctly suggest that you'll find charred meat and malted barley on the menu. While the food isn't particularly memorable, the friendly folks and the desert dive-bar experience certainly are.

Several motels offer clean, cheap, and sometimes eye-opening accommodations. The **Stagecoach Hotel Casino** (900 U.S. 95 N., 775/553-2419, $65–85) is the only true casino in town. Guest rooms are larger than average with sturdy if not overly stylish furnishings. The on-site Rita's Café gets high marks from travelers for the satisfying portions and food quality. The **Atomic Inn** (350 S. 1st St., 775/553-2250, $50–70) is a park-outside-your-room throwback to the 1950s and plays up the Cold War theme with a small museum. Guest rooms are inviting, with lots of golds and honey-blond wood.

Bypassing Tioga Pass

If Tioga Pass is closed—ugh. The only way to Las Vegas is an ugly 8.5-hour, 490-mile ordeal. Take Highway 41 south to Fresno 95 miles (2.5 hours), and then follow Highway 99 south to Bakersfield (1 hour 45 minutes). Continue on Highway 58 east to Barstow (2 hours 15 minutes) before catching U.S. 95 north to Las Vegas (2.5 hours).

STOPPING IN BAKERSFIELD

While far from a tourist destination, Bakersfield is at least a bit of a diversion on the otherwise dreary winter Yosemite–Las Vegas route.

Plenty of vanilla chain hotels such as Holiday Inn, Hampton Inn, and Hilton, in the $90–130 range, as well as America's Best Value Inn, Super 8, and Rodeway Inn, for half as much, can be found in Bakersfield. They all serve their purpose, but travelers looking for a bit of personality in their lodgings will have to look a little harder. The rewards are substantial at the **Padre Hotel** (1702 18th St., 888/443-3387, $109–199), rescued in 2009 and restored to its 1930s grandeur. The hotel's vaguely Spanish colonial exterior gives way to sleek guest rooms with ultramodern furniture. The hotel's fifth-floor Prospect Lounge earns high marks as well, but road-weary travelers fear not: Sound walls and thick insulation ensure a peaceful rest.

A few blocks west, the guest rooms at **Hotel Rosedale** (2400 Camino Del Rio Court, 661/327-0681, $60–120) lure guests with their springy umber, burnt orange, and green decor. The oversize pool is surrounded by plenty of shade and shrubbery. A small playground will keep little tykes busy, while an arcade ensures older children don't lose their video-game dexterity while on vacation. At the on-site **Bull Shed Bar & Grill** (3 P.M.–2 A.M. Mon.–Fri., noon–2 A.M. Sat., noon–midnight Sun., $8–15), you can fill up on burgers, pizza, beer, and deep-fried peaches.

A bit more highbrow, **Uricchio's Trattoria** (1400 17th St., 661/326-8870, 11 A.M.–2 P.M. and 5–9 P.M. Mon.–Thurs., 11 A.M.–2 P.M. and 5–10 P.M. Fri., 5–10 P.M. Sat., $15–25) serves the best lasagna in town, and the lobster ravioli in clam sauce is not bad either.

It's tough to decide among the Caribbean-style chicken, steak, and seafood at **Mama**

Roomba (1814 Eye St., 661/322-6262, 11 A.M.–10 P.M. Mon.–Fri., 5–10 P.M. Sat., $10–15); insist that someone opts for the calamari and another goes for the tri-tip.

Casinos

ORIENTATION

Main Street, Las Vegas Boulevard, and I-15 run roughly parallel through the downtown casino district. Main Street juts due south at Charleston Boulevard and joins Las Vegas Boulevard at the Stratosphere. The Strip and I-15 continue parallel southeast and south out of town.

The corner of Main and Fremont Streets, in the heart of downtown at the Plaza Hotel, is ground zero: All street numbers and directions originate here. Fremont Street, which is technically East Fremont Street because it dead-ends at Main Street, separates north from south until it intersects Charleston Boulevard, which continues east; Fremont Street then cuts south. East of Fremont Street, Charleston Boulevard then separates north from south.

The west side is even vaguer. Here the Las Vegas Expressway (also known as Oran K. Gragson Expressway and U.S. 95) defines north and south, even though it is not a street itself. To further complicate matters, U.S. 95 is a major highway that runs north–south from Canada to Mexico, but in Las Vegas it cuts due east (labeled "South") and west ("North").

UPPER STRIP
Stratosphere Casino, Hotel, and Tower

- **Restaurants:** Top of the World, The Buffet, Roxy's Diner, Fellini's Ristorante Italiano, Mamma Ilardo's, El Nopal Mexican Grill, Tower Pizzeria
- **Entertainment:** *American Superstars, Bite*
- **Attractions:** Top of the Tower thrill rides
- **Nightlife:** The Back Alley Bar, C Bar, Airbar, Images Dueling Pianos

It's altitude with attitude at this 1,149-foot-tall exclamation point on the north end of the Strip. Depending on how nitpicky you want to be, the **Stratosphere Tower** (200 Las Vegas Blvd. S., 702/380-7777 or 800/99-TOWER—800/998-6937, $69–200 d) is either the largest *building* west of Chicago or the largest *tower* west of St. Louis. Entrepreneur, politician, and professional poker player Bob Stupak opened the Stratosphere in 1996 as a marked improvement over his dark and dive-y Vegas World Casino. Daredevils will delight in the vertigo-inducing thrill rides on the tower's

White-knuckle rides at 900 feet lure thrillseekers to the Stratosphere Tower.

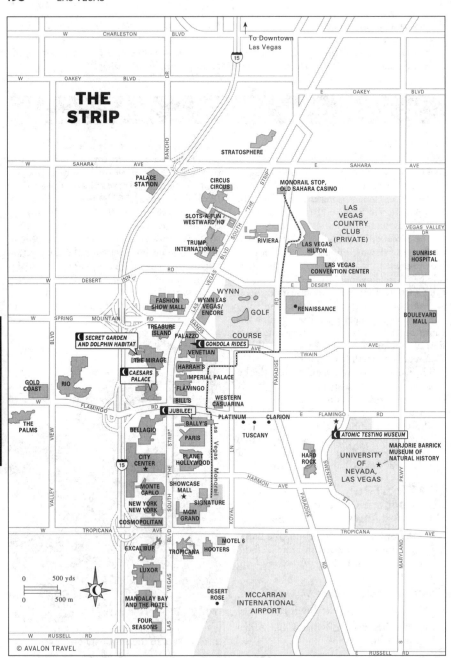

THE STRIP

To Downtown Las Vegas

STRATOSPHERE

PALACE STATION

CIRCUS CIRCUS

MONORAIL STOP, OLD SAHARA CASINO

LAS VEGAS COUNTRY CLUB (PRIVATE)

SLOTS-A-FUN/ WESTWARD HO

RIVIERA

TRUMP INTERNATIONAL

LAS VEGAS HILTON

SUNRISE HOSPITAL

LAS VEGAS CONVENTION CENTER

FASHION SHOW MALL

WYNN LAS VEGAS/ ENCORE

WYNN

GOLF

RENAISSANCE

BOULEVARD MALL

TREASURE ISLAND

PALAZZO

COURSE

◐ SECRET GARDEN AND DOLPHIN HABITAT

◐ GONDOLA RIDES

THE MIRAGE

VENETIAN

◐ CAESARS PALACE

HARRAH'S

IMPERIAL PALACE

GOLD COAST

RIO

FLAMINGO

BILL'S

WESTERN CASUARINA

THE PALMS

◐ JUBILEE!

PLATINUM

CLARION

◐ ATOMIC TESTING MUSEUM

BALLY'S

TUSCANY

MARJORIE BARRICK MUSEUM OF NATURAL HISTORY

BELLAGIO

PARIS

HARD ROCK

UNIVERSITY OF NEVADA, LAS VEGAS

PLANET HOLLYWOOD

CITY CENTER

MONTE CARLO

SHOWCASE MALL

SIGNATURE

NEW YORK NEW YORK

MGM GRAND

COSMOPOLITAN

EXCALIBUR

TROPICANA

HOOTERS

MOTEL 6

LUXOR

0   500 yds

0   500 m

DESERT ROSE

McCARRAN INTERNATIONAL AIRPORT

MANDALAY BAY AND THE HOTEL

FOUR SEASONS

© AVALON TRAVEL

LAS VEGAS

WELCOME TO FABULOUS LAS VEGAS, NEVADA

When someone says "Las Vegas," what image pops into your mind? If you're like many, there's one landmark that encapsulates everything the city represents. Watch any movie or television show set in Las Vegas and you're sure to see it; drive past it at any time of day or night and somebody – road-tripping buddies from Los Angeles or a bachelorette party from Lexington – will be having their pictures taken in front of it.

"It" is The Sign, a beacon that has guided thrill seekers to the Strip for more than 50 years. Its message is simple: "Welcome to Fabulous Las Vegas, Nevada." But the design, imagery, colors, and vocabulary of Betty Willis's creation at 5100 Las Vegas Boulevard South epitomize a trip to the most exciting city in the world. Silver dollars, harking back to a time when slot players actually plunked coins into the machines, pay homage to the precious metal that put Nevada on the map and appear behind the "welcome" letters. The message's

only adjective, *fabulous*, is a distinctly Vegas word: LA may be hip, New York is cosmopolitan, Miami is trendy, but Vegas is "fabulous" – spoken with jazz hands and Liberace enunciation. Bold primary colors and neon flash hint at the visual explosion lying just behind the sign. "Las Vegas" is bold and unapologetic, like the city itself. The sign's diamond shape is a subtle reminder that riches can be yours if Lady Luck smiles. The red-and-gold star promises fun at all hours in a city that never sleeps.

The 25-foot-tall sign even performs double duty: The back reminds motorists to "Drive Carefully; Come Back Soon."

Willis, whose parents were among the first settlers in Las Vegas, considered the sign's design her gift to the city; as a result, she never copyrighted it, so it's in the public domain. You'll see the sign appropriated for souvenirs and event announcements – especially when out-of-towners hold conventions, trade shows, and other happenings in Las Vegas.

observation deck. The more faint-of-heart may want to steer clear not only of the rides but also the resort's double-decker elevators that launch guests to the top of the tower at 1,400 feet per minute. But even agoraphobes should conquer their fears long enough to enjoy the views from the restaurant and bars more than 100 floors up, and the **Chapel in the Clouds** can ensure a heavenly beginning to married life.

If the thrill rides on the observation deck aren't your style, perhaps you'll find the rush of gambling action on the nearly 100,000-square-foot ground-floor casino, two swimming pools (one where you can go topless), and a dozen bars and restaurants more your speed.

Theater of the Stars is home to *American Superstars* (6:30 and 8:30 P.M. Tues.–Wed. and Fri., 7 P.M. Sat.–Sun., $40, $45 including buffet), a song-and-dance tribute show heavy on impressions of recent pop idols and old standbys. It's good, but not as good as *Legends in Concert* at the Imperial Palace. The showroom

also hosts *Bite* (10:30 P.M. Fri.–Wed., $49), a fantasy mix of sexy vampires, hard rock, dancing, and aerial acts. It's a little kitschy, perhaps, but definitely something different.

Roxy's Diner (11 A.M.–11 P.M. Sun.–Thurs., 11 A.M.–midnight Fri.–Sat., $12–20) is a trip back to the malt shop for comfort food and singing waitresses.

Circus Circus

• **Restaurants:** The Garden Grill, Circus Buffet, Casino Café, Pizzeria, Mexitalia X-press, The Steak House, Westside Deli, Rock & Rita's

• **Entertainment:** Circus acts

• **Attractions:** Adventuredome theme park

Quite a contrast to its upscale sister properties in the MGM Mirage family, Circus Circus (2880 Las Vegas Blvd. S., 702/734-0410, $79–200 d) is perhaps the "themiest" of the theme casinos in Las Vegas. While the city briefly

THREE DAYS IN LAS VEGAS

DAY 1

Start at the hotel of your choice, taste, and bankroll. **The Flamingo** (page 209) is a good choice; its room upgrades are hip but moderately priced, and it's in the middle of the action. Get your gambling fix for a few hours before splurging on the **Sterling Brunch** (page 254) at Bally's. Vegas is all about the nightlife, so prepare by taking a nap or at least relaxing by the pool for a couple of hours. Wear sunscreen, and easy on the margaritas!

If you came with your sweetie, head to Paris's **Mon Ami Gabi** (page 255) for a romantic dinner. If it's just you and your pals, a mustardy pastrami sandwich at The Mirage's **Carnegie Deli** (page 205) hits the spot. Only time for one headliner show on this trip, so make it **Blue Man Group** (page 229) at the Venetian.

DAY 2

If the Grand Canyon is on the agenda this trip and the tables were kind on Day 1, book the 7:15 A.M. departure on **Grand Canyon Tour Company**'s 3 in 1 West Rim Air & Ground Voyager Adventure Tour (page 208). You'll see the canyon from above in a plane, from below in a boat, and at eye level on a helicopter descent to the canyon floor. And you'll be back in Vegas by 4 P.M. to take another bite out of the casinos' profit margin.

If the cards and dice didn't fall your way but you still want to visit the Grand Canyon, book **Look Tours** South Rim package (page 209). At $89 including the film at the visitors center's IMAX theater, this tour will give your bankroll a break. And because the bus tour does not drop you off at your hotel until after 10 P.M., you'll be too tuckered to inflict any more damage on your wallet at the craps table.

Rather stay in town? Take in a slice of vintage Vegas. Head downtown, stopping at **Bonanza Gifts** to stock up on Elvis sideburns and Sammy Davis Jr. sunglasses before fueling up with the Gamblers Special breakfast at **Binion's Café** (page 219). While it's daylight, walk over to the **Neon Boneyard** (page 223),

the final resting place of some of Las Vegas's iconic signage. And while you're in the neighborhood, witness the rise and fall of the Mafia in Las Vegas at the Museum of Organized Crime and Law Enforcement, a.k.a. the **Mob Museum** (page 224).

Back at the hotel, change into your tux (or just pretend) and beat it over to the Hilton. Order up a neat bourbon and watch Sinatra try to make it through a rendition of "Luck Be a Lady" while Dino, Joey, and Sammy heckle and cut up from the wings in Sandy Hackett's *Rat Pack Show* (page 233).

DAY 3

It's your last day in Vegas, so live like a high roller. Put in an early wake-up call and submit your breakfast room-service order at the same time. After fresh-squeezed juice and a muffin, go for a swim or a workout in the hotel's gym. You'll want to do justice to that silk shirt or micromini at the club later tonight. Body rejuvenated, it's time to put a dent in the casino's quarterly profit statement. Use the basic optimal blackjack strategy. It's the best way to extend your bankroll, and you might double up if the cards fall your way. Bankroll rejuvenated, you won't feel bad about dropping a few bills at Caesars Palace's **Forum Shops** (page 258). Stock up on club wear, bangles, and baubles for your night on the town.

Never fear if it's Tuesday: Celebrity knows no weeknights at **Pure** (page 207) at Caesars Palace; its Tuesday parties are frequented by national and local stars (be prepared for a long line). **Moon** (page 211), high above the Palms, has plenty to look at, whether you're into cityscape, cheesecake, or beefcake. Locals seem partial to **Blush** (page 201) at Wynn and its themed Tuesday parties. Can't decide where to get your groove on? Caesars Entertainment has got you covered with an all-night pass good for Pure (Caesars Palace), Chateau (Paris), Gallery and Pussycat Dolls Burlesque Salon (Planet Hollywood), Carnival Court (Harrah's), and Crown and VooDoo (Rio).

flirted with selling itself as a family destination in the 1990s, Circus Circus has always courted young families with limited gambling budgets. High above the casino floor, aerialists, clowns, and jugglers regularly entertain children and gambling-weary adults. A carnival-style mid-way lets teenagers test their luck and skill at whacking moles and tossing table-tennis balls while their parents test theirs at splitting aces and rolling sevens downstairs. In keeping with its budget-conscious target market, most of the restaurant and bar selections are cheap and predictable. Circus Circus began life as a casino without a hotel and still hasn't embraced the Vegas-style self-contained vacation experience. Apparently figuring its target customers have traded party time for story time, it eschews Vegas-style shows and nightclubs.

Families with picky eaters will find something for everyone's palate at the **Garden Grill** (2 P.M.–2 A.M. daily, $15–25). In addition to Mexican, Italian, Asian, and American food, a $12 all-you-can-eat prime rib dinner is a good option.

Las Vegas Hilton

• **Restaurants:** Garden of the Dragon, TJ's Steakhouse, The Buffet, Teru Sushi, Casa Nicola, Paradise Café, Benihana, 888 Noodle Bar, Hacienda Margarita, Fortuna
• **Entertainment:** Sandy Hackett's *Rat Pack Show, Sin City Bad Girls, Voices,* Steve Dacri, Andrew Dice Clay, *The King: One Night with You* starring Trent Carlini
• **Attractions:** Sports Zone video arcade
• **Nightlife:** Tempo lounge

The **Hilton** (3000 Paradise Rd., 702/732-5111 or 888/732-7117, $89–300 d) began life as the International in 1969 and has the distinction of being the final stage home to the jumpsuit-and-sideburns Elvis of the 1970s. Today, the Hilton takes advantage of its location adjacent to the Las Vegas Convention Center and its own 220,000 square feet of exhibit and meeting space to cater to the expense-account crowd. The Hilton is gadget-geek

central when the Consumer Electronics Show rolls into town, but bargains can be had when no major conventions reserve blocks of guest rooms, and local horse racing fans brave the convention crowds to soak up the atmosphere of the 30,000-square-foot race and sports book—nearly one-third of the total casino space—and its 30 large-screen TV monitors. The most loyal patrons enjoy reserved parking outside the book, where a larger-than-life statue of Man o' War greets punters. The Hilton's 2008 renovations saw the removal of Star Trek: The Experience, a virtual reality fantasy, and the **Hilton Theater** hosts delightfully eclectic performers. Recent shows have included glam rockers Twisted Sister's Christmas concert, *Carol Burnett Show* alum Tim Conway, and swing-era scion Louis Prima Jr. Sahara Hotel refugee Sandy Hackett's *Rat Pack Show* occupies the **Shimmer Showroom.**

Teru Sushi (5:30–10:30 P.M. Tues.–Sat., $30–40) inside Benihana Village is popular with locals and conventioneers.

CENTER STRIP
Wynn Las Vegas/Encore

• **Restaurants:** Bartolotta Ristorante di Mare, Stratta, The Country Club, Okada, Red 8 Asian Bistro, Pizza Place, Lakeside, SW Steakhouse, Tableau, Terrace Pointe Café, The Buffet, The Café, Wing Lei, Zoozacrackers
• **Entertainment:** *Le Rêve*
• **Attractions:** Penske Wynn Ferrari Maserati, Wynn Country Club
• **Nightlife:** Blush, Tryst

An eponymous monument to indulgence, **Wynn** (3131 Las Vegas Blvd. S., 702/770-7000 or 888/320-9966, $200–400 d) marked the $2.5 billion return of Steve Wynn, "the man who made Las Vegas," to the Strip in 2005. Wynn invites fellow multimillionaires to wallow in the good life and the hoi polloi to sample a taste of how the other half lives: Gaze at Wynn's art, one of the best and most valuable private collections in the world, or drool

LAS VEGAS

© RYAN JERZ

The beautiful and the rich find a home away from home at Steve Wynn's trendy twins.

over the horsepower at the **Ferrari-Maserati dealership** Wynn partly owns. If you're not in the market for an $800,000 ride, also available are logo T-shirts, coffee mugs, and key chains.

Never one to rest on his laurels, Wynn opened the appropriately named Encore Tower next door in 2008. Red must be his favorite color, because the casino area is awash in it. The twins' opulence is matched by the resort's Tom Fazio–designed golf course, open to hotel guests only, of course. Although guests come to explore the privileges of wealth, they can also experience the wonders of nature without the inconvenience of bugs and dirt. Lush plants, waterfalls, lakes, and mountains dominate the pristine landscape.

In addition to the gourmet offerings, don't miss the dim sum at **Red 8 Asian Bistro** (11:30 A.M.–11 P.M. Sun.–Thurs., 11:30 A.M.–1 A.M. Fri.–Sat., $30–45). **Bartolotta** (5:30–10 P.M. daily, $40–55) works as hard on creating a sense of the Mediterranean seaside as it does on its cuisine.

The à la carte menu and especially the tasting menus are quite dear, but the appetizers will give you a sense of Italy for about $25.

Wynn-Encore's formal sophistication belies its location on the site of the old Desert Inn with the unself-conscious swagger Frank, Dino, and Sammy brought to the joint. Both towers boast some of the biggest guest rooms and suites on the Strip, with the usual although better-quality amenities and a few extra touches, like remote-controlled drapes, lights, and air-conditioning. Wynn's guest rooms are appointed in wheat, honey, and other creatively named shades of beige. Encore is a bit more colorful, with the color scheme running toward dark chocolate and cream.

Treasure Island

- **Restaurants:** Isla Mexican Kitchen, Phil's Italian Steak House, Kahunaville, The Buffet at TI, Canter's Deli, Gilley's Saloon, Dance Hall & BBQ, The Coffee Shop, Khotan, Pho, Pizzeria Francesco's, Starbucks, Ben & Jerry's

- **Entertainment:** Treasure Island Theatre, Cirque du Soleil's *Mystère*
- **Attractions:** Sirens of TI
- **Nightlife:** Christian Audigier; Gilley's Saloon, Dance Hall & BBQ; Kahunaville Party Bar; Isla Tequila Bar; Breeze Bar

Much of Treasure Island's (3300 Las Vegas Blvd. S., 702/894-7111 or 800/288-7206, $90–250 d) pirate theme walked the plank when the MGM Mirage property helped Las Vegas shed its family-friendly facade and reclaim its adult playground status. The resort replaced its pirate-skull sign with a more subdued TI logo in a further attempt to distance it from the buccaneer brand that is no longer part of MGM Mirage (Phil Ruffin, owner of the New Frontier, bought it in 2009). The Battle of Buccaneer Bay show out front has been transformed into the sultry **Sirens of TI** (5:30 P.M., 7 P.M., 8:30 P.M., and 10 P.M. daily, free), trading cutlasses for stilettos and swashbuckling for sensuality. Arrive early if you want a good vantage point. Cross Las Vegas Boulevard if you want to get past the hotel during showtime.

Canter's Deli (11 A.M.–midnight Sun.–Thurs., 9 A.M.–midnight Fri.–Sat., $10–20) brings traditional Jewish fare and tradition to Las Vegas from its home base in Los Angles.

The 2,885 standard guest rooms and suites, modernized in 2008, meet Las Vegas resort standards, but nothing more. They're only average in size, but upper floors often sport unforgettable views.

Venetian

- **Restaurants:** AquaKnox, B&B Ristorante, Bouchon, Canaletto, Canyon Ranch Café, Delmonico Steakhouse, Enoteca San Marco, Grand Lux Café Venetian, Noodle Asia, Pinot Brasserie, Postrio, Tao Asian Bistro, Taqueria Cañonita, The Grill at Valentino, Timpano Tavern, Tintoretto's, Trattoria Reggiano, Valentino, Riva Poolside, Zeffirino
- **Entertainment:** Blue Man Group, *Phantom—the Las Vegas Spectacular*
- **Attractions:** Madame Tussauds Las Vegas, Gondola Rides, Streetmosphere
- **Nightlife:** Tao, V Bar, La Scena Lounge

While Caesars Palace bears little resemblance to the realities of ancient Rome and Luxor doesn't really replicate the land of the pharaohs, the **Venetian** (3355 Las Vegas Blvd. S., 702/414-1000 or 866/659-9643, $200–400 d) comes pretty close to capturing the elegance of Venice. An elaborate faux-Renaissance ceiling fresco greets visitors in the hotel lobby, and the sensual treats just keep coming. A life-size streetscape with replicas of the Bridge of Sighs, Doge's Palace, the Grand Canal, and other treasures give the impression that the best of the Queen of the Adriatic has been transplanted in toto. Tranquil rides in authentic gondolas with serenading pilots are perfect for relaxing after a hectic session in the 120,000-square-foot casino. Canal-side, buskers entertain the guests in the **Streetmosphere** (various times and locations daily, free), and the **Grand Canal Shoppes** (10 A.M.–11 P.M. Sun.–Thurs., 10 A.M.–midnight Fri.–Sat.) entice strollers, window shoppers, and serious spenders along winding streetscapes. Don't miss the Fabergé eggs at Regis Galerie and blown-glass figurines at St. Mark's Square.

After you've shopped till you're ready to drop, **Madame Tussauds Interactive Wax Museum** (10 A.M.–10 P.M. daily, adults $25, over age 59 $18, ages 7–12 $15, under age 7 free) invites stargazers for hands-on experiences with their favorite entertainers and sports stars. Then you can dance the night away at **Tao** (nightclub 10 P.M.–late Thurs.–Sat., lounge 5 P.M.–late daily).

Fine dining options abound, but for a change, **Trattorio Reggiano** (11 A.M.–11 P.M. Sun.–Thurs., 11 A.M.–midnight Fri.–Sat., about $20) offers pizza and pasta dishes in a bistro setting. **Canyon Ranch Café** (7 A.M.–3 P.M. daily, $15–25) is a good bet for a light breakfast.

The Venetian spares no expense in the hotel department. Its 4,027 suites are tastefully appointed with Italian (of course) marble, and they're big at 700 square feet. They include

LAS VEGAS

WORLD SERIES OF POKER

Millions of dollars are on the line as the top pros and lucky amateurs bluff, raise, and go all-in for their shot at poker immortality in the **World Series of Poker.** The tournament lasts nearly the whole month of July, with the final table of the main event played in November.

It all began in 1970, after a week of high-stakes poker in Reno, a few dozen gamblers decided Johnny Moss was the best among them and crowned him the poker world champion.

Thirty-three years later, a regular guy, appropriately named Chris Moneymaker, won a no-limit hold 'em poker tournament in Las Vegas and became the newest world champion. These events, separated by a generation and half a state, mark the watershed events in one of the most astonishing gambling revolutions in history. Both brought unprecedented attention to a game of skill and chance that had been played at kitchen tables around the world but had never been seen as a serious casino endeavor. When "Amarillo Slim" Preston won the second World Series of Poker, he bested 11 other players. Fortunately for the "sport," Preston is engaging, intelligent, and likes the sound of his own voice. He relished the role as poker champion and poker promoter, talking up the game and the World

Series with Johnny Carson and appearing as himself in several films.

Moneymaker, a Nashville accountant and pretty good Thursday night poker player with the boys, got into the main event by winning a "satellite tournament" with a $40 entry fee. His winner's share was $2.5 million. Moneymaker's everyman status, his victory over seasoned poker pros, the tournament being televised by ESPN, and the fortune he won spurred other quarter-ante players to try to match his success. The World Series of Poker exploded, as did the World Poker Tour, a series of televised no-limit events, often with million-dollar payouts.

In 2006 the also appropriately named Jamie Gold (we're thinking of changing our name to "Cash" and entering the tournament this year) topped 8,772 other players who ponied up $10,000 each to play in the World Series main event. Gold took home $12 million. That marked the largest field to date, as soon after many online poker sites began barring U.S. players from their satellite tournaments and other real-money games to comply with federal law.

Harrah's Entertainment owns the World Series of Poker, the only asset it kept after buying, then selling, Binion's Horseshoe in 2004.

roomy bedrooms with two queen beds and comfy sitting rooms.

Palazzo

- **Restaurants:** Carnevino, Cut, Lavo, Morels French Steakhouse & Bistro, Table 10, SushiSamba, Zine Noodles Dim Sum, Canyon Ranch Grill, Dal Toro Ristorante, Dos Caminos, Espressamente Illy, First Food & Bar, Grand Lux, Lagasse's Stadium, Solaro, Sweet Surrender
- **Entertainment:** *Jersey Boys,* Palazzo Showroom
- **Attractions:** Lamborghini dealership and showroom

- **Nightlife:** Lavo Nightclub, The Lounge at Dos Caminos, Salute Lounge, Fusion Mixology Bar, Laguna Champagne Bar, Double Helix Wine Bar

In 2007 the colorful Sheldon Adelson, chairman of Las Vegas Sands Corporation, unveiled the Venetian's sister property, The Palazzo (3325 Las Vegas Blvd. S., 702/607-7777 or 866/263-3001, $200–400 d), next door. In the latest broadside in Adelson's rivalry with Steve Wynn, Adelson expanded his vision during construction to ensure the Palazzo towers more than 100 feet over Wynn Las Vegas. In another swipe at Wynn and his Ferrari showroom, the Palazzo houses Las Vegas's Lamborghini dealership.

The hotel lobby is bathed in natural light from an 80-foot dome, and half of the 100,000-square-foot casino is smoke-free, part of the Palazzo's efforts in achieving Leadership in Energy and Environmental Design status.

The smell of Corinthian leather emanates from the high-end boutiques at **The Shoppes at the Palazzo** (10 A.M.–11 P.M. Sun.–Thurs., 10 A.M.–midnight Fri.–Sat.). Prada, Manolo Blahnik, and Barneys New York draw in the fashionistas, and aesthetes of all stripes will find something, from collectible books to haute and hot accessories.

Sugarcane (7 P.M.–2 A.M. Fri.–Sat.) is a mash-up of Brazilian and Asian cultures with a dance floor and eclectic entertainers. The North African bathhouse-themed **Lavo** (10 P.M.–late Tues.–Sun.) will attend to your late-night dining, dancing, and drinking (but not bathing) desires. Lavo's restaurant (702/791-1818) offers patio dining with a view of Sirens of TI across the way.

The Palazzo is a gourmand's dream, with a handful of four-star establishments. The refreshing take on traditional Mexican fare at **Dos Caminos** (11 A.M.–11 P.M. Mon.–Fri., 10 A.M.–4 P.M. Sat.–Sun., $15–25) is highlighted by made-to-order guacamole and tequila tastings.

Accommodations are all suites, with sunken living rooms and sumptuous beds that would make it tough to leave the room if not for the lure of the Strip.

Harrah's

- **Restaurants:** Café at Harrah's, Carnaval Court Bar & Grill, Flavors Buffet, KGB, Ming's Table, Oyster Bar at Harrah's, Starbucks, The Range Steakhouse, Toby Keith's I Love This Bar & Grill
- **Entertainment:** Rita Rudner, Improv Comedy Club, Mac King Comedy Magic Show, *Legends in Concert*
- **Nightlife:** Carnival Court

Once the world's largest Holiday Inn, then an antebellum riverboat, Harrah's (3475 Las Vegas Blvd. S., 800/898-8651, $60–400 d) reinvented itself in 1996 with a Mardi Gras theme. **Carnaval Court,** outside on the Strip's sidewalk, capitalizes on the street-party atmosphere with live bands and juggling bartenders. Just inside, the **Piano Bar** invites aspiring comedians and singers to the karaoke stage weekend evenings, and dueling keyboardists take over at 9 P.M. each night.

The rotating acts at **The Improv Comedy Club** (8:30 P.M. and 10:30 P.M. Tues.–Sun.) offer witty, sometimes gritty, observations on life and relationships.

The country superstar lends his name and unapologetic patriotism to **Toby Keith's I Love This Bar & Grill** (11:30 A.M.–2 A.M. Sun.–Thurs., 11:30 A.M.–3 A.M. Fri.–Sat., $12–20). Try the freedom fries. **Ming's Table** (11:30 A.M.–11 P.M. Sun.–Thurs., 11:30 A.M.–midnight Fri.–Sat., $15–30) features pan-Asian specialties.

For a while it seemed Harrah's was unwilling to engage in the one-upmanship of its colleagues, content instead to carve out a niche as a middle-of-the-action, middle-of-the-road, middle-of-the-price-scale option. But now it's exploring plans to build a pedestrian thoroughfare with bars and shops behind its property—Harrah's own private urban renewal investment. Called Project Linq, it would be highlighted by a 550-foot Ferris wheel, giving riders unimpeded views of the Strip.

The Mirage

- **Restaurants:** B. B. King Blues Club, Blizz Frozen Yogurt, BLT Burger, Stack, Fin, Kokomo's, Samba Brazilian Steakhouse, Onda, Cravings, California Pizza Kitchen, Coconuts Ice Cream Shop, Japonais, Roasted Bean, Roasted Bean Express, Paradise Café, Carnegie Deli, Starbucks
- **Entertainment:** *LOVE,* Terry Fator
- **Attractions:** Secret Garden, Dolphin Habitat, Mirage volcano
- **Nightlife:** 1 Oak, Revolution Lounge, Rhumbar, King Ink Tattoo Studio and Bar

© RYAN JERZ

It's no illusion: Steve Wynn's masterpiece helped return Las Vegas to its grown-up sensibilities.

Steve Wynn reinvented Las Vegas and ushered in a building boom on Las Vegas Boulevard with the opening of his first major Strip property in 1989. While grand and attention-grabbing, the Mirage (3400 Las Vegas Blvd. S., 702/791-7111 or 800/627-6667, $150–300 d) was the first understated megaresort, starting a trend that signifies Las Vegas's return to mature pursuits. This Bali-Ha'i–themed paradise lets guests bask in the wonders of nature alongside the sophistication and pampering of resort life. More an oasis than a mirage, the hotel greets visitors with exotic bamboo, orchids, banana trees, secluded grottoes, and peaceful lagoons. Dolphins, white tigers, stingrays, sharks, and a volcano provide livelier sights.

1 Oak (10:30 A.M.–4 A.M. Fri.–Sat.) has three rooms with two different kinds of music and crowded dance floors. **King Ink Tattoo Studio and Bar** (11 A.M.–4 A.M. daily) doesn't really mix alcohol and needles—Mario Barth's parlor is completely separate from the tattoo art–inspired barroom.

Headliners and a Beatles production show are the high-end entertainment options, but **B. B. King's Blues Club** (6:30 A.M.–2 A.M. Sun.–Thurs., 6:30 A.M.–4 A.M. Fri.–Sat.) dishes out delta blues and other genres nightly, with Cajun and creole fare. **Stack** (5–10 P.M. Sun., Tues., and Thurs., 5 P.M.–midnight Mon. and Fri.–Sat., $35–50) serves variations of what Mom used to make (pigs in a blanket, Shake 'n Bake chicken, a grown-up version of Tater Tots) and what she never would have attempted (sashimi, calamari).

Since a 2008 renovation, the Mirage's guest rooms have jettisoned the South Pacific theme in favor of tasteful appointments and some of the most comfortable beds in town. The facelift gave Mirage guest rooms a modern and relaxing feel in browns, blacks, and splashes of tangerine and ruby.

Imperial Palace

- **Restaurants:** Emperor's Buffet, Pizza Palace, Hash House a Go Go, Embers, Burger

Palace, Quesadilla, Ginseng Barbecue, Betty's Diner

- **Entertainment:** *Human Nature, Matsuri, Divas Las Vegas*
- **Attractions:** Automobile Collection, King's Ransom Museum
- **Nightlife:** Karaoke Club, Rockhouse Bar and Nightclub

Built by the intriguing Ralph Englestad, one of the last holdouts among independent casino owners on the Strip, the Imperial Palace (3535 Las Vegas Blvd. S., 702/731-3311 or 800/351-7400, $74–300 d) was added to the Harrah's family in 2006.

The IP started the trend of entertainment at the tables. Its celebrity look-alikes deal blackjack in the **Dealertainers Pit.** The Imperial Theater is home to *Matsuri* (4 P.M. Sat.–Wed., 7 P.M. and 9:30 P.M. Fri.), a celebration of Japanese athleticism and acrobatics.

Embers (5–10 P.M. Thurs.–Mon., $15–30) is the choice for the meat-and-potatoes crowd, and **Hash House a Go Go** (7 A.M.–11 P.M. Sun.–Thurs., 7 A.M.–2 A.M. Fri.–Sat., $20–35) is the IP's take on comfort food.

Like Harrah's, the Imperial Palace is a low-cost alternative surrounded by upscale neighbors. An unassuming pagoda facade hints at the interior's unassuming Asian decor but gives little clue that it's one of the largest hotels in the world, with 2,640 guest rooms.

(Caesars Palace

- **Restaurants:** Augustus Café, Beijing Noodle #9, Bradley Ogden, Cafe Lago, Cypress Street Marketplace, Guy Savoy, Hyakumi Japanese Restaurant & Sushi Bar, Mesa Grill, Munch, Neros, Payard Pâtisserie & Bistro, Rao's, Sea Harbour, Serendipity 3, Trevi, La Salsa, Max Brenner, Chocolate by a Bald Man, The Palm, Planet Hollywood, Spago, The Cheesecake Factory, BOA Steakhouse, Il Mulino, Joe's Seafood, Prime Steak & Stone Crab, Sushi Roku, Cafe Della Spiga
- **Entertainment:** Céline Dion, Matt Goss

- **Attractions:** *Fall of Atlantis* and *Festival Fountain Show,* aquarium
- **Nightlife:** Pure, Cleopatra's Barge

It's not hard to imagine that Rome would look a lot like Las Vegas had it survived this long. But since the empire doesn't exist, Jay Sarno had to invent Caesars Palace (3570 Las Vegas Blvd. S., 866/227-5938, $200–600 d), incorporating all the ancient civilization's decadence and overindulgence and adding a few thousand slot machines. Sarno's palace—there's no apostrophe in the name because Sarno wanted to treat all his guests like Caesars—opened with great fanfare in 1966. It has ruled the Strip ever since. And like the empire, it continues to expand, now boasting 3,348 guest rooms in six towers and 140,000 square feet of gaming space accented with marble, fountains, gilding, and royal reds. Wander the grounds searching for reproductions of some of the world's most famous statuary. The eagle-eyed might spy Michelangelo's *David* and Giovanni da Bologna's *Rape of the Sabines* as well as the Brahma Shrine.

The casino is so big that the website includes a "slot finder" application so gamblers can navigate to their favorite machines.

Cleopatra's Barge (6 P.M.–3 A.M. daily), a floating lounge, attracts the full spectrum of the 21-and-over crowd for late-night bacchanalias, while **Pure** (10 P.M.–4 A.M. Tues. and Thurs.–Sun.) accommodates a mostly younger crowd of up to 2,400 at a time and keeps them all happy by spinning different dance music in different areas of the club.

All roads lead to the **Forum Shops** (10 A.M.–11 P.M. Sun.–Thurs., 10 A.M.–midnight Fri.–Sat.), a collection of famous designer stores, specialty boutiques, and restaurants. Not all the shops are as froufrou as you might expect, but an hour here can do some serious damage to your bankroll. You'll also find the *Fall of Atlantis* and *Festival Fountain Show* (hourly 10 A.M.–11 P.M. Sun.–Thurs., 10 A.M.–midnight Fri.–Sat., free), a multisensory, multimedia depiction of the gods' wrath. The saltwater **aquarium**

GRAND CANYON TOURS

Nearly a dozen tour companies relay visitors from Vegas to and through the Grand Canyon via a variety of conveyances – buses, airplanes, helicopters, off-road vehicles, and rafts. Coupons and discounts for online reservation and off-season bookings are plentiful; it is not uncommon to book tours at less than half the rack rates listed here. Most bus tours snake through a Joshua tree forest, crossing the Colorado River on the newly constructed Hoover Dam Bypass Bridge with a stop for photos of the dam and Black Canyon below.

GRAND CANYON TOUR COMPANY

Billing itself as the "original," Grand Canyon Tours (702/655-6060 or 800/2-CANYON – 800/222-6966, www.grandcanyontours.com) packs plenty of sightseeing into its 14-hour **National Park South Rim Bus Tour** ($180). A shuttle collects Strip and most other hotel guests at 6:30 A.M., offers them a light snack, and gets them on the road to the canyon by 7:15 A.M. The bus arrives just in time for a buffet lunch (included) at Grand Canyon Railway in Williams, Arizona, then turns passengers loose for four hours before returning to Las Vegas around 9:30 P.M. The **Indian Country West Rim Bus Tour** ($190) features the same sights en route and four hours at the canyon, with lunch on the rim or at **Hualapai Ranch.** The tour begins with hotel pick up at 6:30 A.M.; the bus pulls back into Las Vegas at 5 P.M.

The company's helicopter tours cut down the commute, leaving more time at the canyon and allowing an earlier return. The choppers depart both from Las Vegas and Boulder City, 30 miles south. The "basic" **Grand Canyon and Hoover Dam Helicopter Tour** ($349) takes off up to

nine times 7 A.M.–5:30 P.M. daily, skimming not only Hoover Dam and the canyon but also the Black Mountains, Valley of Fire, and the Strip during the 1.5-hour flight. Most tours are customizable, allowing customers to add tickets to the Grand Canyon Skywalk, Grand Canyon West Ranch, horseback rides, helicopter landings on the canyon floor, and float trips down the Colorado River. Grand Canyon Tour Company's **3 in 1 West Rim Air & Ground Voyager Adventure Tour** ($400) puts all those extras in one 7.5-hour tour. Departing at 7:15 A.M., 9:15 A.M., and noon daily, the excursion begins with an airplane flight to and scenic flight over the Grand Canyon, with views of Hoover Dam, Lake Mead, and the Colorado River valley along the way. After disembarking at Grand Canyon West, customers board a helicopter for the 4,000-foot descent to the canyon floor, where they board a boat for a 20-minute river cruise. Back on the rim, the tour continues by bus to Guano Point.

LOOK TOURS

One of the longest Grand Canyon tours available from Las Vegas, the **North Rim Ground Overnight Trip** ($430-500) from Look (4285 N. Rancho Dr., 702/233-1627 or 800/LOOK-TOURS – 800/566-5868, www.looktours.com) flies guests via fixed-wing aircraft over Lake Mead and through the canyon's inner gorge, landing at the Bar-10 Ranch. Overnight guests bunk down in covered wagons, with all the comforts of the prairie, circa 1880. The North Rim ranch serves as base camp for canyon hikes and serves a hearty dinner and breakfast. As on many of Look's tours, guests can add activities such as horseback riding or ATV safaris for an additional charge.

is also nearby. Feeding times (1:15 P.M. and 5:15 P.M. daily, tours 3:15 P.M. daily) offer the best views of the sharks and other denizens of the deep.

If you (or your wallet) tire of Caesars's high-on-the-hog dining, nosh on a burger or salad at the **Cypress Street Marketplace** (11 A.M.–11 P.M. daily) alfresco, agora-style.

With so many guest rooms in six towers, it seems Caesars is always renovating somewhere. The sixth tower, Octavius, opened in 2010, and the Palace Tower was overhauled in 2009. Most newer guest rooms are done in tan, wood, and marble. Older guest rooms still feature Roman niceties like plaster busts and columns.

Look's "basic" tour to the **South Rim** (6 A.M.–10 P.M. daily, $79) picks you up and drops you off at your hotel and includes a box lunch and three hours of free time after a 15-minute photo-op at the Hoover Dam bypass bridge and the bus ride to the Grand Canyon. Add-ons include admission to the IMAX theater at the canyon's National Geographic Visitors Center ($10) and a 35-minute helicopter ride ($170). Tour-it-yourselfers can rent an SUV from Look ($170 pp, 2-person minimum, 7 A.M., 8 A.M., or 9 A.M. daily) for a leisurely 24-hour exploration of the wonders of the West Rim. Look fetches you from your hotel in the morning and delivers you to your five-passenger vehicle. The tour price includes entry onto Native American land, a Native American buffet or Cowboy Cookout lunch, shuttle transportation from the Grand Canyon West Airport (parking $20) to Guano Point and Eagle Point, an interactive map, literature, coloring books, and a cooler bag with bottled water. Riders are free to spend their 24 hours as they see fit.

MAVERICK HELICOPTER TOURS

Maverick (6075 Las Vegas Blvd. S., 702/261-0007 or 888/261-4414, and 1410 Jet Stream Dr., Suite 100, Henderson, 702/405-4300 or 888/261-4414, www.maverickhelicopter.com) shuttles its customers to the canyon using only Eco-Star helicopters. Its popular **Grand Canyon and Rafting Tour** (7 A.M.–4:30 P.M. daily, $569) begins with the pilot greeting passengers and conducting a quick orientation. Once settled with their voice-activated headsets for clear communication with each other and the pilot, passengers listen as the pilot narrates the journey to, through, and

into the Grand Canyon. Setting down on the canyon floor, passengers enjoy a continental breakfast and champagne (or water) toast. The return flight ends in Boulder City, where Black Canyon River Rafting Company picks up passengers and delivers them downriver from Hoover Dam for a motorized raft trip down the Colorado River. After lunch, the watery portion of the trip continues to Willow Beach, once an Anasazi trading post and current site of a popular marina, campground, and rainbow trout hatchery.

Maverick partners with Pink Jeep Tours for its **Above, Beyond & Below Tour** (6 A.M.–5 P.M. daily, $364), which includes a guided road tour to the West Rim, with a stop on the bypass bridge for Hoover Dam photos. Maverick then takes over, taking guests on a slow descent to the bottom of the Grand Canyon.

GRAND CANYON WEST TOURS

Several other companies in Las Vegas offer guided tours to Grand Canyon West, as well as the South Rim, and other spots. The concierge desk at most of the Strip hotels can help you book a tour and give you directions.

One of the better tours is the 11-hour-plus **Mysterious West** tour ($169–375) of Grand Canyon West offered by **SweeTours** (6363 S. Pecos Rd., Suite 106, Las Vegas, 702/456-9200, http://sweetours.com). Depending on how much you want to pay, you'll travel by bus with about 50 other people, or by SUV with a smaller group, to the West Rim, where you can choose among several packages, including a helicopter and boat tour of the western canyon. SweeTours also offers excellent tours of the South Rim and Hoover Dam.

Flamingo

- **Restaurants:** Tropical Breeze, Paradise Garden Buffet, Jimmy Buffett's Margaritaville, Steakhouse46, Hamada of Japan, Java Coast, food court, Pink Bean, Beach Club, The Burger Joint
- **Entertainment:** George Wallace, Nathan

Burton Comedy Magic, Donny and Marie, Vinnie Favorito, *X Burlesque*
- **Attractions:** Wildlife Habitat
- **Nightlife:** Sin City Brewing Co.

Named for Virginia Hill, the long-legged girlfriend of Benjamin "don't call me Bugsy" Siegel, the Flamingo (3555 Las Vegas Blvd. S.,

702/733-3111 or 800/732-2111, $50–200 d) has at turns embraced and shunned its gangster ties, which stretch back to the 1960s. After Bugsy's (sorry, Mr. Siegel) Flamingo business practices ran afoul of the Cosa Nostra and led to his untimely end, Meyer Lansky took over. Mob ties continued to dog the property even after Kirk Kerkorian bought it to use as a training ground for his pride and joy, the International (now the Las Vegas Hilton). Hilton Hotels bought the Flamingo in 1970, giving the joint the legitimacy it needed. Today, its art deco architecture and pink-and-orange neon beckon pedestrians and conjure images of aging mafiosi lounging by the pool, their tropical shirts half unbuttoned to reveal hairy chests and gold ropes. And that image seems just fine with the current owner, Caesars Entertainment, in a Vegas where the mob era is remembered almost fondly. Siegel's penthouse suite, behind the current hotel, has been replaced by the **Flamingo Wildlife Habitat** (8 A.M.–dusk daily, free), where pheasants, a crane, ibis, swans, and, of course, Chilean flamingos luxuriate amid riparian plants and verdant streams.

Vinnie Favorito (8 P.M. daily, $60–71) channels Don Rickles in Bugsy's Cabaret, followed by the naughty nymphs of *X Burlesque* in the same venue (10 P.M. daily, $54–66). The all-ages crowd will enjoy **Nathan Burton Comedy Magic** (4 P.M. Tues. and Fri.–Sun., $22–49) in the Flamingo Showroom.

Guests can search for their lost shaker of salt in paradise at **Jimmy Buffett's Margaritaville** (8 A.M.–2 A.M. Sun.–Fri., 8 A.M.–3 A.M. Sat., $20–30) while people-watching on the Strip and noshing on jambalaya and cheeseburgers.

The Flamingo recently completed the transformation of many of its guest rooms into "Go Rooms," dressed in swanky mahogany and white with bold swatches of hot pink. The rooms are swank and savvy with high-end entertainment systems. Suite options are just as colorful and include 42-inch TVs, wet bars, and all the other Vegas-sational accoutrements.

Rio

- **Restaurants:** All-American Bar & Grille, Búzios, Café Martorano, Carnival World Buffet, Gaylord, Hamada Asian, Mah Jong, Sao Paulo Cafe, Sports Kitchen, The Village Seafood Buffet, VooDoo Steak & Lounge, McFadden's Irish Pub, Starbucks, Wetzel's Pretzels
- **Entertainment:** Penn & Teller, Chippendales
- **Attractions:** Show in the Sky
- **Nightlife:** I-Bar, Flirt Lounge, VooDoo Lounge

A hit from the beginning, this carnival just off the Strip started expanding almost before its first 400-suite tower was complete in 1990. Three towers and 2,100 more suites later, the party's still raging with terrific buffets, beautiful-people magnet bars, and steamy shows. "Bevertainers" at the Rio (3700 W. Flamingo Rd., 866/746-7671, $80–200 d) push the stereotype of the starving artist as waitress to the hilt, taking turns on mini stages scattered throughout the casino to belt out tunes or gyrate to the music. Dancers and other performers may materialize at your slot machine to take your mind off your losses.

The South American vibe comes to life with the **Show in the Sky** (hourly 7 P.M.–midnight Thurs.–Sun., free). Formerly a pseudo-family-friendly parade of bead tossing and floats, the show has morphed into a naughty, scantily clad writhe fest. For $12.95, guests can get into costume and become part of the show. Three unique productions keep the show fresh. **Flirt Lounge** (6:30 P.M.–late Thurs.–Tues.) and its all-male waitstaff keep the Rio's Ultimate Girls Night Out churning. **VooDoo Lounge** (9 P.M.–late daily), 51 stories up, is just as hip.

Búzio's (5–11 P.M. Wed.–Sun., $30–50) has great crab-shack appetizers and buttery lobster and steak entrées.

All of the Rio's guest rooms are suites—two small sofas and a coffee table replace the uncomfortable easy chair found in most standard guest rooms. Rio suites measure about

650 square feet. The hotel's center-Strip location and room-tall windows make for exciting views. The his-and-hers dressing and vanity areas are a nice touch.

LOWER STRIP
The Palms

• **Restaurants:** Alizé, Blue Agave Oyster & Chile Bar, Garduños, Little Buddha, N9NE, Nove Italiano, 24/Seven, Bistro Buffet, food court
• **Entertainment:** Playboy Comedy Club
• **Nightlife:** Rain, Ghostbar, Moon, Playboy Club

The expression "party like a rock star" could have been invented for The Palms (4321 W. Flamingo Rd., 702/942-7777, $120–400 d). Penthouse views, Playboy bunnies, and starring roles in MTV's *The Real World: Las Vegas* and Bravo's *Celebrity Poker Showdown* have brought notoriety and stars to the property's fantasy suites and recording studio. **The Pearl** regularly hosts rock concerts, and Playmate appearances at the **Playboy Comedy Club** (9 P.M. Thurs.–Fri., 8 P.M. and 10 P.M. Sat., $40–60) add some sex appeal to the stand-up. The **Moon** nightclub (11 P.M.–late Tues., Thurs., and Sat.) is three floors up from the Playboy Club in the same tower, giving it a commanding view of the stars. **Ghostbar** (8 P.M.–late daily) is small, with a capacity of 300, and has vistas of the Strip and a bird's-eye perspective on the pool area through a section of transparent floor. For a more down-to-earth party experience, you can't go wrong with **Rain** (11 P.M.–late Fri.–Sat.) and its light shows and fireballs over the dance floor.

The Palms has plenty of gourmet restaurant choices, but to give your wallet a bit of a break, try the dark, intimate **Little Buddha** (5:30–11 P.M. Sun.–Thurs., 5:30 P.M.–midnight Fri.–Sat., $25–45). The cuisine is French-Chinese fusion.

The Fantasy Tower houses the Playboy section and the fantasy suites, while the original tower offers large guest rooms. They are nothing special to look at, but the feathery beds and luxurious comforters make it easy to roll over and go back to sleep, even if you're not nursing a hangover. The newest tower, Palms Place, is part of the Las Vegas "condotel" trend. Its 599 studios and one-bedrooms are highly recommended.

Bellagio

• **Restaurants:** Café Bellagio, Café Gelato, Circo, FIX, Jasmine, Jean-Philippe Pâtisserie, Le Cirque, Michael Mina, Noodles, Todd English's Olives, Palio, Palio Pronto, Petrossian Bar, Picasso, Pool Café, Prime, Snacks, The Buffet, Sensi, Yellowtail Sushi Restaurant & Bar
• **Entertainment:** Cirque du Soleil's *O*
• **Attractions:** The Fountains at Bellagio, The Conservatory, Bellagio Gallery of Fine Art, Tuscany Kitchen
• **Nightlife:** The Bank, Caramel

With nearly 4,000 guest rooms and suites, Bellagio (3600 Las Vegas Blvd. S., 702/693-7444 or 888/987-6667, $180–500 d) boasts a population larger than the village perched on Lake Como from which it borrows its name. And to keep pace with its Italian namesake, Bellagio created an 8.5-acre lake between the hotel and Las Vegas Boulevard. The view of the lake and its **Fountains at Bellagio** (3 P.M.–midnight Mon.–Fri., noon–midnight Sat.–Sun.) are free, as is the aromatic fantasy that is **Bellagio Conservatory** (24 hours daily). And the **Bellagio Gallery of Fine Art** (10 A.M.–6 P.M. Sun.–Tues. and Thurs., 10 A.M.–7 P.M. Wed. and Fri.–Sat., $10–15) would be a bargain at twice the price—you can spend an edifying day at one of the world's priciest resorts (including a cocktail and lunch) for less than $50. Even if you don't spring for gallery admission, art demands your attention throughout the hotel and casino. The glass flower petals in Dale Chihuly's *Fiori di Como* sculpture bloom from the lobby ceiling, foreshadowing the opulent experiences to come.

The display of artistry continues but the bargains end at **Via Bellagio** (10 A.M.–midnight

Bellagio perches on a lagoon on the Las Vegas Strip.

daily), the resort's shopping district, including heavyweight retailers Armani, Prada, Chanel, Tiffany, and their ilk.

Would you like not only to eat like an Italian but to cook like one too? **The Tuscany Kitchen** (by reservation only, 15-person minimum, $75–150) is your own private Food Network special. World-class chefs demonstrate the preparation of Tuscan delights, and generous samples are included.

Befitting Bellagio's world-class status, intriguing and expensive restaurants abound. **Sensi** (5–10 P.M. Mon.–Thurs., 5–10:30 P.M. Fri.–Sun.) offers a worldwide menu heavy on Italian and seafood for moderate prices. Authentic Asian dishes are the specialty at **Noodles** (11 A.M.–2 A.M. daily), another affordable option.

The Bank (10:30 P.M.–4 A.M. Thurs.–Sun.) is a busy upscale nightclub, with most partiers opting for bottle service and the table space and legroom it buys. **Caramel** (5 P.M.–4 A.M. daily) is a bit more laid-back but no less sophisticated. Primarily a wine and martini bar, it caters to the before- and after-show crowd.

Bellagio's tower rooms are the epitome of luxury, with Italian marble, oversize bathtubs, remote-controlled drapes, Egyptian-cotton sheets, and 510 square feet in which to spread out. The hunter green and mauve decor is a refreshing change from the goes-with-everything beige and the camouflages-all-stains paisley often found on the Strip.

Paris

- **Restaurants:** Café Belle Madeleine, Eiffel Tower Restaurant, Les Artistes Steakhouse, Mon Ami Gabi, Le Provençal, Le Village Buffet, du Parc, Le Café Île St. Louis, JJ's Boulangerie, La Creperie, Sugar Factory, Le Burger Brasserie Sports Grille

- **Entertainment:** Barry Manilow, Anthony Cools

- **Attractions:** Eiffel Tower

- **Nightlife:** Napoleon's Dueling Piano Bar,

© RYAN JERZ

Gustav's Casino Bar, Le Cabaret, Le Central Lobby Bar, Le Bar du Sport

Designers used Gustav Eiffel's original drawings to ensure that the half-size version that anchors Paris Las Vegas (3655 Las Vegas Blvd. S., 877/242-6753, $120–300 d) conformed—down to the last cosmetic rivet—to the original. That attention to detail prevails throughout this property, which works hard to evoke the City of Light, from large-scale reproductions of the Arc de Triomphe, Champs Élysées, and Louvre to more than half a dozen French restaurants. The tower is perhaps the most romantic spot in town to view the Strip; you'll catch your breath as the elevator whisks you to the observation deck 460 feet up, then have it taken away again by the lights of the resorts up and down one of the most famous skylines in the world. Back at street level, the cobblestone lanes and brass streetlights of **Le Boulevard** (10 A.M.–11 P.M. daily) invite shoppers into quaint shops and "sidewalk" patisseries. The casino offers its own attractions, not the least of which is the view of the Eiffel Tower's base jutting through the ceiling.

The **Paris Theatre** hosts headliners. With the showroom named after him, **Anthony Cools—The Uncensored Hypnotist** (9 P.M. Tues. and Thurs.–Sun., $54–75) appears destined for a long run, cajoling his mesmerized subjects through very adult simulations.

Waiters at **Le Provençal** (5–10:30 P.M. daily, $15–30) serenade diners with traditional French and Italian songs between the caprese salad and the bouillabaisse.

Standard guest rooms in the 33-story tower are decorated in a rich earth-tone palette and have marble baths. There's nothing Left Bank bohemian about them, however. The guest rooms exude little flair and little personality, but the simple, quality furnishings make Paris a moderately priced option in the middle of a top-dollar neighborhood.

Hard Rock

- **Restaurants:** Ago, Johnny Smalls, Mr.

Lucky's 24/7, Nobu, Rare 120, Pink Taco, Starbucks, Espumoso
- **Entertainment:** The Rogue Joint
- **Nightlife:** Wasted Space, Vanity

The Palms and a few others have stolen a bit of the Hard Rock's (4455 Paradise Rd., 800/473-7625, $200–500 d) mojo, but young stars and the media-savvy 20-somethings who idolize them contribute to the frat party in the casino and the spring-break atmosphere poolside. The casino is shaped like a record (although if your music collection dates back to records, this probably isn't the place for you), with the gaming tables and machines in the "record label" and the shops and restaurants in the "grooves."

Contemporary and classic rockers regularly grace the stage at the **Rogue Joint** and party with their fans at **Wasted Space** (9 P.M.–4 A.M. Wed.–Sun.). **Vanity** (10 P.M.–4 A.M. Thurs.–Sun.) is a little more refined, with a 20,000-crystal chandelier that showers sparkles on the sunken dance floor.

The provocatively named **Pink Taco** (11 A.M.–10 P.M. Sun.–Thurs., 11 A.M.–midnight Fri.–Sat.) dishes up Mexican and Caribbean specialties.

Undersize and always in demand, the Hard Rock Hotel has undergone major expansion and renovation in the last few years, including construction of HRH Towers, an effort to attract more mature visitors. The resort's 1,500 guest rooms are decorated in warm hues and include Bose CD sound systems and plasma TVs.

Monte Carlo

- **Restaurants:** Andre's, Buffet, BRAND Steakhouse, d.vino, Diablo's Cantina, Dragon Noodle Co., Café, Monaco Garden Food Court, The Pub
- **Entertainment:** Jabbawockeez
- **Nightlife:** BRAND Lounge, Diablo's Lounge

As evidenced by all the marble and chandeliers we've come to expect from a European-themed

Vegas resort, Monte Carlo (3770 Las Vegas Blvd. S., 702/730-7777 or 800/311-8999, $100–300 d) doesn't compromise on quality. But its location, entertainment, dining, and prices make it a good choice for families seeking a happy medium. Parents will appreciate the continental theme, and its flair is understated in comparison to Bellagio and Paris. Kids and teens especially will enjoy the pool, **Easy River,** and the wave pool. The magic and comedy impersonator shows are tame by Vegas standards.

Diablo's Cantina (11 A.M.–1 A.M. daily) opens onto the Strip for terrific people-watching. Margaritas, sangrias, and Mexican-tiled floors carry through the south-of-the-border party atmosphere.

High-end shops dot **Street of Dreams** (10 A.M.–11 P.M. daily), tempting big winners with jewelry and motorcycles and enticing the rest to smother their losses in decadent designer cupcakes.

With 3,000 guest rooms, Monte Carlo provides the casino-resort feel, but room rates are reasonable, especially for families not willing to settle for the bare-bones kitsch of Circus Circus. Standard guest rooms include dark wood furniture, overstuffed chairs, and brass bathroom fixtures. The layout allows you to reach your room without a detour through the casino, so you can more easily resist the urge to drunkenly throw down a Benjamin on the hard four as you stumble through after a night of revelry.

New York New York

- **Restaurants:** America, Chin Chin Café, Coney Island Pavilion, Gallagher's Steakhouse, Gonzalez y Gonzalez, Greenberg's Deli, Il Fornaio, Nine Fine Irishmen, Schrafft's Ice Cream, Village Eateries
- **Entertainment:** Cirque du Soleil's *Zumanity,* The Bar at Times Square
- **Attractions:** The Roller Coaster
- **Nightlife:** Rok Vegas, Coyote Ugly

One look at this loving tribute to the city that never sleeps and you won't be able to fuhgedaboutit. From the city skyline outside (the skyscrapers contain the resort's hotel rooms) to laundry hanging between crowded faux brownstones indoors, New York New York (3790 Las Vegas Blvd. S., 866/815-4365, $200–500 d) will have even grizzled Gothamites feeling like they've come home again. Window air conditioners in the Greenwich Village apartments evoke the city's gritty heat. A more poignant sight, the fence surrounding the replica Statue of Liberty contains tributes to the victims of the World Trade Center attack.

The **Roller Coaster at New York New York** (11 A.M.–11 P.M. Sun.–Thurs., 10:30 A.M.–midnight Fri.–Sat., $14) winds its way around the resort, an experience almost as hair-raising as a ride in a New York City cab, which the coaster cars are painted to resemble. **Coney Island Emporium** (hours vary, daily) has games of skill and luck, motion simulators, and rides.

Dueling pianists keep **The Bar at Times Square** (8 A.M.–2 P.M. daily) rocking into the wee hours, and the sexy bar staff at **Coyote Ugly** (9 P.M.–2 A.M. Sun.–Thurs., 9 P.M.–3 A.M. Fri.–Sat.) defy its name.

New York New York's 2,023 guest rooms are standard size, 350–500 square feet. The roller coaster zooms around the towers, so you might want to ask for a room out of earshot.

MGM Grand

- **Restaurants:** Joël Robuchon, L'Atelier de Joël Robuchon, Seablue, Tom Colicchio's Craftsteak, Pearl, Diego, Fiamma Trattoria, Emeril's New Orleans Fish House, Nobhill Tavern, Rainforest Cafe, Wolfgang Puck Bar & Grill, Grand Wok and Sushi Bar, Shibuya, Studio Café, Stage Deli, Grand Buffet, 'Wichcraft, Cabana Grille, Starbucks, food court
- **Entertainment:** Cirque du Soleil's *Kà,* Crazy Horse Paris
- **Attractions:** Lion Habitat, CBS Television City Research Center, CSI: The Experience
- **Nightlife:** Studio 54, Tabú

CITY WITHIN A CITY

True to its reputation for doing things on a grand scale, Las Vegas recently celebrated the completion of the largest private construction project in U.S. history. Project City Center, a 67-acre complex for hotel, casino, residential, retail, dining, art, and entertainment uses built between Bellagio and Monte Carlo, would have been serious overkill in any other city. In Las Vegas it's impressive, but it's also a natural progression in the city's continuing love affair with grandeur.

City Center employs 12,000 permanent workers, making it the country's largest single hiring effort when it came online in 2009. Its key elements include **Aria,** a more-or-less "traditional" Las Vegas hotel casino: 4,000 guest rooms, 16 restaurants, a spa, nearly a dozen nightclubs and bars, convention space, a pool, 150,000 square feet of slots, table games, and race and sports betting, and *Viva Elvis,* a Cirque du Soleil show.

Vdara is a Euro-chic boutique hotel (no gaming, no smoking, exclusive amenities). The well-heeled can luxuriate in the hotel's health,

beauty, and fitness salons, sip martinis at Bar Vdara, bask in private pool cabanas, and dine in style.

If you have to ask the price, maybe **Crystals** isn't for you. The 500,000-square-foot mall lets you splurge among hanging gardens. Restaurants fronted by Eva Longoria, Wolfgang Puck, and Todd English take the place of Sbarro's and Cinnabon.

Veer Towers and **Mandarin Oriental** are the megaresort's residential spaces. Both come with exclusive pool and spa areas, large condo-style rooms and suites, and a feeling of superiority.

City Center brings another bit of culture to Las Vegas, with its public-area Fine Art Collection. Presented with little fanfare, the art is accessible by anyone strolling the corridors. You can see innovative works by Maya Lin, Jenny Holzer, and Richard Long, among others.

City Center's developers exhibit a concern for the environment, earning six Leadership in Energy and Environmental Design gold designations.

When the MGM Grand (3799 Las Vegas Blvd. S., 888/646-1203, $150–400 d) opened in 1993, guests entered through the gaping maw of the MGM lion. This literal and figurative ingress to the belly of the beast didn't sit well with the superstitious Asian high rollers that the megaresort sought. After renovation, gamblers now enter through portals guarded by the 45-foot-tall king of the jungle. The uninitiated may feel like a gazelle on the savanna, swallowed by the 171,000-square-foot casino floor, the largest in Las Vegas. But the watering hole, MGM's 6.5-acre pool complex, is relatively predator-free.

MGM capitalizes on the movie studio's greatest hits. Even the hotel's emerald facade evokes the magical city in *The Wizard of Oz.*

Boob tube fans can volunteer for studies at the **CBS Television City Research Center** (10 A.M.–8:30 P.M. daily), where they can screen pilots for shows under consideration by

the network. And if your favorite show happens to revolve around solving crimes, don some rubber gloves and search for clues at **CSI: The Experience** (9 A.M.–9 P.M. daily, $30 age 12 and up, not recommended for children under 12). Three crime scenes keep the experience fresh. Patterned on the French classic, **Crazy Horse Paris** (8 P.M. and 10:30 P.M. Wed.–Mon., $61) bills itself as "artistry of the nude." Enough said.

MGM Grand houses enough top restaurants for a week of gourmet dinners. Winning selections include **Diego** (4–10 P.M. Sun.–Fri., 5–10 P.M. Sat., $35–55), for tangy rib eyes in a vibrant setting, and **Pearl** (5:30–10 P.M. daily), for crispy Peking duck in a subtle Asian-Pacific atmosphere.

Standard guest rooms in the Grand Tower are filled with the quality furnishings you'd expect in Las Vegas's posh hotels. The West Tower guest rooms are a bit smaller but exude the swinging style of an upscale Hollywood studio apartment crammed with a CD and DVD player and other high-tech gizmos; those in the Grand Tower are more traditional. All 5,000-plus guest rooms and suites measure more than 440 square feet.

Tropicana

- **Restaurants:** Bacio Pasta & Vino, Legends Steak & Seafood, Havana Go Go Café, South Beach Café & Deli
- **Entertainment:** Hypnosis Unleashed, Brad Garrett's Comedy Club
- **Attractions:** Las Vegas Mob Experience
- **Nightlife:** Nikki Beach, Celebration Lounge

When it opened at Tropicana Avenue and Las Vegas Boulevard in 1959, the Tropicana (801 Las Vegas Blvd. S., 888/381-8767, $75–175 d) was the most luxurious, most expensive, and southernmost resort on the Strip. It has survived several boom-and-bust cycles since then, and its decor reflects the willy-nilly expansion and refurbishment efforts through the years. Another $125 million renovation was completed in 2010, renovating every guest room and the casino while incorporating a new sports book and poker room. Standard guest rooms now reflect the beach theme, with plantation shutters and art deco colors, 42-inch plasma TVs, and iPod docks.

The South Beach–inspired changes in 2011 will see transformation of the Trop's historic four-acre pool area into **Nikki Beach Club** and **Club Nikki,** which will capture the sultry vibe à la South Beach and Saint-Tropez with fruity cocktails, cocoa butter–scented bikini babes, and cool, fresh cuisine.

The renovation will go a long way toward the Tropicana shedding its image as the ugly stepsister to the Luxor, Monte Carlo, MGM Grand, and even Excalibur, which share its intersection. That's good, we suppose, but there was an undeniable charm to the old joint's laid-back atmosphere and commitment to treating low rollers with deference (the casino even

offers free gambling lessons to help guests mitigate their losses). We hope the facelift doesn't give the Trop airs.

Touting "interactive entertainment technology," the **Las Vegas Mob Experience** uses artifacts, photos, and videos to provide a multisensory immersion into the seedy underworld of Las Vegas past and the law enforcement efforts that cleaned up the city. Details were sketchy at press time, but promoters promised visitors "an authentic reach and real perspective into the personal lives and property of the fascinating individuals" who helped create one of Las Vegas's enduring legacies.

The Trop is not big on entertainment, but it did open **Brad Garrett's Comedy Club** (800/829-9034, 8 P.M. Sun.–Thurs., 8 P.M. and 10 P.M. Fri.–Sat., $43–65), and **Hypnosis Unleashed** (800/829-9034, 9 P.M. nightly, $44–66) is performed in The Cellar. It's only a short walk to world-class entertainers at nearby resorts.

Excalibur

- **Restaurants:** The Steakhouse at Camelot, Regale, Dick's Last Resort, Sherwood Forest Cafe, Roundtable Buffet, Krispy Kreme, Starbucks, food court
- **Entertainment:** *Tournament of Kings, Thunder from Down Under, Defending the Caveman*
- **Attractions:** Fantasy Faire Midway, simulated motion rides
- **Nightlife:** Octane Lounge

This bright white castle with vibrant parapets was one of the more interesting designs when it opened on the Strip in 1990, and despite some design changes—a robotic Merlin no longer slays the dragon in a nightly battle—it still clings to the Arthurian legend throughout. It's difficult to shed the whole "quest for the Holy Grail" image when your hotel is a depiction of Camelot. Shops and restaurants are named for the trappings of medieval Europe; minstrels and strolling entertainers transport guests into the realm of fantasy role-play. Sitting between the Luxor and New York New York, Excalibur (3580 Las Vegas Blvd. S., 877/750-5464, $50–200 d) provides a logical (for Las Vegas) progression along the timeline of world civilization. Like the rest of Las Vegas, the resort has grown up, replacing those primary colors with rich burgundies and navies, updating the casino decor and filling the guest rooms with modern conveniences. The clientele is still of the nickel-slot and $5 blackjack ilk, but not every casino can attract the whales. And to its credit, Excalibur doesn't try to be all things for all people. Its entertainment, restaurants, and attractions—the beefcake-y *Thunder from Down Under* (702/597-7600, 9 P.M. Sun.–Thurs., 9 P.M. and 11 P.M. Fri.–Sat., $40–50) notwithstanding—are geared more toward budget-minded families than perk-seeking big spenders.

Little gamers can lose themselves for hours at the **Fantasy Faire Midway** (10 A.M.–midnight Sun.–Thurs., 10 A.M.–1 A.M. Fri.–Sat.), home to carnival games and the SpongeBob SquarePants 4-D ride.

Kevin Burke's witty observations bridge the gender gap at *Defending the Caveman* (3 P.M. Sun.–Thurs., 3 P.M. and 7 P.M. Fri.–Sat., $49–72) in the Down Under Showroom.

Restaurant choices are of the nongourmet variety, but the snarky waitstaff at **Dick's Last Resort** (1 P.M.–late Mon.–Thurs., 11:30 A.M.–late Fri.–Sat.) is good for some laughs. Dig in to some fried finger food and leave your manners at the door.

Standard guest rooms feature hardwood furniture and dark accents. An upgrade can get you a "Widescreen Room" with a 42-inch TV, padded headboard, and the Las Vegas standard marble bath.

Luxor

- **Restaurants:** Backstage Deli, Company Kitchen and Pub House, TENDER Steak & Seafood, Pyramid Cafe, T&T Tacos & Tequila, Luxor Food Court, Starbucks, MORE the Buffet at the Luxor
- **Entertainment:** *Criss Angel Believe,* Carrot Top, *Fantasy, Menopause the Musical*
- **Attractions:** Bodies...the Exhibition, Titanic: The Artifact Exhibition
- **Nightlife:** CatHouse, LAX, Flight, Noir Bar, Aurora, Liquidity, Flight, High Bar, Playbar

With a pyramid shape and a name like Luxor (3900 Las Vegas Blvd. S., 877/386-4658, $50–175 d), it's difficult to imagine this resort without an Egyptian theme, but that's the strategy MGM Mirage has taken over the last few years. Similar to the company's move away from the pirate theme at Treasure Island, beginning in 2007 the parent company moved the resort away from the archeological-dig theme. Much of the mummy-and-scarab decor from the casino, hotel lobby, and public areas was swept away in a $300 million revamp in 2007. In their place are upscale and decidedly postpharaoh nightclubs, restaurants, and shops. The large (120,000-square-foot) casino received a big part of that makeover budget, as did all 2,500 guest rooms in the pyramid and twin 22-story towers.

What remains are the largest atrium in the world, the intense light beam that is visible from space, and inclinators—elevators that move along the building's oblique angles.

Magic meets magic mushrooms in the surrealistic, psychedelic dream sequences of *Mindfreak* Criss Angel in *Believe* (702/262-4400 or 800/557-7428, 7 P.M. and 9:30 P.M. Tues.–Sat., $65–176). The Atrium Showroom (702/262-4400 or 800/557-7428) is home to *Fantasy* (10:30 P.M. daily, $54–70), a typical jiggle-and-tease topless review; *Menopause the Musical* (5 P.M. and 8:30 P.M. Tues., 5:30 P.M. Wed.–Mon., $60–77), a musical salute to the change; and the comedian and prop jockey **Carrot Top** (8 P.M. Mon. and Wed.–Sun., $55–66).

For late-night noshing or traditional dinner, visit **Company Lounge** (5 P.M.–late Wed. and Fri.–Sat., $15–25) for a rustic yet sophisticated atmosphere. A good spot to end the evening after partying is **LAX** (5 P.M.–late Wed. and Fri.–Sat.).

The hotel's pyramid shape makes for interesting room features, such as a slanted exterior wall, as well as a few challenges. Tower rooms are more traditional in their shape, decor, and amenities.

Mandalay Bay

- **Restaurants:** Aureole; Bay Side Buffet; Beach Bar & Grill; Border Grill; China Grill; Fleur de Lys; House of Blues; Mizuya; Raffles Cafe; Red, White and Blue; Red Square; Rumjungle; Sea Breeze Pizza, Ice Cream, and Juices; Shanghai Lilly; StripSteak; Trattoria del Lupo; The Noodle Shop; Turf Club Deli; Hussong's Cantina; Giorgio Caffé & Ristorante; The Burger Bar; Mix; food court

- **Entertainment:** House of Blues, Disney's *The Lion King*

- **Attractions:** Shark Reef, Lion King Exhibit

- **Nightlife:** Rumjungle, Foundation Room, Eyecandy, Mix Lounge

Enter this South Pacific behemoth at the southern tip of the Las Vegas Strip and try to comprehend its mind-boggling statistics.

¢ Mandalay Bay (3950 Las Vegas Blvd. S., 877/632-7800, $120–600 d) has one of the largest casino floors in the world at 135,000 square feet. Wander into Mandalay's beach environment, an 11-acre paradise comprised of three pools, a lazy river, and a 1.6-million-gallon wave pool complete with a real beach made of five million pounds of sand. There's also a tops-optional sunbathing pool deck. You could spend your entire vacation in the pool area, gambling at the beach's three-level casino, eating at its restaurant, shopping for pool gear at the poolside stand, and loading up on sandals and bikinis at the nearby Pearl Moon boutique.

When you're ready to check out the rest of the property, don't miss **House of Blues** (hours and days vary by event), with live blues, rock, and acoustic sets as well as DJs spinning dance tunes.

Mandalay Place (10 A.M.–11 P.M. daily) is a bit smaller and less hectic than other casino

Mandalay Bay is the jewel of Las Vegas's south Strip.

© RYAN JERZ

malls. Unusual shops such as Viva Dogs Vegas, for owners who want to pamper their pooches, share space with eateries and high-concept bars like **Minus 5** (11 A.M.–3 A.M. daily), where barflies don parkas before entering the below-freezing (23°F) establishment. Here the glasses aren't just frosted, they're fashioned completely out of ice. The promenade also houses the **Lion King Exhibit** (10 A.M.–11 P.M. daily), a look into the creative genius behind the Broadway smash that is presented in the Mandalay Bay Theatre.

Sheathed in Indian artifacts and crafts, the **Foundation Room** (11 P.M.–late daily) is just as dark and mysterious as the subcontinent, with private rooms, a dining room, and several bars catering to various musical tastes.

Vegas pays tribute to Paris, Rome, New York, and Venice, so why not Moscow? Round up your comrades for caviar and vodka as well as continental favorites at **Red Square** (5 P.M.–2 A.M. Sun.–Thurs., 4 P.M.–4 A.M. Fri.–Sat., $25–40). Look for the headless Lenin statue at the entrance.

Standard guest rooms are chic and roomy (550 square feet), with warm fabrics and plush bedding. The guest rooms are nothing special visually, but the baths are fit for royalty, with huge tubs, glass-walled showers, and king's-and-queen's commodes. To go upscale, check out Thehotel; for ultraposh, book at the Four Seasons—both are part of the same property.

DOWNTOWN
Main Street Station

• **Restaurants:** Garden Court Buffet, Triple 7 BrewPub

As its full name suggests, Main Street Station Casino, Brewery, and Hotel (200 N. Main St., 800/522-4700, $40–100 d) works hard to provide something for everyone. The result is an eclectic blend of interesting curios, themes, and styles. The casino combines a railroad motif—with Pullman cars belonging to Louisa May Alcott, Buffalo Bill Cody, and Theodore Roosevelt—with European Victorian-era

decor—artifacts from London's Barclay's Bank, Paris's Figaro Opera House, and Belgium's city streets. A hunk of the Berlin Wall graces the men's restroom, and a chandelier from the El Presidente Hotel in Buenos Aires is thrown in for good measure.

Despite these extras, Main Street Station comes up short on amenities that travelers may want. Restaurant choices are limited, but the **Triple 7 Brewpub** (11 A.M.–7 A.M. daily, $10–20) has the hotel's five signature brews on tap as well as pretty good pizza and bargain breakfasts for early risers and late partiers.

Main Street does not offer room service. It also lacks a swimming pool, not unusual for a downtown hotel; but guests have access to the pool at the California just up the street.

Just steps away from the Fremont Street Experience, the hotel's 400 guest rooms are bright and airy, but they are smallish by Las Vegas standards at 400 square feet.

Binion's

• **Restaurants:** Ranch Steakhouse, Binion's Café, Benny's Bullpen

Before Vegas became a destination resort city, it catered to inveterate gamblers, hard drinkers, and others on the fringes of society. Ah, the good old days! A gambler himself, Benny Binion put his place in the middle of downtown, a magnet for the serious player, offering high limits and few frills. Binion's (128 Fremont St., 702/382-1600) still offers single-deck blackjack and a poker room frequented by grizzled veterans. While Binion's and the rest of Las Vegas have been overtaken by Strip megaresorts, the little den on Fremont Street still retains the flavor of Old Vegas, though the Binion family is no longer involved. Harrah's bought the place in 2004 but kept its popular and profitable World Series of Poker.

The hotel at Binion's closed in 2009, but the casino and restaurants remain open, including the **Ranch Steakhouse** (5:30–10:30 P.M. daily, $25–40), famous for its Fremont Street views and primo cuts.

LAS VEGAS

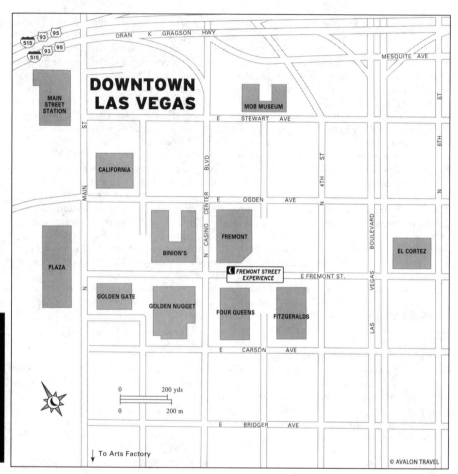

Golden Nugget

- **Restaurants:** The Buffet, Chart House, Lillie's Noodle House, Vic & Anthony's, Grotto Ristorante, Red Sushi, Carson Street Cafe, Starbucks
- **Entertainment:** Gordie Brown
- **Attractions:** Hand of Faith, The Tank
- **Nightlife:** Rush Lounge, Gold Diggers

Considered by many to be the only Strip-worthy resort downtown, the ☾ **Golden**

Nugget (129 E. Fremont St., 800/634-3454, $50–150) has been a fixture for 65 years, beckoning diners and gamblers with gold leaf and a massive gold nugget. Landry's, the restaurant chain and new Nugget owner, has embarked on an ambitious campaign to maintain the hotel's opulence, investing $160 million for casino and guest room upgrades.

If you don't feel like swimming with the sharks in the poker room, you can get up close and personal with their finned namesakes in **The Tank** (10 A.M.–8 P.M. daily, $10–20

LOCALS' FAVORITE CASINOS

Often, frequent Las Vegas visitors will claim they could never live here because they love to gamble too much. Several casinos cater to that local trade, tailoring their offerings to ensure loyal customer bases with locals-only discounts and generous cash-back programs through frequent-player clubs, free poker, video poker, and slot tournaments. They also offer gaming without the traffic and congestion of the Strip and downtown.

THE CANNERY AND EASTSIDE CANNERY

Decor straight out of an Andrews Sisters song attracts military veterans and active-duty flyboys from nearby Nellis Air Force Base. But most locals go here for the deals. The Can Club players program gives cash back for points earned by playing slots and video poker machines and table games. On special days, players earn extra points, and the Cannery (2121 E. Craig Rd., North Las Vegas, 702/507-5700 or 866/999-4899, $40-100 d) and Eastside Cannery (525 Boulder Hwy., 702/507-5700 or 866/999-4899) give special deals for reaching specific point totals. In addition to cash, points can be redeemed for free slot play, show tickets, restaurant meals, and logo merchandise. These casinos also have developed partnership programs allowing players to receive discounts or gift cards good at local merchants.

RED ROCK

The secret of Red Rock casino (11011 W. Charleston Blvd., 702/797-7777, $85-300 d) is spreading beyond locals to high rollers and celebrities who want a more secluded destination with all the resort amenities. Kanye West and Justin Timberlake have stayed here, preferring the "boutique" feel of the 800-room hotel to the megaresorts of the Strip. Westside residents like the something-for-everyone amenities. While the adults belly up to the craps table, teens can take in a movie on one of 16 screens or bowl a few frames in the 72-lane bowling center. Younger kids will have fun climbing, crawling, sliding, and bouncing at Kids Quest, an indoor child care center with lots of ways to burn off excess energy.

SAM'S TOWN

Tranquil Mystic Falls, with its animatronic wildlife and real foliage, suddenly turns into a raging flood punctuated by urgent wolf calls, fountains, and lasers. Locals stroll the park just to see first-timers react to the sudden transformation. Many east-siders also prefer the moseying Old West pace of Sam's Town (5111 Boulder Hwy., 702/456-7777 or 800/897-8696, $26-120 d) and its restaurants and shopping opportunities. Other amenities include 56 lanes of bowling, an 18-screen movie theater, and Sam's Town Live!, an entertainment venue that hosts soft rock, country, and rockabilly acts — perfect for boot-scootin' locals and visitors alike.

SILVERTON

Slot-club points at this south-Strip resort (3333 Blue Diamond Rd., 702/263-7777 or 866/722-4608, $50-160 d) are good for meals, rooms, shows, and even merchandise at the huge Bass Pro Shops located right inside the casino. But the best part of membership is the invitations to members-only events like blackjack tournaments, NASCAR races, and UNLV basketball games. **Twin Creeks** (5-9 P.M. Tues.-Thurs., 5-10 P.M. Fri.-Sat., $30-50) evokes alpine luxury with hardwood floors, exposed beams, subtle lighting, smoky scotch, and small-batch bourbon complementing big ol' steaks. The hotel rooms carry on the lodge feel, with rustic but plush decor and subdued lighting but all the conveniences of home.

nonguests, free for hotel guests), an outdoor pool with a three-story waterslide that takes riders through the hotel's huge aquarium, home to sharks, rays, and other exotic marine life. Bathers can also swim up to the aquarium for a face-to-face with the aquatic predators. Waterfalls and lush landscaping help make this one of the world's best hotel pools.

Gold Diggers nightclub (9 P.M.–late Wed.–Sun.) plays hip-hop, pop, and classic

LAS VEGAS

rock for the dancing pleasure of guests and go-go girls.

When checking in, pause to have your picture taken with the **Hand of Faith,** a 62-pound gold nugget. Rooms are appointed in dark wood and chocolate hues.

The Plaza

- **Restaurants:** Firefly, Downtown Grill, Stuffed Buffet, food court
- **Entertainment:** *The Rat Pack Is Back*
- **Nightlife:** Aqua Lounge

The largest hotel in Las Vegas when it opened in 1971 as the Union Plaza—a nod to the Union

Pacific rail line out back—the Plaza (1 Main St., 702/386-2110 or 800/634-6575, $40–100 d) has held court over Main Street ever since. The hotel's location was the site of the first Las Vegas land auction in 1905. All street numbers in town originate here—1 Main Street—making it the center of modern Las Vegas. In keeping with the hotel's place in history, the *Rat Pack Is Back* (7:30 P.M. daily, $55, $69 with dinner) does a credible job of recreating the heyday of Frank, Dean, and Sammy.

Still one of the larger places downtown, with more than 1,000 guest rooms, the Plaza also offers a variety of suites; expect to get what you pay for.

Sights

DOWNTOWN
◖ Fremont Street Experience

With land at a premium and more and more tourists flocking to the opulence of the Strip, downtown Las Vegas in the last quarter of the 20th century found its lights beginning to flicker. Enter Fremont Street Experience (702/678-5777), an ambitious plan to transform downtown and its tacky "Glitter Gulch" reputation into a pedestrian-friendly enclave. Highlighted by a four-block-long canopy festooned with 12 million light-emitting diodes 90 feet in the air, Fremont Street Experience is downtown's answer to the Strip's erupting volcanoes and fantastic dancing fountains. The canopy, dubbed Viva Vision, runs atop Fremont Street between North Main Street and North 4th Street.

The casinos were slow to embrace the vision at first, concerned that the productions would cause a mass exodus from their slot machines and table games at show time. Viva Vision's backers even wanted the properties to dim their marquees, reducing ambient light, to make the shows more vibrant. But with little else to help them compete with the Strip, they acquiesced.

Urban architect Jon Jerde unveiled his $70

million creation in 1995, and it has been drawing millions of people each year ever since, introducing new generations to "Old Vegas," the casinos that birthed the gambling boom, launched legendary careers, and developed Vegas-style service that makes every gambler feel like a high roller.

A $17 million upgrade in 2004 boosted the resolution of the light show, bringing it nearly to video quality to complement its high-fidelity 550,000-watt sound system.

Once an hour, the promenade goes dark and all heads lift toward the canopy, supported by massive concrete pillars. For six minutes, visitors are enthralled by the multimedia shows that chronicle Western history, span the careers of classic rock bands, or transport viewers to fantasy worlds.

Before and after the light shows, strolling buskers sing for their supper, artists create five-minute masterpieces, and caricaturists airbrush souvenir portraits. Fremont Street hosts top musical acts, including some A-listers during big Las Vegas weekends such as National Finals Rodeo, NASCAR races, and New Year. Viva Vision runs several different shows daily at 8:30 P.M., then on the hour 9 P.M.–midnight.

Las Vegas Natural History Museum

Las Vegas boasts a volcano, a pyramid, and even a Roman coliseum, so it's little wonder that an animatronic *Tyrannosaurus rex* calls the valley home too. Dedicated to "global life forms...from the desert to the ocean, from Nevada to Africa, from prehistoric times to the present," the Las Vegas Natural History Museum (900 Las Vegas Blvd. N., 702/384-3466, 9 A.M.–4 P.M. daily, adults $10, seniors, military, and students $8, ages 3–11 $5) is filled with rotating exhibits that belie the notion that Las Vegas culture begins and ends with neon casino signs.

Visitors to the Treasures of Egypt gallery can enter a realistic depiction of King Tut's tomb to study archeological techniques and discover golden treasures of the pharaohs. The Wild Nevada gallery showcases the raw beauty and surprisingly varied life forms of the Mojave Desert. Interactive exhibits also enlighten visitors on subjects such as marine life, geology, African ecosystems, and more.

The 35-foot-long *T. rex* and his friends (rivals? entrées?)—a triceratops, a raptor, and an ichthyosaur—greet visitors in the Prehistoric Life gallery. And by "greet" we mean a bloodcurdling roar from the *T. rex,* so take precautions with the little ones and the faint of heart.

Neon Museum and Boneyard

The Neon Museum and Boneyard (821 Las Vegas Blvd. N., 702/477-7751), which reopened in late 2010 after construction of Neon Park, is a trip to Las Vegas's more recent past. Housed in the relocated scallop-shaped lobby of the historic La Concha Motel, the museum includes a walking tour north from the Fremont Street Experience. The lamp from the Aladdin Hotel, The Silver Slipper, the Red Barn's martini glass, and the Hacienda's horse and rider, all in glorious twinkling lights, are part of the tour. The self-guided tour is accessible 24 hours a day, but the neighborhood is a bit dubious, so be careful if you go at night.

Neon Park, just behind the clamshell visitors center, is home to some 200 other flashy homages to Old Vegas. Las Vegas doesn't often hold onto its past, so this little walking tour of old signs is an intriguing sight—and it's free.

The small park includes interpretive signage, benches, picnic tables, and a "NEON" sign created from the N's from the Golden Nugget and Desert Inn, the E from Caesar's Palace, and the O from Binion's.

Lied Discovery Children's Museum

Voted Best Museum in Las Vegas by readers of the local newspaper, the Lied Discovery Children's Museum (833 Las Vegas Blvd. N., 702/382-5437, 9 A.M.–4 P.M. Tues.–Fri., 10 A.M.–5 P.M. Sat., noon–5 P.M. Sun., adults $8.50, seniors and minors $7.50) presents more than 100 interactive scientific, artistic, and life-skill activities. Children enjoy themselves so much that they forget they're learning. Among the best permanent exhibits is *It's Your Choice,* which shows kids the importance of eating right and adopting a healthy lifestyle. Exhibits show kids creative ways to explore their world: drama, cooperation, dance, and visual arts. Adult-guided science and arts education programs help open youngsters' imaginations as well, and traveling exhibitions run the gamut from fun and frivolous (a recent special exhibit challenged problem-solvers of all ages to find their way through mazes) to serious and thought-provoking (the museum recently hosted *Torn From Home: My Life as a Refugee*).

Mormon Fort

This tiny museum (500 E. Washington Ave., 702/486-3511, 8 A.M.–4:30 P.M. daily, $1) is the oldest building in Las Vegas. The adobe remnant, constructed by Mormon missionaries in 1855, was part of their original settlement, which they abandoned in 1858. It then served as a store, a barracks, and a shed on the Gass-Stewart Ranch. After that, the railroad leased the old fort to various tenants, including the

Bureau of Reclamation, which stabilized and rebuilt the shed to use as a concrete-testing laboratory for Hoover Dam. In 1955 the railroad sold the old fort to the Elks, who in 1963 bulldozed the whole wooden structure (except the little remnant) into the ranch swimming pool and torched it. The shed was bought by the city in 1971.

Since then, a number of preservation societies have helped keep it in place. The museum includes a visitors center, a re-creation of the original fort built around the remnant. A tour guide presents the history orally while display boards provide it visually. Your visit will not go unrewarded—it's immensely refreshing to see some preservation of the past in this city of the ultimate now.

Mob Museum

The new Museum of Organized Crime and Law Enforcement (300 Stewart Ave., 702/229-2734, http://themobmuseum.org, 10 A.M.–7 P.M. Sun.–Thurs., 10 A.M.–8 P.M. Fri.–Sat., adults $18, ages 5–17 and students $12, Nevada residents $10) celebrates Las Vegas's Mafia past and the cops and agents who finally ran the mob out of town. The museum is located inside the city's downtown post office and courthouse, appropriately the site of the 1951 Kefauver Hearing investigating organized crime.

Displays include "The Skim," an examination of how casinos funneled unreported income to their unacknowledged underworld owners, and "Mob Mayhem," which shows the violence, ceremony, and hidden meanings behind Mafia "hits," all against a grisly background—the wall from Chicago's St. Valentine's Day Massacre that spelled the end of six members of Bugs Moran's crew and one hanger-on. "Bringing Down the Mob" displays the tools federal agents used—wiretaps, surveillance, and weapons—to clean up the town.

Downtown Arts District

Centered at South Main Street and East Charleston Boulevard, the district gives art lovers a concentration of galleries to suit any taste, plus an eclectic mix of shops, eateries, and other surprises. **The Arts Factory** (107 E. Charleston Blvd., 702/383-3133), a two-story redbrick industrial building, is the district's birthplace. Its ground floor is home to **Contemporary Arts Collective,** where artists meet, share ideas, and find creative support and patrons can explore and learn about artists, their media, and their styles. Contemporary Arts Collective hosts shows monthly; performing arts as well as two- and three-dimensional artworks are included—"as long as it can fit through the door," says local artist and volunteer Mark Diederichsen.

Upstairs at **Damned Ink,** you'll find paintings and ink drawings that explore artist Danny Roberts's sometimes hopeful, sometimes heartbreaking examinations of humankind's conflicted relationship with culture, nature, and responsibility. "Each subject is on the verge of an epiphany and facing a new conflict," Roberts says. "It is a brief moment of either acceptance or rebellion."

Make an appointment to stop by **S2 Editions Atelier** (1 E. Charleston Blvd., 702/868-7880), next to the Arts Factory, to see the painstaking process the master printers use to reproduce fine art lithographs on massive 140-year-old presses. Pick up one of the colorful Tom Everhart "Snoopy" lithos printed at S2, or journey north to the **Arts Village** (1039 N. Main St., 702/249-3200) to see Sharon Gainsburg's realist and abstract stone sculptures and wine-rack art.

Virtually all the galleries and other paeans to urban pop culture participate in Las Vegas's First Friday event (6–10 P.M. first Fri. of every month), but otherwise galleries keep limited hours, so if there's something you don't want to miss, call for an appointment.

From here, you can head south to **Commerce Street Studios** (1551 S. Commerce St., 702/678-6278) to browse out the edgy, often avant-garde displays at **The Fallout** and neighboring **Circadian Gallery,** with its aggressive, brooding expressions and impressionistic nudes by Daniel Pearson. Or you can mosey westward to **Gallery P** (231

W. Charleston Blvd., Suite 160, 702/384-8155), where Joseph Palermo displays his modernist art. Or check out the renovated **Holsum Design Center** (241 W. Charleston Blvd.), a former 1950s bakery recently converted to shops, studios, and artist lofts.

CENTER STRIP
Imperial Palace Auto Collection

The exhibits are always changing at this gem hidden atop the parking garage at the Imperial Palace Hotel (3535 Las Vegas Blvd. S., 702/794-3174, 10 A.M.–6 P.M., adults $9, children and seniors $5, under age 3 free). That's because most of the classic muscle and luxury cars are for sale, but this is far from your run-of-the-mill used car lot.

Among the beauties recently on display were two dozen Duesenbergs, Elvis Presley's 1976 Cadillac Eldorado, and a 1957 Jaguar XKSS, appraised at about $7 million.

History buffs and celebrity watchers as well as motor-heads will find plenty to pique their interest. The museum recently featured W. C. Fields's custom-made Fleetwood limousine—complete with electric martini mixer—and one of Johnny Carson's first rides, a 1939 Chrysler Royal sedan that ferried him and his date to Carson's senior prom.

In all, more than 250 cars and a few motorcycles fill several galleries. Discount coupons are plentiful, so don't pay full price.

Madame Tussauds

Ever wanted to dunk over Shaq? Marry George Clooney? Leave Simon Cowell speechless? Madame Tussauds (3377 Las Vegas Blvd. S., 702/862-7800, www.madametussauds.com/lasvegas, 10 A.M.–9 P.M. Sun.–Thurs., 10 A.M.–10 P.M. Fri.–Sat., adults $25, seniors $18, children $15) at the Venetian Hotel gives you your chance. Unlike most other museums, Madame Tussauds encourages guests to get up close and "personal" with the world leaders, sports heroes, and screen stars immortalized in wax. Photo ops and interactive activities abound. With "Karaoke Revolution Presents: American Idol" you can take to the stage and then hear Simon Cowell and Ryan Seacrest's thoughts on your burgeoning singing career. The crowd roars as you take it to the rack and sink the game-winner over Shaquille O'Neal's vainly outstretch arm. You'll feel right at home in the "mansion" as you don bunny ears and lounge on the circular bed with Hugh Hefner.

But it's not all fun and games, especially in the Chamber of Horrors, where the inmates have taken over the asylum. Relax and take a deep breath—all the figures are made of wax, after all. Or are they? Discounts are available on the website.

◖ Gondola Rides

We dare you not to sigh at the grandeur of Venice in the desert as you pass beneath quaint bridges and idyllic sidewalk cafés, your gondolier serenading you with the accompaniment of the Grand Canal's gurgling wavelets.

The indoor gondolas skirt the Grand Canal Shoppes inside the Venetian Hotel (3355 Las

Gondoliers serenade families and couples on the canal at the Venetian.

© RYAN JERZ

LAS VEGAS

Vegas Blvd. S., 702/607-3982, 10 A.M.–11 P.M. Sun.–Thurs., 10 A.M.–midnight Fri.–Sat., $16 for a half mile) under the mall's painted-sky ceiling fresco.

Outdoor gondolas skim the Venetian's 31,000-square-foot lagoon for 12 minutes, giving riders a unique perspective on the Las Vegas Strip.

Plying the waters at regular intervals, the realistic-looking gondolas seat four, but couples who don't want to share a boat can pay double.

◖ Secret Garden and Dolphin Habitat

It's no mirage—those really are pure white tigers lounging in their own plush resort on the Mirage casino floor. Legendary Las Vegas magicians Siegfried and Roy, who have dedicated much of their lives to preserving big cats, opened the Secret Garden (Mirage, 3400 Las Vegas Blvd. S., 702/791-7188, 10 A.M.–7 P.M. daily, adults $15, ages 4–12 $10, under age 4 free) in 1990. In addition to the milky-furred tigers, the garden is home to blue-eyed, black-striped white tigers as well as panthers, lions, and leopards. Although caretakers don't "perform" with the animals, if your visit is well-timed, you could see the cats playing, wrestling, and even swimming in their pristine waterfall-fed pools. The cubs in the specially built nursery are sure to register high on the cuteness meter.

While you're here, visit the Atlantic bottlenoses right next door, also in the middle of the Mirage's palm trees and jungle foliage. The aquatic mammals don't perform on cue either, but they're natural hams, and often interact with their visitors, nodding their heads in response to trainer questions, turning aerial somersaults, and "walking" on their tails across the water. An underwater viewing area provides an unusual perspective on the dolphins' world. Feeding times are a hoot.

Budding naturalists (age 13 and over and willing to part with $550) won't want to miss Dolphin Habitat's Trainer for a Day program, which allows them to feed, swim with, and pose

for photos with some of the aquatic stars while putting them through their daily regimen.

LOWER STRIP
Showcase Mall

"Mall" is an overly ambitious moniker for the Showcase Mall (3785 Las Vegas Blvd. S.), a mini diversion on the Strip. The centerpiece, the original **M&M's World** (702/736-7611, 9 A.M.–11 P.M. Sun.–Thurs., 9 A.M.–midnight Fri.–Sat., free), underwent a 2010 expansion and now includes a printing station where customers can customize their bite-size treats with words and pictures. The 3,300-square-foot expansion on the third floor of the store, which originally opened in 1997, includes additional opportunities to stock up on all things M: Swarovski crystal candy dishes, an M&M guitar, T-shirts, and purses made from authentic M&M wrappers. The addition brings the chocoholic's paradise to more than 30,000 square feet, offering key chains, coffee mugs, lunch boxes, and the addicting treats in every color imaginable. Start with a viewing of the short 3-D film, *I Lost My M in Las Vegas*. A replica of Kyle Busch's M&M-sponsored No. 18 NASCAR stock car is on the fourth floor.

Everything Coca-Cola really should be named "A Few Things Coca-Cola." The small retail outlet has collectibles, free photo ops, and a soda fountain where you can taste Coke products from around the world, but it's a pale vestige of Coke's ambitious marketing ploy, à la M&M's World, that opened in 1997 and closed in 2000. The giant green Coke bottle facade, however, attracts pedestrians into the mall.

GameWorks (702/432-4263, 10 A.M.–midnight Sun.–Thurs., 10 A.M.–1 A.M. Fri.–Sat., games priced individually), with various all-you-can-play options, gives you the chance to work off your sugar rush as you assume the role of hunter, snowboarder, and race-car driver on the virtual gaming floor. The virtual bowling is a kick. You can even go old-school, showing off the Pac-Man and pinball skills that made you an arcade legend. A bar and restaurant are on-site to keep the energy levels up.

Bodies...the Exhibition and *Titanic* Artifacts

Although they are tastefully and respectfully presented, the dissected humans at Bodies... the Exhibition at Luxor (3900 Las Vegas Blvd. S., 702/262-4400 or 800/557-7428, 10 A.M.– 10 P.M. daily, adults $31, over age 64 $29, ages 4–12 $23, under age 4 free) still have a bit of the creepy factor. That uneasiness quickly gives way to wonder and interest as visitors examine 13 full-body specimens, carefully preserved to reveal bone structure and muscular, circulatory, respiratory, and other systems. Other system and organ displays drive home the importance of a healthy lifestyle, with structures showing the damage caused by overeating, alcohol consumption, and sedentary lifestyle. Perhaps the most sobering exhibit is the side-by-side comparisons of healthy and smoke-damaged lungs. A draped-off area contains fetal specimens, showing prenatal development and birth defects.

Luxor also hosts the 300 less surreal but just as poignant artifacts and reproductions commemorating the 1912 sinking of the *Titanic* (3900 Las Vegas Blvd. S., 702/262-4400 or 800/557-7428, 10 A.M.–10 P.M. daily, adults $31, over age 64 $29, ages 4–12 $23, under age 4 free). The 15-ton rusting hunk of the ship's hull is the biggest artifact on display; it not only drives home the *Titanic*'s scale but also helps transport visitors back to that cold April morning a century ago. A section of the *Titanic*'s grand staircase—featured prominently in the 1997 film with Leonardo DiCaprio and Kate Winslet—testifies to the ship's opulence, but it is the passengers' personal effects (a pipe, luggage, an unopened bottle of champagne) and recreated first-class and third-class cabins that provide some of the most heartbreaking discoveries. The individual stories come to life as each patron is given the identity of one of the ship's passengers. At the end of tour they find out the passenger's fate.

Lion Habitat

A descendant of the famed MGM Studios movie lion and a couple of dozen friends cavort in the luxurious MGM Grand Lion Habitat (3799 Las Vegas Blvd. S., 11 A.M.–7 P.M. daily, free). It's a palace fit for a king—of the jungle—in the middle of the casino. Big cat expert Keith Evans designed the habitat to educate and protect the majestic beasts. Evans cares for his 26 lions, three tigers, and two snow leopards at his 8.5-acre Las Vegas compound when they're not entertaining casino guests. The habitat invites visitors to get up close and personal with the lions, separated only by a couple of inches of bulletproof glass. Like your teenage son, lions sleep about 19 hours a day. However, they do rouse themselves twice a day for feeding time—again, just like a high schooler—so it's best to arrive well before the dinner bell rings at 11:15 A.M. and 4:15 P.M. daily to get a good viewing spot. If you come at other times, the handlers may be able to entice the cats into a bit of training or roughhousing. But given the lions' adolescent bent, be prepared to watch a whole lot of snoozing and lazy grooming. Still, it's worth a detour, and posters around the exhibit offer insights into the lion lifestyle.

Shark Reef

Just when you thought it was safe to visit Las Vegas...this 1.6-million-gallon habitat proves not all the sharks in town prowl the poker rooms. Shark Reef (Mandalay Bay, 3950 Las Vegas Blvd. S., 702/632-4555, 10 A.M.–8 P.M. Sun.–Thurs., 10 A.M.–10 P.M. Fri.–Sat., adults $17, ages 5–12 $11, under age 5 free) is home to 2,000 animals—almost all predators. The premise, though a bit farfetched, is pretty cool: Patrons traipse through a slowly sinking ancient temple, coming face to face with some of the most fearsome creatures in the world, such as the sand tiger shark, whose mouth is so crammed with razor-sharp teeth that it doesn't fully close. Fifteen shark species call the reef home, along with golden crocodiles, moray eels, piranhas, giant octopuses, the venomous lion fish, stingrays, jellyfish, water monitors, and the fresh-from-your-nightmares eight-foot-long Komodo dragon.

Mandalay Bay guests with dive certification can dive in the 22-foot-deep shipwreck exhibit at the reef. Commune with eight-foot nurse sharks as well as reef sharks, zebra sharks, rays, sawfish, and other denizens of the deep. Scuba excursions (Tues., Thurs., and Sat.–Sun., age 18 and over, $650) include 3–4 hours underwater, a guided aquarium tour, a video, and admission for up to four guests. Chain mail is required.

OFF STRIP
◖ Las Vegas Springs Preserve
The Springs Preserve (333 S. Valley View Blvd., 702/822-7700, 10 A.M.–6 P.M. daily, adults $19, students and over age 64 $17, ages 5–17 $11, free under age 5) is where Las Vegas began, at least from a Eurocentric viewpoint. More than 100 years ago, the first nonnatives in the Las Vegas Valley—Mormon missionaries from Salt Lake City—stumbled on this clear artesian spring. Of course, the native Paiute and Pueblo people knew about the springs and exploited them millennia before the Mormons arrived. You can see examples of their tools, pottery, and houses at the site, now a 180-acre monument to environmental stewardship, historic preservation, and geographic discovery. The preserve is home to lizards, rabbits, foxes, scorpions, bats, and more. The nature-minded will love the cactus, rose, and herb gardens, and there's even an occasional cooking demonstration using the desert-friendly fruits, vegetables, and herbs grown here.

Las Vegas has become a leader in water conservation, alternative energy, and other environmentally friendly policies. The results of these efforts and tips on how everyone can reduce their carbon footprint are found in the Sustainability Gallery.

Nevada State Museum and Historical Society
Funding secured, the Nevada State Museum (333 S. Valley View Blvd., 702/486-5205, 10 A.M.–6 P.M. Fri.–Mon., $10, included in admission to the Springs Preserve) has finally moved to its permanent home at the Springs Preserve. Visitors can spend hours studying Mojave and Spring Mountains

ecology, southern Nevada history, and local art. Permanent exhibits on the 13,000-square-foot floor describe southern Nevada's role in warfare and atomic weaponry and include skeletons of the Columbian mammoth, which roamed the Nevada deserts 20,000 years ago, and the ichthyosaur, a whalelike remnant of the Triassic Period. The Cahlan Research Library houses Clark County naturalization and Civil Defense records, among other treasures.

◖ Atomic Testing Museum
Kids might not think it's da bomb, but if you were part of the "duck and cover" generation, the Atomic Testing Museum (755 E. Flamingo Rd., 702/794-5161, 10 A.M.–5 P.M. Mon.–Sat., noon–5 P.M. Sun., adults $12, military, over age 64, ages 7–17, and students $9, under age 7 free) provides plenty to spark your memories of the Cold War. Las Vegas embraced its position as ground zero in the development of the nation's atomic and nuclear deterrents after World War II. Business leaders welcomed defense contractors to town, and casinos hosted bomb-watching parties as nukes were detonated at the Nevada Test Site, a huge swath of desert 65 miles away. One ingenious marketer promoted the Miss Atomic Bomb beauty pageant in an era when patriotism overcame concerns about radiation.

The museum presents atomic history without bias, walking a fine line between appreciation of the work of nuclear scientists, politicians, and the military and the catastrophic consequences their activities and decisions could have wrought. The museum's best permanent feature is a short video in the Ground Zero Theatre, a multimedia showing of an actual atomic explosion. The theater, a replica of an observation bunker, is rigged for motion, sound, and rushing air.

One gallery helps visitors put atomic energy milestones in historic perspective along with the age's impact on 1950s and 1960s pop culture. The Today and Tomorrow Gallery examines the artifacts associated with explosives, war, and atomic energy, including a section of I-beam from the World Trade Center. Just as relevant today are the lectures and traveling exhibits that the museum hosts. A recent offering was *Journey through Japan,* a look at the postwar culture and development of the only nation to be attacked with atomic weapons.

Computer simulators, high-speed photographs, Geiger counters, and other testing and safety equipment along with first-person accounts add to the museum's visit-worthiness.

Marjorie Barrick Museum of Natural History

The museum and the adjacent **Donald H. Baepler Xeric Garden** (4505 S. Maryland Pkwy., 702/895-3381, 8 A.M.–4:45 P.M. Mon.–Fri., 10 A.M.–2 P.M. Sat., donation) on

the University of Nevada, Las Vegas (UNLV) campus are good places to bone up on local flora, fauna, and artifacts. First, study the local flora in the arboretum outside the museum entrance, and then step inside for the fauna: small rodents, big snakes, lizards, tortoises, Gila monsters, iguanas, chuckwallas, geckos, spiders, beetles, and cockroaches.

Other displays are full of Native American baskets, kachinas, masks, weaving, pottery, and jewelry from the desert Southwest and Latin America, including Mexican dance masks and traditional Guatemalan textiles.

To find the museum and garden, drive onto the UNLV campus on Harmon Street and follow it around to the right, then turn left into the museum parking lot.

Entertainment

HEADLINERS AND PRODUCTION SHOWS

Production shows are classic Las Vegas–style entertainment, the kind that most people identify with the Entertainment Capital of the World. An American version of French burlesque, the Las Vegas production show has been gracing various stages around town since the late 1950s and usually includes a magic act, acrobats, jugglers, daredevils, and maybe an animal act. The Cirque du Soleil franchise and *Jubilee!* keep the tradition alive, but other variety shows have given way to more one-dimensional, specialized productions of superstar imitators, sexy song-and-dance reviews, and female impersonators. Most of these are large-budget, skillfully produced and presented extravaganzas, and they are highly entertaining diversions.

As Las Vegas has grown into a sophisticated metropolis, with gourmet restaurants, trendy boutiques, and glittering nightlife, it has also attracted Broadway productions to compete with the superstar singers that helped launch the town's legendary status.

Since they're so expensive to produce, the big shows are fairly reliable, and you can count on

them being around for the life of this edition. They do change on occasion; the smaller shows come and go with some frequency, but unless a show bombs and is gone in the first few weeks, it'll usually be around for at least a year. All this big-time entertainment is centered, of course, around Las Vegas's casino resorts, with the occasional concert at the Thomas & Mack Center on the UNLV campus.

Blue Man Group

Bald, blue, and silent (save for homemade PVC musical instruments), Blue Man Group (Venetian, 3355 Las Vegas Blvd. S., 702/414-9000 or 800/258-3626, 7 P.M. and 10 P.M. nightly, $65–149) was one of the hottest things to hit the Strip when it debuted at Luxor in 2000 after successful versions in New York, Boston, and Chicago. It continues to wow audiences with its thought-provoking, quirkily hilarious gags and percussion performances. It is part street performance, part slapstick, and all fun.

Garth Brooks

Steve Wynn lured the country music superstar

out of retirement in 2009 for a series of concerts to run through 2015. Garth and his friends in low places put on a dazzling rock concert–worthy stage show (Encore, 3131 Las Vegas Blvd. S., 702/770-9966, $225) while he delivers his lengthy repertoire of hits with gusto. Shows dates and times for the best-selling solo artist in history are announced a few months in advance.

Céline Dion

Family connections reestablished and vocal cords rested, the ultimate diva returns to the Caesars Palace Colosseum (3570 Las Vegas Blvd. S., 877/4-CELINE—877/423-5463, 7:30 P.M., days vary, $55–250) after a year out of the limelight. The multiplatinum, multi-Grammy songstress is back to deliver pitch-perfect versions of "My Heart Will Go On" and all of her signature hits.

Chippendales

With all the jiggle-and-tease shows on the Strip, Chippendales (Rio, 3700 W. Flamingo Rd., 702/777-7776, 8 P.M. Sun.–Thurs., 8 P.M. and 10:30 P.M. Fri.–Sat., $50–97) delivers a little gender equity. Tight jeans and rippled abs bumping and grinding with their female admirers may be the main attraction, but theirs is a fairly strict hands-off policy. The boys dance their way through sultry and playful renditions of "It's Raining Men" and other tunes with similar themes.

Crazy Horse Paris

A faithful reproduction of the original French "celebration of the nude," Crazy Horse Paris (MGM Grand, 3799 Las Vegas Blvd. S., 702/891-7902 or 866/740-7711, 8 P.M. and 10:30 P.M. Wed.–Mon., from $60) is sensual and alluring but not overtly sexual. The premise is a celebration of women of each astrological sign. Although the dancers are topless and nearly nude, lighting effects and their ballet training put the spotlight on the movement of their bodies rather than on their exposed parts.

Donny and Marie

Donny and Marie Osmond (Flamingo, 3555 Las Vegas Blvd. S., 702/733-3333, 7:30 P.M. Tues.–Sat., $104–285) hurl affectionate put-downs between musical numbers. The most famous members of the talented family perform their solo hits, such as Donny's "Puppy Love" and Marie's "Paper Roses" along with a little bit country, a little bit rock-and-roll duets while their faux sibling rivalry comes through with good-natured ribbing.

Terry Fator

America's Got Talent champion Terry Fator (Mirage, 3400 Las Vegas Blvd. S., 702/792-7777 or 800/963-9634, 7:30 P.M. Tues.–Sat., $59–129) combines two disparate skills—ventriloquism and impersonation—to channel Elvis, Cher, and others. Backed by a live band, Fator sings and trades one-liners with his foam rubber friends. The comedy is fresh, the impressions spot-on, and the ventriloquism accomplished with nary a lip quiver.

Matt Goss

A three-year deal he signed in 2010 means Matt Goss (Caesars Palace, 3570 Las Vegas Blvd. S., 800/745-3000, 10 P.M. Fri.–Sat., $40–95) will be delivering his selections from the great American songbook for some time to come. Backed by a swingin' nine-piece band and the requisite sexy dancers, Goss, in fedora and bow tie, brings his own style to standards like "I've Got the World on a String," "Luck Be a Lady," and other Rat Pack favorites.

Jersey Boys

The rise of Frankie Valli and the Four Seasons from street-corner doo-woppers to superstars gets the full Broadway treatment in *Jersey Boys* (Palazzo, 3325 Las Vegas Blvd. S., 702/411-9000 or 866/641-7469, 7 P.M. Thurs.–Fri. and Sun.–Mon., 6:30 P.M. and 9:30 P.M. Tues. and Sat., $63–200). Unlike, say, *Mamma Mia*, the popular ABBA spectacular, *Jersey Boys* has a true story line, chronicling the lives of the falsetto-warbling Valli and his bandmates.

Terrific sets and lighting create the mood, alternating from the grittiness of the Newark streets to the flash of the concert stage. Remember, it's the story of inner-city teens in the 1950s, so be prepared for more than a few F-bombs in the dialogue.

🅲 Jubilee!

The last of the old-style variety shows, *Jubilee!* (Bally's, 3645 Las Vegas Blvd. S., 800/237-SHOW—800/237-7469, 7:30 P.M. and 10:30 P.M. Sat.–Thurs., $53–113) is showgirl heaven, with dozens of the statuesque, feathered, rhinestoned, topless beauties escorting audiences through seven revue acts that include acrobats, contortionists, aerialists, jugglers, and other specialty acts. Complicated production numbers with intricate dance steps and nearly 100 performers on the 150-foot stage give the showgirls appropriate backdrops for strutting their stuff (the early show is suitable for families; the late show is topless). The climactic sinking of the *Titanic* is a real show-stopper. A Strip must-see for 30 years, *Jubilee!* is a throwback to the swanky Vegas of old.

Kà

Returning to more "traditional" Cirque du Soleil fare, *Kà* (MGM Grand, 3799 Las Vegas Blvd. S., 702/531-3826 or 866/740-7711, 7 P.M. and 9:30 P.M. daily, $69–150) explores the yin and yang of life through the story of two twins' journey to meet their shared fate. Martial arts, acrobatics, plenty of flashy pyrotechnics, and lavish sets and costumes bring cinematic drama to the variety-show acts. The show's title was inspired by the ancient Egyptian *Ka* belief, in which every human has a spiritual duplicate.

Legends in Concert

The best of the celebrity impersonator shows, *Legends in Concert* (Harrah's, 3475 Las Vegas Blvd. S., 702/369-5111, 7:30 P.M. and 10 P.M. Sun.–Fri., $48–70), emceed by "Jay Leno," relies on the tried-and-true superstars, eschewing the flavor-of-the-day pop idols. Elvis is here, of course, for an extended set, as is Madonna.

On any given night, you might hear the Temptations, Garth Brooks, Dolly Parton, or James Brown. A Vegas fixture for 25 years, *Legends* is truly legendary.

Le Rêve

All the spectacle we've come to expect from the creative geniuses behind Cirque du Soleil is present in this stream-of-unconsciousness known as *Le Rêve* (Wynn, 3131 Las Vegas Blvd. S., 702/770-WYNN—702/770-9966 or 888/320-7110, 7 P.M. and 9 P.M. Fri.–Tues., $99–179). The loose concept is a romantically conflicted woman's fevered dream (*rêve* in French). Some 80 perfectly sculpted specimens of human athleticism and beauty cavort, flip, and show off their muscles around a huge aquatic stage. More than 2,000 guests fill the theater in the round, with seats all within 50 feet; those in the first couple of rows are in the "splash zone." Clowns and acrobats complete the package.

The Lion King

The familiar story of Simba's rise from tragedy to his rightful place at the head of his pride comes to life through African beats, glorious costumes, and elaborate choreography in *The Lion King* (Mandalay Bay, 3950 Las Vegas Blvd. S., 877/632-7400, 7:30 P.M. Mon.–Thurs., 4 P.M. and 8 P.M. Sat.–Sun., $77–127). It's based on the Disney animated film, but because it's a resident show, the staging and lighting are tailored for extra appeal.

LOVE

For Beatles fans visiting Las Vegas, all you need is *LOVE* (Mirage, 3400 Las Vegas Blvd. S., 702/792-7777 or 800/963-9634, 7 P.M. and 9:30 P.M. Thurs.–Mon., $94–150). This Cirque du Soleil–produced trip down Penny Lane features dancers, aerial acrobats, and other performers interpreting the Fab Four's lyrics and recordings. With a custom soundscape using the original master tapes from Abbey Road Studios and breathtaking visual artistry, John, Paul, George, and Ringo never sounded so good.

Barry Manilow

Straight men may not appreciate his talent, but Barry Manilow (Paris, 3655 Las Vegas Blvd. S., 800/745-3000, 7:30 P.M. Fri.–Sun., $95–250) sure gives the audience everything he has in every performance. From tear-inducing "Mandy" to the can't-help-but-dance-in-your-seat "Copacabana," Manilow is the consummate showman, professional yet personal. His stage demeanor during spoken interludes between "Looks Like We Made It" and other radio favorites evinces the gratitude and appreciation of his fans.

Mystère

At first glance, Cirque du Soleil production *Mystère* (Treasure Island, 3300 Las Vegas Blvd. S., 702/894-7722 or 800/392-1999, 7 P.M. and 9:30 P.M. Sat.–Wed., $76–120) is like a circus. But it also plays on other performance archetypes, including classical Greek theater, Kabuki, and surrealism. A mix of theater, sport, and art, this production dazzles audiences with its revelations of life's mysteries.

O

Bellagio likes to do everything bigger, better, and more extravagant, and *O* (Bellagio, 3600 Las Vegas Blvd. S., 702/693-7722 or 888/488-7111, 7:30 P.M. and 10 P.M. Wed.–Sun., $94–150) is no exception. This Vegas Cirque du Soleil incarnation involves a $90 million set, 80 artists, and a 1.5-million-gallon pool of water. The title comes from the French word for water, *eau,* pronounced like the letter O in English. The production involves both terrestrial and aquatic feats of human artistry, athleticism, and comedy. It truly must be seen to be believed.

Penn & Teller

The oddball comedy magicians Penn & Teller (Rio, 3700 W. Flamingo Rd., 702/777-7776, 9 P.M. Sat.–Wed., $83–94) have a way of making audiences feel special. Seemingly breaking the magicians' code, they reveal the preparation and sleight-of-hand involved in performing tricks. The hitch is that even when forewarned, observers still often can't catch on. And once

they do, the verbose Penn and silent Teller add a wrinkle no one expects.

Phantom: The Las Vegas Spectacular

From the hauntingly romantic Paris sewers to the famous Paris Opera House above, *Phantom* (Venetian, 3355 Las Vegas Blvd. S., 702/414-9000 or 888/641-7469, 7 P.M. Wed.–Fri., 7 P.M. and 9:30 P.M. Tues. and Sat., $69–165) captures the epic story of Christine's rise to fame and subsequent escape from the clutches of her obsessed patron. The chandelier scene and the heroine's flight from the Phantom's lair are not to be missed; it's probably the best show in town.

Rita Rudner

Showbiz veteran Rita Rudner (Venetian, 3355 Las Vegas Blvd. S., 702/414-9000 or 866/641-7469, 8:30 P.M. Mon.–Wed., 6 P.M. Sat., $49–69) finds humor in the everyday world of wifehood, motherhood, aging, shopping, the gender gap, and life in Las Vegas. Best of all, she elicits laughs with true observational wit, not relying on blue language, bathroom humor, or insults.

Tony n' Tina's Wedding

Feuding future in-laws, a drunken priest, a libidinous nun, and a whole flock of black sheep can't keep Tony and Tina from finding wedded bliss in *Tony n' Tina's Wedding* (Planet Hollywood, 3667 Las Vegas Blvd. S., 702/949-6450, 7:30 P.M. daily, $70–100). Or can they? You play the role of a wedding guest, sitting among the actors, where you learn where the family skeletons are hidden and the bodies are buried. Will you play the peacemaker, or stir up the jealousies and hidden agendas among the family members? Each show is different, based on the audience reaction. So keep your ears peeled; you just might pick up the juiciest gossip between the lasagna and the cannoli.

Tournament of Kings

Pound on the table with your goblet and let loose a hearty "huzzah!" to cheer your king to victory over the other nation's regents at the *Tournament of Kings* (Excalibur, 3580 Las Vegas Blvd. S., 702/597-7600, 6 P.M. Mon.–Thurs., 6 P.M. and 8:30 P.M. Fri.–Sat., $57). Each section of the equestrian theater rallies under separate banners as their hero participates in jousts, sword fights, and riding contests at this festival hosted by King Arthur and Merlin. A regal feast, served medieval style (that is, without utensils), starts with a tureen of dragon's blood (tomato soup). But just as the frivolity hits its climax, an evil lord appears to wreak havoc. Can the kings and Merlin's magic save the day? One of the best family shows in Las Vegas.

Viva Elvis

Nothing says "Elvis" like acrobats and roller skaters. It might be a stretch to fit the King's image into the Cirque du Soleil mold, but *Viva Elvis* (Aria, 3730 Las Vegas Blvd S., 702/590-7760 or 877/25-ELVIS—877/253-5847, 7 P.M. and 9:30 P.M. Fri.–Tues., $99–175) comes close. Building on its success with the Beatles' *LOVE,* Cirque du Soleil lets the music do the talking in a retrospective of Elvis's life through live performances, video and photographic montages, and theater. Of course, it wouldn't be Cirque du Soleil without some displays of athletic and dancing prowess. That's where the skaters come in, with graceful choreography to the accompaniment of "Can't Help Falling in Love."

George Wallace

Hailed as the voice of Las Vegas, George Wallace (Flamingo, 3555 Las Vegas Blvd. S., 702/733-3333 or 800/221-7299, 10 P.M. Tues.–Sat., $60–87) has made a career of snappy one-liners and "yo' mama" jokes. A "don't give a spit what people think" attitude and his ability to blend in interactions with the audience make Wallace a crowd favorite. He got his show business start as a writer for *The Redd Foxx Show,* to give you an idea of the type of hilarious ranting diatribes you can expect.

Zumanity

Cirque du Soleil seems to have succumbed to the titillation craze with the strange melding of sexuality, athleticism, and comedy that is *Zumanity* (New York New York, 3790 Las Vegas Blvd. S., 866/606-7111, 7:30 P.M. and 10 P.M. Fri.–Tues., $69–105). The cabaret-style show makes no pretense of storyline, but instead takes audience members through a succession of sexual and topless fantasies—French maids, schoolgirls, and light autoerotic S and M.

SHOWROOM AND LOUNGE ACTS

Showrooms are another Las Vegas institution, with most hotels providing live entertainment—usually magic, comedy, or tributes to the big stars who played or are playing the big rooms and theaters under the same roofs.

The Vegas lounge act is the butt of a few jokes, but they offer some of the best entertainment values in town—a night's entertainment for the price of a few drinks and a small cover charge. Every hotel in Las Vegas worth its salt has a lounge, and the acts change often enough to make them hangouts for locals. These acts are listed in the free entertainment magazines and the *Las Vegas Review-Journal*'s helpful Friday "Neon" section, but unless you're familiar with the performers, it's the luck of the draw: They list only the entertainer's name, venue, and showtimes.

Rat Pack Show

If we needed any proof that cool transcends generations, Sandy Hackett's *Rat Pack Show* (Hilton, 3000 Paradise Rd., 800/222-5361, 6:45 P.M. and 8:30 P.M. nightly, $50–90) delivers it. The Rat Pack was the epitome of cool when it owned Las Vegas; today, even the ersatz Pack's delivery and singing remains as fresh as ever. And this group plays up Frank, Dean, Sammy, and Joey's camaraderie to the hilt, with the others interrupting Frank's heartfelt renditions of his classics, all the while treating him with the mock deference the Chairman of the Board deserves. And Frank plays right along, pretending to rule his crew with an iron fist. The Hilton version relies more on energetic dancers than the swank of the Sahara rendition.

The Rat Pack Is Back

The Rat Pack Is Back (Plaza, 1 Main St., 702/386-2444, 7:30 P.M. nightly, $57–74) is pretty much the same as the *Rat Pack Show*. In fact, the producers of the two productions are former partners whose messy split in 2009 continues to simmer. The Plaza show offers the option of dinner in the showroom at 6 P.M. for about $15.

Barbra and Frank: The Concert that Never Was

Sinatra and fellow legend Streisand finally share a stage in *The Concert that Never Was* (Riviera, 2901 Las Vegas Blvd. S., 800/634-3420, 7 P.M. Sun.–Thurs., $60–70). At one point in the show the Streisand impersonator, Sharon Owens, sings along with a video of Sinatra, in a Nat–Natalie Cole riff. Owens, especially, and Sebastian Anzaldo both bear striking resemblance to the superstars. The show progresses like you might expect the real thing might have, given the strong personalities of both Sinatra and Streisand. There is little interaction, except in a duet of "Luck Be a Lady," each seemingly content to put on their own separate concerts.

Trent Carlini in The King: One Night With You

Crowned *The Next Big Thing* on the ABC TV contest, Carlini (Las Vegas Hilton, 3000 Paradise Rd., 800/222-5361, 8 P.M. Wed.–Mon., $49–79) is the best of the 245 registered Elvis impersonators in town, combining a strong resemblance to the King with pitch-perfect singing. His show traces Presley's career from rockabilly sensation to "Jailhouse Rock" to Vegas jumpsuit.

The King Lives

Legends in Concert alum Pete Willcox's *The King Lives* (Hooters, 115 E. Tropicana Ave., 702/739-9000, 7:30 P.M. Wed.–Sun., $25) is a close second to fellow alum Trent Carlini in the Elvis impersonator sweepstakes.

Mac King Comedy Magic

The quality of afternoon shows in Las Vegas is spotty at best, but Mac King Comedy Magic (Harrah's, 3475 Las Vegas Blvd. S., 702/369-5222, 1 P.M. and 3 P.M. Tues.–Sat., $25) fits the bill for talent and affordability. King's routine is clean both technically and content-wise. With a plaid suit, good manners, and a silly grin, he cuts a nerdy figure, but his tricks and banter are skewed enough to make even the most jaded teenager laugh.

Human Nature

Blue-eyed soul gets the Down Under treatment with the exhaustingly titled *Human Nature— The Ultimate Celebration of the Motown Sound Presented by Smokey Robinson* (Imperial Palace, 3535 Las Vegas Blvd. S., 888/777-7664, 7:30 P.M. Sat.–Thurs., $60–71). Four clean-cut, well-dressed Aussies, backed by a small live band, belt out Motown classics with enough verve and coordinated dance moves to make Robinson a fan.

Divas Las Vegas

Female impersonator Frank Marino has been headlining on the Strip for nearly 25 years, and he still looks good—with or without eye shadow and falsies. Marino stars as emcee Joan Rivers, leading fellow impersonators who lip-synch their way through cheeky renditions of tunes by Lady Gaga, Cher, Madonna, and others in *Divas Las Vegas* (Imperial Palace, 3535 Las Vegas Blvd. S., 888/777-7664, 10 P.M. Sat.–Thurs., $47–91).

Vinnie Favorito

Vinnie Favorito (Flamingo, 3555 Las Vegas Blvd. S., 702/885-1451, 8 P.M. daily, $55–65) is not impressed, and he'll let you know it. Whatever your profession, level of education, athletic achievement, or other worthy attribute, Favorito will turn it into an instrument of shame. Working with no set material, Favorito is reminiscent of Don Rickles, mingling with and interviewing audience members to find fodder for his quick wit.

Amazing Johnathan

Not much seems to go right for the Amazing Johnathan (Planet Hollywood, 3667 Las Vegas Blvd. S., 702/836-0836, 9 P.M. Tues.–Sat., $60–70), and that's the best part of the comedy magician's act. He panics when he plunges scissors into his assistant's head. Johnathan responds with F-bombs and middle fingers when the audience laughs at—not with—his ineptitude during a magic trick. He takes his revenge on the audience and one volunteer in particular.

Gordie Brown

A terrific song stylist in his own right, Gordie Brown (Golden Nugget, 129 E. Fremont St., 866/946-5336, 8 P.M. Fri.–Tues., $48–70) is the thinking person's singing impressionist. Using his targets' peccadilloes as fodder for his song parodies, Brown pokes serious fun with a surgeon's precision. Props, mannerisms, and absurd vignettes incorporating several celebrity voices at once add to the madcap fun.

Comedy

Comedy is still serious business in Las Vegas, and fans of the genre will find both comedy clubs as well as comedians with permanent gigs. For every Rita Rudner and George Wallace playing regularly in their own showrooms, there are dozens of touring headliners and hundreds of talented up-and-coming comics paying their dues in club stops around town. Among the headliners, veteran Louie Anderson ended a four-year run at Excalibur in 2010 and now waxes nostalgic—and hilarious—as the resident headliner at **Bonkerz** (Palace Station, 2411 Sahara Ave., 8:30 P.M. Mon.–Sat., $30–50).

The up-and-coming have a dozen places to land gigs when they're in town. There's **The Improv** at Harrah's (3475 Las Vegas Blvd. S., 702/369-5223, 8:30 P.M. and 10:30 P.M. Tues.–Sun., $29–45), the **Riviera Comedy Club** (2901 Las Vegas Blvd. S., 702/794-9433 or 877/892-7469, 8 P.M. and 10 P.M. daily, $25–35), and the **Four Queens L.A. Comedy Club** (202 Fremont St., 800/634-6045, 8:30 P.M.

Wed.–Thurs. and Sun., 7:30 P.M. and 9:30 P.M. Fri.–Sat., $16–33).

Magic

Magic shows are nearly as ubiquitous as comedy, with the more accomplished, such as Penn & Teller and **Lance Burton** getting stable long-term contracts. Burton ended a 14-year run at the Monte Carlo in 2010; chances are the master of the big illusion and sleight-of-hand will remain in Las Vegas, but his new home had not been determined at press time. Wherever he ends up, Burton's show is recommended. He shows true reverence for the craft as he perplexes audiences with close-up trickery before engaging in some alchemy, turning a woman into a gold statue. Talent, rather than distracting special effects, rule Burton's kid-friendly shows. He invariably invites youngsters on stage to be part of the act.

Nathan Burton (Flamingo, 3555 Las Vegas Blvd. S., 702/733-3333, 4 P.M. Tues. and Fri.–Sun., $22–49)—no relation—has parlayed his *America's Got Talent* success into a long-term gig as well, and he may be the next big thing to wield the wand in Las Vegas.

Among the other magic shows in town is **Steve Dacri** (Las Vegas Hilton, 3000 Paradise Rd., 800/222-5361, 7 P.M. Sun.–Mon., $49–79).

LIVE MUSIC

With all the entertainment that casinos have to offer—and the budgets to bring in the best—there's some surprising talent lurking in the dives, meat markets, and neighborhood pubs around Las Vegas. Locals who don't want to deal with the hassles of a trip to the Strip and visitors whose musical tastes don't match the often-mainstream pop-rock-country genre of the resort lounges might find a gem or two by venturing away from the neon.

Feelgoods (6750 W. Sahara Ave., 702/220-8849), named for the Mötley Crüe song "Dr. Feelgood" and partly owned by lead singer Vince Neil, brings in the sort of bands you'd expect: hard rock and hair. With more than 20,000 square feet of space and a 2,500-square-foot dance floor, **Stoney's Rockin' Country** (9151 Las Vegas Blvd. S., Suite 300, 702/435-2855) could almost *be* its own country. It's honky-tonk on a grand scale, with a mechanical bull and line dancing lessons. Jeff Healy and B. B. King have graced the stage at the **Sand Dollar** (3355 Spring Mountain Rd., 702/485-5401), where blue-collar blues rule. Bands start around 10 P.M. weekdays, 7:30 P.M. weekends. The people your mama warned you about hang out at the **Double Down Saloon** (4640 Paradise Rd., 702/791-5775), drinking to excess and thrashing to the punk, ska, and psychobilly bands on stage.

THE ARTS

With so much plastic, neon, and reproduction statuary around town, it's easy to accuse Las Vegas of being a soulless, cultureless wasteland, and many have. But Las Vegans don't live in casino hotels and eat every meal in the buffet. We don't all make our living as dealers and cocktail waitresses. Las Vegas, like most others, is a city built of communities. So why shouldn't Las Vegas enjoy and foster the arts? As home to an urban university and many profitable businesses just itching to prove their corporate citizenry, southern Nevada's arts are as viable as any city of comparable size in the country.

The local art scene will receive a big boost in 2012 with the projected opening of the **Smith Center for the Performing Arts,** a major cog in the revitalization of downtown, along with the development of 61 acres of former Union Pacific Railroad land the city has been working to turn into a pedestrian-friendly showplace. It will become home to the Las Vegas Philharmonic, the Nevada Ballet Theatre, local and school performances and classes, and national touring companies.

Classical Music

The **Las Vegas Philharmonic** (702/258-5438) presents a full schedule of pops, masterworks, holiday, and youth performances at the Artemus Ham Concert Hall on the UNLV campus (4505 S. Maryland Pkwy.). The Phil also works with the local school district to develop music education classes.

Ballet

With a 36,000-square-foot training facility, **Nevada Ballet Theatre** (702/243-2623) trains hundreds of aspiring ballerinas aged 18 months through adults and provides practice and performance space for its professional company. The company performs at the Artemus Ham Concert Hall on the UNLV campus (4505 S. Maryland Pkwy.). The fledgling **Las Vegas Ballet Company** (702/240-3263, www.lasvegasballet.org) was founded by former Nevada Ballet Theatre principal dancers as a performance outlet for students at their ballet and modern dance academy.

Theater

Theater abounds in Las Vegas, with various troupes staging mainstream plays, musical comedy, and experimental productions. **Las Vegas Little Theatre** (3920 Schiff Dr., 702/362-7996, www.lvlt.org), the town's oldest community troupe, performs mostly mainstream shows in its Mainstage series and takes a few more chances on productions in its Black Box theater. The repertoire at **Insurgo** (702/771-7331, www.insurgotheater.org) is even more stretched: Its 2010 season included *Macbeth* as well as *Sugar Puppy Comedy Burlesque.*

The highest-quality acting and production values can be found at the University of Nevada, Las Vegas, Performing Arts Center (4505 S. Maryland Pkwy., 702/895-ARTS—702/895-2787, http://pac.unlv.edu), comprising the Artemus Ham Concert Hall, the Judy Bayley Theater, and the Alta Ham Black Box Theater. The **Nevada Conservatory Theatre,** the university's troupe of advanced students and visiting professional actors, performs fall–spring. Shows in the Bayley run from the farcical to the poignant (*Noises Off* and Sam Shepard's *Fool for Love* bookended the 2010–2011 season), while Black Box shows range from Euripides to Lanford Wilson.

Guests become witnesses, sleuths, and even suspects in **Marriage Can Be Murder**

(Fitzgeralds, 301 Fremont St., 702/388-2111, 6:30 P.M. daily, $60–77) interactive dinner theater. Soon the bodies start piling up between the one-liners and slapstick. Dig out your deerstalker and magnifying glass and help catch that killer.

Visual Art

Outside the downtown arts district and the fabulous art collections amassed and displayed by Steve Wynn and other casino magnates, the **Donna Beam Fine Art Gallery** at UNLV (4505 S. Maryland Pkwy., 702/895-3893, 9 A.M.–5 P.M. Mon.–Fri., 10 A.M.–2 P.M. Sat., free) hosts exhibitions by nationally and internationally known painters, sculptors, designers, potters, and other visual artists. In addition to helping visitors enhance their critical thinking and aesthetic sensitivity, the exhibits teach UNLV students the skills needed in gallery management.

Sadly, the Las Vegas Art Museum, which shared space with the West Las Vegas Library, closed in 2009, a victim of the economic downturn. Its board hopes to reopen the gallery when good times return.

RIDES AND GAMES
Top of the Tower

Daredevils will delight in the vertigo-inducing thrill rides on the observation deck at the Stratosphere Tower (200 Las Vegas Blvd. S., 702/380-7711, 10 A.M.–1 A.M. Sun.–Thurs., 10 A.M.–2 A.M. Fri.–Sat., $12–100). The newest ride, Sky Jump Las Vegas, invites the daring to plunge into space for a 15-second free fall. Angled guide wires keep jumpers on target and ease them to gentle landings. This skydive without a parachute costs $100. The other rides are 100-story-high variations on traditional thrill rides: The Big Shot is a sort of 15-person reverse bungee jump; X-Scream sends riders on a gentle (at first) roll off the edge, leaving them suspended over Las Vegas Boulevard; Insanity's giant arms swing over the edge, tilting to suspend riders nearly horizontally. These attractions are about $13 each, plus a charge just to ride the elevator to the top of the tower (adults $16, children $10, seniors, hotel guests, and Nevada residents $12). Multiple-ride packages and all-day passes are available but don't include the Sky Jump.

Adventuredome

Behind Circus Circus, the Adventuredome Theme Park (2880 Las Vegas Blvd. S., 702/794-3939, 10 A.M.–midnight daily summer, 10 A.M.–9 P.M. daily during the school year, over 48 inches tall $25, under 48 inches $15) houses a roller coaster, a log flume, laser tag, and other topsy-turvy and simulated-motion machines—all inside a pink plastic shell. The main teen and adult attractions are the Canyon Blaster, the largest indoor coaster in the world with speeds up to 55 mph, which is pretty rough; and the Rim Runner flume ride, a big drop, a big splash, and you walk around wet the rest of the day. The five-acre fun park can host birthday parties. The all-day passes are a definite bargain over individual ride prices, but carnival games, food vendors, and special rides and games not included in the pass give parents extra chances to spend money. It's not the Magic Kingdom, but it has rides to satisfy all ages and bravery levels. Besides, Las Vegas is supposed to be the *adult* Disneyland.

Indy and NASCAR Driving

If, after your virtual driving practice, you're ready to take the wheel of a 600-hp stock car, check out the **Richard Petty Driving Experience** (Las Vegas Motor Speedway, 7000 Las Vegas Blvd. N., 800/BE-PETTY—800/237-3889, days and times vary, $159–1,299). The "Rookie Experience" ($499) lets NASCAR wannabes put the stock car through its paces for eight laps around the 1.5-mile tri-oval after extensive in-car and on-track safety training. Participants also receive a lap-by-lap breakdown of their run, transportation to and from the Strip, and a tour of the Driving Experience Race Shop. Even more intense—and more expensive—experiences, with more laps and more in-depth instruction, are available. To feel the thrill without the responsibility, opt for the three-lap ride-along

($109) in a two-seat stock car with a professional driver at the wheel.

The **Mario Andretti Driving Experience** (Las Vegas Motor Speedway, 7000 Las Vegas Blvd. N., 877/RACE-LAP—877/722-3527) offers similar high-speed driving using Indy cars.

Primm Attractions

The resorts in Primm, 40 miles south of Las Vegas on I-15, attract families with a lineup of several amusement park–quality thrill rides (702/679-RIDE—702/679-7433, call for hours). The best is the **Desperado** (48 inches or taller, $8), one of the highest and fastest roller coasters in the country. The first hill ferries riders 209 feet almost straight up for an unparalleled view of the flat valley. But look quickly before your car plunges over the precipice on its way to 2.5 minutes of 80-mph twists and turns. There's not much time to catch your breath, because next up is the **Turbo Drop** (48 inches or taller, $6), a 4.5-g plummet from 170 feet up. Riders reach speeds of 45 mph as they hurtle toward earth. Only a bit tamer, **Adventure Canyon Log Flume** (46 inches or taller, $6) challenges riders to shoot not only the rapids but also strategically placed targets using laser light pistols. Waterfall plunges ensure everyone gets wet.

There's plenty of virtual fun in Primm as well. **The Vault** (48–78 inches, $6) lets you choose from eight 3-D thrills: float to Arabia aboard a magic carpet, or careen out of control in an ore cart through an abandoned mine. Another virtual experience awaits in the **Maxflight Cyber Coaster** (48 inches or taller, $5), with motion-simulated rides on roller coasters from around the world. Little thrill seekers get their chance with **Frog Hopper** (36 inches or taller, $3), a tot-size version of Turbo Drop. Cap the evening with a few racing, fighting, and shooting games at **Attraction Zone Arcade.**

SPORTS
Golf

With its climate, endless sunshine, and vacation destination status, it's no wonder that Las Vegas is home to more than 40 golf courses. Virtually all are eminently playable and fair, although the dry heat makes the greens fast and the city's valley location can make for some havoc-wreaking winds in the spring. Las Vegas courses, especially in recent years, have removed extraneous water-loving landscaping, opting for xeriscape and desert landscape, irrigating the fairways and greens with reclaimed water. Greens fees and amenities range from affordable municipal-type courses to some of the most exclusive country clubs anywhere. The following is a selective list in each budget category.

Henderson's **Black Mountain** (500 Greenway Rd., Henderson, 702/565-7933, $50–75) received a $2 million makeover in 2008. Rolling fairways and strategically placed bunkers challenge all skill levels. Black Mountain features three distinct nine-hole sets; mix and match to play your favorite 18. At **Highland Falls** (10201 Sun City Blvd., 702/254-7010 or 800/803-0758, $35–60) you'll be treated to some stunning mountain and city views. Water hazards are tough but infrequent, and flat greens help make up for the challenging 126 slope rating on the 6,512-yard course.

There's much more water to contend with at **Siena Golf Club** (10575 Siena Monte Ave., 702/341-9200 or 888/689-6469, $99–169). Six small lakes, deep fairway bunkers, and desert scrub provide significant challenges off the tee, but five sets of tee boxes even things out for shorter hitters. The large, fairly flat greens are fair and readable. A perfect example of many courses' move toward more ecofriendly design, **Painted Desert** (5555 Painted Mirage Rd., 702/645-2568, $60–149) uses cacti, mesquites, and other desert plants to separate its links-style fairways. The 6,323-yard, par-72 course isn't especially challenging, especially if you're straight off the tee, making it a good choice for getting back to the fundamentals. Bring plenty of balls when you accept the challenge at **Badlands** (9119 Alta Dr., 702/363-0754, $89–140), as you'll routinely be asked to carry beautiful but intimidating desert

RED ROCK CANYON

West of Las Vegas, stretching across the horizon and nestled in the middle of the rugged Spring Mountains, Red Rock Canyon National Conservation Area (702/515-5350, $7 cars, $3 motorcycles, bicycles, and pedestrians) features sandstone in shades of umber, crimson, lavender, and rust vibrant enough to rival the brightest neon.

Drive west on Charleston Boulevard 12 miles from the casinos. The last vestiges of city sprawl give way to desert scrub and Joshua trees as the mountains rise ahead. As you round a final bend, Red Rock Canyon's 200,000 acres of stark yet hospitable wilderness comes into view.

An outstanding interactive **visitors center** (8 A.M.-4:30 P.M. daily), completed in 2009, is the place to get your bearings as well as learn about the trails, animals, plants, and recreational activities the park supports and the history and geography of the colorful cliff faces. Take in the big picture on the **scenic drive** (6 A.M.-7 P.M. daily Mar., 6 A.M.-8 P.M. daily Apr.-Sept., 6 A.M.-7 P.M. daily Oct., 6 A.M.-5 P.M. daily Nov.-Feb.) that circumnavigates the park, with pullouts at popular trailheads, picnic areas, and scenic overlooks. On many warm windless days, you can spot rock climbers clinging to many of the rock faces in designated climbing areas.

When you're ready to stretch your legs, find the trail that fits your mood and fitness level. In the park's northwest corner, the La Madre Spring trailhead at the Willow Springs picnic area leads to a moderate walk through a meandering, narrow, steep-walled canyon. Cool, lush gashes between the cliffs lead up to a trickling spring. For a more taxing scramble, catch the Turtlehead Peak trailhead near the sandstone quarry on the park's northeast side. Five miles of arrow grades and enormous rounded boulders lead to a panoramic summit.

Red Rock Canyon clearly reveals the limestone formed when most of Nevada lay under a warm shallow sea as well as the massive sand dunes that later covered this desert. Chemical and thermal reactions petrified the dunes into polychrome sandstone, and erosion sculpted it into strange and wondrous shapes. When the land began faulting and shifting roughly 100 million years ago, the limestone was thrust up and over the younger sandstone, forming a protective layer that inhibited further erosion, known as the Keystone Thrust. The contact between the limestone and the sandstone accounts for the bands of contrasting colors in the cliffs. Except for the spectacular canyons carved from runoff over the past 60 million years, the 15-mile-long, 3,000-foot-high sandstone escarpment today remains relatively untouched by the march of time.

Camping is available year-round at **Red Rock Campground** (W. Charleston Blvd./Hwy. 159 at Moenkopi Rd., 702/515-5000, $15), two miles east of the visitors center.

gullies and ravines full of lush wildflowers and cacti. This course does not forgive poor tee shots, and even if you do find your ball, hitting from this rough delivers more punishment for golfer and clubface alike.

The only course open to the public on the Strip is **Bali Hai** (5160 Las Vegas Blvd. S., 888/427-6678, $125–295), next to Mandalay Bay on the south end of casino row. The South Pacific theme includes lots of lush green tropical foliage, deep azure ponds, and black volcanic outcroppings. A handful of long par-4s are fully capable of making a disaster of your scorecard even before you reach the sphincter-clinching par-3 16th. Not only does it play to an island green, it comes with a built-in gallery where you can enjoy your discomfort while dining on Bali Hai's restaurant patio.

Reserved only for hotel guests, the **Wynn Golf Club** (3131 Las Vegas Blvd. S., 702/770-3575, $300 and up) transcends indulgences and borders on ostentation. Still, you get what you pay for on the course designed by Tom Fazio with significant input from Steve Wynn.

MOUNT CHARLESTON

In the middle of spring, when Las Vegas temperatures often already flirt with 90°F, many an urbanite gazes wistfully at the white-frosted summit of Mount Charleston, only 35 miles away. As late as mid-May, snow still clings stubbornly to the 12,000-foot-high peak, the jewel of the Spring Mountain range.

Its elevation, resulting cool temperature, and more than 25 inches of precipitation per year make Mount Charleston a summer oasis for Las Vegans and create diverse, distinctive ecosystems that contrast strikingly with that of the desert floor. The Spring Mountains are home to 30 endemic plant species and support a system of six distinct ecological zones. Ascending from Las Vegas to Mount Charleston in terms of altitude is the equivalent of traveling from Mexico to Alaska in terms of latitude. In the valley, creosote bush and Joshua trees thrive. Higher, piñon pine and sagebrush take over before giving way to aspens and finally the hearty bristlecone pine. But even this grizzled veteran of numerous winter campaigns can't survive at Mount Charleston's summit.

Well-maintained roads allow two-wheel-drive vehicles to ascend to about 8,500 feet, high enough for a day of respite from the July heat or a December afternoon of sledding. Nearly a million Las Vegans and others take advantage of the mountain's recreational opportunities, hiking, camping, picnicking, and skiing among its natural wonders.

A little more than 10 miles from U.S. 95, Highway 157 climbs into the forest. For an alpine lodge honeymoon or just a hot chocolate on your way up or down the mountain, stop at the **Resort on Mount Charleston** (2 Kyle Canyon Rd., 702/872-5500 or 888/559-

1888, $60–180), which has a large chalet-like lobby complete with a roaring fireplace, a bar with big TVs, a pool table, slot machines, and a spacious restaurant. Built in 1984, this romantic hideaway received a multimillion-dollar upgrade in 2010, making it a perfect place to propose (you can then return to Las Vegas and get married an hour or two later and come back to check into the resort's bridal suite).

Beyond the hotel, Highway 157 continues another four miles past **Kyle Canyon Campground** (702/872-5577, year-round, $19–34) at 7,100 feet. This is the lowest of five high-mountain campgrounds in the vicinity, roughly 5,000 feet higher in elevation than downtown Las Vegas (and at least 20 degrees cooler). It's also the closest, a mere 45 minutes from the city. Here you'll find 25 campsites for tents or self-contained motor homes up to 40 feet. Reservations are accepted May–September.

A little farther along is **Mount Charleston village,** with a few residences and a U.S. Forest Service district office. Next to it is **Fletcher View Campground** (877/444-6777), with 12 sites (half can be reserved) for tents and trailers. It is smaller and more compact than the Kyle Canyon Campground, with just one road in and out. Sites are a little closer together and a bit shadier. If both campgrounds are full, **Mount Charleston Lodge** (702/872-5408 or 800/955-1314, $135–270) is the main action on the mountain. It is a funky alpine operation with rustic one-room cabins and a restaurant. The cabins come in two sizes, single (500 square feet with a king bed) and double (900 square feet with two kings). The bar is open till midnight, and the restaurant (8 A.M.–9 P.M.

Serenity just steps from the Strip, much of the Wynn sits where the venerable Desert Inn course once resided. It has more than 1,000 mature pine trees salvaged from the previous course, water on 11 holes, a waterfall, and wildly undulating greens and sloping fairways—no small engineering feat on the flat Vegas valley floor and guaranteed to mesmerize and entice players.

Las Vegas Motor Speedway

Home to NASCAR's Sprint Cup and Sam's Town 300 Nationwide Series race, the Las Vegas Motor Speedway (7000 Las Vegas Blvd.

Mon.-Fri., 8 A.M.-10 P.M. Sat.-Sun., $13-28) serves warming fare.

On Highway 157 just before the hotel, Highway 158 heads off to the left and in six miles connects with Highway 156, the Lee Canyon Road. **Robbers Roost** is a short easy hike to a large rock grotto that, if you believe the legend, once sheltered local horse thieves. A mile north is **Hilltop Campground** (702/515-5400, $19-47), at 8,400 feet. It has asphalt pavement, picnic tables and grills, wide staircases from the parking areas to the uphill tent sites, and clean restrooms and shower facilities.

Corn Creek Springs, with its lush environment, three spring-fed ponds, woodland, and pasture, is a fantastic place to have a picnic, view wildlife, or just stroll in the quiet, clean air and meditate. More than 240 species of birds have been observed at the springs; early mornings and evenings are the best time to spot rabbits, squirrels, and occasionally mule deer, coyotes, badgers, and foxes around the field station.

The nearby **Desert National Wildlife Range** (702/646-3401) was established in 1936 to protect the overhunted desert bighorn sheep. It encompasses approximately 1.5 million acres of the Mojave Desert, making it the largest National Wildlife Refuge in the Lower 48.

About four miles up Mormon Well Road, the surrounding mountains offer the best bighorn habitat in the entire range; they visit this area early and late in the year when it is cooler. Their coats blend well with the rugged terrain, so watch the high crags and pinnacles for movement or their telltale white muzzle.

Just before you get to the parking lot for the Las Vegas Ski and Snowboard Resort, you'll pass two campgrounds. At 8,600 feet, **McWilliams Campground** (877/444-6777, $19-34) is 1,600 feet higher than the ones at Kyle Canyon. The trees are still tall but more sparse, and there's less undergrowth, so there's more space among the 40 campsites. There is piped drinking water, picnic tables, grills, fire rings, and a campground host. Slightly up the hill is **Dolomite Campground** (877/444-6777, early May-early Oct., $19), similar to McWilliams but with 31 sites; the higher ones at the back of the campground are more desirable than those terraced below.

At 6,500 feet, **Las Vegas Ski & Snowboard Resort** (Hwy. 156, 702/385-2754, snow conditions 702/593-9500, 8:30 A.M.-4:30 P.M. daily Thanksgiving-Easter, $45-60 adults, $25-35 under age 12 and over 60) is only 45 miles from sizzling Sin City. The base elevation is 8,500 feet, and the top of the chairlift is another 1,000 feet higher, making for some thin air. But cliff walls towering above the slope protect skiers from biting westerlies. A beginner chairlift and ski school feeds the bunny slope; chairlifts ferry skiers to six intermediate runs and four black diamonds. Get here early on the weekend.

There is also a day lodge with a coffee shop and a lounge, a ski shop (702/645-2754) that rents equipment, and a ski school. Snow machines ensure packed and groomed slopes all winter.

Down the mountain from the ski area are plentiful places for tubing, sledding, snowmobiling, and cross-country skiing. The best Nordic skiing is on north-facing slopes in open meadows above 8,000 feet. Scott Canyon, Mack's Canyon, and the Bristlecone Trail are popular Nordic ski areas.

N., 800/644-4444) is a racing omniplex. In addition to the superspeedway, a 1.5-mile trioval for NASCAR races, the site also brings in dragsters to its quarter-mile strip; modifieds, late models, bandoleros, legends, bombers, and more to its paved oval; and off-roaders to its half-mile clay oval.

The speedway underwent a multimillion-dollar renovation project between NASCAR Weekends in 2006 and 2007, resulting in an unprecedented interactive fan experience known as the Neon Garage. Located in the speedway's infield, Neon Garage has unique and gourmet concession stands, live entertainment, and the winner's circle. Fans can get up close or watch drivers and crews from bird's-eye perches.

Boxing and Mixed Martial Arts

Even before Sonny Liston floored Floyd Patterson to retain his heavyweight title at the Las Vegas Convention Center in 1963, Las Vegas had begun to knock out New York City's Madison Square Garden as the undisputed champion of the boxing venues. Boxing, more than the Lennon Sisters, Andy Williams, and the other superstars that played the showroom, established Caesars Palace as the gem of the desert it has become. Ken Norton, Evander Holyfield, Muhammad Ali, and Larry Holmes all fought here. And Sugar Ray Leonard, Thomas Hearns, and Marvin Hagler took turns beating each other up in a classic series of bouts through the 1980s.

The International and its reincarnation as the Las Vegas Hilton jumped into the fight game with both feet, hosting Sonny Liston and George Foreman in separate matches in 1969 and continuing to serve as a major venue until the early 2000s. It was here that Mike Tyson first wrested the heavyweight belt in dominating fashion over Trevor Berbick. Other Las Vegas hotels have been the sites of some of the greatest fights of the century. The fragmenting of the boxing sanctioning bodies, the absence of an engaging heavyweight champion, and the emergence of other venues have taken some of the luster off the fight game in Las Vegas; no longer do the big bouts turn into celebrity fests.

But the sweet science is far from dead in Las Vegas. Nevada's legalized sports betting and the drama surrounding the on-again, off-again Floyd Mayweather Jr.–Manny Pacquiao bout of 2010 rekindled Las Vegas's romance with boxing.

For every Leonard-Hearns or Tyson-Berbick matchup, there are plenty of pugs looking for a payday. Dozens of casinos host occasional or regular fight cards. Cheap tickets, entertaining bouts, occasional former contenders, and lots of punchers working their way up the ladder for a shot at a minor alphabet-soup belt make Las Vegas a boxing fan's Shangri-la.

The advent of mixed martial arts has solidified the city's position as the fight capital of the world. Three separate Las Vegas gyms cater to fighters training to become king of the octagon, and some of the biggest pay-per-view events are held in Las Vegas casinos.

Accommodations

CHOOSING ACCOMMODATIONS

The most important considerations when planning your visit to Vegas are when to go and where to stay. Las Vegas boasts more than 100 hotels and 200 motels, but sometimes that makes it harder, not easier, to choose the perfect place to stay. Also keep in mind that accommodations either sell out or nearly sell out every weekend of the year. Long weekends and holidays, especially New Year's Eve, Valentine's Day, Memorial Day, Fourth of July, Labor Day, and Thanksgiving, along with international holidays such as Cinco de Mayo, Mexican Independence Day, and Chinese New Year, are sold out weeks in advance. Special events such as concerts, title fights, the Super Bowl, the Final Four, NASCAR Weekend, and the National Finals Rodeo are sold out months in advance. Reservations are made for the biggest conventions (Consumer Electronics, Men's Apparel, and so on) a year ahead of time.

The city's 125,000 guest rooms fill up fast—especially the top hotels, the best-value hotels, and the cheapest motels. What's more, the crowds are relentless; Las Vegas rarely gets a break to catch its breath. There are some minor quiet times, such as the three weeks before Christmas and a noticeable downward blip in July–August when the mercury doesn't see fit

THE WORLD'S LARGEST HOTELS

Rank	Name	Location	Size
1.	First World Pahang	Malaysia	6,118 rooms
2.	**MGM Grand**	Las Vegas	5,044 rooms
3.	**Luxor**	Las Vegas	4,408 rooms
4.	Mandalay Bay	including Thehotel Las Vegas	4,341 rooms
5.	Ambassador City	Jomtien, Thailand	4,210 rooms
6.	**Venetian**	Las Vegas	4,027 rooms
7.	**Caesars Palace**	Las Vegas	4,013 rooms
8.	**Excalibur**	Las Vegas	4,008 rooms
9.	**Aria**	Las Vegas	4,004 rooms
10.	**Bellagio**	Las Vegas	3,993 rooms
11.	**Circus Circus**	Las Vegas	3,697 rooms
12.	Planet Hollywood	Tokyo	3,680 rooms
13.	**Shinagawa Prince**	Las Vegas	3,636 rooms
14.	**Flamingo**	Las Vegas	3,565 rooms
15.	**Palazzo**	Las Vegas	3,443 rooms
16.	Hilton Hawaiian Village	Honolulu	3,386 rooms
17.	**The Mirage**	Las Vegas	3,044 rooms
18.	**Monte Carlo**	Las Vegas	3,002 rooms
19.	Venetian Macau	Macau	3,000 rooms
20.	**Las Vegas Hilton**	Las Vegas	2,956 rooms

LAS VEGAS

to drop below 90°F. Also, Sunday–Thursday—when there aren't any large conventions or sporting events—are a little less crazy than usual; almost all the room packages and deep discounts are only available on these days.

If you're just coming for the weekend, keep in mind that most of the major hotels don't even let you check in on a Saturday night. You can stay Friday and Saturday, but not Saturday alone.

Shop around. Casino profits continue to subsidize the other revenue-producing departments, so Las Vegas hotels can afford to discount their rooms up to a whopping 80 percent at times. In Las Vegas, the best way to get deep discounts is to stay where you play. If you play table games with an average bet of at least $25, you should be able to get the "casino rate," a 40–50 percent discount off the rack rate for the room (except for the high-roller casinos, such as Caesars, Mirage, the Venetian, Bellagio, and MGM Grand, where an average bet of $50–100 is often required). If you play slots or video poker, it behooves you to join the slot club at the casino that sees most of your action. The more slot-club points you accumulate in your account, the more free rooms and other free stuff you get.

Of course, your room is where you'll spend the least amount of time during your stay in Las Vegas, so remember the old travelers' axiom: Eat sweet, pay for play, but sleep cheap. Otherwise, as always, it's best to make your room reservations far in advance to ensure the appropriate type, price, and location.

ORIENTATION

Las Vegas hotels congregate in three locations: downtown, the Strip, and off-Strip. The Fremont Street Experience unifies the majority of downtown hotels into one multifarious attraction. Downtown's guest rooms are uniformly less expensive, the food is cheaper with no loss of quality, the gambling can be more positive if you know what you're looking for, and the cast of characters is far more varied and colorful. Henderson has stepped up to the plate with a couple of expansive and luxurious hotels at Lake Las Vegas and a few others in the Green Valley area.

The Strip has the biggest, newest, most themed, and most crowded hotels. Fifteen of the 20 largest hotels in the world are along a four-mile stretch on Las Vegas Boulevard South between Sahara and Tropicana Avenues. These hotels are self-contained mini cities, and although you never have to leave them, you're also somewhat captive in them: It's often hard to find your way out, the distance from your car to your room can be daunting, the distances between the hotels can be prohibitive, and the lines to do anything—eat, drink, play

blackjack, see a show, or catch a cab—can drive you to distraction. But if you want to be right in the thick of the gambling action, the Strip is the ticket.

The off-Strip hotels have the popular casinos, but they often have fewer guest rooms. They're frequented mostly by out-of-towners who specifically like them and by relatives of locals who live nearby. But you can often find good room deals, because even with so few rooms, the locals casinos often have trouble filling them; most visitors want to be in the thick of the neon—on the Strip or downtown.

Note: The casino hotels are covered in the *Casinos* section.

HOTELS
Center Strip

With a name like **Trump** (2000 Fashion Show Dr., 702/982-0000 or 866/939-8786, $99–190), you know that no whim will go unfulfilled. Standard studio suites open onto an Italian marble entryway leading to floor-to-ceiling windows with the requisite magnificent views. In-room amenities include a unique "Euro kitchen" will all appliances, including a stocked refrigerator. Dual sinks, plasma TVs embedded in the mirrors, and spa tubs highlight the marble-studded bathrooms. A bigger plasma TV and a convertible sofa share the living area, and feather comforters and Italian linens make for heavenly restfulness in the bedroom. Dining options include the chic **DJT** steak house and the hip **H2(EAU)** poolside. **The Spa at Trump** offers unique packages such as the "Party Relief Recovery" ($149). The hotel's resort fee includes a $25 spa credit.

One of the newest landmarks on the Las Vegas skyline, **Platinum** (211 E. Flamingo Rd., 702/365-5000 or 877/211-9211, $119–179) treats both guests and the environment with kid gloves. The resort uses the latest technology to reduce its carbon footprint through such measures as low-energy lighting throughout, ecofriendly room thermostats, and motion sensors to turn lights off when restrooms are unoccupied. Suites are an expansive 950 square feet of muted designer furnishings and accents, and they include all modern conveniences, such as high-speed Internet, high-fidelity sound systems, full kitchens, and oversize tubs. **Kilowatt** (6 A.M.–3 P.M. daily, $10–20) with sleek blue and silver decor accented with dark woods, is a feast for the eyes and the palate for breakfast and lunch.

Lower Strip

Offering sophisticated accommodations and amenities without the hubbub of a rowdy casino, the **Renaissance** (3400 Paradise Rd., 702/784-5700 or 800/750-0980, $120–210) has big standard guest rooms that come complete with triple-sheeted 300-thread-count Egyptian cotton beds with down comforters and duvets, walk-in showers, full tubs, 32-inch flat-panel TVs, a business center, and high-speed Internet. Upper-floor guest rooms overlook the Wynn golf course. The pool and whirlpool are outside, and the concierge can score show tickets and tee times. **Envy Steakhouse** (6:30 A.M.–2 P.M. and 5–10 P.M. daily, brunch 11 A.M.–3 P.M. Sun., $30–50) has a few seafood entrées, but the Angus beef gets top billing.

Every guest room is a suite at the **Signature** (45 E. Harmon Ave., 877/612-2121 or 800/452-4520, $95–170) at MGM Grand. Even the junior suite is a roomy 550 square feet and includes a standard king bed, kitchenette, and spa tub. Most of the 1,728 smoke-free guest rooms in the gleaming 40-story tower include private balconies with Strip views, and guests have access to the complimentary 24-hour fitness center, three outdoor pools, a business center, and free wireless Internet throughout the hotel. A gourmet deli and acclaimed room service satisfy noshing needs, and **The Lounge** provides a quiet, intimate spot for discussing business or pleasure over drinks.

Located on the top four floors of Mandalay Bay, **Four Seasons** (3960 Las Vegas Blvd. S., 702/632-5000, $225–375) gives guests its own lobby, exclusive elevators, and a semiprivate entrance, insulating them from the madness of the casino atmosphere. The location on floors 36–39 along with the glass curtain

walls overlooking the pool, mountains, or bustling Strip ensure that guests truly "rise above it all." The 424 guest rooms and suites include 42-inch plasma TVs and DVD players, deep bathtubs, glass showers, and granite throughout the bathroom. The Four Seasons takes care of all its guests, not just those paying the bills. Kids will delight in the complimentary chocolate puzzle awaiting them at check-in. Older kids receive their own welcome gift: popcorn and soda. The **Verandah Lounge** (noon–10 P.M. daily, $25–40) gives comfort food a gourmet tweak, such as oxtail sloppy joes and Kobe beef sliders.

The condominium suites at **Desert Rose** (5051 Duke Ellington Way, 702/739-7000 or 888/732-8099, $100–300) are loaded, with new appliances and granite countertops in the kitchen as well as private balconies or patios outside. One-bedroom suites are quite large, at 650 square feet, and sleep four comfortably. Complimentary continental breakfast is included, as is a manager's reception Monday–Friday. Rates vary widely, but depending on your needs and travel dates, you might find a suite deal.

Although it includes a full-service casino and is just steps from the Strip, the draw of the **Tuscany** (255 E. Flamingo Rd., 702/893-8933 or 877/887-2264, $48–88) is the relaxed atmosphere, from its restaurants and lounges to its lagoon pool. The sprawling 27-acre site with footpaths and impeccable landscaping belies its proximity to the rush-rush of the Strip one block west. A cocktail bar poolside assists the Las Vegas sun in taking the edge off. Dining here is more low-key than at many of Tuscany's neighbors. Although there is a semiformal restaurant, **Tuscany Gardens** (5–10 P.M. daily, $20–35), the casual **Cantina** (11 A.M.–10 P.M. daily, $10–20) and **Marilyn's Café** (24 hours daily, $8–15) are more in keeping with the resort's métier. That's not to say Tuscany is strictly the purview of fuddy-duddies; the 50,000-square-foot casino has all the games you expect in Las Vegas, and there's nightly entertainment in the **Piazza Lounge.** All suites, the Tuscany's guest rooms boast more than 625 square feet and come with galley kitchens, wet bars, 25-inch TVs, and mini fridges.

MOTELS
The Strip

Several good-value motels are located on Las Vegas Boulevard South between the Stratosphere and the Riviera; these places are also good to try for weekly rooms with kitchenettes. When the temperature isn't in the triple digits, they're also within walking distance to the Sahara, Riviera, Circus Circus, and the Adventuredome. **Clarion** (325 E. Flamingo Rd., 800/732-7889, $55–100 d) offers clean doubles.

Motels along the lower Strip, from Bally's below Flamingo Avenue all the way out to the Mandalay Bay at the far south end of the Strip, are well placed to visit all the new big-band casino resorts but have prices that match the cheaper places north of downtown. The independent motels here are hit-and-miss. You're better off sticking with established brands like **Travelodge Las Vegas Strip** (3735 S. Las Vegas Blvd., 702/736-3443, $49–129), which gets a top rating for its reasonable prices; location near the MGM Grand, Luxor, and Mandalay Bay; and little extras like free continental breakfast, newspapers, and heated swimming pool. The supersize **Super 8** (4250 Koval Lane, 702/794-0888, $45–89), just east of Bally's and Paris, is the chain's largest in the world. It offers a heated pool but no other resort amenities; on the other hand, it doesn't charge resort fees. There's free Internet access but not much of a budget for decor in the guest rooms or common areas. If you stay here, order the ribs and a microbrew at the **Ellis Island Casino & Brewery** next door.

Another group of motels clings to the south side of the convention center on Paradise and Desert Inn Roads as well as the west side between Paradise Road and the Strip on Convention Center Drive. If you're attending a convention here and plan well in advance, you can reserve a very reasonable and livable room at any of several motels within a five-minute walk of the convention floor. Most of them have plenty of weekly rooms with kitchenettes, which can save you a bundle. It's a joy to be able to leave the convention floor and walk over to your room and back again if necessary—the shuttle buses to the far-flung hotels are very often crowded, slow, and inconvenient. Even if you're not attending a convention, this is a good part of town to stay in, off the main drag but in the middle of everything. You won't find whirlpool tubs, white-beach pools, or Egyptian cotton at **Rodeway Inn** (220 Convention Center Dr., 702/735-4151, $35–55), but you will find everything the budget traveler could ask for: hot showers, clean beds, and a refreshing pool. You'll also get extras such as a free continental breakfast and Wi-Fi. **Royal Resort** (99 Convention Center Dr., 702/735-6117 or 800/634-6118, $69) is part time-share, part hotel. Its outdoor pool area nestles against tropical landscaping, private cabanas, and a new hot tub. Guests in its 191 rooms receive free newspapers, use of the fitness center, and Internet access.

Downtown

Glitter Gulch fills Fremont Street from South Main Street to South 4th Street, but beyond that and on side streets, bargain-basement motels are numerous. Dozens of places are bunched together in three main groupings. It's not the best part of town, but it's certainly not the worst, and security is usually seen to by the management (but check with them to make sure). Generally speaking, the motels along East Fremont Street and Las Vegas Boulevard North are the least expensive. Motels between downtown and the Strip on Las Vegas Boulevard South are slightly more expensive and in a slightly better neighborhood.

East Fremont Street has plenty of motels, sometimes one right next to another or separated by car dealerships and bars. It's a few minutes' drive to the downtown casinos and an excursion to the Strip. This is also RV country, with RV parks lining the highway past motel row and the big parking lots at the casinos. And with so many possibilities out here, it's a good stretch to cruise if you don't have reservations and most No Vacancy signs are lit.

Two reliable standards in this neighborhood, with guest rooms generally under $50, are **Lucky Cuss** (3305 Fremont St., 702/457-1929) and **Downtowner** (129 N. 8th St., 702/384-1441).

Las Vegas Boulevard North from Fremont Street to East Bonanza Road, along with North Main Street and the north-numbered streets from 6th to 13th, are also packed with motels one after the other. Stay on the lighted streets. It might be a little unnerving to deal with the front desk person through bars, but Glitter Gulch is very handy if that's where you want to spend your time, and these rooms can be amazingly reasonable if a room is not where you want to spend your money. The **Bonanza Lodge** (1808 Fremont St., 702/382-3990, from $38) offers the basics with double rooms with two beds. The **Super 8** (700 Fremont St., 866/539-0036, from $62) is nicer, and the rates are a bit higher.

The motels on Las Vegas Boulevard South between downtown and the north end of the Strip at Sahara Avenue have the most convenient location if you like to float between downtown and the Strip or if you're getting married in one of the wedding chapels that line this stretch of the boulevard. It's also brighter and busier, and right on the main bus routes. Most of these motels also offer weekly room rates with or without kitchenettes. The **High Hat** (1300 Las Vegas Blvd. S., 702/382-8080, $35–95 d) has been around for several years.

Hostels

It's hard to beat these places for budget accommodations. Downtown, **USA Hostels Las Vegas** (1322 Fremont St., 702/385-1150 or 800/550-8958, $24–55) has a swimming pool and a hot tub. The rates include a pancake breakfast, coffee and tea, pool and foosball, and wireless Internet connections. The hostel also arranges trips to the Strip and visits to the Grand Canyon and other outdoorsy attractions.

Reserved only for international student travelers (ID required), the dorms at **Sin City Hostel** (1208 Las Vegas Blvd. S., 702/868-0222, $16–18) fit the starving student's budget

and include breakfast. Located on the Strip, the hostel features a barbecue pit, a basketball court, and Wi-Fi.

CAMPING AND RV PARKING
Camping

Camping options near the city include **Red Rock Campground** (W. Charleston Blvd./ Hwy. 159 at Moenkopi Rd., 702/515-5000, $15), two miles east of the visitors center. Rigs as well as tents are welcome in any of the 71 sites, but there are no water, electrical, or sewer hookups. Potable water is available, and firewood is for sale.

Callville Bay Resort (off Northshore Rd., 702/565-8958 or 800/255-5561, $22), on Lake Mead about 20 miles east of Las Vegas, has five full-hookup sites in its Trailer Village. Campers have access to the resort's gift shop, boat rentals, and snack bar. Nearby, the National Park Service runs **Callville Bay Campground** (702/293-8990, $10) with 80 tent and RV sites with running water, dump stations, picnic grills, and tables.

A half-dozen picturesque campsites dot **Mount Charleston** (Hwy. 157, 800/280-2267), 40 miles north of Las Vegas. Kyle Canyon (elevation 6,900 feet), Dolomite (elevation 8,300 feet), and Hilltop (elevation 8,400 feet) are open May–October. Fletcher View (elevation 7,000 feet) is open year-round. All but Dolomite have vault toilets and potable water, but no hookups.

Casino RV Parking

A number of casinos have attached RV parks. Other casinos allow RVs to park overnight in their parking lots but have no facilities.

Circusland (2800 Las Vegas Blvd. S., 702/794-3757 or 800/562-7270, about $40) is a prime spot for RVers, especially those with kids, who want to be right in the thick of things but also want to take advantage of very good facilities. The big park is all paved, with a few grassy islands here and a shade tree there; the convenience store is open 24 hours. Ten minutes spent learning where the Industrial Road back entrance is will save hours of sitting in traffic on the Strip. The park has 399 spaces operated by KOA. All have full hookups with 20-, 30-, and 50-amp power, and 280 of the spaces are pull-through. Tent sites (about $8) are also available. Wheelchair-accessible restrooms have flush toilets and hot showers, and there's also a laundry, a game room, a fenced playground, a heated swimming pool, a children's pool, a spa, a sauna, and groceries.

Sam's Town Nellis RV Park (4040 S. Nellis Blvd., 702/456-7777 or 800/634-6371, $21–25) has 500 spaces for motor homes, all with full hookups and 20-, 30-, and 50-amp power. It's mostly a paved parking lot with spacious sites, a heated pool, and a spa; the rec hall has a pool table and a kitchen. And, of course, it's near the bowling, dining, and movie theater in the casino.

Arizona Charlie's East (4445 Boulder Hwy., 702/951-5911, $20) has 239 spaces. The **California** (12 E. Ogden Ave., 702/385-1222 or 800/634-6505, $30–35) has 239 spaces, and nearby **Main Street Station** (200 N. Main St., 702/387-1896, $17–22) has 100 sites. Both are essentially parking lots close to the gambling and nothing more.

RV Parks

The best of the RV parks are a bit more expensive than the casino RV parks, but the amenities—especially the atmosphere, views, and landscaping—are generally worth the price.

The **Hitchin' Post** (3640 Las Vegas Blvd. N., 702/644-1043 or 888/433-8402, $29–35) offers free cable TV and Wi-Fi at its 196 spaces. The northern Las Vegas location is perhaps not the most desirable, but security is never a problem at the park. It's clean, and the on-site restaurant-bar rustles up a nice steak.

Oasis RV Park (2711 W. Windmill Lane, 800/566-4707, $30–67) is directly across I-15 from the Silverton Casino (take Exit 33 for Blue Diamond Rd. 3 miles south of Russell Rd., then go east to Las Vegas Blvd. S. Turn right and drive one block to West Windmill, then turn right into the park). Opened in 1996, Oasis has 936 spaces, and huge date palms usher you from the park entrance to the cavernous 24,000-square-foot clubhouse. Each space is wide enough for a car and motor home and comes with a picnic table and patio. The foliage is plentiful and flanks an 18-hole putting course along with family and adult swimming pools. The resort features a full calendar of poker tournaments, movies, karaoke, and bar and restaurant specials. Wheelchair-accessible restrooms have flush toilets and hot showers; there is also a laundry, a grocery store, an exercise room, and an arcade.

Food

Las Vegas buffets have evolved from little better than fast food to lavish spreads of worldwide cuisine complete with fresh salads, comforting soups, and decadent desserts. The exclusive resorts on the Strip have developed their buffets into gourmet presentations, often including delicacies such as crab legs, crème brûlée, and even caviar. Others, especially the locals casinos and those downtown that cater to more down-to-earth tastes, remain low-cost belly-filling options for intense gamblers and budget-conscious families. The typical buffet breakfast presents the usual fruits, juices, croissants, steam-table scrambled eggs, sausages, potatoes, and pastries. Lunch is salads and chicken, pizza, spaghetti, tacos, and more. Dinner is salads, steam-table vegetables, and potatoes with several varieties of meat, including a carving table with prime rib, turkey, and pork.

Buffets are still a big part of the Las Vegas vacation aura, but when the town's swank and swagger came back in the 1990s, it brought sophisticated dining with it. Las Vegas has come a long way from the coffee-and-sandwich shop shoved in a casino corner so players could recharge quickly and rush back to reclaim their slot machine.

Most major hotels have a 24-hour coffee shop, a steak house, and a buffet along with a couple of international restaurants. Noncasino restaurants around town are also proliferating quickly. Best of all, menu prices, like room rates, are consistently less expensive in Las Vegas than in any other major city in the country.

UPPER STRIP
Buffets

Assuming you're not a food snob, the **Garden Court Buffet** (Main Street Station, 200 N. Main St., 702/387-1896 or 800/713-8933, 7 A.M.–3 P.M. and 4–10 P.M. daily, breakfast $7, lunch $8, dinner $11–16, weekend brunch $11) will satisfy your taste buds and your bank account. The weekend brunch is a particular bargain. The fare is standard, with lunch presented in good variety by world region. At (The Buffet (Golden Nugget, 129 E. Fremont St., 800/634-3454, 7 A.M.–10 P.M. daily, breakfast $10, lunch $11, dinner $18, weekend brunch $18), the food leaves nothing to be desired, with extras like Greek salad, perfectly seasoned pork chops, and a delicate fine banana cake putting it a cut above the ordinary buffet, especially for downtown. Glass and brass accents and colorful wall and window treatments make for peaceful digestion.

Just a notch below these two, but still recommended—especially for fans of Mexican and Southwestern staples—**The Feast** (Texas Station, 2101 Texas Star Lane, 702/631-1000, 8 A.M.–9 P.M. daily, breakfast $7, lunch $9, dinner $12, weekend brunch $13) has terrific made-to-order fajitas, great tacos, and barbecue ribs.

Las Vegas Hilton's **The Buffet** (3000 Paradise Rd., 702/732-5111, 7 A.M.–2:30 P.M. and 5–10 P.M. daily, breakfast $14, lunch $15, dinner $20, weekend brunch $19) serves beer and wine at no extra charge during lunch and dinner.

Shrimp Cocktail

The Golden Gate's **Du-Par's** (1 Fremont St., 702/385-1906, 11 A.M.–3 A.M. daily) began

serving a San Francisco–style shrimp cocktail in 1955, and more than 30 million have been served since. The price up until a few years ago was only $0.49, but it's still a number-one value at $1.99. In fact, it's the oldest meal deal in Las Vegas—appropriate for the oldest hotel in Las Vegas. It goes great with a draft beer. Du-Par's Restaurant is also famous locally for melt-in-your-mouth pancakes. The version at the **Westside Deli** (Circus Circus, 2880 Las Vegas Blvd. S., 702/734-0410, 6 A.M.–3 P.M. daily, $3) is pretty good too. The deli still sells a meal's worth of hot dog for $2.95 as well.

Breakfast

Brave the downtown neighborhood (it's a little seedy, but not scary during daylight) to visit the White Cross drug store and belly up to the counter at **Tiffany's** (1700 Las Vegas Blvd. S., 702/444-4459, 24 hours daily, $7–15) where you can watch short-order cooks hard at work at the griddle. The eggs and pancakes are fluffy and the gravy is smooth, so load up—you've got a busy day ahead of you. When you've burned off the biscuits, bacon, and fried eggs, come back for a comfort-food lunch.

It's all about hen fruit at (**The Egg and I** (4533 W. Sahara Ave., 702/368-3447, 6 A.M.–3 P.M. daily, $7–15). They serve other breakfast fare as well, of course—the banana muffins and French toast are notable—but if you don't order an omelet, you're just being stubborn. It has huge portions, fair prices, and on-top-of-it service—go.

Steak

Easily the best steak house downtown, and perhaps in all of Las Vegas, **Vic & Anthony's** (Golden Nugget, 129 E. Fremont St., 702/385-7111, 5–11 P.M. daily, $30–50) isn't the most visually arresting restaurant in town, but that just means there's nothing to distract you from the perfectly cooked rib eyes and generous side dishes. What sets Vic & Anthony's apart from most of the other steak places in town is the way the chefs finish the entrée: Mushroom-wine reductions and an unusual red sauce for the pasta make for memorable meals.

LAS VEGAS

The perfectly cooked steaks and attentive service that once attracted Frank Sinatra, Nat "King" Cole, Natalie Wood, and Elvis are still trademarks at **Golden Steer** (308 W. Sahara Ave., 702/384-4470, 5–11 P.M. daily, $30–50). A gold-rush motif and 1960s swankiness still abide here, but the menu now includes more modern variations on prime rib, filet mignon, and New York strip.

French and Continental

Hugo's Cellar (Four Queens, 202 E. Fremont St., 702/385-4011, 5:30–11 P.M. daily, $35–55) is class from the moment each woman in your party receives her red rose until the last complimentary chocolate-covered strawberry is devoured. Probably the best gourmet room for the money, Hugo's is located below the casino floor (it is a cellar, don't forget), shutting it off from the hubbub above. It is pricy, to be sure, but the inclusion of sides, a mini dessert, and salad—prepared table-side with your choice of ingredients—helps ease the sticker shock. Sorbet is served between courses. The house appetizer is the Hot Rock, four meats sizzling on a lava slab; mix and match the meats with the dipping sauces.

The pink accents at **Pamplemousse** (400 E. Sahara Ave., 702/733-2066, 5:30–10 P.M. daily, $30–45) hint at the name's meaning (grapefruit) and set the stage for cuisine so fresh that the menu changes daily. If you eschew the prix fixe menu and order à la carte, be sure to ask about prices to avoid surprises. Specialties include leg and breast of duck in cranberry-raspberry sauce and a terrific escargot appetizer with mushrooms and red wine sauce.

Italian

Decidedly uncave-like with bright lights and an earthen-tile floor, **The Grotto** (Golden Nugget, 2300 S. Casino Dr., 702/385-7111, 11:30 A.M.–11 P.M. daily, $30–45) offers top-quality northern Italian fare with a view of the Golden Nugget's shark tank (ask for a window table). Portions are large, and the wine list is above average.

Wall frescoes put you on an Italian thoroughfare as you dine on authentic cuisine at

Fellini's (Stratosphere, 200 Las Vegas Blvd. S., 702/383-4859, 5–11 P.M. daily, $20–35). Each smallish dining room has a different fresco. The food is more the American idea of classic Italian than authentic, but only food snobs will find anything to complain about.

Chicago Joe's (820 S. 4th St., 702/382-5637, 11 A.M.–10 P.M. Tues.–Fri., 5–10 P.M. Sat., $15–25) screams Italy, with red-and-white checked table cloths and meats prepared picante, Marsala, Angelo, and more. Its setting is in a tiny Tuscan cottage–like building.

Japanese

Enjoy the chefs' spectacle at **Benihana** (Las Vegas Hilton, 3000 Paradise Rd., 702/732-5821, 5:30–10:30 P.M. daily, $25–45). After you walk through Japanese gardens filled with statues and koi ponds, your chef arrives at your table-side hibachi grill to perform deft feats with his knives. You'll be treated to an onion-ring volcano and other food acrobatics.

Seafood

The prime rib gets raves, but the seafood and the prices are the draw at **Second Street Grill** (Fremont, 200 Fremont St., 702/385-3232 or 800/634-6460, 5–10 P.M. Thurs. and Sun.–Mon., 5–11 P.M. Fri.–Sat., $15–25). The Grill bills itself as "American contemporary with Pacific Rim influence," and the menu reflects this Eastern inspiration with steaks and chops—but do yourself a favor and order the crab legs. The restaurant is not easy to find, but that generally means your table is waiting.

Steaks and seafood get equal billing on the menu at **Triple George** (201 N. 3rd St., 702/384-2761, 11 A.M.–10 P.M. Sun.–Thurs., 11 A.M.–11 P.M. Fri.–Sat., $15–35), but again, the San Francisco–style fish and the martinis are what brings the suave crowd back for more.

Vegas Views

The 360-seat, 360-degree **Top of the World** (Stratosphere, 200 Las Vegas Blvd. S., 702/380-7777 or 800/998-6937, 11 A.M.–11 P.M. daily, $40–60), on the 106th floor of Stratosphere

Tower more than 800 feet above the Strip, makes a complete revolution once every 80 minutes, giving you the full city panorama during dinner. The view of Vegas defies description, and the food is a recommendable complement. Try the tenderloin carpaccio and seafood fettuccine, and be sure to save room for Chocolate Stratosphere—white and dark chocolate with raspberry mousse.

A glass elevator delivers you to the **Ranch Steakhouse** (Binion's, 128 Fremont St., 702/382-1600, ext. 7255, 5:30–10:30 P.M. daily, $30–45) on the 24th floor. Before Stratosphere opened, this was the best view in Las Vegas, and it's still fine. Steaks are the play here—filet mignon, porterhouse, New York—and the Binion's Cut prime rib is as thick as a Michener novel.

CENTER STRIP
Breakfast
Any meal is a treat at **Tableau** (Wynn, 3131 Las Vegas Blvd. S., 702/248-DINE—702/248-3463 or 800/352-DINE—800/352-3463, 8–10:30 A.M. and 11:30 A.M.–2:30 P.M. Mon.–Fri., 8 A.M.–2:30 P.M. Sat.–Sun., bar service 5–9 P.M. daily, $15–25), but the huckleberry pancakes ($16) or white chocolate French toast ($16) in the garden atrium make breakfast the most important meal of the day at Wynn.

Buffets
The best buffet for under $85 in Las Vegas is, without a doubt, the **Village Seafood Buffet** (Rio, 3700 W. Flamingo Rd., 702/967-4000 or 866/462-5982, 4–10 P.M. Sun.–Thurs., 3:30–10 P.M. Fri.–Sat., adults $38, children $24). Extensive remodeling in 2008 added vibrant artwork, a cool sound system, and video screens. You have an incredible choice of seafood preparations: grilled scallops, shrimp, mussels, and calamari with assorted vegetables and sauces, snow crab legs, oysters on the half shell, peel-and-eat shrimp, steamed clams, and lobster tails. There's even hand-carved prime rib for the nonfan of seafood. The Village Buffet also has the highest-quality after-dinner goodies in town. The pies come

in chocolate cream, coconut cream, coconut pineapple, lemon meringue, key lime, apple, blueberry, pecan, cherry, peach, and more, and there's also assorted pound cakes, cheesecakes, pastries, tortes, mousses, cookies, and a terrific gelato selection. It's all quality stuff, but at $38 for dinner, you'd better come hungry to get your money's worth.

Many people give the Rio top marks as the best "traditional" buffet near the center Strip, but we think it has been overtaken by **The Buffet at TI** (3300 Las Vegas Blvd. S., 702/894-7111, 7 A.M.–10 P.M. daily, breakfast $15, lunch $18, dinner $23–27, weekend brunch $24). The offerings are mostly standard—barbecue ribs, pizza, Chinese—but the ingredients are the freshest we've found on a buffet, and the few nontraditional buffet selections (especially the sushi and made-to-order pasta) make the higher-than-average price worthwhile.

Steak
Steak houses—even really good ones—are a dime a dozen in Las Vegas. That makes it a buyer's market. You can be extremely discriminating and patronize only the best few around, or you can shop based on price and still be pretty well assured you'll get a decent meal wherever you go. Among the best, you'll relish **⟨ Del Frisco's** (3925 Paradise Rd., 702/796-0063, 5–11 P.M. Mon.–Sat., 5–10 P.M. Sun., $45–75). We always wonder at people who order chicken, pasta, or seafood at a steak house, but lobster fans will be forgiven here: The Australian cold-water lobster tail beats those at all but the premium seafood restaurants. Still, the rib eye is a must-order. The wine list is formidable and just as pricy as the rest of the menu.

The same accolades and price advisory hold true for **Capital Grille** (3200 Las Vegas Blvd. S., 702/932-6631, 11:30 A.M.–10:30 P.M. Mon.–Fri., noon–10:30 P.M. Sat., 4–10 P.M. Sun., $35–45), in the Fashion Show Mall, but lunch—try the grilled Parmesan sourdough club sandwich with homemade potato chips, or the lobster salad—can be had for less than $20.

Stepping down the fanciness and price ladder, the **All-American Bar and Grille** (Rio, 3700 W. Flamingo Rd., 702/967-4000 or 866/462-5982, 11 A.M.–6 A.M. daily, $25–35) offers casual table and bar dining on choice beef or dry-aged black angus. The sides are big enough to share.

French and Continental

Many times, "bistro food" means French comfort food—hearty, hot, and tasty, yes; imaginative and experimental, no. At first glance, **Pinot Brasserie** (Venetian, 3355 Las Vegas Blvd. S., 702/414-8888, 11:30 A.M.–3 P.M. and 5:30–10 P.M. Sun.–Thurs., 11:30 A.M.–10:30 P.M. Fri.–Sat., $25–45) seems to fit the mold: linguini, chicken, lamb, and so on. But on closer inspection, you'll find West Coast–inspired variations that bring a fresh perspective to these old favorites: the prosciutto-potato hash that accompanies the sea bass and the balsamic vinegar, pepper, and vanilla reduction that accompanies the roasted strawberries and goat cheese. Top it all off with the Belgian chocolate soufflé.

The vanilla mousse–colored banquettes and chocolate swirl of the dark wood grain tables at **Payard Patisserie & Bistro** (Caesars Palace, 3570 Las Vegas Blvd. S., 702/967-4000 or 866/462-5982, 6:30 A.M.–3 P.M. daily, $15–25, pastry counter 6:30 A.M.–11 P.M. daily) evoke the delightful French pastries for which François Payard is famous. Indeed, the bakery takes up most of the restaurant, tantalizing visitors with cakes, tarts, and petits fours. But the restaurant, open only for breakfast and lunch, stands on its own, with the quiches and paninis taking best in show.

Italian

It's no surprise that a casino named after the most romantic of Italian cities would be home to two of the best Italian restaurants around. **Valentino** (Venetian, 3355 Las Vegas Blvd. S., 702/414-3000, 5:30–11 P.M. daily, $25–50) is headed by partner Luciano Pellegrini, recognized as one of the best chefs in the country. The amber and aquamarine interior

foreshadows the golden pasta and treasures *de mare* awaiting your order. If you can't wait till dinner, Valentino's grill is open for lunch. The ravioli with blue cheese fondue is a little heavy for lunch, but perhaps you're up to the challenge. **Canaletto** (11:30 A.M.–11 P.M. Sun.–Thurs., 11:30 A.M.–midnight Fri.–Sat., $15–25) focuses on Venetian cuisine. Chef Gianpaolo Putzu and his crew perform around the grill and rotisserie—a demonstration kitchen—creating sumptuously authentic dishes. The filled pastas—cannelloni filled with chicken and mushrooms, ravioli stuffed with pears—are among the favorites.

You can almost picture Old Blue Eyes himself between shows, twirling linguini and holding court at **Sinatra** (Encore, 3121 Las Vegas Blvd. S., 702/248-DINE—702/248-3463 or 888/352-DINE—888/352-3463, 5:30–10 P.M. daily, $30–50). The Chairman's voice wafts through the speakers, and his photos and awards decorate the walls while you tuck into classic Italian food tinged with Chef Theo Schoenegger's special touches.

Unpretentious and perfectly willing to play into the long-*I* "Italian joint" convention, **Battista's Hole in the Wall** (4041 Audrie St., 702/732-1424, 5–10:30 P.M. daily, $20–35), behind the Flamingo, serves family-style meals with garlic bread, minestrone, all-you-can-eat pasta on the side, and all-you-can-drink wine included. Classic Italian restaurant decor and an accordionist make us long for the old country—and we're not even Italian. From a similar mold is **Maggiano's Little Italy** (Fashion Show Mall, 3200 Las Vegas Blvd. S., Suite 2144, 702/732-2550, 11 A.M.–11 P.M. daily, $15–30). The shareable "large plates" are more than enough for two. Order the eggplant parmesan even if you don't like eggplant.

It's a completely different vibe at **Piero's** (355 Convention Center Dr., 702/369-2305, 5–10 P.M. daily, $25–40). As enchanting as the exotic animal lithographs on the walls, Piero's has attracted celebrities ranging from Dick Van Dyke to Larry Bird. The decor, colorful owner Freddie Glusman, and low-key sophistication give the place a vaguely speakeasy feel.

Seafood

Submerse yourself in the cool, fluid atmosphere at **AquaKnox** (Venetian, 3355 Las Vegas Blvd. S., 702/414-3772, 5:30–11 P.M. Sun.–Thurs., 5:30–11:30 P.M. Fri.–Sat., $30–70). Its cobalt and cerulean tableware and design elements suggest a sea-sprayed embarcadero. The fish soup is chef Tom Moloney's signature entrée, but the crab dishes are the way to go. If you can't bring yourself to order the $69 crab-stuffed lobster, at least treat yourself to the crab cake appetizer for $18.

Adventurous palates are in for a treat at **Sea Harbour** (Caesars Palace, 3570 Las Vegas Blvd. S., 877/346-4642, 3:30–11 P.M. Wed.–Fri., 11:30 A.M.–11 P.M. Sat.–Sun., $30–45). The Chinese import features sea cucumber, jellyfish, shark fin, and other Andrew Zimmern–worthy delicacies. More traditional tastes will find plenty to like here too: Traditional Chinese fare and the boneless chicken are safe options.

Although it's named for the Brazilian beach paradise, **Buzios** (Rio, 3700 W. Flamingo Rd., 702/777-7923, 5–11 P.M. Wed.–Sun., $25–40) serves its fish American and South American style. Hawaiian ahi, Maine lobster, Alaskan crab, and Chilean sea bass are always fresh and presented in perfect complement with tomato reductions, soy emulsions, and butter sauces.

Asian

The Mirage boasts two top center-Strip offerings in this category. A few critics have panned **Japonais** (3400 Las Vegas Blvd. S., 702/792-7979, 5–10 P.M. Thurs. and Sun.–Mon., 5–11 P.M. Fri.–Sat., $25–40) as overpriced, and while we agree the portions tend to be small by American standards, Japonais has several deals that put it solidly in the mid-range for a Japanese dinner. The early-bird lounge dinner ($45) for two includes a pair of appetizers, an entrée, and dessert. Or you could opt for Japanese dim sum (is there such a thing?) with the $7 appetizers and drinks. Japonais's Chinese counterpart is **Fin** (3400 Las Vegas Blvd. S., 866/339-4566, 5–11 P.M. Thurs.–Mon., $25–45). Again, some contend

you pay for the setting as much as for the food, but why not? Sometimes the atmosphere is worth it, especially when you're trying to make an impression on your mate or potential significant other. The metallic-ball curtains evoke a rainstorm in a Chinese garden and set just the right romantic but noncloying mood. Still, we have to agree that while the prices are not outrageous, the food is not gourmet quality either; you can probably find more yum for your yuan elsewhere.

Better value can be had at **Tao** (Venetian, 3355 Las Vegas Blvd. S., 702/388-8338, 5 P.M.–midnight Sun.–Thurs., 5 P.M.–1 A.M. Fri.–Sat., $25–40), where pan-Asian dishes—the roasted Thai Buddha chicken is our pick—and an extensive sake selection are served in decor that is a trip through Asian history, from the Silk Road to Eastern spiritualism, including imperial koi ponds and feng shui aesthetics.

At **Wing Lei** (Wynn, 3131 Las Vegas Blvd. S., 5:30–10:30 P.M. daily, $30–60), French colonialism comes through in chef Ming Yu's Shanghai style.

Vegas Views

Overlooking perfectly manicured fairways and the imposing 18th-green waterfall on Steve Wynn's exclusive course, the view from the glass-partitioned patio at the **Country Club** (Wynn, 3131 Las Vegas Blvd. S., 702/248-DINE—702/248-3463, 11:30 A.M.–3 P.M. Mon.–Tues., 11:30 A.M.–10 P.M. Wed.–Fri., 8 A.M.–3 P.M. Sat.–Sun., $30–60) is enough to make us drool even before we see the menu. The food is perfectly prepared standard steak house fare. The fresh Cobb salad is a lunch favorite.

West Coast fixture **Sushi Roku** (Caesars Palace, 3570 Las Vegas Blvd. S., 702/733-7373, noon–10 P.M. Sun.–Thurs., noon–11 P.M. Fri.–Sat., $25–40) has terrific views both inside and out. Within the restaurant are a veritable Zen garden, bamboo, and shadowy table alcoves. Outside are unparalleled views up and down the Strip. The Imperial Palace's lavender-lit pagoda facade across the street adds to the Japanese fantasy feel.

More Strip views await at **Voodoo Steak** (Rio, 3700 W. Flamingo Rd., 702/777-7923, 5–11 P.M. daily, $30–50) along with steaks with a N'awlins creole and Cajun touch. Getting to the restaurant and the lounge requires a mini thrill ride to the top of the Rio tower in the glass elevator. The Rio contends that the restaurant is on the 51st floor and the lounge is on the 52nd floor, but they're really on the 41st and 42nd floors, respectively— Rio management dropped floors 40–49 as the number 4 has an ominous connotation in Chinese culture. Whatever floors they're on, the Voodoo double-decker provides a great view of the Strip. The food and drink are expensive and a bit tame, but the fun is in the overlook, especially if you eat or drink outside on the decks.

Kokomo's (Mirage, 3400 Las Vegas Blvd. S., 866/339-4566, 5–10:30 P.M. daily, $30–45) sits under hut-like canopies within the rainforest of the Mirage's domed atrium. It's slightly noisy from the casino and the waterfalls, but the hubbub quickly becomes part of the unusual atmosphere. Try the oven-roasted sea bass ($30) and the ahi tartar appetizer ($18).

LOWER STRIP
Breakfast

The **Verandah** (Four Seasons, 3960 Las Vegas Blvd. S., 702/632-5000, $25–40) transforms itself from a light, airy, indoor-outdoor breakfast and lunch nook into a late dinner spot oozing with South Seas ambiance and a check total worthy of a Four Seasons restaurant. As you might expect from the name, dining on the terrace is a favorite among well-to-do locals, especially for brunch on spring and fall weekends.

Buffets

If you think "Las Vegas buffet" means a call to the trough of mediocre cheap prices and get-what-you-pay-for food quality, Bally's would like to invite you and your credit card to the **Sterling Brunch** (702/967-7999, 9:30 A.M.–2:30 P.M. Sun., $85). That's right, $85 for one meal, per person, and you have to fetch your own vittles. But the verdict is almost unanimous: It's worth it, especially if you load up on the grilled lobster, filet mignon, caviar, sushi, Mumm champagne, and other high-dollar offerings. Leave the omelets and salads for IHOP; a plateful of sinful tarts and chocolate indulgence is a must, along with just one more glass of champagne.

On the other hand, for the price of that one brunch at Bally's, you can eat for three days at the **Roundtable Buffet** (Excalibur, 3580 Las Vegas Blvd. S., 7 A.M.–10 P.M. daily, breakfast $15, lunch $16, dinner $20, ages 4–12 get $4 off). The Excalibur started the trend of the all-day-long buffet, and the hotel sells all-day wristbands for $30. If that's not enough gluttony for you, the wristband also serves as a line pass. The **French Market Buffet** (The Orleans, 4500 W. Tropicana Ave., 702/365-7111, 8 A.M.–4 P.M. Mon.–Sat., 8 A.M.–9 P.M. Sun., breakfast $8, lunch $9, dinner $14–19, Sun. brunch $15, ages 4–7 get $3 off) has a similar all-day deal for $24 (Fri. $27).

Steak

The care used by the small farms from which Tom Colicchio's **Craftsteak** (MGM Grand, 3799 Las Vegas Blvd. S., 702/891-7318, 5:30–10 P.M. Tues.–Thurs., 6–10 P.M. Fri.–Mon., $40–60) buys its ingredients is evident in the full flavor of the excellently seasoned steaks and chops. Spacious and bright with red lacquer and light woodwork, Craftsteak's decor is conducive to good times with friends and family and isn't overbearing or intimidating.

The original **Gallagher's Steakhouse** (New York New York, 3790 Las Vegas Blvd. S., 702/740-6450, 4–11 P.M. Sun.–Thurs., 4 P.M.–midnight Fri.–Sat., $30–42) has been an institution in New York City since 1927, and the restaurant here is decorated with memorabilia from the golden age of movies and sports. You'll know why the longevity is deserved after sampling its famed dry-aged beef and notable seafood selection.

Bringing the ultralounge vibe to the restaurant setting is **N9NE** (Palms, 4321 W. Flamingo Rd., 702/933-9900, 5–10 P.M.

Sun.–Thurs., 5–11 P.M. Fri.–Sat., $40–75).
Sleek furnishings of chrome highlighted by
rich colored lighting add accompaniment, but
N9NE never loses focus on its raison d'être:
flawlessly prepared steak and seafood and impeccable service.

French and Continental

Award-winning chef Andre Rochat lays claim
to two top French establishments on this end
of the Strip. **Andre's** (Monte Carlo, 3770 Las
Vegas Blvd. S., 702/798-7151, 5:30–10 P.M.
Tues.–Sun., $35–55) has an up-to-date yet old-
country feel, with smoky glass, silver furnishings, and teal-and-cream accents. The menu
combines favorites from around the world with
French sensibilities to create unique "French
fusion" fare, such as lamb with curried risotto
and goat cheese or a peppercorn and cognac
cream sauce for the delectable fillet of beef.
The cellar is befitting one of the best French
restaurants in town, and the selection of port,
cognac, and other after-dinner drinks is un-
paralleled. Rochat's **Alizé** (Palms, 4321 W.
Flamingo Rd., 702/951-7000, 5:30–10 P.M.
daily, $40–60) is similar but includes a sweet
Strip view from atop the Palms.

The steaks and seafood at **Mon Ami Gabi**
(Paris, 3655 Las Vegas Blvd. S., 702/944-4224,
7 A.M.–11 P.M. Sun.–Fri., 7 A.M.–midnight Sat.,
$20–35) are comparable to those at any fine
Strip establishment—at about half the price.
It's a bistro, so you know the crepes and other
lunch specials are terrific, but you're better off
coming for dinner. Try the trout Grenobloise.

When you name your restaurant after a mae-
stro, you're setting some pretty high standards
for your food. Fortunately, **Picasso** (Bellagio,
3600 Las Vegas Blvd. S., 702/693-7223,
6–9:30 P.M. Wed.–Mon., $113–123) is up to
the self-inflicted challenge. With limited seating in its Picasso-canvassed dining room and a
small dining time window, the restaurant has a
couple of prix fixe menus. They're seriously expensive, and if you include Kobe beef, lobster,
wine pairings, and a cheese course, you and a
mate could easily leave several pounds heavier
and $500 lighter.

Italian

Break out the fedora and wingtips and hoof
it to the **Bootlegger Bistro** (7700 S. Las
Vegas Blvd., 702/736-4939, 24 hours daily,
$15–25), where it's not supper until you slosh
red sauce on your tie. Check out open-mike
night Mondays at 9 P.M. Order the linguini
and clams, sit back in a plush red high-backed
booth, and enjoy the song stylings of up-
and-coming singers and comedians as well as
Strip performers trying out new material. The
Bootlegger's owner, Lorraine Hunt-Bono, is
not only a former Nevada lieutenant governor
but also used to steam up the Vegas lounges
with sultry standards. Husband Dennis Bono
is a veteran of East Coast and Vegas showrooms. Black-and-white photos of their industry friends dot the walls, and the couple's
political and music industry connections are
often in the audience, so if you knock 'em dead
with your own rendition of "That's Amore,"
you might just get discovered.

Seafood

You can go to a lot of restaurants in Las Vegas
and get a pretty good shrimp and crab-leg dinner for $30, but when that dinner comes with
quality all-you-can-eat sushi, $30 is a bar-
gain. That's just what you get at **Todai** (Planet
Hollywood, 3667 Las Vegas Blvd. S., 702/892-
0021, 11:30 A.M.–2:30 P.M. and 5:30–9:30 P.M.
Sun.–Thurs., 11:30 A.M.–2:30 P.M. and 5:30–
10:30 P.M. Fri.–Sat., $30–32, discounts under
age 12 and over age 65). Go during peak dinner
hours—the more people are eating, the fresher
the sashimi is.

Rick Moonen is the "it" chef of the moment, making his **RM Seafood** (Mandalay
Bay, 3950 Las Vegas Blvd. S., 702/632-9300,
11 A.M.–11 P.M. daily, $35–55) the place to
be seen whether you're a seafood junkie or
just another pretty face. You can almost hear
the tide-rigging whirr and the mahogany
creak in the yacht-club restaurant setting.
RM Upstairs delivers a tasty and reasonably priced tasting menu ($75) that recently
featured beef tartare, foie gras, and baked
salmon. You have to try the rabbit trio; it's

available à la carte or on the tasting menu for a supplemental charge.

Asian

Voted one of Zagat's favorite restaurants in Vegas, **China Grill** (Mandalay Bay, 3950 Las Vegas Blvd. S., 702/632-7404, 5–11 P.M. Sun.–Thurs., 5 P.M.–midnight Fri.–Sat., $30–45) is another one of Mandalay Bay's architecturally arresting designer restaurants, using a crystal foot bridge, multiple levels, a light-projected ceiling, and the ubiquitous exhibition kitchen to heighten the dining experience. Signature specialties include exotic twists on traditional Chinese favorites (we suggest the grilled garlic shrimp or lobster pancakes with red curry coconut sauce). More traditional, expensive, and classic is China Grill's next-door neighbor, **Shanghai Lilly** (3950 Las Vegas Blvd. S., 702/632-7409, 5:30–10:30 P.M. Mon., 5:30–11 P.M. Thurs.–Sun., $32–52), where Cantonese and Szechuan creations reign supreme and the decor is understated and elegant.

Chinese art in a Hong Kong bistro setting with fountain and lake views make **Jasmine** (Bellagio, 3600 Las Vegas Blvd. S., 5:30–10:30 P.M. daily, $40–60) one of the most visually striking Chinese restaurants in town. The food is classic European-influenced Cantonese.

Other high-end options include **Pearl** (MGM Grand, 3799 Las Vegas Blvd. S., 702/891-7380, 5:30–10 P.M. Sun.–Thurs., 5:30–11 P.M. Fri.–Sat., $45–60), which specializes in steamed, baked, and fried Cantonese seafood specialties; and **Little Buddha** (Palms, 4321 W. Flamingo Rd., 702/942-7778, 5:30–10:30 P.M. Sun.–Thurs., 5:30–11:30 P.M. Fri.–Sat., $30–45), offering French-inspired Chinese and other Asian classics in a stunning setting. Make sure you get an eyeful, if not a snoot full, at the suave and colorful bar.

Vegas Views

Paris's **Eiffel Tower Restaurant** (3655 Las Vegas Blvd. S., 702/948-6937, 11:30 A.M.–2:30 P.M. and 5–10 P.M. Sun.–Thurs., 11:30 A.M.–2:30 P.M. and 5–10:45 P.M.

Fri.–Sat., $35–55) hovers 100 feet above the Strip. Your first "show" greets you when the glass elevator opens onto the organized chaos of chef Jean Joho's kitchen. Order the soufflé, have a glass of wine, and bask in the romantic piano strains as the bilingual culinary staff performs delicate French culinary feats.

The story goes that that Tony Marnell—the "M" in the M Resort—was frustrated at not finding an Italian restaurant to his liking in Las Vegas, so he built his own. We think Tony must not have looked very hard if he couldn't find good Italian in town, but there's no denying his **Panevino** (246 Via Antonio Ave., 702/222-2400, 11 A.M.–3 P.M. and 5–10 P.M. Mon.–Fri., 5–10 P.M. Sat., $20–40), in the Marnell Corporate Center across Sunset Road from McCarran Airport, has earned its place at least *among* the top Italian places in town, especially considering the terrific view of the McCarran runway across the road. At night, if you have the right table, you can see planes lined up six deep on their descent.

OFF STRIP

There are plenty of fine restaurants outside the resort corridor. Among our favorites: Not only beatniks (or whatever the young whippersnappers are calling themselves these days) will dig the breakfast vibe at **The Beat** (520 E. Fremont St., 702/686-3164, 7 A.M.–7 P.M. Mon.–Thurs., 7 A.M.–10 P.M. Fri., 9 A.M.–10 P.M. Sat., $5–10), in the downtown arts district. Another plus, especially for locals in the know: The Beat's joe is from Colorado River Coffee Roasters in Boulder City, and the bread is from Bon Breads Baking in Las Vegas.

Its delicious dim sum is no secret, so parking and seating are at a premium during lunch at **Cathay House** (5300 W. Spring Mountain Ave., 702/876-3838, 10:30 A.M.–10 P.M. daily, $10–20), in Chinatown. Dim sum is available any time, but be a purist and only order it for lunch. For dinner, opt for orange beef or garlic chicken. **Thai Spice** (4433 W. Flamingo Rd., 702/362-5308, 11:30 A.M.–10 P.M. Mon.–Thurs., 11:30 A.M.–10:30 P.M. Fri.–Sat., $10–17) is the best Thai restaurant in town; the soups, noodle dishes, traditional curries, pad thai, and egg rolls are all well prepared. Tell your waiter how hot you want your food on a scale of 1 to 10. The big numbers peg the needle on the Scoville scale, so macho men beware.

We're sure everything else at **C Dona Maria's** (910 Las Vegas Blvd. S., 702/382-6538, 8 A.M.–10 P.M. Mon.–Fri., 8 A.M.–11 P.M. Sat.–Sun., $6–16) is plenty satisfying, but we wouldn't know. We can't bring ourselves to order anything but the enchilada with green chili. Heck, with prices like these, order two or three enchiladas, tacos, and tostadas—carne, chicken, beef, chorizo, or bean—just make sure they're all slathered in that green sauce. Dona Maria's also serves burgers and traditional Mexican breakfasts. Did we mention the green sauce? Among Las Vegas's other good Mexican restaurants are **Viva Mercado's** (3553 S. Rainbow Blvd., 702/871-8826, 11 A.M.–9:30 P.M. Sun.–Thurs., 11 A.M.–10 P.M. Fri.–Sat., $7–20) and **Lindo Michoacán** (2655 E. Desert Inn Rd., 702/735-6828, 11 A.M.–11 P.M. daily, $10–20). Other restaurants in the Michoacán family dot the valley.

Shopping

MALLS

The most upscale and most Strip-accessible of the traditional indoor shopping complexes, **Fashion Show** (3200 Las Vegas Blvd. S., 702/784-7000, 10 A.M.–9 P.M. Mon.–Sat., 11 A.M.–7 P.M. Sun.), across from the Wynn, is anchored by Saks Fifth Avenue, Dillard's, Neiman Marcus, Macy's, Nordstrom, and Bloomingdale's. The mall gets its name from the 80-foot retractable runway in the Great Hall, where resident retailers put on weekend fashion shows. Unique stores include Futuretronics, to keep you on the cutting edge of technological gadgetry, and Painted with Oil, with thousands of original artworks minus the intimidating gallery atmosphere. The 17-restaurant food court has something for every taste, or better yet, dine alfresco at a Strip-side café, shaded by "the cloud," a 128-foot-tall canopy that doubles as a projection screen.

Parents can reward their children's patience with rides on cartoon animals, spaceships, and other kiddie favorites at two separate play areas in the **Meadows Mall** (4300 Meadows Lane, 702/878-3331, 10 A.M.–9 P.M. Mon.–Sat., 10 A.M.–6 P.M. Sun.). There are more than 140 stores and restaurants—all the usual mall denizens along with some interesting specialty shops. The **Boulevard Mall** (3528 S. Maryland Pkwy., 702/735-8268, 10 A.M.–9 P.M. Mon.–Sat.) is similar but older and in a less trendy setting.

A visit to **Town Square** (6605 Las Vegas Blvd. S., 702/269-5000, 10 A.M.–9:30 P.M. Mon.–Thurs., 10 A.M.–10 P.M. Fri.–Sat., 11 A.M.–8 P.M. Sun.) is like a stroll through a favorite suburb. "Streets" wind between stores in Spanish, Moorish, and Mediterranean-style buildings. Mall stalwarts like Victoria's Secret and Abercrombie & Fitch are here along with some unusual surprises—Tommy Bahama's includes a café. Just like a real town, the retail outlets surround a central park, 13,000 square feet of mazes, tree houses, and performance stages. Around holiday time, machine-made snowflakes drift down through the trees. Nightlife, from laid-back wine and martini bars to rousing live entertainment as well as the 18-screen Rave movie theater, round out a trip into "town."

Easterners and Westerners alike revel in the wares offered at **Chinatown Plaza** (4255 Spring Mountain Rd., 702/221-8448). Despite the name, Chinatown Las Vegas is a pan-Asian clearinghouse where Asians can celebrate their history and heritage while stocking up on favorite reminders of home. Meanwhile, Westerners can submerge themselves in new cultures by sampling the offerings at authentic

Chinese, Thai, Vietnamese, and other Asian restaurants and strolling the plaza reading posters explaining Chinese customs. Tea sets, silk robes, Buddha statuettes, and jade carvings are of particular interest, as is the Diamond Bakery with its elaborate wedding cakes and sublime mango mousse cake.

CASINO PLAZAS

Caesars Palace initiated the concept of Las Vegas as a shopping destination in 1992 when it unveiled the **Forum Shops** (702/893-4800 or 800/CAESARS—800/223-7277, 10 A.M.– 11 P.M. Sun.–Fri., 10 A.M.–midnight Fri.–Sat.). Top brand luxury stores coexist with fashionable hipster boutiques amid some of the best people-watching on the Strip. A stained glass– domed pedestrian plaza greets shoppers as they enter the 175,000-square-foot expansion from the Strip. Here you'll find one of only two spiral escalators in the United States. When you're ready for a break, the gods come alive hourly to extract vengeance in the *Fall of Atlantis* and *Festival Fountain Show*; or check out the feeding of the fish in the big saltwater aquarium twice daily.

Part shopping center, part theater in the round, the **Miracle Mile** (Planet Hollywood, 3667 Las Vegas Blvd. S., 702/866-0703 or 888/800-8284, 10 A.M.–11 P.M. Sun.–Thurs., 10 A.M.–midnight Fri.–Sat.) is a delightful (or vicious, depending on your point of view) circle of shops, eateries, bars, and theaters. If your budget doesn't quite stand up to the Forum Shops, Miracle Mile could be just your speed. The offbeat Amazing Johnathan and *Tony n' Tina's Wedding* showrooms are here too.

Las Vegas icon Rita Rudner loves the **Grand Canal Shoppes** (Venetian, 3355 Las Vegas Blvd. S., 702/414-4500, 10 A.M.–11 P.M. Sun.– Thurs., 10 A.M.–midnight Fri.–Sat.) because "Where else in Vegas can you take a gondola to the Gap?" And where else can you be serenaded by opera singers while trying on shoes? The shops line the canal among streetlamps and cobblestones under a frescoed sky. There's not really a Gap here—the Venetian is way too upscale for such a pedestrian store. Instead, nature gets a digital assist in the photos for sale at Peter Lik gallery, and Mikimoto and Dooney & Bourke compete for your shopping dollar. The "Streetmosphere" includes

© RYAN JERZ

A modern-day agora, the Forum Shops at Caesars Palace tempt shoppers with high fashion and indulgent trinkets.

strolling minstrels and specialty acts, and many of these entertainers find their way to St. Mark's Square for seemingly impromptu performances.

Money attracts money, and Steve Wynn was able to lure Oscar de la Renta and Jean Paul Gaultier to open their first retail stores in the country at the indulgent **Esplanade** (Wynn, 3131 Las Vegas Blvd. S., 702/770-7000, 10 A.M.–11 P.M. daily). A cursory look at the tenant stores is enough to convince you that the Esplanade caters to the wealthy, the lucky, and the reckless: Hermès, Manolo Blahnik, and even Ferrari are at home under stained-glass skylights. Looking around at all the expensive casino-based shopping venues in town, the developers of **Crystal** (City Center, 3730 Las Vegas Blvd. S., 702/590-9299 or 866/754-2489) opted to go in another direction. Rather than going high-end, "We realized this is a niche the market is missing—a selection of retailers under one roof that are *extremely* high-

end," the mall's general manager said. Vuitton, Tiffany, Versace: After viewing the directory, you can't argue with his logic.

The truth is, unless you're looking for a specific item or brand, or you're attracted to the atmosphere, attractions, architecture, or vibe of a particular Strip destination, you can't go wrong simply browsing the one in your hotel. The spots outlined above are our favorites, but you'll find others just as nice at **Le Boulevard** (Paris, 3655 Las Vegas Blvd. S., 702/739-4111, 10 A.M.–11 P.M. daily), **Promenade** (Bally's/Paris, 3645 Las Vegas Blvd. S., 702/739-4111 or 888/266-5687, 10 A.M.–11 P.M. daily), **The Shoppes** (Palazzo, 3325 Las Vegas Blvd. S., 702/414-4525, 10 A.M.–11 P.M. Sun.–Thurs., 10 A.M.–midnight Fri.–Sat.), **Via Bellagio** (Bellagio, 3600 Las Vegas Blvd. S., 702/693-7111 or 888/987-6667, 10 A.M.–midnight daily), or **Mandalay Place** (Mandalay Bay, 3950 Las Vegas Blvd. S., 702/632-7777 or 877/632-7800, 10 A.M.–11 P.M. daily).

Information and Services

INFORMATION BUREAUS

The **Las Vegas Convention and Visitors Authority** (LVCVA, 3150 Paradise Rd., 702/892-0711 or 877/VISIT-LV—877/847-4858, www.lvcva.com, 8 A.M.–5 P.M. daily) maintains a website of special hotel deals and other offers at www.visitlasvegas.com. One of LVCVA's priorities is filling hotel rooms—call its reservations service at 877/VISIT-LV—877/847-4858. You can also call the same number for convention schedules and for an entertainment schedule.

The **Las Vegas Chamber of Commerce** (6671 Las Vegas Blvd. S., 702/735-1616, www.lvchamber.com) has a bunch of travel resources and general fact sheets on its website.

VISITORS GUIDES AND MAGAZINES

Nearly a dozen free periodicals for visitors are available in various places around town—racks in motel lobbies and by the bell desks of the

large hotels are the best bet. They all cover basically the same territory—showrooms, lounges, dining, dancing, buffets, gambling, sports, events, coming attractions—and most have numerous ads that will transport coupon clippers to discount heaven.

Anthony Curtis's monthly **Las Vegas Advisor** (www.lasvegasadvisor.com) is a must for serious and curious Las Vegas visitors. The *Advisor* ferrets out and presents objectively (no advertising or comps accepted) the best dining, entertainment, gambling, and hotel room values, reviews shows and restaurants, and doles out gambling strategies. A year's subscription is only $50 ($37 for an electronic subscription) and includes exclusive coupons worth more than $3,000. The *Advisor* is highly recommended; sign up online.

Today in Las Vegas (www.todayinlv.com) is a 64-page weekly mini magazine bursting its staples with listings, coupons, previews, maps, and restaurant overviews. To get an issue before you leave on your trip, visit www.today-inlv.com/send-for-copy.html.

The digital magazine **What's On** (www.whats-on.com) provides comprehensive information along with entertainer profiles, articles, calendars, phone numbers, and lots of ads. Single issues cost $2.95.

The 150-page **Showbiz Weekly** (http://lasvegasmagazine.com) spotlights performers and has listings and ads for shows, lounges, and buffets. Subscribe or buy single digital online.

The annual publication **Las Vegas Perspective** (www.lvperspective.com) is chock-full of area demographics as well as retail, real estate, and community statistics, updated every year.

SERVICES

If you need the police, the fire department, or an ambulance in an emergency, dial 911.

The centrally located **University Medical Center** (1800 W. Charleston Blvd., at Shadow Lane, 702/383-2000) has 24-hour emergency service, with outpatient and trauma-care facilities. Hospital emergency rooms throughout the valley are open 24 hours, as are many privately run quick-care centers.

Most hotels will have lists of dentists and doctors, and the **Clark County Medical Society** (2590 E. Russell Rd., 702/739-9989, www.clarkcountymedical.org) website lists members based on specialty. You can also get a physician referral from **Desert Springs Hospital** (702/733-6875 or 800/842-5439).

Getting There and Around

BY AIR

Las Vegas is one of the easiest cities in the world to fly to. The number of airlines keeps fares competitive. A Southwest Airlines plane lands every three minutes, it seems. Package deals can be an especially good value if you're only staying for a week or a long weekend, but you might have to do your own research to get the best deals. A good way to start is to look in the Sunday travel supplement in the largest daily newspaper in your area, where many of the airlines, wholesalers, packagers, and hotel specials are advertised. Also, look in the travel supplements of the Los Angeles, Chicago, Dallas, and New York newspapers if you can; although the advertised tour operators and wholesalers might not serve your area, sometimes you can get in on the airfare-only or room-only part of their packages. You can also check the websites of various government agencies charged with promoting Las Vegas and tourism as well as private publishers of Las Vegas guides.

Given the popularity of Las Vegas, it's best to make your reservations as early as possible; last-minute deals are few and far between, and you'll pay through the nose to fly to Vegas on

a whim. Unless your travel agent specializes in Las Vegas, don't count on him or her to help much. Las Vegas prices are so cheap that agents don't make much money selling it, and therefore they don't have much incentive to stay up on the deals, which change with the wind.

McCarran International Airport (LAS, 5757 Wayne Newton Blvd., 702/261-5211, www.mccarran.com) is one of the 10 busiest in the country. The wide-eyed rubbernecking that this town is famous for kicks in the moment you step into the terminal, with its slots, maze of people movers, monorails, advertisements full of showgirls, and Vegas personalities' video admonitions not to leave your luggage unattended.

Las Vegas City Area Transit buses serve the airport. Route 108 runs up Swenson Street, and the closest it comes to Las Vegas Boulevard is the corner of Paradise Road and West Sahara Avenue, but you can connect with the Las Vegas monorail at several stops. Or, if you're headed downtown, take the bus to the end of the line. Alternately, grab the Route 109 bus, which runs east of the 108 up Maryland Parkway. To get to the Strip, you have to transfer at the large cross streets onto westbound buses that cross the Strip. There are stops at Charleston Boulevard, Sahara Avenue, Desert Inn Road, Flamingo Road, and Tropicana Avenue. Route 109 also ends up at the Downtown Transportation Center. Bus fare is $2, with passes of varying duration available.

You can take a **Gray Line** airport shuttle van to your Strip ($12 round-trip) or downtown ($16 round-trip) hotel. These shuttles run continuously, leaving the airport about every 15 minutes. You'll find the shuttles outside the baggage claim area. You don't need reservations from the airport, but you will need reservations from your hotel to return to the airport. Call 702/739-5700 to reserve a spot on an airport-bound shuttle 24 hours in advance.

BY CAR

Downtown Las Vegas crowds around the junction of I-15, U.S. 95, and U.S. 93. I-15 runs from Los Angeles (272 miles, 4–5 hours' drive) to Salt Lake City (419 miles, 6–8 hours). U.S. 95 meanders from Yuma, Arizona, on the Mexican border, up the western side of Nevada, through Coeur D'Alene, Idaho, all the way up to British Columbia, Canada. U.S. 93 starts in Phoenix and hits Las Vegas 285 miles later, then merges with I-15 for a while only to fork off and shoot straight up the east side of Nevada and continue due north all the way up to Alberta, Canada.

Car Rental

When you call around to rent, be sure to ask what the *total* price of your car is going to be. With sales tax, use tax, airport fees, and other miscellaneous charges, you can pay as much as 20 percent over and above the quoted rate. Typical shoulder-season weekly rates run from about $140 for economy and compact cars to $350 for vans and $440 for luxury sedans, but prices increase a third or more during major conventions and holiday periods. One recent holiday week saw economy car rates at about $190 across the board, although the premium for luxury cars and vans was only about 20

percent. Parking is free in casino surface lots and garages. Check with your insurance agent at home about coverage on rental cars; often your insurance covers rental cars (minus your deductible) and you won't need the rental company's. If you rent a car on most credit cards, you get automatic rental-car insurance coverage. Las Vegas rental car rates change as fast as hotel room rates, depending on the season, day of the week, and amount of convention traffic.

Generally, the large car-rental companies have desks at the **McCarran Rent-A-Car Center** (702/261-6001). Dedicated McCarran shuttles leave the main terminal from outside exit doors 10 and 11 about every five minutes bound for the Rent-A-Car Center. Taxicabs are also available at the center. Companies represented at the center include **Advantage** (800/777-9377), **Alamo/National** (800/GO-ALAMO), **Avis** (800/331-1212), **Budget** (800/922-2899), **Dollar** (800/800-4000), **Enterprise** (800/RENTACAR), **Hertz** (800/654-3131), **Payless** (800/729-5377), **Sav-Mor** (800/634-6779), and **Thrifty** (800/367-2277).

RV Rental

Travelers using Las Vegas as their base or departure point can rent virtually any type of recreational vehicle, from pickup truck–mounted coaches to 40-foot Class A rolling mansions. **El Monte RV** (13001 Las Vegas Blvd. S., Henderson, 702/269-8000 or 866/218-6877) south of town (take I-15 south, exiting at St. Rose Parkway; head east to Las Vegas Boulevard and drive south) deals primarily in Class C "cab-over" models and Class A rockstar tour bus behemoths. Base prices for the Class C cab-overs start at about $750 per week, but miles—bundled in 100-mile packages—and incidentals such as kitchenware, pillows, coffeemakers, and toasters can easily increase the total by 75 percent. El Monte's big dog, a 35-foot Fleetwood Fiesta, goes for $1,500 per week before mileage and extras.

Cruise America (6070 Boulder Highway, 702/456-6666 or 888/980-8282) on the east side (from the Strip, head east on Tropicana

HIGH-SPEED TRAINS RACE TO VEGAS

Two competing projects are aiming to give 13 million Las Vegas visitors more time to indulge in the city's gambling, dining, and entertainment. More than one-third of Las Vegas's visitors come from Southern California, but the 300-mile one-day journey and the region's notorious traffic congestion cut deeply into fun time – especially for weekend travelers.

Two high-speed train projects hope to eliminate much of the commute time and a lot of the hassle and stress Angelenos deal with on their voyage east. A maglev train is the more ambitious, more expensive, and more futuristic project. The estimated $12 billion train project would whisk visitors between Anaheim, California, and Las Vegas at some 300 mph, cutting the travel time to about 80 minutes. The project lost funding and the support of Nevada senator Harry Reid, who is unhappy with what he sees as the project's lack of progress. Others are concerned that while maglev trains have been successful in Europe and Asia, the technology is untested in the United States. Still, many support the project because of its potential to create jobs, its linking of two major tourist cities, and the speed of bringing more tourists to town.

Desert Xpress is a more traditional wheels-and-rail train project designed to operate between Las Vegas and Victorville, California. It is expected that Southern California visitors to Las Vegas would park at the Victorville station, to be located just off I-15. The $4 billion train project would parallel I-15, potentially alleviating traffic snarls on that major route. While the project would not continue south through California's Cajon Pass to Los Angeles, it could connect to terminals serving the California high-speed rail line, making it accessible from most population centers in Southern California. It promises to make the trip from Victorville to Las Vegas in 81 minutes.

Ave. and turn right on Boulder Hwy.; from downtown, take U.S. 93 east to Tropicana east, and then right on Boulder Hwy.) touts its exclusively cab-over fleet as having more ready-to-use sleep space and maneuverability. Its RVs range 19–30 feet, suitable for parties of 3–7 people. Seven-night rentals start at $413 for the 19-footers and $553 for the seven-passenger 30-footers. The company adds a mileage estimate (at 32 cents per mile) at the time of rental and adjusts the charges based on actual miles driven when you return the vehicle. Common extra charges include linens, kitchen equipment, and generator use.

Located in the Camping World store for the convenience of stocking up for your trip as you pick up your RV, **Cruise America** (13175 Las Vegas Blvd. S., 877/594-3353) is virtually across the road from El Monte RV. Its 24-foot "standard" rental, at $500 per week, sleeps six if you're all very friendly. A 32-foot Class A goes for $844 per week. Prices include insurance, but mileage and kitchen and linen kits are extra.

LAS VEGAS MONORAIL

Since 2004, the now-defunct Sahara on the north end of the Strip and the MGM Grand near the south end have been connected via the Las Vegas Monorail (702/699-8200, 7 A.M.–2 A.M. Mon.–Thurs., 7 A.M.–3 A.M. Fri.–Sat., $5), with stops at the Las Vegas Hilton, the Convention Center, Harrah's/Imperial Palace, Flamingo/Caesars Palace, and Bally's/Paris. Although the Sahara closed in 2011, the Sahara monorail station remains open. More than 30 major resorts are now within easy reach along the Strip without a car or taxi. Reaching speeds up to 50 mph, the monorail glides above traffic to cover the four-mile route in about 14 minutes. Nine trains with air-conditioned cars carry up to 152 riders along the elevated track running on the east side of the strip, stopping every few minutes at the stations. One-day ($12) and three-day ($28) passes are also available. Tickets are available at vending machines at each station as well as at station properties.

BY BUS

Citizen Area Transit (CAT, 702/228-RIDE—702/228-7433, www.rtcsouthernnevada.com/transit/transitguide), the public bus system, is managed by the Regional Transportation Commission. CAT runs 54 routes all over Las Vegas Valley. Fares are $2–3, half price for seniors, ages 6–17, and people with disabilities. Call or access the ride guide online. Bus service is pretty comprehensive, but even the express routes with fewer stops take a long time to get anywhere.

The **Greyhound Depot** (200 S. Main St., 702/383-9792) is on the south side of the Plaza Hotel. Buses arrive and depart frequently throughout the day and night to and from all points in North America, and they are a reasonable alternative to driving or flying.

BY TAXI

Except for peak periods, taxis are numerous and quite readily available, and drivers are good sources of information (not always accurate) and entertainment (not always wholesome). Of course, Las Vegas operates at peak loads most of the time, so if you're not in a taxi zone right in front of one of the busiest hotels, it might be tough to get one. The 16 companies plying the streets of Las Vegas charge $3 for the flag drop and $2.40 per mile. A $1.80 surcharge is assessed for pickups from the airport. Waiting time is $0.50 per minute. This means that it's cheaper to take the surface streets from the airport to your destination rather than the freeway, which is several miles longer. A taxi ride should run no more than $25 from the airport to a hotel on the Strip or downtown.

BY LIMO

Offering chauffeur-driven domestic and imported sedans, shuttle buses, and SUVs in addition to stretch and superstretch limos, **Las Vegas Limousines** (702/736-1419 or 888/696-4400) can transport up to 20 people per vehicle to and from sporting events, corporate meetings, airport connections, bachelor and bachelorette parties, sightseeing tours, and more. Rates are $55 per hour for a six-seat stretch limo, $75 for a 10-seat superstretch.

Presidential Limousine (702/731-5577 or 800/423-1420) charges $59 per hour for its stretch six-seater, $80 per hour for the superstretch eight-seater; both include TVs and video players, mobile phones, champagne, bottled water, and roses for the women. **Bell Trans** (702/739-7990 or 800/274-7433) has 24- and 29-passenger coaches, a party bus, and a 12-passenger stretch SUV in addition to its fleet of stretch ($52 per hour) and superstretch ($80 per hour) limos.

The distinctive grill and white leather interior will make just the right impression when your chauffeur delivers you in the silver Rolls Royce Phantom offered by **CLS Las Vegas** (702/740-4545). CLS has a full fleet, including Hummer limos and buses that seat up to 36. The stretch goes for $68 per hour, the superstretch for $80 per hour.

TOURS

Several companies offer the chance to see the sights of Las Vegas by bus, helicopter, airplane, or off-road vehicle. The ubiquitous **Gray Line** (702/384-1234 or 800/634-6579) offers tours of the city by night as well as tours of Hoover Dam and the Grand Canyon. City tours (6:30 P.M.–midnight, $55) visit the major Vegas free sights: the Mirage volcano, the Bellagio Conservatory, the "Welcome to Las Vegas" sign, the Fremont Street Experience, and some of the more opulent hotels. You can add a helicopter overview of the neon-lit Vegas skyline to cap your experience. The Hoover Dam tour ($60) can include a luncheon cruise on Lake Mead ($92). To book a lake cruise directly, call **Lake Mead Cruises** (702/293-6180, adults $24, ages 2–11 $12, Sun. brunch cruise adults $39, ages 2–11 $18, dinner cruise adults $49, ages 2–11 $25).

Vegas Tours (866/218-6877) has a full slate of outdoor, adventure, and other tours. Some of the more unusual include soaring in a motorized glider ($129–159) and a visit and tour of the Techatticup gold mine ($113–189). Tours of the Grand Canyon and other state and national parks in the area are available as well. **All Vegas Tours** (702/233-1627 or 800/455-5868) has all the usual tours plus a high-speed you-drive-it dune buggy adventure over the Nellis Dunes ($150–199, drivers must be over age 15). **Pink Jeep Tours** (888/900-4480) takes visitors in rugged but cute and comfortable 10-passenger ATVs to such sites as the Las Vegas Springs Preserve, Eldorado Canyon, the Valley of Fire, and Mount Charleston.

There are plenty of other tour operators offering similar services. Search the Internet to find tours tailored for your needs, the best prices, and the most competent providers.

For history, nature, and entertainment buffs looking for a more focused adventure, themed tours are on the rise in Las Vegas. **Haunted Vegas Tours** (702/339-8744, $66) takes an interesting if macabre trip to the "Motel of Death," where many pseudo-celebrities have met their untimely ends. Guides dressed as undertakers take you to the spot where Tupac Shakur died and where the spirits of Bugsy Siegel and other famous people are still said to walk the earth. The same company offers the **Las Vegas Mob Tour** (702/339-8744, $66), taking visitors to the sites of Mafia hits. Guides, dressed in black pin-striped suits and fedoras, tell tales of the 1970s, when Anthony "The Ant" Spilotro ran the city, and give the scoop on the fate of casino mogul Lefty Rosenthal.

Hoover Dam and Lake Mead

Hoover Dam began detaining the Colorado and Virgin Rivers in 1935. By 1938, Lake Mead was full of three years' worth of river water braced by the monolithic buttress at Black Canyon. The largest artificial lake in the West, Lake Mead measures 110 miles long and 500 feet deep, has 822 miles of shoreline, and contains 28.5 million acre-feet of water (just over nine trillion gallons), a little less than half the water stored along the entire Colorado River system. The reservoir irrigates 2.25 million acres of land in the United States and Mexico and supplies water for more than 14 million people. Nine million people use Lake Mead each year as a recreational resource; it's one of the most-visited National Park Service–managed areas in the country.

For all this, Lake Mead is only incidental to the dam's primary purpose: flood and drought control. In addition, Lake Mead is only the centerpiece of the 1.5-million-acre Lake Mead National Recreation Area, which includes Lake Mojave and the surrounding desert from Davis Dam to the south, Grand Canyon National Park to the east, all the way north to Overton—the largest U.S. Department of the Interior recreational acreage in the Lower 48.

HENDERSON

Only four years after the completion of Hoover Dam, the Germans started dropping terror on England in the form of bombs whose deadly incendiary properties were attributed to magnesium, until then a little-known metal. Lightweight magnesium was also discovered in various components of downed German airplanes. In 1940, Allied scientists and engineers had analyzed the qualities of this metal, and geologists had located huge deposits near Gabbs, Nevada. Since vast amounts of electrical power are required to process magnesium, a site halfway between Hoover Dam and Las Vegas was selected for the magnesium processing plant, and in September 1941 construction started on a massive factory known as Basic Magnesium. More than 10,000 workers spent just a few months erecting the plant, the town, and the transportation systems necessary to aid the war effort. Five thousand people lived in "Basic" by early 1942, and 16 million pounds of magnesium had been produced by 1943. So much magnesium had been shipped from Basic by 1944 that the government had a surplus, and with the war in Europe winding down, the plant was closed.

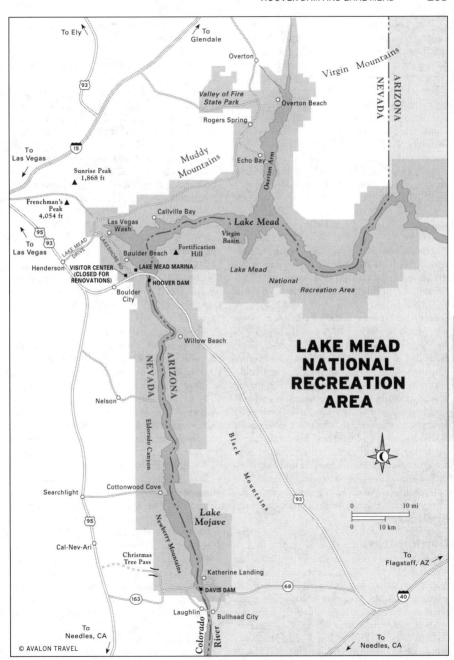

© AVALON TRAVEL

With the town threatened to become yet another ghost in the Nevada desert, the federal government agreed to turn over the property to the state, and the town, renamed to honor Albert Henderson, a local politician and judge who was pivotal in the takeover negotiations, received a new lease on life. By the early 1950s the huge manufacturing complex had been subdivided to accommodate smaller private industry, and by the early 1980s Henderson accounted for half of the state's non–tourist industry output. The town made the national news in 1988 when a huge explosion leveled Pacific Engineering, manufacturer of ammonia perchlorate, the oxidizer in solid rocket fuel, and the Kidd's Marshmallow factory next door.

Henderson is aesthetically...um...interesting, with its huge industrial complex set off from the residential and commercial districts that sprouted up in the last quarter of the 20th century. In early 1994 Henderson joined the Nevada 100,000 Club, an exclusive group of towns with more than 100,000 residents (it now boasts about 250,000), along with Las Vegas, North Las Vegas, and Reno. Until the 2008–2010 recession, Henderson was one of the fastest-growing cities in the fastest-growing state in the country, and it is consistently named among the nation's most livable communities thanks to its jobs, parks, relatively low crime rate, and the development of several new casinos in the Green Valley subdivision. Its excellent location is undeniable—only 15 minutes from Lake Mead, and close enough to Las Vegas to enjoy that city's benefits while far enough away to outdistance the disadvantages.

Getting There

Henderson is 14 miles south of downtown Las Vegas. I-515, which shares the road with U.S. 93 along this section, will get you there in 20 minutes. Boulder Highway south will get you there in 25 minutes. From the Strip, hook up with Boulder Highway by heading east on Sahara Avenue, Desert Inn Road, Flamingo Road, and Tropicana Avenue. If you're south

of the Strip, it is faster to take I-15 south to I-215, the Las Vegas Beltway. The beltway becomes Highway 564 as it crosses I-515 entering Henderson. Two new bus lines shuttle travelers with minimal stops from downtown Las Vegas. The Boulder Highway Express goes from the main transfer station on Bonneville Avenue downtown to Sunset Station. Buses leave every half hour for the 50-minute trip. The Henderson Express goes to downtown Henderson, continuing south to Nevada State College in just over an hour. Rates are $5 for two hours' riding time or $7 for 24 hours. Taxi fare runs about $40 plus tip.

Casinos

Just north of Sam's Town on Boulder Highway is **Boulder Station** (4111 N. Boulder Hwy., 702/432-7777); farther south, just north of Tropicana Avenue, is **Eastside Cannery** (5255 N. Boulder Hwy., 702/507-5700) and **The Longhorn** (5288 N. Boulder Hwy., 702/435-9170). They're all small local joints with a tradition of low limits, good cheap grub, and basic hotel rooms. On Sunset Road near Boulder Highway, the **Skyline** (1741 N. Boulder Hwy., 702/565-9116) is home to The Dumkoffs, a wildly entertaining costumed oompah band. They keep the party going Sunday afternoons with their comedy and music. **Joker's Wild** (920 N. Boulder Hwy., 702/564-8100), near the intersection with Water Street, has no hotel but offers blackjack, Caribbean stud, craps, roulette, a coffee shop, a buffet, and a lounge.

Two major casinos and one minor gambling house are the center of entertainment downtown. The **Eldorado** (140 S. Water St., 702/564-1811) is a typical small Boyd Group property like the California, Main Street Station, and Fremont downtown and Sam's Town and Joker's Wild on the Boulder Strip: a large, bright, classy place with a large pit full of blackjack, crap, and roulette tables along with a sports book, keno, bingo, a couple of bars, a 24-hour coffee shop, and Mariana's Mexican restaurant.

Next door, the **Rainbow Club** (122 S. Water St., 702/565-9777) is dark and gaudy by comparison, with a multicolored facade, startling neon borders, signage inside and out, and crowds around the slots and video poker, giving it the unmistakable signature of Reno's Peppermill.

Classing up the accommodations offerings in Henderson is the **Green Valley Ranch** (2300 Paseo Verde Pkwy., 702/871-7777, $110–180), one of the latest and most upscale of the Station Casinos properties. Located on I-215 just west of town, the property offers a lavish spa and attractive guest rooms packed with amenities such as free newspapers and down comforters. The pool areas offer private cabanas and infinity dipping pools. Guests will also find upscale dining, headliner entertainment, eye-catching bars, and a Regal cinema.

Way west of town, **M Resort** (12300 Las Vegas Blvd. S., 702/797-1000, $150–220) is Henderson's other casino to earn the title "resort." Located far afield from Henderson proper, nearly at Sky Harbor Airport on St. Rose Parkway (take I-215 west to the St. Rose exit and head west to Las Vegas Blvd.), the M is every bit as lavish as Green Valley Ranch, with a strong entertainment schedule and fine dining; the guest rooms are a spacious 550 square feet with all the electronic entertainment you'd expect, including 42-inch TVs. Getting in on the Food Network craze, M hosts *Martini Time with Chef Tina Martini* (noon and 4 P.M. Thurs.–Sun., $40), a cooking show with a live studio audience.

Food

Henderson is no match for Las Vegas when it comes to haute cuisine, but **Todd's Unique Dining** (4350 E. Sunset Rd., 702/430-7544, 4:30–10 P.M. Mon.–Sat., $30–45) holds its own against any in Sin City. With unpretentious decor and food, the seafood is always fresh, but the short ribs are the way to go. The cellar always has just the right accompaniment. From the kitchen to the waitstaff, you'll always be professionally catered to. Other top gourmet choices include **Hank's Fine Steaks & Martinis** (Green Valley Ranch, 2300 Paseo Verde Pkwy., 702/617-7515, 5:30–10 P.M. daily,

$45–65) for steaks with juices sealed in with a perfect charbroil and a sweet South African lobster tail; start with the crabmeat cocktail. Green Valley also has the perfect spot for a late supper, **China Spice** (2300 Paseo Verde Pkwy., 702/617-7515, 5 P.M.–1 A.M. Sun.–Thurs., 5 P.M.–3 A.M. Fri.–Sat., $20–40). Don't miss the crispy duck.

With dinner covered, turn to M Resort for breakfast and lunch. **Studio B** (12300 Las Vegas Blvd. S., 702/797-1000, 7 A.M.–9 P.M. daily, $16–30) brings gourmet to the lunch buffet. Live cooking demonstrations by culinary experts preparing the buffet's dishes are shown on huge video monitors inside the main buffet room. You'll see dedicated professionals preparing delicate pastries, sushi, and Asian cuisine worthy of the top Chinese rooms in town. The beef on the carving station is tender enough to be cut with a plastic knife. Beer and wine is included at no extra charge. To start the day right, bop on into **Hash House a Go-Go** (12300 S. Las Vegas Blvd., 702/797-1000, 7 A.M.–11 P.M. Sun.–Thurs., 7 A.M.–2 A.M. Fri.–Sat., $10–20). Chicken, turkey, and barbecue along with more traditional breakfast meats figure heavily among the scrambled-egg dishes. For a bargain, try the 6–11 A.M. breakfast at **Images** (122 S. Water St., 702/565-9777, 24 hours daily, $7–15) inside the Rainbow Club; $1.89 gets you two eggs, bacon or sausage, and hash browns, toast, or biscuits and gravy.

Lake Las Vegas

Henderson's latest attempt to shed its image as the grittier, less attractive stepsister of Las Vegas seemed headed for epic failure—bankruptcies, lawsuits, and unfinished buildings punctuate the development seven miles east of town. But now Lake Las Vegas, the ambitious, ultraposh Mediterranean-themed housing and resort development, centered on a 320-acre manmade lake, appears poised to snatch prosperity from the jaws of despair. In 2011 alone the resort community saw several improvements. Dolce Hotels and Resorts rebranded and reopened the nongaming Ravella, the former Ritz-Carlton;

Casino Montelago followed suit a few months later; SouthShore Golf Club, designed by Jack Nicklaus, and Montelago Village, a collection of shops on a pedestrian way, have remained open throughout the bankruptcy process. The hotel and casino reopening and the prospect of a stronger economy are cause for optimism that the area can make a go of it.

Loews Hotel (101 Montelago Blvd., 702/567-6000, $130–180) maintains a pride of place and a lakeside getaway for the rich and those who want to dream for a weekend or a week. Loews is Lake Las Vegas for many people, its championship golf courses and water activities the upscale area's most memorable features and inviting locales for weddings and corporate events. Just the right size at about 500 guest rooms and suites, Loews tempts guests with a private white-sand beach and cabanas on two pools, children's activities, kayaks, pedal boats, and electric skiffs for exploring the inlets and lagoons as well as a full-service spa and fitness room. Bright and airy, **Marssa** (6–10 P.M. Tues.–Sat., $30–50) carries on the lakeside theme with sushi and Pacific Rim–inspired seafood, while **Rick's Café** (6 A.M.–3 P.M. daily, $15–30) dishes up delicacies with a continental bent.

Clark County Museum

As you continue east on Boulder Highway, the next attraction is the extensive and fascinating Clark County Museum (1830 S. Boulder Hwy., 702/455-7955, 9 A.M.–4:30 P.M. daily, adults $1.50, seniors and children $1). The main museum exhibit is housed in the new pueblo building, with fine displays tracing Native American cultures from the prehistoric to the contemporary and chronicling nonnative exploration, settlement, and industry: Mormons, the military, mining, ranching, railroading, riverboats, and gambling up through the construction of Hoover Dam and the subsequent founding of Henderson.

The old depot that houses the railroad station and rolling-stock collection has been restored. Also be sure to stroll down to the Heritage Street historical residential and commercial buildings: the **Townsite House,** built in Henderson in the 1940s; the 1890s print shop; the **Babcock and Wilcox House,** one of 12 original residences built in Boulder City in early 1933; and the pièce de résistance **Beckley House,** a simple yet stunning example of the still-popular California bungalow style, built for $2,500 in 1912 by Las Vegas pioneer and entrepreneur Will Beckley.

Other displays include a ghost town trail, a nature trail with a simulated Paiute village, a general store, a jailhouse, and a blacksmith. The gift shop sells some interesting items such as books, magazines, minerals, jewelry, beads, pottery, textiles, and even Joshua tree seeds.

Henderson Bird Viewing Preserve

Southern Nevada's natural side isn't always easy to find, but when you peel back the neon, the discoveries are often surprisingly rich. The Henderson Bird Viewing Preserve (2400 Moser Dr., near Boulder Hwy. and Sunset Rd., 702/267-4180, 6 A.M.–2 P.M. daily Mar.–May, 6 A.M.–noon daily June–Aug., 6 A.M.–2 P.M. daily Sept.–Nov., 7 A.M.–2 P.M. daily Dec.–Feb., free) is a good example. Situated on 140 acres at the city's water treatment center, the preserve is home to hundreds of hummingbirds, ibis, ducks, eagles, roadrunners, and numerous other migratory species. The park, which is managed by the City of Henderson, offers nine ponds with both paved and dirt paths. Don't feed the wildlife.

Railroad Pass

U.S. 93/95 continues southwest up and over a low gate between the River Mountains and the Black Hills known as Railroad Pass (2,367 feet), named for the Union Pacific route to Boulder City and the dam. With a full-service casino, coffee shop, and buffet, **Railroad Pass Hotel and Casino** (2800 Boulder Hwy., 702/294-5000, $39–59) sits at the top of the pass. Just beyond is the junction where U.S. 95 cuts right, south and west of Laughlin, and U.S. 93 heads east into Boulder City.

Information and Services

Past downtown on Water Street are the convention center, city hall, a library, and a park; Water Street runs around to the left and joins Major Street, which heads right back out to Boulder Highway. The **Chamber of Commerce** (590 S. Boulder Hwy., 702/565-8951) is right at the corner.

BOULDER CITY

In 1930, when Congress appropriated the first funds for the Boulder Canyon Project, the Great Depression was in full swing, the dam was to be one of the largest single engineering and public works construction tasks ever undertaken, and urban architects were increasingly leaning toward the social progressiveness of the community planning movement. Boulder City was born of these unique factors and remains the most unusual town in Nevada. In 1930 Saco R. DeBoer, a highly regarded 35-year-old landscape architect from Denver, developed the Boulder City master plan. He set the government buildings at the top of the site's hill. The town radiated out like a fan, and parks, plazas, and perimeters enclosed the neighborhoods in pleasant settings. Construction of the town began in March 1931, only a month before work started at the dam site. The increasing influx of workers, most of whom were housed in a cluster of temporary tent cabins known as Ragtown, forced the government to accelerate construction, and most of DeBoer's more grandiose elements (neighborhood greenbelts, large single-family houses) were abandoned in favor of more economical and expedient dormitories and small cottages. Still, Boulder City became a prettified all-American oasis of security and order in the midst of a great desert and the Great Depression. The U.S. Bureau of Reclamation, charged with constructing the dam, controlled the town down to the smallest detail; a city manager, answerable directly to the Commissioner of Reclamation, oversaw operations with complete authority.

After the dam was completed, the town master plan was further dismantled as workers left and company housing was moved or

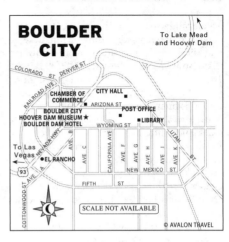

torn down for materials. It seemed Boulder City was in danger of becoming a ghost town, but it gradually became a service center for the recreation area. For 30 years the federal government owned the town and all its buildings, but in 1960 the municipality became independent, the feds began to sell property to longtime residents, and alcohol sales were allowed for the first time. Gambling, however, remains illegal in the only town in the state with laws against it. Boulder City today is far from it's squeaky-clean government origins, but it retains its own atmosphere—especially in contrast to the rest of southern Nevada.

Sights

Coming into Boulder City on U.S. 93 (Nevada Highway) is more like entering a town in Arizona or New Mexico: The downtown streets are lined with Indian and Mexican gift shops and a number of galleries and shops selling crafts, jewelry, antiques, and collectibles as well as businesses catering to the lake-bound crowd. Boulder City has no casinos.

Stop at the **Boulder Dam Hotel** (1305 Arizona St., 702/293-3510, $69–135) for a glimpse at dam-construction and divorce-era Las Vegas. This darling, built in 1933 to accommodate visitors to the construction site, found new life as divorce tourists booked accommodations to wait out Nevada's residency requirements for ending their marriages, and the lobby is now home to the **Boulder City/Hoover Dam Museum** (702/294-1988, 10 A.M.–5 P.M. Mon.–Sat., noon–5 P.M. Sun., adults $2, seniors and children $1). The colonial-style interior looks exactly as it did in 1933 when it was constructed, as you can see in the black-and-white photos that grace the walls. Inside are interesting photos from the 1930s of the Six Companies' rec hall and high scalers working high up on the canyon walls. You can also see the high-scaler chair, and pick up Dennis McBride's excellent book on Boulder City, *In the Beginning*. The restaurant is open for breakfast (included for hotel guests) and lunch. The hotel is also available for tea parties, reunions, and other special events.

Get a walking tour brochure at the hotel and stroll up Arizona Street and then down Nevada Highway to get a feel for the history and design significance of downtown. Then continue on the residential and public-building walks to get an intimate glimpse of DeBoer's plan for the town as modified by the practicalities of government work. You can also head back toward Henderson on Nevada Highway to the Frank T. Crowe Memorial Park (named for the chief dam engineer, immortalized in the book *Big Red*) and take a right onto Cherry Street to see the fine row of bungalows from the 1930s built for dam workers, Boulder City's first residents.

At the Boulder City branch of the **Nevada State Railroad Museum** (600 Yucca St., 702/486-5933), railroad buffs can take a train ride on the **Nevada Southern Railway** (adults $10, ages 4–11 $5, under age 4 free); get a discount coupon at www.nevadasouthern.com/PDFs/Dollar Off Coupon.pdf. The renovated historic cars make treks along the old Boulder Branch Line departing at 10 A.M., 11:30 A.M., 1 P.M., and 2:30 P.M. Saturday–Sunday. The Pullman coaches, some of which date back to 1911, take passengers for a seven-mile, 45-minute round-trip journey across the stark Mojave Desert. All the cars and engines have been refurbished, and the enclosed cars

have been retrofitted with air-conditioning. The spur used for the excursion was donated to the Nevada State Railroad Museum in 1985, and the train still chugs along the original tracks. The ride goes as far as the Railroad Pass Casino, and along the way passengers can expect to see jackrabbits, the occasional bighorn sheep, a variety of desert plant life, and a few historic sites.

Accommodations

Boulder City has a handful of motels, all strung along Nevada Highway (U.S. 93) as you enter town. Coming from the west, bypass the first several inns you come to; you'll be greeted by the impeccable landscaping and the retro-chic sign of the **El Rancho** (725 Nevada Hwy., 702/293-1085, $60–110). The spotless grounds mirror the accommodations. Sparkling microwaves and refrigerators, spacious guest rooms, quilts on the beds, and ceiling fans give the El Rancho a homey feel. Save even more with a cookout on barbecue grills outside, but be sure to eat at least one meal at the Southwest Diner right next door.

If you're looking to save even more on your room, or you crave some nearby gaming action, you could continue even farther, almost to the shore of Lake Mead, to **The Hacienda Hotel & Casino** (U.S. 93, just east of Lakeshore Rd., 702/293-5000 or 800/245-6380, $48–63). The hotel is pet-friendly, which is a plus for folks looking to hike the Lake Mead area with their dogs, but guests who are finicky about sanitary conditions may want to book elsewhere; the room rates are dirt cheap, and while the beds and guest rooms are perfectly clean, the common areas and carpeting are showing signs of age. A Lake Mead and Hoover Dam helicopter tour company and a river rafting concession operate out of the Hacienda, making it a convenient and inexpensive place to stay for sightseers, and there's a decent buffet, a 24-hour café, a steak house, and a lounge with live entertainment.

Canyon Trail RV Park (1200 Industrial Rd., 702/293-1200, $35) has 242 sites. There's no shade and precious little greenery, but craggy sandstone mountains rise from the rear of the place. From the traffic light in Boulder City, take the truck route one block to Canyon Road. Turn left, drive to the end of Canyon Road, and turn left on Industrial Road. The park is half a block down on the right. Another RV park, **Boulder Oaks** (1010 Industrial Rd., 702/294-4425, $38), is quiet despite its in-town location.

Information and Services

The **Chamber of Commerce** (465 Nevada Way, 702/293-2034) has all the local brochures and can answer questions about the town, the dam, and the lake.

HOOVER DAM

The 1,400-mile Colorado River has been carving and gouging great canyons and valleys with red sediment-laden waters for 10 million years. For 10,000 years Native Americans, the Spanish, and Mormon settlers coexisted with the fitful river, rebuilding after spring floods and withstanding the droughts that often reduced the mighty waterway to a muddy trickle in fall. By the turn of the 20th century, irrigation ditches and canals had diverted some of the river water into California's Imperial Valley, west of its natural channel, but in 1905 a wet winter and abnormal spring rains combined to drown everything in sight: Flash floods deepened the artificial canal and actually changed the course of the river to flow through California's low-lying valley. For nearly two years engineers and farmers wrestled the Colorado back into place. The Salton Sea, a lake that had covered 22 square miles, grew to 500 square miles, and 95 years later it still covers more than 200 square miles. But the message was clear to federal overseers: The Colorado had to be tamed, and over the next 15 years the Bureau of Reclamation began to "reclaim" the West, primarily by building dams and canals. By 1923, equitable water distribution for the Colorado River had been negotiated among the states and Mexico, and six years later Congress passed the Boulder Canyon Project Act, authorizing

© KLOTZ/123RF.COM

Hoover Dam and Lake Mead

funds for Boulder Dam to be constructed in Black Canyon; the dam's name was eventually changed to honor Herbert Hoover, then Secretary of Commerce.

The immensity of the undertaking still boggles the mind. The closest settlement was a sleepy railroad town 40 miles west called Las Vegas, and the nearest large power plant was in San Bernardino, more than 200 miles away. Tracks had to be laid, a town built, workers hired, and equipment shipped in just to prepare for construction. Of course, before dam work could begin, the Colorado had to be diverted. That project began in April 1931. Workers hacked four tunnels, each 56 feet across, through the canyon walls. They moved thousands of tons of rock every day for 16 months. Finally, in November 1932, the river water was rerouted around the dam site. Then came the concrete: 40 million cubic yards of it, eight cubic yards at a time. Over the course of the next two years, five million bucketfuls of cement were lowered into the canyon until the dam—660 feet thick at the base, 45 feet thick at the crest, 1,244 feet across, and 726 feet high—was complete.

The top of the dam was built wide enough to accommodate a two-lane highway. Inside this gargantuan wedge were placed 17 massive electricity-generating turbines. The cost of the dam surpassed $175 million. At the peak of construction, more than 5,000 workers toiled day and night to complete the project under extreme conditions of heat, dust, danger from heavy equipment, explosions, falls, and tumbling rocks. An average of 50 injuries per day and a total of 94 deaths were recorded over the 46 months of construction. Contrary to popular legend, none of the dead were entombed in the dam.

The largest construction equipment ever known had to be designed, built, and installed at the site, and miraculously the dam was completed nearly two years ahead of schedule—this was a government project, remember. In February 1935 the diversion tunnels were closed, and Lake Mead began to fill up behind the dam, which was dedicated eight months

later by President Franklin Roosevelt. A month later, the first turbine turned, and electricity started flowing.

Today, the Colorado River system has several dams and reservoirs, storing roughly 60 million acre-feet of water. An acre-foot is just under 326,000 gallons, about as much water as an average U.S. household uses in two years. California is allotted 4.4 million acre-feet, Arizona gets 2.8 million, Nevada 300,000, and Mexico 1.5 million. Hoover Dam, meanwhile, supplies four billion kilowatt-hours of electricity annually, enough to power 500,000 homes.

Getting There

The new bypass bridge siphons through traffic away from Hoover Dam, saving time and headaches for both drivers and dam visitors. Still, the 35-mile drive from central Las Vegas to a parking lot at the dam will take 45 minutes or more. From the Strip, I-15 south connects with I-215 southeast of the airport, and I-215 east takes drivers to U.S. 93 in Henderson. Remember that U.S. 93 shares the roadway with U.S. 95 and I-515 till well past Henderson. Going south on U.S. 93, exit at Highway 172 to the dam. Note that this route is closed on the Arizona side; drivers continuing on to the Grand Canyon must retrace Highway 172 to U.S. 93 and cross the bypass bridge. A parking garage ($7) is convenient to the visitors center and dam tours, but free parking is available at turnouts on both sides of the dam for those willing to walk a bit.

TOURS FROM LAS VEGAS

To avoid driving in traffic, the parking fee, and the walk, many visitors opt for one of the several bus tours from Las Vegas to Hoover Dam. The **Gray Line** (702/384-1234 or 800/634-6579) offers a mini tour (8:30 A.M.–5 P.M. daily, $60) that includes a tour of the dam power plant and additional time to spend exploring the visitors center, watching a film of the dam's construction and checking out the symbolism-rich sculptures. The ride to the dam on the Premium Express tour offered by

Hoover Dam Tour Company (3014 S. Rancho Dr., Bldg. A, 702/361-7628 or 888/512-0075, 9 A.M.–2:30 P.M. daily, $52–60) includes narration of the jaunt through Las Vegas, the Green Valley section of Henderson, and Boulder City. The power plant tour is included in the two-hour stay at the modern-engineering marvel. The trip back includes a stop at Ethel M. Chocolate Factory—there's a short self-guided tour of the candy-making process and a neat desert-landscaped garden outside. The company's Deluxe Tour ($80) includes a dining certificate valid at any of 16 restaurants in Planet Hollywood's Miracle Mile shops. The basic **VegasTours.com** (115 Corporate Park Dr., Henderson, 866/218-6877, 9 A.M.–5 P.M. daily, $52) option does not include the power plant tour, but the company does offer the widest variety of combinations and add-ons to time spent at the dam itself. Examples include a paddlewheel cruise on Lake Mead ($105), a float down the Colorado River through Black Canyon ($132), and a Hummer adventure through Joshua tree forests and searches for kit foxes and gold nuggets ($189).

Visitors Center and Tours

In 1977 the Bureau of Reclamation started to build a new and improved **visitors center** (702/494-2517, 9 A.M.–6 P.M. daily summer, 9 A.M.–4:45 P.M. daily winter, $8, free under age 4, parking $7) to accommodate the 700,000 people who visit every year; more than 32 million visitors have taken the tour of the most-visited dam in the country. Construction on the 44,000-square-foot facility lagged through four presidential administrations until it was completed in 1995 for an estimated cost of $435 million; the Luxor resort in Las Vegas cost only $375 million. To be fair, the project did include building a five-story, 450-car parking garage wedged into a ravine in the mountains, and as visitors centers go, this one is terrific. It has some exhibits, a movie about the Colorado River, and elevators that take you into the bowels of the dam. You can buy tickets for the 35-minute **dam tour** (adults $6, over age 61, ages 4–16, and military $9, military in

uniform and children under age 4 free). Get in line as early as possible to shorten the wait time. The 53-story descent into the dam's interior takes more than a minute. Tunnels lead you to a monumental room housing the monolithic turbines. Next, you step outside to look up to the top of the dam and the magnificently arched bypass bridge downstream. The tour ends with a walk through one of the diversion tunnels, a 30-foot-wide water pipe. The guides pack extensive statistics and stories into the short tour.

LAKE MEAD NATIONAL RECREATION AREA

Three roads provide access to Lake Mead from the Nevada side. From the north, take Highway 147 (Lake Mead Blvd.) as it runs east from North Las Vegas before turning south to the lake and continuing along the east shore to Lake Mead Marina and Boulder Beach. It connects with Highway 167 (Northshore Rd.), which follows the north shore of Las Vegas Bay past Callville Bay and turns north along the Overton Arm.

From Henderson and points south, you can follow Highway 564 (Lake Mead Dr.) northeast past Lake Las Vegas, where it ends at Highway 147. Turn left to hook up with Northshore Road or right to Lakeshore Road. You can also take U.S. 93 to Boulder City, where it takes on an additional name: Nevada Highway. If you stay on this road, you'll wind through canyons and eventually reach Hoover Dam, but just east of Boulder City you can turn left onto Lakeshore Road, which heads north along the eastern shore. Lakeshore Road leads to the **Alan Bible Visitors Center** (702/293-8990, 8:30 A.M.–4:30 P.M. daily) and park headquarters for the recreation area. Named for a popular U.S. senator from Nevada, the center has maps, brochures, knowledgeable rangers, and a 15-minute movie on the lake and its ecosystem.

Across Lakeshore Road from the visitors center is a parking lot for the trailhead to the **U.S. Government Construction Railroad Trail.** The 2.6-mile one-way route follows an

LAS VEGAS

© RYAN JERZ

Lake Mead

abandoned railroad grade along a ledge over-looking the lake. It passes through four tunnels blasted through the hills and ends at the fifth tunnel, which is sealed. This is an enjoyable level stroll that anyone can do. Mountain bikers can get on the **Bootleg Canyon Mountain Bike Trail,** which has 36 miles of cross-country and downhill runs (the "Elevator Shaft" has a 22 percent grade). Trailhead access is off Yucca or Canyon Streets in Boulder City.

Another trail to consider in Boulder City is the **River Mountain Hiking Trail,** a five-mile round-trip hike originally built by the Civilian Conservation Corps in 1935 and recently restored. It has good views of the lake and the valley. The trailhead is on the truck bypass, just beyond the traffic light in downtown Boulder City, on the left as you're heading toward the dam.

Getting There

Lakeshore Road parallels the shoreline of the lake's east side, accessing Las Vegas Bay, Boulder Harbor, Hemmenway Harbor, and Lake Mead Marina. To access it from the south (it's 20 miles or 30 minutes from the I-215–U.S.

93 interchange), turn off U.S. 93 into Lake Mead National Recreation Area at the bottom of a steep downgrade just east of Boulder City. From the north, take I-215 (Hwy. 564/Lake Mead Pkwy.) through Henderson (10 miles, 20 minutes). Near Lake Las Vegas, Lake Mead Parkway splits: The left fork is Lakeshore Road, and the right fork is Northshore Road, which parallels the lake's north shore.

You can also get to Northshore Road by taking Highway 147 (Lake Mead Blvd.) east from North Las Vegas (16 miles, 25 minutes). It dead-ends at Northshore Road. Turning right leads to the intersection of Northshore and Lakeshore Roads; turning left leads to Callville Bay and its marina (a right turn at Callville Bay Rd. after 28 miles, about 45 minutes) and eventually to Valley of Fire State Park and Overton.

Lakeshore Road

Across Lakeshore Road from the Alan Bible Visitors Center is a parking lot for the trailhead to the **U.S. Government Construction Railroad Trail.** The 2.6-mile one-way route follows an abandoned railroad grade along a ledge overlooking the lake. It passes through four tunnels blasted through the hills and ends at the fifth tunnel, which is sealed. This is an enjoyable level stroll that anyone can do. Mountain bikers can get on the **Bootleg Canyon Mountain Bike Trail,** which has 36 miles of cross-country and downhill runs (the "Elevator Shaft" has a 22 percent grade). Trailhead access is off Yucca or Canyon Streets in Boulder City.

Another trail to consider in Boulder City is the **River Mountain Hiking Trail,** a five-mile round-trip hike originally built by the Civilian Conservation Corps in 1935 and recently restored. It has good views of the lake and the valley. The trailhead is on the truck bypass, just beyond the traffic light in downtown Boulder City, on the left as you're heading toward the dam.

On Lakeshore Road about two miles north of the Nevada Highway ingress to the recreation area is the **Lake Mead RV Village** (288 Lakeshore Rd., 702/293-2540, $45), which has many permanent mobiles and trailers but has 115 spaces dedicated to transient RVers, including many pull-throughs (register at the office near the entrance). A Laundromat and groceries are available. Turn right off Lakeshore Road into the entrance and right into the trailer village. If you take a left at the entrance, you enter **Boulder Beach Campground** ($10), a sprawling and somewhat rustic site with water, grills, a dump station, and plenty of shade under cottonwoods and pines, but no hookups. There are 150 campsites for tents or small self-contained motor homes. It's a three-minute walk down to the water, or 0.5 miles' drive north on Lakeshore Road. They don't call it Boulder Beach for nothing: The bottom is rocky and hard on the feet (bring your sandals), but the water is bathtub warm, around 80°F July–September. Sheltered picnic tables and restrooms are available waterside.

Seven miles beyond Boulder Beach is **Las Vegas Bay Campground** (702/293-8907, $10). Turn right into the Las Vegas Marina, then take your first left; the campground is about one mile down the spur road. The campground sits on a bluff over the lake; it's not quite as shady or as large as Boulder Beach. Also, you have to climb down a pretty steep slope to get to the water, and there's no real beach. There are 86 campsites for tents or self-contained motor homes up to 35 feet. Piped drinking water, flush toilets, picnic tables, grills, and fire pits are provided, and there is a campground host.

Continuing north, follow Lakeshore Road around to the left (northwest), then take a right onto Northshore Road (Hwy. 167). In another few miles, turn right at the intersection with Lake Mead Boulevard (Hwy. 147). In another seven miles is the turnoff for Callville Bay.

Callville Bay

From the highway, you rock and roll four miles down to the marina, which is green from oleanders, Russian olives, yuccas, palms, and pines. Callville Bay is the site of Callville, founded by Anson Call in 1865 in response to a directive by Mormon leader Brigham Young. Callville flourished briefly in the 1860s as a landing for Colorado River steamboats and an Army garrison, but the post office closed in 1869. Today the stone ruins of Call's warehouse lie under 400 feet of Lake Mead water and 10 feet of Lake Mead silt.

As you come into the marina, the first left is to **Callville Bay Trailer Village** (702/565-8958, $22), most of which is occupied by permanent mobiles and trailers. There are only five spaces for motor homes to stay overnight, all with full hookups and three with pull-throughs. RVs, along with tent campers, can also park without hookups at the campground across the road.

Callville Bay Campground (702/293-8990, $10) is a little farther down the access road. A beautiful grassy area greets you at the entrance, with stone picnic benches under shelters and a restroom. The sites closer to the front have the taller shade-giving oleanders; those toward the rear are more exposed. A 0.5-mile trail climbs from the dump station near the entrance to a sweeping panorama of the whole area. There are 80 campsites with running water, flush toilets, picnic tables, and grills, and there is a campground host.

The marina has a grocery store with a snack bar, and there is a bar-restaurant with a wall of big picture windows overlooking the lake. Down at the boat launch, you can rent houseboats.

Back on Northshore Road (Hwy. 167), continue east; it's rugged country out here, with the Black Mountains between you and the lake and the dark brooding Muddy Mountains on the left. Eventually the road turns north toward the east edge of the Muddy Mountains. The turnoff to Echo Bay, 24 miles from Callville, is on the right.

Echo Bay

Four bumpy miles down Bitter Spring Valley is **Echo Bay Marina** (702/394-4000, $30). This resort has a similar layout to Callville Bay but is much larger. The trailer village has shaded spots arranged in a horseshoe with restrooms and laundry facilities in the middle. During summer, a shuttle delivers campers to the marina. The marina rents personal watercraft as well as patio, ski, and fishing boats. Recent low water levels have meant that there are no houseboats for rent. Tents are not allowed, but near the upper section is a National Park Service campground (702/394-4066, $10). The lower section, close to the water, has 20-foot-tall oleander bushes for shade and privacy. The upper campground is north, across the road, just inland from the marina.

As you continue down toward the marina, you'll see the **Echo Bay Hotel** (702/394-4000, $70–125). The restaurant next door is open for breakfast, lunch, and dinner.

The great thing about Echo Bay is the beach, the best and most accessible on the Nevada side of the lake. There's no shade, but it's sandy, unlike the rocks at Boulder Beach, and it's not crowded. The bay is shallow for a long distance out, so the swimming is safe; there's no lifeguard.

Overton Beach

Back on Northshore Road, continue north, skirting the east edge of the Muddies. In less than a mile is **Rogers Spring,** which bubbles up clear and warm in a wash that runs east from the Muddy Mountains into Roger's Bay in the Overton Arm of Lake Mead. The warm turquoise pool, outlined by towering palms and sturdy old cottonwoods, overflows into a bubbling creek that meanders down a tree-lined course toward Lake Mead. Tropical fish, the descendants of the denizens of a failed hatchery from the 1950s, dart in the shallows and thrive in its warm waters. This spring has long been a favorite camping spot of southern Nevadans; it was originally developed by the Civilian Conservation Corps in the 1930s under the direction of Thomas W. Miller, the colonel who was instrumental in developing the first facilities at nearby Valley of Fire State Park. The National Park Service has plans to develop 250 campsites with water, sewer, and power. For now, there are chemical toilets and picnic shelters. A sign cautions swimmers not to put their heads under the water. The trailhead for a mile-long trail to an overlook is across the bridge.

A mile up the road from Rogers Spring is **Blue Point Spring,** which provides a grand view of Lake Mead on one side and the back of Valley of Fire on the other. In the early 1900s, farmers near St. Thomas (now at the bottom of the lake) worked to divert the waters of Blue Point and Rogers Springs to irrigate their fields. They dug the canal and hand-mixed concrete to line it. Their work eventually delivered water to the fields, but their health deteriorated; apparently, they drank from the springs, whose mineral content acted as a laxative, resulting in weakness and weight loss. Because of their fate, Blue Point Spring became known as "Slim Creek."

The recent decade-long drought has forced the closure of Overton Beach resort, formerly a terrific spot for fishing for striped bass.

Virgin Basin

Just above Overton Beach, the Virgin River to the northeast and the Muddy River to the northwest empty into Lake Mead. The Virgin Basin is a widening of the Virgin River just before it enters the reservoir. It's a primary habitat for numerous species of wildlife, including mammals, waterfowl, birds of prey, fish, reptiles, and amphibians. In the fall and spring, for example, numerous migrating species use the Virgin Basin as a resting place. Some species, including bald eagles, spend the winter in the Virgin Basin. Because it's accessible only by boat or a jolting primitive access road, it is well protected and offers a habitat safe from most human intervention. If you're careful, the basin provides an excellent opportunity to view and photograph wildlife in one of the few river wilderness areas left near the lake. To get here, you have to boat in from the Overton Arm. Most of the time there isn't enough water in the Virgin River below Riverside (just south of Mesquite) to float anything but an inner tube.

◖ River Tours

Tour operators bus rafters to the restricted side of Hoover Dam, where they board 35-person craft for a 3.5-hour ride with **Black Canyon River Adventures** (800/455-3490, 9 A.M. and 10 A.M. daily year-round, adults $86, youth $83, children $53). The motorized raft trips end at Willow Beach, 13 miles downstream on the Arizona side of the Colorado River. Ospreys and bighorn sheep are often sighted on these trips, and rafters can wade and swim in the chilly water before enjoying the box lunch provided.

The *Desert Princess* (702/293-6180), a 250-passenger Mississippi-style stern-wheeler, and its little sister, the 149-passenger side-wheeler *Desert Princess Too,* cruise Lake Mead from the Lake Mead Cruises Landing (490 Horsepower Cove Rd., off Lakeshore Rd. near the junction with U.S. 93). Ninety-minute cruises (adults $24, children $12) leave at noon and 2 P.M. daily, and there is a two-hour dinner cruise (6:30 P.M. Thurs.–Sun., adults $49, children $25) as well as a two-hour brunch cruise (10 A.M. Sun., adults $39, children $18).

Recreation

Motorized fun is the most obvious recreation on Lake Mead. **Boating** options on the vast lake range from power boats skipping across the surface to houseboats puttering lazily toward hidden coves and personal watercraft jumping wakes and negotiating hairpin turns. **Las Vegas Boat Harbor** (702/293-1191) and **Lake Mead Marina** (702/293-3484), both at Hemenway Harbor (Hemenway Rd., off Lakeshore Rd. near the junction with U.S. 93, 702/293-1191), rent powerboats, pontoons, and WaveRunners for $50–75 per hour, with half-day and daily rates available. **Callville Bay Marina** (off Northshore Rd., 17 miles east of Lake Las Vegas) has all these and houseboat rentals too. For nonmotorized fun, sailing and windsurfing are year-round thrills, and there's plenty of shoreline to explore in a canoe or kayak.

For **anglers,** largemouth bass, rainbow trout, catfish, and black crappie have been mainstays for decades. These days, however, striped bass are the most popular sport fish. Fishing supplies and fishing licenses can be obtained at the marinas.

Sixty miles south of Boulder City, recreation is also abundant at **Lake Mojave,** created by Davis Dam in 1953. This lake backs up almost all the way to Hoover Dam like a southern extension of Lake Mead. The two lakes are similar in climate, desert scenery, vertical-walled canyon enclosures, and a shoreline lined with numerous private coves. There is excellent trout fishing at Willow Beach on the Arizona side, where the water, too cold for swimming, is perfect for serious angling. A few rainbows over 55 pounds have been caught, and 20-pounders are not at all rare. **Cottonwood Cove Resort** (10000 Cottonwood Cove Rd., Searchlight, 702/297-1464), 14 miles east of central Searchlight, sits just north of the widest part of the lake. Access is also available on the Arizona side at Katherine Landing, just north of Davis Dam.

Swimming in Lake Mead requires the least equipment—a bathing suit. Boulder Beach (Lakeshore Rd., Boulder City), just 30 miles from Las Vegas and just down the road from the Alan Bible Visitors Center, is the most popular swimming site. For **divers,** visibility in Lake Mead averages 30 feet, and the water is stable. There is a dive park north of the swimming beach at Boulder Beach. It slopes gently to about 70 feet with placed objects and boats to explore, makes it a good introduction to the sport for novice divers. The sights of the deep are more spectacular elsewhere: the yacht *Tortuga* rests at a depth of 50 feet near the Boulder Islands; Hoover Dam's asphalt factory sits on the canyon floor nearby; the old Mormon town of St. Thomas, inundated by the lake in 1938, has many a watery story to tell; and Castle Cliffs at Gypsum Reef has drop-offs and irregular formations caused by erosion.

THE GRAND CANYON

There's a reason why Arizona's official nickname is "The Grand Canyon State." Any state with one of the true wonders of the world would be keen to advertise its good luck.

The canyon simply must be seen to be believed. If you stand for the first time on one of the South Rim's easily accessible lookouts and don't have to catch your breath, you might need to check your pulse. Staring into the canyon brings up all kinds of existential questions; its brash vastness can't be taken in without conjuring some big ideas and questions about life, humanity, and God. Take your time here—you'll need it.

The more adventurous can make reservations, obtain a permit, and enter the desert depths of the canyon, taking a hike or even a mule ride to the Colorado River, or spending a weekend trekking rim-to-rim with an overnight at the famous Phantom Ranch, deep in the canyon's inner gorge. The really brave can hire a guide and take a once-in-a-lifetime trip down the great river, riding the roiling rapids and camping on its serene beaches.

There are plenty of places to stay and eat, many of them charming and historic, on the canyon's South Rim. If you decide to go to the high, forested, and often snowy North Rim, you'll drive through a corner of the desolate Arizona Strip, which has a beauty and a history all its own.

Water-sports enthusiasts will want to make it up to the far northern reaches of the state to the Glen Canyon Recreation Area to do some waterskiing or maybe rent a houseboat, and anyone interested in the far end of the nation's

© TIM HULL

HIGHLIGHTS

◖ Hermit Road: Make your way west along the forested rim to the enchanting stone cottage called Hermit's Rest, stopping at different view points to see the setting sun turn the canyon walls into fleeting works of art (page 296).

◖ Desert View Watchtower: See one of architect Mary Colter's finest accomplishments – a rock tower standing tall on the edge of the canyon, its design based on mysterious Anasazi structures still standing in the Four Corners region (page 306).

◖ Rim Trail: Park your car, grab a bottle of water and walk along the rim on this easy, accessible trail, past historical buildings, famous lodges, and several of the most breath-taking views in the world (page 306).

◖ Bright Angel Trail: Don't just stand on the rim and stare – hike down Bright Angel Trail, the most popular trail on the South Rim, its construction based on old Native American routes. Or choose one of several additional trails to see the arid grandeur of the inner canyon (page 307).

◖ Grand Canyon Lodge: Even if you're not staying the night at the North Rim, make sure to step inside this rustic old lodge balancing on the edge of the gorge, where you can sink into a chair and gaze out the picture windows at the multicolored canyon (page 315).

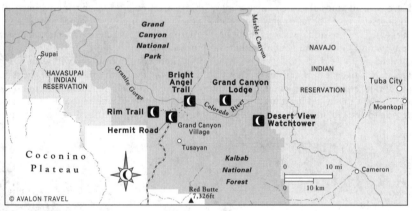

LOOK FOR ◖ TO FIND RECOMMENDED SIGHTS, ACTIVITIES, DINING, AND LODGING.

engineering prowess will want to see Glen Canyon Dam, holding back the once-wild Colorado River.

Seasons

At about 7,000 feet, the South Rim has a temperate climate, warm in the summer months, cool in fall, and cold in the winter. It snows in the deep winter and often rains in the late afternoon in late summer. Summer is the park's busiest season, and it is *very* busy—4–5 million visitors from all over the world will be your companions, which isn't as bad as some make it out to be. People watching and hobnobbing with fellow visitors from the far corners of the globe become legitimate enterprises if you're so inclined. During the summer months (May–Sept.), temperatures often exceed 110°F in the inner canyon, which has a desert climate, but cool by 20–30°F up on the forested rims. There's no reason for anybody to hike deep into the canyon in summer. It's not fun, and it is potentially deadly. It is better to plan a marathon trek in the fall.

Fall is a perfect time to visit the park: It's light-jacket cool on the South Rim and warm but not hot in the inner canyon, where high temperatures during October range 80–90°F, making hiking much more pleasant than it is during the infernal summer months. October–November are the last months of the year during which a rim-to-rim hike from the North Rim is possible, as rim services shut down by the end of October and the only road to the rim is closed by late November, and often before that, due to winter snowstorms. It's quite cold on the North Rim during October, but on the South Rim it's usually clear, cool, and pleasant during the day and snuggle-up chilly at night. Fall is a wonderful time to be just about anywhere in Arizona. A winter visit to the South Rim has its own charms. There is usually snow on the rim January–March, contrasting beautifully with the red, pink, and dusty-green canyon colors. The crowds are thin and more laid-back than in the busy summer months. It is, however, quite cold, even during the day, and you may not want to stand too long at the windy, bone-chilling viewpoints.

Driving to the Grand Canyon

DRIVING TO THE GRAND CANYON FROM LAS VEGAS
South Rim

Las Vegas is 280 miles from the Grand Canyon's South Rim; it's about a five-hour drive, quite breathtaking in some parts and quite boring and monotonous in others. Even if you get a late-morning start and make a few stops along the way, you're still likely to arrive at the park by dinnertime. Most summer weekends, you'll find the route crowded but manageable, unless there's an accident; in that case you'll likely be stuck where you are for some time. At all times of the year, you'll be surrounded by 18-wheelers barreling across the land.

The main and most direct route leaves Sin City, likely a little hungover and shamefaced, south on U.S. 93. After you are free of the city, the road passes near Lake Mead and Hoover Dam and through a barren landscape of jagged rocks and creosote bushes. Before 2010, everybody heading from Vegas to the Grand Canyon had to drive over Hoover Dam, which typically added a bit of extra time to the trip. Today, drivers breeze past the dam over the new Hoover Dam Bypass.

About 100 miles (2 hours) southeast of Vegas you'll hit **Kingman, Arizona.** Here you take I-40, which replaced the old Route 66; drive east to Williams (115 miles), where you pick up Highway 64 for the 60-mile shot across empty, windswept prairie to Grand Canyon National Park. If you feel like stopping overnight—and perhaps it is better to see the great canyon with fresh morning eyes—do so in Williams, just an hour or so from the park's South entrance.

West Rim

Driving from Vegas, you may also want to stop at Grand Canyon West and the Hualapai Reservation's Skywalk; is only 125 miles southwest of Vegas (about a 2.5-hour drive). That being said, it will add at least a full day to your trip, and the view from the South Rim is infinitely better and cheaper. Grand Canyon West charges a $43 entrance fee on top of $32 for the Skywalk, and you'll probably have to ride a shuttle bus part of the way.

To reach Grand Canyon West from Las Vegas, take U.S. 93 out of the city, heading south for about 65 miles to mile marker 42, where you'll see the exit for Dolan Springs, Meadview City, and Pierce Ferry. Turn north onto Pierce Ferry Road. In about 30 miles, turn east on Diamond Bar Road and continue 20 miles, with about seven miles unpaved, to Grand Canyon West.

To continue on to the South Rim, head to

THE GRAND CANYON

THE GRAND CANYON

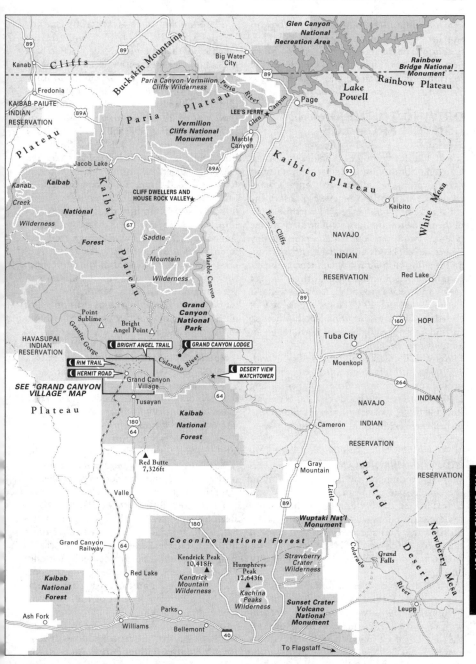

Peach Springs along old Route 66. You can stop here for the night at the Hualapai Lodge, or continue on for about an hour east on Route 66 to Seligman. Then head east on Route 66 to Ashfork, where you can pick up I-40 east to Williams, the gateway to the South Rim.

DRIVING TO THE GRAND CANYON FROM LOS ANGELES

It's 494 miles from Los Angeles to Grand Canyon's South Rim. Most of the 7–8-hour drive is along I-40, across an empty, hard landscape without too much respite save the usual interstate fare. Take I-15 northwest out of the region toward Barstow. The driving time is about two hours, but it takes considerably longer on weekends and during the morning and evening rush hours, which tend to be interminable in Southern California. Expect snarls and delays around Barstow as well. At Barstow, pick up I-40 and for the remainder of the trip to Williams, Arizona (about 5 hours). At Williams, take Highway 64 north for about an hour to the South Rim.

About 320 miles from Los Angeles, but with 173 miles still left to go until you reach the great canyon, Kingman, Arizona, sits along I-40 and offers a few good restaurants and affordable places to sleep—unless you're willing to push on for the final three hours or so to reach the rim in one shot.

STOPPING IN KINGMAN

Proving ground for the manifest destiny of the United States, training ground for World War II heroes, and playground for the postwar middle class, Kingman preserves and proudly displays this heritage at several well-curated museums, such as the Historic Route 66 Museum and the Mohave Museum of History and Arts.

There are several very affordable basic hotels on Andy Devine Avenue (Route 66) in Kingman's downtown area, some of them with retro road-trip neon signs and Route 66 themes. There are many chain hotels in town as well.

The **Ramblin' Rose Motel** (1001 E. Andy Devine Ave., 928/753-4747, $35–42 d) isn't much more than a highway-side place to park and snooze. It's inexpensive, clean, and has big comfy beds. You can check your email using the free wireless Internet, chill your soda in the mini fridge, and warm up a burrito in the microwave. For the price, you can't ask for more.

The small, affordable **Hill Top Motel** (1901 E. Andy Devine Ave., 928/753-2198, www.hilltopmotelaz.com, $47–55) has character, with a 1950s-era neon sign that calls out to Route 66 road-trippers, striking something in the American memory, convincing them to stop and stay. Built in the 1950s but since refurbished, the Hill Top has comfortable standard guest rooms with refrigerators and microwaves as well as free wireless Internet access. Although it's located in the city center, the motel's guest rooms command views of the surrounding Hualapai Mountains and are set back from the main streets, making use of block walls to deflect city noise. Outside is a stylish pool and a well-kept cactus garden.

The best restaurant for miles in any direction is **Mattina's Ristorante Italiano** (318 E. Oak St., 928/753-7504, 5–10 P.M. Tues.–Sat., $13–25), where you can get perfectly prepared Italian food and outstanding beef medallions and rack of lamb. It's difficult to choose from the diverse and outlandishly appetizing selection of pasta dishes, but it's equally difficult to pass up the lobster ravioli or the thick, creamy fettuccini alfredo. Don't leave without trying the tiramisu or the key lime pie, and consider sampling liberally from their well-stocked wine cellar.

Redneck's Southern Pit BBQ (420 E. Beale St., 928/757-8227, 11 A.M.–8 P.M. Mon.–Sat., $10–20), in Kingman's small, often quiet downtown, serves some of the best Southern-style barbecue this side of Memphis, with delicious baked beans and coleslaw on the side. The pulled pork and the brisket should not be missed by connoisseurs of those heaven-sent dishes.

It is widely known throughout this flat and windy region that the retro Route 66 drive-in **Mr. D'z Route 66 Diner** (105 E. Andy Devine

THE GRAND CANYON

Ave., 928/718-0066, www.mrdzrt66diner.com, 7 A.M.–9 P.M. daily, $3–17) serves the best burger in town, but they also have a large menu with all manner of delectable diner and road food, including chili dogs, pizza, hot sandwiches, baby back ribs, chicken fried steak, and a big plate of spaghetti. Breakfast is served all day. The portions are big, but save room for a thick shake or a root-beer float. Don't leave your camera in the car; the turquoise-and-pink interior and the cool old jukebox here are snapshot-ready.

STOPPING IN SELIGMAN

This tiny roadside settlement 87 miles east of Kingman holds on tightly to its Route 66 heritage. There are less than 500 fulltime residents and often, especially on summer weekends, twice that number of travelers. Don't be surprised to see European visitors, classic car nuts, and 60-something bikers passing through town. John Lasseter, codirector of the 2006 Disney-Pixar film *Cars,* has said that he based the movie's fictional town of Radiator Springs partly on Seligman, which, like Radiator Springs, nearly died out when it was bypassed by I-40 in the late 1970s.

Stop at **Delgadillo's Snow Cap Drive-In** (301 E. Chino St./Rte. 66, 928/422-3291, breakfast, lunch, and dinner daily, under $10), off Route 66 on the east end of town, a famous food shack dedicated to feeding, entertaining, and teasing Route 66 travelers for generations. They serve a mean chiliburger, a famous "cheeseburger with cheese," hot dogs, malts, soft ice cream, and much more. Expect a wait, especially on summer weekends, and you will be teased, especially if you have a question that requires a serious answer. The **Roadkill Café** (502 W. Chino St./Rte. 66, 928/422-3554, www.route66seligmanarizona.com, 7 A.M.–9 P.M. daily, $5–24) is more than just a funny name, it's a popular place for buffalo burgers, steaks, and sandwiches.

There are several small, affordable, locally owned motels in Seligman. The **Supai Lodge** (134 W. Chino St./Rte. 66, 928/422-4153, $48–52 d), named for the nearby Grand Canyon village inhabited by the Havasupai people, has clean and comfortable guest rooms at a fair price. The **Historic Route 66 Motel** (500 W. Chino St./Rte. 66, 928/422-3204, www.route66seligmanarizona.com, $57–62 d) offers free wireless Internet and refrigerators in clean, comfortable guest rooms, and the **Canyon Lodge** (114 E. Chino St./Rte. 66, 928/422-3255, www.route66canyonlodge. com, $55 d) has free wireless Internet along with refrigerators and microwaves in its themed guest rooms. They also serve a free continental breakfast.

Gateways to the Canyon

Grand Canyon National Park, especially its South Rim, has some of the best accommodations in the entire national park system, but it's not always possible to get reservations. What's more, while the park's lodging rates are audited annually and generally compare favorably to those offered outside the park, it's possible to find excellent deals at one of several gateway towns around canyon country. Using one of these places as a base for a visit to the canyon makes sense if you're planning on touring the whole of the canyon lands and not just the park. Besides offering affordable, and even

a few luxurious, places to stay and eat, these gateways are often interesting in their own right and deserving of some attention from travelers, especially those interested in the history of this hard and spacious land.

Flagstaff, 79 miles southeast of the park's main South Rim entrance, was the park's first gateway town, and it is still in many ways the best. The home of Northern Arizona University is a fun, laid-back college town with a railroad and Route 66 history. In the old days, eastern tourists detrained at Flagstaff and then faced an all-day stagecoach trip across the forest and the plains, just for a glimpse at the canyon and a few nights in a white canvas tent. These days, you just hop in your rental or your family road-trip wagon and take U.S. 180 northwest for about 90 minutes, and there you are. The route is absolutely (with apologies to desert rats who prefer Desert View) the most scenic of all the approaches to the canyon, passing through Coconino National Forest and beneath the San Francisco Peaks, the state's ruling mountain range.

CAMERON

About 50 miles north of Flagstaff along U.S. 89, near the junction with Highway 64 (the route to the park's east gate), the nearly 100-year-old **(** **Historic Cameron Trading Post and Lodge** (800/338-7385, www.cameronontradingpost.com, $59–179 d) is only about a 30-minute drive from the Desert View area of the park, a good place to start your tour. Starting from the East entrance, you'll see the canyon gradually becoming grand. Before you reach the park, the Little Colorado River drops some 2,000 feet through the arid, scrubby land, cutting through gray rock to create the **Little Colorado Gorge** on its way to its union with the big river. Stop here and get a barrier-free glimpse at this lesser chasm to prime yourself for what is to come. There are usually plenty of booths set up selling Navajo arts and crafts and a lot of touristy souvenirs at two developed pullouts along the road.

The Cameron Lodge is a charming and affordable place to stay, and it is a perfect base for a visit to the Grand Canyon, Indian country, and the Arizona Strip. It has a good restaurant, a Native American art gallery, a visitors center, a huge "trading post" gift shop, and an RV park. A small grocery store sells food and other staples if you don't want to eat at the restaurant, which serves American and Mexican favorites and, of course, huge heaping Navajo tacos, lamb stew, and other local fare. The guest rooms are decorated with a Southwestern Native American style and are very clean and comfortable, some with views of the Little Colorado River and the old 1911

suspension bridge that spans the stream just outside the lodge. There are single-bed rooms, rooms with two beds, and a few suites that are perfect for families. The stone-and-wood buildings and the garden patio, laid out with stacked sandstone bricks with picnic tables and red-stone walkways below the open-corridor guest rooms, create a cozy, history-soaked setting and make the lodge memorable. The vast, empty red plains of the Navajo Reservation spread out all around and create a lonely, isolated atmosphere, especially at night; but the guest rooms have TVs with cable and free wireless Internet, so you can be connected and entertained even way out here.

If you're visiting in winter, the lodge drops its prices significantly during this less-crowded season. In January–February, you can get one of the single-bed guest rooms for about $59 d.

WILLIAMS

This small historic town along I-40, which used to be Route 66, surrounded by the Kaibab National Forest, is the closest interstate town to Highway 64, and thus has branded itself "The Gateway to the Grand Canyon." It has been around since 1874 and was the last Route 66 town to be bypassed by the interstate, in 1984. As a result, and because of resurgence over the last few decades owing to the rebirth of the Grand Canyon Railway, Williams, with about 3,000 full-time residents, has a good bit of small-town charm—the entire downtown area is on the National Register of Historic Places. It's worth a stop and an hour or two of strolling, and there are a few good restaurants. It's only about an hour's drive to the South Rim from Williams, so many consider it a convenient base for exploring the region. The drive is not as scenic as either Highway 64 from Cameron or U.S. 180 from Flagstaff. This is the place to stay if you plan to take the **Grand Canyon Railway** to the South Rim, which is a highly recommended way of reaching the canyon. It's fun, it cuts down on traffic and emissions within the park, and you'll get exercise walking along the rim or renting a bike and cruising the park with the wind in your face.

Sights

On a walk through the **Williams Historic Business District** you'll see how a typical pioneer Southwestern mountain town might have looked from territorial days until the interstate came and the railroad died. Williams wasn't bypassed by I-40 until the 1980s, so many of its old buildings still stand and have been put to use as cafés, boutiques, B&Bs, and gift shops. Walk around and look at the old buildings, shop for Native American and Old West knickknacks, pioneer-era memorabilia, and Route 66 souvenirs you don't need, and maybe stop for a beer, cocktail, or a cup of coffee at an old-school small-town saloon or a dressed-up café. The 250-acre district is bounded on the north by Railroad Avenue, on the south by Grant Avenue, and on the east and west by 1st and 4th Streets, respectively. The district has 44 buildings dating from 1875–1949, and an array of Route 66–era business signs and mid-century commercial architecture worth a few snapshots. Old Route 66 is variously termed Bill Williams Avenue, Grand Canyon Avenue, and Railroad Avenue, and splits into parallel one-way streets through the historic downtown before meeting up to the west and east.

The proposed $25 million 106,500-square-foot **Arizona State Railroad Museum** is slated to open on a 16-acre park in Williams late in 2012. Williams is the ideal spot for the ambitious museum, as it is holy ground to railroad buffs for its popular Grand Canyon Railway. The museum will house and present high-end displays and artifacts related to how the rails won the West in a building that recreates a historic railroad back stop. Railroad enthusiasts and other history buffs should contact the **Arizona State Railroad Museum Foundation** (928/606-2781, www.azstaterrmuseum.org) to check on the progress of what promises to be a major new canyon-area attraction.

Shopping

There's a gathering of boutiques and gift shops in Williams's quaint historic downtown area, bounded Railroad and Grant Avenues and 1st and 4th Streets.

The **Turquoise Tepee** (114 W. Rte. 66, 928/635-4709, 10 A.M.–5 P.M. daily) has been selling top-shelf Native American arts and crafts, Western wear, and regional souvenirs for four generations. There's a lot to see in this store. The same goes for **Native America** (117 E. Rte. 66, 928/635-4600, 8 A.M.–10 P.M. daily summer, 8 A.M.–6 P.M. daily winter), a Native American–owned shop with Hopi and Navajo arts and crafts.

Recreation

The alpine ski runs at the Arizona Snowbowl in the San Francisco Peaks are only a quick hour's drive from downtown Williams, so it's easy to overlook the more modest **Elk Ridge Ski and Outdoor Recreation Area** (Ski Run Rd., 928/814-5038 or 928/814-5027, www.elkridgeski.com, 8 A.M.–10 P.M. daily winter, adults $20–30, children $15–23) in the Kaibab National Forest near town. More laid-back and kid-friendly than the big mountains to the north, Elk Ridge allows skiing, snowboarding, and tubing whenever there's snow to slide on.

Events

In mid-August, perfectly preserved classic cars and low-hung Harleys crowd Williams's narrow downtown streets for the **Cool Country Cruise-In** (928/635-1418, www.route66place.com), a celebration of the town's prominent place along the Mother Road. The two-day festival features a car show, vendors, live music, and the **Miss Route 66 Pageant.**

Northland kids wait all year for the Grand Canyon Railway's celebration of author Chris Van Allsburg's classic holiday story *The Polar Express.* The always sold-out **Polar Express and Mountain Village Holiday** (800/848-3511, www.thetrain.com, departures 6:30 P.M. and 8 P.M. daily mid-Nov.–early Jan., adults $29, ages 2–15 $19) features a one-hour nighttime pajama-party train ride, complete with cookies and hot cocoa, to a lit-up Christmas town that kids ooh and aah at from their train seats. Riders dressed up like characters in the book read the story as kids follow along in their own copies. Then Santa boards the train and

THE GRAND CANYON

gives each kid some individual attention and a free jingle-bell like the one in the famous book. On the return trip, everybody sings Christmas carols, while the younger tykes generally fall asleep. Needless to say, this annual event is *very* popular with kids and their families from all over northern Arizona, and tickets generally sell out as early as August.

Accommodations

Williams has some of the most affordable independent accommodations in the Grand Canyon region as well as several chain hotels.

It's difficult to find a better deal than the clean and basic **El Rancho Motel** (617 E. Rte. 66, 928/635-2552 or 800/228-2370, $35–73 d), an independently owned motel on Route 66 with few frills besides comfort, friendliness, and a heated seasonal pool. The **Canyon Country Inn** (442 W. Rte. 66, 928/635-2349, $39–85 d) is a basic and affordable place to stay, with continental breakfast and high-speed Internet included. The **Grand Canyon Railway Hotel** (235 N. Grand Canyon Blvd., 928/635-4010, $89–179 d) stands now where Williams's old Harvey House once stood. It has a heated indoor pool, two restaurants, a lounge, a hot tub, a workout room, and a huge gift shop. The hotel serves riders on the Grand Canyon Railway and offers the most upscale accommodations in Williams.

The original **◖ Grand Canyon Hotel** (145 W. Rte. 66, 928/635-1419, www.thegrandcanyonhotel.com, $25–125) opened in 1891, even before the railroad arrived and made Grand Canyon tourism something not just the rich could do. New owners refurbished and reopened the charming old redbrick hotel in Williams's historic downtown in 2005, and now it's a very affordable, friendly place to stay with a lot of character and a bit of an international flavor, probably owing to its backpacker dorm ($25). Some of the most distinctive and affordable accommodations in the region include the Spartan single-bed guest rooms with shared baths ($40) and individually named and eclectically decorated double rooms with private baths ($70).

The **Red Garter Bed & Bakery** (137 W. Railroad Ave., 928/635-1484, www.redgarter.com, $120–145) makes much of its original and longtime use as a bordello (which didn't finally close, as in many similar places throughout Arizona's rural regions, until the 1940s), where unlucky women, ever euphemized as "soiled doves," served the town's lonely, uncouth miners, lumberjacks, railway workers, and cowboys from rooms called "cribs." The 1897 frontier-Victorian stone building, with its wide arching entranceway, has been beautifully restored with a lot of authentic charm without skimping on the comforts—like big brass beds along with delightful, homemade baked goods, juice, and coffee in the morning. Famously, this place is haunted by some poor unquiet, regretful soul, so you might want to bring your night-light along.

The **Lodge on Route 66** (200 E. Rte. 66, 877/563-4366, http://thelodgeonroute66.com, $79–179) has stylish, newly renovated guest rooms with sleep-inducing pillow-top mattresses; it also has a few very civilized two-room suites with kitchenettes, dining areas, and fireplaces—perfect for a family that's not necessarily on a budget. The motor court–style grounds, right along Route 66, of course, have a romantic cabana with comfortable seats and an outdoor fireplace.

If you want to get away from Route 66 and into the pine forests around Williams, check out the three-story **FireLight Bed and Breakfast** (175 W. Mead Ave., 928/635-0200, http://firelightbandb.com, $160–250), which rents four eminently comfortable guest rooms, each named and inspired by English counties. They also have delicious breakfasts, a pool table, a cool old juke box, and antique bar-style shuffleboard game that may just keep you from exploring the pinelands and sitting out under the dark, star-laden skies.

RV Camping

The **Canyon Motel & RV Park** (1900 E. Rodeo Dr./Rte. 66, 928/635-9371 or 800/482-3955, www.thecanyonmotel.com, 30-amp RV site $39–46, 50-amp RV site $34–43 Mar.–Oct.,

30-amp RV site $28–37, 50-amp RV site $31–40 Nov.–Feb., hotel $59–169 Mar.–May, $69–169 June–Oct., $45–169 Nov.–Dec., $39–159 Jan.–Feb., plus $2 resort fee per night) inhabits 13 beautiful acres along the road to the Grand Canyon, with the ponderosa pines and long green sweeps of open prairie typical of Arizona's high country. Bill Williams Mountain towers over the charming property. Near the railway, as everything is in Williams, the RV park has two cozy repurposed railcars for rent as well as a few regular motel rooms. The RV park has 47 sites, each with cable TV, Wi-Fi, and the usual amenities. There's an indoor pool and a rec center with a kitchen, outdoor barbecue grills, and much more. The real attraction here is the land itself and all those bright stars you'll see crowding the dark rural sky come nightfall.

Part of the Grand Canyon Railway Hotel complex, the **Grand Canyon Railway RV Park** (601 W. Franklin Ave., 800/843-8724, www.thetrain.com, 50-amp RV site $42) has 124 spaces and can accommodate even the very largest mansion-on-wheels. Each space has cable TV and Wi-Fi, and there's a shower and laundry facility. You can join in a horseshoe game, play volleyball, use the pool and jetted tub in the hotel next door, or sit around the fire pit with a few fellow vagabonds. A smart way to visit the Grand Canyon is to leave your RV at the park and take the **Grand Canyon Railway** to the South Rim.

While many other places to stay in the area accommodate RV parking, it's a good idea to call ahead to make sure.

Food

A northland institution with some of the best steaks in the region, (◀ **Rod's Steak House** (301 E. Rte. 66, 928/635-2671, www.rods-steakhouse.com, 11 A.M.–9:30 P.M. Mon.–Sat., $11.50–35) has been operating at the same site for more than 50 years. The food is excellent, the staff are friendly and professional, and the menus are shaped like steers. The **Pine Country Restaurant** (107 N. Grand Canyon Blvd., 928/635-9718, 5:30 A.M.–9:30 P.M.

daily, $5–10) is a family-style place that serves good food and homemade pies. Check out the beautiful paintings of the Grand Canyon on the walls. **Twisters '50s Soda Fountain and Route 66 Café** (417 E. Rte. 66, 928/635-0266, 8 A.M.–close daily, $5–10) has 1950s music and decor and delicious diner-style food, including memorable root-beer floats. Even if you're not hungry, check out the gift shop selling all kinds of road-culture memorabilia.

You'll find comforting Mexican and Southwestern food at **Pancho McGillicuddy's** (141 Railroad Ave., 928/635-4150, 11 A.M.–10 P.M. daily, $10–17). They serve satisfying burritos, enchiladas, and Navajo tacos, carne asada, New York strip, and fish-and-chips in an 1893 building that used to be the rowdy Cabinet Saloon, on Williams's territorial-era stretch of iniquity known as Saloon Row. They mix a decent margarita, but beer is the drink of choice in this high-country burg. **Cruiser's Route 66 Bar & Grill** (233 W. Rte. 66, 928/635-2445, www.cruisers66.com, 11 A.M.–9 P.M. Mon.–Thurs., 11 A.M.–10 P.M. Fri.–Sun., $6–20) offers a diverse menu, with superior barbecue ribs, burgers, fajitas, pulled-pork sandwiches, and homemade chili.

The vegetarian's best bet this side of downtown Flagstaff is the **Dara Thai Café** (145 W. Rte. 66, 928/635-2201, 11 A.M.–2 P.M. and 5–9 P.M. Mon.–Sat., $3.50–10), an agreeable little spot in the Grand Canyon Hotel. They serve a variety of fresh and flavorful Thai favorites and offer quite a few meat-free dishes.

Information and Services

Stop at the **Williams-Kaibab National Forest Visitors Center** (200 W. Railway Ave., 928/635-1418 or 800/863-0546, 8 A.M.–6:30 P.M. daily summer, 8 A.M.–5 P.M. daily fall–winter) for information about Williams, the Grand Canyon, and camping and hiking in the Kaibab National Forest.

TUSAYAN

Just outside Grand Canyon National Park's south gate, along Highway 64, Tusayan is a collection of hotels, restaurants, and gift shops that has grown side-by-side with the park for nearly a century. The village makes a decent, close-by base for a visit to the park, especially if you can't get reservations at any of the in-park lodges. Although there are a few inexpensive chain hotels here, a stay in Tusayan isn't generally cheaper than lodging in the park; there are many more places to eat here than inside the park, but nonetheless the culinary scene is relatively bleak.

Sights

Tusayan is perhaps best known as the home of the **National Geographic Grand Canyon Visitors Center** (Hwy. 64, 928/638-2468, www.explorethecanyon.com, 8:30 A.M.– 8:30 P.M. daily Mar.–Oct., 10:30 A.M.– 6:30 P.M. daily Nov.–Feb., over age 10 $12.50, ages 6–10 $9.50, under age 6 free), which has been a popular first stop for park visitors since the 1980s. Truth be told, even with the recent addition of the corporate logo–clad **Grand Canyon Base Camp #1,** an interactive display of canyon history, lore, and science, the center wouldn't be worth a stop if not for its **IMAX Theater.** The colossal screen shows the 35-minute movie *Grand Canyon—The Hidden Secrets* every hour. The most popular IMAX film ever—reportedly some 40 million people have seen it—the movie is quite thrilling, affording glimpses of the canyon's more remote corners that feel like real time, if not reality. If you can afford the admission price, this is a fun way to learn about what you're about to see in the park. If you're going budget, skip it and drive a few miles north, where you're likely to forget about both movies and money while staring dumbfounded into that gorge.

Accommodations

Most of Tusayan's accommodations are of the chain variety, and though they are generally clean and comfortable, few of them have any character to speak of and most of them are rather overpriced for what you get. Staying in either Flagstaff or Williams is a better choice if you're looking for an independent hotel or motel with some local color,

and you can definitely find better deals in those gateways.

Before you reach Tusayan you'll pass through Valle, a tiny spot along Highway 64, where you'll find one of the better deals in the whole canyon region. The **Red Lake Campground and Hostel** (8850 N. Hwy. 64, 800/581-4753, $15 pp), where you can rent a bed in a shared room, is a basic but reasonably comfortable place sitting alone on the grasslands; it has shared baths with showers, a common room with a kitchen and a TV, and an RV park ($20) with hookups. If you're going superbudget, you can't beat this place, and it's only about 45 minutes from the park's south gate. The **Red Feather Lodge** (Hwy. 64, 928/638-2414, www.redfeatherlodge.com, $69–159), though more basic than some of the other places in Tusayan, is a comfortable, affordable place to stay with a pool, a hot tub, and clean guest rooms.

The **Grand Hotel** (Hwy. 64, 928/638-3333, www.grandcanyongrandhotel.com, $99–199 d), resembling a kind of Western-themed ski lodge, has very clean and comfortable guest rooms, a pool, a hot tub, a fitness center, and a beautiful lobby featuring a Starbucks coffee kiosk. The **Best Western Grand Canyon Squire Inn** (Hwy. 64, 928/638-2681, www.grandcanyonsquire.com, $75–195 d) has a fitness center, a pool and spa, a salon, a game room, and myriad other amenities—so many that it may be difficult to get out of the hotel to enjoy the natural sights.

Food

Nobody would go to Tusayan specifically to eat, but it makes for a decent emergency stop if you're dying of hunger. One exception: We Cook Pizza would be good in any town, and it is a bright spot in this rather drab and chain-happy commercial parasite of the national park. A lot of tour buses stop in Tusayan, so you may find yourself crowded into waiting for a table at some places, especially during the summer high season. Better to eat in the park, or in Flagstaff or Williams, both of which have many charming and delicious local restaurants worth seeking out. It's only about an hour's drive to either, so you might be better off having a small snack and skipping Tusayan altogether.

One of the better places in Tusayan is the **Canyon Star Restaurant** (Hwy. 64, 928/638-3333, 7–10 A.M. and 11:30 A.M.–10 P.M. daily, $10–25) inside the Grand Hotel, which serves Southwestern food, steaks, and ribs and features a saloon in which you can belly up to the bar on top of an old mule saddle (it's not that comfortable). **The Coronado Room** (Hwy. 64, 928/638-2681, 5–10 P.M. daily, $15–28) inside the Grand

Canyon Squire Inn serves tasty steaks, seafood, Mexican-inspired dishes, and pasta.

If you're craving pizza after a long day exploring the canyon, try **We Cook Pizza & Pasta** (Hwy. 64, 928/638-2278, 11 A.M.–10 P.M. daily Mar.–Oct., 11 A.M.–8 P.M. daily Nov.–Feb., $7–15) for an excellent, high-piled pizza pie. It calls you just as you enter Tusayan coming from the park. The pizza, served in slices or whole pies, is top-notch, and they have a big salad bar with all the fixings, plus beer and wine.

The South Rim

The reality of the Grand Canyon is often suspect even to those standing on its rim. "For a time it is too much like a scale model or an optical illusion," wrote Joseph Wood Krutch, a great observer and writer of the Southwest. The canyon appears at first, Krutch added, "a manmade diorama trying to fool the eye." It is *too big* to be immediately comprehended, especially to visitors used to the gaudy, lesser wonders of the human-made world.

Once you accept its size and understand that a river, stuffed with the dry rocks and sand of this arid country, bore this mile-deep multicolored notch in the Colorado Plateau, the awesome power of just this one natural force—its greatest work here spread before you—is bound to leave you breathless and wondering what you've been doing with your life heretofore. If there are any sacred places in the natural world, this is surely one. The canyon is a water-wrought cathedral, and no matter what beliefs or preconceptions you approach the rim with, they are likely to be challenged, molded, cut away, and revealed like the layers of primordial earth that compose this deep rock labyrinth, telling the history of the planet as if they were a geology textbook for new gods. And it is a story in which humans appear only briefly.

Visitors without a spiritual connection to nature have always been challenged by the Grand

Canyon's size. It takes mythology, magical thinking, and storytelling to see it for what it really is. The first Europeans to see the canyon, a detachment of Spanish conquistadores sent by Coronado in 1540 after hearing rumors of the great gorge from the Hopi, at first thought the spires and buttes rising from the

© TIM HULL

view of the canyon from the South Rim

ONE DAY AT THE GRAND CANYON

The ideal South Rim-only trip lasts three days and two nights, with the first and last days including the trip to and from the rim. This amount of time will allow you to see all the sights on the rim, to take in a sunset and sunrise over the canyon, and even to do a day hike or a mule trip below the rim. If you just have a day, about five hours or so will allow you to see all the sights on the rim and take a very short hike down one of the major trails. But once you stare deep into this natural wonder, you might have trouble pulling yourself away.

MORNING

If you have just one day to see the Grand Canyon, drive to the South Rim and park your car at one of the large, free parking lots inside the National Park. Hop on one of the park's free shuttles or rent a bike or walk along the **Rim Trail** (page 306) and head toward Grand Canyon Village. Spend a few hours looking at the buildings and, of course, the canyon from this central, busy part of the rim. Stop in at the **Yavapai Observation Station** (page 304), check out the history of canyon tourism at the **Bright Angel Lodge** (page 300), watch a movie about the canyon at the visitors center, and have lunch at the **Arizona Room** (page 312) or, better yet, **El Tovar** (page 312).

AFTERNOON

After lunch, take the shuttle along the eastern **Desert View Drive** (page 297), stopping along the way at a few of the eastern viewpoints, especially at Mary Colter's **Desert View Watchtower** (page 306) on the far eastern edge of the park.

EVENING

End your day by heading all the way to the western reaches of the park to see **Hermit's Rest** (page 305). If you time it right, you'll catch a gorgeous canyon sunset from one of the western viewpoints along the way. For dinner, try El Tovar or one of the cafeterias before turning in early. If this is your only day at the canyon, visit Hermit's Rest first, and leave the park via Desert View Drive, stopping at the Watchtower and the **Tusayan Museum and Ruins** (page 305) on your way out.

EXTENDING YOUR STAY

If you're able to spend more time in the park, hit one of the **corridor trails** for a day-hike below the rim. Rest up after rising out of the depths, then check the park newspaper to see what's happening at the **Shrine of the Ages** (page 310), where on most nights there's an entertaining and informative talk by a ranger.

If you include a North Rim or West Rim excursion, add at least 1-2 more days and nights. It takes at least five hours to reach the **North Rim** from the South Rim, perhaps longer if you take the daily shuttle from the south instead of your own vehicle. The **West Rim** and the **Hualapai** and **Havasupai Indian Reservations** are some 250 miles from the South Rim on slow roads, and a trip to these remote places should be planned separately from one to the popular South Rim. The most important thing to remember when planning a trip to the canyon is to plan far ahead, even if, like the vast majority of visitors, you're just planning to spend time on the South Rim. Six months' advance planning is the norm, longer if you are going to ride a mule down or stay overnight at Phantom Ranch in the inner canyon.

bottom were about the size of a person; they were shocked, on gaining a different perspective below the rim, that they were as high or higher than the greatest structures of Seville. Human comparisons do not work here, and preparation is not possible.

Never hospitable, the canyon has nonetheless had a history of human occupation for around 5,000 years, although the settlements have been small and usually seasonal. It was one of the last regions of North America to be explored and mapped. The first expedition through, led by the one-armed genius John Wesley Powell, was completed at the comparatively late date of 1869.

John Hance, the first Anglo to reside at the canyon, in the 1880s, explored its depths and built trails based on ancient Native American routes. A few other tough loners tried to develop mining operations here but soon found out that guiding avant-garde canyon tourists was the only sure financial bet in the canyon lands. It took another 20 years or so and the coming of the railroad before it became possible for the average American to see the gorge.

Though impressive, the black-and-white statistics—repeated ad nauseam throughout the park on displays and interpretive signs along the rim and at the various visitors centers—do little to conjure an image that would do the canyon justice. It is some 277 river miles long, beginning just below Lee's Ferry on the north and ending somewhere around the Grand Wash Cliffs in northwestern Arizona. It is 18 miles across at its widest point, and an average of 10 miles across from the South Rim to the North Rim. It is a mile deep on average; the highest point on the rim, the north's Point Imperial, rises nearly 9,000 feet above the river. Its towers, buttes, and mesas, formed by the falling away of layers undercut by the river's incessant carving, are red and pink, dull brown and green-tipped, although these basic hues are altered and enhanced by the setting and rising of the sun, changed by changes in the light, becoming throwaway works of art that astound and then disappear.

It is folly, though, to try too hard to describe and boost the Grand Canyon. The consensus, from the first person to see it to yesterday's visitor, has generally amounted to "You just have to see it for yourself." Perhaps the most poetic words ever spoken about the Grand Canyon, profound for their obvious simplicity, came from Teddy Roosevelt, speaking on the South Rim in 1903. "Leave it as it is," he said. "You cannot improve on it; not a bit."

GETTING THERE
Air
The **Grand Canyon Airport at Tusayan,** just outside the park's South entrance, has daily flights from Las Vegas and from other major Southwestern airports as well. Both Flagstaff and Williams have small airports, but most visitors fly into **Sky Harbor in Phoenix,** rent a car, and drive about three hours north to the South Rim. You can rent a car at Tusayan, and there are rental places in Flagstaff and Williams as well. A shuttle runs hourly between Tusayan and Grand Canyon Village.

Bus
Arizona Shuttles (928/226-8060, www.arizonashuttle.com) offers comfortable rides from Flagstaff to the Grand Canyon (adults $58 round-trip) three times daily March 1–October 31. The company also goes to and from Phoenix's Sky Harbor Airport ($39 one-way) several times a day, as well as from Flagstaff to Sedona, the Verde Valley, and Williams ($22–29 one-way).

Train
A fun, retro, and environmentally conscious way to reach the park, the **Grand Canyon Railway** (800/843-8724, www.thetrain.com, adults $70–190, depending on accommodations) recreates what it was like to visit the great gorge in the early 20th century. It takes about 2.5 hours to get to the South Rim depot from the station in Williams, where the **Grand Canyon Railway Hotel** (928/635-4010, www.thetrain.com, $89–179 d) and restaurant just beyond the train station makes a good base, attempting as it does to match the atmosphere of the old Santa Fe Railroad Harvey House that once stood on the same ground.

During the trip, one is always wondering when the train is going to speed up, but it never really does, rocking at about 60 mph through pine forests and across a scrubby grassland shared by cattle, elk, pronghorn, coyotes, and red-tailed hawks, all of which can be viewed from a comfortable seat in one of the old refurbished cars. Along the way, there are ruins of the great railroad days, including ancient telegraph posts still lined up along the tracks.

A trip to and from the Grand Canyon on the old train is recommended for anyone who is interested in the heyday of train travel, the

Old West, or the golden age of Southwestern tourism—or for anyone desiring a slower-paced journey across the northland. Besides, the fewer visitors who drive their vehicles to the rim, the better. Kids especially seem to enjoy the train trip, as comedian-fiddlers often stroll through the cars, and on some trips there's even a mock train robbery complete with bandits on horseback with blazing six-shooters.

EXPLORING THE SOUTH RIM

The South Rim is by far the most developed portion of Grand Canyon National Park (928/638-7888, www.nps.gov/grca, 24 hours daily, seven-day pass $25 per car) and should be seen by every American, as Teddy Roosevelt once recommended. Here you'll stand side-by-side with people from all over the globe, each one breathless on his or her initial stare into the canyon and more often than not hit suddenly with an altered perception of time, human history, and even God. Don't let the rustic look of the buildings fool you into thinking you're roughing it. The food here is far above average for a national park. The restaurant at El Tovar offers some of the finest, most romantic dining in the state, and all with one of the great wonders of the world just 25 feet away.

Parking and Shuttle Service

Parking is free throughout Grand Canyon National Park. At the South Rim, there are four large parking lots for visitors. There used to be five, but the large dirt lot near Grand Canyon Village and the train station has recently closed; park officials plan to put the lot to other use. The lots tend to fill up fast, especially during the busy summer months, but there is usually space for everyone.

As you enter, a ranger will give you a free copy of *The Guide,* the park's newspaper, which has a map that includes all the parking options. Try Lot B near **Market Plaza,** the park's largest lot. Another large lot that will typically have open spaces is Lot A, near the **Park Headquarters.** If you're driving an RV or pulling a trailer, head over to the **Back**

Country Information Center, which has a huge lot with spaces for large rigs.

It is not ideal to drive your vehicle to each viewpoint around the park. It fouls the air and is not easy with all the pedestrians everywhere. The best strategy is to park your vehicle for the duration and hop on one the park's free clean-fuel shuttles.

Or better yet, if you have a bit of energy, consider walking along the **Rim Trail,** or bring along a bike (or rent one at the park) and ride through the park without the hassles of driving.

Visitors Centers

Canyon View Information Plaza (9 A.M.–5 P.M. daily), near Mather Point, the first overlook you pass on entering the park's main South entrance, is the perfect place to begin your visit to the park. It is a short walk from the Mather Point parking lot or the free shuttle, for which the plaza serves as a kind of central hub. Throughout the plaza there are displays on the natural and human history of the canyon and suggestions on what to do, and inside the **South Rim Visitors Center,** the park's main welcome and information center, there are displays on canyon history and science, and rangers on duty who are always around to answer questions, give advice, and help you plan your visit.

While at the visitors center, consider attending a free showing of the film *Grand Canyon: A Journey of Wonder* in the park's new 200-seat theater. The film chronicles a full day in the life of the Grand Canyon, providing context that might help you wrap your head around the gorge's astonishing grandeur.

The park's newest information center, **Verkamp's Visitors Center** (8 A.M.–5 P.M. daily), near the El Tovar Hotel and Hopi House in Grand Canyon Village, used to be its oldest souvenir shop.

It's not often that the mere closing of a small family-run curio shop makes the news all over the world, but most such shops haven't been operating for more than 100 years on the edge of one of the great wonders of the world.

©TIM HULL

Verkamp's, one of the first stores in Grand Canyon National Park, is now a visitors center and museum.

In 2008 **Verkamp's Curios** closed its doors for good. The news inspired dozens of feature stories in the media, and canyon visitors from around the world likely remembered the kachina doll, T-shirt, Zuni fetish, or refrigerator magnet they'd bought at the small shop across the parking lot from El Tovar Hotel when they read about it. Visitors had been purchasing mementos from the Verkamps since before the park was a park: The store began in a white canvas tent on the edge of the gorge way back in 1898. Why close now? The current Verkamps told the Associated Press (AP) that they had "bureaucratic process fatigue."

In 1998, Congress passed a law directing the National Park Service to no longer give preference to existing permit holders when renewing permits to operate businesses within the parks. This made the process much more expensive and time-consuming than it had ever been for the Verkamps. Also, "family dynamics" played a role, according to one former store employee. Family matriarch Susie Verkamp said as much when she told AP that there was really nobody left in the family who wanted to be involved in the business. A non-Verkamp manager had been in charge of day-to-day operations at the shop since 1995, although the Verkamps had remained actively involved, AP reported.

Though there are still plenty of gift shops at the Grand Canyon in which to buy your souvenirs, the closing of Verkamp's represented the end of an era. There are few noncorporate permit holders left in the National Parks anymore, and now there is one less.

A few months after it closed, park officials revamped Verkamp's as an information center staffed by rangers and volunteers who can answer your questions and offer advice. There's also a fascinating little museum off in one corner that explains the colorful history of the attempts by early canyon-land settlers and entrepreneurs—the Verkamp family among them, of course—and their hard-won efforts to make a buck in this isolated corner of the world.

The farthest-flung of all the park's information centers, **Desert View Visitors Center and Bookstore** (9 A.M.–5 P.M. daily) sits on Desert View Point about 25 miles east of Grand Canyon Village. It is staffed by helpful rangers and has information and displays on visiting the canyon; this is the natural place to stop for those entering the park from the quieter East entrance.

THE GRAND CANYON

As you enter the park you'll get a copy of *The Guide,* a newsprint guide to the South Rim that is indispensable. Make sure you read through it; it's pretty comprehensive and will likely answer most of your questions.

Entrance Stations

Unless you choose to ride the chugging train from Williams, there are only two ways by road in and out of the park's South Rim section. The vast majority of visitors to Grand Canyon National Park enter through the **South Entrance Station** along Highway 64 from Williams. U.S. 180 from Flagstaff meets up with Highway 64 at Valle, about 30 miles south of the South entrance; it's about 55 miles along scenic U.S. 180 from Flagstaff to Valle. Highway 64 from Williams to the South entrance is 60 miles of flat, dry-grass, and windswept plain dotted with a few isolated trailers, manufactured homes, and gaudy for-sale signs offering cheap "ranchland." Entering through the busy South entrance will ensure that your first look at the Grand Canyon is from **Mather Point,** which as a result is one of the iconic views of the river-molded gorge.

A less used but certainly no less worthy park entrance is the **East Entrance Station,** in the park's **Desert View** section. About 25 miles east of Grand Canyon Village and all the action, this route is a good choice for those who want a more leisurely and comprehensive look at the rim, as there are quite a few stops along the way to the village that you might not otherwise get to if you enter through the South entrance. To reach the East Entrance Station, take U.S. 89 for 46 miles north of Flagstaff, across a wide big-sky landscape covered in volcanic rock, pine forests, and yellow wildflowers, to Cameron, on the red-dirt Navajo Reservation. Then head east on Highway 64 for about 30 miles to the entrance station.

Tours

BUS TOURS

Xanterra, the park's main concessionaire, offers in-park **Motor Coach Tours** (888/297-2757, $20–57). Sunrise tours are available, and longer drives to the eastern and western reaches of the park are offered. This is a comfortable, educational, and entertaining way to see the park, and odds are you will come away with a few new friends—possibly even a new email pal from abroad. Only pay for a tour if you like being around a lot of other people and listening to mildly entertaining banter from the tour guides for hours at a time. It's easy to see and learn about everything the park has to offer without spending extra on a tour. If you like being on your own and getting away from the crowds, this is not for you.

AIRPLANE AND HELICOPTER TOURS

Three companies offer helicopter tours of the canyon of varying lengths. One of the better operators is **Maverick Helicopters** (888/261-4414, www.maverickhelicopter.com, $175 for 25 minutes, $235 for 45 minutes). Though not ideal from the back-to-nature point of view, a helicopter flight over the canyon is an exciting, rare experience, and by most accounts is well worth the rather expensive price. The family-owned **Air Grand Canyon** (928/638-2686 or 800/247-4726, www.airgrandcanyon.com, 50–60 minutes $109–125), one of three companies offering tours in fixed-winged Cessnas, will swoop you over the canyon in one of their small planes—a chance to take some rare photos from a condor's perspective.

Air Grand Canyon, Maverick, and four other plane and helicopter tour operators operate out of **Grand Canyon Airport** (www.grandcanyonairport.org) along Highway 64 in Tusayan. They all prefer reservations, but walk-ins are accepted.

Driving Tours

◖ HERMIT ROAD

March–November the park's free shuttle goes all the way to architect and Southwestern-design queen Mary Colter's **Hermit's Rest,** about seven miles from the village along the park's western scenic drive, called the Hermit Road. It takes approximately two hours to complete the loop, as the bus stops at eight viewpoints along the way. On the return route, buses stop only at Mohave and Hopi Points. A few of the Hermit Road viewpoints are some of the best in the park for viewing the sunsets. To make it in time for such dramatic performances, get on the bus at least an hour before sunset. There is often a long wait at the **Hermit's Rest Transfer Stop** just west of Bright Angel Lodge. The bus drivers will always be able to tell you when sunset is expected, and the times are also listed in *The Guide* newspaper handed to you as you enter the park. In the winter the route is open to cars, and you can drive to most of the viewpoints and stare at your leisure.

Each of the Hermit Road lookouts provides a slightly different perspective on the canyon, whether it be a strange unnoticed outcropping or a brief view of the white-tipped river rapids far, far below. The first stop along the route is the **Trailview Overlook,** from which you can see the Bright Angel Trail twisting down to and across the plateau to overlook the Colorado River. The next major stop along the route is **Maricopa Point,** which provides a vast, mostly unobstructed view of the canyon all the way to the river. The point is on a promontory that juts out into the canyon over 100 feet. To the west you can see the rusted remains of the Orphan Mine, first opened in 1893 as a source of copper and silver—and, for a few busy years during the height of the Cold War, uranium. Consider taking the 10–15-minute hike along the Rim Trail west past the fenced-off Orphan Mine and through the piney rim world to the next point, **Powell Point.** Here stands a memorial to the one-armed explorer and writer John Wesley Powell, who led the first and second river expeditions through the canyon in 1869 and 1871. The memorial is a flat-topped pyramid, which you can ascend and stand tall over the canyon. You can't see the river from here, but the views of the western reaches of the gorge are pretty good, and this is a strong candidate for a sunset-viewing vantage point. About 0.25 miles along the Rim Trail from Powell Point is **Hopi Point,** which offers sweeping and unobstructed views of the western canyon. As a result, it is the most

popular west-end point for viewing the red and orange sun dropping in the west. North across the canyon, look for the famous mesas named after Egyptian gods—Isis Temple, off to the northeast, and the Temple of Osiris to the northwest. The next viewpoint heading west is **Mohave Point,** from which you can see the Colorado River and a few white-tipped rapids. Also visible from here are the 3,000-foot red-and-green cliffs that surround the deep side-canyon, appropriately named **The Abyss.** Right below the viewpoint you can see the red-rock mesa called the Alligator. The last viewpoint before Hermit's Rest is **Pima Point,** a wide-open view to the west and the east, from which you can see the winding Colorado River and the Hermit Trail twisting down into the depths of the canyon.

DESERT VIEW DRIVE

One more Mary Colter construction—arguably her greatest—and a Puebloan ruin are located along Desert View Drive, the 25-mile drive east from the village. The viewpoints along this drive, which one ranger called the "quiet side of the South Rim," have gradually become more desertlike and are typically less crowded. The free shuttle goes only as far as **Yaki Point,** a great place to watch the sunrise and near the popular South Kaibab Trailhead. Yaki Point is at the end of a 1.5-mile side road two miles east of U.S. 180. The area is closed to private vehicles. Along Desert View Drive, make sure not to miss the essential **Grandview Point,** where the original canyon lodge once stood long ago. From here the rough Grandview Trail leads below the rim. The viewpoint sits at 7,400 feet, about 12 miles east of the village and then one mile on a side road. It's considered one of the grandest views of them all, hence the name; the canyon spreads out willingly from here, and the sunrise in the east hits it all strong and happy. To the east, look for the 7,844-foot monument called the Sinking Ship, and to the north below look for Horseshoe Mesa. This is a heavily wooded area, so for the best view, hike a bit down the Grandview Trail. The steep and narrow trail is

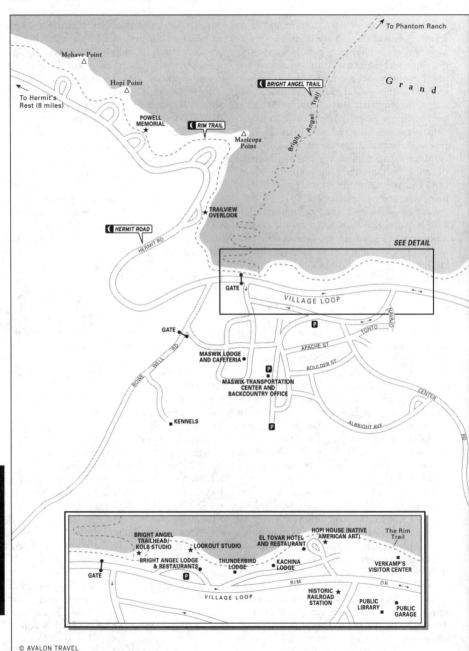

To Phantom Ranch

Mohave Point △

Hopi Point △

☾ BRIGHT ANGEL TRAIL

G r a n d

To Hermit's
Rest (8 miles)

POWELL
MEMORIAL ★

☾ RIM TRAIL

△ Maricopa
Point

Bright Angel Trail

★ TRAILVIEW
OVERLOOK

☾ HERMIT ROAD

HERMIT RD

SEE DETAIL

GATE ↓

VILLAGE LOOP

NAVAJO

GATE

P

TONTO

ROWE WELL RD

APACHE ST

MASWIK LODGE
AND CAFETERIA ●

BOULDER ST.

P

CENTER RD

MASWIK TRANSPORTATION
CENTER AND
BACKCOUNTRY OFFICE

ALBRIGHT AVE.

■ KENNELS

P

BRIGHT ANGEL
TRAILHEAD/
KOLB STUDIO ★

★ LOOKOUT STUDIO

EL TOVAR HOTEL
AND RESTAURANT ■

HOPI HOUSE (NATIVE
AMERICAN ART) ★

The Rim
Trail

BRIGHT ANGEL LODGE
& RESTAURANTS ★

THUNDERBIRD
LODGE ●

KACHINA
LODGE ●

VERKAMP'S
VISITOR CENTER ■

GATE

P

↓

VILLAGE LOOP

RIM

DR

HISTORIC
RAILROAD
STATION ★

PUBLIC
LIBRARY ■

■ PUBLIC
GARAGE

© AVALON TRAVEL

THE GRAND CANYON

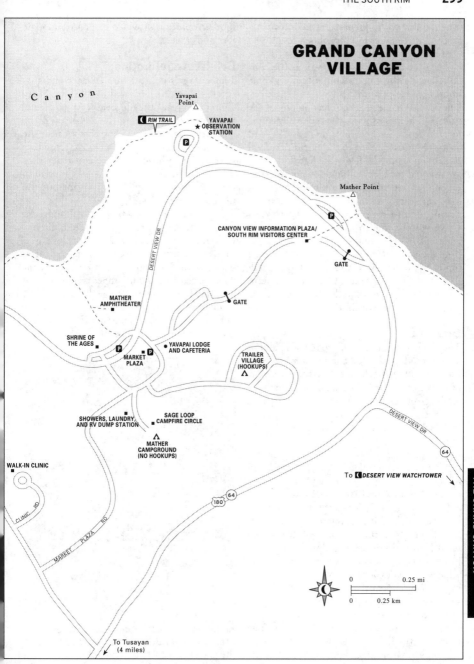

GRAND CANYON VILLAGE

Canyon

Yavapai Point △

RIM TRAIL

★ YAVAPAI OBSERVATION STATION

P

Mather Point △

P

CANYON VIEW INFORMATION PLAZA/ SOUTH RIM VISITORS CENTER ■

GATE

DESERT VIEW DR

GATE

■ MATHER AMPHITHEATER

SHRINE OF THE AGES ■

P MARKET PLAZA P

● YAVAPAI LODGE AND CAFETERIA

△ TRAILER VILLAGE (HOOKUPS)

■ SHOWERS, LAUNDRY, AND RV DUMP STATION

■ SAGE LOOP CAMPFIRE CIRCLE

△ MATHER CAMPGROUND (NO HOOKUPS)

DESERT VIEW DR

64

■ WALK-IN CLINIC

CLINIC RD

MARKET PLAZA RD

To ◖DESERT VIEW WATCHTOWER →

180 64

0   0.25 mi

0   0.25 km

To Tusayan (4 miles) ↙

THE GRAND CANYON

tough, but if you're prepared to hike, you can descend three miles to Horseshoe Mesa.

Moran Point, east of Grandview, is just eight miles south of Cape Royal, as the condor flies, on the North Rim and offers some impressive views of the canyon and the river. The point is named for the great painter of the canyon, Thomas Moran, whose brave attempts to capture the uncapturable on canvas helped create the buzz that led to the canyon's federal protection. Directly below the left side of the point you'll see Hance Rapid, one of the largest on the Colorado. It is three miles away, but if you're quiet, you might be able to hear the rushing and roaring. Farther on Desert View Drive you'll come to **Lipan Point,** with its wide-open vistas and the best view of the river from the South Rim. At Desert View, from the top of the watchtower, you'll be able to catch a faraway glimpse of sacred Navajo Mountain near the Utah-Arizona border, the most distant point visible from within the park.

SIGHTS

Though you wouldn't want to make a habit of it, you could spend a few happy hours at **Grand Canyon Village Historical District** with your back to the canyon. Then again, this small assemblage of hotels, restaurants, gift shops, and lookouts offers some of the best viewpoints from which to gaze comfortably at all that multicolored splendor. Here is a perfect vantage from which to spot the strip of greenery just below the rim called **Indian Gardens,** and follow with your eyes—or even your feet—the famous **Bright Angel Trail** as it twists improbably down the rim's rock face. Here you can also see some of the most interesting and evocative buildings in the region, all of them registered National Historic Landmarks. If you're just visiting for the day, you can drive into the village and park your car in the El Tovar parking lot. More often than not, especially in the summer, the El Tovar lot will be full. You can also park at the large lot at Market Plaza and then take the shuttle bus around the park. The Backcountry Information Office (928/638-7875) also has a rather large parking lot, the

southern portion of which can accommodate RVs and trailers.

Bright Angel Lodge

The village's central hub of activity, this rustic lodge was designed in 1935 by Mary Colter to replace the old Bright Angel Hotel, built by John Hance in the 1890s, and the tent-city Bright Angel Camp that sat near the trail of the same name. The lodge resembles a rough-hewn hunting lodge constructed of materials found nearby and was meant to welcome not the high-toned visitor but the middle-class traveler.

In a room off the lobby is a small museum with fascinating exhibits about Fred Harvey, Colter, and the early years of Southwestern tourism. Here you'll see Colter's "geologic fireplace," a 10-foot-high re-creation of the canyon's varied strata. The stones were collected from the inner canyon by a geologist and then loaded on the backs of mules for the journey out. The fireplace's strata appear exactly like those stacked throughout the canyon walls,

Architect Mary Colter designed the central fireplace in her Bright Angel Lodge to mirror the canyon's strata.

© TIM HULL

THE GRAND CANYON

THE CANYON AND THE RAILROAD

© TIM HULL

The Grand Canyon Railway travels from Williams to the South Rim.

Musing on the Grand Canyon in 1902, John Muir lamented that, thanks to the railroad, "children and tender, pulpy people as well as storm-seasoned travelers" could now see the wonders of the West, including the Grand Canyon, with relative ease. It has always been for storm-seasoned travelers to begrudge us tender, pulpy types a good view. As if all the people who visit the canyon every year couldn't fit in its deep mazes and be fairly out of sight. Muir came to a similar conclusion after actually seeing the railway approach the chasm: "I was glad to discover that in the presence of such stupendous scenery they are nothing," he wrote. "The locomotives and trains are mere beetles and caterpillars, and the noise they make is as little disturbing as the hooting of an owl in the lonely woods."

It wasn't until the Santa Fe Railroad reached the South Rim of the Grand Canyon in 1901 that the great chasm's now-famous tourist trade really got going. Prior to that travelers faced an all-day stagecoach ride from Flagstaff at a cost of $20, a high price to pay for sore bones and cramped quarters.

For half a century or more the Santa Fe line from Williams took millions of tourists to the edge of the canyon. The railroad's main concessionaire, the Fred Harvey Company, enlisted the considerable talents of Arts and Crafts designer and architect Mary Colter to build lodges, lookouts, galleries, and stores on the South Rim that still stand today, now considered to be some of the finest architectural accomplishments in the entire national parks system. Harvey's dedication to simple, high-style elegance and Colter's interest in and understanding of Pueblo Indian architecture and lifeways created an artful human stamp on the rim that nearly lives up to the breathtaking canyon it serves.

The American love affair with the automobile, the rising mythology of the go-west road trip, and finally the Interstate highway killed train travel to Grand Canyon National Park by the late 1960s. In the 1990s, however, entrepreneurs revived the railroad as an excursion and tourist line. Today, the Grand Canyon Railway carries more than 250,000 passengers to the South Rim every year, a phenomenon that has reduced polluting automobile traffic in the cramped park by some 10 percent.

THE GRAND CANYON

equaling a few billion years of earth-building from bottom to rim. The lodge includes a collection of small cabins just to the west of the main building, and the cabin closest to the rim was once the home of Bucky O'Neill, an early canyon resident and prospector who died while fighting with Teddy Roosevelt's Rough Riders in Cuba.

El Tovar

Just east of the lodge is the South Rim's first great hotel and the picture of haute-wilderness style. Designed in 1905 by Charles Whittlesey for the Santa Fe Railroad, El Tovar has the look of a Swiss chalet and a log-house interior, watched over by the wall-hung heads of elk and buffalo; it is at once cozy and elegant. This Harvey Company jewel has hosted dozens of rich and famous canyon visitors over the last century, including George Bernard Shaw and presidents Teddy Roosevelt and William Howard Taft. On the rim side, a gazebo stands near the edge. While it is a wonderfully romantic building up close, El Tovar looks even more picturesque from a few of the viewpoints along the Hermit Road, and you can really get a good idea of just how close the lodge is to the gorge seeing it from far away. Inside you'll find two gift shops and a cozy lounge where you can have a drink or two while looking at the canyon. The El Tovar's restaurant is the best in the park, and it's quite pleasant to sink into one of the arts and crafts leather chairs in the rustic dark-wood lobby.

Hopi House

A few steps from the El Tovar's front porch is Colter's Hopi House, designed and built as if it sat not at the edge of Grand Canyon but on the edge of Hopi land's Third Mesa. Hopi workers used local materials to build this unique gift shop and Native American arts museum. The Harvey Company even hired the famous Hopi-Tewa potter Nampeyo to live here with her family while demonstrating her artistic talents, and by extension Hopi ways of life, to tourists. This is one of the best places in the region for viewing and buying Hopi, Navajo,

El Tovar

and Pueblo art (though most art is quite expensive), and there are even items on view and for sale made by Nampeyo's descendants.

Lookout Studio

Mary Colter also designed the Lookout Studio west of Bright Angel Lodge, a little stacked-stone watch house that seems to be a mysterious extension of the rim itself. The stone patio juts out over the canyon and is a popular place for taking pictures. The Lookout was built in 1914 exactly for that purpose—to provide a comfortable but "indigenous" building and deck from which visitors could gaze at and photograph the canyon. It was fitted with high-powered telescopes and soon became one of the most popular snapshot scenes on the rim. It still is today, and on many days you'll be standing elbow to elbow with camera-carrying travelers clicking away. As she did with her other buildings on the rim, Colter designed the Lookout to be a kind of amalgam of Native American ruins and backcountry pioneer utilitarianism. Her formula of using found and local materials

stacked haphazardly works wonderfully. When it was first built, the little stone hovel was so "authentic" that it even had weeds growing out of the roof. Inside, where you'll find books and canyon souvenirs, the studio looks much as it did when it first opened. The jutting stone patio is still one of the best places from which to view the gorge.

Kolb Studio

This 100-year-old wood house nearly hanging from the rim is significant not so much for its design but for the human story that went on inside. It was the home and studio of the famous Kolb brothers, pioneer canyon photographers, moviemakers, river rafters, and entrepreneurs. Inside there's a gift shop, a gallery, and a display about the brothers, who, in 1912, rode the length of the Colorado River in a boat with a movie camera rolling. The journey resulted in a classic book of exploration and river running, Emery Kolb's 1914 *Through the Grand Canyon from Wyoming to Mexico*. The Kolb Brothers were some of the first entrepreneurs at the canyon, setting up a photography studio, at first in a cave near the rim and then in this house, to sell pictures of travelers atop their mules as early as 1902. After a falling-out between the brothers, the younger Emery Kolb stayed on at the canyon until his death in 1976, showing daily the film of the brothers' river trip to several generations of canyon visitors.

The Viewpoints

While the canyon's unrelenting vastness tends to blur the eyes into forgetting the details, viewing the gorge from many different points seems to cure this. There are some 19 named viewpoints along the South Rim Road, however, from the easternmost Desert View to the westernmost Hermit's Rest. Is it necessary, or even a good idea, to see them all? No, not really. For many it's difficult to pick out the various named buttes, mesas, side-canyons, drainages, and other features that rise and fall and undulate throughout the gorge, and one viewpoint ends up looking not that different from the next. To really get the full experience,

© TIM HULL

Lookout Studio

the best way to see the canyon viewpoints is to park your car and walk along the Rim Trail for a few miles, if not its whole length (if you get tired, you can always hop on the free shuttle at any of its many stops), seeing the gorge from developed points all along as well as from the trail itself. Driving to each and every viewpoint is not that rewarding and tends to speed up your visit and make you miss the subtleties of the different views. Consider really getting to know a few select viewpoints rather than trying to quickly and superficially hit each one. Any of the viewpoints along the Hermit Road and Desert View Drive are ideal candidates for a long love affair. That being said, the views from just outside El Tovar or Bright Angel Lodge, right smack in the middle of all the bustling village action, are as gorgeous as any others, and it can be fun and illuminating to watch people's reactions to what they're seeing. In reality, there isn't a bad view of the canyon, but if you only have so much time, it's never a bad idea to ask a ranger at Canyon View Information Plaza or Yavapai Observation Station what their favorite viewpoint is and why. Everybody is going to have a different answer, but it stands to reason that those who actually *live* at the canyon are going to have a more studied opinion. The shuttle bus drivers are also great sources of information and opinions. Whatever you do, try to get to at least one sunset and one sunrise at one or more of the developed viewpoints; the canyon's colors and details can get a bit monotonous after the initial thrill wears off (if it ever does), but the sun splashing and dancing at different strengths and angles against the multihued buttes, monuments, and sheer shadowy walls cures that rather quickly.

As most South Rim visitors enter through the park's South entrance, it's no surprise that the most visited viewpoint in the park is the first one along that route—**Mather Point,** named for the first National Park Service director, Stephen T. Mather. Although it is crowded, Mather Point offers a typically astounding view of the canyon and is probably the mind's-eye view that most casual visitors take away. It can

get very busy here, especially in the summer. If you're going to the park's main visitors center, **Canyon View Information Plaza** (and you should), you'll park near here and walk a short paved path to the information plaza. At the viewpoint, you can walk out onto two railed-off jutting rocks to feel like you're hovering on the edge of an abyss, but you may have to stand in line to get right up to the edge. A good way to see this part of the park is to leave your car at the large parking area at Mather Point (which is often full, of course) and then walk a short way along the Rim Trail west to **Yavapai Point** and the excellent, newly refurbished **Yavapai Observation Station,** the best place to learn about the canyon's geology and get more than a passing understanding of what you're gazing at. It's a good idea to visit the Yavapai Observation Station before you hit any of the other viewpoints (unless you are coming in from the East entrance).

Yavapai Observation Station

First opened in 1928, this limestone-and-pine museum and bookstore (8 A.M.–7 P.M. daily April 15–fall, 8 A.M.–6 P.M. daily winter, free) hanging off the rim is the best place in the park to learn about the canyon's geology—it is a must-see for visitors interested in learning about what they are seeing. The building itself is of interest; designed by architect Herbert Maier, the stacked-stone structure, like Colter's buildings, merges with the rim itself to appear as an inevitable part of the landscape. The site for the station, which was originally called the Yavapai Trailside Museum, was handpicked by canyon geologists as the very best for viewing the various strata and receiving a rim-side lesson on the region's geologic history. Inside the building you'll find in-depth explanations and displays about canyon geology that are fascinating and easily understood. Too much of the introductory geology found in guidebooks and elsewhere is jargon-laden, confusing, and not very useful to the uninitiated, but not here: Many of the displays are new and use several different approaches, including maps, photographs, and three-dimensional models—coupled with the very rocks and cliffs and canyons and gorges they're talking about right outside the windows—to create fascinating and easy-to-grasp lessons. Particularly helpful is the huge topographic relief map of the canyon inside the observation center. Spend some time looking over the map in detail and you'll get a giant's-eye view of the canyon that really helps discern what you're seeing once you turn into an ant again outside on the ledge.

Hermit's Rest

The final stop on the Hermit Road is the enchanting gift shop and rest house called Hermit's Rest. As you walk up a path through a stacked-boulder entranceway, from which hangs an old mission bell, the little stone cabin comes into view. It looks as if some lonely hermit came out here and stacked rock upon rock until something haphazard but cozy rose from the rim; it is a structure more familiar in the world of fairy tales than the modern world. Inside, the huge yawning fireplace, tall and deep enough to be a room itself, dominates the warm, rustic front room, where there are a few seats chopped out of stumps, a Navajo blanket or two splashing color against the gray stone, and elegant lantern-lamps hanging from the stones. Outside, the views of the canyon and down the Hermit's Trail are spectacular, but something about that little rock shelter makes it hard to leave.

Tusayan Museum and Ruins

The Tusayan Museum (9 A.M.–5 P.M. daily, free) has a small but interesting exhibit on the canyon's early human settlers. The museum is located near an array of 800-year-old Ancestral Pueblo ruins with a self-guided trail and regularly scheduled ranger walks. Since the free shuttle doesn't run this far east, you have to drive to the museum and ruins; it's about three miles west of Desert View and 22 miles east of Grand Canyon Village. It's worth the drive, though, especially if you're going to be heading to the Desert View section anyway (which you should). Although it hasn't been overly hospitable to humans over the aeons,

THE GRAND CANYON

the welcoming entrance to Mary Colter's enchanting Hermit's Rest

the oldest human-made artifacts found in the canyon date back about 12,000 years—little stick-built animal fetishes and other mysterious items. The displays in this museum help put human life on the rim and in the gorge in context, and the small ruins are fascinating. Imagine living here along the rim and walking every day to the great gorge.

Desert View Watchtower
What is perhaps the most mysterious and thrilling of Colter's canyon creations, the Desert View Watchtower is an artful homage to smaller Anasazi-built towers found at Hovenweep National Monument and elsewhere in the Four Corners region, the exact purpose of which is still unknown.

The tower's high windy deck is reached by climbing the twisting steep steps that wind around the open middle, the walls painted with visions of Hopi lore and religion by Hopi artist Fred Kabotie. Pick up the free *Watchtower Guide* in the gift shop on the bottom floor for explanations on the meanings of the paintings and symbols. From the top of the watchtower, the South Rim's highest viewpoint, the evocative power of the whole arid expanse opens up with the rough-edged romanticism of Colter's vision.

RECREATION
Hiking
Something about a well-built trail twisting deep into an unknown territory can spur even the most habitually sedentary canyon visitor to begin an epic trudge. This phenomenon is responsible for both the best and worst of the South Rim's busy recreation. It is not uncommon to see hikers a mile or more below the rim walking along in high heels and sauntering blithely in flip-flops, not a drop of water in hand. It's best to go to the canyon prepared to hike, with the proper footwear and plenty of snacks and water. Just figure that you are, in all probability, going to want to hike a little. And since there's no such thing as an easy hike in Grand Canyon, going in prepared, even if it's just for a few miles, will

make your hike infinitely more pleasurable. Also, remember that there aren't any loop hikes here: If you hike down a mile—and that can happen surprisingly quickly—you also must hike up a mile.

RIM TRAIL
- Distance: about 12 miles
- Duration: all day
- Elevation gain: about 200 feet
- Effort: easy
- Trailhead: Pipe Creek Vista or anywhere along the rim west to Hermit's Rest

If you can manage a 12-mile, relatively easy walk at an altitude of around 7,000 feet, the Rim Trail provides the single best way to see all of the South Rim. The trail, paved for most of its length, runs from the Desert Drive's Pipe Creek Vista through the village and all the way to Hermit's Rest, hitting every major point of interest and beauty along the way. The trail gets a little tough as it rises a bit past the Bright

A stroll along the easy Rim Trail is an ideal way to view the canyon.

HIKING THE GRAND CANYON – THE EASY WAY

One of the first things you notice while journeying through the inner canyon is the advanced age of many of your fellow hikers. It is not uncommon to see men and women in their 70s and 80s hiking along at a good clip, packs on their backs and big smiles on their faces.

At the same time, all over the South Rim you'll see warning signs about overexertion, each featuring a buff young man in incredible shape suffering from heat stroke or exhaustion, with the warning that most of the people who die in the canyon – and people die every year – are people like him. The point here is this: You need not be a wilderness expert or marathon runner to enjoy even a long, 27-mile, rim-to-rim hike through the inner canyon. Don't let your fears hold you back from what is often a life-changing trip.

There are several strategies that can make a canyon hike much easier than a forced march with a 30-pound pack of gear on your back. First of all, don't go in the summer; wait until September or October, when it's cooler, though still quite warm, in the inner canyon. Second, try your best to book a cabin or a dorm room at Phantom Ranch rather than camping. That way, you'll need less equipment, you'll have all or most of your food taken care of, and there will be a shower and a beer waiting for you upon your arrival. Also, for about $50 you can hire a mule to carry up to 30 pounds of gear for you, so all you have to bring is a day pack, some water, and a few snacks. This way, instead of suffering while you descend and ascend the trail, you'll be able to better enjoy the magnificence of this wonder of the world.

Angel Trailhead just west of the village. The trail becomes a thin dirt single track between Powell Point and Monument Creek Vista, but it never gets too difficult. It would be considered an easy, scenic walk by just about anybody, kids included. But perhaps the best thing about the Rim Trail is that you don't have to hike the whole 12 miles; there are at least 16 shuttle stops along way, and you can hop on and off the trail at your pleasure.

◖ BRIGHT ANGEL TRAIL

- Distance: 1.5–9.6 miles
- Duration: a few hours to overnight
- Elevation gain: 4,380 feet
- Effort: moderate to difficult
- Trailhead: Grand Canyon Village, just west of Bright Angel Lodge

Hiking down the Bright Angel, you quickly leave behind the twisted greenery of the rim and enter a sharp and arid landscape, twisting down and around switchbacks on a trail that is sometimes all rock underfoot. Step aside for the many mule trains that go down and up

this route, and watch for the droppings, which are everywhere. Because this trail is so steep, it doesn't take long for the rim to look very far away, and you soon feel like you are deep within a chasm and those rim-top people are mere ants scurrying about.

The most popular trail in the canyon because it starts just to the west of Bright Angel Lodge in the village center, and considered by park staff to be the "safest" trail because of its rest houses, water, and ranger presence, the Bright Angel Trail was once the only easily accessible corridor trail from the South Rim. As such, a $1 hikers' toll was charged by Ralph Cameron, who constructed the trail based on old Native American routes. The trail's general route has always been a kind of inner canyon highway, as it has a few springs. The most verdant of these is Indian Gardens (for centuries exactly that), a welcome slip of green on an otherwise red and rocky land, about 4.5 miles down from the trailhead. Many South Rim visitors choose to walk down Bright Angel a bit just to get a feeling of what it's like to be below the rim.

If you want to do something a little more

THE GRAND CANYON

structured, the three-mile round-trip hike to the **Mile-and-a-Half Resthouse** makes for a good introduction to the steep, twisting trail. A little farther on is **Three-Mile Resthouse,** a six-mile round-trip hike. Both resthouses have water seasonally. One of the best day hikes from the South Rim is the nine-mile round-trip to beautiful **Indian Gardens,** a cool and green oasis in the arid inner canyon. This is a rather punishing day hike, and not recommended in the summer. The same goes for the 12-mile round-trip trudge down to **Plateau Point,** from which you can see the Colorado River winding through the inner gorge. Unless you have somewhere you absolutely have to be, you'll want to consider getting a backcountry permit and camping below the rim rather than trying to do Plateau Point or even Indian Gardens in one day.

SOUTH KAIBAB TRAIL

• Distance: 1.5–7 miles
• Duration: a few hours to all day
• Elevation gain: 4,780 feet
• Effort: moderate to difficult
• Trailhead: Yaki Point

Steep but short, the seven-mile South Kaibab Trail provides the quickest, most direct South Rim route to and from the river. It's popular with day hikers and those looking for the quickest way into the gorge, and many consider it superior to the often-crowded Bright Angel Trail. The trailhead is located a few miles east of the village near Yaki Point; it can easily be reached by shuttle bus on the Kaibab Trail Route. The 1.8-mile round-trip hike to **Ooh Aah Point** provides a great view of the canyon and a relatively easy hike along the steep switchbacks. **Cedar Ridge** is a three-mile round-trip hike down the trail, well worth it for the views of O'Neill Butte and Vishnu Temple. There is no water provided anywhere along the trail, and shade is nonexistent. Bighorn sheep have been known to haunt this trail, and you might feel akin to those dexterous beasts on this rocky, ridgeline route that seems unbearably steep in

some places, especially on the way back up. If you are interested in a longer haul, the six-mile round-trip hike to **Skeleton Point,** from which you can see the Colorado, is probably as far along this trail as you'll want to go in one day, though in summer you might want to reconsider descending so far. Deer and California condors are also regularly seen along the South Kaibab Trail.

HERMIT TRAIL TO DRIPPING SPRINGS

• Distance: 6.2 miles
• Duration: 5–6 hours
• Elevation gain: 1,400 feet
• Effort: moderate
• Trailhead: just west of Hermit's Rest

Built by the Santa Fe Railroad as an antidote to the fee-charging keeper of the Bright Angel Trail, The Hermit Trail just past Hermit's Rest leads to some less visited areas of the canyon. This trail isn't maintained with the same energy as the well-traveled corridor trails are, and there is no potable water to be found. You could take the Hermit Trail 10 miles deep into the canyon to the river, where the first-ever below-rim camp for canyon visitors was built by Fred Harvey 10 years before Phantom Ranch, complete with a tramway from the rim, the ruins of which are still visible. But such a trudge should be left only for fully-geared experts. Not so the 6.2-mile round-trip hike to the secluded and green **Dripping Springs,** which is one of the best day hikes in the canyon for midlevel to expert hikers. Start out on the Hermit Trail's steep, rocky, almost stair-like switchbacks, and then look for the **Dripping Springs Trailhead** after about 1.5 miles, once you reach a more level section dominated by piñon pine and juniper. Veer left on the trail, which begins to rise a bit and leads along a ridgeline across Hermit Basin; the views here are so awesome, and so barrier free, that it's difficult to keep your eyes on the skinny trail. Continue west once you come to the junction with the Boucher Trail after about a mile; then it's about 0.5 miles up a side canyon to the cool and shady rock overhang known as

© TIM HULL

The Hermit Trail leads into the Grand Canyon from the west end of the South Rim.

built first to serve a copper mine at Horseshoe Mesa, and then to entice visitors below the forested rim, the Grandview Trail should be left to midlevel hikers and above. Though you can take the trail all the way to the river and Hance Rapid, more than eight miles in, for day hikers the 6.4-mile round-trip trek to Horseshoe Mesa, where you'll see the remains of an old copper mine, is probably as far as you'll want to go. This trail is definitely not safe for winter hiking. Hiking back up, you won't soon forget the steep slab-rock and cobblestone switchbacks, and hiking down will likely take longer than planned, as the steepest parts of the route are quite technical and require heads-up attention. Park staff are not exactly quick to recommend this route to casual hikers. Don't be surprised if you meet a ranger hanging out along the trail about 1.5 miles in, who may very well tell you to turn around if he or she doesn't think you have the proper gear or enough water to continue on.

Dripping Springs. And it really does drip: A shock of fernlike greenery hangs off the rock overhang, trickling cold, clean spring water at a steady pace into a small collecting pool. Get your head wet, have a picnic, and kick back in this out-of-the-way hard-won oasis. But don't stay too long. The hike up is nothing to take lightly: The switchbacks are punishing, and the end, as it does when one is hiking up all of the canyon trails, seems to get farther away and not closer as your legs begin to gain fatigue weight. There's no water on the trail, so make sure to bring enough along and conserve.

GRANDVIEW TRAIL

- Distance: 8.4 miles to the river
- Duration: a few hours to overnight
- Elevation gain: 4,792 feet
- Effort: difficult
- Trailhead: Grandview Point, 12 miles east of Grand Canyon Village

A steep, rocky, and largely unmaintained route

Biking

Some of us who love the Grand Canyon, its innards and its rim lands alike, look forward to the inevitable day when all cars will be banned from the park. Long leaps have already been made toward this goal: the Grand Canyon Railway is as popular as ever, and a fleet of natural gas–powered shuttles moves thousands of visitors around the park every day. In 2010 the National Park Service took a further stride in the green direction by awarding a long-awaited permit to a bike rental vendor. Of course, you can bring your own bike: Strap it on the back of your SUV, park that gas guzzler, and pedal the rim and the forest at your own pace. There is no better way to get around the park, and you'll be helping keep emissions, traffic, and frustration to a minimum.

For several years the park service has been planning and building an ambitious series of multiuse greenway trails that are perfect for biking. Currently, a 1.7-mile greenway section for hikers and bikers only is open along the Hermit Road, and another is planned for the near future from Mather Point to Yaki Point.

THE GRAND CANYON

BIKE RENTALS AND TOURS

From a kiosk at the Grand Canyon Visitors Center, **Bright Angel Bicycles** (928/814-8704, www.bikegrandcanyon.com, 8 A.M.–6 P.M. daily May–Oct., $10 per hour, $25 for 4 hours, $35 all day) rents comfortable, seven-speed Haro Heartland cruisers on a first-come, first-served basis as well as trailers for the tots and safety equipment. They also offer guided bike tours of the South Rim's sights for $40 pp, $32 under age 17. If you get tired pedaling in the 7,000-foot air, you can strap your bike to a shuttle and have a rest.

MOUNTAIN BIKING ON THE RIM

The **Tusayan Bike Trails** are a series of single-track trails and old mining and logging roads organized into several easy-to-moderate loop trails for mountain bikers near the park's South entrance. The trails wind through a forest of pine, juniper, and piñon, and there are usually plenty of opportunities to see wildlife. The longest loop is just over 11 miles, and the shortest is just under four miles. At the beginning of the trails there's a map of the area showing the various loops. Pick up the trails on the west side of Highway 64 north of Tusayan, about a mile south of the park entrance.

LECTURES AND PROGRAMS

The staff at the South Rim does an above-average job keeping guests comfortable, informed, and entertained. Rangers always seem to be giving lectures, leading walks, and pointing out some little-known canyon fact—and such activities at Grand Canyon are typically far more interesting than they are at other, less spectacular places. It is worth your time to attend at least one of the regularly illuminating lectures held most nights at the **Shrine of the Ages** during your visit to the South Rim. Check *The Guide* for specific times and topics. Every day in summer until late October there are at least 10 ranger programs offered at various sites around the rim. Typically these programs last between 15 minutes and an hour and are always interesting.

SHOPPING

There are at least 16 places to buy gifts, books, souvenirs, supplies, and Native American arts and crafts at the South Rim. Nearly every lodge has a substantial gift shop in its lobby, as do Hermit's Rest, Kolb Studio, Lookout Studio, and the Desert View Watchtower.

For books, the best place to go is **Books & More** at the Canyon View Information Plaza, operated by the nonprofit Grand Canyon Association. Here you'll find all manner of tomes about canyon science and history for both adults and children. All of the gift shops have a small book section, most of them selling the same general selection of popular canyon-related titles. If you're in need of camping and hiking supplies to buy or rent—including top-of-the-line footwear, clothes, and backpacks—try the general store at the **Canyon Village Market Place.** Here you'll also find groceries, toiletries, produce, alcoholic beverages, and myriad other necessities, including "I hiked the Grand Canyon" T-shirts and warm jackets in case you forgot yours.

Whether you're a semiserious collector or a first-time dabbler, the best place on the South Rim to find high-quality Native American arts and crafts is inside Mary Colter's **Hopi House,** where pottery, baskets, overlay jewelry, sand paintings, kachina dolls, and other treasures are for sale. Don't expect to find too many great deals here, though—most of the best pieces are priced accordingly.

ACCOMMODATIONS

There are six lodges within Grand Canyon National Park's South Rim confines. Over the last decade or so most of the guest rooms have been remodeled and upgraded, and you won't find any of them too much more expensive than those outside the park, as the rates are set and controlled by an annual review comparing the park's offerings to similar accommodations elsewhere.

A stay at ◖ **El Tovar** (303/297-2757, $174–426 d), more than 100 years old and one of the most distinctive and memorable hotels in

Mary Colter based her design for Hopi House on Hopi dwellings in northeastern Arizona.

the region, would be the secondary highlight—after the gorge itself—of any trip to the South Rim. The log-and-stone National Historic Landmark standing about 20 feet from the rim has 78 guest rooms and suites, each with cable TV. The hotel's restaurant serves some of the best food in the region for breakfast, lunch, and dinner, and there's a comfortable cocktail lounge off the lobby with a window on the canyon. A mezzanine sitting area overlooks the log-cabin lobby, and a gift shop sells Native American art and crafts and canyon souvenirs. If you're looking to splurge on something truly exceptional, a honeymoon suite ($321–426) overlooking the canyon is available.

When first built in the 1930s, the **Bright Angel Lodge** (303/297-2757, $90–174 d) was meant to serve the middle-class travelers then being lured by the Santa Fe Railroad, and it is still affordable and comfortable while retaining a rustic character that fits perfectly with the wild canyon just outside. Lodge rooms don't have TVs, and there is generally only one bed in each room. Some of the lodge rooms have shared baths, so if that bothers you, make sure to ask for a room with a private bath. The lodge's cabins just west of the main building are a little better equipped, with private baths, TVs, and sitting rooms. There's a gift shop, and drinking and dining options include a small bar; a family-style restaurant serving breakfast, lunch, and dinner; and a more upscale eatery that serves lunch and dinner.

Standing along the rim between El Tovar and Bright Angel, the **Kachina Lodge** (303/297-2757, $170–180 d), a more recent addition to the canyon's accommodations list, offers basic, comfortable guest rooms with TVs, safes, private baths, and refrigerators. There's not a lot of character here, but its location and modern comforts make the Kachina an ideal place for families to stay. The **Thunderbird Lodge** (303/297-2757, $170–180 d) is located in the same area and has very similar offerings.

Maswick Lodge (303/297-2757, $90–170 d) is another nonhistorical lodging option, located just west of the village about 0.25 miles from the rim. The hotel has a cafeteria-style restaurant that serves just about everything you'd want and a sports bar with a large-screen television. The guest rooms are basic and comfortable, with TVs, private baths, and refrigerators. **Yavapai Lodge** (303/297-2757, $107–153 d) is east of the village and is another of the non-historical facilities that offers nice guest rooms with all the comforts but little character or artistic value, although you don't really need any of that when you've got the greatest sculpture garden in the world just half a mile away.

Camping

((Mather Campground (877/444-6777, www.recreation.gov, by reservation up to six months ahead Mar.–Nov., $18, first-come, first-served Dec.–Feb., $15) is located near the village and offers more than 300 basic campsites with grills and fire pits. It has restroom facilities with showers, and laundry facilities are offered for a fee. The campground is open to tents and trailers but has no hookups and cannot accommodate RVs longer than 30 feet.

Even if you aren't an experienced camper, a stay at Mather is a fun and inexpensive alternative to sleeping indoors. Despite its large size and crowds, especially during the summer, the campground gets pretty quiet at night, and there's nothing like sitting back in a camp chair under the dark, starry sky and talking around the campfire—even in summer the night takes on a bit of chill, making a campfire not exactly necessary but not out of the question, and camping without a campfire is missing something. Bring your own wood, or you can buy it at the store nearby. You don't exactly have to rough it at Mather; a large, clean restroom and shower facility is located within walking distance from most of the campsites, and they even have blow-dryers. Everything is coin-operated, and there's an office on site that makes change. Consider bringing your bikes along, especially for the kids. The village is about a 15-minute walk from the campground on forested, paved trails, or you can take the free tram from a stop nearby.

About 25 miles east of the village, near the park's East entrance, is **Desert View Campground** (May–mid-Oct. depending on weather, first-come, first-served, $12), with 50 sites for tents and small trailers only, with no hookups. There's a restroom with no showers, and only two faucets with running water. Each site has a grill but little else.

If you're in a rolling mansion, try next door at **Trailer Village** (888/297-2757, www.xanterra.com, $34), where you'll find hookups.

FOOD

The **((El Tovar Dining Room** (928/638-2631, ext. 6432, reservations required, breakfast 6:30–11 A.M., lunch 11:30 A.M.–2 P.M., dinner 5–10 P.M. daily, lunch $9–16, dinner $7–28) is truly carrying on the Fred Harvey Company traditions on which it was founded more than 100 years ago. Serious, competent staff serve fresh, creative, locally inspired dishes in a cozy, mural-clad dining room that has not been significantly altered from the way it looked back when Teddy Roosevelt and Zane Grey ate here. The wine, entrées, and desserts are all top-notch and would be heartily enjoyed anywhere in the world—but they always seem to be that much more tasty with the sun going down over the canyon. Pay attention to the specials, which usually feature some in-season native edible and are always the best thing to eat within several hundred miles in any direction.

The **Arizona Room** (928/638-2631, lunch 11:30 A.M.–3 P.M. daily Mar.–Oct., dinner 4:30–10 P.M. daily Mar.–Dec., lunch $7–12, dinner $12–25) serves Southwestern-inspired steak, prime rib, fish, and chicken dishes in a stylish but still casual atmosphere. There's a full bar, and the steaks are excellent—hand cut and cooked just right with unexpected sauces and marinades.

If you only have one nice dinner planned for your trip, think about choosing El Tovar over the Arizona Room (but make sure to make a reservation in advance). The food is great at both places, but El Tovar has so much atmosphere and is not that much more expensive than the Arizona Room, which doesn't have the historical and aesthetic interest that's all over El Tovar. Although, thinking about the Arizona Room's baby back ribs with prickly pear barbecue sauce makes one question such a recommendation.

Bright Angel Restaurant (928/638-2631, 6:30 A.M.–10 P.M. daily, $3–9), just off Bright Angel Lodge's lobby, is a perfect place for a big, hearty breakfast before a day hike below the rim. It serves all the standard rib-sticking dishes amid decorations and ephemera recalling the Fred Harvey heyday. At lunch there's stew, chili, salads, sandwiches, and burgers, and for dinner there's steak, pasta, and fish dishes called "Bright Angel Traditions," along with a few offerings from the Arizona Room's menu as well. Nearby is the **Bright Angel Fountain,** which serves hot dogs, ice cream, and other quick treats.

Maswik Cafeteria (928/638-2631, 6 A.M.–10 P.M. daily, $3–9) is an ideal place for a quick, filling, and delicious meal. You can find just about everything here—burgers, salads, country-style mashed potatoes, french fries, sandwiches, prime rib, chili, and soft-serve ice cream, to name just a few of the dozens of offerings. Just grab a tray, pick your favorite dish, and you'll be eating in a matter of a few minutes. There's a similar cafeteria-style restaurant at the Yavapai Lodge to the east of the village.

GETTING AROUND
Shuttles

The park operates an excellent free shuttle service with comfortable buses fueled by natural gas. It's a good idea to park your car for the duration of your visit and use the shuttle. It's nearly impossible to find parking at the various sights, and the traffic through the park is not always easy to navigate—there are a lot of one-way routes and oblivious pedestrians that can lead to needless frustration. Make sure you pick up a copy of the free park newspaper, *The Guide,* which has a map of the various shuttle routes and stops.

Pretty much anywhere you want to go in the park, a shuttle will get you there, and you rarely have to wait more than 10 minutes at any stop. That being said, there is no shuttle that goes all the way to the Tusayan Museum and Ruins or the Watchtower near the East entrance. Shuttle drivers are a good source of information about the park; they are generally very friendly and knowledgeable, and a few of them are genuinely entertaining. The shuttle conveniently runs from around sunrise until about 9 P.M., and drivers always know the expected sunrise and sunset times and seem to be intent on getting people to the best overlooks to view these two popular daily park events.

The North Rim

Standing at Bright Angel Point on the Grand Canyon's North Rim, crowded together with several other gazers as if stranded on a jetty over a wide hazy sea, blurred evergreens growing atop great jagged rock spines banded with white and red, someone whispers, "It looks pretty much the same as the other rim."

It's not true—far from it—but the comment brings up the main question about the North Rim: Should you go? Only about 10 percent of canyon visitors make the trip to the North Rim, which is significantly less developed than the South Rim; there aren't as many activities, other than gazing, unless you are a hiker and a backcountry wilderness lover. The coniferous mountain forests of the Kaibab Plateau, broken by grassy meadows painted with summer wildflowers, populated by often-seen elk and mule deer, dappled with aspens that turn yellow and red in the fall and burst out of the otherwise uniform dark green like solitary flames, are themselves worth the trip. But it is a long trip, and you need to be prepared for a land of scant services and the simple, contemplative pleasures of nature in the raw.

© TOM GRUNDY/123RF.COM

view from the Walhalla overlook on the North Rim

GETTING THERE
From the South Rim

Few South-rim visitors venture the 212-mile, 4.5-hour drive north to the Grand Canyon's somewhat underappreciated North Rim. That's too bad: The rim itself rivals the more popular South Rim in grandeur and beauty, and the drive, though long, is scenic to say the least. It runs through a corner of Navajo land, past the towering Vermillion Cliffs, and deep into the high conifer forests of the Kaibab Plateau. On the plateau, which at its highest reaches above 9,000 feet, Highway 67 from Jacob Lake to the North Rim typically closes to vehicles by late October–early November until May. As you leave the South Rim behind, take Highway 64 east to U.S. 89 north and U.S. 89A. Then pick up Highway 67 south to the North Rim after you climb onto the forested plateau from the stark and lonely valley below.

The **Trans Canyon Shuttle** (928/638-2820, reservations required, $80 one-way, $150 round-trip) makes a daily round-trip excursion between the North and South Rims,

departing the North at 7 A.M. and arriving at the South Rim at 11:30 A.M. The shuttle then leaves the South at 1:30 P.M. and arrives back at the North Rim at 6:30 P.M.

From Las Vegas

It's a long 275-mile drive north and east from Las Vegas to the North Rim. The route passes through the lonely and empty Arizona Strip, a scenic region that's home to much Mormon history and legend. Take I-15 north out of Vegas for 128 miles. Just past St. George, take Highway 9 for 10 miles to Highway 59 through Hurricane to the Utah-Arizona state line. You'll pass Colorado City, in the news these last several years as the home of members of the Fundamentalist Church of Jesus Christ of Latter Day Saints. Highway 59 becomes Highway 389 in Arizona; follow it to U.S. 89A, which heads up onto the Kaibab Plateau. It is then about 30 miles to Highway 67 and the straight 43-mile trip through highland forests and meadows to the North Rim.

EXPLORING THE NORTH RIM

It's all about the scenery here at 8,000 feet and above, and the often misty canyon, and the thick, old-growth forest along its rim, command all of your attention. Some of the people you'll meet here are a bit different from the South Rim tourists, a good portion being hard-core hikers and backpackers waiting for early morning to hit the North Kaibab Trail for a rim-to-rim trek.

That's not to say that there's nothing to do on the North Rim. Spend some time on the lodge's back porch, have an overpriced beer at the cantina, and hike through the highland forest on easy trails to reach uncrowded viewpoints. There are similarly lonely lookouts (at least compared to the often elbow-to-elbow scene at some of the South Rim's spots) at the end of a couple of scenic drives. Only a rare few see the North Rim covered in snow, as it often is past November. The park here closes in mid-October and doesn't open again until mid-May.

Visitors Centers

The **North Rim Visitors Center and Bookstore** (8 A.M.–6 P.M. daily May–Oct.), near the Grand Canyon Lodge, has information, maps, and exhibits on North Rim science and history. The nonprofit Grand Canyon Association operates the well-stocked bookstore. Rangers offer a full program of talks and guided hikes throughout the day and night programs around the campfire. The North Rim edition of the *The Guide* has an up-to-date list of topics, times, and meeting places. Try to attend at least one or two—they are typically interesting and entertaining for both kids and adults, and it tends to deepen your connection with this storied place when you learn about its natural and human history from those who know it best. For the kids, the visitors center has the usual super-fun and educational Junior Rangers Program.

Driving Tours

CAPE ROYAL DRIVE

You can reach Point Imperial and several other lookout spots on the Cape Royal Scenic Drive, one of the most scenic and dramatic roads in the state. From the lodge to Cape Royal is about 30 miles round-trip on a paved road that winds through the mixed conifer and aspen forests of the **Walhalla Plateau.** There are plenty of chances for wildlife spotting and lots of stops and short trails to viewpoints offering breathtaking views of the canyon off to the east and even as far as Navajo land. Plan to spend at least half a day, and take food and water. Go to **Point Imperial** first, reached by a three-mile side road at the beginning of the Cape Royal Road. The best timing is to leave the lodge just before sunrise and watch the show from Point Imperial, and then hit the scenic drive for the rest of the day, stopping often along the way. Binoculars are useful on this drive, as is, of course, a camera. Along the way, **Vista Encantadora** (Charming View) provides just that, rising above Nankoweap Creek. Just beyond that is **Roosevelt Point,** where you can hike the easy 0.2-mile loop trail to a view worthy of the man who saved the Grand Canyon for all of us. When you finally reach the end of the road, **Cape Royal** (elevation 7,865 feet), you'll walk out on a 0.6-mile round-trip paved trail for an expansive and unbounded view of the canyon—one of the very best, from which, on a clear day, you can spot the South Rim's Desert Watchtower way across the gorge and the river far below. Along the short trail you'll pass **Angel's Window,** an unlikely rock arch that seems designed by some overly ambitious god trying to make an already intensely rare and wonderful view even more so.

SIGHTS
⬛ Grand Canyon Lodge

Even if you aren't staying at the 80-year-old Grand Canyon Lodge, a rustic log-and-stone structure perched on the edge of the rim at the very end of the highway, don't make the trip to the North Rim without going into its warm Sun Room to view the gorge through the huge picture windows. You may want to sink into one of the comfortable couches and stare for hours. At sunset, head out to the Adirondack chairs on the lodge's back patio and watch the

Grand Canyon Lodge, perched on the edge of the North Rim

© SHADAY365/123RF.COM

sun sink over the canyon; everybody's quiet, hushed in reverence, and bundled up in jackets and sweaters. Right near the door leading out to the patio, check out sculptor Peter Jepson's charming life-size bronze *Brighty,* a famous canyon burro whose story was told in the 1953 children's book *Brighty of the Grand Canyon* by Marguerite Henry. A display nearby tells the true-life aspects of Brighty's story, and they say if you rub his bronze nose you'll have good luck. The book, along with a movie based on the story, is available at gift shops and bookstores on both the North and South Rims.

Viewpoints

There are three developed viewpoints at the North Rim, each of them offering a slightly different look at the canyon. **Bright Angel Point,** about a 0.5-mile round-trip walk from the lodge's back door, looks over Bright Angel Canyon and provides a view of Roaring Springs, the source of Bright Angel Creek and the freshwater source for the North Rim and the inner canyon. **Point Imperial,** at 8,803

feet, is the highest point on the North Rim and probably has the single best view from the rim, and **Cape Royal,** a view toward the south rim, is a 15-mile one-way drive across the Walhalla Plateau.

RECREATION
Hiking

It's significantly cooler on the high, forested North Rim than it is on the South Rim, making hiking, especially summer hiking, and even more so summer hiking below the rim, much less of a chore. There are a few easy rim trails to choose from, and several tough but unforgettable day hikes into the canyon along the North Kaibab Trail.

Easy trails lead to and from all the developed scenic overlooks on the rim, their trailheads accessible and well marked. *The Guide* has a comprehensive listing of the area's trails and where to pick them up. The three-mile round-trip **Transept Trail** is an easy hike along the forested green rim from the Grand Canyon Lodge to the campground that provides a good overview of the park. Hiking along the rim is an excellent way to see the canyon from many different points of view.

UNCLE JIM TRAIL

- Distance: 5 miles round-trip
- Duration: 3 hours
- Elevation gain: about 200 feet
- Effort: easy
- Trailhead: North Kaibab Trail parking lot, 3 miles north of Grand Canyon Lodge on the main park entrance road

Take this easy, flat trail through the pine forest, where you can watch backpackers winding their way down the North Kaibab Trail's twisting switchbacks, and maybe see a mule train or two along the way. The trail winds through old stands of spruce and fir, sprinkled with quaking aspen, to Uncle Jim Point, where you can let out your best roar into the side notch known as Roaring Springs Canyon.

WIDFORSS TRAIL

- Distance: 10 miles round-trip
- Duration: 5–6 hours
- Elevation gain: negligible
- Effort: easy
- Trailhead: 4 miles north of the lodge; look for the sign

This mostly flat and easy trail leads along the rim of the side canyon called Transept Canyon, and through ponderosa pine, fir, and spruce forest, with a few stands of aspen mixed in, for five miles to Widforss Point, where you can stare across the great chasm and rest before heading back.

NORTH KAIBAB TRAIL

- Distance: varies; 9.4 miles to Roaring Springs
- Duration: a few hours to overnight
- Elevation gain: 5,961 feet from Phantom Ranch

- Effort: moderate to difficult
- Trailhead: North Kaibab Trail parking lot, 3 miles north of Grand Canyon Lodge on the main park entrance road

The North Kaibab Trail starts out among the coniferous heights of the North Rim, a forest trail that soon dries out and becomes a red-rock desert. The trail is cut into the rock face of the cliffs, twisting down improbable routes hard against the cliffs, with nothing but your sanity keeping you away from the gorge. Sooner than you realize, the walls close in and you are deep in the canyon, the trees on the rim just green blurs now. A good introduction to this corridor trail and ancient Native American route is the short, 1.5-mile round-trip jog down to the **Coconino Overlook,** from which, on a clear day, you can see the San Francisco Peaks and the South Rim. A four-mile round-trip hike down will get you to **Supai Tunnel,** blasted out of the red rock in the 1930s by the Civilian Conservation Corps. A little more than a mile farther along and you'll reach **The Bridge in the Redwall** (5.5 miles round-trip), built in 1966 after a flood ruined this portion of the trail. For a tough, all-day hike that will likely have you sore but smiling the next morning, take the North Kaibab Trail five miles to **Roaring Springs,** the source of life-giving Bright Angel Creek. The springs fall headlong out of the cliff-side and spray mist and rainbows into the hot air. Just remember, you have to go five miles back up too. Start hiking early and take plenty of water. A hikers shuttle ($7) leaves every morning from the lodge at 5:45 A.M. and 7:10 A.M.

North Rim Mule Rides

The mules at the North Rim all work for **Canyon Trail Rides** (435/679-8665, www.canyonrides.com, May 15–Oct. 15), the park's north-side trail-riding concessionaire. Guides will take you and your friendly mule on a one-hour rim-side ride ($40), or a half-day ride to Uncle Jim's Point ($75). You can also take a mule down into the canyon along the North Kaibab Trail to the Supai tunnel ($75). Kids have to be at least seven years old to take part in a one-hour ride, at least 10 for the half-day ride, and 12 for the full-day rides. There's a 200-pound weight limit. Call ahead for a reservation if this is something you're set on doing; if you're not sure, you might be able to hop on last-minute, though probably not in June, which is the busiest time at the North Rim.

ACCOMMODATIONS

Built in the late 1930s after the original lodge burned down, ◖ **Grand Canyon Lodge** (928/638-2611 or 888/297-2757, mid-May–mid-Oct., $113–172) has the only in-park accommodations on the North Rim. The rustic but very comfortable log-and-stone lodge has a large central lobby, a high-ceilinged dining room, a deli, a saloon (beer $6), a gift shop, a general store, and a gas station. There are several small, comfortable lodge rooms and dozens of cabins scattered around the property, each with a bath and most with a gas-powered fireplace that makes things very cozy on a cold night. You must book far in advance—at least six months—although there are sometimes cancellations that could allow for a last-minute booking.

The **Kaibab Lodge** (928/638-2389, www.kaibablodge.com, mid-May–early Nov., $95–175) is a small gathering of rustic, cozy cabins behind the tree line at the edge of a meadow along Highway 67, about five miles north of the park boundary. You can rent cabins of varying sizes and enjoy the lounge, gift shop, and warm fireplace in the lobby.

There are also a few accommodations at Jacob Lake, on the Kaibab Plateau about 50 miles north of the park entrance.

Camping

The in-park **North Rim Campground** (877/444-6777, www.recreation.gov, $18–25) has basic camping sites near the rim, with showers and coin-operated laundry. About 25 miles south of Jacob Lake on Highway 67 and about 20 miles north of the park entrance is the **DeMotte Campground** (no reservations, May–Oct., $16), operated by the U.S. Forest Service. It has 38 sites with tables and cooking grills, toilets, and drinking water. Tents, trailers, and motor homes are allowed, but there are no hookups or dump stations available. **Kaibab Camper Village** (Hwy. 67, just south of Jacob Lake, 928/643-7804 or 800/525-0924, full hookup sites $34, basic tent sites $17) also has cabins ($85) and fire pits, tables, toilets, and coin-operated showers.

FOOD

The **Grand Canyon Lodge Dining Room** (928/638-2611, breakfast 6:30–10 A.M., lunch 11:30 A.M.–2:30 P.M., dinner 4:45–9:45 P.M. daily, reservations required for dinner, $8–25) is the only full-service restaurant on the North Rim, serving fish, pasta, and steaks for dinner and soups, sandwiches, and salads for lunch. It's not great, and even less so toward the end of the season (late Oct.), but it is the only thing going for several miles around.

Kaibab Lodge Restaurant (Hwy. 67, 5 miles north of the park boundary, 928/638-2389, breakfast, lunch, and dinner daily, $7–25) serves hearty well-made fare perfect for the high, cool country—much better than the in-park eatery.

GETTING THERE AND AROUND

Although it's only an average of about 10 miles across the canyon from points on the South Rim to points on the North Rim—but only if you're a hawk or a raven or a condor—it's a 215-mile, five-hour drive for those of us who are primarily earthbound. The long route north is something to behold, moving through a corner of Navajo land, past the towering Vermilion Cliffs, and deep into the high conifer forests of the Kaibab Plateau. On the plateau, which at its highest elevation reaches above 9,000 feet, Highway 67 from Jacob Lake to the North Rim typically closes to vehicles by late November until May. In the winter, it's not uncommon for cross-country skiers and snowshoe hikers to take to the closed and snow-covered highway, traveling under their own power toward the canyon and the North Kaibab Trail.

The **Trans Canyon Shuttle** (928/638-2820, reservations required, $70 one-way, $130 round-trip) makes a daily round-trip excursion between the North and South Rims, departing the North Rim at 7 A.M. and arriving at the South Rim at 11:30 A.M. The shuttle then leaves the South Rim at 1:30 P.M. and arrives back at the North Rim at 6:30 P.M.

To get from the Grand Canyon Lodge—the park's only accommodations on the North Rim—to the North Kaibab Trailhead, take the **Hikers Shuttle** ($7 for the first person, $4 for each additional person), which leaves the lodge twice daily first thing in the morning. Tickets must be purchased the day before at the lodge.

If you paid your $25 park entrance fee at the South Rim, it will be honored at the North Rim as long as you go within seven days. If not, you'll have to pay an additional $25. A North Rim edition of the park's helpful newspaper, *The Guide,* is handed out at the North Rim entrance.

The Inner Canyon

Inside the canyon is a desert, red and pink and rocky, its trails lined with cactus and scrub. Hikers are not usually looking down at the ground, though: It's those walls, tight and claustrophobic in the interior's narrowest slots, that make this place a different world altogether. A large part of a canyon-crossing trudge takes place in Bright Angel Canyon along Bright Angel Creek. As you hike along the trail beside the creek, greenery and the cool rushing of the creek clash with the silent heat washing off the cliffs on your other flank.

On any given night there are only a few hundred visitors sleeping below the rim—at either Phantom Ranch, a Mary Colter–designed lodge near the mouth of Bright Angel Canyon, or at three campgrounds along the corridor trails. Until a few decades ago, visiting the inner canyon was something of a free-for-all, but these days access to the interior is strictly controlled; you have to purchase a permit ($10 plus $5 pp per night) to spend the night, and it's not always easy to get a permit—each year the park receives 30,000 requests for a backcountry permit and issues only 13,000.

No matter which trail you use, there's no avoiding an arduous leg- and spirit-punishing hike there and back if you really want to see the inner canyon. It's not easy, but it is worth it: a hard walk, a true accomplishment you'll never forget.

EXPLORING THE INNER CANYON

If you want to be one of the small minority of canyon visitors to spend some quality time below the rim, consider staying at least one full day and night in the inner canyon. Even hikers in excellent shape find that they are sore after trekking down to the river, Phantom Ranch, and beyond. A rim-to-rim hike, either from the south or from the north, pretty much requires at least a day of rest below the rim. The ideal inner canyon trip lasts three days and two nights: one day hiking in, one day of rest, and one day to hike out.

River trips generally last a minimum of three days to up to three weeks and often include a hike down one of the corridor trails to the river. Depending on how long you want to spend on the river, plan far, far in advance and consider making the river trip your only activity on that particular canyon visit. Combining too much strenuous, mind-blowing, and life-changing activity into one trip tends to water down the entire experience.

Permits and Reservations

The earlier you apply for a permit the better, but you can't apply for one prior to the first of the month four months before your proposed trip date. The easiest way to get a permit is to go to the park's website (www.nps.gov/grca/planyourvisit/overnight-hiking.htm), print out a backcountry permit request form, fill it out, and then fax it (928/638-2125) first thing in the morning on the date in question—for example, if you want to hike in October, you would fax your request on June 1. Have patience; on the first day of the month the fax number is usually busy throughout the day—keep trying. On the permit request form you'll indicate where you plan to stay. If you are camping, the permit is your reservation, but if you want to stay at Phantom Ranch, you must get separate reservations, and that is often a close-to-impossible task. For more information on obtaining a backcountry permit, call the South Rim Backcountry Information Center (928/638-7875, 8 A.M.–5 P.M. daily).

HIKING

There are many lesser-known routes into the canyon, but most hikers stick to the corridor trails—Bright Angel, South Kaibab, and North Kaibab. The Bright Angel Trail from the South Rim is the most popular, but the South Kaibab is significantly shorter, though much steeper. The North Kaibab, from the North Rim, is the only trail to the river and Phantom Ranch from the north. The rim-to-rim hike is popular, and you can choose, as long as the season permits, to start either on the north or south. Starting from the South Rim, you may want to go down the Bright Angel to see beautiful Indian Gardens; then again, the South Kaibab provides a faster, more direct route to the river. If you start from the north, you may want to come out of the canyon via the South Kaibab, as it is shorter and faster, and at that point you are probably going to want to take the path of least resistance. Remember though, while it's shorter, the South Kaibab is a good deal steeper than the Bright Angel, and there is no water available.

Day Hikes Around Phantom Ranch

Some people prefer to spend their time in the canyon recovering from the hard walk or mule ride that brought them here, and a day spent cooling your feet in Bright Angel Creek

or drinking beer in the cantina is not a day wasted. However, if you want to do some exploring around Phantom Ranch, there are a few popular day hikes from which to choose. When you arrive, the friendly rangers will usually tell you, unsolicited, all about these hikes and provide detailed directions. If you want to get deeper out in the bush and far from the other hikers, ask one of the rangers to recommend a lesser-known route.

RIVER TRAIL

- Distance: 1.5 miles round-trip
- Duration: 1–2 hours
- Elevation gain: negligible
- Effort: easy
- Trailhead: Phantom Ranch

A highly recommended and rather short hike is along the precipitous River Trail, high above the Colorado just south of Phantom Ranch. The Civilian Conservation Corps (CCC) blasted this skinny cliff-side trail out of the rock walls in the 1930s to provide a link between the Bright Angel and the South Kaibab Trail. Heading out from Phantom Ranch, it's about a 1.5-mile loop that takes you across both suspension bridges and high above the river. It's an easy walk with fantastic views and is a good way to get your sore legs stretched and moving again.

CLEAR CREEK TO PHANTOM OVERLOOK

- Distance: about 1.5 miles
- Duration: 1–2 hours
- Elevation gain: 826 feet
- Effort: easy to moderate
- Trailhead: about 0.25 miles north of Phantom Ranch on the North Kaibab Trail

Another popular CCC-built trail near Phantom Ranch is the 1.5-mile **Clear Creek Loop,** which takes you high above the river to Phantom Overlook, where there's an old stone bench and excellent views of the canyon and of Phantom Ranch below. The rangers seem to recommend this hike the most, but while it's not tough, it can be a little steep and rugged, especially if you're exhausted and sore. Ultimately the views are well worth the pain.

RIBBON FALLS

- Distance: 11 miles round-trip
- Duration: 5–6 hours to all day
- Elevation gain: 1,174 feet
- Effort: easy to moderate
- Trailhead: look for the sign 5.5 miles north of Phantom Ranch on the North Kaibab Trail

If you hiked in from the South Rim and you have a long, approximately 11-mile round-trip day hike in you, head north on the North Kaibab Trail from Phantom Ranch to beautiful **Ribbon Falls,** a mossy, cool-water oasis just off the hot dusty trail. The falls are indeed a ribbon of cold water falling hard off the rock cliffs, and you can scramble up the slickrock and through the green creek-side jungle and stand beneath the shower. This hike will also give you a chance to see the eerie, claustrophobic "Box," one of the strangest and most exhilarating stretches of the North Kaibab Trail.

MULE RIDES

For generations the famous Grand Canyon mules have been dexterously walking along the skinny trails, loaded with packs and people. Even the Brady Bunch rode them, so they come highly recommended. A descent into the canyon on the back of a friendly mule—with an often taciturn cowboy-type leading the train—can be an unforgettable experience, but don't assume because you're riding and not walking that you won't be sore in the morning. A day trip ($139 pp) down the Bright Angel to Plateau Point, from which you can see the Colorado River, includes lunch. One night at Phantom Ranch, meals included, and a ride down on a mule costs $447 pp or $790 for two people. Two nights at Phantom, meals, and a mule ride costs $626 pp or $1,043 for two. Reservations (888/297-2757, www.

grandcanyonlodges.com) should be made six months or more in advance.

RIVER TRIPS

People who have been inside the Grand Canyon often have one of two reactions—they either can't wait to return, or they swear never to return. This is doubly true of those intrepid souls who ride the great river, braving white-water roller coasters while looking forward to a star-filled evening camped, dry, and full of gourmet camp food on a white beach deep in the gorge. To boat the Colorado, one of the last explored regions of North America, is quite simply one of the most exciting and potentially life-changing trips the West has to offer.

Because of this well-known truth, trips are not cheap and not exactly easy to book. Rafting season in the canyon runs April–October, and there are myriad trips possible—from a three-day long-weekend ride to a 21-day full-canyon epic.

Lee's Ferry is the most common launch point for all canyon river trips. In fact, it's the only place for about 700 miles around where you can reach the Colorado River without hiking deep into the canyon. It's a 133-mile drive (about 2.5 hours) from the South Rim. To get here, take Highway 64 east from the park to Cameron on U.S. 89, and then head north for 58 miles to U.S. 89A west. In another 14 miles you're sticking your toes in the mighty river. You can stop at Lee's Ferry on the way from the South Rim to the North Rim, or the other way around. It's 85 miles from the North Rim via Highway 67 to U.S. 89 south and U.S. 89A west.

An Upper Canyon trip will take you from River Mile 0 at Lee's Ferry through the canyon to Phantom Ranch, while a Lower Canyon trip begins at Phantom, requiring a hike down the Bright Angel with your gear on your back. Furthermore, you can choose a motorized pontoon boat, as some three-quarters of rafters do; a paddleboat, a kayak, or some other combination. It all depends on what you want and what you can afford. If you are considering taking a river trip, the best place to start is the website of the **Grand Canyon**

THE GRAND CANYON

LEE'S FERRY

Lee's Ferry (www.nps.gov/glca/planyourvisit/lees-ferry.htm), within the Glen Canyon National Recreation Area is the only spot in hundreds of miles of canyonland where you can drive down to the Colorado River. It's named for a man who occupied the area rather briefly in the early 1870s, Mormon outlaw John D. Lee, one of the leaders of the infamous Mountain Meadows Massacre in Utah. Lee was exiled to this lonely spot after he and others attacked and murdered more than 100 westbound Arkansas emigrants moving through Utah Territory during a period when relations between the Utah Mormons and the U.S. government were strained, to say the least. One of Lee's wives, Emma Lee, ended up running the ferry more than Lee ever did; he soon lit out and lived as a kind of fugitive until he was finally, in 1877, recalled home and sentenced to death.

The Lee family operated a small ranch and orchard near the crossing, the remnants of which can still be seen on a self-guided tour of the **Lonely Dell Ranch Historic Site,** which includes the rusting remains of a mining operation, several old boat ruins, and a graveyard. There are a few rocky hiking trails around the area, but one of the best things to do here is to simply sit on a soggy beach and watch the river flow by the sun-spattered cliffs. There's a nice campground ($12, no hookups) if you feel like staying, and a ranger station and launch ramp as well.

For long before and after Lee lent his name to the crossing, this two-mile break in the Colorado River's canyon-digging, near the mouth of the Paria River, was one of the very few places to cross the river in southern Utah and northern Arizona; in fact, it remained so until the bridging of the Colorado at Marble Canyon in 1929. Today, the area is the starting block for thousands of brave river-trippers who venture into the Grand Canyon atop the Colorado every year. It's also a popular fishing spot, though the trout here have been introduced and were not native to the warm muddy flow before the dam at Glen Canyon changed the Colorado's character. For guides, gear, and any other information about the area, try **Lee's Ferry Anglers** (928/355-2261 or 800/962-9755, www.leesferry.com) located at the Cliff Dweller's Lodge.

Lee's Ferry is also significant because it provides the dividing line between the upper and lower states of the Colorado River's watershed, inasmuch as they were divided by the compact that divvied up the river's water for human use. This has made Lee's Ferry "river mile 0," the gateway and crossroads to both the upper and lower Colorado, and the place where its annual flows are measured and recorded.

Lee's Ferry Lodge at Vermilion Cliffs (U.S. 89A near Marble Canyon, 928/355-2231 or 800/451-2231, www.leesferrylodge.com, $63 d) has comfortable rooms and a delicious restaurant serving hearty fare perfect after a long day of outdoor play, and its beer selection (more than 100 different bottles) is outrageously diverse for such an out-of-the-way place. The steaks are hand cut, and the ribs are outstanding, smothered in the lodge's special homemade sauce. The lodge serves breakfast, lunch, and dinner daily ($10-20).

River Outfitters Association (www.gcroa.org), a nonprofit group of about 16 licensed river outfitters, all of them monitored and approved by the National Park Service, each with a good safety record and relatively similar rates. After you decide what kind of trip you want, the website links to the individual outfitters for booking. If you are one of the majority of river explorers who can't wait to get back on the water once you've landed at the final port, remember that there's a strict rule enforced by the National Park Service allowing one trip per year per person.

ACCOMMODATIONS AND FOOD

Designed by Mary Colter for the Fred Harvey Company in 1922, **Phantom Ranch** (888/297-2757, www.grandcanyonlodges.com, dorm $42 pp), the only noncamping accommodation inside the canyon, is a shady, peaceful place that you're likely to miss and yearn for once you've visited and left it behind. Perhaps Phantom's strong draw, like a Siren wailing from the inner gorge, is less about its intrinsic pleasures and more about it being the only sign of civilization in a deep wilderness that can feel like the end of the world, especially after a 17-mile hike in from the North Rim. But it would probably be an inviting place even if it were easier to get at, and it's all the better because it's not.

As such, it is very difficult to make a reservation. Some people begin calling a year out and still can't get a room, while others show up at the South Rim, ask at Bright Angel Lodge, and find that a cancellation that very day has left a cabin or bed open. This strategy is not recommended, but it has been known to work. Phantom has several cabins and two dormitories, one for men and one for women, both offering restrooms with showers. The lodge's center point is its cantina, a welcoming, air-conditioned, beer- and lemonade-selling sight for anyone who has just descended one of the trails. Two meals a day are served in the cantina—breakfast, comprising eggs, pancakes, and thick slices of bacon ($19.63), and dinner, with a choice of steak ($41.68), stew ($26.10), or vegetarian ($26.10). The cantina also offers a box lunch with a bagel, fruit, and salty snacks ($12.39). Reservations for meals are also difficult to come by.

Most nights and afternoons, a ranger based at Phantom Ranch will give a talk on some aspect of canyon lore, history, or science. These events are always interesting and always well attended, even in the 110°F heat of the summer.

Phantom is located near the mouth of Bright Angel Canyon, within a few yards of clear, babbling Bright Angel Creek, and it is shaded by large cottonwoods planted in the 1930s by the Civilian Conservation Corps. There are several day hikes within easy reach, and the Colorado River and the two awesome suspension bridges that link one bank to the other are only about 0.25 miles from the lodge.

Camping

There are three developed campgrounds in the inner canyon: **Cottonwood Campground,** about seven miles from the North Rim along the North Kaibab Trail; **Bright Angel Campground,** along the creek of the same name near Phantom Ranch; and **Indian Garden,** about 4.5 miles from the South Rim along the Bright Angel Trail. To stay overnight at any of these campgrounds, you must obtain a permit from the Backcountry Office on the South Rim (928/638-7875, $10 plus $5 pp per night). All three campgrounds offer restrooms and a freshwater spigot, picnic tables, and food storage bins to keep the critters out. There are no showers or any other amenities.

The best campground in the inner canyon is Bright Angel, a shady, cottonwood-lined setting along cool Bright Angel Creek. Because of its easy proximity to Phantom Ranch, campers can make use of the cantina, even eating meals there if they can get a reservation, and can attend the ranger talks offered at the lodge. There's nothing quite like sitting on the grassy banks beside your campsite and cooling your worn feet in the creek.

THE GRAND CANYON

Grand Canyon West

Since the Hualapai Tribe's Skywalk opened to much international press coverage a few years ago, the remote western reaches of the Grand Canyon have certainly gotten more attention than in the past. Though no less remote, there has been an uptick in tourism to the Hualapai's portion of the rim, which is about two hours of dirt-road driving from the Hualapai Reservation's capital, Peach Springs, located along Route 66 east of Kingman. At the same time, all that press has led to a little confusion. A few times every hour at the South Rim visitors center, one can usually hear the question "How do we get to the Skywalk?" followed by moans of disbelief and the cancellation of plans when the answer comes that it's about 250 miles away. If you want to experience Grand Canyon West, it's a good idea to plan a separate trip, or else carve out at least two extra days to do so. Along the way, you can drive on the longest remaining portion of Route 66, and if you have a few days on top of that, hike down into Havasupai Canyon and see its famous, fantastical waterfalls.

GETTING THERE
From the South Rim
Grand Canyon West is about 250 miles from the South Rim, a five-hour drive over sometimes rough roads. Take I-40 from Williams to Kingman, then U.S. 93 north to Pierce Ferry Road, about 30 miles from the I-40–U.S. 93 junction. After 28 miles on Pierce Ferry Road, turn right on Diamond Bar Road. About 14 miles of dirt road and seven miles of paved road later, you'll reach Grand Canyon West.

From Las Vegas
Grand Canyon West and the Skywalk are very popular day trips for people visiting Las Vegas, as the Hualapai Reservation is only 125 miles southwest of Vegas, about a 2.5-hour drive. If you want to go on your own, remember that a portion of the route is unpaved, and you have to pay a $43 entrance fee on top of $32 to brave the Skywalk. Take U.S. 93 out of the city, heading south for about 65 miles to mile marker 42, where you'll see the exit for Dolan Springs, Meadview City, and Pierce Ferry. Turn north onto Pierce Ferry Road. In about 30 miles, turn east on Diamond Bar Road and continue 20 miles, with about seven miles unpaved, to Grand Canyon West.

Several companies in Las Vegas offer guided tours to Grand Canyon West, the South Rim, and other spots. The concierge desk at most of the Strip hotels can help you book a tour and give you directions.

One of the better tours is the 11-hour-plus **Mysterious West** tour ($169–375) of Grand Canyon West offered by **SweeTours** (6363 S. Pecos Rd., Suite 106, Las Vegas, 702/456-9200, http://sweetours.com). Depending on how much you want to pay, you'll travel by bus with about 50 other people, or by SUV with a smaller group, to the West Rim, where you can choose among several packages, including a helicopter and boat tour of the western canyon. SweeTours also offers excellent tours of the South Rim and Hoover Dam.

HAVASUPAI INDIAN RESERVATION
Havasu Creek is heavy with lime, which turns the water an almost tropical blue-green. It passes below the weathered red walls of the western Grand Canyon, home these many centuries to the Havasupai (Havsuw' Baaja), the "people of the blue-green water."

The creek falls through the canyon on its way to join the Colorado River, passing briefly by the ramshackle inner-canyon village of Supai, where it is not unusual to see horses running free in the dusty streets, where reggae plays all day through some community speaker, and where the supply helicopter alights and then hops out again every 10 minutes or so in a field across from the post office. Then, about two miles past the village, the creek plunges 120 feet into a misty turquoise pool, and plunges again after another mile, but not before passing peacefully through a cottonwood-shaded campground.

Thousands of people from all over the world (the tribe says 20,000; other sources say half that many) visit Havasupai (928/448-2731, www.havasupai-nsn.gov, entry fee $35 pp) every year just to see these blue-green waterfalls, to swim in their pools, and to see one of the most remote hometowns in the United States. The trip is all the more enticing and memorable because it's more like an expedition. Still, there are those who return year after year as if going home.

The eight-mile one-way hike to the Village of Supai from Hualapai Hilltop is actually one of the easier treks into the Grand Canyon. A few miles of switchbacks lead to a sandy bottomland, where you're surrounded by eroded humps of seemingly melted, pockmarked sandstone. This is not Grand Canyon National Park: You'll know that for sure when you see the trash along the trail. It doesn't ruin the hike, but it nearly breaks the spell. When you reach the village you'll see the twin rock spires, called Wii'Gliva, that tower over the little farms and cluttered-yard homes of Supai. Here you can stay at **Havasupai Lodge** (928/448-2111 or 928/448-2201, $145 d), which has air-conditioning and private baths. The village also has a small café that serves decent breakfast, lunch, and dinner as well as a general store.

What used to be Navajo Falls, about 1.5 miles from the village toward the **campground** (first-come, first-served, $17) was destroyed in a 2008 flash flood. Now there's a wider set of falls and a big pool that sits below a flood-eroded hill. Perhaps the most famous of the canyon's falls, **Havasu Falls** comes up all of a sudden as you get closer to the campground. Few hikers refuse to toss their packs aside and strip to their swimming suits when they see Havasu Falls for the first time. The other major waterfall, **Mooney Falls,** is another mile down the trail through the campground. It's not easy to reach the pool below; it requires a careful walk down a narrow rock-hewn trail with chain handles, but most reasonably dexterous people

© JASON MAEHL/123RF.COM

Havasu Falls, located on the Havasupai Indian Reservation

The Havasupai operate a large campground near the famous waterfalls.

can handle it. **Beaver Falls,** somewhat under-whelming by comparison, is another two miles of creek sloshing toward the Colorado River, which is seven miles from the campground.

A visit to Havasupai takes some planning. It's unbearably hot in the deep summer, and you can't hike except in the very early morning; the best months to visit are September–October and April–June. If you aren't a backpacker, you can hire a packhorse to carry your essentials or you, or both; or you can take the helicopter ($85 one-way). A popular way to visit is to hike in and take the helicopter out. It's a five-minute thrill-ride through the canyon to the rim, and the helipad is only about 50 yards from the trailhead parking lot.

Most visitors stay the night at one of the motels along Historic Route 66 the night be-fore hiking in. You'll want to get an early start, especially during the summer. It's a 60-mile drive to the trailhead at Hualapai Hill from Route 66. The closest hotel is the Hualapai Lodge in Peach Springs, about seven miles west of Indian Route 18, which leads to the trail-head. You'll find cheaper accommodations in Seligman, about 30 miles east. The tribe re-quires a reservation to visit Supai and the falls; call at least six months in advance.

HUALAPAI INDIAN RESERVATION

Although Peach Springs is the capital of the Hualapai (WALL-uh-pie) Reservation, there's not much there but a lodge and a few scat-tered houses. The real attractions are up on the West Rim about 50 miles and two hours away. Peach Springs makes an obvious base for a visit to the West Rim, which has several lookout points, the famous Skywalk, and a kitschy Old West–style tourist attraction called Hualapai Ranch. The tribe's **Hualapai River Runners** (928/769-2219) will take you on a day trip on the river, and there are several all-inclusive package tours to choose from. Check out the tribe's website (www.grandcanyonwest.com) for more information.

THE HUALAPAI

Before the 1850s, northwestern Arizona's small Hualapai Tribe didn't really exist. It was the federal government's idea to group together 13 autonomous bands of Yuman-speaking Pais Indians, who had lived on the high dry plains near Grand Canyon for eons, as the "People of the Tall Pines."

Before the Colonial clampdown and the Hualapai Wars of the 1860s, the Pai bands were independent, though they "followed common rules for marriage and land use, spoke variations of one language, and shared social structures, kin networks, cultural practices, environmental niches, and so on," according to Jeffrey Shepherd's *We Are an Indian Nation: A History of the Hualapai People*, which the scholar spent 10 years researching and writing.

The U.S. Army nearly wiped out the bands during the land wars of the 1860s, and the internment of the survivors almost finished the job. But the bands persisted, and in 1883 the government established the million-acre Hualapai Reservation, with its capital at Peach Springs. Then it spent the next 100 years or so trying to take it away from them for the benefit of white ranchers, the railroad, and the National Park Service.

These days the Hualapai Nation, though still impoverished, is a worldwide brand – Grand Canyon West. How did this happen?

The small, isolated tribe has always been willing to take economic risks, one of the many ways, as Shepherd argues, that the Hualapai have twisted Colonial objectives for their own survival. A few years ago they partnered with Las Vegas entrepreneur David Jin and built the Hualapai Skywalk, a 70-foot-long, glass walkway hanging from the Grand Canyon's western rim. Now you can't walk two steps along the Vegas strip without a tour guide offering to drive you to one of the most isolated sections of Arizona.

Throughout their relatively short history as a nation proper, the Hualapai have consistently tried to make their windy and dry reservation economically viable, sometimes with the assistance of the government but often in direct contradiction to its goals. For generations they were cattle ranchers, but they could never get enough water to make it pay. They successfully sued the Santa Fe Railroad over an important reservation spring in a landmark case for indigenous rights. For a time in the 1980s they even hesitantly explored allowing uranium mining on their reservation. Now, they have bet their future on tourism.

Tour Packages

To visit Grand Canyon West, the Hualapai Tribe requires you to purchase one of its rather overpriced **Legacy Packages** ($43–86 pp), and only the most expensive "Gold" package includes the Skywalk. The lesser packages allow you to ride a shuttle from **Eagle Point,** where the Skywalk juts out, to **Guano Point,** an unobstructed view of the western canyon, and **Hualapai Ranch,** where fake cowboys will entertain you with Old West clichés and take you on a ride in a wagon or on a horseback ride in a corral or to the canyon rim ($10–75). You can stay the night in one of the ranch's rustic cabins ($100). A couple of the packages include a meal, or you can add one ($15 pp). You can also add the Skywalk to your package for $30 if you get up there and decide you really must try it. Frankly, the packages that don't include the Skywalk are definitely not worth the price or the drive. The views from the South and North Rims are much more dramatic and memorable, and it only costs $25 to see those.

The Skywalk

The Skywalk (928/769-2636, www.grandcanyonwest.com) is as much an art installation as it is a tourist attraction. A horseshoe-shaped glass-and-steel platform jutting out 70 feet from the canyon rim, it appears futuristic surrounded by the rugged remote western canyon. It's something to see, for sure, but is it worth the long drive and the high price tag? Not really. If you have time for an off-the-beaten-path portion of your canyon trip, it's better to go to the North Rim and stand out on Bright Angel Point—you'll get a somewhat similar impression, and it's cheaper. There is something of a feeling of a thrill ride to the Skywalk, however. Some people can't handle it: They walk out a few steps, look down through the glass at the canyon 4,000 feet below, and head for more solid ground. It's all perfectly safe, but it doesn't feel that way if you are subject to vertigo. Another drawback of this sight is that they won't let you take your camera out on the Skywalk. If you want a record of this adventure, you have to buy a "professional" photo taken by somebody else. You have to store all of your possessions, including your camera, in a locker before stepping out on the glass, with covers on your shoes like a surgeon entering the operating room.

Recreation

Though the Skywalk may not be worth the high price of admission and the long drive to reach it, the Hualapai Tribe offers one adventure that is worth the steep price tag: the canyon's only one-day river rafting experience (928/769-2636, www.grandcanyonwest.com, May–Oct.). It generally takes up to a year of planning and several days of roughing it to ride the river and the rapids through the inner gorge, making a Colorado River adventure something that the average visitor isn't likely to try. Not so in Grand Canyon West. For about $330 pp, Hualapai river guides will pick you up in a van early in the morning at the Hualapai Lodge in Peach Springs and drive you to the Colorado River via the rough Diamond Creek Road, where you'll float downstream in a motorboat over roiling white-water rapids and smooth and tranquil stretches. You'll stop for lunch on a beach and take a short hike through a watery side canyon to beautiful Travertine Falls. At the end of the trip, a helicopter picks you out of the canyon and drops you on the rim near the Skywalk. It's expensive, yes; but

if you want to ride the river without a lot of preplanning and camping, this is the way to do it. Along the way, the Hualapai guides tell stories about this end of the Grand Canyon, sprinkled with their history and lore.

You can drive to the river's edge yourself along the 19-mile **Diamond Creek Road** through a dry, scrubby landscape scattered with cactus. The road provides the only easy access to the river's edge between Lee's Ferry, not far from the North Rim, and Pearce Ferry, near Lake Mead. The route is best negotiated in a high-clearance SUV; they say you can do it in a regular sedan, but you have to cross Diamond Creek six times as the dirt road winds down through Peach Springs Canyon, dropping some 3,400 feet from its beginning at Peach Springs on Route 66. The creek is susceptible to flash flooding during the summer and winter rainy seasons, so call ahead to check road conditions (928/769-2230). At the end of the road, where Diamond Creek meets the Colorado River, there's a sandy beach and an enchanting lush oasis; and, of course, there's that big river rolling by.

Accommodations and Food

The **Hualapai Lodge** (900 Rte. 66, Peach Springs, 928/769-2230 or 928/769-2636, www. grandcanyonwest.com, $75–105 d) in Peach Springs has a small heated saltwater pool, an exercise room, a gift shop, and 57 comfortable newish guest rooms with soft beds, cable, free wireless Internet, and train tracks right out the back door. The lodge is a good place to stay the night before hiking into Havasupai, as it's only about six miles west of the turnoff to Hualapai Hill and the trailhead.

The lodge's restaurant, **Diamond Creek** (6 A.M.–9 P.M. daily, $7–17), serves American and Native American dishes. They offer a heaping plate of delicious spaghetti if you're carbo-loading for a big hike to Havasupai; the Hualapai taco (similar to the Navajo taco, with beans and meat piled high on a fluffy slab of fry bread) and the Hualapai stew (with luscious sirloin tips and vegetables swimming in a delicious hearty broth) are both recommended. They also have a few vegetarian choices, good chili, and pizza.

For more food and accommodations along old Route 66 in the vicinity of Peach Springs and Grand Canyon West, try Kingman and Seligman.

GETTING THERE AND AROUND

The best way to get to Grand Canyon West is to take I-40 to the Ashfork exit and then drive west on Route 66. Starting at Ashfork and heading west to Peach Springs, the longest remaining portion of Route 66 moves through **Seligman,** a small roadside town that is a reminder of the heyday of the Mother Road. The route through Seligman, which is worth a stop and a walk around if you have the time, is popular with nostalgic motorcyclists, and there are a few eateries and tourist-style stores in town. Once you reach Peach Springs, take Antares Road for 25 miles, then turn right on Pierce Ferry Road for three miles, and then turn east onto Diamond Bar Road for 21 miles; 14 miles of it are dirt. Diamond Bar Road ends at the only entrance to Grand Canyon West. The 49-mile trip takes about two hours. For park-and-ride reservations, call 702/260-6506.

To reach Havasupai Canyon, turn north on Indian Route 18 just before Peach Springs and drive 68 miles north to a parking area at Hualapai Hilltop. From there it's an eight-mile hike in to Supai Village and the lodge, and another two miles to the campground. The trail is moderate and leads through a sandy wash with overhanging canyon walls. For the first two miles or so, rocky, moderately technical switchbacks lead to the canyon floor, then it's easy and beautiful the rest of the way. If you don't want to hike in, you can arrange to rent a horse (928/448-2121, 928/448-2174, or 928/448-2180, www.havasupaitribe.com, $120 round-trip to the lodge, $150 round-trip to the campground), or even hire a helicopter (623/516-2790, $85 pp one-way).

LOS ANGELES AND DISNEYLAND

Los Angeles is the California that the rest of the world envisions. It's true that palm trees line sunny boulevards and the Pacific Ocean starts to warm to a swimmable temperature here—and that traffic is always a mess. But celebrities don't crowd every sidewalk signing autographs, and movies aren't filming on every corner.

Instead, L.A. combines the glitz, crowds, and speed of the big city with an easier, friendlier feel in its suburbs. A soft haze often envelops the warm beaches, which draw lightly clad crowds vying to see and be seen while children play in the water. Power shoppers pound the sparkling pavement lining the ultra-urban city streets. Tourists can catch a premiere at the Chinese Theatre, try their feet on a surfboard at Huntington Beach, and ogle the relics at the La Brea Tar Pits.

For visitors who want a deeper look into the Los Angeles Basin, excellent museums dot the landscape, as do theaters, comedy clubs, and live-music venues. L.A. boasts the best nightlife in California, with options that appeal to star-watchers, hard-core dancers, and cutting-edge music lovers alike.

Out in the suburb of Orange County lies the single most recognizable tourist attraction in California: Disneyland. Even the most jaded native residents tend to soften at the bright colors, cheerful music, sweet smells, and sense of fun that permeate the House of Mouse.

HIGHLIGHTS

◖ Griffith Park: A welcome expanse of greenery, "L.A.'s Central Park" includes the Griffith Observatory, the L.A. Zoo, and the Hollywood sign, as well as several film locations (page 344).

◖ Hollywood Walk of Fame: Since 1960, entertainment legends have wished for a star on this three-mile walk of fame (page 345).

◖ The Chinese Theatre: This Hollywood icon opened in 1927 and has played host to hand- and footprints of the stars, along with premieres of their movies (page 347).

◖ Los Angeles County Museum of Art: LACMA's nine buildings house a diverse and extraordinary array of art in a variety of mediums. Time your visit to coincide with one of their prestigious exhibitions (page 350).

◖ Santa Monica Pier: On a sunny Southern California day, nothing beats a day at the pier. Rides the rides, gorge at the midway-style stands, or simply spread a blanket on the beach (page 354).

◖ Venice Boardwalk: From the freaky to the fantastic, the Venice Boardwalk has it all. Park yourself for people-watching of fantastic proportions or even participate a bit yourself (page 355).

◖ The Gamble House: Take a tour of the Gamble House, a (potentially haunted!) masterpiece of 20th-century craftsman architecture (page 357).

◖ California Adventure: Disneyland may have the mouse, but it's California Adventure – the Golden State-themed park that accompanies it – that has all the rides (page 396).

◖ The *Queen Mary:* This famous former pleasure cruiser is now a famously haunted and historic hotel, museum, and entertainment center. Be sure to book the Paranormal Ship Walk for a highlight of the ship's "most haunted" spots (page 406).

LOOK FOR ◖ TO FIND RECOMMENDED SIGHTS, ACTIVITIES, DINING, AND LODGING.

LOS ANGELES

© NITO500/123RF.COM

the Hollywood Walk of Fame on Hollywood Boulevard

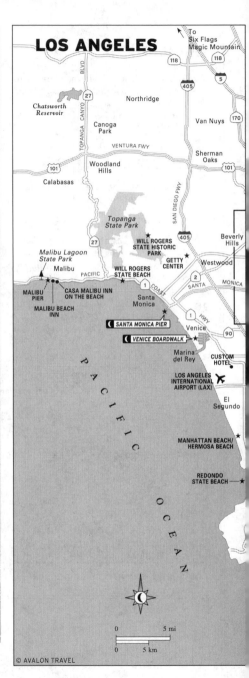

LOS ANGELES

To Six Flags Magic Mountain

118 118

405

5

Chatsworth Reservoir

27

Northridge

Van Nuys 170

Canoga Park

VENTURA FWY

Sherman Oaks

101 Woodland Hills 101

Calabasas

SAN DIEGO FWY

Topanga State Park

405 Beverly Hills

★ WILL ROGERS STATE HISTORIC PARK

Malibu Lagoon State Park

GETTY CENTER ★ Westwood

Malibu

PACIFIC ★ WILL ROGERS STATE BEACH

2

SANTA MONICA

1 COAST

MALIBU PIER ★ CASA MALIBU INN ON THE BEACH

Santa Monica

1 HWY

MALIBU BEACH INN

★

◖ SANTA MONICA PIER

90

Venice

◖ VENICE BOARDWALK ★

Marina del Rey

CUSTOM HOTEL ●

LOS ANGELES INTERNATIONAL AIRPORT (LAX) ✈

El Segundo

P A C I F I C

MANHATTAN BEACH/ HERMOSA BEACH

REDONDO STATE BEACH ★

O C E A N

0   5 mi
0   5 km

© AVALON TRAVEL

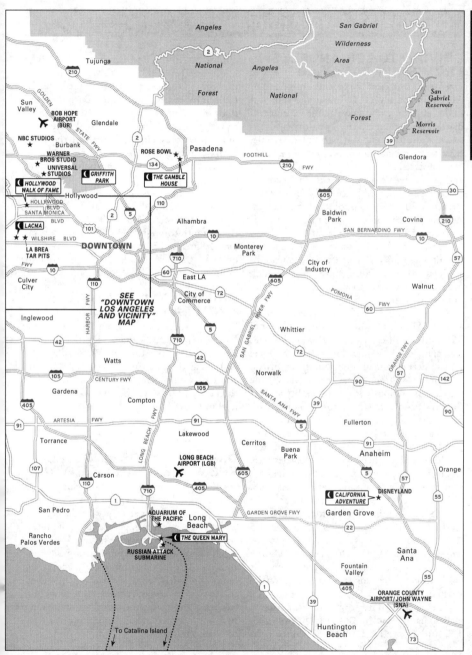

Driving to Los Angeles

DRIVING TO LOS ANGELES FROM SAN FRANCISCO

From San Francisco, the quickest route to Los Angeles is south on **I-5.** This route runs just under 400 miles and takes about six hours of drive time without traffic. The drive on I-5 is straight and flat, and not particularly scenic, filled with trucks and highway patrol cars that can slow traffic considerably. On holiday weekends, the drive time can increase to 10 hours.

To reach I-5, head east on over the Bay Bridge (I-80); there's no toll in this direction. Just on the other side of the bridge, continue east on I-580 toward Livermore and Tracy. Continue on I-580 for 45–50 miles. The I-5 junction appears not long after the outer suburb of Livermore. Head south on I-5, which eventually narrows to two lanes for the next 300 miles or so.

At the south end of California's Central Valley, I-5 ascends through the **Grapevine.** This hilly, high-elevation section of the freeway can close in winter due to snow and ice, and sometimes in summer due to wildfires. November–March, thick, ground-level tule fog can also seriously impede visibility and reduce traffic to a crawl. Before you hit the road, check the Caltrans website (www.dot.ca.gov) for weather and fog reports for the Grapevine and I-5. On the other side of the Grapevine, I-5 descends into the greater Los Angeles area, where it connects with any number of freeways that can be used to continue into the city. U.S. 101 south leads directly into Hollywood; from here, Santa Monica Boulevard can take you west to Beverly Hills. Taking I-210 from I-5 will take you east to Pasadena. The best way to reach Santa Monica, Venice, and Malibu is via U.S. 1. I-10 can get you there from the east, but it will be a long, tedious, and traffic-laden drive.

The coastal route from San Francisco is known as the **Pacific Coast Highway** (U.S. 101 and Hwy. 1). This scenic route runs almost 500 miles and can easily take eight hours to drive. Although it's slower than I-5, the gorgeous coastal scenery that takes in Big Sur, Monterey, and Santa Barbara more than makes up for it. U.S. 101 is long, narrow, and winding; in winter rock slides and mud slides may close portions of the road entirely. Always check Caltrans (www.dot.ca.gov) for traffic conditions before starting your journey.

From San Francisco, take U.S. 101, which runs inland south through San Jose, Gilroy, and Salinas toward Paso Robles. U.S. 101 continues south through Santa Barbara, Ventura, and the greater Los Angeles area. Continuing on U.S. 101 south will lead you directly into Hollywood.

DRIVING TO LOS ANGELES FROM LAS VEGAS

You can expect I-15 to make the drive from Las Vegas fairly quick, at least for the 215 miles through Baker, Barstow, and Victorville, until you reach the junctions with Highway 210 and I-10. From there, the infamous L.A. traffic means all bets are off. Highway 210/I-210 lead west to Highway 134 and the northern suburbs. I-10 makes a beeline for the heart of the city and the beach neighborhoods.

DRIVING TO LOS ANGELES FROM THE GRAND CANYON

It's 494 miles from the Grand Canyon's South Rim to Los Angeles. Most of the 7–8-hour drive is on I-40 across an empty, hard landscape without too much respite save the usual interstate fare. After about five hours' drive, you reach Barstow, I-40's western terminus. From Barstow, take I-15 south into L.A., about two hours through scrub desert and urban sprawl to the city. It can take considerably longer on weekends and during the morning and evening rush hours, which in Southern California tend to be interminable.

DRIVING TO LOS ANGELES FROM YOSEMITE

Los Angeles is a pretty straightforward drive south from Yosemite. The park's South entrance is closest to L.A. and is open year-round via Highway 41. This entrance is also the nearest one to the Badger Pass Ski Area, Glacier Point, and the Bridalveil Creek campground. You can reach the South entrance from Yosemite Valley in about one hour.

Plan about six hours to drive the 300 miles to L.A. Take Highway 41 south for 60 miles to Fresno. Merge onto Highway 99 and follow it through Fresno and Bakersfield (about 130 miles). Highway 99 merges with I-5 south near the Grapevine. Once over the Grapevine, I-5 descends into the greater L.A. area, where it connects with any number of freeways, including U.S. 101 south into the city.

GETTING THERE BY AIR AND TRAIN
Air

L.A. is one of the most commercial airport–dense metropolitan areas in the country. Wherever you're coming from and whichever part of L.A. you're headed for, you can get there by air. **Los Angeles International Airport** (LAX, 1 World Way, Los Angeles, www.lawa. org), known as LAX, has the most flights to and from the most destinations of any area airport. LAX is also the most crowded of the L.A. airports, with the longest security and check-in lines. If you can find a way around flying into LAX, do so. One option is to fly into other airports in the area, including **Bob Hope Airport** (BUR, 2627 N. Hollywood Way, Burbank, 818/840-8840, www.burbankairport.com). It may be a slightly longer drive to your final destination, but it can be well worth it. If you must use LAX, be sure to arrive a minimum of two hours ahead of your domestic flight time for your flight out, and consider three hours on busy holidays.

Train

Amtrak (800/872-7245, www.amtrak.com) has an active rail hub in Los Angeles. Most trains come in to **Union Station** (800 N. Alameda St., 323/466-3876), which has been owned by the Los Angeles Metropolitan Transportation Authority (MTA, www.metro.net) since 2011. From Union Station, you can get to the Bay Area, Redding, and eventually Seattle on the *Coast Starlight* train, or you can take the *Pacific Surfliner* down the coast to San Diego. The *San Joaquin* runs out to Sacramento via the Bay Area. To get to and from L.A. from the East, the *Southwest Chief* comes in from Chicago, Kansas City, and Albuquerque. The famed *Sunset Limited* runs from Jacksonville, Florida, to New Orleans, El Paso, and then Los Angeles.

From Union Station, which also acts as a Metro hub, you can take Metro Rail to various parts of Los Angeles. The **Metro** (www.metro. net, cash fare $1.50, day pass $5) runs both the subway Metro Rail system and a network of buses throughout the L.A. metropolitan area. You can pay on board a bus if you have exact change. Otherwise, purchase a ticket or a day pass from the ticket vending machines at all Metro Rail Stations.

Some buses run 24 hours. The Metro Rail lines start running as early as 4:30 A.M. and don't stop until as late as 1:30 A.M. See the website (www.metro.net) for route maps, timetables, and fare details.

Sights

The only problem you'll have with the sights of Los Angeles and its surrounding towns is finding a way to see enough of them to satisfy you. You'll find museums, streets, ancient art, and modern production studios ready to welcome you throughout the sprawling cityscape.

DOWNTOWN AND VICINITY

Downtown L.A. has tall, glass-coated skyscrapers creating an urban skyline, sports arenas, rich neighborhoods, poor neighborhoods, and endless shopping opportunities. Most of all, it has some of the best and most unique cultural icons in L.A. County.

After years of talk about revitalization, ambitious architectural projects, such as architect Frank Gehry's Walt Disney Concert Hall and the Cathedral of Our Lady of the Angels, have finally made good on hopes for Downtown's renewal. Elsewhere in Downtown, the Museum of Contemporary Art features works by titans of 20th-century art. Koreatown is thriving in the 21st century. Little Tokyo is home to restaurants, shops, an Asian American theater, and the Japanese American National Museum. Neighboring Chinatown, although much less vibrant than other Chinatowns, has spawned a booming gallery scene along Chung King Road. Even kids get a kick out of the museums and parkland of Exposition Park. Downtown makes a great start for any trip to Los Angeles.

El Pueblo de Los Angeles Historical Monument

For a city that is famously berated for lacking a sense of its own past, El Pueblo de Los Angeles (Olvera St. between Spring St. and Alameda St., 213/625-3800, 213/485-6855, or 213/628-1274, elpueblo.lacity.org/elpssmuseums.htm, visitors center daily 10 A.M.–3 P.M.) is a veritable crash course in history. Just a short distance from where Spanish colonists first settled in 1781, the park's 44 acres house 27 buildings—11 of which are open to the public as businesses or museums—dating from 1818 to 1926.

Facing a central courtyard, Our Lady Queen of the Angels Catholic Church still hosts a steady stream of baptisms and other services. On the southern end of the courtyard stands a cluster of historic buildings, the most prominent being Pico House, a hotel built in 1869–1870. The restored Old Plaza Firehouse, which dates to 1884, exhibits firefighting memorabilia from the late 19th–early 20th centuries. And on Main Street, Sepulveda House serves as the Pueblo's visitors center and features period furniture dating to 1887.

Off the central square is Olvera Street, an open-air market packed with mariachis, clothing shops, crafts stalls, and taquerias. Hidden in the midst of this tourist market is the Avila Adobe, a squat adobe structure said to be the oldest standing house in Los Angeles. The home now functions as a museum detailing the lifestyle of the Mexican ranchero culture that thrived here before the Mexican–American War.

Free 50-minute docent-led tours (213/628-1274, www.lasangelitas.org, 10 A.M., 11 A.M., and noon Tues.–Sat.) start at the Las Angelitas del Pueblo office, next to the Old Plaza Firehouse on the southeast end of the Plaza. Some of the best times to visit are during festive annual celebrations like the Blessing of the Animals, around Easter, and, of course, Cinco de Mayo.

Cathedral of Our Lady of the Angels

Standing on a hillside next to the Hollywood Freeway, the colossal concrete Cathedral of Our Lady of the Angels (555 W. Temple St., 213/680-5200, www.olacathedral.org, 6:30 A.M.–6 P.M. Mon.–Fri., 9 A.M.–6 P.M. Sat., 7 A.M.–6 P.M. Sun. Nov.–Apr., 6:30 A.M.–7 P.M. Mon.–Fri., 9 A.M.–7 P.M. Sat., 7 A.M.–7 P.M. Sun. Mar.–Oct., open later for special events)—the first Roman Catholic cathedral to be built in the United States in 25 years and the

THREE DAYS IN LOS ANGELES

Los Angeles is notoriously sprawling, but in a few days, it's possible to hit some of the area's top spots, including the best of the beaches, the Magic Kingdom, and even a dash of Hollywood glamour.

DAY 1

After breakfast, drive to **Hollywood Boulevard.** Check out the movie-star handprints in the cement outside of the historic **Chinese Theatre** (page 347). Poster and memorabilia shops abound, so pick up a still from your favorite movie.

Then it's off to Beverly Hills for a light lunch and an afternoon of window-shopping and star-spotting. Try one of L.A.'s top see-and-be-seen lunch spots, **The Ivy** (page 386), where celebs dine when they want to get photographed. (Call ahead for a reservation.) Fashionistas will want to head to the glamorous designer shopping district anchored by **Rodeo Drive** (page 367). You'll find signs to a number of public parking lots; there's a large one on Beverly Drive.

If you're more interested in high culture, spend the afternoon at **The Getty Center** (page 352). (You'll want to reserve tickets in advance.) Take in dizzying Pacific views, wander through the gardens, and tour the museum's small but outstanding collections.

For dinner, sample the luxurious slices at **Pizzeria Mozza** (page 385) on Highland Avenue, or some luscious pasta at sister restaurant **Osteria Mozza,** located next door.

After dinner, cruise the nightlife scene along the **Sunset Strip,** where revelers flock to legendary music clubs like the **Whisky A Go Go The Roxy Theatre,** and **The Troubadour** (page 362).

Head to Hollywood for a drink at the historic watering hole **Formosa Café** (page 360). With dimly lit booths and photos of legendary screen stars on the walls, the Formosa – one of L.A.'s oldest bars – looks right out of old Hollywood.

If an attack of late-night munchies strikes,

cap off your night with another local tradition – an after-hours hot dog at **Pink's Famous Hot Dogs** (page 385). Rain or shine, this venerable stand draws a line deep into the night.

DAY 2

Start your day with orange pancakes or huevos rancheros and European-style espresso at **Cora's Coffee Shoppe** (page 387) in Santa Monica, a local favorite with a lovely patio. Head south to the **Venice Canals** (page 356) for an after-breakfast stroll. Originally built as a Venetian-themed amusement park, this network of canals is now a quiet residential district of waterways lined with bungalows.

Pack a picnic lunch, hop in the car, and head north for dazzling views and ocean breezes along the gorgeous **Pacific Coast Highway.** The highway connects Santa Monica with Malibu and its beautiful beaches, giving you plenty of opportunity to hit the sand and catch some rays. If you've had your fill of sunshine, spend your time in Malibu touring the small art collection at the **Getty Villa** (page 357) instead. End your day with seaside seafood at **Neptune's Net** (page 390), or go more romantic (and more upscale) at **Catch** (page 390).

Alternately, you may choose to head south to one of the Orange County beaches. Beachcombers might choose **Laguna Beach** (page 410), while surfers will want to experience the world-famous breaks at **Huntington Beach** (page 409). If you spend the night in the O.C., you will be well-situated for Day 3.

DAY 3

Let your inner child run free at **Disneyland** (page 393). Spend the day riding rides, rambling through crowds, and watching parades at the most lovingly crafted theme park in the world. For a full on Disney-riffic experience, enjoy a meal at the **Blue Bayou Restaurant** (page 400) overlooking the Pirates of the Caribbean ride, and spend the night at the **Disneyland Hotel** (page 398).

third largest cathedral in the world—has been a vital part of the revitalization effort in L.A.'s beleaguered Downtown. Since its 2002 opening, the cathedral, which serves as much more than a place of worship, has attracted millions of visitors for free guided tours and such events as Christmas and Chinese New Year.

Every aspect of Spanish architect Rafael Moneo's design is monumental: the 25-ton bronze doors, 27,000 square feet of clerestory windows of translucent alabaster, and the 156-foot-high campanile topped with a 25-foot-tall cross. The cathedral, with seating for 3,000, is merely one part of a larger complex that houses the archbishop's residence, a conference center, and an expansive public courtyard. Critics of the lavish, nearly $190 million price tag dubbed the cathedral the "Taj Mahony" after Cardinal Roger Mahony, who oversaw the project. Others questioned the archdiocese's plan to counter operating expenses by offering crypts in the cathedral's underground mausoleum to wealthy patrons willing to donate $50,000 or more for such a privileged resting place.

The construction of a massive cathedral in the 21st century could have easily been a major anachronism. But the building's sleek design suggests a more forward-looking posture for the Catholic Church. The cathedral is proving to be a monument not just for the more than four million Catholics in L.A.; with events like music recitals, wine tastings, and art exhibitions, it welcomes the city as a whole.

Union Station

When Union Station (800 N. Alameda St., Amtrak 800/872-7245, www.amtrak.com, 24 hours daily) opened in 1939, 1.5 million people supposedly passed through its doors in the first three days, all wanting to witness what is now considered the last of the nation's great rail stations. Architects John and Donald Parkinson's design—an elegant mixture of Spanish mission and modern styles, incorporating vaulted arches, marble floors, and a 135-foot clock tower—was a fitting monument to the soaring aspirations of a burgeoning Los Angeles.

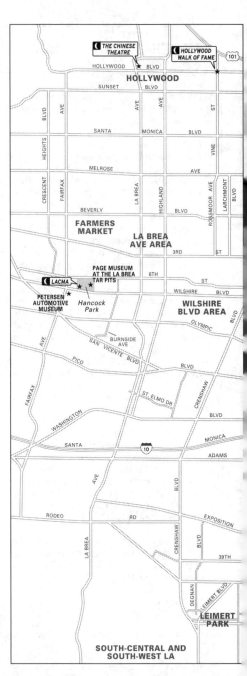

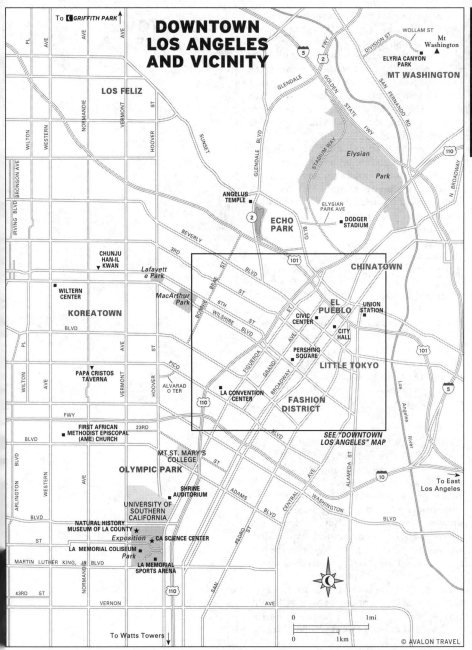

DOWNTOWN LOS ANGELES AND VICINITY

To **GRIFFITH PARK**

WOLLAM ST

Mt Washington ▲

ELYRIA CANYON PARK

MT WASHINGTON

LOS FELIZ

GLENDALE

Elysian

Park

ANGELUS TEMPLE

ECHO PARK

ELYSIAN PARK AVE

DODGER STADIUM

CHINATOWN

CHUNJU HAN-IL KWAN

Lafayette Park

WILTERN CENTER

MacArthur Park

KOREATOWN

BLVD

WILSHIRE BLVD

EL PUEBLO

UNION STATION

CIVIC CENTER

CITY HALL

PERSHING SQUARE

LITTLE TOKYO

PAPA CRISTOS TAVERNA

PICO

ALVARADO TER

LA CONVENTION CENTER

FASHION DISTRICT

FWY

SEE "DOWNTOWN LOS ANGELES" MAP

FIRST AFRICAN METHODIST EPISCOPAL (AME) CHURCH

23RD

MT ST. MARY'S COLLEGE

OLYMPIC PARK

To East Los Angeles

SHRINE AUDITORIUM

ADAMS

WASHINGTON

UNIVERSITY OF SOUTHERN CALIFORNIA

NATURAL HISTORY MUSEUM OF LA COUNTY ★

Exposition Park

★ CA SCIENCE CENTER

LA MEMORIAL COLISEUM

MARTIN LUTHER KING, JR BLVD

LA MEMORIAL SPORTS ARENA

43RD ST

VERNON

AVE

0   1mi

0   1km

To Watts Towers ↓

© AVALON TRAVEL

The station's immediate public success masked a decades-long political struggle over its construction. Civic planners first floated the idea of a unified terminal as early as 1911 but encountered stiff opposition from the major railroads, all of which feared the increased competition that a consolidated terminal would bring. After an entrenched campaign for public opinion, a site was finally approved by voters in 1926.

During the 1940s, Union Station thrived as a hub for both civilian and military traffic, and its stucco facade became a familiar backdrop in scores of classic films. But with the ascendancy of the automobile, the station fell into decline. By the 1970s the terminal was more often populated by pigeons than people.

Since the 1990s, however, the station has experienced a modest renaissance. Today, as the hub for the city's commuter rail network, it houses L.A.'s first modern subway line, which runs from Union Station to the mid-Wilshire and Hollywood districts. In 2003, the Metro Gold Line linked Downtown L.A. to Pasadena, with a future goal of extending east to Montclair. But even if your travel plans aren't locomotive, the station offers a rare glimpse of a more glamorous era of transport.

MOCA

The Museum of Contemporary Art, Los Angeles (250 S. Grand Ave., 213/626-6222 or 213/621-1741, www.moca.org, 11 A.M.–5 P.M. Mon. and Fri., 11 A.M.–8 P.M. Thurs., 11 A.M.–6 P.M. Sat.–Sun., adults $10, students and seniors $5, under age 12 free) is better known to its friends as MOCA. Here you'll see an array of artwork created between 1940 and yesterday afternoon. Highlights of the permanent collections include pop art and abstract expressionism from Europe and the United States. MOCA has two other locations in the area: **The Geffen Contemporary at MOCA** (152 N. Central Ave., Los Angeles) and the **MOCA Pacific Design Center** (8687 Melrose Ave., West Hollywood).

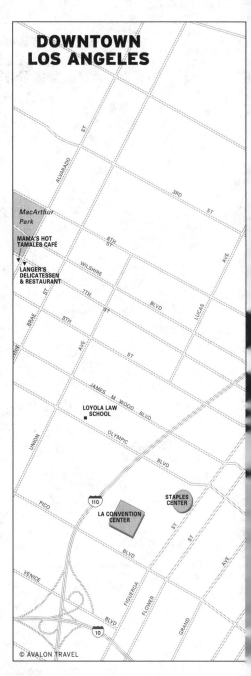

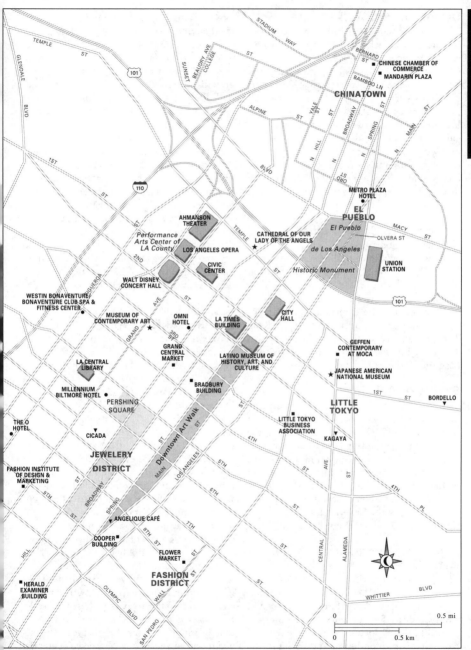

Downtown Art Walk

The dramatic sculptures and fountains adorning these two blocks (300–500 Hope St.) include Alexander Calder's enormous *Four Arches* (1974) beside the Bank of America Plaza and Nancy Graves's whimsical *Sequi* (1986) near the Wells Fargo Center. A free, self-guided, public Downtown Art Walk (213/617-4929, http://downtownartwalk.org, hours vary by gallery but usually noon–9 P.M.) on the second Thursday evening of each month centers predominantly on the galleries in the area bounded by Spring, Main, 2nd, and 9th Streets, but it spreads out to the Calder and Graves pieces on Hope Street.

Los Angeles Central Library

The Central Library (630 W. 5th St., 213/228-7000, www.lapl.org/central, 10 A.M.–5:30 P.M. Mon., Wed., Fri., and Sat., 10 A.M.–8 P.M. Tues. and Thurs., closed Sun.) brings a bit of studious quiet to the business and bustle of Downtown. The exterior's Egyptian influence owes much to the discovery of King Tut's tomb in 1922, the year the library was designed. Enter at Flower Street to visit the Maguire Gardens.

Bradbury Building

One of several historic L.A. structures featured in the movies *Chinatown* (1974), *Blade Runner* (1982), and *(500) Days of Summer* (2009), the 1893 Bradbury Building (304 S. Broadway) is an office building that wows filmmakers with wrought-iron staircases and large skylights in its light-filled atrium. On Saturdays, three-hour docent-led tours (reservations required, $10) are run by the Los Angeles Conservancy (213/623-2489, www.laconservancy.org).

Japanese American National Museum

The Japanese American National Museum (369 E. 1st St., 213/625-0414, www.janm. org, 11 A.M.–5 P.M. Tues.–Sun., 11 A.M.–8 P.M. Thurs., adults $9, students and seniors $5, under age 6 free) focuses on the experience of Japanese people coming to and living in the United States. Japanese immigrants came by the thousands to California—one of the easiest and most pleasant places in the United States to get to from Japan. From the beginning they had a hard time of it, facing unending prejudice, exclusion, fear, and outright hatred. Despite this, the tenacious immigrants persisted, even after the horrific treatment of the Japanese American population by the U.S. government during World War II. Japanese culture has folded into the bizarre mix that is the United States. It is especially influential in California, where sushi bars are almost as common as diners in urban centers, and whole nurseries devoted to bonsai gardening thrive. This museum shows the Japanese American experience in vivid detail, with photos and artifacts telling much of the story. You'll also find galleries sheltering temporary exhibitions, from astonishing displays of ikebana floral art to a show devoted to the *Giant Robot* comic book.

Fashion Institute of Design and Marketing

Have you come to L.A. for the fabulous designer clothes, but your credit cards are screaming in agony? Is your all-time favorite TV show *Project Runway*? Then L.A.'s got the perfect museum for you. The Fashion Institute of Design and Marketing (FIDM) Museum and Galleries (919 S. Grand Ave., 800/624-1200, www.fidm.edu, 10 A.M.–4 P.M. Tues.–Sat., hours vary by exhibit, free) are open to the public, giving costume buffs and clotheshorses a window into high fashion, Hollywood costume design, and the world of a fashion design school. Check the website for current and upcoming exhibitions at the museum. Each winter around award season, the museum shows off a collection of costumes from the previous year's movies, highlighting the film honored with the Oscar for Best Costume Design. Through the rest of the year, FIDM pulls from its collection of more than 10,000 costumes and textiles to create exhibits based on style, era, movie genre, and whatever else the curators dream up. Parking is available in the underground garage for a fee. When you enter the building, tell the folks at the security desk that you're headed for the museum. A small but fun museum shop offers student work, unique accessories, and more.

Also housed in the FIDM building is the **Annette Green Perfume Museum** (10 A.M.–4 P.M. Mon.–Sat., free). This is the world's first museum dedicated to scent and the role of perfume in society.

Natural History Museum

If you'd like your kids to have some fun with an educational purpose, take them to the Natural History Museum (900 Exposition Blvd., 213/763-3466, www.nhm.org, 9:30 A.M.–5 P.M. daily, adults $12, teens and seniors $8, children $5, parking $8). This huge museum features many amazing galleries; some are transformed into examples of mammal habitats, while others display artifacts of various peoples indigenous to the western hemisphere. The Discovery Center welcomes children with a wide array of live animals and insects, plus hands-on displays that let kids learn by touching as well as looking. The chaparral exhibit is a favorite, and it provides a multisensory experience that includes smell as well as sight and sound. Dinosaur lovers can spend a whole day examining the museum's collection of fossils and models, which include a tyrannosaur skull. Be sure to visit the megamouth shark as you walk through; it's one of only 17 examples of this species ever discovered by humans. Rock nuts flock to the Natural History Museum to see the fabulous gem and mineral display, complete with gold and a vault filled with rare precious stones. If you're interested in the natural history and culture of California, be sure to spend some time in the Lando Hall of California History.

The Natural History Museum sits within the larger Exposition Park complex. The Natural History Museum Grill is open 10 A.M.–4 P.M. daily. All exhibits are accessible for both wheelchairs and strollers, but ask at the ticket booths if you need special assistance to tour the museum. Do be aware that the surrounding neighborhood can be rough, so don't plan to explore the area around the museum on foot.

California Science Center

Another gem of Exposition Park, the exhibits at the California Science Center (39th and Figueroa St., 323/724-3623, www.california-sciencecenter.org, 10 A.M.–5 P.M. daily, admission free, parking $10) focus on the notable achievements and gathered knowledge of humankind. Some of the best traveling scientific exhibits stop here, and permanent exhibits start before you even enter the building with the outdoor Science Plaza. Once inside, you'll find galleries dedicated to air and space technology, life as we know it, and human creativity. The central Science Court, not part of the free admission to the center, delights both children and adults with exhibits they can get involved with. Visitors can ride a bike on a three-story-high wire, climb a cliff, or check out a motion-based simulator.

Many people come to the California Science Center for the IMAX theater (adults $8.25,

California Science Center

seniors, teens, and students $6, children $5), which is open daily and shows educational films on its tremendous seven-story screen. Your IMAX tickets also get you onto the rideable attractions of the Science Court.

LOS FELIZ

East of Hollywood, northwest of Downtown, Los Feliz, doggedly pronounced by most locals as "Los FEEL-is," is home to an eclectic mix of retired professionals, Armenian immigrants, and movie-industry hipsters lured by the bohemian vibe, mid-century modern architecture, and the neighborhood's proximity to Griffith Park. Despite gentrification brought by waves of wealthier and more fashionable residents, this enclave and its neighbor to the southeast, Silver Lake, have so far managed to retain their unique, laid-back flavor.

🅒 Griffith Park

Griffith Park (Los Feliz Blvd., Zoo Blvd., or Forest Lawn Dr., 323/913-4688, www.laparks.org, 5 A.M.–10:30 P.M. daily), sometimes called

"L.A.'s Central Park," has an endless array of attractions and amenities to suit every style of visitor. If you love the stars, visit the recently renovated **Griffith Observatory** (2800 East Observatory Rd., 213/473-0800, www.griffithobs.org, noon–10 P.M. Tues.–Fri., 10 A.M.–10 P.M. Sat.–Sun., free), where free telescopes are available and experienced demonstrators help visitors gaze at the stars—the ones in the sky, that is. Golfers can choose among two 18-hole courses, one nine-hole course, and a nine-hole, par-three course located on the parklands. A swimming pool cools visitors in the summer. You'll find a baseball field, basketball and tennis courts, children's playgrounds, and endless miles of hiking and horseback riding trails that thread their way far into the backcountry of the park.

If you prefer a more structured park experience, try the **L.A. Zoo and Botanical Gardens** (5333 Zoo Dr., 323/644-4200, www.lazoo.org, 10 A.M.–5 P.M. daily, adults $14, children $9, free parking). If the weather is poor (yes, it does rain in L.A.), step inside

Griffith Observatory

the **Museum of the American West** at the Autry National Center (4700 Western Heritage Way, 323/667-2000, www.theautry. org, 10 A.M.–4 P.M. Tues.–Fri., 11 A.M.–4 P.M. Sat.–Sun., adults $10, students and seniors $6, children $4). Kids love riding the trains of the operating miniature railroad, both the Travel Town Railroad (5200 Zoo Dr., 323/662-9678, www.griffithparktrainrides. com, 10 A.M.–3:30 P.M. Mon.–Fri., 10 A.M.– 4:30 P.M. Sat.–Sun., $2.50) from the **Travel Town Museum** (5200 Zoo Dr., 323/662-5874, http://traveltown.org, 10 A.M.–4 P.M. Mon.–Fri., 10 A.M.–6 P.M. Sat.–Sun.) and the Griffith Park & Southern Railroad (4400 Crystal Springs Dr., 323/664-6903, www. griffithparktrainrides.com, 10 A.M.–4:15 P.M. Mon.–Fri., 10 A.M.–4:30 P.M. Sat.–Sun., $2.50).

Griffith Park has played host to many production companies over the years, with its land and buildings providing backdrops for many major films. Scenes from *Rebel Without a Cause* were filmed here, as were parts of the first two *Back to the Future* movies. Its use is appropriate to the park's rich history. Much of the land that now makes up the 4,210-acre park was donated by miner and philanthropist Griffith J. Griffith (really). It has changed much over the years, but remains one of Los Angeles's great prizes.

The **Hollywood Sign** sits on Mount Lee, which is part of the park and indelibly part of the mystique of Hollywood. A strenuous five-mile hike will lead you to an overlook just above and behind the sign.

Hollyhock House

Hollyhock House (4800 Hollywood Blvd., 323/644-6269, www.hollyhockhouse.net, $7, seniors $2, under age 18 free) was the first L.A. home designed by Frank Lloyd Wright. Finished in 1923, it was built for Aline Barnsdall, a patron of the arts, and is located in what is now Barnsdall Art Park. Hollyhocks, Barnsdall's favorite flower, are an elemental theme in the decor.

HOLLYWOOD

You won't find blocks of movie studios in Hollywood, and few stars walk its streets except on premiere evenings. It's an odd irony that what the world perceives to be the epicenter of the film industry has little left of that industry beyond its tourist destinations. The only "real" movie business remaining are the blockbuster premieres at the major movie theaters here. Most of the other destinations range from the oversold to the downright kitschy. But still, if you've ever had a soft spot for Hollywood glamour or American camp, come and check out the crowds and bustle of downtown Tinseltown (and be aware that no local would *ever* call it that). Hollywood is also famous for its street corners. While the most stuff sits at Hollywood and Highland, the best-known corner is certainly Hollywood and Vine.

Hollywood Walk of Fame

One of the most recognizable facets of Hollywood is its star-studded Walk of Fame (Hollywood Blvd. from La Brea Ave. to Vine St., 323/469-8311, www.walkoffame.com). This area, portrayed in countless movies, contains more than 2,400 five-pointed stars honoring both real people and fictional characters who have contributed significantly to the entertainment industry and the legend that is Hollywood. Each pink star is set in a charcoal-colored square and has its honoree's name in bronze. The little symbols—movie camera, TV set, record, radio microphone, and tragedy-comedy masks—designate which part of the entertainment industry the honoree is recognized for. Eight stars were laid in August 1958 to demonstrate what the Walk would look like—Olive Borden, Ronald Colman, Louise Fazenda, Preston Foster, Burt Lancaster, Edward Sedgwick, Ernest Torrance, and Joanne Woodward. Legal battles delayed the actual construction until February 1960, and the walk was dedicated in November 1960. Gene Autry has five stars on the walk, one for each industry (film, TV, radio, recording, and

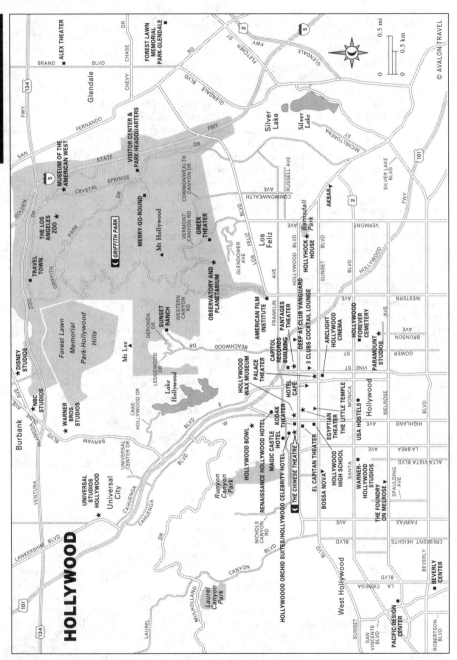

live theater) he contributed to. At each of the four corners of Hollywood and Vine, check out the four moons that honor the three Apollo 11 astronauts—Neil Armstrong, Michael Collins, and Edwin E. "Buzz" Aldrin Jr. Also look for your favorite cartoon characters: Kermit the Frog, Mickey Mouse, and Bugs Bunny are all honored on the Walk of Fame.

You don't need to pay to get into anything, just get out on the sidewalk and start to stroll; the complete walk is about 3.5 miles. You'll be looking down at the stars, so watch out for other pedestrians crowding the sidewalks in this visitor-dense area. At the edges of the Walk of Fame, you'll find blank stars waiting to be filled by up-and-comers making their mark on Tinseltown. If you desperately need to find a specific star and want help doing so, you can take a guided tour of the Walk, but really, it's a waste of money—careful reading and an on-line map (www.gocalifornia.about.com/od/calamenu/a/walkfame.htm) will find you everyone's star you need to see.

Hollywood Wax Museum

It immortalizes your favorite stars, all right. If you want to see the Hollywood heavyweights all dressed up in costume and completely unable to run away, visit the Hollywood Wax Museum (6767 Hollywood Blvd., 323/462-5991, www.hollywoodwaxmuseum.com, 10 A.M.–midnight daily, adults $16, children $9). You can't miss it, since the brilliant sign lights up a good chunk of Hollywood Boulevard, especially at night. Inside, you'll see everyone from Lucille Ball to Captain Jack Sparrow. The shtick of this wax museum is, of course, movies. The exhibits are re-creations of the sets of all sorts of films, and as you pass through you'll be right in the action (if staring at eerie, life-size wax likenesses of real people can be called action). You can even get a glimpse of stars on the red carpet at an awards show–style set.

The Hollywood Wax Museum first opened to amazed crowds in February 1965. To this day, it remains inexplicably popular with visitors and locals alike.

If you need yet another cotton-candy

museum experience, right across the street is the **Guinness World of Records Museum** (6764 Hollywood Blvd., 323/463-6433, www.ripleyattractions.com, 10 A.M.–midnight daily, adults $17, children $9). Here you'll find exhibits describing the records related in the book of the same name.

◖ The Chinese Theatre

You can't miss the Chinese Theatre (6801 Hollywood Blvd., 323/461-3331, www.chinesetheatres.com), perhaps more recognizably known as Grauman's Chinese Theatre, on Hollywood Boulevard. With its elaborate 90-foot-tall Chinese temple gateway and unending crowd of visitors, the Chinese Theatre may be the most visited and recognizable movie theater in the world. Inside the courtyard you'll find handprints and footprints of legendary Hollywood stars. Be sure to stop and admire the bells, dogs, and other Chinese artifacts in the courtyard—most are the genuine article, imported from China by special permit in the 1920s. The theater was built by Sid Grauman

the Chinese Theatre

SEEING STARS

When you hear SoCal denizens talk about "The Valley," they're always talking about the San Fernando Valley. This is the true home of many of the major TV and movie studios. It's also the reputed origin of valley girls, valley speak, and the teen shopping mall culture. Valley suburbs include Burbank, Sun Valley, North Hollywood, and the strangely underwhelming San Fernando.

One of the biggest draws of the Valley is the plethora of major movie and TV studios studding the landscape. Many of these offer tours to visitors who long to see the sets and behind-the-scenes actions of their favorite films and shows. A great place to start is the **Warner Bros. Studio** (3400 Riverside Dr., Burbank, 818/972-8687, www.wbstudiotour.com, 8:30 A.M.-4 P.M. Mon.-Fri., VIP Tour $49 pp, parking at Gate 6 $7). The tour lasts a little over two hours: You'll ride in carts as you go from place to place through the vast spaces of the studio and back lot. Making both movies and TV shows, the WB tour takes you backstage to the sets and scenes of current productions. You'll also get to tour an array of historic sets, and you'll wind up at the Warner Bros. Memorabilia museum. For an even more in-depth look at the inner workings of Warner Bros., check out the Deluxe Tour (10:20 A.M. Mon.-Fri., $250 pp, parking

at Gate 6 $7), which lasts five full hours and includes lunch in the Commissary Fine Dining Room. If you're lucky, you might catch a glimpse of one of your favorite stars eating a sandwich (celebrities – they're just like us). The WB recommends that you purchase your tour tickets in advance; you can call or buy them on the website.

The tour at **NBC Studios** (3000 W. Alameda Ave., Burbank, 818/840-3537, tours 9 A.M.-3 P.M. Mon.-Fri., adults $8.50, seniors $7.50, children $5) takes you into the wide and often obscure world of network television. Unlike the movie studios, NBC films live and daily shows every day – you'll get to see the working sets of *Days of Our Lives* and *The Tonight Show*. In addition, the network has preserved the legendary sets of classic TV shows for your viewing pleasure. Check out the tour-available areas for wardrobe, makeup, and set design. You'll visit the real props- and set-construction departments. The NBC studio tour lasts just over an hour and requires you to walk for the bulk of the time.

If you want to be part of the action, show up early to stand in line for free tickets to *The Tonight Show* (www.nbc.com/the-tonight-show/tickets). Giveaways begin at 8 A.M. daily, or you can send away via snail mail six or more weeks in advance to guarantee yourself seats.

and opened in all its splendor on May 18, 1927, with the premiere of *The King of Kings*. For the first time, stars swanned up the red carpet to the cheers (and eventual riot) of the throng of thousands of fans gathered outside. The next day, the public was allowed into the now hallowed theater.

The studios hold premieres at the Chinese Theatre all the time. Check the website for showtimes and ticket information. The Chinese Theatre has only one screen but seats over 1,000 people per showing. While you're welcome to crowd the sidewalk to try to catch a glimpse of the stars at a premiere, be aware that most of these are private events.

Egyptian Theater

Even before Grauman's Chinese, Hollywood had the Egyptian Theater (6712 Hollywood Blvd., 323/466-3456, www.americancinematheque.com/egyptian/egypt.htm, $10, students and seniors $9). Built by the auspices of the legendary Sid Grauman, the Egyptian was the first of the grandiose movie houses build in Hollywood proper and a follower of those in Downtown Los Angeles. King Tut's tomb had been discovered in 1922, and the glorified Egyptian styling of the theater followed the trend for all things Egyptian that followed. The massive courtyard and the stage both boasted columns, sphinxes, and other

Egyptian-esque decor. The first movie to premiere at the Egyptian was *Robin Hood,* in 1922, followed nine months later by premiere of *The Ten Commandments.* In the 1920s, the showing of a film was preceded by an elaborate live "prologue" featuring real actors in costume on a stage before the screen (the early ancestry of the *Rocky Horror Picture Show*). The Egyptian's stage was second to none, and the prologue of *The Ten Commandments* was billed as the most elaborate to date.

After a haul through the 1950s as a reserved-seat, long-run movie house, the Egyptian fell into disrepair and eventually closed. A massive renovation completed in 1998 restored it to its former glory. Today, you can get tickets to an array of old-time films, or take a morning tour to get a glimpse at the history of this magnificent old theater. Expect to pay $5–20 for parking in one of the nearby lots.

Hollywood Forever Cemetery

The final resting place of such Hollywood legends as Rudolph Valentino, Marion Davies, and Douglas Fairbanks, this formerly run-down cemetery (6000 Santa Monica Blvd., 323/469-1181, www.hollywoodforever.com) received a dramatic makeover and now offers live funeral webcasts.

Paramount Studios

Paramount (5555 Melrose Ave., 323/956-5000, www.paramountstudios.com) is the only major movie studio still operating in Hollywood proper. The wrought-iron gates that greet visitors were erected to deter adoring Rudolph Valentino fans in the 1920s. Call for tour information.

Mulholland Drive

As you drive north out of central Hollywood into the residential part of the neighborhood, you will find folks on street corners hawking maps of stars' homes on Mulholland Drive (entrance west of U.S. 101 via Barham Blvd. exit) and its surrounding neighborhoods. Whether you choose to pay up to $10 for a photocopied sheet of dubious information is up to you.

What's certain is that you can drive the famed road yourself. When you reach the ridge, you'll see why so many of the intensely wealthy in Los Angeles choose to make their homes here. From the ridgeline, on clear days you can see down into the L.A. Basin and the coast to the west, and the fertile land of the San Fernando Valley to the east. Whether you care about movie-star homes or not, the view itself is worth the trip, especially if it has rained recently and the smog is down. You won't see the facade of Britney Spears's multimillion-dollar hideaway facing the street, but a few homes do face the road—most boasting mid-century modern architecture. If you can see them, they probably don't belong to movie stars, who guard their privacy from the endless intrusion of paparazzi and fans.

LA BREA, FAIRFAX, AND MIRACLE MILE

This midtown district can seem a bit of a mishmash, lacking an overarching identity of its own. And yet the area's streets are among the best known and most heavily trafficked in Los Angeles.

Lined with fabric emporiums, antiques dealers, and contemporary furniture design shops, Beverly Boulevard and La Brea Avenue north of Wilshire Boulevard are increasingly trendy haunts for interior decorators. Along bustling and pedestrian-friendly Fairfax Avenue, kosher bakeries and signs in Hebrew announce the presence of the neighborhood's sizable Jewish population. Around the corner on 3rd Street, the Farmers Market is one of L.A.'s historic gathering places. And farther south, Wilshire Boulevard is home to some of the city's many museums, including the Los Angeles County Museum of Art.

La Brea Tar Pits

Even if you've never been within 1,000 miles of California before, you've probably heard of the La Brea Tar Pits and the wonders found within them. But where once tour groups made their stinky way around crude fences protecting them from the pits, now paved paths lead around the most accessible pits, and others (mostly those that are in active excavation) are accessible by guided tour only. Nothing can stop the smell of the tar, or the slow bubbling of the shallow miasma of water that covers the tar.

If what interests you most are the fossilized contents of the tar pits, head for the beautiful **Page Museum** (5801 Wilshire Blvd., 323/934-7243, www.tarpits.org, 9:30 A.M.–5 P.M. daily, adults $11, students and seniors $8, children $5, parking $7–9). The Page contains the bones of many of the untold thousands of animals that became trapped in the sticky tar and met their fate there. The museum's reasonably small size and easy-to-understand interpretive signs make it great for kids and good for a shorter stop for grown-ups. You'll see some amazing skeletal remains, including sloths the size of Clydesdale horses. Genuine mammoths died and were fossilized in the tar pits, as were the tiniest of mice and about a zillion dire wolves. One of the coolest things for science geeks is the big windowed cage housing the paleontologists at work. You can watch them cleaning,

examining, sorting, and cataloging bones from the most recent excavations.

◖ Los Angeles County Museum of Art

Travelers who desperately need a break from the endless, shiny, and mindless entertainments of L.A. can find respite and solace in the Los Angeles County Museum of Art (5905 Wilshire Blvd., 323/857-6000, www.lacma.org, noon–8 P.M. Mon.–Tues. and Thurs., noon–9 P.M. Fri., 11 A.M.–8 P.M. Sat.–Sun., adults $15, seniors and students with ID $10, under age 18 free). Better known to its friends as LACMA, this large museum complex prides itself on a diverse array of collections and exhibitions of art from around the world, from the ancient to the most ultramodern. With nine full-size buildings filled with galleries, don't expect to get through the whole thing in an hour, or even a full day. You'll see all forms of art here, from classic painting and sculpture to all sorts of decorative arts (that is, ceramics, jewelry, metalwork, and more). All major

Los Angeles County Museum of Art

cultural groups are represented, so you can check out Islamic, Southeast Asian, European, and Californian art, plus more. Specialties of LACMA include Japanese art and artifacts in the beautifully designed Pavilion for Japanese Art and the costumes and textiles of the Doris Stein Research Center. Several galleries of LACMA West are dedicated to art and craft for children. Perhaps best of all, some of the world's most prestigious traveling exhibitions come to LACMA; past exhibitions have included the works of Salvador Dalí and a new take on Tutankhamen.

You'll do a lot of walking from gallery to gallery and building to building at LACMA. Inquire at one of the two welcome centers for wheelchairs. Not all the buildings are connected; you must walk outside to get to the Japanese Pavilion and LACMA West. The complex is equipped with two full-service museum cafés, an ATM, and a gift and book shop. And finally, if you're in need of some fine rental artwork, LACMA can hook you up.

If you prefer automotive artistry to more conventional forms, head across the street from LACMA to the **Petersen Automotive Museum** (6060 Wilshire Blvd., 323/930-2277, www.petersen.org, 10 A.M.–6 P.M. Tues.–Sun., adults $10, seniors $8, children $3, students or active military with ID $5, parking $2–8).

Farmers Market
Begun in 1934 as a tailgate co-op for a handful of fruit farmers, the Farmers Market (6333 W. 3rd St., 323/933-9211 or 866/993-9211, www.farmersmarketla.com, 9 A.M.–9 P.M. Mon.–Fri., 9 A.M.–8 P.M. Sat., 10 A.M.–7 P.M. Sun.) quickly became an institution for Angelenos who flocked here to buy produce, flowers, and candy, or just to cool their cars and have a chat.

The market was built by entrepreneurs Roger Dahlhjelm and Fred Beck, who leased the land at 3rd Street and Fairfax from oil tycoon E. B. Gilmore; it quickly grew beyond its initial wooden produce stalls into a bustling arcade. A whitewashed clock tower went up in 1941, signaling the market's growing

importance as an ersatz village square for local residents. During the 1940s and 1950s, the tables at Magee's and Du-par's were crowded with regulars, and over the years the site has hosted circus acts, parades, petting zoos, and Gilmore's "Gas-a-teria," reputedly the world's first self-service gas station.

Today, the market remains a favorite locale for people-watching and, along with the adjacent shopping center, The Grove, now has over 30 restaurants and 50 shops hawking everything from hot sauce to stickers. Gourmands will find fresh fruit, chocolate truffles, sushi, gumbo, Mexican cuisine, and a plethora of other foods. There are even annual events, such as a vintage auto show in early June, free summer concerts, and a fall festival as well as weekly features such as live bands on Saturday evenings.

BEVERLY HILLS AND WEST HOLLYWOOD
Although the truly wealthy live above Hollywood on Mulholland Drive, in Bel Air, or on the beach at Malibu, there's still plenty of money floating around in Beverly Hills. Some of the world's best and most expensive shops sit on the streets of Beverly Hills. You'll also find more than adequate high-end culture in the area, which bleeds into West L.A. The division seems almost seamless now, compared to the tremendous class gash that used to exist between Beverly Hills and the infamous Sunset Strip.

Sunset Strip
A much shorter but equally famous stretch of road, the Sunset Strip really is part of Sunset Boulevard—specifically the part that runs through West Hollywood from the edge of Hollywood to the Beverly Hills city limits. The Strip exemplifies all that's grandiose and tacky about the L.A. entertainment industry. Few other places, even in California, boast about the number and glaring overstatement of their billboards. You'll also find many of the Strip's legendary rock clubs, such as **The Roxy** and the **Whisky a Go Go** and the infamous after-hours hangout **The Rainbow Bar**

& Grill. Decades worth of up-and-coming rock acts first made their names on the Strip and lived at the "Riot Hyatt."

If you last visited the Strip more than a decade ago, you might fear bringing your children to what was once a distinctly seedy neck of the woods. Then again, old-timers might be horrified now by the gentrification of the Strip. Today, a woman alone can stroll the street in comfort in daylight. At night, especially on weekends, no one's alone on the Strip. Don't plan to drive quickly or park on the street after dark; the crowds get big, complete with celebrity hounds hoping for a glimpse of their favorite star out for a night on the town.

WESTWOOD

Designed around the campus of UCLA and the Westwood Village commercial district, this community situated between Santa Monica and Beverly Hills won national recognition in the 1930s as a model of innovative suburban planning. And while the generic faces of nondescript offices and apartment blocks have since encroached on the area, especially to the west, recent slow-growth initiatives have preserved the heart of Westwood as one of L.A.'s most pleasant neighborhoods.

University of California, Los Angeles

From its original quad of 10 buildings, the University of California, Los Angeles (UCLA) campus (tours 310/825-8764, www.ucla.edu) has become the largest in the University of California system, with more than 400 buildings set on and around the 419 beautifully kept acres and a student population of nearly 40,000. Today its facilities include one of the top medical centers in the country, a library of more than eight million volumes, and a number of renowned performance venues, including Royce Hall and Schoenberg Hall.

Running from the south edge of the UCLA campus along Westwood Boulevard toward Wilshire Boulevard, the Westwood Village shopping district caters to a lively mix of students and local residents with a clutch of bookstores, record shops, and cafés. The district also boasts the highest density of movie theaters in the country, with a number of restored landmarks.

Getty Center

Located on a hilltop above the mansions of Brentwood and the 405 freeway, the Getty Center (1200 Getty Center Dr., 310/440-7300, www.getty.edu, 10 A.M.–5:30 P.M. Tues.–Fri. and Sun., 10 A.M.–9 P.M. Sat., admission free, parking $15) is famous for art and culture in Los Angeles. Donated by the family of J. Paul Getty to the people of Los Angeles, this museum features European art, sculpture, manuscripts, and European and American photos. The magnificent works are set in fabulous modern buildings with soaring architecture, and you're guaranteed to find something beautiful to catch your eye and feed your imagination. The spacious galleries have comfy sofas to let you sit back and take in the paintings and drawings. Be sure to take a stroll outdoors to admire the sculpture

TRAVIS CONKLIN/IMAGE COURTESY OF LA INC. THE LOS ANGELES CONVENTION AND VISITORS BUREAU

the Getty Center's Central Garden

collections on the lawns as well as the exterior architecture.

On a clear day, the views from the Getty, which sweep from Downtown L.A. clear west to the Pacific, are remarkable. But the museum pavilions themselves are also stunning. Richard Meier's striking design is multitextured, with exterior grids of metal and unfinished Italian travertine marble, similar to that used by the Romans to build the Colosseum. The blockish buildings have fountains, glass windows several stories high, and an open plan that permits intimate vistas of the city below.

SANTA MONICA, VENICE, AND MALIBU

When many people from around the world think of "L.A.," what they're really picturing are the beach communities skirting the coastline to the west and Los Angeles proper to the east. Some of the most famous and most expensive real estate in the world sits on this stretch of sand and earth. Of the communities that call the northern coast of L.A. County home,

the focal points are Malibu to the north, Santa Monica, and then Venice to the south.

Malibu doesn't look like a town or a city in the conventional sense. If you're searching for the historic downtown or the town center, give up; there isn't one. Instead, the "town" of Malibu stretches for more than 20 miles, hugging the beach the whole way. A few huge homes perch precariously on the mountains rising up over the coastline, also part of Malibu. Many beach-loving superstars make their homes here, and the price of a beach house can easily exceed $20 million.

A few more liberal and social stars prefer to purchase from among the closely packed dwellings of Venice Beach. A bastion of true California liberal-mindedness and the home of several famous landmarks, Venice might be the perfect (if expensive) place to take a movie-style L.A. beach vacation.

Santa Monica comes as close to a community of moderate means as you'll find in this region. With its fun-but-not-fancy pier, its inexpensive off-beach motels, and a huge variety

MICHELE & TOM GRIMM/IMAGE COURTESY OF LA INC. THE LOS ANGELES CONVENTION AND VISITORS BUREAU

Venice Boardwalk

of delicious inexpensive dining options, Santa Monica is a great choice for a family vacation.

◖ Santa Monica Pier

For the ultimate in SoCal beach kitsch, you can't miss the Santa Monica Pier (Ocean Ave. at Colorado Ave., 310/458-8901, www.santa-monicapier.org). As you walk the rather long stretch of concrete out over the water, you'll see an amazing array of carnival-style food stands, an arcade, a small amusement park, the smallest miniature golf course ever paid for by visitors, and restaurants leading out to the fishing area at the tip of the pier. The main attraction

is **Pacific Park** (310/260-8744, www.pacpark. com, 11 A.M.–11 P.M. Sun.–Thurs., 11 A.M.–12:30 A.M. Fri.–Sat., rides priced individually, $3–5 per ride, all-ride pass $16–22, parking $6–12). This park features a roller coaster, a scrambler, and the world's first solar-powered Ferris wheel. Several rides are geared for the younger set, and a 20-game midway provides fun for all ages. Beneath the pier lies a sandy beach with a decent surf break—one of the major attractions of the area in the summer.

You can drive onto the first half of the pier. Parking lots sit both on and beneath it, although your chances aren't great if you're trying

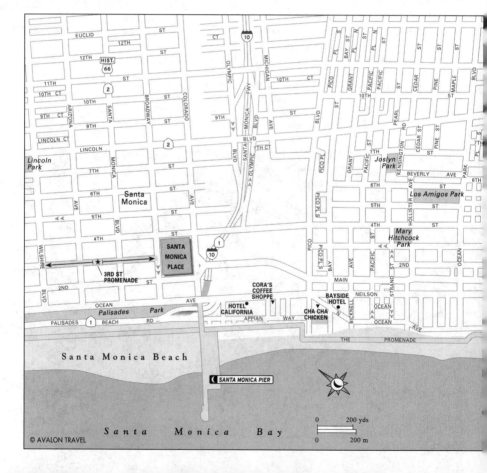

© AVALON TRAVEL

for a spot on a summer weekend. Many hotels and restaurants are within walking distance of the pier, as is the Third Street Promenade shopping district.

⟪ Venice Boardwalk

If the Santa Monica Pier doesn't provide you with enough chaos and kitsch, head on down to the Venice Boardwalk (Ocean Front Walk at Venice Blvd., www.venicebeach.com) for a nearly unlimited supply of both year-round. Locals refer to the Boardwalk as "The Zoo" and tend to shun the area, especially in the frantic summer months. As you shamble down

the tourist-laden path, you'll pass an astonishing array of tacky souvenir stores, tattoo and piercing parlors, walk-up food stands, and more. An honest-to-goodness carnival freak show sits near the middle of the Boardwalk, and a surprisingly good bookstore is tucked in beside a large sidewalk café. On the beach side of the path, dozens of artists create sculptures and hawk their wares. You can watch sculptors creating amazing works of art out of sand, or purchase a piece of locally made jewelry. The dude with the roller skates, the turban, and the guitar is pretty much always here—if you talk to him, he may follow you around until

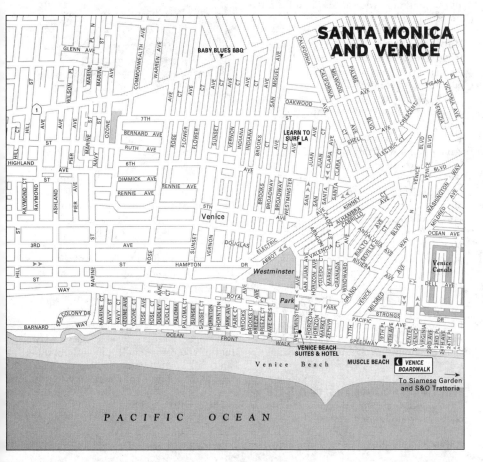

you pay him to leave you alone (he's harmless). The beach side includes the infamous **Muscle Beach** (two blocks north of Venice Blvd., www.musclebeach.net), an easily distinguished chunk of sand filled with modern workout equipment and encircled by a barrier.

The wide, flat beach adjacent to the Boardwalk gets incredibly crowded in the summer. Parking can be nightmarish in this district of car-free walking streets. Expect to park far from the beach and the Boardwalk and to pay for the privilege. The beach at Venice is lifeguard-protected and has restroom and shower facilities built on the sand. You can get all the junk food you can stomach from the Boardwalk stands.

Venice Canals

If you've grown tired of the frenzied Boardwalk (or the idea of those crowds make you break out in hives), consider taking a much more sedate walk along the paths of the Venice Canals (generally bounded by Washington Blvd., Strongs Dr., S. Venice Blvd., and Ocean Ave.). Venice locals seek out the canals when they want to take a stroll or walk their dogs (Venice is a very dog-oriented town), and enjoy the serenity and peace of the quiet waterways. The home gardens and city-maintained landscaping add a lush layer of greenery to the narrow canals. Taking these paths gets you deep into the neighborhood and close to the impressive 20th-century Southern California architecture of Venice. Many of the people who own homes on the canals launch small boats and put on an annual boat parade for the holidays. As you wander this area, marvel at the history of the canals, modeled after those in this beach town's European namesake city. Also, admire the tenacity with which the city saved these last few from the landfill that removed their brethren from the landscape.

Will Rogers State Historic Park

Did you grow up loving the films and culture of the early Hollywood western? If so, one of the best sights in Santa Monica for you is Will Rogers State Historic Park (1501 Will Rogers

JOHN PAUL "BOOMER" IACOANGELO/IMAGE COURTESY OF LA INC. THE LOS ANGELES CONVENTION AND VISITORS BUREAU

Venice canal

State Park Rd., Pacific Palisades, 310/454-8212, www.parks.ca.gov, grounds 8 A.M.–sunset daily, tours 11 A.M., 1 P.M., and 2 P.M. Thurs.–Fri., 10 A.M.–4 P.M. Sat.–Sun., free, fee for parking). This 186-acre ranch with its sprawling 31-room house was the home and retreat of Will Rogers and his family. Rogers's widow, Betty, donated the property to the state on her death in 1944. Today, you can tour the large home and check out some of the facilities of the active working ranch that still exist on the property. Or take a walk around the regulation-size polo field that was Will's joy. If you share Will's love of horses, visit the stables to take a lesson or go out for a ride out on the local range. Travelers who prefer their own two feet can take a three-mile hike to Inspiration Point, or a longer trek on the Backbone Trail out into the Santa Monica Mountains.

Malibu Pier

There are few true "sights" along the long thin stretch of sand that is Malibu. One of those worth checking out is the Malibu Pier (23000

Pacific Coast Hwy., 888/310-7437, www.mali-bupiersportfishing.com). The pier gets busy in the summer and lonely in the winter, though the die-hard surfers plying the adjacent three-point break stick around year-round. A few pier anglers also brave the so-called chilly weather of the Malibu off-season, but you'll feel a sense of some solitude when you walk out across the planks. Some attractions out on the pier include interpretive signs describing the history of Malibu, sportfishing and whale-watching charters, restaurants, and food stands. If you'd prefer to ride the waves yourself, you can rent surf and boogie boards as well as other beach toys on the pier.

The Getty Villa

Perched on the cliffs just east of Malibu in Pacific Palisades, this lush estate (17985 Pacific Coast Hwy., 310/440-7300, www.getty.edu, parking $15) is home to stunning treasures from ancient Greece, Rome, and Etruria. Tickets are free, but you have to reserve them in advance if you want to enjoy this exclusive, intimate, and dazzling experience.

PASADENA

If Venice Beach is the liberal haven of L.A., rockers love the Sunset Strip, and gay people flock to West Hollywood, Pasadena is the elder statesman of Los Angeles neighborhoods and towns. Once a resort-like haven for the very wealthy, Pasadena gently decayed, then was recreated as a charming upper-middle-class residential town. Dotted throughout Pasadena you can still see fabulous examples of the craftsman architecture that was prevalent throughout Southern California in the early 20th century. This older city also lays claim to one of the best-known and most attended parades in the United States, the **Rose Parade** on New Year's Day.

The Huntington

Some of the most beautiful botanical gardens in the world grow in Pasadena. The Huntington (1151 Oxford Ave., San Marino, 626/405-2100, www.huntington.org, noon–4:30 P.M. Mon.

and Wed.–Fri., 10:30 A.M.–4:30 P.M. Sat.–Sun. Labor Day–Memorial Day, 10:30 A.M.–4:30 P.M. Wed.–Mon. Memorial Day–Labor Day, adults $20, seniors $15, ages 12–18 $10, ages 5–11 $6) also includes an amazing library filled with rare and ancient books and manuscripts. Literary travelers and locals come to the Huntington to view and worship the Gutenberg Bible and a manuscript of *The Canterbury Tales*. Art lovers come to view works by Van der Weyden, Gainsborough, Hopper, and more. And everyone comes to explore the 120 acres of gardens, the most popular part of the complex.

More than a dozen different gardens beckon, including the Desert Garden, the Japanese Garden, and the Rose Garden. It takes more than one tour to get a real sense of all that grows here; pick your favorite area and enjoy a peaceful respite from the endless chaos of the L.A. area. Admission to the center includes a docent-led garden tour. Check the website for a look at what will be in bloom when you're in town.

Some of the best museum café food in the state can be had at the **Rose Garden Tea Room and Café** (Tea Room reservations 626/683-8131, no reservations needed for café, hours vary but generally Tea Room noon–4:30 P.M. Mon. and Wed.–Fri., 10:45 A.M.–4:30 P.M. Sat.–Sun., café generally noon–4 P.M. Mon. and Wed.–Fri., 11 A.M.–4 P.M. Sat.–Sun., adults $28, ages 4–8 $15, ages 2–3 $7.50). You can get a scrumptious buffet-style high tea when the museum is open. For a more traditional snack or light lunch, the walk-up café offers salads, sandwiches, and hot soups.

◖ The Gamble House

Where Northern California prides itself on its Victorian architecture, major construction didn't get underway quite as fast in the southern part of the state. Here many of the wealthy residents, such as the Gambles (of Procter & Gamble), built homes in the early 20th century. The Gamble House (4 Westmoreland Pl., 626/793-3334, www.gamblehouse.org, noon–3 P.M. Thurs.–Sun., adults $10, seniors and students with ID $7, under age 12 free) was

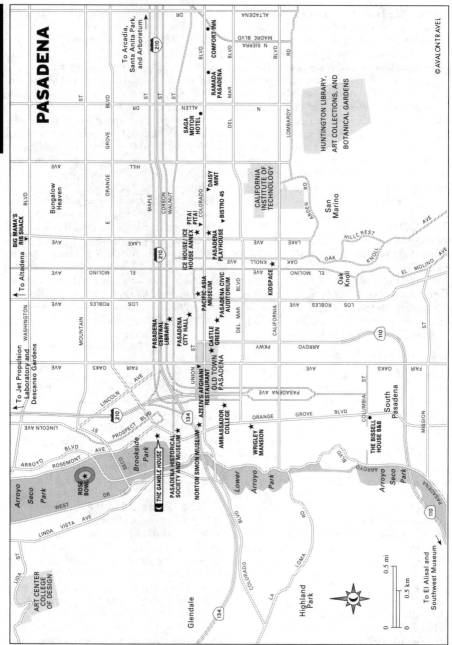

PASADENA

To Arcadia,
Santa Anita Park,
and Arboretum

ALTADENA

COMFORT INN

RAMADA
PASADENA

SAGA
MOTOR
HOTEL

HUNTINGTON LIBRARY,
ART COLLECTIONS, AND
BOTANICAL GARDENS

Bungalow
Heaven

BIG MAMA'S
RIB SHACK

DAISY
MINT

PITAI
PITAI

BISTRO 45

CALIFORNIA
INSTITUTE OF
TECHNOLOGY

San
Marino

To Altadena

ICE HOUSE/ICE
HOUSE ANNEX

PASADENA
PLAYHOUSE

KIDSPACE

Oak
Knoll

PACIFIC ASIA
MUSEUM

PASADENA CIVIC
AUDITORIUM

PASADENA
CENTRAL
LIBRARY

PASADENA
CITY HALL

CASTLE
GREEN

OLD TOWN
PASADENA

To Jet Propulsion
Laboratory and
Descanso Gardens

AZEEN'S AFGHANI
RESTAURANT

AMBASSADOR
COLLEGE

South
Pasadena

WRIGLEY
MANSION

THE BISSELL
HOUSE B&B

THE GAMBLE HOUSE

PASADENA HISTORICAL
SOCIETY AND MUSEUM

NORTON SIMON MUSEUM

ROSE
BOWL

Brookside
Park

Arroyo
Seco
Park

Lower
Arroyo
Seco
Park

Arroyo
Seco
Park

ART CENTER
COLLEGE
OF DESIGN

Glendale

Highland
Park

To El Alisal and
Southwest Museum

0   0.5 mi

0   0.5 km

© AVALON TRAVEL

designed and decorated by legendary SoCal architects Greene and Greene in the American craftsman or American arts and crafts style. The only way to get inside is to take a tour (schedules vary by season). To buy tickets, go to the side of the main mansion and into the garage, built in the same style as the house, that now acts as a bookstore and ticket office.

Inside the house, you'll be led from room to room as the docent describes the construction and decor in detail. The craftsman aesthetic attempted to answer the overly ornate and precious Victorian style with long, clean lines and botanical motifs. The Greenes took this philosophy to heart in the construction of the Gamble house—you'll learn how they created this masterpiece as you view each unique room. You'll also see how the Gambles lived inside the house and hear some of their stories, even that of the house's possible haunting by Aunt Julia. The only place in the mansion that you won't see are two upstairs servants' rooms, now the home of two lucky architecture students who live in the house each school year.

Norton Simon Museum

Believe it or not, much of the nearly two millennia of art displayed at the Norton Simon Museum (411 W. Colorado Blvd., 626/449-6840, www.nortonsimon.org, noon–6 P.M. Wed.–Mon., noon–9 P.M. Fri., adults $10, seniors $5, students free) were once part of a private collection. Wealthy industrialist Norton Simon collected the thousands of works of art over 30 years. He particularly loved the European Renaissance, the works of South and Southeast Asia, and 20th-century sculpture. Several of his most famous Auguste Rodin sculptures decorate the walkway up to the main entrance to the museum. You can visit the lovely modern building housing large, airy galleries to study the beautiful works of fine art. Be sure to head outside to walk through the sculpture gardens in the courtyards behind the building. You can purchase books and reproductions in the museum store or grab a bite to eat at the simple, walk-up Garden Café.

Rose Bowl

The Rose Bowl Stadium (1001 Rose Bowl Dr., 626/577-3101, www.rosebowlstadium.com, office 8:30 A.M.–5:30 P.M. Mon.–Fri.), true to its name, is the home to the famed granddaddy of the bowl games and to the UCLA college football team. Built in 1922, this huge elliptical bowl at first had an open side. It was closed only a few years later, and now seats almost (but not quite) 100,000 people—perfect for the Super Bowl as well as the flea markets and endless parade of college games. In addition to the endless vista of seats, you'll find plenty of restrooms and concessions scattered throughout the stadium—far more than the average college football team's home turf.

You can visit the Rose Bowl anytime, although you might need a ticket during an event, and you'll definitely need to plan in advance to attend the Rose Bowl game. Check the online calendar to find a fun event to attend for the best sense of this National Historic Landmark.

the Rose Bowl Stadium

Entertainment and Events

NIGHTLIFE
Bars

Whatever your taste in bars, whether it tends toward hipster dives, old-school watering holes, or beautiful lounges, L.A. will be able to offer its version.

Golden Gopher (417 W. 8th St., 213/614-8001, http://213nightlife.com/goldengopher, 5 P.M.–2 A.M. Tues.–Fri., 8 P.M.–2 A.M. Sat.–Mon.), which started the Downtown nightlife scene, draws hipsters from all over L.A. For those who don't know the meaning of excess, a liquor store on the premises—allowed by a very, very old liquor license—sells bottles of booze and craft beers to go.

The soaring two-story **Broadway Bar** (830 S. Broadway, 213/614-9909, www.broadway-bar.la, 5 P.M.–2 A.M. Tues.–Fri., 8 P.M.–2 A.M. Sat., available for private parties and special events Sun.–Mon.) looks straight out of the 1920s, with a polished circular bar, gilt walls, spacious balconies, and a crowd that could be coming from the opera or a local punk show.

Sometimes a place doesn't need a huge description or buildup to illuminate its atmosphere and theme. **Bordello** (901 E. 1st St., 213/687-3766, www.bordellobar.com, 7 P.M.–2 A.M. daily, cover $10), with its provocative name and plush red interior, exemplifies such an establishment. Sitting at the former location of Little Pedros, the first bar opened in L.A. with a notorious reputation for its "other" business as a brothel, Bordello strives to be worthy of its historic locale. The interior feels almost cluttered to modern sensibilities; it's crammed with antique glass light fixtures, ornately painted and leafed gewgaws, and velvet lounging couches. Musical offerings are deliberately eclectic. You might hear jazz one night, ska the next, and indie rock the night after that. Bordello also hosts regular burlesque shows. The full bar offers beers on tap as well as club-appropriate pink cocktails. Come in and be seduced.

Featured in films like *L.A. Confidential*, the historic **Formosa Café** (7156 Santa Monica Blvd., 323/850-9050, 4 P.M.–2 A.M. Mon.–Fri., 6 P.M.–2 A.M. Sat.–Sun.) is a landmark that has changed little since 1939. Chinese decor embellishes the dimly lit main bar, and two large patios pack in young hipsters.

A spot for old-school cocktails is **Musso & Frank Grill** (6667 Hollywood Blvd., 323/467-7788, www.mussoandfrank.com, 11 A.M.–11 P.M. daily). Caught in a Hollywood time warp, this L.A. institution—with its hushed lighting, wood-paneled walls, and gruff, red-jacketed barkeeps—has been serving expert martinis and steaks since 1919.

At **The Village Idiot** (7383 Melrose Ave., 323/655-3331, www.villageidiotla.com, 11:30 A.M.–2 A.M. Mon.–Fri., 9 A.M.–2 A.M. Sat.–Sun.), the gastro-pub craze has finally hit the left coast, and the beautiful set has taken notice. Besides the eye candy, the food is pretty delicious too. It's a perfect place for a late-afternoon drink.

With beautiful ocean views, glittering mosaics, marble floors, and romantic piano music, **Casa del Mar Lobby Lounge** (1910 Ocean Way, Santa Monica, 310/581-5533, www.hotelcasadelmar.com, 11 A.M.–12:30 A.M. Sun.–Thurs., 11 A.M.–1 A.M. Fri.–Sat.) is a dramatic real-life sandcastle on Santa Monica Beach and offers perhaps the most elegant cocktail experience in the city.

Clubs

Want to know which of the many dance and nightclubs in the L.A. area is the hottest or hippest or most popular with the stars this week? You'll need to ask the locals or read the alternative weekly papers when you arrive, since these things change almost weekly. What was hot when this guide was written will no doubt be out by the time it's published, so check out the scene when you arrive, or pick one of these reasonably reliable standards.

Know that clubs in L.A. get crowded on weekend nights and that bouncers take joy in selecting only the chicest hipsters in line to allow into the sacred spaces beyond the doors. Women have a slight edge, but in the top L.A. clubs, this can mean little to nothing. Being young and beautiful helps, of course, as does being dressed in the latest designer fashions and knowing a celebrity or the club's owner. So put on your finest and fanciest clubbing outfit, head out, and go for it!

For a good time dancing into the wee hours on a usually sedate Sunday night, head for **Deep at Club Vanguard** (6021 Hollywood Blvd., Hollywood, 323/463-3331, www.deep-la.com, 10 P.M.–4 A.M. Sun., cover $20). This one-night-only monument to the freshest house music was opened in 1998 and has been growing in popularity ever since. Expect top-shelf house DJs from New York, L.A., and anywhere else the best are spinning these days. In addition to the crowded dance floor, you'll find a full bar and a back patio done up in the finest Asian style. For the rest of the week, this space is simply **Club Vanguard** (www.vanguardla.com), hosting DJs in various styles, VIP nights, lingerie fashion shows, and other events that draw in the young and hip on the Hollywood scene.

For serious rockers looking for something a little bit heavier, there's the **Key Club** (9039 W. Sunset Blvd., West Hollywood, 310/274-5800, www.keyclub.com, 7 P.M.–2 A.M. daily, from $12, depending on the band). The Key Club caters to the heavy metal–and–dining crowd (yes, there is definitely such a thing in L.A.), with a full stage that hosts live bands and a full-service restaurant. This club feels like a warren, what with the stage and dance room, the casual and (in theory) quieter room down the hall, and The Plush Lounge VIP suite upstairs. Of course, you'll find more than one full bar inside this multipurpose club.

For an ever-so-slightly more laid-back L.A. clubbing experience, head on down to **The Little Temple** (4519 Santa Monica Blvd., 323/660-4540, www.littletemple.com, 9 P.M.–2 A.M. Wed.–Sun., cover $5–8). This funky, hip space mixes Asian Buddhist decor with deep house, hip-hop, and Latin music for a sometimes dance-heavy, sometimes lounge-centric evening of fun and flirtation. You can get your groove on down on the dance floor, then flop onto the huge communal bed to rest and relax with your oldest and newest friends. The decor mixes the sacred with the profane, and the full bar lubricates an already friendly evening with beer, wine, and cocktails.

The **Three Clubs Cocktail Lounge** (1123 Vine St., Hollywood, 323/462-6441, www.threeclubs.com, 6 P.M.–2 A.M. daily, no cover) acts both as a locals' watering hole and a reasonably priced nightclub catering mostly to the collegiate set. Expect to find the dance floor of the rear club crowded and sweaty, with fairly generic modern dance mixes blaring out over the crush of writhing bodies. Two bars serve up drinks to the masses, and drinks are a bit cheaper here than in the hotter spots. But if you're a lone female, be aware that Three Clubs has no decent parking, and you may have to walk several blocks along Hollywood Boulevard long after dark. Consider bringing a friend or two along with you to up your safety quotient.

Gay and Lesbian

An alternative to glammed-up West Hollywood gay bars, **Akbar** (4356 Sunset Blvd., Silver Lake, 323/665-6810, www.akbarsilverlake.com, 7 P.M.–2 A.M. Mon.–Sun.) pulls in a gay-friendly crowd with its cozy Moroccan-themed decor, neighborhood vibe, and friendly, unpretentious bartenders.

Sleek, glamorous, and candlelit, **The Abbey Food and Bar** (692 N. Robertson Blvd., West Hollywood, 310/289-8410, http://abbeyfoodandbar.com, 9 A.M.–2 A.M. daily) is a popular bar with a great outdoor patio and pillow-strewn private cabanas—all of which are usually jam-packed. Savvy bartenders mix 40 different specialty martinis.

Live Music

Los Angeles has long been one of the biggest destinations for struggling young rockers to come out, live cheap, and struggle to grab a spot on stage to take their shot at that all-important record contract. The clubs in the Sunset district, particularly those on the Sunset Strip, incubated some of the biggest rock acts of all time long before anybody knew who they were. The top three clubs drip rock history from their very walls. You might want to hold your nose when you first walk into the **Whisky a Go Go** (8901 Sunset Blvd., West Hollywood, 310/652-4202, www.whiskyagogo.com, 10 A.M.–2 A.M. Mon.–Fri., 6 P.M.–2 A.M. Sat.–Sun., cover from $10). Despite a stench almost as memorable as its sound, throngs of music fans pack into the Whisky every night of the week. Most nights you'll get a lineup of new bands—sometimes as many as seven in one evening. For those shows, you can pay about $10 in advance or $12 at the door to see groups that might (or might not) be the next big thing. The Whisky also hosts many cover and tribute bands that pay homage to the elders that once played here, such as Led Zeppelin and The Doors. And once in a great while, the Whisky hosts a major event like The Police reunion tour or a performance by a current star.

Almost next door to the Whisky you'll find **The Roxy Theatre** (9009 Sunset Blvd., West Hollywood, 310/278-9457, http://theroxyon-sunset.com, noon–6 P.M. and 8 P.M.–2 A.M. Mon.–Fri., 8 P.M.–2 A.M. Sat.–Sun., cover charge varies). A comparative newcomer to the scene, The Roxy opened in 1973 with Neil Young performing. The second (ish) generation of heavy-duty rock acts made their name here (think Guns N' Roses, Jane's Addiction, and Pearl Jam). Today you'll find the newest acts gracing the stage. Most shows feature 3–5 bands. The Roxy also puts up nonmusical shows, from standup comedy to full-on theatrical productions and performance art. The big black-box theater has an open dance floor, comfy-ish booths (if you can get one), and bare-bones food service during shows. Street parking is nearly nonexistent, and nearby lots will cost $5–15 or more, so think about taking public transit or a cab to the show. You'll find the performance calendar on the website, and tickets are available through major ticket agents. For one of the best after-hours parties

on the Strip, try to get into **On the Rox,** located directly above The Roxy. Or stagger next door to the **Rainbow Bar & Grill** (9015 Sunset Blvd., West Hollywood, 310/278-4232, www.rainbowbarandgrill.com, 11 A.M.–2 A.M. daily).

It's not on the Strip, but its reputation is just as big and bad as its brethren. **The Troubadour** (9081 Santa Monica Blvd., West Hollywood, 310/276-6168, www.troubadour.com, 8 P.M.–2 A.M. daily, cover charge, ticket prices vary) opened its doors in 1957. Over its more than 50 years, Bob Dylan jammed, total unknown comic Steve Martin sang, Tom Waits was discovered, Billy Joel opened for somebody else, Metallica headlined for the very first time, and countless A-list bands have recorded in and even about The Troubadour. Today, it's known for hosting amateur acts and cult favorites (The Mountain Goats, ALO) and even secret shows by mainstream hit-makers like Coldplay. If you're in town past the weekend, come on down for a fabulous "Free Monday" and save your money for drinks. You can check the events calendar in advance to find your favorite bands, and then buy tickets online or via fax. If you've decided on a whim to hit tonight's show, you can buy tickets at the on-site box office on the day of the show only, as long as the show isn't sold out.

If you're looking for something smaller in the way of a semi-underground club, your best bet is to ask around once you're on the ground in L.A. Hot spots turn to cold spots quickly here, and the locals usually know what's up.

Comedy

Not far behind the live music scene, L.A.'s live comedy scene is second only to Manhattan's as a way to see the brightest current stars and the most impressive young new talent. More than a dozen major live comedy clubs make their home in the smog belt. Pick your favorite, sit back, and laugh (or groan) the night away.

Located in the former Ciro's Nightclub on the Strip, **The Comedy Store** (8433 Sunset Blvd., West Hollywood, 323/650-6268, www.thecomedystore.com, 7 P.M.–2 A.M. Mon.,

9 P.M.–2 A.M. Tues.–Sun., age 21 and older, $15–20) is owned by 1980s comedian Pauly Shore's mother, Mitzi. With three separate rooms, you'll find a show going on at The Store every night of the week; most start at 9 P.M. or later, but you can check the website's calendar for both early and late shows. In all three rooms you'll often find a showcase featuring more than a dozen stand-up comics all performing one after another, and leaving space for possible celebrity drop-ins. Local sketch and improv groups also have regular gigs at The Store. Once upon a time, legendary comics got their start here, often on Monday Amateur Nights. Imagine being among the first people ever to see Yakov Smirnoff perform, or getting to see Steve Martin or Whoopi Goldberg 10 feet from your table for less than $20. That's the level of talent you'll find performing here on a nightly basis. You can buy tickets online for bigger shows, and at the door for nonsellouts and The Belly Room. Most shows have a two-drink minimum in addition to the cover; no-cover acts in The Belly Room are your best bet for a bargain.

It seems unlikely that a major comedy club would make its home in peaceful, suburban Pasadena, but that's where you'll find the **Ice House Comedy Club** (24 N. Mentor Ave., off Colorado Blvd., 626/577-1894, www.icehousecomedy.com, show times vary Tues.–Sun., cover $5–20). With shows running nightly and a double-header most Saturday nights, anyone who wants a laugh will enjoy an evening at the Ice House. Comedians who've performed here recently include Louis C.K., Bobby Lee, and Tom Rhodes. You'll also find a focus on female comics and a regular Latino comedy showcase here. The $12.50 newcomers-heavy showcase on Wednesday nights makes for one of the best bargains in the L.A. entertainment scene, and you never know who you'll see. That bouncing hobbit-shaped guy named Daymon Ferguson or the lanky pseudo-depressive comic songster Phil Johnson might be the next ones to hit it big, and you can say you saw them when. If you actually favor a lower-budget, newer-comic evening, hit the

Ice House **Annex,** the smaller ancillary room right next door to the main club.

THE ARTS
Theater
Even with all the hoopla over film in L.A., there's still plenty of room for live theatrical entertainment in and around Tinseltown.

The most notable annual event at the **Kodak Theatre** (6801 Hollywood Blvd., 323/308-6300, www.kodaktheatre.com, box office 10 A.M.–4 P.M. daily, previews $33–203, Saturday previews and evening performances $43–253) is the Academy Awards, often called the Oscars. But for the rest of the year, the Kodak hosts live shows of various types. Many other awards shows make their homes here, and the stage is often graced by major performers such as Eddie Izzard and Ricky Gervais. Also look for classical music concerts and vocal music performances.

Some theatergoers prefer outdoor entertainment to indoor, and the **Ford Theater** (2580 Cahuenga Blvd. E., 323/461-3673, www.fordamphitheater.org, box office noon–5 P.M. Tues.–Sun. and two hours before evening performances, ticket prices vary) certainly takes advantage of Hollywood's temperate climate to bring the shows outdoors. Every sort of theatrical event imaginable can find a stage at the Ford, from classical ballet to experimental theater and postmodern circus acts. Lots of musical acts play the Ford—think jazz, folk, world music, and beyond. Children's shows come to the Ford, and the theater even puts up the occasional film-based multimedia production. Check the events calendar to see what's up during your visit.

The **Ahmanson Theater** (135 N. Grand Ave., 213/628-2772, www.centertheatregroup. org, box office noon–6 P.M. Tues.–Sun. and two hours before performances, ticket prices vary) specializes in big Broadway-style productions. You might see a grandiose musical, heart-wrenching drama, or gut-busting comedy here. Expect to find the names of many familiar shows on the schedule, including Cirque du Soleil's *Iris, A Chorus Line, Death* *of a Salesman,* and *Funny Girl.* With hundreds of seats (all of them expensive), there's usually enough room to provide entertainment even for last-minute visitors.

Classical Music

Although L.A. is better known for its rock than its classical music offerings, you can still find plenty of high-culture concerts as well. If you love the grandiose, get a ticket for a show at the **Los Angeles Opera** (135 N. Grand Ave., 213/972-8001, www.losangelesopera.com, box office 10 A.M.–6 P.M. Tues.–Sun. and matinee Sun., $20–240). The L.A. Opera has only existed since 1986, but in that time it has grown to be one of the largest opera companies in the United States, gaining national recognition for the quality of its work. The dazzling performances held in the Dorothy Chandler Pavilion at the Music Center of Los Angeles County have included such masterworks of the genre as *Don Giovanni, La Bohème,* and *Tristan and Isolde.* Each season includes six or more different operas. The company gets recognition for its amazing production values, which include at least a couple of shows with truly fantastical costumes that in themselves are worth the price of the ticket.

If you prefer your musicians in black and white, take in a show by the **Los Angeles Philharmonic** (111 S. Grand Ave., 323/850-2000 or 800/745-3000, www.laphil.com, box office noon–6 P.M. Tues.–Sun. and two hours before and until 30 minutes after each performance begins, $43–160), better known to its friends as the L.A. Phil. The philharmonic performs primarily at the **Walt Disney Concert Hall** (111 S. Grand Ave.). Concerts can range from classics by famed composers like Tchaikovsky, Bach, and Beethoven to the world music of Asha Bhosle or jazz by Bobby McFerrin. Guest performers can be the modern virtuosi of classical music—Midori plays here on occasion. Whatever style of music you choose to listen to, conductor Esa-Pekka Salonen or one of his guests will lead you on a wonderful aural journey.

With its art deco band shell set against canyon chaparral, the **Hollywood Bowl** (2301 N. Highland Ave., 323/850-2000 or 800/745-3000, www.hollywoodbowl.com, box office noon–6 P.M. Tues.–Sun.) has long been a romantic setting for outdoor summer concerts by the L.A. Philharmonic and other artists.

If you're interested in supporting the work of amateur musicians or just seeing a chamber concert in a more intimate setting, consider getting tickets to the **Los Angeles Doctors Symphony** (424/209-7522, www.ladso.org, $15–20). This lovely community orchestra has been performing regularly since its inception in 1953 and most recently performed concerts at the Wilshire Ebell Theatre (743 S. Lucerne Blvd., just off Wilshire Blvd., 323/939-0126, www.ebell.com, 10 A.M.–5 P.M. Mon.–Fri.). Many, though by no means all, of the musicians you'll hear are members of the medical profession. They play everything from Mozart and Schubert to traditional music of various cultures, depending on the concert venue and the event. Check the website for the annual schedule, programs, and ticket information. If they're playing when you're in town, it's definitely worth your time to support the musical culture of Los Angeles.

Cinema

Movie premieres are a big deal in L.A. for obvious reasons. Crowds throng the streets outside of the Chinese Theatre and the Egyptian, where the stars tromp down the red carpets to enjoy the sight of themselves on the big screen. Even the standard AMC and other theater chains get packed on opening nights, so come early or buy tickets online to assure yourself of seats to your favorite star's latest release.

The current favorite movie house for star sightings is the **ArcLight Hollywood Cinema** (6360 W. Sunset Blvd., Hollywood, 323/464-1478, www.arclightcinemas.com, adults $14–16, seniors $12–14.50, children $10.50–11.50, add $3.50 pp for 3-D movies). Perhaps this is due to the ArcLight's 21-and-older-only screenings of major blockbuster movies, which allow patrons to purchase beer and wine at the Café and bring their drinks into the theater with them. But most of all, the ArcLight complex offers the best visual and sound technologies, all-reserved seating, and the updated geodesic Cinerama Dome theater. Do be sure to make reservations in advance (you can buy tickets online or at the theater) if you want great seats to the latest films. The ArcLight also shows a few art-house flicks and even the occasional "retrospective" (code for old) movie in its hallowed theaters. Ask for parking validation for a discount on the adjacent parking structure. You'll need it, since due to the ArcLight's status as a Hollywood favorite, you'll pay above even the usual high L.A. movie theater rates to see a film here.

Shopping

In Los Angeles, shopping qualifies as a major source of entertainment for locals and visitors alike. Don't worry about being materialistic or a spendthrift here—that's what you're *supposed* to be. If it exists anywhere on earth, you can probably buy it somewhere in L.A., whether "it" is a Smart car, a bunch of flowers, an indie CD, or a pair of pants that cost as much as a Smart car. Different areas and towns have their own unique shopping feel, so decide what kind of retail experience you want and then pick the right spot to find it.

DOWNTOWN AND VICINITY
Flower District

If you have even the slightest love of plants and flowers, you can't miss the world-famous L.A. Flower District (700 block of Wall St., 213/627-3696, 213/622-1966, or 213/627-2482, www.laflowerdistrict.com, www.originallaflower-market.com, and www.bloominnews.com, morning Mon.–Sat., $2 Mon.–Fri., $1 Sat.). Sometimes called "America's Flower Market," this vast sea of color and beauty is a triumph of American multicultural entrepreneurial spirit. The first flower cultivators in Los Angeles were Japanese Americans, and today many growers are of Hispanic descent—perhaps especially fitting for an industry that creates products in all colors of the rainbow. When you visit this vast sea of beauty, you'll find a fun cacophony of different languages being spoken as floral retailers vie for the best products available on any given day. But never fear: Anyone can come and stroll the narrow aisles of the various markets, and you'll find plenty of pre-made bouquets with which to impress your sweetie. Or better yet, find someone who can create a custom arrangement for you, since just about every kind of cut flower, potted plant, and exotic species can be purchased here. You can take away a bouquet filled with flowers you've never even seen before.

Among other major events, the Flower District supplies the unbelievable needs of the Rose Parade each New Year's. Literally millions of flowers go into the creation of the stunning floats (which must incorporate flowers to qualify for most of the awards in the parade). It's hard to image the work necessary to fill the orders for the floats, but the denizens of the flower market do it every year.

One caution: While the flower market itself is safe for visitors, the area to the south is not. Get good directions before you come, and don't plan to wander the neighborhood on foot.

Jewelry District

If you're looking for the bleeding edge of style when you shop for jewelry, you can't do much better than the Los Angeles Jewelry District (bounded by 5th St., 8th St., Broadway, and Olive St., www.lajd.net). With more than 3,000 wholesalers, even the most avid lover of sparkly stones and glittering gold will get his or her fill here. Do be a little bit careful if you're a woman alone, especially at dusk or later, as this isn't the cleanest part of Downtown L.A. But you can shop in reasonable peace here, and even in some confidence that you won't get ripped off as long as you do some preliminary research. The district website provides information on vendor ratings and a map to help you get around more easily. From wholesale dealers of unset gems to professional gem setters who'll create a beautiful piece from the stones you've bought, you can find just about anything you ever dreamed of here.

Chung King Road
A mix of modern art galleries and fun touristy gift shops line the 900 block of Chung King Road, a one-block stretch of Chinatown. Interior decorators often browse the eclectic selection here.

Kinokuniya
This Little Tokyo bookstore Kinokuniya (123 Astronaut E. Onizuka St., 213/687-4480, www.kinokuniya.com) carries both Japanese- and English-language merchandise, including a wide selection of *manga* (Japanese comic books), cookbooks, glossy home-decor and art books, fashion magazines, and stationery.

LOS FELIZ
The shopping options in Los Feliz and Silver Lake reflect the neighborhoods' penchant for variety, with everything from secondhand resale stores to sophisticated boutiques.

Sunset Junction
Artsy, hip boutiques, cafés, and restaurants line Sunset Junction (Sunset Blvd. from Santa Monica Blvd. to Maltman Ave., 213/413-7770, www.sunsetjunction.org), a colorful stretch of Sunset Boulevard concentrated around where Sunset meets Santa Monica Boulevard (or, rather, where Santa Monica Boulevard ends). Weekend mornings bring floods of neighborhood locals down from the hills. Shops here include ecofriendly home accessories purveyor **Kellygreen Home** (4008 Santa Monica Blvd., 323/660-1099, www.kellygreenhome.com), and there's the Silver Lake Certified Farmer's Market (323/661-7771, 8 A.M.–1 P.M. Sat.).

Skylight Books
The "fiercely" independent Skylight Books (1818 N. Vermont Ave., 323/660-1175, www.skylightbooks.com, 10 A.M.–10 P.M. daily) in Los Feliz features alternative literature, literary fiction, Los Angeles–themed books, and an extensive film section. They often have autographed copies of books by authors who have recently spoken here.

HOLLYWOOD
Hollywood and Highland Center
At the center of the efforts to revitalize Hollywood, located next to the Chinese Theatre and connected to the Kodak Theatre, Hollywood and Highland Center (6801 Hollywood Blvd., 323/467-6412 or 323/817-0200, www.hollywoodandhighland.com, 10 A.M.–10 P.M. Mon.–Sat. 10 A.M.–7 P.M. Sun., parking $2–10) flaunts outlandish architecture that's modeled after the set of the 1916 film *Intolerance*. Stroll amid the eateries and boutiques that surround the open-air Babylon Court.

Hollywood and Highland Center

Amoeba Music

Rolling Stone magazine calls Amoeba's branch in Berkeley, California, the world's best record store. If you didn't visit the outpost on Haight Street in San Francisco, you can get another shot at a music geek–worthy selection of CDs, tapes, concert posters, and LPs at the Hollywood branch of Amoeba Music (6400 Sunset Blvd., 323/245-6400, www.amoeba.com, 10:30 A.M.–11 P.M. Mon.–Sat., 11 A.M.–9 P.M. Sun.), located on Sunset Boulevard, two blocks south of Hollywood Boulevard.

LA BREA, FAIRFAX, AND MIRACLE MILE
West 3rd Street

The stretch of charming and eclectic shops on West 3rd Street between Fairfax Avenue and La Cienega Boulevard encompasses one-of-a-kind clothing boutiques, home stores, and bath-and-body shops. At one end you'll find the Farmer's Market and The Grove shopping center; at the other, the Beverly Center.

Among the various home and clothing stores on West 3rd Street, you'll find **Traveler's Bookcase** (8375 W. 3rd St., 323/655-0575, www.travelbooks.com, 11 A.M.–7 P.M. Mon., 10 A.M.–7 P.M. Tues.–Sat., noon–6 P.M. Sun.). Both armchair travelers and true globetrotters browse the extensive selection of guidebooks at this comfortable and friendly bookstore. Travel-oriented literature rounds out the stock.

BEVERLY HILLS AND WEST HOLLYWOOD
Rodeo Drive

If you're reading this book, you probably don't have enough money to go on a serious spree in the shops of Rodeo Drive. The hottest stars and other big spenders come here to purchase the best and most expensive goods the world has to offer.

Have you ever bought a $1,500 pair of pants? Walk into **Chanel** (400 N. Rodeo Dr., Beverly Hills, 310/278-5500, www.chanel. com, 10 A.M.–6 P.M. Mon.–Sat., noon–5 P.M. Sun.) and you'll be able to. You'll see original artwork, catalogs, the very edgiest high-end clothes in existence, and salespeople who will look down their noses at you if your outfit cost less than four figures. Head upstairs for racks of on-sale clothing from last season, although you'll quickly learn that "on sale" is a relative concept. If you're lucky, you might even get dissed by one or more of the überrich women wearing fur hats and carrying yippy little dogs (they're unaware of the irony). Hunt the racks for the classic tweedy Coco Chanel dress—you will find it. Or if you prefer another designer, head outside and find one; all the big leaguers, from Dior to Michael Kors, maintain storefronts on Rodeo Drive.

Although Rodeo Drive is most famous for its designer apparel, many other retailers offer a vast array of expensive things, including sunglasses, jewelry, and housewares. If you're looking for, or just want to look at, the perfect diamond ring, walk past the guards into the huge hallowed halls of **Tiffany's** (210 N. Rodeo Dr., Beverly Hills, 310/273-8880, www.tiffany.com, 10 A.M.–6 P.M. Mon.–Wed. and Fri.–Sat., 10 A.M.–7 P.M. Thurs., 11 A.M.–5 P.M. Sun.). The store has three floors of the most exquisite necklaces, bracelets, rings, watches, and accessories you'll ever find anywhere. This storefront compares easily to its sister store in Manhattan. You'll find the sales help here a bit friendlier than in the clothing stores, since even the middle class of L.A. comes to Tiffany's to purchase special-occasion jewelry.

The wealthy who want to fall asleep with their skin soothed by the softest sheets around go to **Frette** (459 N. Rodeo Dr., Beverly Hills, 310/273-8540 or 800/353-7388, www.frette.com, 10 A.M.–6 P.M. Mon.–Sat., noon–5 P.M. Sun.) to make their purchases. This store doesn't get as crowded as many others on Rodeo Drive, and much of Frette's business is with high-end hotels. But the doors of this open, airy retail store remain defiantly open, beckoning shoppers who love luxury. Salespeople encourage you to pet the merchandise, comparing one set of sheets to another and imagining the feel of the plushy bath sheets after your next shower.

Melrose Avenue

Melrose Avenue (between San Vicente Blvd. and La Brea Ave.) is really two shopping districts. High-end fashion and design showrooms dominate the western end, near La Cienega Boulevard; head east past Fairfax Avenue for tattoo parlors and used clothing.

If you miss 1960s mod, 1970s grooviness, 1980s power-dressing, or even last year's haute couture, drop by **Decades** (8214½ Melrose Ave., 323/655-0223, www.decadesinc.com, 11:30 A.M.–6 P.M. Mon.–Sat., or by appointment) and browse among the prime vintage Courrèges, Hermès, and Pucci castoffs.

If you adore the clothes from *Sex and the City* and *Friends,* stop in at **Ron Robinson at Fred Segal** (8118 Melrose Ave., 323/651-1800, www.ronrobinson.com, 10 A.M.–7 P.M. Mon.–Sat., noon–6 P.M. Sun.), a deluxe department store that has everything from the ridiculously trendy to the severely tasteful.

Futuristic specs from **l.a.Eyeworks** (7407 Melrose Ave., 323/653-8255 or 800/348-3337, ext. 4, www.laeyeworks.com, 10 A.M.–7 P.M. Mon.–Sat., 11 A.M.–5 P.M. Sun., note that they start removing inventory about 30 minutes before closing time) have appeared in films like *The Matrix* and *Blade Runner,* and celebs like Jennifer Aniston and Wesley Snipes are fans of the store's lightweight, trend-defining frames.

The buyers at **Wasteland** (7428 Melrose Ave., 323/653-3028, www.wastelandclothing. com, 11 A.M.–8 P.M. Mon.–Sat., noon–7 P.M. Sun.) carefully pick out merchandise for their club-hopping clientele, so everything at this secondhand store has style. The selection covers a wide range, from Gucci to Gap.

Book Soup

Located on the strip of Sunset Boulevard more famous for nightlife than shopping, the indie bookstore Book Soup (8818 Sunset Blvd., 310/659-3110, www.booksoup.com, 9 A.M.–10 P.M. Mon.–Sat., 9 A.M.–7 P.M. Sun.) crams every nook and cranny of its space, but the film section is particularly strong. Check out the schedule of high-profile readings, or pick up a signed edition.

SANTA MONICA, VENICE, AND MALIBU

Shopping down by the beaches can be as much fun as anyplace else in the L.A. area. Santa Monica offers the best bet for an entertaining retail experience, since Venice Beach and Malibu tend more toward strip malls.

Third Street Promenade

Looking for the place where middle-class locals come to shop in the L.A. area? Head for the Third Street Promenade (3rd St., Santa Monica, 310/393-8355, http://thirdstreet-promenade.org). Much of 3rd Street in Santa Monica is closed to auto traffic to make it easier to walk along the Promenade. This long vertical outdoor mall features all your favorite chain stores for clothing, shoes, jewelry, housewares, computers, and just about anything else you can think of. You'll find people plying the

Melrose Avenue

Promenade day and night, seven days a week. If your goal is a serious retail spree, come out to the Promenade on a weekday during daylight hours to avoid the bigger crushes of people that pile into the area on weekends. On the other hand, if you're looking for a fun social outing, the Promenade gets popular with a younger crowd at night. You can hit one of the movie theaters, stop in at a bar, or just stroll the pedestrian walks enjoying the mild night air and the street performers who work the area. The Promenade is within easy walking distance of the Santa Monica Pier and the adjacent beach.

The Promenade's shops tend toward classic mall fare. You'll find a tremendous three-story Gap offering classic clothes to the masses. The high-end Anthropologie and Armani Exchange can get you looking fine for the remainder of your L.A. vacation and beyond. If you need a new computer or a shiny iPod or iPhone to get you back home in style and entertained, a huge Apple Store can hook you up. There's also a gargantuan Barnes & Noble to pick up some more vacation reading. If you're looking to catch the latest flick, choose from four different movie theaters. On weekends, you can get the freshest and tastiest fruits and vegetables from the legendary farmers market at the Promenade.

PASADENA
Old Town Pasadena

Old Town Pasadena (Colorado Blvd., 626/356-9725, www.oldpasadena.org) was once a quaint downtown area serving a small but wealthy resort community. Today, Old Town essentially acts as a street-based shopping mall, with upscale chain stores inhabiting classic art deco and mid-century modern buildings.

Off the main strip along Colorado Boulevard, one block down Raymond Avenue, is **Distant Lands** (20 S. Raymond Ave., 626/449-3220 or 800/310-3220, www.distantlands.com, 10:30 A.M.–8 P.M. Mon.–Thurs. and Sat., 10:30 A.M.–9 P.M. Fri., 11 A.M.–6 P.M. Sun.), a one-stop shop for travelers that has guidebooks, maps, travel accessories, clothing, and luggage. Even if you're not planning a special trip, the store's ambience is conducive to armchair travel.

Sports and Recreation

You'll find an endless array of ways to get outside and have fun in the L.A. area. Among the most popular recreation options are those that get you out onto the beach or into the Pacific Ocean.

BEACHES

If you're in SoCal for the first time, it's almost a given that one of your destinations is a genuine California beach. You've got plenty to choose from in the L.A. area. From north of Malibu down to Manhattan Beach and Hermosa Beach, you'll find a seemingly endless stretch of public beaches. Most of these have lots of visitor amenities, unlike the Northern California version, such as snack bars, boardwalks, showers, beach toy rental shacks, surf schools, and permanent sports courts. Believe it or not, those listed here are just a drop in the bucket; if none of these beaches do it for you, you can choose from dozens of others that stretch in a nearly unbroken line from one end of the county to the other.

Not all L.A. beaches are created equal. With very few exceptions, you won't find clean, clear water to swim in, since pollution is a major issue on the L.A. coast. Also keep in mind that Los Angeles County is not a tropical zone. The water does warm up in the summer, but not into the 80s like you find in Hawaii. Happily, it's also not in the icy 50s and 60s, as in the northern reaches of the state. Expect to cool off significantly when you dive into the surf, and if you plan to be out in the water for an extended period, get yourself a wetsuit to prevent chills that can turn into hypothermia.

Zuma Beach

If you've ever seen the cult classic film *Earth Girls Are Easy*, you've heard of legendary Zuma Beach (Pacific Coast Hwy., 19 miles north of Malibu, surf report 310/457-9701, http://beaches.lacounty.gov, parking $3–10). This popular surf and boogie-boarding break, complete with a nice big stretch of clean white sand, fills up fast on summer weekends but isn't as crowded on weekdays. Grab a spot on the west side of the Pacific Coast Highway for free parking, or pay for one of the more than 2,000 spots in the beach parking lot. Zuma has all the amenities you need for a full day out at the beach, from restrooms and showers to a kid-friendly snack bar and a beachside boardwalk.

Water lovers can ride the waves or just take a swim in the cool and (unusual for the L.A. area) crystal-clear Pacific waters. Zuma has lifeguards during daylight hours, and for land-lubbers, it's got beach volleyball courts set up and a playground for the kids. Perhaps best of all, this beach doesn't fill up with litter-happy visitors; it's actually a locals' favorite for weekend R&R.

Malibu Lagoon State Beach

In a sea of mansions fronting the beach, Malibu Lagoon State Beach (23200 Pacific Coast Hwy., 818/880-0363, www.parks.ca.gov, 8 A.M.–sunset daily) and its ancillary **Malibu Surfriders Beach** offer public access to the great northern L.A. location. Running alongside the **Malibu Pier** (23000 Pacific Coast Hwy., 310/456-8031 or 888/310-7437, www.malibupiersportfishing.com), this pretty stretch of sugar-like sand offers a wealth of activities as well as pure California relaxation. This beach offers a number of unusual attractions, including both the **Adamson House** (23200 Pacific Coast Hwy., 310/456-8432, www.adamsonhouse.org, 11 A.M.–2 P.M. Wed.–Sat., adults $7, ages 6–16 $2, under age 6 free) and the adjoining **Malibu Lagoon Museum.** You can take a guided tour that goes through the museum and out to the wetlands, butterfly trees, tide pools, and flower gardens. Malibu Creek runs into

Malibu surfer

the ocean here, creating a unique wetlands ecosystem that's well worth exploring. If a beach party is more your style, you can rent beach toys at the pier and stake your spot on the sand. Surfers man the break here year-round; be careful of your fellow riders.

At the intersection that leads to the museum, you can also drive down to the main parking lot. It's likely to fill up fast in the summer, so get there early for a spot.

Will Rogers State Beach

If you're a film buff and a beach bum, you must take a day out of your travel schedule to hang out on the Will Rogers State Beach (17700 Pacific Coast Hwy., Pacific Palisades, http://beaches.co.la.ca.us/bandh/beaches/willrogers.htm, parking $4–12), yet another fabulous full-service L.A. beach. A number of movies have been filmed at Will Rogers. Even if you don't care about that, you'll love the nearly two miles of sandy beach, easy to get to from the parking lot, studded with volleyball courts, playground equipment, restrooms, and picnic tables. The bike path running along the land side of the sand runs for 22 miles or so south. Out in the water, you can swim, skin-dive, and surf. A mild right point break offers a good learning ground for beginners. Lifeguards protect the shores during the day in summer, and the locals think their lifeguards are some of the best-looking in the county. Just be sure to pay attention to the flags and signs, since pollution can be a problem at Will Rogers due to storm drains emptying into the ocean.

Bring cash to pay for parking, but be happy that with more than 1,750 spots, you'll probably find one that's legal and reasonably secure.

Santa Monica State Beach

If you're looking for "The Beach" in Santa Monica, well, it's hard to miss. The waterside edge of town is lined by Santa Monica State Beach (Pacific Coast Hwy., 310/458-8573, http://santa-monica.org, parking from $7), which is operated by the city of Santa Monica. For 3.5 miles, the fine sand gets raked daily

beneath the sun that shines over the beach more than 300 days each year. Flop down in the sand to enjoy the warm sunshine, take a dip in the endless waves of the Pacific, stroll along the boardwalk, or stand at the edge of the water and peer out to see if you can catch sight of a pod of dolphins frolicking in the surf. If you don't mind crowds, hang out on the sand right near the pier. The best people-watching runs south of the pier area and on toward Venice Beach. For a bit more elbow room, head north of the pier to the less populated end of the beach.

Due to its location right "in" town and adjacent to and beneath the Santa Monica Pier, you'll find a near-endless array of services at the beach. On the pier and just across from the beach, you can get snacks and meals, rent surf and boogie boards, hit the arcade, and go shopping. Parking varies, depending on which part of the beach you head for. The north end has spotty parking, the pier area can get really crowded but has more options, and the south probably has the best bet for a good spot.

Santa Monica State Beach

SURFING

If you ask anyone around what the defining sport in California is, they'll tell you it's surfing, and the craze for wave riding in California began in Los Angeles. The mystical athletic endeavor stars in movies and TV shows, yet it's something lots of folks can learn to do. Whether you've been riding waves for decades or you've never touched a surfboard, going surfing will add a touch of real California culture to your L.A. visit.

You'll find a fabulous array of surf breaks in the L.A. area, with waves of all sizes beckoning riders of every ability level. Most folks come out to the beach at Venice to check out the zoo-like boardwalk, but you can ride the waves here on the lifeguard-protected beach too. A great break for all levels, the breakwater at Venice Beach is a favorite spot for locals.

Surf Lessons

If you've never surfed before, your best bet is to sign up for a lesson or two with a reputable surf school. Most schools can get you standing up on your longboard on the very first lesson. One of these, **Learn to Surf LA** (641 Westminster Ave., Suite 5, Venice, 310/663-2479, www.learntosurfla.com, $100–150), has lessons on the beach near the Santa Monica Pier (near lifeguard tower No. 18) and in Dockweiler State Beach (near lifeguard tower No. 49). You can take a private lesson, a semi-private lesson with friends, or join a regularly scheduled group. Each lesson lasts almost two hours and includes all equipment (you'll get a full wetsuit in addition to a board), shore instruction and practice, and plenty of time in the water. No, the brightly colored foam longboards you'll learn on aren't the coolest or most stylish, but they're perfect for new surfers looking for a stable ride on smaller waves. Learn to Surf LA offers lessons for both kids and adults, and this can be a great activity for the whole family to tackle together. Intermediate and advanced surfers can also find great fun with this school, which has advanced instructors capable of helping you improve your skills.

HANG GLIDING

You can pick the kind of ground you want to soar over in L.A.: the ocean or the inland mountains and valleys. If you prefer to see the water slipping past beneath you, head for **Dockweiler State Beach Training Park** (12000 Vista del Mar, Playa del Rey, 11 A.M.–sunset Wed.–Sun.). For a higher-altitude adventure, head to the San Fernando Valley and up to **Sylmar Flight Park** (12601 Gridley St., Sylmar, 818/362-9978, 10 A.M.–sunset daily). For a good school and rental facility, call **Windsports Soaring Center** (12623 Gridley St., Sylmar, 818/367-2430, http://windsports.com, pro shop 10 A.M.–6 P.M. Tues.–Fri., 9 A.M.–noon Sat., $75–200). You can go tandem with an instructor at Sylmar Flight Park (recommended for first-time gliders) or get bold and try a solo ride, which starts at an altitude of five feet out on the beach at Dockweiler. Windsports provides all the equipment and training you need, so all you have to bring are a good pair of athletic shoes, a bottle of water, and, of course, a camera.

SPAS

Inside the Westin Bonaventure Hotel in Downtown L.A., enjoy some good pampering at the **Bonaventure Club and Spa** (404 S. Figueroa St., 213/629-0900, http://bonaventureclub.com, 11 A.M.–11 P.M. daily, from $28). With a focus on beauty as well as health and relaxation, the Bonaventure Club features a number of heavy-duty facials, as well as dermabrasion and collagen treatments. You'll also find a full nail and waxing salon along with an array of massages and body scrubs. The Bonaventure isn't the poshest spa around, but you'll get decent service. The locker rooms, sauna, and other facilities are clean, and the spa is open later than most to accommodate busy travelers. Book in advance if you want a specific treatment at a specific time of day, but you're likely to find a same-day appointment if you aren't too picky about exactly which treatment you want.

For a taste of Beverly Hills luxury, try **Thibiant Beverly Hills** (449 N. Canon Dr.,

310/278-7565 or 800/825-2517, www.thibi-antspa.com), where you can blast yourself clean with a deluge shower, and then have your body slathered with mud, milk, seaweed, or papaya.

Over in Santa Monica, **Exhale** (Fairmont Miramar Hotel and Bungalows, 101 Wilshire Blvd., 310/319-3193, www.exhalespa.com, 6:30 A.M.–9 P.M. Mon.–Fri., 8 A.M.–9 P.M. Sat., 8 A.M.–8 P.M. Sun.) explores the mind-body connection with fusion yoga classes, massage, and ayurvedic therapy. If you don't want to get that deep, you can also just have your nails done.

SPECTATOR SPORTS

Befitting a major American city, Los Angeles boasts a nearly full complement of professional sports teams. L.A. no longer has a National Football League team, but once it had two. Oops!

The **L.A. Kings** (213/742-7100 or 888/546-4752, http://kings.nhl.com, $34.50–465) play lightning-fast NHL ice hockey in Downtown L.A. at the Staples Center (1111 S. Figueroa St., www.staplescenter.com). Well, they try to play lightning fast, anyway; the Kings are more famous for their failures than their successes, but going out to the games is still fun, particularly if your home team is playing the Kings while you're in town.

As great legends of the National Basketball Association, the individual players and the organization as a whole of the **Los Angeles Lakers** (310/426-6031 or 866/381-8924, www.nba.com/lakers) have well and truly earned their places. Although Magic Johnson no longer dunks for the Lakers, Kobe Bryant carries on the star torch for the still-winning team.

Major League Baseball takes advantage of the perfect climate in L.A. to host some of the most beautiful outdoor summer games anywhere in the country. The **Los Angeles Dodgers** (1000 Elysian Park Ave., Los Angeles, 323/224-1507, http://losangeles.dodgers.mlb.com, $12–120) make their home in this hospitable climate, playing often and well throughout the long baseball season. Just one thing: Don't refer to Dodger Stadium (1000 Elysian Park Ave.) as "Chavez Ravine" unless you really mean it. That old field designation has become a derogatory term used primarily by San Francisco Giants fans.

Accommodations

From the cheapest roach-ridden shack motels to the most chichi Beverly Hills hotel, Los Angeles has an endless variety of lodgings to suit every taste and budget.

DOWNTOWN AND VICINITY

If you want to stay overnight in Downtown L.A., plan to pay for the privilege. As expected, most hostelries here run to high-rise towers catering more to businesspeople than the leisure set. Still, if you need a room near the heart of L.A. for less than a month's mortgage, you can find one if you look hard enough. But be aware that once you get into the Jewelry District and farther toward the Flower Market, the neighborhood goes from high-end to sketchy to downright terrifying. If you need a truly cheap room, avoid these areas and head instead for Pasadena or the San Fernando Valley.

Under $150

You won't miss the sign for the **Metro Plaza Hotel** (711 N. Main St., 213/680-0200 or 800/223-2223, http://metroplazahoteldowntownla.com, $90–170). The low-rise hotel with its white facade and big, oddly constructed front marquee sits near Union Station, convenient for rail travelers and public-transit riders. Inside, you'll find your guest room looks like any average, reasonably clean motel room. The bedspreads are floral, the carpets light blue, and the space ample. A complimentary continental breakfast comes with your room, and the Metro Plaza has an on-site fitness center. But the true gems here are the location, central to transportation to all the major L.A. attractions, and the lower-than-average price point for the region.

Since 1923, the **Millennium Biltmore Hotel** (506 S. Grand Ave., 213/624-1011 or 800/245-8673, www.millenniumhotels.com/millenniumlosangeles, $125–600), the grande dame of L.A. hotels, has hosted many dignitaries and heads of state. Guest rooms are impressive, but majestic public spaces—the Rendezvous Court, the Crystal Ballroom, and the Gallery Bar—really dazzle.

Can you imagine staying at a cute B&B only a mile from the towering skyscrapers of Downtown Los Angeles? The **Inn at 657** (657 and 663 W. 23rd St., 213/741-2200, www.patsysinn657.com, $135–225) is two side-by-side buildings with one-bedroom guest accommodations and two-bedroom suites, each individually decorated. You'll find a comfortable antique bed in a room scattered with lovely fabrics and pretty antiques. Each morning, you'll head downstairs to the long, dark table set with fine china for a full breakfast complete with fruit, hot food, great coffee, and fresh juice. The inn has a massage therapist on retainer, a nail salon they love just down the street, Wi-Fi, and a moderate-cost laundry service. You're within easy distance of the Staples Center, the Downtown shopping areas, and the rest of the attractions of Los Angeles.

$150-250

With its red-tiled floor, painted furniture, and lushly landscaped poolside bar, the **Figueroa Hotel** (939 S. Figueroa St., 213/627-8971 or 800/421-9092, www.figueroahotel.com, from $150) is a Spanish-Moroccan oasis in the heart of Downtown.

The **O Hotel** (819 S. Flower St., 213/623-9904 or 855/782-9286, www.ohotelgroup.com, $168–300), formerly known as The Orchid Hotel, is an upscale property that takes the modern urban chic hotel concept and does it L.A.-style. True to its name, orchids are a major theme of this hotel, and you'll find plants both in the common areas and in your room. Guest rooms are done in a modern style, with platform beds, sparkling white linens, and black-and-white baths. A boutique establishment, the O has only 67 guest rooms. You'll find tapas and Mediterranean-inspired cuisine at the on-site restaurant, plus a full bar. The health spa offers both fitness facilities and massage along with other spa services. Perhaps best of all for travelers who come to L.A. for its retail possibilities, you won't need the services of the 24-hour concierge desk to find the Macy's Plaza center just across the street from the hotel.

With **The Standard** (550 S. Flower St., 213/892-8080, www.standardhotels.com, from $245), hipster hotelier André Balazs, of the Chateau Marmont, and the Mercer, transformed the former home of Superior Oil into a mecca for the see-and-be-seen crowd. From its upside-down sign to the minimal aesthetic in the guest rooms, the hotel gives off an ironic-chic vibe. If you're sharing a room, be sure you and your roommate are comfortable with the fishbowl-like showers: The only thing between the showerer and the rest of the room is clear glass. Be sure to visit the rooftop bar, which has spectacular views of the Downtown cityscape.

Over $250

If you're longing for a taste of true L.A. style, get a room at the **Omni Los Angeles at California Plaza** (251 S. Olive St., 213/617-3300 or 888/444-6664, www.omnihotels.com, $290). From the grand exterior to the elegant lobby and on up to your guest room, the light colors, live plants, and lovely accents will make you feel rich, even if just for one night. Your guest room or suite will have plush mattresses and your choice of pillows, stylish decor, plushy towels and robes, and all the right amenities to make your stay perfect. If you're in town for business, you can get a guest room complete with a fax machine, copier, and office supplies. On the other hand, if you're on vacation with your family, you can get a suite specially decorated to delight your children—with a closing door to an adult bedroom to delight you. You can dine at this magnificent hotel, choosing between the **Noé Restaurant** (5–10 P.M. Sun.–Thurs., 5–11 P.M. Fri.–Sat., bar 3 P.M.–2 A.M. daily) and the **Grand Café** (6:30 A.M.–3 P.M. Mon.–Fri., 7 A.M.–3 P.M. Sat.–Sun.). Take a swim in the lap pool or a run on the exercise equipment in the large fitness room. Relax with a massage, hot river rock treatment, or facial at the Spa at Omni. Whatever your pleasure, you'll find it here.

If you're yearning to stay someplace with a movie history, book a room at the **Westin Bonaventure Hotel and Suites** (404 S. Figueroa St., 213/624-1000, www.starwoodhotels.com/westin, $250). The climactic scene of the Clint Eastwood thriller *In the Line of Fire* was filmed in one of the unusual elevators in the glass-enclosed, four leaf clover–shaped high-rise building. This hotel complex has every single thing you'd ever need: shops, restaurants, a day spa, a concierge, and plenty of nice guest rooms. You'll find your room comfortable and convenient, complete with fancy beds and clean spacious baths. Views range from fairly innocuous L.A. streets to panoramic cityscapes. The most fun restaurant and lounge to visit at the Bonaventure is without doubt the **Bona Vista Lounge** (5 P.M.–1 A.M. daily), which slowly rotates through 360 degrees at the top of the building.

The **Hilton Checkers** (535 S. Grand Ave., 213/624-0000 or 800/445-8667, www.hiltoncheckers.com, from $260) is an intimate Downtown boutique hotel. The elegant guest rooms feature marble-floored baths, and there's a classy fusion restaurant and a great rooftop pool on-site.

HOLLYWOOD

If you're star-struck, a serious partier, or a rock music aficionado, you'll want to do more than just visit Hollywood—you'll want to stay the night within staggering distance of the hottest clubs or the hippest music venues. Heck, you might even luck out and find yourself sleeping in the same room where Axl Rose once vomited or David Lee Roth broke all the furniture.

Under $150

Reputed to be one of the best hostels in the state, the **USA Hostels–Hollywood** (1624 Schrader Blvd., 800/524-6783 or 323/462-3777, www.usahostels.com, around $32 dorm, $97 private room) still offers the same great prices you'll find at seedier, more bare-bones hostels. OK, so the exterior doesn't look like much. But in this case, it's what's inside that counts. You can choose between dorm rooms and private guest rooms, but even the larger dorm rooms have baths attached—a nice convenience that's unusual in the hostel world. (You'll also find several common baths in the hallways, helping to diminish the morning shower rush.) Another great boon is the daily all-you-can-make pancake breakfast, which is included with your room along with all the coffee or tea you can drink. Add that to the $5 barbecue nights on Monday, Wednesday, and Friday, and you've got a great start on seriously diminished food costs for this trip. This smaller hostel also goes a long way to fostering a sense of community among its visitors, offering a standard array of area walking tours and a beach shuttle, plus free comedy nights, movie nights, and open mike nights. If you need to make contact with friends back home, hook up to the free Wi-Fi with your own laptop or use one of the complimentary Internet kiosks.

For a nice modestly priced guest room in the Hollywood vicinity, stay at the **Hollywood Orchid Suites** (1753 Orchid Ave., 323/874-9678 or 800/537-3052, www.orchidsuites.com, $110–320). The Orchid's location couldn't be better; it's in the Hollywood and Highland Center, right behind the Chinese Theatre, next door to the Kodak Theatre, and around the corner from Hollywood Boulevard and the Walk of Fame. If you're a film lover or star seeker on a moderate budget, it's tough to do better than this—especially with the free parking and proximity to public transit. Guest rooms are actually suites, with plenty of space and an eye toward sleeping your large family or several friends all in the same suite. All suites but the Juniors have full kitchens. Don't expect tons of luxury in the furnishings or the decor; it all looks like last decade's motel stuff, although you'll get a coffeemaker, free Wi-Fi, and other better-than-average perks. The rectangular pool offers cooling refreshment in the summer, perfect after a long day of stalking Brad or Britney.

Only a few steps away, you can get a room at the **Hollywood Celebrity Hotel** (1775 Orchid Ave., 800/222-7017 or 323/850-6464, www.hotelcelebrity.com, $130–170). This nice budget motel aspires to Hollywood's famed luxury. Guest rooms have satin comforters, Hollywood-flavored black-and-white artwork, and a modern aesthetic in the furnishings and accents. Amenities include free wired high-speed Internet, valet laundry service, a fitness room, and steam rooms. In the morning, come down to the lobby for a complimentary continental breakfast, and in the evenings take advantage of otherwise hard-to-come-by passes to **The Magic Castle** (7001 Franklin Ave., Hollywood, 323/851-3313, www.magiccastle.com). Leave your car in the gated, off-street parking lot.

The **Hollywood Hills Hotel** (1999 N. Sycamore Ave., check-in at the Magic Castle Hotel, 7025 Franklin Ave., at the base of the hill, 800/741-4915 or 323/874-5089, www.hollywoodhillshotel.com, $140–180, parking $8 per day), is not to be confused with the Best Western Hollywood Hills. The Hollywood Hills Hotel offers truth in advertising, set up in the Hollywood Hills offering lovely views of the L.A. skyline on rare smog-free days. The view of the resort itself can be almost as grand, with its Chinese styling and attractive greenery. All guest rooms here, even the studios, have fully equipped kitchens for travelers seeking to save money on meals. The style of these suites is somewhere between a standard motel and a more upscale resort. You'll find floral comforters, warm-toned walls, and attractive if sparse artistic touches. Best of all, the guest rooms facing out over the city have huge windows to help you enjoy the view from the comfort of your bed. On-site, you'll find a cool Chinese pagoda, a prettily landscaped swimming pool, and a grand California-Asian restaurant,

Yamashiro (323/466-5125, www.yamashirorestaurant.com, 5:30–9:30 P.M. Mon.–Thurs., 5:30–10:30 P.M. Fri., 5–10:30 P.M. Sat., 4:30–9:30 P.M. Sun., valet parking $8).

$150-250

If you've got a little bit more cash, you'll find more lodging options in Hollywood. One good spot is the **Magic Castle Hotel** (7025 Franklin Ave., 323/851-0800 or 800/741-4915, www.magiccastlehotel.com, $180–350), named for the world-renowned magic club next door. It boasts the best customer service of any L.A.-area hostelry. You'll have to make that judgment for yourself, but if one of your goals for your visit to the area is to find a way into the exclusive **Magic Castle** (7001 Franklin Ave., Hollywood, 323/851-3313, www.magiccastle.com), their ancillary hotel has your ticket waiting at the desk. If you're just looking for a nice place to relax between days filled with touring, you'll definitely get that here. Sparkling light guest rooms with cushy white comforters and spare, clean decor offer a haven of tranquility. A courtyard pool invites lounging day and night, and you can even enjoy a midnight swim here without breaking the hotel rules (so long as you don't wake the other guests). Many guest rooms at the Magic Castle have their own kitchens. But be sure to enjoy the little luxurious touches, such as high-end coffee, baked goodies in the free continental breakfast, plushy robes, and nightly turn-down service.

Over $250

A lovely upscale hotel is the **Renaissance Hollywood Hotel** (1755 N. Highland Ave., 323/856-1200 or 800/769-4774, www.renaissancehollywood.com, from $280). Right at the corner of Hollywood Boulevard and Highland Avenue, you'll be in the thick of all the action. This hotel has taken the SoCal mid-century modern style and given it some new-millennium touches to create a colorful, high-end property that appeals to well-heeled travelers of many tastes. With more than 600 guest rooms and suites, you'll probably find one to suit you. Expect eye-piercingly bright blue, yellow, and red bedspreads and upholstered chairs in sizeable guest rooms, some with nice city views. Kids are welcome, and the hotel offers child care for parents looking a few hours' respite or more adult attractions. If you're not up for the Walk of Fame or the Wax Museum, grab a chaise longue on the rooftop pool or just order room service. To dine in true style, try **Twist** (323/491-1000, under $30), the on-site California-cuisine restaurant that features small bites to let diners try as many menu items as they can stand. If you're staying at the Renaissance to admire the modern artistic touches, get a brochure from the desk and take a tour of the common spaces, which display more than 70 works of colorful modern art for your admiration, many of them by local artists.

BEVERLY HILLS AND WEST HOLLYWOOD

Most travelers don't come to Beverly Hills looking to stay in a youth hostel. In a town whose name equals wealth, the point is to dive headfirst into the lap of luxury. Although you might have to save up to get a room near Rodeo Drive, if you choose wisely, you might just get a sense of how the other 1 percent lives for just one or two nights.

For budget accommodations in the general vicinity, look to the chain motels in the West Hollywood area, which serves as L.A.'s gay mecca. Lodgings here fall between the Ramada and Beverly Hills–priced unique upscale hotels.

$150-250

The **Hotel Beverly Terrace** (469 N. Doheny Dr., Beverly Hills, 310/274-8141 or 800/842-6401, www.hotelbeverlyterrace.com, $160–182) is a rare affordable alternative in the area. This spruced-up, retro-cool motor hotel enjoys a great spot on the border of Beverly Hills and West Hollywood.

Over $250

A newcomer to the Beverly Hills luxury hotel scene, **The Mosaic Hotel** (125 Spalding Dr., Beverly Hills, 310/278-0303 or 800/463-4466, www.mosaichotel.com, $275–700) offers a laid-back, urban vibe in both its chill common areas and its comfortable guest accommodations. Guest rooms are furnished in contemporary fabrics, with soothing light colors blending into attractive wall art and fluffy white down comforters. Mattresses are topped with feather beds, and the baths sparkle and sooth with Frette towels and Bulgari bath products. If you've got the cash to spring for a suite, you'll be treated to something that feels like your own elegant apartment, with a living room with 42-inch plasma TV, a sofa, and an armchair. Downstairs, a hip bar and small dining room offer top-shelf cocktails and tasty California cuisine. Friendly, helpful staff will serve you tidbits in the bar and can help with any travel or room needs.

The most famous of all the grand hotels of Beverly Hills, the **Beverly Wilshire** (9500 Wilshire Blvd., Beverly Hills, 310/275-5200, www.fourseasons.com/beverlywilshire, from $500) is now a Four Seasons property. But never fear: The recent multimillion-dollar renovation didn't scour away all the classic charm of this historic hotel. Nor did it lower the price of the privilege of sleeping inside these hallowed walls. Even the plainest of guest rooms here feature exquisite appointments such as 42-inch plasma TVs, elegant linens, attractive artwork, and even live plants. Of course, guests with greater resources can rent a suite; the presidential suite resembles nothing so much as a European palace, complete with Corinthian columns. With an in-house spa, a dining room, room service, and every other service you could want, folks who can afford it consider a stay at the Beverly Wilshire well worth the expense.

In West Hollywood, the **Sunset Tower Hotel** (8358 Sunset Blvd., West Hollywood, 323/654-7100, www.sunsettowerhotel.com, $300–2,500) might look familiar to recent visitors to Disney's California Adventure. Indeed, its architecture inspired the "Tower of Terror" ride at the amusement park. But there's no terror in the Sunset Tower today. Instead, you'll find a gorgeous art deco exterior and a fully renovated modern interior. Guest accommodations range from smallish standard queen guest rooms with smooth linens and attractive appointments up to luxurious suites with panoramic views and limestone baths. All guest rooms include flat-screen TVs, 24-hour room service, and free Wi-Fi.

The Loire-esque castle that is **Chateau Marmont** (8221 Sunset Blvd., West Hollywood, 323/656-1010 or 800/242-8328, www.chateaumarmont.com, rooms and suites $415–900, cottages, bungalows, and penthouses $2,000–4,500) looks out on the city from its perch above the Sunset Strip. It has long attracted the in crowd, from Garbo to Leo. The design is eccentric and eclectic, from vintage 1940s suites to Bauhaus bungalows.

The **Le Montrose Suite** (900 Hammond St., West Hollywood, 310/855-1115 or 800/776-0666, www.lemontrose.com, from $250) will give you a taste of the kind of luxury celebrities expect in their accommodations, especially in trendy, gay-friendly West Hollywood. The atmosphere and decor are almost desperately modern, from the silver discs behind the front desk to the neo-patchwork bedspreads in the guest rooms. Happily, you'll find lots of plush comfort in among the primary colors and plain geometric shapes in your guest room. A Berber carpet snuggles your feet, a high-end entertainment system sees to your every audio-visual and gaming need, and a gas fireplace provides just the right romantic atmosphere for an evening spent indoors. Outside your posh suite, you can take a dip in the rooftop saltwater swimming pool and whirlpool, play a set on the lighted tennis courts, or get in a good workout inside the fitness center. Hotel guests alone can enjoy the gourmet delicacies of the private dining room or order from 24-hour room service. If you're dying for some great clubbing or a seat at a show while you're in town, just ask the concierge, who can provide the assistance you need.

SANTA MONICA, VENICE, AND MALIBU

Arguably, the best place to stay in Los Angeles is down by the beach. It seems ironic that you can camp in a park for $25 in exclusive Malibu, and you can pay over $1,000 for a resort room in so-called "working-class" Santa Monica. But whether you choose either of those or a spot in Venice Beach, you'll get some of the best atmosphere is the region.

Under $150

For a bed indoors for cheap, your options near the beach run to youth hostels. The huge **HI-Santa Monica** (1436 2nd St., Santa Monica, 310/393-9913, www.hilosangeles.org, $43–150) offers 260 beds in a building constructed specifically to house the hostel and which recently underwent a $2 million renovation. You'll be right in the thick of downtown Santa Monica in a good neighborhood, within walking distance of the Santa Monica Pier, the Third Street Promenade, and the beach. Plenty of great cheap restaurants cluster in the area, or you can make use of the hostel's open kitchen. This ritzy hostel offers tons of amenities for the price, including a computer room, a game room, a TV room, a movie room, excursions, wheelchair access, sheets with the bed price, and even a complimentary continental breakfast every morning. If you prefer to find your own way around L.A., the local public transit system runs right outside the door.

The **Venice Beach Cotel** (25 Windward Ave., Venice, 310/399-7649 or 888/718-8287, www.venicebeachcotel.com, $30–80 winter, $40–120 summer) claims to be "a hostel with hotel standards." You can make your own judgments on its amenities, which include women's-only and coed dorms with and without in-room baths, private rooms, and private rooms with baths. Rooms get maid service daily (a rarity in the hostelling world), and a computer room and a kick-back lounge welcome guests and encourage them to socialize. But the best part of the Cotel is undoubtedly its location *on* the Boardwalk right across from Muscle Beach. Fall out of your bunk and into the warm sands of Venice's beach every morning. The fabulous restaurants of Washington Street are reached by an easy walk, and the canals sit just a block or two away. Reserve well in advance for summer.

The reasonably priced (for what it is) and fantastically fun ◖ **Custom Hotel** (8639 Lincoln Blvd., Westchester, 310/645-0400 or 877/287-8601, www.customhotel.com, from $125), is south of Venice near LAX. From the herd of sheep in the lobby to the dog-print bedspreads, a sense of whimsy pervades this otherwise ultrastylish hotel. Your guest room might not be the biggest in town, but it will be clean and pristine, with snowy-white linens, comfortable beds, and an attractively appointed bath. On the counter you'll find a basket full of fun favors (for a price, of course); we'll leave it to you to figure out why you'd want to purchase a packet of radish seeds from a high-end hotel. The in-room Wi-Fi is free, as are the views of the city. You'll find the staff incredibly friendly and helpful, ready to help with anything from valet parking to dinner reservations. Fear not if you're seeking food and drink and would rather not leave the hotel: Custom Hotel has six social lounges, each with its own concept, including the VIP lounge-inspired LAX Lounge, the Transonic gaming lounge, the Axis Annex art gallery, and the Duty Free vending machine room; there are places throughout the hotel to relax while gathering with others to share ideas. Want a little more? Try out DECK 33 Bar Restaurant featuring Pacific Rim–influenced cuisine and overlooking the sun deck and pool, or Hanger 39, the event space on the lobby floor with its own entrance and bar.

The **Venice Beach Suites & Hotel** (1305 Ocean Front Walk, 310/396-4559 or 888/877-7602, www.venicebeachsuites.com, $130–260) is a surprisingly lovely and affordable little Venice hotel. It sits right on the beach, but it's far enough from the Boardwalk to acquire a touch of peace and quiet. You can also stroll over to Washington Street to grab a meal or a cup of coffee, or just wander out of the lobby

and straight onto the beach. Inside, the guest rooms and suites all have full kitchens so you can cook for yourself—perfect for budget-conscious travelers and folks staying in Venice for several days. The kitchen is also great for simply coming in from the beach for a quick lunch with ice-cold drinks. The guest room decor is cuter than that of an average motel; you might find exposed brick walls and polished hardwood floors stocked with rattan furniture and cute accessories. Check the website for week-long rental deals.

$150-250

If you're looking for a moderate-priced motel near the beach, look to the 1950s-era motor inns of Santa Monica. One of these that manages to be cute and kitschy is the **Bayside Hotel** (2001 Ocean Ave., Santa Monica, 310/396-6000 or 800/525-4447, www.baysidehotel.com, $210–290). The hotel is not right on the beach, but you can walk there in about two minutes. If you crave elegance along with speedy check-in and checkout, the Bayside isn't for you. But if you're seeking a fun stay in a place that looks like it ought to be in a Gidget movie, the Bayside may be just right.

For a charming hotel experience only a block from the ever-energetic Boardwalk, stay at the **Inn at Venice Beach** (327 Washington Blvd., 800/828-0688, www.innatvenicebeach.com, $180–200, parking $7 per day). The charming yellow-and-blue exterior, complete with a lovely bricked interior courtyard-cum-café, makes all guests feel welcome. Inside, you might be surprised by the brightly colored modern furniture and decor. Common spaces are done in a postmodern blocky style, while the guest rooms pop with brilliant yellows and vibrant accents. The two-story boutique hotel offers only about 20 guest rooms, and its location on Washington Street makes it a perfect base from which to enjoy the best restaurants of Venice. Start each day with a complimentary continental breakfast, either in the dining room or outside in the Courtyard Café. If you need to stay connected, the inn has complimentary Wi-Fi throughout.

If you want to bring your family to stay in legendary Malibu, one of the best hotels going is the **Casa Malibu Inn on the Beach** (22752 Pacific Coast Hwy., 310/456-2219 or 800/831-0858, $170–500). This pleasant and kid-friendly property sits right out on the beach. Many of the guest rooms have ocean views; some also have gas fireplaces for cozy cool winter evenings. White bedsteads match the paint and draperies, while colorful bedspreads add visual appeal to the European styling of each smallish but unique guest room. Some of the gleaming white baths have oversize bathtubs, perfect for a relaxing soak after a long day out on the beach. Head down to the lobby of this unpretentious 1950s-era building for a genuinely fresh continental breakfast each morning. From there, you can stagger right out onto the sand to pick out a prime spot before the crowds descend. You don't even have to worry about parking.

Yes, you really can stay at the **Hotel California** (1670 Ocean Ave., Santa Monica, 310/393-2363 or 866/571-0000, $219–319). Appropriately decorated with classic longboards and electric guitars, this moderate hotel sits a short block from the beach and next to the Santa Monica Pier. You'll be in the perfect spot to enjoy all the best of Santa Monica without ever having to get into a car or worry about finding parking. Inside the hotel, you'll find hardwood floors and matching bedsteads, calming pale yellow walls, and white comforters and linens. Choose between a classic guest room, a suite with a jetted tub, and one- and two-bedroom suites. Outside, enjoy the lush greenery of the oddly named Spanish Courtyard, which looks more like something from the tropics than from Europe. Other perks include free Wi-Fi, a mini fridge, and a smoke-free hotel experience.

Over $250

In Malibu, if you've got silly amounts of cash to spare, stay at the **Malibu Beach Inn** (22878 Pacific Coast Hwy., Malibu, 310/456-6444 or 800/462-5428, www.malibubeachinn.com, $325–1,075). This ocean-side villa offers all the very best furnishings and amenities. Every guest room has a view of the ocean, and the boutique hotel sits on "Billionaire's Beach," an exclusive stretch of sand that's difficult to access unless you're a guest of one of its properties. Your guest room will be done in rare woods, gleaming stone, and the most stylish modern linens and accents. A plasma TV, plush robes, and comfy beds tempt some visitors to stay inside, but equally tempting are the balconies with their own entertainment in the form of endless surf, glorious sunsets, and balmy breezes. The more affordable guest rooms are a bit small but just as attractively turned out as the over-the-top suites. When lunch and dinnertime come, go downstairs to the airy, elegant, on-site Carbon Beach Club ($31–50) to enjoy delicious cuisine in an upscale beach atmosphere.

One of the best-known resort hotels at the beach in L.A. has long been **Shutters on the Beach** (1 Pico Blvd., Santa Monica, 310/458-0030, www.shuttersonthebeach.com, from $495). Make no mistake: You'll pay handsomely for the privilege of laying your head on one of Shutters' hallowed pillows. On the other hand, the gorgeous airy guest rooms will make you feel like you're home, or at least staying at the home you'd have if you could hire a famous designer to decorate for you. Even the most modest guest rooms have not only the comfortable beds, white linens, plasma TVs, and oversize bathtubs of a luxury hotel, you'll also find a comfortable clutter of pretty ornaments on tables and shelves. If you can pry yourself out of your private space, head down to the famed lobby for a drink and a people-watching session. Get a reservation for the elegant One Pico or grab a more casual sandwich or salad at beachside Coast.

The impressive multilevel resort edifice sits right on the beach, so there's no need to find a premium parking spot to enjoy a day in the sand. If you long for more formal relaxation, book a massage at the **ONE Spa.** Art lovers can spend hours just wandering the halls of the hotel, examining the works of many famous modern photographers and painters.

PASADENA

Pasadena lodgings run to the old standard national chains plus a few funky 1950s-era motor lodges and the occasional upscale B&B. If you're planning to stay in Pasadena over the New Year, book early: The town fills up for the legendary Rose Parade. If your aim is to get yourself a guest room from which you can watch the Rose Parade, book earlier still; while you can get the perfect view from a room of your own, such places are at a premium during parade season.

Under $150

The **Ramada Pasadena** (2156 E. Colorado Blvd., 626/793-9339, www.ramada.com, $80–150), formerly the Kingston Inn & Suites, provides good clean guest rooms right along the Rose Parade route for reasonable nightly rates (which go way up for the parade). You're also nice and close to Old Town, restaurants, and museums. The guest rooms have standard dark floral bedspreads and matching deep red carpets, enough room to walk around your two queens or king bed, and average motel baths. A sizeable balcony outside each room offers the perfect Parade vantage point, and a sparkling pool with a hot tub beckons travelers outside. Modern in-room amenities include Wi-Fi, iPod docking stations, coffeemakers, fridges, and more.

The top pick of the quaint motor inns is the **Saga Motor Hotel** (1633 E. Colorado Blvd., 626/795-0431 or 800/793-7242, www.the-sagamotorhotel.com, $92–135). Outside it's all 1950s, from the structure of the low buildings to the Astroturf around the swimming pool. The ambiance extends to the door of your guest room, which includes a doorknob and an actual metal key to open it with. But inside your room, the decor gets a lot more contemporary. The big space has either a king or two double beds, clean if worn carpeting and linens, and a nice bath with a surprisingly good bathtub and nice hot showers. Location-wise, the Saga is right on the Rose Parade route on broad Colorado Boulevard, but it's not right downtown or in Old Town. Sadly, the service is spotty at best, but few people expect concierges at motor hotels.

Of the main chain motels, the best inexpensive one might be the **Comfort Inn** (2462 E. Colorado Blvd., 626/405-0811, www.comfortinn.com, from $85). You'll find comfortable amenities in pleasant standard motel rooms, along with a good set of views of the Rose Parade. Expect room prices to skyrocket for the parade.

$150-250

Once upon a time, Pasadena was the resort haven of wealthy East Coasters. To revisit this wealthy past, stay at **The Bissell House Bed & Breakfast** (201 Orange Grove Ave., 626/441-3535 or 800/441-3530, www.bissellhouse.com, $155–350) on "Millionaire's Row." The tall mint-green Victorian surrounded by the deeper green of lush mature landscaping opens its doors to well-heeled travelers who want a luxurious place to stay while they're in the L.A. area. It is named for one of its residents, Anna Bissell McCay, heiress to the original Bissell vacuum-cleaner fortune. Each of the five guest rooms and two suites has a unique decorating scheme, yet each shares a European floral theme that binds the inn together into a coherent whole. Guest rooms have comfy beds, a luxurious bath (most have claw-foot tubs), and lots of wonderful amenities, and the property has a swimming pool with a hot tub and lots of lovely plants scattered about. Your room rate includes a full breakfast each morning, served at the long table in the downstairs dining room.

Food

You'll find a wide variety of cuisine all over Los Angeles and its surrounding towns. Whatever kind of food you prefer, from fresh sushi to Armenian, you can probably find it in a cool little hole-in-the-wall somewhere in L.A. Local recommendations often make for the best dining experiences, but even just walking down the right street can yield a tasty meal.

DOWNTOWN AND VICINITY

Sure, you can find plenty of bland tourist-friendly restaurants serving American and Americanized food in the Downtown area—but why would you, when one of Downtown L.A.'s greatest strengths is its ethnic diversity and the great range of cuisine that goes along with it? An endless array of fabulous holes-in-the-wall awaits you. Getting local recommendations is the best way to find the current hot spots, or you can choose from among this tiny sampling of what's available.

American

If you're just looking for a good pastrami sandwich, you can get it at **Langer's Delicatessen and Restaurant** (704 S. Alvarado St., 213/483-8050, www.langersdeli.com, 8 A.M.–4 P.M. Mon.–Sat., $12–25). Operating continuously since 1947, the house specialty at Langer's is a hot pastrami sandwich that some say is the best in the world (yes, that includes New York City). Whether you're willing to go that far or not, Langer's serves both hot and cold dishes in the traditional Jewish deli style to satisfy any appetite level or specific craving. Granted, it's still California, so you can get fresh avocado on your tongue sandwich if you really want to. You'll also find a vast breakfast menu and plenty of desserts (noodle kugel, anyone?). If you don't have time to sit down for lunch, order in advance and pick up your meal curbside. If you can dine in, be sure to take a few minutes to gaze at the photos on the walls; the family you'll see has run this deli since it opened in the postwar era.

Located in an old firehouse building, **Engine Co. No. 28** (644 S. Figueroa St., 213/624-6996, www.engineco.com, 7:30 A.M.–10 P.M. Mon.–Fri., 11 A.M.–10 P.M. Sat.–Sun., $14–40) is decked out in classic wood paneling, leather, and brass. Meatloaf and chili are the big sellers.

Asian

One of the largest Asian neighborhoods in Los Angeles is Koreatown. It's only fitting that a city with such a large Korean population has plenty of good Korean restaurants. One of these is **Chunju Han-il Kwan** (3450 W. 6th St., 213/480-1799, 11 A.M.–11 P.M. Mon.–Sat., $10–15). This is an authentic Korean restaurant that caters primarily to the expat Korean community. You won't find English menus here, but you will find helpful waitresses who can guide you through the process of ordering. If your server tells you a dish is very spicy, she means it, but that doesn't mean you won't love it anyway. The menu is eclectic to say the least—you can get a hot dog, octopus, fish soup, Korean stew (thickened with American cheese), kimchi, and much more. Many patrons crave the veggie side dishes that come with the entrées. Don't worry about your standard of dress when you dine here, since this casual restaurant resides in a strip mall and has gas burners on the tables.

There are lots of ramen places in Little Tokyo, but busy, noisy **◖ Daikokuya** (327 E. 1st St., 213/626-1680, www.daikoku-ten.com, 11 A.M.–midnight Mon.–Thurs., 11 A.M.–1 A.M. Fri.–Sat., 11 A.M.–11 P.M. Sun., under $10) is among the very best, hailed by no less an authority than Pulitzer Prize–winning food writer Jonathan Gold. The steaming bowls of hearty pork broth and noodles satisfy even the brawniest appetite.

For a serious authentic Japanese cuisine experience, visit **◖ Kagaya** (418 E. 2nd St., 213/617-1016, 6–10:30 P.M. Tues.–Sat., 6–10 P.M. Sun., $40–128). Even L.A. denizens who've eaten at shabu-shabu places in Japan come back to Kagaya again and again. They make reservations in advance, because the dining room is small and the quality of the food makes it popular even on weeknights. The term *shabu-shabu* refers to paper-thin slices of beef and vegetable that you dip and swish into a pot of boiling *daishi* (broth), then dunk in *ponzu* or other house-made sauces before eating. The shabu-shabu is but one course in the meal you'll get at Kagaya, since all meals include several appetizers (varieties change daily), shabu-shabu with beef and seafood, *udon* noodles, and dessert. You can pay a premium for Wagyu beef if you choose, but the king crab legs in season are part of the regular price of dinner. Even the regular beef here isn't cheap, but the quality makes it worth the price. Sit at the counter if you want to watch all your food being prepared before your eyes.

French

A surprisingly cute little brick-fronted café, the **Angelique Café** (840 S. Spring St., 213/623-8698, www.angeliquebistro.com, 11:30 A.M.–3 P.M. and 5–10 P.M. Tues.–Fri., 8 A.M.–3 P.M. and 5–10 P.M. Sat.–Sun., $11–20) offers a relaxed French atmosphere and good French-style food. The original chef-owner came from France and brought his recipes and his dining aesthetic with him. The large menu has an array of both French and American dishes, heavy on the salads and more traditional hot fare. If you come for breakfast, you can choose from a list of omelets and crepes plus a few American egg dishes, or the more traditional continental breakfast of pastry and coffee. Angelique's small green-and-yellow dining room is open for breakfast and lunch only. If it's a nice day, grab a table outside on the wrought iron–fenced patio, which has almost as many tables as the inside dining room.

Greek

Originally a Greek import company in the 1960s, the **Papa Cristos Taverna** (2771 W. Pico Blvd., 323/737-2970, www.papacristo. com, 10 A.M.–8 P.M. Tues.–Sat., 9 A.M.–4 P.M. Sun., $7–17) restaurant opened in the 1990s.

The import shop still supplies the local Greek community with hard-to-come-by delicacies, which also become ingredients in the cuisine at the Taverna. Dishes are traditionally Greek, from the salads to the kebabs to the baba ghanoush. After you're finished with your meal, wander the aisles of the store to pick up a few unusual Greek delicacies to take with you.

Italian

It seems odd to name a high-end restaurant after a decidedly low-end bug, but that's what the owners of **C Cicada Restaurant** (617 S. Olive St., 213/488-9488, www.cicadarestaurant.com, 5:30–9 P.M. Mon.–Sat., $50–90) did. Set in the 1920s Oviatt building decorated in high French art deco style, the beautiful restaurant glitters with some of its original Lalique glass panels—be sure to check out the elevator doors on your way in or out. The palatial dining room features huge round tables for large parties and balcony seating for intimate duos. The immense space lets Cicada place its tables farther apart than in most restaurants, giving diners a sense of privacy and romance that can be hard to come by.

As for the food, calling it "Italian" isn't quite right, since the cuisine here fuses Italian concepts with California ingredients, techniques, and presentations. Expect a varied seasonal menu of inventive dishes, including pastas and meats in the Italian style with distinct California flavors. Be sure to save room for Cicada's beloved desserts, which many diners declare to be their favorite part of the meal.

Mexican

Everyone in L.A. (and most of the rest of California, for that matter) knows that the best tamales come from the kitchens of Mexican grandmothers and get sold on the streets from carts or trucks. If you're not a local and don't feel able to find the best little sidewalk tamale cart, your best option is **C Mama's Hot Tamales Café** (2124 W. 7th St., 213/487-7474, www.mamashottamales.com, 11 A.M.–3:30 P.M. daily, $6–10). You'll even get a little social justice with your lunch, as Mama's operates as a training ground for "informal" food purveyors to develop the skills they need to become higher-paid employees of the formal food-service world. Open pretty much for lunch only, Mama's serves salads, appetizers, burritos, tostadas, and other simple Latin American dishes. But if you know what's right, you'll order the house namesake: a homemade tamale.

Located on Olvera Street, **La Luz del Dia** (1 W. Olvera St., 213/628-7495, www.luzdeldia. com, 10 A.M.–2:30 P.M. Mon., 10 A.M.–8 P.M. Tues.–Thurs., 10 A.M.–9 P.M. Fri.–Sat., 8:30 A.M.–9 P.M. Sun., $7–10) has been dishing up simple, spicy Mexican food since 1959. Get a beer, a combination plate with delicious homemade corn tortillas, and watch the tourists go by.

Markets
In operation since 1917, the **Grand Central Market** (317 S. Broadway, 213/624-2378, www.grandcentralsquare.com, 9 A.M.–6 P.M. daily) houses dozens of food vendors. Most sell hot prepared foods, but you'll also find stalls selling spices and Latino pantry goods. A $10 or more purchase and validation will get you an hour's free parking at the garage at 308 South Hill Street.

LOS FELIZ
American
French fries in origami bags. Toasters on every table. Dishes with names like Mac Daddy and Cheese. Everything plays into the love-it-or-leave-it hip factor at **Fred 62** (1850 N. Vermont Ave., 323/667-0062, www.fred62. com, 24 hours daily, $7–15), where the booths feel like old Chevy backseats and everyone's a garage-band star.

Asian
Routinely topping critics' lists of the best Thai restaurants in Los Angeles, elegant **Jitlada** (5233½ Sunset Blvd., 323/663-3104, www. jitladala.com, 5–10:30 P.M. Mon., 11 A.M.–10:30 P.M. Tues.–Thurs. and Sun., 11 A.M.–11 P.M. Fri.–Sat.) specializes in the cuisine of southern Thailand, which is rarely seen on

U.S. menus. Order carefully: Some dishes are so spicy you will cry.

Mexican
Not every taco stand wins awards from the James Beard Foundation. ◖ **Yuca's** (2056 Hillhurst Ave., 323/662-1214, www.yucasla. com, 11 A.M.–6 P.M. Mon.–Sat.) received the honor in 2005, but it simply confirmed what Los Feliz locals have known for decades: This shack serves truly memorable (and cheap) tacos and burritos. Vegetarians beware: Even the beans are made with pork fat.

Coffee and Tea
The baristas at **Intelligentsia** (3922 Sunset Blvd., 323/663-6173, www.intelligentsiacoffee. com, 6 A.M.–8 P.M. Sun.–Wed., 6 A.M.–11 P.M. Thurs.–Sat.) are true artisans, pulling shots and steaming milk with cultish reverence. Many of the beans are direct-trade and shade-grown. Linger on the lovely patio, paved with gorgeous blue tiles imported from Nicaragua.

HOLLYWOOD
Hollywood's got just as many tasty treats tucked away in strip malls as other areas of Los Angeles. If you want to rub elbows with rock stars, you're likely to find yourself at a big, slightly raunchy bar and grill. For a chance at glimpsing stars of the silver screen, look for upscale California cuisine or perhaps a high-end sushi bar. If all you need is tasty sustenance, you can choose from a range of restaurants.

American
If you've ever owned a rock album—any rock album—it's worth your time to stop in for a meal at ◖ **The Rainbow Bar & Grill** (9015 W. Sunset Blvd., 310/278-4232, www.rainbowbarandgrill.com, cocktails 11 A.M.–2 A.M. daily, lunch 11 A.M.–4 P.M. Mon.–Fri., dinner 4 P.M.–2 A.M. daily, $13–30). You'll find a lack of fancy sauces and an amazing myriad of rock-and-roll memorabilia in this dark (but no longer smoky) restaurant. To the surprise of some intrepid diners, the hallowed haven, in which countless rockers have been serviced

by innumerable groupies, does serve a darn tasty cheeseburger. If you show up for lunch on a weekday, you're likely to have the cavernous space almost to yourself to enjoy your salad and make your slow way along the walls checking out the endless parade of photos, guitars, newspaper snippets, and other cool stuff. In the even dimmer bar area, you can play a for-real game of authentic table Ms. Pac-Man as you sip your favorite cocktail or quaff a beer.

Nighttime is a whole different story. The crowds start trickling into the Rainbow as the sun goes down. By the time the shows let out at the Roxy and the Whisky, your chances of finding a booth diminish significantly. The good news is that the rockers still gather here after playing shows in the neighborhood. You never know who you'll bump into as you weave your way through the main dining room and outdoor patio to get your next drink. The back rooms also open up late, and you'll find dancing, drinking, smoking (sh!), and fun upstairs in a warren-like space that includes either two or three separate bar-and-club spaces on any given night, depending on whose tales you believe.

As for amenities, expect woefully inadequate and difficult-to-access restrooms, particularly if you happen to be female. Waitstaff runs to cute and buxom young women. You can take your cigarettes just outside of the exits to be legal.

If you prefer to combine your love of live acts and your need for food, head for the **Hotel Café** (1623½ N. Cahuenga Blvd., 323/461-2040, marko@hotelcafe.com, www.hotelcafe.com, 7 P.M.–close daily, 21 and over, $10–30). Food choices run to the casual here—paninis, salads, and desserts, but the restaurant has a beer list, a wine list, and a full bar. The restaurant opens early; it's easiest to secure a table if you show up before the show starts. After 7 P.M., prepare for things to get loud. If you do love yourself some new-to-the-scene music, stick around.

On the more casual end of the spectrum, **[C Pink's Famous Hot Dogs** (709 N. La Brea Ave., 323/931-4223, www.pinkshollywood.

com, 9:30 A.M.–2 A.M. Sun.–Thurs., 9:30 A.M.–3 A.M. Fri.–Sat.) is hot dog heaven. Frankophiles line up at this roadside stand (lit up like a Las Vegas show club into the wee hours of the morning) for variations on a sausage in a bun that range from the basic chili dog to the more elaborate Martha Stewart Dog. It has been at the same location since 1939.

Italian

The warm but clamorous dining room at **[C Pizzeria Mozza** (641 N. Highland Ave., 323/297-0101, www.mozza-la.com, noon–midnight daily, $8–24) has been packed since chef Nancy Silverton, founder of La Brea Bakery, opened the doors in 2006. The wood-fired oven turns out rustic, blistered pizzas with luxurious toppings. Reservations are tough to get, but bar seats are available for walk-ins.

As smashingly popular (and as raucous) as Pizzeria Mozza is the chef's Italian restaurant next door, **Osteria Mozza** (6602 Melrose Ave., 323/297-0100, www.mozza-la.com, noon–midnight daily, $10–40). Serving more than just pizza, the Osteria offers a fuller menu of luscious pastas and adventurous meat dishes. Check out the "mozzarella menu," an assortment of appetizer-size dishes featuring bufala, burrata, and ricotta.

Brazilian

Need food really, really, *really* late? **Bossa Nova** (7181 W. Sunset Blvd., 323/436-7999, www.bossafood.com, 11 A.M.–4 A.M. daily, $10–20) can hook you up. A big menu of inexpensive entrées can satisfy any appetite from lunch to way past dinnertime at Bossa. Some of the dishes bear the spicy flavors of the owners' home country of Brazil, but you'll also find a ton of pastas, plenty of salads, and classic Italian-American build-your-own pizzas. Check out the desserts for some South American specialties if you need sweets after a long night out at the clubs. Not near the Sunset Strip? Bossa Nova has three other L.A. locations: one on Robertson Boulevard, one in Beverly Hills, and one in West L.A. If you've made it back to your hotel room and aren't inclined to leave again, Bossa delivers.

California

It seems right somehow that the spot in L.A. that combines live music with upscale cuisine is on Melrose Avenue. At ◖ **The Foundry on Melrose** (7465 Melrose Ave., 323/651-0915, www.thefoundryonmelrose.com, 6 P.M.–close Mon.–Sat., 5:30 P.M.–close Sun., $25–30), expect to find elegance and art in a style that improbably marries arts and crafts, art deco, and modern industrial. The art extends to the plates, where the chef creates elaborate presentations of an array of ingredients. The dinner menu is small, seasonal, and utterly haute California. You might even see an occasional celebrity dining here, though you'll also remark on the refreshing lack of oh-so-trendy 'tude at this restaurant. At the big curving black bar, you can get a lighter (and less pricey) meal from the bar menu. If you prefer an alfresco dining experience, ask for a table out on the patio (yes, that's an olive tree dangling its streamers in your soup). The third room at the Foundry shelters a small piano bar and a mix of music, from Lunes Latinos on Monday to Bluesy Tuesday and Suds and Songs Sunday.

LA BREA, FAIRFAX, AND MIRACLE MILE
American

Midnight snackers unhinge their jaws on the hulking corned beef sandwiches at **Canter's Deli** (419 N. Fairfax Ave., 323/651-2030, www.cantersdeli.com, 24 hours daily, $12–18), in the heart of the Jewish Fairfax district. This venerable 24-hour deli also boasts its share of star sightings, so watch of noshing rock stars in the wee hours of the morning.

Lunch doesn't get much better than the high-end bounty in the deli cases at **Joan's on Third** (8350 W. 3rd St., 323/655-2285, www.joansonthird.com, 8 A.M.–8 P.M. Mon.–Sat., 8 A.M.–6 P.M. Sun., $10–15). Mix and match fine pasta salads, roasted vegetables, and artisanal cheeses. There are also sidewalk tables,

and a breakfast kitchen serving organic eggs and French toast.

California

Pairing meat and potatoes with a retro-clubby dining room, **Jar** (8225 Beverly Blvd., 323/655-6566, www.thejar.com, dinner from 5:30 P.M. daily, brunch from 10 A.M. Sun., $10–65) puts a Southern California spin on the traditional steak house. Meats and grilled fishes are served à la carte with your choice of sauce, and the side orders serve two. Jar is also known for its Sunday brunch—try the Lobster Benedict.

BEVERLY HILLS AND WEST HOLLYWOOD

Between Beverly Hills and West L.A. you'll find an eclectic choice of restaurants. Unsurprisingly, Beverly Hills tends toward high-end eateries serving European and haute California cuisine. On the other hand, West L.A. boasts a wide array of international restaurants. You'll have to try a few to pick your favorites, since every local has their own take on the area's best eats.

American

The Ivy (113 N. Robertson Blvd., 310/274-8303, 11:30 A.M.–10:30 P.M. Mon.–Sat., 10:30 A.M.–10:30 P.M. Sun., $10–43) is an industry institution: a sun-dappled, cottage-like space where the A-list goes as much to be seen and photographed as to eat. Dishes like chopped salad and soft-shell crab punctuate the new American menu. Call ahead for a prized spot on the sidewalk patio.

Italian

If you're looking for upscale Italian cuisine in a classy environment, enjoy lunch or dinner at **Il Pastaio Restaurant** (400 N. Canon Dr., Beverly Hills, 310/205-5444, www.giacominodrago.com/pastaio.htm, 11:30 A.M.–11 P.M. Mon.–Wed., 11:30 A.M.–midnight Thurs.–Sat., 11:30 A.M.–10 P.M. Sun., $15–30). The bright dining room offers a sunny luncheon experience, and the white tablecloths and shiny glassware lend an elegance to dinner, served reasonably late into the evening even on weekdays. Boasting a large menu for a high-end restaurant, Il Pastaio offers a wide variety of salads, risotto, and pasta dishes as well as some overpriced antipasti and a smaller list of entrées. Preparations and dishes evoke authentic Italy, so you might see osso buco or fettuccine bolognese on the menu. The blue-painted bar offers a tasteful selection of California and Italian vintages, and serious wine lovers will be pleased to see the Italian selections broken out by region.

Happily located right on the Strip, the **Vivoli Cafe & Trattoria** (7994 Sunset Blvd., West Hollywood, 323/656-5050, www.vivolicafe.com, 11 A.M.–10 P.M. Sun.–Thurs., 11 A.M.–11 P.M. Fri.–Sat., $15–30) offers a copious menu of Italian cuisine. Expect white tablecloths, wooden chairs, and friendly service at this locals' favorite. The broad menu focuses on seafood and a surprising variety of salads, but you can also get your favorite cheese-heavy pasta dishes or hearty, meaty entrées. Don't forget dessert—"leave the gun, take the cannoli."

Steak

There's nothing like a good steak dinner, Brazilian style. At **Fogo de Chao** (133 N. La Cienega Blvd., Beverly Hills, 310/289-7755, www.fogodechao.com, 11 A.M.–2 P.M. and 5–10 P.M. Mon.–Thurs., 11 A.M.–2 P.M. and 5–10:30 P.M. Fri., 4:30–10:30 P.M. Sat., 4–9:30 P.M. Sun., $40–80), be prepared for an interactive dining experience. The meat is slow-roasted, then skewered and cut right onto your plate by ever-moving servers. Be sure to use the red-and-green token on your table; if you don't turn it over to the red side occasionally, you will be continuously bombarded with the 15 different kinds of meat the restaurant offers. The fixed-price meal includes endless trips to the salad bar, fresh-cut veggies, and traditional Brazilian side dishes (fried bananas are a starch here, not a dessert). The extensive wine list includes plenty of both California and European vintages, plus a wider-than-average selection of ports and dessert wines. While the food is fabulous, you'll get the most out of a meal

here with a lively group that will enjoy the service as much as the spicy flavors.

Coffee and Tea

A grand afternoon tea in stately Beverly Hills just seems like the right thing to do at least once. You can get some of the best tea in L.A. at (**The Living Room in The Peninsula Hotel** (9882 Santa Monica Blvd., Beverly Hills, 310/975-2736, www.peninsula.com, seatings 2:30 P.M. and 5 P.M. Mon.–Thurs., 12:30 P.M., 2:30 P.M., and 5 P.M. Fri.–Sun., $18–45). The Peninsula has three restaurants, but for tea head to the elegant Living Room and grab a comfy chair near the fireplace. Sit back and enjoy the delicate harp music while admiring the elegant and tasteful furnishings in this posh space. If you skipped lunch or plan to miss dinner, go with the heartier Royal Tea or Imperial Tea. Lighter eaters prefer the Full Tea or the Light Tea. All come with tea sandwiches, scones, pastries, and, of course, a pot of tea. The loose-leaf teas are Peninsula originals; many are flavored. For an extra fee, you can add a glass of champagne to complete your high tea experience.

Dress properly for the occasion: Jackets are required even for tea. Ladies have more latitude, but shouldn't show up in jeans and a T-shirt.

SANTA MONICA, VENICE, AND MALIBU

Yes, there's lots of junky beach food to be found in Santa Monica and Venice Beach, but there are also an amazing number of gems hiding in these towns.

American

(**Cora's Coffee Shoppe** (1802 Ocean Ave., Santa Monica, 310/451-9562, www.corascoffee.com, 7 A.M.–3 P.M. Tues.–Sun., $10) doesn't look like much: It's a tiny building with a smallish sign. But don't be fooled by the unpretentious exterior. The small, exquisite restaurant inside is something of a locals' secret hiding in plain sight, serving breakfast and lunch to diners who are more than willing to pack into the tiny spaces that Cora's calls dining rooms. In addition to the two tiny marble-topped tables and miniature marble counter inside, a small patio area off to one side offers a warm and pleasant atmosphere screened by latticework and venerable bougainvillea vines.

What's best about Cora's is simply the food. The chefs crammed into the tiny kitchen use high-end and sometimes organic ingredients to create breakfast and lunch dishes that don't seem like anything fancy on the menu but will make you rethink your opinion of humble scrambled eggs or lowly oatmeal when they get to your table. The espresso drinks are reminiscent of European coffees—dark, bitter, and served in cups the size of bowls. Perhaps it's the coffee that keeps the staff moving so fast, endlessly serving and busing and serving some more to keep up with the steady flow of diners, many of whom the waiters seem to know quite well.

The lines at the counter of **Urth Caffé** (2327 Main St., 310/314-7040, www.urthcaffe.com, 6:30 A.M.–11 P.M. Mon.–Thurs. and Sun., 6:30 A.M.–midnight Fri.–Sat., $10–15) attest to the popularity of this organic java house's high-quality brew. Mile-high cakes and a vegan-friendly lineup of soups, salads, and sandwiches nourishes the throngs enjoying the outdoor patio.

Asian

If your tastes run to the exotically spicy and romantic, walk across Pacific Avenue from Venice Beach into Marina Del Ray and to the **Siamese Garden** (301 Washington Blvd., Marina Del Rey, 310/821-0098, http://siamese-garden.net, 5–10 P.M. Mon.–Thurs., 4–11 P.M. Fri.–Sat., 4–10 P.M. Sun., $10–30). A favorite of local couples both straight and otherwise looking for a romantic evening out, Siamese Garden boasts outdoor tables set in an overhanging lantern-lit garden, complete with glimpses of the Venice Canals through the foliage and fencing. In the kitchen, Siamese Garden prides itself on creating delightful dishes with only the freshest and best produce and ingredients available. The wide menu offers all of your favorite Thai classics, such as coconut soup, pad

thai, and a rainbow of curries. Mint, lemongrass, peanut sauce, basil, and hot chilies crowd the menu with their strong and distinct flavors. Vegetarians have a great selection of tasty dishes, while carnivores can enjoy plenty of good beef, poultry, and seafood. For dessert, try one of the fun sticky rice and fruit dishes. To accompany your meal, you can get a rich Thai iced tea (ask to see one before you order if you've never had it before) or a light Thai beer.

Barbecue

As is right and proper in California, you have to go to the seedier part of town to get the best authentic Southern barbecue. **Baby Blues BBQ** (444 Lincoln Blvd., Venice, 310/396-7675, www.babybluesvenice.com, 11:30 A.M.–10 P.M. daily, $10–32) disobeys the haute Venice rule of AWOL (Always West of Lincoln), sitting right on Lincoln Boulevard with its grubby sidewalks and elderly strip malls. This disreputable street corner location (it's really not that bad) does not dissuade locals, who line up at lunchtime to grab a plate of ribs or chicken. The menu pays little attention to cholesterol or carb counters. Choose from sausages, pulled pork, beer-braised brisket, barbecued chicken, and pork or beef ribs, all covered in homemade sauces and spice rubs. The cooks know their business, and regional specialties from different parts of the South are created with specific intent and understanding of the cuisine. Fixin's (side dishes) include Baby Blues's famed hot cornbread, baked beans, slaw, mac and cheese, and other appropriate stuff.

Caribbean

How can you not love a restaurant called **Cha Cha Chicken** (1906 Ocean Ave., Santa Monica, 310/581-1684, www.chachachicken.com, 11 A.M.–10 P.M. Mon.–Fri., 10 A.M.–10 P.M. Sat.–Sun., $7–12)? It looks just like it sounds— a slightly decrepit but brightly painted shack only a short walk from the Santa Monica Pier and the Third Street Promenade. You can't miss it even if you're driving quickly down Ocean Avenue. The best place to get a table is definitely the palm tree–strewn patio area outdoors.

A BEGINNER'S GUIDE TO SUSHI

Your first time dining in a sushi restaurant can be an intimidating experience. What to do with the slabs of raw fish, the tentacles, the eggs, the eels, the seaweed – did I mention the raw fish? It's tough to know what's good for a first-timer: The *ebi* or the *unagi*? The *toro* or the *maguro*? Do they cook anything in here?

What follows is a by-no-means-complete beginner's guide to ordering and eating sushi:

Maki (rolls). When most folks think of sushi, they think of seaweed-wrapped circles of rice with fish and vegetables in the middle. This form is called a roll, or *maki*. Almost every sushi place in California will offer certain common rolls, for example the (duh) California roll. This newcomer-friendly roll contains no raw fish; instead, it has cooked crab or crab salad, avocado, and cucumber wrapped in sushi rice and *nori* (seaweed). There are also plain cucumber rolls, Philadelphia rolls (smoked salmon, cream cheese, and avocado), shrimp salad rolls, and tempura rolls at most sushi bars. On the other hand, adventurous diners often eat rolls with raw fish or barbecued eel inside and out, perhaps dusted with flying fish eggs for a touch of salty crunch or a raw quail egg for smoothness.

Nigiri (sushi). *Nigiri*, sometimes called simply "sushi" on restaurant menus, consists of a slice of (usually) raw fish lying on top of a glob of sticky sushi rice, usually with a dab of wasabi paste between the fish and the rice. *Nigiri* are almost always sold in pairs per order. Order *nigiri* with a rectangle of scrambled egg instead of fish, with a whole cooked shrimp, or with smoked salmon to ease yourself into the fishiness of it all. Hardcore sushi-ites munch on seasonal fish, sweet shrimp, and even octopus.

Sashimi. Sashimi refer to slices of raw fish pared to perfection, often arranged in beautiful patterns and designs by the sushi chef. Don't like raw fish? Then don't bother with sashimi. If you want raw fish almost exclusively, then ask for the chef's selection of sashimi.

Wasabi. Important safety tip: That little glob of green stuff on the edge of your plate is not avocado – it's wasabi, a hot Japanese horseradish that has been grated or ground and then mixed into a paste. (In truth, most California wasabi is actually regular ol' Western horseradish mixed with green food coloring.) Take a tiny dab of wasabi and put it into the little empty dish the server brought. Add soy sauce and mix the wasabi in until it dissolves. If you're unaccustomed to spicy foods, use only a tiny fleck of wasabi to start with, and ignore the diners creating a thick sludge with more wasabi in it than soy sauce; they're professionals.

Common raw fish. If you've never had raw fish before and are hesitant to start now, ask for smoked salmon. It's not raw (it's like lox) and it's a good stepping-stone into a world without fire.

Next, consider ordering a couple of common and easy-to-eat fish. *Maguro* is red tuna; it can be served as *nigiri*, but it's often diced fine and mixed with arcane ingredients to create "spicy tuna," which is often more palatable for sushi newcomers who don't mind spicy food. *Sake* is raw salmon. It's often served as *nigiri* and used to decorate the outside of rolls. If you prefer a delicately flavored white fish, try some *hamachi* (yellowtail, a firm white fish) or *tai* (red snapper). To take the next step, order some *unagi*. Hey, it's cooked! In fact, it's barbecued eel.

How to order sushi. While you can order your own plate of rolls and *nigiri*, most sushi fans will tell you that sushi tastes best when shared family-style. Each diner orders a few of their favorite items, all the food comes out on platters, and you and your friends dig in with fingers or chopsticks to try at least one piece of everything.

How to eat sushi. Contrary to popular American belief, it is acceptable to pick up both *nigiri* and roll slices with your fingers. You can then dip your sushi into your dish of wasabi and soy sauce. Be gentle – don't soak your *nigiri* rice in the sauce, or you'll completely cover up the taste of the fish. Next, eat! Chase with hot green tea, sake, or Japanese beer. Repeat until the plate or wooden serving tray empties.

It's the perfect atmosphere to enjoy the wonderful and inexpensive Caribbean dishes that come from the fragrant kitchen. The jerk dishes bring a tangy sweetness to the table, while the *ropa vieja* heats up the plate, and the funky enchiladas put a whole new spin on a Mexican classic. Salads, sandwiches, and wraps are popular with lighter eaters and the lunch crowd. Quaff an imported Jamaican soda or a seasonal *agua fresca* with your meal, since Cha Cha Chicken doesn't have a liquor license.

Italian

A Venice institution, the **C&O Trattoria** (31 Washington Blvd., Venice, 310/823-9491, www.cotrattoria.com, 11:30 A.M.–10 P.M. Mon.–Thurs., 11:30 A.M.–11 P.M. Fri., 8 A.M.–11 P.M. Sat., 8 A.M.–10 P.M. Sun., $13–23) manages to live up to its hype and then some. Pick a seat in the dimly lit indoor dining room with rustic wood furniture and red-checked tablecloths, or sit outside in the big outdoor dining room, enjoying the mild weather and the soft pastel frescoes on the exterior walls surrounding the courtyard. C&O is known for its self-described gargantuan portions, which are best shared family-style among a group of diners. Be sure to start off with the addictive little garlic rolls. Next, seriously consider the pasta list, which includes some truly creative and delectable preparations. If you need help deciding on dishes, be sure to ask your friendly, knowledgeable server, who will be attentive but not overzealous. While C&O has a nice wine list, it's worth trying a jug of the surprisingly tasty house chianti.

Mexican

Looking for good cheap tacos in an unfamiliar town can be a scary proposition, but you have no need to fear **El Tarasco** (109 Washington Blvd., Marina Del Rey, 310/306-8552, 9 A.M.–11 P.M. daily, $5–10). This walk-up dive taqueria has locals' stamp of approval, and it boasts of the freshness of its food. Specialties of the house are the burritos and tostadas, which are big and cheap and yummy. Even the full-fledged dinners that come with rice and beans

and a combination of items please budget diners, since nothing on the menu costs more than $10. You can eat at El Tarasco in the decidedly down-rent but charming dining room, or get your food to go, perhaps for a quick walk down Washington Boulevard to chow down on your burritos at the beach.

Seafood

The dramatic black-and-white–themed dining room at **Catch** (1910 Ocean Way, Santa Monica, 310/581-7714, www.hotelcasadelmar.com, 7–11 A.M., 11:30 A.M.–3 P.M., and 6–10 P.M. daily, $16–45) in the Casa del Mar hotel looks out on spectacular ocean views. The menu offers choices from "land" and "sea," including a nice selection of sushi and sashimi.

Neptune's Net (42505 Pacific Coast Hwy., Malibu, 310/457-3095, www.neptunesnet.com, 10:30 A.M.–8 P.M. Mon.–Thurs., 10 A.M.–8:30 P.M. Fri.–Sun. summer, 10:30 A.M.–7 P.M. Mon.–Fri., 10 A.M.–7 P.M. Sat.–Sun. winter, $10–20) in Malibu catches all kinds of seafood to serve to hungry diners. Locals call it "The Net" and usually order the fish and chips. Situated on the Malibu coastline adjacent to the county line surf break, you'll often find sandy and salt-encrusted local surfers satisfying their enormous appetites after hours out on the waves. Even Midwestern visitors who are put off by the endless raw and rare fish eaten in California will feel comfortable dining in this casual palace of fried seafood. The large menu includes a seemingly endless variety of combinations, à la carte options, and side dishes.

PASADENA
Afghan

For a delicious and upscale dining experience, have lunch or dinner at **Azeen's Afghani Restaurant** (110 E. Union St., 626/683-3310, www.azeensafghanirestaurant.com, lunch 11:30 A.M.–2 P.M. Mon.–Fri., dinner 5:30–9:30 P.M. daily, $20–30). Inside you'll find white tablecloths, black furniture, and unusual paintings. On the menu, the offerings take you into another world—one largely mysterious to Westerners. Trade routes, invasions, religion, ethnicity, and lots and lots of sand all contribute to the way Afghanistan and its cuisine have evolved. Vegetarians, be aware that while you will find some limited options, Afghan food tends heavily toward meat. Kebabs of all kinds are a regional specialty, and the country's proximity to India brings with it a love for truly spicy (and incredibly flavorful) dishes. At Azeen's, you can get kebabs, spicy lamb dishes, dumplings, and traditional desserts.

Asian

If you're just dying for Thai or Vietnamese food, one of the better spots in Pasadena is **Daisy Mint** (1218 E. Colorado Blvd., 626/792-2999, www.daisymint.com, 11 A.M.–9 P.M. Mon.–Fri., noon–9 P.M. Sat.–Sun., $10–30). The tiny green dining room's exposed brick and original artwork speak of SoCal, while the menu items tend to come from Southeast Asia and beyond. You'll find the aforementioned Thai and Vietnamese, plus Korean and uniquely Californian Asian-fusion dishes here. Some of the fun special touches of the house include a variety of steamed rice that you can choose to accompany your meal, and a large selection of unusual and fragrant teas. Pick whatever you think will go best with your satay, curry, seafood, or soup. Reservations are recommended on weekend evenings.

Barbecue

If you're looking for some down-home Southern food, head straight for **Big Mama's Rib Shack** (1453 N. Lake Ave., 626/797-1792, www.bigmamas-ribshack.com, 11:30 A.M.–9 P.M. Tues.–Thurs., 11:30 A.M.–10 P.M. Fri.–Sat., noon–8 P.M. Sun., $10–30). While Big Mama never brewed up the sauce at this Pasadena kitchen, she was a Southern restaurateur who made her way from Georgia across the country to California over her long life. Today, her legacy lives on in the big ol' menu at Big Mama's, which boasts traditional Southern cuisine plus a number of creole and Cajun dishes that speak to a strong New Orleans influence. Whether your poison is a po'boy or good gumbo, you can get it in hearty portions at Big Mama's. Fish lovers

will find oysters and catfish, but strict vegetarians will find their dining options limited. And Big Mama's isn't a diet-friendly establishment since few salads balance out the weight of the fried chicken, smothered ribs, and velvet cake.

California

For an upscale meal without having to fight the crowds on the west side or Downtown, check out **Bistro 45** (45 S. Mentor Ave., 626/795-2478, www.bistro45.com, lunch 11:30 A.M.–2 P.M. Tues.–Fri., dinner 5–9 P.M. Tues.–Thurs., 5–10 P.M. Fri.–Sat., 5–8:30 P.M. Sun., $40–80). This nationally lauded restaurant has beautiful dining rooms: one light and bright with hardwood floors and peach walls with beautiful glass lantern fixtures, and one semi-outdoor space done in gray-blues with distinctive woven chairs and classic French prints. The cuisine is grounded in the French tradition but includes a hearty twist of California in the preparation. Menus change seasonally (or more often), and offer lots of fresh seafood as well as high-end meat and veggie-based dishes. For lunch, lighter appetites can be satisfied with fancy salads, but don't expect much of a midday price break on the bigger entrées. The wine list shifts seasonally to complement the food, and Bistro 45 boasts a full bar with a list of signature martini-esque cocktails.

Greek

For a quick and reasonably healthy lunch in downtown Pasadena, try **Pita! Pita!** (927 E. Colorado Blvd., Suite 101, 626/356-3099, 8 A.M.–9 P.M. Sun.–Thurs., 8 A.M.–10 P.M. Fri.–Sat., $8–10). This walk-up Greek place offers tasty meals with lots of fresh veggies that fill you up without emptying your wallet in the process. If you eat in, you can find your own seat on the uncovered tables in the narrow dining room with its worn tile floor. Fill up your own cup with soda or water while you wait for your pita wrap or falafel and hummus plate to be made up. If you're in a hurry, order your food to go; the pita wrap sandwiches are big and a bit juicy, but properly wrapped, they can be reasonably sidewalk-friendly.

Information and Services

TOURS

If you don't feel up to driving around Los Angeles on your own (and no one will blame you if you don't), dozens of tour operators would love to do the driving for you and let you sit back and enjoy the sights and sounds of Southern California. You can choose between driving tours, walking tours, and even helicopter tours that take you up to get a bird's-eye view of the city, beaches, and the wide Pacific Ocean.

Walking Tours

In among the dozens of cheesy "walking tour" operators who will charge you to walk you over the stars on Hollywood Boulevard (which you can do yourself for free), one organization can give you a better, more in-depth look into the true history of the Los Angeles area. The **Los Angeles Conservancy** (213/623-2489, www. laconservancy.org, tours 10 A.M. Sat., adults $10, children $5) offers more than a dozen different walking tours that explore the architectural history of different parts of Los Angeles in depth. You can pick a style-themed tour, such as Art Deco or Evolving Skyline, or a specific street, area, or major structure, such as Union Station, the Broadway Theaters, or the Biltmore Hotel. Check the website for tour schedules and for a few self-guided tours you can take on your own if you can't make your chosen guided tour. While children are welcome on Conservancy tours, the nature of the entertainment focuses much more on adult visitors; consider leaving the kids elsewhere so they are not bored to bits by all the talk of moldings and archways.

Bus Tours

For bus tours, you can't beat the weight of history provided by **Starline Tours** (800/959-3131, www.starlinetours.com, adults $45–140, children $30–125), which has been in the business of showing L.A. and Hollywood to visitors since 1935. Take a tour of Movie Stars Homes (which actually covers many famous star-studded spots around the region), Hollywood, or try the Grand Tour of Los Angeles (which can be narrated in many languages) for a start. Starline can pick you up at almost any hotel in L.A. Your tour vehicle will be either an air-conditioned minibus, a full-size bus, or a topless "Fun Bus" with a second open-air deck that lets visitors breathe the native smog of L.A. unhindered. Fun Tours also allow passengers to jump on and off at various sights and attractions as they please. Expect your tour to last 2–6 hours, depending on which route you choose. Once you're on board, sit back, relax, and enjoy the sights and stories of Los Angeles.

INFORMATION
Visitor Information

New to L.A.? Make one of your first stops one of the two visitors centers. The Los Angeles Convention and Visitors Bureau (www.discoverlosangeles.com) maintains Visitor Information Centers adjacent to two Metro stations. One of these is in Hollywood at **Hollywood and Highland Visitors Center** (6801 Hollywood Blvd., 323/467-6412) and the other is the **Downtown Visitors Center** (685 S. Figueroa St., 213/689-8822). There are self-serve visitor information centers at the Los Angeles Convention Center and the Port of Los Angeles (Berth 93). L.A. has also created a Mobile Visitors Center, so just look to the streets for the brightly decorated Honda Element. The denizens of this van can give you maps, brochures, information, and advice about visiting the greater L.A. area.

If you're an advance planner, you can take advantage of the Visitors Bureau website to grab half-price tickets to all sorts of shows all around L.A. Visit the website on Tuesday about a week in advance of the date you want to see a show; you'll see all available tickets posted. These tickets are also offered at the bricks-and-mortar Visitor Information Centers in town.

Media and Communications

Los Angeles is home to one of the country's major daily newspapers, the *Los Angeles Times* (www.latimes.com). Pick one up at any newsstand anywhere in the city for a healthy dose of national news, regional current events, and even some good up-to-the-minute restaurant and nightlife information. The Food section comes out once a week, and the Travel section is included with the Sunday edition.

You'll find Wi-Fi at nearly every hotel, a café with Internet access on nearly every corner, and the need to pay a fee for that access in most places. Expect to pay $10–20 per day to connect your laptop to the Internet.

All those Hollywood agents would probably spontaneously combust if they ever lost signal on their cell phones. You'll get coverage pretty much everywhere in L.A., regardless of your provider, with the possible exception of a few minutes going over a mountain pass.

SERVICES
Post Offices
Each separate municipality in the L.A. region has at least one post office (www.usps.com), including Downtown (750 W. 7th St., Suite 33), in Hollywood (1615 Wilcox Ave.), and in Beverly Hills (8383 Wilshire Blvd., Suite 106).

Medical Services

The greater L.A. area offers some of the best medical care options in the world. People come from all over to get novel treatments and plastic surgery in the hospitals frequented by the stars. If you need immediate assistance, **Los Angeles County+USC Medical Center** (1200 N. State St., emergency 911, 323/409-1000, www.ladhs. org) can fix you up no matter what's wrong with you.

Taxis

Taxis aren't cheap but they're quick, easy, and numerous. And in some cases, when you add up gas and parking fees, you'll find that the cab ride isn't that much more expensive than driving yourself.

To call a cab, try **Yellow Cab** (L.A., LAX, Beverly Hills, Hollywood, 800/200-1085) and **City Cab** (San Fernando Valley, Hollywood, LAX, 800/750-4400). Or, for a complete list of franchise providers—not "bandit cabs," in other words—and phone numbers, check out the Taxi Services website (www.taxicab-sla.org) of the Los Angeles Department of Transportation, which also has a consumer complaint line (800/501-0999). You'll also find fare limits listed on the website, so you know what to expect.

Disneyland

The "Happiest Place on Earth" lures millions of visitors of all ages each year with promises of fun and fantasy. During high seasons, waves of humanity flow through Disneyland (1313 S. Disneyland Dr., Anaheim, 714/781-4565, http://disneyland.disney.go.com, 9 A.M.–midnight daily, ticket prices vary, one-day over age 9 $80, ages 3–9 $74, one-day Hopper Ticket for entry to both parks, over age 9 $105, ages 3–9 $99), moving slowly from Land to Land and ride to ride. The park is well set up to handle the often immense crowds. Everything from foot-traffic control to ample restrooms makes even a Christmastime trip to Disneyland

a happy time for the whole family. Despite the undeniable cheese factor, even the most cynical and jaded resident Californians can't quite keep their cantankerous scowls once they're ensconced inside Uncle Walt's dream. It really *is* a happy place.

Disney's rides, put together by the park's "Imagineers," are better than those at any other amusement park in the state—perhaps better than any in the world. The technology of the rides isn't more advanced than other parks, but it's the attention to detail that makes a Disneyland ride experience so enthralling. Even the spaces where you stand in line match the theme of the ride you're waiting for, from the archaeological relics of Indiana Jones to the tombstones of the Haunted Mansion. If you've got several days in the park, try them all, but if you don't, pick from the best of the best in each Land.

Orientation

The Disneyland Resort is a massive kingdom that stretches from Harbor Boulevard on the east to Walnut Street on the west and from Ball Road to the north to Katella Avenue to the south and includes two amusement parks, three hotels, and an outdoor shopping and entertainment complex. The Disneyland-affiliated hotels (Disneyland Hotel, Paradise Pier Hotel, and the Grand Californian) all cluster on the western side of the complex, between Walnut Street and Disneyland Drive (West St.). The area between Disneyland Drive and Harbor Boulevard is shared by the actual Disneyland amusement park in the northern section and the California Adventure amusement park in the southern section, with Downtown Disney between them in the central-west section. There is no admission fee for Downtown Disney. You can reach the amusement park entrances via Downtown Disney (although visitors going to Disneyland or California Adventure should park in the paid lots, rather than the Downtown Disney self-park lot, which is only free for the first three hours) or from the walk-in entrance (for those taking public transportation or being dropped off) on Harbor Boulevard. There are also trams from the parking lot to the entrance.

EXPLORING DISNEYLAND

Your first stop inside the park should be one of the information kiosks near the front entrance gates. Here you can get a map, a schedule of the day's events, and the inside scoop on what's going on in the park during your visit.

New Orleans Square

In New Orleans Square, the unquestioned favorite ride for the 21st century is the revamped **Pirates of the Caribbean.** If you haven't

---

HERE AT DISNEY, WE HAVE A FEW RULES

Think that anything goes at the Happiest Place on Earth? Think again. Uncle Walt had distinct ideas about what his dream theme park would look like, and that vision extended to the dress and manners of his guests. When the park opened in 1950, among the many other restrictions, no man sporting facial hair was allowed into Disneyland. The rules on dress and coiffure have relaxed a bit since the opening, but you still need to mind your manners when you enter the Magic Kingdom.

- Adults may not wear costumes of any kind except on Halloween.

- No shirt, no shoes, no Disneyland.

- If you must use the F word, do it quietly. If staff catches you cussing or cursing in a way that disturbs others, you can be asked to desist or leave.

- The happiest of happiness is strictly prohibited inside the Magic Kingdom. If you're caught having sex on park grounds, not only will you be thrown out, you'll be banned from Disneyland for life (at least that's the rumor).

- Ditto for any illicit substances.

---

visited Disneyland in a few years, you'll notice some major changes to this old favorite. Beginning in the dim swamp overlooked by the Blue Bayou Restaurant, the ride's classic scenes inside have been revamped to tie in more closely to the movies. Look for Jack Sparrow to pop up among your other favorite disreputable characters engaged in all sorts of debauchery. Lines for Pirates can get long, so consider grabbing a Fastpass for this one if you don't want to wait. Even if you don't Fastpass, the line for Pirates moves fast. Pirates is suitable for younger children as well as teens and adults.

For a taste of truly classic Disney, line up in the

graveyard for a tour of the **Haunted Mansion.** Next to Pirates, this ride hasn't changed much in the last 40 years. It hasn't needed to. The sedate motion makes the Haunted Mansion suitable for younger children, but beware: The ghosties and ghoulies that amuse adults can be intense for little kids.

Adventureland

Adventureland sits next to the New Orleans Square area. **Indiana Jones** is arguably one of the best rides in all of Disneyland, and the details make it stunning. As you stand in the line, check out the signs, equipment, and artifacts in mock-dusty tunnels winding toward the ride. The ride itself, in a roller-coaster style variant of an all-terrain vehicle, jostles and jolts you through a landscape that Indy himself might dash through, pursued by booby traps and villains. Hang on to your hat—literally! Use the pouches provided in your seat to secure your unattached things, or they will get jostled out of this exciting ride. This one isn't the best for tiny tots, but the big kids love it, and everyone might want a Fastpass for the endlessly popular attraction.

On the other end of the spectrum, you'll either love the **Tiki Room** or you'll hate it. Up a tree, literally, you'll take a seat and enjoy some classic pseudo-Polynesian tiki entertainment. Even the smallest children love the bright colors and cheerful songs in the Tiki Room, though some adults can't quite hack the cheesiness here.

Frontierland

Take a ride on a Wild West train on the **Big Thunder Mountain Railroad.** This older roller coaster whisks passengers away on a brief but fun thrill-ride through a "dangerous, decrepit" mountain's mine shafts. As you stand in line, be sure to read the names of the locomotives as the trains come rushing by.

Fantasyland

The favorite of many Disneyland visitors, Fantasyland rides tend to cater to the younger set. And for many Disneyphiles, the ultimate expression of Uncle Walt's dream is **It's a Small World.** Toddlers adore this ride, which introduces their favorite Disney characters and the famous (some would say infamous) song. You can almost feel the fairy dust sprinkling down on you as you tour this magical miniature kingdom. (Warning: If ultra-cutesiness makes you gag, you might want to skip this one.)

Kids who are just a little bit older might prefer the crazy fun of **Mr. Toad's Wild Ride.** Even though it's not really a roller coaster, this ride makes for big fun for children and adults alike. What's cool about Mr. Toad's is the wacky scenery you'll get to see along the ride, from a sedate library to the gates of hell.

If it's a faster thrill you're seeking, head for one of the most recognizable landmarks at Disneyland. The **Matterhorn Bobsleds** roller coaster looks like a miniature version of its namesake in the Swiss Alps. Inside, you board a sled-style coaster car and plunge down the mountain on a twisted track that takes you past rivers, glaciers, and the Abominable Snowman.

Tomorrowland

In order to keep up with the realities of the future, many of the rides in this section of the 50-year-old park have been updated or even replaced over the years. An enhanced version of the classic 3-D film musical *Captain EO,* starring Michael Jackson, is back to replace *Honey, I Shrunk the Audience.* Fans of all ages can experience the magic of this innovative film.

Another classic that has been given a makeover to connect it to a Disney blockbuster movie is the **Finding Nemo Submarine Voyage.** On this ride, you and fellow guests board a submarine and descend into an artificial pool. Under the water, you'll find yourself in the brightly colored world of Nemo and his frantic father, filled with an astonishing array of sealife. Help your kids count the number of familiar fish!

Finally, for bigger visitors, the best thrill ride of the main park sits inside a space-age building. **Space Mountain** is a fast roller coaster that whizzes through an almost entirely darkened world. All you'll see are the stars overhead. You will hear your screams and those of your fellow passengers as your "spaceship" swerves and plunges along tracks you cannot see. Despite its age, Space Mountain remains one of the more popular rides in the park. Consider getting a Fastpass to keep out of sometimes-long lines.

◖ CALIFORNIA ADVENTURE

Disney's California Adventure (http://disneyland.disney.go.com/disneys-california-adventure, 10 A.M.–10 P.M. daily, ticket prices vary, one-day over age 9 $80, ages 3–9 $74, one-day Hopper Ticket for entry to both parks, over age 9 $105, ages 3–9 $99) celebrates much of what makes California special. If Disney is your only stop on this trip but you'd like to get a sense of the state as a whole, California Adventure can give you a little taste. (For my money, though, you'd do better to extend your vacation and spend some time exploring California in all its real non-Disneyfied glory.)

Like Disneyland proper, California Adventure is divided into themed areas. Rides in California Adventure tend toward the thrills of other major amusement parks but include the great Disney touches that make the Mouse special.

You'll find two information booths just inside the main park entrance, one off to the left as you walk through the turnstile and one at the opening to Sunshine Plaza. Here's where you'll get your park guide, *Time Guide,* and more information about what's going on in the park that day.

Hollywood Pictures Backlot

Celebrating SoCal's famed film industry, the Backlot holds the ultimate thrill ride inside: **The Twilight Zone Tower of Terror.** Enter the creepy "old hotel," go through the "service area," and take your place inside an elevator straight out of your worst nightmares. This ride aims for teens and adults rather than little kids, and it's not a good one for folks who fear heights or don't do well with free-fall rides.

Less extreme but also fun, **Monsters, Inc.**

Mike & Sully to the Rescue! invites guests into the action of the movie of the same name. You'll help the heroes as they chase the intrepid Boo. This ride jostles you around a bit but can be suitable for smaller kids as well as bigger ones.

A Bug's Land

Want to live like a bug? Get a sample of the world of tiny insects on **It's Tough to Be a Bug!** This big-group, 3-D, multisensory ride offers fun for little kids and adults alike. You'll fly through the air, scuttle through the grass, and get a good idea of what life is like on six little legs. But beware: When they say this ride engages *all your senses,* they mean it.

For the littlest California Adventurers, **Flik's Fun Fair** offers almost half a dozen rides geared toward toddlers and little children. They can ride pint-size hot-air balloons known as Flik's Flyers, climb aboard a bug-themed train, or run around under a gigantic faucet to cool down after hours of hot fun.

Paradise Pier

Paradise Pier mimics the Santa Monica Pier and other waterfront attractions like it, with thrill rides and an old-fashioned midway. Most of the extreme rides cluster in the Paradise Pier area. It seems reasonable that along with everything else, Disney does the best roller coasters in the business. They prove it with **California Screamin',** a high-tech roller coaster designed after the classic wooden coasters of carnivals past. This extra-long ride includes drops, twists, a full loop, and plenty of time and screaming fun. California Screamin' has a four-foot height requirement and is just as popular with nostalgic adults as with kids. **Toy Story Mania!** magnifies the midway mayhem as passengers of all ages use Spring-Action Shooters to take aim at targets in a 4-D ride inspired by Disney-Pixar's *Toy Story.*

Golden State

For a glimpse into other parts of the state, with attractions styled after the Bay Area, Wine Country, and Cannery Row, head to

ALTERNATIVES TO THE MOUSE

The longtime Hollywood-centric alternative to Disneyland is the **Universal Studios Hollywood** (100 Universal City Plaza, Los Angeles, 800/864-8377, www.universalstudios.com, 10 A.M.-6 P.M. daily, adults $77, children under 48 inches tall $69, parking $10-15) theme park. Kids adore this park, which puts them right into the action of their old favorite movies. Flee the carnivorous dinosaurs of *Jurassic Park*, take a rafting adventure on the pseudo-set of *Waterworld,* or quiver in terror of an ancient curse in *Revenge of the Mummy.* If you're the parent rather than the child, you may find some of the effects on the rides pretty cheesy. On the other hand, you may be thrown back to your childhood with memories of your favorite TV shows and movies. One of the major attractions recreates the nightmare world of *Terminator 2: Judgment Day* – in 3-D.

If you're more interested in how the movies are made than the rides made from them, take the Studio Tour. You'll get an extreme close-up of the sets of major blockbuster films like *War of the Worlds.* The *King Kong* set (along with the famed New York set and a number of others) was destroyed in an accidental fire in 2008, but replaced in July 2010 with King Kong: 360 3-D. Better yet, you can get tickets to be part of the studio audience of TV shows currently taping at the Audiences Unlimited Ticket Booth. If you're a serious movie buff, consider getting a VIP pass – you'll get a six-hour tour that takes you onto working sound stages, into the current prop warehouse, and through a variety of working build shops that service films and programs currently filming.

You can enjoy a meal, store your heavier things in a locker, and buy a near-infinite number of souvenirs at Universal Studios. If you need a little help getting yourself or your child around, rent a wheelchair or stroller. Pretty much every ride and show is wheelchair-accessible – ask at the ticket booth for more information about how to get around easily or if you need assisted-listening devices and TTD phones.

For yet another amusement park adventure, hit **Six Flags Magic Mountain** (Magic Mountain Parkway, Valencia, 661/255-4100, www.sixflags.com/magicmountain, hours vary, adults $62, children $37). This park provides good fun for the whole family – even the snarky teenagers who hate almost everything. Magic Mountain has long been the extreme alternative to the Mouse, offering a wide array of thrill rides. You'll need a strong stomach to deal with the g-forces of the major-league roller coasters, the death-defying drops, and the whirling spinners. For the younger set, plenty of "family" style rides offer a less intense but equally fun amusement-park experience. Both littler and bigger kids enjoy interacting with the classic Warner Brothers characters, especially in Bugs Bunny World, and a kids' show features Bugs, Donald, and others. Other than that, Magic Mountain has little in the way of staged entertainment – this park is all about the rides. The park is divided into areas, just like most other major theme parks – get a map at the entrance to help maneuver around and pick your favorite rides.

You'll find services, souvenirs, and snacks galore throughout the park. The food offerings run to burgers, pizza, and international fast food. The highest concentration of snack shacks sits in the Colossus County Fair area – others are evenly distributed throughout the other areas. You can also by tchotchkes in any area, but most of the shopping centers around Cyclone Bay. All major services can be found at the park, including many ATM machines, a first-aid station, ample restrooms, and disability assistance. The Guest Relations office at Six Flags Plaza can help you with just about anything you need.

the aptly named Golden State. Want a bird's-eye view of California? Get on board **Soarin' Over California.** This combination ride and show puts you and dozens of other guests on the world's biggest "glider" and sets you off over the hills and valleys of California. You'll feel the wind in your hair as you see the vineyards, mountains, and beaches of this diverse state. If you prefer water to wind, take a ride down the **Grizzly River Run,** a Disney version of one of the many wild California rivers that rafters love to run.

Smaller visitors can get some exercise and fun in the **Redwood Creek Challenge Trail.** This adventure course mimics the rope courses adults love, but it's sized small enough for kids. Parents can join in on some of the course but must wait and watch for their charges to swing on the ropes.

Parades and Shows

Do you remember the brilliant, colorful **Electric Light Parade** of years past? While bright lights are no longer the biggest or most advanced thing, thousands of people still love the kitsch and fun of this classic parade. So it moved from the main Disney parade route, where newer shows run, to California Adventure, where you can relive your childhood joy most evenings. Check the park's *Time Guide* for the schedule during your visit.

Other regular shows in California Adventure are **Disney Junior–Live on Stage!** and **Disney's Aladdin–A Musical Spectacular.** Both of these shows hark back to favorite children's activities and movies. Your kids can sing along with favorite songs and characters while you take a load off your feet and relax for a while. Check your park guide and *Time Guide* for more information about these and other live shows throughout California Adventure.

DOWNTOWN DISNEY

You don't need an admission ticket to take a stroll through the shops of the Downtown Disney District. In addition to the mammoth World of Disney Store, you'll find RIDEMAKERZ, a Build-a-Bear workshop,

and a LEGO Imagination Center. For adults, the House of Blues Store, Sephora, and the Sunglass Icon boutique beckon. If you need reading material, the small but adequate Compass Books & Café has the most recent best-sellers, travel books, and a few more interesting tomes and titles. You can also have a bite to eat or take in some jazz or a new release movie at Downtown Disney.

ACCOMMODATIONS

The best way to get fully Disneyfied is to stay at one of the park's hotels. Several sit just beside or across the street from the park.

Disney Hotels

For the most iconic Disney resort experience, you must stay at the **Disneyland Hotel** (1150 Magic Way, Anaheim, 714/956-6425 or 714/778-6600, http://disneyland.disney.go.com, from $350). This nearly 1,000-room high-rise monument to brand-specific family entertainment has everything a vacationing Brady-esque bunch could want: themed swimming pools, themed play areas, and even character-themed guest rooms that allow the kids to fully immerse themselves in the Mouse experience. Adults and families on a budget can also get rooms with either a king or two queen beds and more traditional motel fabrics and appointments. The monorail stops inside the hotel, offering guests the easiest way into the park proper without having to deal with parking or even walking.

It's easy to find the **Paradise Pier Hotel** (1717 S. Disneyland Dr., Anaheim, 714/956-6425 or 714/999-0990, http://disneyland.disney.go.com, from $250); it's that high-rise thing just outside the parks on the California Adventure side. This hotel boasts what passes for affordable lodgings within walking distance of California Adventure, Downtown Disney, and Disneyland's main gate. Rooms are cute, colorful, and clean; many have two double or queen beds to accommodate families or couples traveling together on a tighter budget. You'll find a (possibly refreshing) lack of Mickeys in the standard guest accommodations at the Paradise, which has the feel of a beach resort motel.

The **Grand Californian Hotel and Spa** (1600 S. Disneyland Dr., Anaheim, 714/956-6425 or 714/635-2300, http://disneyland.disney.go.com, from $380) is inside California Adventure, attempting to mimic the famous Ahwahnee Lodge in Yosemite. While it doesn't quite succeed (much of what makes the Ahwahnee so great is its views), the big-beam construction and soaring common spaces do feel reminiscent of a great luxury lodge. The hotel is surrounded by gardens and has restaurants, a day spa, and shops attached on the ground floors; it can also get you right out into Downtown Disney and thence to the parks proper. Guest rooms at the Californian offer more luxury than the other Disney resorts, with dark woods and faux-craftsman detailing creating an attractive atmosphere. You can get anything from a standard guest room that sleeps two up to spacious family suites with bunk beds that can easily handle six people. As with all Disney resorts, you can purchase tickets and a meal plan along with your hotel room (in fact, if you book via the website, they'll try to force you to do it that way).

Outside the Parks

The massive park complex is ringed with motels, both popular chains and more interesting independents. **The Anabella** (1030 W. Katella Ave., Anaheim, 714/905-1050 or 800/863-4888, www.anabellahotel.com, $99–199) offers a touch of class along with a three-block walk to the parks. The elegant marble-clad lobby seems like it belongs closer to Downtown L.A. than Downtown Disney. Guest rooms are furnished with an eye toward modern, stylish decor (occasionally at the expense of practicality). Adults looking for an overnight escape from the endless parade of kid-oriented entertainment and attractions will find a welcome respite at the Anabella. A decent restaurant, nail salon, and minimart are on the hotel property, and a fairly lousy diner is right next door. You can get limited room service at the Anabella, and you can leave your car in their parking lot to avoid the expense of parking at Disneyland.

Another nice out-of-park hotel within walking distance of Disneyland is the **Desert Palms Hotel & Suites** (631 W. Katella Ave., 714/535-1133 or 888/788-0466, www.desert-palmshotel.com, from $180). Its spacious and elegant lobby welcomes visitors, the pool and spa provide fun for children and adults alike, and the many amenities make travelers comfortable. Regular guest rooms have one king or two queen beds, a TV, a phone, Internet access, and not a ton of room to walk around after all your luggage is crowded in with the furniture. Bedspreads catch the eye with their bright, multicolored palm design; the rest of the decor is neutral by comparison. Guests with more discretionary income can choose from a number of suites, some designed to delight children and others aimed at couples on a romantic getaway.

Away from the Disneyland complex and surrounding area, the accommodations in Orange County run to chain motels with little character or distinctiveness, but the good news is that you can find a decent room for a reasonable price.

The **Hyatt Regency Orange County** (11999 Harbor Blvd., Garden Grove, 714/750-1234 or 800/492-8804, http://orangecounty.hyatt.com, $130–354) in Garden Grove is about 2.5 miles (10 minutes' drive on Harbor Blvd.) south of the park. The attractive guest rooms are decorated in the latest style inside a tall glass-fronted tower. White linens emphasize the cleanliness of beds and baths, while bright yellows and deep blues provide classy artistic touches. In the sun-drenched atrium, enjoy a cocktail or sit back and read a good book in the attractive atmosphere. Grab a chaise longue by the pool or take a refreshing dip. If you're bringing your family, consider renting one of the "family-friendly suites" that have separate bedrooms with bunk beds and fun decor geared toward younger guests.

The **Red Roof Inn Buena Park** (7121 Beach Blvd., Buena Park, 714/733-6778 or 800/733-7663, www.redroof.com, $64–125) offers a clean bed and bath about seven miles (10 minutes on I-5, more with traffic) north of Disneyland. Amenities include a heated pool and a spa, free Wi-Fi, and a fitness center. Medium-size motel rooms feature a standard motel setup with a variety of bed configurations, dark carpets, and floral bedspreads.

Near John Wayne Airport, the **Best Western Orange County Airport** (2700 Hotel Terr., Santa Ana, 714/432-8888 or 800/432-0053, www.bestwestern-oc.com, $77) offers everything you expect of the popular national chain, including floral and wine-colored decor in the comfortable guest rooms, a pool and hot tub, and a free shuttle to and from the airport. Down in the lobby you'll find a complimentary "cook-to-serve" breakfast each morning (that is, prepackaged heat-and-eat items plus cold cereals, bagels, and coffee).

FOOD
Disneyland

One of the few things the Mouse doesn't do too well is haute cuisine. For a truly good or healthy meal, get a hand stamp and go outside the park. But if you're stuck inside and you absolutely need sustenance, you can get it. The best areas of the park to grab a bite are Main Street, New Orleans, and Frontierland—they offer the most variety in concessions—but you can find at least a snack almost anywhere in the park.

For a sit-down restaurant meal inside the park, make reservations in advance for a table at the **Blue Bayou Restaurant** (New Orleans Square, 714/781-3463, over $36 pp). The best part about this restaurant is its setting in the dimly lit swamp overlooking the Pirates of the Caribbean ride. Appropriately, the Bayou has a reputation for being haunted. The Cajun-ish cuisine matches the junglelike setting, although if you're looking for authenticity, you'd do better to look elsewhere. You will get large portions, and tasty sweet desserts make a fine finish to your meal. Watch your silverware, though—the alleged ghosts in this restaurant like to mess around with diners' tableware.

If you need to grab a quicker bite, *don't* do it at the French Market restaurant in the New Orleans area. It sells what appears to be day-old (or more) food from the Bayou that has been sitting under heat lamps for a good long time. You're better off finding one of the McDonalds Fries carts and getting some greasy food that at least tastes good.

California Adventure

If you need a snack break in California Adventure, you'll find most of the food clustered in the Golden State area. Take a tour of the **Boudin Bakery,** then taste the delectable products of these places in the nearby restaurants. For a Mexican feast, try **Cocina Cucamonga Mexican Grill** (under $15 pp). For more traditional American fare, enjoy the food at the **Pacific Wharf Cafe** (under $15 pp), a Boudin Bakery restaurant, or the **Taste Pilots' Grill** (under $15 pp).

Unlike Disneyland proper, in California Adventure, responsible adults can quaff their thirst with a variety of alcoholic beverages. If you're just dying for a cold beer, get one at the **Pacific Wharf Distribution Co.** Or if your love is for the endless variety of high-quality wines produced in the Golden State, head for the **Golden Vine Winery,** where you can learn the basics of wine creation and production. Have a glass and a pseudo-Italian meal at the sit-down **Wine Country Trattoria at the Golden Vine Winery** (714/781-3463, $15–36).

Downtown Disney

Downtown Disney is outside the amusement parks and offers additional dining options. National chains like **House of Blues** (1530 S. Disneyland Dr., Anaheim, 714/778-2583, www.houseofblues.com, breakfast 8–11 A.M. Mon.–Fri., lunch and dinner 11 A.M.–10 P.M. daily, bar until 1:30 A.M., $15–28) and **Rainforest Café** (1515 S. Disneyland Dr., Anaheim, 714/772-0413, www.rainforestcafe.com, 8 A.M.–11 P.M. Sun.–Thurs., 8 A.M.–midnight Fri.–Sat., $11–18) serve typical menu staples like sandwiches, burgers, pasta, and steak and seafood entrées, with House of Blues putting a Southern spin on these items and adding live-music shows, while kid-friendly Rainforest Café puts on tropical touches like coconut and mango. **ESPN Zone** (1545 Disneyland Dr., Anaheim, 714/300-3776, www.espnzone.com/anaheim, 11 A.M.–11 P.M. Sun.–Thurs., 11 A.M.–midnight Fri.–Sat.) has similar offerings, but due to numerous closures across the country, the Downtown Disney spot is now just one of two locations of this "sports bar on steroids" concept restaurant. The other is at 800 West Olympic Boulevard in Los Angeles (213/765-7070).

There are also more individual restaurants, but even these feel a little like chains. The most distinctive of them, **Ralph Brennan's Jazz Kitchen** (1590 S. Disneyland Dr., Anaheim, 714/776-5200, www.rbjazzkitchen.com, 8 A.M.–10 P.M. Sun.–Thurs., 8 A.M.–11 P.M. Fri.–Sat., $18–30), is meant to replicate the experience of eating in New Orleans's French Quarter. The Cajun menu hits all the staples, including jambalaya, beignets, and various blackened meats and seafood.

The Patina Restaurant Group runs **Catal Restaurant** (1580 Disneyland Dr., Anaheim, 714/774-4442, www.patinagroup.com/catal, usually 8 A.M.–10 P.M. daily, $13–42), with Mediterranean fare, **Naples Ristorante** (1550 Disneyland Dr., Anaheim, 714/776-6200, www.patinagroup.com, 11 A.M.–10 P.M. Sun.–Thurs., 11 A.M.–11 P.M. Fri.–Sat., $15–46) for Italian food, and **Tortilla Joe's** (1510 Disneyland Dr., Anaheim, 714/535-5000, www.patinagroup.com, 11 A.M.–11:30 P.M. Sun.–Thurs., 11 A.M.–1 A.M. Fri.–Sat., $15–21) for Mexican food.

Finally, **La Brea Bakery** (1556 Disneyland Dr., Anaheim, 714/490-0233, www.labreabakery.com, 8 A.M.–10 P.M. Sun.–Fri., 8 A.M.–11 P.M. Sat.) is the Disney outpost of an L.A. favorite. This bakery, founded by Nancy Silverton of the highly touted Campanile restaurant in L.A., supplies numerous markets and restaurants with crusty European-style loaves. The morning scones, sandwiches, and fancy cookies here are superb.

PRACTICALITIES

Tickets

There are as many varied ticket prices and plans as there are themes in the park. A single-day theme park ticket will run you $80, ages 3–9 $74. A variety of other combinations and passes are available online (http://disneyland.disney.go.com).

To buy tickets, go to one of the many kiosks in the central gathering spot that serves as the main entrance to both Disneyland proper and California Adventure. Bring your credit card, since a day at Disney is not cheap. After you've got tickets in hand (or if you've bought them online ahead of time), proceed to the turnstiles for the main park. You'll see the Disneyland Railroad terminal and the large grassy hill with the flowers planted to resemble Mickey's famous face. Pass through, and head under the railroad trestle to get to Main Street and the park center. You can exit and reenter the park on the days your tickets are valid for.

Horrifyingly, the already expensive regular one-day Disneyland ticket doesn't include California Adventure. If you're interested in checking out California Adventure as well as Disneyland proper, your best bet is to buy a **Park Hopper** pass (one-day $99–105, two-day $161–173), which lets you move back and forth between the two parks at will for a slight discount. If you're planning to spend several days touring the Houses of Mouse, buy multiday passes in advance online to save a few more bucks per day. It'll help you feel a little bit better about the wads of cash you'll undoubtedly drop on junk food, giant silly hats, stuffed animals, and an endless array of Disney apparel.

The magical **Fastpasses** are free with park admission and might seem like magic after awhile. The newest and most popular rides offer Fastpass kiosks near the entrances. Feed your ticket into one of the machines and it will spit out both your ticket and a Fastpass with your specified time to take the ride. Come back during your window and enter the always-much-shorter Fastpass line, designated by a sign at the entrance. If you're with a crowd, be sure you all get your Fastpasses at the same time, so you all get the same time window to ride the ride.

Information

Each park has information booths near the park entrance.

For visitor information about Disneyland and the surrounding area, visit the **Anaheim Visitor and Postal Center** (640 W. Katella Ave., Anaheim, 714/817-9733, www.anaheim411.com, 24 hours daily). As the name implies, not only does this facility have the 411 on Orange County, you can also mail a letter or a package here. The office is inside the Jolly Roger Hotel at the corner of Katella Avenue and Harbor Boulevard.

Need a dose of hard news? Get a copy of the *Los Angeles Times* (www.latimes.com) Orange County Edition.

The O.C. has plenty of Internet access, although you'll find few people crouched over laptops inside Disneyland. Look to your hotel, or find a Starbucks outside the park to hook up to the world.

Services

Check your park map or look for signs to the restrooms available in each Land of the park. Restrooms have ample space, so you'll rarely find lines even on the most crowded days.

If mobility is a problem for you or for a small child in your family, consider renting (no, they're not free) a stroller, wheelchair, or scooter. Ask for directions to the rental counter when you enter the park.

Cell phones work inside Disneyland, which is actually a fabulous thing. It's already loud and raucous in the parks, and the ability to use cell phones to connect with lost family or party members at Disneyland is one of *the* finest advances in modern technology in a long, long time.

Disneyland offers its own minor medical facilities, which can dispense first aid for scrapes, cuts, and mild heat exhaustion. They can also call an ambulance if something nastier has

occurred. The **West Anaheim Medical Center** (3033 W. Orange Ave., Anaheim, 714/827-3000, http://wamc.phcs.us) is a full-service hospital with an emergency room.

If you need to stow your bags or hit the restroom before plunging into the fray, banks of lockers and restrooms sit in the main entrance area.

Getting There

The nearest airport to Disneyland, serving all of Orange County, is **John Wayne Airport** (SNA, 18601 Airport Way, Santa Ana, 949/252-5200, www.ocair.com). It's much easier to fly into and out of John Wayne than LAX, though it can be more expensive. John Wayne's terminal has plenty of rental car agencies, and many shuttle services that can get you where you need to go—especially to the House of Mouse.

If you have to fly into LAX for scheduling or budget reasons, you can catch a shuttle straight from the airport to your Disneyland hotel. Among the many companies offering and arranging such transportation, the one with the best name is **MouseSavers** (www.mousesavers.com). Working with various shuttle and van companies, MouseSavers can get you a ride in a van or a bus from LAX or John Wayne to your destination at or near Disneyland.

Disneyland is located on Disneyland Drive in Anaheim and is most accessible from I-5 south where it crosses Ball Road (stay in the left three lanes for parking). The parking lot (1313 S. Disneyland Dr.) costs $15 for a car or motorcycle, $20 for an oversize vehicle such as a motor home or tractor without the trailer, and $25 for buses and tractor-trailer rigs.

If you're coming to the park from elsewhere in Southern California, consider leaving the car (avoiding the parking fees) and taking public transit instead. **Anaheim Resort Transit** (ART, 1280 Anaheim Blvd., Anaheim, 714/563-5287, www.rideart.org) can take you to and from the Amtrak station and all around central Anaheim for $4 per day pass. You can buy passes via the website or at conveniently located kiosks.

Getting Around

Disney's California Adventure sits across the main Disney entry plaza from Disneyland. You can enter from the main parking lots, from Downtown Disney, or you can hop over from Disneyland. Need a tram for the long-distance walk in or out of the park? The **Lion King Tram Route** can get you to and from the main parking areas. The **Mickey & Friends Tram Route** takes you toward Downtown Disney and the resort hotels.

The L.A. and O.C. Coasts

If you're looking for the famed surf beaches of SoCal, look no farther than the coast of Orange County. Sadly, when you look out over the pretty white sands of Huntington and Laguna, you're likely to see the lighted towers of the local oil rigs. Rigs dot the shoreline of Newport and Huntington as well, and as you drive up the legendary Pacific Coast Highway you'll see honest-to-goodness oil fields that will make you wonder if you took a wrong turn into Texas. In truth, the Southern California oil industry has been thriving for many a decade now.

And so you'll surf, sun yourself, bike, in-line skate, eat, drink, and be merry in the sight of the rigs. Despite their unsightliness, the beaches of Los Angeles and Orange Counties and their surrounding resort-oriented towns offer great vacationing potential to all comers.

MANHATTAN BEACH AND HERMOSA BEACH

These South Bay beaches are among the best along the L.A. coast, constituting the quintessential California paradise.

Beaches

Manhattan Beach is centered around the fishing pier that is essentially an extension of Manhattan Beach Boulevard beyond The Strand. **Hermosa Beach** sits just south, along Hermosa Beach Boulevard at 33rd Street. Administered by Los Angeles County Beaches and Harbors (310/305-9503, http://beaches.la-county.gov), both offer volleyball nets, pristine sand, and wave breaks that surfers love. A paved path is packed with bikers and in-line skaters.

Accommodations

For a cute near-the-sand motel in Manhattan Beach, stay at the **Sea View Inn at the Beach** (3400 Highland Ave., Manhattan Beach, 310/545-1504, www.seaview-inn.com, $130–300). Only a block from the sands of the beach, this is a great place to hole up if you're in town for some surfing, volleyball, or sunbathing

IMAGE COURTESY OF LA INC. THE LOS ANGELES CONVENTION AND VISITORS BUREAU

Manhattan Beach Pier

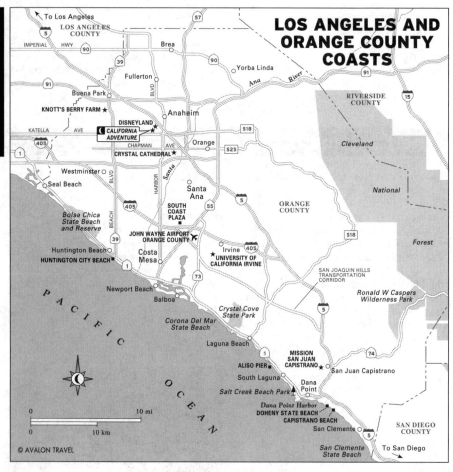

LOS ANGELES AND ORANGE COUNTY COASTS

© AVALON TRAVEL

along the shore. (You'll avoid the traditional summer beach parking nightmare by leaving your car at the motel.) Just grab a boogie board and some beach chairs from the lobby and head out. Inside, guest room appointments are prettier and more coordinated than those of most moderate motels. Guest rooms are done in light blues and whites, with matching prints on the walls and possibly even a live plant to add a homelike touch. The complex of blocky, mid-century modern buildings has its own small swimming pool as well, set in a small,

plant-strewn courtyard. Just around the corner, you'll find an array of restaurants, shops, bars, and clubs.

For a fabulous high-end hotel stay on the beach, go to the **Beach House at Hermosa Beach** (1300 The Strand, Hermosa Beach, 310/374-3001 or 888/895-4559, www.beach-house.com, $299–489). It might be the tiniest bit pretentious, but it's hard not to love this larger boutique hotel that looks right out over the water. The "loft suite" has a cushy king bed with Frette sheets, a big bath with a separate tub and shower, two TVs and a stereo, and a real wood-burning fireplace. The casual, upscale decor makes visitors feel at home, but you'll probably want to spend more time out on the porch or balcony on sunny days. Guests get a free continental breakfast, the use of the outdoor spa, and access to the on-site gym. If you prefer an outdoor workout, enjoy The Strand for a walk, run, or bike ride. Head downstairs to The Strand Café for a bite and a tasty view from the outside tables, or to the spa for a delightful massage or facial.

Food
Have you come to Los Angeles to seek genuine home-style Mexican food? You can find it at **Sion's Mexican Restaurant** (235 N. Sepulveda Blvd., Manhattan Beach, 310/372-4504, 8 A.M.–2 P.M. Sun.–Mon., 8 A.M.–9 P.M. Tues.–Sat., $10). Expect nothing fancy, but everything fresh—from tacos to salsa—in this utterly casual and family-owned hole-in-the-wall.

Getting There
Manhattan Beach is about 12 miles south of Santa Monica. The route along surface streets, with some stretches of coast-side driving, will take about 30 minutes. Hermosa Beach lies about two miles farther south.

REDONDO BEACH
Beaches
Sitting next to the Redondo Beach Pier, Redondo State Beach (400–1700 Esplanade, 310/305-9503, surf report 310/399-8471, http://beaches.lacounty.gov, usually sunrise–sunset, parking $5–12 depending on beach and season) gets really crowded in the summer, so if rubbing elbows with your fellow sun worshippers doesn't work for you, Redondo isn't your best bet. On the other hand, the lack of surfers makes swimming a prime activity here, complete with lifeguards during daytime. You'll also find the usual volleyball and other beach games, the bike path (which is lit at night), and the restaurants of the pier. The beach features

restrooms and showers, and a large multilevel pay parking structure at the pier offers ample space to stow your car for the day.

Entertainment and Events
For a low-key good time, grab a table and a drink at the **Starboard Attitude** (202 The Pier, Redondo Beach, 310/379-5144, www.starboardattitude.com, 4 P.M.–midnight Mon.–Thurs., 5 P.M.–2 A.M. Fri., 3 P.M.–2 A.M. Sat., 2 P.M.–close Sun., no cover) on the Redondo Beach Pier. This cool little locals joint features live music 4–5 nights a week and beer pong and karaoke (8 P.M.–midnight Mon.–Tues. and Thurs., 5:30–9 P.M. Fri., 7 P.M.–close Sun.) nearly every night when musical groups aren't playing. Pro acts tend toward talented classic rock cover bands and soulful blues groups. Expect folks to get up and dance to their favorite songs, and be prepared to be asked to dance if you're a woman on your own. However, the atmosphere here is more friendly than scary, with a mix of younger to middle-aged patrons who all seem to know each other and the servers. Talk up your bartender, and you'll get the whole scoop on the local scene as well as any drink you can imagine and probably one or two you've never heard of. The staff takes good care of the patrons too, so you'll find yourself drinking as much water as liquor as the evening wears on. There's no cover, but you will get hit with a two-drink minimum that's easy to meet, because it's easy to sit down, enjoy the mellow vibe, and stay a good long while at the Attitude.

Accommodations
Of the three Best Westerns that make up much of Redondo Beach's hospitality, the **Best Western Sunrise** (400 N. Harbor Dr., Redondo Beach, 310/376-0746 or 800/334-7384, www.bestwestern-sunrise.com, $160–180) is the best of the lot, with guest rooms overlooking Redondo's King Harbor and the location within walking distance of the pier and its restaurants and bars. Guest rooms are clean and comfortable, and the decor is cute and modern, with earth-tone bedspreads and

Redondo Beach Pier

light wood furniture. You'll get all the standard amenities you'd expect at a Best Western, plus a nice pool and spa, a gym, free Wi-Fi, and a complimentary breakfast.

Food
The **Green Temple Vegetarian Restaurant** (1700 S. Catalina Ave., Redondo Beach, 310/944-4525, www.greentemple.net, 11 A.M.–4 P.M. and 5–9 P.M. Tues.–Thurs., 11 A.M.–4 P.M. and 5–10 P.M. Fri.–Sat., 9 A.M.–4 P.M. and 5–9 P.M. Sun., $10–20) strives for Southern California Zen in both its cuisine and its dining room. All the vegetarian cuisine comes from sustainable and (whenever possible) organic sources, including Trader Joe's and Whole Foods stores.

Getting There
Redondo Beach is about a mile south of Hermosa Beach.

LONG BEACH
◖ The *Queen Mary*
The major visitor attraction of Long Beach is the *Queen Mary* (1126 Queens Hwy., Long Beach, 562/435-3511 or 877/342-0738, www.queenmary.com, 10 A.M.–6 P.M. daily, adults $25, seniors and military $22, children $13, parking $5–15), one of the most famous ships ever to ply the high seas. This great ship, once a magnificent pleasure cruise liner, now sits at permanent anchor (it has been gutted and is no longer seaworthy) in Long Beach Harbor. The *Queen Mary* acts as a hotel (877/342-0742, $140–400), a museum, an entertainment center with several restaurants and bars, and a gathering place for both locals and visitors. You can book a stateroom and stay aboard, come for dinner, or just buy a regular ticket and take a self-guided tour. The museum exhibits describe the history of the ship, with special emphasis on its tour of duty as a troop transport during World War II. You can explore many of the decks at the bow, including the engine room that still boasts much of its massive machinery, the art gallery, and the various upper exterior decks where vacationers once relaxed on their way to Europe.

But it's not just the extensive museum and the attractive hotel that make the *Queen Mary*

Aquarium of the Pacific

famous today. The ship is also one of the most famously haunted places in California. Over its decades of service, a number of unfortunate souls lost their lives aboard the *Queen Mary,* and it is rumored that several of them have stuck with the ship ever since their tragic deaths. If you're most interested in the ghost stories of the *Queen Mary,* book a spot on one of the Attractions at Night, which include the Paranormal Ship Walk (877/342-0738, 8 p.m. Thurs.–Fri. and Sun.), which takes you to the hottest haunted spots, and Dining With the Spirits (7 p.m. Sat.), a combination of dinner and a two-hour haunted tour. For more serious ghost hunters, Paranormal Investigation tours happen on Fridays. Appropriately, the investigations begin at midnight.

The *Queen Mary* offers a large pay parking lot near the ship's berth. You'll walk from the parking area up to a square with a ticket booth and several shops and a snack bar. Purchase your general-admission ticket to get on board the ship. It's also a good idea to buy any guided tour tickets at this point. Night tours can fill up in advance, so consider calling ahead to reserve a spot.

Russian Attack Submarine

Berthed right next to the luxurious *Queen Mary* you'll find a much smaller and more lethal little boat, the Russian Attack Submarine (562/432-0424 or 877/342-0738, www.russiansublongbeach.com, 10 a.m.–6 p.m. daily, adults $11, seniors, military, and children $10, or included in the *Queen Mary*'s First Class Passage package, adults $33, seniors and military $29, children $20). Code-named "The Scorpion," it helped the Soviet Union spy on the United States for more than 20 years during the Cold War. Your admission includes a brief history film and the opportunity to explore the innards of the submarine. Squeeze through the tiny spaces and learn how members of the Soviet Navy lived and worked aboard this attack submarine, which has a history that's still shrouded in secrecy.

Aquarium of the Pacific

Even the locals enjoy the exhibits at Aquarium of the Pacific (100 Aquarium Way, 562/590-3100, www.aquariumofpacific.org, 9 a.m.–6 p.m. daily, adults $25, seniors $22, children $13). The large aquarium hosts animal and plant life native to the Pacific Ocean, from the local residents of SoCal's sea up to the North Pacific and down to the tropics. While the big modern building isn't much to look at from the outside, it's what's inside that's beautiful. Aquarium of the Pacific has far more than the average number of touch-friendly tanks. Kids and adults all love the unusual feel of sea stars, urchins, and rays. More exciting, you can dip your fingers into the Shark Lagoon and "pet" a few of the more than 150 sharks the aquarium cares for. If you prefer tamer and more colorful denizens of the air, spend time in the loud Lorikeet Forest. Overall, there are 11,000 ocean animals representing 500 species on view.

Accommodations

For a quiet, private inn experience in the middle of the big city, try the **The Turret House** (556 Chestnut, Long Beach, 562/624-1991 or 888/488-7738, www.turrethouse.com, $80–100). This cute late-Victorian home sits on a street corner in the densely packed residential section of Long Beach. Each of the five guest rooms has its own decorative theme, an antique bedstead, a claw-foot tub, plenty of knickknacks, and a few pieces of high-end original art—all for a surprisingly reasonable rate. After your breakfast, stroll out into town for more coffee or perhaps a brief downtown shopping spree.

Looking for something completely different? Check in to the **Dockside Boat and Bed** (316 East Shoreline Dr., Dock 5A, Rainbow Harbor, Long Beach, 562/436-3111 or 800/436-2574, www.boatandbed.com, $220–330, overnight parking $24 unless you get the $10 discount parking pass from Dockside). You won't get a regular old hotel room; instead, you'll get one of four yachts. The yachts run 40–54 feet and can sleep four or more people each ($25 pp charge after the first two). The amenities include TVs with DVD players, stereos, kitchen facilities, wet bars, and ample seating. No, you can't actually take your floating accommodations out for a spin; these yachts are permanent residents of Rainbow Harbor.

Food

Combining elegance, fine continental-California cuisine, and great ghost stories, **Sir Winston's Restaurant and Lounge** (1126 Queens Hwy., Long Beach, 562/499-1657, www.queenmary.com, 5:30–10 P.M. daily, $30–50) floats gently on board the *Queen Mary*. For the most beautiful dining experience, request a window table and make reservations for sunset. And dress in your finest; Sir Winston's requests that diners adhere to their semiformal dress code.

A locals' favorite down where the shops and cafés cluster, **Natraj Cuisine of India** (5262 E. 2nd St., Long Beach, 562/930-0930, 11 A.M.–2:30 P.M. and 5–10 P.M. Mon.–Thurs., 11 A.M.–2:30 P.M. and 5–11 P.M. Fri., 11 A.M.–11 P.M. Sat., 11 A.M.–9:30 P.M. Sun., $10–30) offers good food for reasonable (by L.A. standards) prices. Come by for the all-you-can-eat lunch buffet to sample a variety of properly spiced meat and vegetarian dishes created in classic Indian tradition.

Information and Services

For information, maps, brochures, and advice about Long Beach and the surrounding areas, visit the **Long Beach Convention and Visitors Bureau** (301 E. Ocean Blvd., Suite 1900, 562/436-3645 or 800/452-7829, www.visitlongbeach.com, 8 A.M.–5 P.M. Mon.–Fri.).

Long Beach has a **post office** (300 Long Beach Blvd., 562/628-1303 or 800/275-8777).

For medical attention, visit the emergency room at the **Long Beach Memorial Medical Center** (2801 Atlantic Ave., Long Beach, 562/933-2000, www.memorialcare.org).

Getting There

While you can get to the coast easily enough from LAX, the **Long Beach International Airport** (LGB, 4100 Donald Douglas Dr., 562/570-2600, www.lgb.org) is both closer to the Long Beach and less crowded than the LAX.

I-710, which runs north–south, is known as

the Long Beach Freeway. Along the coast, the Pacific Coast Highway can get you from one beach town to the next.

Parking in Long Beach and the other beach towns is just bad as parking anywhere else in L.A. Prepare to pay for the privilege of stuffing your car someplace for the day. Beach parking on summer weekends is the worst, but on weekdays and in the off-season you can occasionally find a decent space down near the beach for reasonable rates.

ORANGE COUNTY COAST

The Orange County coast begins at Huntington Beach and stretches south across a collection of sunny scenic beaches until ending at San Juan Capistrano. Along the way, Newport Beach, Huntington Beach, Laguna Beach, and Dana Point provide surf, sun, and sand galore.

Huntington Beach

The main reason to come to the west edge of Orange County is to hit the beach. The good news is that the coast of the O.C. is rife with wide, flat, sandy beaches. The bad news is that the beaches still get crowded in the summer. If you want a prime spot, come early in the morning and try to avoid having to park a car if you possibly can.

Huntington City Beach (Pacific Coast Hwy. from Beach Blvd. to Seapoint St., beach headquarters 103 Pacific Coast Hwy., 714/536-5281, www.huntingtonbeachca.gov, beach 5 A.M.–10 P.M. daily, office 8 A.M.–5 P.M. Mon.–Fri.) runs the length of the south end of town, petering out toward the oil industry facilities at the north end. This famous beach hosts major sporting events such as the X Games and the U.S. Open of Surfing & Beach Games. But even the average beachgoer can enjoy all sorts of activities on a daily basis, since Huntington City Beach includes a cement walkway for biking, in-line skating, jogging, and walking. On the sand, get up a game of Frisbee or take advantage of the beach volleyball courts. Out in the water, catch a wave at

the famous Huntington surf break or make use of prevailing winds for a thrilling kite-surfing run. Nonriders can boogie board, bodysurf, and skim board closer to the shore. Anglers and lovers prefer the Huntington Beach Pier, which leads out over the water. While dogs aren't allowed on the main portion of Huntington City Beach, the beach offers a dog-friendly section at the north end where dogs can be let off-leash, and you'll even see the occasional surfer riding tandem with a four-legged friend.

This beach offers plenty of services and amenities. In high season, lifeguards keep watch over surfers and swimmers. A number of concession stands make their homes along Huntington City Beach, so you can buy drinks and snacks or rent a wetsuit and surfboard. Buildings with restrooms and outdoor showers also rise from the sand at regular intervals, though lines do form during the most crowded summer weekends and holidays.

Most visitors to the O.C. coast want to stay as close to the beaches as they can. You can have your beachfront room at the **Sun 'N Sands Motel** (1102 Pacific Coast Hwy., Huntington Beach, 714/536-2543, www.sunnsands.com, $130–270). At this tiny place (17 guest rooms) you can expect standard motel-room decor in your king or double-queen guest room, plus an adequate private bath, a TV with movie channels, and Wi-Fi access. But the main attraction lies across the treacherous Pacific Coast Highway: long, sweet Huntington Beach. *Be careful* crossing the highway to get to the sand. Find a traffic light and a crosswalk rather than risking life and limb for the minor convenience of jaywalking.

For a quick bite to eat, stop off at the **Bodhi Tree Vegetarian Cafe** (501 Main St., Suite E, Huntington Beach, 714/969-9500, www.bodhitreehb.com, 11 A.M.–10 P.M. Wed.–Mon., $8–16) for vegetarian soups, salads, and sandwiches. **Sugar Shack Café** (213 Main St., Huntington Beach, 714/536-0355, www.hbsugarshack.com, 6 A.M.–4 P.M. Mon.–Tues. and Thurs., 6 A.M.–8 P.M. Wed., 6 A.M.–5 P.M. Fri.–Sun., $10) is a great place for breakfast.

Newport Beach

Most of the activity in Newport Beach (1200 Newport Center Dr., Suite 120 Newport Beach, 800/942-6278, www.visitnewportbeach.com) centers around Newport Pier (McFadden Pl.) and Main Street on the Balboa Peninsula. Some folks like to hark back to the old days of individual beach houses and long, lazy summer vacations. The **Crystal Cove Beach Cottages** (35 Crystal Cove, Newport Beach, 800/444-7275, www.crystalcovebeachcottages.org, dorm $33–98, cabins $125–191) can help recreate the feeling of another time. Right out on the sands of historic Crystal Cove south of downtown Newport Beach, this collection of cabins offer a delightful and serene beach vacation experience to all who stay here. Ten or so of the cabins are individual rentals where you get the whole house to yourself. The other 10 or so "dorm cottages" offer by-the-room accommodations (linens included, room doors lock) that give even solo budget travelers the opportunity to experience life on a Southern California beach. Another four cottages were restored with disabled guests in mind. Maid service is minimal, with towels changed every four days and trash taken out daily. None of the cottages have TVs or any type of digital entertainment. And all the cottages include a common refrigerator and microwave, but no full kitchen, so you'll need to make plans to eat out—perhaps at the adjacent **Beachcomber Cafe** (15 Crystal Cove, 949/376-6900, www.thebeachombercafe.com, 7 A.M.–9:30 P.M. daily, bar 11 A.M.–9:30 P.M. Mon.–Fri., 10 A.M.–9:30 P.M. Sat.–Sun.) or the concession-style **Shake Shack.**

The Island Hotel Newport Beach (690 Newport Center Dr., Newport Beach, 949/759-0808 or 866/554-4620, www.theislandhotel.com, $200–360) offers perhaps the ultimate O.C. experience. It's a luxury high-rise hotel situated in a giant shopping mall within a few minutes' drive of the beach. No, really. On the bright side, the tropical-themed guest rooms really do have both luxury and comfort in abundance. Expect cushy beds

with white linens, attractive private baths, big TVs, views over the mall (and if you're lucky, out to the ocean beyond the city), and all the best amenities. Perhaps the most innovative of these goodies rests within the room service menu; it's called the "In-Flight Menu" and it's a selection of gourmet box lunches. The idea is to allow air travelers to carry on their own food.

The hotel's **Palm Terrace Restaurant** (690 Newport Center Dr., Newport Beach, 949/760-4920 or 866/554-4619, www.theislandhotel.com, 6:30 A.M.–2 P.M. and 5:30–9 P.M. Sun.–Mon., 6:30 A.M.–2 P.M. and 6–9 P.M. Tues.–Thurs., 6:30 A.M.–2 P.M. and 6–10 P.M. Fri., 7 A.M.–2 P.M. and 6–10 P.M. Sat., $10–35) offers stylish small bites and sophisticated entrées in a picturesque setting. For something French, colorful **Pescadou Bistro** (3325 Newport Blvd., Newport Beach, 949/675-6990, www.pescadoubistro.com, 5:30 P.M.–close Tues.–Sun., $20–35) will fill the bill.

Laguna Beach

Farther south, the town of Laguna Beach has some of the nicest sands in the county. You'll find more than a dozen separate beaches here, though many connect to one another—you just have to choose your favorite. **Heisler Park** and **Main Beach Park** (Pacific Coast Hwy., www.lagunabeachinfo.com) offer protected waterways, with tide pools and plenty of water-based playground equipment. The two parks are connected, so you can walk from one to the other. Both display works of local art in the form of benches and sculptures. Hang out on a bench, pick a spot on the sand to lounge about, or take a swim in the cool Pacific. If you're into scuba diving, you can dive several reefs right off the beach.

You'll find all the facilities and amenities you need at Heisler and Main Beach Parks, including picnic tables, lawns, and restrooms. Use the charcoal grills provided rather than bringing your own. You can park on the street if you find a spot, but be aware that the meters get checked all the time, so feed them well.

THE L.A. AND O.C. COASTS **411**

LOS ANGELES

Dana Point

At the southern tip of the O.C., Dana Point (33282 Golden Lantern, Dana Point, 949/248-3500, www.danapoint.org, 7:30 A.M.–5:30 P.M. Mon.–Thurs., 7:30 A.M.–4:30 P.M. Fri.) has a harbor that has become a recreation marina that draws visitors and locals from all around. It also has several beaches nearby. One of the prettiest is **Capistrano Beach** (35005 Beach Rd., 949/923-2280 or 949/923-2283, www.ocparks.com or www.capistranobeach.com, 6 A.M.–10 P.M. daily, parking $1–2 per hour). You can relax on the soft sand or paddle out and catch a wave. Paths make biking, in-line skating, and walking popular pastimes, while others prefer a rousing game of volleyball out on the sand. You'll find a metered parking lot adjacent to the beach, plus showers and restrooms available.

For travelers looking to escape the endless crowds of the Newport–Huntington Beach scene, options beckon from farther south on the O.C. coast. The **Blue Lantern Inn** (34343 Blue Lantern St., Dana Point, 949/661-1304 or 800/950-1236, www.bluelanterninn.com, $175–600) sits south of San Juan Capistrano, making access to the small mission town easy. This attractive contemporary inn offers beachfront elegance, from the exterior to the downstairs restaurant to the guest rooms. Each of the 29 guest rooms boasts soothing colors, charming appointments, and lush amenities, including a spa tub in every bath and honest-to-goodness free drinks in the mini fridge. All beds come with their own teddy bear, and many of the guest rooms have private patios facing the sea and sunsets.

Mission San Juan Capistrano

One of the most famous and beloved of all the California missions is Mission San Juan Capistrano (26801 Oretga Hwy., 949/234-1300, http://missionsjc.com, 8:30 A.M.–5 P.M. daily, adults $9, seniors $8, ages 4–11 $5, under age 4 free). The lovely little town of San Juan Capistrano hosts flocks of swallows, which return every year at about the same time in the spring to fanfare and celebration by the whole town. These celebrations began during the mission's heyday in the 18th century, and may have been started by Native Americans centuries before that. Swallows are extremely loyal to their nesting grounds.

Today, thanks in part to the famous birds, this mission has a beautiful new Catholic church on-site, extensive gardens and land, and an audio tour of the museum, which was created from the old mission church and buildings. In late fall and early spring, monarch butterflies flutter about in the flower gardens and out by the fountain in the courtyard. Inside the original church, artifacts from the early time of the mission tell the story of its rise and fall. This was the only mission church where Father Junípero Serra, founder of the chain of missions in California, presided over Sunday services. The graveyard outside continues that narrative, as do the bells and other buildings of the compound. If you love stories of times past, you could spend hours wandering Mission San Juan Capistrano, with or without the audio tour. The complex includes adequate restrooms for visitors, plus plenty of garden and courtyard benches for rest, relaxation, and quiet meditation and reflection.

Regrettably, when you exit the mission into the charming town of San Juan Capistrano and stroll back to look at the historic buildings, you'll be standing next to a Starbucks. But if you turn the corner, you'll find yourself on the town's main street, which positively drips Spanish colonial history. Each old adobe building boasts a brass plaque describing its history and use over the years. In names and decor, the swallow is a major theme in the town, which nestles in a tiny valley only minutes from the sea.

Information and Services

Need assistance on arriving on the O.C. coast? A good place to get it is the **Huntington Beach Marketing and Visitors Bureau** (301 Main St., Suite 208, 714/969-3492 or 800/729-6232, www.surfcityusa.com, 9 A.M.–5 P.M.

Mon.–Fri.), which also has a visitor information kiosk (Pacific Coast Hwy. and Main St., noon–5 P.M. Mon.–Fri., 11 A.M.–5 P.M. Sat.–Sun.).

The major newspaper on the O.C. coast is the Orange County edition of the *Los Angeles Times,* which you can pick up at any newsstand.

Each town on the coast has at least one **post office,** including those in Huntington Beach (6671 Warner Ave., 714/843-4200) and in Newport Beach on the inland tip of the bay (1133 Camelback St., 949/640-4663), or down by the ocean (204 Main St., 949/675-1805).

If you need medical care while you're visiting the beach, **Hoag Hospital** (1 Hoag Dr., Newport Beach, 949/764-4624, www.hoaghospital.org) can probably fix whatever's broken.

Getting There

John Wayne Airport (SNA, 18601 Airport Way, Santa Ana, 949/252-5200, www.ocair.com) is the closest airport to the main beaches of the Orange County coast. It's much easier to fly into and out of John Wayne than LAX, though it can be more expensive. John Wayne's terminal has plenty of rental car agencies.

The Orange County Transportation Authority (OCTA, 550 S. Main St., Orange, 714/636-7433, www.octa.net) runs buses along the O.C. coast. The appropriately numbered Route 1 bus runs right along the Pacific Coast Highway from Long Beach down to San Clemente and back. Other routes can get you to and from inland O.C. destinations, including Anaheim. Regular bus fares are $1.50 per local ride, payable in cash on the bus with exact change. You can also buy a day pass from the bus driver for $4.

The one true highway on the O.C. coast is the Pacific Coast Highway, often called "the PCH" for short and officially designated Highway 1. You can get to the PCH from I-405 near Seal Beach, or catch I-710 to Long Beach and then drive south from there. From Disneyland, take I-5 to Highway 55, which takes you into Newport Beach. If you stay on I-5 going south, you'll eventually find yourself in San Juan Capistrano.

Parking along the beaches of the O.C. on a sunny summer day has been compared to one of Dante's circles of hell. You're far better off staying near the beach and walking out to your perfect spot in the sand. Other options include public transit and pay parking, which means "up to $40 per day and still six blocks to the beach."

Catalina Island

For a slice of Greece in Southern California, take a ferry or a helicopter out to Catalina Island (Catalina Island Chamber of Commerce, 310/510-1520, www.catalina.com). You can see Catalina from the shore of Long Beach on a clear day, but for a better view you've got to get onto the island. The port town of Avalon welcomes visitors with plenty of European-inspired hotels, restaurants, and shops. But the main draw of Catalina lies outside the walls of its buildings. With its Mediterranean summer climate, Catalina draws hikers, horseback riders, and ecotourists. Most of all, it beckons to water

lovers of all kinds, from scuba divers and snorkelers to kayakers and anglers.

The climate on Catalina tends toward the temperate, with beautiful, warm, sunny summer days that make getting out into the ocean a pleasure. Even in the winter, you'll find pleasantly warmish days and cool nights. But every once in a while, when the Santa Ana winds come billowing down from the mainland, life in Avalon harbor gets exciting. Storms and winds can whip up the seas, which then come crashing up onto and over the beaches and walkways of Avalon. When you see the yellow sandbags, be aware that the locals are

MICHELE & TOM GRIMM/IMAGE COURTESY OF LA INC.
THE LOS ANGELES CONVENTION AND VISITORS BUREAU

aerial shot of Avalon harbor on Catalina Island

serious. Even on a nonflooding morning, the Pacific can completely engulf the harbor-side beaches, hit the retaining walls, and spray dozens of feet into the air. If you're lucky enough to be around, take a walk down toward the waterside and enjoy the show.

SIGHTS
The Casino

No, it's not that kind of casino. The Casino Building at Avalon harks back to the older Italian meaning of the word, "place of entertainment." The round white art deco building acts as a community gathering place and home for all sorts of different activities. The Avalon Theatre, home to a Page organ, is located on the main level. Be sure to check out the murals by John Gabriel Beckman, of Grauman's Chinese Theatre fame, inside.

Wrigley Memorial and Botanical Garden

Upcountry, the coolest place to visit may be the Wrigley Memorial and Botanical Garden (Avalon Canyon Rd., 1.5 miles west of town,

310/510-2897, www.catalinaconservancy.org, 8 A.M.–5 P.M. daily, adults $7, seniors and veterans with ID $5, ages 5–12 and students with ID $3, under age 5 and active military and their families free), operated by the Catalina Island Conservancy. Stroll through serene gardens planted with flowers, trees, and shrubs that are native to California or even unique to Catalina. You'll see a number of endangered species among the plants that grow nowhere else in the world. The temperate climate on Catalina lends itself to hardy, drought-tolerant species that still manage to produce beautiful colors and fragrances. Just don't eat (or let your kids eat) the wild tomatoes—they're incredibly poisonous. Also, don't bother with the Catalina cherries. They're not deadly, but they don't taste very good.

At the center of the garden you can't miss the Wrigley Memorial, an edifice dedicated to the memory of chewing-gum magnate William Wrigley Jr. Wrigley adored Santa Catalina Island and used his sticky fortune to make many improvements to it; most notably, he funded the building of the Avalon Casino.

The monument is made and decorated with mostly local materials; the crushed stone on the facade comes from the island, as do the blue flagstones, the red roof tiles, and the brightly colored decorative ceramic tiles. All the local-centric construction makes a perfect center-piece to the gardens.

For a more thorough look at the history, culture, and diverse natural abundance of Catalina, visit the **Nature Center at Avalon Canyon** (1202 Avalon Canyon Rd., 310/510-0954, www.catalinaconservancy.org or http://parks.lacounty.gov, 10 A.M.–4 P.M. daily summer, 10 A.M.–4 P.M. Fri.–Wed. winter, free) just down the road from the botanical garden. Here you can learn more about the native plants, indigenous people, and the ocean channel and its islands, of which Catalina is the most visited.

Catalina Island Museum

Another take on the history of Catalina is displayed at the Catalina Island Museum (The Casino, 1 Casino Way, Avalon, 310/510-2414, www.catalinamuseum.org, 10 A.M.–4 P.M. daily Apr.–Dec., 10 A.M.–4 P.M. Fri.–Wed. Jan.–Mar., adults $5, seniors $4, ages 6–15 $2, under age 6 free). Located on the top floor of the landmark Casino, this small museum makes for a great 15–30 minute culture stop in the middle of a beach vacation. Learn about the history of the Chicago Cubs' spring training camp on the island, the short but famed production of Catalina tile and ceramics, the World War II history of Catalina, and more. You'll find a good-size collection of Native American artifacts from the island's original inhabitants, plus a huge collection of historic photos. Look for Hollywood stars enjoying Catalina's natural beauty and luxurious resort amenities among the photographic history of the island. Purchase reproductions of tiles, photos, and more in the museum store, and check the website for museum activities geared to kids and adults.

SPORTS AND RECREATION

Outdoor recreation is the main reason most people venture across the channel to Catalina.

On land or in the water, you'll find the activities that are right for you.

Scuba and Snorkeling

If you want to get out into the water on your own, you'll find plenty of places to kick off from shore. The most popular spot is the **Avalon Underwater Park** (Casino Point). This protected area at the north end of town has buoys and markers to help you find your way around the reefs and keep safe. Not only will you see the famous bright-orange garibaldi fish, you'll get the opportunity to meet jellyfish, anemones, spiny lobsters, and plenty of other sealife. Out at the deeper edge of the park, nearly half a dozen wrecked ships await your examination. Snorkeling and scuba tours groups come here, as do locals and visitors who rent equipment from local shops and shacks or bring their own. Expect big crowds on summer weekends.

If you prefer to take a guided tour, a number of companies offer snorkeling, scuba, kayaking, and combinations all around the island. **Catalina Snorkel & Scuba** (310/510-8558, www.catalinasnorkelscuba.com) is located right on Lover's Cove a short walk from the ferry terminal and offers guided snorkel tours of the Lover's Cove Marine Reserve that include all equipment with the fees. This clear-water preserve sits just southeast of the boat terminal and includes a life-filled kelp forest. If you're a certified scuba diver, you can book a two-hour guided tour of Avalon Underwater Park. If you want to become a scuba diver, Catalina Snorkel & Scuba offers certification classes as well as intro tours that give you a taste of the world underwater. Catalina Snorkel & Scuba also offers equipment rental for snorkelers and divers who want to take off on their own.

Another company to try is **Snorkel Catalina** (107 Pebbly Beach Rd., Avalon, 562/547-4185 or 877/218-9156, www.snorkelingcatalina.com). This company specializes in deeper-water excursions farther away from shore, taking guests out on a custom pontoon boat all year long. If your purpose in coming to Catalina is to swim with the dolphins, Snorkel Catalina can make it happen for you. Standard tours run 2–4 hours and let you check out the prettiest fish, sleekest seals, and friendliest dolphins around the island.

If it's hardcore scuba you're interested in, take a walk out onto the Avalon pier to **Catalina Divers Supply** (800/353-0330, www.catalinadiverssupply.com, 8 A.M.–4 P.M. daily summer, 8 A.M.–noon Sun.–Thurs., 8 A.M.–4 P.M. Sat. Labor Day–Memorial Day). The little blue shack out toward the end of the pier offers everything from certification and referral classes to guided shore dives at the Avalon Marine Preserves to charter trips on the 46-foot *Scuba Cat*. You'll see things that just aren't visible from the surface with a snorkel. The company highly recommends making reservations for any of their tours and trips.

Kayaking

Kayaking is one of the most popular ways to see otherwise unreachable parts of Catalina. Rent a kayak, or if you're not confident in your own navigation abilities, take a tour with a reputable company. **Descanso Beach Ocean Sports/ Catalina Island Kayak & Snorkel** (310/510-1226, www.kayakcatalinaisland.com, $40–60 half-day–full-day) offers several kayak tours to different parts of the island. You don't need previous river or sea kayaking experience to take these tours, since double sit-on-top kayaks make the trip easy and safe even for total beginners and small kids. But if you are a rescue-certified sea kayaker, the folks at Descanso Beach also have an array of lean, sleek, enclosed ocean kayaks for advanced paddlers. This company offers regular year-round trips to Frog Rock (2 hours), Fox Canyon (3 hours, includes a nature walk), and Willow Cove (half-day excursion with snorkeling and hiking). All trips start at Descanso Beach Club, north of Avalon and the Casino.

Another kayak tour provider, **Wet Spot Rentals** (off Pebbly Beach Rd. across the bay from the Casino, 310/510-2229, www.catalinakayaks.com, $35–75 half-day–full-day) specializes in a full-day land and sea tour that includes both kayaking and an auto tour into the Catalina backcountry. After a van trip and nature tour at the airport on top of the hill, you'll travel down to the less-traveled windward side of the island. You'll get a rare opportunity to kayak on the other side of the island from Avalon, exploring the coves and cliffs around Little Harbor. A brief portage and hike takes you to a waterfall. This fabulous, nearly whole-island tour takes all day, and lunch, water, and all equipment, including sit-on-top beginner kayaks, are provided. Wet Spot also offers several shorter kayak expeditions; they're a great operator if you want to combine kayaking with snorkeling the reefs of the leeward (Avalon) side of the island.

These operators also rent kayaks to individuals (you'll have to prove yourself capable to rent an enclosed sea kayak). They also have an array of snorkel equipment, and you can take a kayak out for some fabulous fish watching and even skin diving.

Rafting

For an adventurous ocean tour, head out with **Catalina Ocean Rafting** (103 Pebbly Beach Rd., 310/510-0211 or 800/990-7238, www.catalinaoceanrafting.com, adults $78–140, ages 5–11 and military $67–109, ages 12–18 and get the lower rate when accompanied by two paying adults). From Avalon harbor you'll head out on a two-hour, half-day, or full-day trip on a powered inflatable raft. The small maneuverable craft can take you right up to cliffs and into sea caves, around Eagle Rock and Ribbon Rock, and into reef areas perfect for snorkeling (equipment is provided with your tour). You'll get to harbors beyond Avalon and enjoy lunch, drinks, and snacks as part of your trip. A raft tour is a great way for adventurous newcomers to get the lay of the land and sea before striking off on their own.

Swimming

In the summer, the waters of Catalina can reach more than 70°F—perfect for taking a long, lazy swim in the salty waters of the Pacific. Bring your family out to any one of the charming beaches in the sunny coves for a lazy day on the beach and in the water. The most crowded spots will be at the Avalon Underwater Park, the harbor, and other coves near Avalon. For a more deserted beach, try the windward side of the island; just be aware that it may be, well, windy. Keep a close eye on your children and even adult friends wherever you swim. Catalina's beaches, like most of the California coastline, are subject to dangerous rip currents.

Wildlife-Watching

If you're not keen on swimming in the ocean, but you want a peek at the famous Catalina garibaldi (a bright-orange fish), take a semi-submersible or glass-bottom boat tour. The **Undersea Tour** (310/510-8687 or 800/626-7489, www.visitcatalinaisland.com, on the hour noon–3:30 P.M. Mon.–Fri., 11 A.M.–3 P.M. Sat.–Sun., adults $36, seniors $32, children $26) takes you a few feet underwater for 45 minutes in a comfy cabin to watch the abundant array of aquatic life around Avalon. For a special (and budget-conscious) treat, book a nighttime Undersea Tour to check out a whole different variety of sea species. Every seat on the boat has a great view of the water, and kids love the colorful fish and mysterious bat rays that glide gracefully by.

In the summer, take another boat trip out to see one of the legends of Catalina. A **Flying Fish Boat Trip** (310/510-8687 or 800/626-1496, www.visitcatalinaisland.com, adults $26, seniors $24, children $20) lights up the air just over the waterline, making visible the famous Catalina flying fish as they leap out, putting on a unique show.

Biking

Even most of the locals on Catalina eschew cars in favor of smaller, lighter forms of transportation. A great way to get around and beyond Avalon is on a bicycle. You can bring your own aboard the ferries that travel to and from the airport. If you don't have one, you can rent a bicycle right on the island at **Brown's Bikes** (underneath Holly Hill House, 100 yards from the ferry dock, 310/510-0986, www.catalinabiking.com, 9 A.M.–5 P.M. daily, $8–18 per hour, $20–45 per day). If you're looking for

a simple, one-speed cruiser to putter around downtown Avalon and down to the beach, you can get one for $8 per hour or $20 per day. With no gas to buy, it's the ultimate in affordable transportation. Brown's also has six- and 21-speeds, tandems, an array of mountain bikes, and electric bicycles. You'll also get a map of the bikeable roads and trails in Avalon and around the island.

Mountain bikers, this island's for you: An array of trails from easy to steep and difficult take you up into the hills, providing views and thrills galore. Street bikers will find that Avalon is bike-friendly; the road that runs along the shore on either side of the town is paved, mostly level, and zoned for bicycles. If you've got the legs for it, you can obtain a permit from the Catalina Conservancy to ride farther afield. Call or email Brown's Bikes for more information on biking outside Avalon.

Golf

As most of Catalina Island is devoted to wildlife preservation, you won't find a wealth of golf courses here. But if just can't abide the notion of going for a trip without exercising your clubs, get yourself a tee time at the nine-hole **Catalina Island Golf Course** (1 Country Club Dr., Avalon, 310/510-0530, www.visitcatalinaisland.com, $35–85), which has nine- or 18-hole rounds, discounts for seniors, and higher rates on weekends. You'll be walking on greens built in 1892, used for the Bobby Jones Invitational Tournament from the 1930s through the 1950s, and more recently played on by up-and-coming SoCal junior players such as Craig Stadler and Tiger Woods as they built their skills. Heck, even if you don't play, it's worth walking the course on a sunny day just to enjoy the unbelievable views out to the Casino, the town of Avalon, and the clutch of sailboats bobbing in the harbor. The full-service pro shop provides rental equipment and golf carts as well as a set of **tennis courts** you can rent by the hour.

If your taste in golf runs a little less serious, head for **Golf Gardens** (Sumner Ave., 800/322-3434, www.visitcatalinaisland.com,

10 A.M.–5:30 P.M. Sun.–Fri., 9 A.M.–8:30 P.M. Sat.), a miniature golf course one block inland from the fountain just past the Discovery Tours Plaza and across the street from the City Library. This is a great break for kids tired of sightseeing and ecotouring. This cute 18-hole course has a tropical feel, complete with palm trees and good putting challenges.

Spas

You've got a surprising number of massage and spa options right in and around Avalon. If you prefer your massage in the privacy of your hotel room or condo, call **Catalina Sea Spa** (310/510-8920, www.catalinamassage-bymichelle.net, massage $85–135, spa treatments $120–300), formerly known as In-Room Massage by Michelle. The therapists love to work with couples looking for a relaxing day or evening of romance, and they are trained in a variety of massage techniques and spa therapies, including heated stones and Thai massage. Book a simple Swedish massage or a full spa package with facials, body scrubs, and massages for one or two people. Check the website for a full list of available treatments. Be sure to book in advance to get the date and time you want. Studio sessions are also available.

Whether you're looking for a divine romantic experience with your sweetie or a solo day of spa-induced respite from your busy life, you'll find it at **The Spa at Catalina** (888 Country Club Rd., Avalon, 310/510-9255, www.catalinaspa.com, $55–319). This full-service day spa offers all sorts of massage and treatment packages, from a simple half-hour of bodywork up to nearly three hours of head-to-toe bliss. The spa has dual rooms (many complete with private baths for two) to serve couples or pairs of friends who want to enjoy their treatments together. Choose from the many packages that focus on facials and scalp treatments using lavender, peppermint, and other delicious essential oils. You can also breathe deep and detox with a body wrap or heated stone massage. The spa sits in Falls Canyon outside downtown Avalon; ask about getting a free shuttle from your hotel to the spa at the Best Western

Canyon Hotel when you book your treatments. It's best to make reservations at least a couple of days in advance; even in winter, same-day appointment availability is rare.

Decide for yourself whether the treatments you receive in downtown Avalon live up to the name **A Touch of Heaven** (205 Crescent Ave., 310/510-1633, www.atouchofheavendayspa.com, 9 A.M.–5 P.M. daily, $45–400) at the back of the Metropole Market Place. This day spa echoes the European flavor of the town surrounding it; you'll find an extensive menu of Euro-style facials, from the intense relaxation of a LaStone Facial to the aesthetically focused glycolic–lactic acid peel and facial. Also look for a few unusual treatments, including raindrop therapy and ear candling, as well as practitioners of both Eastern and Western massage modalities. The spa also offers massage for children, and well-behaved young people are welcome to enjoy the treatments here.

ACCOMMODATIONS

You'll find plenty of charming inns and hotels on Catalina; most sit in or near Avalon. You can also camp on Catalina, and ecotourists often prefer to immerse themselves in the natural world of the island by sleeping and eating outdoors.

Camping

Camping is the best way to get away from Avalon and stay on other parts of the island. It's also a great way to get to know the precious Catalina wilderness in an up-close-and-personal way. Check the island's visitors website (www.visitcatalinaisland.com) for a list and descriptions of all the major campgrounds around the island. Also be sure to read the regulations, which are more stringent than at some other camping areas and are strictly enforced. Permits are required for all campsites. Also check out the equipment rentals; if you don't want to bring your own tent and gear, you can rent it at the Two Harbors ranger station (310/510-8368).

You have a choice of more than half a dozen campgrounds, some on the coast and some up the mountains in the interior. One of the largest and most developed campgrounds sits just outside the tiny town of **Two Harbors** (310/510-8368, www.visitcatalinaisland.com/avalon/camp_twoHarbors.php, adults $15, children $8 Mon.–Fri. summer, adults $17, children $9 Sat.–Sun. summer, tent cabins $50–55). Book online to avoid the $25 "administration fee" for reservations phoned in. You can go to the website and see a photo gallery of the campgrounds and check out a map of the campsites before you make a reservation. You can bring your own tent and equipment, rent it, or book one of the tent cabins at this site. The tent cabins come with cots and mattresses, sunshades, and a camp stove and lantern in addition to the usual barbecue grill, fire ring, and picnic table. All campers have access to showers, restroom facilities, and lockers to keep valuables safe while you're out exploring the area.

If you're looking to camp on the beach, check out the **Little Harbor** (310/510-8368, www.visitcatalinaisland.com/avalon/camp_littleHarbor.php, adults $14, children $7 Mon.–Fri. summer, adults $16, children $8 Sat.–Sun. summer, tent cabins $50–55) campground. Located seven miles from the town of Little Harbor, the sandy campsites make a perfect place to sleep if your aim is snorkeling, kayaking (Wet Spot Rentals, 310/510-2229), and playing away from all the casual island visitors. You'll find potable water, showers, and toilets here. The best way to get to the Little Harbor campground is to take the Safari Bus, so be sure to book seats and space for your gear when you book your campsite.

Perhaps the coolest way to stay on Catalina is to bring or rent a kayak and paddle into one of the **boat-in campsites** (adults $12, children $6). These 17 primitive campsites at nine locations can't be accessed by land at all—you must bring and moor your own boat. You'll get a wholly natural experience at any of these beautiful remote locations, with no running water, showers, or toilet facilities, or shade structures. Whatever you want and need, you must pack into your boat with you. A ranger checks each campsite daily, so you're not completely cut off

from the outside world. However, take precautions such as bringing a two-way radio and an above-average first-aid kit just in case an emergency crops up.

Under $150

The **Hotel Atwater** (125 Sumner Ave., 800/626-1496, www.visitcatalinaisland.com, spring–fall, $96–208) has bright, cheerful guest rooms for reasonable rates. Take in the history of a budget hotel that's been hosting guests since the 1920s. Clean, light-colored economy rooms provide the best value for your buck, while the more upscale suites cost more and offer prettier decor and better amenities. Whichever type of room you book, you'll have a TV, a coffeemaker, air-conditioning, and more. You'll find storage for your diving gear and bikes, and a rinse-off area outside for divers, snorkelers, and swimmers. The Atwater closes each winter; call ahead to confirm availability.

$150-250

For inexpensive indoor accommodations, your best bet is the **Hermosa Hotel & Cottages** (131 Metropole St., 310/510-1010 or 877/453-1313, www.hermosahotel.com, $150–225). This simple budget hotel has guest rooms with shared baths in the main building—way off-season, some of these clean guest rooms are dirt cheap if you're willing to walk down the hall to the shower. (Be aware of a two-night minimum for stays involving a Saturday night in the high season.) The cottages have private baths, and some have kitchens and TVs. "Family units" can sleep up to six in the main building and have kitchens—perfect for larger families or groups of friends traveling together on a budget. The 100-plus-year-old building sits only about a block from the harbor beaches and a short walk from the Casino, shops, and restaurants.

Want to stay right on the waterfront? Book a room at the bright yellow **Hotel Mac Rae** (409 Crescent Ave., 310/510-0246 or 800/698-2266, www.hotelmacrae.com, ocean view $209–259 summer, courtyard view $159–259 summer). This bit of Catalina history has been in the Mac Rae family for four generations, and they've been running the hostelry since 1920. The Mediterranean flavor of Avalon follows you into the guest rooms and common spaces of the Mac Rae. Relax with a drink in the bright brick courtyard. You can choose one of the premium guest rooms that looks right out into the harbor, or a more economical courtyard-view room. Grab a complimentary continental breakfast downstairs, and either eat in the courtyard or take your coffee and your pastries back to your pretty Côte d'Azur–styled guest room for more privacy. Catching the afternoon ferry but want to enjoy one last morning in the warm Catalina water? The Mac Rae has luggage storage and even a public shower for use after you check out.

For a European hotel experience in Avalon, stay at the **Hotel Metropole** (205 Crescent Ave., 310/510-1884, www.hotel-metropole.com, $200–500). The comfortably cluttered and warmly decorated guest rooms feel like home almost immediately. You'll find gas fireplaces in some guest rooms and oversize two-person whirlpool bathtubs in a few pretty tiled baths. The beds feel great after a long day of ocean swimming or the ferry ride over from Long Beach. The little extras are nice too, from the nightly turndown service to the L'Occitane toiletries. You can also use the Wi-Fi service in your room and grab a snack from the honor bar. The Metropole is built in a modern style with a pretty gray paint job. On the roof you'll find a whirlpool tub with glass walls enclosing its deck, letting you look out over the rooftops into the harbor. The lower-end guest rooms don't have much in the way of ocean views, so for a window on the water, you have to pay premium rates for an oceanfront room or suites ($500–800). You can walk half a block down the street to the ocean. For extra pampering, make an appointment at the day spa located on the bottom floor of the hotel (A Touch of Heaven, 205 Crescent Ave., 310/510-1633, www.atouchofheavendayspa.com, 9 A.M.–5 P.M. daily, $45–400). Just outside by the back elevator, start a shopping jaunt

in the little Metropole center, where you can grab a cup of coffee, or walk down Crescent Avenue for a meal.

The **Villa Portofino** (111 Crescent Ave., 310/510-0555 or 888/510-0555, www.hotel-villaportofino.com, rooms $125–375, suites $285–550) offers Mediterranean elegance on the Avalon waterfront. The bright-white exterior with red tile roofs invites you inside this 34-room boutique hotel. Guest rooms range from small standard rooms up through immense, lush, individually named suites with fireplaces, soaking tubs, and richly colored furnishings. Amenities include a complimentary continental breakfast, free Wi-Fi, free beach chairs and towels, and an on-site restaurant, Ristorante Villa Portofino (101 Crescent Ave., 310/510-2009, www.ristorantevillaportofino.com, $15–36). The Portofino's location is perfect—right on the main drag running along the harbor-side beach.

FOOD

To be honest, the culinary presence on Catalina isn't much to write home about. While there's certainly no lack of restaurants in Avalon, the trend toward delicious cuisine at both the high and low ends hasn't made it across the island to the channel yet. You might consider getting a guest room or a condo with a kitchen and cooking a few of your own meals to save a bit of cash while you're here. Still, a traveler has to go out to eat sometimes. Here are a few places to try.

American

So where do the locals go? Many of them crowd into **El Galleon** (411 Crescent Ave., 310/510-1188, www.catalinahotspots.com/el_galleon, lunch 11 A.M.–4 P.M. daily, dinner 4–9 P.M. daily, karaoke 9 P.M. Thurs.–Sun., $10–30). It's easy to get to since it's part of the pedestrian-only area on Crescent Avenue, and the porch has a fabulous view out to the harbor. The large menu speaks to hearty American diners with lots of aged steaks, chicken dishes, and fresh fish. Lighter eaters can peruse the selection of salads, soups, and seafood appetizers.

For a major feast, take a look at the prix fixe menu, which, when available, offers a hearty four-course dinner (about $70 pp). The dessert menu offers a few unusual treats, plus a wide array of sweet and strong coffee drinks to round off your evening. El Galleon boasts a full bar and a fun vibe, and live karaoke runs into the night. If you prefer an earlier evening, happy hour is 3–6 P.M. daily.

For a more serious upscale dining experience, get a table in the dining room at the **Catalina Country Club** (1 Country Club Dr., 310/510-7404, www.visitcatalinaisland.com, $21–41). You don't need to be a member to enjoy a refined dinner here or at one of the Country Club's two more casual dining venues. Unlike most of the rest of the island's restaurants, here you'll be served some high-end California cuisine, complete with a focus on organic and sustainable ingredients. Check the online calendar on the website to get the listing for the live entertainment lineup for Thursday-evening Unplugged at the Country Club and Friday-evening Jazz at the Country Club.

Italian

The **Ristorante Villa Portofino** (101 Crescent Ave., 310/510-2009, www.ristorantevillaportofino.com, $15–36), attached to the Villa Portofino hotel, serves tasty pasta and protein dishes with a distinct Italian flare—and you'll get a fabulous harbor view with your cannelloni or calamari. In homage to the locale, the menu here runs to seafood, with some classic and a few inventive preparations. The pastas bring homey comfort food to Catalina, and the hot appetizer menu is well worth a look. For dessert, the Ristorante offers a goodly selection of Italian favorites, such as cannoli and *panna cotta*. In the summer, see if you can get a table on the patio to enjoy the balmy island breezes—you'll feel almost as though you're really on the Mediterranean coast of Italy.

Mexican

Looking for an unpretentious taco? You can get one at the **Catalina Cantina** (313 Crescent Ave., 310/510-0100, $15–25) or its fast-food walk-up neighbor, the **Topless Taco.** Serving a mix of American diner fare (think burgers and fries, wings, and fish-and-chips) and Americanized Mexican staples (burritos, fajitas, combo plates), the Catalina Cantina offers tasty food for decent prices. Better still, if you come in the evening, cool off with one of the Cantina's buckets o' liquor. Rum punch, margaritas, something called the Blue Shark, and more come in either normal human-size glasses or in a 28-ounce bowl that they really hope you'll share with friends.

Seafood

If all you want is a slab of really fresh fish, you can get it down on the Pleasure Pier at **Avalon Seafood and Fish Market** (Pleasure Pier, 310/510-0197). That's the cute blue building at the end of the pier bearing a sign that says "Fish and Chips." It's part fish-and-chips stand, part fresh seafood market, and you can get a casual eat-at-the-picnic-table lunch or barbecued fish dinner. Or if you've got kitchen or barbecue access, pick up the catch of the day and make a fresh fish dinner for yourself and your family or friends.

Steak

All the locals recommend that tourists try **Steve's Steakhouse** (417 Crescent Ave., 310/510-0333, www.stevessteakhouse.com, lunch 11:30 A.M.–2 P.M., dinner from 4:30 P.M. daily summer, lunch 11:30 A.M.–2 P.M., dinner from 4:30 P.M. Fri.–Tues. winter, $15–33). It's possible that the locals are trying to keep the travelers away from their favorite spots by sending them here. Sure, Steve's offers a wide array of classic steak house fare with plenty of seafood options thrown in as a nod to the water lapping the harbor beach just outside. Generous portions of meat or fish are accompanied by traditional steak-house sides, and the desserts up the ante with some tasty sweetness (the mud pie's not half bad). But compared to the lush cuisine you can get on the mainland, the quality of the ingredients and the preparations seem a bit lackluster at Steve's, and the tourist-high prices can be a bit painful.

Coffee

Looking for a cup of coffee and maybe a quick pastry down by the Casino? Stop by **El Encanto Courtyard Coffee** (101 Marilla Ave., 310/510-1652, $1.50–5). In the winter, the hot lattes and chais offer steamy warmth, while the summer sees customers ordering refreshingly icy smoothies and frappés. Courtyard Coffee is in the El Encanto Market Place, across from the Via Casino Arch.

INFORMATION AND SERVICES

If you are camping in a remote location, talk to the rangers at the Two Harbors station before leaving to learn how best to contact them or the police in an emergency. Bring a two-way radio, since cell signal may be unreliable or nonexistent.

For medical assistance, go to the **Catalina Island Medical Center** (100 Falls Canyon Rd., 310/510-0700, www.catalinaislandmedicalcenter.org).

The major local daily newspaper on Catalina is the *Los Angeles Times* (www.latimes.com). Your hotel might have copies. A good website for visitors is www.visitcatalinaisland.com.

Catalina isn't one of Orange County's major shopping destinations; if you're hoping to put a serious dent in your credit cards, you'll want to head back to the mainland. But if you're looking for kitschy souvenirs and reproduction ceramic tiles, you can find them in downtown Avalon in the area sometimes called the **South Coast Plaza.**

GETTING THERE AND AROUND

There are two ways to get to Catalina: by boat and by air.

Boat

Most folks take the ferry over from the mainland coast. The **Catalina Express** (800/481-3470, www.catalinaexpress.com, round-trip adults $73, seniors $66, ages 2–11 $57, under age 2 $5, bikes and surfboards $6) serves as the major carrier, with multiple departures every day, even in the off-season. During the summer high season, you can choose to leave from two docks in Long Beach, one dock in San Pedro, and another in Dana Point. Most ferries dock at Avalon, but you can arrange to travel directly to Two Harbors from San Pedro if you prefer. You can bring your bike, your luggage, and your camping gear aboard for a comfortable hour-long ride on one of eight ferries. Bars on both levels offer snacks and drinks, and TVs help make the cruise go by a little faster. On the way it's worth looking out the window, however: You might spot seals or sea lions, different varieties of pelicans, or even a pod of dolphins playing in the swells. Catalina Express also offers plenty of return cruises to the mainland each day.

An alternate ferry service, the **Catalina Flyer** (Balboa Pavilion, 400 Main St., Newport Beach, 800/831-7744, www.catalinainfo.com, round-trip adults $69, seniors $64, ages 3–12 $52, under age 3 $5, parking $15–25) offers one trip out and one trip back each day. The Flyer operates primarily March–November.

Air

You can also get to Catalina by air. There is a helicopter pad just northwest of Avalon harbor. **Island Express Helicopter Service** (1175 Queens Hwy. S., Long Beach, and Berth 95, San Pedro, 800/228-2566, www.islandexpress.com, 8:30 A.M.–sunset daily, round-trip $201 pp) can fly you from Long Beach or San Pedro to Catalina in about 15 minutes. You can get a cab into town from the helipad. Island Express also offers aerial tours of the island and various travel packages. Or if you prefer to fly your own small plane to Catalina, the **Airport in the Sky** (800/255-8700, 8 A.M.–7 P.M. daily Apr.–Oct., 8 A.M.–5 P.M. daily Nov.–Mar.) offers general aviators a 3,250-foot runway, $10 parking, and a $25 landing fee—there is no gas, though, so fuel up for a round trip before you head out. The Catalina Island Conservancy's **Wildlands Express/Airport Shuttle** (310/510-0143, adults $26, ages 5–11 $21, under age 5 free) is one way to make it the 10 miles or so from the airport to Avalon and back again. Reservations are required, so call ahead.

Car

On Catalina, cars just aren't the fashionable way to get around. Even the locals tend to eschew full cars since they aren't practical in the tiny town of Avalon. Instead, locals and visitors in the know prefer to drive golf carts. Walk from the ferry dock down toward town, and you'll see any number of rental services, complete with herds of carts out and ready for use. The cost runs $80–120 per hour for a 4–6 passenger cart with a $40–60 deposit. A couple of easy-to-find companies include **Island Rentals** (125 Pebbly Beach Rd., 310/510-1456) underneath the Holly Hill House near the ferry dock and **Cartopia** (615 Crescent Ave., 310/510-2493).

You can also grab a taxi if you need to get somewhere in a hurry, especially with your luggage. Taxis hover near the ferry dock when the ferries are due in each day, and it's customary to share your ride with as many people as can fit into the car (which is often a minivan). To get a cab back to the ferry or the helipad when it's time to leave, call **Catalina Transportation Services** (310/510-0025, www.catalinatransportationservices.com, 7 A.M.–11 P.M. Sun.–Thurs., 7 A.M.–midnight Fri.–Sat., rates vary) for a taxi, shuttle, charter, or trolley. It takes only about 10 minutes for a taxi to get to just about anywhere in town.

Bus

Public transit on Catalina includes the **Safari Bus** (310/510-2800, adults $10–32, children $10–26, depending on destination), which runs from Avalon to Two Harbors each day. The bus stops at the southeast corner of Island Plaza in Avalon. You can buy tickets at Visitors Services and the Discovery Tours booth on the Pleasure Pier. Alternately, the **Avalon Trolley** (310/510-0025 or 310/510-0342, 9 A.M.–9 P.M. Fri.–Sat., 9 A.M.–5 P.M. Sun.–Thurs. June 15– Sept. 15, 10 A.M.–4 P.M. Sat.–Sun. and cruise ship days Sept. 16–June 14, $2–7) runs in and around Avalon, hitting most of the major sightseeing and outdoor adventuring spots near town. With two lines that converge inland, you can get where you need to go for a reasonable fare without having to hoof it. The trolley runs approximately every 30–40 minutes, with the entire route taking about an hour.

Tours

One of the main forms of entertainment on the island is touring. You can take a bus tour, a Jeep tour, a glass-bottom boat tour, and more. The Catalina Island Conservancy offers **Jeep Eco-Tours** (310/510-2595, www.catalinaconservancy.org, up to 6 people $495 half-day, $795 full-day) out in the wilds of Catalina. You can go much farther on these tours than you can by yourself—out into the wilderness to see the bison, the wild horses, plant species unique to the island, and more. Be sure to bring your camera, both for close-ups and for views out toward the sea. On the full-day trips, you'll get lunch, drinks, and snacks, while on the half-day trip you'll get snacks and drinks.

For a sedate view of Catalina's more settled areas as well as it's road-viewable wilderness, try a **Inland Motor Tour** (310/510-8687 or 800/626-7489, www.visitcatalinaisland.com, daily year-round, from $76). This 3.5-hour tour aboard a restored 1950s cruising bus takes you away from the coastline and into the island's interior via old stagecoach routes. Along the way you'll see Middle Ranch, the magnificent Arabian horses and Old West mementos of El Rancho Escondido, and the Airport in the Sky Nature Center. A shorter version of this tour is the **Skyline Drive** (310/510-8687 or 800/626-1496, daily year-round, adults $47, seniors $42, children $36), a two-hour trip that takes you up from Avalon to the Airport in the Sky Nature Center along a route cluttered with spectacular vistas of island and ocean.

If you want a guided walking tour of Avalon, try **Catalina Adventure Tours** (877/510-2888, www.catalinaadventuretours.com, adults $22, seniors $18, children $14) for a 90-minute look at Avalon's attractions, past, and architecture. The one-hour tour by **Icons of Avalon** (310/502-6131, www.iconsofavalon.com, $30) is followed by 30 minutes of wine tasting. Of course, this tour is for those age 21 and older. They also offer Ghost Tour of Avalon (http://ghosttoursofcatalina.com, adults $15, children $12). And for the more independent-minded visitor, try **GPS Walking Tours** (310/510-8687, www.visitcatalinaisland.com, $15 per device).

Each device can guide 4–6 people, an ideal money saver for families.

Catalina Adventure Tours also runs the semi-submersible *Nautilus* (877/510-2888, www.catalinaadventuretours.com, adults $39, seniors $34, children $30) and leads 1–2-hour adventure drives around the island.

PACIFIC COAST HIGHWAY

The best and consistently prettiest drive in California runs up the craggy curving coastline on the Pacific Coast Highway (PCH). This is the edge of California—the edge of the continent—where it dramatically meets with the Pacific Ocean. The route itself is sometimes a highway, sometimes a city street, and often a twisty and slow road. Wherever you are, it shows off the edge of California as it meets the Pacific Ocean. If a convertible were appropriate anywhere, this would be the place.

While the stunning vistas are the main attractions along the coastal drive between Los Angeles and San Francisco, PCH also goes through a number of idyllic beachside towns. Eclectic and funky Ventura, a little over an hour north of Los Angeles, serves as a jumping-off point for the pristine and primal Channel Islands National Park. Temperate Santa Barbara has a relaxed yet cultured pace that reflects its mission and university influences as well as its affluence. Seaside Cambria makes a good base from which to visit much of the Central Coast, including San Simeon, home to grand Hearst Castle, an homage to excess.

North of Cambria and south of Carmel, the Big Sur coast is the highlight of Highway 1's scenic tour. This might be the single most beautiful part of California. The rugged cliffs and protected forests have little development to mar their natural charms. It's a sin to remain in your car when such an embarrassment of natural riches await.

To the north, the exclusive moneyed enclave of Carmel rivals Malibu for its charming ocean views, well-traveled beaches and parks,

© MARIUSZ JURGIELEWICZ/123RF

HIGHLIGHTS

◖ **Old Mission Santa Barbara:** Known as the queen of the California missions, this intricately painted church has some of the most lush grounds and landscaping of any mission, making it a routine stopping point (page 455).

◖ **Madonna Inn:** The flamboyant decor is the highlight at the Madonna Inn, which is overrun with pink kitsch. It's a unique place to stay but also a fun spot for lunch, dinner, or even just a photo op (page 496).

◖ **Morro Rock:** Primal, austere, energetic, and endlessly photogenic, this ancient dormant volcano defines Morro Bay and is a refuge for endangered falcons, home of Native American lore, and a visitor's delight (page 510).

◖ **Moonstone Beach:** A perfect stretch of beach for walking, thinking, strolling, and absorbing the beauty of this rugged area, with an accessible boardwalk on the cliffs just above the beach. There are as many otters and sea lions as people (page 520).

◖ **Hearst Castle:** No visit to the Central Coast is complete without a tour of Hearst Castle, the grand mansion on a hill conceived and built by publishing magnate William Randolph Hearst (page 527).

◖ **Elephant Seal Rookery:** Every winter, elephant seals show up on the beaches north of San Simeon to birth their pups. The males fight loudly and spar with each other, the females begin to wean their newborns, and the people get a free show (page 532).

◖ **Big Sur Coast Highway:** This twisty, coastal drive is iconic Big Sur, with jutting cliffs, crashing surf, and epic views all the way (page 535).

◖ **Carmel Art Galleries:** Carmel has more art galleries per capita than anywhere else in the United States; take a look (page 552).

◖ **Monterey Bay Aquarium:** This mammoth aquarium was the first of its kind in the United States and still astonishes with a vast array of sealife and exhibits (page 562).

LOOK FOR ◖ TO FIND RECOMMENDED SIGHTS, ACTIVITIES, DINING, AND LODGING.

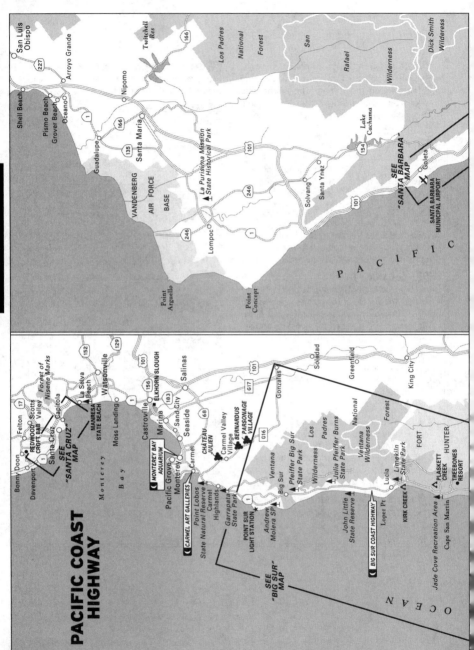

PACIFIC COAST HIGHWAY

San Luis Obispo
Arroyo Grande
227
Shell Beach
Pismo Beach
Grover Beach
Oceano
1
Nipomo
166
Guadalupe
Santa Maria
135
166
VANDENBERG
AIR FORCE
BASE
246
La Purisima Mission
State Historical Park
Lompoc
246
1
Point
Arguello
Point
Concept

Twitchell
Res
166
Los Padres
National
Forest
San
Rafael
Wilderness
Dick Smith
Wilderness

Lake
Cachuma
154
101
246
Santa Ynez
Solvang
Santa Ynez
101
SEE
"SANTA BARBARA"
MAP

Goleta
SANTA BARBARA
MUNICIPAL AIRPORT

P A C I F I C

**PACIFIC COAST
HIGHWAY**

Bonny Doon
Davenport
1
Felton
REDWOOD
CROFT B&B
Scotts
Valley
Santa Cruz
17
Forest of
Nisene Marks
152
129
Capitola
SEE
"SANTA CRUZ"
MAP
La Selva
Beach
Watsonville
MANRESA
STATE BEACH
Moss Landing
101
156
183
ELKHORN SLOUGH
Salinas
Castroville
Marina
Sand City
Seaside
68
Monterey
MONTEREY BAY
AQUARIUM
Pacific Grove
CARMEL ART GALLERIES
Carmel
Point Lobos
State Natural Reserve
Carmel
Highlands
Garrapata
State Park
POINT SUR
LIGHT STATION
Andrew
Molera SP
SEE
"BIG SUR"
MAP

CHÂTEAU
JULIEN
Carmel Valley
Village
BERNARDUS
PARSONAGE
VILLAGE
G16
G17
Gonzales
Soledad
Greenfield
King City
101
101
Ventana
Wilderness
Big Sur
Pfeiffer Big Sur
State Park
Los
Padres
National
Forest
Julia Pfeiffer Burns
State Park
Lucia
Limekiln
State Park
John Little
State Reserve
Lopez Pt
Big Sur Coast Highway
KIRK CREEK
Jade Cove Recreation Area
Cape San Martin
PLASKETT
CREEK
TREEBONES
RESORT
FORT
HUNTER

M o n t e r e y
B a y

O C E A N

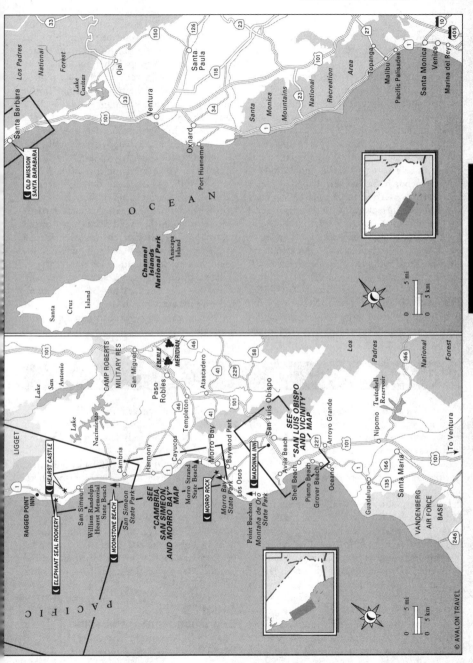

PACIFIC COAST HIGHWAY

© AVALON TRAVEL

and unbelievably expensive real estate. (Clint Eastwood was once mayor here.) The legendary Pebble Beach golf course and resort are just north of downtown.

Gorgeous Monterey Bay is famous for its sealife. Sea otters dive and play at the world-renowned aquarium while sea lions beach themselves on offshore rocks. The historic Cannery Row was immortalized by John Steinbeck in his novel of the same name, but the now-touristy wharf area bears only a superficial resemblance to its fishing past. Around Monterey Bay to the north, Santa Cruz is the last major coastal town south of San Francisco, which is about two hours away. With an ultraliberal culture, redwood-clad university, and general sense of fun, Santa Cruz prides itself on keeping things weird. The beach and Boardwalk are good places to surf and enjoy the sun, as north of here, the waters get ever chillier.

PLANNING YOUR TIME

It is possible to drive from Los Angeles to San Francisco along PCH in one long 12-hour day, but this is one stretch of the grand California tour that you won't want to power through. Spend at least one night on the road somewhere central, such as San Luis Obispo or Pismo Beach, or better yet, take two nights, with one in the southern half and one in the northern half. With three nights and four days, you can explore one or two areas, such as Santa Barbara and Big Sur, in more depth, or take an all-day excursion to a major attraction like the Channel Islands or Hearst Castle.

However you time your trip along PCH, make sure that you are not driving between Cambria and Carmel after dark. Not only are the curvy roads with narrow shoulders particularly harrowing, the magnificent views of the ocean and cliffs that are the highlight of the drive, and possibly of California, will be hidden by the black of night.

The California coast is a big draw, especially in the summer high season. Be sure to book accommodations in advance, particularly if you're planning to spend the night in the Big Sur region.

Ventura

Originally called San Buenaventura, Ventura has long been considered merely a stopping-off point on the way from Los Angeles to Santa Barbara and points north—just a section of the state to use as a rest stop before moving on— but the area has much more to offer. It is rich in natural, cultural, architectural, and historical treasures, with rugged transverse mountain ranges and fertile valleys ranging down to a magnificent coastline with offshore islands.

Despite being so close to Los Angeles, Ventura has retained its seaside charm and indifference to its southern neighbor. In recent years, the city of Ventura has begun to develop a new image and a unique and solid identity as a place with beachfront access, nearby mountains, a growing and impressive arts scene, and a thriving restaurant landscape. The county itself encompasses many different geographic areas, but downtown Ventura is rather compact and easy to walk around; it is three blocks from the beach and still feels somehow unfettered by "progress."

Geographically, water defines Ventura. The Ventura River forms the city's northern boundary, while the Santa Clara River is at its southern edge, and the Pacific Ocean is to the west. The eastern boundary is the Los Padres National Forest. Ventura is also the gateway to the Channel Islands, a series of five undeveloped islands that still retain their primal beauty, with spots to hike, fish, scuba, snorkel, and kayak.

SIGHTS
San Buenaventura Mission
The San Buenaventura Mission (211 E. Main St., 805/643-4318, grounds sunrise–sunset

EL CAMINO REAL: THE KINGS HIGHWAY

As you drive Highway 101 from Ventura up through Paso Robles and beyond, you'll begin to notice signs along the road of what looks like a shepherd's crook with a bell on it, and the words El Camino Real. The signs are peppered along a nearly 600-mile route in California. Here's why: At the same time that the American colonies were rebelling against England, a handful of Spaniards and Mexicans were establishing outposts up the California coast. In 1769, a fortress and the very first mission were established in San Diego. A footpath called the El Camino Real, or the Kings Highway, was created to connect each of the subsequent missions as they were constructed. The missions were situated in areas where large populations of indigenous people lived, and where the soil was fertile enough to sustain a settlement. Each mission was designed to be a day's travel from the next – at least in theory – all linked by El Camino Real. As time progressed and more missions were built, the footpath became a roadway wide enough to accommodate horses and wagons. It was not, however, until the last mission was completed in Sonoma in 1823 that this little pathway became a major road. Ultimately, El Camino Real linked all of California's 21 missions, pueblos, and four presidios, from San Diego to Sonoma. In 1904 the El Camino Real Association was formed to preserve and maintain California's historic road. The first commem-

Historic El Camino Real

© MICHAEL CERVIN

orative bell was placed in 1906 in front of the Old Plaza Church in downtown Los Angeles, and by 1915 approximately 158 bells had been installed along the Camino Real. The bells were made of cast iron, which encouraged theft, and the number of original bells plummeted to about 75. New bells of concrete were then installed in 1974. Highway 101 loosely follows this original footpath.

---

daily, museum 10 A.M.–5 P.M. Mon.–Fri., 9 A.M.–5 P.M. Sat., 10 A.M.–4 P.M. Sun., closed major holidays, self-guided tour adults $2, children $0.50) was established on Easter Sunday, March 31, 1782, and it became the ninth mission founded in the chain of 21 missions in the state. Like most missions, the first structure, which lasted for 10 years, burned to the ground. In part, the mission prospered due to a seven-mile aqueduct that was constructed from the Ventura River to the mission grounds. This allowed a wide variety of crops to grow,

including vegetables, grains, and even exotic fruits such as bananas, coconuts, and figs. The padres often sold these goods to travelers, which helped greatly to raise the funds needed to support mission life.

The mission, like most, was built as a quadrangle. The church was in the southwest corner, with a cemetery on the west side of the church (a grade school now stands where the cemetery was). In 1818, the pirate known as Bouchard was seen off the coast of California and began terrorizing Ventura. The mission

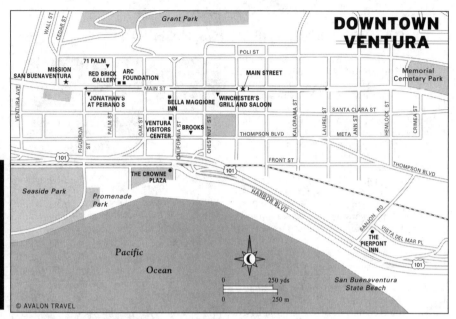

fathers and the Chumash Indians buried some of their valuables and sacred objects and took the rest into the mountains for about a month until the pirate and his band had gone. The church walls of tile, stone, and adobe are just over six feet thick and were built by Indian labor. It's still an active church and one of the most visited sights in Ventura.

To visit today you first pass through the gift shop, with its miniature mission collection and spiritually oriented cards and gifts. Then you'll head up a few steps to the very small museum, which has a few items such as vestments and everyday utensils from the mission period. This is also one of the few missions that still has wooden bells on display. The door then opens to the courtyard, a beautifully landscaped area with a fountain in the center surrounded by a few benches and short interlocking pathways. The church is across the courtyard. The church itself is long and narrow, a neoclassic-looking arch over the altar giving a more modern feel to the interior. Carpet covers much of the original tile floors, unfortunately, and there's a rather

off-putting sign at the center of the altar warning you that you are being videotaped. Behind the church is part of the original brick reservoir and current housing for the staff.

Main Street

The city of Ventura is, basically, Main Street. Of course there are other arteries that cut through town and other things to see and do, but the concentration of these few blocks is what Ventura has become—namely, a city undergoing a renaissance. New and trendy restaurants are opening up, the art scene is showing off talent, and nightlife offerings are improving with a mix of bars, clubs, and live music. Main Street is mainly a collection of one-story storefronts, occasionally punctuated by a few two-story facades, so it keeps a low profile, both literally and figuratively, and in no way feels overwhelming, large, or disproportionate. Unlike other small towns, the city has managed to keep its identity and has not given in to a plethora of corporate chain stores. There are eclectic buildings here forming an

© MICHAEL CERVIN

Downtown Ventura's charming storefronts make it a welcoming place.

amalgam of sorts—brick buildings from the turn of the 20th century, art deco facades, old boarded-up shops next to polished tile-and-glass buildings.

Starting at its westernmost end is the mission, then the old thrift shops, eateries, and art galleries; as you move east you find bars, espresso bars, wine-tasting bars, and a brewery. There is no formal plan to Main Street, no overarching idea of how best to experience it. It has a uniqueness that defies interpretation, and it's best to just wander down one side, exploring and discovering, then come back on the other side of the street. In the middle of it all you might choose to walk to the beach and soak in the low surf before returning to your amble down Main Street.

Ventura Harbor Village

There are many seaport villages along the California coast, but what makes Ventura Harbor Village (1583 Spinnaker Dr., 805/642-8538, www.venturaharborvillage. com) so unique is the abundance of shops and that it is home to working fishing fleets. As you browse the stores, walking right next to the boats, you'll notice the unusual olfactory confluence of just-harvested fish and waffle cones from the ice cream shop. Part working environment, part visitor area, it tries to straddle the two. Some unique spots not to be missed are the Ventura Dive & Sport dive shop and the kid-friendly arcade, which includes plenty of video games as well as a full-size 36-horse carousel. There's also skee ball, race-car driving games, indoor basketball, air hockey, and a large candy counter. The Village is also home to Brophy Brothers Restaurant & Clam Bar seafood restaurant and Harbor Wind & Kite Co. The Village faces the harbor, but if you cross the street, you can walk out onto the sand and face the Pacific Ocean. Parking is free.

BEACHES

People come to Ventura as much to walk along the beach as to walk downtown, and the beach is a core element of a visit here. Beach preferences are very personal: Some people like low and flat, some like rocky and wide. Whatever your taste, Ventura has something to offer. Keep in mind, however, that state-run beaches

© MICHAEL CERVIN

Ventura Harbor Village

and some county-run beaches charge day-use fees averaging about $10.

San Buenaventura State Beach

San Buenaventura State Beach (San Pedro St. and U.S. 101, 805/968-1033, www.parks. ca.gov, dawn–dusk daily) offers two miles of sea and sand for swimming, surfing, and picnicking. Cyclists can take advantage of trails connecting with other nearby beaches, and sports enthusiasts converge on the beach for occasional triathlons and volleyball tournaments. There are also special niche events such as the Pirate Festival. Facilities include a snack bar, an equipment rental shop, and an essential for the 21st-century beach bum, Wi-Fi—although to pick up the signal, you need to be within about 200 feet of the lifeguard tower. You'll find another snack bar, restaurant, and bait shop on the attached pier.

Emma Wood State Beach

Emma Wood State Beach (W. Main St. and Park Access Rd., recorded information 805/585-1850, www.parks.ca.gov, www.reserveamerica. com, dawn–dusk daily, day-use $10 per vehicle)

can be accessed off Main Street. There are no facilities, but a few minutes' walk leads to the campgrounds (one for RVs and one group camp; first-come, first served winter, reservations required spring–fall). At the far eastern side of the parking lot is a small path leading out to the beach that goes under the train tracks. To the right are views up the coast to the Rincon. The beach itself has many rocks—some nearly the size of footballs—strewn about. It is a great spot for windsurfing, as the winds come off Rincon Point just up from the mouth of the Ventura River to create ideal windy conditions. There's a 0.5-mile trail leading through the reeds and underbrush at the far end of the parking lot; although you can hear the surf and the highway, you can't see anything, and you'll feel like you're on safari until you reach the beach where the Ventura River ends.

Harbor Cove Beach

Families flock to Harbor Cove Beach (1900 Spinnaker Dr., dawn–dusk daily), located directly across from the Channel Islands Visitors Center at the end of Spinnaker Drive. The harbor's breakwaters provide children and less

© MICHAEL CERVIN

Emma Wood State Beach

confident swimmers with relative safety from the ocean currents. The wind can kick up at times, but when it's calm it's practically perfect. There's plenty of free parking, lifeguards during peak seasons, restrooms, and foot showers. Food and other amenities can be found across the street at Ventura Harbor Village.

Faria Beach

Farther north, the Ventura County–run Faria Beach (4350 W. U.S. 101, at State Beach exit, 805/654-3951, dawn–dusk daily) is available for tent camping and has 15 RV hookups. The campground has a playground and horseshoe pits, barbecues, and shower facilities but is quite small. It's also very crowded with campers, trucks, and people during nice weather because of its proximity to the water. You might find you have more companions than you care for, but it's a long flat beach, so you can spread out.

ENTERTAINMENT AND EVENTS
Bars and Clubs

As a general rule, the established bars and clubs in Ventura survive while some of the newer

establishments seem to struggle. Those clubs that have tried to emulate Los Angeles venues are not nearly as successful, it seems; Ventura just wants its old-fashioned watering holes.

Winchester's Grill and Saloon (632 E. Main St., 805/653-7446, www.winchesters-ventura.com, 4 P.M.–midnight Mon.–Thurs., 11:30 A.M.–1 A.M. Fri.–Sat., 11:30 A.M.–midnight Sun., food served 4–10 P.M. Mon.–Thurs., 11:30 A.M.–11 P.M. Fri.–Sat.) is just such a watering hole. Maybe it's the 40-foot-long mahogany bar, or the rustic wood-toned feel of the place, or that there are 41 beers on tap, one of the biggest selections between L.A. and San Francisco, but it's just really fun here. It can get loud and rowdy; people seem to step inside and somehow think they instantly become cowboys. Winchester's is open later than many establishments, and the covered patio is more popular than being inside. Wherever you sit, the specialty is game dishes.

Live Music Venues

The Majestic Ventura Theater (26 S. Chestnut St., 805/653-0721, www.venturatheater.net) is a popular live venue that opened in 1928 as a movie house; decades later it was converted into a concert venue. The seats on the main floor have been removed to form a pit, and only the balcony seats remain in place. There is a bar in the rear of the main floor, and some food is served, mainly forgettable sandwiches. The old chandeliers still hang in the auditorium, and other remnants of the 1920s decor remain, creating a unique vibe unlike most new venues. The bands lean toward alternative, although some mainstream groups have played here. It is conveniently located close to the bars and restaurants.

It's All Good Bar and Grill (533 Main St., 805/641-9951 or 805/641-9951, 2 P.M.–2 A.M. Mon.–Fri., 11 A.M.–2 A.M. Sat., 11 A.M.–11 P.M. Sun.), more commonly referred to as Good Bar, is unlike most venues in that all types of people tend to show up here. There's live music most nights, and you can hear it from a few blocks away. There's also dancing, cheap shots of cheap liquor, and inexpensive beer, with a vibe like a controlled frat party. You'll hear all manner of music, but it's not conducive to conversation—you're here to party.

Performing Arts

Rubicon Theatre Company (1006 E. Main St., 805/667-2900, www.rubicontheatre.org) opened in 1998 as a professional theater with stars like Jack Lemmon and John Ritter. The Rubicon has presented original works and shows that have gone on to other venues and won numerous awards. The 200-seat venue is a great place to see top talent and quality productions at a fraction of the prices in larger cities.

Ventura Improv Company (34 N. Palm St., 805/643-5701, www.venturaimprov.com, adults $10, seniors and under age 12 $8) is the place to tickle your funny bone. With performances on Friday–Saturday nights and classes offered throughout the week, there's always something to laugh about. They focus on team comedy improvisation and not solo acts. You can get involved as an audience member and match wits with the county's longest-running comedy group.

Festivals and Events

Westside ArtWalk (http://westsideartwalk. org), held in the summer, is a free self-guided walking tour of several galleries, studios, and eclectic gallery-for-a-day venues all within Ventura's Downtown Cultural District. The all-volunteer event is held just steps from the beach and the Ventura Pier. Participating art venues include restaurants, salons, antiques shops, unique boutiques, and coffee shops—most any place with walls. You might also encounter outdoor multicultural performances. ArtWalk is one of the best ways to check out Ventura's diverse art community.

The annual August ritual of the **Ventura County Fair** (Ventura County Fairgrounds, 10 W. Harbor Blvd., 805/648-3376, www.venturacountyfair.org) has been going strong for well over 100 years. It draws some big-name musicians and comedians, and you can bungee jump, ride the Ferris wheel, eat cotton candy, and sample award-winning beers. It maintains that small-town fair atmosphere, with agriculture still a dominant component, and it's all right near the ocean.

SHOPPING
Outlet Malls

Farther south in Camarillo are the **Camarillo Premium Outlets** (740 E. Ventura Blvd., off Los Posas Ave., 805/445-8520, www.premiumoutlets. com, 10 A.M.–9 P.M. Mon.–Sat., 10 A.M.–8 P.M. Sun., holiday hours vary), with more outlet stores than should be allowed by law. You can find almost anything in this massive complex, including Nike Factory Store, Banana Republic Factory Store, Skechers, J.Crew, Tommy Hilfiger, and Jockey—160 stores in all. Many people spend the entire day here, and large groups are actually bused in. If you're not a shopper, the slow, methodical pace of people meandering from store to store might drive you crazy. If you love to shop, you're guaranteed to find several stores you can't live without.

For nontraditional shopping, **Main Street** in downtown Ventura is home to a surprising number of unique local and specialty stores and has managed to retain a sense of individuality.

Thrift Stores

Although Ventura has long been known for a plethora of inexpensive thrift stores drawing savvy shoppers from surrounding counties, the thrift store scene is changing. Only a handful of stores remain, down significantly from the dozen or so that used to exist here. Many were converted into restaurants or bars. Still, there are bargains to be had. It is worth remembering that these thrift stores were originally designed as a way to bring in revenue for charitable organizations; even now most still only take cash.

Child Abuse and Neglect (CAAN) Thrift Store (340 E. Main St., 805/643-5956, 9:30 A.M.–6 P.M. Mon.–Sat., noon–5 P.M. Sun.) has a wide selection of donated goods, all in good working condition, including some antiques and furniture. The prices lean a little high, and you need to shop carefully, but there are still bargains around the store if you have the time to look.

Treasure Chest Thrift Shop (328 E. Main St., 805/653-0555, 10 A.M.–7:30 P.M. daily) thrives on donations as well and has a larger selection of used furniture and modern beach-cruiser bikes. Some pieces are clearly overpriced since they are newer, but you will find some better deals if you scan the perimeters and especially the back of the store.

The Coalition to End Family Violence/Battered Women's Thrift Store (270 E. Main St., 805/643-4411, 9 A.M.–6 P.M. Mon.–Sat.) has an excess of men's, women's, and children's clothing consuming most of the front section of the store. Their collectibles section is neither collectible nor well-priced, but their general housewares section is terrific. There's also a decent selection of books, toys, and small appliances located in the back.

The **Arc Foundation of Ventura County Thrift Store** (265 E. Main St., 805/650-8611, 9 A.M.–6 P.M. Mon.–Sat., 10 A.M.–5 P.M. Sun.) has more clothes than anything else. The perimeter has a few typical thrift items—cheap

glassware, old stereos, and whatnot, including books and CDs to the right side as you enter. Their clothing selection is varied and quite good, especially for women. The organization's goal is to improve the quality of life for individuals with developmental disabilities, as they have been doing since 1954, so your money is well spent here.

Art Galleries

Ventura is starting to brand itself as a new arts capital, and there are a number of new galleries that have opened. There has always been a strong arts scene here, but it has been overshadowed by Los Angeles, although that is beginning to change.

Red Brick Gallery (315 E. Main St., 805/643-6400, www.redbrickart.com, 11 A.M.–6 P.M. Mon.–Thurs., 10 A.M.–7 P.M. Fri.–Sat., 11 A.M.–5 P.M. Sun.) offers shows that rotate every six weeks. The gallery, logically, is lined with exposed redbrick walls, and it has represented about 150 artists, all from the West Coast, working in paint, wood, glass, and photography, and even jewelry designers and greeting card–makers. There is great diversity, and a variety of art classes are available, from watercolor to mosaics.

Clothing

B. on Main (337 E. Main St., 805/643-9309, www.b-onmain.com, 10:30 A.M.–6 P.M. Mon.–Thurs., 10 A.M.–7 P.M. Fri., 10 A.M.–8 P.M. Sat., 11 A.M.–5 P.M. Sun.) is all about beach clothing with a 1950s retro twist. It is a fun store to browse but can be a little pricey. The fashions and accessories are mainly for women. There is also a full line of retro beach posters as well as an eclectic collection of gift cards and small gift items like soaps and dishware.

At times we all seek a little something special. **Aphrodite's Lingerie & Gift Gallery** (477 E. Main St., 805/652-0082, www.lingerieventura.com, 10:30 A.M.–5:30 P.M. Mon.–Tues., 10:30 A.M.–7 P.M. Wed.–Thurs., 10:30 A.M.–9 or 10 P.M. Fri.–Sat., 11 A.M.–6 P.M. Sun.) has been around for 14 years and offers a great selection of lingerie, teddies, corsets, stocking, games, toys, body products, and even a few fun costumes, all sold by knowledgeable staff who can direct you. Women will feel comfortable, and men won't feel intimidated.

Specialty Stores

Harbor Wind & Kite Co. (1575 Spinnaker Dr., Suite 107B, 805/654-0900, www.harborwindkite.com, 10 A.M.–6 P.M. Sun.–Thurs., 10 A.M.–7 P.M. Fri.–Sat.) has kites literally hanging everywhere. A veteran of Ventura Harbor Village for over 20 years, it has every conceivable type of kite and kite accessories, including items for kite boarding and kite buggies. Harbor Wind also carries wind-oriented toys such as Frisbees and boomerangs. Since the Ventura coast gets its share of wind, a kite can be a lot of fun.

Farmers Markets

There are two farmers markets downtown: the **Downtown Market** (Santa Clara St. and Palm St., 805/529-6266, www.vccfarmersmarkets. com, 8:30 A.M.–noon Sat.) and the **Midtown Ventura Market** (front west parking lot at Pacific View Mall, E. Main St. and Pacific View Dr., 805/529-6266, www.vccfarmersmarkets.com, 9 A.M.–1 P.M. Wed.). These are straightforward produce markets, so you won't find arts and crafts, roving musicians, and the like; people come to shop for food.

SPORTS AND RECREATION
Hiking

With the mountains of Los Padres National Forest as a backdrop, the area has plenty of hiking within a short drive of downtown. The website www.venturacountytrails.org is a good reference for local hikes, and it includes GPS coordinates and photos.

Arroyo Verde Park Trail (Poli St. and Day St., 805/654-7800, www.cityofventura.net, dawn–dusk daily, parking $2 per hour Sat.–Sun. and holidays, maximum $5) is a moderate hike just under four miles out and back. It runs parallel with a popular picnic area, and then quickly turns backcountry, with rugged

terrain and a 300-foot elevation gain that leads to nice views of the Pacific Ocean and Channel Islands. Arroyo Verde Park is a manicured city park with more than four dozen types of trees. A lush green lawn gives way to picnic areas, playgrounds, and a couple of baseball fields. Weekends draw families with young kids. If you look beyond the edges, you'll see hints that there is more to this park than just pretty landscaping. High in the hills surrounding the park, hikers and runners making their way through dense chaparral and semirugged terrain to viewpoints that overlook the park and the Pacific Ocean. From downtown, drive east on Main Street, and turn left on Poli Street near Ventura High School. Poli Street turns into Foothill Road, which goes to the park, located on the left at the corner of Day Road.

Although the majority of the trails at **Grant Park** (Poli St. at Brakey Rd., www.serracrosspark.org, www.cityofventura.net/pw/parks, dawn–dusk daily) are paved, the hiking is a workout, uphill the entire way. Once you reach the summit, you'll have killer views of the ocean and Ventura. A simple up-and-back hike is less than three miles, but you can extend it off-road on the smaller trails. Brakey Road is off Poli Street, near City Hall. Park on Poli Street and walk up, staying on Brakey, which twists and turns. Once at the summit, head left toward the Padre Serra cross (you'll see the sign), which has excellent views of the ocean. From Brakey Road, heading farther into the interior of this 107-acre park, there are smaller side trails, unsigned and nameless, but each is marked by a simple metal gate, that wander the undeveloped hilltop area. There are picnic tables and restrooms at Grant Park as well.

Biking

The Ventura River Trail (Main St. and Peking St., www.ventura-usa.com) follows the Ventura River inland from Main Street just over six miles one-way, ending at Foster Park. From here it joins the **Ojai Trail,** a two-lane bike path that follows Highway 33 into Ojai (16 miles one-way). This trail follows a defunct 100-year-old Southern Pacific Railroad line. At times both of the paths hug the highways, but they also run through beautiful scenery. The elevation gain is close to 1,000 feet, but it's a gentle climb through prime agricultural land.

You can rent a bike at **Ventura Bike Depot** (239 W. Main St., 805/652-1114, www.venturabikedepot.com, 9 A.M.–6 P.M. Mon.–Fri., 8:30 A.M.–6 P.M. Sat., 9 A.M.–5 P.M. Sun.), which rents just about anything mobile, including but not limited to bikes, tandems, in-line skates, and scooters. It's located right where the bike path toward Ojai starts, and there is lots of free parking, so it's very convenient. **Wheel Fun Rentals** is located at the pier (850 Harbor Blvd., 805/765-5795) for in-town cruising or meandering along the promenade by the water.

Matt's Cycling Center (2427 E. Harbor Blvd., 805/477-0933, 11 A.M.–6 P.M. Wed.–Fri., 10 A.M.–5 P.M. Sat., noon–5 P.M. Sun.) rents and sells cruisers, mountain bikes, trailers, tandems, hybrids, and children's bikes—almost anything with wheels.

Whale-Watching and Harbor Cruises

December–March is the ideal time to see Pacific gray whales pass through the channel off the coast of Ventura. Late June–late August has the narrow window for both blue and humpback whales as they feed offshore near the islands. If you visit the Channel Islands during these months, you may see whales on your way out or back. But for straight whale-watching trips, these companies will get you as close as possible. Most whale-watching trips are about three hours. Remember that whale-watching is weather-dependent, so cancellations can occur.

Island Packers Cruises (1691 Spinnaker Dr., Suite 105B, 805/642-1393, www.islandpackers.com, $25–75) has operated whale-watching cruises for years and is the most experienced. It also runs harbor cruises with a variety of options, including dinner cruises and group charters. Their website has the pertinent details for customizing to get exactly what you want.

Ventura Boat Rentals (1575 Spinnaker Dr., 805/642-7753, www.venturaboatrentals.com) offers sunset cruises and dinner cruises starting at the harbor. You can also rent a boat, sailboat, surf bike, or paddle boat. Their hours vary, so it's best to contact them for specific times and rates.

Diving

Ventura Dive & Sport (1559 Spinnaker Dr. Suite 108, 805/650-6500, 10 A.M.–6 P.M. Mon.–Fri., 8 A.M.–6 P.M. Sat., 8 A.M.–5 P.M. Sun., charters $110–125, open-water dive course and certification $550) offers a dive course in their heated pool and in open water, dive trips to the Channel Islands, scuba diving lessons, equipment sales and rentals, and a full line of sports apparel and sunglasses, all best suited to Ventura's outdoor activities.

Surfing

The Rincon (Bates Rd. and U.S. 101) is Ventura's most famous surfing landmark. The name Rincon describes the actual road that is part of U.S. 101, the entire cove, and the surfing area, which is a thin strip of land with a large point that has a long right break. In the early 1920s a road was built to connect Ventura to Santa Barbara, as there was barely any room here because the cliffs plunge directly into the Pacific Ocean. At first the Rincon road was built of rustic logs, and then wood planks between the cliffs and the ocean, but they kept getting washed away by the pounding surf. Finally U.S. 101 was built, the area was extended, and traffic now moves freely, although as you drive by it's clear how little room there is between the cliffs and the ocean. Much of the Rincon portion of the highway still abuts the water, and during storms it's common for the ocean to splash over onto the highway, soaking cyclists and drivers alike.

For surfers it's a great spot, and due to its fame it's almost always crowded. Winter is when the Rincon is at its best, as north and west swells sweep in and wrap around the shallow cobble point, then peel off with an almost predictable evenness around the bend. When conditions are ideal, you can ride the waves in Santa Barbara all the way into Ventura, since the Rincon straddles both counties. To access the Rincon, exit U.S. 101 at Bates Road from the north or south and turn toward the beach. There are city and county parking lots, although they are usually filled early in the morning. There's a small gate that leads down a path behind several residences that drops you at the rocky beach. If you head to the right toward the point, you can jump in the water.

C-Street is the nickname for California Street, which is near what some people call Surfers Point at Seaside Park. For surfers, it's simply C-Street. Early mornings are favored for surfers in this spot close to the pier. There are three distinct zones along this mile-long stretch of beach. At the point is the Pipe, with some pretty fast short breaks. Moving down the beach is the Stables, which continues with the right breaks, with an even low shoulder, and then C-Street, breaking both right and left. Yes, it gets crowded here, and there are a lot of spectators walking along the concrete boardwalk, but you also have a lot of amenities and some free parking at your disposal.

SURF CLASSES

All things considered, surfing is not as difficult as it might seem, so why not get your feet wet? These places can teach you the basics so your time in the water can be a blast.

Surfclass (805/200-8674, www.surfclass. com, two-hour session $90) meets at various beaches around Ventura, depending on weather and swells. They teach everyone from novice landlubbers to rusty shredders. The two-hour class rates are quite reasonable, and they limit class size for individual attention. They will also teach you surf etiquette and lingo.

Ventura Surf School (461 W. Channel Islands Blvd., 805/218-1484, www.ventura-surfschool.com, private two-hour lesson $125, 2 or more $80 pp, 4 or more $75 pp) can also teach you to surf, and they offer a weeklong surf camp and kids-only classes. Beginner lessons are done at Mondos Beach.

SURF RENTALS

If you just need gear, swing by **Seaward Surf and Sport** (1082 S. Seaward Ave., 805/648-4742, www.seawardsurf.com, 10 A.M.–7 P.M. daily winter, 9 A.M.–9 P.M. daily summer, surfboard rental $15–50), which is the place to go to buy or rent most anything for the water: bikinis, body boards, sunglasses, wetsuits, and everything else. It is a half a block from the beach, so you can rent and then head straight to the water.

At **Beach Break Surf Shop** (1557 Spinnaker Dr., Suite 108, 805/650-6641, www.beachbreaksurfshop.com, 10 A.M.–6 P.M. daily, all-day wetsuit rental $20), you're already at the harbor, so you can simply cross the street and hit the beach. You can rent all manner of surf gear, including long boards and boogie boards. The shop has a Hawaiian theme and also carries a lot of Hawaiian shirts.

Spas

Ventura is already a relaxing place to be. If you need further relaxation, check out these spas, which provide a variety of different options.

At **Michael Kelley Salon and Day Spa** (1895 E. Main St., 805/648-7743, www.michaelkelleysalon.com, 8 A.M.–8 P.M. Tues.–Sat., spa packages from $185) you can get a full spectrum of salon services, including Michael Kelley's signature treatment: a 2.5-hour salt-glow exfoliation that includes a steam, a cleanse, a scrub, and a final rinse with the Vichy shower (various water pressures flood over you while you lie in a tiled room). Or get your nails done, perhaps have a massage, or mix and match at this colorful and exuberantly decorated day spa.

Lavender Blue Salon & Fine Gifts (by appointment only, 805/339-0253, www.lavenderblueventura.com, individual treatments $15–55) is a studio that focuses on manicures, pedicures, facial waxing, and hair treatments. The decor is slightly French in essence but warm and intimate, like the service. This is not a large shop with people running everywhere; it provides individual service and attention.

© MICHAEL CERVIN

The Rincon is the best-known surf spot in all of the Central Coast.

ACCOMMODATIONS

There are accommodations downtown, but a drawback to most of them is the unfortunate placement of the freeway and the train tracks. It can't be helped, but it can't be ignored, and many hotels will offer earplugs when you check in—or bring some with you. With your room's window or sliding door shut, you usually only hear vague rumblings, but it's no fun during the summer when you would like the fresh air.

Under $150

Downtown's **Bella Maggiore Inn** (67 S. California St., 805/652-0277, $75–180 d) has a definite European feel. Just three blocks from the beach, the 28 guest rooms in this charmingly peculiar spot are all configured differently and have a quirky quality, some with built-in drawers and cabinets, others with jetted tubs. The furnishings are also varied. Some baths have Formica countertops, and some guest rooms have old chassis TVs—it's

definitely a throwback. The hallways are narrow and quiet, and there is an upstairs sundeck. The attached restaurant is actually a fully covered brick courtyard with old vines climbing the walls. The inn almost feels more like a large bed-and-breakfast than a hotel. The guest rooms are slowly being upgraded, but this isn't the place for state-of-the-art interiors. For some, that's just fine.

If a chain hotel is more your style, the **Best Western Inn of Ventura** (708 E. Thompson Blvd., 805/648-3101, www.bestwesterncalifornia.com, $100–150 d) is a safe and reliable choice. Less than 0.5 miles to the beach and downtown, it's well situated to explore the area. A heated pool and a hot tub, continental breakfast, and microwaves in the guest rooms round out the offerings of the smoke-free property.

The **Vagabond Inn Ventura** (756 E. Thompson Blvd., 805/648-5371, www.vagabondinn-ventura-hotel.com, $70–100 d) is another chain hotel that will go easy on your wallet if you want basic accommodations. Pet-friendly ($10 per pet) and centrally located, this spot is one of the least expensive in town. Don't expect too much, except to save money on accommodations so you can spend it elsewhere.

The **Inn on the Beach** (1175 S. Seaward Ave., 805/652-2000, www.innonthebeachventura.com, $130–180 d) is aptly named, as the hotel is actually pushed up against the sand. The best views are from the second floor, as the first-floor views tend to be obstructed by small mounds of sand. Each of the 24 guest rooms is fancifully decorated with very different antiques. There are parts that could use a face-lift, and it's not the brand-new digs some people may care for, but there's free Wi-Fi and a lot of repeat customers. It's out of the way, somewhat by itself, but within a block's walk of a few restaurants and coffee shops, and downtown is a two-mile drive.

The **Pierpont Inn & Spa** (550 Sanjon Rd., 805/643-6144, www.pierpontinn.com, $101–250) was originally built in 1910, and it still retains its wood-shingled exterior and rich craftsman-style lobby, which looks through to the restaurant and straight out to the ocean. The hotel tends to be frequented by an older crowd, which means that it is quieter. The 77 guest rooms also give a nod to the craftsman style, and all have Tempur-Pedic mattresses. The baths are a bit small, so if you're looking for a long soak, this isn't the place. Unfortunately, the freeway is extremely close, making it a little tough to sit outside by the water feature and have a cocktail, but the guest rooms are relatively quiet. There's a day spa, a restaurant, meeting space, and tennis courts on-site, and though it's a few blocks away, you can walk to the beach by heading under the freeway to reach the sand.

$150-250

The Holiday Inn Express (1080 Navigator Dr., 805/856-9533, www.hiexpress.com, $150–170 d), overlooking the harbor, is a 69-room standard hotel that is more popular with business travelers than with other visitors. It is standard fare and nothing exciting, but it will serve you well for the views and proximity to

other things to do. The guest rooms are larger than most of this type, but not all views reach the harbor, so be advised of that if you have your heart set on seeing the water from your room.

The **Ventura Beach Marriott Hotel** (2055 E. Harbor Blvd., 805/643-6000, www.marriott.com, $150–280 d) has 270 guest rooms and 15 suites, which means that you'll probably always have company at this large hotel near the sand south of downtown. Big is sometimes good, in that Marriott is a trusted name and the prices are reasonable, but keep in mind the $10 daily self-parking rate or $15 for valet parking that is added to your bill. Although there is a large heated pool and a spa with palm trees around them, this is standard hotel fare. Chances are you can more readily find a special deal offered here than at other places.

 The Crowne Plaza (450 E. Harbor Blvd., 805/648-2100, www.crowneplaza.com, $180–250 d) is beautifully positioned right at the beach. There are great views of the pool and the beach from the upper floors, and you're right at the five-mile boardwalk and just steps from the pier. The walk to downtown, over the freeway and train tracks, is a mere three blocks. Being one of the largest hotels, with 258 guest rooms, it can provide better pricing, and it is actually a wonderful place to stay. The guest rooms are very comfortable with a modern feel to them, echoing the overall modern retro feel of the lobby and bar area. There's an in-house restaurant, but you're close enough to downtown that you can find something better within a five-minute walk. There is an outdoor patio that abuts the boardwalk; it's gated and inaccessible to passersby.

FOOD

The culinary scene has taken off in the last few years, and Ventura is seeing its share of excellent restaurants claim center stage. You won't see the sophisticated leanings of Los Angeles, but there are more chefs turning to Ventura to avoid the hype and pressure of Hollywood. There is an abundance of fresh local produce, vegetables, fish, and shellfish.

American

Created by perpetual nice guy Andy Brooks, it's casual at **(Brooks** (545 E. Thompson Blvd., 805/652-7070, www.restaurantbrooks.com, 5 P.M.–close Wed.–Sun., $25), a little gem of a restaurant in an unremarkable location. The exterior looks like a chain store, but the interior is warehouse chic with 1950s accents. Brooks is known for really cool cocktails, like the tequila-sage blood-orange margarita rimmed with chili salt, or the concoction of Blue Coat gin, St. Germain liqueur (made from wild elderflowers), orange, lemon, and lime juice and rimmed with toasted coriander sugar. The food coming out of the kitchen is excellent too: The wild-game chili is earthy, rich, and immensely satisfying, as are the spicy rubbed shrimp. Regardless of what you order, you won't go wrong.

At **Café Zack** (1095 E. Thompson Blvd., 805/643-9445, www.cafezack.com, 11:30 A.M.–2 P.M. and 5:30–9 P.M. Mon.–Fri., 5:30–9 P.M. Sat., $25) you'll find a varied menu that includes boar, pastas, salads, and rotating fish specials. The converted corner house just off Main Street is removed enough that you feel you're in a special place. Well, a special place that borders a lumberyard. But the food and service are routinely wonderful, and the house-made desserts are worth saving some space for. A much-favored local spot, it gets a little cramped on busy nights.

(The Blue Orkid (76 S. Oak St., 805/653-0003, bakery 7 A.M.–3 P.M. Mon.–Fri., 7 A.M.–5 P.M. Sat.–Sun., restaurant 8 A.M.–midnight daily, $10–30) feels like an art deco restaurant wrestling with its identity. There certainly is a throwback feel, with sleek burgundy chairs, couches, a raised performing area with a piano on top, and a very tall silver art deco statue that catches the eye. All that might be irrelevant, though, because the food is quite good. Serving breakfast, lunch, and dinner and offering a full bar and live music, it manages to succeed by being comfortable and slightly sophisticated. The breakfast burrito is a spicy way to begin your day, and all their pastries are baked on-site. The port poached pear and blue cheese salad is a great collection of flavors and textures, as is the miso Meyer lemon salmon. It's one of the few places open early on Sunday mornings—helpful if you're an early riser.

French

71 Palm Restaurant (71 N. Palm St., 805/653-7222, www.71palm.com, lunch 11:30 A.M.–2 P.M. Mon.–Fri., 11 A.M.–2:30 P.M. Sat., dinner 5 P.M.–close Mon.–Sat., $22) is a 100-year-old historic house with a large exterior deck just up from Main Street. The small tables are spaced far enough apart that you feel you have some room to converse. Though billed as French, it's a loose interpretation of French food; the kitchen excels at dishes like chicken ravioli with sage cream sauce and aged New York steak with morel sauce. Cooking classes and private classes are offered by appointment. This is a great spot for quiet conversation and a slow meal. Afterward you can walk the half block to Main Street.

Italian

Cafe Fiore Restaurant and Martini Lounge (66 California St., 805/653-1266, www.fiorerestaurant.net, lunch 11:30 A.M.–3 P.M. daily, dinner 5–10 P.M. Mon.–Thurs., 5–11 P.M. Fri.–Sat., 5–9 P.M. Sun., bar stays open between lunch and dinner, $20) has almost become more about the martini bar scene than anything else. The seductive bar is usually packed, the restaurant area less so. The butternut squash pasta with sage cream sauce and the chicken-stuffed ravioli are favorites.

Mediterranean and Seafood

The brick building that houses **Jonathan's at Peirano's** (204 E. Main St., 805/648-4853, www.jonathansatpeiranos.com, 5 P.M.–close Tues.–Thurs., noon–close Fri.–Sat., noon–9 P.M. Sun., $20) dates from 1877 and is the oldest brick building in Ventura. It was an Italian grocery for well over 100 years and now has new life as one of the top restaurants on Main Street. You're just as likely to find paella as steaks, stuffed dates, and pasta, all with a Middle Eastern flair. Start with the Portuguese crab bisque and move into the eclectic menu. The well-trained staff is always at the ready. You're well positioned to walk along Main Street after dinner.

Near the harbor, **Andria's Seafood Restaurant & Market** (1449 Spinnaker Dr., 805/654-0546, www.andriasseafood.com, 11 A.M.–8 P.M. Sun.–Thurs., 11 A.M.–9 P.M. Fri.–Sat., $12) is known for its clam chowder, fish-and-chips, and an angel shark burger simply called the fish burger. It is also known for its fish market, where you can purchase the same type of fish served in the restaurant. The line for the restaurant is often out the door, but it does move reasonably quickly. Order at the counter first and then find a seat. If you sit outside, watch out for aggressive seagulls.

Mexican

◖ Yolanda's Mexican Cafe (2753 E. Main St., 805/643-2700, www.yolandasmexican-cafe.com, 11 A.M.–9:30 P.M. Mon.–Thurs., 11 A.M.–10 P.M. Fri.–Sat., 10 A.M.–9 P.M. Sun., $10) serves some of the best Mexican food in Ventura in noisy, colorful surroundings. It has efficiently turned out consistently good food for the price since the early 1980s and now has four locations. You will find the expected burritos, tacos, tostadas, and the like along with house specialties such as Shrimp Villa, sautéed shrimp with jalapeños, green onions, and mushrooms blanketed with melted cheese, and the Ventura Veggie Plate of fresh locally grown veggies sautéed in fajita sauce and served on a bed of rice, avocado, tomato, and green onions.

Pub Grub

The **Anacapa Brewing Company** (472 E. Main St., 805/643-2337, www.anacapa-brewing.com, 11:30 A.M.–9 P.M. Sun.–Wed., 11:30 A.M.–midnight Thurs.–Sat., $15) is the only brewpub in Ventura, opened in 2000 in a 115-year-old brick building. Your basic IPA and wheat ales are made here, along with seasonal brews and specialties like the chocolate porter and oatmeal stout. The elongated narrow space and the fully exposed brick walls and fermenters give it that classic pub feel. Anacapa serves up decent food, and the outdoor patio, though small, is always packed—it's prime people-watching territory. Try the black-and-blue chicken sandwich or the asiago cheese dip with your brew.

INFORMATION AND SERVICES

The **Ventura Visitors & Convention Bureau** (101 S. California St., 805/648-2075, www.ventura-usa.com, 8:30 A.M.–5 P.M. Mon.–Fri., 9 A.M.–5 P.M. Sat., 10 A.M.–4 P.M. Sun.) is packed with everything you could want to know about Ventura. There is a surprisingly large amount of information in the large digs, and the staff is eager to help.

Community Memorial Hospital (147 N. Brent St., 805/652-5011) has the only emergency room in the area. The **City of Ventura Police Department** (805/339-4400, www.cityofventura.net/pd) is located at 1425 Dowell Drive. In case of emergency, call **911.**

The only local daily newspaper is the *Ventura County Star,* which can be found all over town. The alternative free weekly, published every Thursday, is the *Ventura County Reporter,* also available everywhere. Both have good entertainment listings, including shows, concerts, theater, and film.

With recent budget cuts, it's best to phone the main branch of the **post office** (675 E. Santa Clara St., 800/275-8777, www.usps.com) for its current hours.

No one likes to do laundry, but if the need arises, you can head over to **Mission Plaza Laundry** (110 N. Olive St., 805/653-9077, www.missionplazalaundry.com). They offer pickup and delivery.

GETTING THERE

Driving from the north or south, Ventura sits squarely along U.S. 101. You can also access Ventura by car from I-5 (the exit is near Six Flags Magic Mountain), taking Highway 126 through Fillmore and Santa Paula. This area, beautiful in its own right, is the agricultural heart of Ventura County, and you'll pass citrus and avocado groves, fruit stands, and probably most of the traffic. But don't exceed the speed limit, which is easy to do on this road.

By air, you'll likely fly into Los Angeles or Burbank, the closest major airports, but the small and efficient **Oxnard Airport** (OXR, 2889 W. 5th St., 805/382-3024, www.iflyoxnard.com) might also be an option if you can get a connection. There are limited flights, but the airport is pretty much hassle-free, and rental cars are available. The drive from Oxnard to Ventura is just 15 minutes.

Assuming you fly into LAX in Los Angeles, the drive is a mere 65 miles, but it can take more than 1.5 hours, depending on traffic. There are commercial shuttle vans from LAX, but keep in mind that these will take longer than if you drove yourself, and they are also subject to traffic delays. The **Ventura County Airporter** (805/650-6600, www.venturashuttle.com) runs a shuttle service to and from LAX every day of the year. Rates start at $35, which is very reasonable. **Roadrunner Shuttle** (800/247-7919, www.rrshuttle.com) also does the LAX airport route with private vans, town cars, and even limos.

Arriving for a day or two in Ventura by train is a great idea as much of the downtown is so compact. **Amtrak**'s (800/872-7245, www.amtrak.com) *Pacific Surfliner,* which runs between San Diego and San Luis Obispo, arrives at a modest Spanish-style building by the county fairgrounds near downtown. Getting to Main Street is a five-minute walk.

Greyhound (291 E. Thompson Blvd., 800/231-2222, www.greyhound.com) takes you to its small station near downtown Ventura from points north or south.

GETTING AROUND

Ventura is designed on a small grid, and downtown is three blocks from the beach, so if you are concentrating on this area, you really don't need a car: Simply park at your hotel and walk. There are many sights outside of

city, however, and driving is simple, as there are three main arteries from which everything is accessible. U.S. 101 runs north–south and is the main transportation route. To access Ojai and the mountains, Highway 33 will take you out of the city into the rural areas, and Highway 126 east toward Santa Paula is a beautiful, easy drive through rich agricultural land and eventually connects with I-5 near Six Flags Magic Mountain.

Downtown parking on Main Street and the surrounding arteries utilizes solar-powered pay stations and costs $2 per hour. The machines accept coin or credit and debit cards.

Gold Coast Transit (GCT, 201 E. 4th St., Oxnard, 805/643-3158, www.goldcoasttransit.org, seniors $0.75, adults $1.50) has bus service in western Ventura County, specifically Route 6, although their main station is in Oxnard. Fares are in the process of being increased, so check the website for specific pricing. The Ojai–Ventura Main Street line, Route 16, runs daily except holidays. GCT connects to the Metrolink and Amtrak rail services as well as Greyhound buses at the Oxnard Transportation Center (201 E. 4th St., Oxnard).

Taxis in Ventura are not exactly ubiquitous; it's best to phone for a taxi. Two of the best companies are **Yellow Cab of Ventura** (805/659-6900) and **Cab4You** (805/850-9200).

Walking Tours

Self-guided walking tours of all types are available free at the **Ventura Visitors Center** (101 S. California St., 805/648-2075, www.ventura-usa.com, 8:30 A.M.–5 P.M. Mon.–Fri., 9 A.M.–5 P.M. Sat., 10 A.M.–4 P.M. Sun.). You can pick up a map for the **Ventura Historic Walking Tour,** highlighting Mission San Buenaventura and historic adobes from the Mexican Rancho era. For the aspiring gumshoe, there's **Perry Mason's Ventura Tour,** which leads visitors to sites throughout the city that inspired Perry Mason creator and novelist Erle Stanley Gardner to pen his classic series. For food lovers, the **Ventura à la Carte Tour** highlights Ventura's farmers markets, nearby farms, fine dining, road food, cooking classes, breweries, and more. Pick up a map and get walking.

If a walking tour is too tame for you, consider a **Ghost Tour** (805/658-4726, www. ghost-stalker.com), hosted by Richard Senate,

who has been studying paranormal activities since 1978. In addition to conducting lectures on the supernatural and leading local ghost tours in Ventura County, he has authored several books and appeared on radio and television programs.

Channel Islands National Park

At the end of Spinnaker Drive in Ventura is the artistically unimpressive two-story headquarters for Channel Islands National Park, called the **Robert J. Lagomarsino Visitors Center** (1901 Spinnaker Dr., 805/658-5730, www.nps. gov/chis, 8:30 A.M.–5 P.M. daily, free), which oversees the islands. There are a few displays about native animals and birds that inhabit the islands, plenty of literature, and a few small touch tanks and a very cool 3-D display of all the islands and their topography. Perhaps best of all, you can climb to the second-story observation deck and look out to sea as well as along the extensive Ventura Harbor. But it's ultimately all about the islands here.

Channel Islands National Park comprises five of the eight islands off the Central Coast of California: Anacapa, Santa Cruz, Santa Rosa, San Miguel, and Santa Barbara. The islands are within sight of the mainland and have been federally protected for just over 30 years. Long before they were a national park they were ranch lands, and archaeological evidence suggests that the islands were inhabited as long as 12,000 years ago. Santa Cruz Island, in particular, was prime grazing land in the 1800s for cattle and sheep without the predators found on the mainland. Santa Cruz was also home to a winery, the remnants of which are still visible.

Although the islands are relatively close to the mainland, most Ventura and Santa Barbara locals have never visited this part of their backyard. To sail to the islands can take 3–4 hours, and motorboats make the trip even faster, yet exploring the islands isn't common. Perhaps it is because they look so far away (although

Anacapa is only 12 miles from Ventura Harbor). True, San Miguel, the farthest west, is not a short trip, nor is the small rock island of Santa Barbara. But Anacapa, Santa Cruz, and to a lesser degree Santa Rosa can be visited as day trips, although only Santa Cruz and Anacapa trips are available year-round. There can be tough weather conditions, and it's often very windy since there's little shelter. These islands are some of the last vestiges of pristine and unadulterated landscape on the West Coast, retaining a purity that many long for. A visit to Ventura merits a day exploring the islands on land or by sea.

Inexpensive day trips allow visitors to explore, hike, kayak, snorkel, camp, and scuba dive at the islands. Multiday trips allow for extended camping excursions into the islands' interiors and for visiting several of the islands.

Getting There

The quickest way to the Channel Islands is via Ventura Harbor. Island Packers is the official concessionaire for the National Park.

Island Packers Cruises (1691 Spinnaker Dr., Suite 105B, 805/642-1393, www.island-packers.com) runs to all five islands in the national park. Bear in mind that when traveling by boat, weather conditions can suspend a planned trip, so you always need to check prior to departure time. These are not always smooth rides, as swells can kick up as you travel the channel, so if you have motion sickness issues, prepare for it before you board.

Trips to Anacapa (daily, adults $56, ages 3–12 $39, over age 54 $51), the closest island, take an average of about 45 minutes.

The most common landing at Santa Cruz (daily May–Oct., Tues. and Fri.–Sun. Nov.–Apr., adults $56, ages 3–12 $39, over age 54 $51) is Scorpion Cove, with a crossing time of 90 minutes.

Santa Rosa trips (adults $78, ages 3–12 $62, over age 54 $70) take 2.5–3 hours and include stops at Santa Cruz. They usually traverse the backside of Santa Cruz Island, which has a more sparse beauty than the mainland side.

The far reaches of San Miguel are unpredictable, and day trips (adults $100, ages 3–12 $80, over age 54 $90) are uncommon due to the 3–4-hour travel time. But there are a few days each year when you can do it, typically September–October.

THE ISLANDS
Anacapa Island

Anacapa is best known for a geologic formation called **Arch Rock,** which is, well, an arched rock. You can't access Arch Rock on foot, but you can sail by it or kayak underneath it. The entrance to the island is at the tediously named Landing Cove, a small harbor where

boats anchor. You have to take an inflatable boat to an old rusted metal ladder to access the island, as the harbor is small and the waters can get rough. There are sheer cliffs almost all the way around Anacapa, and you climb 154 steps to reach the top of the island. Up top, the vegetation is sparse and low, and there are few trees. From the top you can clearly see the "spine" of the island, which curves and bends toward Santa Cruz Island. The stunning volcanic formation almost looks like separate islands, forming a chain that extends five miles. Anacapa has about 130 sea caves and is also home to the largest brown pelican rookery in the country. You'll discover that for yourself once you land, as the stench is obvious in certain spots. Travel time to the island is under an hour, and you're very likely to see dolphins on the way.

Santa Cruz Island

Santa Cruz is the largest of the islands, some 22 miles long. There are more old buildings on this island than the others, and there is a day camp near Scorpion Bay where you can pitch

PACIFIC COAST HIGHWAY

© MICHAEL CERVIN

Arch Rock, Anacapa Island

a tent, store your food in metal lockers, and explore on foot. There are trees here as well as old dried-out creeks and former grasslands that are often barren depending on the amount of winter rainfall. This used to be farmland—hard to believe, but true. So far removed from the mainland, the island's cattle operations dwindled out in the 1920s. The elusive and nimble Channel Islands fox is difficult to spot, but there are beautiful large ravens that make their homes here. This is also the only place in the world to see the endemic island scrub jay. Santa Cruz is by far the most popular island to visit, in part because it most closely resembles the mainland and, frankly, it is the most hospitable. Travel time is 90 minutes, and travelers offload onto a short pier directly connected to shore, though shore landings from a skiff are possible depending on conditions.

Santa Cruz is a vast piece of land, and it's best to visit the center of the island if possible, where the thick, dense vegetation is almost *Jurassic Park*–like; you half expect to find some strange prehistoric animal calmly eating leaves from a tree. The best way to really get a feel for the inherent beauty of the rock formations, the multicolored strata of the rock, the numerous coves, and the tiny beaches that are still relatively unused is to explore by kayak or boat. Seals and sea lions make their homes in some of these coves, and the craggy rocks are home to oystercatchers, eagles, pelicans, and plenty of animals that crave the security and tranquility of these pockets of land.

Santa Rosa Island

Parts of Santa Rosa are a bit more forlorn than Santa Cruz, with low grass and some trees in the once-wet ravines. As with Anacapa, the steep cliffs prohibit landing just anywhere. There are some beautiful white sand beaches as well as coastal lagoons and places that seem virtually untouched. The vistas from the tops of some of the plateaus are beautiful, with views of neighboring Santa Cruz Island and the mainland coastline in the distance. Travel time is about three hours by boat; you'll need to climb a 20-foot steel-rung ladder to reach flat land.

San Miguel Island

San Miguel is visited by the concessionaire's tours only part of the year. It is a remote and

Santa Rosa Island

© MICHAEL CERVIN

desolate place, with fierce winds that sometimes prohibit landing. But the stark beauty is enchanting, and there are more species of birds, plants, and animals here than on the other islands. Stories abound that Juan Rodríguez Cabrillo, the first nonnative to set eyes on the West Coast in 1542, died and was buried here; there is a small memorial to him on land overlooking Cuyler Harbor, a white cross planted firmly in the hard earth. It's true that when Cabrillo landed at the islands (not in Santa Barbara, as many believe—he never set foot on the mainland), he became sick and died, but the specifics on exactly where he was buried are a matter of conjecture. Some say his crew buried him on San Miguel; some say they took his body to Catalina Island, near Long Beach. There is no definitive proof of where Cabrillo's remains were buried.

San Miguel was used for cattle and sheep grazing until just after World War II, when it became a bombing range for military practice. Travel time is about four hours. A skiff will usually run you to shore, but it depends on the weather conditions, which can be hit-and-miss.

Santa Barbara Island
Santa Barbara Island is little more than a small rock in the lonely Pacific, and it's virtually impossible to see from the mainland. There are campsites on these 639 acres, but if you set up camp, you might wonder exactly why you're here. Shut off, secluded, and lonely, it's a rare stop for most people despite of the occasional lush vegetation. Travel time is just over three hours; once here, you have to climb a steel-rung ladder from a skiff, then laboriously trudge up a 0.25-mile set of steps to reach the top. You won't find any shelter, but you will be on one of the least-visited islands. It's a very cool feeling to know that few people have walked this land before you.

SPORTS AND RECREATION
Whale-Watching
Island Packers Cruises (1691 Spinnaker Dr., Suite 105B, 805/642-1393, www. islandpackers.com, $25–35) has operated whale-watching cruises for years and is the most experienced. It also runs harbor cruises with a variety of options, including dinner cruises and group charters. Their website has the pertinent details for customizing to get exactly what you want.

Kayaking Tours
Channel Islands Kayak Center (Channel Islands Harbor, 3600 S. Harbor Blvd., Suite 2-108, Oxnard, 805/984-5995, www.cikayak. com, noon–5 P.M. Mon.–Fri., 10 A.M.–5 P.M. Sat.–Sun., rental $12.50 per hour, kayak tours from $80) rents single or tandem kayaks and a wetsuit if you need one. You can glide around the harbor on your own, or they will take you out to the islands for a guided tour.

Scuba Diving
There are many charter boats that will take divers from Ventura Harbor to the islands and surrounding areas, but it's always best to go on a dive boat with a dive master: someone who knows the islands, the surges, the swells, and the water patterns at any given time of year.

Raptor Dive Charters (1559 Spinnaker Dr., Suite 109, 805/650-7700, www.raptor-dive.com, $110–125) travels to Anacapa and Santa Cruz Islands. It also does night diving. Winter is routinely the best time to dive as the water is the clearest and there are fewer plankton blooms. Yes, the water is colder, but it's worth suffering a little for better visibility.

Peace Boat (2419 Harbor Blvd., 805/650-3483, www.peaceboat.com, $100–135) is a 65-foot dive boat that departs from the harbor for single- and multiple-day dive trips as well as lobster trips; it'll even traverse the waters south to San Nicolas and Santa Catalina Islands. *Peace Boat* has very conscientious staff who know the waters and emergency procedures and are certified and equipped for Nitrox. Plus, soaking in the hot tub with an ice cream is the perfect ending to a long day of diving.

PACIFIC COAST HIGHWAY

Santa Barbara

Santa Barbara's laid-back vibe, inspired by endless waves and eternal sunshine, is complemented by great shopping and recreational opportunities, world-class wine-tasting, and breathtaking Spanish architecture. The city has been referred to as "The American Riviera"— and with good reason. It has an enviable setting, nestled between the Pacific Ocean and the mountains, and incredible views of both— plus fantastic weather. It's an idyllic spot—so much so that if you stay long enough, you probably won't want to leave.

Santa Barbara inspires physical activity and healthy living. With copious sunshine, wide roads, lots of warm sandy beaches, and challenging mountain trails, it's the kind of environment where getting outside is so easy that simply being in Santa Barbara is equated with being outdoors. There are no excuses not to walk, jog, hike, surf, run, bike, dive, or play. Surfing is a favorite activity here, with eager surfers dotting most of the coastline. And along the waterfront, a paved path allows anyone on two feet, two wheels, or anything else that moves to enjoy the coastline alongside grassy areas with palm trees gently swaying in the breeze. At least five area farmers markets held every week make healthy produce abundant and accessible.

To both residents and visitors, Santa Barbara seems almost like a dream. Its natural beauty and great weather, plus stunning geography, creative restaurants, local culture, rich history, a thriving wine industry, and unique festivals, all bookended by the mountains and ocean, make this prime spot enviable beyond belief.

Orientation

Santa Barbara is defined by State Street, the main drag, which runs from the beach through the downtown area. There is only one major artery into and out of Santa Barbara, U.S. 101. Aside from Highway 154 through the San Marcos Pass, which heads from Santa Barbara over the mountains and into the Santa Ynez Valley, no other roads lead here. This can be a problem every once in a while: Fires can shut down U.S. 101, leaving Santa Barbara isolated from its neighbors. If there is a major traffic accident, there simply are no alternate routes.

Aside from that, getting around Santa Barbara is easy, as the city is laid out in a classic grid pattern. State Street does get congested during summer months; unless you enjoy sitting in your car and inching along, it's best to use other arteries on the weekends. The first street east of State Street is Anacapa, which runs one-way toward the ocean. Chapala, the first street west of State Street, runs one-way toward the mountains. Together they allow for quick travel through the city.

Though State Street is not a lengthy street, the 400–600 blocks have become known as "Lower State," and you will hear people refer to this often.

SIGHTS
Downtown

Downtown Santa Barbara covers about 12 blocks. It is a pedestrian-friendly area with more than enough places to grab a bite, get more cash at a bank, or step inside a store to find something of interest. There are even plenty of combination trash cans and recycling bins (the dark green ones). What are lacking, however, are restrooms. Surprisingly, there is only one public facility (914 State St.), and many businesses will not allow noncustomers to use theirs.

EL PRESIDIO DE SANTA BÁRBARA STATE HISTORIC PARK

El Presidio de Santa Bárbara (123 E. Canon Perdido St., 805/965-0093, www.sbthp.org, www.parks.ca.gov, 10:30 A.M.–4:30 P.M. daily, closed major holidays, adults $5, seniors $4, AAA members, students, and military with ID $2.50, includes admission to Casa de la Guerra), founded on April 21, 1782, is the birthplace of Santa Barbara. It was the fourth in a chain of military fortresses built by the Spanish along California's coast. The sun-dried adobe bricks of the buildings were laid on foundations of sandstone boulders. The whitewashed, red tile–roofed buildings are surrounded by an outer wall with two bastions for defense. The most prominent building is the chapel, which was Santa Barbara's second place of worship (the Christianized Chumash population attended services at the mission). Today, only two sections of the original presidio remain: El Cuartel and the Canedo Adobe.

El Cuartel, the family residence of the soldier assigned to guard the western gate into the Plaza de Armas, is right across the street from the chapel. It's a great example of living architecture: The second-oldest building in California, dating from 1782, it can still be touched and experienced today. The massive walls still stand as they have for more than 200 years, with only cosmetic touch-ups to the plaster. It's awesome to stand in the spot where Santa Barbara was founded and feel the connection to history. The presidio is just a block off State Street downtown and can easily be worked into your downtown sightseeing plans.

SANTA BARBARA
HISTORICAL MUSEUM

The Santa Barbara Historical Museum (136 E. De La Guerra St., 805/966-1601, www.santabarbaramuseum.com, 10 A.M.–5 P.M. Tues.–Sat., noon–5 P.M. Sun., donation) houses a beautiful and comprehensive collection of historical artifacts covering the last 600 years of local history, including an 1813 Peruvian mission bell, a three-foot-tall hand-painted wood carving of Saint Barbara, and an exquisitely carved ornate 15-foot Tong shrine from the days when Santa Barbara had a thriving Chinatown. There are also Chumash, Spanish, and Mexican period garments on display as well as guns, swords, and working tools.

The entry foyer hosts rotating exhibits that feature anything from important local artists to designer Kem Weber's industrial work and furnishings from his time spent teaching art and design at a small studio in Santa Barbara. The museum, which also has a small gift store, is one of the great jewels of the city, and a visit is nearly mandatory for anyone who desires an understanding of the multilayered history of this area.

CASA DE LA GUERRA

When its construction was completed in 1827, Casa de la Guerra (15 E. De La Guerra St., 805/965-0093, www.sbthp.org, noon–4 P.M. Sat.–Sun., adults $5, seniors $4, AAA members, students, and military with ID $2.50, includes admission to El Presidio de Santa Bárbara) became the cultural and political heart of Santa Barbara. Construction began in 1919 under the fifth presidio commandant, José de la Guerra, one of the pueblo's wealthiest and most influential citizens. After California became a U.S. state, de la Guerra's son, Pablo, served as both a state senator and as lieutenant governor. In 1874, the first city hall was constructed opposite the Casa in Plaza de la Guerra. In 1922 El Paseo was designed and built around the Casa. Following the devastating 1925 earthquake, the Casa and El Paseo served as models for rebuilding parts of downtown. Visit today and you'll see rooms that were considered ornate at the time, although by today's standards they seem a little crude. Unless you're a history buff, a self-guided tour of the site is sufficient, although the Casa de la Guerra does offer hour-long guided tours, by appointment only.

THE SANTA BARBARA
COUNTY COURTHOUSE

Covering an entire city block, the still-functioning Santa Barbara County Courthouse (1100 Anacapa St., Suite 2, 805/962-6464, www.sbcourts.org, docent-led tours 10:30 A.M. and 2 P.M. Mon.–Wed. and Fri., 2 P.M. Thurs. and Sat.–Sun., free) is a stunning example of Spanish and Moorish design. William Mooser designed this courthouse to replace the earlier 1872 version, a colonial structure with a massive domed cupola. When the courthouse was

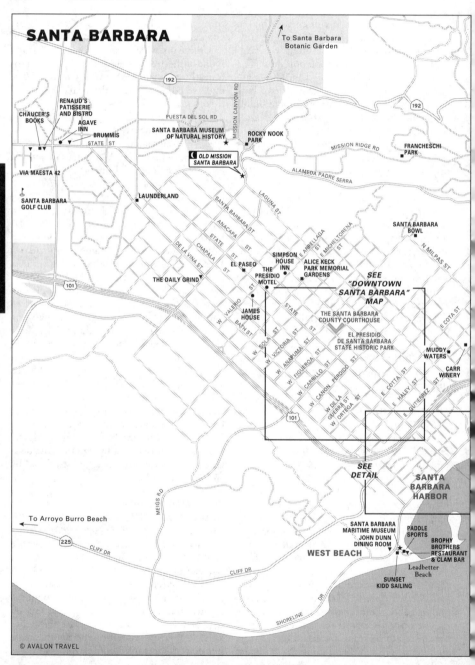

SANTA BARBARA

To Santa Barbara Botanic Garden

RENAUD'S PATISSERIE AND BISTRO

CHAUCER'S BOOKS

AGAVE INN

BRUMMIS

STATE ST

VIA MAESTA 42

SANTA BARBARA GOLF CLUB

MISSION CANYON RD

PUESTA DEL SOL RD

SANTA BARBARA MUSEUM OF NATURAL HISTORY

ROCKY NOOK PARK

OLD MISSION SANTA BARBARA

LAUNDERLAND

MISSION RIDGE RD

FRANCHESCHI PARK

ALAMEDA PADRE SERRA

LAGUNA ST

SANTA BARBARA ST

ANACAPA ST

STATE ST

DE LA VINA ST

CHAPALA ST

EL PASEO

THE DAILY GRIND

SIMPSON HOUSE INN

THE PRESIDIO MOTEL

E ARRELLAGA ST

E MICHELTORENA ST

ALICE KECK PARK MEMORIAL GARDENS

SANTA BARBARA BOWL

N MILPAS ST

SEE "DOWNTOWN SANTA BARBARA" MAP

THE SANTA BARBARA COUNTY COURTHOUSE

EL PRESIDIO DE SANTA BARBARA STATE HISTORIC PARK

JAMES HOUSE

W VALERIO ST

BATH ST

W SOLA ST

W VICTORIA ST

STATE ST

W ANAPAMU ST

W FIGUEROA ST

W CARRILLO ST

W CANON PERDIDO ST

W DE LA GUERRA ST

W ORTEGA ST

E COTA ST

E COTA ST

E HALEY ST

E GUTIERREZ ST

MUDDY WATERS

CARR WINERY

101

SEE DETAIL

SANTA BARBARA HARBOR

MEIGS RD

To Arroyo Burro Beach

225

CLIFF DR

CLIFF DR

SANTA BARBARA MARITIME MUSEUM

JOHN DUNN DINING ROOM

PADDLE SPORTS

BROPHY BROTHERS RESTAURANT & CLAM BAR

WEST BEACH

Leadbetter Beach

SUNSET KIDD SAILING

SHORELINE DR

© AVALON TRAVEL

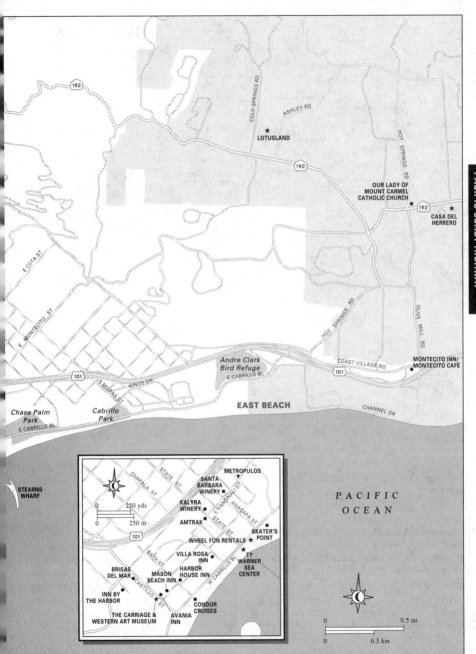

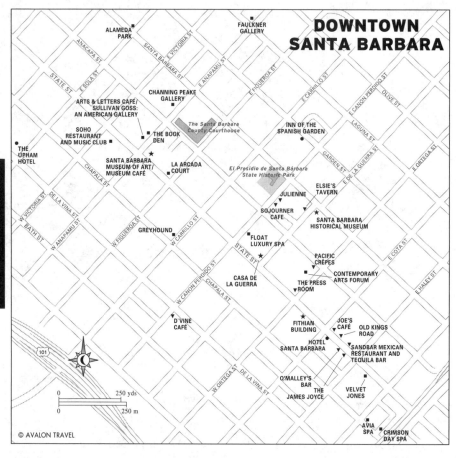

DOWNTOWN SANTA BARBARA

FAULKNER GALLERY

ALAMEDA PARK

CHANNING PEAKE GALLERY

ARTS & LETTERS CAFÉ/ SULLIVAN GOSS: AN AMERICAN GALLERY

The Santa Barbara County Courthouse

INN OF THE SPANISH GARDEN

SOHO RESTAURANT AND MUSIC CLUB

THE BOOK DEN

THE UPHAM HOTEL

SANTA BARBARA MUSEUM OF ART/ MUSEUM CAFÉ

LA ARCADA COURT

El Presidio de Santa Bárbara State Historic Park

ELSIE'S TAVERN

JULIENNE

SOJOURNER CAFÉ

SANTA BARBARA HISTORICAL MUSEUM

GREYHOUND

FLOAT LUXURY SPA

PACIFIC CRÊPES

CONTEMPORARY ARTS FORUM

CASA DE LA GUERRA

THE PRESS ROOM

D'VINE CAFÉ

FITHIAN BUILDING

JOE'S CAFÉ

OLD KINGS ROAD

HOTEL SANTA BARBARA

SANDBAR MEXICAN RESTAURANT AND TEQUILA BAR

O'MALLEY'S BAR

THE JAMES JOYCE

VELVET JONES

AVIA SPA

CRIMSON DAY SPA

0 250 yds
0 250 m

© AVALON TRAVEL

completed in 1929, it was unlike anything in the city. Lush grounds, including the copious lawn and Sunken Garden, provide the foundation for the sandstone building with arabesque windows, archways, hand-painted wood ceilings, walls with intricate designs, and pueblo tile inlays nearly everywhere flashing brilliant colors and Native American designs. Of particular note is the Mural Room, once used by the county board of supervisors. The huge room is covered in a mural depicting the early Chumash people and follows the history of the area leading up to California's statehood. All tours of the building meet in the Mural Room

on the second floor and take approximately one hour.

The clock tower, known as **El Mirador,** juts out of the top of the courthouse, making it one of the tallest structures in the city, although it is just 85 feet tall. The best views of downtown, the mountains, and the ocean from a downtown perspective are here. Take the elevator to the 4th floor, where a dozen steps lead up and out to the platform. You'll be thrilled at the red-tile roofs stretching out in front of you. There are placards describing points of interest in each direction so you can easily get your bearings. You don't need the formal tour

MICHAEL CERVIN

The Santa Barbara County Courthouse has Spanish and Moorish design elements.

to appreciate the sheer beauty and craftsmanship of the building, but taking it will give you more specific information. Ironically, the courthouse doesn't meet the county's current building codes and standards, and would never be approved for construction today.

SANTA BARBARA MUSEUM OF ART

See the power of the visual arts at the Santa Barbara Museum of Art (1130 State St., 805/963-4364, www.sbmuseart.org, 11 A.M.–5 P.M. Tues.–Sun., adults $9, seniors and students $6, under age 6 free, free Sun.) This is an impressive art museum with a good collection for a community this size. Two stories of rotating exhibits always keep visitors intrigued; the museum showcases abstract, postmodern, and other genres in a large diversity of media including print and photography. Of particular note is the collection of Asian art. Nineteen Chinese robes were donated to the museum at its inception in 1941, which encouraged the donation of more Asian works. Today, the Asian collection consists of over 2,600 objects spanning 4,000 years, including 18th–20th-century Japanese woodblock prints.

Admission is free to everyone on Sunday, although a donation is suggested.

Oceanfront

Santa Barbara's oceanfront is defined by Cabrillo Boulevard, which follows the shoreline. With the exception of the wharf and harbor, there are no businesses or shops on the beach side of the street. This undeveloped sandy, grassy area lined with palm trees has created an idyllic setting that people find intoxicating and typically Californian. On clear days the islands hug the horizon and the sounds of the crashing surf, the gulls, and people milling around create a relaxing experience.

This four-mile stretch incorporates Stearns Wharf, the harbor, hotels, and shops; the concrete bike path stretches past a number of beaches and, after Cabrillo Boulevard, is the main access route to the area. Rent a bicycle, a tandem bike, a four-person surrey, or a motorized ScootCoup at **Wheel Fun Rentals** (23 E. Cabrillo Blvd., 805/966-2282, www.wheelfunrentalssb.com, 8 A.M.–8 P.M. daily, $8–49 per hour) and meander the path from Leadbetter Beach at the west end to the zoo in the east. It's actually a lot of fun, even though the surreys seem to have a mind of their own and steering is sometimes challenging. Or use the path as many other people do to stroll, run, or in-line skate while basking in the sunshine.

STEARNS WHARF

Stearns Wharf (State St. and Cabrillo Blvd., 805/564-5530, www.stearnswharf.org, parking $2.50 per hour, first 90 minutes free with validation) is Santa Barbara's most visited landmark. Santa Barbara has no natural harbor, and the shifting sands prohibited large ships from docking here; the wharf was completed in 1872, allowing ships to offload supplies for the burgeoning town. The wharf, which used to extend much farther into the ocean than it does now, has burned completely twice and has been destroyed by storms. The current iteration, scaled back in size, is a favorite for visitors. Frankly, there are a lot of typical tourist shops selling seashells, small personalized license plates, and gift items you can find almost anywhere that have nothing to do with Santa Barbara, but if you walk to the end, you get some of the best views back to the city. There are no railings at the end of the wharf, so keep an eye on little ones.

In addition to the views, there are a few restaurants, an ice cream store, and the Santa Barbara Museum of Natural History's **Ty Warner Sea Center** (211 Stearns Wharf, 805/962-2526, www.sbnature.org, 10 A.M.–5 P.M. daily, adults $8, seniors and ages 13–17 $7, ages 2–12 $5), which is a two-story building devoted to providing a better understanding of how our oceans work. When you first enter, you'll notice the full-size replica of a blue whale hanging from the ceiling. There are touch tanks on the lower level and staff to answer questions and discuss why you should pet the starfish and how sealife coexists with humans. As you move upstairs, you come eye-to-eye with the blue whale, giving you an idea of how massive these creatures really are. There's also a very beautiful little exhibit, nicely backlit, showing jellyfish and how these supple, graceful creatures impact our oceans.

THE SANTA BARBARA HARBOR

The Santa Barbara Harbor (Cabrillo Blvd. and Harbor Way) is home to about 1,100 sailing vessels, a few stores and restaurants, and a museum. A short walk from Stearns Wharf, it is the eye candy most people expect to see when visiting Santa Barbara. One of the best parts of the harbor is the long breakwater wall, often with colorful flags flying in the wind. It's a great walk and terminates on a sand spit, which you can access at low tide. At high tide and during storms, the breakwater is constantly hit by crashing waves that splash over the wall; half the fun is trying to outrun them. There's minimal shopping at the harbor, but you can buy fresh fish every day of the week and smell the catch as it's hauled in.

Interestingly, the area where the harbor is positioned today is not a natural harbor but was built in the 1920s when millionaire Max Fleischmann (of Fleischmann's Yeast) wanted a protected place to moor his yacht and ponied up a lot of money to build the breakwater. Unfortunately, the shifting sands under the water need to be constantly dredged, at a huge cost to taxpayers, to allow boats to enter the harbor, and you'll usually see the rather unsightly dredging equipment sitting near the sand spit.

While at the harbor, stop in to the **Santa Barbara Maritime Museum** (113 Harbor Way, Suite 190, 805/962-8404, www.sbmm. org, 10 A.M.–6 P.M. Thurs.–Tues. Memorial Day–Labor Day, 10 A.M.–5 P.M. Thurs.–Tues. Labor Day–Memorial Day, adults $7, seniors, students, and active military $4, active military in uniform free, ages 1–5 $2, 3rd Thurs. of the month free), which is housed in a 1940s naval building. Inside the two-story structure are exhibits on surfing and shipwrecks and a full-length *tomol*, a wood canoe the Chumash used to cross between the mainland and the Channel Islands. There are rotating exhibits with the sea as a common theme, along with lectures and special screenings in the upstairs theater.

The Mission and the Riviera

One of the older parts of the city, the Riviera sits in the foothills where the mountains cascade down to the lowlands. The area is studded with oak trees and natural waterways and was obviously chosen as a place to build homes because of the views. The main draw of the area is the Mission Santa Barbara, but it is also home to the Santa Barbara Botanic Garden, great hiking opportunities such as the popular Rattlesnake Canyon trail, secluded parks like Franceschi Park, and estates from the 1920s. Some of the estates, including Lotusland and Casa del Herrero, are open to the public.

◖ OLD MISSION SANTA BARBARA

More closely associated with Santa Barbara than any other landmark, Old Mission Santa Barbara (2201 Laguna St., 805/682-4713, www.santabarbaramission.org, 9 A.M.–5 P.M. daily, self-guided tours adults $5, seniors $4, ages 5–15 $1) was founded on December 4, 1786, the Feast of Saint Barbara. Originally there were no plans to build the mission at this site, but after considering the proximity to a source of freshwater, namely Mission Creek, and the defensible position of being able to view the ocean in time to spot unfriendly ships approaching, it was decided the area was ideal. Standing on the church steps, you can immediately understand the importance of this location. Still an active church, it has been a gathering spot for more than 225 years.

Although visually striking, it is one of the least authentic-looking of the missions, and what you see today is the culmination of decades of restoration efforts. The original adobe church was a simple structure that was enlarged twice to accommodate the growth of the population of Chumash and settlers in the area. The fourth and current iteration was built in 1820. The 1925 earthquake inflicted major damage, and the east bell tower was almost completely destroyed. Restoration efforts began in 1926, but within 10 years, signs of further problems began to appear. Cracks

Still an active church, Old Mission Santa Barbara has held its ground for more than 225 years.

emerged in the towers and façade, and conditions continued to worsen until by 1949 it was apparent that something desperately needed to be done. Studies revealed that chemical reactions inside the concrete were fatally weakening the material, rendering the building unsafe. Drastic action—a total reconstruction of both towers and the church facade—began in 1950 and continued until 1953.

Around back of the mission is the Huerta Project, where 6–10 acres of *huertas,* or gardens, were originally established so that there would be food for those living at the mission and presidio. Considered a living museum, the garden today has a variety of fruit trees, grapevines, herbs, and edible plants, all consistent with what would have been grown in mission times. Across the lawn is the rose garden, where over 1,000 different varieties are growing. As you walk across the street, consider that this is where some of the grapevines were planted.

The **Mission Museum** offers a 90-minute docent-guided tour (11 A.M. Thurs.–Fri., 10:30 A.M. Sat., $8) for a maximum of 15 people. You cannot see the church unless you pay for a guided or self-guided tour. On a self-guided tour, you first visit the interior courtyard, where a central fountain is encircled by palm trees. Following the signs you then come upon the cemetery, with a handful of headstones and crypts and a beautiful Moreton Bay fig tree planted around 1890. From there it is a few steps into the church. This is the most decorated of the mission interiors, with lots of vibrant stenciling surrounding the doors and altar and a complete painted wainscot. Large paintings flank both walls; near the formal entrance is a small gated room with the only original altar and tabernacle in the entire mission chain, dating from 1786. After leaving the church you enter the museum section, which houses old photographs of the mission from the 1880s and a few vestments and artifacts from early services. There's also a side room that shows how a typical kitchen looked during the mission's heyday as well as other exhibits dealing with how they constructed the mission and the tools of those times.

SANTA BARBARA BOTANIC GARDEN

Santa Barbara Botanic Garden (1212 Mission Canyon Rd., 805/682-4726, www.sbbg.org, 9 A.M.–6 P.M. daily, closed major holidays, guided tours 11 A.M. and 2 P.M. Sat.–Sun., adults $8, seniors and ages 13–17 $6, ages 2–12 $4), or "The Garden," as it's known, is 78 acres of pristine wilderness, with redwood trees growing in a shaded creek and oaks fanning out everywhere. The garden was founded in 1926 to showcase the rich diversity of Western plants. By 1936 this emphasis had narrowed to plants native to California and now includes flora from northwestern Baja California and southwestern Oregon, which are part of the California Floristic Province. A rich diversity of life is represented here, along with part of the original aqueduct that fed the mission with clean water from the mountains. Today, there are nearly six miles of walking trails and over 1,000 species of plants, and the library contains over 15,000 volumes of works related to botany and horticulture. There is a gift shop, and you can purchase plants directly.

LOTUSLAND

To enjoy the beauty of nature, albeit in a methodically constructed way, visit Lotusland (695 Ashley Rd., 805/969-9990, www.lotusland.org, tours 10 A.M. and 1:30 P.M. Wed.–Sat. mid-Feb.–mid-Nov., adults $35, ages 5–18 $10, reservations required), named for the lotus flowers on the property, 37 acres of the most well-manicured and lovingly tended gardens you may ever see. Given that Lotusland is a public garden operating in a residential neighborhood, reservations are mandatory; tours are docent-led and average just under two hours. There was a commercial nursery on the land in the 1880s, and the garden was last owned by Ganna Walska, a 1920s-era Polish opera singer who routinely rearranged her vast collections of plants into bold color schemes and unusual shapes. She constantly tinkered with her gardens for over four decades, and after her death in 1984, her estate became a nonprofit.

Wander through the moonscape barrenness

of the cactus gardens, the topiary garden, the serenity of the Japanese garden, the olive allée, and the formal English-style gardens. Lotusland is a rare place where you feel you could stay forever—in fact, one of the staff gardeners has been here for over 30 years. It is truly awe-inspiring place and nearly overwhelming in its botanical diversity and beauty. Bring a jacket, as it can get brisk in the heavily wooded areas. The wide walking paths easily accommodate wheelchairs.

CASA DEL HERRERO

At first glance, the entrance to Casa del Herrero (1387 E. Valley Rd., 805/565-5653, www.casadelherrero.com, 90-minute docent-led tours 10 A.M. and 2 P.M. Wed. and Sat., over age 10 $20, reservations required), the "house of the blacksmith," seems like just another Spanish facade in a town replete with them. But the moment you cross the threshold and enter the lobby, you'll see the 18th-century Tibetan wood ceiling and know you're in another world. Designed by owner George Fox Steedman and architect George Washington Smith, the Spanish Colonial Revival structure was completed in 1925 and remains essentially unchanged. The amount of detail and the precise expression of the interior design is overwhelming, from intricate tile work and hand-carved door surrounds to authentic Spanish antiques. Steedman traveled through parts of Europe searching for interiors to embellish his home and had the house altered to fit the doors and windows he purchased. Although it is ornate and elaborate, there is a sense of proportion throughout the house. Steedman also commissioned local artist Channing Peake to provide a Western flair to some of the original art. The house is on the National Register of Historic Places and is a National Historic Landmark.

WINE-TASTING

The wines of Santa Barbara County have been receiving favorable reviews and write-ups in the national media. The area is predominantly known for pinot noir and chardonnay, but with the diversity of microclimates, there are over 50 grape varietals planted here. This means you can find traditional varieties like cabernet sauvignon, merlot, sauvignon blanc, and syrah, but also sangiovese, dolcetto, viognier, cabernet franc, malbec, and others.

Not all wine-tasting is done surrounded by vineyards. On the Urban Wine Trail (www.urbanwinetrailsb.com) you can sample some of the county's best wines without even seeing a vine. Near Lower State Street, a block from the beach, you can walk to six tasting rooms. Visiting others that are part of the trail will require a little driving. Recently passed legislation means that some, but not all, wineries can now offer wines by the glass in addition to wine-tasting, so if you sample something you like, you can purchase a glass to enjoy on the spot or a bottle to take with you.

KALYRA WINERY

Kalyra Winery (212 State St., 805/965-8606, www.kalyrawinery.com, noon–7 P.M. Mon.–Fri., noon–8 P.M. Sat.–Sun.) is famous for having been featured in the 2004 movie *Sideways*. This tasting room wasn't in the film, but you can still sample the California and Australian wines made by Mike Brown, an Aussie and an avid surfer. There's a tropical feel to the interior, with a thatched roof over the tasting bar, and the vibe is relaxed. Kalyra started out making sweet wines, and still offers quite a few, but has a broad portfolio.

SANTA BARBARA WINERY

Once you're done at Kalyra Winery, walk a block down Yanonali Street to Santa Barbara Winery (202 Anacapa St., 805/963-3633, www.sbwinery.com, 10 A.M.–5 P.M. daily), the oldest winery in the county, started in 1962. The chardonnay is delightful and truly expresses a Santa Barbara character with its bright citrus notes. Other varieties include pinot noir, sangiovese, and sauvignon blanc. If you are looking to sample a diverse array of wines, this is your best stop. The tasting bar is just a few feet from the barrel room, and there's a good-size gift shop.

SANTA BARBARA WINE COUNTRY

After Highway 1 splits off from U.S. 101 west of Santa Barbara, the drive north along either highway is largely inland until Pismo Beach. Since you won't be missing any coastal scenery, you could take a detour even farther inland to the Santa Maria Valley to sample wines in the region made famous by the movie *Sideways*. Running roughly parallel to U.S. 101, **Foxen Canyon Road** is a back road hugging the foothills, with multiple wineries along the way.

Foxen Winery (7600 Foxen Canyon Rd., 805/937-4251, 11 A.M.-4 P.M. daily, tasting $10) is known for its rustic wood tasting room – it looks like a run-down shed. But the wines are a far cry from rustic. In addition to chardonnay, syrah, cabernet sauvignon, and pinot noir, the winery is one of the few to produce the underappreciated chenin blanc. Foxen's long-standing reputation goes back six generations, and its 10 acres are the only dry-farmed vineyard in the area, meaning that irrigation is not used.

Set in an old barn, **Rancho Sisquoc** (6600 Foxen Canyon Rd., 805/934-4332, www.ranchosisquoc.com, 10 A.M.-4 P.M. Mon.-Thurs., 10 A.M.-5 P.M. Fri.-Sun., tasting $8) makes a beautiful spot for a picnic. The wood-sided tasting room is rustic but comfortable, and the surrounding setting – a vast field with low hills in the distance – is perfect for some quiet wine-enhanced relaxation.

Located on a little road off Foxen Canyon Road, award-winning **Kenneth Volk Vineyards** (5230 Tepusquet Rd., 805/938-7896, www.volkwines.com, 10:30 A.M.-4:30 P.M. daily, tasting $5) offers all the strange wines you've never tried. In addition to the standard offerings like chardonnay, pinot noir, viognier, cabernet sauvignon, and merlot, Kenneth Volk is a champion of heirloom varieties: funky, wonderfully oddball wines like cabernet pfeiffer, négrette, verdelho, and aglianico. You won't regret the long trek to get to the tranquil 12-acre property along the Tepusquet Creek, surrounded by oak and sycamore trees.

At the southern end of Foxen Canyon is another cluster of wineries, not too far from Los Olivos. One of the oldest wineries in the county, **Zaca Mesa Winery** (6905 Foxen Canyon Rd., 805/688-9339, www.zacamesa.com, 10 A.M.-4 P.M. daily, tasting $10) was the first to plant syrah grapes way back in the 1970s, long before anyone knew what syrah was. Viognier, chardonnay, roussanne, Grenache, and mourvèdre round out the offerings. Check out the large-scale chess set on the property.

GETTING THERE

From the south, take the Alisos Canyon Road turnoff from U.S. 101, about 25 miles north of the Highway 1-U.S. 101 split. Take Alisos Canyon Road 6.5 miles and turn left onto Foxen Canyon Road. Foxen Winery is about 5.5 miles along. Foxen Canyon Road eventually turns into East Betteravia Road and connects back to U.S. 101.

From the north, take the East Betteravia Road exit from U.S. 101, and head east about three miles until it turns into Foxen Canyon Road. From this point, Tepusquet Road, where Kenneth Volk is located, is about 10 miles away.

merlot grapes

© MICHAEL CERVIN

MUNICIPAL WINEMAKERS

Municipal Winemakers (22 Anacapa St., 805/931-6864, www.municipalwinemakers. com, 11 A.M.–6 P.M. Sun.–Wed., 11 A.M.– 11 P.M. Thurs.–Sat., tasting $10) is in an unpretentious small space with an even smaller deck. Inside is rough wood ceilings and plain walls, with a four-top table and standing room at the bar. This is a weekend venture for owner Dave Potter, who will answer your questions and pour his wines. The offerings are Rhône-style wines, including grenache, syrah, and a sparkling shiraz.

CARR WINERY

Carr Winery (414 N. Salsipuedes St., 805/965-7985, www.carrwinery.com, 11 A.M.–6 P.M. Sun.–Wed., 11 A.M.–8 P.M. Thurs.–Sat., tasting $10) focuses on small lots of syrah, grenache, cabernet franc, and pinot noir. The tasting room is in a World War II Quonset hut, with a bar up front and tables in the back. The wine bar (5 P.M.–midnight Thurs.–Sat.) features live music and appetizers along with wines by the glass. It's run by another surfer-winemaker, and you'll see surfboards placed around the tasting room. There's a much younger crowd here, eager to sample the excellent wines and enjoy life.

BEACHES

People flock to Santa Barbara's beaches, which are generally long and flat. Water temperatures in the summer are generally about 61°F, cooling down to about 58°F in the winter months. At low tide you can clearly see the rocks hidden under the waves, which makes for great tide pool exploring. Several creeks run into the ocean, and because it's difficult to keep them clean, there are occasional closures posted at some beaches. Aside from that, swimming in Santa Barbara is a safe endeavor. There are lifeguards during peak summer hours, but they disappear once the crowds do. At Goleta Beach and occasionally at West, East, and Leadbetter Beaches, you might see bulldozers scooping sand back into the ocean. It's a peculiar sight, but it keeps the beaches from eroding too much.

Butterfly Beach

Butterfly Beach (Channel Dr., across from the Four Seasons Hotel, Montecito, sunrise–10 P.M. daily) is accessed by a handful of steps leading to the narrow beach. Many people come here hoping to catch a glimpse of a celebrity from nearby Montecito, but chances are that won't happen. Butterfly is the most west-facing beach in Santa Barbara, meaning that you can actually see the sun set over the Pacific here. To find it, take U.S. 101 to Olive Mill Road in Montecito (a few minutes south of Santa Barbara). At the stop sign, turn toward the ocean (away from the mountains) and follow it 0.25 miles along the coast; Butterfly Beach is on the left. The beach is packed most weekends and often weekdays too, and parking is limited. Park on either side of the street along the beach, or drive up Butterfly Road and park in the nearby neighborhoods. Bring your lunch, water, and sunscreen—there are no public facilities at this beach. Dogs roam freely here.

Carpinteria State Beach

Carpinteria State Beach (5361 6th St., Carpinteria, 805/968-1033, 7 A.M.–sunset daily, day-use $10, camping $35–65) has designated itself the "world's safest beach." Whether that's true or not, this beautiful wide, flat beach is definitely a favorite for locals and visitors alike. With plenty of campgrounds, picnic tables, outdoor showers, RV hookups, telephones, and a short walk to Linden Avenue's restaurants, shops, and grocery store, you'll have everything you need within walking distance. Parts of the campgrounds are tree-lined but right next to the train tracks; passing trains might wake up light sleepers. There is a great sense of community among the campers here.

East Beach

Named because it is east of Stearns Wharf, East Beach (Cabrillo Blvd. at S. Milpas St., sunrise–10 P.M. daily) is all soft sand and wide beach, with a dozen volleyball nets in the sand close to the zoo (if you look closely, you can see the giraffes and lions). It has all the amenities

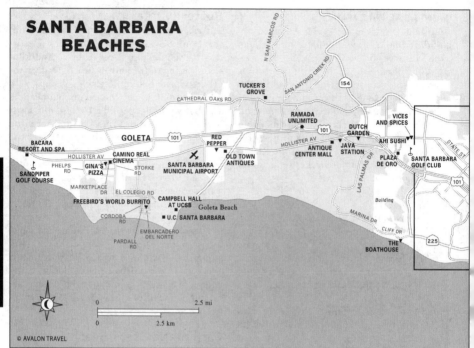

a sun worshipper could hope for: a full beach house, a snack bar, a play area for children, and a path for biking and in-line skating. The beachfront has picnic facilities and a full-service restaurant at the East Beach Grill. The **Cabrillo Pavilion Bathhouse** (1119 East Cabrillo Blvd.), built in 1927, offers showers, lockers, a weight room, a single rentable beach wheelchair, and volleyball rental.

Leadbetter Beach

Leadbetter Beach (Shoreline Dr. and Loma Alta Dr., sunrise–10 P.M. daily) is the best in Santa Barbara. There's a long, flat beach and a large grassy area; Leadbetter Point divides the area's south-facing beaches from the west-facing ones. Sheer cliffs rise from the sand, and trees dot the point. The beach, which is also bounded by the harbor and the breakwater, is ideal for swimming because it's fairly protected, unlike the other flat beaches.

Many catamaran sailors and windsurfers launch from this beach, and you'll occasionally see surfers riding the waves. The grassy picnic areas have barbecue sites that can be reserved for more privacy, but otherwise there is a lot of room. The beach and the park can get packed during the many races and sporting events held here. There are restrooms, a small restaurant, and outdoor showers. Directly across the street is Santa Barbara City College. If you enter the stadium and walk up the many steps, you'll get some terrific views of the harbor, plus a workout.

West Beach

Eleven acres of picturesque sand for sunbathing, swimming, kayaking, windsurfing, and beach volleyball, West Beach (Cabrillo Blvd. and Chapala St., between Stearns Wharf and the harbor, sunrise–10 P.M. daily) has large palm trees, a wide walkway, and a bike path, making it a popular tourist spot. Outrigger canoes also launch from this beach.

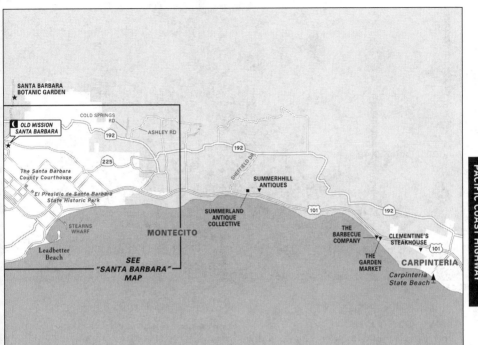

SANTA BARBARA
BOTANIC GARDEN

OLD MISSION
SANTA BARBARA

COLD SPRINGS
RD

ASHLEY RD

192

192

SHEFFIELD DR

225

The Santa Barbara
County Courthouse

El Presidio de Santa Barbara
State Historic Park

SUMMERHHILL
ANTIQUES

SUMMERLAND
ANTIQUE
COLLECTIVE

101

192

STEARNS
WHARF

MONTECITO

THE
BARBECUE
COMPANY

CLEMENTINE'S
STEAKHOUSE

101

Leadbetter
Beach

*SEE
"SANTA BARBARA"
MAP*

THE
GARDEN
MARKET

CARPINTERIA

*Carpinteria
State Beach*

© MICHAEL CERVIN

East Beach

© MICHAEL CERVIN

Leadbetter Beach

Arroyo Burro Beach

Known locally as Hendry's, dog-friendly Arroyo Burro Beach (Cliff Dr. and Las Positas Rd., sunrise–10 P.M. daily) sits at the mouth of Arroyo Burro Creek. A popular spot for surfers and the occasional kayaker or scuba diver, there is a restaurant on-site and a small grassy area for picnics, plus restrooms and outdoor showers. It's very popular with locals and far removed from the downtown beaches, although it can still become very crowded on summer days. At peak times, when the parking lot is full, there's no other parking around. It's flanked by large cliffs, one of which is home to the **Douglas Family Preserve,** still known locally as the Wilcox Property. The 70-acre eucalyptus-studded dog-friendly preserve is popular with locals, but few visitors ever hear about it. The parcel was planned to become housing, but a grassroots campaign raised awareness of the potentially destructive development, and fund-raising efforts to purchase it were bolstered when actor Michael Douglas made a substantial donation, allowing the parcel to remain undeveloped.

He then named it after his father, actor Kirk Douglas.

Goleta Beach

At the base of the University of California, Santa Barbara campus, Goleta Beach Park (5986 Sandspit Rd., sunrise–10 P.M. daily) is popular for its picnic tables, barbecue pits, horseshoes, multiple restrooms, and fishing opportunities. The grassy area is partially shaded by trees, and there's also a small jungle gym for the kids. The pier is popular for fishing, and the low breaks make it an easy entry for kayakers. You can also launch small boats from the pier on weekends, when a crane lowers boats into the water (there is no launch ramp directly into the water). On the mountain-facing side along the bike path are a few platforms for viewing birds in the slough behind the beach.

El Capitán State Beach

Near Refugio State Beach is El Capitán State Beach (off U.S. 101, 17 miles west of Santa Barbara, 805/968-1033, www.parks.ca.gov, sunrise–sunset daily); if you take U.S. 101

© MICHAEL CERVIN

Arroyo Burro Beach

PACIFIC COAST HIGHWAY

north about 15 minutes from downtown, you will see the signs for El Capitán. At the bottom of the exit, turn left and go under the bridge. The road will take you right into the park. El Capitán State Beach offers visitors a sandy beach, rocky tide pools, and stands of sycamore and oak trees along El Capitán Creek. It's a perfect setting for swimming, fishing, surfing, picnicking, and camping. A stairway provides access from the bluffs to the beach area. Amenities include RV hookups, pay showers, restrooms, hiking and biking trails, a fabulous beach, a seasonal general store, and an outdoor arena. Many of the camping sites offer an ocean view.

Refugio State Beach

A state park with a small strip of grass that abuts the water, Refugio State Beach (10 Refugio Beach Rd., Goleta, 805/968-1033, www.parks.ca.gov, sunrise–sunset daily) offers excellent coastal fishing, snorkeling, and scuba diving as well as hiking and biking trails and picnic sites. Palm trees planted near Refugio Creek give a distinctive look to the beach and

camping area. With 1.5 miles of flat shoreline, Refugio is located 20 miles west of Santa Barbara on U.S. 101 at Refugio Beach Road.

ENTERTAINMENT AND EVENTS

Though people flock to Santa Barbara to be outdoors, there's plenty to do inside as well. In bars, clubs, and theaters, Santa Barbara has its own brand of action when the sun goes down. The area is also home to a lively roster of festivals and events year-round.

Nightlife

Every city needs its watering holes, and Santa Barbara is no different. Plenty of bars clog a two-block-long section of State Street; a few more hug the side streets. This is nothing new: Of the first 50 business licenses issued by the city in 1850, 32 were for saloons.

BARS

In the 400–600 blocks of State Street you'll find the majority of Santa Barbara's bars. Frequented mainly by college students, the area has become a hot spot on weekends for flitting in and out of as many bars as possible while taking advantage of cheap drink specials. This has become known as the State Street Crawl, a slow, methodical negotiating of bars and clubs. It's worth remembering that any bar in Santa Barbara leans toward mellow on weeknights and rowdier on weekends. All bars close at 2 A.M., and this is often when trouble occurs, especially on weekend nights; fights are common as far too many intoxicated people converge on the streets at the same time. It's best to be back at your hotel well before that.

Joe's Café (536 State St., 805/966-4638, www.joescafesb.com, 7:30 A.M.–11 P.M. daily) undeniably serves the stiffest drinks in town. A renovation to the interior has produced an old-school feel to the place, harking back to its 1920s origins. It gets packed on weekends and is the only place on State Street with a neon sign.

The James Joyce (513 State St., 805/962-2688, www.sbjamesjoyce.com, 10 A.M.–2 A.M. daily) offers free darts and free peanuts, and the Guinness comes quickly from the tap. There is a great selection of other beers and whiskies as well. The walls are lined with photos of, we assume, Irishmen, and the tin ceiling and rugged feel of the place, not to mention the nice fireplace, means that there's usually an older crowd. A small dance floor in the back doesn't get much use, but the wood bar is a classic drinking spot.

The fairly authentic look and feel of the small **Old Kings Road** (532½ State St., 805/884-4085, http://oldkingsroadsb.com, noon–2 A.M. daily) is as close as you'll get to a British pub on the Central Coast. It's not filled with as many college-age kids and tends to be less rowdy, but that should not suggest a quiet gentlemen's tavern. Wednesday is quiz night, a very popular trivia game, and when darts are flying it's boisterous.

O'Malley's Bar (523 State St., 805/564-8904, noon–2 A.M. daily) has a giant-screen TV and draws big crowds for fight nights. There are plenty of smaller screens ringing the perimeter of the bar. The only drawback is that

no food is served, but they have no problem with patrons bringing in their own grub from one of the many establishments that line State Street. The antique bar at O'Malley's looks like a bar should look—wooden, thick, substantial, and well-worn.

The **Sandbar Mexican Restaurant and Tequila Bar** (514 State St., 805/966-1388, 11:30 A.M.–2 A.M. Sun.–Thurs., 9 A.M.–2 A.M. Fri.–Sat.) is a kind of rustic tequila bar with big cushioned love seats and chairs and at least 50 different tequilas available by the shot. The interior is small, and most people crave the patio fronting State Street, as that's where the action is. But you also might want to stay inside with the 20 plasma TVs and chow down on south-of-the-border food.

Elsie's Tavern (117 E. De La Guerra St., 805/963-4503, noon–2 A.M. Mon.–Fri., 4 P.M.–2 A.M. Sat.–Sun.) is an old garage that was turned into a tavern. There is a funky room with abandoned couches as you first enter, and as you make your way to the back, the space opens up with a bar and a pool table. It's low-key here: No one is really trying to impress anyone else, and the place has an almost lonely feel to it. Rotating shows of local art hang on the walls, and although it is close to downtown, it's a world away.

Located behind the *Santa Barbara News-Press* building is **The Press Room** (15 E. Ortega St., 805/963-8121, 11 A.M.–2 A.M. daily, sometimes earlier on weekends for TV sports), a little English bar with a great juke-box, stiff drinks, British pints, and a fine selection of whiskies. Game nights get noisy and crowded, like any bar, but this spot is usually chill enough for conversation and without the typical on-the-prowl types who make some bars uncomfortable. Posters of British bands like The Who cling to the old walls, and it's still on the inexpensive side.

LIVE MUSIC

Although Santa Barbara is home to a handful of well-known musicians, and there is always some guy with a guitar playing in a corner somewhere, live music is a small scene. One of the better spots is **Velvet Jones** (423 State St., 805/965-8676, www.velvet-jones.com, 8 P.M.–close daily), which offers live music seven nights a week, much of it up-and-comers from the Los Angeles area. The space isn't going for looks, but it does go for hard rock, ska, hip-hop, and anything other than popular and middle-of-the-road music. There is a tiny kitchen, and you can get hot dogs and pizza, but that's it. A small interior balcony and medium-size dance floor provides space so you're not crammed in, and a small gated front patio allows for cooling down.

Muddy Waters (508 E. Haley St., 805/966-9328, 6 A.M.–8 P.M. Mon.–Fri., 8 A.M.–8 P.M. Sat., cash only) has the distinct look of an unsupervised dorm room; it's unkempt and laidback, but it works. Local musicians, mostly playing alternative music, use this as a spot to work out their new songs, and local art hangs on the walls. The have open mike nights as well. Coffee drinks, a few brews, simple sandwiches, and Wi-Fi are on offer, but note that they only take cash. On scheduled performance nights the venue will stay open later, so call ahead for extended hours.

SOhO Restaurant and Music Club (1221 State St., 805/962-7776, www.sohosb.com, 6–10 P.M. daily) is the premier midsize venue in town. There's live music seven nights a week, and every Monday is jazz night. SOhO has seen its share of well-known performers, including David Crosby, Kenny Loggins, Rickie Lee Jones, Jimmy Cliff, the Mad Caddies, Acoustic Alchemy, and many others. The second-floor outdoor patio is a prime location to enjoy tunes under the stars in spring and summer. There is also a full bar and restaurant.

The outdoor **Santa Barbara Bowl** (1122 N. Milpas St., 805/962-7411, www.sbbowl.org), with just over 4,500 seats, is an intimate venue that brings in big A-list talent. It was originally built in the 1930s, but a renovation has greatly expanded the facilities. From its hillside location you can see the ocean and dance under the stars. There is no larger or more important music venue in town, and certainly for live music, this is the most beautiful.

Festivals and Events

SPRING

I Madonnari Italian Street Painting Festival (www.imadonnarifestival.com, free) is held at the Santa Barbara Mission every Memorial Day weekend. Adults aren't often encouraged to use chalk to draw on the sidewalk, but the parking lot in front of the mission is transformed from bleak black with more than 200 chalk paintings as artists, many local and some from across the globe, take chalk to asphalt and create beautiful reproductions of classic works as well as original art. The mission comes alive, and the lawn is crowded with food vendors, live music, picnics, and the chance to watch surprisingly beautiful art being created. For over 20 years it has been a perfect weekend stop if you're in town. Bring a picnic and munch on the lawn, or buy food here.

SUMMER

Woodies at the Beach (www.nationalwoodieclub.com, free) is one of the coolest local festivals, held in mid-August. About 100 woodies (wood-bodied vehicles), including cars, trucks, campers, and a handful of hot rods, grace the grassy bluffs at Santa Barbara City College overlooking Leadbetter Beach. There's live music, a surfboard raffle, and the chance to examine up close some beautifully restored classic cars. It's all free, and even if it's not your thing, it's worth a stop to admire a piece of the past. Everyone is wearing Hawaiian shirts and seems so relaxed that you'll easily end up making friends.

The **Solstice Parade** (www.solsticeparade.com, free) started in 1974 as an homage to local artists and a pseudo-celebration of the summer solstice and has exploded into a free-for-all of color, costume, political incorrectness, dance, music, and just plain summer revelry. Think of it as a family-oriented Mardi Gras, and you'll get the idea. Nearly 100,000 people cram the streets to celebrate the longest day of the year with the parade of funky floats and dancing in the streets, and 1,000 people end up volunteering in the effort. The after-party at Alameda Park is sometimes more fun than the parade itself, with drumming circles, more dancing, food, vendors, two live bands, and people wearing the bare minimum in the summer sun. Grab your tie-dyed T-shirt and join in.

Also known as Old Spanish Days, **Fiesta** (www.oldspanishdays-fiesta.org, some events free) is Santa Barbara's oldest and best-known festival, a five-day extravaganza held the first weekend of August. Started in 1924 to honor the Spanish and Mexican heritage of the city, Fiesta has blossomed into the second-largest equestrian parade in the United States and includes a feast of Mexican food and margaritas and an opportunity to see lots of dance. There are three *mercados* (market-places) around town with tortillas, burritos, tamales, tacos, and other Mexican food. There are also activities for the kids at the *mercados,* like climbing walls, mariachi bands, and carnival rides. During Fiesta, the Sunken Garden at the county courthouse is transformed for a free three-night event known as Las Noches de Ronda ("nights of gaiety"), with a stage where performers from across the globe dance *folklórico,* flamenco, and ballet, and belt out hip-hop and traditional Mexican songs, all under the beautiful evening skies of an August moon. The courthouse, lit up and shining in its magnificence, is a beautiful venue for the free concerts; all you need to do is grab a blanket or chair and a picnic, and you're set. During the Fiesta festivities, you'll see people walking all over town with baskets of hollowed-out eggs that are painted and filled with confetti; it's common to crack them over the heads of friends and loved ones and shout out, "Viva la Fiesta!"

FALL
It's fitting that Santa Barbara should have the **Harbor & Seafood Festival** (805/897-1962, www.harborfestival.org, free) each October; after all, the Santa Barbara Channel is one of the nation's richest sources of bountiful, sustainable seafood. Lobsters, ridgeback shrimps, rock crabs, white sea bass, California halibut, yellowtail, salmon, swordfish, thresher sharks, spot prawns, and sea urchins all thrive here,

and about 100 local anglers catch 6–10 million pounds of seafood annually. This one-day event brings out local fisherfolk, food vendors, and craftspeople, together with cooking demonstrations and U.S. Coast Guard vessels, all to celebrate the sea and our relationship with it and to edify the public about the fish they consume, the water they play in, and the men and women who hit the ocean each day to bring in fresh fish.

SHOPPING
The unique thing about Santa Barbara is that even the malls and shopping districts are visually interesting. These are all outdoor malls, but even in the rain they are still fun for hanging out.

Shopping Centers
La Arcada Court (1114 State St., 805/966-6634, www.laarcadasantabarbara.com) was conceived and built in 1926. Vines climb up walls, tiled fountains beckon you to sit and engage in conversation, colorful flags hang over the walkway, and local shops and sidewalk cafés abound. The mall, a paseo of sorts, has entrances on both State and Figueroa Streets. The mall abuts the Santa Barbara Museum of Art, and the main library is just beyond. You'll notice a few patrons who never move: full-size bronze sculptures, one of which takes up valuable space on a bench. Inside La Arcada are three art galleries, a vintage barber shop, a wine shop, and a few restaurants.

Paseo Nuevo (651 Paseo Nuevo, 805/963-7147, www.paseonuevoshopping.com), an outdoor mall with the ambience of a lazy afternoon, makes shopping fun even if you don't buy anything. The brick pathways meander along, vines climb the white walls, and fountains dispense water. From stores selling knives, candy, or cheese to restaurants and Nordstrom and Macy's, you'll find most everything at two-block-long Paseo Nuevo. This place took its cues and its name from its neighbor across the street, the historic El Paseo, which was Santa Barbara's original, but now obsolete, outdoor shopping complex.

Antiques

As the old saying goes, one person's trash is another's treasure, and antiques shopping is more treasure hunt than anything else.

Old Town Antiques (5799 Hollister Ave., Goleta, 805/967-2528, www.antiquesoldtown. com, 10 A.M.–6 P.M. Mon.–Sat., 11 A.M.–5 P.M. Sun.) in Goleta is a collective of 15 dealers and over 5,000 square feet of eclectic items, especially furniture. The pieces here are clean, unusual, and well-priced, since it is way off State Street. The inventory rotates regularly, with new merchandise coming in frequently.

Also off State Street is the **Antique Center Mall** (4434 Hollister Ave., 805/967-5700, www.antiquecentermall.com, 11 A.M.–6 P.M. Mon.–Sat., noon–5 P.M. Sun.), with nine rooms packed full of everything you can imagine. Of particular note is a very good selection of mid-century modern by a local dealer who knows her stuff; it's located right at the entrance. There is also a lot of wrought iron outdoor pieces and statuary as well as furniture, jewelry, and accessories.

Summerland, just south of Santa Barbara, has become a centralized location for antiques and furnishings. There are a dozen places on or just off Lillie Avenue, Summerland's main drag. The best, and oldest, is the **Summerland Antique Collective** (2192 Ortega Hill Rd., Summerland, 805/565-3189, http://summerlandantiquecollective.com, 10 A.M.–5 P.M. daily). For 30 years they've amassed over 45,000 square feet of everything you can imagine: mid-century modern, jewelry, retro, artworks, and garden furnishings.

More expensive, but with some amazing museum-quality items, **Summerhill Antiques** (2280 Lillie Ave., Summerland, 805/969-3366, www.summerhill-antiques.com, 11 A.M.–5 P.M. daily) has a lot of French and Asian furniture, accent pieces, tables, and unusual pieces such as 17th-century statuary. This is a place for the serious antiques lover.

Art Galleries

Santa Barbara has long been a draw for artists hoping to capture its stunning terrain, landscapes, seascapes, and whitewashed buildings with red-tile roofs. There is a focus in town on plein air, but it is by no means the only genre represented. Most galleries are bunched in the downtown area and have great accessibility, while a few other galleries dot the outer edges of the city. Beyond that, you're likely to see art hanging, and even artist receptions, in restaurants, salons, offices, and other businesses.

Sullivan Goss: An American Gallery (7 E. Anapamu St., 805/730-1460, www.sullivangoss.com, 10 A.M.–5:30 P.M. daily) is the best-known art gallery in town. Owner Frank Goss knows his stuff and hosts constant exhibitions showcasing top talent from across the United States, with an emphasis on 19th–21st-century works. Two side-by-side galleries create enough space to show oversize works. Sullivan Goss has a number of local artists on its large roster of clients and also looks to acquire new works.

The **Contemporary Arts Forum** (CAF, Paseo Nuevo Mall, 653 Paseo Nuevo, 805/966-5373, www.sbcaf.org, 11 A.M.–5 P.M. Tues.–Sat., noon–5 P.M. Sun., $5) is, as the name suggests, devoted to contemporary arts representing a wide range of artistic attitudes. CAF shows new works of local, regional, national, and international artists in a warehouse-size space and pushes the envelope with many of its exhibitions. Multimedia exhibits and performance art are common, if perhaps confusing; but CAF gives Santa Barbara much-needed exposure to diverse expressions.

The **Faulkner Gallery** (40 E. Anapamu St., 805/564-5608, 10 A.M.–8 P.M. Tues.–Thurs., 10 A.M.–5:30 P.M. Fri.–Sat., 1–5 P.M. Sun., free) is one of those places you'd rarely think about going, and if you didn't know it was there, you'd walk right past it. Located in a separate room inside the main branch of the public library, there is a large space with art exhibits rotating every few months, and two small side rooms with even more art. There's always something interesting, and everything is for sale at prices lower than those of traditional galleries. Mainly local artists exhibit here, and you just might make a very cool discovery.

The **Channing Peake Gallery** (105 E. Anapamu St., 1st Fl., 805/568-3994, www. sbartscommission.org, 8 A.M.–6 P.M. Mon.–Fri., free) is located on the ground floor of the County Administration building, which might seem odd if you didn't know that the Arts Commission, which runs the gallery and other artistic endeavors around town, is supported by the county government. The significant works include photography exhibits, art, poetry, and more. And who knows, you might just bump into a county supervisor while you're admiring the work.

BOOKSTORES

Santa Barbara has always been a refuge for literary types; Sue Grafton and T. C. Boyle are two of the writers who currently keep residences here. A couple of independent bookstores have unique charms.

The **Book Den** (15 E. Anapamu St., 805/962-3321, www.bookden.com, 10 A.M.–6 P.M. Mon.–Sat., noon–5 P.M. Sun.) is one of those places that smells a bit musty when you walk in, understandable in this case since it has been a bookstore since 1933. It's great for browsing, with a large selection of used, out of print, and antiquarian books as well as new titles housed on packed floor-to-ceiling shelves; a rolling ladder is needed to reach the top shelves. With 1.4 million volumes, they simply don't have room for them all in this small space.

Chaucer's Books (Loreto Plaza, 3321 State St., 805/682-6787, www.chaucersbooks.com, 9 A.M.–9 P.M. Mon.–Sat., 9 A.M.–8 P.M. Sun.) opened in 1974 and has become the premier independent bookstore in Santa Barbara. The events schedule is busy with book signings by local, regional, and national authors, and there's a huge selection ranging from the well-known to the obscure.

SPORTS AND RECREATION
Parks
Rocky Nook Park (610 Mission Canyon Rd., 805/568-2461, 8 A.M.–sunset daily) is a great spot for watching Mission Creek wander toward the mission. It is covered with, well,

rocks. This 19-acre park is a wonderful respite or place for a picnic with barbecue grills, picnic tables, hiking trails, horseshoes, a small playground, and restrooms.

From here you can head up Alameda Padre Serra to **Franceschi Park** (1510 Mission Ridge Rd., sunrise–sunset daily), home to a dilapidated old estate. The house, named for Italian horticulturist Francesco Franceschi, is closed to the public, but the 18-acre grounds are open and offer some of the best views of the city, harbor, and coast, especially at sunset. There's a small parking lot and a few picnic tables, and even a disturbingly dirty restroom. The view is narrowed by the eucalyptus trees, but they make a perfect frame for photos.

Skater's Point (Cabrillo Blvd. and Garden St., 9 A.M.–sunset daily) was one of those concepts that people decried when the idea was first floated: a concrete skate park at the beach? Over $800,000 later, it has proved a great success. Skateboards and bikes swoop up and down the ramps on nearly 15,000 square feet of concrete in full view of anyone who cares to watch, all within view of the Pacific Ocean. Skater's Point is located just east of Stearns Wharf in Chase Palm Park.

Alameda Park (1400 Santa Barbara St., 8 A.M.–sunset daily) is a wonderful two-block family-oriented picnic and playground spot that hosts the 8,000-square-foot Kids Zone playground, a medieval-looking fort with swings, slides, and climbing equipment. It is close to downtown, and you can usually find plenty of parking and a picnic table if you come early. Don't expect sunbathing, though, as the trees provide plenty of shade. There are restrooms, a small gazebo, and plenty of open spaces for Frisbee. This park is a centerpiece for many citywide celebrations, such as on the summer solstice.

Just across the street is the **Alice Keck Park Memorial Gardens** (1500 Santa Barbara St. at E. Arrellaga St., dawn–dusk daily), which is one of the city's most beautiful spots. The site used to house a grand hotel, and Alice Keck Park (that's her name, not the name of the park) deeded the plot of land to the city. Well-tended gardens surround an artificial pond with koi and turtles. Of special note is that the 75 different plant and tree species can be enjoyed by guests with vision or hearing difficulties, as there are braille signs and audio posts at specific spots to identify what has been planted. The walkway meanders around specialized planting beds that feature low-water-use species. It is a labor of love with a message: Beautiful plants don't have to consume lots of resources. The park is popular with both student and professional photographers, and every Saturday–Sunday you will find brides vying for position in front of the most beautiful flowers or splash of unique foliage to immortalize their big day. There are no facilities here; you'll have to head across the street to Alameda Park.

Golf

The breathtaking views at **Sandpiper Gold Course** (7925 Hollister Ave., 805/968-1541, www.sandpipergolf.com, dawn–dusk daily, $139–159) are classic Santa Barbara. Sandpiper is a par-72 course, which provides expert-level play on the bluffs above the ocean. The only oceanfront course between Los Angeles and Pebble Beach, this must-play course is rarely crowded.

The **Santa Barbara Golf Club** (3500 McCaw Ave., 805/687-7087, www.santabarbaraca.gov, dawn–dusk daily, $40–50) is a par-70 public course sitting on what used to be an airstrip. The course is dotted with eucalyptus trees, and there are peekaboo views of the Channel Islands. It's a beautiful course, and you may forget you're next to the freeway. The greens are a little slow for the avid golfer, but for a municipal course it's one of the best in the area and priced accordingly.

Hiking

Santa Barbara offers hikes for all difficulty levels in a variety of settings. The best place to start to plan a hike is www.santabarbarahikes.com. Here are some suggestions that will get you outside for some of the city's best views.

Rattlesnake Canyon is one of the more popular hikes and is fairly easy—and no, you probably won't come across any rattlesnakes; it was named for its winding canyon location. It's close to downtown, well marked, and less than four miles long. You'll pass pools and streams and eventually come out at the top of a small hill with panoramic views of the ocean. From the mission, take Mission Canyon Road north to Foothill Road. Turn right and make a quick left onto the continuation of Mission Canyon Road. After about 0.5 miles, make a sharp right at Los Conoas Lane, which will take you just over one mile to the old stone Rattlesnake Bridge over the creek. Park in one of the pullouts; the trailhead is clearly marked here.

Seven Falls has an elevation gain of 600 feet over a 2.5-mile path that follows Mission Creek through a gorge and across small waterfalls and deep pools, over boulders and sandstone rocks. It's a moderate hike, and when the creek is flowing unabated, the trail is alive with the sounds of water. To access the trail, from the mission take Mission Canyon Road north to Foothill Road. Turn right and make a quick left onto the continuation of Mission Canyon Road. The road divides—veer left, up the hill, on Tunnel Road. It's about one mile before the road ends. Park and walk to the end of Tunnel Road, staying on the pavement. You'll pass a gate, and the road splits off about 0.5 miles up; stay to the left. You'll cross a wooden bridge over Mission Creek, with Fern Canyon Falls right below. At just under one mile, the road ends at a trail split. The right fork is a fire road, but take the left fork, the Jesusita Trail, which drops into Mission Canyon. Once you cross the next creek, take the narrow path to the right, which runs up the west side of the canyon. This is not a very well-maintained trail and requires scampering over boulders, but you'll soon come to the waterfalls and pools.

Biking

Off-road, on major streets, by the beach—anywhere you go in town you'll see someone on a bike. From flat beachfront rides to tough mountain roads, there is something for every skill level. Lance Armstrong used to train in the mountains here, and there are hard-core cyclists everywhere. Regardless of your skill level, when you come up behind another cyclist, always call out "on your left" to alert the rider to move over to the right. Contact Traffic Solutions (805/963-7283, www.trafficsolutions.info) to obtain a copy of the free and excellent Santa Barbara County bike map. If renting, consider a mountain bike over a touring bike; the slightly beefy tires are perfect for getting off-road and even riding on the sand. Yes, you'll have a slower pace, but you'll be able to go anywhere the mood strikes you.

The **Foothill Route,** also known as Highway 192 or Cathedral Oaks, alternates between narrow stretches of road around Mission Canyon to flat wide streets near Winchester Canyon and the beach in Goleta. It is very popular because of its many hills, and you can ride from the beach in Goleta all the way to Ojai. There is a lot of traffic around the Mission Canyon area; as the road climbs it twists and turns, and cyclists need to be on the lookout for cars coming around blind curves. Between Mission Canyon and Goleta, the road widens and runs past avocado orchards and citrus ranches until it leads into Winchester Canyon by the water.

For the most part, the **Coast Route** bike path hugs the coast near the waterfront, then climbs into a residential area and drops down again near Arroyo Burro Beach. From here, the path climbs into Hope Ranch, a beautiful and well-to-do section of Santa Barbara with a stunning number of mature trees. Eventually you hit the Atascadero Bike Path, which runs through low marshlands before arriving at the University of California, Santa Barbara. You can continue on through campus to hook up with the Foothill Route and make a wide loop, but it's a taxing ride.

Water Activities
WHALE-WATCHING AND SUNSET CRUISES
There is nothing like the thrill of seeing a whale, a pod of dolphins ripping through the surf, or the tranquil simplicity of a sunset cruise. These boats offer a variety of excursions. Most places will offer you another trip if you don't see any whales. But remember, a small break in the water as one of these magnificent creatures takes in air might count as a sighting.

Sunset Kidd Sailing (12 Harbor Way, 805/962-8222, www.sunsetkidd.com, 8 A.M.–7 P.M. daily, from $40) offers private charters and morning, afternoon, evening, and full-moon cruises on its 41-foot sailing yacht. It can accommodate about 18 people, so it's not a crowded outing and you're not fighting to get to the sides to see things. It's a great ship in that on the return to the harbor, they generally cut the motor and rig the sails for a quiet entrance. But remember, this is a sailboat, so there's a lot of up and down movement.

In contrast, **Condor Cruises** (301 W. Cabrillo Blvd., 805/882-0088, www.condorcruises.com, whale-watching tour $50–85) is a 75-foot high-speed catamaran, which means you move across the water quickly rather than sailing. This is a more stable ride for those prone to motion sickness. Whale-watching cruises run about 2.5 hours. Condor also offers a full roster of cruises and excursions, including bird-watching trips. Those trips are usually about two hours and have an open bar and light food.

KAYAKING
Sitting low in a kayak allows you to really experience the water. Kayaking need not be a strenuous activity, and paddling is not difficult. You can rent kayaks for an hour or longer and explore the coast easily and up close—pack food with you and you can choose a beach for a picnic. All rental places will train you in basic safety. If you do launch from the harbor and choose to pass the breakwater, there is a green buoy 0.5 miles straight out that is usually packed with seals basking in the sun. Make a slow approach, and you can easily get within five feet of them. Otherwise, just enjoy the coast, but remember that it's easy to paddle out and it's always longer to come back. Winds, currents, and fatigue could mean it ends up being a

longer day than you had planned. Always take water and sun protection with you.

There are also companies offering guided tours of the Channel Islands, including some of the sea caves on Anacapa and Santa Cruz Islands. Some of the caves go several hundred feet into the islands and are simply spectacular with their soft color palettes of ochers, blues, and greens. Don't ever attempt to kayak into a sea cave without a knowledgeable person with you. The surges can easily lift your kayak up and smash you into the roof or sides of the caves. Yes, the caves are enticing, but if you don't know the area and how the surges affect the caves, you're asking for problems.

Paddle Sports (117B Harbor Way, 805/617-3425, www.kayaksb.com, basic kayak rental $25 for 2 hours) has been around for 20 years and has a great staff. You can rent and get trained in both kayaking and paddle surfing. They also rent pedal kayaks so you can save your arms.

The **Santa Barbara Sailing Center** (Santa Barbara Harbor, 800/350-9090, www.sbsail.com, basic kayak rental $10–15 per hour) will also take you to the islands or just along the coast. They provide single and tandem kayaks and can provide extensive kayak instruction if you want to get really serious.

Spas

Healing Circle Massage (805/680-1984, www.healingcirclemassage.com, 10 A.M.–7 P.M. daily, by appointment only, basic one-hour massage $80) is where you go to get the kinks worked out. This isn't fluffy pampering with hot stones while sipping cocktails; this is serious deep-tissue and trigger-point work. Owner Kathy Gruver works on hard-core athletes and anyone with chronic pain–related problems, and specializes in medical and therapeutic massage—not for the faint of heart. In addition to returning range of motion to stressed-out individuals, she also does prenatal massage, health consultations, Reiki, and Bach flower remedies. While many places actually give you a 50-minute massage and call it an hour, at Healing Circle you get a full hour.

Acupuncture, aromatherapy, spa parties, warm seaweed wraps, and waxing are just some of the offerings from **Crimson Day Spa** (31 Parker Way, 805/563-7546, www.crimsondayspa.com, noon–4 P.M. Mon., 10 A.M.–5:30 P.M. Tues., 10 A.M.–6 P.M. Wed.–Sat., and by appointment, basic one-hour massage $80). The space is uncluttered, with nice decor touches to suggest relaxation. Staff are very professional and have developed a loyal following.

Avia Spa (350 Chapala St., 805/730-7303, www.aviaspa.com, 10 A.M.–6 P.M. Tues.–Sat., noon–5 P.M. Sun.–Mon., basic one-hour massage $100) offers a wealth of services, including tanning beds (both sunless and UV), massage, and salon and spa services like nail and foot care, all housed in a bamboo-accented interior with wood floors and Asian-inspired decor. They also have their own line of skincare products.

Float Luxury Spa (18 E. Canon Perdido St., 805/845-7777, www.floatluxuryspa.com, 9 A.M.–7 P.M. Mon.–Sat., 10 A.M.–6 P.M. Sun., basic 50-minute massage $100) is one of the newest additions to the spa scene, aiming for the day-spa concept where you can stay for hours. Located downtown, the space is surprisingly large, sleek, and uncluttered. They offer the usual treatments, including massage and facials, but out back is a beautiful rectangular tiled reflecting pool, a great spot to get lunch or to take a deep breath. Upstairs is a quiet space, a nearly completely white room with chairs fronting a fireplace where you can sit and detox.

ACCOMMODATIONS

Santa Barbara has never been an inexpensive place to stay. Regardless of time of year, weather, and even the economic downturn, people continue to flock to the area—and they pay for the privilege of hanging out here. Be prepared to spend some cash, and don't expect much negotiating. The bed tax is currently at 12 percent; make sure to factor that into your travel plans and budget. Most properties require a two-night minimum stay during the peak summer season.

Downtown

The great thing about staying downtown is that you don't need a car. You walk out your door and you're close to shopping, restaurants, galleries, and bars. On the flip side, weekend evenings can get noisy, and there's a lot of foot traffic on State Street.

$150-250

The Presidio Motel (1620 State St., 805/963-1355, www.thepresidiomotel.com, $180–230 d) is a very cool motel several blocks up State Street. The 16 guest rooms are minimalist, but each one has unique designs created by University of California, Santa Barbara students, such as abstract stars or a girl holding a parasol as she walks a tightrope above the gaping jaws of an alligator. It's not in the thick of things, but you can still easily access many activities by walking a little farther. They have six complimentary beach cruisers so you can explore on two wheels and an upstairs sun deck from which to watch the happenings on State. Premium coffee and tea and free Wi-Fi add to the allure. The young owners are dedicated to making the motel a must-stop for those who want something different.

At the **Best Western Plus Encina Lodge & Suites** (2220 Bath St., 805/682-7277, www.encinalodge.com, $175–240 d), the 122 good-size guest rooms are decorated with a country motif; the suites are great for extended stays. Located on a residential street near a hospital, it's an out-of-the-way place and fairly quiet. It has a heated pool, a small aviary, free Wi-Fi, and free shuttle service to the airport and train station. It's not really within walking distance of much, so you will probably need a car if you stay here.

Similar in style is the 1894 Queen Anne **Cheshire Cat Inn** (36 W. Valerio St., 805/569-1610, www.cheshirecat.com, $200–350 d), whose 18 guest rooms and cottages have an Alice in Wonderland theme, although not in the wild, goofy colors you might expect. There's a restrained English country feel, and some guest rooms have fireplaces, hot tubs, and balconies. Full breakfasts (weekends)

and continental breakfasts (weekdays) are included, as is an evening wine and cheese reception (5–6 P.M.); there's free Wi-Fi and off-street parking. It's quiet here, in spite of being just a few blocks from the action on State Street.

If being right downtown is what you want, the **Hotel Santa Barbara** (533 State St., 805/957-9300, www.hotelsantabarbara. com, $199–219 d) is a good choice—it's on State Street, where the action is, and everything is within walking distance. The 75 guest rooms are nicely appointed and comfortable, although the standard rooms are a tad small. Copious amounts of tile work inside will give you that Santa Barbara feel. The pillows are either down, feather, or hypoallergenic. There are in-room coffeemakers, but there's also a Starbucks outlet on the premises. There is no on-site workout equipment, but a nearby gym has a $10-per-day rate for hotel guests. Basic continental breakfast is offered 7–10 A.M.

OVER $250

The **(Inn of the Spanish Garden** (915 Garden St., 805/564-4700, www.spanishgardeninn.com, $350–400) is so under the radar that most locals don't even know where it is. Near State Street, this Spanish-style full-service hotel aims for stellar service while keeping a low profile. All 23 guest rooms are beautifully appointed and have either balconies or patios facing a central courtyard. It has high-end linens and French-press coffeemakers, plus large baths. It's an easy three-block walk to the action, but you'll love returning to the luxurious beds, deep bathtubs, and large showers. It's something of a secret that many celebrities stay here because it's so low-key.

(The Upham Hotel (1404 De La Vina St., 805/962-0058, www.uphamhotel.com, $265–280 d) is the oldest continuously operating hotel in Santa Barbara, having opened its doors as the Lincoln House in 1871. A Historic Hotel of America, the property has seven buildings, though it feels much more intimate and is mostly centered around a garden courtyard. There are smaller guest rooms, ideal for a busy weekend, or larger guest rooms with fireplaces for a stay-in weekend. The Upham has an attached restaurant, Louie's, but you're also within walking distance of State Street or a cab ride from the beach. There are varying degrees of antiquity within the hotel, with some guest rooms dating to the 1800s and 1920s.

Also quiet is the remarkable **James House Santa Barbara** (1632 Chapala St., 805/569-5853, www.jameshousesantabarbara.com, $259 d), a historic 1894 Queen Anne property with only five guest rooms, nicely appointed with period-style furnishings and hardwood floors. The baths have all been upgraded to more modern amenities, but the guest rooms will remind you of a time gone by. Breakfast, cooked by the owner, is served each morning. People return again and again for the hospitality, the small size, the walking distance to much of State Street, and the thrill of being in a place where time slows down.

The **Simpson House Inn** (121 E. Arrellaga St., 805/963-7067, www.simpsonhouseinn.com, $350–475 d) bed-and-breakfast features 15 opulent guest rooms on an 1874 estate with a well-manicured and formal English garden—you'll feel like you're in another world. A vegetarian breakfast starts the day, afternoon tea and desserts are available, and there is wine-tasting with four choices in the evening. Simpson House offers a day pass ($20) to a local fitness club, and they boast gratuity-free services. Situated on a corner lot in a residential neighborhood, it's a short walk to State Street.

Oceanfront
$150-250
The **Harbor House Inn** (104 Bath St., 805/962-9745, www.harborhouseinn.com, $175–225 d) is a great little property a block from the water. They'll loan you beach towels, chairs, and umbrellas for lounging at West Beach along with bikes to ride. Other amenities include Wi-Fi and a DVD library. The 17 guest rooms and studios are surprisingly well appointed, with a more home-like feel than most hotels. Best of all, you won't break the bank.

The **Avania Inn** (128 Castillo St., 805/963-4471, www.avaniainnsantabarbara.com, $240–250 d) is just a block up from the beach in an unremarkable two-story motel building, but the 46 guest rooms have a hip pseudo-1950s retro flair, and you'll save some clams. Perhaps the best amenity, in addition to a simple breakfast and proximity to the beach, is the small redwood spa and heated outdoor pool. A free morning paper helps you plan your day.

The **Villa Rosa Inn** (15 Chapala St., 805/966-0851, www.villarosainnsb.com, $229–279 d) is deceptive from the outside: The small door in what looks like someone's house seems nearly hidden, except for the sign. But beyond the door is a beautiful hideaway with a Mediterranean feel and luxurious antiques. The 18 guest rooms are all different, and it's intimate and very comfortable. Most guest rooms have views of the ocean, mountains, harbor, or courtyard, though some are constrained and the baths are a little small. The staff recommends room 13, which has a view of Stearns Wharf and the ocean. Villa Rosa claims to be only 84 steps from the beach. They offer evening port or sherry by the fire and a continental breakfast.

The 43 guest rooms at the **Inn by the Harbor** (433 W. Montecito St., 805/963-7851, www.innbytheharbor.com, $220–250 d) are all decorated slightly differently with Spanish Mediterranean–style furnishings. Many rooms feature full-size kitchens, ideal for budget vacations or extended stays. In addition to a deluxe continental breakfast and afternoon wine and cheese, they serve evening milk and cookies. Bud Bottoms, a local artist who created the bronze dolphins that are at the entrance to Stearns Wharf, created the dolphin sculpture in front of the inn.

Right across from the Carriage Museum, the **Mason Beach Inn** (324 W. Mason St., 805/962-3203, www.masonbeachinn.com, $149–239 d) is a pretty simple whitewashed hotel with 45 guest rooms that feature standard furnishings. It's clean but not fancy and is a fine base for accessing the beach and downtown while saving some cash. Amenities include a heated outdoor pool and hot tub, basic continental breakfast, and free Wi-Fi.

OVER $250

(Brisas del Mar (223 Castillo St., 805/966-2219, www.brisasdelmarinn.com, $250–280 d) is located just two blocks from the beach. Half of the 31 guest rooms are larger suites with full kitchens, great for a longer getaway. Although the exterior is Mediterranean, the interiors have knotty pine furnishings and soft tones. There's covered parking, unusual for most hotels in town, as well as a collection of more than 1,000 DVDs, free Wi-Fi, an exercise room, continental breakfast, bike rental, wine and cheese receptions, and gracious staff.

Upper State Street

Staying just outside the money zone is not necessarily a bad idea. Sure, you don't have the ocean views and are not close to downtown, but if you save some cash on your room, you can spend it elsewhere.

UNDER $150

The delightfully hip and simple **Agave Inn** (3222 State St., 805/687-6009, www.agaveinnsb.com, $119–189 d) uses the Spanish theme a little differently: Spanish movie posters and brightly colored throws as well as various brightly painted walls are the accents that set this place apart. A bit of modern pop flavors each of the 13 guest rooms, where you'll find iPod docks, and some have full kitchens. Agave Inn is directly across from a small park and near Loreto Plaza, a small shopping center with a grocery store and restaurants. The freeway is close, as is downtown.

Goleta
$150-250

Ramada Limited (4770 Calle Real, Santa Barbara, near Goleta, 805/964-3511, www.sbramada.com, $190–220 d) is a locally owned and operated Ramada about 10 minutes' drive from downtown. The best of the 126 guest rooms and suites face the mountains, and every room has a small refrigerator, a microwave,

and a coffeemaker. Near the outdoor pool is an amazing tropical lagoon with water lilies, palms, and koi. The guest rooms are standard, but also less expensive than downtown.

Montecito
$150-250

Charlie Chaplin founded the **(Montecito Inn** (1295 Coast Village Rd., 805/969-7854, www.montecitoinn.com, $220–285 d) in the late 1920s when he wanted a getaway from the hectic Hollywood scene. He built the inn more for his friends to escape with him than as an actual inn. These days the wonderful historic property is as charming as it was intended to be. The 61 guest rooms are small, the halls even smaller, but that's how life was back then. Vintage Chaplin posters line the walls, and there's a collection of Chaplin's films to watch on DVD in your room. Visitors also have free use of the beach cruisers, or jump into the heated pool or sweat in the exercise room. The hotel is only three blocks from the beach and on Coast Village Road, the heart of the tony Montecito shopping district.

FOOD

There's a long-standing claim that Santa Barbara has more restaurants per capita than any other place in the United States. That has never been disproven, but with everything from taco stands to five-star restaurants, you will definitely find something you like. Tourist-oriented places are not always the best choice. There's a lot of average food in town, so seek out the exceptional.

Downtown

Many restaurants in downtown Santa Barbara have outdoor seating, and it's not unusual to see long waits on summer nights. Not all places take reservations, but many do—make reservations if you can. Many of the restaurants serve what is loosely labeled "wine country cuisine," which is to say local fresh foods and ingredients used in lighter dishes that pair well with local wines. Specifically, this means fresh fish from the harbor, fresh veggies and fruits from the many local farmers, and locally sourced meats—not processed foods, but foods that are inherently flavorful.

CHEAP EATS

Quick and easy is always a good option, especially when it's coupled with good prices.

D'Vine Café (205 W. Canon Perdido St., 805/963-9591, www.dvinecafe.com, 8 A.M.–4 P.M. Mon.–Fri., 11 A.M.–3 P.M. Sat., $8) has been crafting sandwiches and salads for years, creating inexpensive, portable food that does not shock your wallet nor offend your taste buds. Insanely popular is the grilled salmon salad, and the chicken salad sandwich is great. They make wraps, and you can customize you sandwich in either whole or half size. The place is basic to look at—indoor and outdoor seating with lots of plastic chairs—but for made-to-order food at these prices, you won't go wrong.

FRENCH

Often overlooked, **Pacific Crêpes** (705 Anacapa St., 805/882-1123, www.pacific-crepe.com, 10 A.M.–3 P.M. and 5:30–9 P.M. Tues.–Fri., 9 A.M.–9 P.M. Sat., 9 A.M.–3 P.M. Sun., $18) is a delightful spot. The interior is laden with French posters, and books line the walls. It's an intimate space with simple French country decor and indoor and outdoor seating. Buckwheat is a main ingredient—traditional for crepes in Brittany, where the owners are from—hence the brown color. The fillings are diverse, and the crepes are surprisingly large. Be sure to try the French onion soup, escargot, and the wonderful profiteroles. A conversational French Club meets 5:30–7 P.M. Wednesday.

HEALTHY FARE

Don't be alarmed by the word *vegetarian* if you're a carnivore. The **Sojourner Cafe** (134 E. Canon Perdido St., 805/965-7922, www.sojournercafe.com, 11 A.M.–10 P.M. Sun.–Wed., 11 A.M.–11 P.M. Thurs.–Sat., $10), or "The Soj," as it's called, will make you rethink how good vegetarian can be. Celebrating

30 years in business, they turn out some of the best food in town, with amazingly flavorful smoothies, fresh-baked cookies, and daily specials. The interior needs a face-lift, but that doesn't detract from the polenta royale, the Cobb salad using hominy, or the cornbread supreme, doused with pinto beans, veggies, garlic butter, and cheese.

WINE COUNTRY CUISINE

At **Julienne** (138 E. Canon Perdido St., 805/845-6488, www.restaurantjulienne.com, 5–10 P.M. Wed.–Sat., 5–9 P.M. Sun., $25), chef Justin West uses vegetables pulled from the ground that day and seafood that arrived on the dock that morning. The small space, with only 12 tables, has a bistro feel to it, and the menu rotates as often as every few days, so you can't usually come back and order the same thing. The menu is limited, and at first you might think you want more options. But the food and service are excellent; be adventurous and let the thoughtfully prepared food work its magic. Things you may have thought you didn't like are masterpieces in the chef's hands.

Arts & Letters Café (7 E. Anapamu St., 805/730-1463, www.sullivangoss.com, lunch 11 A.M.–2:30 P.M. Mon.–Sun. year-round, dinner 5–9 P.M. Wed.–Sun. summer, $18) is behind the Sullivan Goss Art Gallery, and you need to walk through the gallery to reach the secluded back patio. Try their excellent pumpkin soup, written up in the *New York Times,* the smoked-salmon pot stickers, or the very best salad, with warm lamb on top of baby spinach with feta cheese. You'll be looking at beautiful art on the walls, and beautiful food on your plate. You needn't buy any art, but you might be so pleased with your meal that a new painting could be the perfect ending.

COFFEE AND TEA

There are always the ubiquitous national coffee chains, but you can go local: At **The Daily Grind** (2001 De La Vina St., 805/687-4966, 5:30 A.M.–8 P.M. daily, cash only), one of the most popular early morning places, the prime seats on the outside deck always seem to be taken, but there is an indoor seating area near the counter as well. Teas, smoothies, and an abundance of coffee drinks and 11 regular coffees are at the ready. A variety of pastries made on-site and breakfast and lunch options are served.

Oceanfront

For better or worse, the oceanfront offers a collection of average restaurants with great views. The food is standard, and the service is usually hit-or-miss. Most visitors want ocean views, understandably, but you may find it best to search out better food to avoid being frustrated by a bad experience. The ocean is visible from much of Santa Barbara, so save your cash for quality food, then go walk on the beach.

SANDWICHES AND BURGERS

Metropulos (216 E. Yanonali St., 805/899-2300, www.metrofinefoods.com, 8:30 A.M.–6 P.M. Mon.–Fri., 10 A.M.–4 P.M. Sat., $10) is a mere block from the beach and is the best place to stop to gather picnic supplies. Get a sandwich or salad to go, or some of the many olives from Africa, Spain, and Italy. The sandwiches, such as the apple, ham, and brie panini on multigrain sourdough, are wonderful. Or try a cranberry goat cheese salad with spinach and organic mixed greens. There is also a small wine shop, colorful and creative pastas to cook at home, and a really moist chocolate biscotti. There are a handful of prime outdoor seats.

SEAFOOD

◖ **Brophy Brothers Restaurant & Clam Bar** (119 Harbor Way, 805/966-4418, www.brophybros.com, 11 A.M.–10 P.M. Sun.–Thurs., 11 A.M.–11 P.M. Fri.–Sat., $25) is the exception to the oceanfront rule. Located at the harbor, it is eternally busy serving fresh local seafood in a hectic, loud environment. The prime seats are outside on a narrow strip of balcony crowded with people standing at the outdoor bar. Have a sunset dinner of fresh seafood here overlooking the boats. Side dishes such as salad,

coleslaw, and rice seem like afterthoughts, but the entrées are exceptional. There is a raw oyster bar, and the staff, while busy, are efficient. Brophy Brothers doesn't take reservations, so you may find yourself in their downstairs bar waiting to be called.

Upper State Street

Far from the madding crowds—well, not too far—State Street as everyone knows it turns into Upper State Street, a decidedly different place than what most visitors see. It is mainly residential, with some restaurants worth checking out.

BREAKFAST AND BRUNCH

If you've ever been to Paris and eaten a fresh baguette, you know heaven can look like a loaf of bread. Classic French pastries and breads are loaded with real butter, cream, and plenty of calories at **Renaud's Patisserie and Bistro** (3315 State St., 805/569-2400, http://renaudsbakery.com, 7 A.M.–5 P.M. Mon.–Sat., 7 A.M.–3 P.M. Sun., $15), which also has the best croissants in the city. Their classic European breakfast basket, containing a croissant and toasted baguette with butter and jam, plus coffee or tea, will transport you to Paris. For those who need something more, quiche lorraine, *pan-bagnat,* and cheese *ravioletis* will satisfy you. Save room for any of the sweets. It's run by a Frenchman, so you know you're getting authentic French food.

GERMAN

Brummis (3130 State St., 805/687-5916, www.brummis-restaurant.com, 5–9 P.M. Mon.–Sat., $20) has an inside decor as simple as spaetzle—all bare bones with a few posters hanging loosely on the walls. But the restaurant, run by a mother and daughter from Germany, is as authentic as you can get. A few German beers are available to complement your meal, and it's not uncommon to hear conversations in German around you. Schnitzel, sauerbraten, and *kasslerbraten* will put the oompah in you if you have a hankering for German food.

ITALIAN

(◖ Via Maestra 42 (3343 State St., 805/569-6522, 8:30 A.M.–9 P.M. Mon.–Sat., 11 A.M.–5 P.M. Sun., $15), named for the owner's address in his hometown in Italy, is located in an unremarkable strip mall next to the post office but turns out delicious, authentic Italian food, including a wide variety of pastas and cured meats. The space is small, with a few outside seats, so it gets crowded, and the service is a tad slow, but it's worth the wait. You can also buy Italian cheeses, meats, and gelato to go. During truffle season, both white and black truffles are imported from Italy. You can buy them here, as several restaurants in town do.

SUSHI

Kyoto (3232 State St., 805/687-1252, www.kyotosb.com, lunch 11:30 A.M.–2 P.M. Mon.–Fri., noon–2:30 P.M. Sat., dinner 5–10 P.M. Sun.–Thurs., 5–10:30 P.M. Fri.–Sat., $20) is on the opposite end of Upper State Street in a spot that has been a sushi restaurant for 30 years. Eight booths face the four tatami rooms; a separate sushi bar is sequestered behind a pony wall. There's a great price-to-value ratio, enhanced by the nightly sushi happy hour (5–6 P.M.) when the small space gets crowded and 40 rolls and *nigiri* are 50 percent off. For those who don't like sushi, there's plenty of tempura and hibachi, served by a family who is genuinely glad you're here.

Goleta

No longer Santa Barbara's unincorporated sister, Goleta became a city in 2002. Although the area is predominantly residential, there are more and more restaurants moving in to serve the residents who don't want to make the trek downtown.

CHINESE

Red Pepper (282 Orange Ave., 805/964-0995, 11 A.M.–2 P.M. and 5–8:30 P.M. Mon.–Fri., noon–2 P.M. and 5–8:30 P.M. Sat., $15) is a wonderful local Chinese restaurant in Goleta, incongruously located next to a plumber and

a locksmith. Although the ambience is sparse and frankly uninteresting—unless you consider the nine-pound koi in the fish tank an intriguing sight—the food makes up for the decor. The onion pancakes are a great start to any vegetarian or meat dish, and the hot-and-sour soup lives up to its name. As you leave you'll get a hug from the owner.

PIZZA

Pizza may be ubiquitous, but it's not all the same; **Gina's Pizza** (7038 Marketplace Dr., 805/571-6300, www.ginaspizzaingoleta.com, 9 A.M.–10 P.M. Mon.–Fri., 10 A.M.–11 P.M. Sat.–Sun., $15) serves some of the best in the city. Whether you order Hawaiian style, meat lovers, or even vegetarian, what sets this place apart is the copious use of fresh ingredients and an exceptional crust. You can order thick or thin crust, and the sauce is kept to a minimum. The ingredients are well spaced, so each bite gives you comprehensive flavors. They also have pasta dishes such as lasagna as well as minestrone soup.

Carpinteria

Just south of Santa Barbara, Carpinteria is attempting to assert itself as a dining destination along Linden Avenue, and it is going quite well.

AMERICAN

For a throwback to a long-ago dining era, **Clementine's Steakhouse** (4631 Carpinteria Ave., 805/684-5119, 5–9 P.M. Wed.–Sun., $22) is your place. Schmaltzy music plays over the speakers, the older clientele talks quietly, the decor is 1960s country—and you can't help but smile. Burgundy tablecloths contrast with pink scalloped napkins, and nearly everyone leaves with leftovers. All entrées come with a crudités plate; house-baked bread, soup, and salad, along with a choice of side dish; and finally home-baked pie. It's a tremendous amount of food, and they haven't changed their formula in over 30 years. Steaks, fresh fish, chicken, and pastas plus all those sides will make you very full.

Farmers Markets

Santa Barbara County hosts about a dozen farmers markets each week. The markets are just as much for socializing as getting lemon basil or torpedo onions. Strolling musicians entertain while local chefs scour the stalls for what they'll serve that evening. Check out www.sbfarmersmarket.org for a complete schedule. The markets are held all over the county, including Goleta, Montecito, and Carpinteria, but the biggest and best are the Saturday-morning **downtown market** (Santa Barbara St. and Cota St., 8:30 A.M.–1 P.M. Sat.), which is the largest and most social, and the Tuesday-afternoon **State Street market** (500–600 blocks of State St., 4–7:30 P.M. Tues. summer, 3–6:30 P.M. Tues. winter). Be advised that the Tuesday market shuts down parts of State Street, and drivers are rerouted.

INFORMATION AND SERVICES

The **Santa Barbara Chamber of Commerce Visitors Center** (1 Garden St., 805/965-3021, www.sbchamber.org, 9 A.M.–4 P.M. Mon.–Sat., 10 A.M.–4 P.M. Sun.) is located directly across from the beach and offers discounts to many restaurants and sights in town.

John Dickson has put together a most comprehensive website, www.santabarbara.com, that includes things to do and reviews of hotels and restaurant by locals. Some of the information is out of date, but it's still a valuable resource. And www.santabarbaraca.com is the official website for the visitors center, with an up-to-date section of maps you can download as well as the latest specials and deals.

Many local retailers offer the **Axxess Book** (www.sbaxxess.com), a coupon book that costs $30 but allows a number of two-for-one wine tastings and discounts at area restaurants, golf, and sights.

In case of emergency, call **911. Santa Barbara Cottage Hospital** (Bath St. and Pueblo St.) is the only hospital in town and has the only emergency room. The **Santa Barbara Police Department** (805/897-2330) is located at 215 East Figueroa Street.

GETTING THERE

The **Santa Barbara Airport** (SBA, 601 Firestone Rd., 805/967-7111, www.flysba.com) is a small airport that currently has only regional flights from about 10 destinations on four airlines.

Chances are you'll fly into Los Angeles or San Francisco and then connect to Santa Barbara. If you're coming from L.A. and not connecting to Santa Barbara by air, the 90-mile drive takes about two hours. There are commercial shuttle vans and buses from LAX, but keep in mind these will also take two-plus hours, depending on traffic. **Santa Barbara Air Bus** (805/964-7759, www.santabarbaraairbus.com) runs between LAX and Santa Barbara every day and will deliver you in comfort.

By car, the only entrance to Santa Barbara north or south is U.S. 101, a four-lane highway that is reasonably traffic free—at least so far. Exits and off-ramps are clearly marked, and you'll know you are getting close when you see the ocean out your window.

Greyhound (34 W. Carrillo St., 805/965-7551, www.greyhound.com) has a somewhat dingy hub terminal a block off State Street.

Amtrak (209 State St., 805/963-1015, www.amtrak.com) trains *Pacific Surfliner* and *Coast Starlight* pull into Santa Barbara's 1905 depot right on State Street, one block from the beach.

GETTING AROUND

A great resource for bike trails, walking paths, train info, taxi cabs, water excursions, and all manner of transportation is www.santabarbaracarfree.com, which offers downloadable maps and ways to experience Santa Barbara while reducing your carbon footprint.

It's important to make a note about the unusual orientation of Santa Barbara. As you stand at the water's edge near the harbor, it would be easy to assume you are facing west—but you are actually looking southeast. It's a geographical oddity, but it's important to know in order to get your bearings. The city of Goleta is to the west (up the coast), and to the east (down the coast) are the unincorporated areas of Montecito,

© MICHAEL CERVIN

If you arrive in Santa Barbara by train, you'll land at this 1905 train station, a block from the beach.

Summerland, and the City of Carpinteria, which abuts the Ventura county line.

Driving and Parking

Laid out in a grid pattern, the city is easy to navigate, at least the downtown core. Of particular note is that State Street, the defining street, runs northwest from the oceanfront and then makes a 90-degree bend to run east–west, where it's known as Upper State Street. Eventually State Street turns into Hollister Avenue, and by then you are entering Goleta. But all things fan out from State Street, and most directions are given in relationship to it.

The other thing to consider is that although most streets have unique names, three streets can cause confusion: Castillo, Carrillo, and Cabrillo. Here's all you need to know: Cabrillo (think of the *b* as in "beach") runs the length of the waterfront. Carrillo (think of the *r* as in "running right through town") bisects State Street in the middle of downtown. And Castillo (think of the *s* for "State") parallels State Street. If you keep that in mind, it should be easier to get around.

In general, parking is pretty easy. There are a number of parking lots in the downtown area, and street parking is mostly 75 minutes for free. But be advised that parking rules are enforced, and you will be ticketed if you go over your allotted time; parking tickets are $50.

Walking Tours

Seeing Santa Barbara on foot is the best way to experience the city. The **Red Tile Walking Tour** (www.santabarbaraca.com) is a condensed 12-block self-guided tour of all the important buildings in town. You can download a map version to print or a podcast version narrated by John O'Hurley (of TV's *Seinfeld*). You'll see Casa de la Guerra, the county courthouse, and the presidio, among other defining buildings.

For a more structured tour, **Santa Barbara Walking Tours** (800/979-3370, www.santabarawalkingtours.com, $23) has a 90-minute docent-led tour of the visual art and history in town. It combines parts of the Red Tile tour but also shows you some of the city's beautiful paseos, tile work, and public art.

Trolley Tours

If walking just isn't your thing, get an expanded overview of the city by riding through it. The best is the **Land Shark** (805/683-7600, www.out2seesb.com, noon and 2 P.M. daily Nov.–Apr., noon, 2 P.M., and 4 P.M. daily

LA PURISIMA MISSION

Located in a lonely valley between San Luis Obispo and Santa Barbara, Misión La Purísima Concepción de María Santísima (2295 Purísima Rd., Lompoc, 805/733-3713, www.laPurísimamission.org, self-guided tours 9 A.M.–5 P.M. daily, free 60-90-minute guided tours 1 P.M. daily, adults $6, seniors $5) has the most extensive re-creations of the rooms of the times, in-depth explanations of the building's restoration in the 1930s by the Civilian Conservation Corps, and vast grounds that convey a sense of how remote and isolated California must have been.

Founded on December 8, 1787, the Mission of the Immaculate Conception of Most Holy Mary was dedicated and construction began in the spring of 1788. It was constructed in the traditional quadrangle shape, and the converted Chumash lived outside the mission walls in their traditional huts. This first mission was destroyed in a major earthquake in 1812. What was left of the shattered adobe walls dissolved in the heavy winter rains. When they decided to rebuild, the traditional design was abandoned, and the new mission was built with a linear design, making it unique among California missions.

This mission also fell into ruin, a victim of changing times and simple neglect. In 1824 La Purísima was at the center of a failed Chumash revolt. The friction between the military and the missions exploded as the Chumash of the three Santa Barbara missions (La Purísima, Santa Inez, and Santa Barbara) rose up in armed revolt. Soldiers from the presidio at Monterey took the La Purísima mission by force; the attack left 16 Chumash dead and several wounded. One of the elders negotiated surrender terms for the Chumash, but seven of the Chumash who surrendered were executed, and 12 others were sentenced to hard labor at the Santa Barbara presidio.

Secularization of the missions in 1834 was the final nail in the coffin for La Purísima. In 1845 the mission was sold for $1,110, and the church was stripped of its roof tiles and timbers. The walls, exposed to the elements, crumbled. The mission was rescued in 1934, when the site was deeded to the State of California. A resulting restoration project became one of the largest of its kind in the nation.

Today, more than 200,000 visitors enjoy La Purísima State Historic Park each year. The nearly 2,000 acres have trails for simple hikes and walks, and many people bring a picnic. You can examine the five-acre garden that shows native domestic plants typical of a mission garden, including fig and olive trees, sage, and Spanish dagger. There are also mission animals typical of the times, including burros, horses, longhorn cattle, sheep, goats, and turkeys, displayed in a corral in the main compound.

The mission is actually three buildings, and there are well over a dozen rooms to explore, including sleeping quarters for the soldiers, the weaving shop, the candle-making room, the simple church, a chapel, and the priests quarters. Many of the rooms still have their original dirt floors, providing a feel for daily life back then. There are also a few conical huts that the Chumash used to live in. This is one of the only missions that does not have church services now that it's a state park.

La Purísima is about 55 miles (one hour's drive) from Santa Barbara. From U.S. 101 northbound, take Highway 246 west for approximately 18 miles. From San Luis Obispo, it's about 60 miles (1.25 hours' drive) on Highway 1 south; from Highway 1, head east on Purísima Road a few miles south of Vandenberg Air Force Base.

May–Oct., adults $25, under age 10 $10), which is a live-narrated 90-minute tour on the Land Shark, a 15-foot-high amphibious vehicle. You'll see most of the important buildings except the mission. On the plus side, in the last portion of the tour the Land Shark plunges into the ocean and turns into a boat, going past the breakwater for great views of the coast. It's fun and informative, and you can ask all the questions you want. More likely than not, you'll at least see dolphins and seals. All Land Shark tours depart from the entrance to Stearns Wharf.

The **Santa Barbara Trolley Company** (805/965-0353, www.sbtrolley.com, 10 A.M.–5:30 P.M. daily, adults $19, under age 12 $8) offers another live narrated tour that includes the mission and other great locations like Butterfly Beach in Montecito. Tours pick up and drop off at 15 different locations every 60 minutes; see the website for a comprehensive schedule.

Taxi Cabs

Taxis are not abundant in town; it's best to call for one. Assuming you do get a taxi, you're apt to get a leisurely cab ride to your destination. **Santa Barbara Checker Cab** (805/966-6666) is a safe bet.

State Street Trolley

For just 25 cents, you can ride the trolley the length of the waterfront, or the length of State Street. Two electric shuttle routes (www.sbmtd.gov) serve the downtown corridor (State St.) and the waterfront (Cabrillo Blvd.) daily every half hour. Children under 45 inches tall can ride free, and a free transfer is available between the Downtown Shuttle and the Waterfront Shuttle—just ask your driver.

PACIFIC COAST HIGHWAY

Solvang

To some, Solvang might seem like Denmark on steroids, but the colorful and charming village-like town is unlike any other.

Solvang started in 1911 as a Danish retreat. It is still ripe with Scandinavian heritage as well as a new modern sensibility, although the theme park atmosphere is not lacking in kitsch. In the 1950s, far earlier than other themed communities, Solvang decided to seal its fate by keeping a focus on Danish architecture, food, and style, which holds an allure nearly 50 years after its conception. You'll still hear the muted strains of Danish spoken on occasion, and you'll notice storks displayed above many of the stores in town, as they're a traditional symbol of good luck.

Solvang draws nearly two million visitors each year. During peak summer times and holidays, Solvang can be congested, with people clogging the brick sidewalks, riding rented surreys through the streets, and loitering in front of the bakeries and chocolate shops, and it feels uncharacteristic of a small town. Try to visit during off-season, when the simple joys of meandering the lovely shops can still be enjoyed. It's at its best in the fall and early spring when the hills are verdant green and the trees in town are beautiful.

An easily walkable town, Solvang is close to the now-famous ostrich farm from the movie *Sideways*. Solvang is also home to Mission Santa Inés, bakeries, miles of rolling paved roads for bikers and cyclists (Lance Armstrong once trained here), and oak-studded parks. Although not situated on the coast, this recreated Danish town makes a fun if kitschy side trip.

Getting There

Solvang is in a leisurely 50-mile, one-hour from San Luis Obispo on U.S. 101, and it's a lovely drive. You hug the coast through Pismo Beach and then enter the Santa Maria Valley, with plenty of agriculture laid out before you. If you're heading from Santa Barbara north to Solvang, you have two choices. You can drive the back route, Highway 154, also known

Solvang

© MICHAEL CERVIN

as the San Marcos Pass Road, and arrive in Solvang in about 30 minutes. This is a two-lane road, with only a few places to pass slower drivers, but it has some stunning views of the coast as you climb into the hills. You pass Cachuma Lake then turn west on Highway 246 to Solvang. The other option is to take U.S. 101, which affords plenty of coastal driving before you head north into the Gaviota Pass to reach Solvang. This route is longer, about 45 minutes' drive time.

Highway 246 is known as Mission Drive in the town, and it connects both to U.S. 101 and Highway 154, which connects to Santa Barbara in the south and U.S. 101 farther north. It's important to note that Solvang gets crowded on weekends, and getting in and out can be a slow proposition. But since you have little choice but to wait it out, just remind yourself how good a Danish cookie will taste when you finally arrive.

The **MTD Valley Express** (805/683-3702) is a regional commuter bus line run-ning Monday–Friday among Santa Barbara, Buellton, and Solvang.

Amtrak connects to the valley via bus (1630 Mission Dr., Solvang) from Santa Barbara, but trains stop only in Santa Barbara and San Luis Obispo. Bus travel time from the Santa Barbara train station to Solvang is approximately one hour.

Sights and Drives
BALLARD CANYON
Ballard Canyon is not only a great local drive, it's also popular with cyclists and even runners. Just off the main street in Solvang, you can ride, drive, or run the canyon past vineyards, bison, and cattle; the road comes out near Los Olivos. What makes this road so wonderful is the combination of straight segments mixed with gentle curves and occasional steep climbs and, of course, the bucolic scenery from low in the canyon to high atop the ridge, with views of the surrounding areas. To access Ballard Canyon from downtown Solvang, head north on Atterdag Road. The road climbs for a while,

© MICHAEL CERVIN

Mission Santa Inés

then drops down into the canyon. Veer right onto Ballard Canyon Road and take it all the way through the canyon to Highway 154. To the right is Los Olivos; straight ahead is Foxen Canyon Road.

SANTA ROSA ROAD
Santa Rosa Road winds through the Santa Rita Hills, the best-known pinot noir–growing region in the county. The two-lane road meanders past a few wineries, old ranch houses, and lots of gentle sloping hills. Both cars and cyclists share this road, which eventually connects with Highway 1 south of Lompoc. The hills rise to the left; to the right are vineyards and farmland. Early morning and late afternoon are great times to be here, as the sun gently bathes the hills and vineyards in a soft golden hue.

OSTRICHLAND
Made popular by the film *Sideways,* OstrichLand (610 E. Hwy. 246, 805/686-9696,www.ostrichlandusa.com, 10 A.M.–dusk daily, adults $4, under age 12 $1) is on Highway 246 two miles before you reach Solvang from U.S. 101. At first glance it seems somewhat prehistoric; wandering through the shrubs in the distance you'll see the massive birds with thin necks, small heads, and big eyes. They usually keep their distance and only approach when there is food to be had. Should you decided to feed them, you need to hold the food plate firmly in your hand, as they don't eat gingerly but attack the plate with fierce determination, so if you have a loose grip, the plate will fly out of your hand. Aside from feeding them, you can shop for ostrich eggs and ostrich jerky as well as emu eggs and ostrich-feather accoutrements.

MISSION SANTA INÉS
Throughout its 200-plus-year history, Mission Santa Inés (1760 Mission Dr., 805/688-4815, www.missionsantaines.org, 9 A.M.–5 P.M. daily, mass 8 A.M. daily, $4) has overcome natural disasters, political turmoil, and financial hardships and remains a working church to

this day. It is named after Saint Agnes, Santa Inés in Spanish. The town name is spelled Santa Ynez, an anglicization of the Spanish pronunciation. The interior is similar in size to the other missions. A long, tall, narrow church, this one is decorated more simply with hand-painted interiors and without much architectural detail. Of note is the large collection of about 500 church vestments, dating from the 15th century to the early 1700s. Near the Stations of the Cross at the south end of the property are expansive views of the valley below, which used to have orchards for the mission. There is a back entrance few people seem to know about through a parking lot at Mission and Alisal Roads in Solvang. Behind the public restrooms, a brick walkway leads into the backside of the mission grounds.

The mission, established in 1804, was designed to be a stopping point between the missions of Santa Barbara and La Purísima in Lompoc. It was devastated by an earthquake in 1812 but was rebuilt; what is visible today is not original, with the exception of part of the original arch toward the south end of the property. The Chumash population here was reported to be close to 1,000 at its peak. After Mexican independence from Spain in 1821, secularization caused the departure of the Spanish missionaries and most of the Chumash as well as the decline of the mission itself, until it was later rescued by much-needed attention and money.

ELVERHØJ MUSEUM OF HISTORY AND ART

To fully understand Solvang, it's important to visit the Elverhøj Museum (1624 Elverhoy Way, 805/686-1211, www.elverhoj.org, 1–4 P.M. Wed.–Thurs., noon–4 P.M. Fri.–Sun., $3 donation), a delightful and surprisingly cool place. Not only does it have tabletop and kitchen linens and local crafts, there is a comprehensive history of the area with nostalgic photos of the early settlers. Of particular note is the typical Danish kitchen, hand-painted in green with stenciled flowers everywhere and pine floors, countertops, and tables—it gives an idea of

how creatively the Danes made their homes, no doubt in an effort to brighten bleak winters. The winters brightened considerably for those who arrived in this area, but it was a long journey. The museum also features exhibits of traditional folk art from Denmark, including paper-cutting and lace-making, which is clearly evident throughout town. There are displays of wood clogs and the rustic tools used to create them, and rotating exhibits throughout the year focus on the valley. It would be easy to dismiss the museum as a novelty, but clearly the passion of the original settlers and their willingness to come to the United States to continue their way of life from the Old World is inspiring.

HANS CHRISTIAN ANDERSEN MUSEUM

The small Hans Christian Andersen Museum (1680 Mission Dr., 805/688-2052, www.solvangca.com/museum/h1.htm, 10 A.M.–5 P.M. Sun.–Mon., 9 A.M.–8 P.M. Tues.–Thurs., 9 A.M.–9 P.M. Fri.–Sat., free) has a few artifacts of Andersen, including a bronze bust, a copy of which is in the park on Mission Drive; first editions of his books from the 1830s in Danish and English; photographs; and a timeline chronicling his life, work, and impact on literature. It's easy to overlook Andersen as simply a writer of fairy tales, but he also wrote novels, plays, and other works.

MOTORCYCLE MUSEUM

The Motorcycle Museum (320 Alisal Rd., 805/686-9522, www.motosolvang.com, 11 A.M.–5 P.M. Sat.–Sun., by appointment Mon.–Fri., $10) is truly a unique and interesting stop. Ninety-five vintage and new motorcycles are on display on the self-guided tour. Some are downright beautiful, polished and lovingly restored. There are bikes from the 1930s and 1940s, the earliest from 1903, and some are so cool that you'll want to strap on a helmet and take a ride. After 10 years in this spot, the museum has amassed a collection of Ducati, Crocker, Matchless, Nimbus, and many more. Admission is not inexpensive compared to other things to do in town, but if motorcycles are your passion, you should visit.

QUICKSILVER MINIATURE HORSE RANCH

It's free to stop by the Quicksilver Miniature Horse Ranch (1555 Alamo Pintado Rd., 805/686-4002, www.qsminis.com, 10 A.M.–3 P.M. daily, tours by appointment), which serves a growing list of customers from across the globe who want these horses as pets. If you drive by the farm on a spring day, you may catch a glimpse of 25–30 newborn foals, measuring about 20 inches tall, testing out their new legs as they attempt to leap and bound on the grass. Visitors can get up close with the newborns and the adults, but remember that this is not a petting zoo, it's a working ranch. There are usually about 90 horses on the ranch.

Festivals and Events

Danish Days (www.solvangusa.com), held the third weekend in September, is a big draw. Started in 1936, it features clog-wearing Danes dancing in the streets, pastries and coffee everywhere, and even an *aebleskiver* (pancake) eating contest. It's Solvang's annual salute to its cultural heritage, and local women dress in traditional skirts, aprons, and caps despite the heat. The men wear clogs and traditional outfits. The festival is also referred to as Aebleskiver Days, and it has been a tradition for locals to serve *aebleskiver* from pans set up in the streets.

The food and wine event **Taste of Solvang** (www.solvangusa.com), held the third weekend in March, has been held for 18 years, and it keeps growing and becoming more sophisticated. It starts with a dessert reception, and considering the history of pastries and sweets among the Danes, that's enough. Following that is the walking smorgasbord, with 40 stops in town where you pop in and sample what they might be serving—usually Danish food, although some restaurants and stores offer non-Danish food samples. Ten tasting rooms pour their vintages into your souvenir glass, and there's live entertainment in the park, where many people bring a picnic and relax. It's a three-day event that immerses you in the local culture and customs and the new crop of wineries.

The Solvang Century (562/690-9693, www.bikescor.com) is the best-known cycling race in the entire valley. Technically it's a fundraiser, not a race, but it's hard not to be competitive. They added a half-century race to accommodate riders who prefer the shorter distances, but there is still a minimum elevation gain of 2,000 feet, making this a challenging course. The money raised benefits heart-related diseases; the founder of the event used cycling as a way to improve his health after his own heart surgery.

Shopping
BOOKSTORES

Valley Books (1582 Mission Dr., 805/688-7160, www.valleybooks.biz, 9 A.M.–6:30 P.M. daily) sells mostly used books with a small section of new books. There's an abundance of paperbacks, but also magazines, newspapers, and hardcovers. You can sit outside or inside in comfy chairs and read, sip coffee or tea, and enjoy a Danish pastry. This place is made to lounge. The have Wi-Fi, and there's a small kids section with little tables and chairs. It's a quiet respite from all the shopping.

The Book Loft (1680 Mission Dr., 805/688-6010, www.bookloftsolvang.com, 9 A.M.–6 P.M. Sun.–Mon., 9 A.M.–8 P.M. Tues.–Thurs., 9 A.M.–9 P.M. Fri.–Sat.) sells mostly new books, though there's a small section of used books as well. This 35-year-old two-story store has a vast well-organized selection of authors, including locals. The wood stairs creak as you venture upstairs to see even more books. It has the feel of an old bookstore, not sanitized with fancy shelves—in fact, these shelves were all handmade. They also have a nice selection of antiquarian books, and upstairs is the Hans Christian Andersen Museum.

ANTIQUES
The **Solvang Antique Center** (486 1st St., 805/686-2322, www.solvangantiques.com, 10 A.M.–6 P.M. daily) is home to some incredible antiques. In addition to a stellar collection

of magnificent gilded antique clocks, there are music boxes, jewelry, watches, and gorgeous vintage telephones, from old candlestick models to the 1930s and 1940s models. They also have artfully restored antique furniture. The 7,000-square-foot showroom has over 65 specialty dealers from around the globe. It is an expensive place but has such diversity that any antiques lover should stop in, even if just to browse one of the finest stores on the Central Coast.

SPECIALTY STORES

Elna's Dress Shop (1673 Copenhagen Dr., 805/688-4525, 9:30 A.M.–5:30 P.M. daily) is the place to go for a handmade Danish dress or costume as well as more contemporary but conservative and non-Danish-themed dresses for women. If you're searching for that perfect Danish outfit for a young one, you'll find it here. Aprons, caps, and brightly colored simple dresses, some with beautiful lace, are available off the rack, or they will make one for you. They have only a few Danish pieces for young boys, and they're pretty darn cute.

You'll feel a little better from the moment you enter **Jule Hus** (1580 Mission Dr., 805/688-6601, www.solvangschristmashouse. com, 9 A.M.–5 P.M. daily), where it's the holiday season all year long. They offer hand-carved wood ornaments, blown-glass ornaments, traditional Scandinavian ornaments, and standalone decorations as well as a huge selection of nutcrackers. There are also traditional Danish quilts and lace items and plenty of trees fully decked out. Jule Hus has celebrated the Christmas spirit since 1967, and there are always people milling around searching for that ideal ornament. Other stores in town have small sections of Christmas items, but here it's all there is.

Rasmussen's (1697 Copenhagen Dr., 805/688-6636, www.rasmussenssolvang.com, 9 A.M.–5:30 P.M. daily) opened in 1921 and is still going strong five generations later with everything Scandinavian. It's a one-stop shop for gifts, books, souvenirs, Danish packaged food items, and kitchen items.

Nordic Knives (1634 Copenhagen Dr., 805/688-3612, www.nordicknives.com, 10 A.M.–5 P.M. daily) has more knives than you've probably ever seen in one place, including expensive high-end custom-made knives by well-known knife makers and jeweled, engraved, one-of-a-kind knives. There are also hunting and kitchen knives with prices that are much lower than the custom blades. The shop has been in Solvang nearly 40 years, and they know their knives. Whether you need a simple knife or a traditional Swiss Army knife, they'll have it. The display case on the right side as you enter is worth a look, with beautiful knives of all types and pedigree.

Ingeborg's (1679 Copenhagen Dr., 805/688-5612, www.ingeborgs.com, 9 A.M.–5 P.M. daily) has been making traditional Danish chocolates for nearly half a century. There are over 70 varieties of chocolates as well as a large variety of licorice handmade on the premises. It isn't cheap, but it is Danish chocolate made by Danes. They also carry hard-to-find Dutch chocolates. Grab a seat at one of the six round red barstools and enjoy the ice cream.

FARMERS MARKET

Every Wednesday year-round, rain or shine, fresh fruits, veggies, flowers, and local items from surrounding farms make an appearance at the **Solvang Farmer's Market** (Mission Dr. and 1st St., 805/962-5354, 2:30–6 P.M. Wed.). This is not a major farmers market and takes up only two blocks, but the street next to the park is closed, and you can find fresh food harvested from local farms, many of which are within a mile of town. It's hard to get much fresher than that.

Sports and Recreation
PARKS

At 15 acres, **Hans Christian Andersen Park** (500 Chalk Hill Rd.) is the largest park in the area. Enter through a castle gate and you're amid pine and oak trees. Then you come to the skate park, which has cavernous half pipes and is actually well designed, though there are more bikers who use it than boarders. There is a small wooden playground behind the skate park for the younger ones. If you continue driving through the park, you'll come to another playground with tall chute slides embedded in the sand. There are plenty of well-groomed trees and picnic tables. If you drive all the way to the end, there are four tennis courts next to a beautiful gnarled old oak tree. There are restroom facilities and drinking fountains.

Sunny Fields Park (900 Alamo Pintado Rd., 805/688-7529) is almost a pint-size Solvang. There's a Viking ship, swings and slides, monkey bars, a gingerbread house, a faux windmill, and plenty of things to climb around on. Trees offer shade, as it gets hot during the summer. This is a great spot for little kids, and it's reasonably quiet, being just outside of town. There are drinking fountains and restrooms, plenty of parking, and a large flat grassy ball field.

GOLF
The 18-hole, par-72 **River Course at the Alisal** (150 Alisal Rd., 805/688-6042, www.rivercourse.com, $60–70) was featured in *Sideways*. It's a beautiful course on the banks of the Santa Ynez River, punctuated with magnificent oaks. Challenging and beautiful, it features four lakes, open fairways, tricky hazards, and large undulating greens accented by native sycamores. Elevated tees reveal some vistas and occasional vineyards, so bring your best game and your camera.

Accommodations
UNDER $150
Days Inn Windmill (114 E. Hwy. 246, Buellton, 805/688-8448, www.daysinn.com, $90–100 d) was featured in the film *Sideways*—you can even stay in the same room where the main characters stayed in the film (ask for room 234). The 116 guest rooms are pretty standard and basic, with the best feature being the outdoor pool. It's right off U.S. 101, and you can't miss the namesake windmill. It's best to avoid the guest rooms fronting the freeway and go for an interior room to cut down on the noise.

There are no views to speak of, but the prices are good.

$150-250
Solvang Gardens (293 Alisal Rd., 805/688-4404, www.solvanggardens.com, $150–200 d) is a 24-room delight on the edge of town. It feels like a small village. There are stone fireplaces and marble baths, and each guest room is unique and different. Some are decorated with a more modern theme, some have a traditional feel, but all are very well appointed. Beautiful gardens in both the front and center of the property provide peaceful green space. The local owners will do everything they can to ensure your stay is the best it can be. It's quieter here since it's not on the main drag. In the morning you can walk into town or down to the dry riverbed.

◖ Hadsten House Inn & Spa (1450 Mission Dr., 805/688-3210, www.hadstenhouse.com, $164 d) is a nonsmoking property and one of the best places to stay in Solvang. French-style furnishings with custom mattresses, dark-toned furniture, and ample space pull you out of the Danish mentality and into a contemporary and sophisticated setting. A full buffet breakfast and wine and cheese on Friday–Saturday are offered, along with a heated outdoor pool and hot tub. It's one of the closest hotels to U.S. 101 and the first you see as you enter Solvang. Set in a square horseshoe pattern, it offers no views, except across the street to another hotel. Regardless, these are comfortable, well-appointed rooms with European flair.

OVER $250
The 42-room **The Inn at Petersen Village** (1576 Mission Dr., 805/688-3121, www.peterseninn.com, $250–270 d) is unusual in that the rates include dinner and breakfast at the in-house restaurant. The decor is traditional, maybe even a little stuffy, but it is also right on Mission Drive, so you simply walk outside into the thick of things. The inn has been around a long time, and it sees its share of return guests.

Food

There are many places in town that serve traditional Danish food, which doesn't typically conjure images of innovative global fare. But as Solvang is growing, with new hotels and wine-tasting rooms opening, restaurants are looking to stand out from the traditional in what is becoming, albeit slowly, a true destination with farm-fresh food and innovative ways of preparing it. But if you are looking for the traditional, you'll find it here too, occasionally with an accordion player outside the front door enticing you to come in.

AMERICAN

Sleek and sophisticated, **Root 246** (420 Alisal Rd., 805/686-8681, www.root-246. com, 5 P.M.–close daily, bar from 4 P.M. daily, $30), one of the newest additions to the dining scene, has upped the ante. It looks like it belongs in Hollywood, not in rural Solvang, but that's part of the evolution of Solvang and wine country cuisine. Chef and consultant Bradley Ogden has started more than 10 restaurants and knows how to create exciting food. The menu varies, often depending on seasonal ingredients. You'll find oysters, flatbreads, and a variety of fish and game dishes. The crowd is young and urban—you don't see a lot of the old-school Danish residents here.

Firestone Walker Brewing Company Tap Room Restaurant (620 McMurray Rd., Buellton, 805/686-1557, www.firestonewalker.com, 5–8:30 P.M. Mon.–Thurs., 11 A.M.–4:30 P.M. and 5–9 P.M. Fri.–Sat., 11 A.M.–4:30 P.M. and 5–8:30 P.M. Sun., tasting with souvenir pint glass $6.50, food $20) features four Firestone Walker beers in addition to eight alternating beers on tap. You can get it by the pint or the mug, or try a sampler of four beers. The food menu includes pork chops, steaks, burgers, and beer-battered fish-and-chips. Firestone Walker is the best brewery on the Central Coast and right off U.S. 101, just north of Buellton. Grab a brew, and if your picky friend wants wine, they'll pour Firestone wines by the glass.

DANISH

Bit O' Denmark (473 Alisal Rd., 805/688-5426, www.bitodenmark.com, 11 A.M.–9 P.M. daily, $15) is known for its traditional smorgasbord as well as its Monte Cristo sandwich and roast duck. It is the oldest restaurant in Solvang, housed in one of the very first buildings the original settlers built in 1911. It became a restaurant in 1963 and continues to cook up Danish ham, Danish pork, open-faced roast beef sandwiches; the extensive smorgasbord includes *medisterpølse* (Danish sausage), *frikadeller* (meatballs), *rödkål* (red cabbage), *spegesild* (pickled herring), and an array of cold salads. The room to the left as you enter is the best, with large curved booths.

Solvang Restaurant (1672 Copenhagen Dr., 800/654-0541, www.solvangrestaurant. com, 6 A.M.–3 P.M. Mon.–Fri., 6 A.M.–5 P.M. Sat.–Sun., $10) is well known for its *aebleskivers,* round doughy concoctions topped with jam; don't be surprised to see a line out the door. This little diner also dishes up breakfasts in a quaint environment. The overhead wood beams are decorated with Danish proverbs.

One of the top Danish food stops, ◖ **The Red Viking** (1684 Copenhagen Dr., 805/688-6610, http://theredvikingrestaurant.com, 8 A.M.–8 P.M. daily, $10) rolls out Danish dishes such as *hakkebøf* (chopped sirloin and onion topped with a fried egg), wiener schnitzel (veal cutlet), authentic Danish smorgasbord, and a line of Danish cheeses, hams, and beers.

Pea Soup Andersen's (376 Ave. of the Flags, Buellton, 805/688-5881, www.peasoupandersens.net, 7 A.M.–10 P.M. daily, $15) is the granddaddy of Danish restaurants, first opened in 1924, serving standard fare like burgers and milkshakes and, of course, pea soup in a bread bowl. There's a small gift shop, a bakery with fresh daily sweets and fudge, a small art gallery upstairs, and best of all, a mini museum about Rufus T. Buell (as in Buellton), how he started the town, and how Andersen's came into being. It also chronicles some of the changes in the local dining scene. It's just outside of Solvang on U.S. 101 and has the feel of a coffee shop. There are plenty of cans of soup for sale.

BAKERIES
Mortensen's Danish Bakery (1588 Mission Dr., 805/688-8373, www.greenhousesolvang. com/Bakery, 7:45 A.M.–5:30 P.M. Mon.–Fri.) is one of the stalwarts of the Danish bakeries. It's best to visit the low-key interior for a strudel or éclair and a pot of tea or coffee and relax in the subdued environment. The Danish decor is not over-the-top, but it's still good Danish, and this is a great place to start your day.

GROCERIES
El Rancho Marketplace (2886 Mission Dr., 805/688-4300, www.elranchomarket.com, 6 A.M.–10 P.M. daily) is an upscale supermarket that features an old-fashioned full-service meat counter, fresh local organic produce, and a complete selection of local and international wines, champagnes, and spirits. It has very good hot and cold entrées, salads, and fresh baked bread and pies—perfect for putting together a picnic. If you want something quick and easy, there is a great selection here. There's some outdoor seating near the entrance, and on occasion tri-tip is grilled outside.

Information and Services
The **Solvang Visitor Information Center** (1639 Copenhagen Dr., 805/688-6765, www. solvangusa.com) is staffed by locals wearing red vests. They have comprehensive information not just on Solvang but the entire valley as well.

The *Santa Ynez Valley News,* published each Thursday, covers the local angle. For broader national coverage, the *Santa Barbara News-Press* and the *Santa Maria Times* are both dailies available for purchase.

Should you have an emergency, dial **911.** The **Santa Ynez Valley Cottage Hospital** (2050 Viborg Rd., Solvang, 805/688-6431) offers emergency services. Police services are contracted with the Santa Barbara County **Sheriff's Department** (1745 Mission Dr., Solvang, 805/686-5000).

Getting Around
While Solvang is the largest of the small towns in the area, it is still easily navigable and can easily be explored on foot in less than a day. A horse-drawn trolley traverses the streets, taking participants on a narrated tour (www. solvangtrolley.com, noon–6 P.M. Thurs.– Mon., adults $10, seniors $8, children $5) in the Honen Streetcar, a replica of a streetcar dating to the late 1800s or 1915, depending on whom you believe. Two large horses pull you around town as you learn the history and noteworthy spots of Solvang. The tours last about 25 minutes and run every 35 minutes; board at the visitors center (Copenhagen Dr. and 2nd St.).

Santa Ynez Valley Transit (805/688-5452, www.cityofsolvang.com, 7 A.M.–7 P.M. Mon.–Sat., call-in only 8:30 A.M.–4 P.M. Sun.) is a scheduled minibus serving Ballard, Buellton, Los Olivos, Santa Ynez, and Solvang. The Chumash Casino also offers a shuttle service (800/248-6274) serving Solvang, Goleta, Santa Maria, and Lompoc. Riders with a Club Chumash gaming card get preferred seating.

Solvang Taxi (805/688-0069) operates 24 hours daily. You have to call them, however, as taxis are rarely seen in town; wine transportation is also offered. **Promenade Cab Company** (805/717-8400) also operates in Solvang.

Pismo Beach

Pismo Beach is how we imagine classic 1960s California: friendly people, great waves, low-key, easygoing. Located just south of San Luis Obispo, this beach town makes a great place to stop if you're only going to spend one night on the road between San Francisco and Los Angeles.

SIGHTS
Pismo Beach Monarch Grove

The monarch butterfly grove (Hwy. 1, 800/443-7778, www.monarchbutterfly.org, 24 hours daily, docents available 10 A.M.–4 P.M. daily, free), just south of North Pismo State Beach Campground, sees the return of the butterflies November–February, when tens of thousands of monarchs migrate to this small grove of eucalyptus trees near the beach to mate. On average there are about 25,000 of the silent winged creatures, and the trees are often transformed into brilliant shades of orange after their 2,000-mile journey. This is the largest of the gathering spots for the monarchs in California. Docents give brief and fascinating talks (11 A.M. and 2 P.M. daily Nov.–Feb.) about the butterflies and their unique short lives. There's a short boardwalk that leads to the beach and a large picnic area near the low sand dunes and cypress trees. Parking is available at the North Pismo State Beach Campground.

Pismo Beach Winery

It took nearly 10 years for the dream of two brothers to become a reality when Pismo Beach Winery (271B Five Cities Dr., 805/773-9463, www.pismobeachwinery.com, noon–5 P.M. daily, tasting $10) finally opened. Located across from the outlet mall, this urban winery produces about 1,500 cases of wine annually; the portfolio consists of chardonnay, cabernet sauvignon, zinfandel, barbera, pinot noir, and petite sirah. This is a small, family-owned operation, and the corrugated metal exterior belies what's inside. The tasting room is bright and open, with soft yellow walls, wood door trim, a tasting bar, and views into the barrel room. There's a low-key vibe here, and someone from the family is usually behind the counter pouring the wine.

BEACHES
Oceano Dunes

Just south of San Luis Obispo and Pismo Beach are the Oceano Dunes (928 Pacific Blvd., 805/473-7220, www.parks.ca.gov), vast sand dunes that stretch 18 miles from Pismo Beach south to Guadalupe in Santa Barbara County. This is one of the few places left in United States where extensive dunes cover so much coastline. Some are large and domineering, reaching 20 feet or higher. The benefit of visiting Oceano Dunes is that it's relatively uncrowded, and there are flat, wide beaches. It can be breezy here at times, but there is a moonscape beauty to the beaches.

Oceano Dunes is also home to a vehicular recreation area, meaning you can actually drive on certain parts of the beach, although you do need a California state license for off-highway vehicles. There are very specific rules and regulations for this section of the beach, and it's best to visit www.parks.ca.gov for detailed information.

Pismo Beach

Pismo Beach (Pomeroy Ave. and Cypress St.) is best accessed by heading down Pomeroy Avenue straight toward the pier. It features flat, long, and wide stretches of sand. The focal point of this beach is the pier, where you can see the curve of the coastline as it winds around dramatic hills. There are plenty of restrooms, food, and parking nearby.

FESTIVALS AND EVENTS

October is no time to clam up: It's the annual **Pismo Beach Clam Festival** (Pismo Beach pier, 195 Pomeroy Ave., 805/773-4382, www.pismochamber.com). The parade comes first,

THE PISMO CLAM

Pismo Beach was once nearly synony-mous with the word *clam*, as there used to be a thriving clam industry here. Even before the arrival of the Europeans, the Chumash Indians made use of the clams, using the meat for food and the shells for decorative arts.

From the turn of the 20th century until about World War II, the clam industry as defined by Pismo Beach, part of Morro Bay, and into Monterey was substantial. And though the clam population is smaller these days, due to over-fishing and natu-ral predators like otters, the Pismo clam still has good years and bad years. But clamming isn't what it used to be, and though Pismo Beach has its share of clam chowder, few people recall the association between Pismo Beach and its clams.

then clam digging in the sand, and, of course, the clam chowder cook-off, where local restaurants strenuously attempt to defeat whoever was top clam the year before. There's live music, vendors selling arts and crafts, and wine tasting. The festival has been going on for over six decades.

SPORTS AND RECREATION

Fairly new to the Central Coast, **Monarch Dunes** (1606 Trilogy Pkwy., Nipomo, 805/343-9459, www.monarchdunes.com, $30–78) is an 18-hole, par-71 public course. The 12-hole challenge course is becoming a favorite because you can play a little more after the regular course, or just this one if you're short on time. The course is tough: In some cases you're hitting directly into the wind, and the challenge course has five lakes that actually serve as water storage for the nearby housing development. The rugged and raw layout of the course follows the natural sand dunes.

With so many hills in close proximity, there are great hiking trails to try out. The **Oso Flaco Lake** two-mile round-trip trail (Oso

Flaco Rd., off Hwy. 1 north of Guadalupe, www.dunescenter.org, parking $5) is more a walk than a hike. The trail is on a walkway that crosses the lake and reaches the top of the dunes overlooking the ocean, providing great views of the coast. There are a large number of birds, best seen in the morning hours. White pelicans, cormorants, herons, snowy plovers, and California least terns can be seen on the lake; in all, about 200 species have been spotted. From the parking area, walk down the tree-shaded causeway and turn left onto the walkway. There are benches on the walkway over the lake.

ACCOMMODATIONS

The 【 **Dolphin Bay Resort and Spa** (2727 Shell Beach Rd., Pismo Beach, 805/773-4300, www.thedolphinbay.com, $390–480 d) has undoubtedly one of the best locations on the entire Central Coast, perched just yards from the cliffs that drop dramatically to the Pacific Ocean. From ocean-view suites to their well-known Lido Restaurant, the resort not only boasts magnificent views but has proximity to much of what the area offers. You can bicycle (bikes are provided for all guests), kayak, fish, shop, or simply bask in the golden sunset. The one-bedroom suites, at nearly 1,000 square feet, have full kitchens, fireplaces, and flat-screen TVs. All guests have access to the pool and 24-hour workout room. Cooking classes are available throughout the year, and on Tuesday nights, there's a wine-tasting featuring local wineries. If you are traveling with little tykes, there is a Saturday afternoon educational exploration ($55 per child) of the beach's tide pools and sealife that includes lunch, so the adults can have some time off to play.

SeaVenture Resort (100 Ocean View Ave., Pismo Beach, 805/773-4994, www.seaventure. com, $250–330 d) has ocean-view and mountain-view guest rooms, all just steps from the sand. There's covered parking and an in-house restaurant on the second floor with uninterrupted views of the ocean. There are fireplaces in the guest rooms, some have private balconies, and a continental breakfast can be delivered to your room. The guest rooms are intimate and very comfortable, with dark green walls accented by white beach-type furniture with a country flair. You're within walking distance to the center of Pismo Beach and the pier, but you'll need to drive 10 minutes to reach San Luis Obispo. But with these views, you may not want to leave.

FOOD

Jocko's (125 N. Thompson Ave., Nipomo, 805/929-3565, 8 A.M.–10 P.M. Sun.–Thurs., 8 A.M.–11 P.M. Fri.–Sat., $25) is out of the way in Nipomo in an unremarkable building, something like a 1950s Elks lodge that never caught up to the present day. It's known for oak-grilled steaks and the decor, comprised of stackable banquet-type chairs, inexpensive tables, and frankly rather cheap silverware—it's all part of the experience. The steaks and grilled meats are all prime quality, cooked and seasoned by people who know how to grill. On weekends, and often on weeknights as well, there are notoriously long waits. Make reservations, although that doesn't mean you won't still wait.

Steamers of Pismo (1601 Price St., Pismo Beach, 805/773-4711, www.steamerspismobeach.com, 11:30 A.M.–3 P.M. and 4:30–9 P.M. Mon.–Thurs., 11:30 A.M.–3 P.M. and 4:30–10 P.M. Fri., 11:30 A.M.–3 P.M. and 4–10 P.M. Sat., 11:30 A.M.–3 P.M. and 4–9 P.M. Sun., $25) is all about seafood, with dishes like cioppino, Chilean sea bass, and a very good clam chowder. It is also well known for its cocktails, including the (local) award-winning apple coconut mojito martini. The small bar area with great views of the water is available during lunch and for early dinners. If you want a table that looks directly on the Pacific, make

reservations. This is a popular spot for visitors because of the excellent views, and the service and food are equally good.

Splash Cafe (197 Pomeroy Ave., Pismo Beach, 805/773-4653, www.splashcafe.com, 8 A.M.–8:30 P.M. Mon.–Thurs., 8 A.M.–9 P.M. Fri.–Sat., $7) is the place to go for cheap eats by the beach. This is classic Pismo—bright, airy, and rambunctious, with plastic chairs and tables and crudely painted walls with old surfing photos and paraphernalia. Splash is best known for their thick, chunky, and creamy clam chowder, which has recently been picked up by Costco. The fish-and-chips and fish tacos are also worth trying, and burgers and shakes are also served. It does get crowded, so plan to get here early.

The oft-crowded **Cracked Crab** (751 Price St., Pismo Beach, 805/773-2722, www.crackedcrab.com, 11 A.M.–9 P.M. Sun.–Thurs., 11 A.M.–10 P.M. Fri.–Sat., $25) is *the* place to crack open crab, lobster, and other shellfish in a cafeteria-style environment. Old black-and-white photos of fishing days gone by line the walls. Perhaps it's the plastic bibs that give it away, but this is a hands-on joint. Waitstaff dump the shellfish right on your table so you can get to work.

GETTING THERE

Driving U.S. 101 from San Luis Obispo, it's only 12 miles to Pismo Beach, and as you leave San Luis Obispo's low rolling hills, you're heading due west. From points south, the drive time to Pismo from Santa Barbara is about 1.5 hours. U.S. 101 cuts through most towns on the Central Coast, and Pismo is literally right off the freeway, so it's a quick, easy, and pretty drive.

San Luis Obispo

San Luis Obispo is not a coastal town, although the water is less than 10 minutes away. The beauty of its location is that it offers everything within a 15-minute drive: great restaurants, access to hiking and biking trails, wineries, wide-open space, and an ideal climate. Since it is inland, if it's foggy at the beach, more often than not San Luis is warm and sunny. It's one of those spots with great weather. Plus it's about halfway between Los Angeles and San Francisco, making it a good place for an overnight rest stop.

Locals call San Luis Obispo by its nickname, SLO, and a visit to the city will immediately impress on anyone that "slow" is the order of the day. But the secret is out, and an excellent quality of life means that SLO is starting to speed up. With a beautiful downtown fronted by Higuera Street and the accompanying river walk, San Luis Obispo is beginning to receive attention for its idyllic way of life.

SIGHTS
Higuera Street

Higuera Street is the defining artery in San Luis Obispo, and pretty much everything revolves around it. Mature trees, historic turn-of-the-20th-century storefronts, and an absence of large buildings on Higuera Street create a very open and walkable space. It's also a one-way street, which means traffic and congestion is reduced. It follows the same path as San Luis Creek, making it ideal for dining and strolling. Shops and restaurants overlook the creek, and during the spring and summer months these are the best spots to be. The creek is accessible from several points, and kids often play in the water. Bubblegum Alley is on the 700 block, and just across the creek is the mission. Higuera Street even features in a book, *San Luis Obispo: 100 Years of Downtown Business: Higuera Street* (2007). It shows how much the surroundings have changed but how little the storefronts have changed.

PACIFIC COAST HIGHWAY

© MICHAEL CERVIN
Higuera Street

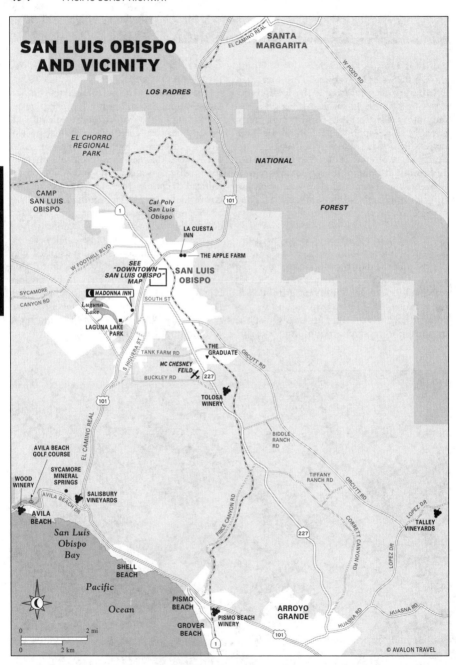

SAN LUIS OBISPO AND VICINITY

SANTA MARGARITA

EL CAMINO REAL

W POZO RD

LOS PADRES

EL CHORRO REGIONAL PARK

NATIONAL

101

FOREST

CAMP SAN LUIS OBISPO

1

Cal Poly San Luis Obispo

LA CUESTA INN

W FOOTHILL BLVD

THE APPLE FARM

SEE "DOWNTOWN SAN LUIS OBISPO" MAP

SAN LUIS OBISPO

SYCAMORE CANYON RD

MADONNA INN

SOUTH ST

Laguna Lake

LAGUNA LAKE PARK

S HIGUERA ST

Tank Farm Rd

THE GRADUATE

ORCUTT RD

MC CHESNEY FEILD

BUCKLEY RD

227

101

TOLOSA WINERY

EL CAMINO REAL

BIDDLE RANCH RD

AVILA BEACH GOLF COURSE

SYCAMORE MINERAL SPRINGS

TIFFANY RANCH RD

ORCUTT RD

WOOD WINERY

AVILA BEACH DR

SALISBURY VINEYARDS

PRICE CANYON RD

227

CORBETT CANYON RD

LOPEZ DR

AVILA BEACH

San Luis Obispo Bay

LOPEZ DR

TALLEY VINEYARDS

SHELL BEACH

Pacific

Ocean

PISMO BEACH

ARROYO GRANDE

PISMO BEACH WINERY

HUASNA RD

0   2 mi

0   2 km

GROVER BEACH

101

1

HUASNA RD

© AVALON TRAVEL

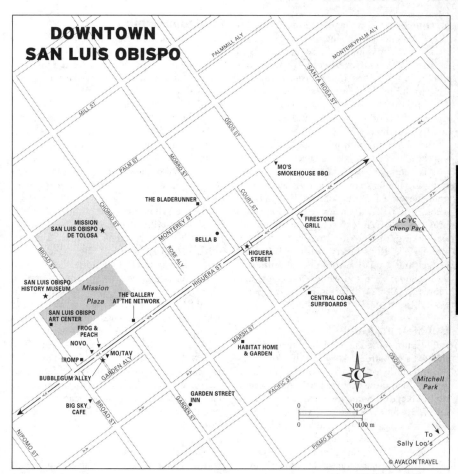

DOWNTOWN SAN LUIS OBISPO

MO'S SMOKEHOUSE BBQ

THE BLADERUNNER

MISSION SAN LUIS OBISPO DE TOLOSA ★

FIRESTONE GRILL

LC YC Cheng Park

BELLA B

HIGUERA STREET

SAN LUIS OBISPO HISTORY MUSEUM ★

Mission Plaza

THE GALLERY AT THE NETWORK

CENTRAL COAST SURFBOARDS

SAN LUIS OBISPO ART CENTER

FROG & PEACH

NOVO

HABITAT HOME & GARDEN

IROMP ■ ▼ MO/TAV

BUBBLEGUM ALLEY

Mitchell Park

GARDEN STREET INN

BIG SKY CAFE

0   100 yds

0   100 m

To Sally Loo's

© AVALON TRAVEL

PALMMILL ALY

MONTEREYPALM ALY

MILL ST

SANTA ROSA ST

PALM ST

MORRO ST

OSOS ST

CHORRO ST

COURT ST

MONTEREY ST

ROSE ALY

HIGUERA ST

BROAD ST

MARSH ST

GARDEN ALY

PACIFIC ST

GARDEN ST

OSOS ST

NIPOMO ST

BROAD ST

PISMO ST

PACIFIC COAST HIGHWAY

Mission San Luis Obispo de Tolosa

The Mission San Luis Obispo de Tolosa (751 Palm St., 805/781-8220, www.missionsanluisobispo.org, 9 A.M.–4 P.M. daily, $3–5 pp donation) was founded in 1772. The region had abundant supplies of food and water, the climate was mild, and the local Chumash were very friendly. To Father Junípero Serra, this seemed like the ideal place for a fifth California mission.

The mission was built over the course of 20 years, primarily by the hard work of local Chumash people. The church and priest's residence were completed by 1794, and other structures at the primitive mission in the early days included storerooms, residences for single women, barracks, and mills. The mission also used the land for farming and raising livestock, and the mission priests, soldiers, and indigenous people depended on the vegetables, fruits, nuts, and meats produced for their survival. Expansion proceeded for a few years with the prosperity of the mission, but like the other missions, it gradually fell into disrepair. When Mexico won independence from Spain in 1821, the missions were secularized, and most mission lands were sold off. Governor Pío Pico sold the San Luis Obispo Mission to Captain John Wilson for a mere $510 in 1845. The building served multiple functions over the years, including as a jail and as the first county courthouse.

Today, the mission fronts Mission Plaza, facing the creek, and Higuera Street. The courtyard is a popular place for small gatherings and festivals. The interior of the mission is minimally decorated, mainly painted by hand, and is long and tall. Still an active church, mass is held each day. While the church itself is modest looking, the interior grounds, also rather simple, are quite pretty, with flowers and hedges and a small arbor. The museum section includes black-and-white photographs and a limited collection of furniture and accessories from mission life.

Bubblegum Alley

Bubblegum started mysteriously appearing on the walls of Garden Alley, on the 700 block of Higuera Street, in the 1960s, when a few people defaced the exposed brick with chewed-up bubblegum. Some assumed it was college kids. Fast forward to today, and Bubblegum Alley is a sticky and unusual landmark in San Luis Obispo. Tens of thousands of wads of multicolored chewing gum are squished one on top of another in a masticated mosaic some 70 feet long and 15 feet high. At the top of the brick-walled alley, the gobs have been blackened by age and weather. This might be sickening to some; to others it is a unique expression of urban pop art. Some people seek to make a statement, spelling out their loves or their hopes, while others merely press gum onto the wall. It's not uncommon to hear people walk by and use adjectives like "disgusting" and "gross" to describe the alley. There are gum dispensers on either side of the alley; for a mere 25 cents, you can get a piece of gum to add your own chewed-up message.

◖ Madonna Inn

The Madonna Inn Resort & Spa (100 Madonna Rd., 805/543-3000, www.madonnainn.com) is truly one of a kind. It's considered a pilgrimage site for lovers of all-American kitsch, but it wasn't planned that way. When Alex and Phyllis Madonna opened the inn in 1958, they wanted it to be different than the typical motel, and made each room special. It started with 12 guest rooms; today there are 110 unique guest rooms, each decorated wildly differently to suit the diverse tastes of the road trippers that converge on the area. The creative names given to each over the years suggest what you will find inside: the Yahoo, Love Nest, Old Mill, Kona Rock, Irish Hills, Cloud Nine, Just Heaven, Hearts & Flowers, Rock Bottom, Austrian Suite, Caveman Room, Daisy Mae, Safari Room, Jungle Rock, and Bridal Falls. Then there is the famous men's restroom downstairs, where the urinal is built out of rock and a waterfall flushes it. Men routinely stand guard so their mothers, sisters, wives, and female friends can go in to gawk at the unusual feature.

Much of the Inn has been custom built. The leaded-glass inserts in the windowed area facing the large fireplace show Alex Madonna's enterprises: construction, lumber, and cattle. The Gold Rush dining room features a marble balustrade from nearby Hearst Castle. The 28-foot gold tree fixture in the main dining room was made from electrical conduit left over from building projects. A team of woodworkers carved the doors, beams, railings, and many other adornments by hand.

And there is the pink, pink, pink everywhere—it was Alex Madonna's favorite color. The gregarious Madonna made his money in the construction business, something he learned when he served in the U.S. Army Corps of Engineers. After he left the service, his company built much of U.S. 101 along the Central Coast. He was known as flamboyant, effervescent, and larger than life, and he never shied away from the bold use of pink. Nowhere is this more robustly expressed than in the beyond-Vegas-style dining room. Most people

the kitschy Madonna Inn

who visit the Madonna don't stay here, which is a shame, since it's a really cool place to stay. The service is excellent. Even if you don't stay the night, stop by to marvel at the extravagant excess. You won't soon forget it.

San Luis Obispo History Museum
The San Luis Obispo History Museum (696 Monterey St., 805/543-0638, www.slochs.org, 10 A.M.–4 P.M. Wed.–Sun., free) is housed in a 1904 Carnegie Library designed by the architect of the Paso Robles Carnegie Library. The museum itself is pretty simple, with a few artifacts and lots of photographs detailing the visual history of the area. Just behind the building on Broad Street is a small portion of wall dating to 1793, the only remaining section of the original mission wall. It's now covered with moss, but gives an idea of how the original buildings were made.

BEACHES
Avila Beach (San Miguel St. and Front St.) has a nice pier and large wide, flat beaches. It tends to have a more family vibe, probably because of the swing sets right on the sand facing the ocean. There are restroom facilities on the beach side of the street and plenty of food and coffee options in the sherbet-colored buildings on the boardwalk. The bay is sheltered, and so the water tends to be warmer and gentler; the weather here is almost always nicer than elsewhere on the Central Coast.

WINE-TASTING
Although Paso Robles is the undisputed leading wine region in the county, the San Luis area, which includes the Edna Valley and Arroyo Grande, has a diverse number of wineries. Don't dismiss this region, which produces some excellent wines. Any exploration of the wine region needs to include San Luis Obispo.

Wood Winery
Taste wine and watch the sunset at the Wood Winery (480 Front St., Avila Beach, 805/595-9663, www.wildwoodwine.com, 11 A.M.–5 P.M.

Sun.–Thurs., 11 A.M.–6 P.M. Fri.–Sat., tasting $7, free with bottle purchase) on Avila Beach boardwalk. It is licensed to sell wines by the glass and offers cheese plates and patio seating. There's a love of syrah here, but also a wide selection of sangiovese, cabernet sauvignon, chardonnay, and zinfandel. The vineyards are at the foot of the Cuesta Grade, just north of downtown San Luis. Wood Winery has one of the few oceanfront tasting rooms in the state, and from the tasting bar you can simply turn around to enjoy the views. The room is decorated in soft aquatic tones, and local artwork hangs on the walls. It's so relaxing here you may not want to leave.

Talley Vineyards

The Talley name has been associated with farming in San Luis Obispo County since 1948. As you drive toward Lopez Lake, on the left you'll immediately notice Talley Vineyards (3031 Lopez Dr., 805/489-0446, www.talleyvineyards.com, 10:30 A.M.–4:30 P.M. daily, tasting $6–12). The Mediterranean and Tuscan-style tasting room sits squarely in the middle of flat cropland, the surrounding hillsides covered in vines. A three-tiered fountain stands sentinel in the courtyard. The interior of the spacious tasting room features floor-to-ceiling glass, a horseshoe-shaped tasting bar, and high vaulted ceilings. You can often purchase some of the fruit and vegetables that grow on the property when it's in the season, including bell peppers, zucchini, tomatoes, and spinach. Pinot noir, chardonnay, syrah, cabernet sauvignon, and pinot gris are the main wines here, but Talley is best-known for producing excellent chardonnay and pinot noir. Talley also has a second label, Bishop's Peak, a line of very good-value wines for under $20.

Tolosa Winery

Imagine James Bond creating a tasting room, and you'll get an idea of what the interior of Tolosa Winery (4910 Edna Rd., 805/782-0500, www.tolosawinery.com, 11 A.M.–5 P.M. daily, tasting $8–15) is like: cork floors, stainless steel ceilings, glass bar, wood panels, and

backlighting, all sleek and sophisticated. A flat-screen TV displays pictures of recent events and the winemaking process, and another screen displays up-to-date specials and wine club information. There's even ambient music playing throughout the tasting room, patio, halls, and bathroom. The tasting room looks out over the gleaming polished stainless steel fermentation tanks. Guests can take a self-guided tour or guided tours (by appointment, $15–35) through the facility as well. Stay and picnic at their tranquil outdoor picnic area, or play a round of boccie ball as you soak in the peaceful surroundings. The focus is on chardonnay and pinot noir, but you'll also find merlot, syrah, viognier, and even grenache blanc.

Salisbury Vineyards

This 104-year-old schoolhouse, now a tasting room and art gallery, underwent a historic interior renovation and opened in 2005. As you enter the tasting room at Salisbury Vineyards (6985 Ontario Rd., 805/595-9463, www.salisburyvineyards.com, noon–5 P.M. Mon.–Thurs., 11 A.M.–6 P.M. Fri.–Sun., tasting $5), you're immediately struck by the openness of the space and the copious amount of wood, most notably the original hardwood floors. A sign by the front door warns that stiletto heels can have a detrimental effect on the old floors, and to walk gently, but that everyone is still welcome. Salisbury aims for the schoolhouse to serve a multitude of functions: besides a tasting room, it's also part art gallery, presenting artwork from around the globe that rotates every 8–10 weeks. Chardonnay, syrah, zinfandel, and cabernet sauvignon are the main wines produced here.

ENTERTAINMENT AND EVENTS
Nightlife
BARS AND CLUBS

San Luis Obispo is a college town, and the college bar is **Frog & Peach** (728 Higuera St., 805/595-3764, noon–2 A.M. daily), a narrow, small space that's usually packed on the weekends. When the bands start playing it gets

PASO ROBLES WINE COUNTRY

A pleasant detour from Cambria or Morro Bay, Paso Robles is being hailed as "the next Napa." Although the accolade is well-intended, this region is similar to Napa in only one respect: It produces world-class wines.

The Paso Robles wine scene is broken down into the east side, west side, and downtown.

Start on the east side by visiting **Eberle Winery** (3810 Hwy. 46 E., 805/238-9607, www.eberlewinery.com, 10 A.M.-5 P.M. daily, free). Gary Eberle is the father of Paso Robles wine, and today, his Eberle Winery is the single most-awarded winery in the country, with top-notch cabernet sauvignons as well as viognier, sangiovese, barbera, zinfandel, and chardonnay – most priced under $25. Bring a picnic and relax on the deck surrounded by vine-covered hills. Don't mind the friendly black poodles that greet you on arrival; they're part of the Eberle family.

Across the road is **Vina Robles** (3700 Mill Rd., 805/227-4812, www.vinarobles.com, 10 A.M.-6 P.M. daily summer, 10 A.M.-5 P.M. daily winter, tasting $5-15), which focuses on Rhône varieties. A voluminous space with stone walls and eclectic artwork, the tasting room has a large fireplace and comfy sofas. The well-priced wines, many under $20, consist of cabernet sauvignon, petite sirah, zinfandel, petite verdot, and blends of these grapes.

Next, head back downtown: Go west on Highway 46, then either take U.S. 101 south toward Paso Robles or continue on 24th Street and turn left on Spring Street, where multiple tasting rooms flank the central park. First, visit the inviting **Pianetta Winery** (829 13th St., 805/226-4005, www.pianettawinery.com, noon-6 P.M. daily, tasting $5), in the late-1880s Grangers Union Building. It feels like a ranch house, with wooden arbors and old family farming photos hanging on the walls. Pianetta's wines, which include sangiovese, syrah, cabernet sauvignon, petite sirah, and several blends, will win you over with lots of up-front fruit and balance.

Walk two blocks south, past the downtown square, to **Vihuela Winery** (840 11th St., 805/226-2010, www.vihuelawinery.com, 11 A.M.-4 P.M. Sun.-Mon., 11 A.M.-7 P.M. Wed.-Sat., tasting $5). Vihuela prefers big reds and Bordeaux varietals, focusing on syrah and cabernet sauvignon, producing only one white wine so far, a chardonnay. Their signature blend, called Concierto del Rojo (Concert of Red), is an unorthodox blend of syrah, merlot, and petite verdot. The tasting room shares an unpretentious space with Vivant Fine Cheese and includes an outdoor patio.

Head toward the coast, back west on Highway 46, accessed from U.S. 101 south of town, to stop by **Windward Vineyard** (1380 Live Oak Rd., 805/239-2565, www.windwardvineyard.com, 10:30 A.M.-5 P.M. daily, tasting $10), which is an anomaly: Normally pinot noir grows better in cooler weather, often near coastal influences. Windward is in Paso Robles, which is hot in the summer and downright cold in the winter. But this small parcel of vines is situated in a pocket of land that protects it. Windward makes only pinot noir, with several vintages to compare and contrast.

Finally, drive along undulating roads to visit **Jada** (5620 Vineyard Dr., 805/226-4200, www.jadavineyard.com, 11 A.M.-5 P.M. daily, tasting $10). The stacked stone walls and arched iron gate that front the highway lead alongside a line of plum trees. The wines have creative names like XCV, a white blend of viognier, roussanne, and grenache blanc; Hell's Kitchen, a mix of syrah, grenache, mourvèdre, and tannat; and Jack of Hearts, a Bordeaux blend of cabernet sauvignon, petit verdot, and merlot. The expansive deck provides lovely views of the vineyards.

GETTING THERE

Paso Robles is right on U.S. 101, and can also be accessed on Highway 46, a 25-mile drive from Highway 1 just south of Cambria. Highway 46 joins U.S. 101 for one mile and leads into downtown Paso Robles from the Spring Street exit.

warm, but the outside patio overlooking the creek is a way to cool down and escape the throngs. Although it calls itself a pub, it's more a pure bar, with basic worn wood and booths that face the long bar. Tuesday evenings are pint nights. If you're looking for a younger crowd, this is the spot.

Koberl at Blue (998 Monterey St., 805/783-1135, www.epkoberl.com, 4–10 P.M. Sun.–Wed., 4–11 P.M. Thurs.–Sat., bar open later) has white tablecloths, exposed brick walls, and more sophisticated flair than Frog & Peach. There are still beers—a wide variety of European brews, in fact—and a stellar wine list. But Koberl is best known for its martini options—locals know it's one of the best places to grab a signature martini after work.

Mo/Tav (725 Higuera St., 805/541-8733, www.motherstavern.com, 11:30 A.M.–9 P.M. Sun.–Wed., 11:30 A.M.–9:30 P.M. Thurs.–Sat., nightclub 9:30 P.M.–1:30 A.M. daily) used to be called Mother's Tavern, but this is not your mother's tavern. In addition to bottle service and a dance floor, there is karaoke every Sunday–Monday and DJs spinning dance tunes the rest of the week. The long wood bar with a massive round mirror echoes the upscale saloon feel of this very popular place.

LIVE MUSIC

The Graduate (900 Industrial Way, 805/541-0969, www.slograd.com, cover $5–10), as the name implies, is aimed at the college and post-college crowd. College night is Wednesday, and there is salsa and merengue on Friday, country music on Thursday, and various other events other nights, along with a large dance floor with a bar and restaurant. Live bands as well as DJs provide a cool place to hang out.

The **Pozo Saloon** (90 W. Pozo Rd., Pozo, 805/438-4225, www.pozosaloon.com) is one of the best venues for live music on the Central Coast. The problem is that it's not near anything: 17 miles off the highway in the all-but-forgotten town of Pozo, it's a 3,000-seat outdoor venue. Many big-name acts have performed here, including the Black Crowes, Ziggy Marley, and Merle Haggard. If you

decide to go with general admission, you need to bring your own chair or blanket. Cell phones don't work here, and there's only one restaurant. It gets packed, in part because it's such a cool venue, away from everything and out among the low hills and oak trees. Check the schedule, as you don't want to head all the way out here on the wrong day.

For a step back in time, the Madonna Inn's **Gold Rush Steakhouse** (100 Madonna Rd., 805/784-2433, www.madonnainn.com) has live swing and ballroom music and dancing most evenings beginning about 7:30 P.M. There is no cover, and the crowd is older, but it's festive and everyone's in a good mood, in part because it's hard to be unhappy in the vibrant pink interior. You don't have to dance, of course—just watch and listen if you like.

At **SLO Brew** (1119 Garden St., 805/543-1843, http://slobrewingco.com) there is a stage with the best acoustics in town, showcasing a diverse range of music that includes acoustic, rock, country, and blues. Food in served upstairs, where there are pool tables, and downstairs is a true entertainment venue; it holds 300 people. Shows begin at 8 P.M. most nights of the week. Cover charge depends on the band, usually about $8–15.

Festivals and Events

Similar to its cousin in Santa Barbara, the **I Madonnari** (805/541-6294, www.aiacentralcoast.org) festival happens each year in September at the plaza of the Old Mission downtown, which is transformed with colorful large-scale street paintings. The 200 squares are divvied up and the labor-intensive work of chalk painting commences. Festival hours are 10 A.M.–6 P.M., and admission is free. Street painting has a long tradition in cities in Western Europe and probably started in Italy in the 16th century. The artists who use chalk to draw on the street are known as *madonnari*, or "Madonna painters," because they originally reproduced icons of the Madonna.

The **City to the Sea Half Marathon, 5K and Kids Fun Run** (www.citytothesea.org) is still the best running event in SLO. It starts downtown and heads all the way to the ocean in Pismo Beach each October, when the weather is just about perfect for a long run. This is one of the largest races in the area and draws all manner of runners, experienced to novice, to the 13.1-mile route.

The Central Coast is home to lots of writers, and once a year they get to showcase all things literary at the **Central Coast Book and Author Festival** (805/546-1392, www.ccbookfestival.org). This festival is by no means just local writers, however. In addition to public readings for kids and adults, the one-day event happens at Mission Plaza, with dance performances and even cooking demonstrations. There are seminars by authors and illustrators, used and new books for sale, and booths to browse and meet your new favorite writer. It's free to attend.

SHOPPING
Bookstores
Many bookstores in San Luis Obispo have closed, but **Phoenix** (990 Monterey St., 805/543-3591, 10 A.M.–9 P.M. Mon–Sat., 11 A.M.–9 P.M. Sun.) still has a large selection of used books. It's actually two stores joined by a doorway, with books wall-to-wall and some just stacked on the floor. The upstairs section has world histories of Ireland and Wales, suggesting a good selection in any category. There is one small case of rare books, and you're more likely to hear NPR than music on the radio.

Clothing
Head to **!Romp** (714 Higuera St., 805/545-7667, www.rompshoes.com, 10 A.M.–6 P.M. Mon.–Sat. 11 A.M.–5 P.M., Sun.) for hand-selected, handmade Italian footwear that isn't carried most places. Owner Karen English offers an exclusive collection of fashionable footwear for women that's worth seeking out for your foot fetish. There are also handbags, belts, and some jewelry. The stylish store carries some styles for men, including boots, sneakers, and loafers.

HepKat (778 Marsh St., 805/596-0360, www.hepkatclothing.com, 10 A.M.–8 P.M. daily) has a focus on 1950s clothes, hats, and accessories. These retro Rat Pack–style looks are not true vintage but rather brand-new modern renditions of men's and women's fashions from that period. Although the store is small, there's a lot to look at here, including Bettie Page–style dresses and hair pomade.

SLO Swim (795 Higuera St., 805/781-9604, 11 A.M.–5:30 P.M. Mon.–Sat., 11 A.M.–5 P.M. Sun.) sells bathing suits and swimwear with an emphasis on full-figured women. There's a tiny selection of suits for men. Shopping for swimwear can be taxing as it is, but here you'll find something that actually fits your body type, especially if you're a hard-to-fit type.

Specialty Stores
The SLO life can best be summed up at these cool stores. **Cloud 9 Smoke Shop & Hookah Lounge** (584 California Blvd., 805/593-0420, www.cloud9slo.com, 11 A.M.–10 P.M. Mon.–Tues., 1 P.M.–midnight Wed., 11 A.M.–2 A.M. Thurs.–Sat., noon–10 P.M. Sun.) has two parts: the smoke shop, with beautiful high-end water pipes and accessories, and next door, through the black curtain, a surprisingly nice hookah lounge with black leather couches and chairs and interesting artwork on the walls. Although it's near campus, it's not child's play, and there are strict regulations. There's a great diversity of flavored tobacco for the hookahs but minimal snack items, mainly candy and chips. It's one of the few hookah lounges between Los Angeles and San Francisco, and they do a nice job keeping it clean and inviting. Rates start at $5 per hookah plus $7 pp.

At **Central Coast Surfboards** (855 Marsh St., 805/541-1129, www.ccsurf.com, 10 A.M.–7 P.M. Sun.–Wed., 10 A.M.–9 P.M. Thurs., 10 A.M.–8 P.M. Fri.–Sat.) you'll find the classic surfboards and boogie boards with which this 30-year-old institution made its name. There are wetsuits upstairs, and downstairs are swimsuits, skate shoes, and a wide selection of clothing, including backpacks for the skater, surfer, or wannabe. They have a huge selection of ugg boots.

Habitat Home & Garden (777 Marsh St., 805/541-4275, 10 A.M.–6 P.M. Mon.–Sat.,

11 A.M.–5 P.M. Sun.) sells furniture and home accessories, with lots of recycled wood and old roots polished into beautiful tables, some capped with metal. There is a Polynesian and Balinese theme and a few antiques mixed in, and some really cool and unique pieces you may not have seen before.

HumanKind (982 Monterey St., 805/594-1220, www.humankindslo.org, 10 A.M.–6 P.M. Mon.–Sat.) is a nonprofit store that deals in clothing, home accessories, books, toys, and jewelry. It's all certified Fair Trade, so you can shop with confidence that your purchase will directly benefit the person who made the item.

Art Galleries

It's no surprise that this area inspires artists, and more galleries are turning up all the time. The choices here provide a great overview of the art scene in town; check out www.sanluisobispogalleries.com for more information on SLO galleries.

Group and solo exhibitions feature Central Coast artists at **San Luis Obispo Art Center** (1010 Broad St., 805/543-8562, www.sloartcenter.org, 11 A.M.–5 P.M. Wed.–Mon. Labor Day–July 3, 11 A.M.–5 P.M. daily July 5–Labor Day, closed major holidays, free), but artists from across the country are also occasionally featured. Four small galleries show new exhibits each month. Also on offer are lectures and art workshops, including stained glass, working with silks, printmaking, and working in a variety of other media. Plans are in the works to turn this into a museum, but that's years away. For now, it continues to occupy the space near Mission Plaza and the river walk.

The Gallery at The Network (778 Higuera St., Suite B, 805/788-0886, www.galleryatthenetwork.com, 11 A.M.–6 P.M. Mon.–Wed. and Fri.–Sat., 11 A.M.–8 P.M. Thurs., 11 A.M.–5 P.M. Sun.) has focused on local arts for a decade and features about 35 artists, some local and some regional, that work with glass, pottery, oil and pastels, wood, and ceramics. The gallery is inside a small indoor mall, which can be easy to miss since there's no storefront on Higuera

Street. If you're looking for local art, this is the stop to buy and also to meet the artists.

RECREATION
Golf

The **Avila Beach Golf Resort** (6464 Ana Bay Dr., Avila Beach, 805/595-4000, www.avilabeachresort.com, $41–70) is an 18-hole, par-71 public course. The front nine holes are situated in peaceful and serene oak-lined valleys. The back nine traverse a tidal estuary. Try not to let the views distract you from the task at hand. There are elevated tees, and the course is a little tight but certainly readable; just don't underestimate it. There's a pro shop and a very good grill on-site.

Hiking

The **Estero Bluffs State Park** (Hwy. 1 at San Geronimo Rd., 805/772-7434) is a four-mile stretch of relatively new state park coastline just north of Cayucos. Access the trail by any of several pullouts on the west side of Highway 1. A trail follows the bluff the entire way, and you can often find short scrambles down to the rocky beaches. It's a great place for seeing sea otters and is mainly level except for heading down to and back from the beach areas. The northern half has better access to beaches and good tide pooling at low tide. Reach the area just 0.5 miles past North Ocean Avenue as you leave Cayucos on Highway 1. Park at any of the pullouts, and head toward the bluff, where you'll find the trails and low sparse vegetation.

Biking

There's no shortage of cyclists in SLO. The **San Luis Obispo Bicycle Club** (805/543-5973, www.slobc.org) organizes weekly rides and has a wealth of information on local routes.

Bob Jones City to the Sea Trail (U.S. 101 at Avila Beach Dr.) is undoubtedly one of the most popular and well-traveled routes, in part because it's separate from the main road and is fully paved, wandering through pretty trees and shrub-lined areas until it terminates at the ocean. The three-mile out-and-back course follows an old railroad line that follows San Luis Obispo Creek. From U.S. 101, exit at Avila Beach Drive and take it 0.25 miles to Ontario Road and turn right. About another 0.25 miles up, you'll see the dirt parking lot; the trailhead is across the street.

In town, **Madonna Mountain** (end of Marsh St. at Fernandez Lane), also known as San Luis Mountain, has short steep trails that are great for a fast, hard bike workout. The wide fire road runs two miles to the top of the hill, which has great views back toward San Luis and of the surrounding hills. The trailhead is at the Maino Open Space, on the west side of U.S. 101 at the end of Marsh Street.

Spas

Sycamore Mineral Springs Resort (1215 Avila Beach Dr., 805/595-7302, www.sycamoresprings.com, massage 8 A.M.–9 P.M. daily, hot tubs 8 A.M.–midnight daily) is best known for its private hot tubs built into the hillside and fed by natural mineral waters. The spa, located near the tubs, is a Tuscan-looking building with treatment rooms facing a central pool. You can get a massage, a facial, a body wrap, and other treatments; incorporate a mineral soak as well. Take a yoga class or simply stroll the grounds and use the labyrinth to detox. This is a one-stop place to find something to soothe you.

The Bladerunner (894 Monterey St., 805/541-5131, www.thebladerunner.com, 9 A.M.–6 P.M. Tues.–Wed. and Fri., 9 A.M.–7 P.M. Thurs., 9 A.M.–5 P.M. Mon. and Sat., 11 A.M.–4 P.M. Sun.) is a spacious full-service salon and spa with tranquil green walls and very competent staff. You can have anything from facials to waxing to a cut and color done here. Bladerunner also offer chair massage in 15-minute increments if you need a quick stress reliever. It is right downtown and has a little waiting area if someone comes with you.

ACCOMMODATIONS

In spite of being so close to the beach, there are still relatively inexpensive places to stay in town. Prices are higher at places near the water.

Under $150

La Cuesta Inn (2074 Monterey St., 805/543-2777, www.lacuestainn.com, $99–159 d) offers great pricing, and although the place is average in appearance, it hardly matters, as you'll be spending most of your time outside. This 72-room property is set near the hills, and in the afternoons they serve tea, coffee, and cookies. The guest rooms are comfortable and nicely decorated but nothing out of the ordinary, and they make a great choice if you're not picky about views. It's one mile to downtown, with a heated outdoor pool and hot tub as well as free Wi-Fi.

Best Western Royal Oak Hotel (214 Madonna Rd., 800/545-4410, www.royaloakhotel.com, $125–180 d) has 99 thoughtfully decorated guest rooms that are larger than most chain hotel rooms. There is a customary continental breakfast, a pool, and a hot tub, and it's close to downtown (although you'll have to drive); you can walk to Laguna Lake Park. This is an independently owned property, and there is a level of service here that exceeds many Best Westerns.

$150-250

Inn at Avila Beach (256 Front St., 805/595-2300, www.hotelsavilabeach.com, $189–245 d) is known locally as the pink hotel because of its faded pink walls. A Mexican theme runs throughout this 31-room property, with tiled walkways and decent-size guest rooms, some of which face the beach. The guest rooms are a little older looking, and some are more decorated than others. The beach is right out the front door, and even if you're not at the beach, you can hear the surf. The sun deck is a favorite hangout with semiprivate cabanas with couches, TVs, and hammocks overlooking everything. There is no air-conditioning, but chances are you won't need it. There is a collection of 300 movies you can rent for in-room evening entertainment, since Avila shuts down early.

Embassy Suites (333 Madonna Rd., 805/549-0800, www.embassysuites.com, $159–190 d) offers comfortable guest rooms, standard in size and decor; the suites provide more room for a longer stay. There is a nice indoor pool and a hot tub, and next door is the fitness room. The lobby is a central courtyard, with guest rooms facing the voluminous space. The restaurant as well as a coffee bar are in the courtyard, and they provide a cooked-to-order complimentary breakfast. Dogs are welcome. It's at the south end of the shopping mall and near Laguna Lake Park, but you'll need to drive to get downtown.

The Apple Farm (2015 Monterey St., 800/255-2040, www.applefarm.com, $150–280 d) has 104 guest rooms spread out over a large area, and the Victorian-country theme and dainty decor draws big crowds because it feels like a hotel your grandmother might run. The clientele tends to be older, and the service is very focused. Fireplaces, large shower tubs, and the daily newspaper are available, and there is an extensive gift shop and in-house restaurant with early-bird dinner specials for seniors. It is right off U.S. 101 just north of downtown and near the site of the very first motel in California. Although it's near the freeway, it's relatively quiet.

Garden Street Inn (1212 Garden St., 805/545-9802, www.gardenstreetinn.com, $219–249 d) is a 13-room bed-and-breakfast right downtown, so you can walk anywhere. It was built in 1887, and though the kitchen has been remodeled, the rest remains pretty much original. The floor-to-ceiling wood-paneled library on the first floor has lots of books to read, and a full breakfast is served each morning. The guest rooms are nicely furnished, all with an eye toward creating a sense of authenticity, even if the room phones are push-button models.

Each of seven rooms at **The Sanitarium** (1716 Osos St., 805/544-4124, www.thesanitariumspa.com, $200–350 d) is different, although each has a deck, a wood-burning stove, and a Moroccan tub. This bed-and-breakfast in a residential neighborhood of well-tended craftsman houses was founded in the 1880s as an actual sanitarium. The owner whitewashed the wood-sided building inside and out and filled it with paintings and sculptures. Breakfasts are made from local produce and include basics such as pancakes, French toast, and scrambled eggs served with fresh organic fruit, unusual jams, fresh-squeezed juice, and coffee.

Over $250

The **Avila La Fonda** (101 San Miguel St., Avila Beach, 805/595-1700, www.avilalafonda.com, $349–449) has a Spanish hacienda feel. A walled waterfall greets guests as they enter. The lobby was patterned after Mission San Miguel in both size and height. If you look at the front of the hotel, you'll see it is meant to resemble a Mexican village, with the mission set in the center. A hospitality suite to the right of the lobby always has chocolate chip cookies, pie, coffee, and tea, and a full spread of cheeses and wine 5–6:30 P.M. daily. There is the chocolate pantry, open 24 hours daily, if you get a craving for something sweet, all included for guests. The 28 guest rooms feature large, deep whirlpool tubs, towel warmers, fireplaces, and wide flat-screen TVs. Some guest rooms have tiled floors, and some are carpeted; the colorful walls and Mexican accents, such as pottery and paintings, do a good job of creating a modern hacienda interpretation. Some guest rooms are spa rooms, some are studio rooms with kitchens, and they can be opened to each other to form a full-size master suite. There is covered parking. Costco members can save 20 percent.

FOOD
American

Mo's Smokehouse BBQ (1005 Monterey St., 805/544-6193, www.smokinmosbbq.com, 11 A.M.–9 P.M. Sun.–Wed., 11 A.M.–10 P.M. Thurs.–Sat., $18) is the spot for barbecue. Forgo the salads and sandwiches, and go for the pork and beef ribs with their special barbecue sauce, which you can purchase on-site (and you'll want to), and get a side of onion rings. All the meats are smoked on-site with hickory wood. The walls are covered with photos of barbecue joints all across the country, an homage to those unsung heroes who create mouthwatering barbecue each and every day.

The **Custom House** (404 Front St., Avila Beach, 805/595-7555, www.oldcustomhouse. com, 8 A.M.–9 P.M. Sun.–Thurs., 8 A.M.–10 P.M. Fri.–Sat., $15), on the boardwalk, provides lots of indoor and outside seating with views of the beach. It's certainly popular, and there is often a wait on weekends. The interior has a nautical theme, with dark wood and large wide windows. For breakfast, there is an excellent eggs Benedict with a large slab of ham and creamy hollandaise sauce. For lunch the mahimahi fish-and-chips can be served either tempura-style or breaded. The dinner has six different steaks, fresh fish, and barbecue dishes with house-made sauce.

At the **Firestone Grill** (1001 Higuera St., 805/783-1001, 11 A.M.–10 P.M. Mon.–Wed., 11 A.M.–11 P.M. Thurs.–Sat., 11 A.M.–10 P.M. Sun., $12), it's all about the tri-tip sandwich. There's a heavy college contingency, and game days can be cumbersome and loud. Most weekends see lines out the door that may move quickly, but seating is at a premium. Don't be alarmed by the wait, but do be prepared for it.

At **Frank's Famous Hot Dogs** (950 California Ave., 805/541-3488, 6 A.M.–9 P.M. daily, $5), the real highlights are the chicken strips and breakfast burritos, not the hot dogs. Crowded because it's pretty cheap, it's also not an overly attractive place, but hey—it's a hot dog stand. For something slightly different, order what the owner calls the pigpen, a hot dog and bun chopped up then doused with chili, cheese, and onions.

Gardens of Avila (1215 Avila Beach Dr., 805/595-7365, www.sycamoresprings.com, 8 A.M.–2 P.M. and 4–9 P.M. Mon–Thurs., 8 A.M.–9 P.M. Fri.–Sun., $25) is tucked into the Sycamore Mineral Springs. The small space has a large glass wall that looks onto the stone wall holding up the back hill, so it feels intimate, almost cave-like. The best spot, however, is a one-table balcony overlooking the dining room. The menu is limited, but the selections cover a wide range of flavors, from niçoise tuna tartar and local snapper to duck confit and traditional steaks. They also always provide a vegetarian option. For breakfast, the sour cream banana pancakes are terrific. Corkage is complimentary on one bottle of local wine.

International Fusion

Novo (726 Higuera St., 805/543-3986, www. novorestaurant.com, food 11 A.M.–9 P.M. Sun.–Thurs., 11 A.M.–10 P.M. Fri.–Sat., cocktails 10 P.M.–midnight Fri.–Sat., $20) was originally a cigar factory in the 1890s. The brick building is located downtown across from Mission Plaza and has a fully heated terraced patio overlooking the creek. In the center of the deck an oak tree provides shade and a bit of tranquility. Downstairs, the Cellar is truly a unique subterranean room; once home to the Old Cigar Factory safe, it is now a must-see wine cellar. Novo specializes in international cuisine, pulling spices and flavors from Brazil, Asia, and the Mediterranean with entrées like lavender lamb chops with sea salt and roasted spring onions as well as *sopes* with slow-roasted *carnitas*.

Italian

Café Roma (1020 Railroad Ave., 805/541-6800, www.caferomaslo.com, lunch 11:30 A.M.–2 P.M. Mon.–Fri., dinner 5–9 P.M. Mon.–Sun., $20) offers a casual dining experience with upscale decor featuring yellow mottled walls with red-accented carpet and drapes and white tablecloths. There's a separate bar and a large outdoor patio for those slow summer evenings, with views of the trains just across the way. Stick with the pasta dishes, like the pumpkin ravioli with sage sauce or the orecchiette with Hearst Ranch beef bolognese, which is what they do best, and everything will be all right. If pasta isn't quite your thing, there are fish, chicken, and beef dishes, all with an Italian flair.

Organic and Farm Fresh

It's not all vegetarian at homey **Sally Loo's** (1804 Osos St., 805/545-5895, 6:30 A.M.–6:30 P.M. Tues.–Sun., $12), but they certainly focus on healthy natural organic ingredients in dishes like strawberry and black pepper scones or goat cheese and asparagus quiche. Live music and even tango lessons are occasionally featured. The venue feels like it belongs in San Francisco and has a community vibe, with communal tables, worn couches, and funky art on the walls. You'll see Sally Loo there too: Just keep your eyes peeled for the content pit bull.

Big Sky Cafe (1121 Broad St., 805/545-5401, www.bigskycafe.com, 7 A.M.–9 P.M. Mon.–Thurs., 7 A.M.–10 P.M. Fri., 8 A.M.–10 P.M. Sat., 8 A.M.–9 P.M. Sun., $15) supports a farm-to-table mentality and offers organic-only dishes like roasted eggplant lasagna as well as dishes like marinated catfish, braised lamb, and a full selection of salads. The ambience is pleasant, and service is very friendly. The wood tables and chairs can be a bit uncomfortable after a while, but after a salad and some organic bread you really won't mind.

Steak Houses

The █ **Gold Rush Steakhouse** (100 Madonna Rd., 805/543-3000, www.madonnainn.com, 5–9 P.M. daily, $25), located inside the Madonna Inn, is an old-school steak house with over-the-top decor. There aren't too many places like this around: The pink booths, surrounded by golden cherubs hanging from the ceiling and red velvet wallpaper, feels like a David Lynch movie. Dine on prime beef grilled over red oak, with salad and a baked potato wrapped in gold foil. Chicken and fish is available. The service is attentive, and the blue cheese dressing is dynamite. Finish the meal with a slice of pink champagne cake, and you'll be close to heaven.

Just down from the Madonna Inn is **Tahoe Joe's Famous Steakhouse** (485 Madonna Rd., 805/543-8383, www.tahoejoes.com, 11 A.M.–10 P.M. Mon.–Thurs., 11 A.M.–11 P.M. Fri.–Sat., 11 A.M.–9 P.M. Sun., $20), where big booths and big portions are the name of the game. It is a small chain, but this is the only coastal location, and they serve excellent prime rib and steaks, not to mention some of the best garlic mashers. It's a hugely popular spot, and

you may have to wait on weekends, but if you're hungry, this is your stop.

Farmers Market

A great farmers market (www.downtownslo.com) kick-starts the weekend every Thursday night year-round. Around 6 P.M. local farmers set up stands along the four blocks of Higuera Street downtown to sell seasonal fruits, specialty herbs, organic vegetables, fresh flowers, and barbecue tri-tip sandwiches. Local musicians provide much of the entertainment, setting up concerts on adjoining streets, and many of the stores and shops extend their hours for the evening. It's more than a farmers market: It's a social and cultural event that has drawn locals, college kids, and travelers for years.

INFORMATION AND SERVICES

The **San Luis Obispo Visitors Center** (1037 Mill St., 800/634-1414) is located right downtown. Free maps and guides for restaurants, wineries, and the like are available, but the authoritative guide to the area costs $4.

The *San Luis Obispo Tribune* is the second-largest daily paper on the Central Coast and is widely distributed. The *New Times* is the free alternative weekly; it appears every Thursday.

In an emergency, dial **911.** Two hospitals serve San Luis Obispo: **French Hospital Medical Center** (1911 Johnson Ave., 805/543-5353, www.frenchmedicalcenter.org) and the smaller **Sierra Vista Regional Medical Center** (1010 Murray Ave., 805/546-7600, www.sierravistaregional.com). **Police services** can be found at the City of San Luis Obispo Police Department (1042 Walnut St., 805/781-7317) and the San Luis Obispo County Sherriff's Office (1585 Kansas Ave., 805/781-4550).

GETTING THERE AND AROUND

As with most towns on the Central Coast, U.S. 101 cuts through town, and access is off this main artery. Traveling north or south, the main exits are Broad and California Streets. You can also reach town by driving south from

Morro Bay on Highway 1, which takes you right downtown. San Luis Obispo is on a grid system with the main drag, Higuera Street, a southbound one-way street; Marsh Street is one-way heading north. Two-hour parking is the norm except on Sunday, when there is free parking all day on city streets.

If you need to travel on someone else's wheels, **234-Taxi** (872 Morro St., 805/234-8294, www.234taxi.com) is a good bet; they serve the area and take all major credit cards. There's also the **SLO Cab Company** (202 Tank Farm Rd., 805/544-1222).

The *Pacific Surfliner,* one of the **Amtrak** (800/872-7245, www.amtrak.com) coastal trains, travels from San Luis Obispo south to San Diego, with stops in Grover Beach, Goleta, Santa Barbara, Los Angeles, and smaller towns, while the *Coast Starlight* runs between Seattle in the north and Los Angeles in the south, with local stops in Paso Robles, San Luis Obispo, and Grover Beach. It has sleeper cars and can be a great way to reach the area from the Pacific Northwest. **Amtrak Thruway Motorcoach Service** (800/872-7245, www.amtrak.com) runs its bus routes 17, 21, and 36 between Oakland in the north and Santa Barbara in the south, with

stops in Paso Robles, San Luis Obispo, and Grover Beach. The buses connect to the *Pacific Surfliner.* The San Luis Obispo Regional Transit Authority (179 Cross St., 805/781-4472, www.slorta.org, 6 A.M.–9:45 P.M. Mon.–Fri., $1.50–3, exact change only) covers the county. All the buses are wheelchair accessible and have bike racks. As a general rule buses do not operate on major holidays, so it's best to check for specific schedules.

The brown and green **Downtown Trolley** (3:30–9 P.M. Thurs., noon–9 P.M. Fri.–Sat., 10 A.M.–3 P.M. Sun.) costs a mere $0.25 to ride. The loop goes from the hotels at the north end of Monterey Street near U.S. 101 to Mission Plaza, down Higuera Street, back up Marsh Street, and back to Monterey Street at Osos Street. It runs every 15–20 minutes.

Located just two miles south of San Luis Obispo, the **San Luis Obispo County Regional Airport** (SBP, 903-5 Airport Dr., 805/781-5205, www.sloairport.com) serves the area from southern Monterey County to northern Santa Barbara County. The airport offers dozens of flights daily; it's currently served by four airlines with flights to Las Vegas, Los Angeles, Phoenix, Salt Lake City, and San Francisco.

Montaña de Oro State Park

It's nearly impossible to describe the inherent beauty of Montaña de Oro State Park (805/528-0513, http://parks.ca.gov, www.slostateparks.com, sunrise–sunset daily, free), a glorious, many-faceted 8,000-acre park with spectacular scenery. As you first enter the park, you're surrounded by a few trees and views of the ocean. But soon you're plummeted into a dense eucalyptus forest. If you stop for just a moment, you can easily inhale the rich aromas of these trees. There are pullouts where small trails wind through the forested section. As you continue on, you're suddenly pulled out of the forest into daylight along bluff-top roads, with the ocean on the right and forested hills on the left.

SIGHTS

Within Montaña de Oro are extensive trails for hiking, walking, and biking. **Spooner's Cove** (805/528-0513, www.parks.ca.gov) is one of the more popular places because of its wide, deep cove of ancient rocks, sandy protected beach, and bluff-top trails that lead up from the beach. The visitors center and park headquarters are also located here at the old **Spooner Ranch House** (3550 Pecho Valley Rd., 805/528-0513, hours vary, call ahead). The beauty of this park is its diversity, with groves of trees, beaches, rocks, and low chaparral. All of this is coupled with tremendous views in a pristine coastal environment. If you do nothing else, drive through this park. Better yet, get a map at the visitors center and spend the day exploring one of the last great coastal regions in the state.

HIKING

Walk the **Bluff Trail at Spooner's Cove** (Pecho Valley Rd., Montaña de Oro), with excellent views of the ocean and back to Montaña de Oro State Park. Spooner's Cove is on the right about four miles in from the official park entrance. There's a clearly marked parking lot at Spooner's Cove. The trail hugs the bluff top and cliffs and the low, flat vegetation allows killer views of the ragged short cliffs and rock. Out and back is about two miles, but there are inland trails that connect to the Rattlesnake–Coon Creek Loop Trail, so you can be out much longer if you want.

The **Valencia Peak-Bluffs Trail** in Montaña de Oro is about 5.5 miles through low scrub and wildflowers. There's an elevation gain of more than 1,000 feet, but it's not overly strenuous, although there is a bit of loose shale here and there. From the top of Valencia, you have 360-degree views as far north as the Piedras Blancas lighthouse in San Simeon. From Highway 1 in Morro Bay, take South Bay Boulevard and follow the signs into Montaña de Oro. Once you pass the official state park sign, it's just over five miles to the turnout for the Valencia Peak Trail, located on the left.

The **Dune Trail,** also in Montaña de Oro, is an easy one-mile round-trip hike. The trailhead is less than 0.5 miles north of Spooner's Cove on Pecho Valley Road, at a small gravel parking lot on the right. This sandy 0.5-mile trail traverses low, dry vegetation and ends at the top of a cliff overlooking the ocean. You can access Spooner's Cove from here as well. It's a steep climb down to the cove, but the views are terrific. This is a great spot when it's sunny or when it's foggy.

BIKING

Barranca Trail Loop (Pecho Valley Rd.) is a dirt single-track and part of the Hazard Peak Trail in Montaña de Oro Sate Park. It has ocean views and some elevation gain, depending on how far you ride. Access the trail from Pecho Valley Road; turn left toward Horse Camp, which puts you on the Hazard Canyon multiuse road. Cycle in from the gate about 0.5 miles on the road, which turns dirt and becomes the Manzanita Trail for another 0.5 miles before meeting Barranca Trail, which is a little over two miles oneway. If you're feeling energetic, you can access the Hazard Trail through the interior portion of Montaña de Oro via elevation gains of 1,000 feet.

GETTING THERE

Access the park via Los Osos Valley Road, off U.S. 101. This road turns into Pecho Valley Road and takes you directly into the park.

Morro Bay

Visitors come to Morro Bay for a slice of coastal California that seems to be vanishing. They want to stroll along the Embarcadero, looking at the boats gently undulating in the calm waters of the bay. They want to hear the call of the sea lions, flit into stores and shops, snack on saltwater taffy, and languidly pass the time in an environment that has not been overbuilt with trendy shops and hotels. And that's what you'll find at Morro Bay. It's not fancy or pretentious, and you're just as likely to see veteran fishermen walking about as you are visitors from all over the world.

The residential section uptown, a few blocks off the Embarcadero, is an odd collection of houses, some new and polished, others from the 1950s, and still others like mobile homes. But Morro Bay maintains its original beach vibe intact, unlike now-swanky Carmel or Monterey. There is plenty of public access to

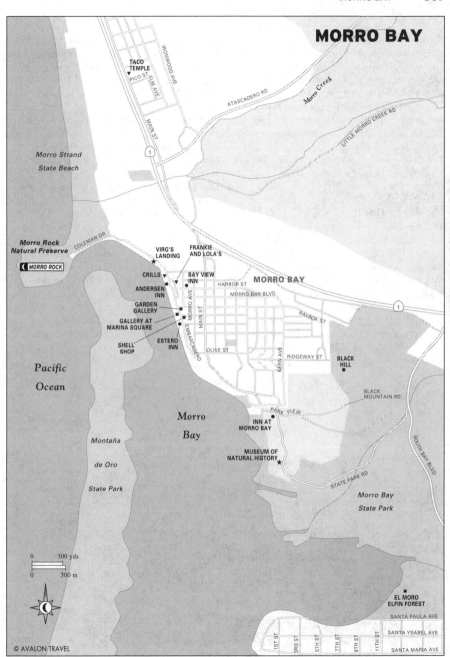

MORRO BAY

IRONWOOD AVE

TACO TEMPLE
PICO ST
ELM AVE
MAIN ST

ATASCADERO RD

Morro Creek

LITTLE MORRO CREEK RD

Morro Strand
State Beach

Morro Rock
Natural Preserve
COLEMAN DR
MORRO ROCK

VIRG'S LANDING
FRANKIE AND LOLA'S
CRILLS
BAY VIEW INN
HARBOR ST
MORRO BAY
ANDERSEN INN
MORRO BAY BLVD
GARDEN GALLERY
MORRO AVE
BALBOA ST
GALLERY AT MARINA SQUARE
EMBARCADERO
MAIN ST
SHELL SHOP
ESTERO INN
OLIVE ST
KERN AVE
RIDGEWAY ST
BLACK HILL

BLACK MOUNTAIN RD

Pacific
Ocean

Morro
Bay

PARK VIEW

INN AT MORRO BAY

SOUTH BAY BLVD

Montaña

de Oro

State Park

MUSEUM OF NATURAL HISTORY

STATE PARK RD

Morro Bay
State Park

0   300 yds
0   300 m

EL MORO ELFIN FOREST
SANTA PAULA AVE
1ST ST
3RD ST
5TH ST
7TH ST
9TH ST
11TH ST
SANTA YSABEL AVE
SANTA MARIA AVE

© AVALON TRAVEL

the water's edge, and nearer to the smokestacks there's a boardwalk, which turns into a concrete sidewalk in the center of town. There are also multiple benches off the main drag where you can sit quietly over the water with a fish taco or saltwater taffy and watch the boats. Morro Bay is also home to a large number of vacation or second-home properties, which undoubtedly helps to sustain its image—people don't want it to change.

The bay tends to have nice weather because it's sheltered from the open water.

SIGHTS
◖ Morro Rock

The defining geographical feature of Morro Bay is the impressive ancient volcanic rock and sacred Chumash site called Morro Rock (www.slostateparks.com, 24 hours daily, free). The rock itself is a collection of nine ancient volcanoes, also known as the Nine Sisters (or seven sisters, depending on who's counting). Morro Rock is one of those spots of incalculable beauty, a sheer rock face with low vegetation

running up parts of it. If you're standing at the base, or if you're in the harbor, there's a nearly palpable energy, a primal beauty, to this ancient volcano. You cannot climb on it because it's home to endangered peregrine falcons. It used to be completely surrounded by water, but now there's a causeway, built mainly of rocks and boulders that fell off the rock or were quarried from it. To access Morro Rock, take Embarcadero Drive north to its end. You can park at the base of the rock for quick access. The breakwater wall connects to the rocks as well, and during storms it's an impressive place to be as the ocean tosses wave after wave over the breakwater.

Black Hill

The second visible volcano in Morro Bay is Black Hill (Morro Bay State Park, State Park Rd., 800/777-0369, www.parks.ca.gov, sunrise–sunset daily, free), which offers stunning panoramas of Morro Rock, the estuary, up the coast toward Cayucos, and down the coast into Baywood Park, a small residential community.

Morro Rock is Morro Bay's defining feature.

© MICHAEL CERVIN

It is accessed by heading into Morro Bay State Park on State Park Road, which is a continuation of Main Street. Immediately after you enter the park, turn left, following a sign for Black Hill Golf Course. This road passes through the golf course and winds up the hill, where it dead-ends. There's a small parking area, and the trail splits in two directions. Take the left fork, which works its way to the summit on a wide path. Once at the top, the views are close to jaw-dropping. You can see the other nearby *morros* (hills), the Nine Sisters, all of Morro Bay, and the surrounding area. Head to the left, where the path quickly turns into a scant trail as you traverse rocks and chaparral, hugging the side of Black Hill. This rugged route is for the adventurous who don't need a clearly marked path. It circles around Black Hill, but it's slow going. Bring a camera. Nonadventurous types can head back the way they came.

Museum of Natural History

The small Museum of Natural History (20 State Park Rd., 805/772-2694, http://mbsp-museum.org, 10 A.M.–5 P.M. daily, adults $3, under age 16 free) at Morro Bay State Park has a great location in the back bay, near the marina. Built on a volcanic point known as White Point, the front section of the facility is very kid-friendly, with lots of touch exhibits about sand, waves, and animals. The back section has a good assortment of stuffed birds, including a peregrine falcon, so you can get a feel for what you'll see in the area. Best of all, there's an albatross dangling from the ceiling, its massive wings like a shelter. There's also a full-size skeleton of a minke whale on the outside deck overlooking the bay. Lectures are occasionally offered. It's a worthy stop to learn more about the area.

Embarcadero

Chances are, while you're in Morro Bay, you will be on the Embarcadero, the main street that faces the ocean, where many of the restaurants and shops are. You can walk all the way to Morro Rock, about a mile away, and stop to get saltwater taffy, watch the fishing boats unload their catch, shop for clothes, check out an art gallery, and even rent a kayak. It gets understandably crowded in the summer months, when everyone wants to be near the water's edge.

BEACHES

There are six miles of flat, uninterrupted sandy beach between Morro Bay and Cayucos to the north. Tide-pooling is a viable sport, at least at low tide. The general catch-all name for this area is **Morro Strand State Beach.** Access is anywhere there are pullouts along Highway 1. The main parking area is at Highway 1 and Toro Creek Road, but this long stretch of beach does not have any facilities until you reach the town of Cayucos. The beach continues past the Cayucos pier and suddenly disappears; then it's all sheer cliffs. There are a few spots on this long stretch, however, that offer more, such as **North Point** (Hwy. 1 at Toro Lane), which has a grassy area for dogs to roam as well as picnic tables, but no restrooms. A short stairway leads to the sand, and at low tide some of the rock formations are exposed. The **Cloisters** (San Jacinto St. and Coral St.) is actually a park set back from the sand, with restrooms, barbecue areas, picnic tables, and a playground. The drawback is that there are no trees for shade. A short path offers direct beach access so you can cool off in the water.

ENTERTAINMENT AND EVENTS
Nightlife

Every night at the **Otter Rock Cafe** (885 Embarcadero, 805/772-1420, www.otter-rockcafe.com, 10 A.M.–midnight Mon.–Fri., 8 A.M.–midnight Sat.–Sun.) there's something musical happening in the rock-themed interior. Every Wednesday is karaoke night, and Otter Rock claims to have over 5,000 songs to choose from. Other evenings feature musicians from around the Central Coast bringing in a mix of jazz and middle-of-the-road rock. It's always festive and upbeat, and you can dance in view of the ocean.

Legends Bar (899 Main St., 805/772-2525, 11 A.M.–2 A.M. daily) has cribbage games, over 60 types of tequila, a jukebox, and even a moose head squarely mounted over the wooden bar. It's small but has a large selection of drinks. There's also a pool table and a shuffleboard court. There is no food service, but you can order from **Sabetta's Pizza** (897 Main St., 805/772-0200) next door. You don't even have to leave the bar: There's a take-out window in the wall. Never mind the goofy statues out front, just head inside. Some weekends there is live music, usually a local band with a blues-rock feel.

The **Bay Club Lounge** (60 State Park Rd., 805/772-5651, 7–10 P.M. Fri.–Sat.), located at the Inn of Morro Bay, has views of the bay and live music on weekends. It's a good low-key nightlife option. Music is more traditional lounge fare and covers of well-known songs. The pace is slower here, and the main clientele are guests of the inn.

Onboard Nautical (docked in the 1200 block of the Embarcadero, 805/771-9916, www.onboardnauticalevents.com) offers custom dinners, wine-pairing dinners, and harbor cruises with live entertainment on the old-school yacht *Papagallo II.* Built in 1964, it was considered the Rolls Royce of yachts at the time, with beautiful teakwood and plenty of interior and exterior space. Prices start at $85 pp with a minimum of 20 people, which is a fantastic deal considering it includes a meal, which is prepared on board. On a perfect day, you can lounge near the bow and watch the world go by while eating sumptuous food, such as pancetta-roasted scallops or coffee- and peppercorn-crusted sirloin steak. Chef-owner Leonard Gentieu trained at the Culinary Institute of America and is a top-notch chef.

Festivals and Events

Every April, the **Morro Bay Kite Festival** (Coleman Park, Embarcadero at Coleman Dr., 805/772-4467, www.morrobay.org, free) transforms the skies around the bay with colorful kites undulating in the breeze. Kites up to 100 feet long and of every size and shape are

welcome. The festival starts off with the ceremonial Blessing of the Wind by local Chumash people, and there are displays, vendor booths, even choreographed kite ballets. Bring a kite, or buy one here, and join the festivities.

The **Cruisin' Morro Bay Car Show** (www.morrobaycarshow.org) takes over the small town each year. It is all about pre-1974 cars of every type, such as hot rods, woodies, vintage passenger cars, and commercial cars and trucks, totaling 500 entries from California and beyond. Trophies are given out on Sunday, and the cars actually do cruise the streets. There's also an ice cream social. It's crowded beyond belief, but it's also a gas.

The **Avocado and Margarita Festival** (714 Embarcadero, 805/772-4467, www.morrobayavocadomargaritafestivalevent.com, free) is a yearly event in September that may seem like it doesn't fit with the context of Morro Bay, but there are actually about 30 avocado farms in the county, where the climate provides a 14-month growing season. The majority of avocados grown are the Haas variety, and the prolonged growing season means that the avocados are creamier and have more oils developed in the fruit. That means better-tasting guacamole. Combined with margaritas, contests, and live music, all within view of the bay, this is a classic California festival.

Each July for more than 40 years, people have done the **Brian Waterbury Memorial Rock to Pier Run** (805/772-6278, www.leaguelineup.com, $20–40). The six-mile beach run begins at Morro Rock and heads up the coast along the water's edge to the pier in Cayucos. The friendly race starts at 7:15 A.M. and has uninterrupted views of the ocean; if you're not concerned about recording your time, you can run even if you haven't registered.

SHOPPING

Morro Bay is great for leisurely wandering in and out of stores. There are a variety of shops on the **Embarcadero,** and many people limit their time to the waterfront, but remember that there are shops three blocks up from the beach along **Main Street** as well.

Home and Garden

From the looks of the exterior of the old wood-shingled building, the **Garden Gallery** (680 Embarcadero, 805/772-4044, www.thegardengalleryinc.com, 11 A.M.–5 P.M. Mon.–Fri., 10 A.M.–5 P.M. Sat.–Sun.) seems like it has been here for years; in fact, it has—it opened in 1974. There is an abundance of garden and home decor, kitchenware, and garden ornamentation. The surprisingly large space is home to succulents in terra-cotta and other pots, and there are bonsai plants and plenty of other things to make you think about your home and garden design.

Clothing

Wavelengths (998 Embarcadero, 805/772-3904, 9 A.M.–6 P.M. daily) has all you'll need for surfing at the beach, skating on the Embarcadero, or just looking cool enough to look like you belong here. They have a huge selection of swim wear and beach attire, including wetsuits, along with skate clothes, shoes, boards, and accessories. If you forgot your flip-flops, they have a large selection of those too.

Art Galleries

Fifty artists, many local and some regional and national, operate the **Gallery at Marina Square** (601 Embarcadero, Suite 10, 805/772-1068, www.galleryatmarinasquare.blogspot.com, 10 A.M.–6 P.M. daily), which opened in 2003, as an artists' co-op. With that many people involved there's a variety of works, including beautiful photography, sculpture, painting, woodcraft, and fabric art in the two-story complex. Once each month, a guest artist is featured; because a majority of the artists are local, you can find works relating to Morro Bay.

Specialty Stores

If you see seashells near the seashore, you're probably standing in the **Shell Shop** (590 Embarcadero, 805/772-8014, www.theshellshop.net, 9:30 A.M.–5:30 P.M. daily). The faded old shell sign in front of the building isn't overly inviting, but this store has been great for shell lovers since 1955. There are the standard shells you can find anywhere, and shell accented pieces for your home like shell mirrors. They also have a vast selection of unique shells like the *Murex salmonea* from Mozambique, a glorious little shell the size of your pinky fingernail, the large New Zealand red abalone shells, coral, and nautilus shells.

SPORTS AND RECREATION
Whale-Watching and Boat Tours

Although no one can promise you a whale sighting, you'll have a good chance with **Virg's Landing** (1169 Market Ave., 805/772-1222, www.virgs.com, 11 A.M.–2 P.M., Fri.–Sun. Dec.–Apr., $29–39). The gray whales pass by Morro on their way to the warmer waters of Baja California. Though the grays are the most commonly sighted, there are 30 species of whales in the waters at various times of the year. Virg's boat is not a luxury cruising craft, it's a fishing boat—but no, there are no dead fish laying around, and it doesn't smell. But it is a working vessel, so don't think you'll be lounging in a recliner. Trips last just under three hours, and you need to be alert, as sometimes a whale comes right alongside the boat. Sand-dab fishing trips and other sportfishing trips are also available.

For a different take on exploring the water, look into **Sub Sea Tours** (699 Embarcadero, 805/772-9463, www.subseatours.com, 11 A.M.–4 P.M. daily summer, adults $14, students and seniors $11, ages 3–12 $7), where you can look into the water from their glass-bottomed boat. This is a Coast Guard–approved boat that mainly stays within the bay or close to the breakwater to see fish, kelp, sea lions, and otters. Of course you can see a lot from the deck too, but the point is to peek below the water's surface. The tours last under an hour.

Kayaking

The best way to experience Morro Bay is to get out on the bay. **Central Coast Outdoors** (888/873-5610, www.centralcoastoutdoors.com) does an amazing job of guiding you to the best spots to view otters, seals, and sea lions and the plethora of birds in and around the bay and providing excellent factual information. Owners John and Virginia Flaherty are passionate about what they do, and it clearly shows. They offer a variety of kayaking excursions, including half-day and full-day trips and dinner on the dunes. Other outdoor adventures can include hiking, biking, and walking—they will customize a tour to fit what you want. But even the standard kayaking trip allows you to get close to the bay's wildlife and a chance to explore the sand spit, something few people ever do. Half-day kayak tours start at $65. This is one of the most professional and knowledgeable tour companies on the Central Coast.

Bird-Watching

The **Morro Bay Estuary** (State Park Rd., www.mbnep.org), also known as the Back Bay, is an 800-acre salt marsh and a prime spots to find birds. A spotting scope or at least very good binoculars are a necessity, as much of the estuary is muddy and inaccessible. There is a huge diversity of birds in Morro Bay, some 250 species at last count; there are 300 different

© MICHAEL CERVIN

bird-watching with a spotting scope

species along the Central Coast, which means the greatest concentration of birds is right here. You'll see songbirds, raptors, white pelicans, herons, egrets, plovers, warblers, and more in the shallow waters of the estuary and all along the back bay and into the bay itself, but the undisturbed estuary sees the greatest concentration of fowl.

Hiking

A word of warning to potential hikers: January–June is tick season. It's not a big deal, really, as long as you check your clothing after a hike and knock them off. Lighter clothing makes it easier to see the annoying pests.

From Cayucos to Montaña de Oro is ripe with great hiking, both moderate walks and hefty mountain hikes.

The **El Moro Elfin Forest** (11th St. to 17th St., Los Osos, www.slostateparks.com, dawn–dusk daily) is a stunted-growth area that includes 90 acres on Morro Bay's back bay where poor, acidic soil has truncated the growth of these plants, including oak trees. A former Chumash site, it looks more like chaparral than forest, and there are hundreds of species of plants, not to mention excellent views of the estuary for birds. You can also get a good feel of the Nine Sisters, as Black Hill is directly in front of you, Morro Rock is in the distance, and the other mountains are behind you. There's about one mile of wide boardwalk for great wheelchair accessibility. From this vantage point, you might notice a few fishing boats in the back bay that don't seem to go anywhere. Chances are they're oyster boats, growing oysters in the waters beneath them. Oysters have been harvested here since the 1950s. From South Bay Boulevard in Los Osos, head west on Santa Ysabel Avenue, then turn right on 14th Street, which ends at the trailhead into the preserve. There are no restroom facilities here.

The **Chumash Trail** begins 0.5 miles past South Bay Boulevard on Turri Road. It starts with a gentle course through grasslands, coastal sage, and native wildflowers within view of Black Hill and the Elfin Forest, and it connects with the Crespi and Park Ridge Trails. Out and back is less than one mile, but you can connect with the other trails for a longer hike.

ACCOMMODATIONS

Some people may assume that it's better to stay in a larger city like San Luis Obispo, but staying in Morro Bay has its own rewards. For starters, you're at the water's edge, and assuming you're not driving all over, Morro Bay is very walkable, so you can leave your car and get out and explore.

Under $150

It may seem hard to believe, but you can indeed stay at the **Sundown Motel** (640 Main St., 805/772-7381, www.sundownmotel.com, $99) for less than any other place in Morro Bay. Yes, this is a true motel, with no amenities except coffeemakers, refrigerators, and microwaves in the guest rooms and Wi-Fi. But for those on a budget, you won't go wrong. Guest rooms are standard size and minimally decorated but clean and comfortable.

Located just south across the back bay, a short drive to downtown Morro Bay, the **Back Bay Inn** (1391 2nd St., Baywood Park, 877/330-2225, www.backbayinn.com, $155–200 d) has 20 guest rooms, 16 of them overlooking the water, with in-room binoculars, coffeemakers, and refrigerators. The majority of the guest rooms are surprisingly large, and the downstairs guest rooms have semiprivate patios accessed by French doors. You will pay extra if you have a third person in your party, as they cater to duos—one of the reasons it's relatively quiet. Breakfast is included in the form of a voucher for the Back Bay Café (1399 2nd St., 805/528-5607) next door. There's a wine and cheese reception (5 to 7 P.M. daily), but they don't serve local wines.

$150-250

The **Embarcadero Inn** (456 Embarcadero, 805/772-2700, www.embarcaderoinn.com, $185–220 d) is a 33-room hotel at the farthest point from Morro Rock. Half of the average-looking guest rooms are equipped with fireplaces, and there are some views of the bay, although you're across the street and there are other buildings in the view. A small continental breakfast is served, but otherwise you're on your own for food. There's no fitness facility, but they have a deal with Fitness Works in town for a $5 day pass, a very good deal. Covered parking is also available, which you don't always see. Children under 12 stay free.

The **Bay View Inn** (225 Harbor St., 805/772-2771, www.bayviewinn.net, $159 d) is a 22-room property set back from the waterfront, so you actually have great views. It is only a block from the bay and boasts Wi-Fi, fireplaces in most of the average-size guest rooms, and nice decor that is part country, part modern. They also have two sundecks in case you want to avoid the sand. This is an older property, so don't expect the newest furnishings and amenities. It is a great value, though, and less expensive than any place right on the Embarcadero.

The **Baywood Inn** (1370 2nd St., Baywood Park, 805/528-8888, www.baywoodinn.com, $150–200 d) has 18 guest rooms, each thematically unique but with an overall Victorian and French country feel with lots of quilted bedding. Located just south across the back bay, it's a short drive to downtown Morro Bay. Billed as a bed-and-breakfast, breakfast is not actually served; you get a voucher for either La Palapa (1346 2nd St., 805/534-1040) or Good Tides Coffee House (1399 2nd St., 805/528-6000), both next to the hotel. The guest rooms are clean and pleasant, and the rates are a very good value. Guest room amenities include microwaves and small refrigerators.

At the end of the Embarcadero is an eight-room property called the **C Estero Inn** (501 Embarcadero, 805/772-1500, www.esteroinn.com, $160–330 d). Designed and owned by a general contractor, an abundance of attention has been paid to detail. Each guest room has a different layout and the furnishings are different, some with a Polynesian theme, others with a mission feel to them, but all with thoughtful appointments. For example, one of the upstairs suites (both have partial wraparound decks) has an angled wall so that when you're in bed, you have a clear view of Morro Rock. The glass is triple-paned, so it's remarkably quiet. A lot of care and attention went into building the place, and that continues with the service.

Over $250

Dead center in Morro Bay and right on the Embarcadero is **(Andersen Inn** (897 Embarcadero, 805/772-3434, www.andersoninnmorrobay.com, $239–349 d), an eight-room property squarely in the middle of the town. Three guest rooms directly facing the water, called the premium rooms, come with fireplaces and deep hot tubs. The other rooms don't directly face the water but have side balconies, so you're not missing anything. A restaurant called the Galley occupied this site for 46 years, and it was torn down to make room for the Andersen Inn and a new Galley restaurant. The inn is clean and sophisticated without being over the top. The soft yellow walls contrast nicely with the wood-toned furnishings. There are large showers, large closets, large flat-screen TVs, Wi-Fi, very comfy beds, and plenty of space in the guest rooms. And when you step out the door, you're in the thick of things on the Embarcadero. Leave your car in their covered parking lot and go explore. There are lots of repeat guests and a large European contingent.

FOOD

Most people equate Morro Bay with seafood, which is understandable, with fresh fish caught locally. While here, definitely seek out local fish dishes, but also make sure you diversify your culinary experiences to include nonfish items, as Morro Bay has a number of excellent eateries.

American

The **Bayside Cafe** (10 State Park Rd., 805/772-1465, www.baysidecafe.com, 11 A.M.–3 P.M. Mon.–Wed., 11 A.M.–8:30 P.M. Thurs.–Sun., $20) is located in Morro Bay State Park at the marina near the back bay. For over 25 years this fun and funky little

place, with both indoor and outdoor seating with views of the boats, has brought in a steady clientele. It's out of the way and more a word-of-mouth place, with a huge following from the Central Valley. It features a winery of the month with very reasonable by-the-glass prices. You'll find an eclectic menu with burgers, salads, sandwiches, pot roast, vegetarian options, and burritos.

Breakfast and Brunch

Frankie and Lola's (1154 Front St., 805/771-9306, www.frankieandlolas.com, 6:30 A.M.–2:30 P.M. daily, $10) serves breakfast and lunch in a small, deliberately low-key space with corrugated wainscoting and marine-influenced lighting fixtures to represent the waterfront. It is one of the few places to open early, should you need breakfast before you leave town. Like most places in town, you can see the rock while you enjoy the creative food, like French toast dipped in crème brûlée and mixed with whole nuts, then baked and served in a bowl—it's excellent and not overly sweet—or chili, which is rich and earthy.

The **Coffee Pot Restaurant** (1001 Front St., 805/772-3176, 7 A.M.–1:30 P.M. daily, $15) has been around a long time. Unpretentious and dated in its decor, it's not aiming to impress. But then, you're here for breakfast. Chances are there will be a wait, as there are few breakfast options in town, but they'll bring you coffee while you wait. The vast menu includes veggie omelets and plenty of meat choices as well as biscuits and gravy, although the service is not optimal.

Mexican

Taco Temple (2680 Main St., 805/772-4965, 11 A.M.–9 P.M. Mon. and Wed.–Sat., noon–8:30 P.M. Sun., $10, cash only), just outside downtown Morro Bay, looks like just another average-looking stop, but that's not the point. It is known for its fish taco, heaped with plenty of ingredients that include moist, spicy, and quite excellent fish. They also have large burritos and tostadas, but go for the fish tacos. It's cash only and there's no ATM on-site.

Seafood

Morro Bay has a multitude of great seafood restaurants to choose from.

(The Galley Seafood Grill & Bar (899 Embarcadero, 805/772-7777, www.galleymorrobay.com, 11 A.M.–2:30 P.M. and 5 P.M.–close daily, $25) sits underneath the Andersen Inn and directly over the water, staring right out at the rock. There's a modern Scandinavian feel to the interior but with the clean lines of Italian design. Multiple semicircular booths face outward, and freestanding tables front the windows. The current owner started at the original Galley restaurant as a busboy. Many years and a brand-new restaurant later, the Galley is better than ever. Pan-seared scallops in beurre blanc capped with shallots is their signature dish, as are the naked fish dishes, like swordfish, ahi tuna, and ono, all simply prepared and served with sauces on the side, so the inherent flavor and quality of the fish come through unhindered. There's a small bar here as well.

Tognazzini's Dockside Restaurant (1245 Embarcadero, 805/772-8100, www.bonniemarietta.com, 11 A.M.–9 P.M. Sun.–Thurs., 11 A.M.–10 P.M. Fri.–Sat. summer, 11 A.M.–8 P.M. Sun.–Thurs., 11 A.M.–9 P.M. Fri.–Sat. winter, $18) is all about ocean-to-table seafood. The restaurant has its own fishing boat that hauls in the catch. You can sit dockside on plastic chairs and under green umbrellas, which is the best way to experience the place, overlooking the boats. Best known for barbecue oysters, which are huge and not barbecued in the sauce sense but slow grilled with garlic and butter, there are also lots of crispy fried foods. This is low-key dining but with some of the freshest seafood around.

Dorn's Original Breakers Cafe (801 Market Ave., 805/772-4415, www.dornscafe.com, 7 A.M.–9 P.M. daily, $25) is a traditional, more formal dining experience with low lighting and a slightly sophisticated environment. Perched on the hill up from the water, there are exceptional views. The clam chowder has been a favorite since the restaurant opened in 1942, and there is a large selection of fresh seafood as well as nonfish entrées, which are all very good, but go for the fish. Dorn's opens early for breakfast.

Vegetarian

Shine Café (415 Morro Bay Blvd., 805/771-8344, www.sunshinehealthfoods-shinecafe.com, 11 A.M.–5 P.M. Mon.–Fri., 9 A.M.–4 P.M. Sat., 10 A.M.–4 P.M. Sun., $10) is located inside the Sunshine Health Foods market. Nothing is over $10, and it's all vegetarian and vegan, with gluten-free options. There is an array of smoothies as well as tempeh tacos, spring rolls, and fresh daily soups, most of which are vegan. Everything is artfully prepared and a feast for the eyes.

Cafés

At **The Rock Espresso Bar** (275 Morro Bay Blvd., 805/772-3411, www.morrobay.com/TheRockEspressoBar, 6 A.M.–5 P.M. daily, $5) you can see Morro Rock, but you're also off the Embarcadero and more among the locals. Coffee is roasted on-site along with pastries, muffins, and scones turned out daily. There are a few computers to check email while you sit on chairs upholstered with old coffee-bean bags. The outdoor patio gives you sun and more glimpses of the rock, or you can let the local artwork inspire you.

Desserts

Crills (903 Embarcadero, 805/772-1679, www.crills.qpg.com, 8 A.M.–9 P.M. Mon.–Fri., 7:30 A.M.–10 P.M. Sat.–Sun., $4) originally started making and pulling saltwater taffy over 40 years ago. The low blue building has two counters to order from. In addition to nearly two dozen varieties of taffy, homemade fudge, peanut brittle, ice cream, and cotton candy are sold. There is a second Crills (1247 Embarcadero) down the road closer to the center of town, but this is the original, right near the smokestacks.

INFORMATION AND SERVICES

The **Morro Bay Chamber of Commerce** (845 Embarcadero, Suite D, 800/231-0592, www.morrobay.org) has a wonderful visitors center overlooking the bay at the end of a small boardwalk. They have a vast array of printed material you can take with you.

French Hospital Medical Center (1911 Johnson Ave., San Luis Obispo, 805/543-5353, www.frenchmedicalcenter.org) is the closest hospital. If you have an emergency, dial **911**. The local police offices (805/772-6225) are located at 870 Morro Bay Boulevard.

The *San Luis Obispo Tribune* is the widely available daily paper covering the county, while the *Bay News* is a free local weekly paper that appears each Thursday.

To get to the **post office** (898 Napa Ave., 805/772-0839), you have to leave the Embarcadero area and head uptown.

American Cleaners & Laundry (365 Quintana Rd.; 1052 Main St., 805/772-6959) has two locations in Morro Bay. Phone for pickup and delivery.

GETTING THERE AND AROUND

As with most towns on the Central Coast, Highway 1 cuts through Morro Bay. If you're traveling south from San Francisco, take U.S. 101 south to Atascadero. Then take Highway 41 west, and head south on Highway 1. Exit at Main Street in Morro Bay. If you're traveling from Los Angeles, the best route is U.S. 101 north to San Luis Obispo, then head north on Highway 1 to Morro Bay and take the Morro Bay Boulevard exit into town.

There is no direct bus service to Morro Bay, although Greyhound travels along U.S. 101 and stops in San Luis Obispo. From there you can connect with various **Regional Transit**

Authority (805/781-4472, www.slorta.com) buses to get into Morro Bay. Likewise, **Amtrak** (800/872-7245, www.amtrak.com) buses travel along the highway and stop in San Luis Obispo.

The small **San Luis Obispo County Regional Airport** (SBP, 903-5 Airport Dr., San Luis Obispo, 805/781-5205, www.sloairport.com) has limited service, as does the **Santa Maria Airport** (SMX, 3217 Terminal Dr., Santa Maria, 805/922-1726, www.santamariaairport.com), but Morro Bay itself has no commercial airport.

Bay Services (805/528-1201) is a 24-hour flat-fee taxi and limousine service. The **Bay Taxi** (1215 Embarcadero, 805/772-1222) provides water-taxi service.

A door-to-door general public transit system, **Call-A-Ride** (535 Harbor St., 805/772-2755, 6:45 A.M.–5:45 P.M. Mon.–Fri.), established in 1977, operates within the city limits. between Call one day before your trip (8 A.M.–10 A.M. Mon.–Fri.) to schedule a ride.

The **Morro Bay Trolley** (595 Harbor St., 805/772-2744, 11 A.M.–5 P.M. Mon., 11 A.M.–7 P.M. Fri.–Sat., 11 A.M.–6 P.M. Sun. Memorial Day–first weekend in Oct.) operates three routes: The **Waterfront Route** runs the length of the Embarcadero, including out to Morro Rock; the **Downtown Route** runs through the uptown area all the way out to Morro Bay State Park; and the **North Morro Bay Route** runs from uptown through the northern part of Morro Bay, north of the rock, along Highway 1. An all-day pass (not a bad idea if you plan on seeing a lot of sights) is $3; one ride is $1.25 over age 12 and $0.50 ages 5–12.

Cambria

Cambria, originally known as Slabtown, retains nothing of its original if uninspired moniker. Divided into east and west villages, it is an easily walkable and charming area of low storefronts with moss-covered pine trees as a backdrop. Many of the buildings date to the 1880s. Travelers meander in and out of the local stores, browse art galleries, or comb Moonstone Beach for souvenir moonstone rocks. The really great thing about Cambria is that aside from the gas stations, you won't find even one chain store in town, and Cambrians like it that way. It truly is an idyllic spot, even during bustling summer months when the crowds swell dramatically. Located within 10 miles of Hearst Castle, Cambria also makes a good place to stay before or after a visit there.

Getting There

The best way to get from Carmel to San Simeon and Cambria is to drive the **Pacific Coast Highway** (PCH), the most idolized drive in California. You pass over the Bixby Bridge, through Big Sur, and hug the stunning tree-lined cliffs and their sheer drop to the ocean. Known as the "Windy Ninety," it's only about a 90-mile drive, but even on a perfect day it will take you nearly three hours. PCH curves so much and has so many hairpin turns that you simply cannot drive fast, nor will you want to. It has been named one of the "Drives of a Lifetime" by *National Geographic* magazine. But since it's so popular, everyone else will be on it too. It is a two-lane road, which can be slow going with campers, motorcycle groups, and everyone jockeying to see the views. On perfect days, a convertible is best.

Your second option is to drive U.S. 101. This means that, leaving Carmel, you need to backtrack through Monterey toward Salinas and drive south. This section of U.S. 101 is not nearly as pretty as the coast route, but it's not bad either, with scattered oak trees and low shrubs. Once at Paso Robles, head west, then

north on the Pacific Coast Highway. It takes about 2.5 hours from Carmel.

SIGHTS
Nitt Witt Ridge

Nitt Witt Ridge (881 Hillcrest Dr., 805/927-2690, by appointment only, $10 adults, $5 children) is a "mansion" of found materials—what we used to call "trash"—offering a stark contrast to the opulence of nearby Hearst Castle. Starting in 1928, Arthur Harold Beal, remembered fondly today as Captain Nitt Witt, collected junk, trash, and recycled goods to use as building materials for this classic American folk-art home. He used washer drums, tire rims, shells from the nearby beaches, tiles, car parts, old stoves, and lots and lots of Busch beer cans (which were apparently plentiful). In a particularly creative move, old toilet seats became picture frames. Beale claimed that most of his materials washed up on the beach or were discarded at local construction sites. It took him over 50 years to complete his dream home.

This is a far cry from a sanitized residence or museum, and it has been left mostly to the forces of nature, so it might not be what you expect. In spite of being registered as a California Historical Landmark, today Nitt Witt Ridge is in disrepair—which somehow seems appropriate. Tours are not offered at regular times, and it may take some persistence to reach the current owners to gain entry, so you'll need to plan ahead. But it's worth stopping to see one man's dedication to his dream: making a home from bits and pieces of society's abandoned materials. Nitt Witt Ridge is on the hill just behind the west village—not a long drive.

BEACHES

The wide sandy beaches of the Central Coast end here, giving way to more rugged beaches with lots of rocks and minimal sand. These are prime areas for tide-pooling. You will occasionally see dolphins and whales from the shore, but you're most likely to see sea otters, seals, and many waterbirds.

Moonstone Beach

Moonstone Beach, accessed from Highway 1 in Cambria at either Windsor Boulevard at the south end or near Moonstone Gardens at the north end, is a mile-long boardwalk on the bluffs with occasional beach access; it is ideal for strolling and is wheelchair accessible. This is the beach that most people associate with Cambria. You can park anywhere along the beach side of the road at the pullouts—it's all free, and there is no time limit. This is a more rugged beach, with less flat sand and more washed-up wood, seaweed, and yes, moonstones. At high tide there's little to no room to walk on the beach, but at low tide there's ample room to tide-pool, watch the otters and the seals, and sit on the wood benches along the boardwalk. These benches were all made by locals, and a dedicated group of locals keeps the area clean, so please do your part by properly disposing of trash. If you look closely, you'll find some areas removed from the boardwalk where you can rest. You'll also notice the ground squirrels that pop out from under the boardwalk, hoping you'll give them food. Feeding them is frowned on, but they are adventurous and curious. Hotels claim the other side of the road, but there are no public facilities here. The closest restrooms are at Leffingwell Landing, a boat and kayak launch ramp at the north end of Moonstone Beach Drive, or at Shamel Park at the south end.

Fiscalini Ranch Preserve/West

Fiscalini Ranch Preserve/West (Windsor Blvd. and Hwy. 1, Cambria) is at the opposite end of town from Moonstone Beach, and though technically there's no beach access, there are boardwalks that grace the property on the low-rolling bluff-top. Much less crowded than Moonstone, this is where the locals go and where you can absorb the sheer beauty of the coastline in relative tranquility. The cliffs drop down to the water, and there is precious little place to walk, even if you wanted to. To

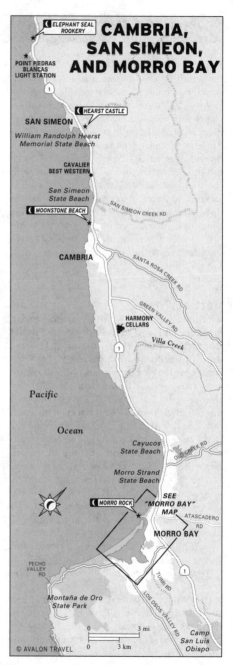

CAMBRIA, SAN SIMEON, AND MORRO BAY

ELEPHANT SEAL ROOKERY

POINT PIEDRAS BLANCAS LIGHT STATION

HEARST CASTLE

SAN SIMEON
William Randolph Hearst Memorial State Beach

CAVALIER BEST WESTERN

San Simeon State Beach

MOONSTONE BEACH

SAN SIMEON CREEK RD

CAMBRIA

SANTA ROSA CREEK RD

GREEN VALLEY RD

HARMONY CELLARS

Villa Creek

Pacific

Ocean

Cayucos State Beach

OLD CREEK RD

Morro Strand State Beach

SEE "MORRO BAY" MAP

MORRO ROCK

ATASCADERO RD

MORRO BAY

PECHO VALLEY RD

TURRI RD

LOS OSOS VALLEY RD

Montaña de Oro State Park

0   3 mi
0   3 km

Camp San Luis Obispo

© AVALON TRAVEL

access West Fiscalini, turn south on Windsor Boulevard at Highway 1 and the entrance to the west village, and follow it through a residential section until the road ends. You can park directly in front of the wood fence to access the trailhead. Turn right and follow the boardwalk to the ocean.

SHOPPING

Part of the draw of Cambria is its shops dotting Main Street. You'll notice that there are no chain stores, and that is by design. Stores and shops are family-run small businesses, which makes shopping here an adventure—you're never exactly sure what you'll find.

Antiques

Antiques on Main (2338 Main St., 805/927-4292, 10 A.M.–5 P.M. Sun.–Thurs., 10 A.M.–8 P.M. Fri.–Sat.) has, among other things, the best selection of vintage and novelty lamps and lighting, including 1930s vanity bullet lamps. The basement contains lots of garden furniture, and upstairs is even more clothes, books, and accessories—just under 10,000 square feet in all. You'll find vintage furniture pieces as well as nonvintage merchandise like rocks and minerals, a collection of sport knives, and lots of women's clothes.

Art Galleries

Seekers Glass Gallery (4090 Burton Dr., 800/841-5250, www.seekersglass.com, 10 A.M.–8 P.M. daily) has an impressive array of all things glass—beautiful vases, sculptures, paperweights, bowls, jewelry, and lamps as well as decorative pieces infused with deep rich colors. These are not inexpensive, but rather masterworks by well-known glass artists from around the world. If you're seeking high-end glassware, then Seekers should be on your radar.

When you walk into **The Vault Gallery** (2289 Main St., 805/927-0300, www.vaultgallery.com, 10:30 A.M.–6 P.M. daily), you just might want to buy everything. An incredibly diverse and eclectic range of artists from Santa Barbara and San Luis Obispo Counties

is represented here. Modern sculpture, photography, and paintings have an edginess that forgoes traditional landscapes and pretty beach scenes. It's worth checking out, and in keeping with the name, a few of the works are displayed in the vault, since the building was formerly a bank.

Wine

Fermentations (4056 Burton Dr., 800/446-7505, www.fermentations.com, 10 A.M.–7 P.M. daily, as late as 10 P.M. Fri.–Sat. and summer, tasting $5, includes glass) used to be a private residence; the cottage is now a wine shop and tasting bar that features a wide variety of local wines and often wines from other regions. Where the tasting bar is now used to be the kitchen of the residence. In addition to tastings, there is a large selection of all things wine, including shirts, gift baskets, wine accessories, and well-known wine publications. They also sell a line of their own olive oils, vinegars, and specialty food items, including a wonderful zinfandel mustard.

Home Furnishings

The Shop Next Door (4063 Burton Dr., 805/927-9600, www.squibbhouse.net, 10 A.M.–9 P.M. daily) sells predominantly Amish-crafted furniture such as beautiful handmade custom rocking chairs, dressers, dining tables, and game tables. Some works have a distinct early American feel; others are craftsman in their approach. Woods used include ash, oak, and cherry. They also carry other house accessories, but it's the finely crafted furniture that is the main draw. Many people sit in the rocking chairs and don't get up for some time.

Bath and Beauty

At **Heart's Ease Herb Shop & Gardens** (4101 Burton Dr., 805/927-5224, www.heartseaseshop.com, 10 A.M.–5 P.M. daily), you can find hand and face lotions, soaps, salt scrubs, potpourri, and about 100 different essential oils in a true 1870s homestead, one of the oldest in the village. There is a large and lovely garden out back, and dried flowers hang from the rafters inside. There are also some garden gift items, books, and a well-stocked selection of fresh and dried herbs.

Farmers Market

The **Cambria Farmers Market** (Veterans Memorial Hall, 1000 Main St., 805/924-1260, 2:30–5 P.M. Fri.) is held at the Veterans Memorial Hall, with a multitude of flowers, fruits, veggies, and nuts from farms all along the coast. You'll also find cookies and pies and a very laid-back environment.

SPORTS AND RECREATION
Lawn Bowling

You're not required to wear white to participate, but you might want to consider stopping at the **Cambria Lawn Bowls Club** (950 Main St., 805/927-3364, www.joslynrec.org, 9:30 A.M.–noon Mon., Wed., and Fri.–Sat., 1–4 P.M. Sun.) to check out all the fuss. You'll get free lessons in the nuances of lawn bowling, and you can't beat hanging out with the locals and engaging in rolling a ball around. It's right on Main Street, so you can wander the town afterward.

Hiking

For a short burst of activity, the **Burton Drive Trail** on East Lodge Hill is 0.5 miles each way. You can start at the Cambria Nursery and Florist (2801 Eton Rd.) at Burton Drive and Eaton Road, and head down the hill toward Santa Rosa Creek. The short trail, which follows the road, is on the opposite side of the guardrail, so you don't need to worry about traffic. A large, shaded, and immensely green wooded and vine-covered ravine is on the left. This trail will take you into town once you cross over the creek. Of course, this is the easy part—then you have to walk back up. The trail is pretty steep, so it's a hearty workout.

Near Burton Drive is the **Fiscalini Ranch Preserve/East,** accessed via a pedestrian bridge near the Bluebird Motel (1880 Main St.). The interconnecting trails here vary between steep unimproved dirt paths and flat,

wide, easy paths. The area is full of moss-covered trees and lush green chaparral. Just beware of poison oak, and don't veer off the paths. There are no great views of the ocean, but this short two-mile hike is more forested and secluded, demonstrating how forested Cambria actually is.

Biking

For an easy ride, **Highway 1 South to Harmony** is a good route. Once you hit the down slope out of Cambria the highway is flat and wide, and the grass-carpeted hills are dotted with cattle. The rock formations are gorgeous. Take your bike to Highway 1 and pedal south from anywhere. You can pedal to the town of Harmony, on the left side, and do a wine-tasting at **Harmony Cellars** (3255 Harmony Valley Rd., Harmony, 805/927-1625, www.harmonycellars.com, 10 A.M.–5 P.M. daily, tasting $4), and then continue on toward Cayucos, which is 15 miles out of Cambria one-way, or return to Cambria.

Spas

The **Moonstone Day Spa** (7432 Exotic Garden Dr., 805/927-5159, www.moonstone-dayspa.com, 9 A.M.–7 P.M. daily and by appointment) is located in the beautiful Hamlet at Moonstone Gardens just north of town. On offer are facials, glycolic peels, face and body waxing, massages, body polishing, manicures, pedicures, and makeovers, many featuring mineral products. The spa also carry a full line of professional beauty and body-care products.

The **Sojourn Spa** (2905 Burton Dr., 805/927-8007, www.sojournspa.com) is located at the Cambria Pines Lodge. In business since 1988, Sojourn offers warm stone massage, Swedish massage, and deep-tissue work for those knots, along with Reiki energy balancing and facials and body treatments that include mud, salt-glow, and pumpkin peels. Perhaps better still, you can have your hands and feet worked on. Side-by-side couples massage is offered, and there is a spa, a sauna, and an outdoor pool.

ENTERTAINMENT AND EVENTS
Nightlife

Being a small town, Cambria has limited choices for things to do at night.

Cambria Pines Lodge (2905 Burton Dr., 805/927-4200, 8–11 P.M. daily) offers entertainment seven nights a week; the majority of talent at its Fireside Lounge is local. There are karaoke nights and small acoustical sets, but ultimately it's about the environment: The fire in the massive stone fireplace, the semi-rustic environment with worn but comfortable couches and chairs, and the laid-back musicians make this a mellow place to relax and hear tunes. There's no charge to sit and listen, but since the bar is right there, you can curl up with a drink and make a night of it.

The Hamlet at Moonstone Gardens (7432 Exotic Gardens Dr., 805/927-3535, www.moonstonegardens.com) has had live jazz since 1991. Currently there are usually two concerts each month, always on Sunday, and on concert nights there are two separate performances by the same group. The first show ($15 pp) begins at 4 P.M. and consists of two sets of music with an intermission and ends around 6:30 P.M. The second show ($12 pp) begins around 7:15 P.M. or later, because the first show can run long, and consists of one long uninterrupted set that ends around 8:30 P.M. The cost for both performances is $20. You'll have views of the ocean and sunset while dulcet tones relax you.

If something more upbeat is your preference, **Las Cambritas** (2336 Main St., 805/927-0175, 11 A.M.–9 P.M. daily) has live music on Thursday evenings and Sunday afternoons; on good weather Sundays they set up on the outside patio, and the music drifts over the rooftops. Usually it's a local solo or duo act, but occasionally a three-piece band will show up, performing music with a Latin feel.

Performing Arts

The **Pewter Plough Playhouse** (824 Main St., 805/927-3877, www.pewterploughplayhouse.org) is a small proscenium-style community theater that produces about four shows each year. Usually two are well-known plays while the others are new works. They also present a series of readers theater throughout the year, where actors read from their scripts and there is little or no stage set. There is no hard and fast formal schedule, so it's best to contact them about performances while you're in town. Shows are usually at 7:30 P.M. Friday–Saturday, with an occasional Thursday performance or Sunday matinee.

Festivals and Events

The **Cambria Art and Wine Festival** (805/927-3624, www.cambriaartwine.org, $10–90) is a January weekend of shopping deals, demonstrating artists, and lots of art for sale throughout the village. The wine-tasting main event is noon–4:30 P.M. Saturday and includes an art show of well over 30 local artists. There's a silent auction, wine tasting, gourmet food, and demonstrations with local artists showing a variety of techniques. About 30 wineries participate. Businesses are open the entire weekend and feature different foods and wines at their stores to draw you in. Tickets can be purchased for the entire weekend, or for separate art or wine events.

ACCOMMODATIONS

While there are quite a few places to stay in Cambria, beachfront lodgings are the most popular. Peak summer months fill up quickly, as does Thanksgiving through New Year's. Plan ahead to get the hotel you want.

Under $150

San Simeon Pines (7200 Moonstone Beach Dr., 866/927-4648, www.sspines.com, $100–180 d) is by itself at the far end of Moonstone Beach Drive, nestled among pine trees on eight acres. San Simeon Beach is right across the street, as is the western entrance to the Moonstone Beach boardwalk. The building is single-story ranch style, and the guest rooms, while standard in size, have a country feel to them. One of the best parts of staying here is that a two-night minimum is not required. Amenities include real wood-burning fireplaces, a pool, Wi-Fi, a shuffleboard court and croquet area, and a nine-hole, par-three golf course—the hotel will loan you clubs to boot.

At **Moonstone Landing** (6240 Moonstone Beach Dr., 805/927-0012, www.moonstonelanding.com, $140–300 d), there are only 29 guest rooms; the 10 facing the ocean are the more expensive, meaning that the value for the other guest rooms is quite good, at least for Moonstone Beach Drive. There's a continental breakfast and a hot tub, and although the standard guest rooms are nothing to write home about, you can access the beach by walking across the street. Staying here allows you to spend your money elsewhere.

$150-250

The **((Olallieberry Inn** (2476 Main St., 805/927-3222, www.olallieberry.com, $150–225 d), built in 1873, is a homey nine-room bed-and-breakfast. The floors creak in certain spots, and the guest rooms with period furniture are larger and laid out differently than standard accommodations. There's a wine reception each evening (5–6 P.M.), which also includes a variety of light food. Sherry in a glass decanter is available in the front hallway whenever you need it. Three guest rooms are located upstairs, two with detached baths, and three rooms are downstairs. The second house has three guest rooms. The property abuts Santa Rosa Creek, and during the summer months you can lounge outside and watch it languidly flow by. Homemade breakfasts are served at 8 A.M. and 9:15 A.M. and include olallieberry jam. Occasionally, cooking classes are available in the large kitchen, and you can walk to the shops in Cambria. The service is beyond gracious—you'll feel like you're the most important person in the world.

The very comfortable **J. Patrick House** (2990 Burton Dr., 800/341-5258, www.jpatrickhouse.com, $175–215 d) has only eight guest rooms, beautifully and authentically decorated with dark woods and unique 1800s antiques. It's located away from the beach in a residential area, but only a 5–10-minute walk

to the east village. There is a lovely back garden area in which to enjoy the fully cooked breakfasts that might include blintzes, soufflé, and homemade bread. Cookies and milk are presented before bedtime, and in classic bed-and-breakfast style, you end up spending time with other guests.

Even further removed is **Fog's End Bed and Breakfast** (2735 Main St., 805/927-7465, www.fogsend.com, $175–195 d), located on eight acres just outside the east village. It's a short 10-minute walk to the east village, but seclusion is part of the charm at the three-room house. You can play boccie ball or walk along Santa Rosa Creek Road, which heads toward orchards in a valley. Breakfasts are served in a formal dining room, and the house has gorgeous hardwood floors; the guest rooms are comfortable and inviting. This isn't an older house that has been converted but a newer building, so it has some modern amenities.

((Cambria Pines Lodge (2905 Burton Dr., 805/927-4200, www.cambriapineslodge.com, $159–199 d) has everything rolled into one: large and small suites and cottages, many with fireplaces, all with Wi-Fi. The lodge is set on 25 acres, most of it woods with hanging moss, and the manicured gardens are well known. The very best parts of the lodge are the gardens and the bar, filled with old couches and stuffed chairs, a few wicker chairs, and a beautiful floor-to-ceiling fireplace made of large round river stones with an old wood hearth. The wide plank floors and knotty pine ceilings make it rustically comfortable. This is an ideal place to hang out and hear live music, or just relax with a glass of local wine. There is an in-house restaurant for breakfast and dinner, and on nice days you can eat outside, facing the small lawn and hedges. The rock grotto is a fairly recent addition to the lodge and provides some seclusion. The guest rooms are generally quite large, and the furnishings have a mountain and woods theme. Some of the older cottages are rather Spartan, whereas some of the newer ones, with private balconies or patios, have more modern touches.

The Lodge is also home to **Sojourn Spa** (2905 Burton Dr., 805/927-8007, www.sojournspa.com), which offers massage, sauna, energy balancing, and facials. The spa is in a renovated cottage right near the indoor pool, making it easy to take advantage of if you're staying at the Lodge, although nonguests can book services too.

The **Blue Dolphin Inn** (6470 Moonstone Beach Dr., 800/222-9157, www.cambriainns.com, $209–349 d) offers that full-on oceanfront experience you crave, and many of the beautifully appointed guest rooms have a view of the ocean. Amenities include a breakfast picnic to go—yes, to go—at the time of your choosing. There's also free Wi-Fi, 32-inch flatscreen TVs, in-room coffeemakers, microwaves, fireplaces, refrigerators, and luxurious bedding and robes that make you feel pampered. The guest rooms are large and each differs in style, with a loose beach theme incorporating American and Asian influences. If you want the full treatment, this might be your spot.

Over $250

The **FogCatcher Inn** (6400 Moonstone Beach Dr., 805/927-1400, www.fogcatcherinn.com, $255–340 d) has an English country motif and a yellow Tudor-style exterior with a classic thatched roof, making it look more like it belongs in the Welsh or English countryside. A full buffet breakfast is enhanced with eggs cooked to order. Like every accommodation on Moonstone Beach Drive, the beach is right across the street. Guest rooms are outfitted with refrigerators, microwaves, and lots of space; the feel here is somewhat upscale rustic, with knotty pine and earthy furnishings. Outside is a heated pool and a spa from which you can see the ocean, and there are cookies at the front desk. The staff is universally helpful.

FOOD

Cambria has its share of touristy places with average and standard food, but there are some wonderful restaurants that take you by surprise.

American

Though the name doesn't imply fine dining, the ◖ **Sow's Ear** (2248 Main St., 805/927-4865, www.thesowsear.com, 5 P.M.–close daily, $20) has been creating fine food for years, with an eye toward comfort food like beef stroganoff, lobster pot pie, and chicken and dumplings. The interior has wood paneling that ties in with the wood chairs and brick fireplace, although it feels a tad heavy in this very small space fronting the street. It's intimate, romantic, and consistently good.

The interior of the ◖ **Black Cat Bistro** (1602 Main St., 805/927-1600, www.blackcatbistro.com, 5 P.M.–close Thurs.–Mon., $20) feels like a 1920s bungalow with vintage light fixtures and hardwood floors; next to the fireplace is the best seating. It's all dim lighting, mustard-colored walls, and tables set close together. The chef's mom decorated the interior and made the cushions on the benches, and the chef herself used to be a TV producer before bolting from L.A. She did it backward, starting the restaurant first, then going to culinary school, but she prepares excellent food. The menu features mostly American dishes with a global influence, like soup with roasted corn, crab, cilantro, and bacon; crispy potatoes with chipotle butter; and seared ahi with crispy mushrooms and shallots. There's a great focus on textures, presented by staff that know exactly what they're doing.

Asian

Wild Ginger (2380 Main St., 805/927-1001, www.wildgingercambria.com, 11 A.M.–2:30 P.M. and 5–9 P.M. Fri.–Wed., $17) is wildly small, with six tables inside and three on a patio, but the Pacific Rim food is flavorful and mixes creative dishes such as smoked salmon–cream cheese wontons with standard Asian cuisine like Hunan beef and spicy calamari. A decent selection of vegetarian options are on offer, and the sorbets are house-made. It's cramped inside, so if you're claustrophobic, sit this one out. Otherwise you're in for a treat.

Breakfast and Brunch

Linn's Fruit Bin (2277 Main St., 805/927-0371, www.linnsfruitbin.com, 8 A.M.–9 P.M. daily, $15) serves breakfast items such as omelets and paninis but for decades has been most famous for its pies. You'll also find cobb salad, beef stroganoff, and house-made pot pies, but it's still about the fruit pies, including strawberry-rhubarb, Dutch apple, and olallieberry. The interior is down-home country, and since this is such a popular place, expect a wait. There is also a small gift shop where you can purchase whole pies and canned fruit.

Cheap Eats

The **Main Street Grill** (603 Main St., 805/927-3194, 11 A.M.–8 P.M. daily, $7) serves simple food done well. It has more of a bar-and-grill feel; you order at the counter and pick up your food when your number is called. There are three flat-screen TVs to watch the game, a small bar, and copious indoor and outdoor seating. It is usually crowded. The chicken tenders and onion rings are consistently good, all prepared while you wait. This is one of the last places to get very good food at good prices before you head north toward Big Sur.

Eclectic

Robin's (4095 Burton Dr., 805/927-5007, www.robinsrestaurant.com, 11 A.M.–9 P.M. daily, $18) is one of the best places to eat in Cambria. The restaurant is in a 1920s cottage that was the home of a construction supervisor for Hearst Castle. The interior is cozy and intimate with a small fireplace. The outdoor enclosed patio is a great spot with views of the garden and is surrounded by a 30-year-old red trumpet vine. The ingredients are fresh and flavorful, with a focus on healthy ingredients. The lobster enchiladas are terrific, as are the espresso-rubbed short ribs. You'll find an eclectic selection of food, including cumin black bean nachos and portobello and spinach lasagna. There are vegetarian items and even some vegan dishes. Reservations are wise for weekends and holidays.

Mexican

At **Medusa's Taqueria** (1053 Main St., 805/927-0135, 7 A.M.–8 P.M. Mon.–Sat., $10) in Cambria, there are a mere half a dozen tables inside the colorful eatery. Though small, it turns out food with big flavors. The chile relleno, fish tacos, and huevos rancheros are some of the best dishes. The chips and salsa are made on-site, and the service is friendly and attentive. It's easy to drive right by this tiny spot, but it's worth a stop.

Cafés and Tearooms

At local haunt the **French Corner Bakery** (2214 Main St., 805/927-8227, www.french-cornerbakery.com, 6:30 A.M.–6 P.M. daily, $10), the five tables are often occupied by people sipping coffee, reading the morning paper, and discussing current events. It's a great stop for a cappuccino or espresso and baked goods, including the chewy cinnamon twists. There are also scones, croissants, breads, sandwiches, and plenty of cakes and cheesecake.

The **Tea Cozy** (4286 Bridge St., 805/927-8765, www.teacozy.com, 11 A.M.–5 P.M. daily, $15) has been serving up British tea and scones since the 1990s. The interior of the small old cottage is all plank wood, a bit rustic in contrast with the idea of a high tea, but the service and food make up for this oversight. The shop also carries a selection of true British foods such as Yorkshire pudding mixes, water crackers, and butterscotch, as well as an assortment of loose teas. The Tea Cozy can also dish up soups and sandwiches for those whose appetite needs more than tea and bread.

The **Cambria Coffee Roasting Company** (761 Main St., 805/927-0670, www.cambria-coffee.com, 7 A.M.–5:30 P.M. daily, $7) not only roasts its own blends, with over 30 years of roasting experience, but has scones, muffins, and pastries as well. Locals keep their mugs here on a separate shelf. The interior is small, so most people sit out front along Main Street, or head up a flight of stairs to a little sundeck to read the paper, chat, and enjoy the morning.

INFORMATION AND SERVICES

The **Cambria Chamber of Commerce** (767 Main St., 805/927-3624, www.cambriachamber.org, 9 A.M.–5 P.M. Mon.–Fri., noon–4 P.M. Sat.–Sun.) is probably the best resource for information on the area and provides a free annual publication that lists many of the stores, restaurants, and lodgings in the area. Pick up a trail guide for additional hikes and walks—Cambria has great places to roam. The Cambria branch of the San Luis Obispo County **public library** (900 Main St., 805/927-4336, 11 A.M.–5 P.M. Tues.–Fri., 11 A.M.–4 P.M. Sat.) offers additional information and local history, including a map of local walking and hiking trails.

Cambria is served by three medical facilities: **Twin Cities Hospital** in Templeton, 25 miles inland, and **Sierra Vista Regional Medical Center** and **French Hospital Medical Center,** both in San Luis Obispo, 35 miles south. Cambria and San Simeon are served by the San Luis Obispo County **sheriff's office** (800/834-3346). If you have an emergency, dial **911.**

The Cambrian (805/927-8652, $0.75) is the local newspaper, published each Thursday. KTEA (103.5 FM) is the local radio station. There is a **post office** (4100 Bridge St.,

805/927-8610, 9 A.M.–4:30 P.M. Mon.–Fri.) in Cambria.

GETTING THERE AND AROUND

Cambria is located on Highway 1 and is only accessible from it, whether you're coming from Monterey or from Morro Bay. You can access Highway 1 from U.S. 101 via scenic Highway 46 west, which meets Highway 1 just south of Cambria. The only driving you'll need to do in Cambria itself is between the east and west villages, out to the coast, or toward Hearst Castle.

The Regional Transit Authority bus system, or **RTA** (805/541-2228, www.slorta.org, $1.50–3), runs buses among San Luis Obispo, Morro Bay, Cayucos, Cambria, and San Simeon.

The Amtrak train station is located in San Luis Obispo, 35 miles south of Cambria; there is no direct train service to Cambria or San Simeon. Car rentals are available in San Luis Obispo, and the county bus system (805/541-2228, www.slorta.org) runs buses between San Luis Obispo and Cambria.

Flights into the region arrive at the **San Luis Obispo County Regional Airport** (SBP, 903-5 Airport Dr., San Luis Obispo, 805/781-5205, www.sloairport.com), 35 miles south of Cambria.

PACIFIC COAST HIGHWAY

San Simeon

San Simeon is less a town and more a stopping point. Stores, hotels, and restaurants flank both sides of Highway 1, with no center of activity, and frankly, there's not much activity at all. This is the last stop before Hearst Castle, and many people stay here due to its proximity, just two miles from the castle. If there's any strolling to be done, it's along the bluffs or on the rocky beaches. Set amid incredible open space between the hills and the ocean, San Simeon is truly a paradise of natural beauty with stunning coastlines. Sunsets are gorgeous as the

amber light casts warm tones on the craggy rocks at the surf line.

SIGHTS
🄲 Hearst Castle

This mammoth compound, on a remote hill on a remote stretch of coastline in a remote part of the state, is virtually indescribable. Nearly 700,000 people flock here each year to experience the grandeur of bygone times. Hearst Castle (750 Hearst Castle Rd., 805/927-2020 or tour info 800/444-4445, www.hearstcastle.org)

is a uniquely American experience. William Randolph Hearst was born into wealth and inherited 270,000 acres in and around San Simeon. He was the first media mogul, operating 26 newspapers, a movie studio, and other endeavors, which he oversaw from his center of operations at the castle during his zenith in the 1920s and 1930s. As gargantuan as the property was, the home Hearst built for himself was also gargantuan. The numbers are staggering: 38 bedrooms, 61 baths, 19 sitting rooms, and 41 fireplaces, all housed in a 90,080-square-foot complex of buildings: a massive main house and three guest "cottages" ranging in size 2,200–5,800 square feet. A fourth and fifth cottage were planned but never built. There are two swimming pools, tennis courts, a private zoo, an airstrip (originally located where the visitor's center is now), a movie theater, and four enormous vaults in the basement that housed guests' valuables, including mink coats and artwork. A bowling alley and a grand ballroom were also planned but never constructed. It may surprise many that the castle was never completely finished. Hearst slowly ran out of money, and you'll see unfinished portions of the exterior to the west side of the main house, a tedious gray concrete that contrasts with the gloss and detail of the rest of the building.

You can certainly experience the castle in one day and with one tour, but that only tells part of the story. It's advisable to visit the castle twice on at least two different tours. You can easily do up to three tours in a day, but it can be overstimulating and make for a long day. If you have the time, it's best to visit over two days, which allows time to explore the rest of the coast and keep things at a reasonable pace. It's impossible to absorb everything on any single tour; there's simply too much detail. Since each of the tours are designed to showcase certain portions of the estate, you would need to take every tour to fully comprehend the castle. There is a 10 percent discount on a second or third daytime tour on the same day, as long as the first tour has been bought at full price; once at the castle, you can purchase additional tours rather than heading back down to the visitors center.

In 2011 the tours changed to allow visitors the chance to complete a 45-minute tour of various parts of the interior, while allowing everyone to spend as much time as they want outside. Formerly off-limits areas are now open to the public, including architect Julia Morgan's minuscule woodshed office, located on the back of the main house. This small, humble, ramshackle shed, which Morgan used for decades while working on the project, stands in stark contrast to the mammoth castle she designed and built; see firsthand the conditions she worked in.

All daytime tours (adults $25, ages 6–17 $12) are priced the same, and evening tours (adults $36, ages 6–17 $18) are slightly higher. The first tour is at 9 A.M., and the castle is open daily year-round except Christmas Day, Thanksgiving Day, and New Year's Day.

THE VISITORS CENTER

Every visit starts at the visitors center, nearly a sight in itself. The large parking lot, operated by the state, provides free parking, but that's the only deal you'll get here. The large domed building houses restrooms and a food area that serves pizza and Hearst Ranch beef hamburgers. There's a patio outside with tables. The airstrip and the airstrip hangar were originally located here, and the current airstrip, still used by the Hearst family, is one mile north of the visitor's center. The nearby theater shows a well-done 40-minute film about Hearst, his past, and how the castle came to be; it is worth seeing if you don't know much about his history. At the very back end of the visitors center are two doors that lead outside to a small viewing area with a few tables and chairs and telescopes to view the castle in the distance. On your way to the viewing area, you'll pass by a few exhibits, including the 1940s fire truck that was once used on the property.

A high-end gift shop sells replica items from the castle as well as everything you can imagine with a Hearst logo on it, even things that have no relation to the castle at all. You'll have your photo taken against the backdrop of the main house, like it or not, but you don't have to buy the photos. Then you'll board the bus and be driven up the winding road while recorded narration gives some preliminary information about the property. The ride up and back is about 30 minutes, which should be factored into your schedule.

THE TOURS

There are three daytime tours available and an evening tour. There is no sitting, except on the bus rides; you'll be standing or walking the entire time, and all tours require visitors to climb stairs. Indoor portions of the tours are 45 minutes, with time allowed afterward to roam freely around the Neptune outdoor pool, which includes the men's and women's dressing rooms, upstairs from the pool, which are nicely adorned. You'll also get time on the patio, where you can imagine a summer cocktail party with eye-catching views of the mountains and ocean. You can walk freely to the magnificent Roman indoor pool, decorated

from floor to ceiling with one-inch-square mosaic tiles, many of which are covered in gold. You'll also have time to peruse the gardens, which feature marble sculptures and flowers in season. Hearst planted many flowering plants and fruit-bearing trees because he liked the color palette, not because he wanted the fruit. This is clearly evident when the gardens are in bloom and the myriad colors interact with their surroundings. Docents are stationed outside to answer questions and provide information.

You'll leave the castle feeling like you've missed seeing some things, and you have. There's no way to assimilate all the visuals, and the information provided, on any tour, and there's really no solid plan that allows you to see more. The best approach is to gravitate to the visuals that you find appealing, perhaps the hand-carved ceiling, the peculiar statuary, the furnishings, or the artwork. No tour guide will describe everything, but there is time for questions, so speak up. The film shown at the visitors center provides useful background information.

PACIFIC COAST HIGHWAY

© HEARST CASTLE/CALIFORNIA STATE PARKS

the Neptune Pool at night

JULIA MORGAN:
A WOMAN OF INDEPENDENT MEANS

Best known for designing and building Hearst Castle over a 21-year period, architect Julia Morgan designed more than 700 buildings in an illustrious career that spanned nearly 50 years. At 5 foot, 2 inches she was a small woman, but never one to be underestimated. On a cool spring morning in 1919, William Randolph Hearst swaggered into Julia Morgan's office in San Francisco. "Miss Morgan, we are tired of camping out in the open at the ranch in San Simeon and I would like to build a little something," Hearst said in his high-pitched voice. And that set in motion events that would catapult her into architectural history.

Julia Morgan never married; she was devoted to her work and she carved out a lasting legacy for women everywhere. She was the first woman to graduate from the prestigious Ecole des Beaux-Arts in Paris and was one of the first (man or woman) to graduate from U.C. Berkeley with a degree in civil engineering.

Her notable California projects included not only the enduring Hearst Castle, but also the Bavarian-style **Wyntoon,** also for W. R. Hearst; **Asilomar,** located in Pacific Grove; the **Los Angeles Herald Examiner Building** in Los Angeles; the **Margaret Baylor Inn** in Santa Barbara; and a plethora of commercial buildings, as well as YWCAs, private residences, apartments, churches, and educational facilities.

Julia Morgan ultimately gave hope to women and girls everywhere, living a life that proved to them that their vision could someday be realized. Today the **Julia Morgan School for Girls,** an all-girls middle school in Berkeley, California, provides girls with education and empowerment. Morgan passed away in 1958 at the age of 85. In 1957, Morgan granted her one and only press interview, stating simply and succinctly: "My buildings will be my legacy. They will speak for me long after I am gone."

Regardless of which indoor tour you choose, pay attention to the details. Ornate and historical artifacts are everywhere: 15th-century ceilings, Flemish tapestries, and art deco influences. Period lamps, clocks, and hand-carved furniture fills the castle, and much of it is a mishmash of different styles and themes, a testament to Hearst's voracious appetite for collecting just about anything.

Grand Rooms Museum Tour (106 steps, 0.7 miles) provides a broad overview of the many facets of Hearst Castle and is the least physically demanding of the tours. Your time is spent solely inside the main house, known as Casa Grande. You visit the best-known large gathering rooms, including the Assembly Room, the largest of the four sitting rooms and once a gathering place for Hearst's guests as they waited for dinner. Interestingly, as massive as this room is, there's little light from the two windows flanking the room or from the main entrance. The Refectory is only dining room at

Hearst Castle, with an unbelievably long table, silver utensils, a massive intricate hand-carved ceiling, and silk flags draped from the vaulted ceiling. Dinner was served here every evening, often around 9 P.M. Note the 28-foot stone mantel that reaches the ceiling. Contrasting the hand-carved silver serving pieces on display, Hearst actually used bottles of ketchup and mustard in their commercial packaging. The Billiard Room features two 1920s billiard tables and a Gothic tapestry. Next you enter the Theater, where Hearst showed movies produced by his film company, often starring girlfriend Marion Davies. The original 50 seats were velvet, and the walls were draped with silk fabric.

The Upstairs Suites Museum Tour (273 steps, 0.75 miles) is the second floor of Casa Grande. This tour includes the Doge's Suite, a Venetian-style room with an open balcony, intended for the "preferred guest" at the ranch. Silk drapes cover the walls, and the ornate

the Gothic Suite

artwork, most from Italy, is both impressive and a little stifling, with heavy bulky furniture and fabrics. The Library has classic wood-paneled walls with nearly every inch given to books—almost 4,000 volumes—and a collection of rare Greek and Roman antiquities, including lots of vases. The Gothic Suite, which occupies the entire third floor and includes Hearst's impressive private suite, library, and office, is the size of a small house. The arches make it almost church-like in appearance. Then you'll visit the Duplex Bedrooms, originally a narrow empty space that Julia Morgan turned into loft bedrooms, utilizing a constrained area to maximize the number of guests who could stay at the house.

The third tour, **Cottages and Kitchen** (176 stairs, 0.75 miles) takes you inside the large kitchen where meals were prepared for Hearst and his guests. It has heated countertops, a new concept back then, as well as early refrigeration units, bread ovens, and tile work and artistic faucets that make it beautiful as well as practical. The Wine Cellar showcases old bottles, ports, and French wines, but compared to the grandeur of rest of the house it's a basic unadorned room and, frankly, a little dull. But hard-core wine lovers will no doubt find labels that interest them. Next are the cottages. House B, called Casa del Monte (House of the Mountains), has 10 rooms lavishly decorated with tapestries, antique furniture, and pieces from the castle's vast art collection. The cottage faces the Santa Lucia mountain range, and in Hearst's time almost everything in sight was his property, extending all the way to present-day U.S. 101. Lastly you visit House A, Casa Del Mar (House of the Sea), where Hearst, in failing health in the postwar years, lived for two years. Of the three cottages, this is the largest and most elaborately decorated, and it was his favorite.

The Evening Museum Tour (308 steps, 0.75 miles, 1 hour 40 minutes) is a special tour that allows visitors to experience the castle at night, as one of Hearst's own guests might have. The evening tour is available in spring and fall and features highlights from the other tours.

Docents in period dress and a newsreel shown in the theater add a touch of authenticity to the magnificent surroundings and takes visitors back to the castle's 1930s heyday. It's similar to a reenactment: You peer into the great rooms to see "guests" dressed in their finest socializing and preparing themselves for dinner. You'll see cooks in the kitchen, though they're not actually cooking anything. These players are not allowed to communicate with the tour groups. It's actually a fun way to spend the evening, adding a unique dimension to touring the castle. It's important to note, however, that since this is an evening tour, there's a different feel to the interiors, bathed in the amber glow of lamps instead of the sunlight that normally illuminates many of the spaces.

There is also an **Accessibly Designed Tour,** an option for visitors who have difficulty using stairs or standing or walking for lengths of time. Companions of anyone with accessibility needs are also welcome to join this tour. Visitors are allowed to use their own wheelchairs, providing the chair can fit through doorways 28 inches wide. Visitors may also borrow wheelchairs at no extra charge. A specially equipped bus takes visitors to the castle for the tour, and trams are then used to escort visitors along the tour route.

◀ Elephant Seal Rookery

The Elephant Seal Rookery (Hwy. 1, www. elephantseal.org, free) is 12 miles north of Cambria or just four miles north of San Simeon. Don't worry about missing it—you will notice the brown Elephant Seal Viewing Area signs, along with a horde of people staring down at the beach over a low wood fence, not to mention the parked cars, buses, and vans. Elephant seals have been known to choose a spot to breed for many years, then leave and find something else. They started appearing on these protected beaches in the early 1990s and haven't left yet. It's still one of those mysteries that scientists can't specifically explain, but this cove does protect them from rough seas and predatory wildlife, and the easy accessibility helps pregnant females get onto land.

In the winter months, the seals come here to breed, and in the summer months they molt.

the Elephant Seal Rookery

© MICHAEL CERVIN

Winter is the best time to view the males, females, and newborn pups. They might seem lazy, sprawled across the sand, but they can dive up to 3,000 feet and swim at three miles an hour, carrying all that blubber with them. The males spar for territorial rights, and the females seem to prefer to be left alone. The seals are here year-round, though not in as great numbers as in summer and winter. Docents, with Friends of the Elephant Seal emblazoned on their blue jackets, are here year-round too. Ask them anything. Information is free, the view is free, and you might spend more time here than you expected.

BEACHES
Little Pico

There is actually no official name for this beach, but locals simply call it Little Pico (Pico St. and Hwy. 1) because the Little Pico Creek meets the ocean here. It is at the end of a dead-end street; to access it, turn west on Pico Street directly off Highway 1 and park. Concrete steps lead down to the shore. Typical of the area, it's not a sandy beach, but one of pulverized rock, sometimes dense and hard, and other times loose enough that you sink a few inches into it. The sunsets, casting an amber glow, are what bring people out. At low tide, you can walk down the coast for quite a distance. Walking up the coast toward the creek and the weathered hills and rocks for tide-pooling on the other side is easy at low tide, but it becomes more difficult at high tide or after rain, when the creek becomes almost impassable. There are little hidden places for sealife in the craggy rocks, and the muddy soil by the mouth of the creek is a great spot for bird-watching.

William Randolph Hearst Memorial State Beach

Opposite the entrance to Hearst Castle is William Randolph Hearst State Beach (750 Hearst Castle Rd., 805/927-2020, www.parks. ca.gov, dawn–dusk daily). The old pier is still here, and the beach is in a small cove with lots of trees on the nearby bluffs. A creek wanders into the ocean, and at low tide it's easy to cross and make your way to the rock formations on the north side, which are teeming with starfish. Although this beach is near Hearst Castle, it's relatively unused, and happily so. There are picnic sites, restrooms, and barbecue grills. Fishing from the San Simeon pier is allowed without a license. As with any state-run park, funding could be cut, and you may find some of these services unavailable.

SHOPPING

Wampum Trading Post (9190 Castillo Dr., 805/927-1866, 10 A.M.–5 P.M. daily) is the place for souvenirs of nearby Hearst Castle such as postcards, key chains, and noncastle merchandise such as Indian jewelry, artifacts, kachinas, and pottery. On the more mundane side, there are sunglasses and even snacks.

SPORTS AND RECREATION
Biking

For those looking for a challenge and with time to spend, the biking route along **Highway 1 North to Ragged Point** will satisfy you. From Cambria or San Simeon, simply start at Highway 1 and begin pedaling north. The route, all along the highway, is a mere 15 miles, but once you're past the low rolling hills near San Simeon, you begin the long ascent up to Ragged Point. The road twists and turns past stunning drop-offs and old trees hugging the cliffs—this is the beginning of the spectacular and scenic drive toward Big Sur. At Ragged Point, there are jaw-dropping vistas of the coast. You can also refuel at the Ragged Point restaurant (19019 Hwy. 1, 805/927-5708, www.raggedpointinn.com), then coast most of the way back.

ACCOMMODATIONS
Under $150

Value is important, and if you're passing through San Simeon for just one night, you might consider the following budget-friendly lodgings.

The **Silver Surf Motel** (9390 Castillo Dr., 805/927-4661, www.silversurfmotel.com,

$90–160 d) has 72 guest rooms on three acres across the street from the beach. There is also a small grass area for pets and kids, and you have easy access to Hearst Castle for a morning tour. The guest rooms are slightly bigger than standard hotel rooms, and they offer an indoor pool and hot tub as well as Wi-Fi.

Just down the road is the **San Simeon Lodge** (9520 Castillo Dr., San Simeon, 805/927-4601, www.sansimeonrestaurant.com, $99–185 d), a 60-unit motel near Hearst Castle and the beach. It's a very good value, although the accommodations are simple and basic. If you're just around for a night and aren't planning on hanging out too much in the room, it's a fine stay. The guest rooms are clean and practical, and there is an outdoor pool. There is a small restaurant (San Simeon Beach Bar & Grill) next to the front desk that has karaoke, a pool table, and a small bar.

$150-250

Best Western Cavalier Oceanfront Resort (9415 Hearst Dr., 805/927-4688, www.cavalierresort.com, $159–319 d) was built in 1965 and is still a family-run operation. The best guest rooms face directly to the ocean; it's one of few hotels where you can simply open your sliding door and hear the beautiful rumblings of the Pacific—for this reason, some of these choice guest rooms are booked over a year in advance. Guest rooms also have wood-burning fireplaces, although they use a disc of compressed wood pulp. There are 90 guest rooms, some without direct ocean views; each has binoculars, plus cedar-lined drawers for your belongings. There's an on-site restaurant offering room service for all three meals. There are two pools, a hot tub, and three outdoor fire pits right on the bluffs.

FOOD
Cheap Eats

Sebastian's (442 San Simeon Rd., 805/927-3307, 11 A.M.–4 P.M. Wed.–Sun., $10) is an amalgam of small restaurant, tiny general store, and post office dating to 1852. The same family has owned it since 1914. It used to serve the fishing boats that docked at the once-busy port in San Simeon; these days it's less busy, but still a world away. The original old wood floors are worn and beat up, demonstrating the long history of service. As you leave Hearst Castle, this is the closet food you'll find. Try the mean French dip sandwich and meatloaf made with Hearst Ranch beef. You can hang out on the side deck, with distant views of the castle, then head down to the pier.

Mexican

You can't miss the dark salmon–colored **El Chorlito Mexican Restaurant** (9155 Hearst Dr., 805/927-3872, www.elchorlito.com, 11:30 A.M.–close daily, $10), the only Mexican place in San Simeon, which has held its ground for over 30 years. It has indoor and ocean-view patio seating with a moderate Mexican decor. House specialties include homemade vegetarian salsa and lamb shanks in mild tomato sauce, and menudo (tripe stew) on Saturday–Sunday. They'll gladly substitute tofu in any meat dishes. It's a fun, simple spot.

GETTING THERE

San Simeon is located on Highway 1 and is only accessible from this route, whether you're coming from the north or the south. From Big Sur, head straight south on Pacific Coast Highway. Given that this is a two-lane road with lots of twists and turns, it will take you over 2.5 hours.

Big Sur

The coastal region north of San Simeon and south of Carmel is for many the highlight of California's Pacific Coast Highway. The two-lane road winds along some of the most dramatic coastal scenery anywhere, with every turn bringing a new view of sheer cliffs plunging into the churning ocean.

Big Sur beckons to many types of visitors. Nature lovers come to camp and hike the pristine wilderness areas, to don thick wetsuits and surf the oft-deserted beaches, and even to hunt for jade in rocky coves.

Some of the wealthiest people in California and beyond visit Big Sur to luxuriate at unbelievably plush hotels and spas with dazzling views of the ocean, flower-strewn meadows, art galleries, and fabulous cuisine.

Whether you prefer a low-cost camping trip or a pampered experience, Big Sur offers its beauty and charm to all comers. Part of the charm is Big Sur's determination to remain peacefully apart from the Information Age—yes, this means that your cell phone won't work in many parts of the region.

Note that the name Big Sur can be confusing: It's both a town and the semiofficial name of this entire coastal region.

SIGHTS AND RECREATION
◖ Big Sur Coast Highway

Even if you're not up to tackling the endless hiking trails and deep wilderness backcountry of Big Sur, you can still get a good sense of the glory of this region just by driving through it. The Big Sur Coast Highway, a 90-mile stretch of Highway 1, runs along jagged cliffs and rocky beaches, through dense redwood forest, over historic bridges, and past innumerable parks. Construction on this stretch of road was completed in the 1930s, connecting Cambria to Carmel. You can start out at either of these towns and spend a whole day making your way to the other end of the road. The road has plenty of wide turnouts set into picturesque

© LIZ HAMILL SCOTT

Big Sur's famous coastline

PACIFIC COAST HIGHWAY

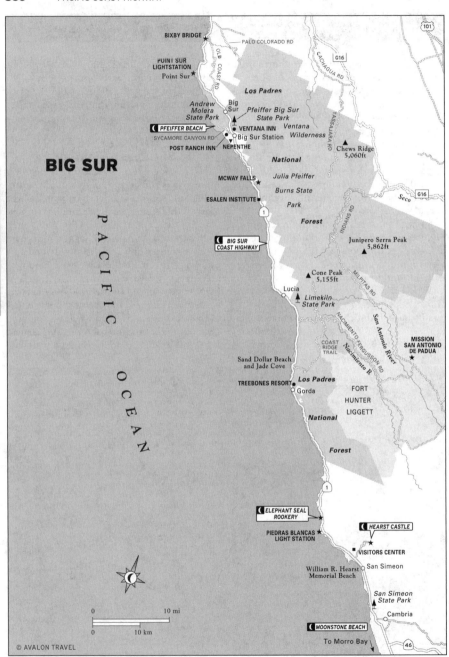

BIG SUR

BIXBY BRIDGE ★
PALO COLORADO RD
OLD COAST RD
101
CACHAGUA RD
G16

POINT SUR
LIGHTSTATION ★
Point Sur ★

Los Padres

TASSAJARA RD

Andrew
Molera
State Park
Big
Sur
*Pfeiffer Big Sur
State Park*
☾ PFEIFFER BEACH
SYCAMORE CANYON RD
POST RANCH INN
● VENTANA INN
○ Big Sur Station
NEPENTHE
*Ventana
Wilderness*
Chews Ridge
5,060ft

National

Julia Pfeiffer

MCWAY FALLS ★

Burns State

ESALEN INSTITUTE ■

Park

1

Forest

G16
Seco

INDIANS RD

Junipero Serra Peak
5,862ft

**☾ BIG SUR
COAST HIGHWAY**

MILPITAS RD

▲ Cone Peak
5,155ft

Lucia ○

*Limekiln
State Park*

NACIMIENTO FERGUSSON RD

San Antonio River

MISSION
SAN ANTONIO
DE PADUA ★

P A C I F I C

O C E A N

COAST
RIDGE
TRAIL

Nacimiento R.

Sand Dollar Beach
and Jade Cove

Los Padres

TREEBONES RESORT ○
○ Gorda

FORT
HUNTER
LIGGETT

National

Forest

1

**☾ ELEPHANT SEAL
ROOKERY** ★

☾ HEARST CASTLE ★

PIEDRAS BLANCAS ★
LIGHT STATION

■ VISITORS CENTER

William R. Hearst
Memorial Beach
○ San Simeon

*San Simeon
State Park*

▲
Cambria

0   10 mi

0   10 km

☾ MOONSTONE BEACH

To Morro Bay ↓

46

© AVALON TRAVEL

cliffs to make it easy to stop to admire the glittering ocean and stunning wooded cliffs running right out to the water. Be sure to bring a camera on your trip along Highway 1—you'll find yourself wanting to take photos every mile for hours on end.

Jade Cove Beach Recreation Area

Jade Cove Beach Recreation Area (Hwy. 1, two miles south of Sand Dollar Beach), is easy to miss as you barrel up Highway 1. A road sign marks the area, but there's no parking lot to denote the treasures of this jagged, rough part of the Big Sur coastline. Park in the dirt and gravel strip off the road and head past the fence into the park. Jade striates the coastline here, and storms tear clumps of jade out of the cliffs and into the sea. Much of it settles just off the shore of the tiny cove, and locals dive here in hopes of finding jewelry-quality stones to sell for huge amounts.

It's fun to read the unusual signs along the narrow well-trodden path that seems to lead to the edge of a cliff. The signs explain that you cannot bring in mining equipment, or take away rocks or minerals obtained from behind the high-tide line. If you're into aerial sports, you can hang-glide off the cliffs here.

Once you get to the edge of the cliff, the short trail gets rough. It's only 0.25 miles, but it's almost straight down a rocky, slippery cliff. Don't try to climb down if you're not in reasonably good physical condition. Even if you are, don't be afraid to use your hands to steady yourself. At the bottom, you'll find huge boulders and smaller rocks and very little sand. You may also see a small herd of locals dressed in wetsuits and scuba gear. But most of all, you'll find the most amazing minerals in the boulders and rocks. Reach out and touch a multiton boulder shot through with jade. Search the smaller rocks beneath your feet for chunks of sea-polished jade. If you're a hard-core rock nut, you can join the locals in **scuba diving** for jewelry-quality jade. As long as you find it in the water or below the high-tide line, it's legal to take what you find.

Jade Cove has no water, no restrooms, no visitors center, and no other services of any kind.

Limekiln State Park

Although not as impressive as the Big Sur parks farther north, Limekiln State Park (Hwy. 1, two miles south of Lucia, 831/667-2403, www.parks.ca.gov) has redwoods, a waterfall, and its namesake kilns to see. The park also includes a day-use area for picnicking and a small but pretty campground.

Esalen Institute

The Esalen Institute (55000 Hwy. 1, 831/667-3000, fax 831/667-2724, www.esalen.org) is known as the home of California massage technique, a forerunner and cutting-edge player in ecological living, and a space to retreat from the world and build a new and better sense of self. Visitors journey from all over to sink into the haven that's sometimes called "The New Age Harvard."

One of the biggest draws of Esalen is the bathhouse, down a rocky path on the edge of the coastal cliffs. It includes a motley collection of mineral-fed hot tubs looking out over the ocean. This isn't a day spa: You have to make an appointment for a massage ($165), which grants you access to the hot tubs for an hour before and an hour after your 75-minute treatment session. If you just want to sit in the mineral water, you'll have to stay up very late. Inexpensive ($20) open access to the Esalen tubs begins on a first-come, first-serve basis at 1 A.M. and ends at 3 A.M. Many locals consider the sleep deprivation well worth it to get the chance to enjoy the healing mineral waters and the stunning astronomical shows.

You can choose the Quiet Side or the Silent Side to sink into the water and contemplate the Pacific Ocean's limitless expanse, meditate on a perfect sunset or stars, or (on the Quiet Side) get to know your fellow bathers.

Esalen's bathhouse area is clothing optional; its philosophy emphasizes the essence of nature, and it encourages openness and sharing among its guests—to the point of chatting nude with total strangers in a smallish hot tub. You'll also find a distinct absence of staff to help you find your way around. Once you've parked and been given directions, it's up to you to find your way down to the cliffs. You'll have to ferret out a cubby for your clothes in the changing rooms, grab a shower, then wander out to find your favorite of the hot tubs. Towels are supplied. Be sure you go all the way outside past the individual claw-foot tubs to the glorious shallow cement tubs that sit on the edge of the cliff with the surf crashing just below.

If you're not comfortable with your own nudity or that of others, or you find it impossible to lower your voice or stop talking for more than 10 minutes, Esalen is not for you. But if this description of a California experience sounds fabulous to you, make your reservations now, as they fill up fast.

Julia Pfeiffer Burns State Park

Julia Pfeiffer Burns State Park (Hwy. 1, 12 miles south of Pfeiffer Big Sur State Park, 831/667-2315, www.parks.ca.gov, sunrise–sunset daily) overlooks the dramatic coastline and provides some great photo ops. The visitors center is easily accessible from the main parking lot. Rangers can advise you about hiking and activities both in their park and at other parks in the region.

HIKING

One of the best-known and easiest hikes in the region is in Julia Pfeiffer Burns State Park. The **Overlook Trail** is only 0.7 miles round-trip along a level wheelchair-friendly boardwalk. Stroll under Highway 1, past the Pelton wheel, and out to the observation deck and the stunning view of McWay Falls, an 80-foot year-round waterfall that cascades off a cliff and onto the beach of a remote cove, where the water wets the sand and trickles to the sea. The water of the cove gleams bright blue against the off-white sand—it looks more like the South Pacific than Northern California. Anyone with any love for the ocean will want to be on the beach beside the waterfall, but you

McWay Falls

© LIZ HAMILL SCOTT

can't—there's no way down to the cove that's even remotely safe.

The tiny Pelton wheel exhibit along the Overlook Trail isn't much unless you're a fan of hydraulic engineering history. It does have an interpretive exhibit that includes an old Pelton wheel, describing what it is and what it does. Besides the museum there's a small visitors center adjacent to the parking lot.

If you want to spend all day at Julia Pfeiffer Burns State Park, drive north from the park entrance to the Partington Cove pullout and park along the highway. On the east side of the highway is the trailhead for the difficult **Tan Bark Trail** (6.4 miles round-trip). It goes through redwood groves and up steep switchbacks to the top of the coastal ridge. Be sure to bring your camera to record the stunning views before you head back down the fire road to your car.

DIVING

The biggest and most interesting **dive site** along the Big Sur coast is in Julia Pfeiffer Burns

State Park. You have to get a special permit at Big Sur Station and prove your experience to dive at this protected underwater park, which is part of the Monterey Bay National Marine Sanctuary, along with the rest of the Big Sur coast. You enter the water from the shore, which gives you the chance to check out all the ecosystems, beginning with the busy life of the beach, then the rocky reefs, and then into the lush green kelp forests. Water temperatures are in the mid-50s in the shallows, dipping into the 40s as you dive deeper. Visibility is 20–30 feet, although rough conditions can diminish it significantly; the best season for clear water is September–November.

Henry Miller Memorial Library

A number of authors have spent time in Big Sur, soaking in the remote wilderness and sea air to gather inspiration for their work. Henry Miller lived and wrote in Big Sur for 18 years, and one of his works is named for the area. Today, the Henry Miller Memorial Library (Hwy. 1, 0.25 miles north of Deetjens, 831/667-2574, www.henrymiller.org, 11 A.M.–6 P.M. Wed.–Mon.) celebrates the life and work of Miller and his brethren in this quirky community center, museum, coffee shop, and gathering place. The library is easy to find on Highway 1—look for the hand-painted sign and funky fence decorations. What you won't find is a typical lending library, bookshop, or slicked-up museum. Instead, wander the lovely sun-dappled meadow soaking in the essence of Miller's life here, come inside and talk to the docents about the racy novels Miller wrote, and sit back with a cup of coffee to meditate on life and art and isolated gorgeous scenery. The library offers a glimpse into the "real" world of Big Sur as a spread-out artists colony that has inspired countless works by hundreds of people.

Big Sur Station

If you haven't yet stopped at one of the larger state parks in the area and hit the visitors center, pull in at Big Sur Station (Hwy. 1, south of Pfeiffer Big Sur State Park, 831/667-2315,

9 A.M.–4 P.M. daily). The ranger station offers maps and brochures for all the major parks and trails, plus a minimal bookshop. Frankly, the visitors center and attendant services at Pfeiffer Big Sur State Park have the same or better information, so if you're planning to visit that park, skip this stop. Several of the smaller parks and beaches (Limekiln, Garrapata, Sand Dollar) have no visitors services, so Big Sur Station serves visitors to those less-traveled spots. You can also get a free backcountry permit for the Ventana Wilderness here.

Ventana Wilderness

If you long for the lonely peace of backcountry camping, the Ventana Wilderness (www.ventanawild.org) area is ideal, comprising the peaks of the Santa Lucia Mountains and the dense growth of the northern reaches of the Los Padres National Forest. You'll find many trails beyond the popular day hikes of the state parks, especially toward the south. Check the website to find reports on the conditions of the trails in advance, and stop in at Big Sur Station or the ranger station at Pfeiffer Big Sur State Park to get the latest news on backcountry areas.

Pfeiffer Big Sur State Park

The biggest, most developed park in Big Sur is Pfeiffer Big Sur State Park (47225 Hwy. 1, 831/667-2315, www.parks.ca.gov, day use $10). It's got the Big Sur Lodge, a restaurant and café, a shop, an amphitheater, a somewhat incongruous softball field, plenty of hiking-only trails, and lovely redwood-shaded campsites. This park isn't situated by the beach; it's up in the coastal redwoods forest, with a network of roads up into the trees and along the Big Sur River that can be driven or biked.

Pfeiffer Big Sur has the tiny **Ernst Ewoldsen Memorial Nature Center,** which features stuffed examples of local wildlife. It's open seasonally; call the park for days and hours. Another historic exhibit is the **Homestead Cabin,** once the home of part of the Pfeiffer family—the first European immigrants to settle in Big Sur. Day-trippers and overnight visitors can take a stroll through the cabins of the **Big Sur Lodge,** built by the Civilian Conservation Corps during the Great Depression.

This is one of the few Big Sur parks to offer a full array of services. There's a **visitors center** in with the Big Sur Lodge Restaurant, the hotel check-in, and a small store. This visitors center is a good spot to get maps and information for hiking here and at other Big Sur parks that don't have staffed visitors centers. This large park also offers laundry facilities, some basic staples at the store, and food all day long at the restaurant and attached espresso bar. Before you head out into the woods, stop to get a meal and some water, and load up on snacks and sweatshirts. Between the towering trees and the summer fog, it can get quite chilly and somewhat damp on the trails.

HIKING

No bikes or horses are allowed on trails in this park, which makes it quite peaceful for hikers. For a starter walk, take the easy 0.7-mile **Nature Trail** in a loop from Day Use Parking Lot 2. Grab a brochure at the lodge to learn about the park's plant life as you walk the trail. For a longer, more difficult, and interesting hike deeper into the Big Sur wilderness, start at the Homestead Cabin and head to the difficult **Mount Manuel Trail** (10 miles round-trip). From the Y intersection with Oak Grove Trail, it's four miles of strenuous hiking to Mount Manuel, one of the most strenuous peaks in the area. The popular Pfeiffer Falls Trail was damaged in the 2008 Basin Complex Fire and remains closed.

Need to cool off after hiking? Scramble out to the entirely undeveloped Big Sur River Gorge, where the river slows and creates pools that are great for swimming. Relax and enjoy the water, but don't try to dive here.

FISHING

Steelhead run up the Big Sur River to spawn each year, and a limited **fishing** season follows them up the river into Pfeiffer Big Sur State Park and other accessible areas. Check with Fernwood Resort (831/667-2422,

www.fernwoodbigsur.com) and the other lodges around Highway 1 for the best spots this season.

The numerous creeks that feed into the Big Sur River are also places to cast for trout. The California Department of Fish and Game (www.dfg.ca.gov) can give you specific locations for legal fishing, season information, and rules and regulations.

Big Sur Spirit Garden

A favorite among local art lovers, the Big Sur Spirit Garden (47540 Hwy. 1, at Loma Vista, 831/238-1056, www.bigsurspiritgarden.com, 9 A.M.–6 P.M. daily, 9 A.M.–midnight when there's a show) changes a little almost every day. The "garden" includes a variety of exotic plants, while the "spirit" section is devoted to modern and postmodern Fair Trade art from around the world. The artwork tends toward brightly colored small sculptures done in exuberant childlike style. The Spirit Garden offers educational programs, community celebrations, musical events, and more; call ahead for information on upcoming events.

Andrew Molera State Park

The "Big Sur" park closest to Carmel is Andrew Molera State Park (Hwy. 1, 21 miles south of Carmel, 831/667-2315, www.parks.ca.gov, day use $10). Once home to small camps of Esselen Native Americans, then a Spanish land grant, this chunk of Big Sur eventually became the Molera ranch. The land was used to grow crops and ranch animals, and as a hunting and fishing retreat for family and friends. In 1965, Frances Molera sold the land to the Nature Conservancy, and when she died, three years later the ranch was sold to the California State Park system per her will. Today, the **Molera Ranch House Museum** (831/667-2956, info@bigsurhistory.org, http://bigsurhistory.org/museum.html, 11 A.M.–3 P.M. Sat.–Sun. when a docent is available) displays stories of the life and times of Big Sur's human pioneers and artists as well as the wildlife and plants of the region. Take the road toward the horse tours to get to the ranch house.

BIRD-WATCHING IN BIG SUR

Many visitors come to Big Sur just to see the birds. The Big Sur coast is home to innumerable species, from the tiniest bush tits up to grand pelicans and beyond. The most famous avian residents of this area are no doubt the rare and endangered California condors. Once upon a time, condors were all but extinct, with only a few left alive in captivity and conservationists struggling to help them breed. Today, more than 30 birds soar above the trails and beaches of Big Sur. You might even see one swooping low over your car as you drive down Highway 1. You'll know it if one does this – a condor's wingspan can exceed nine feet. Check with the park rangers for the best times and places to see condors during your visit.

The **Ventana Wilderness Society** (VWS,

www.ventanaws.org) watches over many of the endangered and protected avian species in Big Sur. As part of their mission to raise awareness of the condors and other birds, the VWS offers bird-watching expeditions; these can be simple two-hour tours or overnight wilderness camping trips, depending on your interest. Check the website for schedules and prices.

One of the hot spots of VWS conservation efforts and tours is Andrew Molera State Park. You can head out on your own to take a look around for some of the most interesting species in the Big Sur area. But wherever you choose to hike, on the beach or in the forest, you're likely to see a variety of feathered critters fluttering about.

At the park entrance, you'll find restrooms but no drinkable water and no food concessions. If you're camping here, be sure to bring plenty of your own water for washing dishes as well as drinking. If you're hiking for the day, pack in bottled water and snacks.

HIKING

The park has numerous hiking trails that run down to the beach and up into the forest along the river—many are open to biking and horseback riding as well. Most of the park trails are west of the highway. The beach is a one-mile walk down the easy multiuse **Trail Camp Beach Trail.** From there, climb on out on the **Headlands Trail,** a 0.25-mile loop, for a beautiful view from the headlands. If you prefer to get a better look at the Big Sur River, take the flat, moderate **Bobcat Trail** (5.5 miles roundtrip) and perhaps a few of its ancillary loops. The walk is along the riverbanks and the local microhabitats. Watch out for bicycles and the occasional horse and rider.

For an even longer and more difficult trek up the mountains and down to the beach, take the eight-mile **Ridge Bluff Loop.** Start at the parking lot on the Creamery Meadow Beach

Trail, then make a left onto the long and fairly steep Ridge Trail to get a sense of the local ecosystem. Turn left again onto the Panorama Trail, which runs down to the coastal scrublands, and finally out to the Bluff Trail, which leads back to Creamery Meadow.

HORSEBACK RIDING

You can take a guided horseback ride into the forests or out onto the beaches of Andrew Molera State Park with **Molera Horseback Tours** (831/625-5486, http://molerahorsebacktours.com, $50–70). Tours of 1–2.5 hours depart each day starting at 9 A.M.—call ahead to guarantee a spot, or take a chance and just show up at the stables 15 minutes ahead of the ride you want to take. You can also book a private guided ride for your group. Each ride leads from the modest corral area along multiuse trails through forests or meadows, or along the Big Sur River and down to Molera Beach. Your horse walks along the solid sands as you admire the beauty of the wild Pacific Ocean.

Molera Horseback Tours are suitable for children ages six and older, as well as riders of all ability levels; you'll be matched to the right horse for you. All rides go down to the beach. Tours can be seasonal, so call ahead if you want to ride in the fall or winter. Guides share their knowledge of the Big Sur region and wildlife, and they welcome questions about the plants you see on the trail. Early morning and sunset rides tend to be the prettiest and most popular.

Point Sur Light Station

Lonely and isolated on its cliff, the Point Sur Light Station (Hwy. 1, 0.25 miles north of Point Sur Naval Facility, 831/625-4419, tours 1 P.M. Wed., 10 A.M. Sat.–Sun. Nov.–Mar., 10 A.M., 1 P.M., and 2 P.M. Wed., 10 A.M. Sat.–Sun. Apr.–June and Sept.–Oct., 10 A.M., 1 P.M., and 2 P.M. Wed., 10 A.M. Thurs., 10 A.M. Sat.–Sun. July–Aug., adults $10, ages 6–17 $5, under age 6 free) keeps watch over ships navigating near the rocky waters of Big Sur. It's the only complete 19th-century light station in California that you can visit, and even here access is severely limited. First lit in 1889, the now fully automated light station still provides navigational aid to ships off the coast; people stopped living and working in the tiny stone-built compound in 1974. But is the lighthouse truly uninhabited? Take one of the moonlight tours (call for information) to learn about the haunted history of the light station buildings.

You can't make a reservation for a Point Sur tour, so park on the west side of Highway 1 by the farm gate. Your guide will meet you here and lead you up the paved road 0.5 miles to the light station. Once here, climb the stairs to the light, explore the restored keepers' homes and service buildings, and walk out to the cliff's edge. Expect to see a great variety of flora and fauna, from brilliant wildflowers in the spring to gray whales in the winter and flocks of pelicans flying in formation any time of year. Be sure to dress in layers; it can be sunny and hot or foggy and cold in winter or summer, and sometimes both on the same tour. Tours last three hours and require more than one mile of walking, with a bit of slope and more than 100 stairs.

The farm gate is locked, and there's no access to the light station without a tour. Tour schedules can vary from year to year and season to season; check in advance. If you need special assistance for your tour or have questions about accessibility, call 831/667-0528 as far in advance as possible of your visit to make arrangements. Strollers, food, pets, and smoking are not allowed on light station property.

Bixby Bridge

You'll probably recognize the Bixby Bridge when you come to it on Highway 1 in Big Sur. The picturesque cement open-spandrel arched bridge is one of the most photographed in the nation, and it has been used in countless car commercials over the years. The bridge was built in the early 1930s as part of the massive government works project that completed Highway 1 through Big Sur to connect roads in the north to those in the south. Today, you can pull out north or south of the bridge to take photos or just admire the attractive span and Bixby Creek flowing into the Pacific far below.

Are there two Bixby Bridges? Nope, but the Rocky Creek Bridge (north of Bixby Bridge on Hwy. 1) is similar in design, if not quite as grand and picturesque.

Garrapata State Park

A narrow, two-mile-long band of pretty light sand creates the beach at Garrapata State Park (Hwy. 1, gate 18 or 19, 831/624-4909, www.parks.ca.gov), north of the Point Sur Light Station. Stroll along the beach, scramble up the cliffs for a better view of the ocean, or check out the seals, sea otters, and sea lions near Soberanes Point. In the winter, grab a pair of binoculars to look for migrating gray whales passing quite close to shore. The **Soberanes Canyon Trail** east of the highway is one of the more challenging and fun hikes to tackle at Garrapata. The beach is also good for **shore fishing.**

Expect little in the way of facilities—parking is in a wide spot on Highway 1, and if you're lucky, you might find a pit toilet open for use.

ACCOMMODATIONS

Many visitors to Big Sur want to experience the unspoiled beauty of the landscape. The accommodations options along the Big Sur coast range from forest lodges to grand destination resorts.

Ragged Point Inn

Despite the forbidding name, Ragged Point Inn (19019 Hwy. 1, 805/927-4502, http://ragged-pointinn.net, $200–480) takes advantage of its location to create an anything-but-ragged hotel experience for its guests. If you've come to Big Sur to bask in the grandeur of the Pacific Ocean, this is your hotel. It perches on one of Big Sur's famous cliffs, offering stellar views from the purpose-built glass walls and private balconies or patios of almost every guest room. Budget-friendly guest rooms still have plenty of space, a comfy king bed or two doubles, and those unreal ocean views. If you've got a bit more cash to burn, go for a luxury room, with optimal views, soaring interior spaces, plush amenities, and romantic two-person spa bathtubs. Outside your room, enjoy a meal in the full-service restaurant or get picnic supplies from the snack bar or the minimart, fill up for a day trip at the on-site gas station, or peruse the works of local artists in the gift shop or jewelry gallery. A special treat is the hotel's own hiking trail, which drops 400 vertical feet past a waterfall to Ragged Point's private beach.

Treebones Resort

For the ultimate high-end California green lodging-cum-camping experience, book a yurt (a circular structure made with a wood frame covered by cloth) at the Treebones Resort (71895 Hwy. 1, 877/424-4787, www.treebones-resort.com). The resort got its name from the a local's description of this scrap of land, once a wood recycling plant with sun-bleached logs—"tree bones"—lying around. The yurts ($179–309) tend to be spacious and charming, with polished wood floors, queen beds, seating areas, and outdoor decks for lounging. There are also five walk-in **campsites** ($70 for two people). In the central lodge, you'll find nice hot showers

and usually clean restroom facilities. Treebones offers a somewhat pricey casual dinner each night (entrées $26–33) and basic linens. If you like extra pillows and towels, you'll have to bring your own. Check the website for a list of items to bring and the FAQ about the resort facilities to make your stay more fun. Treebones allows only children older than age six to stay at its property; children ages 6–12 may not be left alone in the yurts.

Deetjens Big Sur Inn

When locals speak of Deetjens, they could be referring to the inn, the restaurant, or the family that created both. Deetjens operates as a nonprofit organization dedicated to offering visitors to the Big Sur region great hospitality for reasonable rates. To stay at Deetjens Big Sur Inn (48865 Hwy. 1, 831/667-2377, www.deetjens.com, $90–250) is to become a small part of Big Sur's history and culture. It doesn't look like a spot where legions of famous writers, artists, and Hollywood stars have laid their heads, but Deetjens can indeed boast a guest register that many hostelries in Beverly Hills would kill for. And yet the motley collection of buildings has also welcomed transient artists, San Francisco bohemians, and the occasional criminal looking for a spot to sleep as they traveled the coast on bicycles or even on foot.

Your guest room will be unique, still decorated with the art and collectibles chosen and arranged by Grandpa Deetjen many moons ago. The inn prides itself on its rustic historic construction—expect thin weathered walls, funky cabin construction, no outdoor locks on the doors, and an altogether unique experience. Many guest rooms have shared baths, but you can request a room with a private bath when you make reservations. Deetjens prefers to offer a serene environment, and to that end does not permit children under 12 unless you rent both rooms of a two-room building. Deetjens has no TVs or stereos, no phones in the guest rooms, and no cell phone service. A pay phone is available for emergencies, but other than that you're truly cut off from the outside world. Decide for yourself whether this sounds terrifying or wonderful.

Ventana

If money is no object, you cannot possibly beat the lodgings at **(Ventana** (48123 Hwy. 1, 800/628-6500, www.ventanainn.com, $400), a place where the panoramic ocean views begin in the parking lot. This might well be the best hotel in California. Picture home-baked pastries, fresh yogurt, in-season fruit, and organic coffee delivered to your room in the morning, then enjoying that sumptuous breakfast outdoors on your own private patio, overlooking a wildflower-strewn meadow that sweeps out toward the blue-gray waters of the ocean. And that's just the beginning of an unbelievable day at the Ventana. Next, don your plush spa robe and rubber slippers (all you are required to wear on the grounds of the hotel and spa) and head for one of the Japanese bathhouses at each end of the property. Both are clothing-optional and gender segregated, and the upper house has glass and open-air windows that let you look out to the ocean. Two swimming pools offer a cooler hydro-respite; the lower pool is clothing-optional, and the upper pool perches on a high spot for enthralling views. Almost every other amenity imaginable, including daily complimentary yoga classes, can be yours for the asking.

The guest rooms range from the "modest" standard rooms with king beds, tasteful exposed cedar walls and ceilings, and attractive green and earth tone appointments up through generous and gorgeous suites to full-size multiple-bedroom houses. If you have the money available, the Vista Suites boast the most beauteous hotel accommodations imaginable. You'll reach your room by walking along the paved paths crowded with lush landscaping, primarily California native plants that complement the wild lands of the trails behind the main hotel buildings. You can also take an evening stroll down to the restaurant—the only spot on the property where you need to wear more than your robe and flip-flops.

The **Spa at Ventana** (831/667-4222, http://www.ventanainn.com/spa.aspx, 9 A.M.–6 P.M. daily fall–spring, until 9 A.M.–8 P.M. daily summer, $120 for a 50-minute massage) offers a large menu of spa treatments to both hotel guests and visitors. You'll love the serene atmosphere of the treatment and waiting areas. Greenery and weathered wood create a unique space that helps to put you in a tranquil state of mind, ready for your body to follow into a state of relaxation. Indulge in a soothing massage, purifying body treatment, or rejuvenating or beautifying facial. Take your spa experience a step further in true Big Sur fashion with a Reiki or craniosacral treatment. Or go for a private New Age reading, a personal yoga or meditation session, or a private guided hike. If you're a hotel guest, you can choose to have your spa treatment in the comfort of your own room or out on your private deck.

Post Ranch Inn

Just across the highway from the Ventana, Post Ranch Inn (47900 Hwy. 1, 888/524-4787, www.postranchinn.com, $550–2,185) is another exclusive luxury resort perched on the cliffs of Big Sur. Spa, yoga, and a unique rustic atmosphere are just a few of its perks.

At the **Post Ranch Inn Spa** (831/667-2200, $140 for a one-hour massage), body, facial, and massage work focuses on organics and gem and crystal therapies. You can also indulge in private sessions, including shamanic meetings that focus on indigenous techniques that are said to enhance your life.

Big Sur Lodge

If you want to stay inside one of the parks but tents just aren't your style, book a cabin at the Big Sur Lodge (47225 Hwy. 1, 800/424-4787, www.bigsurlodge.com, $199–399) in Pfeiffer Big Sur State Park. The lodge was built in the 1930s as a government works project to create jobs during the Great Depression; by then Big Sur's astounding beauty and peace had been recognized by both federal and state governments, and much of the land was protected as parks. The amenities have been updated, but the cabins of Big Sur Lodge still evoke the classic woodsy vacation cabin. Set in the redwood forest along an array of paths and small roads, the cabins feature patchwork quilts, rustic furniture, understated decor, and simple but clean baths. Many cabins have lots of beds—perfect for larger families or groups of adults traveling together. The largest cabins have fireplaces and kitchens. You can stock your kitchen at the on-site grocery store, or just get a meal at the lodge's restaurant or café.

The lodge has a swimming pool for those rare sunny summer days in the Big Sur forest, but the real attraction is its doorstep access to the Pfeiffer Big Sur trails. You can leave your car outside your room and hike all day inside the park. Or take a short drive to one of the other state parks and enjoy their charms for free with proof of occupancy at Big Sur Lodge.

Fernwood Resort

Along Highway 1 in the town of Big Sur, you'll find a couple of small motels. One of the most popular is the Fernwood Resort (47200 Hwy. 1, 831/667-2422, www.fernwoodbig-sur.com, $99–165). The low sprawl of buildings includes a 12-room motel, a small general store, a restaurant, and a tavern that passes for the local nighttime hot spot. Farther down the small road are the campgrounds, which include a number of tent cabins as well as tent and RV sites. If all this makes a "resort," so be it. Your motel room will be a modest space in a blocky, one-level building off to the side of the main store and restaurant buildings. Not too much sunlight gets into the guest rooms, but the decor is lightly colored and reasonably attractive. Guest rooms have queen beds and attached private baths but no TVs. If you tend to get chilly in the winter (or in the summer fog), ask for a room with a gas stove. One room has a two-person hot tub just outside on the back deck. In summer, book in advance to be sure of getting a room, especially on weekends.

Big Sur River Inn

Another lodge-style motel set in the redwood forest, the Big Sur River Inn (46840 Hwy. 1, at Pheneger Creek, 800/548-3610, www.big-surriverinn.com, $125–270) is in one of the "populated" parts of Big Sur. First opened in the 1930s by a member of the Pfeiffer

family, the inn has been in continuous operation ever since. Today, it boasts 20 motel rooms, a restaurant, and a gift shop. Guest rooms are small but comfortable, with a juxtaposition of chain-motel comforters and curtains with rustic, lodge-style wooden interior paneling. Budget-conscious guest rooms have one queen bed. Families and small groups can choose among standard rooms with two queen beds, two-room suites with multiple beds, and attractive back decks that look out over the Big Sur River. All guests can enjoy the attractively landscaped outdoor pool with its surrounding lawn leading down to the river. The attached restaurant offers three meals a day. Be sure to make reservations in advance for summer weekends.

CAMPING

For true outdoors lovers, many of the parks and lodges in the area have overnight campgrounds. You'll find all types of camping, from full-service RV-accessible areas to environmental tent campsites to wilderness backpacking. You can camp in a state park or out behind one of the small resort motels near a restaurant and a store or the cool Big Sur River.

Treebones Resort

At the Treebones Resort (71895 Hwy. 1, 877/424-4787, www.treebonesresort.com) there are five walk-in **campsites** ($70 for two people). Facilities at the central lodge—hot showers and usually clean restrooms—are included.

Limekiln State Park

The small but pretty campground at Limekiln State Park (63025 Hwy. 1, 831/667-2403, www.parks.ca.gov, summer only, $35), two miles south of Lucia, offers 28 developed campsites with hot showers and flush toilets out along an attractive creek that runs toward the nearby ocean. RVs and trailers can stay here (call for maximum length restrictions), although hookups and dump stations aren't available. In summer, the park recommends making reservations early. In winter, no reservations are available, and many sites are closed. Call for more information if you want to camp off-season.

Pfeiffer Big Sur State Park

The biggest and most developed campground in Big Sur sits at Pfeiffer Big Sur State Park (Hwy. 1, 831/667-2315, www.parks.ca.gov, $35–50). With 212 individual sites, each of which can take two vehicles and eight people or an RV (up to 32 feet, trailers up to 27 feet, dump station on-site), there's enough room for almost everyone. During the summer, a grocery store and laundry facilities operate within the campground for those who don't want to hike down to the lodge, and plenty of flush toilets and hot showers are scattered throughout the campground. In the evening, walk down to the campfire center for entertaining and educational programs. If you prefer a quieter and less asphalt-oriented camping experience, check out the hike-in and bike-in campgrounds that make up part of the Pfeiffer Big Sur complex.

Pfeiffer Big Sur fills up fast in the summer, especially on weekends. Advance reservations (800/444-7275, www.reserveamerica.com) are strongly recommended.

Fernwood Resort

The large campground area at this popular resort (47200 Hwy. 1, 831/667-2422, www.fernwoodbigsur.com, campsites $40–45, tent cabins $70) occupies both sides of the Big Sur River. You can choose between pitching your own tent, pulling in an RV, or renting a tent cabin. The resort has easy access to the river, where you can swim, inner tube, and hike.

Tent cabins offer small canvas-constructed spaces with room for four people in a double and two twin beds. You can pull your car right up to the back of your cabin. Bring your own linens or sleeping bags, pillows, and towels. Hot showers and restrooms are a short walk away. Tent campsites are scattered in great places—tucked in down by the river under vast shady redwood trees. You can even park your RV under a tree, then hook it up to water and electricity.

Andrew Molera State Park

Andrew Molera State Park (Hwy. 1, 21 miles south of Carmel, 831/667-2315, www.parks.ca.gov, $25 per night) offers 24 walk-in, tent-only campsites located 0.25–0.5 miles from the parking lot via a level, well-maintained trail. Pitch your tent in a pretty meadow near the Big Sur River at a site that includes a picnic table and a fire ring. No reservations are taken, so come early in summer to get one of the prime spots under a tree. While you're camping, look for bobcats, foxes, deer, raccoons (stow your food securely), and lots of birds.

As of 2007, no potable water was available at Andrew Molera. Toilets are a short walk from the camping area, but you cannot shower here.

FOOD

As you travel famed Highway 1 through Big Sur, you'll quickly realize that a ready meal isn't something to take for granted here. You'll see no McDonald's, Starbucks, 7-Elevens, or Safeways lining the road. While you can find groceries, they tend to appear in small markets attached to motels. The motels and resorts usually have restaurants attached as well, but they're not all-meals or 24-hour kinds of places. Plan in advance to make it to meals during standard hours, and expect to have dinner fairly early. Pick up staple supplies before you enter the area if you don't plan to leave again for a few days to avoid paying a premium at the minimarts.

Deetjens

According to Big Sur locals, the best breakfast in the area can be had at **Deetjens** (48865 Hwy. 1, 831/667-2377, www.deetjens.com, breakfast and dinner daily, $10–30). The funky dining room with its mismatched tables, dark wooden chairs, and cluttered wall decor belies the high quality of the cuisine served here. Enjoy delectable dishes created from the freshest local ingredients for breakfast and then again at dinnertime.

Nepenthe and Café Kevah

When you dine at **Nepenthe** (48510 Hwy. 1,

831/667-2345, www.nepenthebigsur.com, 11:30 A.M.–4:30 P.M. and 5–10 P.M. daily, lunch $15, dinner $32), be sure to ask for a table outdoors on even partly sunny days. That way you get to enjoy both your Ambrosia Burger and the phenomenal cliff-top views. Open for lunch and dinner, the restaurant offers a short but tasty menu of meat, fish, and plenty of vegetarian dishes.

Outside at the Nepenthe, the seasonal **Café Kevah** (breakfast and lunch 9 A.M.–2:30 or 3:30 P.M. daily Feb.–Dec., $11–15) patio offers a similar sampling at slightly lower prices. Munch on your Café Kevah Benedict or sandwich as you drape your arms over the wrought-iron railing and stare out into the mesmerizing blue-gray of the Pacific below.

Ventana

You don't need to be a guest at the gorgeous Ventana to enjoy a fine gourmet dinner at **The Restaurant at Ventana** (48123 Hwy. 1, 831/667-4242, www.ventanainn.com/dining.asp, 11:30 A.M.–4:30 P.M. and 6–9 P.M. daily, lunch $14, dinner $33). The spacious dining room boasts a warm wood fire, an open kitchen, and comfortable banquettes with plenty of throw pillows to lounge against as you peruse the menu. If you're visiting for lunch or an early supper on a sunny day, be sure to request a table outside so you can enjoy the stunning views with your meal. The inside dining room has great views from the bay windows too, along with pristine white tablecloths and pretty light wooden furniture. Even with such a setting, the real star at this restaurant is the cuisine. The chef offers a changing spread of California haute cuisine dishes, many of which feature organic or homegrown produce and local meats. To go with the seascape theme, the menu is heavy on sustainable seafood offerings. Be sure to tell your server if you're vegetarian or have dietary limitations—the chefs can whip up something special for you. The best value is the prix fixe menu, from which you can choose several courses. A pricier option is to get a wine pairing with each course, and be sure to save room for dessert.

Post Ranch Inn and Spa

The **Sierra Mar** (47900 Hwy. 1, 831/667-2800, www.postranchinn.com, 8–10:30 A.M., 12:15–3 P.M., and 3–9 P.M. daily, lunch $26, dinner $110) restaurant at the Post Ranch Inn offers a decadent four-course prix fixe dinner menu in a stunning ocean-view setting. Lunch and snacks are served through the afternoon to casual travelers, but expect to put on the ritz for a formal white-tablecloth dining experience at this over-the-top upscale restaurant.

Big Sur Bakery and Restaurant

The **Big Sur Bakery and Restaurant** (47540 Hwy. 1, 831/667-0520, www.bigsurbakery.com, 11 A.M.–2:30 P.M. Mon., 11 A.M.–2:30 P.M. and 5:30 P.M.–close Tues.–Fri., 10:30 A.M.–2:30 P.M. and 5:30 P.M.–close Sat.–Sun., $25) might sound like a casual walk-up eating establishment, and the bakery part of it is: You can stop in from 8 A.M. every day to grab a fresh-baked scone, a homemade jelly doughnut, or a flaky croissant sandwich to go. But on the dining room side, an elegant surprise awaits diners who've spent the day hiking the redwoods and strolling the beaches. Be sure to make reservations or you're unlikely to get a table, and you'd miss out on the amazing clam chowder (with whole clams in their shells) and other unique California takes on classic American cuisine.

Big Sur Lodge

Serving three meals each day to lodge guests and travelers, the **Big Sur Lodge Espresso House and Restaurant** (47225 Hwy. 1, 800/242-4787, www.bigsurlodge.com, 7:30 A.M.–9 P.M. daily, $23) has a dining room as well as a cute espresso and ice cream bar out front. The dining room dishes up a full menu of American classic for every meal, and you can grab a quick sandwich to go from the Espresso House.

Fernwood

The **Redwood Grill Restaurant** (47200 Hwy. 1, 831/667-2129, www.fernwoodbigsur.com,

11:30 A.M.–9 P.M. daily, $20) at Fernwood Resort looks and feels like a grill in the woods ought to. Even in the middle of the afternoon, the aging wood-paneled interior is dimly lit and strewn with slightly saggy couches and casual tables and chairs. Walk up to the counter to order somewhat overpriced burgers and sandwiches, then on to the bar to grab a soda or a beer.

In the evening, you can find some fun at the **Fernwood Tavern** (Hwy. 1, 831/667-2422, noon–midnight Sun.–Thurs., noon–1 A.M. Fri.–Sat.). Live music acts entertain locals and visitors alike, and you might hear country, folk, or even indie rock from the small stage. Most live music happens on weekends, especially Saturday nights, starting at 9 P.M. and ending at about midnight. Even without the music, the tavern can get lively in the evening (it's good to be the only game in town), with locals drinking from the full bar, eating, and holding parties in the meandering dim rooms.

The Fernwood also has a **general store** where you can stock up on staples.

Rocky Point Restaurant

The northernmost dining on the Big Sur coast, **Rocky Point Restaurant** (36700 Hwy. 1, 831/624-2933, www.rocky-point. com, 9 A.M.–3 P.M. and 5 P.M.–close daily, $35) offers decent food and great views. Enjoy the smell of mesquite from the grill as you wait for your steak or fish. Meat-eaters will find all the good solid dishes they want for breakfast, lunch, and dinner, but vegetarian options are limited.

INFORMATION AND SERVICES

The two most comprehensive visitors centers in Big Sur lie within **Pfeiffer Big Sur State Park** (47225 Hwy. 1, 831/667-2315, www. parks.ca.gov) and **Julia Pfeiffer Burns State Park** (Hwy. 1, 12 miles south of Pfeiffer Big Sur State Park, 831/667-2315, www.parks. ca.gov). At Pfeiffer Big Sur State Park, the visitors center is a good spot to get maps and information for hiking here and at other Big Sur

parks that don't have staffed visitors centers. This large park also offers laundry facilities and some basic staples at the store.

Farther south at Julia Pfeiffer Burns State Park, rangers can advise you about hiking and activities in any park in the region. You'll find fewer services here than at Pfeiffer Big Sur State Park—head north if you need to shop, do laundry, or gas up.

Be aware that your cell phone may not work in all of Big Sur, especially out in the undeveloped reaches of forest and on Highway 1 away from the town of Big Sur and the Post Ranch. Call boxes appear at regular intervals along the highway.

For health matters, the **Big Sur Health Center** (46896 Hwy. 1, Big Sur, 831/667-2580, http://bigsurhealthcenter.org, 10 A.M.–1 P.M. and 2–5 P.M. Mon.–Fri.) can take care of minor medical needs and provide ambulance service and limited emergency care. The nearest full-service hospital is the **Community Hospital of the Monterey Peninsula** (23625 Holman Hwy., Monterey, 831/624-5311, http://www. chomp.org).

GETTING THERE AND AROUND

The name Highway 1 may make it sound like a major freeway to many visitors, and down south it does get big and flat and straight. But along Big Sur, Highway 1 is a narrow, twisting, cliff-carved track that's breathtaking both because of its beauty and because of its dangers. Once you get five miles or so south of Carmel, expect to slow down—in some spots north of the town of Big Sur you'll be driving no more than 20 mph on hairpin turns carved into vertical cliffs. If you're coming up from the south, Ragged Point is the southern end of the Big Sur region, 15 miles (20 minutes' drive) north of San Simeon and 25 miles (35 minutes' drive) north of Cambria along Highway 1. Highway 1 is fairly wide and friendly north of Cambria, only narrowing into its more hazardous form as the cliffs get higher and the woods thicker. Be aware that fog often comes in on the Big Sur coast at sunset, making the drive even more hazardous (and much less attractive). If you must drive at night, take it slow.

Plan to spend several hours driving from Carmel to Cambria, partly to negotiate the difficult road and partly to make use of the many convenient turnouts to take photos of the spectacular scenery. Most of the major parks in the Big Sur region are right along Highway 1, making it easy to spend a couple of days meandering along the road, stopping at Julia Pfeiffer or Andrew Molera to hike for a few hours or have a picnic on the beach.

Carmel

Carmel's landscape is divided into two distinct parts. The adorable village of Carmel-by-the-Sea perches on the cliffs above the Pacific, surrounded to the north and the south by golf courses and beach parks. Carmel-by-the-Sea boasts the highest number of art galleries per capita in the United States. When most Californians talk about Carmel, they mean Carmel-by-the-Sea. The streets are perfect for strolling; in fact, some street signs are wooden posts with names written vertically, to be read while walking along the sidewalk, rather than driving down the street. There are no house numbers in Carmel-by-the-Sea, so locations are always given as "on 7th between San Carlos and Delores" or "the northwest corner of Ocean Avenue." There are lots of trees and just a few streetlights. There's little to do at night, and as recently as a few years ago, live music was outlawed in the evenings. The city even requires a no-fee permit for shoes with high heels measuring more than two inches high. These are a few clues as to how this village facing the Pacific Ocean maintains its lost-in-time charm.

Inland, the far less-traveled Carmel Valley

© LIZ HAMILL SCOTT

the view along 17 Mile Drive

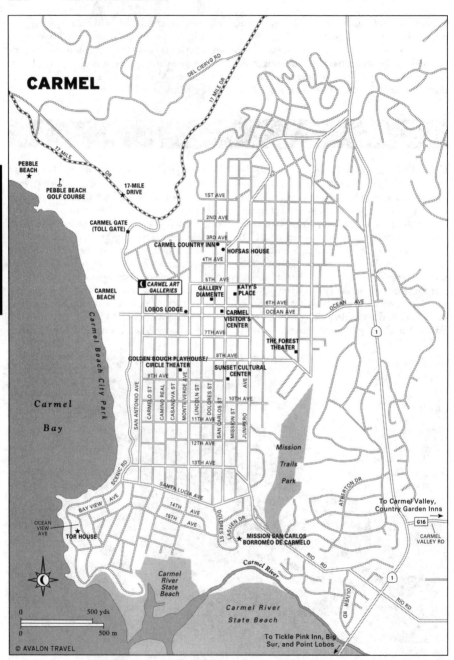

CARMEL

DEL CIERVO RD

17 MILE DR

PEBBLE BEACH ★

17 MILE

PEBBLE BEACH GOLF COURSE

17-MILE DRIVE

CARMEL GATE (TOLL GATE)

DR

1ST AVE

2ND AVE

3RD AVE

CARMEL COUNTRY INN ● ● HOFSAS HOUSE

4TH AVE

5TH AVE

CARMEL ART GALLERIES

CARMEL BEACH

GALLERY DIAMENTE ■ KATY'S PLACE ■

6TH AVE

OCEAN AVE

OCEAN AVE

LOBOS LODGE ● ■ CARMEL VISITOR'S CENTER

Carmel Beach City Park

7TH AVE

THE FOREST THEATER ●

Carmel Bay

GOLDEN BOUGH PLAYHOUSE/ CIRCLE THEATER

8TH AVE

9TH AVE

SUNSET CULTURAL CENTER ■

SAN ANTONIO ST

CARMELO ST

CAMINO REAL

CASANOVA ST

MONTE VERDE AVE

LINCOLN ST

DOLORES ST

SAN CARLOS ST

MISSION ST

JUNIPERO

10TH AVE

11TH AVE

12TH AVE

13TH AVE

SCENIC RD

Mission Trails Park

BAY VIEW AVE

SANTA LUCIA AVE

14TH AVE

15TH AVE

ATHERTON DR

To Carmel Valley, Country Garden Inns

G16

CARMEL VALLEY RD

OCEAN VIEW AVE

TOR HOUSE ★

DOLORES ST

LASUEN DR

MISSION SAN CARLOS ★ BORROMEO DE CARMELO

RIO RD

Carmel River

1

Carmel River State Beach

Carmel River

OLIVER RD

RIO RD

0   500 yds

0   500 m

Carmel River State Beach

To Tickle Pink Inn, Big Sur, and Point Lobos

© AVALON TRAVEL

has its share of huge estates owned by some of the wealthiest folks in the state. The narrow valley, surrounded by verdant hillsides, has recently discovered its footing as a niche wine region. Visitors can also play a few holes at the inevitable golf courses and check out the tiny hamlets that line the lone main road through the valley. The valley is far enough inland to benefit from diurnal swings, with much warmer and consistent daytime temperatures. When it's still foggy in Carmel, the fog will probably have burned off in the Carmel Valley, which will be basking in sunshine.

Both Carmel by-the-Sea and Carmel Valley, residents love dogs. Your pooch is welcome at many establishments, and a number of stores and restaurants offer doggie treats and keep fresh water outside for the canine set.

SIGHTS
17 Mile Drive
You can't come to Carmel and not succumb to 17 Mile Drive (www.pebblebeach.com, daily sunrise–sunset, $9.50, no motorcycles), the private road of luxury homes that hugs the rugged coastline. This road offers the only access to Pebble Beach and the Lone Cypress, the landmark so often depicted in paintings, photos, and postcards. From Highway 1, take Highway 68 west for Pacific Grove and Pebble Beach. At the exit, go straight through the light to the Pebble Beach gate. After you pay the admission fee, bear right.

The best time to view this scenic seascape is at dusk, when the pinks of the fading sun accent the blues of the ocean. This quintessential Carmel experience comes with a cost: It's a toll road, and motorcycles are not allowed. A map at the entry gate will lead you through the area; if you take your time and bring a picnic, it will take you about two hours. The best picnic spots are between Point Joe and Seal Rock. There are also golf courses, hotels, and restaurants along the way, so you won't be stranded without services.

Pebble Beach
While the legends of Pebble Beach (Palmero Way, www.pebblebeach.com) surround its championship golf course, there's a lot more

© LIZ HAMILL SCOTT

Pebble Beach

PACIFIC COAST HIGHWAY

to it than just greens and sand traps. A gated community surrounding the course and spreading back toward the trees has some of the most expensive homes in California. From 17-Mile Drive, turn onto the lengthy driveway to visit the high-end resort. Any visitor can park and walk into the main lobby of the hotel area. Most walk right through and out onto the immense multilevel patio area to take in the priceless and often-photographed views. Whether you stay on the flagstones and enjoy a drink from the lobby bar or take a walk out onto the wide lawns, your eyes will be caught by the dramatic cliffs plummeting down to the small blue-gray bay. The golf course is right next to the lawns, allowing even casual visitors to check out a couple of the hallowed greens and fairways dotted with cypress trees. The lodge itself is worth touring; you can take footpaths to see the outsides of the posh accommodations, walk in to the lobby of the exclusive spa, and peer at the tables of the gourmet dining room.

◖ Art Galleries

Carmel boasts more art galleries per capita than any other town in the United States. Accordingly, shopping in the downtown pedestrian area means "checking out the galleries." Of the many galleries in Carmel, none have the breadth of local talent you'll find at the **Carmel Art Association** (Dolores St. between 5th Ave. and 6th Ave., 831/624-6176, www.carmelart.org, 10 A.M.–5 P.M. daily), a co-op of over 120 talented artists, all of whom live within a 30-mile radius of Carmel. The association was founded in 1927 and bought this space in 1933. The majority of the pieces are oil and pastel paintings, but there are other media too, such as wood and sculpture. Artists bring in new works on the first Wednesday of each month, ensuring constant rotation.

Gallery Diamante (Dolores St. between 5th Ave. and 6th Ave., 831/624-0852, www.gallerydiamante.com) represents a typical Carmel gallery, with a large collection of landscape paintings by different artists and interesting sculptures scattered around. The most popular modern styles in painting, sculpture, and even art glass and jewelry are on display. Jewelry here can be reasonably priced, but expect to spend more for an original painting.

Bucking the current trends in Carmel art is Boban Bursac, sole owner of the tiny **Extempore Gallery** (Dolores St. between 5th Ave. and 6th Ave., 831/626-1298, www.ex-temporegallery.com). Burasac's amazing large-format paintings evoke feelings in even the most casual passerby; lucky visitors might even get to talk with the artist. Sadly, these works of art do not come cheap, understandable given their size and the skill and devotion with which they are painted.

Mission San Carlos Borroméo de Carmelo

More popularly known as Carmel Mission, the Mission San Carlos Borroméo de Carmelo (3080 Rio Rd., 831/624-1271, www.carmelmission.org, 9:30 A.M.–5 P.M. Mon.–Sat., 10:30 A.M.–5 P.M. Sun., adults $6.50, seniors $4, children $2, under age 7 free) was Father Junípero Serra's personal favorite among his California mission churches. He lived, worked, and eventually died here, and visitors today can see a replica of his cell. A working Catholic parish remains part of the complex, so be respectful when taking the self-guided tour. The rambling buildings and courtyard gardens show some wear, but enough restoration work has gone into the church and living quarters to make them attractive. The Carmel Mission has a small memorial museum in a building off the second courtyard, but don't make the mistake of thinking that this small and outdated space is the only historical display. In fact, the "museum" runs through many of the buildings, showing a small slice of the lives of the 18th- and 19th-century friars. The highlight of the complex is the church, with its gilded altar front, its shrine to the Virgin Mary, the grave of Father Serra, and an ancillary chapel dedicated to the memory of Father Serra. Round out your visit by walking out into the gardens to admire the flowers and fountains and to read the grave markers in the small cemetery. The mission can get crowded, making parking out front difficult.

Tor House

Local poet Robinson Jeffers built this rugged-looking castle on the Carmel coast in 1919. He named it Tor House (26304 Ocean View Ave., 831/624-1813, www.torhouse.org, tours 10 A.M.–3 P.M. Fri.–Sat., adults $10, ages 12–18 $5, under age 12 not permitted, maximum six people per tour), after its rocky setting, and added the majestic Hawk Tower a year later. The granite stone structure exists today as an example of the Carmel ethos that Jeffers embodied and as a monument to his work and poetry.

Earthbound Farm's Farm Stand

One of the largest purveyors of organic produce in the United States, Earthbound Farm (7250 Carmel Valley Rd., 831/625-6219, www.ebfarm.com, 8 A.M.–6:30 P.M. Mon.–Sat., 9 A.M.–6 P.M. Sun.) offers visitors easy access to its smallish facility in the Carmel Valley. Drive up to the farm stand and browse a variety of organic fruits, veggies, and flowers. Outdoors, you can ramble into the fields, checking out the chamomile labyrinth and the kids garden (yes, kids can look *and* touch). Select and harvest your own fresh herbs from the cut-your-own garden, or leave the cooking to the experts and purchase delicious prepared organic dishes at the farm stand. If you're interested in a more in-depth guided tour of the farm, check the website for a schedule of walks, which will take you, a group, and an expert guide—perhaps a chef or local famous foodie—out into the fields for a look at what's growing and how to use it.

Point Lobos State Natural Reserve

Four miles south of Carmel is Point Lobos State Natural Reserve (Hwy. 1 and Riley Ranch Rd., 831/624-4909, www.pointlobos.org, 8 A.M.–sunset daily, day-use $10), a stunning piece of land abutting the sea. The rugged, ragged cliffs and rocks, beautiful and malformed, are

dotted with pine and cypress trees, so the scent of pine is as strong as the fresh ocean breeze. Spanish moss hangs languidly from many of the branches.

Point Lobos offers hiking through forestland and along the beach, scuba diving (831/624-8413) off the shore, picnicking, and nature study. Take a walk through unique ecosystems and observe the indigenous wildlife while strolling through the rugged landscape (it's important to stay on the paths to avoid the plentiful poison oak). Be aware that July–September fog often dims the summer sun at Point Lobos, even in the middle of the day. In terms of weather, spring and fall are the best times to visit.

WINE-TASTING

The majority of tasting rooms are located in Carmel Valley; however, you can start in downtown Carmel and work your way east.

Carmel-by-the-Sea
CIMA COLLINA

Cima Collina (San Carlos St. between Ocean Ave. and 7th Ave., 831/620-0645, www.cimacollina.com, 1–7 P.M. daily June–Sept., noon–6 P.M. daily Oct.–May, tasting $1.25 per glass) is located back in a courtyard, which makes it a little hard to find. A beautiful curved wooden bar takes up most of the small tasting room. Wines include a light crisp sauvignon blanc and a semisweet riesling. But the winery excels at reds: The pinot noirs are loaded with bright raspberry fruit, and a surprisingly good Meritage blend and Bordeaux blend prove that you can get excellent cabernet sauvignon fruit from this area. Also worthwhile is their Howling Good Red, a kitchen-sink blend of whatever red grapes might be available. This is a nonvintage wine, but very good.

MORGAN WINERY

Morgan Winery (204 Crossroads Blvd., 831/626-3700, www.morganwinery.com, 11 A.M.–6 P.M. daily, tasting $5) is a beautiful tasting room, surprising given that it's in a shopping center. Located between Carmel proper and Carmel Valley, it's a great stop to combine with lunch since nearby dining options abound. The dark amber walls and warm woods, along with the leather couches and chairs, make it very inviting. Owner Dan Morgan has been part of the Monterey wine scene for a number of years; his pinot noirs and chardonnays, all made with local grapes, are top-notch. The first two tastes are free, then you pay for the next five. If you divide it up, make sure you try the Hat Trick chardonnay and pinot. These wines are taken from Morgan's best three barrels of each wine and the best grapes. Also sample the sauvignon blanc and the Rio Tinto, a table wine made from port grapes.

Carmel Valley

CHÂTEAU JULIEN

Winemaker Bill Anderson has been at Château Julien (8940 Carmel Valley Rd., Carmel Valley, 831/624-2600, www.chateaujulien. com, 8 A.M.–5 P.M. Mon.–Fri., 11 A.M.–5 P.M. Sat.–Sun., tasting $7) since it first started in 1982. The château-style tasting room, the first you encounter in Carmel Valley, has a huge reception area. The central tasting table allows people to mingle freely. Notable wines include chardonnay and a merlot-malbec blend called La Conviviance, as well as a port and Carmel Cream Sherry, blended from palomino, madera, and tokay grapes. This is one of the few tasting rooms located on vineyard property; twice-daily tours (10:30 A.M. and 2:30 P.M. Mon.–Fri., 12:30 P.M. and 2:30 P.M. Sat.–Sun.) of the 16-acre estate are offered by reservation.

HELLER ESTATE ORGANIC VINEYARDS

Heller Estate Organic Vineyards (69 W. Carmel Valley Rd., Carmel Valley, 800/625-8466, www.hellerestate.com, 11 A.M.–5:30 P.M. Mon.–Thurs., 11 A.M.–6 P.M. Fri.–Sun., tasting $7–15) is the only local winery growing organically certified grapes. Some wine drinkers are prejudiced against organic wines; the uninitiated seem uncertain of the quality. Everything is estate-grown on 120 acres and

dry-farmed: The stressed roots dip 30 feet into the earth searching for water, which ultimately creates more flavorful wines. Heller produces about 18,000 cases annually. The red wines are nicely balanced and hefty, and chenin blanc and chardonnay are produced, but the estate cabernet sauvignons and Meritage blends are their best wines. Wines by the glass are $5–10. The tasting room is located in a former ranch house, along with a series of restaurants and a small art gallery. Owner Toby Heller is a noted sculptor; a sculpture garden alongside the tasting room features her work.

TALBOTT VINEYARDS

You will not go wrong at Talbott Vineyards (53 W. Carmel Valley Rd., Carmel Valley, 831/659-3500, www.talbottvineyards.com, 11 A.M.–4:30 P.M. Mon.–Fri., 11 A.M.–5 P.M. Sat.–Sun., tasting $7.50), which showcases some of the best of what the land in Monterey County can produce. The pinot noirs and chardonnays are universally excellent. The vineyards produce wines under the Talbott label, and although the top-end wines are very expensive, the very good secondary label, Kali Hart, offers pinot noir and chardonnay for about $20. They sell wines by the glass for $6–15. There are two tasting bars and shelves of bottled wine in what looks more like a nice hotel lobby than a tasting room; it's a bit formal and lacks much identity. Fortunately the wine takes center stage. There is a small dog-friendly outdoor patio.

BOEKENOOGEN VINEYARD & WINERY

The property at Boekenoogen Vineyard & Winery (24 W. Carmel Valley Rd., Carmel Valley, 831/659-4215, www.boekenoogen-wines.com, 11 A.M.–5 P.M. daily, tasting $5–10) began as cattle-farming land in the late 1880s. These days the family sells most of their grapes to about eight other wineries and makes less than 3,000 cases of wine, but what they do make is excellent. The chardonnays and pinot noirs are very impressive, and the syrah and petite sirah are coming along. The tasting room is completely unadorned (better to focus on the wines, they'll tell you). The tiled space can get terribly loud when more than four people are tasting. There's also a small outdoor patio with half a dozen tables and a fire pit. Wines by the glass are $10–12.

BERNARDUS WINERY
Bernardus Winery (5 W. Carmel Valley Rd., Carmel Valley, 800/223-2533, www.bernardus. com, 11 A.M.–5 P.M. daily, tasting $7.50–15) makes an astounding 55,000 cases per year and manages to do it well. Although there are two lists, standard and reserve, the best choice is to sample both; that way you can compare the sauvignon blanc, chardonnay, pinot noir, and Bordeaux blends side by side. Local Monterey County grapes are used to produce these uniformly excellent wines, although the reserve wines are not inexpensive. The tasting room is small and proper, if a little boring, catering mainly to guests at Bernardus Lodge.

PARSONAGE VILLAGE VINEYARD
Family-owned and operated, Parsonage Village Vineyard (19 E. Carmel Valley Rd., Carmel Valley, 831/659-7322, www.parsonagewine. com, 11 A.M.–5 P.M. daily, tasting $10) is part tasting room and part art gallery. The tasting room is simple and low-key, with a brightly polished copper-topped bar. Many of the labels on the wine bottles are photographs of quilts made by Mary Ellen Parsons, and some of these are available for sale, along with other art. Most of the wines are minimal case production, usually under 500 cases. The pinot noir and chardonnay are nice, but the syrah, merlot, and Bordeaux blends are the standouts.

ENTERTAINMENT AND EVENTS
Nightlife
Even though live music after dark is no longer against the law, as it was in Carmel for many years, the village still closes down after sunset. But there are a few places to hear live performances, with everything wrapping up by 10 P.M.

Terry's Restaurant & Lounge (Cypress Inn, Lincoln St. and 7th Ave., 831/624-3871, 11 A.M.–11 P.M. daily, live music 6–9 P.M. Thurs. and Sun., 7–10 P.M. Fri.–Sat.) offers a variety of vocals, guitar, piano, and soft jazz. The fireplace and wood trusses give the small space an intimate feel, but during the summer the doors to the patio are opened and the crowds swell.

Jack London's Neighborhood Pub & Grill (Dolores St. between 5th Ave. and 6th Ave., 831/624-2336, www.jacklondons.com, 11 A.M.–close daily, live music 8–10 P.M. Fri.–Sat.) offers live guitar in the wood-toned bar. The spot is popular, and the bar is small enough that seating is at a premium. On warmer nights the crowds spill into the courtyard.

With boots, saddles, and other Western paraphernalia hanging from the ceiling, the **Running Iron Saloon** (24 E. Carmel Valley Rd., Carmel Valley, 831/659-4633, 11 A.M.–2 A.M. Mon.–Fri., 10 A.M.–2 A.M. Sat., 9 A.M.–2 A.M. Sun.) is true to its name, even if it's rather out of place for the ritzy Carmel Valley. (Of course, that's partly the point.) Call ahead for the live music schedule and off-season closing hours, which can vary.

Performing Arts
The outdoor **Forest Theater** (Mountain View St. and Santa Rita Ave., 831/626-1681, www. foresttheaterguild.org) was started in 1910. Productions include musicals by traveling off-Broadway troupes and the Films in the Forest series, with a variety of movies to enjoy under the stars. The indoor **Sunset Center** (San Carlos St. at 9th Ave., 831/620-2048, www.sunsetcenter.org) hosts the Monterey Symphony as well as other live performers and comedians.

Festivals and Events
Held in mid-April, in its short life **Pebble Beach Wine & Food** (26364 Carmel Rancho Lane, Pebble Beach, 866/907-3663, www. pebblebeachfoodandwine.com) has become the predominant culinary event between Los Angeles and San Francisco. Master chefs and high-end winemakers from across the nation converge on Pebble Beach for a four-day

celebration of eating and drinking. There are cooking demonstrations, wine symposia, and special vertical tastings of rare vintages, all against the gorgeous backdrop of Pebble Beach and the Pacific Ocean.

Each May, the **Carmel Art Festival** (www. carmelartfestival.org, free) showcases the talent of local artists at Devendorf Park. Competitions and exhibitions focus on plein air paintings, watercolors, and a sculpture garden. There are also live and silent auctions, live music, and painting demonstrations for the kids.

During the first two weeks of August, the **Concours d'Elegance** (www.pebblebeachconcours.net) celebrates the automobile. Hundreds of cars—vintage, unusual, and just plain beautiful—congregate on the 18th green at Pebble Beach, while others line the streets in Carmel. Cars are judged for their historical accuracy; you'll see some stunning, expensive, mint-condition vehicles. Some sell at auction for nearly $500,000. This is one of the largest events in the area, second only to the Monterey Jazz Festival, with nearly 10,000 people swamping the tiny hamlet of Carmel. Getting reservations anywhere during this time is nearly impossible unless you plan well in advance.

Each October, the **Carmel Art and Film Festival** (www.carmelartandfilm.com, $10–50, unlimited pass $245) contrasts the quiet sophistication of Carmel with cutting-edge art and film through five days of screenings, exhibitions, panel discussions, and tech expos. Of course, there's also food and wine (this is Carmel!). Some 75 independent films are presented.

SHOPPING

Carmel is a shopper's heaven. Fashionable people stroll quaint streets ripe with high-end stores. In contrast, shopping in Carmel Valley is geared to the practical needs of valley residents.

Antiques

You'll find two floors of furniture for sale at **Carmel Antiques** (Ocean Ave. and Dolores St., 831/624-6100, 10 A.M.–5:30 P.M. daily),

including wardrobes, desks and sideboards, many of them French and English pieces from the 1930s. Lamps and other small items round out an overall good selection.

The focus at **Robertson's Antiques** (Delores St. and 7th Ave., 831/624-7517, www. robertsonsantiquescarmel.com, 10 A.M.–5 P.M. Mon.–Sat., 11 A.M.–5 P.M. Sun.) is on mid-19th–mid-20th-century pieces. You'll find lots of porcelain and silver plates, but they also carry some more unusual items, including Asian pieces, small sterling silver tea sets, and even a small collection of swords. They have a strong reputation, having been in business for nearly 40 years.

Bookstore

Founded in 1969, **Pilgrim's Way** (Dolores St. between 5th Ave. and 6th Ave., 800/549-9922, www.pilgrimsway.com, 11 A.M.–6 P.M. Mon.–Thurs., 11 A.M.–7 P.M. Fri.–Sun.) is the only remaining bookstore in Carmel. It's a small store with a good selection of books with spiritual themes, along with current best-sellers and biographies. The shop will gladly special-order anything you might need. Be sure to take a peek at the secret garden in back, which is filled with water fountains, wind chimes, and plants—as well as peace and quiet.

Clothing

"Clean sportswear" is the motto at **Pacific Tweed** (129 Crossroads Blvd., 831/625-9100, www.pacifictweed.com, 10 A.M.–7 P.M. Mon.–Sat., 11 A.M.–5 P.M. Sun.), one of the best-known clothing stores in Carmel. The clothes are slightly traditional, slightly trendy, casual, and subdued—aimed more toward the locals than travelers.

Conversely, **Carmel Forecast** (Ocean Ave. and Dolores St., 831/626-1735, 8 A.M.–8 P.M. daily) is all about casual wear and souvenirs, the best place to buy a gift for someone who wants the word "Carmel" emblazoned on their hat. There are two floors of clothes: hats, sweatshirts, flip-flops, and jeans, along with mugs and knickknacks. This is the place to go if your goal is comfort, affordability, or finding something to toss on your back when the weather turns.

Gourmet

Cow, goat, sheep, and triple crème: it's all here under one roof. For 38 years, **The Cheese Shop** (Ocean Ave. and Junipero St., 800/828-9463, www.thecheeseshopinc.com, 10 a.m.–6 p.m. Mon.–Sat., 11 a.m.–5:30 p.m. Sun.) has offered some 300 cheeses for sale, with selections from France, Italy, Norway, Greece, Belgium, and the United States. They also carry a small section of wines to go with all that beautiful cheese.

And now for something completely different: Check out **Fine H2O** (San Carlos St. between Ocean Ave. and 7th Ave., 831/625-6800, www.fineh2o-bottled-water-store.com, 10 a.m.–6 p.m. Mon.–Wed., 10:30 a.m.–6 p.m. Thurs.–Sat.), the only place to taste and buy bottled waters from across the globe—from places like Switzerland, England, Norway, and Hawaii—about 20 different varieties in all. You can sample the various waters to try to distinguish the subtle differences in taste, and perhaps find something unique. Bottle prices range $2–9. It's tucked in the back of a narrow courtyard, in a space that's white and clean, and feels a little sanitized (although that's appropriate for water, isn't it?).

RECREATION
Parks

The wide white sand and low waves at **Carmel City Beach** (Ocean Ave., dawn–dusk daily) are immensely popular; the small parking lot fills up quickly. It's also an easy walk (about eight blocks) from the center of Carmel. Dogs are allowed to roam off-leash; you'll see many happy dogs running freely along the water's edge. The view to the north is Pebble Beach; to the south is Point Lobos.

In contrast, **Devendorf Park** (Ocean Ave. and Junipero St., dawn–dusk daily) is one of the few spots in Carmel where dogs are not allowed; of course, you're not allowed to toss a football either. It occupies a full block, shielded from view by hedges and trees. The verdant

grass, benches, and stone pathways that line the perimeter make it a pretty little refuge. There are restrooms but no picnic tables.

Golf

Located in Carmel Valley, **Rancho Canada Golf Club** (4860 Carmel Valley Rd., 800/536-9459, www.ranchocanada.com, $40–70) consists of two 18-hole courses, known as the East Course and the West Course. The East Course is longer, but both have wide and narrow fairways that cross the Carmel River. There's a pro shop, dining, and bunkered chipping greens.

Quail Lodge Golf Club (8000 Valley Greens Dr., 831/620-8866 www.quaillodge.com, $125–150) is a par-71 course tucked between the hills of Carmel Valley. The verdant greens meander languidly between the mountains rising on either side. It's quiet, despite being close to Highway 1. This is a traditional course, with three sets of tees at each hole and a seven-acre driving range. The presence of 10 lakes and the Carmel River on the property provide some challenge. PGA-certified pros are available to help improve your game.

Spas

At **The Spa at Bernardus Lodge** (415 W. Carmel Valley Rd., 831/658-3560, www.bernardus.com), you'll find all kinds of services, from the traditional—massages and wraps, pedicures and manicures—to the exotic, such as the rosemary-cabernet full-body exfoliation and the Aqua Float, where you are stretched as you float in 101°F water. All treatments include complimentary visits to the eucalyptus steam sauna.

ACCOMMODATIONS

Carmel has an eclectic collection of places to stay. Most are smaller properties, without amenities like pools or exercise rooms. Another thing you won't find are parking lots; street parking is common, so beware of parking time limits. Since Carmel is so dog-friendly, it's a good idea to check to see which lodgings allow pets. During peak season, rooms go fast, so booking more than six weeks out is a smart idea.

$150-250

Lobos Lodge (Monte Verde Ave. and Ocean Ave., 831/624-3874, www.loboslodge.com, $160) is right in the middle of downtown Carmel-by-the-Sea, making it a perfect spot from which to dine, shop, and admire the endless array of art in the upscale town. Each of the 30 guest rooms and suites offers a gas fireplace, a sofa and table, a bed in an alcove, and enough space to stroll around and enjoy the quiet romantic setting. Do be aware that Lobos Lodge bills itself as an adult retreat. While families with children can stay here, expect to pay extra for more than two guests in your room, and there is little in the way of child-friendly amenities.

Family-owned and operated, **⟨ Hofsas House** (San Carlos St. between 3rd Ave. and 4th Ave., 831/624-2745, www.hofsashouse.com, $170–205 d) is a large, pink hotel. The Hofsas's Bavarian heritage is evident in the hand-painted mural near the front of the hotel. The third floor guest rooms have nice views of the ocean. The lodging options are some of the most diverse in Carmel: There are king and queen guest rooms and suites to accommodate families and groups, some with full kitchens, kitchenettes, fridges, and microwaves. There is also a heated pool and men's and women's dry saunas. There's even a large meeting room with a full dedicated kitchen, which is often used for family reunions. Some guest rooms are pet friendly. There is a continental breakfast (8–10 A.M.), and free Wi-Fi throughout the property. There's a convenient trolley stop in front of the hotel.

Edgemere Cottages (San Antonio St. between 13th Ave. and Santa Lucia Ave., 866/241-4575, www.edgemerecottages.com, $149–199 d) is removed from the hustle of downtown Carmel and only two minutes to the beach. There are three cottages located in the back of a private residence and one room inside the house; all guest rooms are reasonably large, with comfortable everyday furnishings.

The three cottages all have kitchenettes, and all four rooms have Wi-Fi. Breakfast is served 8:30–10 A.M. in the dining room. Edgemere is pet-friendly, but the two house cats, Riff-Raff and Magenta, rule the backyard (dogs beware).

For folks who come to Carmel to taste wine, hike in the woods, and enjoy the less-expensive golf courses, **Country Garden Inns** (102 W. Carmel Valley Rd., Carmel Valley, 831/659-5361, www.countrygardeninns.com, $189) offers a perfect spot to rest and relax. Actually comprising two inns, the Acacia Lodge and the Hidden Valley Inn, Country Garden's small B&Bs offer violet and taupe French country–style charm in the guest rooms as well as a pool, a self-serve breakfast bar, and strolling gardens outdoors. Guest rooms range from romantic king-bed studios to big family suites, and most sleep at least four people, with daybeds in the window nooks.

The casual country feel of **Carmel Country Inn** (Dolores St. and 3rd Ave., 800/215-6343, www.carmelcountryinn.com, $225–295 d) makes it a comfortable everyday spot, and people like it that way. Most guests leave the top portion of their Dutch doors open, creating a neighborly atmosphere. All the guest rooms include a fridge, in-room coffee, tea, cream sherry, and DVD players (with 250 movies available). Breakfast is available 8–10 A.M. There's a communal microwave in the lobby, along with a communal computer, though Wi-Fi is available throughout the property. This is another pet-friendly spot: Tescher, the longtime black-and-white resident cat, is such a fixture that people send him cards. The parking lot, rare in Carmel, is another plus.

Doris Day is one of the owners of the **Cypress Inn** (Lincoln St. at 7th Ave., 831/624-3871, www.cypress-inn.com, $235–575 d), one of the oldest and classiest places to stay in Carmel. Her Hollywood memorabilia is on display throughout the property. Given Day's love of animals, it's no surprise that the inn is very pet friendly. The midsize guest rooms are well-appointed, with fresh flowers, fruit, and cream sherry to welcome you. Many rooms have whirlpool tubs, and all have Wi-Fi. You can hear the ocean, five blocks away, from the charming outdoor patio.

Over $250

Set amid seven acres of grapes, the **(** **Bernardus Lodge** (415 W. Carmel Valley Rd., 888/648-9463, www.bernardus.com, $555 d) is one of the nicest properties in Carmel Valley, with first-rate service and furnishings. Small bottles of Bernardus wines welcome you to your room, along with complimentary bottled water, a small fridge, and a spacious bed. Some guest rooms look out over the pool; others face the boccie ball and croquet lawn. There are two restaurants on-site; go for the Chef's Table, a small half booth right in the kitchen, where the chef will prepare your meal in front of you. The walls have been signed by well-known guests, including Julia Child. This is one of those places you just don't want to leave.

Built in 1929, **L'Auberge Carmel** (Monte Verde St. and 7th Ave., 831/624-8578, www.laubergecarmel.com, $295–700 d) defines luxury. This is the place to come if you like to be pampered: Virtually anything you want will be provided. The brick courtyard, where the horses were once brought in after a ride, is the best feature of this European-style hotel. The furnishings are beautiful but not stuffy. All 20 guest rooms have fridges and Wi-Fi. Pets are not allowed.

Despite its ghastly name, the cliff-top **Tickle Pink Inn** (155 Highland Dr., 831/624-1244, www.ticklepinkinn.com, $390) offers tasteful luxury south of Carmel. Each guest room has a view of the ocean, an array of high-end furniture and linens, and all the top-end amenities you'd expect from a distinctive Carmel hostelry. For a special treat, shell out for the spa-bath suite and watch the ocean while you soak in the tub with your sweetie.

FOOD
American

The funky **(** **Cachagua General Store** (18840 Cachagua Rd., Carmel Valley, 831/659-1857, dinner Mon., $25) defies description. The

location is a run-down old general store, a piecemeal building that you wouldn't notice if you drove by. Not that you would drive by it, since it's out in the middle of nowhere—it will take at least 45 minutes to drive from Carmel, past Carmel Valley up and down winding roads. Dinner is served only on Monday nights, and reservations must be made three weeks in advance. Menus are printed as guests show up and are sometimes incomplete. There are two seatings, 6:30 P.M. and 8:30 P.M., but those are only approximate. If the kitchen isn't ready to serve at 6:30 P.M., you wait. It's like an occasionally oiled, makeshift machine. So why is it worth all the trouble? Because Michael Jones's food is superb. The ever-changing menu offers dishes like rabbit five ways, pumpkin basil ravioli, or local sardines. Many of the ingredients come from the surrounding farms. Sometimes there's live music. There's no decor to speak of, the chairs are mismatched, and the servers wear whatever suits their mood, but that's all part of the charm. Don't fight it, just go with the flow.

The outdoor patio at **Corkscrew Café** (55 W. Carmel Valley Rd., Carmel Valley, 831/659-8888, www.corkscrewcafe.com, 11:30 A.M.–4:30 P.M. Mon.–Sun., $18), with its brightly colored chairs and umbrellas, is perfect on spring days. The interior has a soft Tuscan feel, with tiled floors and ocher walls. The menu is limited but good: Meals begin with hummus and toasted bread and continue with items like calamari, halibut tostadas, sandwiches, and salads. They also carry a decent list of Monterey County wines.

Em Le's (Dolores St. between 5th Ave. and 6th Ave., 831/625-6780, http://emlescarmel.com, 7 A.M.–3 P.M. Mon.–Tues., 7 A.M.–3 P.M. and 4:30–8 P.M. Wed.–Sun., $10–20) focuses on comfort foods like meatloaf, Caesar salad, pasta dishes, triple-decker clubs, and patty melts. The food is simple but fresh and fairly inexpensive compared to surrounding restaurants. Unfortunately, the wine list doesn't match the food. The decor is country comfortable and the service attentive. This is one of the older restaurants in Carmel, having opened its doors in 1955.

Breakfast

Need breakfast? Get it at **Katy's Place** (Mission St. and between 5th Ave. and 6th Ave., 831/624-0199, www.katysplacecarmel.com, 7 A.M.–2 P.M. daily, $10–20), a self-described "Carmel Tradition" that can get quite crowded on weekend mornings. Whether you love heavy eggs Benedict or light Belgian waffles, you can get your favorite breakfast until 2 P.M.

From Scratch (3626 Barnyard Shopping Village, Hwy. 1, 831/625-2448, 7:30 A.M.–2:30 P.M. Mon.–Fri., 7 A.M.–3 P.M. Sat.–Sun., $10) makes their breakfasts—including corned beef and hash, cheese blintzes, crab eggs Benedict, granola, and oatmeal—well, from scratch. There's a country feel to the small dining room, tucked downstairs from street level, but the best seats are out front under the vine-covered arbor.

Cheap Eats

When you just want a good burger, go for **r.g. Burgers** (201 Crossroads Shopping Village, Hwy. 1, 831/626-8054, 11 A.M.–8:30 P.M. Sun.–Thurs., 11 A.M.–9 P.M. Fri.–Sat., $10). All the burgers can be made with beef, bison, turkey, chicken, or veggie falafel, with variations like the black-and-bleu, the jalapeño cheddar, and even a Reuben, so no one gets left out. They also offer 21 varieties of milkshakes, including mint chip, strawberry, banana, or mocha; while they aren't thick, they are flavorful. Since it gets loud inside, the few tables outside are better choices.

Brophy's Tavern (4th Ave. and San Carlos St., 831/624-2476, www.brophystavern.com, 11:30 A.M.–11 P.M. daily, $10) serves basic pub food like potato skins, sliders, BLTs, French dip sandwiches, and hot dogs smothered with sauerkraut, all in a golf-themed, wood-paneled environment. There's a good selection of beers as well as tequilas, and they're open late—unusual for Carmel.

Italian

The King of Jordan has dined at **Casanova** (5th Ave. between San Carlos St. and Mission St., 831/625-0501, www.casanovarestaurant.

com, 11:30 A.M.–10 P.M. Mon.–Thurs., 11:30 A.M.–10:30 P.M. Fri.–Sat., 10 A.M.–10 P.M. Sun., cheese, dessert and cocktails only 3–5 P.M. daily, $39, five-course menu $65–85), a Carmel fixture. It's deceptively small from the outside; the restaurant unfolds into several dining areas, including a fine dining section, a large arbor-covered outdoor patio, several small intimate spaces, and the Van Gogh room—where you eat your meal at a table once used by artist Vincent Van Gogh. An excellent wine list complements the country French and Italian menu, with options like niçoise salad, linguini with lobster, bacon-wrapped rabbit, and house-made cannelloni.

Mexican

The walls and ceilings at **Baja Cantina** (7166 Carmel Valley Rd., 831/625-2252, www.bajacantina.com/carmel.htm, 11:30 A.M.–9 P.M. Mon.–Thurs., 11:30 A.M.–10 P.M. Fri., 11 A.M.–10 P.M. Sat., 11 A.M.–9 P.M. Sun. Nov.–Apr., 11:30 A.M.–10 P.M. Mon.–Thurs., 11:30 A.M.–11 P.M. Fri., 11 A.M.–11 P.M. Sat., 11 A.M.–10 P.M. Sun. May–Oct., $15) are decorated with everything imaginable, as if you just walked into a very festive yard sale. It's an upbeat environment, with an outside deck that's perfect for sunny days and a fireplace near the bar that's perfect when the fog rolls in. The tequila selection will also keep you warmed up; most shots are in the $10 range. Menu favorites include the rosemary chicken burrito, mango chicken enchiladas, and halibut fish tacos. The chips and salsa are excellent.

Sweets

People gather at the storefront window of **Pieces of Heaven** (3686 Barnyard Shopping Village, Hwy. 1, 831/625-3368, 10 A.M.–6 P.M. Mon.–Thurs., 10 A.M.–8 P.M. Fri.–Sat., 11 A.M.–5 P.M. Sun., $3) to watch owners Peg and Bob Whitted make candy and pull taffy. Peg and Bob are that rare breed of chocolatier that actually makes almost everything on site. They've been turning out two dozen kinds of truffles, English toffee, caramel-covered marshmallows, and plenty of other candies since 1995. Real cream and butter make the taste far superior to factory-manufactured chocolates.

Farmers Markets

You'll find fruits, veggies, honey, meats, cheeses, and flowers—many of them organically farmed or produced at the **Carmel Certified Farmers Market** (3690 Barnyard Shopping Village, Hwy. 1, www.montereybay-farmers.org/carmel.html, 9 A.M.–1 P.M. Tues. May–Sept.).

INFORMATION AND SERVICES

The **Carmel Visitors Center** (San Carlos St. between 5th Ave. and 6th Ave., 800/550-4333, www.carmelcalifornia.com, 9 A.M.–5 P.M. daily) has maps and brochures of the area and of the greater Central Coast. There is two-hour street parking throughout Carmel, and they keep tabs on it, so don't overstay. Parking can get cramped; there are long-term lots, but they aren't cheap.

For more information about the town and current events, pick up a copy of the weekly *Carmel Pine Cone* (www.pineconearchive. com), the local newspaper.

In case of emergency, dial **911**. The **Carmel-by-the-Sea Police Department** (Junipero St. and 4th Ave., 831/624-6403, http://ci.carmel. ca.us) is centrally located. The **Community Hospital of the Monterey Peninsula** (23625 Holman Hwy., 888/452-4667, www. chomp.org) has 233 beds and every service imaginable.

GETTING THERE AND AROUND

The much-preferred coastal routes into Carmel are via Highway 1, which runs north–south.

You can access Carmel via Highway 1 from San Francisco or Santa Barbara, slow but incredibly beautiful routes. Most people travel north–south on U.S. 101 and then take Highway 68 at Salinas through Monterey to Carmel. This can also be a slow road, heavily congested during weekends and peak summer times.

Monterey-Salinas Transit (888/678-2871, www.mst.org) has service all around the peninsula and can transport you from Monterey to Carmel. It also operates a green and wood shuttle service through Carmel every 60 minutes. The **Carmel Valley Grapevine Express** (888/678-2871, www.mst.org, 6:45 A.M.–7 P.M. daily year-round, $4 round-trip) shuttle picks up downtown at the Monterey Conference Center and again at the Monterey Transit Plaza before heading to The Barnyard Shopping Village in Carmel and to the Carmel Valley wineries. Buses run every hour. This is a great idea to avoid the hassle of driving and finding parking.

Coast Starlight, the **Amtrak** (800/872-7245, www.amtrak.com) Seattle–Los Angeles train, stops in Salinas. To reach Carmel, you'll first need to take the bus to the Aquarium Bus Stop in Monterey, which is a curbside-only stop. From there, switch to the Monterey-Salinas Transit (MST) bus to Carmel.

The **Monterey Regional Airport** (MRY, 200 Fred Kane Dr., Monterey, 831/648-7000, www.montereyairport.com) has non-stop flights from Los Angeles's LAX, San Diego, Phoenix, Denver, Las Vegas, and San Francisco, but airfares to Monterey and Carmel are high. Another option is to fly into San Jose International Airport (SJC, 2077 Airport Blvd., San Jose, 408/392-3600, www.sjc.org), an hour's drive away, and then rent a car and drive to Carmel.

Monterey

The best days in Monterey are picture-perfect. It's no wonder so many artists have been inspired to paint this area. The blue of the ocean beckons you to wander the twisting coastline, taking in the boats, kayaks, and otters playing along the bay. Nearly four million people heed this call annually.

There are two distinct sections of Monterey, about one mile apart: the waterfront area around Cannery Row, and downtown. The six blocks of Cannery Row retain much of the sardine-cannery look described in John Steinbeck's novel *Cannery Row,* although the buildings have been spruced up (and in some cases, completely rebuilt) since the 1940s. The canneries are long gone, and today the Row is packed with businesses, including the must-see Monterey Bay Aquarium, terrific seafood restaurants, shops, galleries, and wine-tasting rooms. As you walk the street, you have direct access to the beach and the ocean. Downtown Monterey is somewhat neglected by travelers, but it offers more unique stores, some historic buildings, and fewer crowds. With the exception of a few streets, it's laid out on a grid, with new buildings plopped next to historic structures from the 1850s. Slightly east is Pacific Grove, a quiet community that receives its share of overflow traffic.

SIGHTS
◖ Monterey Bay Aquarium
There is no better aquarium on the West Coast, possibly even in the country, than the Monterey Bay Aquarium (886 Cannery Row, 831/648-4800, www.montereybayaquarium.org, 10 A.M.–6 P.M. Mon.–Fri., 9:30 A.M.–8 P.M. Sat.–Sun. summer, 10 A.M.–5 P.M. daily winter, adults $30, students and seniors $28, ages 3–12 $20), located right on the bay. Don't miss the Outer Bay section to see the beautifully lit jellyfish, their graceful movements like a ballet. The penguin exhibit is another popular show, more so when they dive into the water and you can see their agility. Other must-see exhibits include the kelp forest, a two-story-high view into an ethereal underwater world. Divers feed the fish and give informative talks (11:30 A.M. and 4 P.M. daily). Other exhibits showcase sharks, sheepshead, and schools of anchovies that move as a single unit. But the otter exhibit is often the most crowded, especially at feeding time (10:30 A.M., 1:30 P.M., and 3:30 P.M. daily). More often than not they are playing and acting up for the crowds; everyone loves otters. There's also the Splash Zone, a series of open rooms with touch tanks and moving exhibits that keep kids entertained and, hopefully, informed. With so many wonderful exhibits, not to mention the crowds, the aquarium will take more time than you may anticipate; plan at least 2–3 hours to explore. Facilities include a rather pricey on-site restaurant and gift shop as well as outdoor decks with views of the bay.

Cannery Row
The fishing canneries and warehouses that lined Cannery Row (www.canneryrow.com) were successful in the 1930s and 1940s and were made famous by John Steinbeck's novel. But as overfishing took its toll on the bay and the fishing industry, they fell into disrepair. By the late 1950s, Cannery Row was deserted; some buildings actually fell into the ocean. A slow renaissance began in the 1960s, driven by new interest in preserving the historic integrity of the area as well as a few savvy entrepreneurs who understood the value of beachfront property. Today, the fabled street, similar architecturally to the way it was in its fishing days, is one of the most popular destinations in California. The corrugated metal siding of the canneries is still here, as are the squared block industrial buildings and crossovers that connected them to the nearby railway. Now there's a bike and walking path where the trains once stopped to load up sardines for transport. The smells of fish and a hard day's work are gone, and everything is painted and

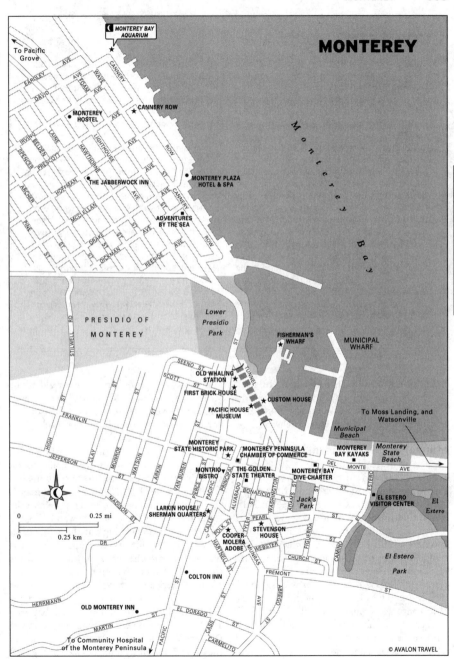

MONTEREY

To Pacific Grove

MONTEREY BAY AQUARIUM

EARDLEY AVE
DAVID AVE
WAVE AVE
FOAM AVE
CANNERY ROW
IRVING
BELDEN
LAINE
PRESCOTT
SPENCER
HAWTHORNE
LIGHTHOUSE AVE
MONTEREY HOSTEL
CANNERY ROW
HOFFMAN
THE JABBERWOCK INN
MONTEREY PLAZA HOTEL & SPA
ARCHER
McCLELLAN
CANNERY ROW
PINE ST
DRAKE AVE
REESIDE
DICKMAN AVE
ADVENTURES BY THE SEA

Monterey Bay

PACIFIC COAST HIGHWAY

STILWELL RD

PRESIDIO OF MONTEREY

Lower Presidio Park

FISHERMAN'S WHARF

MUNICIPAL WHARF

FRANKLIN

SEENO ST
SCOTT ST
TUNNEL
OLD WHALING STATION
FIRST BRICK HOUSE
CUSTOM HOUSE
PACIFIC HOUSE MUSEUM

To Moss Landing, and Watsonville

Municipal Beach

HIGH
CLAY
MONROE
WATSON
LARKIN
VAN BUREN
PIERCE
PACIFIC
PRINCIPAL
ALVARADO
BONAFACIO PL
WASHINGTON
ADAMS ST
DEL MONTE AVE

JEFFERSON

MONTEREY STATE HISTORIC PARK
MONTEREY PENINSULA CHAMBER OF COMMERCE
MONTEREY BAY KAYAKS

Monterey State Beach

MONTRIO BISTRO
THE GOLDEN STATE THEATER
MONTEREY BAY DIVE CHARTER

Jack's Park

EL ESTERO VISITOR CENTER

El Estero

MADISON ST
CALLE PRINCIPAL
POLK
TYLER
PEARL
WEBSTER
FIGUEROA
ESTERO ST
CAMINO

LARKIN HOUSE/ SHERMAN QUARTERS
STEVENSON HOUSE
COOPER-MOLERA ADOBE

DR

0   0.25 mi
0   0.25 km

MUNRAS
CHURCH ST

El Estero Park

COLTON INN

FREMONT
ABREGO

HERRMANN

OLD MONTEREY INN

MARTIN
EL DORADO
PACIFIC ST
CASS ST
CARMELITO

To Community Hospital of the Monterey Peninsula

© AVALON TRAVEL

JOHN STEINBECK

John Ernst Steinbeck was born in Salinas, California in 1902 and grew up in its tiny, isolated agricultural community. He somehow managed to escape life as a farmer, a sardine fisherman, or a fish canner, and ended up living the glamorous life of a writer for his too-short 66 years.

Steinbeck's experiences in the Salinas Valley farming community and in the fishing town of Monterey informed many of his novels. The best known of these is *Cannery Row*, but *Tortilla Flat* is also set in working-class Monterey (though no one knows exactly where the fictional "Tortilla Flat" neighborhood was supposed to be). The Pulitzer Prize-winning novel *The Grapes of Wrath* takes more of its inspiration from the nearby Salinas Valley. Steinbeck used the Valley as a model for farming in the Dust Bowl – the wretched, impoverished era that was the Great Depression.

In fact, Steinbeck was fascinated by the plight of working men and women; his novels and stories generally depict ordinary folks

going through tough and terrible times. Steinbeck lived and worked through the Great Depression – thus it's not surprising that many of his stories do *not* feature happy Hollywood endings. Steinbeck was a realist in almost all of his novels, portraying the good, the bad, and the ugly of human life and society. His work gained almost immediate respect – in addition to his Pulitzer, Steinbeck also won the Nobel Prize for Literature in 1962. Almost every American high school student from the 1950s onward has read at least one of Steinbeck's novels or short stories; his body of work forms part of the enduring American literary canon.

Steinbeck's name can be found all over now-commercial Cannery Row. More serious scholars of Steinbeck should investigate the **National Steinbeck Center** (1 Main St., Salinas, 831/796-3833, www.steinbeck.org, daily 10 A.M.-5 P.M., $10.95), which also hosts the annual **Steinbeck Festival** (www.steinbeck.org) in August to celebrate the great man's life and works in fine style.

clean, ready to show off for visitors. In addition to the Monterey Bay Aquarium, the Row is home to dozens of shops, tasting rooms, and restaurants, with easy access to the water.

Monterey State Historic Park

Monterey State Historic Park (20 Custom House Plaza, 831/649-7136, www.parks. ca.gov, gardens 9 A.M.–5 P.M. daily May–Sept., 10 A.M.–4 P.M. daily Oct.–Apr., free), usually called Old Monterey by locals, pays homage to the long and colorful history of the city of Monterey. This busy port town acted as the capital of California when it was under Spanish rule, and then later when the area became U.S. territory. Today, this park provides a peek into Monterey as it was in the middle of the 19th century—a busy place filled with dock workers, fisherfolk, bureaucrats, and soldiers. And yet it blends into the modern town of Monterey as well, and modern stores, galleries,

and restaurants sit next to 150-year-old adobe structures. Several buildings have been closed, and tours have been stopped, especially during the winter, due to state budget cutbacks. Call ahead for tour information.

It's tough to see everything in just one visit to Old Monterey. If you only get to one spot on your first trip, make it the **Custom House.** It's California State Historic Landmark Number 1, the oldest bureaucratic building known in the state. You can spend some time wandering the adobe building, checking out the artifacts on display, or even just looking out the upstairs window toward the sea. Also on the plaza is the **Pacific House Museum,** with exhibits of Native American artifacts.

There are 10 other buildings in the park; most were built with adobe or brick between 1834 and 1847. These include the **Casa del Oro,** the **Cooper Molera Adobe** (525 Polk St.), the **First Brick House,** the **Larkin House** (510

Calle Principal), the **Old Whaling Station,** the **Sherman Quarters,** and the **Stevenson House** (530 Houston St.), the former residence of Robert Louis Stevenson.

Famous artists, writers, and military men have stayed in some of these spots, most of which have long histories playing several different roles. Look down as you walk to see if you're stepping on antique whalebone sidewalks. And be sure to take a few minutes to admire the many beautiful gardens surrounding the adobes, which are lovingly maintained by local groups.

Museum of Monterey

Part of Old Monterey, the Stanton Center includes the Museum of Monterey (5 Custom House Plaza, 831/372-2608, www.monterey-history.org, 10 A.M.–5 P.M. Tues.–Sat., noon–5 P.M. Sun.). The large modern facilities provide plenty of space for the art and historical artifacts collected over the decades, most of which pertain directly to the area's history, maritime or otherwise. In the museum, explore the history of the native Rumisen and Ohlone people, the Spanish exploration and conquistador era, and the U.S. military and fishing presence on the Central Coast. The original Fresnel lens from the Point Sur light station is here, as is an array of sardine fishing equipment.

Elkhorn Slough

Some of the best birding in the state can be had at Elkhorn Slough (1700 Elkhorn Rd., Watsonville, 831/728-2822, www.elkhorn-slough.org, 9 A.M.–5 P.M. Wed.–Sun., adults $4), a few miles north of Monterey in Moss Landing. This large waterway and wetland area is incongruously marked by the mammoth smokestacks of the Moss Landing power plant. While you can access the wetlands and bird habitats from Highway 1 in Moss Landing, to get to the visitors center you must drive several miles into the agricultural backcountry. But once you're here, knowledgeable and dedicated rangers can provide you with all the information you need to spot your favorite birds, plus find a few you've never seen before.

ENTERTAINMENT AND EVENTS
Nightlife

If live piano is your gig, then the bar at **The Sardine Factory** (701 Wave St., 831/373-3775, www.sardinefactory.com, 7:30–10:30 P.M. Tues.–Sat.) is your best bet. Expect to hear ballads and renditions of current popular songs. Say hi to Big Mike, the bartender—he's been slinging drinks here for 36 years. Specialty cocktails include the Blue Sardine, the Pink Sardine, and Misty's Kiss, inspired by the Clint Eastwood movie *Play Misty for Me,* part of which was filmed here. Tapas are also on the bar menu.

Six nights a week you can find live music at **Cibo Ristorante Italiano** (301 Alvarado St., 831/649-8151, www.cibo.com, 7–10:30 P.M. Tues.–Sun.). On Sunday nights, dinner is accompanied by light jazz music. Things heat up the rest of the week, with dancing to Latin jazz, R&B, salsa, soul, funk, and swing. Both the decor and the menu are Italian, with soft yellow Tuscan walls creating a nice environment for enjoying pizza, pastas, and scampi along with the music.

Shoot some pool at **Blue Fin** (685 Cannery Row, 831/717-4280, www.bluefinbilliards.com, 11 A.M.–2 A.M. daily, tables $12 per hour), which offers 11 tournament-size pool tables as well as arcade games, darts, and even a small dance floor. There are also 16 draft beers on tap.

Sly McFly's Refueling Station (700 A Cannery Row, 831/649-8050, www.slymc-flys.net, 11 A.M.–2 A.M. daily, no cover) is the best venue for live music on Cannery Row, bringing in a wide variety of artists, some very well known, to play rock, blues, and soul seven nights a week. The stage is small, and the ambience is a little tired, but the music and the crowds spill out into the streets. Forget the food; come for the tunes.

If you want a late-night brew, the **Cannery Row Brewing Company** (95 Prescott Ave., 831/643-2722, www.canneryrowbrewingcom-pany.com, 11:30 A.M.–11 P.M. Mon.–Thurs., 11:30 A.M.–midnight Fri.–Sun., from 9 A.M. Sun. during football season) is a choice spot, with 73 beers on tap and 25 in bottles. The industrial decor and concrete floors give it a bit of a rough feel—and can also make it quite loud.

If old school bars are your thing, it's worth stopping in at **Segovia's Cocktails** (650 Lighthouse Ave., 831/646-3154, noon–2 A.M. daily), the oldest bar in Monterey, opened in 1937. Located away from downtown a few blocks up from Cannery Row, it's populated mostly by locals. The interior is dated, with a padded bar and stools and 1960s decor that now make it feel retro. There's no food, just drinks, and the most popular concoction is the Tennis Ball: orange vodka, melon schnapps, pineapple juice, and sweet and sour mixes.

Performing Arts

The **Monterey Symphony** (831/646-8511, www.montereysymphony.org) has provided a wealth of concerts for more than 65 years, focusing on traditional classical music, with works by Bach and Mozart as well as a few operatic offerings.

The **Bruce Ariss Wharf Theatre** (Old Fisherman's Wharf No. 1, 831/649-2332, www.mctaweb.org, adults $25, under age 13 $10) has been putting on lighthearted shows and musicals for 35 years, with occasional dramas and Broadway reviews. Community-based shows run Thursday–Saturday evenings with a Sunday matinee.

Festivals and Events

The **Best of the Blue** (831/375-9400, www.montereywines.org, $60–120), held each November, mixes wine pairings with food and cooking demonstrations from chefs like Robert Bleifer, an executive chef at the Food Network. There are also multiple wine tastings around the county, such as pinot noir tastings highlighting the diverse soil and growing conditions from the different American Viticultural Areas around Monterey.

The **Winemakers' Celebration** (Barnyard Shopping Village, Hwy. 1, Carmel, 831/375-9400, www.montereywines.org, $30–40) held one day each August, is an inexpensive tasting event that remains true to its humble roots, making it the best gateway to over 40 Monterey County wineries. There's live music, dancing, food, and, of course, wine, including reserve tastings. But the celebration is small enough to make it easy to chat—not only with the people pouring the wines but also the many winemakers and winery owners in attendance.

For over half a century, the **Monterey Jazz Festival** (Monterey Fairgrounds, 831/373-3366, www.montereyjazzfestival.org, from $40), held one weekend in September, has brought together a who's who of jazz greats, both vocalists and musicians. If you are a jazz fan, this is heaven. This is the biggest annual event in Monterey, drawing in some 40,000 people. Plan ahead, as tickets go quickly.

SHOPPING
Antiques

If you're looking for antiques, you'll find something to suit your fancy at the **Cannery Row Antique Mall** (471 Wave St., 831/655-0264, 10 A.M.–5:30 P.M. Mon.–Fri., 10 A.M.–6 P.M. Sat., 10 A.M.–5 P.M. Sun.), with 150 vendors in a massive two-story warehouse filled with sterling silver, vintage dolls, china, and furniture in mission, country, and art deco styles.

Art

Housed in an old green shingle-covered home, the **Monterey Peninsula Art Foundation** (425 Cannery Row, 831/655-1267, www.mpaf.org, 11 A.M.–4:30 P.M. daily) is a cooperative of about 30 local artists working in watercolor, acrylics, ceramics, jewelry, and sculpture. It's one of the few Monterey galleries that exhibit exclusively local art. They also have a good selection of greeting cards featuring the works of their artists.

Clothing

At **Carmel Yacht Club** (751 Cannery Row, 831/643-9482, www.boatworkscarmel.com, 10 A.M.–6 P.M. daily) you can find men's and women's clothes with a nautical bent, mainly nice, fairly conservative resort wear from names like Tommy Bahama and Bugatchi, with some souvenir clothes mixed in. There are also hats, sweaters, books, and gifts.

California Classics (750 Cannery Row, 831/324-0528, 9 A.M.–9 P.M. daily) sells men's, women's, and kid's clothing with Monterey and California motifs. You can buy souvenir sweatshirts and T-shirts to remind you that you were indeed on Cannery Row.

Bookstore

BookBuyers (600 Lighthouse Ave., 831/375-4208, www.bookbuyers.com, 11 A.M.–7 P.M. daily) is sadly one of the last independent used bookstores in the area. They have over 30,000 titles, an even mix of hardbacks and paperbacks. The tight maze of books is surprisingly well organized, with a diverse selection, including a large children's section.

RECREATION
Dennis the Menace Park

Originally envisioned by Hank Ketcham, the creator of the comic strip, Dennis the Menace Park (777 Pearl St., Monterey 831/646-3860, 10 A.M.–dusk daily July–Aug., 10 A.M.–dusk Wed.–Mon. Sept.–June) opened in 1956. Ketcham was heavily involved in the design process; he moved to the area after World War II and lived here until his death in 2001. There's a nine-foot climbing wall, a suspension bridge, a long green curvy slide attached to brightly colored jungle gyms, a real black locomotive, and a whole lot more, as well as a bronze sculpture of the little menace near the entrance.

Lover's Point Park

Located near Cannery Row in Pacific Grove, Lover's Point Park (Ocean View Blvd. and 17th St., Pacific Grove, dawn–dusk daily) juts out to offer views of Monterey to the right, Pacific Grove to the left, and Santa Cruz directly across the bay. It's one of the most beautiful spots on the Peninsula. There's access to sandy coves and stunning rock formations, including displaced shards of granite. Climb up for even better views of the coastline. It's a great spot for a picnic, with a large grassy area,

tables, a beach volleyball court, and restrooms just above the water. It's also a popular location for weddings.

Bella on the Bay

To be near Monterey Bay is a treat; to be on it is a delight. Because the 47-foot sailboat *Bella on the Bay* (32 Cannery Row, Suite 8, 818/822-2390, www.bellamontereybay.com, two-hour cruise from $69) only seats six people, it offers more of a relaxed, intimate cruise than an organized tour. The quiet of the boat under sail will take you far from the crowds on Cannery Row: You'll feel like the bay is yours. Captain Christian is happy to tailor the experience to your interests. Once in a while, he'll pull up his crab traps out at sea and grill his catch on the boat. You can also ask him to put up the hammock on the bow so you can sway with the waves. Or bring your own picnic if you like. Typical cruises last 2–4 hours. The shorter cruises go out just 4–5 miles from shore, then return along the Cannery Row coast. Of course, since this is a sailboat, speed depends on the weather, sometimes reaching 25 knots when the wind is up.

Diving

Yes it's cold to scuba dive in the bay, but with the wealth of sealife present, it's worth it. Explore the bay and all it has to offer with **Monterey Bay Dive Charters** (250 Figueroa St., 831/383-9276, www.mbdcscuba.com, from $49), which offers guided beach diving right off Cannery Row. They also offer scuba lessons.

Another of your many dive shop options is the **Aquarius Dive Shop** (2040 Del Monte Ave., 831/375-1933, www.aquariusdivers.com). Aquarius offers everything you need to go diving out in Monterey Bay, including air and nitrox fills, equipment rental, certification courses, and help with guided dive tours.

Kayaking and Paddle Boating

Adventures by the Sea (299 Cannery Row, 831/372-1807, www.adventuresbythesea.com, 9 A.M.–sunset daily, rentals $20–30 per day) rents kayaks and stand-up paddle boats for the whole day to let you choose your own route in and around the magnificent Monterey Bay kelp forest. If you're not confident enough to go off on your own, Adventures offers tours (2.5 hours, 10 A.M. and 2 P.M. daily summer, $50 pp) from Cannery Row. Your guide can tell you all about the wildlife you're seeing: harbor seals, sea otters, pelicans, seagulls, and maybe even a whale in the winter. The tandem sit-on-top kayaks make it a great experience for school-age children. Adventures by the Sea also runs a tour of Stillwater Cove at Pebble Beach. Reservations are recommended for all tours, but during summer you can stop by on a whim to see if there's a spot available on the Cannery Row tour.

Monterey Bay Kayaks (693 Del Monte Ave., 831/373-5357 or 800/649-5357, www.montereybaykayaks.com, 9 A.M.–7 P.M. daily) specializes in tours of both central Monterey and Elkhorn Slough to the north. You can choose between open-deck and closed-deck tour groups, beginning tours perfect for kids, romantic sunset or full moon paddles, or even long paddles designed for more experienced sea kayakers. Most tours cost $50–60 pp; check the website for specific tour prices, times, and reservation information. If you prefer to rent a kayak and explore the bay or slough on your own, rentals start at $30 and include wetsuits, life vests, and a quick intro if you've never kayaked before. Single, double, or triple-seat kayaks are available. If you really get into it, you can also sign up for closed-deck sea kayaking classes to learn about safety, rescue techniques, tides, currents, and paddling techniques.

Since 1966, family-owned **El Estero Boating** (Camino El Estero and Camino Aguajito, 831/375-1484, 10 A.M.–sunset daily) rents colorful paddle boats ($16 for 30 min., $21 per hour) on the U-shaped El Estero Lake around Dennis the Menace Park. The water on the lake is typically calmer than on the bay, which makes for a relaxing experience. Your legs will thank you.

Whale-Watching

The **Monterey Bay Whale Watch Center**
(84 Fisherman's Wharf, 831/375-4658, www.gowhales.com, from $39) offers whale-watching trips year-round, but December–March is the best time to see some of the 7,000 gray whales that make their annual migration to Baja California. You may also see dolphins, sea lions, seals, and otters as well as a few other whales, such as humpbacks and blues. A marine biologist is on board to answer questions about the sealife. Because the bay is sheltered, the water usually doesn't get too rough.

Princess Monterey Whale Watching (96 Fisherman's Wharf, 800/979-3370, www.montereywhalewatching.com, adults $40, seniors $35, ages 3–12 $30) prides itself on its knowledgeable marine biologist guides and its comfortable, spacious cruising vessels. The *Princess Monterey* offers morning and afternoon tours, and you can buy tickets online or by phone.

Golf

Known locally as the Navy course because it's owned by the U.S. Navy, the **Monterey Pines Golf Club** (1250 Garden Rd., 831/656-2167, www.thegolfcourses.net, dawn–dusk daily, $34–49 Mon.–Fri., $37–52 Sat.–Sun.) is a short and sweet 18-hole, par-69 course. Redesigned in 2009, it's the most inexpensive course in the area, ideal for beginners or for someone who wants to work on their short game. **Del Monte Golf Course** (1300 Sylvan Rd., Pebble Beach, 800/654-9300, www.pebblebeach.com, dawn–dusk daily, $110) is one of the oldest courses on the West Coast, originally designed in 1897. This uncrowded 18-hole, par-72 course is less difficult than more modern courses, but its fairways are studded with mature trees, making them a little challenging to negotiate.

Spas

The **Spa on the Plaza** (2 Portola Plaza, 831/647-9000, www.spaontheplaza.com, 9 A.M.–9 P.M. daily) has 10 treatment rooms, including two couples massage rooms, one of which has whirlpool tubs. The spa also offers body wraps, Japanese soaking tubs, wet steam rooms with rock-lined walls, and a large relaxation room for detoxing prior to your treatment. If you choose to make it a daylong adventure, you can order food from the Portola Plaza Hotel across the street.

Vista Blue Spa (400 Cannery Row, 800/334-3999, www.montereyplazahotel.com/spa.html, 8 A.M.–6 P.M. Sun.–Thurs., 8 A.M.–7 P.M. Fri.–Sat.) performs massages on their fourth-floor sun deck overlooking the bay—not a bad way to relax. But it's the bath rituals that are the big draw: They last 25–45 minutes, with four different essential oils and minerals in the water, including arnica, rosemary, and basil.

ACCOMMODATIONS
Under $150
The **Monterey Hostel** (778 Hawthorne St., 831/649-0375, http://montereyhostel.com, dorm $25, private room $65) offers inexpensive accommodations within walking distance of the major attractions of Monterey. Frankly, when it comes to rooms and amenities, this isn't the best hostel in California. Lockers are free for those who bring their own locks, there's no laundry facility on-site, and the dorm rooms can be pretty crowded. On the other hand, the hostel puts on a free pancake breakfast every morning, linens are included with your bed, and there are comfy, casual common spaces with couches and musical instruments. And then there's that location. You can walk to the aquarium and Cannery Row, stroll the Monterey Bay Coastal Trail, or drive over to Carmel to see a different set of sights.

The **Best Western De Anza** (2141 Freemont St., 831/646-8300, www.bestwesterncalifornia.com, $129–149 d) is within driving distance of Cannery Row and downtown, but it's one of the least expensive and nicest of the chain hotels in the Monterey area. Off-season rates drop to under $100, which can't be beat in Monterey. Forty-three guest rooms include microwaves, fridges, and coffeemakers, and there's an outdoor heated pool and a hot tub.

Closer to the ocean, the **Inn at Del Monte Beach** (1110 Del Monte Blvd., 831/655-0515, www.theinnatdelmontebeach.com, $125–210 d) offers 16 guest rooms in a unique boutique property with a 1960s–meets–beaux arts feel. Amenities include Wi-Fi in the guest rooms, DVD players, electric fireplaces, a full breakfast in the communal dining room, afternoon tea, and wine and cheese in the early evenings on the deck overlooking the Pacific, all included in the rates. You can park on the street, or pay a small fee for the valet. A nice rooftop deck offers great views of the bay and downtown, which is just a five-block walk.

$150-250
A small, cute budget motel, the **Monterey Bay Lodge** (55 Camino Aguajito, 831/372-8057, www.montereybaylodge.com, $169) brings a bit of the Côte d'Azur to the equally beautiful coastal town of Monterey. With small guest rooms decorated in classic yellows and blues, a sparkling pool with a fountain in the shallow end, and an on-site restaurant serving breakfast and lunch, the Lodge makes a perfect base for budget-minded families.

The **Colton Inn** (707 Pacific St, 831/649-6500, www.coltoninn.com, $165) offers a touch of class above that of a standard beachtown motel. Located in the middle of downtown Monterey, the queen and king guest rooms boast attractive fabrics, designer baths, and pretty appointments. While you'll find restaurants and historic adobe buildings adjacent to the Colton, expect to drive or take public transit to Cannery Row and the Aquarium.

Designed by architect Julia Morgan of Hearst Castle fame, ◖ **Asilomar** (800 Asilomar Ave., Pacific Grove, 888/635-5310, www.visitasilomar.com, $148–180 d) was originally commissioned as a YWCA by William Randolph Hearst's mother. The original 65 guest rooms, built between 1913 and 1928, are true to their historic roots: They're small—quaint, really—and face an outdoor courtyard. Built separately from the original building, 259 larger, more modern guest rooms are Spartan, with no telephones or TVs. There is an outdoor pool, Wi-Fi in the communal areas, and a business center. The overall vibe is log-cabin rustic: A park ranger offers talks around a campfire in the early evenings. It's a very short walk across the dunes to the beach in Pacific Grove, so it's not unusual to see deer wandering among the pines that grow throughout the property.

Built as a private residence in 1911, **Jabberwock Inn** (598 Laine St., 888/428-7253, www.jabberwockinn.com, $169–309) was used as a convent for 35 years. Now it's the B&B with the best views of the bay, as it is perched up on the hills, a 10-minute walk downhill to Cannery Row. Breakfast (8:30–9:30 A.M.) is served in the dining room, which has a large window with a view, just above the boccie ball court. Wine and hors d'oeuvres are served 5–7 P.M., every afternoon milk and home-baked cookies appear, and there is always homemade *limoncello* available. There is Wi-Fi on the property.

The woodwork is spectacular at the **Inn at 213 Seventeen Mile Drive** (213 17-Mile Dr., Pacific Grove, 800/526-5666, www.innat17.com, $200), a classic craftsman home built in 1925. There are four upstairs guest rooms in the house and an additional 10 guest rooms in the separate coach house. Breakfast is served at 8 A.M., and each evening wine and hors d'oeuvres are served at 5:30 P.M. The guest rooms are large, each with its own theme. There is also off-street parking, Wi-Fi, and a small hot tub in the garden.

Over $250

If you're looking for a traditional high-end hotel, this is it: The **Monterey Plaza Hotel & Spa** (400 Cannery Row, 800/334-3999, www.montereyplazahotel.com, $259–349 d) has a prime location at the end of Cannery Row, with Monterey Bay and beach access in its front yard. Many of the large, nicely appointed guest rooms face the bay with private balconies. Other amenities include in-room coffeemakers, refrigerators, and turndown service. The service is first-rate, and it's far enough away from the center of Cannery Row to avoid the noise that accompanies the usual goings-on.

Although the **Portola Hotel** (2 Portola Plaza, 831/649-4511, www.portolahotel.com, $270–330 d) is a big hotel, it feels smaller than it is. About 40 percent of its 379 guest rooms offer prime views of the bay. There is also an on-site fitness room (5 A.M.–11 P.M. daily), a large round outdoor pool, and a hot tub. The hotel is conveniently located between downtown Monterey and Cannery Row: The walk to downtown is five minutes, and to Cannery Row about 20 minutes along the coast (more if you stop to watch the sea lions). The guest rooms and baths are large and comfortable, with in-room coffeemakers, and fridges on request. Many packages include local restaurants and attractions, but you have to pay extra for parking and Wi-Fi.

◖ Old Monterey Inn (500 Martin St., 800/350-2344, www.oldmontereyinn.com, $269–379 d) is a delightful spot, perfect for a romantic getaway. It was built as a residence by the first mayor of Monterey in 1929. Thick vines cling to the entrance of this beautiful Tudor-style property, with an oak tree shading the front. There are extensive gardens on the side and in the back. Breakfasts start with parfait and an entrée such as orange blossom French toast, served at 9 A.M. in the formal dining room (with a beautiful coffered ceiling) or in your room at 9:15 A.M. Wine and cheese is served 4–6 P.M., but coffee, tea, sodas, and water are available all the time. The guest rooms are large, with comfortable beds, hot tubs, and carpeting throughout, which adds to the quiet atmosphere. Choose from over 100 DVDs to watch in your room. There is Wi-Fi, but the signal is weak; you can use the communal computer in the living room.

The **◖ Intercontinental Clement Monterey** (750 Cannery Row, 831/375-4500, www.ichotelsgroup.com, $289) is a comfortable, minimalist hideaway. The modernist, Asian-inspired interior belies the pragmatic Cannery Row exterior. Tiles and woods are blended with woven fabric and inset rugs to create a dynamic play of materials and surfaces that honors its cannery past. Every guest room has its own orchids, and the furnishings are clean and sleek. There are 110 guest rooms on the bay side of Cannery Row and another 98 on the inland side, connected by a covered walking bridge. The hotel includes a full-service spa, a Kids Club with supervised day care so that parents can slip away for a while, and a 350-car covered garage. This is the newest and probably last oceanfront hotel that will be built on Cannery Row due to stringent building regulations.

FOOD
American
Montrio Bistro (411 Calle Principal, 831/648-8880, 5–10 P.M. Sun.–Thurs., 5–11 P.M. Fri.–Sat., $25) is in an old firehouse, but you'd never know it once you walk inside, thanks to the high ceilings, graceful curved walls, and custom lighting. The menu emphasizes local and organic foods in dishes like artichoke ravioli, seared diver scallops on parsnip puree, and rosemary roasted portobello mushroom. It gets very busy, so the noise level can get high. Reservations are recommended.

Breakfast
For 60 years people have been flooding into **Red's Donuts** (433 Alvarado St., 831/372-9761, 6:30 A.M.–1:30 P.M. Mon.–Sat., 6:30 A.M.–12:30 P.M. Sun., $2) in downtown Monterey to grab an old fashioned, a bear claw, or any of 20 different varieties. This is a local classic, with old yellow Formica countertops, simple stools, and walls lined with old photos and paintings of clowns. There are no fancy coffee drinks or French pastries—nothing but doughnuts and basic coffee. Sometimes all you need is a glazed doughnut to go.

Around the corner is the **East Village Coffee Lounge** (498 Washington St., 831/373-5601, www.eastvillagecoffeelounge.com, 6 A.M.–close Mon.–Fri., 7 A.M.–close Sat.–Sun., $5), which has a comfortable lounge vibe as well as outdoor seating. There are plenty of coffee and tea drinks, and they use organic milk. Pastry options include a tasty and moist chocolate scone and organic peach coffeecake. Parfaits, ham and cheese

croissants, and tomato and basil paninis are also available. Free Wi-Fi means lots of people hunker down with laptops.

British
The **Crown & Anchor** (150 W. Franklin St., 831/649-6496, www.crownandanchor.net, 11 A.M.–2 A.M. daily, $12) is about as British as you'll get, at least in downtown Monterey. It's located below street level; as you walk downstairs you'll see walls lined with images of kings, queens, lords, and guns. Twenty British and international beers on tap complement lamb shanks, cottage pie, corned beef and cabbage, and, of course, fish and chips. It's very popular with the locals, mainly an older crowd.

Cheap Eats
On the far south end of Cannery Row, the **Cannery Row Deli** (101 Drake St., 831/645-9549, 7 A.M.–5 P.M. daily, $8) offers massive breakfast burritos stuffed with eggs, chorizo, and potatoes as well as pancakes; lunch options like tuna melts and tofu pitas; and hot and iced coffee drinks. The space is tiny, with just three small tables, but the wood deck outside facing the bike path surrounded by ivy makes for a nice respite.

Pino's Café (211 Alvarado St., 831/649-1930, 6:30 A.M.–6:30 P.M. daily, $8) offers daily pasta dishes and traditional salads like chicken and tuna as well as Italian meatball sandwiches, salami, and turkey. There are also about 16 different gelatos. The simple interior makes it a great spot for kids or for a grab-and-go breakfast. It's right near Cannery Row for a waterside stroll.

French
At **Bistro Moulin** (867 Wave St., 831/333-1200, www.bistromoulin.com, 5 P.M.–close daily, $20), you'll think you're in France, even though you're just steps away from the Monterey Bay Aquarium. It's a true European bistro with intimate tables, a casual environment, and a menu that includes classics like coq au vin, crepes, and pâté. The wine list

showcases local wineries but has a good selection of French wines too.

Mediterranean

Petra (477 Lighthouse Ave., Pacific Grove, 831/649-2530, 11 A.M.–9 P.M. Mon.–Thurs., 11 A.M.–9:30 P.M. Fri.–Sat., $14) has been making kebabs, gyros, lentil soup, and stuffed grape leaves since 1984. The interior isn't much, with an upscale cafeteria vibe, but the Mediterranean menu is packed with flavor. There is a separate entrance, just to the left of the main door, for take-out orders.

The **Persian Grill** (675 Lighthouse Ave., 831/372-3720, www.persiangril.com, 11:30 A.M.–2:30 P.M. and 5–9:30 P.M. Wed.–Mon., $20) smells amazing as soon as you walk in the door. The potent flavors of Iran are well represented with kebabs, lamb, walnut stew, feta cheese and herbs, and stuffed vine leaves. Traditional belly dancing (7 P.M. and 8 P.M. Fri.–Sat.) add to the authentic atmosphere.

Spanish and Mexican

Estéban (700 Munras Ave., 831/375-0176, www.estebanrestaurant.com, 5–9 P.M. Sun.–Wed., 5–10 P.M. Thurs.–Sat. winter, 5–10 P.M. daily summer, $15) focuses on small plates or tapas, and there is plenty to choose from. Traditional Spanish Serrano hams share the spotlight with crab cakes, chorizo dishes, and paella. Outdoor dining in the large wood chairs near the fire pit is the best, but the interior, all sleek and sophisticated, offers views of the kitchen.

The colorful eatery **Turtle Bay Taqueria** (431 Tyler St., 831/333-1500, http://fishwife.com/turtlebay.htm, 11 A.M.–8:30 P.M. Mon.–Thurs., 11 A.M.–9 P.M. Fri.–Sat., 11:30 A.M.–8:30 P.M. Sun., $10) focuses on foods and flavors of coastal Mexico. You'll find Yucatán-style soups, charbroiled tilapia, *carnitas,* tacos, and burritos. The very good salsa, as well as the Mayan chocolate mousse, are made in-house.

Seafood

▟ The Sardine Factory (701 Wave St., 831/373-3775, www.sardinefactory.com, 5 P.M.–midnight daily, $30) kicked off the resurgence of Cannery Row over four decades ago and remains a must-stop restaurant. There are several dining rooms: The Captain's Room pays tribute to the brave sailors who ruled the sea, the Conservatory is a glass room surrounded by greenery, and the Wine Cellar is the more exclusive private dining room downstairs. The abalone bisque, served at both of President Ronald Reagan's inaugural dinners, is a must, and the fish entrées are tremendous—consider Alaskan salmon topped with artichoke hearts and hollandaise sauce. Wine enthusiasts won't be disappointed either; the Sardine Factory has received many awards for its impressive wine list, and the wine collection comprises over 35,000 bottles. The cellar below the dining room includes the only vertical collection of Inglenook cabernet sauvignons from 1949 to 1958 (No, you can't buy them, but you can take a peek). Nearby are the private wine lockers of Clint Eastwood and Arnold Schwarzenegger, among others, who can pull their wines when they dine here. Desserts are simple: Skip the ice cream, take the cannoli.

The newest addition to the Cannery Row dining scene is also one of the best: **▟ C Restaurant & Bar** (750 Cannery Row, 831/375-4500, www.thecrestaurant-monterey.com, 6:30 A.M.–10 P.M. daily, $30). The sleek, minimalist interior offers unencumbered views of the bay. The clean lines also extend to the menu, which is heavy on seafood, but also includes rack of lamb, or pasta mixed with local sardines. The lobster bisque is the best and creamiest you'll find in the county. Also worthwhile is the local red abalone with angel hair pasta, harvested just steps from the restaurant. All of the fish is sustainable, in concert with the Monterey Bay Aquarium's seafood watch list, and fresh local ingredients rotate seasonally. Finish off with a staggeringly large sundae: a concoction of pistachio and chocolate gelato with caramelized banana. You'll need multiple spoons.

Located in one of the original sardine cannery buildings, **The Fish Hopper** (700 Cannery Row, 831/372-8543, www.fishhopper.com,

10:30 A.M.–9 P.M. Sun.–Thurs., 10:30 A.M.–10 P.M. Fri.–Sat., $25) is right over the bay, with a great deck that gets crowded quickly. Around 15 daily specials include fresh fish, pasta, and steaks. Dishes worth sampling include the crab ravioli, seafood Louie salad, and maple soy-marinated skirt steak. There is also a good-size kids menu.

Located away from the tourist haunts, **Monterey's Fish House** (2114 Del Monte Ave., 831/373-4647, lunch 11:30 A.M.–2:30 P.M. Mon.–Fri., dinner 5–9:30 P.M. daily, $20) has long been a locals favorite, serving up all manner of seafood, including sole, oysters, calamari, and swordfish. The best versions of any of the fish are oak-grilled, with a delicate smoky note. Reservations are advised.

If sushi is more to your liking, **Crystal Fish** (514 Lighthouse Ave., 831/649-3474, http://crystalfishsushi.com, 11:30 A.M.–2 P.M. and 5–9 P.M. Mon.–Fri., 1–9 P.M. Sat.–Sun., $20) is your place. From rolls to *nigiri* and sashimi, the fish is fresh and artfully prepared and served, and there is a selection of vegetarian rolls. Noodles and tempura are available as well, but stick with the sushi and you won't go wrong.

Farmers Market
The often-crowded **Monterey Farmers Market** (930 Freemont St., www.montereybayfarmers.org, 10 A.M.–2 P.M. Fri. year-round) is located at the Monterey Peninsula College and includes a very large selection of fruits, veggies, honey, meats, and flowers along with cheeses, many of them organically farmed or produced within the region.

INFORMATION AND SERVICES
Housed in the old French Consulate building from the mid-1800s, the **Lake El Estero Visitors Center** (401 Camino El Estero, 877/666-8373, www.seemonterey.com, 9 A.M.–6 P.M. Mon.–Sat., 9 A.M.–5 P.M. Sun. summer, 9 A.M.–5 P.M. Mon.–Sat., 10 A.M.–4 P.M. Sun. winter) has a wealth of information on every conceivable thing to do in the county, even things you may not have considered.

The **Monterey County Herald** (www.montereyherald.com) is the daily newspaper. **Monterey County Weekly** (www.montereycountyweekly.com) is a free arts and entertainment paper. Both offer information on local activities and events.

In case of emergency, dial **911.** The **Community Hospital of the Monterey Peninsula** (23625 Holman Hwy., 888/452-4667, www.chomp.org) has 233 beds and every service imaginable. The **Monterey Police Department** (351 Madison St., 831/646-3824, www.monterey.org) is located near downtown.

GETTING THERE AND AROUND
Like many attractive towns, Monterey has retained its identity in part because it is difficult to reach. There are only two direct routes: Highway 1 along the coast from the north or south, and Highway 68, which runs west from U.S. 101 and Salinas. Either way, it tends to be slow going during peak seasons.

The only bus service via **Greyhound** (19 W. Gabilan St., Salinas, 831/424-4418, www.greyhound.com) stops in Salinas. From there, you have to take a connecting **Monterey-Salinas Transit** (888/678-2871, www.mst.org, $2) bus to Monterey.

Coast Starlight, the **Amtrak** (800/872-7245, www.amtrak.com) Seattle–Los Angeles train, stops in Salinas; to reach Monterey, take the bus to the Aquarium Bus Stop, a curbside-only stop right on Cannery Row. **Monterey-Salinas Transit** (888/678-2871, www.mst.org, $2) covers the Monterey Peninsula, including Carmel Valley to the south and Salinas to the east.

Cab 33 (1056 7th St., 831/373-8294) and **Yellow Cab** (831/646-1234) are two of the best taxi companies serving Monterey.

The **Monterey Regional Airport** (MRY, 200 Fred Kane Dr., 831/648-7000, www.montereyairport.com) has nonstop flights from Los Angeles's LAX, San Diego, Phoenix, Denver, Las Vegas, and San Francisco, but

PACIFIC COAST HIGHWAY

airfares to Monterey are high. Another option is to fly into **San Jose International Airport** (SJC, 2077 Airport Blvd., San Jose, 408/392-3600, www.sjc.org), an hour's drive away, and then rent a car and drive to Monterey.

Parking is a perpetual problem in Monterey. Expect to pay no matter where you go. There are eight parking lots near Cannery Row, and all-day fees run $10–20. The streets closest to

Cannery Row have 12-hour metered parking. The farther away you go, the cheaper it gets. If you cross Lighthouse Avenue and are willing to walk the six blocks to Cannery Row, you can find free parking in the residential neighborhood. When you're downtown, there is free two-hour street parking and a handful of lots as well, but most charge about $1.50 per hour.

Santa Cruz

There's no place like Santa Cruz. Not even elsewhere in the wacky Bay Area can you find another town that has embraced the radical fringe of the nation and made it into a municipal-cultural statement quite like this. In Santa Cruz you'll find surfers on the waves, nudists on the beaches, tree-huggers in the

redwood forests, tattooed and pierced punks on the main drag, and families walking the dog along West Cliff Drive. Oh, and by the way, that purple-haired woman with the tongue stud might well be a dedicated volunteer at the local PTA. With the kind of irony only Santa Cruz can produce, a massive

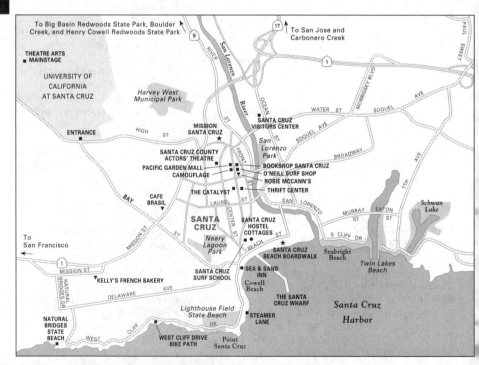

illegal fireworks storm erupts over the beaches in patriotic celebration each Fourth of July.

Most visitors come to Santa Cruz to hit the Boardwalk and the beaches. Locals and University of California, Santa Cruz students tend to hang at the Pacific Garden Mall and stroll on West Cliff Drive. The east side of town can get dicey, especially a few blocks from the Boardwalk, while the west side tends more toward families with children. The food of Santa Cruz qualifies as a hidden treasure, with myriad ethnicities represented.

The Santa Cruz area includes several tiny towns that aren't inside Santa Cruz proper but blend into each other with the feeling of beach-town suburbs. Aptos, Capitola, and Soquel are south of Santa Cruz along the coast. Each has its own small shopping districts, restaurants, and lodgings. They've also got charming beaches, which can be as

foggy, as crowded, or as nice to visit as their northern neighbors.

SIGHTS
Santa Cruz Beach Boardwalk

The Santa Cruz Beach Boardwalk (400 Beach St., 831/423-5590, www.beachboardwalk.com, 11 A.M.–close Mon.–Fri., 9 A.M.–close Sat.–Sun., parking $12), or just "the Boardwalk," as it's called by the locals, has a rare appeal that beckons to young children, too-cool teenagers, and adults of all ages.

The amusement park rambles along each side of the south end of the Boardwalk; entry is free, but you must buy either per-ride tickets or an unlimited-ride wristband. The Giant Dipper boasts a history as the oldest wooden roller coaster in the state, still giving riders a thrill. The Spinner and the Zipper tend to be more fun for kids (or at least folks with hardy inner ears). In summer, a log ride cools down

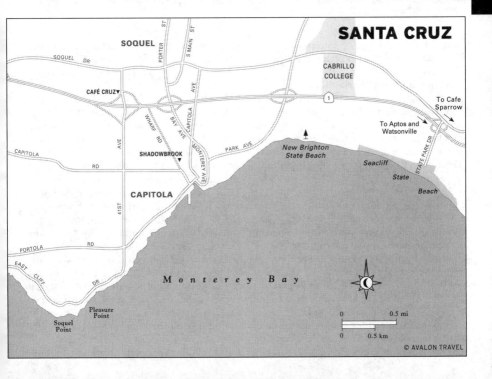

© AVALON TRAVEL

Santa Cruz Beach Boardwalk

© MARK RASMUSSEN/123RF

PACIFIC COAST HIGHWAY

visitors hot from hours of tromping around. The Boardwalk also offers several rides for toddlers and little kids.

At the other end of the Boardwalk, avid gamesters choose between the lure of prizes from the traditional midway games and the large arcade. Throw baseballs at things, try your arm at skee ball, or take a pass at classic or newer video games. The traditional carousel actually has a brass ring you or your children can try to grab.

After you've worn yourself out playing games and riding rides, you can take the stairs down to the broad, sandy beach below the Boardwalk. It's a great place to flop down in the sun, or brave a dip in the cool Pacific surf. Granted, it gets a bit crowded in the summer, but you've got all the services you could ever want right here at the Boardwalk, plus the sand and the water (and the occasional strand of kelp). What could be more perfect?

Looking for something tasty to munch on or a drink to cool you off? You can definitely find it at the Boardwalk. An old-fashioned candy shop sells sweets, while the snack stands offer corn dogs, burgers, fries, lemonade, and other generally unhealthy traditional carnival food.

Mission Santa Cruz

Believe it or not, weird and funky Santa Cruz started out as a mission town. Mission Santa Cruz (126 High St., 831/425-5849, www.parks.ca.gov, www.holycrosssantacruz.com, 10 A.M.–4 P.M. Thurs.–Sat., free) was one of the later California missions, dedicated in 1791. Today, the attractive white of the building with its classic red-tiled roof welcomes parishioners to the active Holy Cross Church and students from around the Bay Area to the historic museum areas of the old mission. In fact, the buildings you can visit today, like many others in the chain of missions, are not the original complex built by the Spanish priests in the 18th century. Indeed, none of the first mission and only one wall from the second mission remain today—the rest was destroyed in an earthquake. The church you'll tour today is the fourth one, built in 1889.

After a tour of the complex and grounds, stop in at the Galeria, which houses the mission gift shop and a stunning collection of religious vestments—something you won't see in many other California missions.

Seymour Marine Discovery Center at the Long Marine Laboratory

If you love the sea and all the critters that live in it, be sure to take a tour of the Seymour Marine Discovery Center at the Long Marine Laboratory (Delaware Ave., 831/459-3800, www2.ucsc.edu/seymourcenter, 10 A.M.–5 P.M. Tues.–Sat., noon–5 P.M. Sun., adults $6, seniors and children $4). The large, attractive gray building complex at the end of Delaware Avenue sits on the edge of the cliff overlooking the ocean—convenient for the research done primarily by students and faculty of the University of California, Santa Cruz. Your visit will be to the Seymour Marine Discovery Center, the part of the lab that's open to the public. You'll be greeted outside the door by a full blue whale skeleton that's lit up at night. Inside, instead of a standard aquarium setup, you'll find a marine laboratory similar to those used by the scientists elsewhere in the complex. Expect to see pipes and machinery around the tanks, which are designed to display their residents rather than to mimic habitats. Kids especially love the touch tanks, while curious adults enjoy checking out the seasonal tank that contains the wildlife that's swimming around outside in the bay right now.

If you've never been to Long-Seymour before, take a tour (1 P.M., 2 P.M., and 3 P.M. daily); there are also family tours (11 A.M. Tues.–Sat., 12:30 P.M. Sun.). Sign up an hour in advance to be sure of getting a slot.

University of California, Santa Cruz

The University of California, Santa Cruz (UCSC, 1156 High St., 831/459-0111, www.ucsc.edu) might be the single most beautiful college campus in the country. Set in the hills above downtown Santa Cruz, the classrooms and dorms sit underneath groves of coastal redwood trees, among tangles of ferns and vines and cute woodland creatures. It is possible to tour the campus (groups of six or more, 831/459-4118, reservations required). Or just find a parking lot and wander out into the woods like the students do, perhaps finding a perfect circle of trees to sit in and meditate.

ENTERTAINMENT AND EVENTS
Bars and Clubs

Down on the Pacific Garden Mall, you can stroll upstairs to **Rosie McCann's** (1220 Pacific Ave., 831/426-9930, www.rosiemccanns.com) for a pint and a bite. This dark-paneled Irish-style saloon serves Guinness, black and tan, snakebites, and several tasty draft beers. You can also get a hefty meal at Rosie's, where the menu runs to sausage, mashed potatoes, and other weighty pub foods. A largely local crowd hangs out here, and you'll find the bar crowded and noisy, but the vibe is friendly and entertaining.

Live Music

The Catalyst (1011 Pacific Ave., advance tickets 866/384-3060, door tickets 831/423-1338, www.catalystclub.com, $12–35), right downtown on the Pacific Garden Mall, is *the* Santa Cruz nightclub. This live rock venue hosts all sorts of big-name national acts that now play clubs rather than stadiums. The Catalyst is completely democratic in its booking—you might see Ted Nugent one week, the Indigo Girls the next, and a ska band the week after that. In between, the Catalyst hosts DJ dance nights, teen nights, and other fun events. Be sure to check the calendar when you buy tickets—some shows are age 21 and over only (with music, dancing, and a full bar). The main concert hall is a standing-room-only space, while the balconies offer seating. The bar is downstairs next to the concert space. The vibe at the Catalyst tends to be low-key, but it depends on the night and the event. Some of the more retro acts definitely draw an older crowd, while the techno-DJ dance parties cater to the university set. You can buy tickets online or by phone; purchasing in advance is recommended, especially for national acts.

The **Crow's Nest** (2218 E. Cliff Dr., 831/476-4560, www.crowsnest-santacruz. com, from 8:30 P.M. Wed.–Sun.) functions as a venue for all kinds of live musical acts. You might see a contemporary reggae-rock group one night and a Latin dance band the next. Lots of funk bands play the Nest, which is appropriate to the Santa Cruz ethos. A few tribute bands, usually to hippie 1960s and 1970s legends like Jimi Hendrix and Santana, perform on occasion as well. Most shows are free, but if there's a popular act or comedy night on Sunday, you'll be charged $3–7 at the door. Check the website for the calendar, but it's a good bet that you'll get live musical entertainment here every night Wednesday–Saturday.

Comedy

For a good laugh in Santa Cruz, the **Crow's Nest** (2218 E. Cliff Dr., 831/476-4560, www. crowsnest-santacruz.com, comedy 8:30 P.M. Sun., $7) also hosts a weekly stand-up show. Because the show runs on Sunday nights, the Crow's Nest takes advantage of the opportunity to hire big-name comics who have been in San Francisco or San Jose for weekend engagements. This allows headliners to play in a more casual setting for a fraction of the cost of the big-city clubs. The Crow's Nest, with its great views out over the Pacific, also has a full bar and restaurant. You can enjoy drinks and dinner while you get your giggle on.

Theater

Santa Cruz is home to several community theaters and an outdoor summer Shakespeare festival that draws theatergoers from around the Bay Area.

The **Santa Cruz County Actors' Theatre** (1001 Center St., 831/479-8101, www.actorssc. org) acts as Santa Cruz's permanent local theater company. The Actors' Theatre does it all: performs a subscription season, holds theater arts workshops, sponsors playwriting contests for kids and adults, and stages improv shows.

All shows at this low-cost theater are contemporary works, including the full-production series plays. But the most exciting (though not necessarily the highest quality) shows you can see here are the new-works festivals, featuring completely new plays, mostly by local authors, that have won Actors' Theatre contests. If one of these, especially the "Eight Tens at Eight," appears during your stay, consider getting tickets so you can see something completely different.

If you prefer historic theater to modern, UCSC puts on an annual summer Shakespeare festival, **Shakespeare Santa Cruz** (831/459-2121, http://shakespearesantacruz.org, adults $15–44, seniors and students $15, children $14). This six-week festival usually runs in the second half of July and through August. Venues are on the UCSC campus, one indoors at the Theatre Arts Main Stage (1156 High St.) and the other out in the redwood forests at the Festival Glen (Meyer Dr.). Each year the festival puts on at least two Shakespeare plays—2011 selections included *The Comedy of Errors* and *Henry IV, Part 1*—plus at least one other production (often a more contemporary play). At the outdoor Festival Glen, audience members are encouraged to bring their own picnics. This can make for the perfect romantic date, or a fun outing for the whole family.

SHOPPING

There's no shopping area in California quite like the **Pacific Garden Mall** (Pacific Ave., 831/429-8433). Hanging out "on the Mall," as the locals call it, is a pastime for many teens and adults from Santa Cruz and beyond. The Mall runs along Pacific Avenue and its side streets, and it is usually open to (very slow) auto traffic. Park in one of the structures a block or two off the Mall proper and walk. At the north end, shoppers peruse antiques, boutique clothing, and kitchenware. Down at the seedier south end, visitors can get shiny new body jewelry, a great new tattoo, or a silicone sex toy. In the middle (and to a lesser degree throughout the Mall), you can grab a bite to eat, a cappuccino, or a cocktail in one of the many independent eateries. You'll find only a few chain stores on the Mall, and those are uniformly reviled by the fiercely anticorporate residents of Santa Cruz. The Borders across the street from the **Bookshop Santa Cruz** (1520 Pacific Ave., 831/423-0900, www.bookshopsantacruz.com, 9 A.M.–10 P.M. Sun.–Thurs., 9 A.M.–11 P.M. Fri.–Sat.) takes shockingly little business away from its local independent rival.

Sure, you will find an **O'Neill Surf Shop** (110 Cooper St., 831/469-4377, www.oneill. com) on the Mall, but surf shops are a staple of Santa Cruz. This one specializes in surfboards, wetsuits, and brand-name clothing. If your trip to California has got you hooked on riding the waves, and you just have to invest in your own equipment, O'Neill can be a good place to start. (If you're an expert who prefers custom work, you already know that prefab chain stuff isn't for you.) You can also buy a T-shirt or some sweats here—handy if you didn't pack quite right for Central Coast summer fog.

If you want to buy clothes in Santa Cruz, chances are you're looking for a secondhand store. This town has plenty of 'em. One of the largest of these is only a block off Pacific Avenue—the aptly if redundantly named **Thrift Center Thrift Store** (504 Front St., 831/429-6975). This big, somewhat dirty retail space offers a wide array of cheap secondhand clothes. You'll need to hunt a bit to find that one perfect vintage item that's just too perfect, but isn't that the fun of thrift store shopping?

Down toward the great divide between the "good side" and the "less good side" of the Mall, you can price some more adult merchandise. **Camouflage** (1329 Pacific Ave., 831/423-7613, www.shopcamouflage.com, 10 A.M.–9 P.M. Mon.–Thurs., 10 A.M.–10 P.M. Fri.–Sat., 11 A.M.–7 P.M. Sun.) is an independent, women-operated and women-friendly adult store. The first room contains mostly lingerie and less-shocking items. Dare to walk through the narrow black-curtained passage, and you'll find the *other* room, filled with grown-up toys designed to please women of every taste and proclivity. (A few cool gizmos and gadgets can make things fun for the men as well.) As many women as men shop here and will feel comfortable doing so.

SPORTS AND RECREATION
Beaches
At the tip of the west side, **Natural Bridges State Park** (W. Cliff Dr., 831/423-4609, www.parks.ca.gov, 8 A.M.–sunset daily) offers nearly every kind of beach recreation possible. The sand strip doesn't stretch wide, but falls back deep, crossed by a creek flowing into the sea. An inconsistent break makes surfing at Natural Bridges fun on occasion, while the near-constant winds that sweep the sands bring out windsurfers nearly every weekend. Hardy sun-worshippers brave the breezes, bringing out their beach blankets, umbrellas, and sunscreen on rare sunny days (usually in late spring and fall). Back from the beach, a wooded picnic area has tables and grills for groups small and large. Even farther back, the visitors center can provide great stories about the various national wonders of this surprisingly diverse state park. Rangers offer guided tours of the tide pools on the west side of the beach. You can access these by a somewhat scrambling short hike (0.25–0.5 miles) on the rocks cliffs. These odd little holes filled with sealife aren't like most tide pools; many are nearly perfect round depressions in the sandstone cliffs worn away by harder stones as the tides move tirelessly back and forth. Don't touch the residents of these pools, since human hands can hurt delicate tide pool creatures.

At **Cowell Beach** (350 W. Cliff Dr.) on the west side, it's all about surfing. This beach is right at a crook in the coastline, which combines with underwater features to create a reliable small break that lures new surfers by the dozens.

At the south end of Santa Cruz, down by the harbor, beachgoers flock to **Seabright State Beach** (E. Cliff Dr. and Seabright Ave., 831/685-6500, www.thatsmypark.org, 6 A.M.–10 P.M. daily, free) all summer long. This miles-long stretch of sand, protected by the cliffs from the worst of the winds, is a favorite retreat for sunbathers and loungers. While there's little in the way of snack bars, permanent volleyball courts, or other facilities, you can still have a great time at Seabright. There's lots of soft sand to lie in, plenty of room to play football or set up your own volleyball net, and, of course, easy access to the chilly Pacific Ocean. There's no surfing here—Seabright has a shore break that delights skim-boarders but makes wave riding impossible.

Each Fourth of July, the Santa Cruz police cordon off the area surrounding Seabright Beach. No one can park nearby or even walk in after a certain time in the afternoon (which seems to change annually). But if you show up early to cart your stuff down onto the sand, you can participate in the unbelievable fireworks extravaganza that starts almost as soon as the sun goes down. Though it's technically illegal, amateurs still create professional-grade pyrotechnical productions and launch them from Seabright. The effect quickly becomes overwhelming, but for those who can handle it, the night is truly magical.

Down in Capitola, one of the favorite sandy spots is **New Brighton State Beach** (1500 Park Ave., Capitola, 831/464-6330, www.parks.ca.gov). This forest-backed beach has everything: a strip of sand that's perfect for lounging and cold-water swimming, a forest-shaded campground for both tents and RVs, hiking trails, and ranger-led nature programs. If you plan to camp, call in advance to make reservations at this popular state park, or just come for the day and set up on the sand. New Brighton can get crowded on rare sunny summer days, but it's nothing like the wall-to-wall humanity of the popular beaches in Southern California.

Surfing

The coastline of Santa Cruz has more than its share of great surf breaks. The water is cold, demanding full wetsuits year-round, and the shoreline is rough and rocky—nothing at all like the flat sandy beaches of SoCal. But that doesn't deter the hordes of locals who

ply the waves every day they can. Surfing culture pervades the town—if you walk the cliff, you'll likely pass the *To Honor Surfing* sculpture. Santa Cruz loves this statue: It's often dressed up and always gets a costume for Halloween.

If you're a beginner, the best place to start surfing Santa Cruz is **Cowell's** (stairs at W. Cliff Dr. and Cowell Beach). The waves are low and long, making for fun long-board rides perfect for surfers just getting their balance. Because the Cowell's break is acknowledged as the newbie spot, the often sizeable crowd tends to be polite to newcomers and visitors.

For more advanced surfers looking for smaller crowds in the water, **Manresa State Beach** (San Andreas Rd., Aptos, www.parks.ca.gov) offers fun rides under the right conditions. Manresa is several minutes' drive south of Aptos. You'll usually find a good beach break, and the waves can get big when there's a north swell.

Visitors who know their surfing lore will want to surf the more famous spots along the Santa Cruz shore. **Pleasure Point** (between 32nd Ave. and 41st Ave., Soquel) encompasses a number of different breaks. You may have heard of The Hook (steps at 41st Ave.), a well-known experienced long-boarder's paradise. But don't mistake The Hook for a beginner's break; the locals feel protective of the waves here and aren't always friendly toward inexperienced outsiders. The break at 36th Avenue and East Cliff Drive (steps at 36th Ave.) can be a better place to go on weekdays—on the weekends, the intense crowding makes catching your own wave a challenge. Up at 30th Avenue and East Cliff Drive (steps at 36th Ave.), you'll find challenging sets and hot-dogging short-boarders.

The most famous break in Santa Cruz can also be the most hostile to newcomers. **Steamer Lane** (W. Cliff Dr. between Cowell's and the Lighthouse) has both a fiercely protective crew of locals and a dangerous break that actually kills someone about every other year. But if you're into adrenaline and there's a swell coming in, you'll be hard-pressed to find a more exciting ride on the Central Coast or indeed in California.

Yes, you can learn to surf in Santa Cruz, despite the distinct local flavor at some of the breaks. Check out either the **Santa Cruz Surf School** (131 Center St., Suite 1, 831/426-7072, www.santacruzsurfschool.com) or the **Richard Schmidt Surf School** (849 Almar Ave., 831/423-0928, www.richardschmidt.com) to sign up for lessons. Who knows, maybe one day the locals will mistake you for one of their own.

Windsurfing and Parasurfing

If you prefer to let the wind help you catch the waves, you probably already know that Santa Cruz has some prize windsurfing and parasurfing locales. Beginning windsurfers vie with long-boarders for space at **Cowell's,** right next to the Santa Cruz Wharf (stairs at W. Cliff Dr. and Cowell Beach). For a bigger breeze, head up West Cliff Drive to **Natural Bridges State Park** (W. Cliff Dr., www.parks.ca.gov, parking $6). Natural Bridges offers the best spot to set up, along with restroom facilities and ample parking. Serious sailors head farther north to **Davenport Landing** (Hwy. 1, 15 miles north of Santa Cruz). You'll be able to discern that you've found the right rugged and windswept stretch of coast by the endless crowd of sailors and parasurfers out on the waves. Parking can be a bit haphazard here, but even if you're just stopping by to watch, it can be worth your time since the sight of these athletes using both wind and waves to create fast rides is nothing short of amazing.

If you want to try your luck at windsurfing for the first time, contact **Club Ed** (831/464-0177, www.club-ed.com) to set up a lesson. They operate in the gentle breezes and small swells at Cowell's and make it easy for first-timers to gain confidence and have a great time.

Hiking and Biking

To walk or bike where the locals do, head out to **West Cliff Drive.** This winding street with a full-fledged sidewalk-trail running its length on the ocean side is the town's favorite walking, dog-walking, jogging, skating, scootering, and biking route. You can start at Natural Bridges (the west end of W. Cliff Dr.) and go for miles. The *To Honor Surfing* statue is several miles down the road, along with plenty of fabulous views. Bring your camera if you're strolling West Cliff Drive on a clear day—you won't be able to resist taking photos of the sea, cliffs, and sunset. Just be sure to watch out for your fellow path users. What with the bicyclists and skaters and such, it can get a bit treacherous if you don't watch where you're going.

ACCOMMODATIONS
Under $150

Staying at a hostel in Santa Cruz just feels right. The **Santa Cruz Hostel Carmelita Cottages** (321 Main St., 831/423-8304, www.hi-santa-cruz.org, dorm $25, private room $60, cottage $150–290) offers great local atmosphere. Like most historic Santa Cruz edifices, it doesn't look like much from the outside, and certainly the interior doesn't have the newest furniture and paint. But it's clean, cheap, friendly, and close to the beach. You'll find a spot to store your surfboard or bike for free, and car parking is $2 per day. The big homey kitchen is open for guest use and might even be hiding some extra free food in its cupboards. Expect all the usual hostel-style amenities along with a nice garden out back, free linens, laundry facilities, and a free Internet kiosk.

$150-250

The four-room **Adobe on Green Street** (103 Green St., 831/469-9866, www.adobeongreen.com, $189–219) offers lovely bed-and-breakfast accommodations close to the heart of downtown Santa Cruz. The location, within walking distance of the Pacific Garden Mall, lets you soak in the unique local atmosphere to your heart's content. A unifying decorative scheme runs through all four guest rooms—a dark and minimalist Spanish mission style befitting Santa Cruz's history as a mission town. Each guest room has a queen bed, a private bath (most with tubs), a small TV with a DVD player, and lots of other amenities that can make you comfortable even over a long stay. An expanded continental breakfast is set out in the dining room 8–11 A.M. each morning. Expect yummy local pastries, organic and soy yogurts, and multicolored eggs laid by a neighbor's flock of chickens. In keeping with the Santa Cruz ethos, the Adobe runs on solar power.

For a room overlooking the ocean, stay at the **C Sea & Sand Inn** (201 W. Cliff Dr., 831/427-3400, www.santacruzmotels.com/sea_and_sand.html, $229). In an unbeatable location on the ocean side of West Cliff Drive at Bay Street, you'll be close enough to downtown and the Boardwalk to enjoy the action of Santa Cruz, but you'll also have more quiet in a neighborhood that's starting to tend toward residential. Every guest room in the house comes with an ocean view (hence the high price for what's really a pretty basic motel room), and suites with hot tubs and private patios make for a wonderful seaside vacation. Guest rooms and suites do have nicer-than-average decor with pretty furniture, private baths, and free Internet access.

Some travelers prefer to stay in the woods rather than downtown or out by the busy Boardwalk. **Redwood Croft Bed and Breakfast** (275 Northwest Dr., 831/458-1939, www.redwoodcroft.com, $155–275) is a funky B&B set back in the recently charred ruins of the redwood forest to the northwest of Santa Cruz. The inn itself takes the woodsy theme indoors, using natural wood in the walls and furniture to create a serene retreat-house feeling. Each of the three guest rooms, as well as the cottage, bursts with beautiful appointments, lovely stone baths, and views out into the recovering woods.

FOOD
American
At **Café Cruz** (2621 41st Ave., Soquel, 831/476-3801, www.cafecruz.com, 11:30 A.M.–2:30 P.M., 3–5 P.M., and 5:30 P.M.–close Mon.–Sat., 5 P.M.–close Sun., $16–30), the menu runs toward homey American favorites done

up with a California twist (ribs, rotisserie chicken, bowls of pasta, and crunchy fresh salads). Café Cruz purchases the freshest local produce, meats, seafood, and even drinks that they can find. You can munch locally caught fish with goat cheese from Half Moon Bay and an organic soda from Monterey. The attractive white-tablecloth dining room welcomes casual and elegant diners alike, and if you choose wisely, you can get an upscale meal for medium-scale prices.

Asian
When locals who love their sushi get that craving for raw fish, they head for **Shogun Restaurant** (1123 Pacific Ave., 831/469-4477, noon–2:30 P.M. and 5–9 P.M. Mon.–Wed., noon–2:30 P.M. and 5–10 P.M. Thurs.–Fri., 3–10 P.M. Sat., $25). Right on the Pacific Garden Mall, Shogun serves big fresh slabs of *nigiri* and an interesting collection of *maki* (rolls). The fish served here is some of the freshest you'll find in this coastal city. Meats and other dishes also please diners with fresh ingredients and tasty preparations. While service can be spotty, usually it's efficient—you'll get your order quickly, and it will be right on. If you're not used to sushi prices, you may find Shogun expensive, but if you're a connoisseur, you'll feel that they're quite reasonable. There's often a wait for a table in the evenings, especially on weekends.

California
The Santa Cruz region boasts one serious upscale eatery. The **C Shadowbrook** (1750 Wharf Rd., Capitola-by-the-Sea, 831/475-1511, www.shadowbrook-capitola.com, 5–8:45 P.M. Mon.–Fri., 4–9:45 P.M. Sat., 4–8:45 P.M. Sun., $26) has long been worth driving over the hill for. The cliff-side location, complete with an entrance that can be reached by cable car, has perhaps the most impressive views and atmosphere of any restaurant in the area. The Shadowbrook is a perfect spot to stage the ultimate romantic date, complete with roses, candlelight, and fine chocolate desserts.

French

In Aptos Village, **Cafe Sparrow** (8042 Soquel Dr., Aptos Village, 831/688-6238, www. cafesparrow.com, 11:30 A.M.–2 P.M. and 5:30 P.M.–close Mon.–Fri., 11 A.M.–2 P.M. and 5:30 P.M.–close Sat., 9 A.M.–2 P.M. and 5:30 P.M.–close Sun., $20) serves country French cuisine that's consistently tasty. Whatever you order, it will be fantastic. The seafood is noteworthy (especially the Friday-night bouillabaisse), as are the steaks. Cafe Sparrow's kitchen prepares all the dishes with fresh ingredients, and the chef, who can sometimes be seen out in the dining room checking on customer satisfaction with the food, thinks up innovative preparations and creates tasty sauces. He's also willing to accommodate special requests and dietary restrictions with good cheer. The best deal for your money is the daily-changing prix-fixe menu. For dessert, treat yourself to the profiteroles, which can be created with either ice cream or pastry cream.

South American

Cafe Brasil (1410 Mission St., 831/429-1855, www.cafebrasil.us, 8 A.M.–2:45 P.M. daily, $10–20) serves up the Brazilian fare its name promises. Painted jungle green with bright yellow and blue trim, you can't miss this totally Santa Cruz breakfast and lunch joint. In the morning, the fare runs to omelets and international specialties, while lunch includes pressed sandwiches, meat and tofu dishes, and Brazilian house specials. A juice bar provides rich but healthy meal accompaniments that can act as light meals on their own. To try something different: get an *açaí* bowl—*açaí* is a South American fruit—or an Amazon cherry juice and OJ blend.

Coffee and Bakeries

For a casual sandwich or pastry, head for **Kelly's French Bakery** (402 Ingalls St., 831/423-9059, www.kellysfrenchbakery.com, 7 A.M.–7 P.M. Sat.–Thurs., 7 A.M.–8 P.M. Fri., $10). This popular bakery is in an old industrial warehouse-style space. Its dome shape, constructed of corrugated metal, looks nothing

like a restaurant. It's got both indoor and outdoor seating and serves full breakfasts and luncheon sandwiches. You can order to eat in or to go, and pick up a breakfast or sweet pastry, some bread, or a cake while you're here.

INFORMATION AND SERVICES

While it can be fun to explore Santa Cruz just by using your innate sense of direction and the bizarre, those who want a bit more structure on their travels can hit the **Santa Cruz Visitors Center** (303 Water St., Suite 100, 800/833-3494, www.santacruzca.org) for maps, advice, and information.

Santa Cruz has its own daily newspaper, the *Santa Cruz Sentinel* (www.santacruzsentinel. com), with a daily dose of national wire-service news and current events, local news, and some good stuff for visitors. The *Sentinel* has a Food section, a Sunday Travel section, and plenty of up-to-date entertainment information.

You can get your mail on at the **post office** (850 Front St., 831/426-0144) near the Mall.

Santa Cruz is, like, totally wired, man. You'll definitely be able to access the Internet in a variety of cafés and hotels. There are Starbucks locations here, and the many indie cafés often compete with their own (sometimes free) Wi-Fi.

Santa Cruz has plenty of banks and ATMs, including some ATMs on the arcade at the Boardwalk. Bank branches congregate downtown near the Pacific Garden Mall. The west side is mostly residential, so you'll find a few ATMs in supermarkets and gas stations but little else.

Despite its rep as a funky bohemian beach town, Santa Cruz's dense population dictates that it have at least one full-fledged hospital. You can get medical treatment and care at **Dominican Hospital** (1555 Soquel Ave., 831/426-7700, www.dominicanhospital.org).

GETTING THERE AND AROUND

If you're driving to Santa Cruz from Silicon Valley, you've got two choices: Most drivers take fast, dangerous Highway 17. This narrow road doesn't have any switchbacks and is the main truck route "over the hill." Most locals drive this 50 mph corridor faster than they should; each year several people die in accidents on Highway 17, and I once crashed my vehicle into an overturned pickup truck on Big Moody curve. So if you're new to the road, keep to the right and take it slow, no matter what the traffic to the left is doing. Check traffic reports before you head out; Highway 17 is known to be one of the worst commuting roads in the Bay Area, and the weekend beach traffic in the summer jams it up fast in both directions.

For a more leisurely drive, you can opt for two-lane Highway 9. The tight curves and endless switchbacks will keep you at a reasonable speed; use the turnouts to let the locals pass. On Highway 9, the biggest obstacles tend to be groups of bicyclists and motorcyclists, both of whom adore the slopes and curves of this technical drive. The good news is that you'll get an up-close-and-personal view of the gorgeously forested Santa Cruz Mountains, complete with views of the valley to the north and ocean vistas to the south.

To drive or bike around Santa Cruz, get a good map, either before you arrive or at the visitors center in town. Navigating the winding, occasionally broken-up streets of this

oddly shaped town isn't for the faint of heart. Highway 1, which becomes Mission Street on the west side, acts as the main artery through Santa Cruz and down to Capitola, Soquel, Aptos, and coastal points farther south. You'll find that Highway 1 at the interchange to Highway 17, and sometimes several miles to the south, is heavily congested most of the time.

Parking

Parking in Santa Cruz can be its own special sort of horror. Downtown, head straight for the parking structures one block from Pacific Avenue on either side. They're much easier to deal with than trying to find street parking. The same goes for the beach and Boardwalk areas. At the Boardwalk, pay the fee to park in the big parking lot adjacent to the attractions; you'll save an hour and possibly a break-in or theft trying to find street parking in the sketchy neighborhoods that surround the Boardwalk.

Bus

In town, the buses are run by **Santa Cruz Metro** (831/425-8600, www.scmtd.com, adults $2 per ride, passes available). With dozens of routes in Santa Cruz County, you can probably find a way to get nearly anywhere you want to go.

ESSENTIALS

Getting There

FLYING INTO SAN FRANCISCO

San Francisco has one major airport surrounded by a few ancillary and less-crowded airports. **San Francisco International Airport** (SFO, www.flysfo.com) isn't in San Francisco proper—it's actually located approximately 13 miles south of the City.

Several public and private transportation options can get you into the City: rental car, taxi, BART, or even Caltrain. As in Los Angeles, if your flight is out of SFO, plan to arrive at the airport up to three hours before your flight leaves. Airport lines, especially on weekends and holidays, are notoriously long.

To avoid the SFO crowds, consider booking a flight into **Oakland International Airport** (OAK, 1 Airport Dr., Oakland, 510/563-3300, www.flyoakland.com), which services the East Bay with access to San Francisco across the Bay Bridge, or **San Jose International Airport** (SJC, Airport Blvd., San Jose, www.sjc.org), south of San Francisco in the heart of Silicon Valley. These airports are quite a bit smaller than SFO, but service is brisk from many U.S. destinations.

Bay Area Rapid Transit (BART, www.bart.gov) connects directly with SFO's international terminal, providing a simple and relatively fast trip to downtown San Francisco

(under an hour). The BART station is an easy walk or free shuttle ride from any point in the airport, and a one-way ticket to any downtown station costs $5.35.

Shuttle vans are also a cost-effective option for door-to-door service, although these include several stops along the way. From the airport to downtown, the average one-way fare is $15–20 pp. Shuttle vans congregate on the second level of SFO above the baggage claim area for domestic flights, and on the third level for international flights. Advance reservations guarantee a seat, but they aren't required and don't necessarily speed the process. Some companies to try: Bay Shuttle (415/564-3400, www.bayshuttle.com), Quake City Shuttle (415/255-4899, www.quakecityshuttle.com), and SuperShuttle (800/258-3826, www.supershuttle.com).

For **taxis,** the average fare to downtown is around $40.

FLYING INTO LOS ANGELES

The greater Los Angeles area is thick with airports. **Los Angeles International Airport** (LAX, 1 World Way, www.lawa.org) serves the greater Los Angeles area, and is located about 10 miles south of the city of Santa Monica. If you're coming in from another country or from across the continent, you're likely to find your flight coming into this endlessly crowded hub. If you're flying home from LAX, plan plenty of time to get through security and the check-in lines—up to three hours for a domestic flight on a holiday weekend.

To miss the major crowds, consider flying into one of the many suburban airports. **John Wayne Airport** (SNA, 18601 Airport Way, Santa Ana, 949/252-5200, www.ocair.com) serves Disneyland perfectly, and the **Long Beach Airport** (LGB, 4100 Donald Douglas Dr., 562/570-2600, www.lgb.org) is convenient to the beaches. **Ontario Airport** (ONT, www.lawa.org) is farther out but a good option for travelers planning to divide their time between Los Angeles, Palm Springs, and the deserts.

In Los Angeles, free shuttle buses provide service to the Los Angeles County Metropolitan Transportation Authority **Metro Rail** (800/266-6883, www.mta.net), accessible at the Green Line Aviation Station. Metro Rail trains connect Long Beach, Hollywood, North Hollywood, downtown Los Angeles, and Pasadena. Passengers should wait under the blue "LAX Shuttle Airline Connection" signs outside the lower-level terminals and board the "G" shuttle. Passengers may also take the "C" shuttle to the **Metro Bus Center** (800/266-6883, www.mta.net), which connects to buses that serve the entire L.A. area. Information about bus service is provided via telephones on the Information Display Board inside each terminal.

Shuttle services are also available if you want to share a ride. **Prime Time Shuttle** (800/733-8267, www.primetimeshuttle.com) and SuperShuttle (800/258-3826, www.supershuttle.com) are authorized to serve the entire Los Angeles area out of LAX. These vans can be found on the lower arrivals deck in front of each terminal, under the orange "Shared Ride Vans" signs. Average fares for two people are about $32 to downtown Los Angeles, $34 to West Hollywood, and $30 to Santa Monica.

Taxis can be found on the lower arrivals level islands in front of each terminal, below the yellow "Taxi" signs. Only licensed taxis are allowed into the airport; they have standard rates of about $40 to downtown and $30 to West Los Angeles.

FLYING INTO LAS VEGAS

Las Vegas's **McCarran International Airport** (LAS, 5757 Wayne Newton Blvd., 702/261-5211, www.mccarran.com) is one of the 10 busiest in the country. The wide-eyed rubbernecking that this town is famous for kicks in the moment you step into the terminal, with its slots, maze of people movers, monorails, advertisements full of showgirls, and Vegas personalities' video admonitions not to leave your luggage unattended.

Las Vegas City Area Transit buses serve the airport. Route 108 runs up Swenson Street, and the closest it comes to Las Vegas Boulevard is the corner of Paradise Road and

West Sahara Avenue, but you can connect with the Las Vegas monorail at several stops. Or, if you're headed downtown, take Route 108 to the end of the line. Alternately, grab the Route 109 bus, which runs east of the 108 up Maryland Parkway. To get to the Strip, you have to transfer at the large cross streets onto westbound buses that cross the Strip. There are stops at Charleston Boulevard, Sahara Avenue, Desert Inn Road, Flamingo Road, and Tropicana Avenue. Route 109 also ends up at the Downtown Transportation Center. Bus fare is $2, with passes of varying duration available.

You can take a **Gray Line** airport shuttle van to your hotel on the Strip ($12 round-trip) or downtown ($16 round-trip). These shuttles run continuously, leaving the airport about every 15 minutes. You'll find the shuttles outside the baggage claim area. You don't need reservations from the airport, but you will need reservations from your hotel to return to the airport. Call 702/739-5700 to reserve a spot on an airport-bound shuttle 24 hours in advance.

TRAVELING BY TRAIN
Several cross-country **Amtrak** (800/USA-RAIL—800/872-7245, www.amtrak.com) trains rumble into California each day. If you're arriving from another part of the country, the train can be a relaxing way to make the journey to the Golden State; long-distance train routes usually include dining and lounge cars. There are eight train routes that serve California, southern Nevada, and northern Arizona. The *California Zephyr* travels to Chicago, Denver, and Emervyille (just across the bay from San Francisco). Note that while this train stops in Nevada in Reno, Winnemucca, and Elko, Amtrak no longer runs through Las Vegas. The *Capitol Corridor* serves Bay Area cities Emeryville, Oakland, and San Jose. The *Coast Starlight* travels down the West Coast, from Seattle to Portland and ending in Los Angeles.

The *Pacific Surfliner* will get you to the central coast, Los Angeles, and San Diego, while the *Southwest Chief* runs from Los Angeles to Flagstaff, for access to the Grand Canyon, and on to Chicago. The *Sunset Limited* runs to Los Angeles from Texas, New Orleans, and Florida.

TRAVELING BY CAR
Many Americans visit the Southwest by driving here. A number of interstate highways run into the state from points east and north. From the Pacific Northwest, I-5 runs north–south through the state and will get you here quickly. The coastal routes along Highway 1 and U.S. 101 are longer but prettier. I-10 and I-15 allow access from the southeast.

Traffic jams, accidents, mudslides, fires, and snow can affect highways and interstates at any time. Before heading out on your adventure, check road conditions online at the California Department of Transportation (Caltrans, www.dot.ca.gov). Updates on Nevada road conditions are available by calling for a Road Condition Report (877/NV-ROADS—877/687-6237). Note that in winter weather, mountain passes may require snow tires or chains. In rural areas and in the deserts, gas stations may be few and far between.

Common-sense maintenance consciousness is required on the road. If the car gets hot or overheats, stop for a while to cool it off. Never open the radiator cap if the engine is steaming. After it has sat, squeeze the top radiator hose to see if there's any pressure in it; if there isn't, it's safe to open. Never pour water into a hot radiator—you could crack your block. If you start to smell rubber, your tires are overheating, and that's a good way to have a blowout. Stop and let them cool off. In winter in the high country, a can of silicone lubricant such as WD-40 will unfreeze door locks, dry off humid wiring, and keep your hinges in shape.

Visas and Officialdom

PASSPORTS AND VISAS

If you're visiting from another country, you must present a valid passport on entry into the United States. You must also hold a return plane or cruise ticket to your country of origin dated less than 90 days from your date of entry (Canada excepted).

If you hold a passport from one of the following, you do not need a visa to enter the United States: Australia, New Zealand, Japan, South Korea, Singapore, Brunei, and western European countries.

In most other countries, the local U.S. embassy should be able to provide a free tourist visa, often within 24 hours. Plan more time for visa processing if you're requesting travel in the summer high season (June–Aug.).

EMBASSIES

San Francisco and Los Angeles both have consulates from many countries around the globe. If you should lose your passport or find yourself in some other trouble while visiting the region, contact your country's offices for assistance. To find a consulate, check www.travel.state.gov for a list.

CUSTOMS

Before you enter the United States from another country by sea or by air, you'll be required to fill out a customs form. Check with the U.S. embassy in your country or U.S. Customs and Border Protection (www.cbp.gov) for an updated list of items you must declare.

If you require medication administered by injection, you must pack your syringes in a checked bag; syringes are not permitted in carry-on bags coming into the United States.

Also pack documentation describing your need for any narcotic medications you've brought with you. Failure to produce documentation for narcotics on request can result in severe penalties in the United States.

If you're driving into California along I-5 or another major highway, prepare to stop at Agricultural Inspection stations a few miles inside the state line. You don't need to present a passport, a visa, or even a driver's license; instead, you must be prepared to present all your fruits and vegetables.

California's largest economic sector is agriculture, and a number of the major crops grown here are sensitive to pests and diseases. In an effort to prevent known pests from entering the state and endangering crops, travelers are asked to identify all produce they're carrying in from other states or from Mexico. If you've got produce, especially homegrown or from a farm stand, which might be infected by a known problem pest or disease, expect it to be confiscated on the spot.

You'll also be asked about fruits and veggies on your customs form, which you'll be asked to fill out on the airplane or ship before you reach the United States.

Tips for Travelers

CONDUCT AND CUSTOMS

The legal drinking age nationwide is 21. Expect to have your ID checked if you look under 30, especially in bars and clubs, but also in restaurants and wineries.

Most California bars and clubs close at 2 A.M.; you'll find the occasional after-hours nightspot in Los Angeles and San Francisco. There are no time restrictions on drinking in Las Vegas.

Cigarette smoking has been all but criminalized throughout the state of California. Don't expect to find a smoking section in any restaurant or an ashtray in the bars. Smoking is illegal in all bars and clubs, but your new favorite watering hole might have an outdoor patio where smokers can huddle. Taking the ban one step further, many hotels, motels, and inns throughout the state are strictly nonsmoking, and you'll be subject to fees of several hundred dollars if your room smells of smoke when you leave.

There's no smoking in any public building, and even some state parks don't allow cigarettes. There's often good reason for this; fire danger in California is extreme in the summer, and one carelessly thrown lit butt can cause a genuine catastrophe.

TRAVELING WITH CHILDREN

Many spots in the region are ideal destinations for families with children of all ages. In both the San Francisco Bay Area and the Los Angeles region, amusement parks, interactive museums, zoos, parks, beaches, and playgrounds all make for family-friendly fun. Even some of the upscale hotels offer great programs for young people, and many Southern California resorts designate at least one swimming pool as "family" or "loud" to accommodate rambunctious fun and outside voices.

On the other hand, there are a few spots in the Golden State that beckon more to adults than to children. Frankly, there aren't many family activities in Wine Country. This adult playground is all about alcoholic beverages and high-end dining.

Before you book a room at a B&B that you expect to share with your kids, check to be sure that the inn can accommodate extra people in their guest rooms and that it allows guests under age 16.

WOMEN TRAVELERS

California is a pretty friendly place for women traveling alone. Most of the major outdoor attractions are incredibly safe, and even many of the urban areas boast pleasant neighborhoods that welcome lone female travelers.

But you'll need to take some basic precautions and pay attention to your surroundings just as you would in any unfamiliar place. Carry your car keys in your hand when walking out to your car. Don't sit in your parked car in a lonely parking lot at night; just get in, turn on the engine, and drive away. When you're walking down a city street, be alert and keep an eye on your surroundings and on anyone who might be following you. In rural areas, don't go tromping into unlit wooded areas or out into grassy fields alone at night without a flashlight; many of the region's critters are nocturnal. (Actually, this caution applies to men traveling alone as well. Mountain lions and rattlesnakes don't tend to discriminate.)

Some neighborhoods in the big cities are best avoided by lone women, especially at night. Besides the obvious—the Tenderloin in San Francisco and the Compton and Watts neighborhoods of Los Angeles—some other streets and neighborhoods can turn distinctly hostile after dark.

SENIOR TRAVELERS

California makes an ideal destination for retired folks looking to relax and have a great time. You'll find senior discounts nearly every place you go, from restaurants to golf courses to major attractions, and even at some hotels, although the minimum age can range 50–65.

Just ask, and be prepared to produce ID if you look young or are requesting an AARP discount. For landlubbers, RV parks abound throughout the state, and even many of the state and national parks can accommodate RVs and trailers. Check with the parks you want to visit for size and location restrictions, hookup and dump-station information, and RV slot prices.

GAY AND LESBIAN TRAVELERS

California is known for its thriving gay and lesbian communities. In fact, the Golden State is a golden place for gay travel—especially in the bigger cities and even in some of the smaller towns. As with much of the country, the farther you venture into more rural and agricultural regions, the less likely you are to experience the liberal acceptance the state is known for.

In Northern California, San Francisco has the biggest and arguably best Gay Pride Festival (www.sfpride.org) in the nation, usually held on Market Street the last weekend in June. All year round, the Castro District offers fun of all kinds, from theater to clubs to shopping, mostly targeted at gay men but with a few places sprinkled in for lesbians. If the Castro is your primary destination, you can even find a place to stay right in the middle of the action.

Both gay men and women flock to Santa Cruz, on the coast, although the quirky town is specially known for its lesbian-friendly culture. A relaxed vibe informs everything from underground clubs to unofficial nude beaches to live-action role-playing games in the middle of town. Even the lingerie and adult toy shops tend to be female-owned and operated.

West Hollywood in Los Angeles has its own upscale gay culture. Just like the rest of L.A.'s clubs, the gay clubs are havens of the see-and-be-seen crowd.

Information and Services

When visiting California, you might be tempted to stop in at one of several Golden State Welcome Centers scattered throughout the state. In all honesty, these visitors centers aren't that great. If you are in an area that doesn't have its own visitors center or tourism bureau, the State Welcome Center might be a useful place to pick up maps and brochures. Check www.visitcwc.com to find a local Welcome Center wherever you're visiting. Otherwise, stick with local, regional, and national park visitors centers, which tend to be staffed by volunteers or rangers who feel a real passion for their locale.

MAPS AND VISITOR INFORMATION

Almost all gas stations and drugstores sell maps both of the locale you're traversing and of the whole state. AAA Northern California (CSAA, www.csaa.com) and the Automobile Club of Southern California (www.calif.aaa.

com) offices offer maps to auto club members for free.

Many local and regional visitors centers also offer maps, but you'll need to pay a few dollars for the bigger and better ones. But if all you need is a wine-tasting map in a known wine region, you can probably get one for free (plus a few tasting coupons) at the nearest regional visitors center. Basic national park maps come with your admission fee. State park maps can be free or can cost a few dollars at the visitors centers.

HEALTH AND SAFETY

Have an emergency anywhere in the region? Dial 911. Inside hotels and resorts, check your emergency number as soon as you get into your guest room. In urban and suburban areas, full-service hospitals and medical centers abound. But in more remote regions, help can be more than an hour away.

If you're planning a backcountry expedition, follow all rules and guidelines for obtaining wilderness permits and for self-registration at trailheads. These are for your safety, letting the rangers know roughly where you plan to be and when to expect you back. National and state park visitors centers can advise in more detail as to any health or wilderness alerts in the area.

MONEY
Businesses here accept the U.S. dollar ($). Most businesses also accept major credit cards: Visa, MasterCard, Discover, Diner's Club, and American Express. ATM and check cards work at many stores and restaurants, and you're likely to find ATMs in every town of any size.

You can change currency at any international airport. Currency-exchange points also crop up in downtown San Francisco and Los Angeles and at some of the major business hotels in urban areas.

Internet Resources

It should come as no surprise that the California travel industry leads the way in the use of the Internet as a marketing, communications, and sales tool. The overwhelming majority of destinations have their own websites—even tiny towns in the middle of nowhere proudly tout their attractions on the Web.

CALIFORNIA
California Department of Transportation
www.dot.ca.gov/hq/roadinfo/statemap.htm
Contains state map and highway information.

Visit California
www.visitcalifornia.com
The official tourism site of the state of California.

LATourist.com
www.latourist.com
An informative Los Angeles tourist website.

Los Angeles Convention and Visitors Bureau
www.lacvb.com
The official website of the Los Angeles Convention and Visitors Bureau.

NapaValley.com
www.napavalley.com
A Napa Valley tourism website from WineCountry.com.

California Outdoor and Recreational Information
www.caoutdoors.com
A recreation-focused website that includes links to maps, local newspapers, festivals, and events as well as a wide variety of recreational activities throughout the state.

California State Parks
www.parks.ca.gov
The official website lists hours, accessibility, activities, camping areas, fees, and more information for all parks in the state system.

Disneyland
http:/disneyland.disney.go.com
The official website for Disneyland and all Disney attractions.

State of California
www.ca.gov/tourism/greatoutdoors.html
Outdoor resources for California state and government organizations. Check for information about fishing and hunting licenses, backcountry permits, boating regulations, and more.

Yosemite National Park
www.nps.gov/yose
The National Park Service website for Yosemite National Park.

Yosemite National Park Vacation and Lodging Information
www.yosemitepark.com
The concessionaire's website for Yosemite National Park lodging, dining, and reservations.

LAS VEGAS
Visit Las Vegas
www.visitlasvegas.com,
www.vegas.com
Lots of information on staying and playing in Las Vegas.

Las Vegas Convention and Visitors Authority
www.lvcva.com
The authority works to fill southern Nevada's 150,000 hotel rooms with vacationers, conventioneers, and business travelers. It runs the massive and technologically advanced Las Vegas Convention Center.

GRAND CANYON
Grand Canyon National Park
www.nps.gov/grca
The Grand Canyon's official website has basic information on the park; go here for information about backcountry permits.

Xanterra South Rim
www.grandcanyonlodges.com
Information on the park's accommodations as well as reservations.

Index

List of Maps

Contributors

MICHAEL CERVIN

For Michael Cervin, writing about coastal California is like a dream come true. Having lived on the coast for over a decade — exploring the beaches and mountains, boating on the water, diving off the Channel Islands, tasting the food, and sampling the wine — the joy is in sharing those experiences with others.

Michael Cervin grew up in La Cañada, a suburb of Los Angeles. After a brief acting career on TV shows including *3rd Rock from the Sun, Grace Under Fire,* and *The Young and the Restless,* he relocated to Santa Barbara, where wine quickly became one of his passions.

Michael has written for major wine publications including *Decanter, Wine & Spirits, Wine Enthusiast,* and *The Tasting Panel.* His work has also appeared in *Skywest, Westways, Fido Friendly, Food & Beverage World, Vine Times,* and more than sixty other publications. He has served as a wine judge at the Santa Barbara County Fair, the Central Coast Wine Competition, the Monterey Wine Competition, and the El Dorado and Amador County Fair Wine Competitions.

Michael is the author of one other guidebook, *Moon Santa Barbara & the Central Coast.* His book of poetry, *Generous Fiction,* was published in 2009. He is currently the restaurant critic for the *Santa Barbara News-Press.* Find more information about his works at www.MichaelCervin.com.

LIZ HAMILL

Liz Hamill was born and raised in the San Francisco Bay Area. After getting her English degree at local institution Stanford University, she pursued her love of dining and travel throughout the Golden State and beyond. Her exploits included everything from whitewater rafting on the Kaweah River to dining at the French Laundry. When a battle with chronic pain put an end to her rafting and camping trips, Liz discovered wine tasting and spa resorts. To this day, she's not sure which style of vacation she likes better.

In 2008, Liz made the terrifying leap from overpaid high-tech employee to almost broke full-time freelance travel and food writer. You can read about her adventures in national magazines, Bay Area newspapers, and on the web at www.travelswithpain.com.

Liz lives and writes, often chasing her cats away from her computer so she can get some work done, in San Jose.

TIM HULL

Born on a U.S. Air Force base in South Carolina, *Moon Arizona* author Tim Hull was brought to Arizona when he was just six months old and has since left only rarely. He grew up in Prescott, a small town in the state's north-central pinelands, where his mother's family has lived since the 1870s. Tim graduated from Arizona State University and has traveled extensively throughout the Southwest and Mexico.

Currently, Tim is a freelance writer based in Tucson, Arizona. He has been a staff writer and editor for *Green Valley News* in southern Arizona's Santa Cruz Valley and *Inside Tucson Business*. He has also written for *Tucson Weekly, High Country News,* CourthouseNews.com, and various other publications and websites. His fiction writing has been published in *Santa Monica Review, Blue Mesa Review,* and other arts journals. Tim is also the author of *Moon Tucson*.

HEATHER C. LISTON

Journalist Heather C. Liston has lived in San Francisco for almost ten years. During that time, she has traveled extensively and often throughout Northern California, spending many weekends in Calistoga, Big Sur, Lake County, Napa, Mendocino, and beyond.

Heather has written about Northern California for *California Wild, San Jose* magazine, RoadandTravel.com, *Running Times, Trail Runner,* and the *Albuquerque Journal*.

SCOTT SMITH

Moon Nevada author Scott Smith has lived in Nevada for 20-plus years, making him — by Las Vegas standards — a native. He earned his journalism degree from Ball State University, and an MBA at the University of Nevada, Las Vegas.

Scott enjoys exploring his adopted home state with his wife and four sons. His favorite Nevada memories include battling gale-force winds to keep the family tent anchored near Sunnyside and digging two toddlers out of knee-deep muck along the shores of Lake Mead.

During his travels, Scott seeks out the unexpected — and enjoys finding evidence that contradicts most people's stereotypes. He has written about a selfless pioneer's heroic trek to save his friends in the Nevada desert; the flourishing arts scene in "vacuous" Las Vegas; and the state's brief embrace of Progressive values in the early 1900s that saw it outlaw gambling and liquor. A frequent contributor to *Nevada* magazine, Smith's writing has also appeared in *American History* and *WildWest*.

www.moon.com